Heritage Signature® Auction #1116
Long Beach U.S. Coin
September 17-19, 2008 | Long Beach, California

Featuring: The Nora Bailey Collection • The Bell Collection • The Davis Conway Collection • The Morton J. Greene Collection
The Hamous Collection of California Gold • The Laredo Collection • The Malibu Collection • The Mississippi Collection
The Menlo Park Collection • The Nevada Collection of Seated Quarters • The Sundance Collection

LOT VIEWING
Long Beach Convention Center
100 South Pine Ave. • Room 104A
Long Beach, CA 90802

Tuesday, September 16 • 11:00 AM PT - 7:00 PM PT

Wednesday, September 17 • 8:00 AM PT - 7:00 PM PT

Thursday, September 18 • 8:00 AM PT - 7:00 PM PT

Friday, September 19 • 8:00 AM PT - 7:00 PM PT

Saturday, September 20 • 8:00 AM PT -12:00 PM PT
(Lot viewing for Sessions 7-8)

View lots online at HA.com/Coins

LIVE FLOOR BIDDING
Bid in person during the floor sessions.

LIVE TELEPHONE BIDDING *(floor sessions only)*
Phone bidding must be arranged on or before
Tuesday, September 16, 2008, by 12:00 PM CT.
Client Service: 866-835-3243.

"HERITAGE LIVE" BIDDING
Bid live from your location, anywhere in the world,
during the Auction using our "Heritage Live" program
at HA.com/Live

INTERNET BIDDING
Internet absentee bidding ends at 10:00 PM CT the evening
before each session. HA.com/Coins

FAX BIDDING
Fax bids must be received on or before Tuesday,
September 16, 2008, by 12:00 PM CT. Fax: 214-409-1425

MAIL BIDDING
Mail bids must be received on or before
Tuesday, September 16, 2008.

*Please see "Choose Your Bidding Method" in the back of this
catalog for specific details about each of these bidding methods.*

LIVE AUCTION
SIGNATURE® FLOOR SESSIONS 1-6
(Floor, Telephone, Heritage Live, Internet, Fax, and Mail)
Long Beach Convention Center
100 South Pine Ave. • Room 103B
Long Beach, CA 90802

SESSION 1
Wednesday, September 17, 2008 • 6:00 PM PT • Lots 1–873

SESSION 2
Thursday, September 18, 2008 • 1:00 PM PT • Lots 874–1505

SESSION 3
Thursday, September 18, 2008 • 6:00 PM PT • Lots 1506–2558

SESSION 4
Friday, September 19, 2008 • 9:30 AM PT • Lots 2559–3104

SESSION 5
Friday, September 19, 2008 • 3:00 PM PT • Lots 3105–3422

SESSION 6
Friday, September 19, 2008 • 6:00 PM PT • Lots 3423–4546

NON FLOOR/NON PHONE BIDDING SESSIONS 7-8
(Heritage Live, Internet, Fax, and Mail only) See separate catalog
Dallas, Texas • September 20-21, 2008

SESSION 7
Saturday, September 20 • 9:30 AM CT • Lots 7001-9554

SESSION 8
Sunday, September 21 • 9:30 AM CT • Lots 9555-11554

AUCTION RESULTS
Immediately available at HA.com/Coins

LOT SETTLEMENT AND PICK-UP - ROOM 104A
Thursday, September 18 • 10:00 AM PT - 1:00 PM PT
Friday, September 19 • 10:00 AM PT - 1:00 PM PT
Saturday, September 20 • 9:00 AM PT - 12:00 PM PT

Extended Payment Terms available. See details in the back of this catalog.

*Lots are sold at an approximate rate of 200 lots per hour, but it
is not uncommon to sell 150 lots or 250 lots in any given hour.*

This auction is subject to a 15% Buyer's Premium.

THIS AUCTION IS PRESENTED AND CATALOGED BY HERITAGE NUMISMATIC AUCTIONS, INC.

Heritage World Headquarters

HERITAGE HA.com
Auction Galleries

Home Office • 3500 Maple Avenue, 17th Floor • Dallas, Texas 75219
Design District Annex • 1518 Slocum Street • Dallas, Texas 75207
214.528.3500 | 800.872.6467 | 214.409.1425 (fax)
Direct Client Service Line: Toll Free 1.866.835.3243 • Email: Bid@HA.com

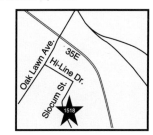

Heritage Design District Annex

Auctioneer licenses: Heritage Numismatic Auctions, Inc.: CA Bond #RSB2004175; CA Auctioneer Bonds: Samuel Foose #RSB2004178; Robert Korver #RSB2004179;
Bob Merrill #RSB2004177; Leo Frese #RSB2004176; Jeff Engelken #RSB2004180.

FL LICENSES: HERITAGE NUMISMATIC AUCTIONS, INC.: AB665; CURRENCY AUCTIONS OF AMERICA: AB2218;
FL AUCTIONEER LICENSES: SAMUEL FOOSE AU3244; ROBERT KORVER AU2916; SCOTT PETERSON AU3021; MIKE SADLER AU3795.

Consignor #	Client #
Name:	
Address:	
Phone No.	Email	Fax No.

SCHEDULE 1 – CONSIGNED PROPERTIES

	Date	MM	Den.	Service	Grade	Cert. ID#	Notes
1.							
2.							
3.							
4.							
5.							
6.							
7.							
8.							
9.							
10.							
11.							
12.							
13.							
14.							
15.							
16.							
17.							
18.							
19.							
20.							

	Received by Heritage Auction Galleries
	Name:
Consignor:	
Date:	Date:

Mail to: Consignments, Heritage Auction Galleries, 3500 Maple Avenue, 17th Floor, Dallas, TX 75219-3941

U.S. COIN AUCTION

*1916 Walking Liberty Half
in Silver, Judd-1994
PR64 NGC*

*1879 Schoolgirl Dollar
in Silver
Judd-1608, High R.6
PR65 Cameo NGC*

*1877 Large Head Fifty Dollar
in Copper Gilt
Judd-1547, Low R.7
PR65 NGC*

*1792 Birch Cent, Lettered Edge
TO BE ESTEEMED BE USEFUL*
Judd-5, R.8
FA 2BN NGC*

*1792 Silver Center Cent
Judd-1, High R.6
VF 30 BN NGC*

*1882 Shield Earring
Half Dollar
in Silver
Judd-1700, Low R.7
PR64 Cameo NGC*

*1916 Walking Liberty Half
Judd-1992, R.8
PR58 NGC*

*1877 Morgan Head,
Defiant Eagle Half in Silver
Judd-1512, High R.7
PR62 NGC*

*1882 Shield Earring Quarter
in Silver, Judd-1698
PR67 ★ NGC*

*1864 Indian Head
Flying Eagle Cent
Judd-362, R.8
PR65 Cameo NGC*

*1882 Shield Earring Dollar
in Copper
Judd-1703, High R.7
PF66 ★ RB Cameo NGC*

*1880 Coiled Hair Stella in Copper
Judd-1661, Low R.7
PR64 RB NGC*

*1872 Amazonian Half
in Silver, Judd-1200
PR64 NGC*

*1879 Coiled Hair Stella
in Aluminum
Judd-1640, High R.7
PR66 Cameo NGC*

*1880 Flowing Hair Stella in Copper
Judd-1658, Low R.7
PR66 RB NGC*

*1915 No S Panama-Pacific
Half Dollar in Gold
Judd-1960, R.8
PR64 NGC*

The Greatest Pattern Collection to be Auctioned in Our Generation

*Will be sold by Heritage Auction Galleries in FUN 2009 Orlando — January 7-10, 2009
The Lemus Collection – Queller Part Two of American Pattern Coinage is one of the finest to ever come on
the market: 485 different Patterns, world-class in aesthetic appeal and numismatic breadth.*

Call 800-872-6467 ext. 1000 to speak with a Consignment Director today or fill in the form on the reverse.

MAIL/FAX BID SHEET

Heritage Auction Galleries
Direct Client Service Line—Toll Free:
866-835-3243
HA.com
3500 Maple Avenue, 17th Floor
Dallas, Texas 75219-3941
(All information must be completed.)

NAME _____ CUSTOMER # (if known) _____

ADDRESS _____ E-MAIL ADDRESS _____

CITY/STATE/ZIP _____

DAYTIME PHONE (A/C) _____ EVENING PHONE (A/C) _____

Would you like a FAX or e-mail confirming receipt of your bids? If so, please print your FAX # or e-mail address here: _____

REFERENCES: New bidders who are unknown to us must furnish satisfactory industry references or a valid credit card in advance of the sale date.

Dealer References (City, State) and/or Credit Card Information

_____

_____

_____

_____

You are authorized to release payment history information to other dealers and auctioneers so that I may establish proper credit in the industry. (Line out this statement if you do not authorize release.)

Non-Internet bids (including but not limited to, podium, fax, phone and mail bids) may be submitted at any time and are treated similar to floor bids. These types of bids must be on-increment or at a half increment (called a cut bid). Any podium, fax, phone or mail bids that do not conform to a full or half increment will be rounded up or down to the nearest full or half increment and will be considered your high bid.

Current Bid	Bid Increment		
< - $10	$1	$10,000 - $19,999	$1,000
$10 - $29	$2	$20,000 - $29,999	$2,000
$30 - $49	$3	$30,000 - $49,999	$2,500
$50 - $99	$5	$50,000 - $99,999	$5,000
$100 - $199	$10	$100,000 - $199,999	$10,000
$200 - $299	$20	$200,000 - $299,999	$20,000
$300 - $499	$25	$300,000 - $499,999	$25,000
$500 - $999	$50	$500,000 - $999,999	$50,000
$1,000 - $1,999	$100	$1,000,000 - $1,999,999	$100,000
$2,000 - $2,999	$200	$2,000,000- $2,999,999	$200,000
$3,000 - $4,999	$250	$3,000,000- $4,999,999	$250,000
$5,000 - $9,999	$500	$5,000,000 - $9,999,999	$500,000
		>$10,000,000	$1,000,000

(Bid in whole dollar amounts only.)

LOT NO.	AMOUNT	LOT NO.	AMOUNT	LOT NO.	AMOUNT	LOT NO.	AMOUNT

PLEASE COMPLETE THIS INFORMATION:

1. IF NECESSARY, PLEASE INCREASE MY BIDS BY:
    ☐ 10%   ☐ 20%   ☐ 30%
    Lots will be purchased as much below bids as possible.

2. ☐ I HAVE BOUGHT COINS FROM YOU BEFORE (references are listed above)

I have read and agree to all of the Terms and Conditions of Auction: inclusive of paying interest at the lesser of 1.5% per month (18% per annum) or the maximum contract interest rate under applicable state law from the date of sale (if the account is not timely paid), and the submission of disputes to arbitration.

_____
(Signature required) Please make a copy of your bid sheet for your records.

SUBTOTAL	
TOTAL from other side	
TOTAL BID	

FAX HOTLINE: 214-409-1425   REV. 01-15-08

TOTAL, this side

LOT NO.	AMOUNT	LOT NO.	AMOUNT	LOT NO.	AMOUNT	LOT NO.	AMOUNT

TOTAL, this side

LOT NO.	AMOUNT	LOT NO.	AMOUNT	LOT NO.	AMOUNT	LOT NO.	AMOUNT

DIRECTORY FOR DEPARTMENT SPECIALISTS AND SERVICES

COINS & CURRENCY

COINS – UNITED STATES

HA.com/Coins
U.S. Coins

Leo Frese, Ext. 1294
Leo@HA.com
Charles Clifford, Ext. 1477
CharlesC@HA.com
Sam Foose, Ext. 1227
SamF@HA.com
Jim Jelinski, Ext. 1257
JimJ@HA.com
Katherine Kurachek, Ext. 1389
KKurachek@HA.com
David Lewis, Ext. 1520
DLewis@HA.com
David Lisot, Ext. 1303
DavidL@HA.com
Bob Marino, Ext. 1374
BobMarino@HA.com
David Mayfield, Ext. 1277
DavidM@HA.com
Mike Sadler, Ext. 1332
MikeS@HA.com
Doug Nyholm, Ext. 1598
DNyholm@HA.com
Eugene Nowell, Ext. 1517
EugeneN@HA.com
Dave Lindvall, Ext. 1231
David@HA.com
Jason Friedman, Ext. 1582
JasonF@HA.com
Amber Dinh Ext. 1634
AmberD@HA.com

COINS – WORLD

HA.com/Coins
World Coins & Currencies

Warren Tucker, Ext. 1287
WTucker@HA.com
Scott Cordry, Ext. 1369
ScottC@HA.com
Cristiano Bierrenbach, Ext. 1661
CrisB@HA.com

CURRENCY

HA.com/Currency
Paper Money

Len Glazer, Ext. 1390
Len@HA.com
Allen Mincho, Ext. 1327
Allen@HA.com
Dustin Johnston, Ext. 1302
Dustin@HA.com
Jim Fitzgerald, Ext. 1348
JimF@HA.com
Michael Moczalla, Ext. 1481
MichaelM@HA.com

TOKENS & MEDALS

HA.com/Coins

David Lisot, Ext. 1303
DavidL@HA.com

UNITED STATES COINS PRIVATE TREATY SALES

HA.com/Coins

Todd Imhof, Ext. 1313
Todd@HA.com

COMICS

HA.com/Comics
Comics, Original Comic Art and Related Memorabilia

Ed Jaster, Ext. 1288
EdJ@HA.com
Lon Allen, Ext. 1261
LonA@HA.com
Barry Sandoval, Ext. 1377
BarryS@HA.com

FINE ART & JEWELRY

ART OF THE AMERICAN WEST & TEXAS ART

HA.com/TexasArt
Michael Duty, Ext. 1712
MichaelD@HA.com

DECORATIVE ARTS

HA.com/FineArt
Sculpture, European & American Silver Antique Furniture, Art Glass & Ceramics

Michael Wolf, Ext. 1541
MWolf@HA.com
Tim Rigdon, Ext. 1119
TimR@HA.com
Meredith Meuwly, Ext. 1631
MeredithM@HA.com

FINE ART

HA.com/FineArt
Impressionist, Old Masters and Contemporary Drawings, Paintings, Sculpture and Photography

Edmund P. Pillsbury, Ph.D., Ext. 1533
EPP@HA.com
Michael Duty, Ext. 1712
MichaelD@HA.com
Kathleen Guzman, Ext. 1672
KathleenG@HA.com
Ed Jaster, Ext. 1288
EdJ@HA.com
Courtney Case, Ext. 1293
CourtneyC@HA.com

ILLUSTRATION ART

HA.com/FineArt
Pinups and Illustration Art

Ed Jaster, Ext. 1288
EdJ@HA.com

JEWELRY

HA.com/Jewelry

Jill Burgum, Ext. 1697
JillB@HA.com

PHOTOGRAPHY

HA.com/FineArt

Lorraine Davis, Ext. 1714
LorraineD@HA.com

RUSSIAN ART

HA.com/FineArt

Douglass Brown, Ext. 1165
DouglassB@HA.com

TIMEPIECES

HA.com/Timepieces

Jim Wolf, Ext. 1659
JWolf@HA.com

20TH CENTURY ART & DESIGN

HA.com/FineArt

Thom Pegg, Ext. 1742
ThomP@HA.com

HISTORICAL

AMERICAN INDIAN ART

HA.com/Historical

Delia Sullivan, Ext. 1343
DeliaS@HA.com

AMERICANA & POLITICAL

HA.com/Historical
Historical & Pop Culture Americana, Vintage Toys, Presidential & Political Memorabilia, Buttons & Medals, Books & Manuscripts, First Editions and Collectible Autographs

Tom Slater, Ext. 1441
TomS@HA.com
Marsha Dixey, Ext. 1455
MarshaD@HA.com
John Hickey, Ext. 1264
JohnH@HA.com
Michael Riley, Ext. 1467
MichaelR@HA.com

CIVIL WAR ARTIFACTS

HA.com/Civil War
Artifacts, Documents and Memorabilia Related to the American Civil War

Douglass Brown, Ext. 1165
DouglassB@HA.com
Dennis Lowe, Ext. 1182
DennisL@HA.com

RARE BOOKS

HA.com/Books

James Gannon, Ext. 1609
JamesG@HA.com
Joe Fay, Ext. 1544
JoeF@HA.com

MANUSCRIPTS

HA.com/Manuscripts

Sandra Palomino, Ext. 1107
SandraP@HA.com

TEXANA

HA.com/Texana

Sandra Palomino, Ext. 1107
SandraP@HA.com

WESTERN AMERICANA

HA.com/Historical

Russ Jorzig, Ext. 1633
RussJ@HA.com

MOVIE POSTERS

HA.com/MoviePosters
Posters, Lobby Cards, and Hollywood Ephemera

Grey Smith, Ext. 1367
GreySm@HA.com
Bruce Carteron, Ext. 1551
BruceC@HA.com

MUSIC & ENTERTAINMENT MEMORABILIA

HA.com/Entertainment
Autographs, Stage-worn Costumes, Film and Television-used Props and Wardrobe, Celebrity-played Instruments, Pop-Culture Memorabilia, Rare Records and Acetates.
Doug Norwine, Ext. 1452
DougN@HA.com

John Hickey, Ext. 1264
JohnH@HA.com
Garry Shrum, Ext. 1585
GarryS@HA.com
Jim Steele, Ext. 1328
JimSt@HA.com

NATURAL HISTORY

HA.com/NaturalHistory

David Herskowitz, Ext. 1610
DavidH@HA.com

SPORTS COLLECTIBLES

HA.com/Sports
Sports Cards, Artifacts, Game-Used Jerseys & Equipment

Chris Ivy, Ext. 1319
CIvy@HA.com
Stephen Carlisle, Ext. 1292
StephenC@HA.com
Mike Gutierrez, Ext. 1183
MikeG@HA.com
Lee Iskowitz, Ext. 1601
LeeI@HA.com
Mark Jordan, Ext. 1187
MarkJ@HA.com
Jonathan Scheier, Ext. 1314
JonathanS@HA.com

STAMPS

HA.com/Stamps

Steven Crippe, Ext.1777
StevenC@HA.com
Brian Degen, Ext.1767
BrianD@HA.com
Leo Frese, Ext.1294
Leo@HA.com

CORPORATE & INSTITUTIONAL COLLECTIONS/VENTURES

Jared Green, Ext. 1279
Jared@HA.com

AUCTION OPERATONS

Norma Gonzalez, Ext. 1242
V.P. Auction Operations
Norma@HA.com

CREDIT DEPARTMENT

Marti Korver, Ext 1248
Marti@HA.com
Eric Thomas, Ext. 1241
EricT@HA.com

MARKETING

Debbie Rexing, Ext. 1356
DebbieR@HA.com

MEDIA & PUBLIC RELATIONS

Kelley Norwine, Ext. 1583
KelleyN@HA.com

CORPORATE OFFICERS

R. Steven Ivy, Co-Chairman
James L. Halperin, Co-Chairman
Gregory J. Rohan, President
Paul Minshull, Chief Operating Officer
Todd Imhof, Executive Vice President
Leo Frese, Executive Vice President

WIRING INSTRUCTIONS

Bank Information:
JP Morgan Chase Bank, N.A.
270 Park Avenue, New York, NY 10017
Account Name:
Heritage Numismatic Auctions
Master Account
ABA Number: 021000021
Account Number: 1884827674
Swift Code: CHASUS33

Dear Bidder,

What a wonderful series of Long Beach auctions is about to take place! Heritage is offering catalogs featuring U.S. Coins, U.S. Currency, Tokens & Medals, and Ancient & World Coins. Literally, there is something of interest for every collector.

We continue to be gratified by the number of Registry collections and coins being sold through Heritage's exciting auctions. We are proud to be involved in every aspect of managing so many important collections, whether the collectors are assembling, upgrading, adjusting, or selling their numismatic treasures.

I invite you to read about our many anchor consignors. They share fascinating stories of their collecting histories, motivations, and successes.

The Nora Bailey Collection

The Nora Bailey Collection of Half Cents contains many wonderful early half cents, led by the census level 1805 C-2, B-2 Small 5, Stems rarity (certified XF40 by PCGS). This low R.6 is the rarest 1805 half cent as well as one of the rarest Draped Bust half cent varieties. This series is much beloved by specialists, but these coins, collected over four decades, will have enormous appeal to type collectors, the lovers of early copper, and those seeking "trophy coins." Many of these rare varieties could easily be found at coin shows in the early years, but even today there are still treasures to be found there, and the consignor recommends that "every collector educate himself enough to be able to find them."

The Bell Collection

Kevin Bell's father started him on his lifelong hobby of coin collecting; together they attended the monthly coin club meetings in Erie, Pennsylvania. Father and son both enjoyed the coins and the camaraderie, and both found the coins continually interesting. Mr. Bell continued to search circulating coins through High School, but with financial success came more sophisticated coin buying. In this auction are included two PCGS Registry sets: 1) Basic Type Set with gold (as the Bell Collection), #2 Current, #3 All-Time (and winner of the 2008 Category award); and 2) Gold Type Set, 12 Pieces, Circulation Strikes 1839-1933 (as the Indiana Gold Collection), #5 Current Finest.

The Davis Conway Collection

Davis Conway's father started buying gold and silver out of the storefront of his copier repair business in the late 1970s, and eventually he sold that business to focus on a coin and jewelry store in 1980. Davis was allowed to set up his own coin supplies section at the age 10, and with developing passion, "bought as many coins as I could from him and other dealers with my profits from selling supplies." A promising career was cut short by a family crisis in 1982, and his coins went into storage.

"In 2006, my original collection was discovered during house archaeology, and my seven year-old daughter was so fascinated that we decided to start collecting together. Shortly thereafter, my father was diagnosed with cancer, and all three of us worked to complete an Indian Head cent collection before his passing in early 2007. I soon began a PCGS-certified Lincoln collection, continually amazed at how coin collecting had changed in 25 years, including the amazing availability of coins online. Just as we were closing in on the top Registry spot on the Lincoln Date set, the family nature of the collection took precedence – the proceeds from this auction are supporting building our new home! But I am far from giving up, and there will be other Registry sets in the future."

The Morton J. Greene Collection

Morton J. Greene has been collecting coins for more than six decades, starting in the 1920s. At first, like all collectors, he collected out of circulation, and collected the oldest coins he could find. Fortunately, he also learned that quality was important, and he began to save newly issued coins. He focused on minor coinage, although he also developed a fondness for the classic commemoratives (due to all of the history that they represented). While coins were always a relaxing hobby for Mr. Greene, the circumstances of life meant variations in his levels of interest, but busy periods were always followed by collecting periods. Mr. Greene especially enjoyed the educational aspects of collecting, and thinks that that aspect alone would be of great benefit to today's younger generation.

The Hamous Collection of California Gold

James Hamous and his best friend started collecting coins at the age of eight; his friend's mother would front $5 for their weekly trip to the bank for rolls to search (after they found coins of interest, they had to return the entire $5 to their 'backer' for the following week!). Monthly, they would attend the active coin club in Chadron, Nebraska, which offered additional opportunities to spend their entire allowance. After graduating with his medical degree from the University of Nebraska, Dr. Hamous ultimately became a pathologist, and coins offered a respite from the pressure of his profession. Serious interest in California Gold began around 1990, inspired by an advertisement of Jay Roe. Dr. Hamous ordered a few of the diminutive coins, and got really hooked on their history. Small in size but large in history, they would hold his fascination for nearly two decades.

The Laredo Collection

The Laredo Collection is an eclectic holding of numismatic masterpieces, reflecting the interests of a collector who chose not to specialize, but rather to buy beauty and rarity when they most appealed to him. The collector began his interest in rare coins around the age of eight when he inherited his grandmother's coin collection but real participation in the hobby had to be postponed for decades of hard work in real estate development. Financial success there finally allowed the consignor to obtain these treasures, coins that he could never have imagined owning as a child. After delighting in them for many years, he is now presented with a golden opportunity to use the capital for his largest development ever. "Real estate bought me these wonderful coins, and now they will help fund a new and wonderful project."

The Malibu Collection

These selections from The Malibu Collection may be small in number, but they are large in quality and eye-appeal – many among the finest known. Among the Proof Liberty Seated quarters being offered: 1864 PR66 Cameo NGC; 1872 PR68 NGC; 1880 PR68 Cameo NGC; 1889 PR68 Star NGC; 1891 PR67 Cameo NGC. Among the Seated half dollars: an 1849 PR66 NGC from the Pittman and Byers Collections. Specialists and type collectors alike will be thrilled to add this pedigree to their collections.

The consignor has been in love with rare coins since the age of eight, when he received a Fair Standing Liberty quarter "of indeterminate date in change from a Coke machine at a country gas station in Lake George, New York – sometimes numismatic memories share camping and fishing trips with Dad! I began putting aside old coins from circulation in a Mason jar, and loved every coin." Serious collecting began around 2000 as financial success encouraged the pursuit of rarer items. The consignor is still in love with the Standing Liberty design, but as he approached completing his set in top grade, his interests widened to include the Seated Liberty issues. "The Seated Liberty coins represent such a long and fascinating period of American history – with all of the tales of westward expansion, the taming of the Old West, the Civil War, and Reconstruction during the nineteenth century. Additionally, the Seated design is spectacularly beautiful in its simplicity. He encourages all collectors to buy quality and hold the coins for an appropriate length of time, and fully share in this great hobby of history.

The Menlo Park Collection

The very private collector who formed the Menlo Park Collection has had an "'on again, off again' affair with rare coins for more than sixty years – mostly on again!" There were times in his life that called for selling coins, such as when he got married, and many more times for collecting. Over so many decades, his interests naturally evolved. His collection of Sheldon varieties was sold many years ago, and over recent decades he has been diligently working to diversify his wonderful type collection. That collection is very nearly complete, and will provide many exciting coins to collectors seeking the same goal.

The Mississippi Collection

The collector's interest in rare coins began while he was helping his five children work on modest collections involving their birth date. As he became more interested he also began to pursue more sophisticated rarities. The selections from his larger collection included in this auction reflect his general concentration on gold rarities, with an emphasis on Dahlonega and Charlotte pieces.

The Nevada Collection of Seated Quarters

The Nevada Collection of Seated Quarters is the result of a most unusual arrangement. More than two decades ago, two dedicated numismatists who had come to know and appreciate each other's talents decided to combine their efforts instead of compete. Two collectors, living in different western states, collecting with different styles (one was advised by Julian Leidman, while the other worked alone) working together to form a single great collection. Heritage is pleased to offer selections from this important achievement.

The Sundance Collection

The Sundance Collection was formed by a very private collector from the Midwest with an eye for quality coins. While he enjoys many series, his original intention over more than a decade was to pursue Seated halves - but enormous price increases in that series for top quality pieces have convinced him to be a seller instead of a buyer! His acquisitions in other series will continue.

We invite you to peruse our many offerings; we are offering such an incredible array of important material that it only makes sense to start your bidding research now! Our free Permanent Auction Archives at HA.com are available around the clock, wherever you may find yourself around the globe, so you have a continual opportunity to determine your favorite lots from more than 10,000 items being offered. Concentrating on your favorite pieces will maximize your chances of adding to your important collection; our interactive system allows you to easily determine when any lot becomes too expensive, allowing you to concentrate on other lots. The Archives contain amazing images, lot descriptions, and prices realized data from more than a decade of past numismatic auctions – some 1.5 million numismatic items! This is the most incredible free resource on the Web!

We look forward to receiving your bids, whether you bid by mail, fax, e-mail, Interactive Internet, Heritage Live, by agent, by telephone, or best of all – in person! We expect that more than two thousand bidders will be successful in these auctions, and there is no reason you cannot be among those happy collectors! I invite you to join us in Long Beach – if you can, please stop by and say "Hello" at the Heritage tables.

Good luck with your bidding.

Sincerely,

Greg Rohan
President

NATURAL HISTORY AUCTION

Saber-toothed Cat, South Dakota

Gem Ammolite, Canada

Yellow, Blue & Purple Fluorite, Illinois

Amber Scorpion, Dominican Republic

Green Fluorite, China

Barite & Fluorite on Sphalerite, Tennesse

Calcite, Tennessee

Golden Calcite, Kazakhstan

Heritage Auction Galleries has become the World leader in Natural History Auctions.

These unique auctions feature a variety of Museum Quality Specimens from around the world including Rare & Exotic Gems, Minerals, Meteorites, Zoology and Fossils.

Whether you wish to sell an entire collection or just one valuable item, only Heritage, the unchallenged world leader in the sale of Natural History can help you do that.

Our next Natural History Auction will be conducted on January 18th at our Dallas, Texas Headquarters and will feature the collection of Daniel Trinchillo Sr. Mr. Trinchillo has been avidly collecting fine specimens for over 20 years. His collection reflects his passion for aesthetics and quality.

A fully illustrated color catalogue will be available for this auction as well as online previews.

Denomination Index

SESSION ONE

Live, Internet, and Mail Bid Signature® Auction #1116
Wednesday, September 17, 2008, 6:00 PM PT, Lots 1-873
Long Beach, California

A 15% Buyer's Premium ($9 minimum) Will Be Added To All Lots

Visit HA.com to view full-color images and bid.

COLONIALS

1   **1662 Oak Tree Twopence—Bent —NCS, Fine Details.** Crosby 1-A3, Noe-31, High R.6. 12.3 gn. Wear is concentrated on the date, but the telltale horizontal break from the top of the 2 through the A in ENGLAND confirms the rare Noe variety. Bent at 6 o'clock, causing a flan crack through the E in NEW. The obverse is misaligned toward 7 o'clock, as usual for Noe-31. Listed on page 36 of the 2009 *Guide Book*. (#17)

Appealing Choice VF 1652 Oak Tree Shilling Noe-10, 'Ghost Tree' Variety

2   **1652 Oak Tree Shilling VF35 PCGS.** Noe-10. 70.3 grains. The tree is weakly struck as always; hence the "Ghost Tree" moniker. The Wurtzbach plate coin, as noted in the Ford sale. Still-luminous surfaces show warm gold, pink, and reddish-violet shadings over silver-gray surfaces. Immense eye appeal.
Ex: Virgil Brand; Carl Wurtzbach; T. James Clarke; F.C.C. Boyd Collections; Ford XII (Stack's, 10/05), lot 33. (#20)

Pleasing XF45 Noe-13 1652 Oak Tree Shilling

3   **1652 Oak Tree Shilling XF45 PCGS.** Noe-13. 71.9 grains. The Wurtzbach plate coin, according to the Ford catalog. Deep green-gray surfaces overall with occasional glints of gold. Well-defined, minimally marked, and desirable.
Ex: A.H. Woods; Charles E. Clapp; Carl Wurtzbach; T. James Clarke; F.C.C. Boyd Collections; Ford XII (Stack's, 10/05), lot 40. (#20)

4   **1652 Pine Tree Sixpence—Environmental Damage—NCS. XF Details.** Noe-33, R.3. 32.4 gn. Although Noe-33 is the more common variety, all Pine Tree sixpences can rightfully be described as scarce. Silver and gunmetal-gray patina covers both sides, with areas of corrosion that give a brownish appearance. Nonetheless, the details are bold and the letters are particularly sharp. This popular Colonial is the "pellets at trunk" variety, and is listed on page 37 of the 2009 *Guide Book*. (#22)

Lovely XF Noe-6 1652 Pine Tree Shilling, Large Planchet

5   **1652 Pine Tree Shilling, Large Planchet XF40 PCGS.** Noe-6. 68.5 grains. Each side shows a pronounced wavy appearance from the rocker press, though the centers are well-defined nonetheless. Luminous and pleasing with intermingled gray-gold and silver-blue shadings across each side.
Ex: F.C.C. Boyd Collection; Ford XII (Stack's, 10/05), lot 91. (#23)

Extraordinary 1652 Pine Tree Shilling
Large Planchet, Noe-1, AU50

6   **1652 Pine Tree Shilling, Large Planchet AU50 PCGS.** Noe-1. 71.30 grains. The tree points to the second S in MASATHVSETS and the 5 in the date is centered below the second N in ENGLAND. The XII is closely spaced, while the 6 in the date is large, which is diagnostic for this variety. Pleasing gunmetal-gray patina covers the remarkably smooth and unabraded surfaces. This impressive piece has the typical wavy texture seen because of the rocker press used at the Massachusetts Mint. Besides being almost fully centered on the planchet, the strike is exceptionally sharp, with only trivial weakness at the bottom of each side. An attractive and above-average representative of this famous colonial issue. Listed on page 37 of the 2009 *Guide Book*. (#23)

Attractive AU 1652 Noe-2 Pine Tree Shilling

7   **1652 Pine Tree Shilling, Large Planchet AU50 PCGS.** Noe-2. 72.5 grains. Subtle silver-blue, violet, and green-gold tints embrace much of each side. Strongly lustrous beneath the toning and well-defined. Excellent quality in virtually every respect for a Noe-2 Pine Tree shilling, particularly in strike and centering, a theme also noted in the Ford catalog.
Ex: F.C.C. Boyd Collection; Ford XII (Stack's, 10/05), lot 78. (#23)

XF Details Pine Tree Shilling, Noe-29

8   **1652 Pine Tree Shilling, Small Planchet—Environmental Damage—NCS. XF Details.** Crosby 14-R, Noe-29, R.3. 71.0 gn. Deep olive-gray with peripheral dark russet patina. Mildly granular, and the central reverse has a few wispy hairlines. Some of the upper letters are softly brought up and are partly off the flan, but the overall strike is good. Listed on page 37 of the 2009 *Guide Book*. (#24)

Elusive American Plantations Restrike MS62

9   **(c. 1828) American Plantations 1/24 Part Real, Restrike MS62 NGC.** Newman 5-D. The die break through the A in FRAN is associated with the scarce restrike variety. Much of the initial silvery color is present, although the open fields and the horseman and rider are toned dark gray. Evenly impressed and only mildly granular. Struck a few degrees off center toward 3:30, affecting only the right-side dentils. Listed on page 39 of the 2009 *Guide Book*. (#52)

Popular (1694) London Elephant Token, Thick Flan, VF35

10 (1694) London Elephant Token, Thick Planchet VF35 PCGS. Breen-186, Hodder 2-B. Pleasing medium brown with streaks of darker steel toning on both sides. Traces of lamination are visible on the reverse, and both sides have a few rim bruises that are only mildly distracting. Listed on page 44 of the 2009 *Guide Book*. (#55)

11 1722 Rosa Americana Penny, UTILE AU50 PCGS. Breen-115. Rosette after 1722. A deep dove-gray penny with light wear on the king's cheek and other design highpoints. The surfaces have a few pinpoint mint-made flaws, but no marks are obvious. Listed on page 40 of the 2009 *Guide Book*. (#113)

12 1723 Rosa Americana Twopence AU50 PCGS. Breen-92. Stop after REX, no stop after date. Briefly circulated with substantial glimmers of luster on the golden-brown brass surfaces. Well-defined with only modest wear across the high points. Listed on page 41 of the 2009 *Guide Book*. (#128)

13 1722 Hibernia Halfpenny, Type One, Harp Left VF35 PCGS. Harp at Left. Breen-144. Nelson-3. Perfectly centered, the medium brown surfaces show even wear over the highpoints and are pleasing and abrasion-free. Listed on page 42 of the 2009 *Guide Book*. (#167)

14 1723 Hibernia Farthing, D:G:REX MS62 Brown PCGS. Nelson-6, Breen-169. The heavily abbreviated reverse is easily recognized. Well-defined with glossy chocolate-brown surfaces and rich eye appeal. Population: 7 in 62 Brown, 14 finer (8/08). (#173)

15 1723 Hibernia Farthing, DEI GRATIA MS63 Brown PCGS. Martin 2.1-Bc.1, R.5. The first G in GEORGIUS always has a small die break in the middle, and the E in HIBERNIA has the upper and lower serifs joined to the middle. There is also the usual die crack through the NIA in HIBERNIA that ends at the 1 in the date. These die flaws can typically identify this variety. Pleasing mahogany patina covers each side of the present piece, with a few patches of darker toning at the perimeter. The strike is sharp, and there are no marks visible to the unaided eye. A couple of slight blemishes are noted at the top of the reverse, but they do not affect the central design elements. Listed on page 42 of the 2009 *Guide Book*. (#176)

16 1723 Hibernia Farthing, DEI GRATIA MS64 Brown PCGS. Martin 2.1-Bc.4, R.4. Pleasing mahogany patina covers the surfaces with some small patches of coffee color near the legends. Although the luster is subdued by the brown patina, the harp is fully struck, which is exceptional considering that these pieces often have mushy details on the seated figure. Listed on page 42 of the 2009 *Guide Book*. (#176)

17 1723 Hibernia Halfpenny VF30 PCGS. Nelson-8, Breen-157. No pellet before H, small 3. Luminous walnut-brown surfaces are minimally marked with moderate wear. Solid eye appeal. Listed on page 43 of the 2009 *Guide Book*. (#180)

18 1723 Hibernia Halfpenny VF35 PCGS. Nelson-8, Breen-157, No pellet before H, small 3. A lovely Choice VF piece that shows only light to moderate wear across the well struck high points of the teak-brown surfaces. Listed on page 43 of the 2009 *Guide Book*. (#180)

19 1723 Hibernia Halfpenny XF45 PCGS. Nelson-8, Breen-157. No pellet before H, small 3. Rich chocolate-brown patina with only minor striking softness and trifling wear on the high points. The fields are well-preserved. Listed on page 43 of the 2009 *Guide Book*. (#180)

Exceptional Select 1724 Hibernia Halfpenny Martin 4.67-K.3, Stop After Date

20 1724 Hibernia Halfpenny MS63 Brown PCGS. Martin 4.67-K.3, R.2. Outstanding from the technical perspective, since the chocolate-brown fields and devices are essentially unabraded. A good strike with minor incompleteness on the tops of Hibernia's legs. A vertical flan flaw at 12:30 affects only the obverse. Lesser flaws are noted at 11 o'clock on the obverse and to the left of Hibernia's head. The obverse die is lightly clashed. Listed on page 43 of the 2009 *Guide Book*. Population: 1 in 63 Brown, 1 finer (4/08). (#190)

Important 1710-D French Colonies Double Sol, MS63

21 1710-D French Colonies 30 Deniers MS63 PCGS. Breen-280, Vlack-2, R.2. The present 30 deniers piece, also known as a "Mousquetaire" or double sol, is the only 1710-D certified as Mint State by PCGS. The John J. Ford Collection contained 32 double sols of various dates and mints from 1709 to 1713, yet only two of those were cataloged as Uncirculated. The finest 1710-D double sol in the Ford sale was just AU. While these French 30 deniers coins are seemingly commonplace in today's numismatic marketplace, we cannot overemphasize the importance of such a high quality example.

Evenly struck and satiny with ice-blue, tan-gold, and olive toning. The upper right obverse field is minutely granular and displays wispy marks, possibly as struck, but the remainder of this French colonies example is well preserved. Listed on page 51 of the 2009 *Guide Book*. (#158635)

22 1711-D French Colonies 30 Deniers AU55 PCGS. Only a trace of wear visits the mildly granular surfaces, which are draped in rich tan, green-gray, and umber shadings. Minimally marked and pleasing. Listed on pages 50-51 of the 2009 *Guide Book*. Population: 4 in 55, 1 finer (8/08). (#158686)

23 1712-AA French Colonies 15 Deniers AU55 PCGS. Breen-294, Vlack-13, R.4. Elements of silvering blend with copper-violet and steel-gray shadings. Pleasingly detailed with only a trace of actual wear. Listed on page 51 of the 2009 *Guide Book*. Population: 1 in 55, 2 finer (4/08). (#158628)

24 1738-A French Colonies Sou Marque AU53 PCGS. Light powder-gray peripheral elements cede to steel and violet-silver shadings in the centers. Well struck and highly attractive with only modest wear. Listed on pages 50-51 of the 2009 *Guide Book*. Population: 2 in 53, 7 finer (8/08). (#158658)

25 **1758-A French Colonies Sou Marque VF35 PCGS.** Breen-417, V-39a, R.5. Second semester with dot under the D in LUD. Problem-free for the grade, with ample silvering within the legends and design. A few flecks of debris ensure the originality. Listed on page 51 of the 2009 *Guide Book*. (#158604)

26 **1763-A French Colonies Sou Marque AU55 PCGS.** Breen-424, Vlack-47b, R.4. 2nd semester. A difficult date and mintmark combination, none were in the Ford auctions. Substantial almond-gold silvering remains. The open fields are steel-blue. The centers show slight inexactness of strike, but the peripheral legends and symbols are sharply impressed. Listed on page 51 of the 2009 *Guide Book*. (#158680)

27 **1767-A French Colonies Copper Sou VF20 PCGS.** Breen-700. Two-tone light and medium brown patina. Slight darkening outlines the legends, a few letters of which are faint due to the indifferent strike and subsequent wear. Not countermarked, an unusual state according to Breen. Listed on page 51 of the 2009 *Guide Book*. (#158651)

Remarkable 1767 French Colonies Sou, AU58 Uncounterstamped Example

28 **1767-A French Colonies Copper Sou AU58 PCGS. CAC.** Breen-700. No RF counterstamp. The 1767 copper sous primarily circulated in Louisiana and in the Caribbean. Those lacking the RF counterstamp are especially difficult to locate in any grade. Attractive medium brown surfaces with only slight high point wear, this piece is somewhat finer than Ford XIII, lot 27 that was called "far nicer than the vast majority of these known," although clearly lower quality than the "Choice Brilliant Proof" of lot 26 in that sale. Listed on page 51 of the 2009 *Guide Book*. (#158651)

29 **1773 Virginia Halfpenny, Period AU58 NGC.** Reverse with seven harpstrings. A lovely near-Mint example with smooth and lustrous chocolate-brown surfaces. (#240)

1773 Virginia Halfpenny, Period Newman 27-J, MS65 Brown

30 **1773 Virginia Halfpenny, Period MS65 Brown NGC.** Newman 27-J. Seven harp strings. The A in VIRGINIA is repunched. Despite the Brown designation, there is plenty of red remaining, especially on the reverse. A late die state of both dies, with the top of the first I in III mostly effaced and the 73 eroding away. Lustrous and essentially mark-free, listed on page 43 of the 2009 *Guide Book*. (#240)

31 **1773 Virginia Halfpenny, Period MS64 Red and Brown PCGS.** Newman 23-Q. More red than brown, although the king's cheek and the lower right corner of the shield are toned dark gray. Nicely struck and nearly unabraded. Listed on page 43 of the 2009 *Guide Book*. (#241)

32 **1760 Hibernia-Voce Populi Halfpenny XF40 PCGS.** Z. 4-B, N.2, R.3. The "corrected date" variety with the 6 changed from a 0. The violet-accented surfaces exhibit a degree of original luster; this minimally marked piece is graded from the surfaces rather than the strike, which is soft in the centers. Listed on page 47 of the 2009 *Guide Book*. (#262)

33 **1760 Hibernia-Voce Populi Halfpenny AU50 PCGS.** Z. 1-A, N.1, R.6. The very rare 'Child's Bust' variety. Evenly struck and well centered with all design details bold. The maroon fields are unabraded and only moderately granular. Listed on page 47 of the 2009 *Guide Book*. (#262)

34 **1760 Hibernia-Voce Populi Halfpenny AU50 PCGS.** Z. 2-A, N.4, R.1. A glossy mahogany-brown import copper with surfaces that appear undisturbed to the unaided eye. Thorough evaluation reveals inconspicuous wispy marks on the field near the harp. Listed on page 47 of the 2009 *Guide Book*. (#262)

35 **1760 Hibernia-Voce Populi Halfpenny AU53 PCGS.** Z. 2-A, N-4, R.1. Briefly circulated with heavy die crumbling at the periphery of the obverse. Pleasing olive-brown patina covers each side, with a few areas of darker color to the left of the bust. The obverse is well-centered but the last few letters of HIBERNIA are partially obscured at the edge. Listed on page 47 of the 2009 *Guide Book*. (#262)

36 **1788 Massachusetts Half Cent XF40 PCGS.** Ryder 1-B, R.2. This chocolate-brown half cent has moderate wear, but HALF CENT is clear. Minor laminations and minute planchet flaws are of mint origin. Listed on page 57 of the 2009 *Guide Book*. (#308)

37 **1788 Massachusetts Cent, Period VF35 PCGS.** Ryder 7-M, High R.4. A pleasing Choice VF example of this very scarce variety, well struck with few marks and attractive woodgrain patina. A lamination is noted at the L of WEALTH, and a light crack crosses the obverse figure. Listed on page 57 of the 2009 *Guide Book*. (#311)

38 **1788 Massachusetts Cent, Period AU53 PCGS.** Ryder 3-A, Low R.4. A charming walnut-brown commonwealth copper. Free from marks and evenly struck. The borders exhibit minor granularity, and a thin obverse planchet defect connects 4:30 to 6 o'clock. Listed on page 57 of the 2009 *Guide Book*. (#311)

39 **1785 Connecticut Copper, Bust Right AU50 NGC.** M. 4.4-C, R.3. A mahogany-brown piece with pleasing sharpness on the major devices. Well centered, all legends are intact aside from the very bottom of the date. The strike is soft on the lower left obverse and opposite on the upper right reverse. A minor rim bruise at 4 o'clock is noted, and the seated effigy has a number of small pits. Listed on page 58 of the 2009 *Guide Book*. (#316)

40 **1785 Connecticut Copper, African Head VF25 PCGS.** M. 4.1-F.4, R.1. Chocolate-brown fields contrast against lighter olive-gray devices. This well-centered piece has mostly smooth surfaces and is clearly defined save for the date. A lovely example of this popular variety. Listed on page 58 of the 2009 *Guide Book*. (#319)

41 **1787 Connecticut Copper, Horned Bust Left XF45 PCGS.** M. 4-L, R.1. Designated as a generic Mailed Bust Left variety by PCGS, but the "horn" is faintly evident in the lower left obverse field. In this relatively early die state, the horn is unattached to the bust. This ebony-brown piece is well centered and only moderately granular. Listed on page 59 of the 2009 *Guide Book*. (#349)

42 **1787 Connecticut Copper, Draped Bust Left VF25 PCGS.** M. 32.3-X.4, R.2. This well centered example has clear legends and a consistent strike. The fields are faintly granular but unabraded. The major devices have a couple of faded pinscratches. A suitable representative of the type. Listed on page 60 of the 2009 *Guide Book*. (#370)

43 **1787 Connecticut Copper, Draped Bust Left VF25 PCGS.** M. 33.20-Z.9, R.5. A rare variety which has the lower half of the colon following ETLIB on the edge of Liberty's gown. All legends are complete aside from the bottom of the date. A wispy flaw on the lower half of the Seated Liberty, but otherwise a splendid example for the grade. Listed on page 60 of the 2009 *Guide Book*. (#370)

44 **1787 Connecticut Copper, Draped Bust Left VF35 PCGS.** M. 33.16-Z.15, R.3. This unabraded state copper is mostly chocolate-brown, although the reverse border between 4 and 10 o'clock is lavender. Mildly granular in places, as made, but definition is clear aside from minor planchet voids near the head and waist of the seated Liberty. Listed on page 60 of the 2009 *Guide Book*. (#370)

45 **1787 Connecticut Copper, Draped Bust Left XF40 PCGS.** M. 37.8-HH, High R.5. This olive-brown representative has less circulation wear than the third party grade implies, but the strike is uneven, affecting the drapery of the bust and the head of the seated Liberty. The date is partly off the flan, but the surfaces are pleasing, without any abrasions or corrosion. Listed on page 60 of the 2009 *Guide Book*. *Ex: Pre-Long Beach Sale (Superior, 6/2000), lot 22.* (#370)

46 **1788 Connecticut Copper, Draped Bust Left XF40 PCGS.** M. 16.1-H, R.4. A close ET LIB helps identify the reverse, while the obverse has several diagnostics including a period after AUCTORI. Lovely medium brown patina drapes the surfaces, which have moderate porosity and a few minor marks. The lower left of the obverse is soft and INDE is partly obscured, but the rest of the details are crisp. Listed on page 60 of the 2009 *Guide Book*. (#409)

47 **1787 New Jersey Copper, Outlined Shield XF40 PCGS.** Maris 46-e, R.1. One of the more available New Jersey copper die pairs, notable for the wide legend NOVA CAESAREA. The surfaces are deep walnut-brown with striking areas of lighter mocha at the worn high points. Population: 26 in 40, 56 finer (8/08). (#503)

48 **1787 New Jersey Copper, Large Planchet, Plain Shield XF45 NGC.** Maris 62-q, R.3. A deep chestnut-brown state copper that has soft centers but is otherwise well struck. A thin streak beneath the horse's head was on the planchet before the strike. Listed on page 66 of the 2009 *Guide Book*. (#509)

Scarce AU PLURIBS 1787 New Jersey, Maris 60-p

49 **1787 New Jersey Copper, PLURIBS AU50 PCGS.** Maris 60-p, High R.4. The PLURIBS designation is absent on the PCGS insert. A high grade for this very scarce error legend subtype. Toned deep golden-brown and medium brown. The centers and right shield corner show the surface of the planchet prior to the strike. Listed on page 66 of the 2009 *Guide Book*. Population: 9 in 50, 19 finer (8/08). (#512)

50 **1788 New Jersey Copper, Head Left—Environmental Damage—NCS. Fine Details.** Maris 50-f, R.2. This well centered and boldly detailed medium brown example lacks any notable abrasions. Both sides are granular, but the central devices and legends are clear. A scarce Head Facing Left subtype. Listed on page 67 of the 2009 *Guide Book*. (#527)

51 **1786 Vermont Copper, VERMONTENSIUM—Damaged—NCS. XF Details.** RR-6, Bressett 4-D, R.2. The mahogany-brown fields and tan devices are moderately granular in places, and there are a few planchet flaws on each side. A shallow dig through the 8 in the date accounts for the "Damaged" modifier. Still, a crisply struck and affordable representative. Listed on page 68 of the 2009 *Guide Book*. (#545)

52 **1783 Nova Constellatio Copper, Pointed Rays, Small US XF40 PCGS.** Crosby 2-B, R.2. Boldly defined with pleasing medium olive surfaces. A few minor surface marks are expected for the grade, especially on these old colonials. Housed in a green-label holder. (#801)

53 **1783 Nova Constellatio Copper, Pointed Rays, Small US XF45 PCGS.** Crosby 2-B, R.2. A chocolate-brown piece that displays traces of luster within design recesses. The fields are nearly mark-free, although minute planchet defects are distributed. Listed on page 52 of the 2009 *Guide Book*. (#801)

54 **1787 Fugio Cent, STATES UNITED, 4 Cinquefoils, Pointed Rays Fine 15 PCGS. CAC.** Newman 6-W, R.4. A heavy die break near 7 o'clock on the reverse is characteristic of this scarce variety. A second die break nearly consumes the U in YOUR. A golden-brown circulated Fugio cent with inconspicuous gray verdigris on the reverse. Listed on page 83 of the 2009 *Guide Book*. (#883)

Important 1787 Newman 14-O Fugio, VF30

55 **1787 Fugio Cent, STATES UNITED, 4 Cinquefoils, Pointed Rays VF30 PCGS.** Newman 14-O, R.4. Although the surfaces are a bit dark, and slightly rough, the sharpness of this piece is clearly better than usual for the variety that normally comes only in Fine or lower grades. This example is only the third 14-O that we have handled since 1993, and the finest of the three coins. (#883)

56 **1787 Fugio Cent, STATES UNITED, 4 Cinquefoils, Pointed Rays VF30 PCGS. CAC.** Newman 22-M, R.5. This better variety walnut-brown representative is richly defined for the grade. A faded thin mark within the sun's rays is difficult to find. Struck several degrees off center toward 2 o'clock. The dies are widely rotated. Listed on page 83 of the 2009 *Guide Book*. (#883)

57 **1787 Fugio Cent, STATES UNITED, 4 Cinquefoils, Pointed Rays AU55 NGC.** Newman 13-X, R.2. The famous X or "WE / A RE / ONE" reverse. A luminous and minimally worn medium-brown example struck from a prominently clashed obverse. (#883)

Lovely 1787 Newman 13-X Fugio, MS65 Brown

58 **1787 Fugio Cent, STATES UNITED, 4 Cinquefoils, Pointed Rays MS65 Brown PCGS.** Newman 13-X, R.2. Undoubtedly the most plentiful single Fugio cent variety today, thanks to the New York Hoard that contained 726 examples of this die variety (44% of the entire hoard). It is probably the case that many of these coins, discovered in the 1850s, still survive in or near Mint State, providing many collectors with an opportunity to obtain a high quality example.

In *United States Fugio Copper Coinage of 1787* [Ypsilanti, MI: Jon Lusk, 2008], Eric Newman comments on the hoard: "Today, while Mint State Fugio coppers are seen as a glorious addition to a numismatist's cabinet, their very existence underlines their failure as a circulating medium."

This lovely copper has highly lustrous surfaces with deep chocolate color that is blended with considerable original red color, nearly enough to qualify for a "RB" designation. (#883)

Desirable 1787 Newman 10-T Fugio
AU50 1 over Horizontal 1

59   **1787 Fugio Cent, STATES UNITED, 1/Horizontal 1 AU50
PCGS.** Newman 10-T, R.5. The 1 over Horizontal 1 obverse is an
important and integral part of any Fugio cent collection, carrying its
own listing in the *Guide Book*. A late die state with heavy obverse
clash marks and a strong reverse crack from the border at 7 o'clock
across the ring to the label at the first S. Pleasing dark brown and
steel surfaces, the obverse and center of the reverse are sharp, the
peripheral reverse weaker, as usual for the variety. Superior quality
to John Ford's, lot 262 in Part I of the Stack's sales devoted to
the Ford Collection. Listed on page 83 of the 2009 *Guide Book*.
(#886)

MS62 Brown 1787 Fugio Cent
UNITED STATES, Cinquefoils, Newman 8-B

60   **1787 Fugio Cent, UNITED STATES, Cinquefoils MS62 Brown
NGC.** Newman 8-B, R.3. This satiny Fugio cent is medium brown
with tinges of faded red near design outlines. The strike is generally
sharp, with weakness isolated to the lower obverse margin and the
upper reverse border. The obverse has a couple of minor laminations,
as made. Listed on page 83 of the 2009 *Guide Book*. (#889)

Desirable 1787 Fugio Cent, UNITED STATES
Cinquefoils, Newman 8-B, MS64 Red and Brown

61   **1787 Fugio Cent, UNITED STATES, Cinquefoils MS64 Red
and Brown PCGS.** Newman 8-B. The O in FUGIO is low and
an ornament is located above the left side of the I in BUSINESS,
distinguishing the obverse. On the reverse, UNITED is left and
STATES is right, and the AR in ARE is recut. This piece, like all
others of this variety, shows heavy clash marks inside of the rings.
Charming mahogany and cherry-red patina graces both sides of this
carefully preserved representative. The strike is sharp, although
slightly off-center (perhaps 10%). An excellent example of the
famed Fugio Cent—one of the most popular and important issues in
the Colonial series, if not in all of American numismatics. Listed on
page 83 of the 2009 *Guide Book*. (#890)

Attractive 1787 Newman 19-Z Fugio, VF20

62   **1787 Fugio Cent, STATES UNITED, Raised Rim VF20 PCGS.**
Newman 19-Z, R.5. The Ford cataloger calls the reverse a "Production
Pattern Reverse," noting: "This reverse has been called a production
pattern because its design elements seem to have been entered into
the die by hand, unlike those on other Fugio reverses, suggesting
that it represents a stage in the development of the Fugio design
somewhere between the original hub layout and the regular run."
    Despite considerable wear, this surfaces are smooth with a two-
tone appearance, deeper brown in the fields and lighter brown on
the devices. (#895)

Scarce 1787 Newman 19-Z Fugio, VF25

63 **1787 Fugio Cent, STATES UNITED, Raised Rim VF25 PCGS. CAC.** Newman 19-Z, R.5. The reverse label has raised inner and outer rims. The Ford cataloger calls this the "So-Called 'Production Pattern' Reverse," but fails to explain further at lot 310 of the Ford catalog, Part I. The full explanation is actually found at lot 233 in the same catalog, an example of Newman 1-Z, called the "Production Pattern Issue."

This example has smooth surfaces with nicely blended olive and steel patina. Although somewhat worn, the major motifs are visible and complete. A few scattered surface marks and rim bruises are of little consequence. (#895)

64 **1787 Fugio Cent, Club Rays, Rounded Ends VF25 PCGS. CAC.** Newman 3-D, R.3. A moderately worn cocoa-brown example of this scarce subtype. A minute rim bruise is noted near 10 o'clock on the obverse, and a minor lamination is present near the F in FUGIO. Listed on page 84 of the 2009 Guide Book. (#904)

65 **1787 Fugio Cent, Club Rays, Rounded Ends VF30 NGC.** Newman 4-E, R.3. The O in YOUR is over the first S of BUSINESS. Despite moderate wear across the chocolate-brown surfaces, the overall eye appeal is strong. Listed on page 84 of the 2009 Guide Book. (#904)

66 **1787 Fugio Cent, Club Rays, Rounded Ends VF30 NGC.** Newman 3-D, R.3. This medium brown Fugio has pleasing detail, and the surfaces are unmarked aside from a minor rim nick on the reverse at 12:30. Listed on page 84 of the 2009 Guide Book. (#904)

67 **1787 Fugio Cent, Club Rays, Rounded Ends VF30 PCGS. CAC.** Newman 3-D. This impressively detailed Club Rays Fugio has medium brown centers and olive-gray borders. Slightly off center toward 3 o'clock, but all legends are intact. Both sides are evenly microgranular. Listed on page 84 of the 2009 Guide Book. Population: 18 in 30, 36 finer (8/08). (#904)

Lovely 1787 New Haven Restrike Fugio, MS65 Brown

68 **1787 Fugio Cent, New Haven Restrike, Copper MS65 Brown PCGS. CAC.** Newman 104-FF, copper, R.2. About a dozen 19th century "restrikes" of the Fugio cents were produced, and today they are highly desirable. Only the Newman 104-FF is generally available to collectors, as all other 19th century pieces are extremely rare. This wonderful Gem has lustrous olive surfaces with considerable original red color at the borders. The obverse is noticeably bulged from die sinking. A lovely a desirable colonial associated piece. (#916)

Choice VF 1787 Immunis Columbia, Eagle Reverse

69 **1787 Immunis Columbia Piece, Eagle Reverse VF35 PCGS.** Crosby Pl. VIII, 8. Breen-1137. An attractively detailed medium brown example of this very scarce Early American copper. Thorough study beneath a loupe locates occasional small marks. Listed on page 53 of the 2009 Guide Book. (#841)

70 **1789 Mott Token, Thick Planchet, Plain Edge AU58 PCGS.** Breen-1020. Well-defined on the obverse, though the reverse shows a degree of weakness and granularity, as usual. The chocolate-brown surfaces are glossy. Population: 13 in 58, 31 finer (8/08). (#603)

71 **1789 Mott Token, Thick Planchet, Plain Edge MS61 Brown PCGS.** Breen-1020. Once considered an 18th-century issue, the Mott Token has since been punch-linked to the Hard Times era of the 1830s. The golden-brown surfaces are well preserved aside from a solitary faded pinscratch in the right obverse field. The die break on the northwest corner of the clock is well advanced, and consumes the D in GOLD and a nearby ampersand. Well struck from rusted dies, as made. Listed on page 70 of the 2009 Guide Book. (#603)

Impressive MS64 Red Kentucky Token LANCASTER Edge, Breen-1156

72 **(1792-94) Kentucky Token, LANCASTER Edge MS64 Red PCGS.** Breen-1156. A beautiful dusky orange-gold near-Gem that has a few dashes of brown within the starry pyramid. No abrasions are present, although a thin, faint diagonal streak (as made) crosses JUST. Satiny and high grade for this widely collected 18th century token. Listed on page 71 of the 2009 Guide Book. *From The Aspen Collection.* (#625)

73 **1794 Franklin Press Token MS63 Brown PCGS.** Breen-1165. From early dies without any breaks within the press, although die chips are present near the R in LIBERTAS. Olive-brown with ample faded rose-gold and a couple of gray areas on the press. Listed on page 72 of the 2009 Guide Book. Population: 17 in 63 Brown, 6 finer (8/08). (#630)

74 **1783 Washington & Independence Cent, Large Military Bust AU58 PCGS.** Baker-4, R.1. Chocolate-brown patina covers both sides, which are mostly unmarked except for a trace of friction on the high points. Obverse Die Four, as indicated by the die crack through part of the legend that radiates from a larger break from the first N of INDEPENDENCE. The strike is razor sharp except for a little weakness on the seated figure on the reverse. Listed on page 75 of the 2009 Guide Book. (#667)

75 1783 **Washington Unity States Cent** AU58 PCGS. Baker-1, R.1. This chocolate-brown Washington piece is richly detailed, and has an attractively undisturbed obverse. The reverse field has faint pinscratches that do not fully remove the eye appeal. The borders have moderate roller marks, as made. Population: 14 in 58, 11 finer (3/08). (#689)

76 1793 **Washington Ship Halfpenny, Copper, Lettered Edge** AU53 PCGS. Baker-18, R.3. This chocolate-brown representative is pleasantly unabraded, and also lacks consequential carbon. The reverse die was apparently improperly annealed, since all examples seen have a bulged appearance on the central reverse and a raised border near 4 o'clock. Listed on page 79 of the 2009 *Guide Book*. (#734)

77 1795 **Washington Grate Halfpenny, Large Buttons, Reeded Edge** AU53 NGC. Baker-29AA. This well struck halfpenny is toned dark brown and has smooth surfaces save for a few thin marks on the field near the forehead. Listed on page 79 of the 2009 *Guide Book*. (#746)

Lovely (1795) Washington
Liberty & Security Penny, MS62 Brown

78 **Undated Washington Liberty & Security Penny** MS62 Brown NGC. Baker-30. Pleasing chocolate-brown patina endows the lightly abraded surfaces of this attractive specimen. The right obverse rim and the corresponding area on the reverse are flat, as typical seen, but the rest of the details are crisply defined. A popular piece designed by Thomas Wyon for Kempson & Sons in Birmingham, England. Listed on page 80 of the 2009 *Guide Book*. (#767)

Silvered Large Size Success Medal
Reeded Edge, Borderline Uncirculated

79 **Undated Washington Success Medal, Large Size, Reeded Edge, Silvered** AU58 PCGS. Baker-265B without the lengthy obverse die break through the nose, unlike most original large planchet examples. A bold dove-gray Washington piece with a pair of minor peripheral flan cracks and an area of dark toning on the central reverse. Listed on page 80 of the 2009 *Guide Book*, which states, "specimens with original silvering are rare and are valued 20% to 50% higher." (#788)

Select Mint State Success Medal
Small Size, Reeded Edge, Baker-267

80 **Undated Washington Success Medal, Small Size, Reeded Edge** MS63 Brown NGC. Baker-267. The present lot is the single finest certified reeded edge small size Washington Success medal. Light golden-brown and dove-gray toning drapes the nicely struck surfaces. Thin marks on the reverse border near SUCCESS TO THE emerge beneath a loupe. Listed on page 80 of the 2009 *Guide Book*. (#783)

Garrett's '1796' Washington Repub
Ameri Cent, MS64 Brown

81 1796 **REPUB AMERI** MS64 Brown PCGS. CAC. Baker-69. Closely related to the American colonial series, the Repub Ameri pieces are named for the lettering that appears on the scroll at the center of the reverse. The obverse has a bust of Washington facing right, with GEORGE WASHINGTON in large letters above, and BORN FEB 11 1732 DIED Dc 21 1799 in small letters below. The reverse has three lines of inscription around the small central motif: GENl OF THE AMERICAN ARMIES 1775, RESIGNd THE COMMd [sic] 1783 / ELECd PRESIDENT OF THE UNITED STATES 1789 / RESIGNED THE PRESIDENCY 1796.

Perhaps the latest date on the reverse led the Garrett cataloger to conclude that these pieces "were first issued in 1796," but that is clearly incorrect, as the date of Washington's death would have been unknown at the time. At least one example of Baker-69 is seen struck over a 1797 British penny, and they were apparently struck early in the 19th century.

A splendid, lightly mirrored Proof, as issued, with deep brown surfaces and a few minor spots. An attractive and highly desirable Washington piece.

Ex: Garrett Collection; Johns Hopkins University (Bowers and Ruddy, 3/1981), lot 1759.

Brasher Regulated 1747 Brazil 6400 Reis, VG

82 **Undated Brasher New York Regulation Counterstamp, VG, holed, Uncertified.** Stamped on a 1747 Brazil 6400 reis gold coin, 195.4 grains, and holed at the center, probably by someone at a later date to remove a quantity of gold, much like other pieces were clipped for the same purpose. The hole in this piece seems to have removed approximately 25 grains of gold. That would place the earlier weight at just a few grains over the 216-grain New York standard for an $8 gold coin. The EB counterstamped gold coins are an integral part of the 18th century colonial series.

Important EB Counterstamped 1749 British Guinea, VF

83 **Undated Brasher New York Regulation Counterstamp, VF Uncertified.** Stamped on a 1749 British Guinea, 125 grains, VF, clipped at the bottom edge. Most or all known EB counterstamped coins have some type of clipping, or other damage such as the holed piece in this sale. Brasher was clearly accomplished and careful in his regulation skills, but soon afterwards, contemporary persons set about removing small amounts of the metal as a sort of savings plan. Since these coins traded at weight, such activities hardly affected future valuations. Today, all of the EB counterstamped gold coins, whether holed, clipped, or perfect, are highly collectible windows into the 18th century commercial world.

Desirable 1820 North West Company Token, VG10

84 **1820 North West Brass VG10 PCGS. CAC.** Breen-1083. Holed at 12 o'clock, as issued. Nearly every known survivor has a hole at 12 o'clock to aid suspension on a ribbon or neckpiece. Furthermore, nearly every known survivor is well worn and somewhat corroded like this piece. About evenly divided into brassy olive-yellow and deep steel-gray, with the latter present on the devices and nearby portions of the fields. Listed on page 74 of the 2009 *Guide Book*. (#952)

HALF CENTS

85 **1793—Corroded—ANACS. VG Details, Net AG3.** C-2, B-2, R.3. A popular first-year half cent, the Cohen-2 is also the second scarcest variety of the year. Although corroded, this piece has fully visible details and letters save for a partially obscured LIBERTY. The fields are deep brown, which contrasts against the lighter devices. Despite corrosion, this piece would make a nice and relatively affordable type coin. EAC 3. (#1000)

Popular 1793 Half Cent, C-3, Fine Sharpness

86 **1793—Corroded—NCS. Fine Details.** C-3, B-3, R.3. Although difficult to discern because of the corrosion, the fraction in the denomination is crowded between the ribbons, and the second A in AMERICA touches the right stem. The obverse is identified by the small 7 in the date and the low L in LIBERTY, which is closely spaced to the hair. Deep chocolate-brown covers the surfaces, with lighter areas of patination on the devices. This piece exhibits heavy corrosion, but a lot of the details are still visible. EAC 2. (#1000)

Lovely 1793 Half Cent, VF20 Details, C-4

Popular 1793 Half Cent, C-3, VF30

87 **1793—Corroded, Cleaned—ANACS. VF20 Details.** C-4, B-4, R.3. LIBERTY is positioned low on this variety, and the wreath's stems are the longest of any variety for the year. Delightful mahogany patina covers both sides of this first-year issue. Pitting is visible around LIBERTY, which accounts for the corroded moniker. Evenly worn, there is outstanding detail particularly on the reverse, where every berry is fully defined. EAC 10.
From The Jerry Kochel Collection. (#1000)

88 **1793 VF30 NGC.** C-3, B-3, R.3. Only four varieties of 1793 half cents are known, and Cohen-3 is considered to be third in the emission sequence. The obverse of this variety is identified by a small 7 in the date and a low L in LIBERTY. On the reverse, the fraction bar is long and crowded between the ribbons. A total 35,334 half cents were struck in 1793 for all four varieties, and the C-3 ranks behind the C-4 in terms of availability. All examples are highly desirable because of their status as the first half cents struck at the newly opened Mint.

This specimen has lovely olive-brown surfaces with scattered abrasions and minimal porosity. There are no marks of any significance, with a small planchet defect on the reverse at the first T in STATES noted. Despite traces of localized weakness and a few areas of die rust, this is a crisply struck and well-preserved example with nearly full border beads on each side. EAC 12.
From The Menlo Park Collection. (#1000)

18   Please visit *HA.com* to view other collectibles auctions

A 15% Buyer's Premium ($9 min.) Applies To All Lots

Exceptional 1793 C-3, B-3 Half Cent, MS60 Brown

89 **1793 MS60 Brown NGC.** C-3, B-3, R.3. Breen State III with considerable reverse die rust through much of the wreath. Manley only records a single die state for the variety. The bust of Liberty on the obverse has a hooked bust line, and the reverse has the U and A crowding the stems. These features combine for immediate attribution of the variety.

The 1793 half cents were the first of the denomination coined at a young Philadelphia Mint, and they followed the Chain and Wreath cents into production. Mint records indicate that 35,334 pieces were minted, and each of the four die varieties were probably struck in about equal numbers, considering that the rarities are nearly identical.

Breen believed that the 7,000 coins delivered on July 20, 1793, represented the entire production of C-1, and that the 3,400 of September 18, 1793, represented the final examples of C-4. That left 24,934 coins delivered on July 26, for all of C-2, C-3, and the balance of C-4. A mintage of about 9,500 to 10,000 coins each seems to be about right for C-2 and C-3.

This delightful example has satiny medium brown surfaces with a few tiny rim bumps, but no other problems on either side. Some might consider the obverse planchet marks and laminations to be "problems," but they are exclusively mint-made and have no actual affect on the grade. This piece almost reaches the Condition Census for the variety, and is easily among the top 10. EAC 50. (#1000)

90 **1794—Damaged—NCS. VG Details.** Large Letters Edge, C-1a, B-1a, R.3. A well worn example that someone apparently attempted to puncture, with a circular device, unsuccessfully; presumably in order to create a piece of jewelry. Light porosity is noted across both sides. EAC 2. (#1003)

Late State 1794 C-4, B-6b Half Cent, VF20

91 **1794 VF20 PCGS.** C-4, B-6b, R.3. Apparently one of the latest die states with heavy clash marks and evidence of reverse cracks, although the die crack from M to a berry is not apparent. Relatively plentiful as a variety, but generally only found in lower grades. Pleasing medium olive surfaces with some minor marks attributed solely to circulation, and entirely consistent with the grade. EAC 12. *From The Nora Bailey Collection.* (#1003)

Wonderful 1794 Half Cent, C-9, XF40

92 **1794 XF40 NGC.** B-9, C-9, R.2. The Cohen-7, 8, and 9 varieties are peculiar in that the head is struck in noticeably high relief, which is apparent even on worn specimens. The reverse is identified by the T in CENT, which leans left, and by the "heavy" (tightly spaced) wreath. Wonderful light brown patina endows the surfaces of this lovely representative. Myriad abrasions cover both sides, but none merit specific mention. The high points are soft, as often seen, but the details are fully outlined. An attractive example of this interesting variety. EAC 20. *From The Menlo Park Collection.* (#1003)

93 **1795 Plain Edge, Punctuated Date VG8 NGC.** C-4, B-4, R.3. Manley Die State 2.0 with HALF CENT illegible. Medium brown with a slightly darker shade on the lower right obverse. Remarkably problem-free for the grade. EAC 6. (#1012)

94 **1795 Plain Edge, Punctuated Date VF20 PCGS.** C-4, B-4, R.3. The central reverse is weak as almost always on this variety. Both sides have pleasing medium brown surfaces with deeper steel and pale bluish-gray toning. EAC 12. *From The Menlo Park Collection.* (#1012)

95 **1795 Plain Edge, No Pole—Improperly Cleaned—NCS. VG Details.** Thin Planchet, C-6a, B-6a, R.2. A smooth, evenly toned example with the date moderately worn but still faintly evident. The NCS assessment of the piece as "improperly cleaned" seems overly harsh, but there is light porosity noted on the upper reverse. Other than a pitted indention along the lower reverse edge, near 7 o'clock, there are no other individually notable marks on either side. EAC 5. (#1018)

Lovely 1795 C-6a, B-6a Half Cent, XF45

96 **1795 Plain Edge XF45 PCGS.** C-6a, B-6a, R.3. The obverse has a faint trace of a bulge right of Y. This lovely piece has smooth olive surfaces with a few splashes of darker steel and lighter tan. The surfaces are remarkably free of imperfections for the grade. Apparently on "rolled copper" stock, with no trace of undertype. EAC 25. *From The Nora Bailey Collection.* (#1018)

Desirable 1796 C-2, B-2 With Pole Half Cent, AG3

97 **1796 With Pole AG3 PCGS.** C-2, B-2, R.4. The 1796 half cents, both the With Pole and No Pole varieties, are the classic key-date issues of the denomination. Only about 100 With Pole coins and a couple dozen No Pole coins are known in all grades, and they are seldom seen above Good. The example that is now offered is a delightful piece for the grade, with dark brown surfaces and a few old obverse and reverse scratches that are entirely blended with the surrounding surface. The obverse is absolutely full Good, while the reverse is nearly smooth, typical of the issue with a strong obverse and weaker reverse. PCGS has assigned a grade that undoubtedly takes into account the appearance of both sides, and in this regard is the same approach used for our grade of EAC 3. (#1027)

Late State 1797 C-1, B-1a Half Cent, VF20

98 **1797 1 Above 1, Plain Edge VF20 PCGS.** C-1, B-1a, R.2. Late die states of this variety are extremely difficult to grade, due to the weakness associated with the extensive die cracks and bulges. The obverse die is shattered with TY of LIBERTY entirely absent. The lower right reverse is similarly absent due to the obverse die damage. This is a delightful dark olive example with excellent surfaces. EAC 20. *From The Nora Bailey Collection.* (#1042)

Important 1797 C-3a, B-3c Half Cent, Fine 12 Struck Over Spoiled Cent

99 **1797 Plain Edge Fine 12 PCGS.** C-3a, B-3c, R.4. The same die combination with the Low Head obverse was used for three sub-varieties, with either a plain edge, lettered edge, or gripped edge. Breen claims that all of those coins were actually struck in 1800, from backdated dies. They were apparently all struck on spoiled cent stock (misstruck or error large cents that were unsuitable for use). Indeed, this piece shows just such an undertype in the form of large dentils on Liberty's neck and inside the wreath. The surfaces are pleasing with light olive color, deeper brown on the devices. The surfaces are smooth with few imperfections on each side. *From The Nora Bailey Collection.* EAC 8. (#1036)

100 **1797 Plain Edge VF25 NGC.** C-1, B-1, R.2. Manley Die State 3.0. This interesting variety is easily identified by the second 1 that is punched directly above the 1 in the date due to an engraver's miscalculations. Smooth tan-brown fields show lovely contrast against the slightly deeper chocolate-brown devices. HALF is a little weak, but the rest of the legends are sharp, as are most of the denticles. A charming piece with no bothersome marks or blemishes. *From The Menlo Park Collection.* EAC 12. (#1036)

Fascinating 1797 C-2, B-2 Half Cent, VF30

101 **1797 Plain Edge VF30 PCGS.** C-2, B-2, R.4. A late die state with a reverse crack extending from below the 2 to the tops of UN and the border over I. An intriguing mark at the top of the Y in LIBERTY may deserve close study, as it is possibly an undertype from a cut-down large cent. Wonderful light tan and pale blue toning on both sides accompany the smooth and pleasing surfaces of this piece. EAC 20. *From The Nora Bailey Collection.* (#1036)

Debut 1800 Draped Bust Half Cent, C-1, B-1, AU58

102 **1800 AU58 PCGS.** C-1, B-1, R.1. The first year of Draped Bust half cent coinage is readily available due to hoard discoveries, nearly all in late die states such as this piece. The surfaces are dark steel with considerable luster still remaining on both sides. The central obverse and reverse are nicely struck up, with typical weakness at the borders. A few minor imperfections are evident on each side. EAC 45. (#1051)

Outstanding 1802/0 C-2, B-2 Half Cent, Fine 12

103 **1802/0 Reverse of 1802 Fine 12 PCGS.** C-2, B-2, R.3. A single 1802/0 obverse die was used for both varieties, the extremely rare Reverse of 1800 and the scarce Reverse of 1802. Typically, examples of either variety are low grade, dark, and porous, but this coin is hardly typical. It has extremely smooth medium brown surfaces with traces of maroon in the fields. As always, the reverse has HALF CENT weak, but it is mostly readable. EAC 10. *From The Nora Bailey Collection.* (#1057)

Rare Late State 1803 C-2, B-2 Half Cent, VG8

104 **1803 VG8 PCGS.** C-2, B-2, R.4. Breen Die State IV, Manley State 2.0. The reverse has a faint crack through the tops of ATES OF AMERIC, a die state called "extremely rare" by Walter Breen, and "Rare" by Ron Manley. Although it appears recolored, this is a wonderful example for the grade, with smooth, problem free surfaces, aside from the usual grade-consistent abrasions. EAC 5.
From The Nora Bailey Collection. (#1060)

Elusive 1803 C-1, B-1 Half Cent, MS65 Brown

105 **1803 MS65 Brown NGC.** C-1, B-1, R.1. Among coins that are part of the Draped Bust half cent series, 1800, 1804, and 1806 are the only dates that regularly come in Mint State grades. The best 1802 is XF, and 1803, 1805, and 1808 are each about equally rare in MS60 or finer, while 1807 is a bit more plentiful.

This 1803 C-1 variety, NGC certified MS65 Brown, is an amazing example of the date and variety. Both sides have a nice impression, and the surfaces are exceptional, with dark olive color and splashes of deeper steel patina. Census: 2 in 65 Brown, 0 finer (7/08). EAC 55. (#1060)

106 **1804 Plain 4, No Stems AU58 NGC.** C-13, B-10, R.1. Chocolate-brown with mottled olive and steel color. A pleasing example of this popular *Guide Book* variety. EAC 45.
From The Menlo Park Collection. (#1063)

107 **1804 Spiked Chin—Cleaned—ANACS. VF20 Details.** C-6, B-6, R.2. Braig State 9.0, Manley State 12. The latest state known for the 1804 C-6 half cent, with extensive rim breaks around the reverse. Perhaps cleaned and recolored, now with pleasing tan surfaces. EAC 12.
From The Jerry Kochel Collection. (#1066)

108 **1804 Spiked Chin VF35 ANACS.** C-6, B-6, R.2. Braig State 7.2, Manley State 10.2. A late intermediate die state. Pleasing dark brown surfaces with slightly lighter tan on the devices. EAC 20.
From The Jerry Kochel Collection. (#1066)

109 **1804 Spiked Chin VG10 PCGS.** C-7, B-5, High R.4. Manley Die State 3.0, "extremely rare." The rarest of the Spiked Chin die marriages. A lovely collector-grade medium brown half cent with pleasing surfaces. All legends are bold, and some hair detail is present. EAC 6. Population: 1 in 10, 1 finer (8/08). (#1075)

110 **1804 Spiked Chin AU53 PCGS.** C-6, B-6, R.2. Braig State 8.0. Manley State 11.0. Manley calls this the "second most common state." Pleasing medium brown is blended with some olive and steel, darker patina at the fraction. EAC 30.
From The Nora Bailey Collection. (#1075)

1805 C-3, B-3 Small 5, Stems, Fine 15

111 **1805 Small 5, Stems Fine 15 PCGS.** C-3, B-3, R.4. Manley State 2.0. A bulge in the right obverse field is clearly visible, indicative of the later die state. A glass reveals a few faint lines and marks, but the overall appearance is excellent, especially for this elusive issue that is normally found in low grade, with rough and porous surfaces. A splendid specimen. EAC 10.
From The Nora Bailey Collection. (#1087)

Census Level 1805 C-2, B-2 Small 5 Stems Half Cent, XF40

112   1805 Small 5, Stems XF40 PCGS. C-2, B-2, Low R.6. This is an important example of the rarest 1805 half cent. It is also one of the rarest Draped Bust half cent varieties. Only five varieties in the 1800 to 1808 series are considered Rarity-6 or 7, including 1802 C-1 (about 20 known), 1804 C-2 (13 or 14 known), 1805 C-2 (perhaps 27 or 28 known), 1806 C-3 (about 25 known), and 1808 C-1 (seven known).

One other listing, the 1804 C-3, is known by a total of just five or six pieces. However, this die combination is considered by most to be an early die state of 1804 C-5, and not a legitimate variety.

This specimen ranks high in the Condition Census, possibly second finest known but certainly third finest. A single example approaches XF, serves as the Breen plate coin, and remains tucked away in an advanced private collection. Next in line is an example that is almost as sharp, but has been cleaned, according to Breen. That piece is also plated in Breen's *Half Cent Encyclopedia*, for State I.

The piece that is offered here is nearly as sharp as the second example listed in Breen, but has not been cleaned. Rather, the surfaces are fully original with light tan and olive on the obverse, and mahogany and tan on the reverse. This piece does have a few minor dents on Liberty, and minor hairlines on each side, so it is unclear if it is second or third finest known in the absence of side-by-side comparison of the two coins. Slight doubling is visible on the obverse, along Liberty's neck and chin, the hair ribbons, and the bottoms of LIBERTY, essentially the same as a double profile. EAC 20.
From The Nora Bailey Collection. (#1087)

Pleasing 1805 Half Cent, Large 5, Stems, C-4, MS63 Brown

113   1805 Large 5, Stems MS63 Brown PCGS. C-4, B-4, R.2. A large 5 in the date and stems at the bottom of the wreath identify this variety. This piece is Breen Die State VI, as evidenced by the numerous cracks and die rust spots on the obverse and the multiple clash marks on the reverse. Charming mahogany patina drapes the surfaces of this remarkably clean specimen. A small blemish on Liberty's cheek is barely worthy of mention. The strike is bold and the eye appeal is great. Breen (1983) wrote that this variety is "common enough in ordinary grade, but of the highest rarity in true mint state." Population: 1 in 63 Brown, 2 finer (8/08). EAC 55. (#1090)

114   1806 Small 6, No Stems AU58 PCGS. C-1, B-3, R.1. Peripheral weakness is typical of the variety. The obverse has pleasing light tan and medium olive, with tan and darker olive on the reverse. A lovely example. EAC 50.
From The Nora Bailey Collection. (#1093)

115   1806 Large 6, Stems MS61 Brown PCGS. C-4, B-4, R.1. Manley Die State 1.0 with clear repunching on the top of the 6. A lustrous half cent with lovely olive-green, gold, lavender, and powder-blue patina. A few leaves and the final S in STATES are incompletely brought up, and the right obverse has a few small dark gray planchet flaws. EAC 50. (#1099)

116   1806 Large 6, Stems MS61 Brown NGC. C-4, B-4, R.1. Localized strike weakness is evident on the end of the drapery and on the forehead is opposite similar reverse weakness at the upper left and lower right branch. An attractive light brown example with deeper steel patina on the highpoints, and faint traces of original mint red close to the devices. EAC 55.
From The Menlo Park Collection. (#1099)

117   1807 XF45 PCGS. C-1, B-1, R.1. A typical late die state with absent border dentils, and prominent flowlines. Dark brown with hints of maroon patina. EAC 25.
From The Nora Bailey Collection. (#1104)

118   1808/7—Obverse Scratched—NCS. VF Details. C-2, B-2, R.3. Manley Die State 1.0. A faded diagonal obverse scratch from 9 o'clock to 6 o'clock corresponds to the NCS designation. A less important pinscratch extends from the ear to the eye. A nicely detailed medium brown half cent. EAC 8. (#1110)

119   1808/7 VF25 PCGS. C-2, B-2, R.3. Incorrectly labeled by PCGS as an 1808 Normal Date half Cent. A pleasing piece with medium olive surfaces. EAC 12.
From The Nora Bailey Collection. (#1110)

120   1808 AU53 NGC. C-3, B-3, R.1. A lovely late state example with olive and darker brown patina on each side. EAC 25. (#1107)

121   1809/6 AU58 PCGS. C-5, B-5, R.1. Technically an 1809 over Inverted 9, but the "1809/6" labeled has been associated with the variety for too many years to change now. Splendid light tan surfaces with a circle of darker olive on the obverse. EAC 50.
From The Nora Bailey Collection. (#1126)

122   1810 XF45 PCGS. C-1, B-1, R.2. Dark brown with traces of surface roughness, as often seen on these pieces. A lovely example of a single-variety date. EAC 35.
From The Nora Bailey Collection. (#1132)

123 **1810 AU55 NGC.** C-1, B-1, R.2. The only variety known. Pleasing chocolate-brown patina covers the surfaces of this sharply defined piece. Close inspection reveals no significant marks or blemishes. An attractive representative. EAC 40. (#1132)

124 **1811 Fine 15 PCGS.** C-2, B-2, R.3. A delightful 1811 half cent, representing a key-date in the Classic Head series. Pleasing surfaces exhibit dark olive and steel toning. EAC 12.
From The Nora Bailey Collection. (#1135)

125 **1828 13 Stars MS65 Brown PCGS.** C-3, B-2, R.1. A lustrous light olive example with prominent dark steel on the obverse and iridescence on the reverse. EAC 55.
From The Menlo Park Collection. (#1147)

126 **1855 MS64 Red and Brown PCGS.** C-1, B-1, R.1. This crisply struck near-Gem has a mostly brown obverse, although crimson-red outlines the stars and portrait. The reverse is principally orange-red, although portions of the field have mellowed to lilac-gray. A small spot in front of the nose is the sole detraction. EAC 60+. (#1234)

127 **1855 MS65 Red and Brown PCGS.** C-1, B-1, R.1. Crimson color is especially extensive on the reverse. Well struck in the centers, while the right obverse border has minor softness. A virtually unabraded Gem. Absolutely free of the usual spots associated with the hoard examples. Encapsulated in a first generation PCGS holder. EAC 63. Population: 18 in 65, 0 finer (8/08).
From The Menlo Park Collection. (#1234)

128 **1855 MS65 Red and Brown PCGS.** C-1, B-1, R.1. Primarily violet-brown, though enough reddish-orange shows at the margins to justify the Red and Brown designation. Smooth surfaces host pleasingly detailed central devices. Population: 18 in 65 Red and Brown, 0 finer (8/08). EAC 60.
From The Bell Collection. (#1234)

129 **1855 MS63 Red PCGS. CAC.** C-1, B-1, R.1. The only variety known. Attractive red patina covers both sides of this lustrous piece. A couple of small blemishes on the obverse and a number of flecks on the reverse are noted, although there are virtually no abrasions on each side. Encapsulated in a first generation PCGS holder. EAC 63. (#1235)

130 **1855 MS64 Red PCGS.** C-1, B-1, R.1. Bright orange and red patina drapes both sides, with charming cherry-red luster in the fields. There are several grade-defining blemishes and flecks, but a loupe reveals only a few nearly imperceptible handling marks. A couple of stars are weakly struck, but the details are otherwise fully defined. One of just 56,500 pieces minted. EAC 65. (#1235)

Bright Red 1856 C-1 Half Cent, MS64 Red

131 **1856 MS64 Red PCGS.** C-1, B-2a, R.1. Among the 1849 to 1857 series of circulation strike half cents, only 1854, 1855, and 1857 are seen with any frequency in fully brilliant red Mint State preservation, due to several hoards of those dates. All other dates are major rarities in full red. PCGS has only certified nine submissions as MS64 Red, and just two finer examples, including resubmissions over 22 years. This piece is fully brilliant and sharply detailed with a few minor spots on each side to prevent a higher grade. EAC 63. (#1238)

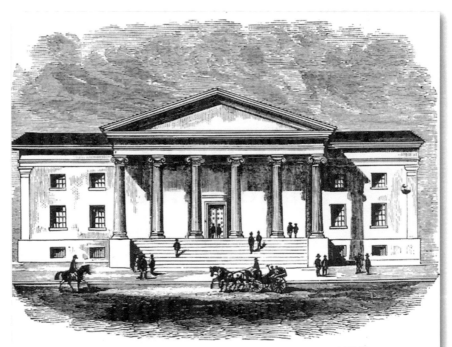

THE UNITED STATES MINT, PHILADELPHIA.—Erected 1829–30.

A view of the Philadelphia Mint, the second Mint building, erected in 1829 and 1830 and used until 1901.

Extremely Rare 1832 C-2, B-2 Half Cent, PR64 Brown

132 **1832 PR64 Brown PCGS.** C-2, B-2, R.7 as a proof. Housed in a first-generation PCGS holder. Only seven or eight proofs of this variety are known, and less than 20 proofs of all three varieties exist, according to information in Walter Breen's *Half Cent Encyclopedia.* While that reference is out-of-date today, the Census information still provides an excellent indication of rarity.

Breen lists the following in his Census:

1. Mougey Collection (Thomas Elder, 9/1910), lot 316; Lyman H. Low; Essex Numismatics; later, Breen Plate Coin.
2. Alison Jackman (Henry Chapman (2/1918), lot 887; David W. Valentine (Thomas Elder, 12/1927), lot 536a; Hillyer Ryder (New Netherlands, 44th Sale, 6/1954); , lot 310; Philip Showers; Willis duPont; private collection.
3. New Netherlands, 51st Sale; Stack's (3/1975), lot 851; Missouri Cabinet.
4. T. James Clarke (Abe Kosoff (4/1956), lot 464; Norweb Collection.
5. Brobston Collection; Stack's, 1/1963 FPL.
6. Connecticut State Library.
7. Henry C. Miller Collection (Thomas Elder, 4/1917), lot 1058.
8. Bruce Abrash.

We are certain that this piece is different from numbers 1, 3, 4, and 6. It should be easy to identify, with several toning spots on both sides. The fields are mildly reflective, with light cameo contrast. An exquisite example that is sharply struck from perfect dies, this piece has amazing lime-green, gold, and lilac toning. EAC PR60. (.#1195)

Desirable 1843 B-1a Original Half Cent, PR58

133   **1843 Original PR58 NGC.** B-1a, R.6. Two different die states are described in Breen's *Half Cent Encyclopedia* for the Large Berries proofs, and classified as Originals or Series VII Restrikes depending on the die state, early or late respectively. The only difference between the die states involves short die file marks near stars 2 and 12, either bold or faint. Breen also discusses a early and late reverse states, and refers the reader to page 424 of his reference, but page 424 describes an entirely different die.

This piece appears to be an earlier die state with bold obverse file marks. The coin is boldly struck with dark brown surfaces, slightly lighter on the reverse. The fields are slightly reflective, and the overall appearance is pleasing. EAC PR55. (#1266)

Elusive 1843 'Original' Half Cent, PR64 Brown

134   **1843 Original PR64 Brown PCGS.** B-1a, R.6. The large berries in the wreath identify the "Original" Braided Hair half cents, a group that also includes some coins that Breen called "Series VII" restrikes. The strength of die file marks at stars 2, 3, and 12 were the distinguishing feature, and they are quite bold on this piece. It is boldly detailed, although with somewhat dull fields that only show slight reflectivity. Some minor surface marks should aid in provenance research. It is believed that less than two dozen of these coins still exist today. EAC PR60. (#1266)

Seldom-Offered 1855 Half Cent, PR62 Brown

135   **1855 PR62 Brown PCGS.** C-1, B-1, R.5 as a proof. The only variety known. Breen (1983) estimates that just 35 to 40 proofs survive. Lovely olive-brown patina envelops both sides of this fully struck representative. The highly reflective fields have a few minuscule contact marks, along with scattered flecks. In nearly 15 years of record-keeping, this will be only the 12th offering of this rare issue by Heritage at auction. A wonderful opportunity to acquire a seldom-seen proof half cent. Population: 2 in 62, 10 finer (7/08). EAC PR60. (#1326)

136   **1793 Chain AMERICA—Corroded—NCS. XF Details.** S-3, B-4, Low R.3. This variety is distinguished by a high R in LIBERTY, which is closely spaced to the T. On the reverse, AMERICA is spelled out. Although corroded on both sides, there are areas where the surfaces are remarkably smooth or only minutely porous. The sharpness is impressive, and corrosion does not obscure any of the design elements. The chain and denomination are boldly impressed, and Liberty is fully defined. At first glance the chocolate-brown surfaces appear quite pleasing, and only under a loupe does the corrosion appear significant. Scattered marks are typical for the grade, and none merit individual mention. Chain cents, the nation's first regular issue coins, were struck for just a few months in 1793 until they were replaced by the Wreath design. While contemporaries complained that the chain was emblematic of slavery, modern day collectors treasure these important pieces of numismatic history. EAC 20. (#1341)

137   **1793 Chain, AMERICA, Periods, S-4, B-5, R.3—Corroded—NCS. XF Details.** The initial type struck by the First Philadelphia Mint was the Chain cent. Within a few short months, a wreath replaced the chain, which had been criticized as "an ill omen for Liberty." East Coast denizens of the day spent the pieces, and those continued to circulate until the design was nearly unrecognizable. Relatively few Chain cents have bold legends. The date, in particular, rapidly became faint upon repeated use in commerce. The present dark brown piece has minor marks on the profile, and the fields are finely granular with occasional small clumps of verdigris. However, it has full legends and rich hair detail, features prized by the Early American collector. EAC 8. (#91341)

138   **1793 Wreath, Vine and Bars, S-8, B-13, R.3—Corroded, Damaged—ANACS. AG3 Details.** Horizontal stem parallel to the date. The bow is high and triangular. Semi-bright reddish-yellow surfaces are porous and have been polished, and reveal a few digs on each side. An outline of most of the central devices shows. EAC 2. (#1347)

Popular 1793 Vine & Bars Wreath Cent, S-8, VF Details

139 **1793 Wreath Cent, Vine and Bars, S-8, B-13, R.3—Corroded— NCS. VF Details.** The stem of the sprig is mostly horizontal, which is diagnostic for the obverse. A triangular bow with a slightly concave top identifies the reverse. Deep mahogany patina endows the surfaces and complements the well-detailed devices. Both sides are moderately porous for the most part, although there are several areas of pronounced corrosion. A relatively affordable example of this popular early cent. EAC 5. (#1347)

Delightful 1793 Wreath Cent, Vine and Bars, S-9, VF20

140 **1793 Wreath Cent, Vine and Bars VF20 ANACS.** S-9, B-12, R.2. An excellent choice for a type collector, Sheldon-9 is the most frequently encountered Wreath cent variety and can be obtained at a relatively affordable price. The obverse of S-9 is easily identified by the stem of the sprig below the bust, which runs parallel the top of the date. On the reverse, the bow has a distinctive kidney shape. The charming mahogany surfaces of the present piece exhibit uniform light to moderate porosity, which is typical of many early coppers. A minor rim bruise at 7 o'clock on the reverse is barely worthy of note. All of the design elements are nicely detailed and well-centered on the planchet. EAC 12.
From The Menlo Park Collection. (#1347)

Lovely 1793 S-9 Wreath Cent, AU58

141 **1793 Wreath Cent, Vine and Bars AU58 PCGS.** S-9, R.2. Ex: Hesselgesser. The S-9 die marriage combines the horizontal stem obverse with a kidney-shaped ribbon bow on the reverse. It is clearly the most plentiful Wreath cent variety, an excellent choice for type collectors. This early die state example has minor die cracks on Liberty's temple, and no signs of any clash marks or die cracks on the reverse. Examples are usually seen with die cracks at the lower right part of the reverse. The olive and dark brown surfaces have microscopic roughness with few other imperfections of any sort. While imperfectly centered, full beaded borders are visible on both sides. EAC 45. (#1347)

142 **1793 Wreath Cent, Vine and Bars—Damaged—NCS. Good Details.** S-10, B-10, R.4. The position of the three leaves identifies the obverse, while the reverse has the diagnostic period after AMERICA, which is faint due to corrosion. Overall, this chocolate-brown representative has minimal porosity and just a couple of minor digs. The bottom of the reverse is more corroded than the rest of the piece and causes the fraction to be partially obscured, but the rest of the details are fully visible. EAC 3. (#1347)

Interesting 1793 Lettered Edge Wreath Cent
S-11b, Fine Sharpness

143 **1793 Wreath, Lettered Edge, S-11b, B-16b, R.4—Scratched—NCS. Fine Details.** On the obverse all three leaves in the spring lean right, and the reverse is identified by a "period" after the last A in AMERICA that is formed by the line of berries. This variety is distinguished because it features a lettered edge with two leaves. Breen and Borckardt (2000) estimate that this interesting variety comprised 2,500 to 3,000 of the 11,825 cents delivered by the coiner on July 6, 1793. The planchets were often defective, and this piece exhibits mottled toning with streaks of medium brown and chestnut patina. Several shallow scratches on both sides account for the designation by NCS. The details are bold and the strike is only slightly off-center. EAC 7.

1793 S-13 Liberty Cap Cent, AG

144 **1793 Liberty Cap AG3 PCGS.** S-13, B-20, Low R.4. A wonderful example for the grade with smooth medium brown surfaces, lighter on the devices. Both sides are free of significant abrasions. The obverse has the bust, date, and LIBERTY fully visible, the 1 slightly weak. About half of the reverse design features. EAC 3.

Important 1793 S-13 Cent, VG Details

145 **1793 Liberty Cap—Corroded—NCS. VG Details.** S-13, B-20, Low R.4. All of the motifs, including the date, LIBERTY, legend, denomination, and border are entirely outlined with little internal detail remaining. Both sides are noticeably corroded, yet the overall appearance is excellent. EAC 5.

Pleasing 1794, Head of 1794 Cent, S-41, VF30

146 **1794 Head of 1794 VF30 PCGS.** S-41, B-30, R.3. Although faint on the present piece, the uppermost lock of Liberty's hair is separated in the middle, which identifies the obverse. The reverse has the diagnostic of a triangular notch in the left ribbon, just below the stem. This piece is Die State V, as evidenced by the reverse die cracks through the D in UNITED to the CE in CENTS, and between the AT in STATES. Both sides of this desirable cent have pleasing mahogany patina with hints of olive color. The surfaces are lightly abraded, but have no significant marks. A tiny green spot is noted on Liberty's top braid, above eye level. The reverse has a minor corrosion spot above the A in STATES. This is an attractive piece with only minor faults. EAC 10. (#901374)

Exquisite 1794 Cent, Head of 1794, S-57, Extremely Fine

147 **1794 Head of 1794 XF40 NGC.** S-57, B-55, R.1. This piece has been misattributed by NGC as Sheldon-58. It is difficult to see a "button" on the lower left corner of the hat, which is normally diagnostic for the obverse, so this variety can be identified by the fifth lock being severed and the end of the Liberty pole nearly touching a dentil. A berry touches the left side of the bow, which identifies the reverse. Lovely chocolate-brown patina embraces the minimally marked surfaces of the present specimen. The hair is weakly defined, as almost always seen, but the rest of the details are crisp. A pleasing example of this transitional variety. EAC 15. (#901374)

148 **1794 Head of 1794, S-49, B-41, R.2—Corroded—NCS. XF Details.** A bold die break through the upright of the E in LIBERTY helps identify the Sheldon marriage. A richly detailed cent whose dark mahogany-brown surfaces are evenly microgranular. The reverse has a minor rim ding at 8:30. EAC 15. (#901374)

Interesting 1794, Head of 1794, Cent, S-32, XF45

149 **1794 Head of 1794 XF45 PCGS.** S-32, B-18, Low R.3. A die break above the LI in LIBERTY and a pronounced die crack through the first S in STATES help distinguish this variety. The left half of the reverse features multiple clash marks, which identify this piece as Breen die state IV. Pleasing medium brown patina endows the fairly smooth surfaces of the present piece. Faint graffiti, which appears to read "946003," is visible along the obverse border near 9 o'clock, but the are no other noteworthy marks. This charming piece would make a lovely type coin. EAC 20. *From The Menlo Park Collection.* (#901374)

Scarce AU Details 1794 Cent S-43, Head of 1794

150 **1794 Head of 1794, S-43, B-32, R.2—Damaged—NCS. AU Details.** A splendidly detailed gunmetal-gray example of the Liberty Cap type. A rim ding at 2 o'clock on the reverse explains the NCS designation, and the obverse has a few unimportant pits. Most 1794 cents are well worn or corroded, unlike the present piece. EAC 20. (#901374)

Splendid 1794 S-67 Cent, VF30

151 **1794 Head of 1795, S-67, B-59, R.3 VF30 PCGS.** PCGS incorrectly calls this a Head of 1794 obverse. The large circular curl and defects in the hair and on the jaw identify the obverse, although it is usually recognized by the prominent leaf tip clash marked at the junction of the hair and forehead. The reverse has a double leaf below ED. and a double parallel leaf below OF. Fine, line-like planchet laminations on the reverse resemble die cracks. This pleasing piece has medium olive and darker brown color with smooth surfaces. EAC 20. (#1365)

AU 1794 Head of 1795 Cent, S-70

152 **1794 Head of 1795, S-70, B-62, R.2, AU50 NGC.** Breen Die State IV with heavy crack across Liberty's temple and a clashmark to the F in OF. A high grade example of this scarce Head of 1795 subtype. The olive-brown surfaces are refreshingly free from blemishes, and the portrait is richly detailed. EAC 25. (#1365)

Desirable 1795 S-76b, B-4b Cent, Unc Details

153 **1795 Plain Edge—Improperly Cleaned—NCS. Unc Details.** S-76b, B-4b, R.1. Smooth olive-brown surfaces with traces of cartwheel luster. considerable deep orange color is the result of cleaning, and yet it is an outstanding, attractive example. Many original planchet marks are evident in the fields and on the devices, but few other blemishes are visible. EAC 40. (#1380)

154 **1796 Liberty Cap Fine 15 PCGS.** S-89, B-10, R.3. The so-called "crowded head" obverse, with the 1 nearly touching the hair and the top of the 6 joined to the bust. The L in LIBERTY is connected to the cap, while the BE leans right and is distant from the LI. A pair of berries on each side of CENT is diagnostic for the reverse, as well as the single leaf below the R in AMERICA. Lovely chocolate-brown patina covers both sides of this final Liberty Cap issue. There is significant detail remaining although the OF and ONE CENT are slightly softer. A charming type coin. EAC 8. (#1392)

155 **1797 Reverse of 1797, Stems, S-139, B-21, R.1—Scratched—NCS. Fine Details.** A tan-brown cent with several dull scratches on the lower right obverse field and above CENT. Late dies with a swollen area above Liberty's shoulder, as made. EAC 5. (#1422)

Lovely 1797 S-123 Nichols Find Cent
MS64 Brown

Impressive 1797 Cent,
Reverse of 1797, No Stems, S-131, XF40

156   **1797 Reverse of 1797, Stems, S-123, B-12, R.4 MS64 Brown PCGS.** The die chip just below Liberty's eye identified this Nichols Find variety that is usually found in or near Mint State grades. Considered R.4, meaning between 80 and 200 examples survive, well over half of the known examples grade AU or better. In fact, the variety would probably be a solid R.5 or perhaps even R.6 if that hoard never existed.

Like nearly all coins from the Nichols Find, the surfaces are pleasing medium brown with smooth, slightly reflective fields. Most of the few marks in the right obverse field and elsewhere actually remain from the original planchet before the coin was struck. This is an outstanding example that provides date and type collectors an excellent opportunity to acquire a high grade Draped Bust cent. EAC 60. (#1422)

157   **1797 Reverse of 1797, No Stems XF40 NGC.** S-131, B-27, R.3. The prominent die break behind Liberty's ribbon identifies the obverse die, while the stemless wreath helps distinguish the reverse. This variety differs from Sheldon NC-8, which is also stemless, because the point of a leaf is located below the upright of the D in UNITED on S-131. This boldly detailed example exhibits lovely medium brown patina across both sides. There are no particularly bothersome abrasions and the eye appeal is great. EAC 20. *From The Menlo Park Collection.* (#1425)

158   **1798 First Hair Style, S-145, B-2, R.3 Good 4 Counterstamped, Lightly Corroded Uncertified.** Counterstamped D V V on the central reverse. The Brunk-unlisted counterstamp is rectangular and in recessed relief. The host large cent is chocolate-brown and has moderately granular fields. All legends are bold aside from OF. EAC 4.

159   **1798 First Hair Style—Flip-Over Double Strike, Second Strike 10% Off-Center—Fine 12 PCGS.** S-154, B-8, High R.4. A pleasing, evenly worn chocolate-brown example of this very scarce variety. On the obverse, dentils from the off-center impression appear to the left of the L in LIBERTY, and the faint letters STA(TES) appear to the right of the tip of the bust. EAC 8. (#1431)

160   **1798 First Hair Style XF45 NGC.** S-166, R.1. Die State VI, late dies with a heavy reverse crack and reverse breaks at 10:30 and on the C in CENT. A bold dark brown piece. Only the first A in AMERICA is not evenly struck. A few moderate obverse marks are not worthy of further elaboration. EAC 25. *From The Menlo Park Collection.* (#1431)

161   **1798 Second Hair Style, S-184, B-45, R.1—Improperly Cleaned—NCS. AU Details.** An attractive large cent with deep chocolate-brown and cobalt-blue patina across each side. A series of shallow planchet laminations are noted in the right obverse fields, and a raised die defect resides just above the right edge of 7 in the date. Die clash marks are noticeable on the lower reverse. There are minimal signs of improper cleaning, despite the NCS caveat. EAC 25. (#1434)

Lovely 1800 S-204 Cent, MS62 Brown

162 **1800 MS62 Brown NGC.** S-204, B-25, High R.3. Breen Die State VI. A die crack and heavy clash marks are visible along the right obverse border, weakening the border from 1 o'clock to 3 o'clock. The reverse is rotated a few degrees counterclockwise. Deep steel surfaces serve as a backdrop for hints of original red color near the devices. This piece ranks in the Condition Census, probably fifth finest known. It is clearly finer than the Rasmussen coin, and just misses the quality of the Husak coin. An extraordinary example with amazing eye appeal. It is an important piece for the advanced specialist. EAC 50. (#1449)

Alluring 1800/79 Cent, S-194, VF30

163 **1800/79 VF30 PCGS.** S-194, B-8, Low R.3. An overdate helps distinguish the obverse, while the reverse features a high fraction bar that is closer to the numerator than to the denominator. This piece is Breen Die State V, as evidenced by the rim break between the IC in AMERICA. Pleasing medium brown patination in the fields contrasts nicely against the chestnut patina that drapes the devices. A shallow mark on Liberty's neck is mentioned for future identification purposes. An appealing, semi-glossy, and crisply defined representative. EAC 12.
From The Menlo Park Collection. (#1455)

164 **1803 Small Date, Small Fraction XF40 PCGS.** S-251, R.2. An early to intermediate die state. The surfaces are dark brown overall with much lighter accents over the highpoints on each side. Close examination reveals fine, pebbly surfaces with no major impairments. EAC 20. *From The Menlo Park Collection.* (#1482)

165 **1803 Small Date, Small Fraction, S-254, B-13, R.1, XF40 NGC.** The die crack along the bust tip and bold clashmarks near the fraction help identify the Sheldon marriage. Sharper than the assigned grade and much luster persists, but the deep brown toning conceals verdigris near the R in LIBERTY, a thin mark above the ear, and pinscratches on the reverse border at 6:30, 7:30, and 9:30. EAC 30. (#1482)

Pleasing Late State 1804 S-266, B-1 Cent, VG8

166 **1804 VG8 NGC.** S-266, B-1, R.2. The late die state, sometimes called S-266c, represents the last of the 1804 large cents coined from a single die pair for the date. Pleasing medium olive surfaces with a small rim void at 10 o'clock on the reverse. Minor verdigris hidden in the reverse devices can probably be removed, except the coin is sealed in its holder. EAC 6. (#1504)

Lovely 1804 Cent, S-266, VF25

167 **1804 VF25 PCGS.** S-266, B-1, R.2. The only variety known. Obvious repunching is visible to the right of the 4 in the date. This piece is Die State I, with no die defects on either side. Lovely chocolate-brown patina drapes the surfaces and complements the crisply outlined devices. Scattered marks define the grade, but none merit individual mention. Population: 3 in 25, 30 finer (8/08). EAC 10. *From The Menlo Park Collection.* (#1504)

168 **1804 Restrike MS63 Brown NGC.** Judd-28a. This restrike issue is of uncertain origin, with Joseph Mickley and John W. Haseltine both named as possible suspects. This Select example exhibits rich reddish-mahogany coloration and no obvious post-strike imperfections. The usual thick die cracks and heavy die rust are noted on both sides. EAC 50. (#45344)

169 **1804 Restrike MS64 Brown NGC.** Generous glimpses of mint red surround the deep steel-brown centers. The 'restrike' 1804 is a notorious issue struck circa-1860 from muled Mint dies sold as steel scrap. The rarity of the official 1804 cent, known from a single die pair, created demand that was partly met by this contemporaneously condemned private restrike. Struck from broken and heavily rusted dies. EAC 63. (#45344)

170 **1805 VF35 NGC.** S-267, B-1, R.1. This medium-brown representative displays glimpses of luster in protected areas. A faint horizontal pinscratch crosses the portrait just beneath the mouth, and the obverse rim between 4 and 7 o'clock is moderately abraded. EAC 12. *From The Menlo Park Collection.* (#1510)

171 **1805 S-269, B-3, R.1, VF35 NGC.** This deep brown Choice VF cent offers smooth surfaces and substantial hair definition. Clashed near the profile, and a die crack passes through Liberty's upper neck curls. EAC 20. (#1510)

172 **1806 XF40 PCGS.** S-270, R.1. The only dies. This glossy mahogany-brown piece has a few distributed small marks along with a hint of verdigris, but remaining luster is substantial, and the sharpness is impressive. Most survivors of this date are well worn. Housed in a green label holder. EAC 25.
From The Menlo Park Collection. (#1513)

Remarkable MS64 Brown S-270 1806 Cent
Single Finest NGC-Certified

173 **1806 S-270, B-1, R.1, MS64 Brown NGC.** On Valentine's Day, 2008, Heritage auctioned the Walter Husak Collection, one of the finest holdings of early large cents ever assembled. His Sheldon-270 was certified by PCGS as AU50. The present example is eight grades finer, and is the single finest certified by NGC. It has little company in Mint State, where NGC has certified just seven pieces between MS61 and MS63. None have been certified as Red or Red and Brown. PCGS has certified six Brown Mint State coins, the single finest as MS64, along with a solitary MS66 Red and Brown. Thus, the present coin ranks among the finest certified, and is the highest graded by NGC.

The 1806 is one of only three years in the large cent series represented by just one variety. (The 1804 and 1809 are the other two dates). S-270 is plentiful in well worn condition, but better grade examples are very scarce and are subject to strong date demand. The present lustrous near-Gem would be the centerpiece of most specialized collections. It has dazzling cartwheel luster, and the toning is a pleasing light golden-brown with glimpses of aqua and rose. The strike is crisp, although the curl near the date lacks complete detail. There are no visible marks, further ensuring the eye appeal. An important acquisition for the connoisseur who demands the best. EAC 60+. (#1513)

Splendid 1810 Cent, S-282, Choice AU

174 **1810 AU55 PCGS. CAC.** S-282, B-3, R.2. The E and T in LIBERTY are low and lean left, and the sixth star is noticeably closer to the fifth than the seventh. A berry is located below the right foot of the first A in AMERICA, which is a helpful diagnostic for the reverse. Pleasing medium brown patina covers both sides, with a few darker spots noted on both sides. The stars and Liberty's hair are a trifle weak, but the reverse is sharply defined. This splendid piece is housed in a first generation PCGS holder. EAC 45. (#1550)

175 **1810/09 VF30 PCGS.** S-281, B-1, R.1. Mottled steel and dark brown surfaces with excellent details and a few minor marks. EAC 20. (#1552)

176 **1811 S-287, B-1, R.2—Corroded-NCS. VF Details.** The level of design detail on this piece actually seems better than VF, and more like XF. The surfaces are highly porous, however, on both sides. An affordable representative of this somewhat scarce Sheldon variety. EAC 10. (#1555)

177 **1812 Large Date, S-289, B-4, R.1—Corroded—NCS. AU Details.** S-289 is readily identified by the location of the second S in STATES relative to the leaf below. This Classic Head cent has a wealth of detail, although the deep brown surfaces are evenly granular. The Classic type is notoriously elusive in better grades. EAC 20. (#1564)

178 **1814 Crosslet 4 AU55 NGC.** S-294, B-1, R.1. The only Crosslet 4 variety. Traces of luster shimmer beneath the attractive mahogany patina. Numerous deep brown spots are noted on the reverse, but the obverse is remarkably free of any blemishes or abrasions. Both sides exhibit light porosity and there are a few minuscule patches of verdigris. A boldly defined example with pleasing eye appeal. EAC 40.
From The Menlo Park Collection. (#1573)

179 **1818 MS64 Brown NGC.** N-10, R.1. A Randall Hoard variety and found in large numbers in mint condition. For more than a century this variety has been a type coin of choice for the Matron Head type. An attractive coin that retains a considerable amount of original mint red, although faded now, for a coin that has been classed as Brown. Sharply defined on the hair of Liberty, but several stars are incompletely brought up. A few subtle spots determine the grade. EAC 60. (#1600)

180 **1818 MS64 Red and Brown PCGS.** N-10, R.1. A lovely Randall Hoard cent that is ideal for a date or type collector. The 1818 and 1820 cents from the famous hoard are the easiest dates of the 1816 to 1839 series to acquire with partial or full red color. This attractive piece exhibits about 50% red with light brown toning and a few minor spots. EAC 63.
From The Mississippi Collection. (#1601)

181 **1820 Large Date MS65 Brown NGC.** N-13, R.1. A lovely toned example from the Randall Hoard, with fully lustrous surfaces. Both sides show pale gold, lilac, and bright blue over the satiny obverse and reverse surfaces. EAC 55.
From The Menlo Park Collection. (#1615)

182 **1822 AU58 NGC.** N-4, R.2. A bold inner circle, which is significantly sharper than typically seen on this variety, is nearly complete on the obverse, and the bottom of the L in LIBERTY is recut. The obverse also has the diagnostic plain center dot to the left of the ear. The position of the leaves helps identify the reverse, and the E's in ONE and CENT are noticeably large and lean to the left. This interesting piece has a mix of tan and medium brown patina on both sides. A small spot is noted on Liberty's neck, but all of the abrasions are minor. Crisply struck save for some weakness on the stars. EAC 40. (#1624)

183 **1822 AU58 NGC.** N-11, R.3. Dusky gray toning with faded golden-brown about the reverse lettering. A thin mark on the hairbun, but abrasions are otherwise minimal. EAC 40. (#1624)

184 **1829 Large Letters MS62 Brown NGC.** N-2, R.2. Stars 1, 2, and 3 point between the denticles, and this variety always has a die crack through the first four stars. This sharply defined example has mostly minor marks, with a few tiny digs noted around the AME in AMERICA. A small spot below the wreath minimally affects the great eye appeal of this mahogany patinated representative. EAC 50. (#1663)

185 **1830 Large Letters MS62 Brown NGC.** N-4, Low R.3. Noyes Die State B. The portrait and the central reverse field are medium brown, while lighter golden-brown accompanies design recesses. Smooth aside from a pair of trivial ticks on the cheek. The 1830 has never appeared in hoards, unlike certain earlier Matron Head dates, yet remains affordable in nice Mint State. Census: 10 in 62 Brown, 17 finer (7/08). EAC 55. (#1672)

186 **1838 MS65 Brown NGC.** N-3, R.1. Two center dots on the reverse, resembling a colon, identify this variety. The denticles at the lower right of the obverse are weakly struck ("smeared"), as typically seen, and the stars are soft, also as usual. A wonderfully preserved piece with traces of original red luster in the protected areas of the date and wreath. EAC 60. (#1741)

187 **1847 MS66 Brown NGC.** N-29, R.3. Grellman die state b, as evidenced by the die crack through the top of AMERIC, but there are also the beginnings of a crack through UNITED, which is indicative of die state c. This variety is identified by a point above the right upright of the N in CENT, as well as several die lines through the E in ONE. Numerous other die lines can be used to aid in attribution. Although mostly mahogany colored, significant amounts of mint red are visible throughout the protected areas. The surfaces are nearly pristine and there is just a trace of weakness on a couple of stars. EAC 60+. (#1877)

188 **1850 MS66 Brown PCGS.** Ex: Jules Reiver Collection. N-25, R.4. A strong die dot below the eye identifies the obverse, while several faint die lines from the rim to the R in AMERICA are diagnostic for the reverse. Lovely mahogany patina graces each side, with traces of red luster in the protected areas. Sharply struck with virtually no marks and only a couple of tiny blemishes. EAC 60. (#1889)

189 **1850 MS65 Red and Brown NGC.** N-7, R.2. Grellman Die State b. A satiny representative with nearly equal amounts of brick-red and olive-green on each side. A small spot above the hair bun, but free from marks. EAC 60+. (#1890)

190 **1850 MS64 Red NGC.** N-7, R.2. Grellman State b. The usual late die state for the variety, with numerous Mint State pieces in existence from a hoard discovered long ago. This specimen has deep orange luster with minor spots on each side, typical of nearly all known survivors. EAC 63. (#1891)

191 **1853 MS65 Brown NGC.** N-25, R.1. Attractive walnut-brown surfaces with traces of faded mint color around the peripheral stars and lettering. Sharply defined in the centers, while nearly all of the stars lack complete centrils. EAC 55. (#1901)

192 **1853 MS66 Brown NGC.** N-19, R.1. Grellman Die State b. Liberty and the open fields are deep brown, but orange-red nonetheless surrounds many peripheral elements. Well struck save for the stars. Essentially void of marks and carbon. EAC 63. (#1901)

193 **1853 MS65 Red and Brown PCGS.** N-26, R.2. Grellman Die State c. Orange-gold dominates the reverse and much of the obverse, although the open fields and cheek are brown. Well struck aside from a few star centers. EAC 63. (#1902)

194 **1853 MS63 Red PCGS.** N-13, R.1. Grellman Die State b. This pumpkin-gold Mature Head cent has boldly struck central devices, although several stars are soft and UNITED STATES OF is affected by a sinking reverse die. A couple of small spots along the lower obverse border decide the grade. EAC 63. (#1903)

195 **1854 MS66 ★ Brown NGC.** N-8, R.1. Crisply struck and nearly unabraded with potent luster and lovely blended mahogany-brown and aqua toning. Arguably the finest example that NGC has certified as N-8, since none have been certified in higher grades, and among the four MS66 Brown pieces, only the present coin has received a Star designation (8/08). EAC 63. (#1904)

196 **1855 Upright 5s MS64 Red PCGS.** N-4, R.1. Grellman state a. The reverse is almost entirely bright orange and red, while the obverse has traces of light brown on Liberty's cheek and in the fields. Several tiny marks and a couple of nearly microscopic corrosion specks at the date are noted. The stars are weakly defined, as typically seen, but the rest of the details are bold. EAC 63. (#1909)

Attractive 1855 N-4 Cent, MS65 Red

197 **1855 Upright 5s MS65 Red NGC.** N-4, R.1. Grellman Die State a. The strike is exacting on the portrait, although selected stars have central softness. Generally orange-gold, with slight mellowing on the neck, the jaw, and the reverse margin at 7 o'clock. Nearly unabraded, and carbon is relegated to the left obverse field. Certified in a former generation holder. EAC 63. (#1909)

198 **1855 Slanting 5s MS66 Brown NGC.** N-10, R.1. Italic 5s in the date, as well as a tiny point from the left side of Liberty's coronet, identify this variety. Pleasing mahogany patina with accents of deep cherry-red graces both sides of this highly lustrous piece. The strike is razor-sharp, and there are virtually no marks save for a small dig on the rim above the O in OF. Census: 6 in 66, 0 finer (7/08). EAC 63. (#1910)

Red Gem 1855 Slanted 5s Cent, N-10

199 **1855 Slanting 5s MS65 Red PCGS.** N-10, R.1. Grellman Die State e. This lustrous brick-red Gem has an exacting strike and unabraded surfaces. Minor obverse carbon has little impact on the imposing eye appeal. One of only three 1855 varieties with slanted 5s in the date. Certified in a first generation holder. Population: 79 in 65 Red, 13 finer (8/08). EAC 63.
From The Bell Collection. (#1912)

200 **1856 Upright 5 MS65 Brown NGC.** N-10, R.1. Grellman Die State a. The obverse is olive-brown with glimpses of fire-red, while the reverse has apple-green fields and tan legends and devices. A few stars are softly impressed, but the strike is otherwise bold. A strike-through is noted beneath ONE. Smooth save for a tiny reverse rim nick at 1:30. EAC 60. (#1919)

201 **1856 Upright 5 MS65 Red and Brown PCGS. CAC.** N-6, R.1. Grellman state a. A notable die lump off the lower left tip of the bust identifies the obverse, while the reverse has several faint die lines, including one from the second A in AMERICA to the rim. A lovely distribution of red and light brown covers the surfaces. Nearly all of the stars are weakly struck, but the rest of the details are razor-sharp. A couple of insignificant blemishes and abrasions keep this piece from an even higher grade. Certified in a first generation PCGS holder. PCGS has certified only one Red and Brown example finer (7/08). EAC 63. (#1920)

202 **1856 Slanted 5 MS65 Brown NGC.** N-4, High R.2. Grellman Die State b. Orange-gold outlines design elements on the central reverse, but this unblemished Gem is primarily chocolate-brown. The wreath and portrait are well struck. EAC 60. (#1922)

203 **1857 Small Date MS65 Red and Brown NGC.** N-2, High R.1. The reverse is mostly red, while the obverse retains the initial fiery luster around the stars and along the border of the portrait. This is a nearly unabraded Gem, well struck save for the centers of stars 2 to 8. EAC 63. (#1932)

Impressive 1857 N-2 Small Date Cent, MS65 Red and Brown

204 **1857 Small Date MS65 Red and Brown PCGS. CAC.** N-2, R.1. Grellman State a. Faint lines are visible from the dentils to some letters in UNITED, the usual die state for the variety. The surfaces are smooth and attractive with pleasing medium brown surfaces, blended with considerable deep orange luster. A wonderful example of the final large cent issue. EAC 63. (#1932)

FLYING EAGLE CENTS

AU Details Proof 1856 Flying Eagle Cent

205 **1856—Whizzed—NCS. Proof, AU Details.** Snow-9. A needle-sharp proof that at first glance appears to be Gem. The open obverse field has been carefully smoothed, and the reverse is slightly glossy. A faded mark is noted above the N in ONE, and a thin abrasion is seen beneath the first A in AMERICA. A collectible example of this legendary rarity. (#2013)

Famous 1856 Flying Eagle Cent AU53
Desirable Business Strike Snow-3

206 **1856 AU53 PCGS. Eagle Eye Photo Seal, Card Included.** Snow-3. This variety is often pursued by knowledgeable collectors as the "Mint State" 1856 Flying Eagle cent. The diagnostic die scratches on each side are faint on this piece, but the variety is confirmed by the date location and the strike doubling seen on the date, a feature that is seen on a significant number of coins from this variety.

Snow estimates that "probably no more than 700 pieces" were struck. Further, he states "it is nearly certain that this issue makes up most or all of the 634 specimens originally distributed to Congress to help promote passage of the pending coinage bill." These coins were struck as test pieces to try and anticipate what problems might occur with the new size, metal, and design. This example shows the production problem that did occur the following year: the head and tail feathers of the eagle are weakly struck as are many of the design elements on the reverse wreath. The surfaces have a honey-golden color overall with darker accents scattered irregularly on each side.
From The Menlo Park Collection. (#2013)

207 **1857 MS63 PCGS.** Light chestnut patina graces both sides, with a darker area on the eagle's wings. A couple of minor marks and several tiny flecks define the grade. Encapsulated in a first generation PCGS holder. (#2016)

208 **1857 MS63 PCGS.** A shimmering golden-tan representative of this briefly issued type. The strike is virtually unimprovable, and the preservation is exemplary aside from a hair-thin obverse mark at 7:30.
From The Menlo Park Collection. (#2016)

209 **1857 MS64 PCGS.** A lustrous and boldly struck representative with especially crisp details on the reverse. Only the letters of UNITED STATES are slightly weak, and die doubling is noted along the upper edges. Pleasing accents of champagne and gold modify the tan coloration. Scattered carbon flecks on each side and minor abrasions in the obverse field limit the grade. Housed in a green label PCGS holder. (#2016)

210 **1857 MS64 NGC.** A dusting of darker toning spots covers the tan and orange surfaces of this crisply defined representative. Several abrasions are nearly imperceptible and do not affect the flow of the flashy luster. (#2016)

211 **1857 MS64 PCGS.** A powerfully struck Choice type coin that boasts smooth fields, light tan-gold toning, and coruscating luster. The date exhibits light strike doubling. (#2016)

212 **1857 MS64 NGC.** A splendid mark-free near-Gem with unencumbered luster and no conspicuous carbon. The strike is crisp, with incompleteness limited to a corner of the lower left cotton leaf. (#2016)

Colorful Gem 1857 Flying Eagle Cent

213 **1857 MS65 NGC.** A sharply struck Gem with exquisite peach-red obverse toning. The rose-gold and lime-green reverse is also attractive. Lustrous and unabraded with the occasional minute carbon fleck. Certified in a prior generation holder. NGC has certified only 13 pieces finer. (#2016)

Pleasing 1857 Gem Flying Eagle Cent

214 **1857 MS65 NGC.** This lustrous Gem displays crisp definition on the design elements, including the tail feathers and leaf ribbing. A mix of light tan and gold patina graces both sides, each of which is devoid of mentionable contacts. Some tiny light flecks do not detract from the pleasing overall eye appeal. NGC has seen only 13 pieces grading higher (8/08). (#2016)

215 **1858 Large Letters MS64 NGC.** Low Leaves, Closed E in ONE. Beautifully toned in lime-gold, apricot, lilac-rose, and sky-blue. Booming luster and a crisp strike combine with mark-free surfaces. One small spot is east of the T in CENT. (#2019)

216 **1858 Large Letters MS64 PCGS.** Low Leaves, Closed E in ONE. Slight doubling is evident on ICA. Well struck on all of the design details, except for the tip of the eagle's tail, with even olive-brown toning over both sides, and accents of red-orange luster clinging to some of the devices. Blemish-free on both sides.
From The Menlo Park Collection. (#2019)

Well Struck 1858 Large Letters Cent, MS65

217 **1858 Large Letters MS65 NGC.** A well executed strike imparts sharp delineation to this highly attractive Gem. Lustrous surfaces display occasional whispers of light tan, along with splashes of lavender on portions of the eagle. A few light marks visible only under high magnification may well preclude an even higher grade. (#2019)

Bold 1858 Large Letters Cent, MS65

218 **1858 Large Letters MS65 PCGS.** Closed E in ONE, open E in CENT. High leaves below CENT. An engaging Gem with fully defined and bold design elements on both sides. Although a few spots are present as usual, the light tan surfaces and brilliant luster trump those spots. An exceptional example for the connoisseur. PCGS has only graded 28 finer pieces.
From The Bell Collection. (#2019)

219 **1858 Small Letters MS63 PCGS.** Low Leaves, Open E in ONE. A precisely struck and mildly prooflike rose-tan example. A few subtle gray obverse spots fail to distract.
From The Menlo Park Collection. (#2020)

220 **1858 Small Letters MS64 NGC.** A lovely Choice representative of the popular Small Letters variety, well-defined with considerable fire in the lavender-accented copper-orange fields. NGC has graded 82 numerically finer pieces (8/08). (#2020)

221 **1858/7 AU50 NGC.** Snow 1, Die Stage C. The diagnostic triangular dot midway between the 8 in the date and the eagle stands out, but the "flag" or upper right corner of a 7 above the second 8 is not readily apparent. Dark brown surfaces exhibit some light roughness, especially in the lower right reverse quadrant. (#2022)

222 **1858/7 MS63 NGC.** Snow-1. This early die state example has a bold overdate feature, with the right corner of the 7 clearly visible above the right side of the final 8, and traces of the top of the 7 visible to the left, extending over the 8. Boldly defined with lustrous light tan surfaces and only a few tiny marks on the reverse. Early die states such as this piece command the highest premiums for the variety. (#2022)

PROOF FLYING EAGLE CENTS

Legendary 1856 Flying Eagle Cent PR40

223 **1856 PR40 NGC.** Snow-9. The 1 is centered over a denticle and a small die gouge extends from the left ribbon stem, both characteristics of the proof Snow-9 pairing. The eagle's breast and tail feathers display moderate wear, and the chocolate-brown surfaces are smooth. Protected areas on the reverse exhibit minor buildup. *From The Laredo Collection.* (#2037)

224 **1856 PR63 PCGS.** Snow-9. A proof-only issue, Snow-9 is the most available Flying Eagle variety and is a perfect representative for a type collector. Although the 1856 Flying Eagle cent is technically a pattern, numismatic scholars have debated whether Mint State or Proof pieces are originals or restrikes. It is now generally believed that the proofs were struck for collectors shortly after 1856. Either way, the 1856 Flying Eagle ranks as one of the most popular 19th century issues.

Dusted light brown patina intermingles with the deeply reflective orange-tan fields. The strike is razor-sharp, and there are virtually no marks on each side. A couple of small blemishes on the obverse are noted. This attractive piece would make a wonderful representative. (#2037)

Lovely Snow-9 Select Proof
1856 Flying Eagle Cent

Colorful Choice Proof 1856 Flying Eagle Cent

225 **1856 PR63 PCGS.** Snow-9. The 1856 Flying Eagle cent is perhaps the most widely collected pattern issue in American numismatics, thanks in part to a longstanding listing in the *Guide Book*. The issue was restruck in the years after its original production, and as a result, it is available to collectors in a wide range of grades, albeit at a price.

This exquisitely detailed Select proof specimen is uncommonly appealing for the grade. Dappled rose, violet, and mahogany-orange shadings enrich each side. Aside from a hairline over the eagle's head and a few tiny points of contact in the field above the date, this is a carefully preserved coin. (#2037)

226 **1856 PR64 PCGS.** Snow-9. Rich orange, navy-blue, and ruby-red emblazon this penetratingly struck and unabraded Choice proof. The obverse is satiny, while the reverse field is reflective. A high quality example of the rarest small cent date. For more than a century, collectors pursued the famous 1856 Flying Eagle cent whether it originated as a proof or business strike. In recent decades, numismatists have favored the commercial strikes, even though a strike doubled Snow-3 with softly brought up devices has substantially less eye appeal than a fully struck Snow-9 with clean and moderately reflective fields. Perhaps one day, collectors will again spurn Uncirculated examples of average quality and instead favor well made proofs. (#2037)

INDIAN CENTS

227 **1859 MS64 PCGS.** A boldly detailed and highly lustrous piece with rich gold and tan toning on both sides. First year of the Indian design, and the only variety without a shield at the top of the wreath, a one-year type coin.
From The Menlo Park Collection. (#2052)

228 **1859 MS64 NGC.** This is a pleasing near-Gem example of the first-year 1859 Indian cent, the only issue in the series with the Laurel Wreath Without Shield reverse. Well struck and lustrous with rich reddish coppery-brown coloration and minimal surface marks. (#2052)

229 **1859 MS64 PCGS.** This boldly struck single year type coin has an unmarked appearance and only a whisper of carbon. The walnut-brown toning is slightly deeper on the reverse. (#2052)

230 **1859 MS65 NGC.** An impressive first-year Indian cent. This lovely Gem has splendid satiny luster with glowing rose-orange fields and powerfully impressed devices. The surfaces are free of any significant abrasions, and a small planchet flaw is noted near the upper right reverse border. (#2052)

231 **1860 MS65 NGC.** Lovely tan patina has accents of chestnut on both sides. The surfaces appear pristine to the unaided eye with no noticeable abrasions or blemishes. A couple of feathers of Liberty's headdress are a trifle weak, as usual. An attractive and highly lustrous example. NGC has certified just 38 examples finer (7/08). (#2058)

232 **1860 MS65 PCGS.** Rounded Bust. Lovely chestnut patina graces the surfaces of this attractive Gem. Several nearly microscopic flecks limit the grade, but there are virtually no marks. A crisply struck and highly lustrous example. Housed in a first generation PCGS holder. (#2058)

233 **1860 MS65 NGC.** This sharply impressed Gem has good luster and an absence of marks. Unimportant carbon is all that limits the grade. From the year of the Pony Express and Lincoln's first Presidential election. (#2058)

234 **1861 MS65 PCGS.** Light chestnut patina at the center of the obverse contrasts nicely against the orange-gold perimeter and rose-tan reverse. This charming piece is free of any blemishes save for a lone fleck near the wreath, and there are just a couple of minor abrasions on each side. Housed in a first generation PCGS holder. (#2061)

235 **1861 MS65 PCGS.** An impeccably preserved representative with lovely tan patina on both sides. The first few feathers in the headdress are soft, but the rest of the details are boldly impressed. A number of minuscule flecks and a small blemish keep this lustrous piece from an even higher grade. Encapsulated in an early PCGS holder. (#2061)

236 **1861 MS65 NGC.** Booming luster and light golden-tan toning combine with a mark-free appearance and a good strike to confirm the quality of this handsome Gem. A subtle lamination on the reverse at 5 o'clock is of mint origin. Encapsulated in a prior generation holder. (#2061)

237 **1862 MS65 NGC.** Delightful orange-tan patina overlies the remarkably clean surfaces. Close inspection with a loupe reveals only a couple of minor flyspecks and virtually no marks. This nearly fully struck Gem is encapsulated in an old NGC holder. (#2064)

238 **1862 MS65 PCGS.** Olive-gold iridescence endows the obverse, while the reverse is apricot-gold. Intricately struck and mark-free with a fleck on the neck and a faint fingerprint fragment on the lower reverse. Encapsulated in a green label holder. (#2064)

Wonderful 1862 Indian Cent, MS66

239 **1862 MS66 NGC.** Highly lustrous with satiny golden-tan surfaces, the fields slightly reflective. Faint orange and iridescent toning splashes add to its eye appeal. Despite the common nature of 1862 and 1863 Indian cents, neither date is plentiful in Gem or finer grade. Census: 30 in 66, 5 finer (7/08). (#2064)

240 **1863 MS65 NGC.** Delightful orange-red patina drapes the surfaces of this remarkably clean and lustrous Gem. A few tiny flecks on the obverse are visible under magnification, but they do not detract from the flow of the impressive luster. NGC has certified a mere 16 pieces finer (7/08). (#2067)

241 **1864 Copper-Nickel MS65 NGC.** Lustrous tan-colored surfaces have excellent eye appeal and show virtually no marks. Scattered flecks on the reverse are nearly invisible without a glass. NGC has certified a mere 14 pieces finer (7/08). (#2070)

Attractive 1864 Bronze No L Indian Cent, MS65 Red

242 **1864 Bronze No L MS65 Red NGC.** Dusted rose-red patina accents the mostly tan surfaces of this resplendent Gem. The surfaces are remarkably unabraded for the grade, and only a couple of minuscule flecks are visible. Faint clash marks are noted on each side. This lovely specimen is housed in an old NGC holder. NGC reports just 27 examples finer (8/08). (#2078)

243 **1864 Bronze No L MS66 Red PCGS. CAC.** Bright red drapes the surfaces of this fully struck Premium Gem. The surfaces appear to have no marks, and there are only a few small blemishes. Housed in a first generation PCGS holder. Population: 31 in 66 Red, 1 finer (7/08). (#2078)

244 **1864 L On Ribbon MS64 Brown PCGS.** The With L variety is significantly scarcer than its No L counterpart. Charming mahogany patina drapes the surfaces, with traces of red luster in the protected areas. The tips of the first few feathers on Liberty's headdress are soft, as usual, but the rest of the details are sharp. An unblemished, minimally marked, and attractive representative. Population: 50 in 64 Brown, 5 finer (7/08). (#2079)

245 **1864 L On Ribbon MS64 Red and Brown PCGS.** FS-006.73, Snow-10b. A well struck and lightly shimmering near-Gem with generous portions of original gold iridescence. Brown elements are generally limited to the upper left obverse. A great example of this popular semi-key issue. (#2080)

246 **1864 L On Ribbon MS65 Red and Brown NGC.** Peppered medium brown patina mixes with the bright red that radiates throughout. This attractive piece has virtually no marks or blemishes. The second T in STATES is weak, and the first few feathers on the headdress are a trifle soft, as typically seen. NGC has certified a mere 21 examples finer (7/08). (#2080)

Sharp 1864 L On Ribbon Cent, MS64 Red

247 **1864 L On Ribbon MS64 Red PCGS.** Nice fully Red 1864 L On Ribbon cents are difficult to come by. This near-Gem specimen exhibits copper-gold luster, and a hint or two of faded red. A solid strike leaves sharp definition on the design features, including clarity on all four diamonds and on some of the feather tips. What appear to be faint remnants of a fingerprint on the left obverse likely precludes Gem status. Housed in a first generation PCGS holder. Population: 46 in 64 Red, 38 finer (8/08). (#2081)

248 **1866 MS64 Red and Brown PCGS.** Charming mahogany patina on the devices yields to rose and orange patina around the perimeter. Liberty's hair is a trifle soft and a few flecks are noted in the fields, but there are no marks visible to the unaided eye. Certified in a first generation PCGS holder. (#2086)

249 **1866 MS65 Red and Brown NGC.** Light mahogany patina at the centers is surrounded by vivid red luster. The strike is nearly full, and only slight abrasions and flecks become visible under a glass. NGC has certified just 22 pieces finer (7/08). Encapsulated in an old holder. (#2086)

250 **1867 MS65 Red and Brown NGC.** Eye-catching red-orange patina surrounds the mahogany colored centers. The surfaces are remarkably pristine, with a peppering of nearly imperceptible flyspecks on the reverse. Fairly prominent clashmarks from the bust of Liberty are noted on the reverse. (#2089)

Lustrous 1869/69 Cent, MS65 Red

251 **1869/69 MS65 Red NGC.** FS-008.3, Snow-3. Fivaz and Stanton (2000) state that this variety was once attributed as an 1869/8, but has recently been confirmed as an 1869/69. This is one of the finest examples of this type we have recently seen. The reddish-orange surfaces are wholly original with a full complement of mint luster. The strike is razor sharp over the Indian's portrait, and the balance of the features are at least bold in detail. A few speckles of carbon have gathered on both sides, but these are really not distracting to the naked eye. We are confident that this coin will elicit strong bids from advanced Indian Cent specialists. (#2095)

Impressive 1869 Cent, Premium Gem Red and Brown

252 **1869 MS66 Red and Brown NGC.** Enticing chestnut and cherry-red colors intermingle on both sides of this outstanding representative. The surfaces appear to have no marks, and only a couple of minor blemishes are visible under magnification. A sharply struck and conditionally scarce example. Census: 30 in 66 Red and Brown, 0 finer (7/08). Encapsulated in an old NGC holder. (#2095)

253 **1870 MS65 Red and Brown PCGS.** Light brown patina drapes the devices, which contrast nicely against the rose-red fields. The strike is nearly full, and a loupe locates only minor handling marks. Several die cracks are noted on the reverse. Population: 47 in 65 Red and Brown, 4 finer (7/08). (#2098)

254 **1871 MS65 Red and Brown NGC.** A 50/50 mix of lovely red and brown patina graces both sides of this carefully preserved Gem. There are no notable areas of weakness or any blemishes. Several light grazes barely affect the great eye appeal. NGC has certified just six Red and Brown pieces finer (7/08). Housed in an old holder. (#2101)

255 **1872 MS62 Brown NGC.** Deep brown patina covers the smooth, mark-free surfaces that are somewhat lackluster, which explains the lower grade assigned to this example. Nonetheless, this is a sharply struck example that can be difficult to locate in higher Mint State grades. (#2103)

256 **1872 MS62 Brown NGC.** Bold N in ONE. This low mintage cent is sharply struck and has only minimal contact for the grade. Generally medium brown with glimpses of lighter golden-brown. (#2103)

257 **1872 MS63 Brown PCGS.** Hints of mint red on the perimeter contrast against the chocolate-brown centers. Some softness is noted on the tips of Liberty's headdress, as typically seen. Although the surfaces are mostly unmarked, a shallow abrasion below the first S in STATES is noted. Population: 28 in 63 Brown, 38 finer (7/08). (#2103)

258 **1873 Open 3 MS65 Red and Brown NGC.** Captivating red-orange patina surrounds the mahogany centers of this minimally marked example. The flashy luster is barely affected by several carbon spots on the obverse. A sharply struck and conditionally scarce representative; housed in an old NGC holder. NGC has certified only two Red and Brown pieces finer (8/08). (#2107)

259 **1873 Open 3 MS65 Red and Brown NGC.** Delightful orange-red recesses contrast against medium brown devices. Both sides are essentially unmarked, but there is a peppering of minuscule flecks around the perimeter. A faint fingerprint in the field above Liberty's head is noted. NGC has certified just two Red and Brown examples finer (7/08). Certified in an old holder. (#2107)

260 **1873 Open 3 MS64 Red PCGS.** Considerable fire graces the vibrant orange surfaces of this Choice coin, struck from dies with the later Open 3 logotype. Minimally marked and attractive. Population: 48 in 64 Red, 25 finer (8/08). (#2108)

Sharply Struck 1873 Doubled LIBERTY, Closed 3 MS62 Brown, FS-9.1, Snow-2

261 **1873 Doubled LIBERTY, Closed 3 MS62 Brown NGC.** FS-9.1, Snow-2. LIBERTY, especially BERT, is lightly die doubled east. While not as spectacular as the Guide Book variety FS-9, which is die doubled southwest, this variety nonetheless commands a five star interest designation in Cherrypickers'. Sharply struck, with pleasing brown surfaces. (#2115)

262 **1873 Closed 3 MS64 Red and Brown PCGS.** A lustrous and sharply struck Choice Indian cent that is closer to Red than Brown. The cheek is gunmetal-blue, but orange-gold otherwise dominates. Well preserved aside from faded marks on the face. (#2109)

Challenging 1873 MS64 Red Closed 3 Cent

263 **1873 Closed 3 MS64 Red PCGS.** Locating full Red examples of the Closed 3 is challenging. The surfaces of this near-Gem are a light copper-gold , and an impressive strike results in sharp definition on the design elements, save for softness on some of the feather tips. A few light carbon flecks are noted on each side, but this piece has good eye appeal nonetheless. Population: 16 in 64 Red, 16 finer (8/08). (#2111)

264 **1873 Doubled LIBERTY, Closed 3 VG10 PCGS.** Snow-1, FS-009. Although this piece has seen extensive circulation, the doubling is still apparent below Liberty's nose and on several of the visible letters in LIBERTY. The surfaces are fairly smooth and have no noteworthy marks. A look at the population data shows how scarce this variety is in any grade. (#2115)

Important 1873 Snow-1 Doubled LIBERTY Cent, XF45

265 **1873 Doubled LIBERTY, Closed 3 XF45 PCGS.** Snow-1, FS-009. This is the variety with every letter of LIBERTY boldly doubled. Doubling is also visible on portions of the profile, the L, and feather tips. A second doubled die variety is known, with only the L in LIBERTY doubled, and it is much less desirable than Snow-1. This piece is lovely with deep brown patina and pleasing surfaces. The usual light circulation marks expected for the grade are evident on this example. (#2115)

266 **1874 MS64 Red NGC.** Peach and rose colors intermingle on this intricately struck and lustrous representative. A strike-through on the reverse border at 10 o'clock and a faint pinscratch east of the date are noted. Census: 20 in 64, 22 finer (7/08). (#2120)

Appealing 1874 Cent, MS65 Red

267 **1874 MS65 Red PCGS.** Copper-gold luster adorns both sides of this Gem, and an attentive strike leaves strong definition on the design elements, including fully delineated diamonds. A few tiny flecks are noted, more so on the reverse, but these do not take away from the coin's overall appeal. A die crack runs through the bottom of the digits in the date. Population: 29 in 65 Red, 5 finer (8/08). (#2120)

Scarce MS65 Red 1874 Indian Cent

268 **1874 MS65 Red PCGS.** This Gem Uncirculated Indian cent has survived more than 130 years with no discernible spotting, a testament to its remarkable state of preservation. The 1874 is among the elusive Indian cent issues from the 1870s, and NGC and PCGS together have certified only eight Red pieces finer (8/08). The strike is sharp throughout, and the surfaces display lovely orange-red color that is evenly matched from one side to the other. (#2120)

269 **1875 MS65 Red and Brown PCGS.** The obverse is mostly light brown and contrasts sharply against the bright orange and rose-red reverse. This fully struck piece is devoid of any marks and has only a couple of microscopic carbon spots. PCGS has certified just three Red and Brown pieces finer (7/08). Housed in a first generation holder. (#2122)

270 **1876 MS65 Red and Brown NGC.** Mostly red-orange with mottled light brown patina at the centers. The obverse has numerous die cracks in the periphery, but the strike is crisp. A lightly marked and unblemished representative. NGC has certified only 14 pieces finer (7/08). (#2125)

271 **1877—Corroded—ICG. Very Good Details.** As the undisputed key to the series, the 1877 is highly desirable in any condition. The obverse of this piece shows a few patches of shallow corrosion, but the reverse is clean and attractive. Significant detail remains, making this coin a nice example of this popular issue. (#2127)

272 **1877 VG10 NGC.** Subtle caramel and lavender overtones grace the otherwise chocolate-brown surfaces, which show considerable gloss. Mildly abraded with the L and RTY of LIBERTY plain on the headband. (#2127)

273 **1877 Fine 12 PCGS.** This deep brown key date cent is without any distracting marks, and has only unimportant granularity. All letters in LIBERTY are at least partially visible, with two letters bold. (#2127)

274 **1877 XF45 ANACS.** Subtle lavender-rose overtones enrich the chocolate-brown surfaces of this lightly circulated key-date cent. Minimally marked and well-defined with striking visual appeal. (#2127)

Desirable AU50 1877 Cent

275 **1877 AU50 NGC.** Between its famous mintage of under a million pieces and collectors' general ignorance of the issue until decades later, the 1877 cent has become one of the greatest prizes in its series. Rich chocolate-brown and walnut-brown surfaces show only light, even wear and few flaws. An attractive example of this famous key in a better circulated state. (#2127)

276 **1877—Improperly Cleaned—NCS. Unc. Details.** Shallow N in ONE, characteristic of the business strike. Sharply struck and smooth. Recolored at one time but now partly retoned gunmetal-gray and caramel-gold with a slightly brighter area on the lower left obverse. (#2127)

277 **1877—Improperly Cleaned—NCS. Unc. Details.** Shallow N in ONE. This recolored key date cent is principally lilac-red, although lemon-gold occasionally emerges and most of the portrait is olive-brown. The left obverse has a few thin marks. (#2127)

Magnificent MS66 Red 1878 Cent

278 **1878 MS66 Red NGC.** This peach-red Premium Gem has booming luster, and the strike is intricate save for the upper right corner of the shield. Only microscopic flecks and ticks deny technical perfection. Mintages had yet to recover from the 1877 drought, since the 1878 is the final Philadelphia issue with a mintage of less than 6 million pieces. Census: 4 in 66 Red, 0 finer (7/08). (#2132)

279 **1881 MS65 Red PCGS.** Eye-catching rose-orange surfaces show lovely yellow accents around the perimeter. A couple of tiny abrasions are noted on Liberty's cheek. PCGS has certified just 26 pieces finer (7/08). Encapsulated in a green label holder. (#2141)

Incredible 1882 Indian Cent, MS66 Red

280 **1882 MS66 Red PCGS.** An absolutely stunning Premium Gem, this cent has bold design features on each side with no evidence of weakness anywhere. The obverse is satiny and fully brilliant with light orange color. The reverse has deeper orange-red color with fully brilliant mint frost. This is an amazing example with few peers. Population: 21 in 66, 2 finer (7/08). (#2144)

281 **1883 MS65 Red NGC.** A delightful rose-red and orange piece with excellent eye appeal. The strike is nearly full, and there are only a few minor flyspecks. NGC has certified just 21 examples finer (7/08). (#2147)

Gorgeous MS66 Red 1883 Cent

282 **1883 MS66 Red NGC. CAC.** Dazzling luster and an undisturbed appearance confirm the quality of this crisply struck Premium Gem. Apricot-gold overall with a blush of rose on the cheek and the obverse border near 5 o'clock. Housed in an older generation holder. Census: 18 in 66 Red, 3 finer (7/08). (#2147)

Popular 1886 Type Two Cent, MS65 Red and Brown

283 **1886 Type Two MS65 Red and Brown NGC.** Close to full red, although this orange-red Gem has slightly mellowed color on the portrait. Boldly struck and lustrous with a sublime obverse and minuscule flecks on the reverse field. The 1886 Type Two is a popular semi-key identified by the location of the lowest headdress feather relative to the CA in AMERICA. (#92155)

284 **1892 MS65 Red NGC.** Bright red-orange patina covers the surfaces of this impeccably preserved Gem. The top feathers of Liberty's headdress are a trifle soft, as usual, but the rest of the details are bold. This virtually unmarked piece has a number of tiny flecks that limit the grade. Census: 36 in 65 Red, 4 finer (7/08). (#2183)

285 **1893 MS65 Red NGC.** FS-10.95, Snow-2. Described as "scarce." The 893 in the date is widely repunched, and remnants are visible east of the date. This lustrous, cherry-red Gem is sharply struck aside from the typical softness on the tips of the uppermost headdress feathers. Both sides have just a few wispy grazes, and the reverse has a couple of small toning flecks. (#2186)

Essential Registry Set Variety
1894 Doubled Date Snow-1, MS65 Red
Tied for Finest PCGS-Certified

286 **1894 Doubled Date MS65 Red PCGS.** Snow-1. The 1894/94 Doubled Date is collected with the regular issues alongside a few other varieties including the 1873 Doubled LIBERTY, the 1867/67, and 1869/69. The variety features the most prominently repunched date in the entire series, and this piece is currently one of only 11 Gem Red pieces certified at PCGS, with none finer (8/08). The lustrous brick-red surfaces show wonderful eye appeal and a bold strike. An essential acquisition for Registry Set collectors, this rare PCGS-certified Gem Red coin is also worth a whopping seven-point bonus in the PCGS Indian Cents with Varieties, Circulation Strikes collection. Certified in a green-label holder and accompanied by an Eagle Eye Photo Seal and certificate.

Gorgeous 1900 Indian Cent, MS66 Red

287 **1900 MS66 Red PCGS.** A splendid Premium Gem with rich orange mint luster and frosty surfaces. Four individual feather tips are slightly flat, but all other details on both sides are boldly brought up. The spot-free surfaces are pristine. A lovely example. Population: 56 in 66, 6 finer (8/08). (#2207)

288 **1903 MS66 Red NGC.** Sharply struck with luscious copper-red and lime-green toning, and intense coruscating luster across both sides. Other than a minor mark in the upper left obverse field, the surfaces are impressively preserved. Census: 55 in 66, 7 finer (7/08). (#2216)

Attractive 1903 Cent, Premium Gem Red

289 **1903 MS66 Red PCGS.** Appealing cherry-red patina endows the resplendent surfaces. Flashy mint luster shimmers across both sides and highlights the boldly struck devices. The reverse is nearly perfect, and only a couple of marks are visible under magnification on the obverse. An impressive high-grade example. NGC and PCGS combined report just 12 pieces finer (8/08). (#2216)

290 **1908 MS66 Red PCGS.** Pleasing red-orange patina envelops the surfaces of this lustrous Premium Gem. Careful inspection with a loupe reveals a few insignificant flyspecks and only a couple of microscopic handling marks. Fully struck with great eye appeal. Population: 40 in 66, 0 finer (8/08). (#2231)

Flashy 1908-S Cent, MS66 Red

291 **1908-S MS66 Red PCGS.** The popular 1908-S is a semi-key at all levels of preservation. This fully Red Premium Gem displays unbelievable flash. Copper-gold luster adorns both sides, and a well executed strike brings out crisp definition on the design features, including sharpness on all four diamonds. Close examination reveals no marks or spots worthy of note. Housed in a first generation holder. Population: 33 in 66 Red, 0 finer (8/08). (#2234)

292 **1909 MS66 Red PCGS.** Well struck and remarkably clean. The fiery copper-orange color is virtually unperturbed despite the passage of nearly a century. Splendid eye appeal. PCGS has graded a mere four finer Red examples (8/08).
From The Bell Collection. (#2237)

293 **1909 MS66 Red PCGS.** The shimmering luster and mint-red coloration are even and unbroken across the two sides of this impressive example, struck in the final year of the Indian cent series. A tiny nick directly above the third feather tip in Liberty's headdress, and a faint toning streak on her neck, are too trivial to preclude the Premium Gem grade assessment. (#2237)

294 **1909-S VG8 PCGS.** The obverse of this significantly circulated final-year Indian cent shows streaks of caramel and chocolate, while the latter shade is uniform on the obverse. The letters RTY of LIBERTY are plain. (#2238)

295 **1909-S MS64 Red and Brown PCGS.** With the lowest mintage in the series (309,000 pieces), the 1909-S is a popular scarcity from the final year of Indian cents. A delightful mix of bright red and medium brown patina covers both sides of this carefully preserved specimen. Just a couple of tiny flecks and handling marks are visible on each side. This boldly defined example is encapsulated in a first generation PCGS holder. (#2239)

296 **1909-S MS64 Red and Brown PCGS.** The reverse is nearly fully red, while the obverse is brick-red aside from gunmetal-gray on the portrait and left obverse field. Crisply struck save for the feathertips, and no marks are visible. (#2239)

297 **1909-S MS65 Red and Brown NGC.** An impressive, exceptionally clean, and highly lustrous representative of this desirable key date. The obverse is almost entirely red and orange, which contrasts nicely against the interesting pattern of orange and medium brown streaks on the reverse. A mere eight examples have been certified finer by NGC (7/08). Housed in an old NGC holder. (#2239)

298 **1909-S MS63 Red PCGS.** Crisply struck and satiny with orange-red color and a smattering of minute obverse flecks. A famous key date that has an even lower mintage than its 1909-S VDB Lincoln cent successor. (#2240)

PROOF INDIAN CENTS

Impressive 1859 Indian Cent, Gem Proof

299 **1859 PR65 NGC.** Delightful rose and orange colors intermingle across the surfaces of this razor-sharp Gem. Peppered flyspecks are particularly evident on the reverse of this otherwise unmarked specimen. A powerfully lustrous example of the first Indian Head cent. Only about 800 proofs are estimated to have been struck. Census: 31 in 65, 22 finer (8/08). (#2247)

300 **1862 PR64 PCGS.** The 1862 is one of just five years of Variety Two (Copper-Nickel with Shield) Indian cents issued, and it boasts a diminutive mintage of approximately 550 proofs. Bright red and orange intermingle on the surfaces of this resplendent specimen. A couple of tiny flecks and abrasions are noted. (#2259)

301 **1862 PR65 PCGS.** The original "white" surfaces have mellowed slightly, with an even overlay of tan patina. A few tiny specks of carbon can be found with a magnifier on each side. The most frequently encountered date in the copper-nickel series and thus an obvious choice for a type set. (#2259)

Exceptional PR67 1862 Indian Cent

302 **1862 PR67 NGC.** Despite a limited mintage of approximately 550 pieces, the 1862 is the most readily obtainable proof issue in the copper-nickel Indian cent series. Nevertheless, many of these coins were mishandled during the war years, and the present Superb Gem is rare from a condition standpoint. Warm, champagne-tan color dominates this coin's outward appearance, and significant reflectivity is seen in the fields. There are no areas of noticeable striking softness, and the surfaces are expectantly hairline-free for the grade. This coin shares the PR67 grade level with only five examples at NGC and PCGS, and it is bettered by none (8/08). (#2259)

303 **1864 Copper Nickel PR64 Cameo PCGS.** This outstanding specimen is nearly covered with bright orange and red luster, and has only the slightest traces of brown patina. The devices are lightly frosted and contrast sharply against the highly reflective fields. A few microscopic flecks are noted on the reverse, but each side is virtually devoid of abrasions. The obverse has an interesting weblike array of die cracks at the center, which indicates the beginning of significant die failure. (#82265)

Splendid 1864 Copper-Nickel Cent, Snow-PR1 PR65 ★ Cameo

304 **1864 Copper Nickel PR65 ★ Cameo NGC.** Snow-PR1. TA are firmly joined, and all of the A's and the date digits show frosty (unpolished) centers. On the reverse, there is a small diagonal file mark at the base of the T in CENT. One seldom sees copper or copper-nickel certified proof coinage from NGC with the Star and Cameo designations, but they are incredibly apt here. This piece displays splendid tan-on-black surfaces, along with a remarkably sharp strike and premium eye appeal. Only a few tiny obverse flecks that appear under a loupe apparently prevent an even finer grade. A couple of areas of brilliance appear just before and behind the Indian's ear, standing out against the otherwise-frosted devices. Interestingly, the reverse is rotated perhaps 15 degrees counterclockwise from the obverse, a feature Snow notes on "25% of known examples." Simply splendid quality for this popular type coin, from an estimated proof mintage of only 370 pieces. (#82265)

Iridescently Toned 1864 No L Indian Cent PR65 Red and Brown

305 **1864 Bronze No L PR65 Red and Brown NGC.** Predictably, the 1864 is scarce in high grade and with some red color simply because it is the first year of issue for the new bronze alloy. Unlike other first year of issue coins, this one does not appear to have been saved in any appreciable numbers. The surfaces of this piece are extraordinarily lovely. There is significant red color present in addition to lime-green and slight brown, producing an iridescent effect. Deeply mirrored fields. Census: 16 in 65, 17 finer (7/08). (#2277)

306 **1865 PR64 Red PCGS.** A dusting of deep red patina covers the otherwise bright orange surfaces. The fields appear deeply mirrored when put under a lamp, and there are virtually no abrasions on either side save for a tiny lint mark by Liberty's ear. A couple of nearly microscopic flecks limit the grade. Approximately 500 proofs were minted. (#2284)

Charming 1865 Cent, PR64 Red

307 **1865 PR64 Red PCGS.** Powerful luster radiates beneath lovely red-orange and yellow patina, with a patch of deep maroon above Liberty's head. A number of small carbon spots limit the grade, but the surfaces are virtually devoid of any marks. This charming piece is one of approximately 500 proofs struck and is housed in a green label holder. Population: 14 in 64 Red, 9 finer (8/08). (#2284)

308 **1865 PR64 Red NGC.** Plain 5. Mostly honey-gold, save for variegated orange and lilac on the central reverse. Sharply struck and devoid of marks. Census: 8 in 64 Red, 6 finer (7/08). (#2284)

309 **1868 PR64 Red NGC.** An attractive red and orange specimen with a nearly medallic alignment, which is typical for proof 1868 cents. Several faint hairlines in the fields preclude a higher grade. One of approximately 600 proofs minted. Census: 7 in 64 Red, 6 finer (7/08). (#2293)

310 **1871 PR65 Brown NGC.** Crisply struck with deep lilac, purple-blue, and amber-gold toning over the two sides. Well preserved and free of hairlines or bothersome contact marks. Census: 8 in 65 Brown, 2 finer in Brown (7/08). (#2300)

311 **1871 PR65 Red and Brown PCGS.** Though the peripheral elements are generally unturned reddish-orange, deeper violet-brown shadings characterize the centers. Boldly impressed and carefully preserved, and housed in a small-format holder. (#2301)

312 **1872 PR64 Red and Brown PCGS.** This sharply struck piece deserves a designation of Red, as its bright rose-orange surfaces have only a trace of brown. Several carbon spots limit the grade, but there are virtually no marks. One of approximately 950 proofs minted. (#2304)

Remarkable 1872 Cent
PR66 Red and Brown

313 **1872 PR66 Red and Brown NGC.** A remarkable Premium Gem example of this scarce proof issue. Light tan patina adorns the motifs that are nicely highlighted against the copper-gold fields that show occasional splashes of crimson and sky-blue. An attentive strike leaves strong definition on the design elements. Both sides are devoid of significant contacts or spots. Census: 8 in 66 Red and Brown, 0 finer (7/08). (#2304)

314 **1873 Closed 3 PR64 Cameo NGC.** The intricate design elements are all crisply delineated, including the feather tips of Liberty's headdress. A touch cloudy in the fields, but expertly preserved and free of contact marks or hairlines. One of just two pieces graded as Red and Brown Cameo by NGC (the other is a PR65), as of (8/08). (#82308)

315 **1874 PR65 Red and Brown Cameo NGC.** This pinpoint-sharp Gem has green-gold centers bounded by cherry-red. The devices display obvious contrast with the flashy fields. A splendid Gem that must be seen in person to be best appreciated. (#2310)

Extraordinary 1874 Indian Cent, PR66 Red Cameo

316 **1874 PR66 Red Cameo NGC.** Snow-PR1. This scarce proof issue has the diagonal of the 4 extending into the field past the crossbar. This is the only proof die marriage for the year, according to Snow, and the result of a defective digit punch rather than die repunching. (The same digit punch occurs on nonproof examples of the year.)

Because of the scarcity of 1874 business strikes, proofs of this date enjoy added demand from collectors. This exceptional Premium Gem has bright, unmellowed golden-tan surfaces overall and mildly frosted devices contrasted over highly reflective fields. The piece is sharply struck, well preserved, and free of hairlines or contact marks. (#82311)

Key-Date 1877 Cent, PR65 Red and Brown

317 **1877 PR65 Red and Brown PCGS.** While no precise mintage figures are available for this key issue, it is believed that some 900 proofs were produced, as part of both "silver" proof sets and "nickel" proof sets and sold as singles over the counter at the Mint. This is very well preserved example that has deeply reflective proof mirrors in the fields. Both original mint red and bright lime-green compete for color dominance on this exceptionally attractive coin. Fully struck throughout. Population: 59 in 65, 5 finer (8/08). (#2319)

318 **1878 PR65 Red NGC.** Attractive rose-red devices contrast nicely against the vivid yellow-orange fields. This fully struck Gem has only a couple of insignificant contact marks, but there are number of tiny flyspecks on the obverse. A mere 2,350 proofs were minted. Certified in an old NGC holder. Census: 20 in 65 Red, 7 finer (7/08). (#2323)

319 **1880 PR65 Red PCGS.** Vivid rose-red and orange patina endows the highly reflective surfaces of this attractive Gem. Careful examination reveals a couple of minor handling marks and scattered flecks. Nonetheless, this nearly fully struck piece has excellent eye appeal and is housed in a green label PCGS holder. One of just 3,955 proofs struck. Population: 62 in 65, 24 finer (7/08). (#2329)

320 **1880 PR65 Red PCGS.** Orange-red and butter-gold grace this needle-sharp and unmarked Gem. A couple of minor peripheral spots are of little account. In a green label holder. Population: 62 in 65 Red, 24 finer (8/08). (#2329)

321 **1881 PR65 Cameo NGC.** A wonderful Gem proof with mellow red surfaces and excellent contrast between the mirrored fields and frosty devices. Minor spots on each side prevent a higher grade. (#82332)

322 **1883 PR65 Red PCGS.** Rose and bright orange colors intermingle on the surfaces of this powerfully struck Gem. A tiny spot is noted above the upper arrow shaft, but there are virtually no imperfections otherwise. A mere 6,609 proofs were minted. Population: 16 in 65 Red, 6 finer (7/08). (#2338)

323 **1884 PR65 Red PCGS.** Intricately struck and prominently mirrored with mark-free surfaces. A solitary speck northwest of the C in CENT will identify future appearances of the present Gem. Encased in an old green label holder. Population: 48 in 65 Red, 41 finer (8/08). (#2341)

324 **1885 PR65 Red NGC.** Vivid red and orange covers the intricately detailed surfaces. This well-preserved and fully struck Gem shows only a couple of tiny lint marks under magnification. One of only 3,790 proofs minted. Census: 4 in 65 Red, 4 finer (7/08). (#2344)

Near-Gem Proof Red 1886 Type Two Indian Cent

325 **1886 Type Two PR64 Red PCGS.** Bowers' *Guide Book of Flying Eagle and Indian Cents* estimates that perhaps 40% of the total proofs for this year were of the new Type Two hub variety, introduced this year and lasting through the end of the series. Only in 1954 did collectors begin discriminating between the two variants. This piece displays plenty of dusky orange-red coloration, with some waves of light olive toning in the left obverse field. Seldom seen finer. Population: 10 in 64 Red, 3 finer (8/08). (#92347)

326 **1889 PR65 Red PCGS.** Enticing bright orange and red patina drapes each side, with highly reflective fields that enhance the spectacular eye appeal. Speckled copper spots in the fields are minor. A mere 3,336 proofs were struck. Population: 16 in 65 Red, 8 finer (7/08). (#2356)

327 **1891 PR64 Cameo NGC.** Watery fields and sharply frosted devices characterize this attractive near-Gem proof. This issue had a fairly high mintage of 2,350 pieces, but apparently has a low survival ratio, as examples are very scarce either with or without the Cameo designation. Census: 2 in 64 Cameo, 2 finer (7/08). (#82362)

Amazing Full Red PR67 1892 Indian Cent

328 **1892 PR67 Red NGC.** This beautiful Superb Gem proof seems to be virtually without flaws. Sharply struck and pristine with lovely, even, fire-red coloration, a few mint-green high point accents, and pleasingly reflective fields. Just seven pieces have been graded PR67 by NGC and PCGS combined, with none finer (8/08). (#2365)

329 **1897 PR65 Red and Brown Cameo NGC.** This meticulously struck Gem displays beautiful sun-gold, ruby-red, ocean-blue, and lime shades when it is rotated beneath a light. No carbon is visible, and the portrait exhibits obvious contrast with the glassy obverse field. (#2379)

330 **1902 PR66 Red PCGS.** Snow-PR1. Lime, deep red, and pale rose hues endow this bright orange, intricately struck Premium Gem. A small spot of carbon is noted in front of the headband. Only a couple of minor handling marks are visible under magnification. (#2395)

331 **1909 PR65 Red NGC.** Whispers of light green and crimson visit the copper-gold surfaces of this Gem proof cent. Nice field-motif contrast is evident when the coin is tilted slightly under a light source. Sharply struck and well preserved. Census: 17 in 65 Red, 10 finer (7/08). (#2416)

LINCOLN CENTS

332 **1909 VDB MS67 Red PCGS.** An impressive example of this popular and relatively affordable one-year type. Fully struck with excellent detail and frosty pale orange luster. An appealing representative. PCGS has certified only one piece finer (7/08). (#2425)

333 **1909 VDB MS67 Red PCGS.** Smooth wheat and copper-gold surfaces offer crisp detail and striking luster. A seemingly unimprovable survivor, housed in a green label holder. PCGS has graded just one finer Red representative (8/08). *From The Davis Conway Collection.* (#2425)

Red Gem 1909 VDB Cent
Doubled Die Obverse, FS-1101

334 **1909 VDB Doubled Die Obverse MS65 Red PCGS.** FS-1101, formerly FS-012. Most of LIBERTY and the date are die doubled to the northwest. This is a beautiful Gem with dazzling luster and attractive orange-red and olive-gold color. Intricately struck, and separated from a higher grade by only a faint graze near the face.

335 **1909 VDB DDO MS64 Red and Brown PCGS.** FS-1101, previously FS-012. The date and the RTY in LIBERTY are nicely die doubled. This satiny near-Gem is crisply struck and offers variegated lilac and steel-gray toning. (#82424)

336 **1909-S VDB—Environmental Damage—NCS. XF Details.** A lightly circulated chocolate-brown key date cent that has peripheral gray verdigris, somewhat more prominent on the reverse. Inspection beneath a lens reveals a few trivial marks. *From The Morton J. Greene Collection.* (#2426)

337 **1909-S VDB—Cleaned—ANACS. XF45 Details.** The oddly lustrous copper-pink and olive-green surfaces show significant streakiness and a handful of hairlines. Minimally flawed otherwise with few marks and only light wear. (#2426)

338 **1909-S VDB—Improperly Cleaned—NCS. AU Details.** A lightly circulated golden-brown example of this popular series key. No hairlines are readily evident, and the color appears natural. Faint parallel marks, likely of mint origin, extend from UNUM to the VDB initials. The field near the profile has a wood-grain texture. (#2426)

339 **1909-S VDB—Improperly Cleaned—NCS. AU Details.** Authentication by one of the major third-party grading companies is always advisable when dealing with a famous key date issue like the 1877 Indian cent, the 1916-D Mercury dime, or the 1909-S VDB Lincoln cent. This example has been improperly cleaned, and exhibits highpoint wear consistent with the AU Details assessment by NCS, but lacks any appreciable surface marks. (#2426)

340 **1909-S VDB AU58 NGC.** A touch of light rub limits the grade of this crisply defined representative. Streaks of medium brown and chestnut toning cover both sides. The surfaces are remarkably unabraded and have great eye appeal. (#2426)

1909-S VDB Cent, MS64 Brown

341 **1909-S VDB MS64 Brown NGC.** This key-date cent, in an older NGC holder, is interestingly tagged thereon as a "1909 VDB S 1C," but it is a no-questions 1909-S VDB, with sharp designer's initials showing all three periods. The obverse shows mottled woodgrain toning in shades of blue and pinkish-orange, while the reverse is a more lustrous and consistent pinkish-blue. (#2426)

342 **1909-S VDB MS62 Red and Brown ICG.** A mostly red example of this famous key-date Lincoln cent. The reverse exhibits especially pleasing satiny luster. There are only a couple of minor marks and flyspecks, although mention is needed of a fairly prominent carbon spot to the left of the bust near the rim. Overall, a nice and crisply struck piece. (#2427)

Attractive MS64 Red and Brown 1909-S VDB

343 **1909-S VDB MS64 Red and Brown PCGS.** A satiny near-Gem with olive-brown centers and red-gold peripheries. Sharply struck, particularly on the VDB initials, which on many examples are blurry or in low relief. A worthy representative of this perennial collector favorite. Encapsulated in an old green label holder. (#2427)

Lustrous Near-Gem Red and Brown 1909-S VDB Cent

344 **1909-S VDB MS64 Red and Brown NGC.** All three designer's initials show boldly on this near-Gem Red and Brown coin, which offers lustrous burnt-orange surfaces and good eye appeal. A loupe reveals a couple of nicks on Lincoln's beard that prevent a finer grade, but carbon is minimal, and elsewhere there are few singular distractions. (#2427)

Delightful 1909-S VDB Lincoln Cent, MS64 Red and Brown

345 **1909-S VDB MS64 Red and Brown NGC.** At first glance the surfaces appear entirely cherry-red, but a close inspection reveals streaks of medium brown patina, particularly on the reverse. Dazzling satiny luster shimmers across the minimally abraded surfaces and accents the powerfully impressed design elements. An attractive example of this popular first-year issue. (#2427)

Popular 1909-S VDB Cent, MS64 Red and Brown

346 **1909-S VDB MS64 Red and Brown PCGS.** A well struck and gently shimmering orange and sea-green near-Gem. Light spotting is seen on the reverse including minor spots at 7 o'clock and on the left inside edge of the O in ONE. The VDB initials are softly defined but readable. Housed in a first generation holder. (#2427)

Appealing 1909-S VDB, Gem Mint State Red and Brown

347 **1909-S VDB MS65 Red and Brown PCGS. CAC.** An enticing example of this popular key date Lincoln cent. Bright red and orange luster shows streaks of chestnut brown patina on each side. A few scattered flecks around the perimeter of the obverse are the only noticeable imperfections on this delightful Gem. Close examination with a loupe reveals only insignificant marks. An appealing example of one of the most famous U.S. coins. (#2427)

Bold 1909-S VDB Cent, MS65 Red and Brown

348   **1909-S VDB MS65 Red and Brown PCGS.** This frosty piece has light golden-brown luster with a few splashes of lilac and iridescent toning. It is boldly struck with pristine surfaces. The S-VDB cent is well known to collectors, and to many non-collectors as well. It ranks as one of the most popular 20th century American coins. (#2427)

349   **1909-S VDB—Environmental Damage—NCS. XF Details.** Lincoln's cheekbone and jaw show wear, but most design details are bold. Golden-brown and olive-green with an attractive obverse and scattered small gray spots on the reverse. (#2428)

Lovely 1909-S VDB Cent, MS64 Red

350   **1909-S VDB MS64 Red NGC. CAC.** Boldly detailed and fully lustrous with satiny surfaces, this exceptional example exhibits brilliant orange and gold surfaces with speckled deeper orange toning on both sides. Despite a substantial population, the "SVDB" is always in demand, and examples routinely find a ready market, even when multiple pieces are offered in a single auction event. (#2428)

Key Gem Red 1909-S VDB Cent

351   **1909-S VDB MS65 Red PCGS.** The surfaces of this attractive Gem coin show sandy golden-tan coloration, with radiant luster and good eye appeal. All three designer's initials and the periods are plain, and the strike elsewhere is boldly brought up. For many collectors, the Gem Red level is about as nice as can be expected to be found (and afforded). Certified in a green-label holder. (#2428)

Radiant MS66 Red 1909-S VDB Cent

352   **1909-S VDB MS66 Red PCGS.** The 1909-S VDB enjoys a constant level of popularity from Lincoln cent collectors because of its relatively low mintage, its status as the first year of issue, and as a one-year subtype, the only year in which the designer's initials were placed on the lower reverse. All of the 1909 issues have seen unrelenting price pressure with the impending release in 2009 of several new 1809-2009 bicentennial Lincoln cent commemorative issues from the Mint. As such, this Premium Gem 1909-S VDB must be considered as the ultimate acquisition (barring an MS67 Red piece) among the 1909 issues. The Premium Gem offered here combines radiant luster with attractive rose and lemon-yellow highlights. A paper-thin blemish above the N in ONE is useful for future attribution. This piece shows all three periods in the designer's initials, for those who collect the VDB issues according to the classification in Dr. Sol Taylor's *The Standard Guide to the Lincoln Cent.* (#2428)

Beautiful MS67 Red 1909 Cent

353 **1909 MS67 Red PCGS.** A bright orange Superb Gem that boasts brief splashes of yellow-green patina. Well struck with fiery luster. A gorgeous and practically unimprovable representative of this first-year issue. Population: 54 in 67 red, 0 finer (7/08).
From The Kendall Marie PCGS Registry Set (Heritage, 4/2006), lot 467.
From The Davis Conway Collection. (#2431)

354 **1909-S XF40 ICG.** Light to medium brown patina shows on both sides, and the design elements are nicely detailed. There are no mentionable contacts or spots. (#2433)

355 **1909-S MS65 Red and Brown PCGS. CAC.** Although designated Red and Brown by PCGS, this piece is mostly bright orange and red, with a dusting of brown across the devices. There are a couple of microscopic flecks, but overall the surfaces are exceptionally clean. A sharply struck example with impressive eye appeal. (#2433)

356 **1909-S MS65 Red and Brown PCGS.** Copper-gold and tan patina decorates the lustrous surfaces that exhibit sharply struck design elements. We note a few slight, inoffensive flecks. (#2433)

Delightful 1909-S Lincoln Cent MS66 Red

357 **1909-S MS66 Red PCGS.** Although not as widely recognized as the 1909-S VDB, the 1909-S is still a low mintage (1.8 million pieces) issue whose certified population falls off rapidly above the MS65 grade level. This premium example boasts clean surfaces and intriguing pink-red luster. A frosty example, the devices display pinpoint striking detail throughout. Only four pieces have been certified finer by PCGS (7/08).
From The Davis Conway Collection. (#2434)

Lustrous 1909-S Cent, MS66 Red

358 **1909-S MS66 Red PCGS.** Bright copper-gold hues dominate the surfaces of this incredible Lincoln, glowing with rich, satiny luster. Close examination turns up a mere handful of minute toning specks that are absolutely lost in the luster. An attentive strike complements these attributes, enhancing the overall eye appeal. This coin deserves a new owner who appreciates only the finest. (#2434)

359 **1910 MS66 Red PCGS.** The surfaces of this second-year Lincoln cent are generally pale copper-gold, though areas of more overt orange are present near the margins. A small carbon fleck is noted below the L of LIBERTY. PCGS has graded 18 finer Red pieces (8/08). (#2437)

360 **1910 MS67 Red PCGS.** This is a simply gorgeous survivor with frosty, textured surfaces bursting with reddish-orange luster. The color lightens slightly to a lime-green shade at the border areas on each side. Every feature is sharply struck. Population: 18 in 67 Red, 0 finer (8/08).
From The Davis Conway Collection. (#2437)

361 **1911 MS66 Red PCGS.** This radiant apricot-copper Premium Gem is intricately struck and highly lustrous. Marvelous eye appeal and minimal carbon. PCGS has graded only eight finer Red pieces (8/08).
From The Davis Conway Collection. (#2443)

362 **1911-D MS65 Red PCGS.** Generally fresh copper-orange with only the slightest hint of mellowing at the margins. A crisply struck Gem example of the first cent issue coined at Denver. PCGS has graded 18 finer Red pieces (8/08).
From The Davis Conway Collection. (#2446)

Attractive 1911-S Gem Brown Cent

363 **1911-S MS65 Brown NGC.** Delicate reddish-blue patina graces the semi-gloss surfaces of this early Lincoln. The design elements exhibit strong detail, including full separation in the lines of the wheat stalks. Both faces have been well cared for, further enhancing the coin's eye appeal. Census: 14 in 65 Brown, 1 finer (7/08). (#2447)

Charming 1911-S Cent MS65 Red

364 1911-S MS65 Red PCGS. This orange and khaki-gold Gem is essentially devoid of abrasions, and flyspecks are refreshingly few. The strike is good despite minor blending of detail opposite Lincoln's shoulder. A low mintage semi-key that ranks highly on many want lists. Population: 58 in 65 Red, 11 finer (7/08). *From The Davis Conway Collection.* (#2449)

365 1912 MS66 Red PCGS. The obverse shows varying degrees of mint-copper and peach, while the latter color prevails on the well-defined reverse. Highly appealing. PCGS has graded just seven finer Red examples (8/08). *From The Davis Conway Collection.* (#2452)

366 1912 MS66 Red PCGS. Rich reddish-orange surfaces prevail, with occasional dots of lemon-gold appearing close to the portrait. Pleasingly detailed with remarkable eye appeal for this early Lincoln cent issue. PCGS has graded only seven finer Red representatives (8/08). *From The Bell Collection.* (#2452)

367 1912-D MS65 Red and Brown NGC. Pleasing cherry-red and mahogany colors intermingle on the surfaces of this lustrous Gem. Scattered minor flecks limit the grade, and a couple of tiny abrasions are visible under magnification. Powerfully struck and housed in an old NGC holder. (#2454)

Splendid Gem Red 1912-D Lincoln Cent

368 1912-D MS65 Red PCGS. Although not so difficult as some of the later S-mint entries in the Lincoln cent series, the 1912-D is considerably more elusive in Gem Red condition than, for example, the 1910-S or 1911-D in equal grade. This example boasts splendid luster radiating from brick-red surfaces, characteristic of the issue. PCGS has certified only eight Red pieces finer (8/08). (#2455)

Sharp 1912-D Cent, MS66 Red

369 1912-D MS66 Red PCGS. The 1912-D, with a mintage of 4.431 million pieces, is a semi-key date in the Lincoln cent series. David Lange, in *The Complete Guide to Lincoln Cents*, says: "... choice and gem examples having original, fully red or even red/brown color are scarce and always in demand."

Original orange-gold luster exudes from both sides of this Red Premium Gem, and an attentive strike leaves crisp definition on the design elements, including the bow tie and lines in the wheat stalks. A couple of tiny light flecks are noted, but these do not disturb. Population: 8 in 66 Red, 0 finer (8/08). (#2455)

Desirable Red Gem 1912-S Cent

370 1912-S MS65 Red PCGS. Reddish-orange cascades over the top two-thirds of the obverse and most of the reverse on this superb San Francisco example of an early Gem Lincoln. With fully lustrous and virtually mark-free surfaces, this piece exhibits clashed-die features on the reverse. Difficult to obtain in all grades and even more so in Mint State. Housed in a green label holder. Population: 42 in 65 Red, 0 finer (7/08). *Ex: Mike Sadler Collection (Heritage, 1/2004), lot 4600, which realized $5,175. From The Davis Conway Collection.* (#2458)

Charming 1913 Cent MS66 Red

371 **1913 MS66 Red PCGS.** A boldly impressed peach-red and olive Premium Gem. Luster dominates the fields and devices, and marks are virtually non-existent. Minor carbon near 10 o'clock on the reverse is of little concern. The right obverse field has a faint wood-grain appearance, as made. Population: 60 in 66 Red, 4 finer (7/08). *From The Davis Conway Collection.* (#2461)

Elusive Red Gem 1913-D Cent

372 **1913-D MS65 Red PCGS.** This shimmering brick-red Gem has a penetrating strike and an impeccably unabraded appearance. The occasional minute fleck is all that determines the grade. Only the third Denver Mint issue, struck the same year the Buffalo nickel was introduced. Population: 95 in 65 Red, 10 finer (7/08). *From The Davis Conway Collection.* (#2464)

373 **1914-D AU53 PCGS.** Blended olive-gold and tan embraces this well defined and unblemished key date cent. Scarcer than the heralded 1909-S VDB in better grades. Housed in an old green label holder. (#2471)

374 **1914-D AU55 PCGS.** This is an impressively detailed Choice AU example of the vaunted '14-D Lincoln cent, one of the most important key dates in the entire series. Well struck with rather dark violet-brown toning, light wear on the highest design points, and few marks on either side. (#2471)

Lustrous MS64 Red and Brown 1914-D Cent

375 **1914-D MS64 Red and Brown ANACS.** Like many Mint State examples of this key date, the surfaces are actually a pinkish-red with blue on the high points of the obverse. The reverse is a more consistent orange-red with sprinkles of brown, but both sides offer much appeal. Several different mintmark positions are known for the issue, and this piece is one with the mintmark fairly close to the date. The good luster more than compensates for a few minor obverse flecks that appear under a loupe. (#2472)

Key 1914-D Cent, MS64 Red

376 **1914-D MS64 Red PCGS.** A crisply struck near-Gem without any consequential marks. Generally medium orange-gold, with moderate mellowing on the central reverse. The 1914-D has one of the lowest mintages of the entire series, and is among the keys to acquiring a complete set. Encased in a green label holder. *From The Davis Conway Collection.* (#2473)

377 **1914-S MS64 Red and Brown ICG.** The obverse is almost entirely red, while the reverse is light brown. Scattered flecks and minuscule abrasions are typical of the grade. A lovely example of a rather elusive S-mint Lincoln cent. (#2475)

Laudable MS66 Red 1915 Cent

378 **1915 MS66 Red PCGS.** The 1915 has by far the lowest production of any Philadelphia Mint issue from the teens, a little over 29 million pieces. This example has bright orange-gold luster across exemplary surfaces. The design features are crisply struck throughout, with no areas revealing hints of weakness. Virtually devoid of mentionable abrasions or carbon spots. Population: 79 in 66 Red, 6 finer (7/08). *Ex: San Francisco ANA Signature (Heritage, 7/2005), lot 5253, which realized $2,530.* *From The Davis Conway Collection.* (#2479)

379 **1915-D MS65 Red PCGS.** Vibrant lemon-gold surfaces show slight pebbling in the fields, close to subtle orange accents. A boldly struck and appealing Red Gem. PCGS has graded only 17 finer pieces in the color category (8/08). *From The Davis Conway Collection.* (#2482)

Appealing 1915-S Cent, MS64 Red and Brown

380 **1915-S MS64 Red and Brown PCGS.** An elusive S-mint issue in the Lincoln cent series in Gem and finer condition, albeit a well-produced one when encountered in the higher Mint State grades. This 1915-S near-Gem Red and Brown piece boasts plenty of eye appeal, with fiery red lying under a coating of ice-blue on the obverse and plenty of luster throughout. The reverse on its own would garner a Red ranking, and in terms of contact and eye appeal, the piece appears high-end for the MS64 grade. (#2484)

381 **1915-S MS64 Red PCGS.** Elements of lime and copper-orange combine with a hint of violet on this intriguing Choice S-mint piece. Well struck and pleasingly preserved for the grade. Population: 48 in 64 Red, 33 finer (8/08).
From The Davis Conway Collection. (#2485)

382 **1916 MS66 Red PCGS. CAC.** An appealing apricot and rose representative with charming satiny luster throughout. Scattered yet nearly microscopic flecks are the only flaws with this otherwise outstanding specimen. PCGS has certified only 34 pieces finer (7/08). (#2488)

383 **1916 MS66 Red PCGS.** Bright apricot and rose colors intermingle across the surfaces, which have a distinct orange-peel texture. A few wispy handling marks keep this impressive piece from an even higher grade. PCGS has certified just 34 pieces finer (8/08). (#2488)

Red Superb Gem 1916 Cent

384 **1916 MS67 Red PCGS.** A precisely struck and highly lustrous Superb Gem with orange and pale lime hues. A loupe is required to locate distributed minute carbon. Superior eye appeal confirms the lofty certified grade. A popular Philadelphia issue. Population: 34 in 67 Red, 0 finer (7/08).
From The Davis Conway Collection. (#2488)

Widely Pursued MS65 Red 1916-D Cent

385 **1916-D MS65 Red PCGS.** A lustrous brick-red beauty. Despite its branch mint status, the strike is penetrating, and both sides have only minimal carbon. The 1916-D is easily located in most circulated grades, but attractive full red examples are difficult to acquire. Population: 39 in 65 Red, 4 finer (7/08).
From The Davis Conway Collection. (#2491)

386 **1916-S MS64 Red NGC.** Light tan patina shows accents of rose-red in the fields. A couple of minuscule abrasions and flecks limit the grade, but overall the surfaces are remarkably clean. Boldly struck with great eye appeal. The 1916-S is seldom seen fully Red, but this piece is exceptional. Census: 27 in 64, 6 finer (7/08). (#2494)

387 **1917 Doubled Die Obverse XF45 ANACS.** FS-013. Doubling is most apparent on the date and WE TRUST. Charming mahogany patina graces the surfaces of this minimally marked representative. Handsome, well detailed, and listed in the *Guide Book.* (#2495)

388 **1917 MS66 Red PCGS.** Bright orange-red patina endows the surfaces of this carefully preserved Premium Gem. There is a tiny "flake," possibly a lamination from another planchet, stuck to the rim below the bust. A couple of tiny spots limit the grade, but this piece is virtually devoid of any marks. PCGS has certified only 16 Red examples finer (8/08). (#2497)

389 **1917 MS66 Red PCGS.** Fire-red and pale olive alternate across this high-end example. The strike is unimprovably sharp, and only a handful of tiny flyspecks appear close to the portrait.
From The Davis Conway Collection. (#2497)

Satiny Red Gem 1917-D Cent

390 **1917-D MS65 Red PCGS.** This brick-red Gem has barely mellowed despite the passing of more than 70 years. A mark-free Gem that has good luster and a suitable strike. Patience and a loupe eventually locates infrequent pinpoint carbon. Population: 42 in 65 Red, 5 finer (7/08).
Ex: Francis Sullivan Collection (Heritage, 11/2002), lot 5426, which realized $2,185.
From The Davis Conway Collection. (#2500)

391 **1917-S MS64 Red PCGS.** Dusky reddish-orange and peach shadings prevail on this Red near-Gem. Well-defined with excellent overall eye appeal. Population: 57 in 64 Red, 17 finer (8/08).
From The Davis Conway Collection. (#2503)

Exquisite 1918 Cent, MS67 Red

392 **1918 MS67 Red NGC.** With 288 million plus pieces produced, one has to wonder why no more than a mere handful of coins were saved in Superb Red condition. NGC has certified a mere two MS67 Red pieces and none finer (8/08). The surfaces have a warm reddish glow with just a touch of lilac over the portrait of Lincoln. There are no obvious abrasions on either side and the coin displays the finely granular texture often seen. The design elements are exquisitely brought up. (#2506)

393 **1918-S MS65 Red and Brown PCGS.** Streaks of brown patina mix with bright mint red across both sides. A couple of light abrasions on Lincoln and a tiny fleck on the reverse are barely noticeable. A fully struck and conditionally scarce representative. Population: 18 in 65 Red and Brown, 0 finer (7/08). (#2511)

Exquisite Red Near-Gem 1918-S Cent

394 **1918-S MS64 Red PCGS.** A satiny Choice early branch mint cent that lacks any visible marks. The golden-orange surfaces show occasional hints of olive-gray. The strike is impeccable aside from unimportant incompleteness along the right reverse border. Population: 65 in 64 Red, 15 finer (7/08).
From The Davis Conway Collection. (#2512)

Eye-Catching MS67 Red 1919 Cent

395 **1919 MS67 Red PCGS.** The peach centers are framed by greenish yellow-gold. Dynamic luster brightens this fully struck Superb Gem. Strong magnification is necessary to locate even trivial imperfections. A ravishing example from the final Philly issue of the teens. Population: 55 in 67 Red, 15 finer (7/08).
From The Davis Conway Collection. (#2515)

Spectacular 1919 Cent, MS67 Red

396 **1919 MS67 Red NGC.** A spectacular example of this early issue. The surfaces display bright copper-gold luster and exquisitely defined design elements. Impeccably preserved, with no apparent marks or spots. Great overall eye appeal! Housed in a prior generation holder. Census: 11 in 67 Red , 0 finer (7/08). (#2515)

Exceptional Red Gem 1919-D Cent

397 **1919-D MS65 Red NGC.** Like other branch mint issues from the teens, the 1919-D is difficult to locate in full red above the MS64 level. This Gem has scintillating luster and is sharply struck. Carbon is essentially absent, and the obverse appears pristine. Population: 19 in 65 Red, 0 finer (7/08).
Ex: Common Cents Collection (Heritage, 11/2003), lot 204. (#2518)

Challenging 1919-D Cent MS65 Red

398 **1919-D MS65 Red PCGS.** Impressive cartwheel sheen dominates this nicely struck and unabraded Gem. Radiant pumpkin-gold fields occasionally cede to olive or rose shades. Like so many branch mint issues from the teens, the 1919-D is difficult to find in such exemplary quality. Population: 56 in 65 Red, 12 finer (7/08).
Ex: FUN Signature (Heritage, 1/2007), lot 1784, which realized $4,025.
From The Davis Conway Collection. (#2518)

399 **1920 MS66 Red PCGS.** The obverse is primarily copper-yellow, while the well struck reverse is more orange. Carefully preserved and pleasing. PCGS has graded just five finer Red pieces (8/08).
From The Davis Conway Collection. (#2524)

Red Premium Gem 1921 Cent

400 **1921 MS66 Red PCGS.** Coruscating luster endows this splendidly preserved Premium Gem. Well struck and thoroughly attractive. The 1921 is low mintage for a Philadelphia issue, probably due to unprecedented Morgan dollar production. Population: 59 in 66 Red, 11 finer (7/08).
From The Davis Conway Collection. (#2533)

Challenging 1921-S Cent, MS64 Red

401   **1921-S MS64 Red PCGS.** A nicely struck straw-gold Choice cent with gray highpoints on the portrait and a couple of faint, thin streaks on the lower reverse. Minor obverse carbon appears beneath a loupe. Population: 87 in 64 Red, 17 finer (7/08).
Ex: Rafael Romero Collection (Heritage, 11/2004), lot 5511.
From The Davis Conway Collection. (#2536)

Elusive MS65 Red 1922-D Cent

402   **1922-D MS65 Red PCGS.** A gorgeous olive-red Gem that lacks the usually seen flyspecks. Sharply struck save for the final 2 in the date. The Denver Mint was the only facility that struck cents in 1922, presumably because of heavy silver dollar production at Philadelphia and San Francisco. Population: 83 in 65 Red, 10 finer (7/08).
From The Davis Conway Collection. (#2539)

403   **1922 No D Strong Reverse Fine 12 NGC.** FS-013.2. Die Pair 2. A chocolate-brown representative of this famous variety. The lines in the wheat ears are mostly separated, and while the obverse is a bit bright, the fields are smooth aside from faded thin marks near the O in ONE. (#3285)

404   **1922 No D Strong Reverse Fine 12 NGC.** FS-013.2. Die Pair 2. Attractive light brown surfaces with excellent eye appeal, the reverse appearing finer than the grade assigned. An important opportunity.
From The Morton J. Greene Collection. (#3285)

405   **1922 No D Strong Reverse Fine 12 PCGS.** FS-013.2. Die Pair 2. IN GOD WE and LIBERTY are blurry but readable. The lines in the wheat ears are generally separated. Sea-green and tan with no mentionable marks. (#3285)

406   **1922 No D Strong Reverse VF20 PCGS.** FS-013.2. Die Pair 2. Well struck with a pleasing woodgrain pattern in chocolate and walnut across the reverse. Even with the moderate wear on the reverse, the lines in the wheat ears are readily visible. (#3285)

407   **1922 No D Strong Reverse VF20 PCGS.** This tan-brown cent has pleasing definition on the wheat ears, and the obverse legends are clear. Nearly mark-free, although faint laminations (as made) are noted near the Y in LIBERTY. Housed in a green label holder. (#3285)

408   **1922 No D Strong Reverse VF25 NGC.** FS-013.2. Die Pair 2. This die marriage is the most desirable of the three known die pairs, and features a strong reverse die. Lovely chocolate-brown patina covers the surfaces of this immensely popular *Guide Book* variety. Scattered marks define the grade, but none merit individual mention. (#3285)

409   **1922 No D Strong Reverse VF30 NGC.** FS-013.2. Die Pair 2. This key date chocolate-brown cent has pleasing surfaces aside from a curvy thin mark above the date. The lines within the wheat ears are sharply defined. (#3285)

1922 No D Die Pair Two Cent, AU50

410   **1922 No D Strong Reverse AU50 PCGS.** The important Die Pair Two of the 1922 No D cent varieties is the most desirable and collectible of the three known die pairings. This example has subdued olive surfaces with mahogany on the reverse. Traces of luster remain on both sides. (#3285)

Handsome Choice AU
Strong Reverse 1922 No D Cent

411   **1922 No D Strong Reverse AU55 NGC. CAC.** FS-013.2. Die Pair 2. Sharp definition on the wheat ears, and a bold second 2 in the date, confirms this desirable variety. A key date cent with consistently smooth chocolate-brown surfaces. Carbon is uncommonly absent, and there are no consequential marks. (#3285)

Red Superb Gem 1923 Cent

412   **1923 MS67 Red PCGS.** Ex: Tom Mershon. The quintessential 1923 Lincoln, both in terms of aesthetics and technical merit. Razor-sharp features show no obvious abrasions and each side is covered with shimmering mint luster. This luster still retains the bright, original orange-red color in some places, but much of each side is also framed in a deep cherry-red patina, which gives the coin dazzling eye appeal. Two tiny spots on Lincoln's beard are easily overlooked. Population: 12 in 67 Red, 1 finer (7/08).
Ex: Tom Mershon #2 All-Time PCGS Registry Set (Heritage, 5/2005), lot 5342.
From The Davis Conway Collection. (#2545)

413   1924 MS66 Red PCGS. Orange, rose-red, and sea-green enrich the obverse, while the reverse is sun-yellow with glimpses of ruby-red near the rim. Booming luster and undisturbed surfaces ensure the quality of this exactingly impressed Premium Gem. Population: 63 in 66 Red, 4 finer (7/08).
From The Davis Conway Collection. (#2551)

Spectacular MS67 Red 1925 Cent

414   1925 MS67 Red PCGS. Dazzling luster sweeps this gorgeous apricot-gold Superb Gem. Meticulously struck and remarkably devoid of abrasions or spots. Only the most inconsequential reverse pinpoint flecks deny perfection. Nearly 140 million pieces were struck, but only a handful remain with such exemplary quality. Population: 50 in 67 Red, 0 finer (7/08).
From The Davis Conway Collection. (#2560)

Lovely Red Gem 1925-D Cent

415   1925-D MS65 Red PCGS. This beautiful pumpkin-gold Gem has an impressive strike, especially on Lincoln's shoulder and opposite on the O in ONE. The surfaces are essentially unabraded, and carbon is virtually absent. Exemplary quality for this scarce branch mint issue. Population: 38 in 65, 1 finer (7/08).
From The Davis Conway Collection. (#2563)

Choice Red 1925-S Cent

416   1925-S MS64 Red PCGS. This satiny near-Gem has pleasing sharpness and surprisingly consistent dusky rose-gold color. Carbon and abrasions are inconsequential. Like all branch mint cents from its decade, the 1925-S is difficult to locate in full Red. Population: 52 in 64 Red, 10 finer (7/08).
From The Davis Conway Collection. (#2566)

Exhilarating Red Superb Gem 1926 Cent

417   1926 MS67 Red PCGS. A boldly struck and thoroughly lustrous honey-gold Superb Gem with seamless color and exemplary surfaces. Locating a superior piece would prove an arduous task. Population: 53 in 67 Red, 0 finer (3/06).
Ex: Central States Signature (Heritage, 4/2006), lot 647, which realized $2,530.
From The Davis Conway Collection. (#2569)

418   1926-D MS64 Red PCGS. CAC. Rich copper-orange surfaces show occasional glints of honey and peach. Well-defined with few flaws aside from a handful of flecks on the reverse. PCGS has graded 45 finer Red coins (8/08). (#2572)

Conditionally Rare Red Gem 1926-D Cent

419   1926-D MS65 Red PCGS. Rich, even orange-red fills the obverse margin and the entire reverse. The central obverse has a brass-yellow appearance. This lustrous and unabraded Gem is well struck aside from slight merging on the first A in AMERICA and the lower right border of the right wheat ear. Population: 43 in 65 Red, 2 finer (7/08).
Ex: FUN Signature (Heritage, 1/2003), lot 5720.
From The Davis Conway Collection. (#2572)

Choice Red 1926-S Cent

420 **1926-S MS64 Red PCGS.** If the 1922 No D Strong Reverse is excluded, the 1926-S is the rarest Lincoln cent issue in MS65 Red. PCGS and NGC have each certified exactly one example in that grade, with none finer. The present near-Gem comes close to the Holy Grail grade, held back only by a few inconsequential ticks on the EN in CENT and a slightly subdued appearance. The satiny pumpkin-gold fields and devices are impressively free from spots or marks, and the strike is crisp. Specialists are well aware of the rarity of the 1926-S in full Red, and are certain to compete vigorously for this Choice representative.
From The Davis Conway Collection. (#2575)

Enticing Red Gem 1927-D Cent

421 **1927-D MS65 Red PCGS.** This lustrous Gem is sharply struck aside from minor inexactness on the LU in PLURIBUS. Campfire-red overall with a hint of aqua on the left obverse. A brief mark after UNITED is perhaps all that prevents an even higher grade. Population: 50 in 65 Red, 2 finer (7/08).
From The Davis Conway Collection. (#2581)

422 **1927-S MS64 Red PCGS.** A surprisingly low number of full red cents survive today out of a substantial mintage of 14.2 million pieces. This example has bright, shimmering orange-red surfaces and no obvious or mentionable defects. (#2584)

423 **1928 MS67 Red PCGS.** An exceptional copper coin that exhibits bright red color on each side with lighter orange coloration in the center of the obverse. Sharply struck with slight evidence of metal flow around the margins. A spectacular and nearly flawless example of this popular Roaring Twenties issue. Tied for the finest Red example graded by NGC or PCGS (8/08).
From The Davis Conway Collection. (#2587)

424 **1928-D MS65 Red PCGS.** Luminous copper-orange and peach surfaces show occasional elements of mint. Well struck and pleasingly preserved for the Gem designation. PCGS has graded just 11 finer Red pieces (8/08).
From The Davis Conway Collection. (#2590)

Scintillating Red Gem 1928-S Cent

425 **1928-S MS65 Red PCGS.** This honey-gold Gem has scintillating luster and a precise strike. Occasional hints of blue-gray and a small tick on the forehead are all that limit the grade. A scarce lot mintage issue. Housed in an old green label holder. Population: 40 in 65 Red, 5 finer (7/08).
From The Davis Conway Collection. (#2593)

Magnificent MS67 Red 1929 Cent

426 **1929 MS67 Red PCGS.** An exquisite yellow-green and orange-gold Superb Gem with remarkably unperturbed fields and devices. Both carbon and contact are absent, and the quality and eye appeal are formidable. 1929 was a bad year for the stock market, but whoever set aside this beauty made a much better investment. Population: 31 in 67, 0 finer (7/08).
From The Davis Conway Collection. (#2596)

427 **1929-D MS65 Red PCGS.** Bright lemon-gold centers show slight fading to copper-orange close to the margins. A well-defined Gem example of this turn-of-the-decade issue. PCGS has graded 19 finer Red pieces (8/08).
From The Davis Conway Collection. (#2599)

428 **1930 MS67 Red PCGS.** A boldly struck and beautifully preserved orange-gold Superb Gem. There is a tiny fleck above the A in STATES, but this Lincoln cent is worthy of a demanding specialist. Population: 73 in 67 Red, 1 finer (8/08).
From The Davis Conway Collection. (#2605)

Outstanding 1931-D Cent, MS66 Red

429 **1931-D MS66 Red PCGS.** A sharply struck Gem with undisturbed cartwheel luster and rich orange-gold color. Well preserved and problem-free. Although long overshadowed by the low mintage 1931-S, the 1931-D is actually much more elusive in Mint State. A scarce issue with full Red color, the 1931-D is undeniably rare as a premium Gem. Population: 29 in 66, 1 finer (8/08).
From The Davis Conway Collection. (#2617)

430 **1931-S MS65 Red NGC.** This popular low-mintage representative displays vibrant orange-gold luster and well struck devices. Some light toning spots are visible on each side. (#2620)

431 **1931-S MS66 Red PCGS.** A well-defined example of this popular lower-mintage issue, tied for the finest Red example known to PCGS (8/08). Attractive copper-orange surfaces show occasional rose shadings.
From The Davis Conway Collection. (#2620)

Impressive 1936 Type Two Doubled Die Cent, MS65 Red

432 **1936 Doubled Die Obverse Type Two MS65 Red PCGS.** A gorgeous example of the popular 1936 Type Two Doubled Die cent, with bold doubling on the date, and minor doubling on LIBERTY and the motto. Both sides are frosty and highly lustrous with brilliant orange mint color. Population: 16 in 65, 10 finer (8/08) (#92650)

433 **1937-S MS67 Red PCGS.** Occasional pink accents flicker across the primarily peach-gold surfaces. Well-defined with fresh luster and excellent eye appeal. Tied for the finest Red representative known to PCGS (8/08).
From The Davis Conway Collection. (#2665)

Pristine 1939-D Cent, MS68 Red

434 **1939-D MS68 Red PCGS.** Almost as sharply struck as a proof, with intense luster and a pleasing mix of mint-green and copper-red coloration across both sides, this Lincoln cent displays a seemingly unimprovable combination of technical and visual assets. A mere trace of carbon is noted on the upper right obverse field. Housed in an older, green label PCGS holder, this coin is worthy of a strong bid. Population: 8 in 68, 0 finer (8/08).
From The Davis Conway Collection. (#2680)

435 **1943 MS68 PCGS.** A crisply struck and seemingly pristine example of the popular "steel" cent, a one-year type produced in response to World War II shortages of copper. This is a lovely, lustrous piece without any noticeable flaws.
From The Davis Conway Collection. (#2711)

436 **1943-D MS68 PCGS.** A great example, with shimmering steel-blue surfaces that display crisply designed devices and undisturbed surfaces. Many "steel" cents were produced in 1943, but few still exist in such a lofty state of preservation.
From The Davis Conway Collection. (#2714)

437 **1943-D/D MS65 PCGS.** FS-019. The most dramatic repunched mintmark variety for the 1943-dated zinc-plated steel cents. The secondary mintmark is fully outlined and widely shifted southwest. The variety is both listed and photographed in the 2009 *Guide Book*. Lustrous and undisturbed with a sharp strike and exemplary eye appeal. Population: 34 in 65, 31 finer (8/08). (#2715)

438 **1943-S MS68 PCGS.** Well struck and radiantly lustrous, with die striations (as struck) in the fields on each side, and a tiny spot in the right obverse field. The bright surfaces seem entirely free of contact marks. Population: 51 in 68, 0 finer (8/08).
From The Davis Conway Collection. (#2717)

439 **1944-D/S MS64 Red PCGS.** FS-020. OMM #1. The dramatic overmintmark with much of the curve of an S above the prominent D. A lustrous and beautiful peach-red near-Gem. The obverse has a few subtle gray spots, and the reverse exhibits minor contact. Housed in a green label holder. (#2728)

440 **1945 MS67 Red PCGS.** Primarily pale copper-gold, though crescents of deeper peach-orange grace the right obverse and reverse. Crisply struck with excellent luster. Tied for the finest Red example known to PCGS (8/08).
From The Davis Conway Collection. (#2734)

441 **1946-S MS67 Red PCGS.** Beautifully detailed with warm, delightful luster across the copper-orange surfaces. Carefully preserved with pillowy-strong detail on Lincoln's portrait. Tied for the finest Red example known to PCGS (8/08).
From The Davis Conway Collection. (#2749)

442 **1947-D MS67 Red PCGS.** Primarily peach-gold, though beguiling mint accents visit the right obverse and reverse. Fresh luster and crisp detail contribute to the eye appeal. Tied for the finest Red example known to PCGS (8/08).
From The Davis Conway Collection. (#2755)

443 **1948-D MS67 Red PCGS.** Warm copper-orange surfaces offer occasional hints of peach and rose. Crisply struck and vibrant with undeniable eye appeal. PCGS has graded no finer Red representatives (8/08).
From The Davis Conway Collection. (#2764)

Scintillating 1949-D Lincoln, MS67 Red

444 **1949-D MS67 Red PCGS.** A fantastic orange-gold example that is aglow with scintillating luster. A curved die crack crosses Lincoln's forehead. The rarity and importance of top-grade coins from the 1940s and 1950s should surprise no one who was actually active 50 years ago. Population: 31 in 67, 0 finer (8/08).
From The Davis Conway Collection. (#2773)

Pedigreed 1950 Cent, MS67 Red

445 **1950 MS67 Red PCGS.** Ex: Joshua and Ally Walsh. A beautiful, blazing orange-gold coin. The design elements are well brought up throughout, and the well preserved surfaces are devoid of mentionable abrasions or fly specks. Numerous as-struck die striations traverse each side. Population: 18 in 67 Red, 0 finer (4/07).
Ex: Long Beach Signature (Heritage, 5/2007), lot 266, which realized $3,737.50.
From The Davis Conway Collection. (#2779)

446 **1951-D MS67 Red PCGS.** Solid overall detail and smooth copper-orange surfaces with swirling luster combine for great eye appeal. Tied for the finest Red example known to PCGS (8/08).
From The Davis Conway Collection. (#2791)

Important 1952 Cent, MS67 Red

447 **1952 MS67 Red PCGS.** Frosty deep orange luster and bold design motifs characterize this Superb Gem 1952 cent. The surfaces are remarkable with just a single tiny spot on the reverse. While fully brilliant Gems are readily available, MS67 pieces are extremely rare. Through E PL at the upper left reverse is a small bulge that probably represents a faint bubble beneath the surface from the original planchet. Population: 8 in 67, 0 finer (8/08).
From The Davis Conway Collection. (#2797)

448 **1952-D MS67 Red PCGS.** Light copper-gold and peach shadings form a subtle woodgrain pattern on the reverse. Well-defined and pleasingly preserved. Neither NGC nor PCGS has graded a finer Red example (8/08).
From The Davis Conway Collection. (#2800)

Unexpectedly Rare MS67 Red 1953-D Cent

449 **1953-D MS67 Red PCGS.** A peach-red beauty with dynamic luster and a fresh, original appearance. Although the 1953-D was set aside by the roll, the issue is surprisingly rare as a Superb Gem. Unlike the present piece, most examples have acquired noticeable flyspecks or toning over the past 55 years. Population: 12 in 67 Red, 0 finer (7/08).
From The Davis Conway Collection. (#2809)

450 **1955 Doubled Die Obverse AU50 PCGS.** Delicate blue accents grace the teak-brown surfaces of this briefly circulated cent. The doubling is prominent as always for this variety, particularly on the date and IN GOD WE TRUST. (#2825)

451 **1955 Doubled Die Obverse—Improperly Cleaned—NCS. AU Details.** FS-101, formerly FS-021.8. This momentarily circulated key date cent was recolored to pass as Mint State, although the orange-gold surfaces have mellowed and the borders exhibit forest-green toning. A dramatic die variety. (#2825)

452 **1955 Doubled Die Obverse AU58 PCGS.** FS-101, formerly FS-021.8. This is an exceptionally nice doubled die Lincoln cent, showing mere traces of highpoint wear and just a few minuscule nicks on each side. The surfaces show even, saddle-brown coloration. One of the most popular and important doubled die varieties in all of U.S. numismatics. (#2825)

453 **1955 Doubled Die Obverse AU58 ANACS.** FS-101, formerly FS-021.8. A splendid mahogany-brown representative of this popular error, easily spotted even from a distance. The surfaces are remarkably clean and a loupe reveals only a couple of light marks. (#2825)

454 **1955 Doubled Die Obverse AU58 PCGS.** FS-101, formerly FS-021.8. This satiny golden-brown near-Mint key date cent appears to be free from wear, and was perhaps restrained in grade by an inconspicuous thin mark beneath LIBERTY. (#2825)

Glossy MS62 Brown 1955 Doubled Die Cent

455 **1955 Doubled Die Obverse MS62 Brown PCGS.** FS-101. This is a nice, solid, collector-grade example of this always-popular doubled-die error, one that was discovered almost immediately upon its release. The details of the 1955 Doubled Die Obverse being found so quickly are a testament to its boldly doubled obverse, one that is startlingly "wrong," both to the noncollectors and collectors who came across examples soon after their release. This example shows glossy brown fields with an overall clean appearance, although a couple of dark toning spots are noted on the lower reverse that likely prevent a finer grade. (#2825)

Splendid 1955 Doubled Die Obverse Cent, MS62 Brown

456 **1955 Doubled Die Obverse MS62 Brown PCGS.** FS-101, formerly FS-021.8. Lovely mahogany patina drapes the surfaces of this attractive piece. The surfaces appear remarkably clean to the unaided eye, and a loupe reveals only minuscule abrasions. A tiny blemish at the bottom of the reverse is barely worthy of mention. A charming representative of this popular error. (#2825)

Delightful 1955 Doubled Die Cent, MS63 Brown

457 **1955 Doubled Die Obverse MS63 Brown PCGS.** Glossy brown patina drapes both sides of this highly lustrous and sharply struck piece. There are no mentionable marks, and the scattered flecks on the reverse are nearly imperceptible without a loupe. This handsome specimen would make a wonderful addition to any Lincoln cent collection. (#2825)

Pleasing 1955 Doubled Die Cent, MS63 Brown

458 **1955 Doubled Die Obverse MS63 Brown PCGS.** FS-101, formerly FS-021.8. Charming medium brown patina drapes the surfaces of this carefully preserved specimen. A number of tiny toning spots on both sides barely affect the great eye appeal. Interestingly, while this piece features the pronounced doubling on the obverse, it also has a small lamination above the ONE on the reverse. This lovely specimen is housed in a first generation PCGS holder. (#2825)

Exquisite 1955 Doubled Die Obverse, MS63 Brown

459 **1955 Doubled Die Obverse MS63 Brown ANACS.** A touch of lilac patina accents the medium brown that covers the surfaces. Several minor abrasions limit the grade, but none are worthy of individual mention. Crisply struck with excellent eye appeal. This intriguing and vividly pronounced error will always be a favorite among collectors. (#2825)

Impressive 1955 Doubled Die Cent, MS64 Brown

460 **1955 Doubled Die Obverse MS64 Brown NGC. CAC.** FS-101, formerly FS-021.8. An impressive example of this popular error. Traces of mint red in the protected areas enhance the mahogany patina that graces both sides. The doubling is extremely pronounced, as usual, and the strike is also razor-sharp. A couple of minor abrasions keep this piece from an even higher grade. NGC reports just 11 Brown pieces finer (7/08). (#2825)

Charming 1955 Doubled Die Cent, MS64 Brown

461 **1955 Doubled Die Obverse MS64 Brown PCGS. CAC.** FS-101, formerly FS-021.8. Delightful luster radiates from the medium brown surfaces. The fields are virtually pristine, and only a few minor marks on the devices preclude a higher grade. The 1955 doubled die ranks as one of the most famous U.S. coin varieties, and is known even among many non-collectors. This sharply struck example would make an excellent representative of this sought-after error. (#2825)

462   **1955 Doubled Die Obverse MS63 Red and Brown PCGS. CAC.** Although PCGS has certified this piece Red and Brown, it is mostly reddish-orange, with just a touch of light brown in the fields and on Lincoln's jacket. Scattered flecks and tiny blemishes on both sides limit the grade, but there are no marks visible to the unaided eye. A sharply defined example of this desirable variety. (#2826)

Excellent 1955 Doubled Die Cent
MS65 Red and Brown

463   **1955 Doubled Die Obverse MS65 Red and Brown PCGS.** This is the variety that everyone mentions when a discussion of doubled die coinage takes place. Although the hunt for doubled die varieties is widespread and sophisticated today, few took notice of such coins 50 years ago. It was only because the doubling is so prominent, and visible without magnification, that this 1955 Doubled Die cent variety was noticed within a year after its production. Soon thereafter, listings appeared in the popular *Red Book* and in other guides. The variety was eventually included in coin albums, and that publicity made it famous. The example offered here is a lovely Gem with considerable deep orange mint color, blended with pale olive and blue toning. Although a few tiny ticks are visible on Lincoln's head, this is an excellent quality example. The diagnostic, authenticating narrow "X"-shaped double die line just left of the T in CENT is the most prominent that this cataloger (GH) has seen. Population: 4 in 65 Red and Brown, 0 finer (8/08). (#2826)

464   **1958-D MS67 Red PCGS.** Well struck with dynamic luster and lovely peach and mint-green toning. The obverse is virtually flawless, and only a trivial field mark below the N in CENT is visible on the reverse. Population: 62 in 67 Red, 0 finer (8/08). *From The Davis Conway Collection.* (#2851)

465   **1971 MS67 Red PCGS.** Warm copper-orange surfaces offer subtle radiance and delightful eye appeal. The carefully preserved devices are exactly struck. Population: 29 in 67 Red, 0 finer (8/08). *From The Davis Conway Collection.* (#2941)

466   **1972 MS67 Red PCGS.** Cherry-red and bright orange intermingle across the surfaces, with grayish accents along the perimeter. Incredible satiny luster gives this piece impressive eye appeal. The strike is full excepting a touch of weakness on the second S in STATES and OF. Tied for the finest certified (7/08). (#2953)

467   **1972 Doubled Die Obverse MS65 Red PCGS.** FS-103, formerly FS-033.53. Not the most famous variety, but still interesting with considerable spread, particularly on the L and B of LIBERTY. (#2950)

468   **1972 Doubled Die Obverse MS66 Red PCGS.** FS-033.3. Die #1. The dramatic die doubling on the obverse legends has nearly as wide a spread as the even more famous 1955 DDO. This satiny peach-gold cent appears immaculate, and surely challenges the mere 16 pieces that PCGS has certified finer (8/08). (#2950)

469   **1972 Doubled Die Obverse MS66 Red PCGS.** FS-033.3. Of the several die combinations for this variety, FS-033.3 features the most pronounced doubling on all the obverse letters and the date. Pale red patina graces the nearly pristine surfaces, with dazzling satiny luster throughout. (#2950)

470   **1973 MS67 Red PCGS.** Elegant copper-lemon surfaces show only occasional glimpses of peach. Razor-sharp striking definition and seemingly unimprovable surfaces combine for winning eye appeal. Population: 27 in 67 Red, 0 finer (8/08). *From The Davis Conway Collection.* (#2965)

471   **1975-D MS67 Red PCGS.** Lemon-gold centers cede to peach at the margins, and intriguing glimpses of magenta and silver grace the lower obverse and reverse. Excellent definition and eye appeal to match. Population: 33 in 67 Red, 0 finer (8/08). *From The Davis Conway Collection.* (#2979)

472   **1976-D MS66 Red PCGS.** Splashes of peach grace otherwise copper-gold surfaces. A strikingly attractive Premium Gem, well-defined with fields that fall just shy of a finer grade. PCGS has certified just 15 finer Red representatives (8/08). *From The Davis Conway Collection.* (#2985)

473   **1978 MS67 Red PCGS.** Delightful copper-gold and reddish-orange surfaces are carefully preserved. Well-defined with uncommon quality for a Lincoln cent of the 1970s. Population: 37 in 67 Red, 0 finer (8/08). *From The Davis Conway Collection.* (#2992)

474   **1980-D MS67 Red PCGS.** Excellent definition on the central devices. This luminous orange-gold Superb Gem is carefully preserved and attractive. Population: 25 in 67 Red, 0 finer (8/08). *From The Davis Conway Collection.* (#3004)

475   **1982 MS68 Red PCGS.** Satiny luster shimmers beneath the eye-catching orange patina, with patches of medium red in the fields. Fully struck with virtually no marks. Population: 23 in 68 Red, 0 finer (7/08). (#3047)

476   **1982 MS68 Red PCGS.** Not identified by variety, though this otherwise flawless copper-peach Large Date example has tiny, telltale air bubbles beneath the plating, characteristic of copper-plated zinc examples from this transitional year. Striking eye appeal, suitable for one of the finest examples known to PCGS. *From The Davis Conway Collection.* (#3047)

477   **1982-D MS68 Red PCGS.** Nearly perfect but for a few microscopic handling marks. The strike is razor-sharp, and flashy luster enhances the eye appeal of this bright red representative. Population: 23 in 68 Red, 0 finer (7/08). (#3050)

478 **1982-D MS68 Red PCGS.** Square Base 2. A pristine orange-gold Superb Gem. Only STATES lacks a crisp impression. No air bubbles are visible beneath the fields, a rarity for this initial copper-plated zinc issue. Population: 23 in 68 Red, 0 finer (8/08). *From The Davis Conway Collection.* (#3050)

Deep Red MS67 1983 Doubled Die Reverse Cent

479 **1983 Doubled Die Reverse MS67 Red PCGS.** The 1983 Doubled Die Reverse Lincoln cent is one of the more obvious mint errors of the modern era, with strong doubling on all peripheral letters. In MS67 Red, the present piece is not only a bold Doubled Die, but also a conditionally rare coin. PCGS has certified no examples of the variety finer (8/08). Both sides display deep cherry-red color. An exceptionally attractive example of this popular Doubled Die. (#3056)

480 **1983-D MS68 Red PCGS.** Lovely cherry-red patina endows the surfaces of this resplendent specimen. A couple of nearly invisible blemishes keep this piece from being absolutely perfect. Population: 20 in 68 Red, 0 finer (7/08). (#3051)

481 **1983-D MS68 Red PCGS.** Light copper-gold, orange, and peach shadings embrace each side of this lovely D-mint modern. Excellent strike and eye appeal to match. Population: 20 in 68 Red, 0 finer (8/08). *From The Davis Conway Collection.* (#3051)

482 **1984 Doubled Die Obverse MS67 Red PCGS.** FS-037. The ear is prominently doubled, and Lincoln's beard also shows notable doubling. A few patches of deep red accent the rosy surfaces. Several tiny specks keep this satiny Superb Gem from an even higher grade. (#3062)

483 **1984-D MS68 Red PCGS.** All of the design elements are boldly defined, and the surfaces seem pristine, even under close inspection with a magnifier. This bright, essentially flawless example displays light coral-red color across both sides. Population: 15 in 68 Red, 0 finer (8/08). *From The Davis Conway Collection.* (#3068)

484 **1985 MS68 Red PCGS.** Captivating satiny luster shimmers over each side of this bright orange and fully struck representative. The surfaces have a rippled texture, and a close inspection yields only a few tiny spots. Population: 19 in 68 Red, 0 finer (7/08). (#3071)

485 **1987-D MS68 Red PCGS.** Pale copper-gold centers cede to vibrant orange at the shining margins. Beautifully preserved with exacting detail. Population: 20 in 68 Red, 0 finer (8/08). *From The Davis Conway Collection.* (#3080)

486 **1988-D MS68 Red PCGS.** Delightfully preserved with attractive peach accents against the otherwise lemon-yellow surfaces. Bright and crisply struck. Population: 23 in 68 Red, 1 finer (8/08). *From The Davis Conway Collection.* (#3105)

PROOF LINCOLN CENTS

487 **1909 PR64 Brown ICG.** Despite the "Brown" designation, this pleasing matte proof is primarily violet with glimmers of copper-orange at the muted margins. Crisply detailed with great eye appeal. (#3303)

488 **1912—Cleaned—ICG. PR60 Details.** Matte proofs were only struck for a few years and are highly desirable today. Only a couple of tiny marks are visible on the splendid chestnut-brown surfaces, and there is just a small blemish to the right of Lincoln's face. A delightful example despite cleaning. One of just 2,172 proofs minted. (#3312)

489 **1913 PR65 Red and Brown PCGS. CAC.** Sharply struck and intensely lustrous, with bright fire-red and mint-green toning, and just a couple of minor carbon flecks that prevent an even loftier grade. A lovely, conditionally scarce early Lincoln cent. (#3316)

490 **1916 PR64 Red and Brown NGC.** A lovely Choice Red and Brown representative of the last readily available matte proof Lincoln cent issue. Rich reddish-orange, violet-brown, and magenta shadings grace the finely granular surfaces. (#3325)

Desirable 1936 Type One—Satin Finish Lincoln Cent, PR66 Red

491 **1936 Type One—Satin Finish PR66 Red PCGS.** Ex: Tom Mershon Collection. Pleasing apricot patina overlies the lustrous surfaces of this carefully preserved Premium Gem. A few minor flecks limit the grade, but none are particularly bothersome. Only 5,569 proofs were issued of both Satin and Brilliant finishes, and although the Satin pieces were struck in greater quantities, they are less often seen in high grades. Population: 24 in 66 Red, 1 finer (8/08). (#3332)

492 **1936 Type Two—Brilliant Finish PR65 Red and Brown NGC.** This Brilliant Finish proof Gem displays exquisite sunset-red and gold toning. Crisply struck without any surface distractions. Proof strikings of the Lincoln cent type occurred for the first time in twenty years in 1936, in both Satin and Brilliant proof formats. Census: 33 in 65 Red and Brown, 11 finer (7/08). (#3334)

Wonderful Gem Proof 1936 Brilliant Finish Cent

493 **1936 Type Two—Brilliant Finish PR65 Red PCGS.** This Brilliant Finish coin shows wonderful brick-red coloration, with a sharp strike and only the most insignificant, tiny distractions that go entirely unseen save under a high-power loupe. PCGS has graded 30 Red coins finer of this first-year issue (8/08). (#3335)

Blazing PR67 Red 1937 Cent

494 **1937 PR67 Red NGC.** Although the 1937 is not nearly as rare as the 1936, it is still an elusive coin as a Superb Gem. One of only 24 so graded specimens at NGC and PCGS (10/02), this is a fire-red survivor whose surfaces are undiminished by either toning or grade-limiting blemishes. Fully struck with uniformly reflective features. (#3338)

Phenomenal PR67 Red 1937 Lincoln

495 **1937 PR67 Red PCGS.** Phenomenally clean surfaces and premium eye appeal are the hallmarks of this blazing Superb Gem Red 1937 proof, one of only 10 coins so certified at PCGS, with none finer (8/08). Even a diligent search under a loupe fails to reveal any mentionable distractions, although a hue of lighter mint-green appears near the left reverse rim. (#3338)

Stunning PR67 Red Cameo 1937 Cent

496 **1937 PR67 Red Cameo PCGS.** Ex: Tom Mershon Collection. Although a handful of 1937 proof Lincolns, with a total mintage of 9,320 coins, are certified at PCGS in grades up to PR67 Red, in PR67 Red Cameo this piece is tied for finest certified with only one other coin—or else this piece has been submitted twice. Considerable contrast that appears to verge on Deep Cameo appears on each side of this stunning sunset-orange piece, and the effect is especially noticeable on the wheat ears and lettering of the reverse. A likely candidate for acquisition by Registry Set collectors of the popular Lincoln cent series. (#83338)

Flawless PR67 Red 1938 Lincoln Cent

497 **1938 PR67 Red PCGS.** Ex: Tom Mershon Collection. Unimprovable from the standpoint of technical quality and eye appeal, this originally preserved, fiery orange-red example is smooth from rim to rim. Even under a high-powered loupe, there are no mentionable flaws. Another proof from the same die, showing counterclockwise reverse die rotation of about 15 degrees with respect to the obverse. Population: 28 in 67 Red, 0 finer (8/08). (#3341)

Gem Red Cameo Proof 1938 Lincoln Cent

498 **1938 PR65 Red Cameo NGC.** Interestingly for a proof issue of so recent vintage, this Gem Red Cameo 1938 Lincoln cent shows the reverse die rotated counterclockwise about 15 degrees from the obverse. Only the tiniest flecks appearing under a loupe seem to keep this piece from a finer grade. The orange-red surfaces show considerable contrast, and much eye appeal. (#83341)

499 **1939 PR67 Red PCGS.** Ex: Tom Mershon Collection. PCGS has graded only 28 specimens in PR67 Red, with none finer (8/08). Impressive luster radiates from both sides in well-blended orange-red and cherry-red hues. The smooth, fully brilliant features are as close to pristine as one can expect for the date. (#3344)

Bright, Full Red PR67 1940 Lincoln Cent

500 **1940 PR67 Red PCGS.** Ex: Tom Mershon Collection. Bright and highly reflective, the surfaces display undiminished bright red color over each side. This Superb proof is virtually flawless. In fact, the only flaw we see is Mint-made, a shallow strike-through in the field to the left of Lincoln's head. None are graded finer at either service. Population: 10 in 67 (8/08). (#3347)

Marvelous 1941 Cent, PR67 Red

501 **1941 PR67 Red PCGS.** Ex: Tom Mershon Collection. Glowing orange-gold surfaces make up this marvelous Superb Gem proof, and a well executed strike results in completeness on the design elements. A few tiny flecks are noted on each side. Population: 3 in 67 Red, 0 finer (8/08). (#3350)

1942 Cent, PR66 Red Cameo

502 **1942 PR66 Red Cameo PCGS.** Ex: Tom Mershon Collection. The 1942 Lincoln cent is a difficult issue to find with any degree of cameo contrast. The present example boasts good contrast, with bright gold color with a reasonable strike. The upper obverse has a couple of tiny spots that appear only under a loupe. Population: 3 in 66 Red Cameo, 1 finer (8/08). (#83353)

503 **1950 PR66 Red Ultra Cameo NGC.** A splendid pumpkin-gold Premium Gem with pleasing contrast between the glassy fields and the frosted motifs. An interesting lintmark on the reverse exergue identifies the present piece. Census: 13 in 66 Red Ultra Cameo, 13 finer (7/08). (#93359)

504 **1953 Doubled Die Obverse PR68 Red Ultra Cameo NGC.** FS-021.7. The 19 in the date is die doubled. The pumpkin-gold fields are virtually pristine, and the portrait and wheat ears are frosty. For the variety, the single finest certified by NGC (8/08). (#93368)

505 **1955 PR67 Deep Cameo PCGS.** Captivating deeply mirrored fields show strong cameo contrast against the heavily frosted devices. The surfaces are virtually pristine for the grade and the eye appeal is extraordinary. This piece would be perfect for inclusion in a registry set. Population: 23 in 67 Deep Cameo, 6 finer (8/08). (#93374)

506 **1956 PR67 Deep Cameo PCGS.** A bright orange representative with captivating deeply mirrored fields and frosted devices that create a startling cameo appearance. Several tiny flecks and light blemishes limit the grade, but the surfaces are virtually free of any contact marks. Population: 33 in 67 Deep Cameo, 6 finer (7/08). (#93377)

Breathtaking 1956 Cent
PR68 Deep Cameo

507 **1956 PR68 Deep Cameo PCGS.** The mintage of 1956 proof cents (669,384 pieces) was increased significantly over that of previous years. Consequently, proof cents in all grades are readily available. Cameos are more elusive, however, especially Deep/Ultra Cameos in the higher grades. PCGS and NGC have certified about 100 Gem and finer Deep/Ultra examples.

 The satiny motifs of this PR68 Deep Cameo appear to float over deep watery fields. Indeed, both sides yield an orange-gold-on-black appearance from several angles. An attentive strike sharpens the design elements, and close inspection reveals no mentionable flaws. In short, this is a breathtaking coin with superior technical quality and aesthetic appeal. Population: 6 in 68 Deep Cameo, 0 finer (8/08). (#93377)

508 **1957 PR67 Red Ultra Cameo NGC.** This outstanding Superb Gem has pristine yellow-gold fields that change to dark mirrors when rotated beneath a light. The portrait is radiant, and the strike is meticulous throughout. Census: 2 in 67 Red Ultra Cameo, 3 finer (7/08). (#93380)

509 **1960 Large Over Small Date PR66 Red PCGS.** FS-025. DDO-1. This interesting variety is the product of a doubled die and features evidence of doubling in LIBERTY and the date, with the 0 particularly obvious. A small milk spot on the right rim of the obverse is the only imperfection visible to the unaided eye. Attractive bright orange patina highlights the fully struck details. (#3410)

Outstanding 1961 Cent, PR69 Deep Cameo

510 **1961 PR69 Deep Cameo PCGS.** Deeply mirrored orange-red fields show dazzling cameo contrast against the heavily frosted devices. Careful examination yields just a couple of tiny lint marks. Neither NGC nor PCGS have certified any examples in PR70, and PCGS reports just nine PR69 Deep Cameo specimens (8/08). (#93395)

511 **1962 PR69 Deep Cameo PCGS.** Deeply mirrored fields and frosty devices create a fantastic cameo appearance on this fully struck example. A loupe reveals a couple of nearly imperceptible carbon spots, but this piece appears perfect to the unaided eye. PCGS has certified no pieces finer (7/08). (#93398)

512 **1970-S Large Date PR69 Deep Cameo PCGS.** It is nearly impossible to locate any flaw that could keep this spectacular piece from PR70. Orange and red patina covers the surfaces, which have outstanding cameo contrast. Neither NGC nor PCGS has certified any pieces finer (7/08). (#93430)

Gleaming 1990 No S Cent, PR68 Deep Cameo

513 **1990 No S PR68 Deep Cameo PCGS.** As the lone No S proof variety to appear in the Lincoln Memorial series, the 1990 No S is highly popular with series enthusiasts. This Superb Gem has impressively mirrored copper-orange surfaces that offer delightful contrast with the sharp, richly frosted devices. Population: 61 in 68 Deep Cameo, 19 finer (8/08). (#93506)

514 **1990 No S PR68 Deep Cameo PCGS.** On several occasions from the late 1960s to the 1990s, proof dies that were made in Philadelphia and sent to San Francisco for the year's production, did not actually get stamped with a mintmark punch. In most instances, only a few proofs were struck and sent out with proof sets before the error was spotted and the die pulled from service. Of course, this type of die error was only possible once San Francisco started coining proofs in 1968. In the Lincoln cent series, only the 1990 No S proofs were coined without a mintmark. Other examples include the 1971 nickel, and the 1968, 1970, 1975, and 1983 dimes. This amazing and superlative piece has gorgeous orange luster with brilliant devices and deeply mirrored fields. (#93506)

TWO CENT PIECES

515 **1864 Small Motto MS64 Brown NGC.** FS-000.5. This key date shows faded red and light blue patina, is sharply struck, and devoid of significant blemishes. Census: 62 in 64, 33 finer (7/08). *From The Menlo Park Collection.* (#3579)

Gem 1864 Small Motto Two Cent Piece, MS65 Brown

516 **1864 Small Motto MS65 Brown PCGS.** Is it technically a pattern or a short-lived regular issue? The jury is still out on this question, but it is certainly an intriguing one. Even if it is a pattern, the Small Motto has traditionally been considered a regular part of the two cent series and will continue to be. This is a brown coin, as PCGS has stated, but much of the original red is still apparent just beneath the thin veneer of brown patina. Sharply defined throughout. Population: 14 in 65, 0 finer (8/08). (#3579)

517 **1864 Large Motto MS65 Red PCGS. CAC.** Lovely pumpkin-orange and red patina drapes the surfaces of this nearly unmarked and lustrous Gem. Several minor flecks are noted on each side. A few letters on the reverse are a little soft, but the rest of the details are sharp. PCGS has certified 47 pieces finer (7/08). (#3578)

518 **1864 Large Motto MS65 Red NGC.** Peach and straw-gold shades endow this lustrous and exactingly impressed Gem. Carbon and contact are inconsequential. A pleasing first year type coin, encased in a prior generation holder. (#3578)

519 **1864 Large Motto MS66 Red PCGS.** Vibrant copper-orange with occasional glints of lemon-gold near the margins. A well-defined and delightfully preserved example of this popular odd-denomination type issue. PCGS has graded just one finer Red piece (8/08). *From The Bell Collection.* (#3578)

520 **1864 Large Motto MS66 Red NGC.** Fresh copper-orange surfaces prevail on this wonderful Large Motto type piece. Overall detail is excellent, if slightly soft at the lower shield, and the fields are carefully preserved with minimal carbon. Elusive in this condition with fully Red surfaces and prohibitively rare any finer, with just two such pieces in the combined certified population (6/08). (#3578)

521 **1865 MS64 Red PCGS. CAC.** Fancy 5. Delightful rose and orange colors intermingle on each side of this lustrous near-Gem representative. Scattered flecks on the obverse limit the grade, but the surfaces are remarkably clean with only a couple of minor abrasions on the reverse. Housed in a first generation PCGS holder. (#3584)

522 **1865 MS65 Red PCGS. CAC.** Eye-catching satiny luster shimmers beneath the pleasing tan patina. The surfaces have virtually no marks save for a tiny scrape to the left of the date, but a number of tiny flecks are noted. PCGS has certified just 42 pieces finer (7/08). (#3584)

523 **1865 MS65 Red PCGS.** Plain 5. Variegated cherry-red and orange patina endows the surfaces of this highly lustrous specimen. Prominent clash marks from the shield are visible on the reverse. A loupe locates a few minuscule marks, but overall this crisply struck piece has been carefully preserved. (#3584)

524 **1865 MS65 Red NGC.** Fancy 5. This boldly struck Gem has alternating shades of orange-gold and rose patina. The surfaces are virtually free of any marks, and there are only a few pinpoint flecks along the reverse border. (#3584)

525 **1867 MS64 Red PCGS. CAC.** A dusting of red patina covers the brighter orange beneath on this conditionally scarce example. Several flyspecks and a couple of light marks keep this piece from an even higher grade. Certified in a first generation PCGS holder. Population: 34 in 64 Red, 20 finer (7/08). (#3593)

526 **1868 MS65 Red and Brown PCGS. CAC.** The obverse has lovely mahogany patina with cherry-red accents around the perimeter, which contrasts nicely against the deep red reverse. There are virtually no marks on each side and just a couple of tiny blemishes. Encapsulated in a first generation PCGS holder. PCGS has certified only three Red and Brown examples finer (7/08). (#3598)

527 **1872 XF45 PCGS.** Medium tan surfaces are devoid of mentionable abrasions, and reveal just a tiny fleck in the lower part of the right wreath. The design elements are nicely detailed throughout. *From The Menlo Park Collection.* (#3612)

528 **1872 AU55 PCGS.** Rich chocolate-brown surfaces show occasional violet accents and only a trace of wear. Solidly struck with strong eye appeal for this final circulation-strike two cent issue. Population: 10 in 55, 42 finer (8/08). (#3612)

PROOF TWO CENT PIECES

529 1868 PR65 Red and Brown PCGS. CAC. A 50/50 mix of bright red and light brown patina covers both sides of this carefully preserved specimen. The eye-catching fields have minor flecks but virtually no marks. This impressive piece is housed in a first generation PCGS holder and is one of approximately 600 proofs struck. (#3637)

Impressive 1868 Two Cent, Gem Proof Red

530 1868 PR65 Red PCGS. Vivid red patina coats the surfaces of this resplendent Gem. The details are nearly fully struck and the surfaces are virtually immaculate. A couple of flecks are visible only under magnification and barely affect the outstanding eye appeal. Slightly more than 600 proofs are estimated to have been struck. Population: 20 in 65 Red, 11 finer (7/08). (#3638)

Delightful 1869 Two Cent, PR67 Red and Brown

531 1869 PR67 Red and Brown PCGS. CAC. Housed in a first-generation PCGS holder, this Superb Gem proof is almost entirely faded orange, with some traces of light brown. It is an exceptional example that appears the same as the day it was slabbed.

When grading services first started encapsulating coins, there was concern that copper coins would change color after they were slabbed. Now more than 20 years later, the concern is unfounded. Population: 2 in 67 Red and Brown, 0 finer (8/08). (#3640)

532 1870 PR64 Red PCGS. Splendid pumpkin-orange patina graces both sides of this lustrous near-Gem piece from near the series end. A number of flecks on each side limit the grade, but only a couple of inconsequential marks are visible under magnification. One of an approximate mintage of just 1,000 pieces. (#3644)

Resplendent 1872 Two Cent, Premium Proof Red and Brown

533 1872 PR66 Red and Brown PCGS. Lovely medium brown patina is surrounded by pleasing rose-orange in the periphery. The strike is essentially full, and it is difficult to locate any abrasions, even with a glass. Several minuscule flecks are noted, but they barely affect the dazzling satiny surfaces. Housed in a green label PCGS holder. One of approximately 950 proofs struck. Population: 16 in 66, 1 finer (7/08). (#3649)

First-Rate 1873 Closed 3 Two Cent, PR65 Red and Brown

534 1873 Closed 3 PR65 Red and Brown PCGS. Even though PCGS has called this amazing Gem a Red and Brown example, the obverse is virtually full red with exceptional eye appeal. It is boldly defined with fully mirrored and pleasing fields. The reverse is much the same, with deep lilac and emerald toning at the center. Population: 78 in 65 RB, 15 finer (8/08).
From The Mississippi Collection. (#3652)

THREE CENT SILVER

535 1851 MS66 NGC. Satiny luster radiates from the white surfaces of this carefully preserved piece. A couple of light grazes in the fields are nearly imperceptible, and a few specks of russet on the reverse are the only signs of toning throughout. A splendid example of this popular first-year issue. NGC has certified only eight coins finer (7/08). (#3664)

536 1851 MS66 NGC. Glowing luster is evident beneath the layer of attractive bluish-gray and beige-gold patina. An unobtrusive hair-thin reverse mark is noted on otherwise impeccably preserved surfaces. We mention some localized design softness, typical of Type One trimes.
From The Menlo Park Collection. (#3664)

537 1851 MS66 PCGS. The strike is uncommonly sharp, since the shield is fully brought up, and the stars have crisp centers. Booming luster and gentle tan-gray toning provide further eye appeal. Only a wispy diagonal mark above the 51 in the date denies perfection. PCGS has certified a mere 11 finer pieces (8/08).
From The Bell Collection. (#3664)

538 1851 MS66 NGC. Enticing satiny luster shines throughout the lightly toned silver-gray surfaces. The strike is razor-sharp save for a trace of softness on several stars. NGC has certified only eight coins finer (8/08). (#3664)

539 **1851-O MS65 NGC.** This was the first and only three cent piece made in New Orleans, and the only branch Mint silver three cent piece produced during the entire history of the denomination from 1851 to 1873. Light gold toning is evident over frosty luster with hints of lilac toning. This is an elusive issue in Mint State grades, and especially difficult to locate in Gem quality. Census: 52 in 65, 16 finer (7/08). (#3665)

540 **1852 MS66 NGC.** Seemingly pristine and essentially white with coruscant luster, this trime has a pebbly texture towards much of the peripheries and smoother textured centers. Striking characteristics are typical for the issue with slight weakness noted on some of the reverse stars. Census: 69 in 66, 12 finer (7/08). (#3666)

541 **1854 MS64 PCGS.** Cobalt-blue, steel-gray, lilac, and rose colors intermingle across the lustrous and remarkably clean surfaces. Clash marks are readily apparent on both sides under magnification. Sharply struck with impressive eye appeal. (#3670)

542 **1856 MS64 NGC.** A charming near-Gem example of this date, with pleasing luster and vibrant toning throughout. Attractive shades of green, gold, purple, and gray cover both sides. A couple of wispy abrasions on the obverse are entirely imperceptible to the unaided eye. NGC has certified a mere 18 pieces finer (8/08). (#3672)

543 **1857 MS64 NGC.** Mottled multicolored toning is deeper on the obverse of this three cent silver. Generally well struck, with no significant marks. Census: 90 in 64, 44 finer (7/08). *From The Menlo Park Collection.* (#3673)

544 **1858 MS64 PCGS.** Light yellow toning surrounds the silver-gray centers of this satiny Choice representative. A clash mark from the C is visible at the top of the obverse. The surfaces are remarkably clean for the grade, and there is great eye appeal. (#3674)

545 **1858 MS64 ANACS.** This is an intriguing example that has the striking sharpness of a proof, but shows heavy die clash marks on each side, making it much more likely to be a business strike. It is deeply toned in shades of cobalt-blue and rose-gray, but there are no obvious distractions on either side. (#3674)

546 **1858 MS67 ★ NGC.** Rarely is a Type Two three cent silver seen in such a superior state of preservation. One would think more would exist since more than 1.6 million pieces were produced of this date alone, but attrition and melting obviously took a heavy toll. This is a curious coin when closely examined. The striking details are unusually sharp, almost full, which is most unusual for a Type Two. The obverse is, in fact, fully detailed. The upper part of the reverse shows just a bit of softness, suggesting that die might have been slightly out of alignment. Another obverse / reverse difference is apparent: the obverse fields show heavy die striations which have imparted prooflikeness on that side, while the reverse shows none of these striations. Both sides are richly toned in shades of rose and teal, and the only mark worthy of mention is on the reverse to the left of the denomination. Census: 14 in 67, 0 finer (7/08). (#3674)

547 **1861 MS66 NGC.** A wonderfully patinated Premium Gem with consistently bold design details and shimmering mint luster. Clash marks occur near the reverse center, but post-strike distractions are absent on both sides. Census: 70 in 66, 30 finer (7/08). (#3679)

548 **1862 MS65 PCGS.** This unabraded Civil War Gem features dusky lime-green, champagne-rose, and straw-gold toning. The upper reverse is minutely die doubled, visible on the star points. Encapsulated in an old green label holder. (#3680)

549 **1862 MS65 PCGS.** This lovely three cent silver piece is well struck, save for minor softness in the central areas. Dapples of olive-green, golden-tan, and sky-blue are more extensive and deeper on the reverse. The reverse shows a couple of insignificant contact marks, but for the most part the lustrous surfaces are well preserved. Housed in a green-label holder. *From The Menlo Park Collection.* (#3680)

550 **1862/1 MS65 PCGS.** FS-301, formerly FS-007. A popular Civil War-era overdate, listed in the *Guide Book.* There are exceptionally pronounced clashmarks noted on each side. The shield is a little weak, but the rest of the details are boldly defined. Dramatic lavender and gray toning drapes the minimally marked and lustrous surfaces. (#3681)

551 **1862/1 MS66 PCGS. CAC.** FS-301, formerly FS-007. A delightfully toned representative of this popular overdated trime variant. Peach, blue-green, and silver-white predominate with powerful luster throughout the patina. Incredibly appealing and a delightful coin for the assigned grade. Population: 59 in 66, 11 finer (8/08). (#3681)

552 **1862/1 MS66 PCGS.** FS-301, formerly FS-007. A pinpoint-sharp Civil War Premium Gem with attractive chestnut-tan toning and impeccably smooth surfaces. In a green label holder. Population: 59 in 66, 11 finer (8/08). (#3681)

553 **1862/1 MS66 NGC.** FS-301, formerly FS-007. Apple-green and rose-red enrich this thoroughly lustrous and exactingly struck Premium Gem. Produced from clashed dies, but void of abrasions. Encased in a former generation holder. Census: 62 in 66, 11 finer (7/08). (#3681)

554 **1862/1 MS66 PCGS.** FS-301, formerly FS-007. The underdigit 1 is visible along the left side of the 2. Both sides are bathed in cartwheel luster, and display the faintest touch of light tan color. Well struck, save for softness in the leaves. Devoid of mentionable marks. *Ex: Dallas Signature (Heritage, 7/2006), lot 270, which realized $4,887.50.* (#3681)

Deeply Toned 1867 Silver Three Cent, MS65

555 **1867 MS65 NGC.** Mirrored fields and cameo contrast are visible underneath the deep gold, blue, and iridescent toning. At first glance, one could mistake this piece for a proof, but close inspection clearly reveals its nature as a true and rare business strike. Census: 5 in 65, 4 finer (7/08). (#3687)

556 **1871 MS66 NGC.** One of the final silver three cent pieces, the 1871 has a low mintage of just 2,400 coins. Deeply mirrored fields are apparent beneath the dramatic violet and crimson toning that encircles the lightly frosted devices. The centers are a little soft, but the rest of the details are powerfully impressed. Census: 34 in 66, 20 finer (7/08). (#3692)

PROOF THREE CENT SILVER

Deeply Mirrored PR64 1858 Three Cent Silver

557 **1858 PR64 NGC.** This is a splendid near-Gem proof that represents the Type Two design of the silver three cent series. This second design modification, distinguished by a double outline around the star on the obverse, was only coined from 1855 to 1858, and few proofs were produced. All four dates exist in proof format, yet each is a rarity. This example is sharply struck with light cameo contrast and fully brilliant obverse and reverse surfaces. The fields are fully mirrored. A few of the stars on the reverse of this three cent silver have raised outlines. Census: 42 in 64, 45 finer (7/08). (#3705)

558 **1860 PR64 NGC.** A glittering near-Gem proof with fully mirrored fields and light contrast beneath rich blue, gold, russet, and sea-green toning. (#3709)

Attractive 1860 Three Cent, PR66 Cameo

559 **1860 PR66 Cameo NGC. CAC.** Fantastic rainbow toning is particularly appealing on the reverse, and both sides feature cobalt-blue, violet, orange, and rose colors. The deeply mirrored fields show splendid cameo contrast against the frosted devices. Boldly struck save for softness on several stars and a touch of weakness at the centers. An impeccably preserved and attractive example. Census: 3 in 66 Cameo, 0 finer (7/08). (#83709)

560 **1864 PR64 Cameo PCGS.** The 1864 is a scarce issue with a low business strike mintage of just 12,000 pieces, which is complemented by a meager 470 proofs. Dramatic rings of violet, lime-green, rose-red, and russet toning encircle the brilliant centers. The frosted devices show vibrant cameo contrast against the highly reflective fields. This razor-sharp near-Gem representative exhibits remarkably clean surfaces. Population: 8 in 64 Cameo, 18 finer (8/08). (#83714)

561 **1867 PR64 NGC.** The 1867 silver three cent had a low mintage of business strikes (4,000 pieces), which was coupled with a diminutive proof issue of just 625 specimens. Pleasing pearl-gray frost covers the glassy surfaces of this carefully preserved and sharply struck near-Gem representative. (#3717)

562 **1867 PR64 PCGS.** The fields show exceptionally deep reflectivity and the devices are noticeably frosted. A cameo effect is definitely present, but probably remains unacknowledged because of the even gray toning that covers each side. (#3717)

563 **1867 PR65 PCGS.** Appealing blue-gray and russet-gold toning adorns the highly reflective surfaces of this sharply struck Gem. A tiny contact mark in the lower right obverse field, and a shallow planchet flaw (as struck) just to the left of A in STATES are the only minor detractions. Population: 55 in 65, 22 finer (8/08). (#3717)

Lovely PR66 ★ Cameo 1867 Three Cent Silver

564 **1867 PR66 ★ Cameo NGC.** With the introduction of the three cent nickel in 1865, the silver version of that denomination was on its way out, though it would hang on for several more low-mintage years. This gorgeous, boldly contrasted Premium Gem is one such survivor, hailing from an issue of just 625 proofs. Census: 7 in 66 Cameo, 4 finer (7/08). (#83717)

565 **1868 PR65 NGC.** Dappled forest-green, golden-brown, navy-blue, and salmon-pink endow this mirrored Gem. The strike is precise, and the preservation is unassailable. Census: 46 in 65, 17 finer (7/08). (#3718)

Impressive 1870 Silver Three Cent, PR65 Cameo

566 **1870 PR65 Cameo NGC.** A gorgeous proof with fully mirrored fields and lustrous, contrasting devices, beneath concentric album toning, a term devised for coins that have lighter centers and deeper toning at the borders, forming rings of rainbow color. The heavier toning at the border is a result of the sulphur content in the cardboard of old coin albums. Census: 4 in 65 Cameo, 4 finer (7/08). (#83721)

Wonderful 1871 Silver Three Cent, PR65 Cameo

567 **1871 PR65 Cameo NGC.** A fully brilliant, untoned Gem with excellent contrast and outstanding eye appeal. This lovely proof survives from a mintage of 960 coins. Breen described three different obverse dies in his Proof Encyclopedia. This pieces appears to be from the third obverse with the 7 and 1 slightly separated, the star point over the right edge of the 8, and horizontal striae along the left border. (#83722)

568 **1872 PR64 NGC.** Mottled golden-red toning around the perimeter accents the mostly brilliant surfaces. A little softness on the tips of the shield is noted, and there is a trace of softness on several stars. The deeply mirrored fields show numerous die polish lines, but are virtually devoid of any contact marks. Only 950 proofs were struck. (#3723)

Pretty, Toned 1872 Three Cent Silver, PR67

569 **1872 PR67 NGC.** Although there was some overlap, the three cent nickel replaced the hated three cent silver (a.k.a. "fish scales") denomination, and certainly by 1872, when the three cent silver saw a proof mintage of 950 pieces accompanied by only 1,000 business strikes, the writing was on the wall. This pretty Superb Gem proof has pearl, gold, and lavender obverse toning, with sage and burnt orange predominating on the reverse. As expected, there are no contact marks of any import. Census: 8 in 67, 2 finer (7/08). (#3723)

Gleaming 1872 Trime, PR66 Cameo

570 **1872 PR66 Cameo NGC.** Sharply struck with glassy mirrored fields and mildly frosted devices that together create an attractive degree of cameo contrast on both sides. This exceptionally well preserved piece is free of marks, except for a few tiny planchet flaws on each side. Faint die striations (as struck) are noted on the reverse. A conditionally scarce offering at the current grade level. Census: 4 in 66 Cameo, 2 finer (7/08). (#83723)

Superb Cameo Gem Proof 1872 Three Cent Silver

571   **1872 PR67 Cameo NGC.** A single die pair was used to coin the business strikes and proofs of 1872. Business strikes are extremely rare, while proofs are scarce but available. Soon after they were struck, and continuing into the early 20th century, collector demand was for proof coins, so most Philadelphia Mint business strikes simply entered circulation. Today, emphasis is on separate collections that are consistent, either business strike or proof. For the advanced specialist who desires a complete set of proof three cent silver coins, this is an excellent opportunity. Census: 2 in 67 Cameo, 0 finer (7/08). (#83723)

Brilliant 1873 Trime, PR65 Cameo

572   **1873 PR65 Cameo NGC.** The 1873 silver three-cent pieces were only coined in proof, with a mintage of just 600 coins. Perhaps half of those exist today, mostly in grades below Gem. They were struck early in the year, and a considerable number of pieces were melted on July 10, 1873, according to information that Walter Breen published. This wonderful Gem is a brilliant and glittering proof with entirely untoned surfaces, displaying its full cameo contrast. Census: 11 in 65 Cameo, 15 finer (7/08). (#83724)

THREE CENT NICKELS

Gem 1873 Open 3 Three Cent Nickel

573   **1873 Open 3 MS65 PCGS.** The Open 3 1873 is a true sleeper. The *Guide Book* reports a mintage of 783,000 pieces, and prices the issue as only a slightly better date. Yet both NGC and PCGS have certified relatively few pieces in Mint State. Gems are unquestionably rare. Presumably, the published mintage is incorrect, and includes a large delivery of Closed 3 pieces. No Open 3 proofs were struck. This is a lustrous and lightly toned Gem with pleasing surfaces and a crisp strike. Population: 11 in 65, 0 finer (7/08). (#3740)

574   **1879 MS66 NGC.** The 9 and the lower loop of the 8 in the date are filled. This Premium Gem displays an exceedingly sharp strike on all of the design elements, including the obverse and reverse denticles. Essentially untoned, with bright, satiny surfaces that are impressively preserved. Census: 21 in 66, 4 finer (7/08). (#3747)

575   **1883 MS62 PCGS.** Boldly defined with lovely light gray surfaces and satin luster. A minor lint mark is visible in the left obverse field, and a few faint scratches are visible on the reverse. Designated as a circulation strike and extremely rare as such. Population: 6 in 62, 18 finer (8/08). (#3751)

576   **1887 MS65 NGC.** One of only 2,960 proofs minted. Silver-gray toning covers the obverse, while the reverse has accents of light hazel patina. Scintillating luster highlights the sharply struck design elements. Census: 22 in 65, 4 finer (7/08). (#3755)

Golden Toned 1888 Three Cent Nickel MS67

577   **1888 MS67 PCGS.** Beautiful apricot-gold toning endows this lustrous and meticulously struck Superb Gem. Immaculate aside from the infrequent minute carbon fleck. Business strikes are scarce due to a low mintage of 36,501 pieces. In a green label holder. Population: 32 in 67, 1 finer (8/08).
From The Bell Collection. (#3757)

PROOF THREE CENT NICKELS

Choice Cameo Proof 1865 Three Cent Nickel

578   **1865 PR64 Cameo NGC.** Ex: W.J. Skiles Collection. Pleasing contrast shines through light layers of lavender, champagne, and peach patina. Strongly appealing despite a handful of minor hairlines and a delightful representative of this popular first-year three cent nickel issue. Census: 5 in 64 Cameo, 29 finer (7/08). (#83761)

Desirable 1865 Three Cent Nickel, PR66 Cameo

579   **1865 PR66 Cameo PCGS.** The number of circulation strike three cent nickels minted in 1865 was the highest for any year of the series, but the mintage of 400-500 proofs was the lowest. Bronze toning with a hint of rose highlights the lustrous surfaces of this scarce first-year proof example. NGC and PCGS combined have certified less than 40 Premium Gem coins. Population: 23 in 66 Cameo, 1 finer (7/08). (#83761)

580   **1869 PR65 Deep Cameo PCGS.** Though the minor base-metal coinage of the era is not known for strong cameo effects, this nickel-white piece shows rich frost on the portrait and distinct contrast with the gleaming fields. A delightful Gem. Population: 14 in 65 Deep Cameo, 2 finer (8/08). (#93765)

581   **1872 PR65 Cameo PCGS.** Starkly contrasted on each side and untoned. This is a splendid Gem type coin. Population: 16 in 65 Cameo, 5 finer (8/08). (#83768)

582   **1872 PR66 Cameo NGC. CAC.** Brilliant and highly reflective fields create startling cameo contrast against the frosted devices, which have a hint of orange toning. Several light grazes are visible under magnification, and a number of die lines are noted on the reverse. It is estimated that less than 1,000 proofs were minted. Census: 19 in 66 Cameo, 2 finer (7/08). (#83768)

583   **1873 Closed 3 PR66 NGC.** Virtually untoned with moderately reflective fields. Both sides display a trace amount of milky patina in the fields. Sharply struck, exquisitely preserved, and free of hairlines or contact marks. Census: 24 in 66, 4 finer (7/08). (#3769)

584   **1873 Closed 3 PR65 Cameo PCGS.** This nicely struck Gem appears brilliant at first glance, but faint gold toning is evident. A couple of pinpoint flecks on the neck are all that limit the grade. Like all pre-1878 dates, the 1873 is scarce in proof format. Population: 40 in 65 Cameo, 10 finer (8/08). (#83769)

585   **1874 PR65 NGC.** Subtle golden tints grace the impressive mirrors of this well-defined, carefully preserved specimen. An attractive Gem, housed in a prior-generation holder. (#3770)

586   **1874 PR65 Cameo PCGS.** Deeply reflective fields show pleasing cameo contrast against the frosted devices, with a touch of golden toning over the surfaces. A number of microscopic flecks on each side limit the grade, but there are virtually no abrasions. Many planchet striations in the fields are visible under magnification. Just over 700 proofs are estimated to have been struck. (#83770)

587   **1874 PR65 Cameo PCGS.** This silver-gray and almond-gold Gem has satin luster and a penetrating strike. The *Guide Book* reports a mintage of just 700+ pieces. Population: 25 in 65 Cameo, 13 finer (8/08). *Ex: FUN Signature (Heritage, 1/2005), lot 5628, which realized $805.* (#83770)

588   **1876 PR65 NGC.** A dusting of yellow-gray patina graces the centers of this lustrous Gem. A prominent die dot is visible above the truncation of Liberty's bust, and there are several other small die defects on Liberty's neck and hair. This nearly pristine specimen is one of about 1,150 proofs struck. (#3772)

Brilliant Choice Cameo Proof-Only 1877 Three Cent Nickel

589   **1877 PR64 Cameo NGC. CAC.** A brilliant proof-only near-Gem with cameo frost throughout the major devices and obverse legends. A small strike-through northwest of the wreath ribbon is of mint origin. The key to the series, along with the proof 1865. The mintage of 510+ pieces is a fraction of its 1878 proof-only successor. (#83773)

Essential 1877 Three Cent Nickel, PR64 Cameo

590   **1877 PR64 Cameo PCGS.** Only proofs were struck for three cent nickels in 1877, 1878, and 1886. The 1877 mintage was the lowest of the 25-year series, with an estimated 510 coins produced. It is a necessary date for the collector who wants an example of every year. This pleasing coin has reflective silver surfaces accented by a few minor toning spots. (#83773)

A 15% Buyer's Premium ($9 min.) Applies To All Lots

Amazing PR66 Cameo 1877 Three Cent Nickel

591 **1877 PR66 Cameo PCGS.** Essentially untoned with crisp contrast between the shining fields and the moderately frosted devices. Sharply struck throughout with no mentionable distractions. A great example of this immensely popular proof-only three cent nickel issue. Population: 34 in 66 Cameo, 8 finer (8/08). (#83773)

592 **1878 PR65 Cameo PCGS.** The 1878 is a proof-only issue with a mintage of just 2,350 specimens. Peppered hazel toning covers both sides and accents the light gray devices. Boldly struck with a splendid cameo appearance. (#83774)

593 **1878 PR65 Cameo PCGS.** Light golden-gray surfaces exhibit excellent field-device contrast, and are sharply defined, including all lines of the III. A few minute flecks are visible on the reverse. (#83774)

594 **1879 PR67 ★ NGC. CAC.** The deeply mirrored fields of this nearly immaculate specimen show moderate cameo contrast against the frosty devices, but apparently not enough to earn the designation from NGC. It is difficult to locate any handling marks on this Superb Gem, even with the aid of a loupe. This brilliant specimen is one of only 3,200 proofs struck in a year when business strikes numbered a relatively low 38,000 pieces. NGC has certified only six pieces finer (7/08). (#3775)

595 **1879 PR66 Cameo PCGS.** A well struck and unabraded Premium Gem that has light golden toning and displays noticeable contrast between the devices and fields. Population: 56 in 66 Cameo, 31 finer (8/08). (#83775)

596 **1880 PR67 NGC.** Sharply struck with pristine nickel-gray surfaces. Although not reflective or mirrored, the surfaces have satiny luster and the overall eye appeal is exceptional. Traces of recutting appear within the upper loop of the second 8. Census: 39 in 67, 2 finer (7/08). (#3776)

Superlative 1880 Three Cent Nickel, PR68

597 **1880 PR68 NGC.** Minor repunching is visible inside the loops of the second 8 in the date, with the lower loop of that digit unpolished, apparently diagnostic for the 1880 proofs. The reverse die was lapped or overpolished, with several fragmented leaves, and the ribbon ends almost entirely missing. This amazing Superb Gem proof has full contrast between the lustrous devices and mirrored fields, perhaps deserving to be called a Cameo proof. The surfaces are pristine and entirely untoned. (#3776)

598 **1881 PR66 Cameo NGC.** This essentially untoned piece displays frosty motifs against a background of mirrored fields. A well executed strike brings out complete definition on the design elements. Impeccably preserved. Census: 44 in 66 Cameo, 39 finer (7/08). (#83777)

599 **1882 PR66 NGC.** Powerful luster emanates from the nearly pristine surfaces of this sharply struck Premium Gem. Just 22,200 business strikes were produced in 1882, which followed the enormous mintage of over one million pieces the previous year. A mere 3,100 proofs were struck. (#3778)

600 **1882 PR67 PCGS.** Powder-blue and almond-gold invigorate this precisely struck and unabraded Superb Gem. A few minute flecks are noted east of the denomination. Encased in a doily label holder. Population: 86 in 67, 7 finer (8/08). (#3778)

601 **1882 PR67 ★ NGC. CAC.** A wonderful Superb Gem proof with light champagne toning over nickel-gray surfaces. Hints of gold and iridescent toning add to the eye appeal. This is an exceptional piece with light cameo contrast. (#3778)

602 **1883 PR66 PCGS.** While the obverse is mostly untoned, the gleaming reverse of this carefully preserved Premium Gem displays lovely golden patina. Fully struck and highly reflective with virtually no marks. (#3779)

603 **1883 PR66 NGC.** Caramel-gold and olive endow this intricately struck and undisturbed Premium Gem. A wonderful and affordable 19th century proof type coin. Housed in a prior generation holder. (#3779)

604 **1883 PR67 PCGS.** A dusting of russet toning around the rims accents the mostly bright gray surfaces. Liberty's hair is a trifle soft, but the rest of the details are razor-sharp. A couple of tiny spots barely affect the outstanding luster and impressive eye appeal. One of 6,609 proofs struck. Housed in a green label PCGS holder. Population: 63 in 67, 4 finer (8/08). (#3779)

605 **1883 PR67 Cameo PCGS.** Mild field-motif contrast is evident on both sides of this Superb Gem Cameo. An exacting strike leaves bold definition on the untoned surfaces, including complete delineation in the lines of the III. Impeccably preserved throughout. Population: 31 in 67 Cameo, 0 finer (8/08). (#83779)

606 **1884 PR66 NGC.** Lovely streaks of autumn-brown are particularly prominent on the obverse. Flashy fields and a penetrating strike provide exemplary eye appeal. Certified in an older generation holder. (#3780)

607 **1884 PR66 PCGS. CAC.** A satiny Premium Gem that displays pastel powder-blue, gold, and apricot toning. Meticulously struck and without any visible imperfections. (#3780)

608 **1886 PR66 NGC.** The reverse shows moderate cameo contrast, while the obverse is nicely frosted throughout. Both sides appear pristine to the unaided eye, and a close inspection yields just a few microscopic blemishes. Only 4,290 proofs were issued. NGC has certified a mere 33 examples finer (8/08). (#3782)

609 **1886 PR66 Cameo PCGS.** The 1886 was a proof-only issue with a mintage of just 4,290 pieces. This piece has nearly pristine surfaces that exhibit magnificent contrast and have a hint of golden toning. A couple of tiny copper spots are noted on the reverse. Population: 33 in 66 Cameo, 16 finer (7/08). (#83782)

610 **1887/6 PR64 Cameo PCGS.** Strong Overdate. The undertype of the 6 is especially prominent, and there is also a trace of an 8 below the second 8. Peppered light tan toning covers both sides, and splendid cameo contrast enhances the eye appeal. Faint clashmarks are visible in the right reverse field. A popular, *Guide Book*-listed variety. (#83784)

Heavily Contrasted 1887/6 Three Cent Nickel
PR66 Ultra Cameo
The Only Ultra Cameo in Any Grade

611   1887/6 PR66 Ultra Cameo NGC. A superlative example of this popular and distinctive overdate, the only one in the three cent nickel series. This brilliant example has exceptionally deep mirrors in the fields that set up a strong contrast against the thickly frosted devices. A few tiny lint marks and planchet voids can be seen with strong magnification, but no contact marks are apparent. This is the only Ultra Cameo certified by NGC in any grade (8/08). (#93784)

612   1889 PR66 Cameo PCGS. Light chestnut-gold toning graces this precisely struck final year proof type coin. Thorough inspection locates several pinpoint aqua flecks. Population: 35 in 66 Cameo, 19 finer (8/08). (#83786)

613   1889 PR67 Cameo PCGS. The deeply mirrored fields of this virtually pristine representative show outstanding cameo contrast against the ivory-white devices. This fully struck Superb Gem exhibits impressive eye appeal. One of 3,436 proofs struck in the final year of the series and denomination. Population: 18 in 67 Cameo, 1 finer (8/08). (#83786)

SHIELD NICKELS

Amazing Gem 1866 Rays Nickel

614   1866 Rays MS65 NGC. Untoned with a rather shallow, satiny luster and an inconsistent strike resulting from visible stress on the dies. An advanced die crack arcs under IN GOD on the obverse. First year of issue for the Shield nickels, and for the nickel denomination. NGC has only certified 22 finer pieces (8/08).
From The Menlo Park Collection. (#3790)

Spectacular 1866 Rays Shield Nickel, Premium Gem

615   1866 Rays MS66 PCGS. Ex: Larry Shapiro. A desirable example from the first year of the Shield Nickel series. Only the 1866 and 1867 issues feature rays between the stars on the reverse, which puts additional demand on this date from type collectors. Light rose and yellow patina graces the centers, which contrast nicely against the pale gray margins. Among other die cracks, a circular crack goes through the stars on the reverse, which exhibit minor softness. Otherwise, this piece is decisively struck with captivating luster. Neither NGC nor PCGS has certified any pieces finer (8/08). (#3790)

616   1868 MS65 NGC. The date is lightly repunched south. A shimmering gunmetal-gray and straw-gold Gem with pleasing surfaces and a suitable strike. NGC has certified only 32 pieces finer (7/08). (#3795)

617   1869 MS65 NGC. A veneer of champagne-gray patina rests on the lustrous surfaces of this Gem nickel, and an attentive strike brings out strong delineation on the design elements. A few grade-consistent, trivial marks do not disturb. Census: 84 in 65, 16 finer (7/08). *From The Menlo Park Collection.* (#3796)

618   1875 MS65 PCGS. Vibrant luster sweeps the unabraded honey-gold surfaces. Portions of the shield stripes are inexactly brought up, but the remainder of the designs are crisp. Certified in an old green label holder. Population: 22 in 65, 9 finer (8/08). (#3804)

619   1876 MS65 NGC. A wisp or two of light gold visits the nickel-gray surfaces of this attractive Gem. The design elements are well defined, and there are no mentionable contacts or spots. Some peripheral cracks are noted over each side. Census: 34 in 65, 6 finer (7/08). (#3805)

620   1881 MS65 PCGS. With a mintage of only 68,800 pieces, the 1881 is elusive in most grades, especially in the upper echelon of Mint State. Mottled slate-gray patina graces both sides of this lustrous and fully struck Gem. Population: 31 in 65, 18 finer (7/08). (#3811)

621   1882 MS65 PCGS. A brilliant and fully struck Gem. This interesting piece has a number of die cracks on both sides, with several extremely pronounced cracks on the obverse and a couple through the reverse lettering. Dazzling satiny luster enhances the eye appeal of this magnificent late-series representative. (#3812)

622   1882 MS66 ★ NGC. Exactingly struck with a radiant satiny sheen across both sides and essentially untoned surfaces that have a slight bluish-gray tint in the fields. A conditionally scarce Premium Gem that is also the only business strike 1882 Shield nickel that currently has the coveted "Star" designation from NGC, which denotes exceptional eye appeal. (#3812)

623   1882 MS66 NGC. Impressively lustrous with solid detail for the series. Light gold, orange, and pink shadings drape each side, and the reverse shows a number of light die striations. Census: 50 in 66, 5 finer (7/08). (#3812)

624   1883 MS66 PCGS. Carefully preserved with untoned surfaces that reveal numerous die cracks upon close inspection. A wonderful example of the final Shield nickel issue. PCGS has graded just nine finer pieces (8/08). *From The Bell Collection.* (#3813)

PROOF SHIELD NICKELS

1866 Rays Shield Nickel, PR66 Cameo

625 **1866 Rays PR66 Cameo PCGS.** A popular first-year type coin, the 1866 Rays Shield nickel is many times more common than the 1867 Rays. The obverse has a tiny center dot in the shield, and the reverse is Reverse Style A, with prominent center dot and 5 repunched at the upper left. This silver-gray specimen has just a glint of golden toning, with minimal evidence of contact. Population: 27 in 66 Cameo, 3 finer (8/08). (#83817)

626 **1867 No Rays PR64 PCGS.** A minimally marked and nearly brilliant piece that would make an excellent type coin. Streaks of yellow toning accent the sharply struck details. Several tiny flecks are noted on each side. It is estimated that slightly more than 600 proofs were struck of the No Rays type. (#3821)

Magnificent 1868 Shield Nickel, PR66 Cameo

627 **1868 PR66 Cameo PCGS.** The 1868 is elusive in PR66 and is virtually impossible to locate in a higher grade. This specimen is entirely brilliant with a stunning cameo appearance. Numerous die polish lines are visible in the fields, which accounts for the deep reflectivity. A fully struck and appealing Premium Gem. Only about 600 proofs were struck. Population: 9 in 66 Cameo, 0 finer (8/08). (#83822)

628 **1869 PR66 PCGS.** Whispers of pastel rose and blue color bathe both sides, and a well executed strike leaves strong definition on the design features. A nicely cared for proof. Population: 21 in 66, 1 finer (8/08). (#3823)

629 **1870 PR65 NGC.** Dusted pearl-white toning accents the mostly silver-gray surfaces of this intricately struck Gem. Several minuscule contact marks keep this highly lustrous piece from an even higher grade. Only about 1,000 proofs are estimated to have been struck. NGC reports just 16 examples finer (8/08). (#3824)

Outstanding 1870 Shield Nickel Premium Gem Proof Cameo

630 **1870 PR66 Cameo PCGS.** A splendidly preserved cameo that is nicely mirrored in the fields. The reverse displays subtle shadings of lilac and rose, while there is almost no color to be seen on the obverse. Contrast on coins from this era is more a matter of chance than design, but this piece is exceptional. Population: 14 in 66 Cameo, 0 finer (8/08). (#83824)

Conditionally Scarce 1871 Shield Nickel, PR66 Cameo

631 **1871 PR66 Cameo PCGS.** This is a remarkable and highly desirable example with fully brilliant silver-gray surfaces. The fields are deeply mirrored with excellent contrast against the fully detailed design elements. Business strikes of this year are scarce, which places additional demand on high quality proof examples. Fewer than 1,000 proofs are estimated to have been struck. Population: 10 in 66 Cameo, 0 finer (8/08). (#83825)

632 **1872 PR66 Cameo PCGS.** A veneer of champagne color bathes the Cameo surfaces of this Premium Gem, and an impressive strike completes the design elements. A few tiny flecks are noted over each side. (#83826)

633 **1873 Closed 3 PR66 Cameo PCGS.** The 1 in the date is repunched north. Sharply struck and essentially untoned, with a bright frosty appearance and shimmering, impeccably preserved surfaces. All proof 1873 Shield nickels display a Closed 3 in the date. Population: 15 in 66 Cameo, 0 finer (8/08). (#83827)

634 **1878 PR66 PCGS.** A powerful strike lends bold definition to this Premium Gem proof. Light tan-gold color imbued with traces of ice-blue visits both sides, each of which reveals a few light flecks. (#3832)

635 **1878 PR66 NGC.** A pristine proof, one of a few hundred of this proof-only date that survive today, with brilliant light gray surfaces. Faint traces of iridescent toning accent this boldly defined proof. Some raised metal inside the lower loop of the second 8 prompted Breen to call this obverse an overdate, but it appears to be a repunched 8, in our opinion. (#3832)

PR66 Cameo 1879 Shield Nickel

636 **1879 PR66 Cameo PCGS.** Considerable contrast between the mirrored fields and frosty devices produces the desired Cameo designation. Mostly under a loupe, the surfaces show myriad microscopic planchet flaws that appear to be bubble from improper planchet production, as made. While such criteria do not affect a technical grade, they must be considered as aesthetic considerations, even though they are not overly distracting. Population: 13 in 66 Cameo, 3 finer (8/08). (#83833)

637 **1879/8 PR66 Cameo PCGS.** This shimmering example, a no-questions Premium Gem, possesses a rather unique appearance due to its unusual toning. The typical olive-gold color is modified somewhat by a thin layer of milky patina. The highly reflective fields provide an exquisite backdrop for the cameo contrast on each side, and the frosted devices stand out. Population: 29 in 66 Cameo, 7 finer (8/08). (#83834)

638 **1880 PR64 NGC.** Films of pastel golden-tan and bluish-violet color cover each side of this near-Gem proof, and well defined devices stand out against the mirrored fields when the coin is tilted slightly under a light source. A handful of light flecks are noted on the obverse. Housed in a prior generation holder.
From The Morton J. Greene Collection. (#3835)

Brilliant PR67 1881 Shield Nickel

639 **1881 PR67 PCGS.** The second 8 in the date is recut, and the outline of the ball ornament is incomplete near the first 8 in the date. This piece is fully struck, with beautiful olive coloration on both sides and near-pristine surfaces disturbed only by a few tiny planchet flaws on the reverse and a wispy lintmark on the lower left obverse, just beneath the left arrowhead. The proof brilliance of this impeccable Superb Gem is undiminished. (#3836)

640 **1882 PR66 PCGS.** A halo of peripheral multicolored toning frames pale violet centers, and an attentive strike leaves sharp definition on the design elements. Both sides are free of significant contacts or spots. Housed in a green-label holder. (#3837)

641 **1882 PR67 PCGS.** The obverse and reverse fields of this Superb Gem proof are moderately reflective around frosty devices. It is sharply struck and enhanced by wispy gold toning. Population: 39 in 67, 0 finer (8/08). (#3837)

642 **1882 PR66 Cameo PCGS.** This brilliant and fully struck Premium Gem has impressive deeply mirrored fields that create pleasing cameo contrast against the snowy devices. Close inspections with a loupe yields a few scattered lint marks (as made), and there are also a couple of small die dots on the shield. Population: 59 in 66 Cameo, 14 finer (7/08). (#83837)

643 **1883 PR66 NGC.** A gleaming lightly gold-toned exemplar of the final Shield nickel issue, crisply struck with minimal carbon and impressive luster. This carefully preserved specimen is nearly free of any marks. NGC has graded only 43 pieces finer (7/08). (#3838)

644 **1883 PR66 Cameo PCGS.** A gorgeous final-year piece that displays moderate contrast and elegant golden tints. The boldly mirrored fields are carefully preserved and greatly enhance the overall visual appeal. Population: 40 in 66 Cameo, 5 finer (8/08). (#83838)

LIBERTY NICKELS

Outstanding 1883 No Cents Liberty Nickel, Superb Gem

645 **1883 No Cents MS67 NGC.** This spectacular Superb Gem is tied for finest certified and would make a great addition to a registry set. Untoned and attractive, this piece boasts captivating satiny luster throughout. Several stars are a trifle soft, as usual, but the central design elements are powerfully impressed. Numerous die cracks are noted around the perimeter of both sides. Neither NGC nor PCGS have certified any examples finer (7/08). (#3841)

Remarkable 1883 No Cents Liberty Nickel, MS67

646 **1883 No Cents MS67 NGC.** An extraordinary, impeccably preserved, and highly lustrous representative. A touch of lemon-yellow on both sides complements the eye-catching satiny luster in the fields. Numerous die cracks are noted on the obverse, but there are no marks worthy of mention. Neither NGC nor PCGS has certified any coins finer (8/08). (#3841)

647 **1883 No Cents MS67 ★ NGC.** Semi-prooflike fields establish pleasing contrast with the lightly frosted motifs. An exacting strike emboldens the design elements, and close examination reveals no marks of consequence. Census: 3 in 67 ★, 0 finer (7/08). (#3841)

648 **1883 With Cents MS66 PCGS.** A rose and golden tint imbues the surfaces of this nearly pristine representative. The strike is sharp save for trivial softness on a few stars. Numerous die cracks encircle the obverse. The 1883 With Cents is nearly impossible to find in a finer grade. (#3844)

649 **1883 With Cents MS66 PCGS.** Eye-catching cartwheel luster graces both sides of this carefully preserved Premium Gem. Wafts of lemon color accent the light-gray patina, and the strike is sharp save for minimal weakness on a couple of stars. Several pronounced die cracks are noted around the perimeter of the obverse, with a particularly noteworthy one through the date. PCGS has certified just one piece finer (7/08). (#3844)

650 **1884 MS65 NGC.** Uncommonly fine striking definition and luster combine for great eye appeal on this well-preserved, minimally toned Gem. A minor disturbance at 8 o'clock on the obverse rim has the appearance of a tiny clip. Census: 58 in 65, 15 finer (7/08). (#3845)

Lightly Toned 1886 Select Nickel

651 **1886 MS63 PCGS.** Soft violet patina mingles with light champagne-gold. Liberty's hair detail is quite strong, while softness is noted on some of the star centers and on the leaves left of the bow knot. A few minute flecks are visible on each side, as are some peripheral cracks. Housed in a green label holder. (#3847)

Beautiful and Elusive 1886 Nickel, MS65

652 **1886 MS65 PCGS.** Key dates in the Liberty nickel series, aside from the ultra-rare 1913, include 1885, 1886, and 1912-S. The 1885 and 1886 are both relatively available in proof format, but are elusive in circulation strike format. Of course, such circulation strikes are the only coins available for the 1912-S.

This Gem has brilliant white surfaces with sharp design definition and frosty luster. The obverse has faint die cracks, while the reverse is shattered with numerous peripheral cracks. An amazing piece for the Liberty nickel enthusiast. Population: 32 in 65, 4 finer (8/08). (#3847)

Sharp Gem 1886 Liberty Nickel

653 **1886 MS65 PCGS.** The business strike 1886 Liberty nickel is closely tied to the more illustrious 1885 issue, and both are keys to the series. The 1885 saw a mintage of nearly 1.5 million pieces, increasing to 3.3 the following year. However, in Gem condition the 1886 is even more elusive than the 1885, and the prices for the two dates are not far apart. This example offers frosty olive-gray surfaces with considerable field-device contrast, and a strike that is sharp, save for a couple of obverse stars and the lower left ear of corn. Some wispy die cracks appear on both sides. A nice acquisition for a Gem set. Population: 33 in 65, 4 finer (8/08). (#3847)

654 **1889 MS65 PCGS.** Bright, satiny luster stands out on this Gem Liberty nickel. It is mostly well struck, except for some softness on the wreath. A shallow luster graze is noted just to the right of the date, but it has little impact on the overall attractiveness of the coin. (#3850)

655 **1890 MS65 PCGS.** Boldly struck with just a hint of weakness on the reverse left ear of corn. A faint coating of streaky russet patina crosses the olive-gray surfaces on both obverse and reverse. Well preserved and blemish-free; a highly attractive Gem. Population: 44 in 65, 10 finer (8/08). (#3851)

Conditionally Scarce 1891 Liberty Nickel, Premium Gem

656 **1891 MS66 NGC.** This lovely piece is well-defined in the centers, although the stars show slight softness. The surfaces offer pleasing luster beneath thin olive-green, rose, and lavender toning. It is virtually impossible to locate an example nicer than the present coin. Census: 14 in 66, 1 finer (8/08). (#3852)

657 **1896 MS65 PCGS.** Light tan toning accents the silver-gray surfaces of this carefully preserved piece. The surfaces are remarkably unabraded, but there are a number of tiny carbon spots. Splendid luster accents the sharply struck details. Population: 53 in 65, 7 finer (7/08). (#3857)

Frosty Key 1896 Nickel, MS66

658 **1896 MS66 PCGS.** The mintage for 1896 was a paltry 8.8 million Liberty Head nickels, a figure reflecting that the nation had not yet recovered from the Panic of 1893. The issue thus became a key in the series, and sharply struck examples are seldom seen. This is one such piece, however, which shows good detailing on the obverse star centrils, the hair above Liberty's brow, and on the left ear of corn on the lower reverse. The silver-gray surfaces show no discernible color, but there is considerable mint frost throughout, adding to the premium appeal. PCGS has certified only six examples in MS66, with none finer (8/08). (#3857)

659 **1898 MS65 PCGS.** The 189 in the date is repunched. A shimmering, splendidly lustrous Gem, untoned and free of distracting marks. The obverse stars and reverse left ear of corn are softly struck, but the overall Gem quality and eye appeal of the piece seems assured. Population: 72 in 65, 19 finer (8/08). (#3859)

660 **1898 MS65 NGC.** Vibrant pink, nickel-blue, and gold-orange patina graces the highly lustrous surfaces of this well struck Gem. Excellent visual appeal. Census: 61 in 65, 16 finer (7/08). *From The Menlo Park Collection.* (#3859)

661 **1899 MS66 NGC.** The strike of this untoned Premium Gem is so sharp that even the ear of corn left of the ribbon bow is boldly defined. The surfaces have frosty luster with subliminal champagne toning. An impressive example. Census: 37 in 66, 4 finer (7/08). (#3860)

662 **1899 MS66 NGC.** Gorgeous gold and iridescent toning will appeal to the aficionado, while the relatively sharp design features will be of interest to specialists. Only the ear of corn left of the ribbon bow is weak. Census: 37 in 66, 4 finer (7/08). (#3860)

663 **1903 MS66 NGC.** Hints of golden-tan color adhere to the lustrous surfaces of this Premium Gem nickel. A sharp strike leaves its mark on the design elements, save for minor softness on the corn ear left of the bow knot. Well preserved, with no mentionable contacts. Census: 60 in 66, 2 finer (7/08). (#3864)

664 **1904 MS66 PCGS. CAC.** A veneer of soft champagne-gold patina rests on the lustrous surfaces of this Premium Gem. Sharply struck, save for weakness in a couple of the star centers and on the leaves left of the bow knot. This is a well cared for piece. Population: 64 in 66, 0 finer (8/08). (#3865)

665 **1905 MS66 NGC. CAC.** Potent luster and cream-gray toning confirm the originality of this unabraded Premium Gem. The strike is good except for the left ear of corn. Census: 32 in 66, 1 finer (7/08). (#3866)

Magnificent 1906 Liberty Nickel, Premium Gem

666 **1906 MS66 PCGS.** Splashes of gold toning add color to the mostly silver-gray surfaces. The strike is nearly full, and there are no mentionable marks on either side. Vibrant luster enhances the wonderful eye appeal. Neither NGC nor PCGS has certified any coins finer than the present piece (8/08). (#3867)

667 **1911 MS66 PCGS.** Light reddish-orange patina overlies each side of this impeccably preserved specimen. A couple of stars show traces of weakness, but the rest of the details are full. The surfaces have almost no marks save for a few tiny abrasions in the obverse field. NGC and PCGS combined have certified just three pieces finer (7/08). (#3872)

668 **1911 MS66 PCGS.** Light golden tints grace the centers, while the margins are pale nickel-gray. A well-defined piece overall with only isolated, trifling softness. Population: 37 in 66, 2 finer (8/08). *From The Bell Collection.* (#3872)

Highly Lustrous MS66 1912 'V' Nickel

669 **1912 MS66 PCGS. CAC.** Exceptionally bright and lustrous for this often dull date. Typically softly struck on the obverse stars, and on the reverse left ear of corn, but exceptionally clean and well preserved. A small depression near the bottom of the large Roman numeral V, on the reverse, appears to be a planchet flaw (as struck). Population: 33 in 66, 0 finer at either service (8/08). (#3873)

Near-Gem 1912-S Liberty Nickel

670   1912-S MS64 NGC. Khaki-gold and cobalt-blue swaths alternate across this suitably struck and unperturbed near-Gem. San Francisco first struck cents in 1908, but waited until the waning days of the Liberty nickel to strike the low mintage 1912-S. Housed in a prior generation holder. (#3875)

Well Struck Gem 1912-S Nickel

671   1912-S MS65 NGC. The San Francisco Mint waited until the final year of the type, but managed to strike 238,000 Liberty nickels in 1912. That mintage is less than that of the more famous 1916-D dime, which trades for multiples of the 1912-S nickel in every grade. This is an impressive Gem with an uncommonly sharp strike, especially on the forehead curls and the left ear of corn. Lushly toned in rose-red and pearl-gray with smooth, satiny surfaces. (#3875)

PROOF LIBERTY NICKELS

672   1883 No Cents PR65 Cameo PCGS. Vividly frosted devices show remarkable black-on-white cameo contrast against the deeply mirrored fields. Careful examination reveals a couple of tiny milk spots, but there are virtually no marks on either side. This fully struck piece is one of just 5,219 proofs minted. (#83878)

673   1883 No Cents PR65 Cameo NGC. Impressive cameo contrast is apparent between the captivating glassy fields and the icy-frosted devices. A shallow mark on Liberty's jaw is noted for future identification purposes. An appealing and powerfully struck Gem. (#83878)

674   1883 No Cents PR66 Cameo PCGS. Freckles of tan-gold and pale purple race over the well preserved surfaces of this proof nickel. Great field-motif contrast, with the latter sharply struck, save for the elements immediately left of the bow knot. Population: 52 in 66 Cameo, 11 finer (8/08). (#83878)

675   1883 With Cents PR66 Cameo PCGS. CAC. Both sides of this first-year With Cents specimen show mild, yet distinct contrast. Rich blue-green and gold shadings drape the well-preserved surfaces. Sharply struck throughout. Population: 23 in 66 Cameo, 1 finer (8/08). (#83881)

676   1884 PR66 Cameo NGC. Pastel powder-blue and golden-tan patina adorns both sides of this lovely Cameo. Exquisitely preserved and struck. Census: 25 in 66 Cameo, 15 finer (7/08). (#83882)

677   1884 PR66 Cameo PCGS. Light gold and orange patina enriches the Cameo surfaces of this Premium Gem proof nickel. An attentive strike imparts crisp delineation to the design features. Well preserved throughout. Population: 27 in 66 Cameo, 2 finer (8/08). (#83882)

678   1885 PR64 PCGS. Elegant nickel-blue shadings grace the fields, while the portrait and the area within the wreath exhibit pink elements. Well-defined and pleasingly mirrored with only a handful of minor hairlines. (#3883)

Wonderful 1885 Liberty Nickel, PR67

679   1885 PR67 PCGS. The key date in the Liberty nickel series, although in business strike format, since the proof 1885 is no more elusive than any other date in the series—just in greater demand, to replace the elusive business strikes. This wonderful Superb Gem proof boasts an incredibly strong strike, with needle-sharp detail in the hair and obverse stars, and throughout the wreath on the reverse. Couple that with superlative luster and a near-cameo appearance, then add glints of olive, gold, pink, and ice-blue. Simply a wonderful coin. Population: 15 in 67, 1 finer (8/08). (#3883)

Spectacular 1885 Liberty Nickel, PR68

680   1885 PR68 NGC. Proof 1885 Liberty nickels are quite popular because of the relative scarcity of their business strike counterpart. A mere 3,790 proofs were struck, and neither NGC nor PCGS has certified any pieces finer than the present coin. In fact, just three pieces have been certified at the PR68 level by both services combined, and it is possible that that number represents resubmissions of the same coin (8/08). A golden tint accents the light gray surfaces of this impeccably preserved specimen. Careful inspection with a loupe locates only the most minor abrasions, with a tiny mark between the 1 and the 8 in the date noted for future identification purposes. The first two stars are a trifle soft, but the rest of the details are fully struck. This nearly immaculate specimen would make a spectacular addition to a registry set. (#3883)

681   1886 PR65 NGC. Lemon-gold, sky-blue, and plum-red embrace this Gem proof semi-key nickel. The fields are flashy, and the devices are exactly struck. Encased in a prior generation holder. (#3884)

682   1886 PR66 PCGS. Lightly toned with flashy mirrored fields. The surfaces appear pristine to the unaided eye, and only a couple of light abrasions are visible under a glass. This fully struck Premium Gem is housed in a green label PCGS holder. One of just 4,290 proofs minted. (#3884)

683   1886 PR66 PCGS. This is a sharply struck Premium Gem proof with light gold and gray patina. Both sides are impeccably preserved. Population: 69 in 66, 16 finer (8/08). (#3884)

Gorgeous 1886 Liberty Nickel, PR67 ★ NGC

684   **1886 PR67 ★ NGC.** The 1886 proof issue's association with the low-mintage business strikes of that year makes it one of the most desirable dates in the specimen series. This colorfully toned representative, gold and pink with elements of mint at the centers, shows excellent central detail, though the upper and right obverse stars show a degree of softness. No finer examples have been certified by either NGC or PCGS. (#3884)

Frosty 1886 Liberty Nickel, PR67

685   **1886 PR67 PCGS.** This Superb Gem example displays essentially flawless, pristine surfaces and just a hint of light golden patina over silver-gray fields. As is often seen on the issue, this example has a frosty appearance, not the typical mirrored fields of a proof. However, the strike is full and sharp, a clear indication of proof manufacture. It is difficult to conceive of a finer example, and indeed none are graded finer. Population: 16 in 67, 0 finer at either service (8/08). (#3884)

Eye-Catching 1886 Liberty Nickel, Superb Proof Cameo

686   **1886 PR67 Cameo NGC.** A splash of yellow toning accents the mostly silver-gray centers of this carefully preserved specimen. Deeply mirrored fields show stunning cameo contrast against the icy-frosted devices. The surfaces appear immaculate to the unaided eye, and a close inspection with a loupe reveals only a couple of minuscule abrasions. A fully struck and attractive representative. Census: 4 in 67 Cameo, 0 finer (7/08). (#83884)

687   **1888 PR66 Cameo NGC.** Brightly mirrored with appreciable, if not stark contrast between fields and devices. Even after several years of the major grading services recognizing the cameo designation, precious few 1888 Nickels have been certified as such. Population: 2 in 66 Cameo, 1 finer (7/08). (#83886)

Fabulous 1888 Liberty Nickel, Premium Gem Proof Cameo

688   **1888 PR66 Cameo PCGS.** A brilliant and highly lustrous Premium Gem. The 1888 is seldom seen with such a tremendous level of preservation. Deeply mirrored fields exude eye-catching luster and contrast sharply against the frosted devices. Sharply struck with outstanding eye appeal. Population: 3 in 66 Cameo, 0 finer (8/08). (#83886)

PR67 Cameo 1888 Liberty Nickel

689   **1888 PR67 Cameo NGC.** This pearl-gray example is nearly devoid of color, although tilting it at the proper angle displays the desired black-on-silver contrast of Cameo proof nickel or silver coinage. The piece is almost devoid of contact as well, save for a single contact mark well-hidden in the hair just above the ear. The single finest Cameo example of the issue certified at NGC. (#83886)

Spectacular 1891 Liberty Nickel, PR66 Ultra Cameo

690   **1891 PR66 Ultra Cameo NGC.** Whispers of gold patina visit the margins of this mostly untoned Liberty nickel proof, which features immense contrast between the frosty devices and glassy fields. The sharp strike further enhances this attractive piece. This issue is seldom seen with such deep cameo contrast. Census: 2 in 66 Ultra Cameo, 2 finer (8/08). (#93889)

691   **1892 PR66 Cameo PCGS.** Wisps of light gold-tan visit the well cared for surfaces of this Premium Gem. A powerful strike results in crisp delineation non the design elements. Population: 16 in 66 Cameo, 0 finer (8/08). (#83890)

Impressive 1893 Liberty Nickel, Superb Proof Cameo

692 **1893 PR67 Cameo NGC. CAC.** Deeply mirrored fields create a stunning black-on-white cameo appearance with the pearl-white devices. The contrast is so vivid that it makes one wonder what more must be necessary to achieve an Ultra Cameo designation from NGC. Regardless of the answer, this virtually flawless piece would make an outstanding addition to any collection. Fully struck with only a couple of microscopic blemishes. NGC and PCGS report a combined 15 pieces in PR67 Cameo, and neither has certified any coins finer (8/08). (#83891)

693 **1897 PR66 PCGS. CAC.** This glassy, untoned Premium Gem is fully struck and highly attractive. The surfaces are distraction-free on both sides. This issue is not rare, but it is somewhat scarce at the current grade level or finer. Population: 57 in 66, 20 finer (8/08). (#3895)

694 **1899 PR67 PCGS.** An outstanding, impeccably preserved, and deeply mirrored Superb Gem. The only apparent mark is a shallow dig at the lower reverse rim. This fully struck specimen is one of only 2,031 proofs minted. Population: 7 in 67, 1 finer (7/08). (#3897)

695 **1900 PR67 NGC.** Beautiful lemon-gold and powder-blue patina embraces this satiny and needle-sharp Superb Gem. Devoid of carbon, and encased in a former generation holder. Census: 26 in 67, 1 finer (7/08). (#3898)

Fantastic 1900 Liberty Nickel, PR67 Cameo

696 **1900 PR67 Cameo PCGS.** Just over 2,200 proof nickels were struck in 1900. Only about 60 have been designated Cameo, however, and just a few pieces have been graded PR67. This Superb Gem is nearly untoned, save for a barely discernible wisp or two of gold color. Immaculately preserved surfaces exhibit boldly impressed design features. Population: 9 in 67 Cameo, 0 finer (8/08). (#83898)

697 **1906 PR66 ★ Cameo NGC.** Spectacular cameo contrast is apparent between the frosted devices and the highly reflective surfaces. The reverse has a lovely hazel center, and a few streaks of light toning accent the brilliant obverse. Sharply struck with virtually no marks. One of only 1,725 proofs struck. NGC has certified only two in 66 Star Cameo, with none finer (7/08). (#83904)

698 **1909 PR66 PCGS.** Lightly toned with highly reflective fields that show remarkable contrast against the frosted devices, although PCGS has not given this piece a Cameo designation. Liberty's hair is a trifle weak, but the rest of the strike is razor-sharp. There are virtually no marks, and just a few tiny blemishes in the right obverse field. A mere 4,763 proofs were struck. Certified in a first generation PCGS holder. (#3907)

699 **1909 PR67 NGC. CAC.** This brilliant and deeply mirrored proof appears immaculate to the unaided eye, and a loupe reveals a faint graze or two. The devices are lightly frosted, but not quite enough for a Cameo designation. NGC has certified only six coins finer (7/08). (#3907)

700 **1909 PR65 Cameo NGC.** Warm golden shadings grace the immensely reflective fields of this later Liberty nickel. Beautifully frosted, decisively struck devices supply amazing contrast. Census: 22 in 65 Cameo, 74 finer (7/08). (#83907)

701 **1909 PR66 Cameo PCGS.** The contrast on the surfaces of this brilliant issue is impressive, with vivid orange and rose-violet patina on the portrait and the left side of the reverse. Boldly impressed and carefully preserved. Population: 49 in 66 Cameo, 11 finer (8/08). (#83907)

Stunning 1909 Liberty Nickel, Superb Proof Cameo

702 **1909 PR67 Cameo PCGS.** A virtually flawless representative with an impressive cameo appearance. Even with a glass it is difficult to locate any imperfection on the highly reflective surfaces. A touch of softness and a few pinpoint handling marks keep this piece from an even higher grade. Pleasing lilac patina in the margins encircles the lovely silver-gray centers. One of only 4,763 proofs struck. Population: 11 in 67 Cameo, 0 finer (8/08). (#83907)

703 **1910 PR66 Cameo PCGS.** Minimally toned with amazing preservation and eye appeal. While the mirrors are not particularly strong and neither is the frost on the devices, the two elements combine for distinct contrast. Population: 24 in 66 Cameo, 13 finer (8/08). (#83908)

704 **1911 PR66 Cameo PCGS.** Peppered hazel patina graces the surfaces of this fully struck Premium Gem. The deeply mirrored fields show unmistakable cameo contrast against the frosted devices. Careful searching under magnification locates only a couple of tiny contact marks. Only 1,733 proofs were minted. Population: 25 in 66 Cameo, 7 finer (8/08). (#83909)

BUFFALO NICKELS

705 **1913 Type One MS66 PCGS.** A veneer of light champagne patina resides on the lustrous surfaces of this Premium Gem nickel, and a well executed strike leaves sharp definition on the design elements. Both sides are well cared for. (#3915)

706 **1913 Type One MS67 NGC.** This piece's later die state has granted it frosty, fascinating luster. A wonderful Superb Gem that offers glints of golden-tan toning close to the margins. (#3915)

707 **1913 Type One MS67 PCGS.** Boldly struck and fully lustrous with only a hint of toning. An amazing Superb Gem with brilliant mint frost that generates exceptional aesthetic appeal. PCGS has only graded 12 finer examples of the issue. (#3915)

708 **1913 Type One MS67 PCGS.** A majestic and immensely appealing Superb Gem example that has remarkable texture, particularly in the fields. Highly lustrous with traces of gold and blue toning. (#3915)

709 **1913 Type One MS67 NGC.** This impeccably preserved and highly lustrous example would make a perfect addition to a registry set. Eye-catching satiny luster graces the fields and complements the razor-sharp design elements. Both sides appear pristine to the unaided eye. NGC has certified a mere 10 pieces finer (8/08). (#3915)

710 **1913 Type One MS67 PCGS.** Delicate ice-blue, violet, and gold-beige patina adorns the immaculately preserved surfaces of this Superb Gem. Well impressed throughout. The reverse is rotated a few degrees counterclockwise. (#3915)

Enticing 1913-D Type One Buffalo Nickel, MS67

711 **1913-D Type One MS67 NGC.** A true condition rarity, the 1913-D Type One Buffalo nickel is easily located in virtually any grade. Of course, as one would except, only a select few specimens have been certified in MS67. The present piece has delightful steel-gray patina with alluring satiny luster throughout. A number of die cracks are noted on the reverse. Carefully preserved with great eye appeal. Census: 12 in 67, 0 finer (8/08). (#3916)

Resplendent 1913-D Type One Nickel, MS67

712 **1913-D Type One MS67 PCGS.** An amazing example of the Type One design, with the bison standing on a mound or bluff, overlooking the plain below. This piece is sharply struck with exceptional gold, pale blue, and iridescent toning on both sides. It is a remarkable specimen. Population: 41 in 67, 2 finer (8/08). (#3916)

713 **1913-S Type One MS66 NGC.** This impeccably preserved Premium Gem features light yellow and blue accents across each side, with pleasing satiny luster throughout. A sharply struck piece that would make a splendid Type One representative. (#3917)

714 **1913-S Type One MS66 PCGS.** Rich yellow-orange patina with glimmers of pink drapes the immensely lustrous surfaces. Crisply detailed with striking eye appeal for this issue of just over 2.1 million pieces. PCGS has graded 17 finer examples (8/08). (#3917)

715 **1913 Type Two MS66 PCGS.** Champagne-gold patina bathes the radiantly lustrous surfaces of this Premium Gem. Better struck than most examples of this issue, though the letters in LIBERTY are a tad soft. A couple of minute marks are noted on each side. (#3921)

Amazing 1913-D Type Two Nickel, MS66

716 **1913-D Type Two MS66 PCGS.** An impeccable example of the elusive 1913 Type Two issue from Denver, this piece is boldly defined with frosty luster. The obverse has light nickel-gray surfaces and the reverse has subtle champagne toning. Population: 60 in 66, 10 finer (8/08). (#3922)

Sharp 1913-D Type Two Nickel, MS66

717 **1913-D Type Two MS66 PCGS.** The 1913-D Type Two nickel is scarce in all grades. The lustrous, light gray surfaces of this Premium Gem exhibits a sharp strike, which is characteristic of the issue. A scattering of tiny, light flecks on each side do not disturb. Population: 60 in 66, 10 finer (8/08). (#3922)

718 **1913-S Type Two MS63 NGC.** Dusky pearl-gray with glimpses of lavender near the right-side borders. Satiny and unmarked with the expected incompleteness in the centers and on the curve of the tail. Among the lowest mintage issues in the series, and popular in all grades. (#3923)

Desirable 1913-S Type Two Nickel, MS64

719 **1913-S Type Two MS64 PCGS.** The Type Two design modification has the buffalo standing on flat ground, rather than the mound of the Type One design. While Type One coins are common, branch mint Type Two examples are elusive. This near-Gem has pale gold toning over satiny nickel-gray luster, slightly brighter on the reverse. (#3923)

Impressive 1913-S Type Two Buffalo Nickel, MS65

720 **1913-S Type Two MS65 NGC.** A wonderful representative of this key Buffalo nickel issue. Delightful lemon and lilac toning in the periphery accents the silver-gray patina that covers the central design elements. A dusting of russet toning spots is visible under magnification, as are only a few tiny marks. This sharply struck Gem features enticing satiny luster throughout. NGC has certified just 20 examples finer (8/08). (#3923)

Splendid 1913-S Type Two Buffalo Nickel, MS66
Key to the 1913 Series

721 **1913-S Type Two MS66 PCGS.** The most challenging of the Buffalo nickel issues from 1913, the 1913-S Type Two was little saved in the year it was minted, and the vast majority of survivors show various degrees of wear. By contrast, this amazing Premium Gem, strongly lustrous with delicate champagne and gold-green patina across the surfaces, offers bold and undisturbed devices. Finer examples of this issue are exceedingly rare; NGC has graded only five such pieces, while PCGS acknowledges only one (8/08). (#3923)

Superb 1913-S Type Two Buffalo Nickel
Tied for Finest Certified

722 **1913-S Type Two MS67 NGC.** The 1913-S Type Two Buffalo nickel, with the buffalo standing on a thinner mound of grass with a straight line at the base, is the first acknowledged series key, and one that is popular and available in all grades, from the many low-grade circulated pieces available at coin shows to the Gems that are occasionally available, albeit for a price.

In MS67 grade, however, this piece is tied with a half-dozen other examples at NGC and PCGS combined for the finest certified (and likely the finest known, as it is extremely unlikely that there are any uncertified examples so fine remaining undiscovered, ungraded, and unauthenticated of this elusive issue). Splendid lilac and hazel low points accent the golden high points on the obverse, and the reverse offers lilac and golden coloration throughout. The coin appears to be an early die state, as it lacks the "beard" die clash that so many later examples show. Both sides are expectedly free of distractions, and the strike is excellent for the issue. Census: 6 in 67, 0 finer (8/08). (#3923)

723 **1914 MS66 NGC.** Carefully struck with vibrant luster and eye appeal. Delicate rose-gold shadings drape the subtly textured, pleasingly preserved surfaces. Census: 46 in 66, 9 finer (7/08). (#3924)

724 **1914/3 AU58 ANACS.** Late Die State. FS-101, formerly FS-014.87. The upper crossbar of the 3 is barely perceptible but is still visible under magnification. Wafts of gold color accent the slate-gray patina. The strike is crisp, and there are only a few light abrasions on each side. (#93924)

Pleasing 1914/3 Five Cent, AU58

725 **1914/3 AU58 PCGS.** FS-101, formerly FS-014.87. The top stroke of the 3 is clearly visible on this lightly circulated representative. Both sides display a good amount of luster, and are bathed in light gray, sky-blue, and gold patina. Devoid of mentionable contact marks or spots. Population: 14 in 58, 27 finer (8/08). (#93924)

726 **1914-D MS65 PCGS.** A scarce and highly respected issue that has traditionally been linked to the 1914-D cent. While not as difficult as that key date issue, the '14-D nickel is elusive in high grades and with problem-free surfaces. The reverse of this piece is especially well defined, and there is just the slightest bit of softness noted above the Indian's braid on the obverse. The original gray patina has soft olive undertones, and the surfaces are almost free of marks. (#3925)

727 **1914-D MS65 NGC.** A softly struck Gem that offers subdued, yet pleasing luster. Gold and nickel-rose tints across much of each side show a degree of streakiness. Census: 63 in 65, 13 finer (7/08). (#3925)

728 **1914-S MS65 NGC.** This second-year Buffalo nickel offers a striking chromelike gleam in the fields. Well-defined with occasional golden-tan tints that grace the peripheries. Census: 51 in 65, 28 finer (7/08). (#3926)

729 **1914/3-S AU55 ANACS.** FS-101, formerly FS-014.89. In *The Complete Guide to Buffalo Nickels*, David Lange writes that the 1914/3 overdate from the San Francisco Mint is extremely difficult to identify, and this piece it no exception. It does, however, feature the characteristic faint die crack beneath the denomination, and has a faint trace of the top of the 3. Medium gray patina covers both sides of this briefly circulated piece, which Lange states is significantly less available than its P-mint counterpart. A small spot to the left of the bison's head is noted. (#93926)

Lovely 1915-D Buffalo Nickel, Gem Mint State

730 **1915-D MS65 PCGS. CAC.** An interesting, crisply struck, late die state example of this early Buffalo nickel issue. Numerous die cracks cover the obverse, which is nearly shattered, while the reverse rim is crumbled. Magnificent satiny luster radiates from the brilliant and minimally marked surfaces. PCGS has certified just 28 pieces finer (8/08). (#3928)

Fully Struck MS66 1915-D Buffalo Nickel

731 **1915-D MS66 PCGS.** Sparkling luster exudes from well preserved surfaces that displays sharply impressed design elements, especially on the braid, date, LIBERTY, the bison's hair, horn, and tail, and the mintmark. Occasional wisps of gold-tan color are visible under magnification. Population: 26 in 66, 2 finer (8/08). (#3928)

Brilliant 1915-S Buffalo, MS65

732 **1915-S MS65 NGC.** The surfaces of this sharply defined 1915-S nickel are fully brilliant and satiny with exceptional white luster. The obverse has a strong hair braid, and LIBERTY is completely separated from the strong border. The reverse is bold with an excellent coat on the bison, and with a sharp and split tail. Save for a couple tiny flecks, all aspects suggest an excellent coin for the grade. (#3929)

Impressive 1915-S Nickel, MS66

733 **1915-S MS66 NGC.** Tied for the finest we have offered in the last 15 years, this lovely Buffalo has exquisite olive, gold, and iridescent toning over satiny luster. The underlying fields have a slightly reflective appearance. Although the tops of LIBERTY are slightly indistinct, it is otherwise boldly detailed. Census: 23 in 66, 0 finer (7/08). (#3929)

Low Mintage 1915-S Nickel, MS66

734 **1915-S MS66 PCGS.** This impressively struck Premium Gem has shimmering luster and original olive and chestnut-gold toning. Carbon is minimal, and neither side shows any noticeable abrasions. The bison's head, shoulder, and tail are boldly defined, as is the mintmark and date. Outstanding quality for this low mintage issue. Population: 27 in 66, 3 finer (8/08). (#3929)

735 **1916 MS66 PCGS.** Delicate gold and sage shadings mingle on the carefully preserved surfaces of this softly lustrous Premium Gem. Pleasingly detailed and highly elusive any finer, with just 10 such coins graded by PCGS (8/08). (#3930)

736 **1916-D MS65 PCGS.** Delicate golden tints visit parts of the generally nickel-gray surfaces. A luminous and well-defined survivor from this underrated Denver issue. PCGS has graded only 10 finer pieces (8/08). (#3932)

737 **1916-S MS65 NGC.** A delightful Gem example of this underrated S-mint issue. The generally nickel-white surfaces show glimpses of violet and gold patina. Census: 33 in 65, 14 finer (7/08). (#3933)

738 **1917 MS66 PCGS.** Sharply struck, with attractive golden-gray patina and pleasing luster. Devoid of mentionable marks or spots. (#3934)

739 **1917-D MS64 NGC.** A sharply struck example with pale blue and gold patina over each side. Lovely for the near-Gem grade with remarkable eye appeal for an issue that seldom comes so nice. (#3935)

Sharp Gem 1917-D Buffalo Nickel

740 **1917-D MS65 PCGS.** Although the 1917-D is not quite as elusive in Gem condition as some of the later-series S-mint condition rarities, it is seldom seen finer than MS65; PCGS has certified only 13 examples finer (8/08). This example boasts quicksilver surfaces that are largely gold-tinged silver, save for an interesting swath of ice-blue down the buffalo's midsection. A well-struck and thoroughly delightful coin. (#3935)

Bright, Satiny MS65 1917-D Buffalo Nickel

741 **1917-D MS65 PCGS.** The bright, satin-like surfaces are free from any noticeable abrasions. Most of the 9.1 million coins struck are sub-par in the striking category. That is only the case with the obverse on this piece, the reverse is fully detailed. Generally brilliant, there is just a hint of light golden color around the margins on each side. (#3935)

742 **1917-S MS64 NGC.** A gorgeous example with highly lustrous and brilliant mint frost on each side. The strike is bold and the surfaces are untoned. (#3936)

Charming 1917-S Buffalo Nickel, MS66 PCGS

743 **1917-S MS66 PCGS.** This charming example features satiny luster with lovely lilac, blue, and gold toning on each side. The strike is sharp with full details, even at the usual soft spots of the design. Overall, an above-average representative of the issue. Population: 22 in 66, 0 finer (8/08). (#3936)

Attractive 1918-S Nickel, MS63

754   **1918-S MS63 PCGS.** The 1918-S Buffalo is one of the most elusive series issues in the higher Mint State grades, and almost never seen in Gem or finer condition. Although this example displays a typical weak strike, both date and lettering are clear, and the bison's horn and mintmark are crisply outlined. The surfaces show few abrasions for the grade, certainly none that demand attention. Subtle copper and rose accents along the rims contrast with silver-gray surfaces. An eye-appealing example. (#3940)

Elusive, Sharply Struck Gem
1918-S Buffalo Nickel

755   **1918-S MS65 NGC.** The 1918-S is among the most elusive of the mintmarked Buffalo nickel issues from the teens, and in Gem condition it is seldom seen. Many of the NGC and PCGS Registry Sets featuring Gem or finer coins have an MS64 example for the 1918-S nickel. That is borne out by the grading service figures, which show a total of only three and a half dozen Gems at both combined, with two pieces finer (8/08).

This lustrous silver-gold Gem example shows tinges of sky-blue on both sides, with a marvelous strike on the high points, the horn, and the split tail. The eye appeal is every bit what one would expect from the Gem ranking. This is an issue that has seen a considerable surge in price in recent years, recognition of both its popularity and rarity. Census: 12 in 65, 1 finer (8/08). (#3940)

756   **1919 MS66 PCGS.** Well struck with shimmering luster and clean, virtually pristine surfaces. An immaculately preserved Premium Gem example of this early, conditionally scarce issue in the Buffalo nickel series. (#3941)

757   **1919 MS66 PCGS.** Beautifully detailed with delightful, dusky golden shadings over much of the otherwise nickel-gray surfaces. Luminous and carefully preserved. PCGS has graded eight finer examples (8/08). (#3941)

758   **1919-D MS63 PCGS.** Although the luster is subdued by pale yellow toning, this piece is highly desirable for its exceptional strike. LIBERTY and the reverse legend are both bold and fully separated from the rim. (#3942)

Near-Gem 1919-D Buffalo Nickel

759   **1919-D MS64 PCGS.** The 1919-D is a challenging (and challenged) issue, one that is seldom seen with attractive toning and a sharp strike. The present piece is lustrous throughout, although it is below-par in terms of the series if not the issue. The strike is somewhat indistinct, as usually seen; although the hindquarters of the buffalo are fairly sharp, the head and horn are not. Appealing amber-gold peripheral toning appears on the obverse. (#3942)

Scarce 1919-D Buffalo Nickel, Gem Mint State

760   **1919-D MS65 PCGS.** Although not generally thought of in the same league with the S-mint keys, the 1919-D is a difficult issue in its own right. Lange calls this issue "one of the last holes filled by a discriminating collector, regardless of whether one is collecting XF-AU or gem uncirculated." This charming, boldly struck Gem offers attractive, lightly toned hazel-olive surfaces with accents of rose-copper. PCGS has certified only 14 examples finer (8/08). (#3942)

Impressive 1915-S Nickel, MS66

733 **1915-S MS66 NGC.** Tied for the finest we have offered in the last 15 years, this lovely Buffalo has exquisite olive, gold, and iridescent toning over satiny luster. The underlying fields have a slightly reflective appearance. Although the tops of LIBERTY are slightly indistinct, it is otherwise boldly detailed. Census: 23 in 66, 0 finer (7/08). (#3929)

Low Mintage 1915-S Nickel, MS66

734 **1915-S MS66 PCGS.** This impressively struck Premium Gem has shimmering luster and original olive and chestnut-gold toning. Carbon is minimal, and neither side shows any noticeable abrasions. The bison's head, shoulder, and tail are boldly defined, as is the mintmark and date. Outstanding quality for this low mintage issue. Population: 27 in 66, 3 finer (8/08). (#3929)

735 **1916 MS66 PCGS.** Delicate gold and sage shadings mingle on the carefully preserved surfaces of this softly lustrous Premium Gem. Pleasingly detailed and highly elusive any finer, with just 10 such coins graded by PCGS (8/08). (#3930)

736 **1916-D MS65 PCGS.** Delicate golden tints visit parts of the generally nickel-gray surfaces. A luminous and well-defined survivor from this underrated Denver issue. PCGS has graded only 10 finer pieces (8/08). (#3932)

737 **1916-S MS65 NGC.** A delightful Gem example of this underrated S-mint issue. The generally nickel-white surfaces show glimpses of violet and gold patina. Census: 33 in 65, 14 finer (7/08). (#3933)

738 **1917 MS66 PCGS.** Sharply struck, with attractive golden-gray patina and pleasing luster. Devoid of mentionable marks or spots. (#3934)

739 **1917-D MS64 NGC.** A sharply struck example with pale blue and gold patina over each side. Lovely for the near-Gem grade with remarkable eye appeal for an issue that seldom comes so nice. (#3935)

Sharp Gem 1917-D Buffalo Nickel

740 **1917-D MS65 PCGS.** Although the 1917-D is not quite as elusive in Gem condition as some of the later-series S-mint condition rarities, it is seldom seen finer than MS65; PCGS has certified only 13 examples finer (8/08). This example boasts quicksilver surfaces that are largely gold-tinged silver, save for an interesting swath of ice-blue down the buffalo's midsection. A well-struck and thoroughly delightful coin. (#3935)

Bright, Satiny MS65 1917-D Buffalo Nickel

741 **1917-D MS65 PCGS.** The bright, satin-like surfaces are free from any noticeable abrasions. Most of the 9.1 million coins struck are sub-par in the striking category. That is only the case with the obverse on this piece, the reverse is fully detailed. Generally brilliant, there is just a hint of light golden color around the margins on each side. (#3935)

742 **1917-S MS64 NGC.** A gorgeous example with highly lustrous and brilliant mint frost on each side. The strike is bold and the surfaces are untoned. (#3936)

Charming 1917-S Buffalo Nickel, MS66 PCGS

743 **1917-S MS66 PCGS.** This charming example features satiny luster with lovely lilac, blue, and gold toning on each side. The strike is sharp with full details, even at the usual soft spots of the design. Overall, an above-average representative of the issue. Population: 22 in 66, 0 finer (8/08). (#3936)

744 **1918 MS65 PCGS. CAC.** Delicate golden tints grace the otherwise nickel-white surfaces of this delightful Gem. Well struck, minimally marked, and attractive. PCGS has certified 49 finer examples (8/08). (#3937)

Sharp, High Grade 1918 Buffalo Nickel, MS66

745 **1918 MS66 PCGS.** Mostly brilliant with intense luster and only a whisper of golden color splashed on either side. As one would expect from a coin in this lofty grade, the surfaces show no noticeable abrasions. Despite its high mintage, the 1918 is a difficult P-mint Buffalo nickel in Gem condition. Population: 42 in 66, 7 finer (8/08). (#3937)

746 **1918-D MS64 PCGS.** Light beige-gold and powder-blue patina coats lustrous surfaces. Nicely struck, except for minor softness in the hair over the bison's forehead. (#3938)

Outstanding 1918-D Buffalo Nickel, MS65

747 **1918-D MS65 NGC.** The *Guide Book of Buffalo and Jefferson Nickels* succinctly summarizes this issue: "Although the 1918-D is common in lower grades, in gem Mint State (MS-65 or higher) and with a decent strike, it is a rarity." Despite a little softness on the Indian, this piece is certainly above-average in terms of sharpness, and its strong satiny luster adds to the appeal. The surfaces appear pristine to the unaided eye, and only a few minor handling marks are visible under a glass. NGC has certified just six examples finer (8/08). (#3938)

748 **1918/7-D Good 6 PCGS.** FS-016.5. This stone-gray example has a clear legends and a fully readable date. The thickness on the 8, particularly near the upper right corner, confirms the valuable overdate. (#3939)

749 **1918/7-D VG10 PCGS.** FS-016.5. This piece is evenly worn throughout, with the date somewhat faint but the overdate readily apparent under a glass. Several shallow marks on the Indian are the only abrasions visible to the unaided eye. A lovely representative of this popular variety. (#3939)

750 **1918/7-D—Scratched—ICG. Fine 12 Details.** FS-016.5. The crossbar and downstroke of the underdigit 7 are apparent as extra thickness on the 8 in the date. This key date nickel is slate-gray and generally attractive but does have a light curved pinscratch concealed within the Indian's upper hair. (#3939)

Popular 1918/7-D Nickel, Fine 12

751 **1918/7-D Fine 12 NGC.** FS-016.5. The underdigit is clear on this popular Fine overdate. Light gray patina shows over each side. A well defined piece, with about two-thirds of the horn showing. The mintmark is sharp. There are no significant marks or spots. (#3939)

Desirable 1918/7-D Buffalo Nickel, VF25

752 **1918/7-D VF25 PCGS.** FS-016.5. Lange (2006) writes that the "1918/7-D overdate certainly rivals the 1916 DDO and 1937-D 3-leg nickel for the title of most popular and highly sought variety in the series." Despite wear associated with the VF25 grade, the overdate on this piece is clear even to the unaided eye. The remainder of the details are boldly outlined as well. Light gray patina covers both sides of this minimally marked representative. (#3939)

Late Die State 1918/7-D Buffalo Nickel, MS62
Rare in Mint State

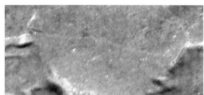

753 **1918/7-D MS62 PCGS.** The history of U.S. numismatics in the 20th century reveals a number of wartime overdates, including the 1918/7-S Standing Liberty quarter, the 1918/7-D Buffalo nickel, and the 1942/1-P and D Mercury dimes. Each of those coins was produced apparently as the result of a dual-hubbing error, in which two differently dated working hubs are used in the sinking of a single working die. At an earlier time in numismatics—and even still today—many collectors wrongly believed that such coins were simply the result of a working die being reengraved toward the end of the year. The slightly more complex truth is that working dies require several blows from a working hub and are "hardened" or annealed by heat between those blows, so that the possibility exists for blows from two different-dated hubs on a single die.

Although the 1918/7-D Buffalo nickel is a popular variety collected alongside the 1916 Doubled Die Obverse and the 1937-D Three Legged Buffalo, it is many times scarcer in Mint State than the latter. David Lange's third edition (2006) of his reference on the series places the estimate of Mint State pieces at two dozen, accounting for resubmissions. Given the current number of Mint State "submission events"—91 coins at NGC and PCGS together—we would place the estimate somewhat higher, between three dozen and four dozen, still placing Mint State examples squarely within the R.5 (or "rare") ranking.

This piece, as all Mint State examples we have offered, shows the diagonal downstroke of the 7 boldly underneath the loops of the 8. This piece is somewhat softly struck and shows signs of considerable die erosion, an interesting characteristic reinforcing the urgency with which the Mint was responding to a wartime shortage of minor coins that resulted in this error's production in the first place. Two other diagnostics are also present: the designer's initial, F, looks like a P. Most examples, except for perhaps those in the earliest die states, have a fine die crack just above and in front of the Indian's braid knot, on the cheek.

The present example, as we mentioned, shows significant die erosion, and the die crack here runs all the way down to the corner of the Indian's mouth, the most advanced state of the dies we have ever seen for this particular error (see closeup). Although the strike is somewhat soft on the high points, full luster is present throughout both sides, and pretty golden-orange patina with a touch of ice-blue at the lower reverse complements the clean surfaces. For any Buffalo nickel die state specialists, this coin is a must-have Uncirculated example of this rare error. (#3939)

Attractive 1918-S Nickel, MS63

754   1918-S MS63 PCGS. The 1918-S Buffalo is one of the most elusive series issues in the higher Mint State grades, and almost never seen in Gem or finer condition. Although this example displays a typical weak strike, both date and lettering are clear, and the bison's horn and mintmark are crisply outlined. The surfaces show few abrasions for the grade, certainly none that demand attention. Subtle copper and rose accents along the rims contrast with silver-gray surfaces. An eye-appealing example. (#3940)

Elusive, Sharply Struck Gem 1918-S Buffalo Nickel

755   1918-S MS65 NGC. The 1918-S is among the most elusive of the mintmarked Buffalo nickel issues from the teens, and in Gem condition it is seldom seen. Many of the NGC and PCGS Registry Sets featuring Gem or finer coins have an MS64 example for the 1918-S nickel. That is borne out by the grading service figures, which show a total of only three-and-a-half-dozen Gems at both combined, with two pieces finer (8/08).

This lustrous silver-gold Gem example shows tinges of sky-blue on both sides, with a marvelous strike on the high points, the horn, and the split tail. The eye appeal is every bit what one would expect from the Gem ranking. This is an issue that has seen a considerable surge in price in recent years, recognition of both its popularity and rarity. Census: 12 in 65, 1 finer (8/08). (#3940)

756   1919 MS66 PCGS. Well struck with shimmering luster and clean, virtually pristine surfaces. An immaculately preserved Premium Gem example of this early, conditionally scarce issue in the Buffalo nickel series. (#3941)

757   1919 MS66 PCGS. Beautifully detailed with delightful, dusky golden shadings over much of the otherwise nickel-gray surfaces. Luminous and carefully preserved. PCGS has graded eight finer examples (8/08). (#3941)

758   1919-D MS63 PCGS. Although the luster is subdued by pale yellow toning, this piece is highly desirable for its exceptional strike. LIBERTY and the reverse legend are both bold and fully separated from the rim. (#3942)

Near-Gem 1919-D Buffalo Nickel

759   1919-D MS64 PCGS. The 1919-D is a challenging (and challenged) issue, one that is seldom seen with attractive toning and a sharp strike. The present piece is lustrous throughout, although it is below-par in terms of the series if not the issue. The strike is somewhat indistinct, as usually seen; although the hindquarters of the buffalo are fairly sharp, the head and horn are not. Appealing amber-gold peripheral toning appears on the obverse. (#3942)

Scarce 1919-D Buffalo Nickel, Gem Mint State

760   1919-D MS65 PCGS. Although not generally thought of in the same league with the S-mint keys, the 1919-D is a difficult issue in its own right. Lange calls this issue "one of the last holes filled by a discriminating collector, regardless of whether one is collecting XF-AU or gem uncirculated." This charming, boldly struck Gem offers attractive, lightly toned hazel-olive surfaces with accents of rose-copper. PCGS has certified only 14 examples finer (8/08). (#3942)

Delightful 1919-S Buffalo Nickel, MS64

761 **1919-S MS64 PCGS. CAC.** Despite a mintage of over 7 million pieces, the 1919-S is seldom seen in Choice Uncirculated grades, and is rare any finer. This highly lustrous example exhibits incredibly reflective fields that are entirely brilliant. The strike is crisp, and the abrasions are all minor. PCGS has certified just 33 pieces finer (7/08). (#3943)

Conditionally Rare 1919-S Nickel, MS64

762 **1919-S MS64 PCGS.** The 1919-D and 1919-S nickels rank among the tough condition rarities. Although PCGS has certified 173 examples as MS64, they have only graded 33 finer Gem specimens. Both sides have satiny and lustrous gray surfaces with traces of gold toning. Only slight weakness is evident, primarily on the reverse. (#3943)

Exquisite 1919-S Buffalo Nickel, MS64

763 **1919-S MS64 NGC.** Pleasing silver-gray surfaces show hints of yellow patina in the fields. The strike is sharp save for the typical weakness on the Indian's hair. Magnificent satiny luster drapes the fields and gives this piece excellent eye appeal. NGC has certified a mere 15 pieces finer (8/08). (#3943)

764 **1920 MS66 PCGS.** The 1920 is one of the most consistently well produced early Buffalo nickels. This piece displays bright mint luster that is overlaid with blue and golden toning of varying configurations on each side. Boldly struck. (#3944)

765 **1920-D MS62 PCGS.** Housed in an older green-label holder, this pleasing Mint State piece has exceptional surfaces for the grade, but it is noticeably weak at the centers. (#3945)

Gem 1920-D Buffalo Nickel

766 **1920-D MS65 PCGS.** Delicate orange-gold patina with hints of light green bathe the highly lustrous surfaces of this '20-D Buffalo nickel. A well executed strike brings out sharp definition on the design elements, save for the typical softness in the hair at the bison's forehead. There are no mentionable marks or spots to report. Housed in a green label holder. Population: 48 in 65, 1 finer (8/08). (#3945)

Pleasing 1920-S Buffalo, MS63

767 **1920-S MS63 PCGS.** Lustrous light gray surfaces with excellent eye appeal for the grade, this 1920-S Buffalo features a typical strike with some central design weakness, but other design elements are much sharper. Faint gold toning adds to its eye appeal. An excellent coin for the Buffalo enthusiast. (#3946)

Glossy, Well Struck MS64 1920-S Buffalo Nickel

768 **1920-S MS64 PCGS.** Glossy, generally unmarked surfaces are well defined for this challenging S-mint Buffalo, with each side coated in pastel blue and golden patina. The opportunity to acquire a Gem 1920-S almost never occurs and would prove too costly for many collectors, thus the appealing near-Gem offered here is an especially viable alternative. (#3946)

769 **1921 MS66 NGC.** Boldly struck and satiny, with lovely olive, apricot-yellow, and rose toning, and seemingly blemish-free surfaces. There are noticeable die clash marks (as struck) on the lower obverse, and over the reverse motto, and a rather sizeable planchet flaw (as made), resides near the left reverse rim, a bit below 9 o'clock. (#3947)

Lustrous 1921-S Nickel, MS64

770 1921-S MS64 PCGS. Lovely golden-tan, sky-blue, russet, and steel-gray toning adorns the satiny, highly lustrous surfaces of this pleasing, conditionally scarce near-Gem. Well detailed on the obverse, but mushy on the reverse, especially on the bison's head and shoulder areas. Impressively preserved and mark-free on both sides. Housed in a green label holder. (#3948)

771 1923 MS66 PCGS. Delicate champagne and aqua tints visit the shining surfaces of this attractive P-mint piece. Solidly struck overall, though the bison's shoulder shows a touch of softness. Nicely preserved throughout. (#3949)

772 1923-S MS64 PCGS. While common in circulated grades, the 1923-S is surprisingly scarce in Mint State. The typical '23-S has poorly defined details, especially on the reverse, but the present specimen exhibits above-average sharpness, although the hair on the bison's head is a trifle soft. Lustrous hazel-gray surfaces are endowed with traces of ice-blue and lilac. A couple of minuscule light green spots are noted. PCGS has certified just 32 pieces finer (8/08). (#3950)

773 1923-S MS64 NGC. This piece is very softly struck, with especially mushy details near the peripheries. A satiny near-Gem without any distracting surface marks. (#3950)

774 1923-S MS64 PCGS. Marvelous yellow patina drapes both sides of this crisply struck near-Gem representative. There are no mentionable marks on either side and the eye appeal is excellent. The 1923-S is seldom seen finer than this lovely piece. (#3950)

775 1923-S MS64 PCGS. Although some weakness is evident on each side, this is a lovely example of the date with brilliant, satiny luster beneath pale champagne and heather toning. PCGS has only graded 32 finer pieces (8/08). (#3950)

Remarkable 1923-S Buffalo Nickel, Gem Mint State

776 1923-S MS65 NGC. This piece exhibits above-average sharpness for the issue, which is often seen rather soft. The obverse is nearly full, and the reverse shows just a touch of softness on the highpoints. Richly frosted surfaces have light golden and lilac patina. A remarkably clean piece that would be perfect for a high grade Buffalo nickel set. Census: 25 in 65, 5 finer (8/08). (#3950)

777 1924 MS66 PCGS. Occasional splashes of gold visit the quicksilver surfaces of this Philadelphia Premium Gem. Well struck and elusive any finer, with just four such coins known to PCGS (8/08). (#3951)

778 1924-D MS64 PCGS. Pale gold toning blends with the satiny gray luster of this pleasing Buffalo. It has an excellent strike for the date and possesses considerable eye appeal. (#3952)

Vivid Gem 1924-D Buffalo Nickel

779 1924-D MS65 PCGS. This coin commands both the viewer's attention and the Gem ranking by virtue of its pristine surfaces and excellent eye appeal. Glimpses of lilac and pinkish-blue glint from the obverse, and while the strike is typical for the issue, with softness on the bison's head, the strong luster and good overall surface preservation more than compensate. PCGS has certified a single coin finer (8/08). (#3952)

Lovely 1924-S Buffalo, MS63

780 1924-S MS63 PCGS. Typically struck with some central weakness that prevents a higher grade, this beauty has satiny blue-gray luster with traces of gold and lilac toning. The mintmark is bold and the rims are complete on both sides. An impressive piece for the budget-minded connoisseur, with the general appearance of a higher grade. (#3953)

Upper-End MS64 1924-S Nickel

781 1924-S MS64 PCGS. CAC. The 1924-S Buffalo nickel is regarded as one of the key dates in the series, especially in Mint State. This near-Gem is lustrous and typically struck, with noticeable softness on the bison. The rose-gray and tan-gold surfaces are remarkably clean and abrasion-free, and the coin has a very pleasing appearance overall. (#3953)

Desirable 1924-S Buffalo Nickel, MS65

782 1924-S MS65 NGC. A key date in one of the most popular series in American numismatics. The low mintage of 1.4 million coins makes this issue difficult to locate in all grades. David Lange estimates that MS65 examples are quite rare, and David Bowers reports that he has never seen a coin with full details. The present coin is a particularly attractive and sharply struck example of this scarce date.

From a design by James Earle Fraser, the Buffalo nickel has been called the most "American" of all U.S. coins. Collector enthusiasm for the design has always been high, and the series was studied closely from its inception. Numismatists recognized the scarcity of the 1924-S early on, and virtually all examples were garnered from circulation during the 1930s. As a date, only the celebrated 1926-S has been more sought after.

This piece show delightful surface coloration on both sides in shades of silver-gold, and the notably sharp strike extends even to the often-weak letter tops of LIBERTY and the split tail on the bison. A memorable collector example, exceeded by only three pieces at NGC and one at PCGS (7/08). (#3953)

783 1925 MS66 PCGS. Beautiful sky-blue patina rests atop predominately smooth, satiny surfaces, with flashes of lemon-yellow and orange at the margins. Inspection with a glass yields a few minuscule grade-consistent ticks. (#3954)

784 1925-D MS64 NGC. CAC. This interesting piece features a 45-degree die rotation. Light yellow patina graces the surfaces, which feature vibrant satiny luster throughout. A few minuscule flecks are barely worthy of mention. (#3955)

785 1925-D MS64 PCGS. Highly lustrous and fully brilliant with untoned light gray surfaces. Both sides are exceptionally well detailed for the issue. (#3955)

786 1925-D MS64 PCGS. CAC. Primarily soft lavender-gray with splashes of fiery champagne-gold that grace parts of the fields. Softly struck, yet pleasing. PCGS has graded 72 finer examples (8/08). (#3955)

787 1925-D MS64 PCGS. CAC. Although somewhat weakly struck, the existing details are still sharper than usual for the issue. This brilliant near-Gem is fully lustrous with light champagne toning. A delightful example for the grade. (#3955)

Lustrous Gem 1925-D Nickel

788 1925-D MS65 NGC. The surfaces are silver-gray with considerable dollops of gold added into the mix, and much luster gleams from each side. The strike is typical for the issue, however, with weakness on LIBERTY and the high points of the bison. The reverse die, not unsurprisingly, shows some rather advanced orange-peel effect from erosion and overuse. (#3955)

789 1925-S MS63 PCGS. Hints of golden luster combine with pleasing gray patina on the devices. This issue is usually poorly struck, and a soft strike is apparent on this piece, but not overly so. A minimally marked and lustrous example. (#3956)

790 1925-S MS63 PCGS. Deep russet, olive, and stone-gray toning embraces this satiny and unmarked example. Struck from worn dies, as made, with an 'orange peel' texture to the fields near the borders. The top half of the mintmark is apparent when viewed with the naked eye. Certified in a green label holder. (#3956)

Attractive MS64 1925-S Nickel

791 1925-S MS64 PCGS. This challenging issue is seen here with slightly above average striking definition, especially on the reverse. Superb mint frost covers each side of this attractive near-Gem. Light reddish-lilac toning gives this piece an appearance of untampered originality. Minimally abraded for the grade. (#3956)

792 1926-D MS64 ANACS. A pale yellow tint accents the soft luster of this lovely representative. There is a trace of softness on the bison's head, but the rest of the details are fully defined. A couple of insignificant abrasions are apparent only under a glass. (#3958)

793 1926-D MS64 PCGS. Pale amber and gold are blended with faint blue tones over satiny luster. Both sides have brilliant surfaces and above average design definition. (#3958)

Sharply Defined MS65 1926-D Nickel

794 **1926-D MS65 PCGS.** Lilac and apricot patina envelopes the unabraded surfaces. The mintmark is sharp on this satiny, well-struck Gem, which shows much better details than the typical example of this notoriously weakly struck issue. Highly lustrous with noteworthy eye appeal. Population: 83 in 65, 24 finer (8/08). (#3958)

Choice AU 1926-S Buffalo Nickel

795 **1926-S AU55 PCGS.** Just a whisper away from Mint State, this 1926-S is high-end in terms of its luster, surfaces, and planchet. Both sides offer golden toning with patches of ice-blue, and the strike is better than average for this challenged issue. There are none of the planchet problems for which the 1926-S is so well-known, and this piece would fit nicely in a Mint State set. Certified in a green-label holder. (#3959)

Near-Mint 1926-S Buffalo Nickel

796 **1926-S AU58 PCGS.** This low-mintage Roaring Twenties San Francisco issue is one of the most popular Buffalo nickels, and the minimally marked near-Mint coin offered here has excellent eye appeal. Light orange and gold-gray toning drapes luminous fields and devices that offer surprisingly strong detail. (#3959)

Near-Gem 1926-S Buffalo Nickel

797 **1926-S MS64 NGC.** The 1926-S is considered the key-date in the Buffalo nickel series, from a mintage of just 970,000 coins, the only Buffalo date-mintmark issue with a mintage of less than 1 million coins. This satiny Mint State piece has soft luster with lovely pale gray and gold toning, blended with hints of pale blue. While the strike is a little soft as usual, the overall eye appeal is most impressive. At first glance this piece has the appearance of a full MS65 grade. Perhaps it is only the inadequate strike that prevented such a grade. Census: 84 in 64, 8 finer (7/08). (#3959)

Attractive Near-Gem 1926-S Nickel

798 **1926-S MS64 PCGS.** The low-mintage 1926-S nickel was not recognized as particularly elusive until nearly a decade after its release, when cardboard coin folders with printed mintage statistics became popular. As a result, the vast majority of survivors are circulated, and Mint State pieces better than Select are elusive. This Choice example is well-defined for the issue with particular sharpness on the horn, though the bison's shoulder and the Indian's braid show trifling softness. Luminous gold-orange patina drapes minimally marked surfaces with quicksilver luster. PCGS has graded just 11 finer representatives (8/08). (#3959)

Pleasing 1927-D Buffalo Nickel, MS65

799 **1927-D MS65 NGC.** Attractive gold and slate-gray toning endows the surfaces of this carefully preserved Gem. Lange (2006) writes that he still believes this issue is undervalued in Gem and considers well-struck examples to be particularly elusive. This piece is sharply struck save for a touch of weakness on the Indian's hair. Satiny luster on both sides enhances the eye appeal of this charming piece. Census: 32 in 65, 2 finer (7/08). (#3961)

Condition Scarcity 1927-S Nickel, MS64

800 **1927-S MS64 NGC.** The 1927-S is scarce in Mint State. The lustrous surfaces of this near-Gem example are covered in pastel hues of golden-tan and powder-blue, and a well executed strike leaves strong definition on the design features. Close inspection reveals no significant marks. NGC has graded only 20 coins finer. (#3962)

Lustrous Semi-Key 1927-S Buffalo Nickel, MS64

801 **1927-S MS64 NGC.** With the eighth lowest mintage for the Buffalo nickel series, the 1927-S is considered a semi-key issue. Warm gray coloration covers lustrous surfaces, with darker accents and a hint of ice-blue on the lower reverse. Though softly struck in the centers, this example shows no marks worthy of mention. Scarce in Choice Uncirculated; NGC has certified just 20 coins finer (8/08). (#3962)

Sharply Defined, Upper End MS64 1927-S Buffalo Nickel

802 **1927-S MS64 PCGS. CAC.** The CAC sticker on this piece speaks volumes. The coin is clearly upper end for the issue, meaning the striking details are above average for this usually lightly struck issue. The surfaces are also rich and satiny with minimal abrasions, all of which adds up to a better-than-average coin. (#3962)

Lustrous 1928-S Buffalo, MS65

803 **1928-S MS65 PCGS.** The 1928-S is one of those dates that receives far less attention than it deserves, as it is truly scarce, especially in top grades. This piece has a nice strike with lovely light gray luster and champagne accents. Only a slight lack of brilliance seems to keep it from an even higher grade. An outstanding opportunity. Population: 60 in 65, 5 finer (8/08). (#3965)

804 **1929 MS66 PCGS.** With a mintage of more than 36 million pieces, the 1929 nickel is readily available in all but the higher Mint State grades. This sharply struck Premium Gem exhibits great luster, and is toned in golden-tan with dabs of lavender and sky-blue on the reverse. Both sides are impeccably preserved. Challenging in this level of preservation, and virtually unobtainable any finer. (#3966)

805 **1929-D MS65 PCGS.** Nickel-gray surfaces display pleasing luster and are nicely preserved. This Gem exhibits a somewhat better-than-average strike, though minor softness is visible on some of the letters in LIBERTY and the hair over the bison's forehead. (#3967)

806 **1930-S MS66 PCGS.** Autumn-gold shades embrace this shimmering and nearly unabraded Premium Gem. Well struck for the issue, since only the hair near the braid shows any incompleteness. PCGS has only certified four finer pieces (8/08). (#3970)

807 **1930-S MS66 PCGS.** The light golden tints that surround a nickel-gray center on the quicksilver obverse consume the reverse. Softly struck as usually seen, yet attractive. PCGS has graded four finer examples (8/08). (#3970)

808 **1931-S MS66 PCGS.** Coinage production was extremely limited in 1931, consisting only of cents, nickels, dimes, and double eagles. Buffalo nickels were only coined in San Francisco, with production limited to 1.2 million coins. This piece has exquisite luster with faint gold toning over brilliant gray surfaces. PCGS has only certified two finer examples of the date. (#3971)

809 **1931-S MS66 PCGS.** Subtle shades of olive-green, steel-gray, and gold endow this lustrous and mark-free Premium Gem. A popular low mintage Great Depression issue. Encased in an old green label holder. Only two pieces have been certified finer by PCGS (8/08). (#3971)

810 **1931-S MS66 PCGS.** Pale violet and light gold patina resides on the highly lustrous surfaces of this Premium Gem, and the design elements exhibit nice detail. Well preserved over both sides. (#3971)

Bill Fivaz's 1934-D Nickel MS66

811 **1934-D MS66 PCGS.** Ex: Fivaz Collection. While weak strikes are the rule for this date, this Premium Gem has a good strike with only minor blending at the centers. Delicate blue-green, violet-pink, and champagne patina ensures the eye appeal. The luster is pleasing, and the fields and devices are beautifully preserved. Population: 41 in 66, 0 finer (8/08). (#3973)

Bright 1934-D Small D Nickel, MS66

812 **1934-D MS66 NGC.** Small D. Splashes of pale violet and golden-orange patina bathe both sides of this Premium Gem, each of which is awash in bright luster. Fairly well struck, or at least in relation to most examples of this typically weak date. The Indian's hair is a tad soft. Well preserved throughout. The date is strike doubled. Census: 6 in 66, 0 finer (7/08). (#3973)

813 **1935-D MS66 PCGS.** Interesting die lines are evident near and beneath the date. This highly lustrous Premium Gem evinces deep amber-gold, rose, and electric-blue toning on both sides. Sharply struck and nearly pristine. Only nine examples of this Denver Mint issue have been graded finer than MS66, by NGC and PCGS combined (8/08). (#3975)

814 **1935-D MS66 PCGS.** Satiny and well struck with only occasional softness. The gray-green surfaces exhibit subtle rose accents near the reverse center. A great, unblemished Premium Gem. PCGS has graded just five finer pieces (8/08). (#3975)

815 **1937-D MS67 PCGS.** This highly lustrous Superb Gem displays soft champagne-gold and violet patination. Immaculately preserved, and sharply struck. (#3981)

816 **1937-D Three-Legged Fine 15 NGC.** FS-020.2. The famous 1937-D Three-Legged nickel is highly desirable in any grade. Hints of brown accent the mostly medium gray surfaces. The details are well-outlined and there are no mentionable marks on either side. *From The Morton J. Greene Collection.* (#3982)

817 **1937-D Three-Legged—Improperly Cleaned—NCS. VF20 Details.** FS-020.2. Perhaps the most famous variety of any American coin, the Three-Legged Buffalo nickel is desirable in any grade. Numerous abrasions are visible, but none are worthy of specific mention. A lovely example despite cleaning. (#3982)

818 **1937-D Three-Legged VF25 NGC.** Subtle sage elements grace the otherwise nickel-gray surfaces of this mid-range example. From an earlier die state with the usual diagnostics weak, yet present. (#3982)

819 **1937-D Three-Legged—Corroded—ANACS. VF30 Details.** FS-020.2. Each side has a couple of tiny spots and an occasional hint of granularity, but this collector grade slate-gray key date nickel will appeal to many collectors. (#3982)

820 **1937-D Three-Legged—Cleaned—ANACS. XF40 Details.** Luminous mustard-gold and orange shadings blanket the moderately hairlined surfaces of this oddly lustrous Three-Legged piece. Well struck with few significant abrasions. (#3982)

821 **1937-D Three-Legged XF40 NGC.** Luminous gray-gold elements grace the margins on this lightly circulated Three-Legged nickel. The bison's horn is intact, though the tip is beginning to merge with the rest of the head. (#3982)

822 **1937-D Three-Legged AU53 NGC.** FS-020.2. A moderately circulated slate-gray key date that has a smooth obverse and only minute marks throughout the reverse. The granular back leg and other diagnostics are evident. (#3982)

823 **1937-D Three-Legged AU55 NGC.** FS-020.2. A lightly worn Choice AU example of this famous, immensely popular Buffalo nickel variety, created by excess polishing of the die. Satiny with ivory-gray color and faint bluish-green field accents. Just one abrasion is noticeable, below the Indian's jawline. (#3982)

824 **1937-D Three-Legged AU55 NGC.** Subtle rose and gold tints add color to the otherwise nickel-gray surfaces of this briefly circulated Three-Legged piece. From an early die state with the reverse diagnostics weak, yet visible. (#3982)

825 **1937-D Three-Legged AU55 PCGS.** FS-020.2. This gunmetal-gray and chestnut-tan key date nickel shows light wear on the hipbone and other device highpoints, but marks are minimal and all major design details are bold. (#3982)

Famous Three-Legged 1937-D Nickel MS62

826 **1937-D Three-Legged MS62 NGC.** FS-020.2. Olive-gray and almond-gold encompass this satiny and nearly unabraded representative. The strike is generally bold, with inexactness relegated to the base of the 19 in the date and the outer curve of the bison's tail. The trail of minute die dots below the bison's flank, diagnostic for this key variety, are present and accounted for. (#3982)

Wonderful 1937-D Three-Legged Buffalo Nickel, MS62

827 **1937-D Three-Legged MS62 NGC.** Delightful silver-gray patina coats both sides, with sparkling satiny luster throughout. The surfaces appear remarkably clean to the unaided eye and a loupe fails to locate any noteworthy marks. This attractive piece is sure to be a welcome addition to a Buffalo nickel collection. (#3982)

Enticing 1937-D Three-Legged Buffalo Nickel, MS62

828 **1937-D Three-Legged MS62 NGC.** FS-020.2. A marvelous example of this popular key Buffalo nickel variety. The obverse is sharply struck, while the reverse exhibits the typical softness. Splendid satiny luster accents the medium gray patina that embraces the surfaces. Scattered abrasions define the grade, but all are insignificant. (#3982)

Always-Popular 1937-D Three-Legged Buffalo Nickel, MS62

829 **1937-D Three-Legged MS62 NGC.** FS-020.2. Lovely hazel and rose patina drapes both sides, with alluring satiny luster in the fields. Attractive patches of teal on the reverse enhance the eye appeal. The immense desirability of the three-legged Buffalo nickel cannot be overstated, and this well-detailed piece would make a wonderful example. (#3982)

Lustrous 1937-D Three-Legged Select Nickel

830 **1937-D Three-Legged MS63 NGC.** Lustrous golden-gray surfaces greet the observer of this popular variety. Well struck, except for minor weakness in the hair over the bison's forehead. A few minute contact marks and flecks are noted. Housed in a prior generation holder. (#3982)

Elegant Select 1937-D Three-Legged Nickel

831 **1937-D Three-Legged MS63 PCGS.** The major reverse diagnostics, including the die rust below the bison's body and the weakened back leg, are faint but visible. A luminous Select piece, lightly gold-toned on the reverse with splashes of rose and orange at the margins of the reverse. Excellent overall eye appeal. (#3982)

Colorful 1937-D Three-Legged Nickel, MS63

832 **1937-D Three-Legged MS63 NGC.** FS-020.2. This lustrous key date nickel is bathed in honey-gold and lilac-red toning. Careful inspection reveals only trivial contact. The strike is precise, particularly on the diagnostic trail of tiny die dots beneath the bison's flank. Along with the 1922 No D, Strong Reverse cent, the most widely collected die abrasion error. (#3982)

Magnificent 1937-D Three Legged Gem Nickel

833 **1937-D Three-Legged MS65 PCGS.** The 1937-D Three-Legged nickel is one of the more significant varieties in American numismatics. It is especially noteworthy when a Gem-quality piece appears for sale; most offerings are in the Very Fine to lower-level Mint State grade range. The present MS65 example should therefore elicit considerable bidder interest.

The Three-Legged variety was caused by excessive die polishing to remove clash marks and/or die erosion furrows. David Lange, in his *Complete Guide to Buffalo Nickels* reference, writes that these disfigurements, when discovered, usually result in die replacement. In the case of the '37-D, however, the urgency of completing a coinage run precluded this customary practice. Lange cites Breen, who recounts that a mint employee, in the course of grinding off evidence of clashing, also removed the element of lowest relief in the die, the bison's right foreleg between hoof and thigh. This went unnoticed until the coins had already been distributed to banks.

Iridescent multicolored toning bathes the radiantly lustrous surfaces of this magnificent Gem, and an attentive strike leaves strong definition on the design elements, including the braid, horn, and tail. Both sides are nicely preserved, with no mentionable abrasions or spots. Population: 45 in 65, 4 finer (8/08). (#3982)

PROOF BUFFALO NICKELS

Delicately Toned 1914 Five Cent, PR66

834 **1914 PR66 NGC.** Occasional streaks of golden-tan cross the obverse of this Premium Gem proof, while splashes of powder-blue, lavender, and golden-tan cover the reverse. The design elements exhibit sharp definition, befitting a proof strike. Luminous surfaces reveal no mentionable marks or spots. Housed in a prior generation holder. (#3991)

Lovely Superb Gem Proof 1914 Buffalo Nickel

835 **1914 PR67 PCGS.** The design elements are crisply produced and the surfaces are utterly pristine, with satiny textures typical of Buffalo nickel proofs. Pale green and rose toning are intermingled on the obverse, while the reverse shows dramatic steel-green, purple-rose, and gold patina. A lovely Superb Gem example of the most commonly-seen issue for the 1914 through 1916 Buffalo proofs. Population: 67 in 67, 9 finer (8/08). (#3991)

Vibrant 1914 Buffalo Nickel, PR67

836 **1914 PR67 PCGS.** An exciting example of this second year of issue for the Buffalo nickel series. The surfaces are vibrant and nearly brilliant, with just a hint of light gold over each side. The surfaces show a lovely orange-peel texture and satiny luster on each side, as one would expect on a matte proof. PCGS has certified only nine pieces finer (8/08). (#3991)

837 **1915 PR64 PCGS.** There were only a handful of proof Buffalo nickel issues, and the mintages for all of them were stingy, by modern standards. Just 1,050 pieces were struck in 1915, an amazingly small number considering the huge popularity of this series with collectors. This specimen has a typically satiny appearance, with boldly struck devices and light olive, steel-green, and gold toning. A lovely near-Gem proof, with distraction-free surfaces. (#3992)

838 **1936 Type One—Satin Finish PR66 PCGS.** The coinage of proofs was interrupted in 1916 by World War One, and they would not be struck again at the Philadelphia Mint until 1936. One of two types produced that year, the Satin Finish specimens closely resembled the matte proofs struck from 1913 to 1916. A hint of light yellow toning accents the crisply struck devices. Both sides are virtually pristine save for a few tiny flecks. (#3994)

Impressive 1936 Buffalo Nickel Type One—Satin Finish, PR67

839 **1936 Type One—Satin Finish PR67 PCGS.** After a hiatus of 20 years, the coinage of proof nickels resumed with the 1936, which was the only issue that was given a satin finish. This highly lustrous specimen has a hint of gold toning that highlights the razor-sharp devices. The surfaces appear unabraded, and a close inspection reveals only a few minuscule flecks. One of just 4,420 proofs minted. PCGS reports a mere 27 examples finer (7/08). (#3994)

Pristine 1936 Type One—Satin Finish Buffalo Nickel, PR67

840 **1936 Type One—Satin Finish PR67 PCGS.** Wafts of gold patina accent the mostly brilliant surfaces. The strike is nearly full, and the surfaces are remarkably pristine for the grade. Only 4,420 proofs were minted of both Satin and Brilliant finishes. The Satin pieces were sold first and accounted for approximately two-thirds of the total mintage. (#3994)

Gorgeous 1936 Satin Finish Buffalo, PR68

841 **1936 Type One—Satin Finish PR68 PCGS.** Ex: Tom Mershon Collection. Gorgeous ice-blue patina covers both sides, with a splash of pale lilac toward the left obverse rim. The full strike is all that one would expect for a proof, and there are no distracting blemishes on either side. The Philadelphia Mint resumed proof Buffalo nickel coinage in 1936 after a hiatus of two decades. About two-thirds of the 4,420-piece delivery are believed to have been produced with a Satin Finish. Population: 26 in 68, with one finer (8/08). (#3994)

Impressive 1936 Buffalo Nickel
Type Two—Brilliant Finish, PR67

842 **1936 Type Two—Brilliant Finish PR67 NGC.** Fully struck with an attractive mixture of pastel colors across each side. The design features are produced with impressive sharpness, as expected for a proof specimen. Some watery reflectivity graces the fields. Neither side shows any evidence of contact. Interesting die lines occur along the tops and bottoms of 36 in the date, a mint-made feature that looks like guidelines for the date. The Brilliant Finish proofs of 1936 are much scarcer than their Satin Finish counterparts in Superb Gem condition. (#3995)

Wonderful 1936 Buffalo, Brilliant PR67

843 **1936 Type Two—Brilliant Finish PR67 PCGS. CAC.** Unlike most proof Buffalo nickels, close examination with a glass fails to reveal any flecks that normally adhere to the surface of these coins. Both sides are virtually flawless, with bold design features. An exceptional example, clearly one of the finest imaginable. PCGS has only certified eight finer submissions (8/08). (#3995)

Splendid Brilliant Finish 1936 Buffalo, PR67

844 **1936 Type Two—Brilliant Finish PR67 PCGS. Ex: Tom Mershon Collection.** The quicksilver surfaces of this Buffalo nickel proof variety hold a peculiar fascination for many collectors, as optimal representations of the coiner's art in this beloved and historic series. The present coin boasts splendid flash and luster, with silver-gold coloration on both sides and no discernible distractions. (#3995)

845 **1937 PR65 NGC. CAC.** Vivid yellow and tan patina drapes the surfaces and is particularly deep on the reverse. Scattered tiny toning spots cover both sides, with accents of purple around the perimeter. The luster is especially eye-catching on the obverse of this lightly marked specimen. A mere 5,769 proofs were struck. Housed in an old NGC holder. (#3996)

846 **1937 PR66 PCGS.** The 1937 was the last of the proof Buffalo nickel issues. This brilliant piece has deeply mirrored fields and remarkably pristine surfaces. A top quality specimen with full details. (#3996)

847 **1937 PR66 NGC.** Uniformly brilliant, the pale powder-blue tinged surfaces are devoid of any bothersome hairlines and contact marks. This is a perfect coin to represent the Buffalo nickel in a high grade proof type set. (#3996)

Dazzling 1937 Buffalo Nickel, Superb Proof

848 **1937 PR67 PCGS. CAC.** An untoned and deeply mirrored representative of the penultimate Buffalo nickel issue. The highly lustrous fields are virtually pristine save for a couple of tiny toning specks. This fully struck piece exhibits outstanding eye appeal and is one of just 5,769 proofs minted. PCGS has certified only 11 pieces finer (8/08). (#3996)

Nearly Perfect PR68 1937 Buffalo Nickel

849 **1937 PR68 PCGS. Ex: Tom Mershon Collection.** The desirability of this particular coin is derived from several factors. The general preservation of the surfaces is paramount, of course; but a close second is the complete absence of carbon spotting. Eye appeal counts for a great deal of this coin's grade and desirability, and that in turn is based on the ice-blue centers that are surrounded by deep russet at the margins. A fabulous coin that is only bettered by one piece (a PCGS PR69), but it would be difficult to imagine a more strikingly impressive type coin than this one. (#3996)

JEFFERSON NICKELS

850 **1940 MS67 Full Steps PCGS.** Hints of yellow patina grace the mostly silver-gray surfaces. Magnificent satiny luster highlights the fully struck details, and only a couple of minuscule marks keep this Superb Gem from an even higher grade. (#84007)

851 **1941 MS67 Full Steps PCGS.** Lilac and apricot toning drapes this lustrous and precisely struck Superb Gem. The surfaces are remarkably smooth and there is immense eye appeal. The 1941 is surprisingly scarce in such exemplary condition, given the mintage of more than 200 million pieces. Population: 15 in 67 Full Steps, 0 finer (8/08). (#84010)

852 **1942-D—D Over Horizontal D—AU58 ANACS.** FS-027. A briefly circulated and lustrous example of this popular *Guide Book* variety. The horizontal D is readily apparent under magnification. Scattered abrasions are typical for the grade, but all are minor. Fivaz and Stanton (2000) consider this RPM to be "very rare" in any grade. (#4015)

853 **1942-D D Over Horizontal D AU55 PCGS.** FS-501, previously FS-027. The errant initial mintmark is visible left of the prominent mintmark, and within its loop. This lustrous Choice AU mint error has streaky chestnut-gold toning. Population: 10 in 55, 26 finer (8/08). (#4015)

Seldom-Seen 1942-D, D Over Horizontal D Jefferson Nickel, Mint State

854 **1942-D D Over Horizontal D MS60 NGC.** FS-501, previously FS-027. In *A Guide Book of Buffalo and Jefferson Nickels*, Bowers (2007) remarks that the D Over Horizontal D variety is "very rare, even a worn example would be a prize." Certainly, this Mint State specimen would be a wonderful addition to any Jefferson nickel collection. Light yellow and rose patina covers the surfaces, with a darker area noted at the top of the obverse. The mintmark error is bold under magnification. A lustrous and well-preserved example. (#4015)

855 **1943-P—Doubled Die Obverse—MS67 NGC.** VP-002. The doubling is most evident around Jefferson's eye, but LIBERTY and the date are also slightly doubled. Satiny luster gleams from the lightly toned and minimally marked surfaces. A boldly struck example of this popular doubled die. Listed on page 131 of the 2009 *Guide Book*. (#4018)

Elusive 1946-D D Over Horizontal D Nickel MS64

856 **1946-D D Over Horizontal D MS64 PCGS.** FS-301, formerly FS-031. A curve west of the upright of the primary mintmark is diagnostic for this rare variety. The upper obverse is honey-gold while most of this shimmering near-Gem is cream-gray. Impressively devoid of marks. Population: 6 in 64, 3 finer (8/08). (#94029)

857 **1957-D MS66 Five Full Steps NGC.** Ex: Omaha Bank Hoard. Light gold toning accents the highly lustrous surfaces of this carefully preserved Premium Gem. This powerfully struck piece exhibits great eye appeal. Census: 7 in 66 Five Full Steps, 0 finer (8/08). (#84062)

SMS JEFFERSON NICKEL

858 **1997-P SMS MS70 Full Steps NGC.** Special "frosted" uncirculated pieces were included in the 1997 Botanic garden sets. Whispers of light gold color adorn the reverse of this exquisitely struck specimen. Both faces are pristine. Census: 81 in 70 (7/08). (#84140)

PROOF JEFFERSON NICKELS

859 **1938 PR68 PCGS.** Ex: Tom Mershon Collection. A pleasing lemon-yellow and lilac tint graces the surfaces and complements the powerfully impressed design elements. Deeply reflective with great eye appeal. Population: 11 in 68, 0 finer (8/08). (#4175)

860 **1939 Reverse of 1938 PR67 PCGS.** Ex: Tom Mershon Collection. Pale lilac and gold patina embraces this marvelously undisturbed and needle-sharp Superb Gem. An outstanding example of this second-year issue. PCGS has certified just seven coins finer (8/08). (#4176)

Outstanding PR68 ★ 1939 Nickel Reverse of 1938

861 **1939 Reverse of 1938 PR68 ★ NGC.** Struck with the so-called "wavy steps" die leftover from 1938. The fields are deeply mirrored, and the obverse even shows a slight cameo effect. Essentially a brilliant coin, one must look closely to discern color on this piece. A superlative example of this second-year issue. Census: 3 in 68, 0 finer (7/08). (#4176)

862 **1940 Reverse of 1940 PR67 PCGS.** This is a vividly reflective Superb Gem with pristine surfaces and a dusting of iridescent pastel-gold. It is virtually impossible to find a representative finer than the present piece. NGC has not certified any coins above PR67, while PCGS reports just two examples in PR68 (8/08). (#4177)

Unsurpassed 1940 Reverse of 1940 Nickel, PR68

Beautifully Toned PR68 1941 Jefferson Nickel Tied With Only Two Others for Finest Certified

863   **1940 Reverse of 1940 PR68 PCGS.** Though the Reverse of 1938 pieces command most of the attention for this early proof Jefferson nickel issue, the Reverse of 1940 pieces present their own challenges, particularly in the Superb Gem grades; for non-Cameo coins, NGC has graded no pieces above PR67 and PCGS has certified just two, one of which is the present coin (8/08).

    The virtually flawless fields offer impressive reflectivity, and the devices offer razor-sharp detail, particularly on the crisp, straight steps. Generally nickel-white centers show golden overtones at the obverse margins, while the reverse shows a subtle rainbow pattern with the addition of yellow and cyan. An important specimen for the Registry enthusiast. (#4177)

864   **1941 PR68 PCGS.** Ex: Tom Mershon Collection. Close examination with a loupe confirms the nearly perfect status of this coin as indicated by the grade. But the desirability of this piece is not limited to mere preservation of the surfaces. The untampered originality of the surfaces are demonstrated by the streaks of rose, ice-blue, and green iridescent toning seen over each side. Only 18,720 proofs were struck in 1941, but surprisingly few were set aside and remain in the ultimate grade. In PR67, this date is relatively common with a total of 138 pieces certified by both of the major services. However, there is a steep drop off in PR68 with only this and two other coins that have been so graded (none are finer). Undoubtedly this proof will be avidly sought after by Registry Set collectors. (#4178)

865   **1942 Type One PR68 NGC.** Pale blue-gray color with lilac accents over deeply mirrored fields and lustrous devices. This is an amazing quality example, tied for the finest certified of the issue. Both varieties of the 1942 Jefferson nickel were coined in proof format during the year, after which no more proof examples were coined until 1950. Census: 9 in 68, 0 finer (8/08). (#4179)

866   **1942 Type One PR68 PCGS.** Neither NGC nor PCGS has certified any coins finer than this resplendent specimen, and PCGS reports just eight pieces at the PR68 level (8/08). Vibrant yellow toning encircles the perimeter and contrasts nicely against the light blue patina that covers the centers. This decisively struck piece would be an excellent addition to a registry set. (#4179)

867 **1942-P Type Two PR68 NGC.** Bright and exceedingly sharp with a light coating of "oil slick" patina. This usually develops from years of storage in an old cello envelope. A fully original example of this silver wartime issue. Census: 19 in 68, 0 finer (7/08). (#4180)

Iridescently Toned PR68 1942 Type Two Nickel

868 **1942-P Type Two PR68 PCGS.** Ex: Tom Mershon Collection. This silver issue has a different texture and striking quality than the previous nickel issues. Since silver is a softer metal it naturally strikes up better than nickel, a general characteristic that continues through the war years. This fabulous piece is brilliant in the centers and surrounded by thin bands of multicolored iridescence at the margins. Population: 10 in 68, 1 finer (8/08). (#4180)

Marvelous 1951 Jefferson Nickel, PR66 Deep Cameo

869 **1951 PR66 Deep Cameo PCGS.** Impeccable, fully brilliant surfaces with a degree of contrast one looks for on later-date S-mint proofs, but almost never sees on the early issues. For identification purposes, a tiny inverted U-shaped lintmark is seen below Jefferson's ear. Population: 2 in 66 Deep Cameo, 8 finer (8/08). (#94183)

870 **1952 PR68 Cameo PCGS.** A fully struck and virtually immaculate specimen. Although not designated Deep Cameo by PCGS, it is hard to envision a piece with more reflective fields than the present example. Population: 14 in 68 Cameo, 0 finer (7/08). (#84184)

871 **1953 PR67 NGC.** A fully brilliant Superb Gem proof. Nicely struck, with flawless surfaces. (#4185)

Seldom-Seen Deep Mirror PR68 1955 Jefferson Nickel

872 **1955 PR68 Deep Cameo PCGS.** Magnificent white-on-black contrast leaves no doubt concerning the Deep Cameo status of this impressive specimen. A hint of chestnut toning is draped over the portrait of Jefferson. Although current proof Jefferson nickels are invariably Deep Cameo, this was not the case for 1950s proofs. Generally, only the initial pieces struck from a pair of fresh dies displayed cameo contrast. Population: 15 in 68 Deep Cameo, 0 finer (8/08). (#94187)

873 **1971 No S PR67 Deep Cameo PCGS.** In his *Encyclopedia*, Breen (1988) writes that this rare variety was discovered in a proof set on December 29, 1971. The Mint confirmed the error and provided a mintage of 1,655 pieces. Deeply mirrored fields on this piece show stunning cameo contrast against the frosted devices. The surfaces are virtually pristine, and the appeal of this interesting issue is outstanding. Population: 9 in 67 Deep Cameo, 7 finer (8/08). (#94204)

End of Session 1

SESSION TWO

Live, Internet, and Mail Bid Signature® Auction #1116
Thursday, September 18, 2008, 1:00 PM PT, Lots 874-1505
Long Beach, California

A 15% Buyer's Premium ($9 minimum) Will Be Added To All Lots

Visit HA.com to view full-color images and bid.

WASHINGTON QUARTERS

874 **1932-D—Improperly Cleaned—NCS. Unc Details.** Patches of light purple toning cover the obverse and contrast nicely against the arc of deep violet toning that encircles the brilliant center of the reverse. Both sides have only a few minuscule marks and exhibit impressive Choice sharpness. This lustrous piece is a great representative despite cleaning. (#5791)

Appealing 1932-D Quarter, MS63

875 **1932-D MS63 PCGS.** The 1932-D Quarter has been at the forefront of collectors' attention ever since it was issued, as only 436,800 pieces were issued at the Denver facility in this first year of production. This is a lustrous and especially attractive example with just a hint of faint toning over both sides. A few light grazes keep this lovely '32-D from easily advancing into a higher grade. (#5791)

Wonderful 1932-D Quarter, MS63

876 **1932-D MS63 PCGS. CAC.** Vibrant maroon and gold toning in the periphery yields to a dusting of colors across the mostly silver-gray centers. Several minuscule marks are entirely insignificant. Delightful satiny luster accents the crisply struck design elements and gives this desirable piece excellent eye appeal. Housed in a green label PCGS holder. (#5791)

Frosty 1932-D Quarter, MS64

877 **1932-D MS64 PCGS.** Light ice-blue toning, especially on the reverse, is complemented by subtle dabs of sienna and magenta coloration on both sides. Thick patination and uninterrupted luster confirms the pleasant fact that this piece has been properly handled by all of its past owners. A few marks on the neck, although well hidden by the patina, may be what precluded an even higher grade. PCGS has only graded 64 finer examples (8/08). (#5791)

Gold Toned Near-Gem 1932-D Quarter

878 **1932-D MS64 NGC.** A satiny near-Gem, this brilliant piece has light gold toning on both sides. It is boldly detailed, although the mintmark is weak and mushy as usual. The 1932-D and S quarters are both low-mintage key issues in the series. NGC has only certified 16 finer examples of the date (8/08). (#5791)

Brilliant 1932-D Quarter, MS64

879 **1932-D MS64 PCGS.** An impressive near-Gem that displays bold design definition with frosty and untoned silver surfaces. Both sides are highly lustrous with excellent eye appeal. Intended as a commemorative, the Washington quarters were struck at all three mints with just 436,800 coined at Denver. The design and subject was apparently popular enough that these pieces remained in production as a regular issue. (#5791)

880 **1932-S—Improperly Cleaned—NCS. AU Details.** With its 1932-D counterpart, the 1932-S ranks as one of the two keys in the Washington quarter series, and although the '32-S is slightly more available, it actually has the lower mintage. This well-defined example has touches of russet toning and just a few marks or tiny spots. A lovely example despite light cleaning. (#5792)

881 **1932-S MS63 ANACS.** A boldly struck and intensely lustrous Select Mint State specimen. Both sides display a layer of dappled olive-drab and russet patina. One of two first-year Washington quarter key issues, along with the 1932-D. (#5792)

882 **1932-S MS63 PCGS.** The minimally toned centers give way to splashes of crimson, golden-tan, and cloud-white patina close to the margins. Softly lustrous and well struck with few flaws. (#5792)

883 **1932-S MS64 PCGS.** Peppered charcoal and russet toning begins at the rims and gets lighter as it approaches the centers. The strike is crisp and there is significant luster throughout. A minimally marked and well-preserved example of this key-date Washington quarter. (#5792)

884 **1932-S MS64 PCGS.** Deep tan and crimson toning accents the mostly silver-gray centers. Enticing luster highlights the boldly impressed details. An appealing Choice representative of this desirable key issue. (#5792)

885 **1932-S MS64 PCGS.** Rich violet and amber toning covers the obverse, which contrasts nicely against the mostly brilliant reverse. Eye-catching satiny luster sparkles throughout and highlights the crisply struck details. (#5792)

886 **1932-S MS64 PCGS.** An attractive Choice example of this West Coast Washington quarter key, highly lustrous beneath dappled blue and gold patina over the upper obverse and champagne toning on the reverse. Well-defined with excellent visual appeal for the grade. (#5792)

887 **1932-S MS64 PCGS.** An impressive Choice Mint State piece, this '32-S quarter has frosty silver luster and sharp design motifs. Both sides are awash with pale lilac-gold toning. (#5792)

888 **1932-S MS64 NGC.** An incredible satiny Mint State piece with fully brilliant, untoned silver surfaces. All design elements are bold, and the surfaces are virtually mark-free. So close to Gem quality, this piece will easily please nearly any Washington collector. (#5792)

Magnificent 1932-S Quarter, Gem Mint State

889 **1932-S MS65 PCGS. CAC.** The 1932-S is one of the key issues in the Washington quarter series and boasts a diminutive mintage of just 408,000 pieces. Patches of russet and hazel toning cover the obverse, which contrasts nicely against the lightly toned reverse. Both sides show splendid accents of lilac and golden toning around the periphery. Several die cracks are noted at the truncation of the bust. Flashy luster radiates beneath the lovely toning and gives this piece impressive eye appeal. NGC and PCGS combined have certified fewer than 10 pieces finer (8/08). (#5792)

Gorgeous MS65 1932-S Washington Quarter

890 **1932-S MS65 PCGS.** One of the finest existing 1932-S quarters, as PCGS has only has graded 92 similar pieces, and just four better ones. Both sides are fully brilliant and highly lustrous, without any trace of toning. The connoisseur will appreciate this piece and the opportunity to bid on it. (#5792)

Impressive 1932-S Quarter, Gem Uncirculated

891 **1932-S MS65 PCGS.** A brilliant example of this key issue, which is virtually impossible to locate in a higher grade. The powerful strike is complemented by dazzling satiny luster in the fields. A few minor marks are nearly imperceptible to the unaided eye. This piece would make a great addition to a Washington quarter collection. NGC and PCGS combined report just nine examples finer (8/08). (#5792)

Highly Lustrous 1934 Doubled Die Obverse Quarter, MS64

892 **1934 Doubled Die Obverse MS64 PCGS.** FS-025-1934-101. Previously FS-009. Pronounced doubling is noted on IN GOD WE TRUST; separation is also visible on the E of LIBERTY. Splashes of tan-gold color adhere to the highly lustrous surfaces of this well struck example. A few minute marks preclude Gem status. Population: 26 in 64, 26 finer (8/08). (#5795)

893 **1935-D MS66 PCGS.** Freckles of russet, gold, purple, and light blue run over the lustrous surfaces of this Premium Gem D-mint quarter, and a well directed strike sharpens the design elements. Free of significant contacts. (#5798)

894 **1935-D MS67 NGC.** A touch of hazel and violet toning surrounds the brilliant centers of this razor-sharp Superb Gem. Several minuscule handling marks are nearly imperceptible without a loupe. Magnificent cartwheel luster graces both sides and gives this piece outstanding eye appeal. A delicate die crack is noted at the truncation of the bust. Neither NGC nor PCGS have certified any pieces finer, and both services combined have certified just 21 examples at the MS67 level (8/08). (#5798)

Gorgeous MS67 1935-D Quarter

895 **1935-D MS67 NGC.** Immensely lustrous with fantastic eye appeal. The strike is bold, and dots of blue-green and gold-orange patina enliven the obverse margins. Despite a mintage of nearly 5.8 million pieces, the 1935-D is highly elusive at this level of preservation. Census: 9 in 67, 0 finer (7/08). (#5798)

Shining Superb Gem 1935-D Quarter

896 **1935-D MS67 NGC.** The most striking aspect of this earlier D-mint quarter is its impressive luster, which shines unimpeded in the centers and through peach and orange patina at parts of the margins. Well-defined and beautifully preserved, even by the standards of the grade. Neither NGC nor PCGS has graded a numerically finer example (8/08). (#5798)

897 **1935-S MS67 NGC.** Like many of the early S-mint Washington quarters, the 1935-S is challenging in high grades. Enticing gold, violet, and teal toning accents the pearl-gray surfaces of this powerfully struck Superb Gem. Close examination under a glass yields only a couple of nearly imperceptible handling marks. Neither NGC nor PCGS has certified any examples finer (8/08). (#5799)

898 **1936-D MS65 PCGS.** Mostly brilliant with soft, frosted luster and an impressive strike. Q. David Bowers has speculated that demand for the many commemorative issues of 1936 caused collectors to neglect setting aside this conditionally rare Denver issue. In an old green label holder.
Ex: Paul Bolyard Collection (Heritage, 1/2005), lot 6819, which realized $1,495. (#5801)

899 **1936-D MS66 PCGS.** While common in low grades, the 1936-D is seldom seen in Premium Gem and is rare any finer. Peppered hazel toning around the rims accents the brilliant centers. There are several tiny marks but all are nearly imperceptible. PCGS has certified just nine pieces finer (7/08). (#5801)

900 **1937 Doubled Die Obverse AU50 PCGS.** FS-101, formerly FS-012. A lovely, lightly circulated example of this *Guide Book* variety, well struck with silver-gray patina overall and splashes of olive and violet-blue at the margins. Highly appealing. Population: 3 in 50, 13 finer (8/08). (#95803)

Captivating 1937-D Quarter, Superb Mint State

901 **1937-D MS67 PCGS.** A touch of amber toning around the perimeter of the obverse accents the pleasing silver-gray that covers the center. The reverse is fully brilliant with impressive eye appeal. Magnificent satiny luster glimmers across both sides of this impeccably preserved specimen. Neither NGC nor PCGS has certified any pieces finer (8/08). (#5804)

Superlative 1939 Washington Quarter, MS68

902 **1939 MS68 NGC. CAC.** This assertively struck early Washington Quarter features golden-brown, lavender, lime-green, and olive toning, which is especially iridescent throughout the reverse. As expected of the grade, the lustrous surfaces are virtually unblemished. The combined forces of NGC and PCGS have certified six pieces as MS68, and none have achieved a higher grade. (#5808)

903 **1940-D MS67 NGC.** A lustrous Superb Gem with above-average definition for a Denver issue of this era. Reddish-orange patina surrounds the margins, while the rest of the coin is silver-gray. Carefully preserved and housed in an old NGC holder. NGC has certified only one piece finer (7/08). (#5812)

904 **1941-S MS67 PCGS.** Delightful flashy luster shines from each side of this carefully preserved Superb Gem. An arc of deep orange and magenta toning encircles the right side of the obverse, with accents of pale blue adding to the wonderful eye appeal. The reverse is mostly brilliant with a only a hint of russet toning near the rim. A fully struck example with excellent eye appeal. Neither NGC nor PCGS has certified any pieces finer (7/08). (#5816)

905 **1948-D MS67 PCGS. CAC.** The 8 in the date appears to be repunched; possibly over a previous numeral 7. This is a lovely Superb Gem quarter with splendid satiny luster and appealing red-brown peripheral toning on both sides. Boldly struck and impressively preserved, with just a few ticks noted under magnification. Population: 25 in 67, 0 finer (7/08). (#5837)

906 **1948-D MS67 PCGS.** Peppered amber toning envelops both sides, with accents of violet in the margins. Impressive satiny luster graces the surfaces and highlights the boldly struck design elements. Neither NGC nor PCGS has certified any examples finer (8/08). (#5837)

907 **1949-D MS67 NGC.** A lustrous and solidly struck example with mottled bronze-olive patina over each side. Without magnification, finding any sort of flaw is practically impossible. NGC has certified just two pieces finer (8/08). (#5840)

908 **1950-D/S MS64 PCGS.** FS-601, formerly FS-021. Traces of an S mintmark are present above and northwest of the Denver mintmark. A 1950-S/D is also known, and one has to wonder if both dies were mintmarked by the same person near the same time. A beautiful and lustrous near-Gem with peripheral golden-brown and sea-green toning. Population: 25 in 64, 22 finer (8/08). (#5843)

PROOF WASHINGTON QUARTERS

909 **1936 PR62 NGC.** The first proof issue in the Washington quarter series had a scant mintage of 3,837 pieces; not nearly enough to satisfy the many collectors of this immensely popular type. This specimen has a light layer of milky patina over each side, and a pinscratch across the eagle's breast, limiting the NGC grade to PR62. (#5975)

910 **1936 PR62 PCGS.** An example from the first year of Washington quarter proof coinage, showing some grade-limiting milkiness on the obverse. Housed in a green label PCGS holder. (#5975)

911 **1936 PR64 PCGS.** A peppering of russet and golden toning accents the mostly silver-gray devices. The strike is razor-sharp, and there are virtually no marks on each side. One of just 3,837 proofs struck. Housed in a first-generation PCGS holder. (#5975)

912 **1936 PR65 NGC.** Pleasing slate-gray toning is surrounded by hints of light blue, olive-green, and lemon-yellow. A few minor contact marks barely affect the impressive eye appeal of the highly reflective surfaces. Only 3,837 proofs were struck. (#5975)

Incredible Superb Gem Proof 1936 Quarter

913 **1936 PR67 PCGS.** Ex: Tom Mershon Collection. Impressive reflectivity with rich silver-gray patina that drapes much of the centers. Deeper orange and tan shadings appear at parts of the margins. An excellent specimen from the first proof Washington quarter issue. Population: 8 in 67, 0 finer (8/08). (#5975)

Superb 1937 Washington Quarter
PR68 Tied for Finest-Certified by PCGS

914 **1937 PR68 PCGS.** Ex: Tom Mershon Collection. A Superb example of this scarcer, low mintage issue. In just the second year of proof coinage for the Washington quarter series, a mere 5,542 pieces were produced; a tiny number compared to modern issues. The fields are nicely mirrored and there are no mentionable contact marks on either side of this wonderfully preserved piece. The undeniably exquisite eye appeal of the coin is generated, in part, by the delicate gold-tan and turquoise-blue coloration that adorns the pristine surfaces. Tied with one other specimen as the finest-certified by PCGS (8/08). (#5976)

Fantastic PR68 1938 Quarter

915 **1938 PR68 PCGS.** Ex: Tom Mershon Collection. Boldly impressed with surprisingly strong mirrors that shine through the rich silver-gray and gold-orange patina that drapes most of each side. Hints of crimson-violet grace the upper reverse rim. One of just two PR68 coins graded by PCGS, with none finer (8/08). (#5977)

Notable 1938 Quarter, PR68

916 **1938 PR68 NGC.** One of the finest survivors imaginable from this earlier proof Washington quarter issue of just over 8,000 pieces. The surfaces are virtually flawless beneath gold, orange, and silver-gray patina. Boldly impressed and blessed with considerable mirrors that shine through the toning. Census: 12 in 68, 0 finer (7/08). (#5977)

Fabulous 1940 Quarter, PR68

917 **1940 PR68 PCGS.** Ex: Tom Mershon Collection. Beautifully preserved, boldly detailed, and shining. A delicate layer of subtly iridescent patina does not impede the impressive luster. Practically unrivalled quality for this early proof Washington quarter issue. Population: 2 in 68, 0 finer (8/08). (#5979)

918 **1941 PR67 PCGS.** Ex: Tom Mershon Collection. A brilliant and bright Superb Gem proof that has a razor sharp strike and virtually pristine surfaces. Great overall eye appeal! (#5980)

Gleaming PR68 1942 Washington Quarter

919 **1942 PR68 PCGS.** Ex: Tom Mershon Collection. A fantastically reflective, decisively struck example from the last of the brilliant-era proof Washington quarter issues. The obverse offers subtle blue and gold shadings, while the reverse is generally gleaming silver-gray. Population: 5 in 68, 0 finer (8/08). (#5981)

Gorgeous 1951 Quarter, PR68 Cameo

920 **1951 PR68 Cameo PCGS.** Ex: Daniel D. Biddle Collection. An impressively mirrored specimen that sports moderate contrast between the fields and the pleasingly frosted, sharply struck devices. Carefully preserved and notably appealing. One of just four Cameo examples at this level known to PCGS, with none finer (8/08). (#85983)

Desirable 1952 Superbird Quarter, PR66 Deep Cameo

921 **1952 Superbird FS-901 PR66 Deep Cameo PCGS.** The so-called "Superbird" quarter has a tiny raised "S" on the center of the eagle's breast. Fivaz-Stanton state the cause of the mark is unknown, although it seems to be a tiny lintmark on the hub, leaving a depression in the coinage die, leading to the raised mark on the finished coin. Fully brilliant with outstanding contrast. (#144444)

Incredible 1954 Washington Quarter, PR68 Deep Cameo

922 **1954 PR68 Deep Cameo PCGS.** An absolutely stunning Deep Cameo proof with amazing, watery contrast between the fields and devices. Undoubtedly one of the finest existing proofs of this or any other date in the silver Washington series. Population: 13 in 68 Deep Cameo, 0 finer (8/08). (#95986)

923 **1955 PR68 Deep Cameo PCGS.** Boldly struck with frosted devices and exceptionally deep, glassy fields that combine for a strong cameo effect. Occasional specks of milky toning appear to either side of the portrait. Population: 18 in 68 Deep Cameo, 0 finer (8/08). (#95987)

924 **1956 PR69 Deep Cameo PCGS.** The stunning white-on-black contrast between watery fields and bright, silver devices confirms the Deep Cameo assessment by PCGS. The devices are sharply struck and the surfaces are virtually pristine. Population: 40 in 69 Deep Cameo, 0 finer (8/08). (#95988)

925 **1958 PR68 Deep Cameo PCGS.** Icy-frosted devices show impressive cameo contrast against the deeply mirrored fields. The surfaces are mostly brilliant with a light peppering of yellow on each side. A virtually perfect representative. Population: 19 in 68 Deep Cameo, 5 finer (7/08). (#95990)

926 **1959 PR68 Deep Cameo PCGS.** The U.S. Mint produced nearly 1.5 million examples of this proof Washington quarter issue, but it seems doubtful that many remain in such an excellent state of preservation. Watery, jet-black fields and intensely frosted devices create a stark white-on-black visual effect, on both sides. Population: 34 in 68 Deep Cameo, 0 finer (8/08). (#95991)

927 **1961 PR70 PCGS.** Fully struck with seemingly pristine surfaces that include tremendously deep mirror fields and lightly frosted central devices. Just misses having enough contrast on the obverse for a Cameo designation. (#5993)

928 **1976-S Silver PR70 Deep Cameo PCGS.** Impressive black and white cameo contrast is created between the deeply mirrored fields and the heavily frosted devices. This piece is technically perfect and has wonderful eye appeal. (#96008)

WALKING LIBERTY HALF DOLLARS

Impressive MS66 1916 Half

929 **1916 MS66 PCGS.** This first-year Walking Liberty half offers smooth, satiny luster beneath delightful, dusky champagne and crimson patina. Well-defined, particularly on the branch hand, and a Premium Gem with undeniable eye appeal. Highly elusive any finer, with only six such pieces certified by PCGS (8/08). (#6566)

930 **1916-D MS65 NGC.** Splendid gold toning accents the frosty and vibrantly lustrous surfaces. Liberty's dress is a trifle weak, but the rest of the details are boldly defined. An attractive first-year representative. (#6567)

Choice 1916-S Walking Liberty Half

931 **1916-S MS64 NGC.** Well-defined for this initial S-mint Walking Liberty issue with soft, pleasing luster and delightful patina. Subtle gold and silver-white shadings prevail on the obverse, while the reverse shows deeper silver-blue and peach patina. Carefully preserved for the grade. NGC has certified 61 numerically finer pieces (8/08). (#6568)

Luminous Gem 1916-S Walking Liberty Half

932 **1916-S MS65 PCGS.** A well struck Gem that offers soft, delightful luster beneath colorful, yet low-key patina. Rose, gold-orange, and violet shadings drape the beautifully preserved surfaces. This early S-mint Walker issue is a rarity any finer, with just 14 such pieces certified by PCGS (8/08). (#6568)

933 **1917 MS65 PCGS.** Well-defined for this second-year issue with appreciable detail on Liberty's branch hand. The luster is strong and satiny, and dots of crimson and tan toning appear at the peripheries of the otherwise silver-gray surfaces. (#6569)

934 **1917 MS65 NGC.** Potent luster graces both sides of this lovely Gem, and a penetrating strike leaves sharp definition on the design elements. Minimally marked surfaces are visited by whispers of light brown color. (#6569)

935 **1917-D Obverse MS62 PCGS.** Splashes of russet and deep purple concentrate mainly around the borders of this Obverse mintmark example. Nicely struck, with just a few minute obverse marks. (#6570)

936 **1917-D Obverse MS63 PCGS.** The 1917-D Mintmark on Obverse variety has a mintage of less than half of its Mintmark on Reverse counterpart. This lustrous Gem exhibits a dusting of violet and russet around the rims, with streaks of hazel throughout. A faint vertical die crack passes below the eagle's neck and bisects most of the reverse. Scattered abrasions define the grade, but none are worthy of individual mention. Crisply struck save for a touch of softness on the centers, as usual. Housed in a green label PCGS holder. (#6570)

937 **1917-D Obverse MS63 NGC.** This is a brief two-year type with the mintmark located on the obverse, just below WE TRUST. Later in 1917, it was moved to the reverse. This is a satiny Select uncirculated piece with slight notes of lavender and russet patina noted near the peripheries. (#6570)

938 **1917-D Obverse MS63 PCGS.** Whispers of ocean-blue and russet gravitate to the margins of this lustrous Select half. Adequately struck, and a few light grade-defining marks. (#6570)

939 **1917-D Obverse MS64 PCGS.** Splashes of medium brown toning accent the obverse, which contrasts nicely against the mostly brilliant reverse. Several of Liberty's dress lines are softly defined, as typically seen, but the rest of the details are sharp. PCGS has certified 63 pieces finer (8/08). (#6570)

940 **1917-D Reverse AU58 NGC.** Subtle gold and blue tints grace the immensely lustrous surfaces. Well struck overall with only a trace of friction on the uppermost parts of the design. (#6571)

1917-S Obverse Mintmark Walker AU58

941 **1917-S Obverse AU58 NGC.** Although San Francisco struck more than 6.5 million halves in 1917, most bore the mintmark on the reverse. Fewer than 1 million pieces were coined prior to the changeover in mintmark position. This is a lustrous Borderline Uncirculated example with unblemished surfaces and little indication of friction. (#6572)

942 **1917-S Obverse MS62 PCGS.** The 1917-S Mintmark on Obverse is a relatively scarce date with a mintage of fewer than a million pieces, which is less than one-fifth of that for the Mintmark on Reverse issue. Peppered light brown toning complements the mostly silver-gray surfaces. There are no marks of any significance and the strike is sharp save for a touch of weakness on Liberty's body. (#6572)

Select 1917-S Obverse Mintmark Half

943 **1917-S Obverse MS63 PCGS.** An attractive silver-gray Select example of this challenging San Francisco issue, well struck with occasional dustings of golden-tan patina at the margins. Pleasingly lustrous with only a handful of wispy abrasions that account for the assigned grade.
From The Sundance Collection. (#6572)

944 **1917-S Reverse MS62 PCGS.** According to Jeff Ambio (2008), the 1917-S Mintmark on Reverse is a "scarce-to-rare issue in all Mint State grades." This untoned piece boasts enticing satiny luster. The surfaces have scattered abrasions typical for the grade, but none merit individual mention. Well-struck save for the usual softness on Liberty's head and dress. (#6573)

945 **1917-S Reverse MS63 PCGS.** Wafts of light orange-brown toning accent the mostly silver-gray surfaces. A couple of minor marks define the grade, but all are inconsequential. Sharply struck save for the usual weakness on the highest points of Liberty. (#6573)

Charming 1917-S Half Dollar, Mintmark on Reverse, MS64

946 **1917-S Reverse MS64 PCGS.** An often underrated issue, the 1917-S Mintmark on Reverse issue can actually be quite difficult to locate in high Uncirculated grades. This untoned and highly lustrous near-Gem representative has only a few minor abrasions and exhibits a bold strike. An attractive piece for a collector. PCGS has certified 44 examples finer (8/08). (#6573)

Lovely 1917-S Mintmark on Reverse Half Dollar, MS64

947 **1917-S Reverse MS64 PCGS.** Light gold toning is surrounded by delightful violet color in the margins. Scintillating luster graces the surfaces and highlights the boldly struck design elements. Scattered abrasions define the grade, but all are insignificant. PCGS has certified just 44 examples finer (8/08). (#6573)

Sharp, Frosty Gem 1918 Walking Liberty Half

948 **1918 MS65 PCGS.** The 1918 Walking Liberty half dollar is one of the better-produced early halves in the series, but despite a mintage exceeding 6.6 million coins, few examples are found in grades above MS65. The present piece shows frosty surfaces that are typical for the date, with a sharp strike and just a few light, grade-consistent abrasions. PCGS has certified seven examples finer (8/08). (#6574)

949 **1918-D—Cleaned—ICG. MS60 Details.** Although common in low grades, the 1918-D can be difficult to locate in Mint State. This mostly untoned piece has just a touch of russet at the top of the obverse and virtually no marks. A nice representative despite cleaning. (#6575)

Shining MS64 1918-S Half

950   **1918-S MS64 NGC.** Immensely lustrous with occasional whispers of subtle golden patina across parts of the otherwise silver-white surfaces. Well struck with a degree of definition on the thumb of Liberty's branch hand. This issue is challenging at the Gem level, with just 38 pieces graded MS65 or better known to NGC (8/08). (#6576)

Attractive 1919 Half Dollar, Gem Uncirculated

951   **1919 MS65 NGC.** Enchanting satiny luster shimmers beneath the attractive toning. Pleasing lilac, rose, and gold colors in the margins give way to light gray across the centers. Liberty's dress is a trifle soft, as typically seen, but most of the details are decisively impressed. A charming example of this early Walker. Census: 27 in 65, 11 finer (8/08). (#6577)

952   **1919-D XF45 PCGS.** A luminous and well struck representative of this early mintmarked Walker key, minimally marked and bathed in delightful gold-rose, greenish-gold, and violet patina. Eminently appealing. (#6578)

Lustrous AU53 1919-D Half

953   **1919-D AU53 ICG.** This earlier Denver issue was little-appreciated at the time of release, and today, even better circulated examples are elusive. This still-lustrous survivor is well struck with lovely pink, lavender, and gold shadings across each side. Only minor wear is noted on the high points.
From The Morton J. Greene Collection. (#6578)

Pleasing AU53 1919-D Half

954   **1919-D AU53 NGC.** A lightly circulated, still-lustrous gold-gray survivor from this challenging earlier D-mint issue. Despite light wear, the coin's original strong strike still shows, particularly on the well-defined branch hand. The luminous rose-accented fields show surprisingly few flaws of any note. (#6578)

Remarkable 1919-D Walking Liberty Half, MS64

955   **1919-D MS64 NGC.** The 1919-D is the rarest coin in the Walking Liberty half dollar series in grades above MS65. In his new book *Collecting & Investing Strategies for Walking Liberty Half Dollars,* Jeff Ambio estimates only 10-15 examples survive at this level, with a single MS66 coin known. Because of the huge jump in price between MS64 and MS65 coins, Ambio recommends premium quality MS64 as a sensible buy for this issue.

    The present coin has all the elements of a high end MS64. The strike is far above average with sharp detail on Liberty's gown up to the knee. Liberty's hand is strongly outlined and the peripheral elements are crisp. Liberty's head is weak, as almost always seen. There is strong detail on the eagle's breast feathers. Intense luster complements the strong strike. The surfaces are brilliant and free of distracting abrasions. Superior eye appeal for this date. (#6578)

Lovely 1919-S Half, MS65

956 **1919-S MS65 PCGS. CAC.** In his new reference Collecting & Investing Strategies for Walking Liberty Half Dollars, Jeff Ambio writes: "I really like the 1919-S in MS-65. Such coins are decidedly rare in an absolute sense, but enough exist that you should be able to acquire an attractive piece after a year or so of diligent searching."

Although it is shy of a full strike, enough of Liberty's thumb is still visible to assure interest from specialists who have been searching for a selected Gem. This piece has excellent luster and frosty surfaces, with light champagne toning on the obverse and heavier iridescent toning on the reverse. Population: 38 in 65, 11 finer (8/08). (#6579)

957 **1920 MS64 PCGS.** Vibrant green and violet toning around the rims accents the brilliant centers. Enticing satiny luster ripples across the surfaces and is barely affected by a few scattered abrasions. A fully struck example with impressive eye appeal. (#6580)

Sharply Struck 1920-D Walker, MS66

958 **1920-D MS66 NGC.** The 1920-D is a notable strike rarity among early Walkers. This piece is far above average for the issue, with nearly complete definition on Liberty's head, and close to two-thirds of the skirt lines are also complete. Walking Liberty specialists have noted that subdued mint luster is often a problem with this issue. The surfaces of this coin are highly lustrous, with coruscating mint frost and just a trace of light golden toning around the margins. The 1920-D is elusive in all Uncirculated grades, and only a handful of examples are known above the Gem level. NGC Census: 1 in 66, 0 finer (7/08).
From The Laredo Collection. (#6581)

Delightful 1920-S Half Dollar, MS64

959 **1920-S MS64 PCGS.** Charming pearl-gray surfaces have hints of hazel and charcoal around the perimeter. The reverse is fully struck, while the obverse has minor softness at the center, which is typical for S-mint halves from the 1920s. Soft satiny luster shines throughout this minimally abraded piece. PCGS has certified 48 pieces finer (7/08). (#6582)

Amazing MS66 1920-S Half

960 **1920-S MS66 NGC. CAC.** Like its D-mint counterpart from the same year, the 1920-S half is elusive in Mint State grades despite a high mintage compared to a number of other issues. Moreover, though the 1920-S may be available for a price in grades through Choice or even Gem, Premium Gems such as the coin offered here are top-drawer rarities. This immensely lustrous survivor offers pleasing detail for the issue and soft, lovely luster beneath occasional golden shadings. The beautifully preserved surfaces are silver-gray otherwise. One of just nine pieces at this level known to NGC, with just two numerically finer (8/08). (#6582)

Attractive and Desirable 1921 Half Dollar, MS63

961 **1921 MS63 PCGS.** Philadelphia and Denver mintage totals for 1921 were the lowest of the Liberty Walking half dollar series. Guth and Garrett (2005) call these two issues rare, noting that both are "... extremely difficult to locate in Mint State condition." This is an attractive and eye-catching coin, displaying a dusting of sepia toning over a lustrous silver backdrop. (#6583)

Spectacular Gem 1921 Half

962 **1921 MS65 NGC.** The post-World War I recession year of 1921 saw a substantial drop in the quantity of coins produced for circulation, and though almost all denominations experienced this fall to some degree, the half dollar was affected more dramatically than most. Between the three active mints of the time, total production of half dollars amounted to only slightly over a million pieces, and fewer than a quarter-million halves were struck at Philadelphia. The Gem offered here is one of the best-preserved survivors from that low-mintage issue, well-defined with occasional whispers of golden toning over immensely lustrous silver-white surfaces. Census: 30 in 65, 2 finer (7/08). (#6583)

Choice XF 1921-D Half Dollar

963 **1921-D XF45 NGC.** The 1921-D is the lowest business strike issue of the Walking Liberty half series. This Choice XF example displays light to medium gray patina and hints of luster. The design elements retain nice definition, including partial detail in Liberty's branch hand. Both sides are quite clean.
From The Morton J. Greene Collection. (#6584)

Important 1921-S Half Dollar, Choice AU

964   1921-S AU55 PCGS. After World War I, the mintage of half dollars dropped precipitously, and all three 1921 Walkers are scarce in any grade. Although five different dates have lower mintages, the 1921-S ranks as the rarest issue in the series in grades above Fine. This date seems to have been largely ignored by contemporary collectors and is now quite rare in high grades.

The present piece has a lovely ring of hazel toning on the rims that contrasts nicely against the brilliant centers. There are no mentionable marks on either side, and eye-catching luster flashes in the fields. Liberty's head and the centers are a trifle soft, but the rest of the details are boldly defined. An attractive example of this highly desirable key date. (#6585)

965   1929-S MS64 NGC. A frosty, near-Gem specimen with remarkably clean surfaces and splendid satiny luster throughout. This piece is mostly brilliant, although the reverse has a peppering of hazel and lilac toning at the top. A trace of softness is noted on the figure of Liberty. (#6590)

Resplendent 1933-S Half Dollar, Gem Mint State

966   1933-S MS65 PCGS. CAC. An eye-catching, brilliant, and carefully preserved Gem. Outstanding satiny luster drapes both sides and complements the crisply defined details. Liberty's dress lines are nearly full and there is just a trace of softness on the right (facing) hand. Scattered abrasions limit the grade, but none are worthy of individual mention. This attractive example would make a wonderful addition to any collection. (#6591)

967   1936-D MS66 PCGS. This lustrous Premium Gem appears brilliant at first glance, but wisps of golden toning are here and there. Exactingly struck and only minimally abraded. PCGS has certified only 20 pieces finer. (#6599)

968   1937-D MS66 NGC. Whispers of light tan color make occasional visits to the lustrous surfaces of this Premium Gem. Adequately struck, and well preserved. (#6602)

969   1937-S MS66 NGC. White surfaces possess coruscating luster, and are nicely preserved. The design elements are typically struck. Rare in this level of preservation. (#6603)

970   1938-D MS64 PCGS. Patches of violet surround the silver-gray centers of this minimally marked piece. The strike is sharp save for the usual weakness on Liberty's dress. Splendid satiny luster shimmers across the surfaces and enhances the appeal of this attractive specimen. (#6605)

971   1938-D MS65 PCGS. Wafts of tan toning mix with silver-gray across the satiny surfaces of this carefully preserved Gem. Liberty's dress lines are a trifle weak, as usual, but the rest of the details are fully defined. (#6605)

972   1938-D MS65 NGC. Highly lustrous surfaces display a couple dabs of olive green. Generally well struck, with especially crisp gown lines. Some grade-consistent marks are not bothersome. (#6605)

973   1938-D MS66 PCGS. Well-defined with soft, pleasing luster beneath elegant silver-gray and champagne shadings. Excellent eye appeal. PCGS has graded 23 finer pieces (8/08). (#6605)

974   1939-D MS66 PCGS. Frosty silver-white surfaces are free of distracting abrasions, and although the strike is less than full, there is a suggestion of a split thumb on Liberty's branch hand, and the head details are well-impressed. A much rarer issue only one grade point finer.

Superlative 1941 Walker, MS68

975 **1941 MS68 NGC.** What a pleasure it is to examine this remarkable half dollar. The nearly perfect surfaces show pinpoint striking definition and there is just a slight degree of peripheral toning present, including a faintly perceptible arc of rainbow coloration near the left obverse border. There are certainly no distractions on either side of the piece, and a beautiful satiny sheen perfectly highlights the nearly immaculate fields and devices. A splendid example of one of the best produced issues in the entire series, in a state of preservation that has never been exceeded. Census: 16 in 68, 0 finer (7/08). (#6611)

976 **1941-S MS65 PCGS.** An excellent strike for this often mushy issue, with impressive detail on Liberty's head and skirt lines. Lightly toned and thoroughly lustrous. The key to the 1941 to 1947 short set, unless the die doubled reverse 1946 is included. (#6613)

Appealing 1941-S Half Dollar, Premium Gem

977 **1941-S MS66 PCGS.** An exciting piece with impressive eye appeal. Incredible satiny luster shimmers across the surfaces, which are entirely brilliant save for a hint of gold and a splash of charcoal toning on the rims. The strike is razor-sharp except for a trace of softness on Liberty's dress lines. A carefully preserved specimen with virtually pristine fields. PCGS has certified just six examples finer (7/08). (#6613)

Sharp MS66 1941-S Walker

978 **1941-S MS66 PCGS.** An attractive ring of amber toning surrounds the brilliant centers of this resplendent Premium Gem. The strike is sharp save for the usual weakness on several of Liberty's dress lines. Dazzling satiny luster gives this piece great eye appeal. PCGS has certified just six pieces finer (8/08). (#6613)

Vibrant 1941-S Walking Liberty MS66

979 **1941-S MS66 NGC. CAC.** Pastel ice-blue and honey-gold endow this shimmering Premium Gem. Well preserved, since a loupe locates only minor contact on the cheek. An above average strike for this short set key, with full head detail and a separated thumb on the branch hand. NGC has certified just 16 pieces finer (7/08). (#6613)

Lovely 1941-S Half Dollar, Premium Gem

980 **1941-S MS66 NGC. CAC.** Spectacular satiny luster shimmers throughout this lightly toned and powerfully struck piece. Only part of Liberty's dress is soft, which is typical for the issue. A few nearly imperceptible abrasions keep this attractive piece from an even higher grade. NGC has certified just 16 examples finer (7/08). (#6613)

Outstanding 1945-S Half Dollar, Superb Gem

981 **1945-S MS67 PCGS.** The 1945-S is a perfect example of a condition rarity: with a mintage of over 10 million pieces it is common even in MS66, but it is virtually unobtainable in MS67. This Superb Gem, however, not only ranks among the finest certified, but also has extraordinary eye appeal. The satiny surfaces are accented by a ring of maroon, rose-gold, and violet toning in the periphery. Nearly full struck, this piece has only a couple of nearly imperceptible grazes on Liberty's dress. This outstanding representative would make a wonderful addition to a registry set. Population: 3 in 67, 0 finer (7/08). (#6626)

982 **1946-S MS67 NGC.** Though a degree of typical softness affects the high points, the delightful frostiness on the central devices and the impressive luster on the fields are immensely appealing. Carefully preserved, as befits the Superb Gem designation. (#6629)

983 **1947 MS67 NGC.** Wafts of lovely medium brown toning grace the obverse, which contrasts sharply against the entirely brilliant reverse. A loupe locates only a few tiny abrasions on Liberty's dress. A lustrous and fully struck Superb Gem. (#6630)

Dazzling 1947 Half Dollar, Superb Gem

984 **1947 MS67 NGC.** A brilliant and satiny representative of the final year of the Walking Liberty series. The strike is nearly full, and only a couple of minor marks on Liberty's body keep this piece from an even higher grade. This carefully preserved and conditionally scarce piece would make an ideal type coin. Census: 55 in 67, 0 finer (7/08). (#6630)

985 **1947-D MS65 ICG.** A lustrous and essentially untoned Gem with an above average strike and smooth fields.
From The Jerry Kochel Collection. (#6631)

PROOF WALKING LIBERTY HALF DOLLARS

In-Demand 1936 Walking Liberty Half, PR64

986 **1936 PR64 NGC.** An in-demand issue as the start of modern proof coinage, the 1936 Walking Liberty half dollar has seen remarkable price appreciation over the years as a first-year type. This is a well-struck near-Gem example with silver-white centers and golden-ringed rims. Excellent eye appeal. (#6636)

987 **1936 PR67 PCGS.** Ex: Tom Mershon Collection. With a mintage of just 3,901 pieces, the 1936 proof Walking Liberty half issue is widely desired, and pieces in top grades are particularly prized. The obverse of this Superb Gem specimen displays a blush of pale violet patina across the center, while thin flashes of orange and lime-green color along the lower third of the border provide a glimpse of things to come on the reverse. Here the multicolored hues expand to a wide crescent of green and rose iridescence that is sure to excite the toning enthusiast. Population: 18 in 67, 1 finer (8/08). (#6636)

988 **1937 PR67 NGC.** The 1937 Walking Liberty proof issue had a relatively low mintage of 5,728 pieces, and survivors are not numerous at the Superb Gem grade level. This example is well struck and essentially untoned, with deep mirror fields and immaculately preserved surfaces. (#6637)

Eye-Catching 1937 Half Dollar, PR67

989 **1937 PR67 NGC.** Entirely brilliant with deeply mirrored fields that appear glassy under a lamp. The strike is nearly full, and there are only a couple of minuscule contact marks at the centers. This attractive example is one of just 5,728 proofs struck. NGC has certified a mere 19 pieces finer (8/08). (#6637)

PR68 1937 Walking Liberty Half Dollar

990 **1937 PR68 PCGS.** Ex: Tom Mershon Collection. This Superb Gem coin from the second year of Walking Liberty proof coinage is lightly patinated in streaky olive-gold and pale violet hues, with underlying mirror surfaces that come temptingly close to sheer perfection. Population: 9 in 68, 0 finer (8/08). (#6637)

991 **1938 PR65 NGC.** A frosty and vividly lustrous Gem. Patches of russet on the rims accent the untoned centers. Several light grazes and microscopic spots keep this piece from an even higher grade. (#6638)

992 **1938 PR65 PCGS.** Strong reflectivity, detail, and eye appeal. The mirrors shine through shallow silver-gray patina that shows occasional splashes of milky olive toning. (#6638)

993 **1938 PR66 PCGS.** Subtle silver-gray shadings at the margins leave the powerful mirrors essentially undimmed. A well-defined piece that offers excellent visual appeal. (#6638)

994 **1938 PR67 NGC. CAC.** Dusted gold and russet toning in the periphery adds color to the mostly pearl-gray surfaces. Glassy reflectivity complements the nearly full design elements. An immensely appealing superb Gem. (#6638)

995 **1938 PR67 NGC. CAC.** A fully brilliant and powerfully impressed Superb Gem. Several microscopic marks are entirely imperceptible without magnification. A mere 8,152 proofs were struck. NGC has certified just 45 examples finer (8/08). (#6638)

996 **1938 PR67 PCGS.** A thin layer of translucent olive patina clings to the margins of this carefully preserved Superb Gem. Crisply detailed with strong reflectivity through the toning. PCGS has graded 10 coins finer (8/08). (#6638)

Sharp PR68 1938 Walking Liberty Half

997 **1938 PR68 PCGS.** Ex: Tom Mershon Collection. A loupe reveals the slight suggestion of color at the obverse border, a combination of iridescent fuchsia, copper, and blue shades, both otherwise the centers are silvery. The eye appeal is enormous, as expected, with a razor-sharp strike and total absence of contact. Population: 10 in 68, 0 finer (8/08). (#6638)

998 **1939 PR67 NGC.** Deep amber and russet toning encircles the obverse of this fully struck Superb Gem. Lovely milky patina overlies the glassy and deeply mirrored surfaces. A couple of minor contact marks on Liberty's dress are visible under magnification. One of 8,808 proofs struck. (#6639)

Extraordinary 1939 Walking Liberty Half, PR68

999 **1939 PR68 PCGS.** Ex: Tom Mershon Collection. Simply extraordinary quality for the issue. Both sides are virtually pristine, with an exactness of strike that can only be the result of proof production methods. The uniformly reflective features shine forcefully through light copper-gold patination. Population: 24 in 68, 0 finer (8/08). (#6639)

1000 **1940 PR65 PCGS.** Beautifully detailed with impressive mirrors that shine through faint whispers of green-gold patina. Pleasingly preserved, as befits the Gem designation. (#6640)

1001 **1940 PR67 NGC.** This is a brilliant Superb Gem proof with amazingly clean surfaces and razor-sharp striking details. In terms of both eye appeal and overall technical merit, this piece is exceptional for the grade. (#6640)

Splendid PR68 1940 Walking Liberty Half

1002 **1940 PR68 PCGS.** Ex: Tom Mershon Collection. This is another splendid Superb Gem from the Tom Mershon Collection, with silvery centers and just a touch of iridescence at the obverse rim in rainbow shades of yellow, copper, mint, and fuchsia. One of less than three dozen certified PR68 at PCGS, with none finer (8/08). (#6640)

1003 **1941 PR66 PCGS.** Toned delicate olive-gold aside from a dash of golden-tan near the I in LIBERTY. Precisely struck and unabraded with good field reflectivity. Encased in an old green label holder. (#6641)

1004 **1941 PR67 NGC. CAC.** No AW. According to Breen (1988), proofs minted from January to October 1941 were struck from dies that were excessively polished, which unintentionally removed the designer's monogram. A deeply mirrored and frosted Superb Gem. Traces of russet and hazel toning encircle the perimeter of this nearly perfect example. A lovely and appealing specimen. (#6641)

1005 **1941 PR67 NGC.** Strongly mirrored as always with the astonishing striking sharpness found only on proofs. Minimally toned and carefully preserved. NGC has graded 62 finer examples (8/08). (#6641)

Exquisite PR68 ★ 1941 Half Dollar

1006 **1941 PR68 ★ NGC. CAC.** No AW. Lovely pastel ice-blue, rose-red, lime-green, and honey-gold adorn the obverse, and confirm the Star designation awarded by NGC. Pinpoint-sharp and gorgeously preserved. As is the case with a majority of 1941 proofs, the designer's monogram is absent, inadvertently removed when the reverse die was lapped at the Mint prior to coinage. No AW Census: 11 in 68 ★, 0 finer (7/08). (#6641)

Lightly Toned PR68 1941 Walking Liberty Half Dollar

1007 **1941 PR68 PCGS.** Ex: Tom Mershon Collection. This piece is tied with another dozen pieces as the finest certified of the 1941 issue at PCGS, and there are none finer (8/08). Both sides are silver, with suggestions of gold and ice-blue patina on both sides, but a bit more obvious on the obverse than the reverse. (#6641)

1008 **1942 PR66 PCGS.** Deep, watery reflectivity is seen in the fields of this Premium Gem specimen, from the final year of proof coinage in the Walking Liberty half dollar series. The striking details are razor-sharp. (#6642)

1009 **1942 PR66 PCGS.** Bright surfaces exhibit impressively struck design features, and are exquisitely struck. A few small toning spots occur on the obverse. (#6642)

1010 **1942 PR67 NGC.** Fully white surfaces exude powerful reflectivity. The strike is nearly full, and there are only a few minuscule contact marks on either side. This enticing example is one of 21,120 proofs minted. (#6642)

1011 **1942 PR67 ★ NGC.** Dazzling, fully brilliant surfaces with moderate cameo contrast. The U.S. entry into World War II ended proof production of the type in 1942. Census: 17 in 67 ★, 15 finer with a Star designation (7/08).
Ex: Mike Jacobson Collection (Heritage, 2/2005), lot 8250, which realized $1,092. (#6642)

Enticing 1942 Half Dollar, PR68

1012 **1942 PR68 NGC.** One of 21,120 proofs struck. The present piece is entirely white and untoned, with eye-catching satiny luster beneath light mint frost. Both sides appear to be unmarked, even with the aid of a loupe. Only a touch of weakness on Liberty's dress keeps this piece from being absolutely perfect. NGC has certified just four examples finer (8/08). (#6642)

Wonderful Rim-Toned 1942 Walking Liberty Half, PR68

1013 1942 PR68 PCGS. Ex: Tom Mershon Collection. Another wonderful Superb Gem Walking Liberty half dollar, the present piece also features delicate rim toning, here in shades of gold, sage, and fuchsia, with silver centers and the astonishing appeal high-grade proofs of this series are known for. (#6642)

FRANKLIN HALF DOLLARS

1014 1949-D MS64 Full Bell Lines NGC. Lustrous and lightly toned with a crisp strike, clean fields, and a couple of thin marks on the bell. (#86654)

1015 1949-S MS64 Prooflike NGC. Before the days of third party grading, the 1949-S was considered to be a key to Franklin half series. Despite its San Francisco mintmark, this near-Gem has moderately flashy fields, and is essentially bereft of toning. For the entire series, NGC has certified just six pieces as prooflike (8/08). (#6655)

Brilliant Prooflike 1949-S Franklin Half MS65 Full Bell Lines

1016 1949-S MS65 Full Bell Lines Prooflike NGC. In the days before full bell lines became important to collectors, the 1949-S was considered the key to the series. It remains a scarce and popular low mintage issue. The present Gem has noticeably flashy fields and is fully brilliant. Marks are minimal, and the eye appeal is substantial. (#86655)

1017 1949-S MS65 Full Bell Lines NGC. CAC. This scarce date Gem has original dappled cream-gray and forest-green toning. Highly lustrous and impressively unabraded. NGC has certified a mere 14 pieces finer with Full Bell Lines (7/08). (#86655)

1018 1950-D MS66 Full Bell Lines PCGS. Subtle gray-gold shadings invigorate the immensely lustrous surfaces of this solidly struck Premium Gem. Bold, impressive eye appeal. Population: 47 in 66 Full Bell Lines, 0 finer (8/08). (#86657)

1019 1950-D MS66 Full Bell Lines PCGS. Ex: Chesapeake Collection. The dappled apple-green and copper-red patina competes for territory with the underlying dove-gray color. This is a Premium Gem that has it all: a bold strike, dynamic luster, and exquisite preservation. A wonderful example that would improve even the finest specialized collection. Population: 47 in 66 full Bell Lines, 0 finer (8/08). (#86657)

1020 1951-D MS66 Full Bell Lines PCGS. CAC. A lovely dusting of lilac toning covers the centers, while a ring of gold surrounds the perimeter. Vivid satiny luster gives this razor-sharp Premium Gem outstanding eye appeal. Neither NGC nor PCGS has certified any examples finer (8/08). (#86659)

1021 1951-S MS65 Full Bell Lines PCGS. CAC. Splendid luster radiates from each side of this Gem, which boasts mottled russet and amber-gold toning more prominently on the obverse, with the reverse adding pink champagne to the heady mix. The bell lines are bold and well-detailed. (#86660)

1022 1951-S MS66 Full Bell Lines PCGS. Both sides show radiant, brilliant cartwheel luster, and the bell is exceptionally mark-free with pleasing line definition. PCGS has graded no finer Full Bell Lines pieces (8/08). (#86660)

1023 1952 MS67 NGC. Well struck, with essentially full definition on the lower lines of the Liberty Bell. Lovely olive-gray patina drapes the impressively preserved surfaces that display only a couple of small contact marks. Census: 6 in 67, 0 finer (8/08). (#6661)

1024 1952-S MS64 Full Bell Lines NGC. Pleasing violet, silver-gray, and olive-green intermingle across the remarkably clean surfaces. The razor-sharp strike is complemented by impressive luster throughout. Census: 26 in 64 Full Bell Lines, 15 finer (8/08). (#86663)

1025 1952-S MS65 Full Bell Lines PCGS. Solidly struck for this issue and quite lustrous, with deep bronze and lavender patina on the obverse, which contrasts sharply against the ring of russet that encircles the reverse. A few minor marks keep this piece from an even higher grade. PCGS has certified only 28 examples finer (8/08). (#86663)

1026 1954-D MS66 Full Bell Lines PCGS. Strong, swirling luster with only occasional whispers of champagne close to the margins. The beautifully preserved surfaces are brilliant otherwise, and the lines on the bell are particularly crisp. PCGS has graded only two finer Full Bell Lines pieces (8/08). *From The Bell Collection.* (#86668)

Attractively Toned 1958-D Half Dollar, MS67 ★

1027 1958-D MS67 ★ NGC. Vibrant rainbow toning envelops both sides, with lime-green, amber, gold, and lavender all present throughout this attractive piece. Flashy luster penetrates the toning and highlights the powerfully impressed design elements. NGC has graded only four pieces as MS67★, with none finer (8/08). (#6675)

Colorful 1958-D Half Dollar, MS67 Full Bell Lines

1028 **1958-D MS67 Full Bell Lines PCGS.** Lovely reddish-gray toning covers the surfaces, with accents of gold and lavender around the periphery. The reverse is especially colorful, and both sides feature shimmering luster beneath the vibrant toning. A couple of minuscule handling marks keep this attractive piece from an even higher grade. Neither NGC nor PCGS have certified any examples finer. Population: 26 in 67, 0 finer (7/08). (#86675)

Lushly Toned 1959 Franklin Half MS66 Full Bell Lines

1029 **1959 MS66 Full Bell Lines PCGS.** Type One Reverse. Lovely sea-green and gold toning adorns this thoroughly lustrous and assertively struck Premium Gem. Beautifully preserved and worthy of a commanding bid. Population: 30 in 66, 0 finer (8/08).
Ex: Alex & Nan Registry Sets (Heritage, 4/2006), lot 3123. (#86676)

1030 **1962 MS64 Full Bell Lines NGC.** Peppered violet toning covers the obverse, which contrasts sharply to the entirely brilliant reverse. Dazzling luster enhances the eye appeal of this sharply struck piece, and there are no mentionable marks on either side. Census: 44 in 64, 10 finer (8/08). (#86682)

1031 **1963-D MS65 Full Bell Lines ANACS.** Although the 1963-D is the last issue in the series and have by far the highest mintage, Full Bell Lines specimens are elusive. This piece displays light russet and ice-blue shades on surfaces that are still mostly silver-white. (#6685)

1032 **1963-D MS66 Full Bell Lines PCGS.** Pleasingly detailed for this final Denver Franklin half dollar issue with strong luster. Warm gold-orange and cool silver-gray shadings embrace each side. Tied for the finest Full Bell Lines coin known to NGC or PCGS (8/08). (#86685)

PROOF FRANKLIN HALF DOLLARS

1033 **1950 PR67 NGC. CAC.** Wafts of gold and lilac accent this impeccably preserved Superb Gem. The strike is nearly full, and the deeply mirrored surfaces appear pristine to the unaided eye. NGC has certified just one example finer, and PCGS reports none above PR67 (7/08). (#6691)

1034 **1950 PR67 NGC.** A boldly impressed example of this initial proof Franklin half dollar issue, moderately reflective with dappled green-gold and cloud-gray patina across much of each side. NGC has graded just one finer example for the contrast category (8/08). (#6691)

Extraordinary 1950 Franklin, PR66 Cameo

1035 **1950 PR66 Cameo PCGS. CAC.** Fully struck with marvelously clean, virtually untouched surfaces. The lettering and the steps of the Liberty Bell are more crisply defined than usual, even for a proof specimen. The field-to-device contrast is extraordinary, on both obverse and reverse. Population: 20 in 66 Cameo, 2 finer (8/08). (#86691)

1036 **1951 PR66 Cameo PCGS.** Fully struck and exquisitely preserved with attractive sky-blue toning on both sides, deeply reflective fields, and frosted devices. Faint die polish lines (as struck) cross the central devices, but few post-striking marks are evident on either side of this lovely Premium Gem proof. Population: 52 in 66 Cameo, 6 finer (8/08). (#86692)

1037 **1951 PR64 Deep Cameo PCGS.** Proof 1951 half dollars are seldom seen in Deep Cameo, which is partially attributable to their having the second lowest proof issue of the series. A dusting of purple toning around the perimeter accents the brilliant fields and frosted devices. This fully struck piece would make an excellent representative. Population: 12 in 64 Deep Cameo, 21 finer (7/08). (#96692)

Exemplary 1951 Franklin Half, PR65 Deep Cameo

1038 **1951 PR65 Deep Cameo PCGS.** This early proof Franklin half issue is relatively available in non-cameo condition, but Deep Cameo pieces are extremely scarce. This Gem example is well struck and shows jet-black fields and heavily frosted devices. Exemplary preservation has left the coin free of any contact marks or other distractions. Population: 8 in 65 Deep Cameo, 13 finer (8/08). (#96692)

1039 **1952 PR67 Cameo NGC.** This is a gorgeous Superb Gem proof, with intense reflectivity in the fields and softly frosted central devices. A conditionally scarce specimen, fully struck and free of surface distractions. Census: 73 in 67 Cameo, 1 finer (7/08). (#86693)

1045 **1957 PR67 Deep Cameo PCGS.** Snowy devices create spectacular black and white cameo contrast against the deeply mirrored fields. There are virtually no contact marks visible to the unaided eye, and the strike is full. Population: 57 in 67 Deep Cameo, 50 finer (7/08). (#96698)

Superb 1952 Franklin Half, PR67 Cameo

1040 **1952 PR67 Cameo PCGS.** Mintages for proof Franklin half dollars began to increase this year, eventually exceeding one million pieces for the first time in 1957. At 81,980 coins, however, the 1952 production figure was still small by modern standards. This Superb Gem is crisply struck and immaculately preserved, with deeply reflective fields and mildly frosted devices. Population: 26 in 67 Cameo, 1 finer (8/08). (#86693)

Eye-Catching 1953 Half Dollar, PR66 Deep Cameo

1041 **1953 PR66 Deep Cameo PCGS.** The 1953 is a condition rarity in the Franklin half dollar series and while Cameo examples are scarce, Deep Cameo specimens are even more difficult to locate. Intensely mirrored fields show remarkable black-on-white contrast against the snow-white devices. A number of milk spots in the fields limit the grade, but there are virtually no marks on either side. PCGS reports just seven Deep Cameo pieces finer than this sharply struck specimen. (#96694)

1042 **1954 PR68 NGC.** This is an awesome proof representative, with crisp striking definition on all of the design details, including the frequently blurry lettering on the upper section of the Liberty Bell. The fields are dark and deeply reflective, and the surfaces are virtually pristine. (#6695)

1043 **1954 PR68 Cameo PCGS.** An awesome cameo Superb Gem with stark white-on-black contrast observed on both sides. The design details are sharply struck, including the lettering on the Liberty Bell. A marvelously well preserved example of this earlier Franklin half proof issue. Population: 27 in 68 Cameo, 0 finer (8/08). (#86695)

1044 **1954 PR67 Ultra Cameo NGC.** This is an essentially perfect specimen that is very impressive for the date. The inky-black fields display immense reflectivity, and the devices are nicely frosted. A conditionally scarce early proof Franklin half. Census: 19 in 67 Ultra Cameo, 9 finer (7/08). (#96695)

Great 1959 Franklin Half, PR68 Cameo

1046 **1959 PR68 Cameo PCGS.** This Superb example has a dramatic black-and-white appearance, with stark contrast observed between the inky-black fields and intensely frosted devices. The design details are reproduced with pinpoint sharpness, and both sides of the coin are essentially pristine. Population: 29 in 68 Cameo, 0 finer (8/08). (#86700)

Incredible 1959 Franklin, PR67 Ultra Cameo

1047 **1959 PR67 Ultra Cameo NGC.** A Superb Gem proof with amazing contrast between the deeply mirrored fields and highly lustrous devices. The obverse and reverse surfaces are fully pristine, providing exceptional aesthetic appeal for the connoisseur. Census: 4 in 67 Ultra Cameo, 0 finer (7/08). (#96700)

Popular 1961 Doubled Die Reverse Half, PR66

1048 **1961 Doubled Die Reverse PR66 PCGS.** FS-801, formerly FS-013. Doubled Die Reverse. There is prominent doubling on E PLURIBUS UNUM and UNITED. Sharply struck and fully brilliant, with deeply watery fields and well preserved surfaces. Listed on page 198 of the 2008 *Guide Book*. Population: 19 in 66, 9 finer (8/08). (#6689)

SMS KENNEDY HALF DOLLAR

Remarkable 1965 SMS Half Dollar, MS66 Deep Cameo

1049 **1965 SMS MS66 Deep Cameo PCGS.** This exquisitely preserved specimen has an excellent cameo appearance that enhances the eye appeal. A few faint toning spots add color to the almost entirely brilliant surfaces. Several minuscule contact marks are nearly imperceptible without a glass. This impressive piece would be a great addition to a registry set. Population: 10 in 66 Deep Cameo, 8 finer (8/08). (#96845)

PROOF KENNEDY HALF DOLLARS

1050 **1964 PR68 Ultra Cameo NGC.** Ivory-white devices show intense black-on-white cameo contrast against the virtually pristine surfaces. An outstanding representative with a full strike and tremendous eye appeal. (#96800)

1051 **1964 PR69 Deep Cameo PCGS.** Type Two Reverse. A brilliant and essentially flawless proof Half Dollar. The frosted devices demonstrate obvious contrast with the powerfully mirrored fields. Neither NGC nor PCGS has certified any pieces in PR70 Deep Cameo (8/08). (#96800)

1052 **1964 PR69 Ultra Cameo NGC.** Watery deeply mirrored fields show startling cameo contrast against the white devices. Both sides are virtually immaculate and the eye appeal is tremendous. This wonderful example would be an excellent addition to a registry set. (#96800)

1053 **1964 Accented Hair PR67 Deep Cameo PCGS.** Magnificent black and white cameo contrast gives this virtually pristine piece outstanding eye appeal. The surfaces appear brilliant, but a loupe locates a couple of tiny toning spots. Population: 17 in 67 Deep Cameo, 8 finer (8/08). (#96801)

1054 **1964 Accented Hair PR67 Ultra Cameo NGC.** The surfaces of this Superb Gem appear flawless, even with the aid of a loupe. The deeply mirrored fields and exquisitely frosted devices create a spectacular cameo appearance. Census: 14 in 67 Ultra Cameo, 10 finer (8/08). (#96801)

1055 **1964 Accented Hair PR68 Cameo PCGS.** An elusive variety, this half dollar features an especially pronounced part in Kennedy's hair. The surfaces are brilliant save for a couple of yellow toning spots on the obverse. Impressive black and white cameo contrast is apparent between the deeply mirrored fields and frosted devices. Population: 55 in 68 Cameo, 0 finer (8/08). (#86801)

COMMEMORATIVE SILVER

1056 **1893 Isabella Quarter MS64 PCGS.** This popular commemorative honors Queen Isabella of Spain on the obverse and has a figure emblematic of women's industry on the reverse. With a distribution of only 24,214 pieces, these quarters are significantly rarer than their Columbian Exposition half dollar counterparts. Cobalt-blue toning at the top of the obverse accents the rose and gold that covers the rest of the surface. The untoned center of the reverse is surrounded by deep purple and russet along the rim. Remarkable satiny luster gives this sharply struck and carefully preserved specimen outstanding eye appeal. (#9220)

1057 **1893 Isabella Quarter MS64 PCGS. CAC.** A highly lustrous and razor-sharp specimen. The obverse is entirely brilliant, which contrasts nicely against the light ring of lilac that encircles the silver-gray center of the reverse. The surfaces appear pristine, with only a couple of minor grazes visible under a glass. (#9220)

1058 **1893 Isabella Quarter MS64 PCGS.** Deep toning envelops both sides, with pearl-gray centers that contrast nicely against the dramatic violet in the margins. This powerfully impressed example displays lovely satiny luster beneath the appealing toning. (#9220)

1059 **1893 Isabella Quarter MS64 PCGS.** A delicate mix of light gray and ivory patina rests on the lustrous surfaces of this near-Gem commemorative. Nicely struck, with no mentionable marks. (#9220)

Popular 1893 Isabella Quarter, Gem Mint State

1060 **1893 Isabella Quarter MS65 PCGS.** Streaks of cream and silver-gray intermingle across the surfaces of this popular early commemorative. Queen Isabella's hair is a trifle soft, as usually seen, but the rest of the details are boldly defined. Alluring satiny luster graces both sides and enhances the great eye appeal. Housed in a first generation PCGS holder. (#9220)

Magnificent 1893 Isabella Quarter, Gem Uncirculated

1061 **1893 Isabella Quarter MS65 NGC.** A vibrantly toned and highly lustrous Gem. This piece features dusted gold, russet, and violet across the obverse, which contrasts sharply against the light rose and lavender that encircles the brilliant center of the reverse. Powerful satiny luster graces both sides and highlights the sharply defined design elements. (#9220)

1062 **1893 Isabella Quarter MS65 PCGS.** The rich layers of purple-rose and cobalt-blue toning over both sides of this well struck Gem are illuminated by intense, coruscant luster. Just one or two trivial nicks are found on the surfaces, under magnification. A lovely, conditionally scarce Isabella quarter. (#9220)

Appealing 1893 Isabella Quarter, MS65

1063 **1893 Isabella Quarter MS65 PCGS.** Delicate shades of pastel violet, electric-blue, and golden-tan bathes the highly lustrous surfaces of this Gem commemorative quarter. An attentive strike leaves razor-sharp, even definition on the motifs, and both sides are devoid of mentionable marks. Super all around eye appeal! (#9220)

1064 **1900 Lafayette Dollar MS61 NGC.** DuVall 1-B. This stone-white silver dollar has satin luster and nearly unabraded fields. Careful inspection finally locates a few trivial slide marks on Washington. (#9222)

1065 **1900 Lafayette Dollar MS61 NGC.** DuVall 1-B. An unworn piece with soft, creamy luster beneath rich copper-mocha peripheral toning and silver-gray patina across the centers. Well struck with several long, shallow abrasions across the portraits that account for the grade. (#9222)

1066 **1900 Lafayette Dollar MS62 PCGS.** DuVall 3-D, an elusive variety characterized by repunching of (ST)AT(ES) on the obverse and a thin-stemmed branch with a leaf over the 9 in the date on the reverse. Light, dappled gold and violet patina dots the otherwise silver-gray surfaces. A well struck piece that shows several slide marks on the portrait that account for the grade. (#9222)

Lovely MS64 ★ Lafayette Dollar

1067 **1900 Lafayette Dollar MS64 ★ NGC.** DuVall 1-B. As of (8/08), only two Lafayette dollars have garnered the coveted Star designation from NGC, the present piece and an MS66. The designation is due to the eye-catching patina, which features peripheral bands of ocean-blue, autumn-gold, and plum-mauve toning that surrounds the cream-gray fields and devices. Lustrous with smooth fields and minimally abraded portraits. (#9222)

Original Near-Gem 1900 Lafayette Dollar

1068 **1900 Lafayette Dollar MS64 PCGS.** DuVall 1-B. A chestnut-brown near-Gem with original toning and vigorous satin luster. The strike is precise, and the fields are well preserved. Two minor reeding marks on Washington's face are all that limit the grade. Curiously, the Lafayette dollar is the only pre-1983 silver dollar commemorative, despite the traditional collector preference for crown-sized coins. (#9222)

Lustrous Gem Lafayette Dollar

1069 **1900 Lafayette Dollar MS65 NGC.** DuVall 1-B. A nearly brilliant Gem that boasts intense cartwheel sheen. Specialists know that it is difficult to locate Lafayette dollars with vibrant luster, since so many have been dipped or wiped over the years. It is also unusual to find an example with essentially unabraded surfaces. Washington's cheek has a couple of faint ticks, but these are from the planchet prior to the strike and are invariably present on the type. The strike is bold with only trivial incompleteness on Lafayette's book. Although Lafayette dollars are available in lower Mint State grades, it is a frustrating task to locate high quality examples. Save the hard work, and instead simply view the present lot. (#9222)

Peripherally Toned Gem Lafayette Dollar

1070 **1900 Lafayette Dollar MS65 PCGS.** DuVall 1-B. Lovely tobacco-brown and aquamarine toning adorns the borders of this thoroughly lustrous and crisply impressed silver dollar. The fields are gorgeously preserved, while contact is minor and limited to small marks on Washington's jaw and the lower front of the horse. All Lafayette dollars were struck on a single day, December 14, 1899, to commemorate the exact centennial of Washington's passing. Perhaps the Mint struggled to reach the deadline, which helps explain the existence of several positional die varieties involving the lettering and branch. (#9222)

Dramatically Toned Lafayette Dollar MS65

1071 **1900 Lafayette Dollar MS65 PCGS. CAC.** DuVall 2-C. This slightly better DuVall variety is identified by a recut second S in STATES on the obverse. Beautiful golden-brown, apple-green, gold, and cherry-red enrich this satiny Gem. The strike is exemplary, and the only visible imperfection is a subtle graze on the left reverse field. Among the many curious incidents in the history of the Lafayette dollar is a Treasury melting of 14,000 pieces in 1945, decades after the 14 sealed bags first occupied government vaults, but shortly before Chicago dealer Aubrey Bebee attempted to purchase the hoard from the Treasury. (#9222)

Appealing 1900 Lafayette Gem Dollar

Lustrous 1900 Lafayette Dollar, MS65

1072 **1900 Lafayette Dollar MS65 PCGS.** DuVall 1-B. The leaf points between the 1 and 9 in the date, and the A in DOLLAR is low and leans left. John Winkelmann writes in the August 2007 *Numismatist* that Congress presented an equestrian statue of Major General Lafayette to France. To help fund the monument, Congress authorized the minting and sale of a commemorative dollar, with the busts of Lafayette and George Washington on the obverse and a mounted Lafayette on the reverse.

Soft luster exudes from the silver-gray surfaces of this Gem specimen, and an attentive strike imparts sharp definition to the design feathers. A few light handling marks are consistent with the grade designation. Great overall technical quality and aesthetic appeal. (#9222)

1073 **1900 Lafayette Dollar MS65 PCGS.** DuVall 2-C. The second S in STATES is repunched east. The obverse has conjoined busts of Washington and Lafayette, while the reverse depicts Lafayette on horseback. It is one of very few coinage issues to depict the same person on both sides. Housed in an older green-label holder, this wonderful Gem is fully brilliant with pristine surfaces beneath faint champagne toning. It is also sharply struck with excellent design definition on both sides. PCGS has only certified 85 finer examples of the Lafayette dollar (8/08). (#9222)

1074 **1921 Alabama MS65 PCGS.** The obverse is mostly silver-gray with light yellow accents, and contrasts sharply to the reverse, which has a pleasing arc of amber and violet toning at the bottom. Magnificent satiny luster shimmers across this carefully preserved specimen. (#9224)

1075 **1921 Alabama MS65 NGC.** Alabama half dollars are not rare in the absolute sense, but they are surprisingly scarce in high grades. This sharply struck piece has just a few minor abrasions and a couple of microscopic spots. The brilliant surfaces have captivating satiny luster throughout. (#9224)

1076 **1921 Alabama MS65 PCGS.** A lustrous Gem, minimally marked with powder-blue peripheral toning and hints of plum on the obverse. The softly struck eagle offers a trace of golden patina. (#9224)

1077 **1921 Alabama MS65 PCGS.** A frosty and fully lustrous Gem with the overall appearance somewhat muted due to light champagne toning. A pleasing and desirable piece that is seldom found any finer. (#9224)

1078 **1921 Alabama MS65 PCGS.** This satiny Gem has olive-gold toning and is nearly unabraded. A small spot beneath the eagle's breast, and the left obverse field has a few pinpoint flecks. The eagle's legs show minor weakness, but the overall strike is good. Encapsulated in a green label holder. (#9224)

1079　**1921 Alabama 2x2 MS65 NGC.** Electric-blue and reddish-gold patina gravitates to the margins of this lovely Gem, and a solid strike imparts strong detail to the motifs. A couple of unobtrusive marks are noted on the obverse. (#9225)

1080　**1921 Alabama 2x2 MS65 PCGS.** Vibrant russet and light green toning encircle the silver-gray centers. The satiny luster is truly extraordinary, and there are just a few minor marks on each side. The "2X2" Alabama half dollar is significantly scarcer than its plain counterpart, and has a distribution of just 6,006 pieces. (#9225)

Well Struck 1921 Alabama 2x2 Half Dollar, MS66

1081　**1921 Alabama 2x2 MS66 NGC.** Dappled olive-green, reddish-gold, gray, and greenish-gold patination races over the lustrous surfaces of this Premium Gem commemorative half. A well executed strike sharpens the design features, and both sides are nicely preserved. Census: 66 in 66, 1 finer (7/08). (#9225)

1082　**1937 Antietam MS65 PCGS.** The popular Antietam half dollar, struck to honor the 75th anniversary of the most gruesome single-day battle of the Civil War, had a distribution of just over 18,000 pieces. Splendid rose, gold, and lilac toning drapes the surfaces of this sharply struck Gem. Several insignificant abrasions limit the grade. (#9229)

1083　**1937 Antietam MS66 PCGS.** Brilliant and sharply struck, this carefully preserved specimen would make a wonderful representative. Several minor handling marks are typical for the grade, but all are inconsequential, and there are no blemishes to report. Impressive satiny luster gives this piece great eye appeal. (#9229)

1084　**1937 Antietam MS66 NGC.** Delicate ice-blue and cream toning enriches this satiny and sharply struck Civil War commemorative. Inspection beneath a lens locates a few pinpoint reverse marks. (#9229)

1085　**1937 Antietam MS66 NGC.** Delicate gold patina visits this satiny and virtually unabraded Premium Gem. Crisply struck, and desirable in such exemplary condition. Antietam had the largest single day death toll of any Civil War battle. (#9229)

1086　**1937 Antietam MS67 PCGS.** Superbly struck and vibrantly lustrous, with a brilliant reverse that contrasts sharply against a lovely ring of russet-gold toning around the obverse. Other than two or three tiny contact marks, near the center of the obverse, the satiny surfaces appear pristine. (#9229)

1087　**1937 Antietam MS67 PCGS.** Streaks of russet grace the surfaces of this satiny Superb Gem. A couple of light abrasions on McClellan and Lee are nearly imperceptible. This fully struck representative is one of a mere 18,028 pieces minted. PCGS has graded only 13 examples finer (7/08). (#9229)

1088　**1937 Antietam MS67 NGC.** Mostly brilliant with a touch of light yellow toning on the obverse. A few nearly imperceptible marks keep this sharply struck piece from being absolutely flawless. Vivid satiny luster gives this piece great eye appeal. NGC reports just 19 examples finer (8/08). (#9229)

1089　**1935-D Arkansas MS67 NGC.** Ex: Bingham Collection. Attractive dappled golden-brown, rose-red, and slate-gray adorn this shimmering and crisply struck Superb Gem. Undisturbed, original, and desirable in such quality. Houston Oilers linebacker Greg Bingham's commemorative collection was certified by NGC in 2002. Census: 26 in 67, 1 finer (7/08). (#9234)

Impressive Superb Gem 1937-D Arkansas Half

1090　**1937-D Arkansas MS67 PCGS.** This is one of the scarcer issues in the early silver commemorative series, which is understandable considering its low mintage of 5,505 coins. This Superb Gem piece is sharply struck, and the design elements are noticeably better-defined than usual, on both sides. Mottled olive and orange-gold patina occurs near the obverse periphery, and to a lesser extent near the reverse margins. Impressively preserved and nearly pristine. Population: 13 in 67, 1 finer (8/08). (#9242)

1091　**1939 Arkansas MS65 NGC.** A golden brown tint in the periphery accents the brilliant and lustrous centers. Several light grazes limit the grade, but all are insignificant. This final-year Arkansas half dollar has great eye appeal and is one of a distribution of a mere 2,104 pieces. (#9249)

1092　**1939-S Arkansas MS65 NGC.** Although the Arkansas Centennial was celebrated in 1936, commemoratives were issued until 1939 of one design, while a second design was struck in 1936. Eye-catching satiny luster radiates from the untoned and minimally marked surfaces. A mere 2,105 pieces were issued. (#9251)

1093　**1935/34-D Boone MS65 PCGS.** The important variety with the small 1934 on the reverse is an elusive issue that was created to boost sales of the Boone half dollars. While the Philadelphia version is common, both the D and S pieces are rare. This example has brilliant, satin luster with excellent eye appeal. (#9263)

1094　**1935/34-D Boone MS67 PCGS.** A shining Superb Gem example of this famous low-mintage classic silver commemorative issue. The centers are generally pale silver-gray, while pink, champagne, and violet-rose shadings grace much of the obverse and reverse periphery. PCGS has graded just five finer examples (8/08). (#9263)

Attractive 1938 Boone Half Dollar, Superb Gem

1095　**1938 Boone MS67 PCGS.** The Boone commemorative series came to an end in 1938 after a production run of five years. During that period, only 86,600 examples made their way to collectors and speculators, compared to the authorized mintage of 600,000 pieces from all mints. Of that total, just 6,300 coins—2,100 from each mint—are dated 1938. This is a beautifully toned Superb Gem with silver-gray centers and deep rose, russet, antique-gold, and lime-green toning over most of the surfaces. Crisply struck with immense luster and powerful visual appeal. NGC has certified no examples finer and PCGS reports just one such coin (8/08). (#9274)

1096　**1938-D Boone MS66 PCGS.** Wafts of medium brown toning intermingle with the mostly light gray surfaces. The strike is bold, and there are a few minor abrasions on the bust of Boone. NGC has certified just 39 pieces finer (7/08). (#9275)

1097 1938-D Boone MS67 PCGS. Though the branch-mint Boone halves dual-dated 1934 and 1935 get far more attention, the 1938 issues had net production of just 2,100 pieces each. This Superb Gem from Denver offers vibrant luster beneath occasional golden-tan toning. Population: 43 in 67, 3 finer (8/08). (#9275)

1098 1938-S Boone MS66 NGC. Magnificent satiny luster is barely affected by a few light grazes. This sharply struck example is entirely brilliant and has great eye appeal. Census: 88 in 66, 23 finer (7/08). (#9276)

1099 1938-S Boone MS67 NGC. The almond-gold toning is faint but deepens slightly near the rims. Well struck and essentially pristine with coruscating surfaces. Among the lowest mintage silver commemoratives, since only 2,100 pieces were coined. Census: 23 in 67, 1 finer (7/08). (#9276)

1100 1925-S California MS65 NGC. A carefully preserved example of this popular commemorative, struck to honor California's 75th anniversary as a state. Several dots of medium brown toning accent the mostly brilliant surfaces. Magnificent satiny luster shimmers on both sides. (#9281)

1101 1925-S California MS66 PCGS. Dazzling satiny luster radiates from the surfaces of this brilliant, light gray example. The surfaces are nearly pristine and the details are razor-sharp. A truly stunning representative. (#9281)

1102 1925-S California MS66 NGC. Bright, essentially untoned surfaces showcase radiant luster. A well-defined California coin, carefully preserved with delightful visual appeal. (#9281)

1103 1925-S California MS66 PCGS. Generally silver-gray in the centers with strong luster and captivating blue, gold, tan, and orange patina in varying quantities at the margins. Minimally marked and pleasing. (#9281)

1104 1936 Cincinnati MS66 PCGS. Delicate pastel multicolored toning runs over the lustrous surfaces of each side. A nicely struck and well preserved piece. Population: 91 in 66, 2 finer (8/08). (#9283)

1105 1936 Cincinnati MS66 NGC. A conditionally scarce example of the Cincinnati half dollar, which has a diminutive distribution of just 5,005 pieces. Several light grazes and minuscule spots keep this lustrous Premium Gem from an even higher grade. The surfaces are mostly brilliant with hints of russet and gold toning on the reverse. Census: 54 in 66, 4 finer (7/08). (#9283)

1106 1936 Cincinnati MS66 NGC. Radiantly lustrous surfaces exhibit whispers of greenish-gold patina, that becomes slightly deeper at the reverse periphery. The design features are well impressed. A few minuscule marks do not detract. Census: 54 in 66, 4 finer (7/08). (#9283)

1107 1936-D Cincinnati MS66 PCGS. With a distribution of just over 5,000 pieces for each mint, the Cincinnati Music Center half dollar is one of the scarcest classic commemoratives. Satiny luster shimmers beneath the lightly frosted slate-gray and pale yellow surfaces. Several nearly imperceptible abrasions are noted on each side. (#9284)

1108 1936-D Cincinnati MS66 NGC. Light to dusky peach-gold patina confirms the originality of this lustrous Premium Gem. The Cincinnati ranks among the most elusive types, and exemplary examples are subject to strong demand. (#9284)

1109 1936-S Cincinnati MS66 PCGS. An arc of hazel covers the top of the obverse, while a dusting of gold and russet toning surrounds the perimeter of the reverse. Nearly fully struck with only a couple of light abrasions. (#9285)

1110 1936 Cleveland MS67 NGC. An impressive, deeply toned Superb Gem with extraordinary luster under gray-brown, green, russet, lilac, and blue toning. Census: 49 in 67, 3 finer (7/08). (#9288)

1111 1892 Columbian MS66 PCGS. This popular issue was the first United States commemorative ever struck. A ring of russet encircles the pleasing silver-gray centers. Magnificent satiny luster gleams throughout and gives this piece great eye appeal. PCGS has certified just nine examples finer (7/08). (#9296)

1112 1893 Columbian MS66 NGC. Intense electric-blue and red-brown iridescence is evenly distributed along the obverse and reverse peripheries of this satiny, lustrous near-Gem, ensuring a high degree of eye appeal. Boldly struck and minimally abraded, as expected for the Premium Gem grade. (#9297)

1113 1893 Columbian MS66 NGC. Both sides of this premium quality Gem have a pleasing array of colors. Rich cobalt-blue, maroon, and golden-orange shades are present, and there are only minor handling marks visible under magnification. NGC has certified just 27 pieces finer (7/08). (#9297)

1114 1893 Columbian MS66 PCGS. CAC. Pleasing detail and captivating luster are just two of the attractive attributes of this Premium Gem. Both sides also exhibit lovely patina, silver-gray at the center of the obverse with a melange of blue, gold, rose, and orange elsewhere. PCGS has graded just six finer examples (8/08). (#9297)

Enthralling 1893 Columbian Half, MS67

1115 1893 Columbian MS67 NGC. The 1893 Columbian is the first of only three classic commemorative issues to have an original mintage in excess of a million pieces. This well struck example offers shining luster beneath amethyst and sapphire colors that alternate between hazy and clear. A gorgeous Superb Gem. Census: 25 in 67, 2 finer (7/08). (#9297)

1116 1893 Columbian MS64 Prooflike NGC. Faint tan-gray toning visits this flashy and crisply struck near-Gem. A pleasing example of the introductory commemorative type. Census: 67 in 64 Prooflike, 25 finer (7/08). (#89297)

1117 1935 Connecticut MS66 PCGS. Dots of violet toning accent the silver-gray surfaces of this impeccably preserved specimen. Flashy luster enhances the eye appeal, and there are just a couple of light abrasions on this fully struck Premium Gem. (#9299)

1118 1935 Connecticut MS66 PCGS. Subtle golden overtones grace the immensely lustrous surfaces of this captivating Premium Gem. Well-defined and attractive. PCGS has graded 43 finer pieces (8/08). (#9299)

1119 1936 Elgin MS67 ★ NGC. CAC. A dusting of russet covers the silver-gray centers, which are surrounded by deep gold and violet toning. The obverse is especially eye-catching, but both sides exhibit remarkable satiny luster. This issue is notorious for a weak strike, but the people on the reverse have softly struck heads, the obverse has above-average definition. A minimally marked and appealing example. (#9303)

1120 1936 Gettysburg MS66 PCGS. A handsome Premium Gem example of this popular commemorative. Both sides are mostly brilliant with a dusting of hazel toning in the fields. Alluring satiny luster graces the surfaces and gives this nearly pristine piece impressive eye appeal. (#9305)

1121 1922 Grant no Star MS66 NGC. Pleasing luster rests on the silver surfaces of this Grant No Star Premium Gem, and an attentive strike leaves strong impressions on the design elements. A couple of minute spots are visible on the obverse. (#9306)

1122 **1922 Grant no Star MS66 PCGS. CAC.** Golden-gray patination becomes a tad deeper at the margins. This is a well struck, lustrous piece that reveals well preserved surfaces. (#9306)

1123 **1922 Grant no Star MS66 PCGS.** Vivid tan, russet, and sky-blue toning graces the periphery of each side. The fields and centers are pearl-gray, and there is satiny luster throughout. Generally sharp save for slight weakness on the lower half of the reverse. Impeccably preserved and nearly pristine. (#9306)

Premium Gem 1922 Grant No Star Half

1124 **1922 Grant no Star MS66 PCGS.** Delightful gold and russet toning surrounds the outer reaches of each side. There is only slight weakness on Grant's hair, and the rest of the details fully struck. Lots of luster is present throughout. Although Grant half dollars without the star are fairly common with a distribution of 67,405 pieces, they are seldom seen finer than MS64. (#9306)

1125 **1922 Grant with Star—Genuine—PCGS. In-House Graded AU50.** Light tan-gray surfaces reveal fine hairlines under magnification. Well struck, with no significant marks. We grade the piece AU50. (#9307)

1126 **1922 Grant with Star MS62 NGC.** Mistaken orders at the Philadelphia Mint resulted in this notable low-mintage variety, one that has been the subject of much fakery over the years. The lustrous, minimally toned surfaces of this piece show scattered marks, including several reed marks on Grant's forehead. (#9307)

1127 **1922 Grant with Star MS63 NGC.** An unintentional variety of sorts, the With Star half was created when Mint officials interpreted the promoters' request for two gold dollar variants to include two half dollar versions as well. This minimally toned and lustrous piece is well struck with only occasional faint abrasions. (#9307)

Low Mintage 1922 Grant With Star Half Dollar, MS64

1128 **1922 Grant with Star MS64 NGC.** This is a satiny, lightly toned near-Gem with semi-reflective fields and carefully preserved surfaces. A light golden-gray cast over each side is enhanced by russet specks near the peripheries. Boldly struck and attractive, with few surface marks of any kind. From a low mintage of 4,256 pieces, and one of the scarcer issues in the early silver commemorative series. (#9307)

Desirable 1922 Grant With Star Half Dollar, MS65

1129 **1922 Grant with Star MS65 NGC.** The Grant Memorial commemorative with the star in the obverse field is one of the most elusive issues in the classic series with a distribution of just 4,256 pieces. That figure is many multiples lower than the 67,405 examples issued without the star. This vibrantly toned Gem has an arc of gold around the perimeter with charming accents of lilac on the reverse. Pleasing mint frost covers both sides. There are no mentionable marks on either side and the strike is razor-sharp. (#9307)

Marvelously Lustrous 1922 Grant With Star, MS65

1130 **1922 Grant with Star MS65 PCGS.** A series key to the silver commemorative set, the 1922 Grant with Star is seldom seen above Gem condition, and even in MS65 it will be an expensive acquisition, compared to most pieces in the set. This piece offers silver-white surfaces lightly kissed with gold and ice-blue patina, but it is the marvelous luster that is this coin's chief attribute. PCGS has certified 33 specimens finer (8/08). (#9307)

Attractive 1922 Grant With Star Half Dollar, MS65

1131 **1922 Grant with Star MS65 PCGS.** Pastel shades of violet and light golden-tan patina reside over each side of this Grant With Star Gem. The fields are bright, reflecting numerous swirling die polishing marks. Sharply struck on the motifs, and revealing no mentionable abrasions. A nice looking specimen overall. (#9307)

1132 **1928 Hawaiian AU58 ANACS.** Soft bluish-gray and yellow-orange patina resides on both sides of this near-Mint commemorative half. Lustrous surfaces exhibit well struck design elements, and are quite clean.
From The Morton J. Greene Collection. (#9309)

1133 **1928 Hawaiian—Improperly Cleaned—NCS. Unc Details.** Struck for the 150th anniversary of Captain Cook's arrival at Hawaii, these half dollars had a low distribution of just 9,958 pieces. This sharply defined piece has mottled tan and silver toning on each side. Only a couple of insignificant marks are visible under magnification. (#9309)

1134 **1928 Hawaiian—Improperly Cleaned—NCS. Unc Details.** This nearly untoned example has diminished luster and a subdued appearance, but there are no obvious patches of hairlines and other abrasions are minimal. The key to the 50 piece classic silver commemorative type set. (#9309)

1135 **1928 Hawaiian—Improperly Cleaned—NCS. Unc. Details.** Light almond-gold with wisps of powder-blue. A satiny representative with faint hairlines but few contact marks. The most coveted type of the silver commemorative series. (#9309)

Lustrous Near-Gem 1928 Hawaiian Commemorative Half

1136 **1928 Hawaiian MS64 PCGS.** This lustrous near-Gem example of one of the most elusive and hotly sought-after silver commemoratives from the classic era (1892-1954) offers most silver surfaces, with a coating of golden and deeper amber coloration near the rims on the obverse. The reverse offers dappled ice-blue toning around the Hawaiian chieftain, and generous eye appeal appears throughout. (#9309)

Delightful 1928 Hawaiian Half Dollar, Choice Mint State

1137 **1928 Hawaiian MS64 NGC.** Bright gray toning covers the surfaces of this resplendent specimen. Scintillating mint luster graces both sides and is not affected by a couple of minuscule handling marks. This piece is boldly struck and exhibits great eye appeal. One of a distribution of only 9,958 examples. (#9309)

Popular 1928 Hawaiian Commemorative Gem Half Dollar

1138 **1928 Hawaiian MS65 PCGS.** The ever-popular Hawaiian commemorative becomes quite challenging in Gem condition. The satiny, essentially untoned surfaces of this specimen exhibit sharply struck design elements, including the intricacies of the reverse beach environment. A couple of unobtrusive reverse marks do not detract. Housed in a green label holder. (#9309)

Outstanding High-End MS65 1928 Hawaiian Half

1139 **1928 Hawaiian MS65 PCGS. CAC.** Advanced commemorative half collectors will appreciate the subtleties of this lovely piece. The surfaces are softly frosted and appear nearly brilliant at first glance. However, closer examination shows pale golden and lilac color interspersed over both obverse and reverse. Exceptionally clean. (#9309)

1140 **1935 Hudson MS64 NGC.** A Choice example of this popular one-off silver commemorative design, softly struck and lustrous beneath variable gold and peach shadings. Minimally marked and fundamentally pleasing. (#9312)

1141 **1935 Hudson MS65 NGC.** Colorful apple-green, apricot, and rose-red illuminate this lustrous and suitably struck Gem. Careful evaluation locates only faint and unimportant contact. (#9312)

1142 **1935 Hudson MS65 NGC.** Delicate gold-gray patina drapes much of each side. The immensely lustrous surfaces of this Gem exhibit a delightful blend of frostiness and satin. (#9312)

1143 **1935 Hudson MS65 PCGS.** Softly lustrous, well struck, and minimally toned. Though a small abrasion is noted to the right of Neptune's leg, the surfaces are virtually mark-free otherwise. (#9312)

1144 **1935 Hudson MS65 NGC.** Peppered hazel toning surrounds the perimeter of this attractive specimen. The strike is a trifle weak at the centers, but the alluring satiny luster adds to the eye appeal. A well-preserved and attractive representative. (#9312)

1145 **1935 Hudson MS65 NGC.** A light dusting of russet toning in the periphery accents the mostly brilliant design elements. The strike is a trifle weak at the centers, as typically seen, but the rest of the details are sharply defined. One of a distribution of just 10,008 pieces. Housed in an old NGC holder. (#9312)

Impressive 1935 Hudson Half Dollar, MS66

1146 1935 Hudson MS66 NGC. The Hudson commemorative half Dollar ranks among the scarce commemorative types, with a mintage of just 10,000 coins, along with eight additional pieces that were reserved for the next annual assay meeting. This gorgeous representative embodies the quality that every commemorative collector should strive for. The surfaces are frosty and lustrous with light peripheral gold toning. (#9312)

Desirable 1935 Hudson Commemorative Half, MS66

1147 1935 Hudson MS66 NGC. Intense luster radiates from both sides of this Premium Gem commemorative half, each of which is nicely preserved. An impressive strike leaves relatively strong delineation on the design features, further enhancing the overall eye appeal. Hudson is a small city on the eastern bank of the Hudson river, and is about 40 miles south of Albany. (#9312)

Radiant MS66 1935 Hudson Half Dollar

1148 1935 Hudson MS66 PCGS. CAC. The Hudson half dollar was widely criticized after its release. Despite its depiction of explorer Henry Hudson's ship the *Half Moon* on the obverse, the commemorative had nothing to do with the navigator; rather, it celebrated the 150th anniversary of the founding of Hudson, New York—a town of some 14,000 residents in the early 1930s. This piece offers splendid silver-white surfaces that are essentially untouched by any mentionable distraction, with radiant luster and just the barest hint of golden patina. Certified in a green-label holder. PCGS has graded only six pieces finer (8/08). *From The Sundance Collection.* (#9312)

1149 1924 Huguenot MS66 PCGS. Well-defined and softly lustrous beneath generally even patina. The obverse is primarily silver-gray with arcs of orange and golden-brown at the upper and right margin, while the reverse is essentially gold-gray. PCGS has graded 37 finer pieces (8/08). (#9314)

1150 1925 Lexington MS66 NGC. A lightly toned and highly lustrous Premium Gem. The surfaces are minimally marked with a dusting of russet toning on each side. While this commemorative has a distribution of an incredible 162,013 pieces, it can be difficult to locate in MS66 and is virtually impossible to find in higher grades. NGC has certified just 10 pieces finer (7/08). (#9318)

1151 1925 Lexington MS66 PCGS. Powerful luster and solid detail combine with pleasing preservation on this notable Premium Gem. Subtle golden shadings drape much of the centers. (#9318)

1152 1918 Lincoln MS66 PCGS. Immensely lustrous with occasional whispers of lemon-yellow patina at the margins of the otherwise silver-white surfaces. Only a handful of shallow flaws in the fields preclude an even finer designation. (#9320)

1153 1936 Long Island MS66 NGC. Magenta and yellow-green patination covers both sides of this lustrous Premium Gem, and a solid strike leaves strong definition on the design elements. Devoid of mentionable marks. (#9322)

1154 1936 Lynchburg MS67 NGC. A light coating of yellowish-green and iridescent toning masks the satiny mint luster on both sides of this attractive commemorative half dollar. Census: 88 in 67, 6 finer (7/08). (#9324)

1155 1920 Maine MS66 PCGS. CAC. Highly lustrous and boldly impressed with smooth surfaces and light gold toning. Anthony de Francisci provided the models for this commemorative type, shortly before he received greater recognition for his Peace dollar design. Housed in a green label holder. (#9326)

1156 1920 Maine MS66 PCGS. A creamy, lightly toned Premium Gem with impressive satiny luster throughout. The strike is nearly full, and a loupe locates only a couple of nearly imperceptible grazes. PCGS has certified just 16 examples finer (7/08). (#9326)

1157 1920 Maine MS66 NGC. Splashes of aqua-blue, reddish-gold, and russet concentrate at the margins of this Premium Gem, and an attentive strike leaves strong definition on the intricate design elements. Lustrous surfaces are well preserved. (#9326)

1158 1934 Maryland MS67 NGC. Swirling luster emanates from the well preserved, silver-gray surfaces of this Superb Gem commemorative. An attentive strike leaves sharp definition on the design elements. (#9328)

1159 1921 Missouri MS64 NGC. Lightly toned rims accent the mostly brilliant surfaces of this highly lustrous piece. Only a few minuscule abrasions are visible under magnification. Boldly impressed save for a trace of weakness on the frontiersman. (#9330)

1160 1921 Missouri MS64 PCGS. A blend of bronze and pinkish-gray patina covers both sides of this near-Gem. This attractive statehood centennial commemorative issue was heavily marketed at the state fair in Sedalia, and the town's name appears within the exergue on the reverse. (#9330)

Attractive MS65 1921 Missouri Half

1161 1921 Missouri MS65 NGC. High grade Missouri halves are known for exceptional mint luster. This piece is certainly among those select coins and additionally the fields have a faint glimmer of semireflectivity. As one would expect, and is so difficult to find on this early commemorative, the surfaces are nearly abrasion-free. Mostly brilliant, there is just a hint of light golden-brown color around the devices. (#9330)

1162 **1921 Missouri 2x4 MS63 NGC.** Well struck for the often-weak Missouri design with soft luster beneath omnipresent gold and silver-blue patina. A handful of wispy abrasions on each side account for the grade. (#9331)

1163 **1921 Missouri 2x4 MS64 PCGS.** Dapples of olive-green are unevenly distributed over the lustrous, minimally marked surfaces of this near-Gem. Well struck throughout. (#9331)

1164 **1921 Missouri 2x4 MS64 NGC.** Hints of gold highlight the impressive satiny surfaces of this resplendent near-Gem specimen. Close examination reveals only insignificant abrasions. Boldly struck with excellent eye appeal. (#9331)

Desirable Gem 1921 Missouri 2x4

1165 **1921 Missouri 2x4 MS65 NGC.** A desirable Gem example of this key issue in the classic commemorative series. The surfaces are mostly powder-gray, with hints of gold and tinges of cinnamon in the peripheral lettering. But the eye appeal is generous throughout. NGC has certified only 14 pieces finer (8/08). (#9331)

Remarkable 1921 2x4 Missouri Half Dollar, MS65

1166 **1921 Missouri 2x4 MS65 NGC.** If one looks at the combined mintage for both types of the Missouri Centennial commemorative—20,428 pieces—less than one-quarter of that number comprises the popular 2x4 variety. Dusted lilac toning graces the surfaces of this resplendent Gem. The strike is nearly full and the eye appeal is excellent. (#9331)

Impressive 1921 Missouri 2x4 Half Dollar, Gem Mint State

1167 **1921 Missouri 2x4 MS65 PCGS.** The 2x4 Missouri half dollar is considerably scarcer than its plain counterpart, and has a distribution of just 5,000 pieces. This lightly toned Gem has remarkable satiny luster that highlights the nearly full strike, with only a trace of weakness on the high points. Numerous planchet striations are visible under a glass, and there are a few minor marks on each side. An appealing example of this elusive issue. (#9331)

Flashy MS65 1921 Missouri 2x4

1168 **1921 Missouri 2x4 MS65 NGC.** Gem examples of the 1921 Missouri 2x4 should be one of the first "holes" that collectors should fill in their sets, but due to their scarcity they are often the last, along with the Hawaiian, Grant With Star, and a few other series keys. This MS65 example offers plenty of flashy luster over silvery surfaces accented by gold, with cinnamon sprinkles at the obverse rim. NGC has certified 14 pieces finer (8/08). (#9331)

Lovely Gem 1921 Missouri 2x4 Commemorative Half

1169 **1921 Missouri 2x4 MS65 PCGS.** This vibrantly lustrous, richly toned piece is a no-questions Gem, by virtue of impeccable striking definition and outstanding surface preservation. The deep shades of patina on both sides include cobalt-blue and russet-red near the obverse margins, and appealing tan-gold accents near the reverse periphery. A great Gem example of this scarce, early commemorative key issue; housed in a green label PCGS holder. (#9331)

1170 **1923-S Monroe MS65 PCGS.** Consistent cream-gray toning embraces this lustrous and refreshingly unabraded Gem. A fingerprint may be present on the portrait of Adams, but the overall quality is outstanding. The Monroe is notorious as a conditional rarity, common in Select Mint State but increasingly difficult any finer. Housed in a first generation holder. (#9333)

1171 **1923-S Monroe MS65 NGC.** Outstanding satiny luster radiates beneath the lightly frosted and untoned surfaces. The strike is weak at the centers, as typically seen, but there are no marks of any significance. NGC reports just 51 numerically finer examples. (#9333)

1172 **1923-S Monroe MS65 NGC.** Dappled sun-gold and silver-blue endows the obverse, although the reverse has only faint chestnut toning. A hair-thin mark is noted beneath the bust of Adams. The Monroe type is conditionally rare. (#9333)

1173 **1938 New Rochelle MS67 PCGS.** Excellent detail for a New Rochelle half with only trifling softness on the iris. Subtle golden accents at the margins yield to virtually brilliant centers. PCGS has graded only two finer pieces (8/08). (#9335)

1174 **1938 New Rochelle MS67 PCGS.** Soft gold and violet shadings in varying measure drape the smooth, lustrous surfaces of this New Rochelle Superb Gem. Pleasingly detailed and attractive. (#9335)

1175 **1936 Norfolk MS68 PCGS. CAC.** An impeccable example with light gold and iridescent toning over frosty surfaces. Norfolk commemoratives are often found in higher grades due to the lack of open field space to gather marks. None have been graded finer. (#9337)

1176 **1926 Oregon MS67 PCGS.** Charming silver-gray surfaces are accented at the perimeter by olive and reddish-brown toning that is likely due to long-term storage in an album. This first-year Oregon issue, although minted in significant quantities, is actually more difficult at this high grade level than nearly all of its lower mintage counterparts. PCGS has certified only three pieces finer (7/08). (#9340)

1177 **1926-S Oregon MS67 NGC.** A handsome representative of the first issue in the long-lived Oregon Trail commemorative series. Eye-catching satiny luster drapes the surfaces, with pleasing yellow, rose-red, and violet toning in the margins. NGC has certified a mere seven coins finer (8/08). (#9341)

1178 **1928 Oregon MS67 PCGS. CAC.** The obverse of this Superb Gem has pleasing ivory surfaces with splashes of deep gold, russet, and steel toning around the perimeter, while the reverse is brilliant and satiny. One of a distribution of just 6,028 pieces. Population: 62 in 67, 0 finer (7/08). (#9342)

1179 **1933-D Oregon MS67 PCGS.** An eye-catching and entirely brilliant Superb Gem. Close inspection with a loupe reveals only trivial handling marks. Impressive satiny luster shimmers throughout, and the strike is powerfully impressed. Not a single piece has been certified finer by PCGS (7/08). (#9343)

1180 **1936 Oregon MS67 NGC.** Impressive luster and a solid strike are the norm for this issue, and the Superb Gem offered here does not deviate from those strengths. Amber and orange peripheral shadings yield to silver-gray in the centers. NGC has graded three finer examples (8/08). (#9345)

1181 **1936 Oregon MS67 PCGS. CAC.** The Oregon Trail coins were issued sporadically from 1926 to 1939. After coins were struck in 1934 in Denver, no 1935-dated coins were struck before coinage resumed in 1936 at Philadelphia and San Francisco. This piece offers greenish-gold patina over the well-struck and problem-free, highly lustrous surfaces. (#9345)

1182 **1938-D Oregon MS67 NGC.** Crisply struck, softly lustrous, and minimally toned. Only a handful of incidental flaws appear in out-of-the-way areas on this Superb Gem. One of just 6,005 pieces struck. (#9349)

1183 **1939 Oregon MS67 NGC.** Whispers of gold patina gravitate to the margins of this Superb Gem. Remarkably well preserved, lustrous surfaces exhibit strong design detail. Census: 88 in 67, 5 finer (7/08). (#9352)

1184 **1939-D Oregon MS66 NGC.** A brilliant and lustrous representative of the final-year Oregon Trail half dollar, which had been intermittently struck since 1926! This sharply struck piece has only a couple of inconsequential marks. The 1939-D had a distribution of just 3,004 pieces. (#9353)

1185 **1939-D Oregon MS67 NGC.** Pastel steel-blue and caramel-gold visit this satiny and virtually pristine Superb Gem. Sharply struck and pleasing. Tied with the 1939 for the honor of lowest mintage Oregon issue. (#9353)

1186 **1939-S Oregon MS66 NGC.** The Oregon half dollar showcases the outstanding engraving abilities of James Earle Fraser and his wife, Laura Gardin Fraser. This lightly toned Premium Gem appears pristine to the unaided eye and has impressive satiny luster. A mere 3,005 pieces were distributed. (#9354)

1187 **1939-S Oregon MS67 NGC.** Light gold and powder-blue toning visits this shimmering and gorgeously unabraded Superb Gem. The three 1939-dated issues are the lowest mintage of the long-running Oregon Trail type. Census: 77 in 67, 7 finer (7/08). (#9354)

1188 **1939 Oregon PDS Set MS66 PCGS.** A pleasing PDS set of the three low-mintage Oregon Trail issues. All three pieces are satiny and impressively preserved, with creamy coloration and unmarked surfaces. Includes: **the 1939, the 1939-D, and the 1939-S.** (#9355)

1189 **1915-S Panama-Pacific MS64 NGC.** Lovely golden-russet and sea-green toning embraces this expertly struck and satiny near-Gem. No marks appear to limit the grade. A better type, scarcer than its mintage suggests since many buyers were non-numismatist exposition attendees. (#9357)

1190 **1915-S Panama-Pacific MS64 NGC.** Sky-blue, brown, and gray patination adheres to the lustrous surfaces of this near-Gem commemorative. Sharply struck, and well preserved. (#9357)

1191 **1915-S Panama-Pacific MS65 NGC.** A ring of light reddish toning encircles the perimeter of both sides, probably the result of long-term storage in an album. Several small dark toning spots are noted on the obverse. The lustrous surfaces are minimally marked and have sharply detailed devices. (#9357)

Iridescent 1915-S Panama-Pacific Half Dollar, MS66

1192 **1915-S Panama-Pacific MS66 NGC.** A remarkable, gorgeous Premium Gem, this 1915-S Panama-Pacific half dollar is fully lustrous with frosty surfaces beneath pale gold toning, framed by peripheral iridescence on each side. NGC has only graded 63 finer examples of this issue (8/08). (#9357)

Richly and Originally Toned 1915-S Panama-Pacific Half, MS66

1193 **1915-S Panama-Pacific MS66 PCGS. CAC.** The softly frosted surfaces are nearly free from post-striking impairments on each side. The obverse and reverse both have the same color, but the distribution is quite different. The obverse has light gray-silver centers that are surrounded by a margin of cobalt-blue. The reverse, on the other hand, has the same colors but they are evenly intermixed. An exceptional, high grade Pan-Pac half. (#9357)

1194 1915-S Panama-Pacific MS67 PCGS. Despite Farran Zerbe's high hopes for the Panama-Pacific commemorative coin program, sales were a disappointment, even for the most affordable denomination, the silver half dollar. As noted by Q. David Bowers in his *A Guide Book of United States Commemorative Coins*, "[t]he coins themselves, as beautiful as they are to contemplate and own today, followed the usual Zerbe pattern of hype and overblown expectations. Vast quantities remained unsold and were melted ... "

This carefully preserved half dollar survivor offers soft, pleasing luster beneath ample lavender and orange patina. The strike is solid, and the eye appeal is magnificent. Housed in a green label holder. PCGS has graded a mere two finer examples (8/08). (#9357)

1195 1915-S Panama-Pacific MS67 NGC. CAC. As Chief Engraver Charles Barber's life drew to a close, he worked with his eventual successor, George T. Morgan, on several patterns and other side-projects not linked to the mainstream of circulation coinage. The reverse design of the Panama-Pacific half dollar, which includes contributions from both men, was one of their last true collaborations.

This amazing representative is tied for numerically finest certified by NGC (8/08). It offers pleasingly detailed devices with whispers of frostiness at the high points, as well as subtle luster beneath light blue and orange peripheral toning on the obverse. The reverse shows broader coverage with violet, rose, and golden-tan shadings. A single minuscule mark on Columbia's wrist is the only appreciable barrier to an even finer designation. (#9357)

Radiant 1920 Pilgrim Half Dollar, Superb Gem

1196 1920 Pilgrim MS67 NGC. Outstanding luster is complemented by a thin veil of gray and golden patina on the obverse. Speckled russet toning in the periphery of the reverse highlights the razor-sharp details and incredible radiance. A resplendent and highly appealing specimen. Neither NGC nor PCGS has certified any coins finer (8/08). (#9359)

1197 **1921 Pilgrim MS66 PCGS.** A lovely Premium Gem example of the second, lower-mintage Pilgrim half. Strongly lustrous surfaces are silver-gray in the centers with elements of deeper crimson close to the margins. (#9360)

1198 **1921 Pilgrim MS66 PCGS.** A brilliant and nearly pristine specimen with magnificent satiny luster on both sides. This fully struck Premium Gem is one of a distribution of just 20,053 pieces. A semicircular die crack is noted above the ship. Housed in a green label PCGS holder. (#9360)

1199 **1921 Pilgrim MS66 PCGS.** A well-defined Premium Gem that offers delightful, frosty luster. The obverse is essentially silver-white, though hints of gold, blue, and iridescence grace parts of the reverse margins. (#9360)

1200 **1936 Rhode Island MS67 NGC.** This Superb Gem Rhode Island half dollar is entirely brilliant white with the exception of iridescent toning at the extreme obverse border. Census: 20 in 67, 1 finer (7/08). (#9363)

Sumptuous Superb Gem 1936-S Rhode Island Half

1201 **1936-S Rhode Island MS67 NGC. CAC.** Subtle violet and tan elements at the margins yield to silver-white in the centers of this S-mint Superb Gem. The piece is well struck with the soft, finely textured luster peculiar to the Rhode Island design. Neither NGC nor PCGS has graded a numerically finer example (8/08). (#9365)

1202 **1935-S San Diego MS67 NGC.** An exquisitely struck, virtually pristine, and conditionally scarce representative. Delightful satiny luster shimmers beneath the wafts of russet and lemon-yellow that encircle the margins. NGC has certified only five examples finer (8/08). (#9371)

Splendid 1926 Sesquicentennial Half Dollar, Gem Mint State

1203 **1926 Sesquicentennial MS65 PCGS.** The Sesquicentennial half dollars are notable as the first U.S. issue to feature a portrait of a living president: Calvin Coolidge. Deep charcoal and hazel toning surrounds the perimeter of this delightfully lustrous specimen. The details are a little soft, as typically seen for this issue, but the surfaces are nearly unabraded. PCGS has certified only eight pieces finer (7/08). (#9374)

Captivating 1926 Sesquicentennial Half Dollar
Gem Mint State

1204 **1926 Sesquicentennial MS65 PCGS.** A highly lustrous and boldly struck representative. The surfaces are mostly brilliant with a golden tint on the rims. This carefully preserved specimen has numerous planchet striations that radiate from the centers, and only a couple of tiny abrasions. Although common in lower grades, it is virtually impossible to find an example better than Gem. PCGS has certified a mere eight pieces finer (7/08). (#9374)

1205 **1935 Spanish Trail—Improperly Cleaned—NCS. Unc. Details.** A slightly bright and minutely granular representative with dull luster. The strike is bold, and there are no relevant marks. Among the lowest mintage silver types. (#9376)

1206 **1935 Spanish Trail MS63 NGC.** Faint tan toning accents the vibrantly lustrous surfaces. Several tiny marks limit the grade, but none are of any significance. Only 10,008 examples of this popular commemorative were sold. (#9376)

1207 **1935 Spanish Trail MS64 ANACS.** Deep amber toning yields to patches of silver-gray at the centers. Strong luster shines throughout this remarkably clean specimen. A sharply struck example of this popular commemorative. (#9376)

1208 **1935 Spanish Trail MS64 PCGS.** This is a sparkling, satiny, untoned near-Gem. The design details are uniformly well struck, and the surfaces are nearly-blemish-free. A conservatively graded example of this popular commemorative type. (#9376)

1209 **1935 Spanish Trail MS64 NGC.** Lustrous, untoned surfaces exhibit well struck design elements. A shallow hair-thin mark is visible on the left reverse. (#9376)

1210 **1935 Spanish Trail MS65 NGC.** A brilliant and highly lustrous Gem. Scattered light abrasions limit the grade, but none merit individual mention. This boldly struck piece is one of just 10,008 pieces sold. (#9376)

1211 **1935 Spanish Trail MS66 PCGS. CAC.** Soft luster issues from both sides of this Premium Gem commemorative, and an exacting strike brings about strong definition on the design elements. The broad, expansive fields of this coin reveal just a few minor marks, slightly more so on the reverse. Delicately toned in nearly imperceptible light gray. (#9376)

1212 **1935 Spanish Trail MS66 PCGS.** Exciting satiny luster shimmers on both sides of this untoned and remarkably pristine specimen. The strike is razor-sharp and only a couple of tiny abrasions are visible under magnification. (#9376)

1213 **1935 Spanish Trail MS66 NGC.** Each side offers soft, pleasing luster beneath subtle rose and silver-gray shadings. A well struck, pleasing piece that is carefully preserved.
From The Morton J. Greene Collection. (#9376)

1214 **1935 Spanish Trail MS66 NGC.** Pastel ice-blue and apricot patina endows this thoroughly lustrous and meticulously struck Premium Gem. The Spanish Trail ranks among the lowest mintage types, and unblemished examples are very scarce. (#9376)

1215 **1935 Spanish Trail MS66 PCGS.** Well-defined with smooth, subdued luster. Faint golden accents grace the generally silver-gray surfaces, and speckles of deeper crimson-violet are visible on the rims. (#9376)

1216 1925 Stone Mountain MS67 PCGS. Deep rose-bronze toning covers about half of each side and contrasts sharply against the greenish-gray patina that graces the rest of the surfaces. Flashy luster radiates from both sides and enhances the eye appeal. PCGS has certified only six piece finer (8/08). (#9378)

1217 1934 Texas MS67 NGC. Apricot-gold and olive-gray embrace this virtually pristine state commemorative. The strike is above average, with only a hint of incompleteness on the knee and hand of the Winged Victory. Census: 41 in 67, 0 finer (7/08). (#9381)

Amazing MS68 1935 Texas Half

1218 1935 Texas MS68 NGC. Fabulous preservation and eye appeal to match. This well-defined survivor exhibits strong "halo" luster through a light dusting of tan, gold, and silver-white patina. By a narrow margin, the Philadelphia edition of the 1935 Texas half has the lowest mintage for the design and year. Census: 11 in 68, 0 finer (7/08). (#9382)

1219 1936-D Texas MS67 PCGS. An arc of golden-brown toning drapes the left half of both sides, with pleasing streaks of color that extend across the remaining surfaces. This virtually pristine Superb Gem is nearly fully struck and exhibits outstanding satiny luster. PCGS has certified just 12 examples finer (7/08). (#9387)

1220 1936 Texas PDS Set MS67 NGC. Each Superb Gem offers pleasing detail and the striking "halo" luster peculiar to the Texas design. Varied tan-gold, violet, and silver-blue shadings embrace the coins' surfaces. (Total: 3 coins) (#9389)

1221 1938-D Texas MS66 PCGS. Impressively lustrous with solid detail. This Premium Gem has generally silver-white centers with touches of gold-orange toning near the rims. PCGS has graded 59 finer pieces (8/08). (#9395)

1222 1925 Vancouver MS65 PCGS. It is interesting that although these pieces were struck in San Francisco, the mintmark was omitted, which makes them appear as if they were struck in Philadelphia. A dusting of hazel toning around the perimeter of the reverse accents the mostly brilliant surfaces. Pleasing satiny luster highlights the sharply struck details. (#9399)

1223 1925 Vancouver MS65 PCGS. Luminous violet, gold-orange, and silver-blue shadings embrace each side of this well struck Vancouver Gem. Solid eye appeal for the grade assigned. (#9399)

1224 1925 Vancouver MS65 NGC. Decisively struck with marvelous satiny luster throughout. Several minuscule grazes are entirely insignificant and do not affect the great eye appeal. Dotted light tan toning accents the mostly brilliant surfaces. (#9399)

1225 1925 Vancouver MS66 PCGS. Hints of auburn and violet-gray toning dot the periphery of this attractive Premium Gem. The details are sharply defined and are accented by captivating satiny luster. PCGS has certified 46 pieces finer (7/08). (#9399)

1226 1925 Vancouver MS66 PCGS. Generally silver-gray centers show hints of blue, while the lustrous margins exhibit ample amber-tan and umber patina. Well struck and carefully preserved. (#9399)

1227 1927 Vermont MS66 PCGS. Well struck with soft, pleasing luster beneath milky gold-orange patina that crosses the obverse. More subtle champagne shadings embrace parts of the reverse. PCGS has graded 21 finer examples (8/08). (#9401)

1228 1927 Vermont MS66 NGC. The upper obverse and lower reverse have charming mustard toning, and the remainder of the surfaces is brilliant. A pleasing piece with plenty of flashy luster. NGC has only certified 20 coins finer (8/08). (#9401)

1229 1927 Vermont MS66 PCGS. A sharply struck example of the impressive high relief Vermont Sesquicentennial half dollar. Peppered charcoal and rose toning in the recesses accent the silver-gray remainder. Delightful satiny luster enhances the eye appeal of this impeccably preserved specimen. (#9401)

1230 1927 Vermont MS66 PCGS. The green-gold toning that covers much of the right half of the obverse consumes the reverse. Pleasingly lustrous with solid detail for the issue. PCGS has graded 21 finer examples (8/08). (#9401)

Vividly Toned MS67 1927 Vermont Half

1231 1927 Vermont MS67 PCGS. Linking the lynx on the reverse of the Vermont half with the Catamount Tavern, a famous meeting place for revolutionaries of that state, and thence to Ira Allen and the Green Mountain Boys proved too much for many numismatists, and the visual pun goes down as one of the most obscure in American commemorative history. The practically flawless surfaces display powerful luster beneath dappled russet and apple-green toning on the obverse, though such patina appears only at the margins on the reverse. This highly appealing piece is tied for the finest certified by PCGS and is housed in a first-generation holder (8/08).
Ex: New York Signature (Heritage, 7/2002), lot 5115; Cary & Cheryl Porter Collection (Heritage, 5/2007), lot 2633. (#9401)

1232 1946-S Booker T. Washington MS67 PCGS. Intense amber, gold, lilac, and emerald toning on each side of this Superb Gem masks the frosty luster. The virtually pristine surfaces are nearly flawless, and even Washington's face is free of the usual heavy marks. PCGS has certified none finer (7/08). (#9406)

1233 1946-S Booker T. Washington MS67 NGC. CAC. Deep amber toning surrounds the slate-gray and ruby centers. The dramatic colors are highlighted by the outstanding satiny luster that flows across the surfaces. This sharply struck Superb Gem has only microscopic imperfections, none of which affect the impressive eye appeal. (#9406)

1234 1946-S Booker T. Washington MS67 PCGS. Remarkable sea-green, rose-red, and golden-brown embraces this lustrous and exceptionally preserved Superb Gem. Better struck than is customary for the type, with only a hint of planchet striations above the jaw. A lovely piece from the initial year of the six-year Booker T. Washington program. (#9406)

1235 1947-S Booker T. Washington MS67 NGC. This mostly brilliant and fully struck Superb Gem exhibits powerful satiny luster on both sides. A few tiny maroon toning dots on the reverse accent the bright silver-gray surfaces. The fields are virtually pristine, and several microscopic abrasions on Washington's cheek and the memorial preclude an even higher grade. Neither NGC nor PCGS have certified any pieces finer (7/08). A splendid example of this popular commemorative. (#9410)

1236 1948-S Booker T. Washington MS67 NGC. Essentially untoned with as sharp a strike as this cataloger has seen on a BTW half. Carefully preserved and impressive. NGC has graded only one numerically finer piece (8/08). (#9414)

1237 1949-S Booker T. Washington MS67 NGC. Brilliant aside from a dash or two of autumn-gold along the right obverse margin. Highly lustrous, unmarked, and the strike is above average. A scant 6,004 pieces were struck, with the extra four pieces presumably destined for assay. (#9418)

1238 1950 Booker T. Washington MS67 NGC. A veneer of champagne-gold color is slightly deeper at the margins, where it is joined by freckles of russet. A sharply struck piece, with no mentionable marks. (#9420)

1239 1950-S Booker T. Washington MS67 NGC. Peppered hazel toning around the rims accents the untoned and frosty centers. Several insignificant marks become visible under a loupe, but otherwise the surfaces are pleasantly smooth. A lustrous and handsome representative of this popular commemorative. (#9422)

1240 1951-S Booker T. Washington MS67 PCGS. The surfaces of this Superb Gem are brilliant in the centers, with glints of gold and amber near the rims on each side. A couple of trivial marks in the reverse fields are consistent with the grade. Tied for the finest certified by either NGC or PCGS (8/08). (#9426)

1241 1953 Washington-Carver MS66 PCGS. The popular Washington/Carver half dollar was the final commemorative of the classic series, and the 1953 had the lowest distribution (8,003 pieces) of all four years. This razor-sharp Premium Gem has a few grade-defining handling marks on the devices, but none are significant. Enticing satiny luster gives this brilliant piece great eye appeal. Population: 36 in 66, 0 finer (7/08). (#9438)

1242 1936 York MS68 NGC. The 1936 York commemorative is one of the few silver commemoratives that can be occasionally encountered in this "Superb Gem Plus" certified grade. Of the more than 200,000 silver commemoratives that NGC has certified, currently 648, or about one-quarter of 1%, are MS68s, and many series issues show only one or two MS68s certified, at most. The York, on the other hand, has 50 examples in this grade. The present example boasts splendid luster over silver centers, with the rims deeply toned in ocher, amber, and fuchsia. (#9449)

COMMEMORATIVE GOLD

Pretty Near-Gem 1903
Louisiana Purchase/Jefferson Gold Dollar

1243 1903 Louisiana Purchase/Jefferson MS64 PCGS. A single curving contact mark on Jefferson's cheek is all that likely limits the grade on this nonetheless-pretty near-Gem, with orange-gold coloration accenting tinges of hazel on the high points. This boldly struck commemorative gold piece is certified in a green-label holder. (#7443)

Deeply Patinated 1903 Louisiana Purchase/Jefferson
Gold Dollar, MS65

1244 1903 Louisiana Purchase/Jefferson MS65 PCGS. The pumpkin-gold centers are framed by olive and powder-blue tints. A sharply struck and fully lustrous Gem. The first appearance of the third President on a U.S. coin. Jefferson later appeared on the Jefferson Nickel, the 1991 Mount Rushmore commemoratives, the 1993 Monticello dollar, and the 2007 Jefferson Presidential dollar. (#7443)

Exquisite 1903 Jefferson Gold Dollar, MS66

1245 **1903 Louisiana Purchase/Jefferson MS66 PCGS.** Beautiful lime-green and orange toning alternates across this highly lustrous and razor-sharp Premium Gem. Well preserved despite a brief hair-thin mark beneath the first T in STATES. Scarce in such outstanding quality, and certain to grace a high grade collection of gold commemoratives. (#7443)

1246 **1903 Louisiana Purchase/McKinley MS64 NGC.** Stunning brass-gold surfaces yield strong luster, and exhibit well struck devices. A couple of light reverse marks define the grade. (#7444)

Gem 1903 Louisiana Purchase/McKinley Gold Dollar

1247 **1903 Louisiana Purchase/McKinley MS65 NGC.** This lustrous canary-gold Gem example of the nation's first commemorative gold dollar displays an immaculate obverse and good eye appeal. The strike is exquisite save for slight softness on the HA in PURCHASE, and it is apparently only a couple of tiny contact marks nearby that keep this coin from an even finer grade (8/08). (#7444)

Remarkable 1903 Louisiana Purchase/McKinley Gold Dollar, Premium Gem

1248 **1903 Louisiana Purchase/McKinley MS66 NGC.** Outstanding lemon-yellow patina embraces the virtually pristine surfaces. Eye-catching satiny luster enhances the eye appeal and complements the boldly struck details. An attractive representative of the first United States gold commemorative. One of a distribution of only 17,500 pieces. (#7444)

Gorgeous 1903 Louisiana Purchase/McKinley Dollar, MS66

1249 **1903 Louisiana Purchase/McKinley MS66 PCGS.** This gorgeously toned Premium Gem McKinley dollar displays yellow and orange-gold patina on the obverse, splashed with lavender and ice-blue, while the reverse is a medley of apricot and mint-green. Well preserved surfaces exhibit sharply struck design elements. Die polish lines are visible in the obverse fields. (#7444)

Wonderful MS66 1903 Louisiana Purchase/McKinley Gold Dollar

1250 **1903 Louisiana Purchase/McKinley MS66 PCGS.** The time was 1803. For a price of about $28 per square mile (4.5 cents an acre), the United States bought from France an area of 828,000 square miles. Doubling the United States in size, the purchase comprised basically all of the territory between the Mississippi River and the Rocky Mountains, an event known in America as the Louisiana Purchase—and in French as "*la vente de la Louisiane*," or "Louisiana sale."

To celebrate the centennial of this seminal event in U.S. history, the Mint in 1903 issued its first gold commemorative coin in two versions, one depicting Thomas Jefferson, president at the time of the purchase, the other portraying recently martyred President William McKinley. From the authorized mintage of 250,000 gold dollars between the two varieties, all but 17,500 of each were melted. This lustrous piece has wonderful golden-orange color with tinges of hazel. Tiny die cracks from the rim to peripheral letters are noted on each side. Certified in a green-label holder. (#7444)

Appealing 1904 Lewis and Clark Gem Gold Dollar

1251 **1904 Lewis and Clark MS65 NGC.** Apricot-gold surfaces are imbued with traces of light green, and display pleasing deep mint luster. This is a well struck and nicely cared for Gem that generates considerable eye appeal. As the first year of issue for the Lewis and Clark, the 1904 is considerably less expensive than its 1905 counterpart. (#7447)

Lustrous 1904 Lewis and Clark Gold Dollar MS66

1252 **1904 Lewis and Clark MS66 NGC.** A blazingly lustrous and scintillating peach-gold representative of this popular issue. As of (8/08), NGC has certified a scant 24 pieces at a higher technical grade. These Charles Barber-designed commemoratives are the only two-headed coins officially struck by a U.S. mint. Money generated from the sale of 1904 and 1905 Lewis and Clark gold dollars—together with donations for national women's organizations—financed the creation of a large bronze statue of Sacagawea for the Lewis and Clark Centennial Exposition in 1905. The statue proudly stands today in Portland, Oregon's Washington Park. (#7447)

1253 **1905 Lewis and Clark AU58 ICG.** Only a trace of friction affects the high points on this mildly reflective near-Mint survivor. An attractive and affordable lemon-gold representative of this famously challenging commemorative gold issue. (#7448)

1254 **1905 Lewis and Clark—Improperly Cleaned—NCS. Unc Details.** Lots of luster shines beneath the lovely yellow-gold patina. Although cleaning has given the fields an altered appearance, both sides show no prominent marks. This boldly struck piece is a relatively affordable example of this popular classic commemorative. (#7448)

Lovely 1905 Lewis and Clark Gold Dollar, MS63

1255 **1905 Lewis and Clark MS63 PCGS.** Both Lewis and Clark gold dollars had similar distributions of just over 10,000 pieces, although it is generally believed that the 1905 had a lower survival rate than its 1904 counterpart. A couple of tiny spots of verdigris are noted, but the surfaces are remarkably unabraded for the grade. Vibrant yellow patina covers both sides, with accents on rose-gold in the periphery. Pleasing satiny luster complements the sharply struck details. (#7448)

Pleasing Gem 1905 Lewis and Clark Dollar

Fantastic Gem 1905 Lewis and Clark Gold Dollar

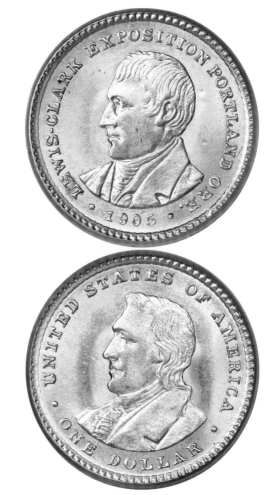

1256 **1905 Lewis and Clark MS65 NGC.** It is interesting to note that both NGC and PCGS have certified more 1905 Lewis and Clark gold dollars than examples dated 1904, although the population of Gem pieces—such as the current offering—is substantially lower for the 1905-dated commemoratives. The reason for this anomaly is likely due to the fact that the 1904 gold dollars, being the inaugural release, were saved with more fervor than the subsequent issue. This rose-gold representative boasts rich luster and pleasing surface quality. A minute toning spot is observed in the field adjacent to IC of AMERICA on Clark's side of the coin. As of (8/08), NGC has certified only 49 pieces at a finer designation. (#7448)

1257 **1905 Lewis and Clark MS65 PCGS.** Following the disappointing sales of the 1904-dated Lewis and Clark gold dollars, their promoter, Farran Zerbe, made the only logical move: he ordered thousands more strikings dated 1905. These sold even more poorly than their 1904 counterparts, many were melted, and high-end survivors are among the most prized classic gold commemoratives today. This solidly struck Gem has vibrant yellow-gold surfaces with a touch of flashiness. Minimally marked, even by the standards of the grade, with excellent eye appeal. PCGS has graded 70 finer examples (8/08). (#7448)

Memorable 1905 Lewis & Clark Dollar
MS66 Prooflike
Finest Certified by Two Grade Points

1258 **1905 Lewis & Clark MS66 Prooflike NGC.** The 1903 Louisiana Purchase gold dollars depicting Jefferson and McKinley, the first two commemorative gold U.S. coin issues, were followed in 1904 and 1905 by the Lewis and Clark Louisiana Purchase issues. The former commemorated the 100th anniversary of the actual land purchase from France, while the latter pieces commemorated the centenary of the two-year trek of Meriwether Lewis, William Clark, and the Corps of Discovery as they set out to explore the Missouri River and the Louisiana Territory, and to discover the mythic Northwest Passage. This distinction was apparently not sustainable enough to support the issue, and most were later melted, leading to a net mintage just over 10,000 of each issue, as compared to the 17,500 each of the 1903 Jefferson and McKinley gold dollars.

Today in the higher Mint State grades, the 1904 and 1905 Lewis and Clark issues show a huge price differential compared to the more-available 1903 pieces. But this is truly a *special coin*, as of the hundreds of Mint State 1905 Lewis & Clarks, NGC has certified only *nine pieces as Prooflike, and this is the finest of those by two grade points.* The orange-gold surfaces are expectedly abrasion-free on each side, and with the deep frost on the devices and highly mirrored fields, this piece could easily pass for a true proof. Only a loupe reveals its status as a circulation strike. A truly memorable coin. (#77448)

1259 **1915-S Panama-Pacific Gold Dollar MS64 PCGS.** An occasional wisp of copper-orange visits the yellow-gold surfaces of this near-Gem commemorative gold dollar. Well struck and nicely preserved. (#7449)

1260 **1915-S Panama-Pacific Gold Dollar MS64 NGC.** Scintillating luster radiates beneath the yellow-gold patina that drapes both sides. A few wispy abrasions are nearly imperceptible without a loupe. An appealing and boldly struck representative. (#7449)

1261 **1915-S Panama-Pacific Gold Dollar MS64 PCGS.** Wonderful buttery-gold patina covers this example, with pleasant lilac on the obverse devices. The outstanding color is further enhanced by the remarkably pristine surfaces. This spectacular gold commemorative had a distribution of only 15,000 pieces. (#7449)

1262 **1915-S Panama-Pacific Gold Dollar MS65 PCGS.** Smooth, softly lustrous butter-yellow surfaces show occasional golden variations. Solidly struck with hardly any flaws visible to the unaided eye. (#7449)

Exciting 1915-S Panama-Pacific Gold Dollar, MS66

1263 **1915-S Panama-Pacific Gold Dollar MS66 NGC.** The attractive design of this popular commemorative features the head of a canal laborer on the obverse along with two dolphins on the reverse, which signify the linking of the Atlantic and Pacific oceans. Charming apricot-gold patina endows the surfaces of this frosty Premium Gem. Both sides are nearly pristine and the eye appeal is excellent. (#7449)

Gorgeous 1915-S Panama-Pacific Gold Dollar, MS66 PCGS

1264 **1915-S Panama-Pacific Gold Dollar MS66 PCGS.** Sealed in an older green-label is this Premium Gem that exhibits light yellow-gold surfaces with splashes of copper toning and traces of pale green patina. PCGS has only graded 47 finer examples of this particular issue. Numismatist Farran Zerbe, master promoter of the early gold commemorative coins, issued four different denominations, including a massive $50 piece for the Exposition. (#7449)

Wonderful 1915-S Panama-Pacific Gold Dollar, MS66 NGC

1265 **1915-S Panama-Pacific Gold Dollar MS66 NGC. CAC.** Issued in connection with the Panama-Pacific Exposition in San Francisco, this fully brilliant Premium Gem exhibits wonderful lemon-yellow luster with attractive splashes of orange patina. NGC has only certified 50 finer examples of this issue (8/08). (#7449)

Luminous 1915-S Pan-Pac Quarter Eagle, MS62

1266 **1915-S Panama-Pacific Quarter Eagle MS62 NGC.** Luminous peach-gold surfaces display a few splashes of greenish-gray, and a well directed strike brings out strong definition on the design elements. A few minute marks on each side do not unduly detract. This is a rather nice piece for the grade designation. (#7450)

Extraordinary 1915-S Panama-Pacific $2.50, MS66

1267 **1915-S Panama-Pacific Quarter Eagle MS66 NGC. CAC.** A gorgeous Panama-Pacific quarter eagle, undoubtedly exactly what Farran Zerbe expected when he originally created his special four denomination series of coins for the Exposition that marked completion of the Panama Canal. Rich orange-gold luster with pristine, frosty surfaces. (#7450)

Amazing 1915-S Panama-Pacific Quarter Eagle, MS67

1268 **1915-S Panama-Pacific Quarter Eagle MS67 NGC.** Out of all the classic gold commemorative issues, only one, the 1922 Grant dollar, was the creation of a lady designer (Laura Gardin Fraser). Seven years earlier, in 1915, another artist, Evelyn Beatrice Longman of New York City, was awarded the commission to design the Panama-Pacific quarter eagle, but she fell ill and her ideas were abandoned at the sketch stage. In their place went a collaboration between Charles Barber and George T. Morgan, one of several among the nation's earliest commemoratives.

This strongly lustrous Superb Gem is primarily butter-yellow with hints of peach and rose close to the rims. Though Columbia's head shows a degree of softness, the overall preservation is wonderful, and the coin's visual appeal is a match. Tied for the numerically finest certified by NGC or PCGS (8/08). (#7450)

1269 1915-S Panama-Pacific 50 Dollar Round MS62 PCGS. The Panama-Pacific International Exposition, held in 1915 in San Francisco, was the product of many years of planning. New Orleans was the chief rival contending for the honor of hosting the expo, and it was four years before the expo started, in 1911, that President William Howard Taft named San Francisco as the host city.

While the "Panama" portion of the exposition is well-remembered today—a commemoration of the completion of the Panama Canal, linking for the first time the Eastern and Western Hemispheres—the "Pacific" portion of the name is sometimes forgotten. Of course the Panama Canal did join the Pacific with the Atlantic oceans, but the "Pacific" also referred to the 400th anniversary of the discovery of the Pacific Ocean by the navigator Vasco Nuñez de Balboa. The Panama-Pacific International Exposition in San Francisco ran from Feb. 20 through Dec. 4, 1915, on a 635-acre site near the present-day Marina, while the complementary but distinct Panama-California International Exposition in San Diego's 1,200-acre Balboa Park ran from March 9, 1915, until Jan. 1, 1917. The latter also touted San Diego's status as the first port of call for ships after their passage through the Panama Canal. Today Balboa Park in the latter city is the nation's largest urban cultural park, home to 15 major museums, performing arts venues, civic gardens, and the San Diego Zoo.

While the 1915-S Panama-Pacific commemorative coins are commonly associated only with the former (and due partly to their striking at the San Francisco Mint), the San Diego exposition has only so-called dollars to commemorate it, listed in the Hibler-Kappen reference as HK-426 through HK-434.

This example of the Panama-Pacific fifty dollar round commemorative displays wonderful luster radiating from the deep orange-gold-colored surfaces. This piece shows excellent eye appeal overall and there are few signs of visible contact. A couple of dark spots near the reverse rim, above the P in PANAMA, likely keep the coin from an even finer grade. A small reddish-colored area near the reverse rim at 6 o'clock appears to be an alloy spot. (#7451)

1270 **1915-S Panama-Pacific 50 Dollar Round MS64 NGC. CAC.** As described elsewhere herein, although outside sculptor-designers were engaged to model concepts for the various medals and coins proposed for the Panama-Pacific Exposition, Charles Barber ended up, rightly or wrongly, with some of the final designs. They include both sides of the half dollar and the obverse of the gold quarter eagle, with a figure of Columbia riding a seahorse through the waves and holding a caduceus. According to Taxay, "Assistant engraver George Morgan prepared the reverse, modeling one of his usual unsightly eagles. Regarding [Treasury Secretary William G.] McAdoo's objection to Minerva and Poseidon [originally proposed by Charles Keck for the gold dollar], it is noteworthy that Barber's own allegorical design was heartily approved."

Expediency was definitely a factor in the decisions—both those rejected and those approved—as the actual Panama-Pacific Exposition opened on Feb. 20, 1915, in San Francisco, and closed on Dec. 20 of that same year. President Woodrow Wilson, pressing a gold key in Arlington, Virginia, caused doors and mechanical exhibits at the San Francisco exposition to operate.

Only on March 22 were the final designs for the Panama-Pacific coinage approved—more than a month after the exposition had already opened. While numismatists of the present day can overlook the Pan-Pac half dollar design of Charles Barber in the company of so many other silver commemorative halves that came before and after, we can only thank our lucky stars that designer Robert Aitken's fifty dollar commemorative designs remained largely intact. Taxay says of the Barber commemorative, "Barber's half dollar depicts a figure of Columbia scattering flowers. Behind her is a child holding an overflowing cornucopia, in front the Golden Gate bridge surmounted by a setting sun. Though not unattractive, the design is indefinitely modeled and has an unfinished appearance. The reverse features an heraldic eagle and at best is commonplace."

Imagine if Barber had attempted to "dash off" a fifty dollar design in both round and octagonal versions. American numismatics would have lost one of the most unusual coinage designs ever executed. It is certainly appropriate to question whether the design is derivative rather than original, but there is little question about its superlative execution.

It is worth noting that designer Aitken also won the commission for the official medals of the Pan-Pac Exposition, now collected as so-called dollars, listed in Hibler-Kappen as HK-399 through HK-401, produced in silver, bronze, and gilt. On those medals a full-length, nude Mercury, sporting a winged hat (a la "Mercury" dime), opens the locks of the Panama Canal, with the ship *Argo*, the symbol of navigation, passing through and reflecting the setting sun off of her sails. On the reverse two female figures entwine about a globe, representing the joining of Earth's two hemispheres.

Finally, it must be noted that Aitken's wonderful designs not only continued, with their classical allusions, a renaissance that began with Augustus Saint-Gaudens' gold coinage designs in 1907, but, being struck in San Francisco, they also celebrated the renaissance of the "City by the Bay" itself and its recovery from the devastating Great Earthquake and Fire of less than a decade earlier.

The present specimen of the Round variety is actually somewhat rarer than the Octagonal pieces, due to greater meltings of the former after they remained unsold at the exposition. This piece offers bold cartwheel luster that is unusually rich for the issue, along with delightful yellow-gold coloration and a relative absence of distracting marks. A high-end and thoroughly delightful example. (#7451)

Remarkable Near-Gem 1915-S Panama-Pacific
Fifty Dollar Octagonal

1271 **1915-S Panama-Pacific 50 Dollar Octagonal MS64 NGC. CAC.** Due to the urgency with which coinage designs were needed for the various issues proposed for the Panama-Pacific Exposition, Mint Director George Roberts fortunately (and wisely) enlisted, with the approval of Treasury Secretary William G. McAdoo, the aid of the Commission of Fine Arts. The commission recommended various artists to submit sketches for different coins and medals, and the Mint engaged Robert Aitken to design the fifty dollar gold pieces, along with Charles Keck for the gold dollar, Evelyn Longman for the quarter eagle, and Paul Manship for the half dollar.

According to Don Taxay's useful *An Illustrated History of U.S. Commemorative Coinage,* Aitken wrote, in forwarding his preliminary designs to Acting Mint Director T.P. Dewey:

"Dear Sir: Enclosed please to find sketches for the obverse and reverse of the new Fifty-Dollar piece. They are so arranged as to show the application of the circular form to the octagonal.

"By way of an explanation of my design, permit me to state that in order to express in my design the fact that this coin is struck to commemorate the Panama-Pacific Exposition, and as the Exposition stands for all that Wisdom and Industry have produced, I have used as the central motive of the obverse the head of the virgin goddess Minerva. She is the goddess of wisdom, of skill, of contemplation, of spinning and of weaving, of horticulture and agriculture. Moreover she figures prominently upon the seal of the State of California. This head will make a beautiful pattern in the circle and the use of the Dolphins on the octagonal coin do much to add to its charm, as well as express the uninterrupted water route made possible by the Canal.

"Upon the reverse I use the owl, the bird sacred to Minerva, also the symbol of wisdom, perched upon a branch of western pine, behind which is seen the web of the spider, suggesting industry.

"With these simple symbols, all full of beauty in themselves, I feel that I have expressed the larger meaning of the Exposition, its appeal to the intellect.

"I trust that these designs will meet with the approval of the Secretary of the Treasury."

Unfortunately, they did not.

While the Fine Arts Commission approved the designs, Assistant Treasury Secretary William Malburn, reversing all previous governmental signals, recommended to Secretary McAdoo that the Treasury Department reject all submissions by "outside" artists. When the artists were so notified, the understandably shocked members of the Fine Arts Commission intervened, asking for specific critiques of the designs. Regarding the fifty dollar gold, McAdoo objected to the spider web, the appropriateness of the figure of Minerva (Pallas Athena), and the "floating dolphins."

A few days later Aitken submitted a revised design that did little more than remove the offending spider web behind the owl. Mint Engraver Charles Barber, ever eager to prove his capacity against superior outside talent, ended up designing the half dollar and one side of the quarter eagle, but Charles Keck, submitting radically revised designs, kept the one dollar gold. Despite the minor modifications to the fifty dollar gold (and undoubtedly with considerable behind-the-scenes intervention), the revised Aitken design was also approved, despite McAdoo's objections.

The present specimen is a wonderful realization of that design, with brilliant luster cascading from the surfaces, which are predominantly orange-gold on each side. Only under a loupe do a few minor contact marks appear, completely undistracting and not easily seen otherwise. The Aitken design is as remarkable and fresh today as it was when launched nearly a century ago (one wonders what the Mint will produce in the year 2015?), and this coin remains a remarkable representation of that historic aquatic event. (#7452)

1272 **1916 McKinley MS64 NGC.** Light terra cotta-orange toning and bold striking detail characterize this attractive near-Gem. There are no significant marks on either side of the coin. (#7454)

1273 **1916 McKinley MS64 PCGS.** Strong, satiny luster adds life to the butter-yellow and green-gold surfaces. A well struck Choice example that shows just a handful of scattered flaws. (#7454)

1274 **1916 McKinley MS65 PCGS.** Solidly struck with surprisingly flashy luster for a McKinley dollar. Yellow-gold at the centers and margins with circles of subtle green-gold visible between the two. (#7454)

Marvelous 1916 McKinley Gold Dollar, Premium Gem

1275 **1916 McKinley MS66 NGC.** McKinley gold dollars were struck in 1916 and 1917 to help finance the construction of a memorial to the slain president in his birthplace of Niles, Ohio. The 1916 had an distribution of approximately 15,000 pieces, which is about three times the number of pieces struck in 1917. Charming apricot-yellow patina endows the virtually pristine surfaces of the present example. Exquisite satiny luster shimmers from both sides and gives this piece great eye appeal. NGC reports just 59 finer examples (7/08). (#7454)

1276 **1917 McKinley MS61 ICG.** Surprisingly bright and reflective for a second-year McKinley dollar. The lemon-gold surfaces offer solid overall detail, and minor blemishes generally do not distract. (#7455)

1277 **1917 McKinley MS63 PCGS.** Warm sun-gold and yellow-gold shadings cede to green-gold within the columns of the memorial. Pleasingly detailed for this often-weak issue with only wispy abrasions. (#7455)

Bright MS65 1917 McKinley Gold Dollar

1278 **1917 McKinley MS65 NGC.** The buttery-gold surfaces display crisply struck design features and pleasing satin luster. Distracting marks or blemishes are not found on either side of the coin. The McKinley commemorative gold dollars of 1916 and 1917 were intended to help defray the cost of constructing a McKinley birthplace memorial in the assassinated president's hometown of Niles, Ohio. (#7455)

Attractive Premium Gem 1922 Grant no Star Dollar

1279 **1922 Grant no Star MS66 NGC.** In the higher grades of Mint State, the Grant no Star is among the more available issues, although in terms of absolute numbers the 1915-S is probably the most frequently seen. This attractive Premium Gem Grant no Star offers lustrous yellow-gold surfaces with good eye appeal. Relatively few contact marks appear, even under a loupe. (#7458)

Splendid 1922 Grant With Star Gold Dollar, MS64

1280 **1922 Grant with Star MS64 NGC.** An affordable Grant Star gold dollar is combined with exceptional quality for the grade to present a good value. This piece has amazing lemon-yellow luster with stunning design features. This was the final commemorative gold dollar issued at the Mint. (#7459)

Popular 1922 Grant With Star Gold Dollar, MS66

1281 **1922 Grant with Star MS66 PCGS.** Both sides of this popular issue are awash with full luster, and draped with peach-gold patina with light green undertones. An attentive strike delivers nice definition to the design elements. The With Star is scarcer than its Without Star counterpart. (#7459)

Premium Gem 1922 Grant With Star Gold Dollar

1282 1922 Grant with Star MS66 PCGS. This Premium Gem 1922 Grant Star gold dollar is housed in an older generation green-label PCGS holder, and it appears to be remarkable quality for the grade. Grant half dollars and Grant gold dollars were both coined in two varieties, with identical designs (except the denomination) on each. (#7459)

1283 1926 Sesquicentennial MS63 NGC. A satiny and lustrous Select example of this commemorative gold quarter eagle, from a celebration of the 150th anniversary of the United States. There are a couple of small abrasions on each side, but the overall appearance of the piece is quite attractive for the grade. (#7466)

1284 1926 Sesquicentennial MS64 PCGS. Splendid apricot-gold patina covers the surfaces of this attractive and popular commemorative. A couple of pinprick-sized marks preclude a Gem designation, but the impressive luster adds to the eye appeal. (#7466)

1285 1926 Sesquicentennial MS64 PCGS. Magnificent yellow-orange patina drapes the surfaces of this carefully preserved Choice specimen. Although these pieces are typically soft because they were struck in such low relief, this example has above-average definition throughout. Several minor grazes are noted, but they barely affect the delightful luster. (#7466)

1286 1926 Sesquicentennial MS64 PCGS. Dazzling luster radiates from each side of this near-Gem Sesqui commemorative. Peach-gold surfaces reveal a few minute obverse marks. Well struck throughout. (#7466)

1287 1926 Sesquicentennial MS64 PCGS. Uncharacteristically strong luster is the most impressive element of this Choice Sesquicentennial quarter eagle. Boldly struck with a hint of frostiness on the high points. (#7466)

1288 1926 Sesquicentennial MS64 PCGS. Rich orange-gold coloration shows occasional hints of honey. Spectacular strike and luster, though a handful of tiny marks on each side preclude Gem status. (#7466)

1289 1926 Sesquicentennial MS64 NGC. Remarkable luster sparkles beneath the charming apricot-gold patina that covers both sides. This decisively struck specimen has no prominent abrasions on either side and exhibits great eye appeal. (#7466)

1290 1926 Sesquicentennial MS64 PCGS. An appealing near-Gem with a very balanced appearance between the obverse and the reverse. Satiny and well preserved, with nice yellow-gold and rose toning. (#7466)

1291 1926 Sesquicentennial MS64 NGC. CAC. The luminous orange-gold surfaces offer strong, satiny luster. A well-defined piece that shows only a handful of minor flaws scattered in the fields. (#7466)

1292 1926 Sesquicentennial MS64 PCGS. Vibrantly lustrous yellow-gold surfaces offer occasional elements of honey. Well-preserved for the grade, if a trifle softly struck on the high points. (#7466)

1293 1926 Sesquicentennial MS64 NGC. Lustrous peach-gold surfaces are laced with tints of light green, and exhibit well struck devices. A handful of obverse marks limits the grade. (#7466)

1294 1926 Sesquicentennial MS64 PCGS. Primarily yellow-gold with a degree of green-gold on either side of Independence Hall. Immensely lustrous with strong eye appeal, though a handful of trivial faults preclude Gem status. (#7466)

Gem 1926 Sesquicentennial Two and a Half

1295 1926 Sesquicentennial MS65 NGC. It is difficult to believe that the quarter-millennium mark of American independence is only 18 years away, in the year 2026. And yet so it is. Perhaps the 1926 Sesquicentennial quarter eagle will be more popular at that time than it was when issued. Of the authorized maximum mintage of 200,000 coins—and despite the patriotic portrayal of Independence Hall and a modern, stylized Liberty—more than 150,000 examples of the production were melted. This piece offers radiant luster emanating from orange-gold surfaces, with lots of eye appeal. (#7466)

Splendid Gem 1926 Sesquicentennial Quarter Eagle

1296 1926 Sesquicentennial MS65 NGC. The low-relief design of the 1926 Sesquicentennial quarter eagles and half dollars made them unpopular at the time, and today both issues are difficult to grade and seldom found at the Gem level. This coin offers splendidly lustrous orange-gold surfaces that are remarkably free of the numerous ticks and abrasions that so frequently plague the issue. (#7466)

Eye-Catching 1926 Sesquicentennial Quarter Eagle, MS65

1297 1926 Sesquicentennial MS65 PCGS. Commemorative half dollars and quarter eagles were issued to help finance a celebration in Philadelphia of the 150th anniversary of the Declaration of Independence. John R. Sinnock, who would later model the Roosevelt dime, designed these popular pieces. This apricot-gold Gem exhibits dazzling satiny luster with accents of rose and olive in the fields. Crisply struck and housed in a green label PCGS holder. (#7466)

Astounding 1926 Sesquicentennial Quarter Eagle, MS66 ★

Impressive 1926 Sesquicentennial Quarter Eagle, MS66

1298 **1926 Sesquicentennial MS66 ★ NGC.** Only five 1926 Sesquicentennial quarter eagle commemoratives have been awarded the coveted ★ designation by NGC, with the finest being two MS66 specimens, and without the ★ notation, only three have been certified at a higher level—those being MS67 examples (8/08). NGC will only bestow a ★ upon those coins that display exceptional eye appeal for the assigned grade and the current offering is undeniably deserving of the distinction. Rich, apricot-gold coloration is brought to life by blazingly lustrous surfaces. Considering the aesthetically pleasing qualities of this coin, serious collectors must ask the question: which is more desirable—an MS67 piece or an astounding MS66 ★ specimen? (#7466)

1299 **1926 Sesquicentennial MS66 PCGS.** As the nation celebrated its 150th anniversary, a great celebration was held in Philadelphia, with commemorative half dollars and quarter eagles minted as souvenirs. With high expectations, the Congressional legislation for these coins far exceeded the actual demand. A total of 1 million half dollars and 200,000 quarter eagles were authorized, and the entire quantity of each was actually struck at the Philadelphia Mint, yet only 141,120 half dollars, and 46,019 quarter eagles were distributed, including a small number of each that were examined by the Assay Commission early the next year.

This piece, tied for the finest Sesquicentennial quarter eagles certified by PCGS (8/08), has sharp design features with creamy yellow-gold luster and faint rose highlights. A few barely perceptible surface marks are evident on each side. (#7466)

Rare and Impressive 1903 Jefferson Gold Dollar
Superb Proof Ultra Cameo

1300 **1903 Jefferson PR67 Ultra Cameo NGC.** Two different gold commemoratives were struck to help offset the cost of the Louisiana Purchase Exposition, which was held in St. Louis to celebrate the 100th anniversary of this monumental event. Although the anniversary actually took place in 1903, hence the date on each of these pieces, the fair was delayed until the next year because of the enormity of the undertaking. These pieces hold the distinction of being the first gold commemoratives struck by the United States. While both varieties feature a common reverse, one has a bust of Thomas Jefferson, who was president at the time of the Louisiana Purchase, and the other depicts William McKinley, who sanctioned the event.

Attractive yellow-gold patina drapes the surfaces of this carefully preserved specimen. The devices have a splendid frost, which shows outstanding cameo contrast against the deeply mirrored fields. Close inspection with a loupe reveals only a couple of nearly imperceptible handling marks. This dazzling piece has tremendous eye appeal and would suit even the most discerning eye.

Each of the two types had a total distribution of 17,500 pieces and were offered for sale to collectors or attendees of the exposition. The first 100 pieces of each variety were proofs and, rather than being sold, they were given to important individuals and officials. PCGS has certified only 33 proof Jefferson specimens, of which just two have been certified as Cameo. NGC reports a total of 25 proof Jefferson dollars in all grades, and only five have received the coveted Ultra Cameo designation. A mere two examples have been certified in PR67 Ultra Cameo, and neither grading service reports any finer (8/08). (#97482)

MODERN ISSUES

1301 **1996-W Smithsonian Gold Five Dollar MS69 PCGS.** Orange and lemon-yellow patina intermingle on this carefully preserved specimen. With a mintage of just 9,068 pieces, the Smithsonian half eagle is one of the more elusive modern commemoratives. (#9744)

1302 **Four-Piece 1997 Jackie Robinson Commemorative Set.** This Uncertified set includes the key date Uncirculated 1997-W gold five dollar; a proof 1997-W gold five dollar; an Uncirculated 1997-S silver dollar; and a proof 1997-S silver dollar. The coins are housed in the box and case of mint issue, and the certificate of authenticity accompanies. (Total: 4 coins)

MS69 1997-W Jackie Robinson Half Eagle

1303 **1997-W Jackie Robinson Gold Five Dollar MS69 PCGS.** The key date of the modern commemorative series. It seems that buyers concentrated on proofs, which are comparatively available, while the Uncirculated finish was neglected by collectors. Only 5,174 pieces were sold. This sun-gold Superb Gem is intricately struck, and flawless aside from a trivial graze on the cheekbone. (#9759)

Beautiful 1997-W Jackie Robinson Five Dollar, MS69

1304 **1997-W Jackie Robinson Gold Five Dollar MS69 PCGS.** With its mintage of 5,174 pieces (per the 2009 *Guide Book*), the Jackie Robinson five dollar gold in Uncirculated format has emerged as the key to the modern gold commemorative series. This highly lustrous example displays a blend of yellow and orange-gold color, and reveals immaculately preserved surfaces. A powerful strike results in complete definition on the design features. (#9759)

1305 **1997-W Jackie Robinson Gold Five Dollar MS70 NGC.** Ex: U.S. Vault Collection. The famous key issue of the modern commemorative series. Although the proof version has a reasonable mintage, the Uncirculated finish Jackie Robinson five had a net production of just 5,174 pieces. This shimmering example is perfect aside from a pinpoint flake within the baseball above the O in OF. (#9759)

1306 **1997 Jackie Robinson Four Piece Set** The four piece Mint issued set of Jackie Robinson commemorative coins includes Uncirculated and Proof examples of the silver dollar and the five-dollar gold piece. These are as struck, and housed in the original custom velveteen case, with the outer box and certificate. (Total: 4 coins)

1307 **2000-W Library of Congress Bimetallic Ten Dollars MS69 PCGS.** This distinctive piece features a platinum center enclosed in a ring of yellow-gold, and is the first and only bimetallic commemorative issue by the United States. Careful examination under a loupe yields no answer as to why this piece was not graded MS70. (#9784)

1308 **2000-W Library of Congress Bimetallic Ten Dollars MS69 PCGS.** A virtually immaculate, thoroughly frosted piece. In addition to being the lone bimetallic commemorative, this piece also features a peculiar eagle on the reverse, which has fanlike wings as opposed to feathers. (#9784)

1309 **2000-W Library of Congress Bimetallic Ten Dollars MS69 ICG.** A well-defined representative of this distinctive bimetallic issue with the satiny surfaces associated with the Mint State finish. No marks are perceptible to the unaided eye. (#9784)

MS70 2000-W Library of Congress Ten

1310 **2000-W Library of Congress Bimetallic Ten Dollars MS70 NGC.** Ex: U.S. Vault Collection. The 2000-W Library of Congress is currently the sole bimetallic U.S. type, and has an outer ring of gold and an inner platinum inset. Sales of the Uncirculated finish were low, limited to 7,261 pieces. This exemplary example has flawless satin surfaces and a needle-sharp strike. (#9784)

1311 **2000-W Library of Congress PR69 Deep Cameo PCGS.** A gorgeous butter-yellow ring surrounds the brilliant platinum inner disk. Tremendous cameo contrast is created between the deeply mirrored fields and frosty devices. A couple of microscopic lint marks keep this attractive piece from being absolutely perfect. (#99784)

1312 **2000-W Library of Congress PR69 Deep Cameo PCGS.** This popular bimetallic commemorative has a magnificent cameo appearance and tremendous eye appeal. Even under magnification it is difficult to locate whatever tiny imperfection that keeps this piece from MS70. (#99784)

1313 **2001-W Capitol Visitor's Center Half Eagle MS69 PCGS.** The Capitol Visitor Center half eagle had a distribution of just 6,781 Mint State-finish pieces, which ranks it among the least available modern commemoratives. This nearly perfect, bright yellow specimen exudes satiny luster and has spectacular eye appeal. (#9792)

1314 **2001-W Capitol Visitor's Center Half Eagle MS69 PCGS.** Satiny, smooth, and seemingly pristine surfaces are brassy-gold and yield exquisitely struck design elements. These lovely pieces were minted to finance the construction of a Capitol Visitor Center in Washington, D.C. (#9792)

MODERN BULLION COINS

1315 **1986-S Silver Eagle PR70 Ultra Cameo NGC.** A technically perfect exemplar from the first of the proof silver American Eagle issues. The fields offer absolute reflectivity, and the silver-white frost of the devices is unusually creamy. (#9802)

1316 **1986-W $50 One-Ounce Gold Eagle PR69 Ultra Cameo NGC,** flawless; **1987-P $25 Half-Ounce Gold Eagle PR69 Ultra Cameo NGC,** exquisite; **1987-W $50 One-Ounce Gold Eagle PR69 Ultra Cameo NGC,** fully struck; **1988-P Tenth-Ounce Gold Eagle PR69 Ultra Cameo NGC,** beautiful; **1988-P Quarter-Ounce Gold Eagle PR69 Ultra Cameo NGC,** gorgeous; **1988-P $25 Half-Ounce Gold Eagle PR69 Ultra Cameo NGC,** essentially perfect; **1988-W $50 One-Ounce Gold Eagle PR69 Ultra Cameo NGC,** magnificent; **1989-P Tenth-Ounce Gold Eagle PR69 Ultra Cameo NGC,** only minute imperfections; **1989-P Quarter-Ounce Gold Eagle PR69 Ultra Cameo NGC,** a few pinpoint flaws; **1989-P $25 Half-Ounce Gold Eagle PR69 Ultra Cameo NGC,** outstanding; and a **1989-W $50 One-Ounce Gold Eagle PR69 Ultra Cameo NGC,** pristine. (Total: 11 coins)

1317 **1987-S Silver Eagle PR70 Ultra Cameo NGC.** Technically perfect, with enticing frosted devices that have spectacular contrast against the deeply mirrored and flawless fields. A gorgeous representative of the second year of the Silver Eagle bullion series. (#9809)

1318 **1987-S Silver Eagle PR70 Ultra Cameo NGC.** A starkly contrasted, utterly unimpeachable example of this earlier proof silver American Eagle issue. The mirrors on each side are flawless and deep, and the richly frosted devices are exactingly struck. (#9809)

1319 **1993-P Silver Eagle PR70 Ultra Cameo NGC.** A flawless, beautifully contrasted example of this popular proof Philadelphia silver American Eagle issue. The broad fields offer absolute reflectivity. (#9867)

1320 **1994-P Silver Eagle PR70 Ultra Cameo NGC.** An entirely pristine specimen with watery and unblemished fields that create an eye-catching cameo contrast against the frosted devices. This appealing piece is the pinnacle of perfection. (#9877)

1321 **1994-P Silver Eagle PR70 Ultra Cameo NGC.** No amount of searching will turn up a perceptible flaw on this amazing 1994-P proof. It offers spectacular reflectivity and contrast with eye appeal to match. (#9877)

1322 **1994-P Silver Eagle PR70 Ultra Cameo NGC.** Outstanding reflectivity in the flawless fields and magnificent visual appeal. Rich frost on the crisply struck central devices supplies spectacular contrast on each side. (#9877)

Breathtaking 1995-W Silver Eagle, PR69
Part of a Five-Piece American Eagle Set

1323 **1995-W Five-Piece Proof Set PR69 PCGS.** The main attraction (pictured) is the **1995-W One-Ounce Silver American Eagle,** which offers breathtaking white-on-black contrast. A powerful strike lends bold definition to the design elements, which along with immaculately preserved surfaces, enhances the coin's eye appeal. The proof-only issue saw only 30,125 pieces struck. Housed in a green-label holder.

Also included are the four corresponding gold American Eagle issues of the same year, each graded PR69 Deep Cameo: the **tenth-ounce, quarter-ounce, half-ounce,** and **one-ounce.** (#9887)

Impressive 1995-W Silver Eagle, PR69 Deep Cameo

1324 **1995-W Silver Eagle PR69 Deep Cameo PCGS.** The 1995-W was the first Silver Eagle struck at West Point and remains the only issue to feature the W mintmark. With a mintage of just 30,125 pieces, many multiples below the typical Silver Eagle, the 1995-W is easily the key issue in the series. Impressive black and white cameo contrast gives this virtually flawless piece spectacular eye appeal. (#9887)

1325 **2005-W Platinum Eagle Set PR70 Ultra Cameo NGC.** The set includes the **tenth-ounce $10, quarter-ounce $25, half-ounce $50, and one-ounce $100.** Housed in separate NGC holders bearing the ultimate grade. All four pieces appear immaculate and exhibit unimprovable cameo contrast. (Total: 4 coins)

1326 **Four-Piece 2005-W Platinum Eagle Proof Set.** The tenth-ounce $10, quarter-ounce $25, half-ounce $50, and one-ounce $100 proof 2005-W platinum eagles appear immaculate. The coins are Uncertified, and reside in the box and case of Treasury issue. The certificate of authenticity is absent. (Total: 4 coins)

1327 **2006-P Reverse Proof Silver Eagle, 20th Anniversary PR70 PCGS.** A numerically perfect and breathtaking proof, featuring the unusual reverse finish that was used only for the 20th anniversary of U.S. bullion coins. Close examination shows a couple of wispy patches of tan toning in the right obverse field of this otherwise brilliant specimen. (#799977)

1328 **2006-W One-Ounce Gold Eagle Reverse Proof PR70 NGC.** Certified by NGC with a special Gold Eagle 20th anniversary insert. This immaculate specimen has the distinctive reverse finish, with heavily polished devices and frosted fields. A low distribution issue that was originally sold only as part of a three-piece set. (#89994)

1329 **2006-W One-Ounce Gold Eagle Reverse Proof PR70 NGC.** The 20th Anniversary gold American Eagles included the striking reverse proof one-ounce pieces, such as the present coin. The central devices gleam, the fields show excellent frost, and nary a flaw is present. (#89994)

1330 **2006-W One-Ounce Gold Eagle Reverse Proof PR70 NGC.** A flawless piece with absolute contrast between the high sheen of the central devices and the finely granular frost of the fields. Appealing and noteworthy. (#89994)

1331 **2006-W 20th Anniversary One-Ounce Gold Reverse Proof PR70 PCGS.** "First Strike." A technically perfect exemplar that displays absolute contrast between the frost of the fields and the startling brilliance of the devices. Notable and attractive. (#89995)

1332 **2006-W Buffalo One-Ounce Gold PR70 Deep Cameo PCGS.** A perfect representative of this popular bullion piece, which was the first American coin struck in .9999 fine gold. James Earle Fraser's Buffalo nickel design has been reproduced with impressive precision, and it even has the distinctive orange-peel texture in the fields that was seen on the first 1913 issues. The frosted devices and deeply mirrored fields give this specimen an outstanding cameo appearance. (#9990)

1333 **2006-W Platinum American Eagle Uncirculated Set.** This four-piece set is uncertified in the original box of issue with outer casing and literature. The quality of the coins, which show the year's reverse with classical Liberty seated and writing with eagles perched atop columns on either side, is uniformly excellent. (Total: 4 coins)

1334 **2007-W One-Ounce Gold Eagle MS70 PCGS.** Splendid mint frost overlies the pleasing butter-yellow surfaces of this utterly flawless representative. The obverse of this attractive piece features Augustus Saint-Gaudens' famous design for the double eagle that debuted in 1907. (#150432)

1335 **2007-W One-Ounce Platinum Eagle MS70 PCGS.** A technically perfect, vividly frosted, and attractive Platinum Eagle. Pale gray toning covers both sides, and a careful inspection with a loupe locates no marks or blemishes. (#150439)

1336 **Two 2007-W 10th Anniversary Half-Ounce Platinum American Eagles.** The two pieces are housed in a foam-lined tray in cherrywood-simulating plastic with brass-finish accents and magnetic clasp. Includes the **2007-W Reverse Proof Half-Ounce Platinum American Eagle PR70** and the **2007-W Half-Ounce Platinum American Eagle PR70 Ultra Cameo,** each technically perfect with remarkable field-device contrast. A fascinating study in opposites. (Total: 2 coins)

1337 **2007-W One-Ounce Platinum Eagle PR70 Deep Cameo PCGS.** This remarkable specimen appears flawless in every respect. The spectacular eye appeal is enhanced by the vivid cameo contrast between the deeply mirrored fields and icy-frosted devices. (#149579)

1338 **2007-W One-Ounce Platinum Eagle PR70 Ultra Cameo NGC.** The deeply mirrored fields appear black under a lamp and create a startling cameo appearance with the snow-white frosted devices. Both sides appear perfect, even with the aid of a glass. (#149579)

CALIFORNIA FRACTIONAL GOLD

1339 **1854 Liberty Octagonal 25 Cents, BG-104, R.4, MS63 PCGS.** The obverse is prooflike, and the reverse field is nearly as flashy. Crisply impressed and attractive. Faint handling beneath the date requires a loupe to locate. Certified in a green label holder. Population: 14 in 63, 15 finer (7/08).
From The Hamous Collection of California Gold. (#10373)

Lovely, High Grade (MS63) 1852-3 Narrow Head Quarter Round Liberty Head, BG-201, High R.7

1340 **Undated Liberty Round 25 Cents, BG-201, High R.7, MS63 PCGS.** This is a part of a string of controversial 1852-3 Narrow Head quarters. Generally attributed to Joseph Brothers, but there is no clear indication that these were made by that company or Frontier, Deviercy & Co. Either the BG-201 or 202 were referred to in the *Sacramento Daily Union* on April 29, 1853 as having "lately" appeared in circulation. The BG reference notes that this variety was discovered by Kenneth W. Lee before 1970. The obverse stars are from a punch with one broken point, and many of the stars are double punched. BG lists six coins, ranging from MS63 to a plugged (and presumably circulated) piece. Of those pieces listed, this is most likely the # 2 piece, only identified as "Another coin certified by PCGS as MS-63." The surfaces are bright yellow-gold with semiprooflikeness on the obverse only. Identifiable by an irregular planchet flake out of the obverse near the rim at 4 o'clock. The Jay Roe specimen graded MS62 and brought $9775 in Bowers' 2003 sale of his collection. (#10386)

1341 1854 Liberty Round 25 Cents, BG-216, R.6, MS62 PCGS. Lovely deep orange toning graces this unabraded and evenly struck fractional gold piece. The surfaces are granular because of the die preparation, which also weakened portions of the reverse legends. Housed in a green label holder. Population: 8 in 62, 8 finer (7/08). *Ex: Superior, 5/1995, lot 3874.*
From The Hamous Collection of California Gold. (#10401)

Near-Mint State 1853 Peacock Reverse
Octagonal Half Dollar, BG-302

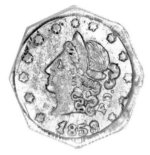

1342 1853 Peacock Reverse 50 Cents, BG-302, Low R.4, AU58 PCGS. Considerable die rust marks this as a Die State II piece, and the minor circulation evident on this piece is consistent with its stint in commerce during the historic 1850s Gold Rush in California. Unlike many later issues, this issue served for making change during the recurring shortages of minor coins of the era. There is a retained rim cud joining the star behind Liberty's head. Some luster remains on the golden-smoky surfaces. (#10422)

Famous Peacock Reverse 1853 Octagonal Half
BG-302, Borderline Uncirculated

1343 1853 Peacock Reverse 50 Cents, BG-302, Low R.4, AU58 PCGS. A popular variety due to the reverse design, which depicts an eagle with glory rays reminiscent of a peacock. The rays may be a reference to those seen on Federal 1853 quarters and half dollars. This is a lustrous and well struck green-gold piece with smooth surfaces and little indication of actual wear. Encapsulated in a green label holder.
From The Hamous Collection of California Gold. (#10422)

Exotic Peacock Reverse BG-302
1853 Octagonal Half MS62

1344 1853 Peacock Reverse 50 Cents, BG-302, Low R.4, MS62 PCGS. The charming 'Peacock' reverse subtype, distinctive from the lengthy parade of wreaths that occupy the majority of California small denomination gold reverses. This canary-gold example has moderately mirrored fields and a consistent strike. Population: 18 in 62, 39 finer (8/08). (#10422)

Lustrous 1853 Peacock Reverse
Octagonal Half, BG-302, MS63

1345 1853 Peacock Reverse 50 Cents, BG-302, Low R.4, MS63 PCGS. An example of the popular Peacock reverse, struck by Frontier, Deviercy & Co. and in a finer grade than usually seen, as this is one of those pieces that actually filled in for change-making during the California Gold Rush. The lustrous surfaces show pretty yellow-gold color and are Die State I, with extra outlines around the 50 and T in CENTS that fade with time. Population: 25 in 63, 14 finer (8/08). (#10422)

Pleasing 1853 Peacock Reverse
Half Dollar Gold Fractional, BG-302, MS63

1346 1853 Peacock Reverse 50 Cents, BG-302, Low R.4, MS63 PCGS. The famous "Peacock" reverse was possibly made to mimic the federal coins that were struck with rays that year. A small blemish on the reverse minimally affects the appeal of this yellow-gold and lustrous representative. Numerous die rust spots indicate that this piece is Die State II. Encapsulated in a green label PCGS holder.
Ex: Harold Rothenberger Collection (Superior, 1/31-2/1/1994), lot 2803.
From The Hamous Collection of California Gold. (#10422)

Very Rare Peacock Reverse BG-303
1853 Octagonal Half AU58

Key Date 1853 Round Half Dollar
BG-435, MS62

1347   **1853 Peacock Reverse 50 Cents, BG-303, Low R.7, AU58 NGC.**
A very rare variety of the popular Peacock reverse subtype. The F.D.
initials (for Frontier and Deviercy) are located above the date rather
than beneath the hair bun, although die lapping has weakened the
initials and date. A satiny near-Mint example with original olive,
peach, and ruby-red toning. Unabraded and problem-free. Census: 1
in 58, 1 finer (7/08).
From The Hamous Collection of California Gold. (#10423)

1348   **1854 Liberty Octagonal 50 Cents, BG-306, R.4, MS64 PCGS.**
Distinctly reflective yellow-gold fields supply a degree of contrast
with the devices. Well struck for the issue with a degree of trifling
haze on the reverse. (#10426)

1349   **1854 Liberty Octagonal 50 Cents, BG-306, R.4, MS65 PCGS.** A
beautiful Gem that has dazzling mirrored fields and a precise strike.
A pass beneath a loupe fails to locate marks. The central portion
of the portrait has missing detail due to a lapped die, as made.
Population: 4 in 65, 1 finer (8/08). (#10426)

1350   **1853 Liberty Round 50 Cents, BG-408, R.6, MS62 PCGS.**
The D.N. below the bust is almost certainly meant to denote the
brief partnership of Deriberpie and Nouizillet sometime in late
1852 or early 1853, which places this piece is among the earliest
fractional issues. Mottled olive-green and yellow-gold toning covers
both sides of this interesting representative. Pleasing luster shines
throughout and is barely affected by a couple of light grazes and tiny
patches of detritus. The reverse shows faint clashmarks, and there
are numerous die cracks on the obverse. (#10444)

1351   **1856 Liberty Round 50 Cents, BG-434, Low R.4, MS63
Prooflike NGC.** A lovely piece struck by Antoine Louis Nouizillet.
Bright yellow patina drapes the highly reflective surfaces. This piece
is Die State III, with a small clash mark visible on the reverse after
the heavy clash marks were lapped away. (#710470)

1352   **1853 Arms of California 50 Cents, BG-435, Low R.5, MS62
PCGS.** This date has always been one of the most sought-after in
the popular California fractional gold series. The distinctive obverse
is modeled after the state arms, with a seated Minerva holding a
shield and spear. A bear appears at her feet, and mountains loom in
the background. The reverse features an eagle with shield, scroll and
olive branch, reminiscent of the contemporary Humbert fifty dollar
slugs. Neither die appears on any other issue, making this a key date
for the type collector, as well as the specialist. The maker of this
unique design type is unknown. This specimen is sharply struck,
with fine detail in all the design elements. Lustrous, yellow-gold
surfaces make this example especially attractive.
From The Hamous Collection of California Gold. (#10471)

Uncirculated Assay Office Motif
BG-501 Octagonal Dollar

1353 **Undated Liberty Octagonal 1 Dollar, BG-501, Low R.5, MS60 PCGS.** The only undated octagonal dollar variety, but even more noteworthy for its reverse design, which imitates the then-contemporary logo of the U.S. Assay Office of Gold. Attractive lemon-gold toning enriches this sharply struck and lustrous piece. The reverse has a thin mark at 1 o'clock. Housed in an old green label holder. Population: 2 in 60, 11 finer (8/08). *From The Hamous Collection of California Gold.* (#10478)

BG-504 1854 Octagonal Dollar AU53
Popular 'Humbert Fifty' Motif Reverse

1354 **1854 Large Eagle Octagonal 1 Dollar, BG-504, Low R.5, AU53 PCGS.** The popular Period One type with the eagle, shield, and ribbon reverse, a design based upon the Humbert fifty dollar 'slugs' that dominated West Coast commerce in 1854. Splashes of orange and lime-green ensure the eye appeal of this well defined and generally lustrous example. Housed in an old green label holder. *Ex: Baltimore ANA Signature (Heritage, 7/1993), lot 7638. From The Hamous Collection of California Gold.* (#10481)

1355 **1854 Liberty Octagonal 1 Dollar, BG-508, High R.4, AU53 PCGS.** Although Liberty's curls possess moderate wear, the olive-gold surfaces are unblemished aside from a faint diagonal mark below the 4 in the date. *Ex: Long Beach Signature (Heritage, 6/2004), lot 10248. From The Hamous Collection of California Gold.* (#10485)

1356 **1854 Liberty Octagonal 1 Dollar, BG-508, High R.4, MS62 PCGS.** Lovely orange-gold patina graces the surfaces of this carefully preserved piece. A loupe locates a few trivial marks, and there is the typical weakness on the high points. Struck by Frontier, Deviercy & Co. Encapsulated in a green label PCGS holder. (#10485)

Important 1854 BG-508 Dollar, MS63 Prooflike

1357 **1854 Liberty Octagonal 1 Dollar, BG-508, High R.4, MS63 Prooflike NGC.** A gorgeous greenish-gold example with bright yellow luster, fully mirrored fields, and exceptional cameo contrast. California Fractional gold dollars from the first issuing period are in extreme demand. Census: 2 in 63 Prooflike, 2 finer (7/08). (#710485)

1358 **1854 Liberty Octagonal 1 Dollar, BG-510, Low R.5, AU58 PCGS.** A lustrous lime-green octagonal dollar with only faint indications of wear on the highpoints of the coronet and hair. An early variety with a majority of certified examples in circulated grades, including a VF35. In a green label holder. Population: 12 in 58, 14 finer (7/08). *From The Hamous Collection of California Gold.* (#10487)

1359 **1853 Liberty Octagonal 1 Dollar, BG-514, High R.5, MS62 PCGS.** Highly lustrous with satiny green-gold surfaces. This attractive piece is a desirable "fractional" gold dollar from Period One. While Period Two pieces were considered to be mere tokens, the first period pieces were actually intended to serve as small change during the California Gold Rush days. A charming piece issued by M. Deriberpie. Population: 10 in 62, 10 finer (7/08). (#10491)

1360 **1853 Liberty Octagonal 1 Dollar, BG-519, Low R.4, MS62 PCGS.** A pleasing Mint State example with semi-reflective fields and rich coloration. Typically softly struck on the peripheral elements, but free of any major problems. Population: 25 in 62, 11 finer (8/08). (#10496)

Difficult BG-522 1853 Octagonal Dollar
From the Jay Roe Collection

1361 **1853 Liberty Octagonal 1 Dollar, BG-522, High R.6, Genuine PCGS.** Ex: Jay Roe. Die State II with a diagonal die crack down from the base of the hairbun, and the plate coin for the die state in the second edition of Breen-Gillio. This example has little if any wear and is attractive to the unaided eye, but a strong loupe reveals extensive hairlines. *Ex: Jay Roe Collection (Bowers and Merena, 9/2003), lot 120. From The Hamous Collection of California Gold.* (#10499)

1362 **1853 Liberty Octagonal 1 Dollar, BG-523, R.5, AU55 NGC.** This briefly circulated Period One octagonal dollar has orange-red toning and smooth surfaces. Although its designs are generic, BG-523 is very scarce. Census: 1 in 55, 3 finer (7/08). *From The Hamous Collection of California Gold.* (#10500)

1363 **1853 Liberty Octagonal 1 Dollar, BG-524, High R.6, XF40 Cleaned Uncertified.** Ex: Jay Roe. This canary-gold representative is glossy from a cleaning, but all design details are bold and there are no detrimental marks. Lightly buckled, as produced. Encapsulated in a PCGS-style holder by Collectors Universe.
Ex: Jay Roe Collection (Bowers and Merena, 9/2003), lot 122.
From The Hamous Collection of California Gold. (#10501)

1364 **1853 Liberty Octagonal 1 Dollar, BG-530, R.2, MS61 NGC.** This sharply struck piece by Antoine Louis Nouizillet has eye-catching semiprooflike luster beneath yellow-gold patina. A few wispy marks define the grade and minimally affect the delightful eye appeal. (#10507)

1365 **1853 Liberty Octagonal 1 Dollar, BG-530, R.2, MS62 PCGS.** The original first period fractional dollars are undoubtedly the most popular pieces as they are the ones that were actually coined for use in the 1850s. This lustrous piece has a lovely blend of light yellow and pale green patina. (#10507)

1366 **1853 Liberty Octagonal 1 Dollar, BG-530, R.2, MS63 NGC.** It is interesting that more than a dozen examples of this issue were recovered from the wreck of the *S.S. Winfield Scott*, which indicates that Nouizillet had the intent to circulate these pieces. This boldly struck specimen features impressive prooflike reflectivity, although NGC has not designated this piece as such. Numerous die polish lines are noted in the fields, but there are no bothersome abrasions. (#10507)

1367 **1853 Liberty Octagonal 1 Dollar, BG-531, R.4, AU58 PCGS.** An original and well struck green-gold representative, attractive despite a V-shaped mark near the lower right portion of the portrait. A popular Period One octagonal dollar variety that must have passed in circulation, since PCGS has certified 54 pieces in grades of less than MS60. Encased in a green label holder.
From The Hamous Collection of California Gold. (#10508)

1368 **1854 Liberty Octagonal 1 Dollar, BG-532, Low R.4, AU58 PCGS.** A lustrous and sharply impressed green-gold example with a couple of tiny, roundish sunken marks near star 12 and above the O in DOLLAR. Certified in a green label holder. Population: 28 in 58, 28 finer (7/08).
Ex: Anaheim ANA Signature (Heritage, 8/1995), lot 8177.
From The Hamous Collection of California Gold. (#10509)

Important 1854 BG-534 Eagle Reverse Dollar, AU Details

1369 **1854 Large Eagle Octagonal 1 Dollar, BG-534, High R.6—Mount Removed—NCS. AU Details.** This important variety has the eagle reverse that was patterned after contemporary territorial gold issues. The obverse has evidence of an old jewelry mount at the top.
From The Hamous Collection of California Gold. (#10511)

Extremely Rare BG-601
Round Liberty 1854 Dollar
Formerly From the Jay Roe Collection

1370 **1854 Liberty Round 1 Dollar, BG-601, R.8, Genuine PCGS.** Ex: Jay Roe. An extremely rare Frontier, Deviercy, & Co. variety. The second edition of Breen-Gillio notes only three known examples, with the present piece listed first as the "finest known." The sharpness of XF, but kept out of a graded PCGS holder by a slightly granular appearance and a cluster of light pinscratches through the RNIA in CALIFORNIA.
Ex: Robert Lecce, 7/1991; Goliad Corporation, to Jay Roe via Mike Brownlee, 8/1991; Jay Roe Collection (Bowers and Merena, 9/2003), lot 134, which realized $12,650.
From The Hamous Collection of California Gold. (#10512)

1371 **1854 Liberty Round 1 Dollar, BG-602, High R.6—Damaged—NCS. AU Details.** This rare Period One dollar retains most of its initial luster, but a scrape on the wreath near 3 o'clock has slightly bent the coin and flattened portions of the hairbun opposite. The reverse has other abrasions, including a scratch on the upper field.
From The Hamous Collection of California Gold. (#10518)

Rare BG-603 1854 Liberty Round Dollar AU53

1372 **1854 Liberty Round 1 Dollar, BG-603, High R.6, AU53 PCGS.** A rarely-seen Period One variety with the Frontier and Deviercy initials separated by a star. The portrait of Liberty is unusually expressive for the series. Problem-free despite light circulation. Ample luster remains.
From The Hamous Collection of California Gold. (#10519)

Prohibitively Rare BG-607 1857 Round Dollar
One of Only Two Known, Ex: Jay Roe

1373 **1857 BG-607, R.8, VF20 Polished, Solder Residue, Lightly Corroded, Clogged Dies Uncertified.** Ex: Jay Roe. The plate coin for both editions of the standard Breen-Gillio reference, which states "plating separation resulted in severe clogging of the date elements, probably leading Frontier, Deviercy & Co. to abandon the issue immediately." One of only two known. This piece is bright from polishing, and has minor granularity and a spot of dark solder on the obverse at 12 o'clock. Housed in a PCGS-style Collectors Universe holder without a serial number.
Ex: Liberty Coin Service, 6/1977; Jay Roe Collection (Bowers and Merena, 9/2003), lot 139.
From The Hamous Collection of California Gold.

1374 **1859 Liberty Octagonal 25 Cents, BG-705, High R.6, Genuine PCGS.** Ex: Jay Roe. A lightly cleaned sun-gold example of this challenging variety. The reverse is concave and the date and denomination lack a crisp strike. The devices display only slight rub. The plate coin for the second edition of Breen-Gillio.
Ex: Jay Roe Collection (Bowers and Merena, 9/2003), lot 146.
From The Hamous Collection of California Gold. (#10532)

1375 **1871 Liberty Octagonal 25 Cents, BG-717, R.3, MS65 PCGS.** A prooflike Gem with undisturbed fields and nicely frosted motifs. Well struck, and worthy of the advanced specialized collection. Population: 49 in 65, 21 finer (8/08). (#10544)

1872 Washington Quarter, BG-722, MS62

1376 **1872 Washington Octagonal 25 Cents, BG-722, Low R.4, MS62 PCGS.** Part of the popular Washington portrait subset of California small denomination gold, which is a change of pace from the usual Indian and Liberty heads. Well engraved for the series. The satiny yellow-gold fields are free from grade-limiting marks. Certified in a green label holder.
From The Hamous Collection of California Gold. (#10549)

Lustrous 1872 BG-722 Washington Quarter Dollar, MS65

1377 **1872 Washington Octagonal 25 Cents, BG-722, Low R.4, MS65 NGC.** The popular and highly collectible Washington fractional gold pieces bridge collecting categories between California gold pieces and Washingtoniana. This is a lovely example with satiny green and orange-gold. Census: 3 in 65, 2 finer (7/08). (#10549)

1872 Washington Head Octagonal Quarter
Rare BG-723 Variety, AU55

1378 **1872 Washington Octagonal 25 Cents, BG-723, Low R.6, AU55 PCGS.** Fully lustrous, although a slight color change on the highpoints suggests momentary non-numismatic handling. Evenly struck and blemish-free with radiant sun-gold fields. A popular "Washington quarter" variety. Housed in a green label holder.
From The Hamous Collection of California Gold. (#10550)

Rare BG-723 1872 Washington Quarter MS61

1379 **1872 Washington Octagonal 25 Cents, BG-723, Low R.6, MS61 PCGS.** An elusive variety of the popular Washington type. Much scarcer than BG-722, which lacks berries on the wreath. A lustrous yellow-gold example. The portrait has linear marks, and the central reverse is glossy and has slightly blurry detail. Population: 6 in 61, 12 finer (8/08). (#10550)

Rare BG-724 1872 Washington Quarter MS62

1380 **1872 Washington Octagonal 25 Cents, BG-724, High R.6, MS62 PCGS.** The Small Date Washington Head variety with berries on the reverse wreath. Richly toned in variegated orange and lilac shades. There are few singular detractions, and the overall appeal is high for this rare variety. Population: 3 in 62, 5 finer (8/08). *From The Hamous Collection of California Gold.* (#10551)

Very Rare 1863 Octagonal Quarter, BG-733 MS62, Tied for Finest Certified

1381 **1863 Liberty Octagonal 25 Cents, BG-733, High R.7, MS62 PCGS.** Extremely rare. The second edition of Breen-Gillio enumerates only five known survivors, one of which permanently reposes in the Smithsonian. A prooflike example with a few faint obverse field marks and an ascending lintmark above the DO in DOLLAR. In a green label holder. Population: 3 in 62, 0 finer (7/08). *Ex: Grafton Collection (Kurt Krueger, 5/1980), lot 434; Jay Roe; Lee Collection (9/1988), lot 145; Mike Brownlee; Texas Collection (Bowers and Merena, 1/1992), lot 4043; Detroit ANA Signature (Heritage, 7/1994), lot 8031; Superior, 5/1995, lot 3952. From The Hamous Collection of California Gold.* (#10560)

Desirable 1867 BG-742 Quarter Dollar, MS62

1382 **1867 Liberty Octagonal 25 Cents, BG-742, Low R.7, MS62 NGC.** A delightful Mint State piece with reflective gold surfaces beneath orange, gold, violet, and blue toning on each side. The obverse shows extensive die rust and light cracks while the reverse shows slight die rust. The date has the 1 entirely missing and the 7 doubled. *From The Hamous Collection of California Gold.* (#10569)

Rare BG-742 1867 Octagonal Quarter MS62

1383 **1867 Liberty Octagonal 25 Cents, BG-742, Low R.7, MS62 PCGS.** A lustrous representative without noticeable marks, although the reverse has minute strike-throughs. Slightly wavy, as produced. Tied as the finest certified, and encapsulated in a green label holder. Population: 4 in 62, 0 finer (7/08). (#10569)

1384 **1868 Liberty Octagonal 25 Cents, BG-745, Low R.6, MS62 PCGS.** The flashy fields are ruby-red and sun-gold. A crisply struck example, held back from a higher grade by a couple of thin vertical marks on the reverse. Housed in a green label holder. Population: 11 in 62, 1 finer (7/08). *Ex: Superior, 5/1995, lot 3960. From The Hamous Collection of California Gold.* (#10572)

Interesting 1871 Liberty Octagonal 25 Cents, BG-765, MS66

1385 **1871 Liberty Octagonal 25 Cents, BG-765, R.3, MS66 NGC.** An eye-catching yellow-gold piece struck by Robert B. Gray & Co. The obverse die has begun to shatter, and there are numerous die cracks that radiate from the center. With its highly mirrored surfaces, this specimen deserves recognition from NGC as Prooflike. The reverse shows a tiny crack at 8 o'clock, and it is interesting that there are still guidelines below DOLLAR and CAL, which were not removed by lapping. It is also peculiar that despite these guidelines, the C in CAL was punched significantly lower than the other letters. The stars and some of the dentils are weak, but the rest of the details are powerfully impressed. (#10592)

1386 **1873 Liberty Octagonal 25 Cents, BG-772, High R.6, Genuine PCGS.** Ex: Jay Roe. A few hair-thin marks prevent assignment of a numerical grade by PCGS, but the fields shimmer with luster and there is no obvious wear. The plate coin for the variety in the second edition of Breen-Gillio. *Ex: Jay Roe Collection (Bowers and Merena, 9/2003), lot 217. From The Hamous Collection of California Gold.* (#10599)

Impressive 1876 Liberty Octagonal 25 Cents, BG-780, Superb Gem

1387 **1876 Liberty Octagonal 25 Cents, BG-780, R.4, MS67 NGC.** It is amazing that this minuscule piece has been so carefully preserved for more than 130 years. Although it is not known for certain who struck these specimens, recent die and punch linking has led some researchers to believe that they were produced by Herman J. Brand of San Francisco. This splendid yellow-gold piece has numerous die polish lines in the fields and as a result it exhibits dazzling reflectivity throughout, although NGC has neglected to designate it Prooflike. The strike is razor-sharp, with full dentilation on both sides, save for just a touch of weakness on the AR in DOLLAR, as usual. This variety features a repunched C in CAL, after the first C was punched too low. Close examination with a loupe reveals clash marks from Liberty on the reverse. A spectacular representative. Census: 1 in 67, 0 finer (7/08). (#10607)

1388 **1870 Goofy Head Octagonal 25 Cents, BG-789, R.4, MS64 PCGS.** A well struck and unblemished olive-tinted near-Gem of the popular 'Goofy Head' subtype, noted for its prominent jaw. Most certified examples grade MS61 to MS63. Population: 9 in 64, 1 finer (7/08). *From The Hamous Collection of California Gold.* (#10616)

1389 **1876 Indian Octagonal 25 Cents, BG-799D, R.6, MS64 Deep Prooflike NGC.** A lovely, prooflike example with glassy fields and several die striations noted on the lower obverse. A couple of faint pinscratches prevent an even finer grade. A scarce octagonal quarter variety that is especially rare at this lofty grade level. (#710630)

1390 **1878/6 Indian Octagonal 25 Cents, BG-799G, R.5, MS64 PCGS.** Well struck aside from unimportant softness on the DO in DOLLAR. The reverse field is slightly wavy, as made. A few pinpoint aqua flecks are noted on the portrait. Population: 17 in 64, 7 finer (7/08). *From The Hamous Collection of California Gold.* (#10633)

1391 **1868 Indian Octagonal 25 Cents, BG-799T, High R.5, MS64 PCGS.** A flashy near-Gem with consistent apricot-gold color. Intricately struck and void of detractions. Similar to BG-799R and BG-799S, but the numerator has a different style. Ensconced in a green label holder. Population: 13 in 64, 4 finer (7/08). *From The Hamous Collection of California Gold.* (#10646)

1392 **1865 Liberty Round 25 Cents, BG-802, Low R.5, MS64 NGC.** Although undesignated as Prooflike, the fields are flashy and lack noticeable contact. Primarily pale gold with hints of lilac patina on the highpoints of the portrait. The denomination resembles the word LOLA due to extensive lapping of the reverse die prior to the strike. Census: 1 in 64, 0 finer (7/08). *From The Hamous Collection of California Gold.* (#10663)

1872 Washington Round Quarter, BG-818, MS62

1393 **1872 Washington Round 25 Cents, BG-818, Low R.4, MS62 PCGS.** This round Washington quarter is generally sun-gold, although glimpses of lime iridescence are also present. The central reverse has a few slightly soft letters, but the overall strike is good. Popular with collectors of Washingtonia, and a change of pace from the usual Indian and Liberty types. Encased in an old green label holder. *From The Hamous Collection of California Gold.* (#10679)

Choice 1872 Washington Round Quarter, BG-818

1394 **1872 Washington Round 25 Cents, BG-818, Low R.4, MS64 NGC.** A radiant canary-gold near-Gem that boasts a blemish-free appearance. Minor incompleteness of strike in the centers is all that precludes an even higher grade. BG-818 is the only round Washington quarter variety, although three octagonal Washington varieties exist, BG-722 to BG-724. (Census: 2 in 64, 3 finer (7/08). (#10679)

1395 **1870 Liberty Round 25 Cents, BG-832, Low R.6, MS64 PCGS.** A prominently mirrored canary-gold near-Gem that exhibits obvious cameo contrast. Faint marks near the R in DOLLAR merit only passing mention. Certified in a green label holder. Population: 1 in 64, 1 finer (7/08). *From The Hamous Collection of California Gold.* (#10693)

Rarely Seen BG-836 1870 Round Quarter MS61

1396 **1870 Liberty Round 25 Cents, BG-836, High R.7, MS61 NGC.** An extremely rare variety. The second edition of Breen-Gillio (2003) lists just four known examples, nonetheless enough to discern two important die states. The present piece is State One, the "Fresh Reverse" prior to die polishing that removed stems to create floating berries. This semi-prooflike yellow-gold example is undisturbed save for a few faint slide marks on each side. Stars 4 and 11 are softly struck. *From The Hamous Collection of California Gold.* (#10697)

1397 **1871 Liberty Round 25 Cents, BG-839, Low R.4, MS63 PCGS.** A boldly struck gold quarter with flashy fields and predominant honey-gold color. A few trivial hairlines determine the grade. The reverse field is slightly concave, as struck. Population: 19 in 63, 6 finer (7/08). *From The Hamous Collection of California Gold.* (#10700)

1398 **1874 Liberty Round 25 Cents, BG-845, R.6, MS60 PCGS.** Dusky orange-gold with satin luster and an even strike. Like most examples of this rare variety, the obverse field exhibits recessed 'ghosts' from the wreath. The reverse is concave, usual for the series. Encapsulated in a green label holder. *From The Hamous Collection of California Gold.* (#10706)

1399 **1875 Liberty Round 25 Cents, BG-846, R.6, MS62 PCGS.** A proof-like yellow-gold piece with unabraded and reflective fields. The usually seen 'ghosts' (faint incused and reversed images from the opposite design) are of mint origin. Encased in a green label holder. Population: 6 in 62, 2 finer (7/08). *Ex: Superior, 5/1995, lot 4064.* *From The Hamous Collection of California Gold.* (#10707)

1400 **1880/76 Indian Round 25 Cents, BG-885, R.3, MS66 PCGS.** Although not designated as such by PCGS, this piece is decidedly proof-like with deeply mirrored fields that show excellent cameo contrast against the frosted devices. This interesting variety features an obviously hand-engraved date, with a remnant of the 6 plain inside of the opening of the 0. Numerous die cracks are noted on the obverse. A charming minimally marked piece, struck by Christopher Ferdinand Mohrig of San Francisco. (#10746)

1401 **1867 Liberty Octagonal 50 Cents, BG-905, Low R.5, MS65 PCGS.** This proof-like representative is principally yellow-gold, although dashes of steel-blue and autumn-brown are also present. Devoid of detectable marks. Encased in a green label holder. Population: 8 in 65, 6 finer (7/08). *Ex: Superior, 5/1995, lot 4108.* *From The Hamous Collection of California Gold.* (#10763)

1402 **1870 Liberty Octagonal 50 Cents, BG-909, R.6, MS64 PCGS.** The bright apricot-gold luster is augmented with dashes of powder-blue toning. The D in DOLLAR is soft as usual, since it is opposite Liberty's high relief hair. Population: 5 in 64, 3 finer (3/07). *From The Diamond K Collection of California Fractional Gold.* (#10767)

1403 **1872 Liberty Octagonal 50 Cents, BG-913, R.4, MS66 PCGS.** A decidedly proof-like piece with uncommonly clean surfaces and outstanding eye appeal. Evenly struck, and worthy of the finest collection. Population: 4 in 66, 1 finer (8/08). (#10771)

1404 **1870 Liberty Octagonal 50 Cents, BG-921, Low R.5, MS64 Prooflike NGC.** This "mouthless" variety was the result of heavy die polishing, which removed the mouth and weakened part of the bust and nose. Struck by Robert B. Gray & Co., this prooflike specimen shows a few minor handling marks under magnification. This piece features the typical die buckling behind the head, as well as the die cracks through the final four stars. An interesting and attractive example.

1405 **1871 Liberty Octagonal 50 Cents, BG-924, R.3, MS64 Prooflike NGC.** Die State I. A magnificent, meticulously preserved fractional from the final year of Robert B. Gray & Co. The G beneath the bust was originally punched too low and was subsequently corrected. There are a number of raised die lines on Liberty, which Breen and Gillio describe as file marks. A few stars and several letters are weakly struck, as typically seen. (#710782)

1406 **1872/1 Indian Octagonal 50 Cents, BG-937, High R4, MS65 PCGS.** Deeply mirrored fields show pleasing cameo contrast against the frosted devices. The stars are soft, as typically seen, but the central design elements are boldly impressed. This piece features a 90-degree die rotation. (#10795)

1407 **1873 Indian Octagonal 50 Cents, BG-942, Low R.5, MS64 PCGS.** A beautiful near-Gem that has canary-gold toning with occasional dashes of peach and rose. Sharply struck, prooflike, and encapsulated in a green label holder. Population: 9 in 64, 2 finer (7/08). *Ex: Superior, 5/1995, lot 4144.* *From The Hamous Collection of California Gold.* (#10800)

Deep Mirror Prooflike Gem BG-946
1875 Octagonal Indian Half Dollar

1408 **1875 Indian Octagonal 50 Cents, BG-946, R.4, MS65 Deep Mirror Prooflike NGC.** Prominently reflective fields provide pleasing cameo contrast and exemplary eye appeal. A sharply struck Gem with only a few trivial grazes on the reverse field. Struck from widely rotated dies. Census: 1 in 65 Deep Mirror Prooflike, 2 finer (7/08). (#710804)

Important BG-947 Octagonal 1875 Indian Half MS62

1409 **1875 Indian Octagonal 50 Cents, BG-947, High R.7, MS62 PCGS.** BG-947 is very rare. The second edition of Breen-Gillio was able to enumerate only five distinct examples. Apart from the present coin, the last appearance of BG-947 in a Heritage Signature auction was in 1996. A crisply struck green-gold representative that has glimpses of lacquer in protected areas. *Ex: Diamond K Collection of California Fractional Gold (Heritage, 5/2007), lot 3007.* *From The Hamous Collection of California Gold.* (#10805)

1410 **1881 Indian Octagonal 50 Cents, BG-957, Low R.6, MS65 Prooflike NGC.** Decidedly proof-like fields show a lovely cameo contrast against the frosted devices. A touch of apricot patina in the margins intermingles with the butter-yellow centers. Struck by Christopher Ferdinand Mohrig of San Francisco. (#710815)

Deep Mirror Prooflike MS67
1874 Indian Octagonal Half, BG-958

1411 **1874 Indian Octagonal 50 Cents, BG-958, High R.6, MS67 Deep Mirror Prooflike NGC.** Double struck on both sides with a slight counter-clockwise spread. Otherwise, a well impressed sun-gold Superb Gem with dazzling field reflectivity and pleasing cameo contrast. NGC has certified only two octagonal halves as BG-958, and the present piece is the sole Deep Mirror Prooflike example (8/08). (#710816)

1412 **1871 Liberty Round 50 Cents, BG-1011, R.2, MS66 PCGS.** A magnificent and essentially immaculate example that boasts semi-prooflike fields and attractive green-gold and apricot patina. Population: 11 in 66, 0 finer (8/08). (#10840)

Finest Certified and Extremely Rare
1864 Round Half Fractional, BG-1016A, MS63

1413 **1864 Liberty Round 50 Cents, BG-1016A, R.8 MS63 PCGS.** In the first edition of Breen-Gillio, this variety was misidentified as Die State I of BG-1016. It is now known that this is a different reverse die, with a much shorter left stem on the wreath. PCGS has certified just three examples of BG-1016A, and the present piece is the single finest graded by two points. This piece is well struck, unlike the MS61 PCGS Jay Roe specimen, which has weakness on the portrait and the 8 in the date. Pleasing rose-red patina encircles the yellow-gold devices. A magnificent opportunity for the dedicated fractional gold collector. (#10908)

1414 **1866 Liberty Round 50 Cents, BG-1017, High R.6—Mount Removed—NCS. AU Details.** A rare, crude round half variety. Breen-Gillio Die State I without the heavy die cracks seen on the Roe example. The present piece has little if any wear, but is harshly cleaned and has solder residue at 6 o'clock on the reverse.
From The Hamous Collection of California Gold. (#10846)

1415 **1869 Liberty Round 50 Cents, BG-1021, High R.6, AU58 PCGS.** The 18 in the date is softly struck, although the remainder of the legends and devices are crisp. A golden-brown example with pleasantly smooth surfaces. Population: 3 in 58, 8 finer (7/08).
Ex: New York Signature (Heritage, 11/2003), lot 8222.
From The Hamous Collection of California Gold. (#10850)

1416 **1870 Liberty Round 50 Cents, BG-1022, High R.6, MS62 PCGS.** A moderately prooflike piece with glimpses of navy-blue and mauve across the open fields. Nicely struck and devoid of detrimental abrasions. Housed in a green label holder. Population: 2 in 62, 4 finer (7/08).
Ex: East Coast Expo (Heritage, 9/1994), lot 739.
From The Hamous Collection of California Gold. (#10851)

1417 **1871 Liberty Round 50 Cents, BG-1044, High R.6, MS62 PCGS.** A lustrous canary-gold round half that has a well struck portrait and a typically brought up wreath. A pass beneath a loupe fails to locate any marks. Encased in a green label holder. Population: 3 in 62, 4 finer (7/08).
Ex: Superior, 5/1995, lot 4192.
From The Hamous Collection of California Gold. (#10873)

1418 **1871 Liberty Round 50 Cents, BG-1045, R.5, MS61 PCGS.** A charming semi-prooflike piece that boasts a bold strike and relatively smooth fields. The tiny H beneath the bust represents the maker, Hershfield & Mitchell of Leavenworth, Kansas. Encapsulated in a green label holder.
From The Hamous Collection of California Gold. (#10874)

1419 **1870 Liberty Head Round 50 Cents, BG-1047, High R.4, MS63 PCGS.** This obverse is sometimes called the "Goofy Head" for the unusual engraving style. Looking at the profile of Liberty suggests another name: the "Angry Head." An attractive piece with prooflike fields and brilliant green-gold surfaces, housed in an older green-label holder. (#10876)

1420 **1874/3 Indian Round 50 Cents, BG-1052, High R.4, MS62 PCGS.** A prooflike round half with pleasing yellow-gold surfaces. The reverse appears slightly buckled, as made. Certified in a green label holder. Population: 22 in 62, 28 finer (7/08).
From The Hamous Collection of California Gold. (#10881)

1421 **1874 Indian Round 50 Cents, BG-1055, High R.4, MS61 Prooflike NGC.** Bright lemon-gold surfaces have outstanding prooflike reflectivity. While the Indian is sharp, the rest of the details are soft or unevenly struck, as typically seen. The fields have numerous die polish lines and no significant marks. An impressive issue by Christopher Ferdinand Mohrig of San Francisco. (#710884)

1422 **1876 Indian Round 50 Cents, BG-1060, High R.5, MS64 PCGS.** A beautiful Choice fractional gold piece that has alternating peach and lime patina. An unimportant spot is concealed within the Indian's hair. Encapsulated in a green label holder. Population: 8 in 64, 2 finer (7/08).
From The Hamous Collection of California Gold. (#10889)

1423 **1876 Indian Round 50 Cents, BG-1063, Low R.6, MS62 PCGS.** The yellow-gold fields are reflective and mildly contrast with the olive-tinted devices. A hair-thin mark ascends through the O in DOLLAR. Struck from widely rotated dies, and housed in a green label holder. Population: 4 in 62, 11 finer (7/08).
From The Hamous Collection of California Gold. (#10892)

1424 **1876 Indian Round 50 Cents, BG-1064, R.6, MS64 PCGS.** This rare variety near-Gem has unabraded prooflike fields and consistent canary-gold color. The centers show slight incompleteness, and the reverse has the usual star 'ghosts.' Population: 9 in 64, 0 finer (8/08). (#10893)

1425 **1880/70 Indian Round 50 Cents, BG-1067, Low R.4, MS65 PCGS.** Prominently mirrored fields and unblemished surfaces ensure the eye appeal of this nicely struck Gem. The 'overdate' is a horn from the upper right corner of the second 8. Population: 4 in 65, 0 finer (8/08). (#10896)

1426 1881 Indian Round 50 Cents, BG-1070, R.5, MS65 NGC.
The nearly pristine orange-gold surfaces have glittering prooflike reflectivity, which is typical for this issue. Weakly struck at the centers, as usual, and this piece lacks the "ghost" at the opening of the wreath described by Breen and Gillio. A number of die lines are noted around the denomination. Census: 2 in 65, 0 finer (7/08). (#10899)

1427 1871 Liberty Octagonal 1 Dollar, BG-1104, High R.4, MS63 NGC. The color is more greenish-gold than usually seen, typically an indication of a higher content of silver alloy. This piece offers relatively few abrasions with good luster. A couple of minuscule dark spots appear under a loupe, but they are scarcely seen otherwise. (#10915)

1428 1871 Liberty Octagonal 1 Dollar, BG-1109, Low R.4, MS62 PCGS. The reflective, radiant fields are sun-gold. This precisely struck piece has a slightly concave reverse and only a few faint, unimportant marks near the denomination. Certified in a green label holder. Population: 23 in 62, 19 finer (7/08).
From The Hamous Collection of California Gold. (#10920)

1429 1870 Goofy Head Octagonal 1 Dollar, BG-1118, Low R.5, MS61 NGC. This semi-prooflike straw-gold representative has a typical strike and a few faint field hairlines. The distinctive lantern-jawed "Goofy Head" bust, whose maker is unknown. Census: 2 in 61, 1 finer (7/08).
From The Hamous Collection of California Gold. (#10929)

1430 1872 Indian Octagonal 1 Dollar, BG-1120, Low R.5, MS63 PCGS. This handsome octagonal dollar has prooflike fields and a penetrating strike. Study beneath a loupe locates no noticeable marks. Encapsulated in a green label holder. Population: 7 in 63, 13 finer (7/08).
From The Hamous Collection of California Gold. (#10931)

Rare and Attractive 1873/2 Indian Octagonal Gold Dollar, BG-1122, MS62

1431 1873/2 Indian Octagonal 1 Dollar, BG-1122, High R.6, MS62 NGC. This interesting piece was struck by Christopher Ferdinand Mohrig in San Francisco and features an obviously hand-engraved date. The highly reflective surfaces are decidedly prooflike and show splendid contrast against the frosted devices, although NGC has neglected Prooflike or Cameo designations. A pleasing example of this rare issue. (#10933)

1432 1874 Indian Octagonal 1 Dollar, BG-1124, High R.4, MS64 Prooflike NGC. An appealing octagonal "fractional" gold dollar, struck by Christopher Ferdinand Mohrig in San Francisco. The deeply prooflike yellow-gold surfaces have only a couple of microscopic handling marks. Nearly fully struck save for minor weakness at the centers. (#710935)

1433 1875 Indian Octagonal 1 Dollar, BG-1127, R.4, AU58 PCGS. A lightly circulated aquamarine octagonal dollar with moderate incompleteness of strike at the centers. A wispy mark or two above DOLLAR fails to distract. Housed in a green label holder.
Ex: Long Beach Signature (Heritage, 9/2004), lot 8223, which realized $978.
From The Hamous Collection of California Gold. (#10938)

Deep Mirror Prooflike MS64 BG-1128 1876/5 Indian Octagonal Dollar

1434 1876/5 Indian Octagonal 1 Dollar, BG-1128, R.5, MS64 Deep Mirror Prooflike NGC. Incorrectly designated as BG-1129 on the NGC insert. Both varieties are from the same dies, but the R.4 BG-1129 was re-engraved by the maker and has a berry left of the wreath bow. The sun-gold fields are mirrored and exhibit blatant contrast with the frosty devices. Well struck and unblemished. No examples of BG-1128 have been given a Deep Cameo designation by NGC. (#710939)

1435 1876/5 Indian Octagonal 1 Dollar, BG-1129, R.4 AU58 PCGS. Subtle rose highlights visit the devices and legends. The olive-gold fields retain much mint flash. A brief, faint pinscratch is seen above the headdress. The dies are rotated 90 degrees from coin turn.
From The Hamous Collection of California Gold. (#10940)

Alluring 1876/5 BG-1129 Dollar MS65 Deep Mirror Prooflike

1436 1876/5 Indian Octagonal 1 Dollar, BG-1129, R.4 MS65 Deep Mirror Prooflike NGC. The final digit is crudely overdated with a blob at the lower left of that digit. An absolutely stunning green-gold Gem with full prooflike surfaces and exceptional cameo contrast. Census: 2 in 65 Deep Mirror Prooflike, 0 finer (7/08). (#710940)

Exquisite 1871 Liberty Round Gold Dollar, BG-1201, MS61

1437 1871 Liberty Round 1 Dollar, BG-1201, High R.6, MS61 PCGS. A seldom-seen variety struck by Frontier & Co. Deep olive-gold patina envelops the fields, which contrast sharply against the yellow-gold devices. The surfaces show startling prooflike reflectivity, although PCGS has not designated this piece as such. Only a few microscopic hairlines keep this sharply struck piece from a higher grade. Housed in a green label PCGS holder.
From The Hamous Collection of California Gold. (#10946)

1438 **1870 Liberty Round 1 Dollar, BG-1203, Low R.5—Improperly Cleaned—NCS. AU Details.** This olive-gold example is luminous and mildly granular. The lower left obverse field, the field to the left of the prominent 1, and the reverse border at 2, 5, and 7 o'clock appear to have been wiped.
From The Hamous Collection of California Gold. (#10948)

1439 **1870 Goofy Head Round 1 Dollar, BG-1205, High R.4, AU53 PCGS.** Rose-red borders frame the orange centers. An evenly struck example that has a few brief, thin field marks. There are only eight varieties of round Period Two dollars. Encased in a green label holder.
From The Hamous Collection of California Gold. (#10950)

1440 **1872 Indian Round 1 Dollar, BG-1206, High R.6, AU55 NGC.** The devices show slight wear, presumably from non-numismatic handling instead of a brief stay in circulation. Ample honey-gold luster remains, and there are no apparent marks. Struck from widely rotated dies.
From The Hamous Collection of California Gold. (#10951)

Impeccable BG-1207 1872 Round Dollar MS62

1441 **1872 Indian Round 1 Dollar, BG-1207, R.4, MS62 PCGS.** A precisely struck orange-gold example with clean surfaces and a slender lintmark through the final star. The penultimate Period Two variety, followed only by the famous TOKEN reverse BG-1208. Certified in a green label holder. Population: 22 in 62, 28 finer (8/08).
From The Hamous Collection of California Gold. (#10952)

CALIFORNIA GOLD CHARM

1442 **"1853" California Gold Charm MS64 NGC.** The obverse depicts the California state arms and the legend EUREKA. The reverse displays a wreath with 1853 nestled inside and CALIFORNIA GOLD about. The I in CALIFORNIA is boldly repunched. Presumably made for souvenir sale during the first half of the 20th century.
From The Hamous Collection of California Gold.

COINS OF HAWAII

1443 **1847 Hawaii Cent MS62 Brown PCGS.** Plain 4, 17 berries. Medcalf 2CC-3, a scarce die variety. Dusky medium brown with distributed small areas of deep gray toning. The lower reverse rim has a wire-shaped indentation. (#10965)

Sharp 1883 Hawaii Ten Cent, MS66
Tied for Finest Certified

1444 **1883 Hawaii Ten Cents MS66 PCGS.** The 1883 Hawaii dime is much more elusive in the higher Mint State grades than the quarter of the same year. This sparkling Premium Gem is virtually silver-white, with just a whisper of original golden toning, and the piece is quite high-end for the assigned grade. In MS66 this is one of the 10 finest examples (less duplicates) certified at PCGS, and it is difficult to imagine a finer specimen. A wonderful acquisition for a Registry Set or a complete Hawaiian collection. This piece is blessed by a needle-sharp strike, and certified in a green-label holder. (#10979)

Splendid 1883 Hawaii Quarter, MS66

1445 **1883 Hawaii Quarter MS66 PCGS.** Tinges of ice-blue and pinkish-gold grace both sides of this splendid 1883 Hawaii quarter, which shows surfaces that are virtually devoid of contact. This Premium Gem represents nearly the finest quality obtainable, as PCGS has certified only a dozen pieces finer of this popular issue (8/08). (#10987)

Premium Gem 1883 Hawaii Quarter

1446 **1883 Hawaii Quarter MS66 PCGS.** A boldly detailed example of the popular 1883 Hawaii quarter that was struck at the San Francisco Mint on behalf of King Kalakaua I, who is depicted on the obverse. Both sides have frosty silver luster with wispy iridescence. Population: 85 in 66, 12 finer (8/08). (#10987)

Delightful Premium Gem 1883 Hawaii Quarter

1447 **1883 Hawaii Quarter MS66 PCGS.** Each side has crisply detailed, carefully preserved surfaces with vibrant luster. The obverse exhibits rich, dappled rose and green-gold toning, while the reverse shows only minimal patina at the margins. An exceptionally delightful hapaha. Population: 85 in 66, 12 finer (8/08). (#10987)

Impressive 1883 Hawaii Quarter, MS66

1448 **1883 Hawaii Quarter MS66 PCGS. CAC.** The breathtaking pastel coloration consists of fuchsia centers accented with jade-green and ice-blue at the margins on both sides. Much luster emerges from underneath the light layer of toning. A nice piece for the grade, and a definite keeper for the color aficionados. (#10987)

Flashy MS66 1883 Hawaii Quarter

1449 **1883 Hawaii Quarter MS66 PCGS. CAC.** Untoned surfaces show flashy mint luster on this wonderful Premium Gem coin. The surfaces are more satiny than brilliant, with tremendous eye appeal. PCGS and NGC combined have certified several dozen in this grade, but there are few finer at either service (8/08). (#10987)

Scintillating 1883 Hawaiian Quarter, Superb Gem

1450 **1883 Hawaii Quarter MS67 PCGS. CAC.** Variegated sea-green and russet coloration atop scintillating luster defines this Superb Gem Hawaiian quarter. As of (8/08), only 12 examples of this issue have earned the MS67 grade at PCGS, with none grading finer. The population at NGC is even lower with just six Superb Gem pieces. Fortunately, the quarter dollar issues of Hawaii saw less attrition through melting than the larger half dollar and dollar coins, so high grade examples are readily available in near-Gem or better condition. However, the handful of extant MS67 pieces occupy only the most fortunate of cabinets. (#10987)

1451 **1883 Hawaii Dollar XF45 PCGS.** A lightly circulated example of the largest Hawaiian denomination of 1883, luminous beneath deep rose-gray patina. The fields and devices show surprisingly few marks. (#10995)

Choice AU 1879 Thomas Hobron One Real Token

1452 **1879 T. Hobron AU55 NGC.** Medcalf-Russell 2TE-8. The copper "one real" railroad tokens from Wailuku Plantation were redeemable at Thomas Hobron's general store in Kahului, Maui, Hawaii. The Kahului and Wailuku Railroad carried sugar cane to the port of Kahului for export. Today Kahului, host to the Maui airport and a deep-draft harbor, is the largest town on the island of Maui, the site of several shopping centers and home to more than 20,000 inhabitants. This chocolate-brown piece is well-struck through the centers, softly struck at the rims, as typical for the issue, and shows good eye appeal. Listed on page 391 of the 2009 *Guide Book*. (#600515)

1882 Haiku Plantation One Rial, AU58

1453 **1882 Haiku Plantation One Rial AU58 PCGS.** Medcalf-Russell TE-15. The Haiku Plantation tokens are among the better-produced issues from the plantation token days in Hawaii during the 19th century. This piece is no exception, and was well cared-for after its release, adding to its appeal. The glossy brown surfaces display much luster remaining, and only a few tiny contact marks appear under a loupe. Listed on page 391 of the 2009 *Guide Book*. Population: 3 in 58, 2 finer (8/08). (#600518)

ERRORS

1454 **1826 Large Cent—Triple Struck with Brockage on Reverse—VG8 NGC.** N-5, R.2, but perhaps a unique error. The obverse is triple struck, and the reverse shows a partial brockage at 10 o'clock. Attractive medium to dark olive surfaces. EAC 8.

1455 **1865 Fancy 5 Indian Cent—Struck 45% Off Center—XF45 NGC.** This chocolate-brown Civil War cent is struck widely off center toward 12 o'clock. The date is full, as is Liberty's profile, the shield, and most of the denomination. Noticeable luster remains despite light wear on the Indian's ribbon.

1456 **1904 Indian Cent—Double Struck, Second Strike 30% Off Center—XF45 NGC.** The second strike is widely off center toward 10:30, at 10 o'clock relative to the first strike. The dates from both strikes are clear and complete. The obverse is golden-brown, and the reverse has slightly deeper steel-gray toning.

1457 **1916-D Lincoln Cent—Struck 15% Off Center—MS63 Red and Brown NGC.** Moderately off center toward 11 o'clock, taking a portion of IN GOD WE off the flan. This early branch mint Lincoln cent has good luster and substantial sun-gold is present. The open fields are blended cherry-red and medium brown.

1943 Cent Struck on a Silver Dime Planchet AU58

1458 **1943 Lincoln Cent—Struck on a Silver Dime Planchet—AU58 PCGS.** While a bronze 1943 cent in this grade is worth perhaps $100,000, the present off-metal error should be significantly more affordable. A lustrous cream-gray example with striking softness on the O in ONE and the LIB in LIBERTY, typical sharpness for an undersized planchet.

1459 **1964 Lincoln Cent—Deep Die Cap—MS66 Red PCGS.** This cent clung to the obverse die instead of getting ejected. It was struck repeatedly against a series of fed planchets, none of which are included, causing the obverse to wrap partly around the die while the reverse design became expanded and distorted from strikes against incoming flans.

1460 **1966 Lincoln Cent—Staple Struck in Obverse—MS62 Red and Brown NGC.** An interesting error with a wire staple struck into the center of the obverse. The staple is still present.

Fascinating MS64 1967 Cent Struck on a Clad Dime Layer

1461 **1967 Lincoln Cent—Struck on a Clad Dime Outer Layer—MS64 PCGS.** 6 grains. Likely a clad layer from a 1967 cent struck on a dime that later separated, since the detail is sharp and the back of the piece shows a strong inverse impression. Whispers of light golden toning add hints of color to the otherwise essentially brilliant surfaces. A fascinating and noteworthy error.

1462 **1973-S Lincoln Cent—Double Struck, Flipover Second Strike 60% Off Center—MS64 Red and Brown NGC.** The first strike was normal, but the piece failed to complete eject from the dies, and was struck a second time. The second strike was 60% off center toward 10:30, at 4:30 relative to the reverse of the first strike. The second strike was uniface obverse, since a newly fed planchet blocked the reverse die. The coin flipped over between strikes, which greatly adds to the value. Both dates and mintmarks are intact. There is a faint thin mark above the 19 in the date of the first strike.

1463 **1989 Lincoln Cent—Struck on a 1988 Dime—MS65 NGC.** A 1988 dime somehow ended up being struck by the next year's cent dies, with the obverse of the dime rotated 45 degrees clockwise on the obverse of the cent. Significant undertype remains, and there is lots of luster throughout. A fascinating and carefully preserved error.

Mated Pair Obverse and Reverse Die Cap
1997 Lincoln Cents, MS67 Red and MS68 Red

1464 **1997 Lincoln Cent—Obverse Die Cap, Matched Pair 1 of 2—MS68 Red NGC; and a 1997 Lincoln Cent—Reverse Die Cap, Matched Pair 2 of 2—MS67 Red NGC.** This remarkable error combination began when coin #2 stuck to the reverse die. It was then struck repeatedly against a series of newly fed planchets, which caused the obverse portrait of Lincoln to become blurry, low relief, and expanded. The final strike was against coin #1, which became an obverse die cap. Coin #1 has a brockage impression from coin #2. (Total: 2 coins)

MS63 Liberty Nickel Struck on a Fragment

1465 **Undated Liberty Nickel—Struck Fragment—MS63 ANACS.** A planchet split prior to the strike, and a portion representing 25% of the original planchet was struck. Stars 1 through 5 are visible, as is a portion of Liberty's profile. The reverse includes UNITED ST and a few elements from the left border of the wreath. Lustrous, and toned light golden-brown.

1466 **1898 Liberty Nickel—Struck on a Foreign Planchet—AU55 NGC.** Possibly struck on a Nicaragua five centavos planchet, a world coin struck at the U.S. Mint in 1898. A briefly circulated pearl-gray piece that is smooth aside from a hair-thin mark beneath the UN in UNUM.

1467 **1902 Liberty Nickel—Struck on a Columbia Five Centavos Planchet—VF20 ANACS.** The U.S. struck 1902 five centavo pieces for Columbia in 1902 in an alloy of 835 fine silver. At least one five centavo planchet, the present coin, made it between Liberty nickel dies. This lightly toned piece is slightly uncentered toward 1 o'clock, where the rim is absent. Problem-free for the grade aside from a pair of faint russet streaks on the portrait.

MS64 Buffalo Nickel
Struck on a 26% Clipped Planchet

1468 **Undated Philadelphia Mint Buffalo Nickel—26% Clipped Planchet—MS64 PCGS.** A large curved clip is centered at 5:30 and prevents most of the date from appearing on this satiny and unabraded near-Gem. Golden-brown and dove-gray toning confirms the originality. A visually impressive mint error.

1924 Buffalo Nickel Struck on
Lincoln Cent Planchet, MS64

1469 **1924 Buffalo Nickel—Struck on a Cent Planchet—MS64 Brown PCGS.** 3.05 gm. Because the Buffalo nickel is slightly larger than the Lincoln cent—21.2 mm versus 19 mm—the edges of the well-centered strike are off the flan, including the bison's extreme head and tail, and the mintmark below FIVE CENTS. This coin could technically be from any of the three mints—Philadelphia, Denver, San Francisco—that struck both cents and nickels during 1924. Glossy chocolate surfaces with tinges of red in protected areas.

1470 **1925-D Buffalo Nickel Struck On a Blank—Improperly Cleaned—NCS. AU Details.** 3.09 gms. The dies have produced a nearly complete reproduction of the Buffalo nickel design on this Lincoln cent planchet. Only the edges of the peripheral devices and the tops of the peripheral letters are absent. The surfaces display deep cocoa-tan color, with an area of dark-green verdigris noted on the bison's chin and chest. A few faint hairlines are evident, from a light cleaning.

40% Off Center 1929-Dated Buffalo Nickel MS64

1471   **1929-? Buffalo Nickel—Struck 40% Off Center—MS64 PCGS.** Struck widely off center toward 2 o'clock. The date is complete, as is the left two-thirds of the bison. The mintmark area and the Indian's profile are off the flan. Lightly toned and well preserved. A desirable off center mint error on a popular obsolete type.

1472   **1935 Buffalo Nickel—20% Straight Clip—MS64 NGC.** 4 grams. A straight clip from 10 o'clock to 12:30 prevents the mintmark (if any) from appearing on the lower reverse. This satiny, cream-gray, and chestnut-tan nickel has the expected softness of strike on the eagle's front leg. An interesting and unmarked error.

Double Clipped Planchet 1935 Nickel 8% and 2% Clips, MS64

1473   **1935 Buffalo Nickel—10% Double Clipped Planchet—MS64 PCGS.** This satiny Buffalo nickel has a slightly curved 2% clip at 3:30 and an 8% curved clip at 6 o'clock. The latter clip affects a minor portion of the 35 in the date. Olive and steel-gray toning visits nearly unabraded surfaces.

1974 Jefferson Nickel—Struck on Cent Planchet—MS66

1474   **1974 Jefferson Nickel—Struck on Cent Planchet—MS66 Red and Brown NGC.** This is a fascinating mint error that features a 1974 Jefferson nickel, struck on a Lincoln cent planchet. Even more unusual is the fact that the reverse impression, from the Jefferson nickel die, has been diagonally struck over the obverse portrait impression of our nation's third president. Deep purple-rose and electric-blue toning across both sides is highlighted by intense, satiny mint luster.

1475   **Undated Jefferson Nickel—Obverse Die Cap—MS64 NGC.** The cataloger suspects the date is 1981, but the final two digits are heavily distorted from metal flow to the cap, and are also affected by a small split at 4 o'clock. The cap is uneven in height, quite deep near 9 o'clock but less dished near 3 o'clock. The reverse is expanded, distorted from impressions against a series of planchets fed between strikes.

1476   **Undated Jefferson Nickel—Reverse Die Cap—MS66 NGC.** This nickel has a die cap sufficiently thick that it barely fits within its NGC holder. The obverse shows an expanded, distorted, reversed image of Monticello, which suggests that during the first strike, the planchet rested between the obverse die and a previously struck coin.

Massive 1999-P Jefferson Nickel Bonded Die Cap, MS66

1477   **1999-P Jefferson Nickel—2-Piece Bonded Die Cap—MS66 PCGS.** At least two, and possibly three, planchets are bonded together to form this amazing capped die error. The maximum outside height is 15.3 mm. and the maximum diameter is 29.1 mm. Needless to say, the Jefferson obverse design inside the cap is bold, and the reverse design outside is a mere shadow of Monticello, although it is fascinating that every one of the six steps are complete and sharp. It is difficult to estimate how many strikes were involved, although judging from the rings inside the cap, it is probably in the order of 15 to 20 individual cycles of the press, and perhaps even more.

1478   **1944 Roosevelt Dime—Struck 15% Off Center—MS64 Full Bands PCGS.** The off-center strike, positioned toward 12:30, is responsible for the bold strike of this lovely piece. Both sides are fully brilliant and lustrous, with only faint golden toning.

1479   **1964 Roosevelt Dime—Flipover Double Strike, Second Strike 50% Off Center—MS64 PCGS.** The first strike appears to be normal, but the piece failed to leave the coinage chamber. It flipped over and was struck a second time, 50% off center toward 2 o'clock. The second strike is at 4:30 relative to the reverse of the first strike. The second strike is uniface obverse, with the reverse die blocked by a fed planchet (not included). The force of the second strike caused a tornado-shaped split, which makes much of the first date illegible. The second strike shows only the 196 in the date.

1480   **1979-D Roosevelt Dime—Triple Struck, One Strike Flipover—MS64 PCGS.** The first strike was double-sided, but was apparently already a mint error since the rim appears irregular. Struck a second time 70% off center toward 2 o'clock, at 12 o'clock relative to the first strike. The second strike is uniface obverse. The third strike was a uniface obverse flipover, 60% off center toward 2:30, at 2 o'clock relative to the reverse of the first strike. The date and mintmark is present on the first strike, and the second strike has a partial date.

1481   **1988-D Roosevelt Dime—Struck 95% Off Center—MS63 PCGS.** Although struck 95% off center, this dime has a complete date and mintmark. The unstruck area of the coin has the expected number of tiny planchet abrasions, but the struck portion is lustrous and well preserved.

Impressive Gem 1964 Quarter
Struck on a Cent Planchet

1482 1964 Quarter—Struck on a Cent Planchet—MS65 Brown NGC.
3.09 gm. The small planchet has cut off many peripheral elements,
though enough appears of the tops of the digits in the date to
identify the year. Swirling violet, blue, and olive iridescence drapes
the well-preserved surfaces, and the portrait shows strong detail,
considering the undersized, underweight flan.

**1483 1973 Washington Quarter—Flipover, Double-Struck in Collar—
MS64 PCGS.** This remarkable error was struck, flipped over inside
of the coining chamber, and then struck a second time. The original
striking is most apparent around the perimeter, but the outline of
Washington's head is visible on the reverse. A couple of small grease
spots in the lower right of the obverse are the only areas of color on
this silver-gray representative. The obverse is somewhat dull, but the
reverse is brilliant and highly lustrous.

**1484 1973 Washington Quarter—Struck on a Cent Planchet—MS64
PCGS.** Bright red surfaces with deeper orange and pale blue
toning. Enough of the date is visible for positive year identification,
although the mintmark (if any) is not present.

**1485 1977-D Washington Quarter—Struck on CentPlanchet—MS63
Red and Brown NGC.** 3.07 gms. An impressive mint error with
boldly struck Washington quarter design elements that are nearly
complete, despite being produced on a Lincoln cent planchet. The
planchet appears to be clipped between 9 and 11 o'clock on the
obverse. Lustrous with dense purple-violet and cobalt-blue toning.
Free of any coin-to-coin or circulation marks.

**1486 1981-P Washington Quarter—Struck on a 1981 Nickel—AU58
PCGS.** Golden, light brown, and violet toning accents this
impressive error, which was struck over a 1981 nickel. A couple of
light marks limit the grade, but the details are exceptionally sharp.
The top of LIBERTY and the bottom of the denomination are
obscured. An interesting error with no noteworthy blemishes and
plenty of luster.

Amazing 1999-P Connecticut Quarter Error
Struck on a Feeder Finger Fragment, 0.13 gm

**1487 1999-P Connecticut Quarter—Struck on a Feeder Finger
Fragment—MS65 NGC.** 0.13 gm. A surprising, tiny error piece
that is nonetheless fully identifiable by date and mint. The obverse
of this fragment shows the "P" mintmark prominently, and on the
reverse, the rightmost branches of a tree and the letters (C)UT are
present; these could only correspond to the Connecticut design,
struck only in 1999.

**1488 1969-D Kennedy Half—Double Struck, Second Strike Flipover,
85% Off Center—AU58 NGC.** The first strike was normal. Struck
a second time 85% off center, but the 69 in the date is present on the
second strike, which is uniface because a fed planchet (not
included) blocked the reverse die. The coin flipped between strikes.
The second strike is toward 10:30, and is located at 10:30 relative to
the reverse of the first strike.

**1489 1971-D Kennedy Half—Struck on a Foreign Planchet—
Environmental Damage—NCS. AU Details.** 4.57 gm. Struck
55% off center toward 10:30 on what appears to be a nickel alloy
planchet. The mintmark and the 71 in the date are intact. The
unstruck portion is toned light golden-brown and has the expected
moderate marks, along with a hint of granularity. (#6717)

Interesting AU58 Undated Kennedy Half
Struck 30% Off-Center On a Clad Layer

**1490 Undated Kennedy Half—Struck 30% Off-Center On a Clad
Layer—AU58 PCGS.** An intriguing piece, struck 30% off-center
toward 5 o'clock on a single clad layer. Though the front shows solid
overall detail, particularly on the visible letters of LIBERTY, the
reverse shows merely a ghost image of Kennedy's head. A fantastic
compound error that should delight the enthusiast.

**1491 Undated S-Mint 40% Silver Kennedy Half—Die Adjustment
Strike—PR63 ANACS.** This die adjustment strike shows strong
detail on the portrait and nearby lettering (including the S
mintmark), though the reflective fields taper away to planchet
roughness at the periphery, with the date unidentifiable. Gold and
tan shadings visit the ill-defined areas.

Gem 1978 Eisenhower Dollar Error
Missing Reverse Clad Layer

**1492 1978 Eisenhower Dollar—Missing Reverse Clad Layer—MS65
PCGS.** The depth of the missing reverse clad layer is uneven on this
example, ranging from substantial voids to either side of the eagle
to hints of the clad layer being visible in the center. The obverse
shows subtle gold shadings, while the reverse is generally mahogany-
orange with elements of violet and nickel-white.

1493 **1979-S Anthony Dollar—Broadstruck on a 33% Straight Clip Planchet—MS65 PCGS.** Type One mintmark. The clip is slightly curved and extends from 10 o'clock to 3 o'clock. Due to the broadstrike, the rims have a stretched appearance, as do the letters in UNITED STATES OF AMERICA.

2000-P Sacagawea Dollar Struck on Anthony Dollar Planchet, AU58

1494 **2000-P Sacagawea Dollar—Struck on a Susan B. Anthony Planchet—AU58 ANACS.** Apparently a clad Susan B. Anthony one dollar planchet from the 1999-P issue was retained in a storage hopper, producing this error after the changeover to the first-year Sacagawea design in the year 2000. Lightly circulated with a few contact marks. The ANACS Clearview holder allows easy viewing of the clad layer on the edge.

Choice 2000-P Sacagawea Dollar Struck on a Maryland Quarter

1495 **2000-P Sacagawea Dollar—Double Denomination on a Struck Maryland Quarter—MS64 PCGS.** The lower portion of the left branch of the Maryland quarter undertype is apparent between 12 and 1 o'clock on the reverse. The 2000 date of the undertype is also legible. A lustrous example with light chestnut-gold and ice-blue toning. An important piece that appeals to both Statehood quarter and Sacagawea dollar error collectors.

HARD TIMES TOKEN

1496 **1837 Feuchtwanger Cent MS64 NGC.** Low-120, NY HT-268, Breen 5-G, R.2. NGC has incorrectly certified the variety as Breen 5-H. Exquisitely toned with golden-brown, aquamarine, and ruby-red hues. Mark-free, with a retained lamination present at 3 o'clock on the obverse. Listed on page 385 of the 2009 *Guide Book*. (#20001)

MINT SETS

1497 **Uncertified 1947 Double Mint Set.** The coins individually grade between MS62 and MS65. Most of the silver coins display light to moderate original toning. No 1947-S Walking Liberty halves were struck. (Total: 28 coins)

1498 **Uncertified 1947 Double Mint Set.** The coins are lustrous, and most display attractive moderate original toning. Grades range between MS63 and MS65. No 1947-S Walking Liberty halves were produced. (Total: 28 coins)

1499 **Uncertified 1948 Double Mint Set.** The coins individually grade between MS63 and MS65, and are still housed in the cardboard folders of mint issue. The cents are mostly red, and the silver coins exhibit light to moderate toning. No 1948-S half dollars were struck. (Total: 28 coins)

1500 **Uncertified 1949 Double Mint Set.** The coins grade between MS63 and MS65. The cents are red and brown, and the silver coins have rich and attractive original toning. One of the 1949 Philadelphia nickels is missing, and no 1949-S quarters were struck. (Total: 27 coins)

1501 **1956 through 1958 Mint Sets. Uncertified.** Three double mint sets, one of each year, in the original cardboard holders and later white envelopes. All of the silver coins in each holder have matching toning, indicating that the coins have probably remained together since they were issued. (Total: 3 sets) (#2836)

PROOF SET

Rare 1990 No S Proof Cent

1502 **Uncertified 1990 No S Proof Set.** The set contains a 1990 No S proof cent in addition to the 1990-S proof nickel, dime, quarter, and half. The cent appears pristine at first glance, but has minor corrosion on the rims from contact with the felt insert. The set is still sealed in its plastic holder of mint issue. The outer purple cardboard holder and certificate of authenticity are included. (Total: 5 coins) (#3506)

GSA DOLLARS

1503 **1881-CC GSA HOARD MS63 NGC.** An essentially untoned, minimally abraded Select piece with light frost across the high points, band-certified in the holder of issue. Comes with original box and paper ephemera. (#407126)

1504 **1885-CC GSA HOARD MS65 NGC.** Band-certified in the original holder of issue. This essentially untoned Gem offers vibrant, frosty luster, bold detail, and amazing eye appeal. A great example of this popular GSA issue. (#407160)

Mint and Treasury Archive

1505 **Mint and Treasury Related Financial Documents.** Five early documents pertinent to the U.S. Mint or Treasury:

(1) ALS dated August 2, 1809 by Albert Gallatin, signed as Secretary of the Treasury (Gallatin served that position from 1801 to 1814), to Nathaniel Williams, Esq., Collector of Dighton (MA), pertaining to a petition of Abel Borden, regarding his vessels, with a note on the back, in the pen of Williams, "From the Sec'y, August 2, 1809, that if the facts in Abel Borden petition be true his vessel ought to be released. I answered that they were not."

(2) Mint of the United States, Assistant Treasurer's Office, Philadelphia, March 16, 1848, deposit receipt signed by James Ross Snowden.

(3) Printed report dated June 23, 1854, providing a report of the Register of the Treasury "to communicate to the Senate copies of all quarterly or other accounts of the expenditures of the mint, which have been returned since the 3d of March, 1853," 21 pp.

(4) Printed report of July 5, 1854, transmitting "information respecting the present condition of the building of the United States branch mint at New Orleans," 4 pp.

(5) Report dated September 21, 1874, from the Melter and Refiner itemizing "small sales of sundry residues," signed as received by J.A. Pollock, Superintendent of the Mint.

The five items provide a remarkable and eclectic view of the Mint and Treasury at different points in the 19th century, and will undoubtedly provide much enjoyment for the history buff. Overall condition is excellent. (Total: 5 items)

End of Session Two

SESSION THREE

Live, Internet, and Mail Bid Signature® Auction #1116
Thursday, September 18, 2008, 6:00 PM PT, Lots 1506 - 2558
Long Beach, California

A 15% Buyer's Premium ($9 minimum) Will Be Added To All Lots

Visit HA.com to view full-color images and bid.

THE NEVADA COLLECTION OF SEATED QUARTERS

Richly Toned 1838 No Drapery Seated Quarter, MS63

1506 **1838 No Drapery MS63 NGC.** Open Claws. Briggs 1-A. Rich silver-gray and blue-green toning blankets each side of this lustrous Select Mint State example. While other specimens of this issue have been certified in higher numeric grades, few can reach this example in terms of originality or eye appeal. No individually distracting abrasions are apparent, and the strike is above average for the issue. Popular as the first year of the type, and the only Seated denomination introduced in 1838, following 1837's half dimes and dimes, and preceding 1839 and 1840's halves and silver dollars, respectively.
Ex: Harry Laibstain, private transaction.
From The Nevada Collection of Seated Quarters. (#5391)

1507 **1840-O No Drapery AU58 PCGS.** Briggs 1-A. Mintmark Placed Left. This well struck O-mint quarter offers soft, swirling luster beneath effusive orange and rose patina. Remarkable eye appeal with only slight evidence of brief circulation. Population: 12 in 58, 10 finer (8/08).
Ex: Hoffecker Collection (Superior, 2/1987).
From The Nevada Collection of Seated Quarters. (#5393)

Gorgeous 1840-O Quarter
Drapery MS63 ★, Briggs 2-C, Small O
Finest Certified With Star

1508 **1840-O Drapery MS63 ★ NGC.** Briggs 2-C, Small O. Attributed by a die scratch in the lower obverse shield, the mintmark centered over the R of QUAR, and the 7th vertical line of the reverse shield extending to the 4th horizontal line. Briggs rates the Small O R.6 in Uncirculated. This Select example with the coveted Star displays deep electric-blue, purple, and golden brown peripheral toning framing nearly untoned centers. Sharply struck, with lustrous surfaces revealing just a few trivial handling marks. Census: 1 in 63 ★, 0 finer (7/08).
Ex: Auction '90 (8/1990), lot 647.
From The Nevada Collection of Seated Quarters. (#5398)

Seldom Encountered 1842-O Large Date Quarter, MS64

1509 **1842-O Large Date MS64 PCGS.** Briggs 2-A. The upper part of the top loop of the 8 is heavily recut. The reverse is easily distinguished by the lower positioning of the mintmark. By far the more frequently encountered of the two date size variants. The 1842-O is generally well struck for an O-mint quarter, and this piece certainly bears out that generalization. There are no traces of softness on either side of this splendid piece; in fact, if the mintmark were covered the strike on this coin would be indistinguishable from a P-mint quarter. The bright satiny surfaces are toned on each side but a couple of shades deeper on the reverse. In spite of the mintage of more than three-quarters of a million pieces, the 1842-O is a rare coin in mint condition. Population: 16 in 64, 0 finer (8/08).
Ex: Casterline and Hall Collections (Superior, 5/1989), lot 1451.
From The Nevada Collection of Seated Quarters. (#5402)

1510 **1843-O XF40 PCGS.** Large O. Briggs 3-F, the only known dies. This Large O specimen displays the characteristic die rust lumps scattered throughout the reverse field. Somewhat available in grades up to VF, and rare in higher grades. Indeed, Briggs (1991) assigns an R.7 rating to the large O variety. Dappled olive-green and gray patina covers both sides of this XF specimen, and sharp detail is apparent on the design elements. Both obverse and reverse are quite clean.
Ex: Dick Osburn.
From The Nevada Collection of Seated Quarters. (#5405)

1511 **1844 MS62 PCGS.** Briggs 1-B. The 1844 (421,200 pieces produced) is typically encountered in well worn condition. To date (4/08), PCGS and NGC have seen 50 Mint State examples. This MS62 specimen displays soft silver-white luster imbued with occasional hints of light tan. Well struck, except for softness in most of the star centers. A few minute handling marks show up under magnification.
From The Nevada Collection of Seated Quarters. (#5406)

1512 **1845 MS63 PCGS.** Exquisitely detailed with bright, semiprooflike fields and rich mint-green, yellow, rose, and violet-blue patina over each side.. Strong eye appeal for the Select designation. Very scarce in mint condition, as are all quarters from the 1840s. Population: 12 in 63, 11 finer (8/08).
Ex: Auction '89 (Akers' Session, 7/1989), lot 1059.
From The Nevada Collection of Seated Quarters. (#5408)

1847 Quarter With Repunched Date and Doubled Die Reverse FS-801, MS63

1513 **1847 RPD & DDR MS63 PCGS.** FS-801 (FS-002). The 7 in the date is especially noticeable with the first punch widely to the left. But the more important feature is on the reverse with die doubling seen most notably on UNITED STATES OF AMERICA and QUAR. DOL. At the time the Briggs reference was published (1991) no 1847/47 coins were known in Unc. Apparently several are known today but these are still rare in mint condition. This is a well struck coin that has pronounced die striations in the fields. Rose-purple and gray toning is seen over each side but is deeper on the reverse.
Ex: Auction '86 (Stack's Session, 7/1986), lot 134.
From The Nevada Collection of Seated Quarters. (#5410)

1514 **1848 AU58 PCGS.** Briggs 1-A. Doubled Date. Softly lustrous beneath captivating patina that shows elements of slate-gray, violet, and blue. A well-defined coin that has just a whisper of friction on the uppermost design elements. The population data for this scarce variant is not relevant as the doubled date is not noted on the insert and it does not have a separate PCGS number.
Ex: Norweb Collection (Bowers and Merena, 3/1988), lot 1584.
From The Nevada Collection of Seated Quarters.

Pretty, Low-Mintage 1848 Quarter, MS63

1515 **1848 MS63 NGC.** Briggs 2-B, 1/1/1-8/8. The first digit shows the base of a superfluous 1 near the base, with a horizontal line from another 1 about halfway up the upright. The last 8 is repunched, with doubling showing at the bottom left loop. Wispy die cracks touch the bottoms of the date digits, several of the stars (some of which show recutting), and the liberty cap. The reverse is the "plain shield" variety (per Briggs) with large thick letters, although, unusually, there are few "spider cracks" connecting the peripheral legends. The obverse is silver with a ring of gold, while the reverse shows iridescent almond and steel-blue tones. An interesting and pretty example of this low-mintage issue, seldom seen finer.
Ex: Harmer Rooke, 1986.
From The Nevada Collection of Seated Quarters. (#5412)

1516 **1849 MS61 NGC.** Well struck with varying shades of charcoal-gray and steel-gray, and hints of coral near the peripheries. An appealingly lustrous example with a few tiny marks on each side.
Ex: Four Landmark Collections (Bowers and Merena, 3/1989), lot 247.
From The Nevada Collection of Seated Quarters. (#5413)

Select Mint State 1850-O Seated Quarter

1517 1850-O MS63 PCGS. Briggs 1-B. Liberty's rock, the shield, and date area all show heavy die rust, as well as on the reverse under the eagle's right (facing) wing. The large O mintmark is low and to the right of center under the eagle, thinner at the bottom than at the top. The lowest horizontal shield line is heavily doubled at the right side.

It is uncertain how many 1849-O and 1850-O quarters were struck—and how many survived the mass meltings of the 1850s, when silver rose as reckoned in gold dollars, due to the vast California discoveries. The 1849-O delivery was included in the 1850-O number, but the 1849-O is much rarer. Grayish-pink patina covers most of both sides, a bit heavier on the obverse. The coin has a good strike, but the deep coloration subdues the luster to a degree. Certified in an old-style small holder. Only one piece finer is certified at PCGS. Population: 6 in 63, 1 finer (8/08).
From The Nevada Collection of Seated Quarters. (#5416)

Elusive, Lustrous MS63 1852 Seated Quarter

1518 1852 MS63 NGC. Briggs 2-B. Throw away the reported mintage figures for the 1849-1853 No Arrows coinage. No one today truly knows how many of each issue escaped the smelters in 1853-1855 or so, when the silver content of those pieces, as measured in gold dollars, rose sufficiently above their face value to make melting not only profitable, but predictable. This well-struck, golden-pink example boasts bountiful luster and premium appeal, although an undistracting bit of die grease near the final A in AMERICA is noted. Census: 8 in 63, 10 finer (8/08).
Ex: J.D Garrett / ANA Mid-Winter Sale (Heritage, 2/1986), lot 893, where it realized $950.
From The Nevada Collection of Seated Quarters. (#5419)

Remarkable 1852-O Quarter, MS62
Tied for Second Finest Certified

1519 1852-O MS62 PCGS. Only 96,000 pieces were struck of the 1852-O and remarkably few are known today, especially above VF. Those that are seen are generally weakly struck and many have a "saltwater" surface. This piece shows some softness of details on the obverse, but the reverse is remarkably well defined. The obverse also shows some porosity, but again the reverse is smooth and sparkles with mint luster. The obverse has smoky golden and lilac toning, while again the reverse presents a stark contrast and is nearly brilliant. This piece is tied for second finest certified with one NGC coin. The finest known is an NGC MS63 that sold in our November 2007 Dallas Auction for an unprecedented $126,500.
Ex: Auction '88 (Superior's Session, 7/1988), lot 119.
From The Nevada Collection of Seated Quarters. (#5420)

Lustrous MS64 1853 Arrows and Rays Quarter

1520 1853 Arrows and Rays MS64 PCGS. Struck for only one year, the 1853 Arrows and Rays has an enduring popularity with collectors. While the arrows device was used through 1855 and then resurrected again in 1873-74, the glory of rays on the reverse is unique to this one year alone. As with most of the higher grade pieces known, this piece has lovely soft, frosted mint luster. The surfaces are overlaid with streaky deep and lighter gray toning on the obverse, while the reverse is generally light gray overall. Sharply struck throughout.
From The Nevada Collection of Seated Quarters. (#5426)

Sharply Contrasted
1853/4 Arrows and Rays Quarter, MS64
Tied for Finest Certified

1521 **1853/4 Arrows and Rays MS64 PCGS.** Briggs 1-A. This enigmatic overdate shows a mistaken final-digit punch from the next year rather than the previous year. This die state shows the upper portion of the 4 within the top of the 3, and it also plainly displays the repunching above the right arrow shaft. Only 20 pieces have been certified in mint condition by both of the major grading services. At the MS64 level, this coin is tied with two others as finest certified (8/08). This is a lovely coin that has the usual strong mint luster one would expect on an 1853 quarter. This lustrous finish serves to backlight the gray-olive surfaces that have a strong contrast of charcoal-gray over the devices. Sharply struck and seemingly defect-free.
Ex: Auction '89 (Superior's Session, 7/1989), lot 577.
From The Nevada Collection of Seated Quarters. (#5427)

Condition Rarity 1854-O Arrows Quarter, MS62

1522 **1854-O Arrows MS62 NGC.** The 1854-O Arrows quarter is common through VF, but becomes scarce in XF and AU. Mint State pieces are very rare; Larry Briggs (1991) assigns an R.6 rating to Uncirculated coins. Delicate gold-tan patina concentrates at the borders of this luminous MS62 specimen, and an attentive strike leaves sharp definition on the design elements. A few minute marks are visible in the fields of both sides.
From The Nevada Collection of Seated Quarters. (#5433)

Lustrous, Richly Toned 1855 Arrows Quarter, MS64

1523 **1855 Arrows MS64 PCGS.** While the 1855 Arrows is a common coin in the lower circulated grades, it is surprisingly difficult in mint condition. Only 18 other pieces have been so graded by both of the major services combined, with 17 finer (4/08). This is a sharply struck example that shows the date with notably weakly impressed digits. Deep, swirling multicolored toning is seen over each side with strong underlying mint luster. There are no surface defects visible without the use of a magnifier. Population: 9 in 64, 7 finer (8/08).
Ex: Norweb II (Bowers and Merena, 3/1988), lot 1600.
From The Nevada Collection of Seated Quarters. (#5435)

1524 **1855-S Arrows AU53 ANACS.** The 1855-S was the first quarter dollar issued in the newly-opened San Francisco mint. Almost 400,000 pieces were struck but attrition took a heavy toll on this issue, as small change was so badly needed in the channels of commerce in California at the time. The surfaces are light-gray, with even wear, and a few wispy field blemishes. Well struck throughout. What appears to be die crumbling occurs around the wings.
From The Nevada Collection of Seated Quarters. (#5437)

1525 **1857 MS64 NGC.** Ex: Richmond Collection. Wisps of faint gold-tan patina adhere to the lustrous surfaces of this near-Gem, and a well executed strike sharpens the design features, save for softness in the arrow feathers. A few minute marks preclude Gem status.
From The Nevada Collection of Seated Quarters. (#5442)

1526 **1857-O MS61 NGC.** Despite a sizeable mintage of nearly 1.2 million pieces, this O-mint Seated quarter issue is surprisingly elusive in Uncirculated grades. The present example is richly toned over both sides in deep russet-red and purple patina. Liberty's head is typically weak, but most of the other design elements are sharply defined. Vibrantly lustrous and free of severe marks; a fingerprint fragment is noted across the upper reverse field.
Ex: Stack's, private transaction.
From The Nevada Collection of Seated Quarters. (#5443)

Low-Mintage 1857-S Quarter, MS63
Seldom Seen Finer

1527 **1857-S MS63 PCGS.** Briggs 1-A. The initial mintage was a skimpy 82,000 pieces, and most apparently entered circulation immediately, as the average grade of certified pieces is only slightly better than Choice XF. In MS63 this is one of only two examples at PCGS, with two finer (8/08). The date slopes downward slightly left to right, and the large S mintmark on the reverse is barely free of a feather on the left, and tilts to the left. The lustrous silver-gold surfaces show good field-device contrast, with lots of eye appeal. A well struck and pleasing coin, seldom seen finer. Certified in an old-style small holder.
Ex: Auction '89 (RARCOA, 7/1989), lot 156.
From The Nevada Collection of Seated Quarters. (#5444)

1528 **1859-O MS61 PCGS.** Silver-white, gold-orange, and tan elements converge on each side of this unworn and shining New Orleans quarter. Well defined with few overt marks, though wispy abrasions are present in the fields. Population: 3 in 61, 7 finer (8/08).
Ex: Stack's (1/1987), lot 187.
From The Nevada Collection of Seated Quarters. (#5449)

Rare XF 1859-S Seated Quarter

1529 **1859-S XF40 NGC.** Briggs 1-A, the only known dies. This is a scarce issue in all grades, and no true Mint State examples are known, although a few AU coins are certified at NGC and PCGS. This piece shows deep smoke-gray toning evenly covering both sides, with the usual die crumbling around several of the obverse stars. A few shallow scrapes appear to the left of the date, but otherwise the coin is characterized by even wear with no singular distractions. Briggs calls the issue "rare" in XF and "extremely rare" in AU. Census: 4 in 40, 5 finer (8/08).
Ex: Jim Gray Collection (Bowers and Merena, 7/2004), lot 2237.
From The Nevada Collection of Seated Quarters. (#5450)

1530 **1860 MS62 PCGS.** One of the more available No Motto quarters with a mintage of 804,000 pieces. This sharply struck example is almost totally brilliant with just a hint of pale rose color on each side. Only the slightest abrasions account for the grade of this attractive quarter. Population: 8 in 62, 31 finer (8/08).
Purchased from Bowers and Merena, 1987.
From The Nevada Collection of Seated Quarters. (#5451)

Scarce 1860-S Quarter, VF35

1531 **1860-S VF35 PCGS.** The 1860-S quarter is similar to most of the other S-mint denominations from this decade. The mintage was not notably low, in this case 56,000 pieces produced, but it was apparently calculated to fulfill the needs for regional commerce. Only 30 coins have been certified in all grades by both PCGS and NGC combined (8/08), and only one piece has been graded in mint condition (an NGC MS61). Most of the coins certified grade lower than this piece with the average grade only 21.2. Problem coins are also frequently seen on this issue. This is a problem-free coin for the grade. The devices show the usual softness that this issue is known for, and the high points are light rose-gray and contrast sharply against the deep charcoal gray seen in the fields and recesses of the design elements.
Ex: Wiley Collection.
From The Nevada Collection of Seated Quarters. (#5453)

1532 **1864 MS62 NGC.** Ex: Richmond Collection. Well struck with intense mint frost across both sides, and lovely olive and champagne peripheral toning. A couple of faint pinscratches, on the lower left obverse, restrict the grade. Census: 5 in 62, 28 finer (8/08).
Ex: Richmond Sale, Part III (David Lawrence), lot 1458.
From The Nevada Collection of Seated Quarters. (#5459)

1533 **1864-S MS64 PCGS.** In a *Coin World* article from January 29, 2002, Paul Green analyzed the 1864-S quarter and came to the conclusion that its rarity is based on heavy circulation and lack of a collector base in the West, not merely that only 20,000 pieces were struck.

> "San Francisco only made silver and gold coins, but there seemed to be a general feeling in the West that anything other than gold and silver was not really welcome. Apparently, if change of less than five cents was needed, people just compensated with a free donkey ride."

In all grades only 69 of these pieces have been certified by PCGS and NGC, minus an uncertain number of resubmissions. The breaking point of availability, such as it is, for the '64-S seems to be at the XF45 level. Above that only 18 pieces have been certified. The number of high grade 1864-S quarters is paltry indeed. A mere 10 pieces have been graded by both services. In MS64 only five others have been certified. The finest is a remarkable NGC MS68!

The surfaces on this piece are bright and sparkling with deeper accents of golden-brown toning in the fields. Overall the strike is strong, but is lacking on the peripheral obverse stars. With only 20,000 pieces struck, virtually no collector base, and a high attrition rate, when a high grade 1864-S such as this one can be located, it is well worth owning and certainly a coin that many advanced collections lack.

Ex: R.L. Miles Collection (Stack's, 4/1969); Auction '86 (Stack's Session, 7/1986), lot 142.

From The Nevada Collection of Seated Quarters. (#5460)

Lustrous and Rare Near-Gem 1866 Motto Quarter

1534 **1866 Motto MS64 NGC.** This is the first year that Mint added
the motto IN GOD WE TRUST to the nation's larger coinage,
where it retains it to this day (even if sometimes in awkward places).
But the Philadelphia Mint in this year was chiefly concerned with
pumping out vast quantities of minor coins and Seated halves, and
the mintage figures for the Seated half dime, dime, and quarter are
decidedly on the skimpy side. The quarter saw a production of only
26,800 pieces, and today Briggs rates the issue rare in all grades. This
is a nice piece with no singular distractions or hairlines, although a
small scrape downward from the Liberty cap likely limits a finer
grade. The lustrous silver-gray surfaces show considerable contrast,
and generate plenty of appeal. Census: 4 in 64, 17 finer (8/08).
Ex: Westchester Collection (Bowers and Merena, 2/1987), lot 1692.
From The Nevada Collection of Seated Quarters. (#5468)

Seldom Seen 1868-S Quarter, MS64

1535 **1868-S MS64 PCGS.** The 1868-S continues the tradition of
scarcity from the West coast facility in spite of a mintage that should
indicate greater availability. The end of the Civil War seemed to
have no impact on the high attrition rate of S-mint silver coins, as
indeed they continued to circulate just as heavily after the War as
they had during it. The 1868-S had a mintage of only 96,000 pieces,
but its availability in better grades is equal to a Philadelphia Mint
coin with only a fraction of that production. A paltry five pieces
have been certified of the '68-S in MS64 by both of the major
services, and another five have been graded higher (8/08). This is
a lovely piece with creamy mint luster and nearly untoned surfaces.
Strongly struck, except on the upper two stars on the obverse, there
are no noticeable abrasions on either side.
*Ex: R.L. Miles (Stack's, 4/1969); Auction '86 (Stack's Session, 7/1986),
lot 146.*
From The Nevada Collection of Seated Quarters. (#5473)

Very Rare MS63 1869 Seated Quarter

1536 **1869 MS63 PCGS.** Briggs 1-A. The year 1869 is another one in which the small mintage of Liberty Seated quarters took a distant back seat in Philadelphia to various other coinage preoccupations. While the quarters were produced to the extent of only 16,000 pieces, the Seated halves comprised nearly 800,000 examples. This piece shows a triple-punched 1 in the date, with remaining digits double-punched. On the reverse there are crisscrossing die polish lines, including one starting at the period after DOL., past arrowheads, touching the tip of the second arrowhead, and intersecting a right-angle die line from the dentils. The surfaces display generous luster with light pink-champagne patina on the obverse, while the reverse is mostly brilliant. A very rare issue in Mint State. Population: 5 in 63, 3 finer (8/08).
Ex: Robert Michael Prescott Collection (ANR, 1/2006), lot 378.
From The Nevada Collection of Seated Quarters. (#5474)

1537 **1872 MS63 NGC.** More difficult to locate than its mintage of 182,000 would imply, as many were probably melted in the 1873 silver melt. Splashes of purple and electric-blue are more prominent on the obverse of this Select quarter. Lustrous surfaces exhibit sharply struck devices, and reveal a few minor grade-defining handling marks.
Ex: Stack's (6/1991).
From The Nevada Collection of Seated Quarters. (#5481)

Sketch for Gobrecht's Long-Running Eagle Reverse

Spectacular 1872-S Quarter, MS66
The Incomparable Norweb Specimen

1538 **1872-S MS66 PCGS.** The 1872-S ranks among the most challenging Motto Seated quarters. Larry Briggs, in *The Comprehensive Encyclopedia of United States Liberty Seated Quarters*, offers brief comments on the issue: "Rarest 'S' mint. Rare and very hard to locate in any condition. Most probably melted in 1873 creating a far greater demand than supply." The original production of 83,000 pieces is consistent with the yearly nominal mintages for quarters at San Francisco between 1866 and 1872, the first years for the Motto Above Eagle, No Arrows design variant. Passage of the Act of February 12, 1873, resulted in numerous changes to American coinage, one of which was a slight increase in the weights of the dime, quarter, and half dollar. San Francisco did not issue any old-tenor quarters in that year; in addition, any quarters of previous years still on hand were likely melted and recoined to the new standard. Such melting could explain why the 1872-S is less available today than other issues with lower published mintages.

When this coin sold as part of the second sale of the Norweb Collection in March 1988, the cataloging staff described it as "... unsurpassed by any other example we have ever seen or heard of." Three years later, Larry Briggs specifically referred to this remarkable coin as the finest known survivor in his *Comprehensive Encyclopedia*. Just 40 examples of the 1872-S quarter appear in the combined certified populations of NGC and PCGS, with 18 coins graded by the former firm and 22 by the latter. These figures likely include resubmissions and crossovers, further narrowing the pool of unimpaired survivors. Neither NGC nor PCGS has certified an example that is numerically finer than the MS66 designation awarded to this coin. Of the 40 listings in the August PCGS *Population Report*, 12 are Mint State (with several apparent resubmissions); two are graded MS65, and there is now another MS66 (we believe this represents a crossover at this grade level).

In its aforementioned appearance as part of Norweb II, this coin's description began: "**1872-S MS-65.** A superb specimen with brilliant surfaces overlaid by delicate lilac toning." More specifically, the obverse offers the appearance of lilac to the unaided eye, while subtle champagne and turquoise shadings are visible under magnification. On the reverse, gold patina prevails, and occasional whispers of peach grace the margins. This coin offers powerful luster and strong definition for the issue, with the central details particularly impressive. The stars above and to the right of Liberty display slight softness, but the effect is minor. The fields of each side show numerous die polish lines; while the obverse displays little (if any) evidence of clash marks, a curving line to the left of IN and a strong, straight line below WE on the ribbon above the eagle correspond exactly to the contours of Liberty on the opposite side. Astonishingly well-preserved, with only trivial and well-hidden flaws on each side. A pair of markers permit easy plate-matching with the Norweb specimen. To the left of Liberty is a faint fingerprint, and a minor planchet flaw at the upper reverse offers a further diagnostic.

When this piece was offered as part of the Stack's sale of the Empire Collection in November 1957, the brief description concluded that it was "[w]orthy of a premium bid." As part of Norweb II, it received even more effusive praise: "Here indeed is a major rarity. ... a memorable Liberty Seated quarter, a piece which, when sold, could probably not be duplicated the morning after for double the price." The eloquence of numismatists can do little more than pay tribute to this amazing piece, but its beauty can speak for itself.

Ex: Empire Collection (Stack's, November 1957), lot 1112; Norweb II (Bowers and Merena, March 1988).

From The Nevada Collection of Seated Quarters. (#5483)

Deeply Toned MS64 1873-S Arrows Quarter Tied for Second Finest Certified

1539 1873-S Arrows MS64 PCGS. Briggs 1-A. Open 3, as are both variants of the 1873-S quarter. Obverse 1 has an irregular date that slopes downward, and on Reverse A the mintmark is small, clearly defined, and positioned above the upright of the R in QUAR. Only 156,000 pieces were struck in the West Coast facility, and as usual, most were circulated with few examples set aside in mint condition. Only 23 pieces have been certified in Mint State by both of the major services, minus an unknown number of resubmissions. At the MS64 level, this is the only piece certified by PCGS, while NGC has certified three (8/08). Only one coin is finer, a PCGS MS65. Deep scarlet, blue, and gray toning is seen over each side. Sharply defined in all areas, there are no obvious abrasions, and the mint luster glows strongly beneath the deep toning.
Ex: B. Max Mehl, November 18, 1955; Norweb II (Bowers and Merena, 3/1988), lot 1650; Auction '89 (Superior's Session, 7/89), lot 583.
From The Nevada Collection of Seated Quarters. (#5493)

1540 1874-S Arrows MS60 PCGS. Splashes of light olive-green patina are seen on both sides of this S-mint quarter, each of which exhibits well struck devices. A few light handling marks are noted. Housed in a first generation holder.
From The Nevada Collection of Seated Quarters. (#5495)

1541 1875-S MS62 NGC. Well struck and lustrous, with pale steel-blue and speckled tan coloration over both sides. Free of distracting marks, with slightly subdued luster that seemingly limits the grade. A scarce, lower-mintage issue with a total business strike mintage of just 680,000 pieces. Census: 14 in 62, 38 finer (7/08).
Ex: Stack's (1/1987), lot 209.
From The Nevada Collection of Seated Quarters. (#5500)

1542 1876 MS63 PCGS. Brilliant except for a few dabs of golden on the reverse rim, and showing strong semireflective fields on each side. Fully struck. A lovely type coin.
Ex: Stack's (6/1989), lot 1594.
From The Nevada Collection of Seated Quarters. (#5501)

1543 1877-S Over Horizontal S MS63 NGC. Briggs 4-D, a popular and elusive variety, this example readily reveals traces of its undermintmark. Cobalt-blue, purple, and gold-tan patina dances over the lustrous surfaces of this well struck Select quarter. A few trivial marks limit the grade.
Ex: Westchester Collection and other consignments (Bowers and Merena, 2/1987), lot 1708.
From The Nevada Collection of Seated Quarters. (#5507)

Reflective MS64 1880 Quarter Mintage: 13,600 Pieces

1544 1880 MS64 PCGS. While the fields are bright and flashy with ample reflectivity, they are not strong enough to confuse this coin with a proof—a problem that frequently occurred before third-party grading. Both sides are brilliant and completely untoned, and strong striking details are seen throughout. Always popular because of the low emission of business strikes, only 13,600 pieces were produced.
From The Nevada Collection of Seated Quarters. (#5512)

1545 1884 MS62 Prooflike NGC. Rich red-brown, lavender, and cobalt-blue toning adorns the obverse and reverse margins of this prooflike Mint State specimen. Well struck with few surface marks, all of which are trivial in nature.
Ex: Auction '89 (Stack's Session, 7/89), lot 1687.
From The Nevada Collection of Seated Quarters. (#5516)

1546 1886 MS64 PCGS. Sharply struck with powerful, flashy luster. The minimally toned centers yield to delightful peach, gold, and violet-blue patina at the margins. Population: 21 in 64, 19 finer (8/08). *Ex: Fenn Collection (Stack's, 10/1976), lot 639; Stack's (1/1987), lot 229.*
From The Nevada Collection of Seated Quarters. (#5518)

1547 1890 MS64 PCGS. Electric-blue, purple, and gold-tan patina at the margins frame the silver-gray centers of this near-Gem. Satiny luster adorns both sides, each of which displays sharply struck design elements. Nicely preserved, and residing in a first generation holder.
From The Nevada Collection of Seated Quarters. (#5523)

1548 1891-S MS64 NGC. Glowing luster emanates from both sides of this near-Gem, each of which is bathed by dapples of light gray patina. Impressively struck, with just a few trivial obverse marks. Census: 48 in 64, 15 finer (8/08). *Ex: Jascha Heifetz Collection (Superior, 10/1989), lot 3653.*
From The Nevada Collection of Seated Quarters. (#5526)

PROOF SEATED QUARTERS FROM THE NEVADA COLLECTION

1549 1858 PR63 NGC. The 2009 *Guide Book* gives a mintage of 300 proof 1858 quarters. Warm orange-gold patina is accented with sky-blue and lavender, and a full strike results in bold definition on the design elements. A few faint hairlines in the fields limit the grade. *Ex: The Charles Kramer Collection Sale (Superior, 11/1988), lot 1289.*
From The Nevada Collection of Seated Quarters. (#5554)

Richly Toned PR64 1873 Arrows Quarter

1550 1873 Arrows PR64 PCGS. Always popular with collectors, the Arrows type was only struck for two years. In 1873 a mere 540 proofs were produced. Several dozen are known today in PR64 and finer—apparently the significance of the arrowheads in relation to the normally seen design type was appreciated by a number of collectors at the time. The deeply mirrored fields on this proof flash strongly through the deep scarlet-rose centers and sea-green peripheral color. A splendid example of this important type coin. *Ex: Auction '88 (Superior's Session, 7/1988), lot 122.*
From The Nevada Collection of Seated Quarters. (#5574)

1551 1875 PR62 Cameo PCGS. Sharply struck with outstanding contrast between the moderately hairlined fields and the richly frosted devices. Reddish-orange peripheral patina highlights the minimally toned centers. Population: 5 in 62 Cameo, 26 finer (8/08).
From The Nevada Collection of Seated Quarters. (#85576)

1552 1881 PR63 NGC. Beautiful multicolored toning bathes both sides of this Select proof, and an attentive strike brings out virtually complete definition on the design elements. The grade is limited by some faint handling marks. *Ex: The Charles Kramer Collection (Superior, 11/1988), lot 1307.*
From The Nevada Collection of Seated Quarters. (#5582)

Iridescently Toned Gem Proof 1885 Seated Quarter

1553 1885 PR65 PCGS. While the proofs were produced to their usual degree (940 pieces), the business strikes, like so many Seated denominations of the era, were produced in minuscule quantities (13,600 coins), so many collectors must turn to proof coinage for a nice, problem-free piece. This Gem proof offers iridescent steel-blue and champagne-pink patina on each side, with good field-device contrast and plenty of appeal. Certified in an old-style small holder. *Ex: L.W. Hoffecker Collection (Superior, 2/1987), lot 2877.*
From The Nevada Collection of Seated Quarters. (#5586)

Additional Seated Quarters Begin With Lot 1841

PCGS-Certified 15 Piece 1873 Proof Set
Complete From Cent Through Trade Dollar

1554 **15-Piece 1873 Proof Set PCGS.**

Closed 3 Cent PR65 Red. Well struck and unabraded. Straw-gold aside from variegated rose-red on the central reverse. Very scarce in full red. Population: 27 in 65 Red, 3 finer (7/08).

Closed 3 Two Cent Piece PR65 Brown. Substantial orange-red remains, although the open fields are gunmetal-blue. Boldly struck and carbon-free. A popular proof-only date with a Closed 3 mintage of 600 pieces.

Open 3 Two Cent Piece PR64 Brown. A sharply struck and mark-free near-Gem with dusky tan toning. Just 500 Open 3 proofs were struck. Population: 26 in 64 Brown, 4 finer (7/08).

Three Cent Silver PR63. An untoned example with moderate contrast between the devices and the slightly subdued fields. The upper reverse is mildly granular. A proof-only date with a mintage of just 600 pieces, all struck with a Closed 3.

Closed 3 Three Cent Nickel PR64. Ice-blue and honey-gold illuminates this suitably struck and unmarked near-Gem. A charming example in a grade that provides excellent value.

Closed 3 Shield Nickel PR65 Cameo. This nicely mirrored Gem is delicately toned in caramel-gold and steel-blue. Refreshingly free from marks or carbon. Population: 22 in 65 Cameo, 15 finer (7/08).

Half Dime PR64. Closed 3, as are all 1873 half dimes. Aquamarine and golden-brown with clean surfaces and minor inexactness of strike on the upper left portion of the wreath. The final year of the denomination, made unnecessary by the Shield nickel. Just 600 proofs were struck.

No Arrows, Closed 3 Dime PR65 Cameo. Ocean-blue and golden-brown bands hug the obverse border. The reverse is untoned aside from a couple of russet freckles. Reasonably struck with good obverse contrast. Population: 10 in 65 Cameo, 1 finer (7/08).

Arrows Dime PR64 Cameo. The fields and devices are untoned, while the obverse border is navy-blue. A suitably struck near-Gem with attractive preservation. A scarce and popular two-year type with a combined proof mintage of 1,500 pieces. Population: 5 in 64 Cameo, 4 finer (5/08).

No Arrows Quarter PR64. Light gold toning visits this precisely struck and mark-free Choice proof dime. Although undesignated as Cameo, white on black contrast is perceptible. Only 600 proofs were struck. Population: 37 in 64, 18 finer (7/08).

Arrows Quarter PR64 Cameo. Peripheral rose patina encompasses the nearly brilliant fields and devices. Intricately struck and attractive. The major devices display obvious contrast. Only 540 proofs were struck for the first of only two proof Arrows issues. Population: 10 in 64 Cameo, 2 finer (7/08).

No Arrows, Closed 3 Half Dollar PR64 Cameo. Blushes of pale apricot grace this exquisitely struck and undisturbed near-Gem. Only 600 proofs were struck, and quality survivors are very scarce. Population: 11 in 64 Cameo, 4 finer (7/08).

Arrows Half Dollar PR63 Cameo. A good strike with only minor blending on the eagle's left (facing) ankle. The lightly frosted devices contrast with the slightly subdued fields. Just 550 proofs were struck, and only 1,250 proofs were issued for the entire two-year subtype.

Seated Dollar PR64 Cameo. Medium apricot-gold and apple-green adorns this nicely struck near-Gem. IN GOD WE is moderately die doubled. The final date of the type, since silver dollars were replaced with the Trade dollar by the "Crime of 1873" legislation. A scant 600 proofs were struck. Population: 20 in 64 Cameo, 1 finer (7/08).

Trade Dollar PR63 Cameo. Icy motifs provide good contrast with the minimally toned and glassy fields. The strike is precise save for blending on the eagle's right (facing) leg. A lengthy, bold die line (as made) passes through the lower obverse drapery. A mere 865 proofs were issued. Population: 11 in 63 Cameo, 6 finer (7/08). (Total: 15 coins) (#2308)

Choice VF 1792 Half Disme, Judd-7, Pollock-7

1555 **1792 Half Disme, Judd-7, Pollock-7, R.4, VF35 NGC. CAC.** Silver. Diagonally reeded edge. 17.5 mm. The famous 1792 half disme is one of the most coveted issues in all of American numismatics, and rightly so. It was (possibly) designed by British engraver Robert Russell Birch, and (probably) struck in the coachhouse cellar of John Harper, a Philadelphia sawmaker. The original issue of 1,500 (or 2,000) pieces was allegedly made using silver bullion contributed by George Washington, perhaps even from his own personal silverware. This story is, alas, unconfirmed.

Such is the history of the 1792 half disme. Many of the facts about these fascinating pieces are simply unknown, but can be reasonably deduced: like the name of their designer. Robert Russell Birch executed other coin designs very similar to that of the half disme, making him the most likely candidate for authorship. Other facts (like the original number produced) are likely to remain uncertain; possibly forever. That will not reduce the ongoing fascination of numismatists with these coins, however. They are simply too interesting to ignore.

The current example is an attractive and well detailed specimen that is sure to elicit a great deal of attention. The toning over both sides is quite dark, but not unattractive. Shades of emerald-green, amber, blue-gray and gold are among the most prominent colors to be featured on the coin's surfaces. There are a few wispy pinscratches and hairlines on each side, but the only noticeable mark is a shallow abrasion that extends from the upper obverse rim, across the right edge of the P in PAR, to a point that is just above the centering dot over Liberty's ear. A small carbon spot is noted directly beneath the Y in INDUSTRY.

An important piece of history, and a highly desirable numismatic rarity. (#11020)

1556 1795—Improperly Cleaned—NCS. AU50 Details. V-4, LM-10, R.3. The first star is joined to the tip of the second hair curl, identifying the obverse, and the reverse has five berries on each side. Cleaning has left the surfaces a somewhat unnatural deep gray, but there is impressive detail throughout. Several shallow scratches are noted in the fields, and there is also a tiny rim nick between stars 5 and 6. Still, a sharply defined and minimally abraded representative. (#4251)

Impressive 1795 Half Dime
MS62, V-5, LM-8

1557 1795 MS62 PCGS. V-5, LM-8, R.3. Most easily attributed by the lack of berries around the lower left portion of the wreath and the relative position of the lowest outside left leaf relative to the U in UNITED. The die crack through the Y in LIBERTY, familiar to specialists, also confirms this die pairing. Among the finest known examples of this variety is the MS67 Prooflike piece we sold in our November 2006 Dallas Signature. The present example has striking details that are less well defined as that coin, with some weakness evident in the center of each side. Brilliant throughout, the surfaces show satin-like mint luster, and there are surprisingly few abrasions on either side. *From The Menlo Park Collection.* (#4251)

Lustrous 1795 LM-8 Half Dime, MS63

1558 1795 MS63 PCGS. V-5, LM-8, R.3. Relatively few Mint State 1795 half dimes exist, and those that do survive are most apt to be examples of either LM-8 or LM-10. They are the two most plentiful die varieties, and the pieces that are most often available to type collectors. The obverse has a ring of golden-brown on the bust, with brilliant silver luster inside the ring, and pale gray outside. The reverse has smooth gray luster with hints of ivory. Reverse adjustment marks slant down to the right and left, and they are primarily visible on the eagle. This lovely half dime will undoubtedly please the connoisseur. Population: 44 in 63, 37 finer (8/08). (#4251)

1559 1796 LIKERTY VG8 NGC. V-1, LM-1, R.3. A well worn but easily identifiable example of this scarce, popular early half-dime variety. A few shallow adjustment marks extend through Liberty's hair, but there are no large or distracting abrasions on either side. (#94254)

Rare XF 1797 13 Stars Half Dime

Splendid 1797 LM-1 15 Stars Half Dime, AU55

1560 **1797 13 Stars XF40 PCGS.** V-1, LM-4, R.6. The sole 13 stars variety, and quite rare although Heritage has auctioned several in recent years, including an NGC AU58 that brought $40,250 in June 2006. This is an attractively toned example with rich golden-brown, sun-gold, plum-red, and jade-green toning. A small mark near the nose and a brief hair-thin mark behind the hair ribbon, but otherwise unabraded. The strike is good, and the eye appeal is imposing. The key *Guide Book* variety to a collection of Draped Bust, Small Eagle half dimes. Population: 3 in 40, 6 finer (8/08). (#4260)

1561 **1797 15 Stars AU55 NGC.** V-2, LM-1, R.3. Four die marriages are known for 1797-dated half dimes, but these exhibit three different obverse star counts. LM-1 is the sole 15 Star variety for the year, and hence merits its own *Guide Book* listing. Apple-gray and lavender colors proclaim the originality of this pleasing early half dime, which retains most of its original shimmering luster. The centers have minor softness of strike, as is usual for the type, but rub is generally limited to Liberty's drapery. As of August 2008, NGC has certified 23 examples of LM-1 in all grades, but only two in AU55 and nine in higher grades. An extremely important opportunity is presented to the advanced specialist.
From The Menlo Park Collection. (#4258)

Nicely Defined 1800 Half Dime
VF30, V-1, LM-1

1562 **1800 VF30 NGC.** V-1, LM-1, R.3. A somewhat thick 8 and a leaf joined to the second A in AMERICA identify this die marriage. Also, a die break develops through the dentils below 00 in the date. Variegated pale violet and bluish-gray patina bathes both sides, each of which is devoid of serious marks. A nicely defined piece. Housed in a prior generation holder.
From The Morton J. Greene Collection. (#4264)

Elusive 1800 Half Dime AU53, V-1, LM-1

1563 **1800 AU53 PCGS.** V-1, LM-1, R.3. A prominent die break (as made) within the denticles below the 00 in the date confirms the die marriage. This sharply struck early Half Dime has deep lavender and olive-green patina. Very close to Mint State, but moderate abrasions are noted near the L in LIBERTY and on Liberty's forehead, cheek, and chin. A sharp example of this scarce early silver type.
Ex: Portland Signature (Heritage, 3/2004), lot 5467.
From The Menlo Park Collection. (#4264)

1564 **1800 LIBEKTY—Reverse Scratched, Improperly Cleaned—NCS. XF Details.** The reverse has three noticeable pinscratches, one from the left shield tip through UNUM and two others northeast of the eagle's head. A small obverse edge flaw at 9 o'clock is as made. Some luster remains, and the obverse ocean-blue and rose-gold toning is attractive.
From The Morton J. Greene Collection. (#4265)

Colorful AU 1800 Half Dime LIBEKTY
V-2, LM-3

1565 **1800 LIBEKTY AU50 NGC.** V-2, LM-3, R.4. The collectible LIBEKTY variety, since its alternative, LM-4, is extremely rare. The letter punch for R had a broken upper crossbar when it was selected by obverse die engraver, and with a little imagination it resembles the letter K. The variety is sometimes confused with the 1796 LIKERTY, caused by a broken and softly impressed B punch.

Of course, any 1800 half dime is desirable, as a representative of the difficult Draped Bust, Heraldic Reverse type. The present example will be warmly welcomed by bidders, since it is splendidly detailed and displays attractive cream-gray, golden-brown, and cobalt-blue patina. From a later state with localized die failure beneath the eagle's beak, as made. (#4265)

Desirable 1803 Large 8 Half Dime MS62
V-1, LM-2

1566 1803 Large 8 MS62 NGC. V-1, LM-2, R.4. LM-2 is the scarcer of the two Large 8 varieties, and is distinguished by a leaf tip touching the C in AMERICA. A splendid Uncirculated Draped Bust dime. Light caramel-gold and cream-gray embrace this satiny representative. The only discernible mark is a minute tick on the shoulder. Well struck in the centers, while the upper reverse areas opposite the drapery show the moderate incompleteness customary for the type. A wonderful opportunity for the early silver specialist. Large 8 Census: 5 in 62, 2 finer (7/08). (#4269)

1567 1803 Small 8—Repaired—NCS. XF Details. V-3, LM-1, R.5. The 1803 Small 8 half dime is an unheralded rarity in U.S. numismatics. It is significantly rarer than the Large 8. This example is repaired on Liberty's neck and beneath the bust truncation. Both sides are thickly hairlined, and the left reverse has several pinscratches. *From The Morton J. Greene Collection.* (#4270)

Rare XF 1805 Half Dime, V-1, LM-1

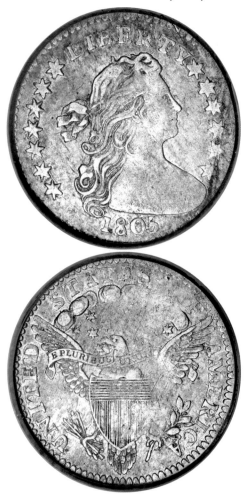

1568 1805 XF40 PCGS. V-1, LM-1, R.4. The only dies for this difficult date. Pleasing tobacco-brown and powder-blue enriches the surfaces, which are smooth aside from a couple of faded thin marks on the field beneath the chin. Luster brightens the hair, wings, and legends. The usual strike for the 1805, with softness noted on the bust truncation and opposite on the upper right reverse. A scant 15,600 pieces were struck, since bullion depositors preferred the more convenient half dollar. The final date of the Draped Bust type, and the rarest date with the exception of the famous 1802. Population: 5 in 40, 10 finer (8/08). (#4272)

BUST HALF DIMES

1569 **1831 MS64 NGC. CAC.** V-3, LM-7, R.2. This is a well struck example that is nicely preserved and beautifully toned, in shades of reddish-gold, gray, and electric-blue. Other than a faint pinscratch, in the left obverse field between star 5 and the tip of Liberty's nose, the satiny surfaces are essentially distraction-free. (#4278)

1570 **1831 MS64 NGC.** V-6, LM-1.3, R.1. This is the earliest stage of the LM-1.3 remarriage with a crack through the tops of NIT that has not yet advanced to form a retained cud over these letters. The present example has satiny silver luster with sea-green, red, and deep orange toning across the obverse, and apricot-gold along the reverse border. A faint vertical mark on the cheek is all that prevents a finer grade. *Ex: Bowers and Merena, 1/1986, lot 1748; William A. Harmon Collection (Heritage, 9/2005), lot 2028; Long Beach Signature (Heritage, 2/2006), lot 667.* (#4278)

1571 **1832 MS63 NGC.** V-9, LM-7, R.2. Stars 6 and 7 are relatively close on this variety, and there is a die line from the inner pair of leaves. Gray-blue patina rests on lustrous surfaces. A hair-thin mark is visible in the left obverse field. (#4279)

1572 **1832 MS64 NGC.** V-1, LM-3, R.1. Sharply struck, with vibrant luster and occasional very faint speckles of light tan color. Marks are minimal, and the eye appeal is exceptional. (#4279)

Impressive 1832 Half Dime, V-8, LM-5, Gem Mint State

1573 **1832 MS65 NGC.** V-8, LM-5, R.1. This variety is best identified by the reverse, which has a large period in the denomination centered above two dentils, and in AMERICA the base of R is slightly higher than the I. The highly lustrous fields are nearly prooflike and complement the boldly defined design elements. An early die state example, only the second S in STATES is filled in the upper loop and there are faint clash marks above the eagle. This brilliant specimen has great eye appeal and would make a wonderful representative. (#4279)

Important MS66 1832 Half Dime
Challenging V-5, LM-8.2 Variety

1574 **1832 MS66 PCGS.** V-5, LM-8.2, R.3. This is an important opportunity for the advanced die state specialist, and it was described by Logan and McCloskey as the rarest of the five LM-8 die remarriages. The authors further noted that only a few high-grade examples of this die marriage had been found. The present example is far finer than the Reiver specimen, and is possibly the finest known example of the LM-8.2 variety. *Ex: Atlanta ANA Signature (Heritage, 4/2006), lot 348. From The Bell Collection.* (#4279)

1575 **1833 MS63 NGC.** V-1, LM-10, R.1. A well struck representative with bright luster and moderate golden-russet toning. The fields have their share of thin marks, but the piece is attractive to the unaided eye. (#4280)

Beautiful Toned 1833 V-5, LM-7 Half Dime, MS65

1576 **1833 MS65 PCGS.** V-5, LM-7, R.2. An original, deeply toned Gem with underlying satin luster. The design types on both sides are bold, except for the usual central weakness characteristic of the Capped Bust design. Both sides have intermingled steel, lilac, russet, sea-green, and iridescent toning with splashes of lighter ivory. A lovely and highly appealing piece. Population: 35 in 65, 23 finer (8/08). (#4280)

1577 **1834 MS62 NGC.** V-1, LM-2, R.1. Deep golden-brown and iridescent toning flow over the soft, satiny luster on this piece. An excellent example for the grade. (#4281)

1578 **1834 3 Over Inverted 3 MS63 Prooflike NGC.** V-5, LM-1, R.2. The 3 Over Inverted 3 feature is undesignated on the NGC insert. This is a flashy representative that offers light autumn-gold toning and an impeccable strike. No marks are present aside from inconsequential hairlines. (#94281)

1579 **1836 Large MS62 NGC.** V-4, LM-3, R.1. The date has the 3 punched over an inverted 3, with the appearance of possible doubling on other digits. The surfaces of this attractive piece have satin luster beneath deep iridescent toning. (#4287)

Stunning MS66 1836 Half Dime, V-6, LM-5

1580 **1836 Small MS66 NGC.** V-6, LM-5, R.2. Representing the penultimate year of the series, this half dime can be a showcase for a high-end type set. Splashes of azure and copper highlight the obverse, while the reverse displays crimson, sky-blue, and copper patina. The strike is sharp, and the surfaces are clean. Clash marks appear on the obverse both before and behind Liberty's head, between the date and the lower bust, and in the reverse fields, as frequently seen on this variety. Although this coin is unattributed by NGC, that service currently shows only two MS65 LM-5s that are attributed, and none finer. PCGS shows one Small 5 1836 in MS66 (all varieties), with two finer (7/08). (#4288)

1581 **1837 No Stars, Large Date (Curl Top 1) MS64 NGC.** Medium golden-brown patina graces this lustrous and intricately struck first year Seated dime. Well preserved aside from a faint X near the profile. The popular No Stars subtype was only struck in 1837, with the exception of the very scarce 1838-O. (#4311)

SEATED HALF DIMES

Splendid 1837 No Stars
Large Date Half Dime, V-2, MS67

1584 1837 No Stars, Small Date (Flat Top 1) MS65 NGC. This important issue is considered to be much scarcer than its Large Date counterpart. Both sides exhibit fully original deep turquoise-blue, gold, and rose patination. A couple of minuscule grazes in the right obverse field are imperceptible without magnification and do not affect the powerful luster. The sharply impressed devices showcase Christian Gobrecht's original Liberty Seated design. *From The Menlo Park Collection.* (#4312)

Late State 1837 No Stars Half Dime, MS65

1585 1837 No Stars, Small Date (Flat Top 1) MS65 NGC. One of the latest die states we have seen, with heavy die rust in the field along Liberty's forearm and shin. Other small rust spots are evident in the right obverse field, with heavy peripheral flow lines. The reverse is cracked from the border to R of AMERICA. Fully brilliant and boldly struck with faint champagne toning. (#4312)

Toned 1837 No Stars Half Dime, MS66

1586 1837 No Stars, Small Date (Flat Top 1) MS66 NGC. This attractive Premium Gem has frosty silver luster beneath deep bluish-green and iridescent luster. The surfaces are smooth and the strike is bold. The reverse is rotated about 45 degrees clockwise. Census: 80 in 66, 16 finer (7/08). The NGC Census figures include both coins designated as a Small Date and others that are undesignated. (#4312)

1582 1837 No Stars, Large Date (Curl Top 1) MS67 NGC. V-2. This is the famous No Stars, Large Date issue, which has a curl-top 1 in the date and the entire date arcs in the exergue, unlike the 1837 Small Date, with date in a straight line and a flat-top 1. In early die states of the Large Date, the date shows triple-punching, which fades in later states. Valentine recognized three distinct die states, and this piece matches V-2 state/die pairing, with die cracks from the rim through Liberty cap and downward along the pole across Liberty's thighs, through the shield, and out through the rock to the rim again at 8 o'clock. A second crack joins the toe to the rim, and on the reverse the lettering is heavy, with the lower left serif of T double-punched.

This piece displays deep, splendid toning in shades of russet and ice-blue near the rims on both sides. The strike is sharply executed, and even a loupe reveals no marks of any size whatsoever. NGC has certified 15 pieces in MS67, with two finer (8/08). (#4311)

1583 1837 No Stars, Small Date (Flat Top 1) MS63 PCGS. Gobrecht's Seated Liberty half dimes debuted without stars around the obverse, and were struck with Small and Large Date variations. Both types had a combined mintage of about 1.4 million pieces, and the Small Date variety is generally considered to be the rarer of the two. Mottled gunmetal and light gray toning coats both sides of this impressive example. Several insignificant abrasions are visible under magnification. A sharply struck representative of this one-year type. Population: 17 in 63, 50 finer (7/08). (#4312)

1587 **1838 Large Stars, No Drapery MS65 NGC.** Deeply toned in shades of electric-blue and rose-gray on the obverse, and tan-gray and electric-blue on the reverse. Well struck and essentially unmarked, with noticeable clash marks near Liberty's right (facing) arm and elbow, and on the lower right reverse quadrant. A lustrous and highly attractive Gem. (#4317)

Scintillating 1838 Half Dime, MS66

1588 **1838 Large Stars, No Drapery MS66 PCGS. CAC.** Star 8 is recut and the reverse has light clash marks within the wreath. Stars were introduced to the obverse in 1838, and every one is bold and complete on this Premium Gem. All other design elements on both sides are similarly sharp. Highly lustrous and frosty silver surfaces shine through light gold toning. An exceptional, aesthetically desirable example. (#4317)

1589 **1842 MS66 PCGS.** Tall Date. V-3. A delightful Gem Stars half dime that is well struck and shows rich, frosty luster. The gray-lilac centers change to mint-green at the rims on each side. A sharp, appealing, and almost unimprovable example of this better issue. Population: 3 in 66, 0 finer (8/08).
From The Bell Collection. (#4330)

1590 **1842-O AU58 NGC.** This splendid Variety 2 representative has lots of flashy luster throughout. A couple of stars on the left are soft, but most of the details are well-defined. The lightly toned fields have minimal abrasions. Census: 3 in 58, 10 finer (7/08). (#4331)

1591 **1843 MS65 PCGS.** A lustrous, conditionally scarce Gem. Close inspection with a loupe reveals only minor grazes, and there are fairly pronounced clashmarks visible on the reverse, most notably between STATES and OF. Population: 14 in 65, 10 finer (7/08). (#4332)

1592 **1843 MS65 PCGS.** Struck from an essentially shattered reverse die, with several die cracks that radiate from the center. A few trivial abrasions on Liberty's body keep this piece from an even higher grade. The surfaces are mostly untoned, and there is delightful luster throughout. Population: 14 in 65, 10 finer (7/08). (#4332)

1593 **1843 MS65 NGC.** Sharply detailed and brilliant overall with a single dot of charcoal patina above the seventh star and small fragments of similar toning nearby on the rim. The carefully preserved, lustrous surfaces exhibit great eye appeal. Census: 24 in 65, 10 finer (7/08). (#4332)

1594 **1844 MS65 NGC.** A well-defined and impressively lustrous Gem that offers subtle tan shadings across much of the otherwise pale silver-gray surfaces. Strong visual appeal. Census: 24 in 65, 11 finer (7/08). (#4333)

1595 **1844-O—Whizzed, Retoned—ICG. AU50 Details.** V-2, Small O. This variety is often seen with a 180-degree rotation, but this piece has a proper coin turn. Deep gunmetal-gray patina coats the surfaces of this well-defined representative. The fields show moderate granularity, and there are scattered marks throughout. Some weakness is noted on the upper left of the wreath and on several stars. (#4334)

Noteworthy AU 1844-O Half Dime

1596 **1844-O AU50 PCGS.** Medium O, rarer than its Small O counterpart. A dove-gray and olive-gold example with smooth surfaces and minimal wear. A good strike overall, despite a few incompletely brought up left-side elements. The 1844-O is even more difficult to locate than implied by its low mintage of 220,000 pieces, and most survivors are well worn. Population: 6 in 50, 16 finer (7/08). (#4334)

Key-Date 1846 Half Dime, XF45

1597 **1846 XF45 NGC.** Ex: Pittman. The 1846 is one of the keys to the series. Al Blythe assigns a rating of R.6 in XF-AU. Splashes of sky-blue, lavender, and gold-brown toning reside in the obverse fields of this Choice XF specimen, leaving the obverse motif and most of the reverse in silver-tan hues. Generally well struck, except for the usual softness on Liberty's head. A horizontal hair-thin mark below the breasts identifies the coin. Census: 6 in 45, 15 finer (7/08). (#4336)

1598 **1849 MS65 NGC.** Deep red-violet toning covers both sides of this powerfully impressed Gem. The surfaces are nearly immaculate with significant luster throughout. Census: 7 in 65, 11 finer (7/08). (#4341)

1599 **1851 MS65 PCGS.** The date is high, and there are a number of clashmarks visible on the reverse. This brilliant and highly lustrous Gem has nearly pristine surfaces and exhibits razor-sharp details. Housed in a green label PCGS holder. Population: 11 in 65, 18 finer (7/08). (#4347)

1600 **1851-O MS63 NGC.** Subtle silver-blue and gold shadings visit the lustrous surfaces of this Select O-mint half dime. Well struck and attractive for the grade. Census: 11 in 63, 36 finer (7/08).
From The Menlo Park Collection. (#4348)

1601 **1853 Arrows MS65 PCGS.** Mottled russet and silver-gray toning drapes each side of this impeccably preserved specimen. This issue features arrows at the date to indicate the reduction of weight that effectively moved the United States to the gold standard. A sharply struck representative of this three-year type. (#4356)

1602 **1853 Arrows MS65 NGC.** Silver-gray lustrous surfaces display freckles of deeper gray on the obverse. Well struck, and devoid of significant contacts. The surfaces are somewhat grainy, likely due to extended die use.
From The Menlo Park Collection. (#4356)

1603 **1855-O Arrows AU58 ICG.** V-1a. Die rust, cracks, and clash marks are present on this brilliant near-Mint specimen. Only a trace of high point wear is evident on each side. (#4361)

Intriguing 1856 Half Dime, MS66

1604 **1856 MS66 NGC.** High date. The date is placed high in the space below the base, and would actually be joined to the base except for the curved, cut-outs that accommodate the tops of each digit. Both sides of this frosty, iridescent Premium Gem are well-struck, except for the borders that are missing nearly all of the dentils.

We are unable to explain the peculiar border appearance. A hub problem would yield dentil-less borders on one side or the other, but not on both dies. A filled die would normally affect one die, or might affect both dies, but would probably have some adverse affect on other details as well. This leaves a striking problem as the likely source of the undetailed border, but what striking problem would only affect the borders, leaving all remaining details sharp? Perhaps this is a topic for a advanced student to address. (#4363)

1605 **1856 MS66 NGC.** Centered date with the 1 about equally spaced from the base of Liberty and the border. A fully brilliant example with frosty silver luster. The head is nearly flat, and the obverse and reverse borders are almost entirely absent of dentils. These missing dentils are characteristic of most or all 1856 half dimes, including pieces from different die marriages. Another 1856 half dime in the present sale, from a different obverse die, has an identical border appearance. (#4363)

1606 **1857-O MS65 PCGS.** This is a lovely untoned Gem, with shining silver-gray surfaces that are remarkably clean and well preserved. The design elements are sharply struck, including Liberty's head and the obverse stars. Population: 19 in 65, 14 finer (8/08). (#4366)

1607 **1858 MS65 NGC.** Nearly untoned, save for whispers of light tan at the right obverse margin. Die polish lines in the fields give rise to prooflike characteristics. Nicely struck throughout. (#4367)

Mind-Blowing 1860 Half Dime, MS68 ★

1608 **1860 MS68 ★ NGC.** A stunning ice-blue Superb Gem with variegated patches of cobalt and russet coloration throughout. Areas of darker patination cling to the rims on both sides and the luster is phenomenal, as one would expect for such a lofty coin. All attributes combined, the current offering seems unimprovable. As of (8/08) NGC has certified only two 1860 half dimes at the MS68 level with the coveted ★ designation and none finer-understandably so. The population for the same technical grade at PCGS is two pieces. A coin for the connoisseur of Seated half dimes and for those who simply appreciate uncommonly attractive type coins. (#4377)

1609 **1861/0 MS64 PCGS.** V-4, Breen-3102. A trace of another digit is most evident at the lower left serif of the 1 in the date. The exact cause of this variety is the subject of much debate, with some numismatists arguing that it is not a true overdate, while others believe it is the result of an overdated date punch. Regardless, it is highly popular among collectors. Medium-gray toning covers the obverse, which contrasts nicely against the silver-gray reverse. The surfaces are remarkably clean, and there is lots of luster throughout. A charming, minimally marked, and excellent study piece. (#4380)

Dramatic 1862 Half Dime, Superb Gem

1610 **1862 MS67 NGC.** Slate-steel toning covers the fields, which contrast nicely against yellow, red, and lilac that encircle the perimeter. The devices have a pleasing dove-gray frost, which is complemented by highly reflective fields. Both sides show traces of clash marks, although they are more evident at the center of the reverse. A fully struck and virtually pristine representative. Census: 19 in 67, 5 finer (7/08). (#4381)

1611 **1865 MS64 PCGS.** A Civil War date with a tiny mintage of 13,000 pieces, since fractional currency replaced the half dime in East Coast circulation. Sharply struck and satiny with deep gunmetal-blue and tawny-gold toning. Encapsulated in a first generation holder. Population: 11 in 64, 15 finer (8/08). (#4386)

Extraordinary MS66 1868 Half Dime

1612 **1868 MS66 PCGS. CAC.** After the start of the Civil War, half dimes circulated in the West, but rarely east of the Mississippi River; many were eventually melted. While the half dime was produced concurrently with Shield nickels starting in 1866, the nickel survived the coinage changes of the Mint Act of 1873, but the half dime did not. This well struck half dime is one of nine coins certified MS66 at both services combined, with only eight finer. The coin has clean, silver-gray surfaces that display a hint of sepia toning. Population: 5 in 66, 2 finer (7/08). (#4392)

Splendid Gem 1868-S Half Dime, Late Die State

1613 **1868-S MS65 NGC.** Coinage dies were produced at the Philadelphia Mint for more than 200 years, a monopoly that ended only 1996, when the Denver Mint opened its own die shop. Coinage dies at the branch mints were often used until they shattered, as in the case of this splendid silver-gold Gem, which shows numerous die cracks and bulging on each side. Incredibly, it is one of two in the present sale in the same die state, prizes for the Seated Liberty die state specialists. (#4393)

Scarce 1868-S Half Dime, MS65

1614 **1868-S MS65 NGC.** This wonderful Gem has rich, lustrous obverse and reverse surfaces beneath light ivory-gray toning that is accented by splashes of gold and iridescent coloration. Although the borders are a trifle weak, the remaining design elements are boldly defined. Census: 16 in 65, 4 finer (7/08). (#4393)

Late Die State 1868-S Half Dime, MS65

1615 **1868-S MS65 NGC.** San Francisco Mint coinage from the era circulated extensively, making high quality Mint State pieces elusive. Pleasing champagne toning subdues the frosty mint luster of this lovely Gem. Design details are mostly bold with only slight peripheral weakness. Both dies are shattered, each with several die cracks. Census: 16 in 65, 4 finer (7/08). (#4393)

1616 **1870 MS66 PCGS.** Semi-prooflike fields display mild contrast with motifs. Well struck, and devoid of mentionable contacts. Some minute spots are visible on the lower obverse. Population: 7 in 66, 4 finer (8/08). (#4396)

PROOF SEATED HALF DIMES

1617 **1862 PR65 Cameo NGC.** Delightfully frosted devices and highly reflective fields create an eye-catching cameo appearance. This brilliant representative has only a couple of light grazes and a lone fleck above Liberty's head. One of just 550 proofs struck. Census: 4 in 65 Cameo, 11 finer (7/08). (#84445)

1618 **1864 PR65 Cameo NGC.** A brilliant and needle-sharp Gem that possesses blatant Cameo frost on the devices. Outstanding from a technical viewpoint, minuscule mint-made strike-throughs limit the grade but not the eye appeal. Just 470 proofs were struck. (#84447)

1619 1864 PR66 Cameo PCGS. A mere 470 proof half dimes were struck in 1864. Approximately 250 have been seen by PCGS and NGC; only 31, however, have been assigned the Cameo designation. The Premium Gem Cameo offered here displays somewhat dusky light gray color, and frosted, well impressed design features stand out against reflective fields. An all-around attractive coin. Population: 4 in 66 Cameo, 0 finer (8/08). (#84447)

1620 1870 PR66 NGC. Deep blue and amber toning covers the fields of the obverse, which contrasts nicely against the dramatic lilac, gold, and orange on the reverse. The figure of Liberty is essentially untoned and frosted, and is particularly eye-catching next to the dark toning around it. A loupe reveals only a couple of light hairlines. One of just 1,000 proofs struck. (#4453)

1621 1870 PR64 Cameo PCGS. Barely discernible tan-gold color shows up under magnification. Well struck, with pleasing field-motif contrast. A couple of minute toning spots are visible on the obverse. Population: 3 in 64 Cameo, 8 finer (8/08). (#84453)

1622 1871 PR66 Cameo NGC. Deep iridescent sunset orange, fuchsia, yellow, and sage grace the obverse, without impeding the considerable contrast between the reflective fields and the devices. The color is even more intense on the reverse, but from the same color palette. One of 960 examples made. Census: 4 in 66 Cameo, 5 finer (7/08). (#84454)

1623 1871 PR67 Ultra Cameo NGC. This stunning Superb Gem proof offers silver-white surfaces on both sides that meld into the desired silver-on-black contrast when turned to the proper angle. Under a high-power loupe both some die rust on the Liberty device and tiny pebbles in the planchet appear. Neither should be considered grade-affecting, although we note them for accuracy. The strike is essentially unimprovable. Census: 2 in 67 Ultra Cameo, 0 finer (7/08). (#94454)

1624 1873 PR66 NGC. Razor-sharp detail for this final proof half dime issue. Each side offers rich blueberry and grass-green patina that embraces the mirrors and devices. Census: 21 in 66, 8 finer (7/08). (#4456)

EARLY DIMES

1625 1796 Fair 2 PCGS. JR-2, R.4. Light silver surfaces with faint roughness and considerable wear. The date is entirely visible and complete, with a few stars remaining. The eagle is complete, including a few wing details, and part of the legend and wreath are still evident. (#4461)

Very Fine 1796 Dime, JR-2

1626 1796 VF20 PCGS. JR-2, R.4. Only faintly toned aside from splashes of russet beneath the IB in LIBERTY and on the right wreath stem. The eagle's breast is smooth, but the wings display considerable plumage. The first year of the denomination if the pattern dismes are excluded. Housed in a green label holder. *From The Morton J. Greene Collection.* (#4461)

Scarce 1796 Dime, JR-5, Choice XF

Choice AU 1796 Dime, JR-1

1627 **1796 XF45 PCGS.** JR-5, R.5. The obverse is identified by a close Liberty and the position of star 1, which touches the second hair curl. On the reverse, there are two berries below the upright of the E in UNITED, and a leaf tip is located under the right side of the A in STATES. According to *Early United States Dimes, 1796-1837*, JR-5 is the rarest 1796 variety and accounts for less than 5% of this date's appearance on the market.

The present piece is boldly struck (except for MERIC and the right obverse stars) and lightly circulated, with a lovely original appearance. A few faint adjustment marks are noted on the obverse, but these are nearly imperceptible without a loupe. Several shallow scratches are noted on the reverse. An evenly worn and well-struck example that boasts an attractive obverse for the grade. Housed in a green label PCGS holder.

From The Menlo Park Collection. (#4461)

1628 **1796 AU55 PCGS.** JR-1, R.3. The usual die state with clashmarks along the profile and a prominent cud beneath star 1. This is a generally lustrous Choice AU example from the first year of dime production. Golden-brown and emerald-green embrace the borders, while the open fields and devices are only lightly toned. Devoid of mentionable marks, and recommended for both its beauty and its quality. Die progression studies of 1796 dimes have come up with four candidates for the honor of first variety struck: JR-1, JR-2, JR-3, and JR-6. We know that JR-4, JR-5, and JR-7 succeeded JR-3. (#4461)

Lustrous Mint State Details 1796 Dime, JR-4

1629 **1796—Improperly Cleaned—NCS. Unc. Details.** JR-4, R.4. Attractive peach, ice-blue, and plum-mauve enrich this boldly struck and gently shimmering first year dime. The 96 in the date is lightly recut, and a die crack extends from the upper right leaf tip. A second die crack is noted to the left of the first S in STATES. A bit bright from a mild cleaning, but there are no visible marks except for a brief vertical line beneath the Y in LIBERTY. The strike is sharp aside from minor merging of detail on the eagle's breast and front leg. The Small Eagle type was only struck in 1796 and 1797, similar to its half dollar counterpart. (#4461)

Pleasing 1797 JR-2 13 Stars Dime, VG Details

1630 **1797 13—Genuine—PCGS.** JR-2, R.4. Certified as Genuine by PCGS, and graded VG8 by Heritage. This example is deeply toned, but slightly lighter at the center of the reverse. A few faint reverse scratches were apparently disagreeable to PCGS, but they are of little actual consequence. (#4463)

Wonderful 1802 JR-4 Dime, AU55

1631 **1802 AU55 PCGS.** JR-4, R.4. The JR-4 die combination is the most plentiful of four known varieties of 1802 dimes, yet it is still rated R.4, meaning that less than 200 are known. It is probably accurate to say that about half that number actually exist. In fact, there are perhaps just 200 known 1802 dimes of all varieties, and nearly every one of those is well worn, and/or damaged.

This beautiful dime bright silver surfaces with satin luster and hints of gold toning along the borders. The central obverse and reverse of this nicely centered piece are weakly defined, as nearly always for the issue, and faint surface marks are consistent with the grade. An outstanding opportunity for the advanced date or variety collector. Population: 4 in 55, 5 finer (8/08). (#4472)

Challenging AU 1803 Dime, JR-3

Rarely Seen JR-2 1804 14 Stars Dime, XF40

1632 **1803 AU50 PCGS.** JR-3, R.4. Dark gunmetal and olive-gray surfaces with glimpses of lighter silver-gray on the reverse. The richness of the toning tends to mute the underlying luster. The reverse appears slightly buckled near the right shield border. This is a fascinating late die state of this variety. An arcing die crack extends from the rim through the 3 and Liberty to the fourth star. A heavier die crack splits the 0 of the date and curls around to the first star, and this die section has sunk, forming a retained cud. A third die crack splits the retained cud from the rim to Liberty's lowest curl. On the reverse, there is a die crack through the T of UNITED to the eagle's wing, just missing the lower point of the ribbon. Boldly clashed between the chin and cleavage. Population: 3 in 50, 7 finer (8/08). (#4473)

1634 **1804 14 Stars on Reverse XF40 NGC.** JR-2, R.5. A wonderful example of this rare coin. While the mintage of the 1804 dimes rests at a disputed 8,265 pieces, it is likely that fewer than 60 14 Star examples exist today. Moreover, the JR-2 is the scarcer of the two 1804 varieties, and the last to be minted. It is interesting to note that the reverse die of this coin was also used to strike the 1804 BD-2 14 Stars quarter eagle, which is also very scarce. Collectors of the Heraldic Eagle dime series should note that we have offered only four finer examples of the JR-2 over the past five years, making the appearance of this specimen especially significant. Attractive deep blue and tan-gold toning covers each side. There are a few shallow pinscratches on the lower portion of the obverse that one only notices with magnification. (#4475)

Scarce 1804 Dime, 13 Stars on Reverse, JR-1, Fine Details

Charming 1807 Dime, JR-1, Choice Extremely Fine

1633 **1804 13 Stars on Reverse—Genuine—PCGS.** JR-1, R.5. This variety is easily distinguished because it has the normal 13 star reverse. Light cleaning has caused PCGS to certify this piece only as genuine, but we believe that it shows Fine-12 details. A small patch of pinpoint abrasions to the right of Liberty is noted, but there are no mentionable marks otherwise. The obverse is a trifle weak at the center, but the reverse is crisply defined. A total of just 8,265 pieces were minted for both 1804 varieties, with perhaps two-thirds of that number accounting for 13 Star Reverse examples. (#4474)

1635 **1807 XF45 PCGS.** JR-1, R-2. The only variety known. This piece exhibits a remarkable amount of luster for the grade, with a pleasing sparkle throughout the fields. A ring of deep charcoal toning encircles the lovely silver-gray centers. Numerous clash marks are apparent on the obverse, most notably between the date and the bust. A faint pinscratch near the final star is the only mentionable handling mark.
From The Menlo Park Collection. (#4480)

1636 **1807—Improperly Cleaned—NCS. AU Details.** JR-1, R.2. Splendidly detailed, but the dusky olive-gray surfaces are unnaturally matte-like and lackluster. A thin mark affects the reverse rim at 5 o'clock.
From The Morton J. Greene Collection. (#4480)

BUST DIMES

1637 **1821 Large Date AU55 NGC.** JR-8, R.2. A pleasing Choice AU dime with considerable luster and smooth surfaces under deep iridescent toning. (#4496)

1638 **1821 Large Date MS61 NGC.** JR-1, R.2. Medium sea-green and lavender patina. Well struck aside from a couple of lower left side stars. A moderately abraded representative of this popular Large Date variety, which is surprisingly challenging in Mint State.
From The Menlo Park Collection. (#4496)

Impressive 1823/2 Small Es Dime, JR-1, Choice Mint State

1639 **1823/2 Small Es MS64 NGC.** Ex: Eliasberg. JR-1, R.3. This is the only variety with small E's in the reverse legend. Mottled violet and silver-gray mix across the surfaces of this lustrous specimen. The strike is nearly full, and there are no marks of any significance. Over time, the two distinct varieties of this year have gained recognition, and both Small and Large Es types are now listed in the *Guide Book*. (#4498)

1640 **1827 AU58 NGC.** JR-3, R.1. A luminous near-Mint example of this popular and available variety. The softly struck high points show only a trace of friction, and delicate lemon-gray tints visit the margins. (#4504)

Wonderful 1827 Gem Dime, JR-3

1641 **1827 MS65 NGC.** JR-3, R.1. A faint die crack connects the top of Liberty's cap to the rim, and the eagle's shield displays solid gules stripes, both characteristic of the die marriage. Beautiful white surfaces are frosty throughout the reverse and on the obverse portrait, which offers pleasing contrast with glassy, partially prooflike fields. An attentive strike leaves bold definition on the design elements, heightening even more the coin's eye appeal. A few trivial obverse handling marks might well preclude an even higher grade. Census: 23 in 65, 7 finer (8/08). (#4504)

Prooflike 1829 JR-3 Dime, MS65

1642 **1829 Small MS65 NGC.** JR-3, R.4. An amazing prooflike example with fully mirrored fields beneath delightful gold and iridescent toning. The devices are generally bold with only a trace of weakness on a few of the curls. Frosty highpoint luster contrasts nicely with the reflective fields. The present piece undoubtedly qualifies in the Condition Census for this scarce variety. (#4511)

1643 **1830 Medium MS62 NGC.** JR-6, R.2. Both sides are sharply defined with complete borders, although some dentils are extremely short. The surfaces are lustrous beneath blue-green, gold, and iridescent toning. (#4516)

1830 Small 10C Dime, JR-2, Choice Uncirculated

1644 **1830 Small 10C MS64 NGC.** JR-2, R.1. The 0 in the denomination is noticeably small, which is diagnostic for this variety. Light gray toning endows the surfaces of this minimally marked representative. The strike is sharp save for a touch of softness on several strands of Liberty's hair. Plenty of luster on both sides gives this piece splendid eye appeal.
From The Menlo Park Collection. (#4517)

1645 **1835 MS61 ANACS.** JR-3, R.2. Fancy 8, 8 low at top, 10 C high in field. Light tan-gold color visits each side. Well struck, with just a few minute marks. Nice for grade designation. (#4527)

Patinated Choice 1836 Dime, JR-3

1646 **1836 MS64 PCGS.** JR-3, R.3. The second T in STATES is recut, diagnostic for the variety. Deep blue-green toning embraces this nicely struck Choice Capped Bust dime. Inspection beneath a loupe fails to locate any obverse abrasions, and the reverse is nearly as undisturbed. Population: 15 in 64, 13 finer (8/08).
From The Bell Collection. (#4528)

SEATED DIMES

1647 1837 No Stars, Small Date MS62 PCGS. The 1837 Small Date is distinguished from the Large Date by the curved top of the 3 versus the Large Date's flat-topped 3. This essentially untoned and satiny example possesses clean fields and a sharp strike. A bold die crack ventures from the E in UNITED to the M in DIME. Struck from moderately rotated dies. This introductory No Stars issue is elusive in Mint State. Population: 9 in 62, 26 finer (8/08). *From The Menlo Park Collection.* (#4562)

1648 1838-O No Stars XF45 NGC. Light violet and gold overtones grace the still-lustrous silver-gray surfaces of this briefly circulated dime. An excellent example from the New Orleans Mint's debut year. Census: 16 in 45, 73 finer (7/08). (#4564)

1649 1838 Small Stars MS62 NGC. Fortin-101. Die doubling on the D in DIME and a slender die crack through the left-side stars helps attribute this scarce variety. Lightly toned and well struck with smooth surfaces. (#4569)

Splendid 1839 No Drapery Dime, MS66

1650 1839 No Drapery MS66 NGC. Fortin-106. This die is characterized by the vertical die crack directly above Liberty's head and several die striations in the left obverse field above the rock. More than a million pieces were struck of this three-year type coin. As such, it is available in mint condition but, of course, it is rare in MS66. This is a richly toned coin whose pale violet centers are surrounded by deep blue at the margins. Bright underlying mint luster further enhances the tonal qualities. Fully struck in all areas. Census: 14 in 66, 20 finer (7/08). (#4571)

Condition Scarcity 1840-O No Drapery Dime, AU58

1651 1840-O No Drapery AU58 PCGS. Large O. A touch of violet toning accents the mostly silver-gray surfaces. A number of die cracks on the reverse connect the rim to the lettering. The strike is sharp, and the abrasions are entirely minor. Conditionally scarce at this grade level, and rare in Mint State. Population: 4 in 58, 10 finer (7/08). (#4574)

Seldom-Seen 1842-O Dime, MS63

1652 1842-O MS63 NGC. Medium O. Conditionally scarce in Mint State, despite its mintage of more than 2 million coins. The 1842-O is known in both Medium O and Small O varieties. This example is well struck and nearly free of marks, with reduced luster seeming to limit the grade. Attractive speckled red-brown patina occurs near the obverse periphery, with lighter tan color appearing over most of the reverse. Census: 6 in 63, 7 finer (7/08). (#4582)

1653 1844 XF40 ICG. Hints of orange accent the gunmetal-gray patina that covers the surfaces. There are no mentionable marks on either side and the details are boldly defined. One of only 72,500 pieces struck. (#4585)

1654 1845 MS64 PCGS. Pleasing hazel and lavender toning graces the surfaces of this conditionally scarce example. Close inspection with a loupe reveals no marks of any significance. An excellent opportunity to acquire a virtually pristine Variety Two Seated Liberty dime. Population: 24 in 64, 2 finer (7/08). (#4586)

1655 1850 MS64 PCGS. Fully struck with complete detail on Liberty's head and on all of the obverse stars. Deep green-gray toning covers nicely preserved surfaces. The only minor detraction is a shallow pinscratch beneath 850 in the date. Population: 17 in 64, 4 finer (8/08). (#4593)

1656 1850-O AU58 PCGS. The luminous surfaces of this New Orleans specimen exhibit well defined design features. Both faces are untoned and devoid of significant abrasions. (#4594)

1657 1854 Arrows MS64 NGC. Elegant peach-gold accents enliven the lustrous surfaces of this elegant Choice survivor. A well struck Arrows piece that would fit well in a similarly graded type set. Census: 39 in 64, 32 finer (7/08). *From The Menlo Park Collection.* (#4605)

1658 1856-S AU55 NGC. Fortin-101. Light caramel-gold toning embraces the borders of this sharply struck example. For the initial S-mint dime issue, a mere 70,000 pieces were struck, and survivors with substantial mint luster are rare. Census: 1 in 55, 5 finer (7/08). (#4613)

1659 1858 MS65 NGC. Though the obverse of this minimally toned Gem shows pillowy detail, the reverse is sharp. The luster is soft and highly appealing. Census: 14 in 65, 11 finer (7/08). (#4616)

R.6 1859-S Seated Liberty Dime, Choice AU

Key Date 1873-CC Arrows Dime, VF Details

1660 **1859-S AU55 NGC.** Low R.6. According to Gerry Fortin's www.
seateddimevarieties.com website, the 1859-S, with a mintage of
only 60,000 pieces, is the second-rarest S-mint dime above VF after
the 1858-S, and rated low R.6 in AU and R.8 (unique or nearly so)
in Mint State. This example has pale gray surfaces with brownish
toning and a few surface marks on each side. Fortin also notes that
"determining an accurate pricing for AU specimens is difficult since
few examples are ever sold." (#4621)

1661 **1860 MS65 NGC.** In 1860 the design of the dime was slightly
altered, and this first-year type is seldom encountered in high
Uncirculated grades. There are a couple of light handling marks
on this handsome Gem, but none are particularly detracting. A
brilliant and lustrous piece with pronounced clashmarks on the
reverse. Census: 17 in 65, 12 finer (7/08). (#4631)

1662 **1865-S—Genuine—PCGS.** Fortin-101. This better date S-mint
dime has AU58 details, but the luster is subdued, and the steel-gray
left obverse field is scuffed. The obverse rim appears slightly bent at
8 o'clock, and the central reverse has faint hairlines. We believe this
piece grades AU, with a few contact marks. (#4642)

1663 **1866-S Weak S—Improperly Cleaned—NCS. AU Details.**
Fortin-101. The date location and the slender vertical die crack on
the seated Liberty confirm the variety, even though the mintmark is
faint and accompanied by light marks. This cream-gray example has
ample luster and is only mildly cleaned. (#4644)

1664 **1867-S AU58 PCGS.** Soft blue and light orange colors compete for
territory on this near-Mint dime. Clean surfaces retain considerable
luster, and are well struck. (#4646)

1665 **1868 MS63 NGC.** A frosty representative with accents of hazel
toning around the perimeter. Several light marks define the grade,
but none merit individual mention. Liberty's head and the left
branch of the wreath are weakly struck, but the remaining design
elements are crisp. (#4647)

1666 **1873 Arrows MS63 ANACS.** Deep navy-blue and mauve-red colors
consume this crisply struck, attractively preserved, and moderately
prooflike Seated Arrows dime. Struck from clashed dies.
From The Menlo Park Collection. (#4665)

1667 **1873-CC Arrows—Improperly Cleaned—NCS. VF Details.** The
minuscule mintage of 18,791 pieces, along with a low survival rate,
makes the 1873-CC Arrows a key date in the Seated Liberty dime
series. This VF Details specimen displays fairly nice overall detail.
Close examination reveals some surface grooves and minor metal
movement, suggesting mechanical cleaning. The fields have retoned
a medium gray, and the motifs a lighter gray.
From The Morton J. Greene Collection. (#4666)

1668 **1873-S Arrows MS63 PCGS.** Peppered violet toning surrounds
the mostly untoned center of the obverse, while the reverse is
entirely brilliant. A number of light marks limit the grade, and a
few tiny digs on Liberty's knees are barely worthy of note. Dazzling
satiny luster graces both sides of this conditionally scarce two-year
type coin. Population: 11 in 63, 15 finer (7/08).1 (#4667)

1669 **1873-S Arrows MS63 NGC.** A satiny example, with ivory-
beige color and a few wispy field marks on the obverse. Liberty's
head is typically softly struck, but the other design elements are
produced with decent sharpness. Census: 7 in 63, 14 finer (7/08).
(#4667)

1670 **1875 MS66 NGC.** A lustrous and essentially brilliant Gem with a
pleasing strike and carefully preserved surfaces. The upper reverse
has a pair of wispy die cracks, as made. Struck from clashed dies.
(#4672)

1671 **1875-CC Mintmark Above Bow MS64 NGC.** Deep bluish
lavender toning covers the majority of each side with accents of
russet near the perimeters. The strike is sharp, and a couple of
minor abrasions are masked by the dramatic colors. (#4673)

Stunning 1879 Seated Dime, MS67 ★

1672 **1879 MS67 ★ NGC.** The lower loop of the 8 is widely repunched.
Golden-brown and cobalt-blue perimeters frame the brilliant fields
and devices. Lustrous and nicely struck with clean surfaces. A low
mintage date because of heavy Morgan dollar production. Only four
finer pieces have been NGC certified, including a prooflike MS68
★ specimen. (#4687)

1673 **1881 MS63 PCGS.** Satiny and well struck, with bold definition on Liberty's hair and shield. Both sides are abrasion-free, and display natural greenish-gray and tan coloration. One of only 24,000 business strikes produced in 1881. Population: 18 in 63, 29 finer (8/08). (#4689)

1674 **1881 MS65 NGC.** Hints of champagne-gold patina are visible on the lustrous surfaces of this Gem. The usual softness is noted in the hair on Liberty's head and on the upper left part of the wreath. A couple of grade-consistent marks do not detract. A scarce date, from a mintage of 24,000 business strikes. Census: 11 in 65, 8 finer (7/08). (#4689)

1675 **1882 MS66 NGC.** This Premium Gem exhibits a better-than-average strike, particularly on Liberty's head. Silver-gray surfaces exhibit pleasing luster, and are nicely preserved. (#4690)

Pleasing 1882 Dime, Superb Gem

1676 **1882 MS67 NGC.** Patches of aquamarine and deep steel-gray intermingle with the silver-gray and gold toning that covers the rest of the surfaces. Splendid satiny luster accents the razor-sharp details. Scattered delicate die cracks are noted around the perimeter of this charming, conditionally scarce piece. Census: 26 in 67, 2 finer (7/08). (#4690)

1677 **1884 MS66 ANACS.** Surprisingly vibrant luster shines through green-gold, violet, and pale silver-gray patina. Solidly detailed and beautifully preserved with striking visual appeal. (#4692)

1678 **1886 MS66 NGC.** Both sides of this Premium Gem are awash with thick mint frost. Well struck, except for softness in Liberty's hair. Impeccably preserved. Census: 50 in 66, 9 finer (7/08). (#4696)

1679 **1887 MS65 PCGS.** Gold toning with accents of burgundy drapes both sides of this impeccably preserved Gem. Liberty's head, OF, and the first A in AMERICA are a trifle soft, but the rest of the details are boldly impressed. Enticing satiny luster gives this piece great eye appeal. PCGS has certified just 24 pieces finer (7/08). Housed in a green label holder. (#4698)

Incredible 1887 Seated Dime, MS68 ★

1680 **1887 MS68 ★ NGC.** In the entire Seated dime series from 1837 to 1891, NGC has only certified 16 coins as MS68 ★, and only two finer MS69 pieces. PCGS has graded another 20 MS68 examples, but nary an MS69. It seems safe to suggest that this beauty is one of the 20 finest Seated dimes, regardless of date.

A few faint clash marks and die cracks are faintly visible. Both sides have exceptional mint frost with ivory luster, accented by peripheral lilac, sea-green, and gold. The strike is bold, and this dime presents exceptional aesthetic appeal. Census: 2 in 68 ★, 0 finer (7/08). (#4698)

1681 **1888 MS66 NGC.** Well struck, fully brilliant, and highly lustrous, there are a pair of small ticks on the obverse, but the reverse seems to be pristine. Rare at this level. Census: 25 in 66, 1 finer (7/08). (#4700)

1682 **1888 MS66 NGC.** Strongly lustrous surfaces are generally silver-white with only occasional traces of patina. This Premium Gem is well struck in the centers. NGC has graded one finer example (8/08). (#4700)

1683 **1890 MS65 PCGS.** A medley of medium violet, sky-blue, yellow-gold, and purple toning runs over the lustrous surfaces of this late-date Gem dime. Well struck, except for the hair atop Liberty's head. Devoid of significant marks. Population: 55 in 65, 35 finer (8/08). *From The Menlo Park Collection.* (#4704)

1684 **1891 MS66 NGC.** Alluring satiny luster shimmers beneath the icy frosted surfaces. Faint clash marks on the reverse are most noticeable around the E in DIME. A couple of tiny abrasions do not affect the splendid eye appeal of this fully struck Premium Gem. This final-year issue would make a lovely addition to any collection. Census: 56 in 66, 19 finer (7/08). (#4706)

1685 **1891 MS66 PCGS.** The yellow-gold and peach toning that is prominent on the obverse is less prominent on the highly lustrous reverse. A well-defined Premium Gem example of this final-year Seated dime issue. Population: 50 in 66, 6 finer (8/08). *From The Bell Collection.* (#4706)

Important 1891-O/O Seated Dime, MS66

1686 **1891-O MS66 NGC.** Greer-106 obverse with repunched 189; and Greer-107 reverse with a boldly repunched mintmark. A lustrous and untoned Premium Gem example combining two different varieties. Clash marks are noticeable on the upper obverse, but post-striking marks are nonexistent on both sides. (#4707)

PROOF SEATED DIMES

Gorgeous 1859 Seated Dime, PR65 Cameo

1687 **1859 PR65 Cameo NGC.** An extremely important and elusive Gem Cameo proof of the Stars Obverse design type. Indeed, NGC has only certified 51 Cameo proofs of the entire design type, and 26 of those are dated 1859. Tiny raised die chips are visible near the outside points of stars 3 through 9 and star 13. The shield point is left of the serifs of the 1, and the pendant is over the right half of the 5. This brilliant Gem is untoned with exquisite contrast between the mirrored fields and lustrous devices. Census: 7 in 65 Cameo, 8 finer (7/08). (#84748)

1688 **1865 PR64 NGC.** A sharply struck, near-Gem proof, displaying light to medium gray patina. Some surfaces roughness on the obverse. Census: 36 in 64, 25 finer (7/08). *From The Morton J. Greene Collection.* (#4758)

Seldom-Seen 1865 Dime, PR66

1689 **1865 PR66 NGC.** Fortin-102. The date slopes slightly upward, there is prominent die rust in the shield, and a pronounced die scratch is located above the shield. This frosty Premium Gem has strong reflectivity in the fields that gives it great eye appeal. Only a few minor hairlines keep this razor-sharp piece from an even higher grade. A mere 10,000 business strikes were produced along with just 500 proofs. Census: 8 in 66, 2 finer (8/08). (#4758)

Splendid PR67 ★ 1866 Dime

1690 **1866 PR67 ★ NGC.** Attractively patinated in rose-red, emerald-green, and sun-gold. Intricately struck and devoid of lintmarks or abrasions. The date is lightly repunched near the first and final digits. A meager 625 proofs were struck. Census: 2 in 67 ★, 1 finer with a star designation (7/08). (#4759)

1691 **1869 PR64 ANACS.** This is an attractive near-Gem, with lovely electric-blue, gold-tan, and red-brown iridescence over contact-free surfaces. Sharply struck with a few grade-limiting hairlines in the fields. A scarce proof dime issue, as just 600 pieces were struck. (#4762)

1692 **1873 No Arrows PR65 Cameo NGC.** An essentially untoned piece with bright silver-white devices and watery, silver-gray fields that engender a pleasing cameo effect on each side. A decidedly attractive Gem proof specimen, and conditionally scarce at the current grade level. Census: 2 in 65 Cameo, 6 finer (7/08). (#84766)

Spectacular Superb Gem Proof 1873 Arrows Dime

1693 1873 Arrows PR67 NGC. The shift in weight for dimes to 2.5 gm was the last such change for the denomination until the end of 90% silver coinage in the United States. To mark the occasion, the Mint resurrected the arrows it had used for the last substantial change in weight; the arrows lasted just two years in the 1870s, compared to three in the 1850s. While both sides of this incredible Arrows proof dime show pleasing mirrors and frost on the central design elements, the piece falls just shy of Cameo contrast. It is impressively appealing nonetheless, with subtle hints of golden toning near the rims. For the contrast designation, Census: 3 in 67, 0 finer (8/08). *From The Aspen Collection.* (#4769)

1694 1874 Arrows PR63 NGC. As one of the proof Arrows dime issues, the 1874 attracts substantial collector interest. This crisply detailed, strongly mirrored piece has elegant golden toning with occasional splashes of green against the lightly hairlined surfaces. (#4770)

1695 1876 PR65 NGC. Splashes of blue-green and beige-gold patina bathe both sides of this Gem proof. Some minor, localized softness is noted on the design elements. Well preserved throughout. Census: 16 in 65, 9 finer (7/08). (#4773)

1696 1880 PR64 PCGS. The richly frosted devices and gleaming mirrors supply obvious contrast on this Choice specimen, which is housed in a green label holder. Only a few faint hairlines are present in the fields. (#4777)

Marvelous 1880 Dime, PR67 Cameo

1697 1880 PR67 Cameo NGC. CAC. Fortin-101. The business-strike 1880 Seated dime is a key coin in all grades, putting added pressure on the proofs made during the year. This piece offers marvelous, untoned silver-white surfaces with much contrast and generous eye appeal. Some of the deep folds of Liberty's gown are brilliant rather than frosty, from die overpolishing. The second loop of the 8 is broken at the bottom, a characteristic of this die pairing. On the reverse a small, triangular die chip is noted on the right upright of the M in DIME, and a tiny dark spot is noted on the left half of that letter. Nonetheless a lovely, rare, and interesting piece of this elusive issue. Census: 12 in 67 Cameo, 1 finer (7/08). (#84777)

1698 1884 PR64 Cameo NGC. A touch of russet toning near the rims accents the mostly brilliant surfaces. The vibrantly reflective fields have a couple of insignificant hairlines and contrast sharply against the frosted devices. This fully struck example is one of just 875 proofs minted. (#84781)

Stunning 1885 Dime, PR69 Cameo

1699   **1885 PR69 Cameo NGC.** Breen-3429. From a proof mintage of 930 pieces, this spectacular coin is a numismatic miracle. For a present-day proof coin to attain the PR69 Cameo designation is not startling, due to technological advances in the minting process, but it is still not taken for granted. For a coin minted 123 years ago to achieve this level of perfection is nothing short of marvelous. The brilliant, reflective fields shimmer under delicate shades of green and gold toning, with dark azure at the rims. The beautiful play of colors creates impressive eye appeal. This pattern of toning is often seen on coins that were housed in Wayte Raymond holders. The strike is unusually strong for this date; most examples have little detail on Liberty's head. The devices on this example have the crisp detail and sharp contrast expected from a Cameo designation. This variety has a recut numeral 1 in the date. Walter Breen erroneously believed that only business strikes were produced with this die, but many proof examples have also been certified. A fabulous opportunity for the advanced collector. Census: 1 in 69 Cameo, 0 finer (7/08). (#84782)

Patinated PR67 1888 Seated Dime

1700   **1888 PR67 NGC.** Deep ocean-blue patina envelops most of this exactingly struck Superb Gem, although the centers are plum-red. Those who covet richly toned proof Seated type coins will cherish this colorful representative. A scant 832 proofs were struck. Census: 6 in 67, 1 finer (7/08). (#4785)

1701   **1888 PR65 Cameo NGC.** A crisply struck, untoned proof dime with watery reflectivity in the fields and mild frost on the central devices. Well preserved and free of distractions. Census: 6 in 65 Cameo, 15 finer (7/08). (#84785)

1702   **1889 PR66 NGC.** Impressive reflectivity and mild contrast combine with vibrant gold-orange peripheral toning for winning eye appeal. Carefully preserved save for a single hairline in the right obverse field. Census: 35 in 66, 9 finer (7/08). (#4786)

Pristine 1891 Dime, PR67 Cameo

1703   **1891 PR67 Cameo NGC.** The last year of the Seated Liberty dime coinage. This is a beautiful untoned specimen, perfect for the collector who prefers coins that look the same as they did the day they left the mint. Proof dime mintage in 1891 was 600 pieces, and of the 26 Superb Gems NGC has certified, only four have received the Cameo designation (7/08). (#84788)

BARBER DIMES

1704   **1892 MS65 NGC.** Rich gray-green toning graces Gem quality surfaces with occasional blushes of reddish-gold and cobalt-blue. This sharply impressed example would make a lovely addition to a first-year type set that highlights originality as well as technical quality. *From The Menlo Park Collection.* (#4796)

1705   **1892 MS66 PCGS.** Excellent detail for this first-year issue with effusive luster that shines through ample emerald, rose, and gold patina. A notable choice for the discerning type collector. Population: 59 in 66, 9 finer (8/08). (#4796)

1706 1892 MS66 PCGS. An impressive Premium Gem, this lovely first-year Barber dime has attractive iridescent toning with bold and complete design elements. Population: 59 in 66, 9 finer (8/08). (#4796)

Lustrous 1893-O Gem Dime

1707 1893-O MS65 PCGS. This better date dime is tough to find in grades higher than MS64. The current Gem is brightly lustrous, with silver surfaces giving way to bold burgundy-gold color on the left side of the reverse. Sharply struck overall, with the few visible surface marks providing no distractions. Population: 8 in 65, 9 finer (8/08). (#4801)

Elusive Toned Gem 1893-S Barber Dime

1708 1893-S MS65 PCGS. The 1893-S Barber dime is considerably more elusive in Gem condition than the mintage approaching 2.5 million pieces would lead one to believe. PCGS has certified only a dozen examples in Gem grade, with another half-dozen finer (8/08). This piece offers mottled rainbow toning on both sides, with copper-gold and mint-green predominating over the lustrous, clean surfaces. (#4802)

1709 1894 MS63 Prooflike NGC. This brilliant and highly reflective specimen is remarkably clean for the grade, with only a couple of minuscule handling marks and a tiny spot between OF and AMERICA. The strike is sharp and the eye appeal is excellent. Census: 19 in 63, 69 finer (7/08). (#4803)

1710 1897 MS66 PCGS. Softly lustrous beneath colorful patina and well-defined. Warm gold-orange, peach, and blue shadings embrace the carefully preserved surfaces. Population: 37 in 66, 4 finer (8/08). (#4812)

Delightful Gem 1897-S Dime

1711 1897-S MS65 PCGS. CAC. Light gold toning graces this lustrous and boldly impressed Gem. Thorough inspection fails to locate any remotely relevant abrasions, although light parallel roller marks cross the cheek and right obverse field, as made. Population: 8 in 65, 6 finer (8/08). (#4814)

1712 1898-O MS64 PCGS. This impeccably preserved example has pleasing wafts of rose-red toning around the perimeter. The top of Liberty's head and the bottom of the wreath are weakly struck, but the rest of the details are sharp. Only a couple of tiny marks are visible under magnification. Population: 6 in 64, 12 finer (7/08). (#4816)

1713 1903 MS65 PCGS. A bold specimen with satiny luster beneath lovely lilac, gold, and blue toning, somewhat deeper on the reverse. Population: 26 in 65, 11 finer (8/08). (#4830)

1714 1905-S MS65 NGC. Aquamarine and tan-gold enrich both sides, although the reverse has the deeper toning. Well struck and only minimally abraded. In an old pre-hologram holder. (#4837)

1715 1906-O MS65 PCGS. CAC. Red and gold toning around the obverse accents the brilliant and frosty center. The reverse is entirely untoned, and both sides exhibit impressive satiny luster. This sharply struck Gem is virtually devoid of any marks. Population: 30 in 65, 20 finer (7/08). (#4840)

1716 1906-O MS66 PCGS. Russet borders frame the silver-gray centers. This intricately detailed and highly lustrous Premium Gem is remarkably clean and attractive. Population: 15 in 66, 5 finer (7/08). (#4840)

1717 1907-D MS64 PCGS. Each side offers soft, pleasing luster beneath dappled cornflower-blue, violet, green-gold, and silver-gray patina. The well-defined portrait shows few overt flaws. Population: 13 in 64, 12 finer (8/08). (#4843)

1718 1909 MS66 PCGS. Delightfully lustrous and well-defined with swirls of gold and champagne across otherwise silver-white devices. Beautifully preserved, as expected of the grade, with remarkable eye appeal. Population: 8 in 66, 3 finer (8/08). *From The Bell Collection.* (#4850)

1719 1909-D MS64 PCGS. Charcoal-gray patina concentrates at the obverse margins, and olive-green graces those on the reverse. Lustrous surfaces exhibit well struck devices. Some unobtrusive marks define the grade. (#4851)

Ebullient Superb Gem 1911-S Dime

1720 **1911-S MS67 NGC.** Thick mint frost and ebullient luster are the chief attributes of this remarkable Superb Gem coin. The silver-white surfaces are remarkable attractive, and even a loupe reveals only a couple of hair-thin, undistracting marks in the left obverse field that fail to detract. Nearly the finest certified at both services, save for a single NGC piece finer (8/08). (#4859)

1721 **1916 MS66 NGC.** A lightly frosted Premium Gem with remarkable satiny luster. The surfaces are virtually pristine, and the strike is razor-sharp. A conditionally scarce representative of the final Barber dime issue. Census: 42 in 66, 7 finer (7/08). (#4870)

1722 **1916 MS66 PCGS.** The bright, brassy-copper and amber-rose color on the obverse of this highly lustrous Gem is its most distinctive feature. The reverse is virtually untoned. Boldly struck, with repunching noted on the date, and well preserved surfaces on both sides. Population: 42 in 66, 5 finer (8/08). (#4870)

PROOF BARBER DIMES

1723 **1894 PR66 NGC.** Powerful mirrors and bold detail combine for winning eye appeal. This delightful Premium Gem proof is essentially untoned and carefully preserved. Census: 43 in 66, 35 finer (7/08). (#4878)

1724 **1896 PR66 Cameo NGC.** Delightful contrast shines through intermittent pink-gold and silver-gray patina. This earlier proof Barber dime is well-defined and attractive. Census: 14 in 66 Cameo, 11 finer (7/08). (#84880)

Amazing 1898 Barber Dime, PR66 Cameo

1725 **1898 PR66 Cameo NGC.** Both sides of this amazing Premium Gem proof have entirely brilliant and untoned silver surfaces with exceptionally deep mirrors around frosty and highly lustrous silver luster. The strike is bold and the surfaces are pristine. Census: 13 in 66 Cameo, 21 finer (7/08). (#84882)

1726 **1901 PR65 PCGS.** Cobalt-blue and lavender visits the obverse of this Gem proof, ceding to apple-green and orange-gold dappled with blue-gray on the reverse. Well struck design elements stand out against the mirrored fields. Well preserved, and housed in a green label holder. Population: 31 in 65, 30 finer (8/08). (#4885)

1727 **1901 PR66 Cameo NGC.** Icy-frosted devices create a startling cameo appearance with the deeply mirrored fields. This piece is mostly brilliant and a careful inspection with a loupe reveals only a few minuscule spots and abrasions. Census: 9 in 66 Cameo, 7 finer (7/08). (#84885)

1728 **1903 PR66 NGC.** The obverse of this Premium Gem proof has deep steel and blue toning, with vivid cobalt-blue on the reverse. Both sides have deeply mirrored underlying surfaces with evidence of light cameo contrast. Census: 35 in 66, 11 finer (7/08). (#4887)

Beautifully Toned 1905 Dime, PR67

1729 **1905 PR67 PCGS.** A striking mix of peach, sky-blue, ruby, and indigo on the obverse of this midseries Barber dime entry contrasts with a subtle covering of rose-tinted slate on the reverse. A couple of small spots to the left of Liberty do not detract from the bold strike and lustrous surfaces. NGC and PCGS have certified fewer than 30 coins combined, with just seven pieces finer (7/08). (#4889)

Lavishly Toned PR67 1907 Dime

1730 **1907 PR67 NGC.** This Superb Proof is for the aficionado of colorfully toned coins. Variegated cobalt-blue, orange-gold, and lavender patina adorns each side, but does not in the least interfere with the reflectivity from the mirrored fields. Exquisitely struck design elements appear to be suspended over glassy fields when the coin is tilted beneath a light source. Only 575 proofs were struck. Census: 18 in 67, 0 finer (4/08). (#4891)

Exquisitely Toned PR67 1910 Dime

1731 **1910 PR67 NGC.** Lovely chestnut-gold and aquamarine toning adorns this penetratingly struck Superb Gem. The central reverse remains brilliant. Gorgeously preserved as well as aesthetically pleasing. Among the lower mintage proofs, since only 551 pieces were coined. Census: 13 in 67, 4 finer (7/08). (#4894)

MERCURY DIMES

1732   1916-D Good 4 PCGS. This smooth cream-gray key date dime has a bold date and a distinct mintmark. The right reverse legend touches the rim, but remains legible. (#4906)

1733   1916-D Good 6 PCGS. The 1916-D is the only issue in the Mercury dime series with a six-figure mintage (264,000 pieces) and is one of the most famous rarities of 20th century numismatics. Pleasing light gray patina graces the surfaces of this well-defined piece. A couple of shallow scratches are barely worthy of note. (#4906)

1734   1916-D Good 6 PCGS. Bluish-gray and ivory patina rests on the semi-bright surfaces of this key date representative. The design elements retain nice detail, and the rims are full, except for a slightly weak area above AMER. Both sides are quite clean. Housed in a green-label holder. (#4906)

1735   1916-D Good 6 PCGS. The '16-D has been regarded as the key date to the Mercury dime series since at least the 1930s, and it undoubtedly always will be. This well worn example shows a few hints of patina, mainly near the peripheries; and a few faint pinscratches and hairlines. (#4906)

1736   1916-D—Damaged—NCS. VG Details. An original appearing example with medium gray surfaces, and also with the appearance of being bent and straightened. (#4906)

1737   1916-D VG8 PCGS. The peripheral legends are bold, and the top of the fasces is sharp for the grade. Dusky lavender-gray toning embraces unblemished surfaces. Housed in a green label holder. (#4906)

1738   1916-D VG8 PCGS. Mostly medium gray, but splashes of golden-brown and aqua invigorate the peripheries. All legends are crisp, and this key date dime is problem-free for its grade. (#4906)

1739   1916-D VG10 PCGS. Deep pearl-gray patina graces this charming series key dime. No marks are worthy of discussion, and all legends are well delineated. Traces of vertical lines are present above the central bands. (#4906)

Appealing AU 1916-D Mercury Dime

1740   1916-D AU50 NGC. All of the vertical fasces sticks are split on this AU example, which reveals golden-gray patina on both sides and considerable luster remaining. A single thin contact mark is noted behind Liberty's head, but much appeal is present on this satisfying example. A promising candidate for the budget-minded collector building a Mint State set. (#4906)

Select Full Bands 1916-D Dime

1741   1916-D MS63 Full Bands PCGS. The 1916-D dime was saved in small quantities when it was delivered to banks; though it was the first-year issue, casual-collector interest was low compared to the West and East Coasts, and as a result, Mint State survivors make up only a small portion of the existing issue. This lovely Select piece is a notable exception, crisply detailed with luminous peach-gold and rose shadings that drape each side. Liberty's portrait offers solid detail, and the bands on the reverse, though a touch flat, are cleanly separated. Minor, scattered marks account for the grade. (#4907)

1742 **1916-D MS65 Full Bands NGC.** The relative availability of 1916-D quarters is directly related to the unavailability and low mintage of 1916-D dimes. The entire mintage of 264,000 dimes was produced in November. At a meeting of mint superintendents and the director at the end of November, it was decided that the striking of all other denominations should be suspended at the Denver Mint until the Treasury Department's order for 4 million quarters could be satisfied. This placed considerable pressure on the 10-year-old Denver Mint, and as a result, by the time Treasury's order could be fulfilled, the calendar year was over and it was time to move on to coins dated 1917.

Knowledgeable collectors are aware that the 1916-D dime is not rare in the absolute sense. However, like the 1909-S VDB cent, its low mintage and *perception* of rarity are far more important than an actual lack of coins in the marketplace—those two factors being the primary motivators that have consistently increased the price of the 1916-D dime in all grades over the past 70 years. In Gem condition and with full central cross bands on the reverse, though, the 1916-D is an important condition scarcity, and there are never enough coins available to satisfy collector demand.

This is an all-brilliant coin that displays the usual granular, mattelike texture with an overlay of satiny mint luster. There are no singularly mentionable abrasions on either side of this lovely piece, and the cross bands are deeply split and rounded on the reverse, as are the diagonals. Only 23 pieces have been so graded by NGC, with another 32 certified by PCGS (8/08), and only 31 coins are known in higher grades. This is an impressive and lustrous example of this important 20th century key. (#4907)

1743 **1917 MS66 Full Bands PCGS.** Highly lustrous surfaces exhibit a few speckles of gold-tan under magnification. Sharply defined throughout, culminating in Full Bands. A light mark or two is noted on each side. Population: 74 in 66 Full Bands, 13 finer (8/08). (#4911)

Conditionally Scarce 1918-D Dime, MS64 Full Bands

1744 **1918-D MS64 Full Bands PCGS.** Well struck and lustrous, with clean surfaces that are free of any serious marks or abrasions. Satiny and essentially untoned, save for faint gold and tan hints in the fields and near the margins. A minor luster graze on Liberty's neck prevents a finer grade. The 1918-D is one of the scarcest Mercury dime issues with full band detail in high grades. (#4919)

Rarely Encountered Full Bands
1918-D Dime, MS65

1745 **1918-D MS65 Full Bands NGC.** Even though more than 22 million pieces were struck, the 1918-D is generally acknowledged today as the most challenging strike rarity in the Mercury dime series, probably as a result of hurried wartime conditions. Gems are very elusive and plagued by peripheral weakness, which is accompanied by indistinct central bands on all but a few of the Uncirculated population. The current specimen is a notable exception. Its design elements are sharply struck throughout, not just on the bands. Excellent definition is seen in the peripheral lettering (save for minor softness on the base of E in ONE), on the numerals of the date, and on the mintmark. The surfaces have a grainy-textured appearance with soft, glowing luster, and are nearly untoned, except for a whisper of gold color in limited areas. There are no obvious or distracting blemishes on either side of this exceptional coin. Census: 8 in 65, 1 finer (7/08). (#4919)

1746 **1919 MS66 Full Bands PCGS.** Delicate gold and rose tints visit the margins, while the centers are largely subtle silver-blue. Excellent definition and preservation. Population: 44 in 66 Full Bands, 9 finer (8/08). (#4923)

Extraordinary 1920-D Dime, MS67

1747 **1920-D MS67 NGC.** An absolutely stunning 1920-D dime that could only be finer had the strike been a little stronger. The central bands are flat, but all other details are quite bold. As of August 2008, NGC had only certified two MS67's, and two other MS67 FB's. Both sides have intensely frosty silver luster with full brilliance, sans toning. (#4930)

Attractive 1920-D Dime, MS66 Full Bands

1748 **1920-D MS66 Full Bands NGC.** Attractive rose-orange and yellow toning endows the surfaces of this minimally abraded piece, with wafts of lilac and hazel around the perimeter. Enticing satiny luster graces both sides and is complemented razor-sharp design details. This spectacular piece would make a great addition to even the finest collection. Census: 7 in 66 Full Bands, 2 finer (7/08). (#4931)

Semikey 1920-S Dime, MS65 Full Bands

1749 **1920-S MS65 Full Bands NGC.** The 1920-S is a scarce, semikey issue in the Mercury dime series that is much more challenging than its mintage of 13.8 million pieces would suggest. It is also scarcer than several other, better-known issues. Only 18 pieces have been so graded by NGC with a mere four coins finer (8/08). This is a solid Gem example that has rich, frosted mint luster and an even overlay of rose and lilac toning. Some fadeaway is seen on the peripheral lettering, and the final digit of the date is weak as usual—described by Lange as "shy." An exceptionally pleasing and problem-free 1920-S dime. (#4933)

Splendid 1921-D Dime, Choice Mint State

1750 **1921-D MS64 PCGS.** The Philadelphia and Denver dimes of 1921 were underappreciated when minted, and as a result they are now elusive in any grade. After the famous 1916-D, the 1921-D ranks as the most difficult issue in the series with a comparatively low mintage of just over 1 million pieces. Satiny luster radiates from the untoned surfaces, and is unaffected by a few microscopic abrasions. The bands are fully defined, and there is only slight weakness in the hair above Liberty's forehead. A couple of tiny copper spots are noted on the reverse. A dazzling example of this desirable issue. PCGS has certified only 23 pieces finer (7/08). (#4936)

1751 **1923 MS67 Full Bands NGC. CAC.** Decisively struck with captivating satiny luster beneath rich green-gold and lilac patina. Impeccably preserved, even by Superb Gem standards, and housed in a old holder. NGC has certified only one numerically finer representative (8/08). (#4939)

1752 **1924 MS66 Full Bands PCGS.** The obverse is close to brilliant, while peach-gold and stone-gray blend throughout the reverse. Lustrous and impeccably preserved with a penetrating strike. Population: 68 in 66 Full Bands, 11 finer (8/08). (#4943)

1753 **1925 MS65 Full Bands PCGS.** Vibrantly lustrous with crisp detail on the central devices. Light golden toning graces much of the otherwise silver-white surfaces. PCGS has graded 30 finer Full Bands pieces (8/08). (#4949)

1754 **1925 MS66 Full Bands PCGS.** Crisply struck with minimal patina and vibrant luster. This often ill-produced Roaring Twenties issue is highly elusive any finer, with just three such Full Bands pieces known to PCGS (8/08). (#4949)

1755 **1925-D MS64 Full Bands NGC.** Crisply struck except for minor peripheral fadeaway in a few areas. The central reverse bands are fully rounded and fully separated. A satiny, untoned example without any serious flaws. Census: 56 in 64 Full Bands, 32 finer (7/08). (#4951)

1756 **1927-D MS66 NGC.** Speckled purple toning adds color to the mostly silver-gray surfaces. Scintillating luster radiates from the virtually pristine fields. Encapsulated in an old NGC holder. Census: 9 in 66, 0 finer (8/08). (#4962)

1757 **1927-D MS66 NGC.** Pleasing luster adorns both sides, and a well executed leaves sharp definition on the design elements, including strong (though not full) separation of the middle bands. A few minute marks are visible on the reverse. Scarce in Mint State. Census: 9 in 66, 0 finer (7/08). (#4962)

1758 **1927-D MS64 Full Bands PCGS.** Ex: Larry Shapiro. Original luster interspersed with hazy hints of toning. This better date dime has a few minor marks only visible beneath a loupe. Population: 38 in 64 Full Bands, 32 finer (8/08).
Ex: Velma & Bowie Lynch Collection, Part Four (Heritage, 8/2004), lot 5789; Larry Shapiro Collection of Mercury Dimes (Heritage, 1/2006), lot 2032. (#4963)

Splendid 1927-S Mercury Dime, MS65 Full Bands

1759 **1927-S MS65 Full Bands PCGS.** David Lange (1993) states that fully struck, Gem quality 1927-S Mercury dimes are among the key dates for this immensely popular series. This bright, satiny example displays pristine surfaces that have a pale gold cast, along with faint touches of speckled russet on both sides. Faint die clash marks and a couple of spidery die cracks are noted on the obverse, but they do nothing to decrease the eye appeal of this intensely lustrous Gem. Population: 29 in 65 Full Bands, 11 finer (8/08). (#4965)

1760 **1930 MS66 Full Bands PCGS.** Ex: Bassano Collection. Boldly impressed with light, lovely silver-blue patina over much of the obverse and mint-green iridescence at the reverse border. Excellent preservation and visual appeal. PCGS has graded just 12 finer Full Bands coins (8/08). (#4979)

Superb Gem Full Bands 1931-D Dime

1761 **1931-D MS67 Full Bands PCGS.** A lightly toned Superb Gem with delicate blue and golden pastel overtones. Refreshingly devoid of abrasions. The low mintage 1931-D is generally available in Mint State, but it appears only infrequently as a Superb Gem. None have been certified finer by either NGC or PCGS (8/08). (#4985)

1762 **1935-S MS67 Full Bands PCGS.** Impressively lustrous, effectively silver-white surfaces are carefully preserved. A sharply struck Superb Gem, tied for the finest Full Bands example known to NGC or PCGS (8/08). (#4997)

1763 **1937 MS68 Full Bands PCGS.** Deep violet, russet, and silver-gray toning embraces the obverse, which contrasts sharply against the minimally toned reverse. Captivating satiny luster radiates beneath the light frost. Neither NGC nor PCGS has certified any examples finer than the present piece, and this appealing specimen would make a spectacular addition to a registry set. (#5005)

Formidable MS68 Full Bands 1938-D Dime

1764 **1938-D MS68 Full Bands PCGS.** Formidable luster and exquisite sun-gold peripheral obverse toning combine with immaculate surfaces to confirm the lofty third party grade. A sharply struck and gorgeous example of this low mintage issue from the tail end of the Great Depression. Population: 9 in 68 Full Bands, 0 finer (8/08). (#5013)

1765 **1939-D MS68 Full Bands PCGS.** This gorgeous piece displays beautiful iridescent toning on obverse and reverse alike, which includes shades of chartreuse, gold, crimson, and electric-green. The striking details are flawless, and the expertly preserved surfaces are nearly pristine. A spectacular type piece. Population: 84 in 68 Full Bands, 14 finer (8/08).
From The Bell Collection. (#5019)

1766 **1939-D MS68 Full Bands PCGS.** Beautiful and essentially brilliant. The strike is needle-sharp, and a loupe fails to locate any abrasions. Population: 84 in 68 Full Bands, 14 finer (8/08). (#5019)

Rainbow-Toned 1941-D Dime, MS68 Full Bands

1767 **1941-D MS68 Full Bands PCGS.** Eye-catching rainbow toning graces the obverse of this nearly perfect specimen. An arc of lime green at the bottom of the obverse is the outermost color, and subsequently yields to deep green, violet, lilac, and bright yellow. The top of the obverse, along with the entire reverse, features a dusting of violet and red toning. A loupe locates only a couple of nearly imperceptible handling marks. Population: 18 in 68 Full Bands, 0 finer (7/08). (#5031)

1768 **1942/1 AU50 NGC.** Luminous green-gold and silver-blue shadings drape the well-preserved surfaces of this briefly circulated overdate dime. Minimally marked with the overdigit bold. (#5036)

1769 **1942/1 AU55 ICG.** FS-101, formerly FS-010.7. Golden-brown and cream-gray embrace this satiny and unblemished key date dime. Evidence of circulation is minimal, and as always, the underdigit 1 is obvious. (#5036)

1770 **1942/1 AU58 NGC.** FS-101, formerly FS-010.7. This lustrous green-gold slider has slight rub on the central bands, but would pass as Uncirculated in many circles. No marks of any relevance are detected. A charming key date dime. (#5036)

1771 **1942/1 MS60 Details ICG.** FS-101, formerly FS-010.7. After the 1916-D, the 1942/1 (and its Denver Mint counterpart) ranks as the key date in the Mercury dime series. Although the obverse is somewhat dull, the reverse exhibits eye-catching luster beneath dusted gold toning. A well-detailed and desirable piece. (#5036)

Phenomenal 1942/1 Mercury Dime Overdate
MS66 Full Bands, Tied for Finest Certified

1772 **1942/1 MS66 Full Bands PCGS.** FS-101. At an earlier time, many numismatists understood little about the mechanism that produces such startling overdate errors as the 1918/7-D Buffalo nickel, the 1918/7-S Standing Liberty quarter, the 1943/2-P Jefferson nickel, and the 1942/1-P and D Mercury dimes. Lacking a detailed knowledge of the process of hub, die, and coin production and the procedures involved in moving from one calendar year's coinage to the next, it was a simplistic but understandable assumption that many numismatists made, that the errors were produced simply by reengraving a digit for the later year over that of the earlier. Today there is little excuse, with the wealth of information available both online and in print to researchers, to make such a leap.

When the 1942/1-P and D errors were produced, the P-mint version, being much more bold and obvious, was recognized outside the Mint within a short time. The D-mint, a subtler overdate, went unrecognized for nearly 20 years; according to Lange, it was first mentioned in *Numismatic Scrapbook* in November 1960. When news of the 1942/1-P issue earlier surfaced in that same publication, in March 1943, among the more preposterous theories propounded—by no less a luminary than Chief Engraver John R. Sinnock—was that the error was produced when a 1941 dime was overstruck with a 1942 die! According to Lange, "Perhaps realizing the incredible nature of this explanation, he [Sinnock] then presented readers of [*Numismatic Scrapbook* editor Lee] Hewitt's publication with a streamlined rendition of what is now known to have been the actual cause—the use of two differently dated working hubs in the sinking of a single working die."

Lange continues with a direct quote from Sinnock, more credibly disputing the theory that a 1941 die might have been reengraved to read 1942:

In September of each year we start engraving the numeral in the new master die for the following year. We have no punches for these numerals since they were sculptured in the first place we follow the individual style of each sculptor. From this master die a working "hub" is drawn. This is re-touched if necessary, then hardened. This hub is used to fabricate all the working dies for that year. About one thousand dies with new date must be ready by January 1st of each year.

Because the error was published so soon after its creation, hobbyists began examining all 1942 dimes they encountered, leading to the many AU examples known today. Lange points out, however, that true Mint State coins are rare. The certified population data bear that out: While NGC and PCGS have each certified a few dozen Uncirculated examples, that is a far smaller number than those who desire an example of this popular variety.

Of course, Full Bands examples are rarer yet, and in MS66 Full Bands, this splendid example is one of only a half-dozen so certified at PCGS, and there are none finer (8/08). NGC has graded two coins MS66 Full Bands.

For starters, the overdate is incredibly bold on this piece, a naked-eye variety nearly as obvious as the 1955 Doubled Die cent. Not only the central horizontal bands on the reverse are split and rounded, but also the top and bottom bands. The top diagonal is full and, as often seen, the lower diagonal shows slight weakness where it joins the nearby olive leaf. The silver-white surfaces exhibit just a hint of golden-gray toning; radiant luster washes from both sides in copious quantities. The surfaces are almost entirely frosty, although under a loupe small patches in the left obverse field and behind Liberty's head display the shiny prooflike attributes that Lange calls "die burn," the result of die overpolishing.

This piece is simply the finest quality either obtainable or imaginable, a prize for the Registry Set collector or 20th century series enthusiast. (#5037)

1773 **1942/1-D XF40 PCGS.** Light silver-blue shadings grace much of each side, while the margins show glimpses of green-gold. A pleasing, modestly circulated example of this famous *Guide Book* overdate. (#5040)

Lustrous Near-Mint 1942/1-D Dime

1774 **1942/1-D AU58 NGC. CAC.** This double-hub error is not as obvious as its 1942/1 P-mint counterpart, and as a consequence it is rarer in all grades and more likely to show considerable wear, having escaped detection for more than 20 years. Interestingly, however, unlike the 1942/1-P, the double-hubbing is also visible on the 1942/1-D on IN GOD WE TRUST, especially along the left sides of RU. The D mintmark is also repunched to the south on all genuine specimens, as here.

This piece displays just a trace of highpoint rub that separates it from Mint State. A couple of minor scrapes appear on Liberty's neck under a loupe, not terribly distracting but mentioned for accuracy. The obverse is pearl-gray while the reverse is deeper amber-gold, but much luster remains on both sides. (#5040)

Appealing 1942/1-D Dime, AU58

1775 **1942/1-D AU58 NGC.** FS-101, formerly FS-010.8. Very scarce in all grades, and rare in Mint State, having escaped detection for about twenty years. The silver-gray surfaces of this near-Mint example retain considerable luster, and exhibit well defined design features. The middle bands, while not full, display a good amount of separation, and the two diagonal bands are strong. A few inoffensive marks are scattered about. Overall, a highly pleasing coin. Census: 43 in 58, 8 finer (7/08). (#5040)

Lustrous Select 1942/1-D Dime

1776 **1942/1-D MS63 NGC.** FS-101, formerly FS-010.8. The bands are very close to full, and the overall strike is sharp. This is a lustrous key date dime with attractive honey-gold, ivory-gray, and aqua-blue toning. No marks are remotely of interest. It will take a premium bid to acquire the present delicacy. (#5040)

Beautiful Full Bands MS62 1942/1-D Dime

1777 **1942/1-D MS62 Full Bands PCGS. CAC.** Brilliant, satiny luster in the centers cedes to smoke-gray and copper hues at the extreme rims and around the devices. This key date dime is quite attractive and the details are well brought up, including the crucial central band separation, but there are a few minor abrasions that define the grade. Population: 16 in 62, 82 finer (8/08).
Ex: Dallas Signature (Heritage, 7/2006), lot 738, which realized $4,887.50. (#5041)

Choice Full Bands 1942/1-D Dime

1778 **1942/1-D MS64 Full Bands PCGS.** FS-101, formerly FS-010.8. This exactingly struck near-Gem has enervating luster and unblemished surfaces. Attractively toned in olive-green and rose-red. The bases of the prior 41 are visible directly west of the 42. Population: 34 in 64 Full Bands, 28 finer (8/08). (#5041)

1779 **1944-D MS68 Full Bands PCGS. CAC.** Wafts of gold and deep red accent the mostly untoned surfaces. The strike is full, and a glass locates only a couple of minuscule handling marks on this nearly perfect specimen. Neither NGC nor PCGS have certified any pieces finer (7/08). (#5053)

1780 **1945 MS62 Full Bands PCGS.** An untoned and highly lustrous example of the final Mercury dime issue. Several wispy abrasions keep this piece from an even higher grade, but the strike is remarkably sharp for the grade. (#5057)

PROOF MERCURY DIMES

1781 **1936 PR63 NGC.** Sharply struck and free of bothersome contact marks, with slight milkiness in the fields and a fingerprint across the obverse that limits the grade. From the first Mercury dime proof issue, consisting of 4,130 pieces. (#5071)

Wonderful 1936 Mercury Dime, PR67

1782 **1936 PR67 PCGS.** Ex: Tom Mershon Collection. A few years ago the Heritage catalogers had the pleasure of describing the phenomenal Tom Mershon #2 All-Time PCGS Registry Set of Lincoln Wheat Cents, so it is a pleasure to see some other Registry Set-caliber denominations with the famed Mershon provenance. This wonderful Superb Gem, like many of the Mershon proof coins, has splendid original rim toning, here in shades of iridescent violet, aquamarine, and fuchsia, with silver centers and premium appeal. Population: 43 in 67, 1 finer (8/08). (#5071)

Lustrous PR68 1937 Mercury Dime

1783 **1937 PR68 PCGS.** Ex: Tom Mershon Collection. This virtually perfect proof Mercury dime boasts brilliant surfaces and just a whisper of even golden toning. The fields and devices have comparable luster, with a full cartwheel effect. This example is tied for finest certified by PCGS, although we can imagine no other with finer appeal than the present example. Population: 21 in 68, 0 finer (8/08). (#5072)

1784 **1938 PR67 PCGS.** Ex: Tom Mershon Collection. A few tiny speckles of golden-brown grace both sides, but the exquisitely preserved surfaces are otherwise brilliant. The uppermost portion of Liberty's nose is absent because of overzealous die polishing. (#5073)

Needle-Sharp 1939 Mercury Dime, PR68

1785 **1939 PR68 PCGS.** Ex: Tom Mershon Collection. The 1939 is of medium rarity among proof Mercury dimes, but precious few examples grade as fine as the present Superb Gem. This seemingly flawless representative is smooth from rim to rim, with just a hint of powder-gray iridescence. The needle-sharp strike is all that one would expect of a proof specimen. Population: 30 in 68, 0 finer (8/08). (#5074)

1786 **1940 PR67 NGC. CAC.** This is a fully struck proof that is entirely brilliant and untoned. The fields are deeply reflective, and both sides of the piece are essentially pristine. A great Mercury dime specimen that will please even the most demanding collector. (#5075)

1787 **1940 PR68 PCGS.** Fully and crisply struck on all of the design elements, with none of the bothersome peripheral "fadeaway" common to business strikes. There is slight milkiness in the fields, and trace amounts of tan color occur near the left-side peripheries, but the overall presentation and quality of this proof Mercury dime are Superb. Population: 18 in 68, 0 finer (8/08). (#5075)

Vibrant 1941 Dime, PR68 ★

1788 **1941 PR68 ★ NGC.** Dramatic lilac, yellow-gold, and lime-green patina envelops the obverse, which contrasts nicely against the dusted hazel toning on the reverse. The surfaces appear perfect to the unaided eye, and a loupe locates only a couple of tiny spots. Splendid watery and highly lustrous fields give this razor-sharp piece excellent eye appeal. NGC has certified 10 pieces in PR68 ★, with none finer (7/08). (#5076)

Outstanding 1941 Dime, PR68

1789 **1941 PR68 PCGS.** Ex: Tom Mershon Collection. Faint hazel toning visits the margins of this mostly brilliant specimen. The surfaces are virtually immaculate, and even with a loupe it is difficult to locate anything that keeps this razor-sharp piece from being absolutely perfect. Neither NGC nor PCGS has certified any coins finer (8/08). (#5076)

Superlative 1941 Dime, PR68

1790   1941 PR68 NGC. This bold and beautiful proof Mercury is just shy of a Cameo designation with brilliant silver surfaces and exceptionally deep mirrored fields. It is tied for the finest 1941 proof dime certified by NGC or PCGS, with just 63 examples graded. Census: 48 in 68, 0 finer (7/08). (#5076)

1791   1942 PR68 PCGS. Ex: Tom Mershon Collection. Essentially a flawless coin, the brilliant, deeply reflective surfaces are only disturbed by the slightest overlay of hazy, pale reddish patina on each side. A virtually unimprovable type coin. Population: 37 in 68, 0 finer (8/08). (#5077)

ROOSEVELT DIME

Exceptional 1951-S Dime, MS68 Full Bands

1792   1951-S MS68 Full Bands PCGS. Ex: Larry Shapiro. Both sides are highly frosted and silver-white, with iridescent patina in shades of amber, magenta, and mint-green. Both sets of horizontal lines that bind the fasces are fully split all along their length, and the vertical lines are outlined as well. The eye appeal is exceptional. Population: 5 in 68 Full Bands, 0 finer (8/08).
Ex: Denver Signature (Heritage, 8/2006), lot 1032, which realized $5,175. (#85099)

PROOF ROOSEVELT DIMES

Incredible 1951 Dime, PR66 Deep Cameo

1793   1951 PR66 Deep Cameo PCGS. This untoned and splendidly preserved specimen features river rock-white devices and flawless fields. Both sides exhibit extraordinary contrast for an early proof Roosevelt dime, created through a combination of deep mirrored fields and frosty devices. Population: 2 in 66 Deep Cameo, 2 finer (8/08). (#95226)

1794   1951 PR67 Cameo NGC. Dappled sky-blue, purple, and aqua-green are deeper in hue on the obverse of this Superb Gem Cameo proof. Exceptionally well struck, with no mentionable marks. (#85226)

Rare Deep Cameo Superb Gem Proof 1954 Roosevelt Dime

1795   1954 PR67 Deep Cameo PCGS. Although proof Roosevelt dimes with heavy cameo contrast, as on the present coin, are scarce, they do appear on the market from time to time. Superb Gem Deep Cameo coins, however, are a different story. Slight hints of milky toning occur on the deeply reflective fields. Nicely struck, and virtually blemish-free. Population: 4 in 67, 0 finer (3/04). (#95229)

Important PR68 1968 No S Dime

1796 **1968 No S PR68 PCGS.** Proof production resumed in 1968 after a three-year experiment with special mint sets. San Francisco took over the duty of proof coinage from Philadelphia, and the S mintmark was supposed to appear on all proofs, moved to the obverse. The very first year, however, one proof dime obverse die failed to receive a mintmark, and some (but not many) coins struck from the die made it past all mint quality control inspectors. The dime is the smallest diameter circulating coin, and was prone to the missing S error, which happened again to the dime in 1970, 1975, and 1983. Now, the mintmark is hubbed, and the era of No S proof sets is over. This is a brilliant and crisply struck Superb Gem of this rare error. The portrait has a hint of frost and contrasts slightly with the glassy field. Population: 5 in 68, 0 finer (8/08). (#5245)

1797 **1970 No S PR69 Cameo NGC.** This Superb example of the second No S proof Roosevelt dime error is knocking on the door of a perfect rating. There is not a single outwardly noticeable blemish or contact mark. The coin is deeply contrasted, and tied with nine other pieces as the finest NGC-certified specimen with a Cameo designation (8/08). (#85248)

1798 **1983 No S PR69 Deep Cameo PCGS.** A virtually flawless, boldly contrasted example of the fourth and (presumably) final No S error among proof Roosevelt dimes. Beautiful frost across the devices contrasts strongly with the fathomless mirrors. Population: 67 in 69 Deep Cameo, 0 finer (8/08). (#95265)

1799 **1983 No S PR69 Deep Cameo PCGS.** Virtually flawless with absolute field-to-device contrast. This snow-white No S specimen is second to none, with neither NGC nor PCGS recognizing a perfect example at the highest contrast level (8/08). (#95265)

TWENTY CENT PIECES

1800 **1875 AU58 NGC.** Only a hint of rub appears on the high points of this first-year Philadelphia twenty cent piece. Deep blue-violet and green-gold shadings consume each side.
From The Menlo Park Collection. (#5296)

Exquisite 1875 Twenty Cent, MS64

1801 **1875 MS64 PCGS.** First year of issue for the brief cent series, struck only from 1875 to 1878, the last two years only in proof format. An amazing, nearly prooflike example with satiny silver luster and full brilliance. While each of the obverse stars is small in stature, they are all boldly detailed through the entire circumference of the die. Although shy of Gem quality, the surfaces are exceptional for the grade. The inside edge of the eagle's right (facing) wing is minutely doubled, and it may be a doubled die, however, it is more likely strike doubling.
From The Bell Collection.

1802 **1875 MS64 PCGS.** A beautifully detailed Choice example of this popular twenty cent issue, strongly lustrous beneath dappled green-gold and violet-silver patina. Highly attractive. Population: 62 in 64, 29 finer (8/08). (#5296)

1803 **1875-CC—Scratched—ICG. Fine 15 Details.** A moderate-length vertical scratch is noted in the right obverse field. Pleasing otherwise with appreciable detail and generally slate-gray surfaces that lighten to pearl-gray at the worn devices. (#5297)

1804 **1875-CC AU50 PCGS.** The 1875-CC is the only collectible CC-mint issue of this short-lived denomination. This unblemished golden-brown and slate-gray representative is softly defined on the devices, but has no prominent marks. Encased in a green label holder. (#5297)

1805 **1875-S MS62 ICG.** A splendid example of this short-lived denomination. Flashy luster enhances the eye appeal of this boldly defined representative. The surfaces are mostly medium gray save for a peppering of hazel toning in the periphery. A faded streak of a grease stain is noted on the reverse. (#5298)

1806 **1875-S MS63 PCGS.** Deep blue, violet, and russet toning surrounds the golden centers. There are traces of weakness on the stars, head, and eagle, but the surfaces are remarkably clean with only a couple of insignificant marks. A charming type coin. (#5298)

1807 **1875-S MS63 NGC.** A relatively high number of these odd-denomination pieces were struck at the San Francisco Mint in 1875. The total mintage was 1,155,000 business strikes, and Mint State survivors are fairly numerous. This example is rather weakly struck, especially on the obverse, and displays subdued satin luster. Surface marks are minimal for the grade, however. (#5298)

1808 **1875-S MS63 PCGS.** Smoky light to medium patina adheres to lustrous surfaces that exhibit well struck design elements. Some minute grade-defining marks are concealed within the toning. *From The Menlo Park Collection.* (#5298)

1809 **1875-S MS64 PCGS.** Rose, gold, and silver-gray toning overlies the surfaces of this lustrous piece. There is a trace of softness on Liberty's head and the adjacent stars, but the rest of the details are fully defined. A few microscopic spots and abrasions limit the grade. (#5298)

1810 **1876 MS62 NGC.** The 1876 is the last of the generally available business strike twenty cent pieces, with a mintage of just 14,600 pieces. Both sides show solid definition and minimal patina, and the eagle offers ample frostiness. Strongly lustrous with a handful of fine marks in the fields that account for the grade. *From The Menlo Park Collection.* (#5299)

Low-Mintage 1876 Twenty Cent, Choice Uncirculated

1811 **1876 MS64 NGC.** A golden tint graces the surfaces of this powerfully impressed Choice representative. This piece is remarkably clean for the grade, and exhibits strong satiny luster that enhances the great eye appeal. The 1876 is a scarce issue with a mintage of just 14,640 pieces. Census: 66 in 64, 57 finer (7/08). (#5299)

PROOF TWENTY CENT PIECES

Silver-White PR62 1875 Twenty Cent Piece

1812 **1875 PR62 PCGS.** Numismatic riddle: What do the twenty cent piece and the Susan B. Anthony dollar have in common? They both had short lives because in appearance and size they were too easily confused with a quarter. The 1875 has the highest mintage of the four proof twenty cent issues, although the 1878 seems to have been saved in slightly greater numbers. This piece displays silver-white surfaces with near-Cameo contrast, and only the numerous small contact marks appearing under a loupe appear to keep the piece from an even finer grade (8/08). (#5303)

Lovely PR64 Cameo 1875 Twenty Cent

1813 **1875 PR64 Cameo NGC.** Proof production for this odd denomination began with a rush, with 2,790 specimens struck in 1875. Mintages tapered off swiftly thereafter, and 1875-dated proofs are the most available today. This attractive type piece offers minimally toned surfaces with strong contrast between the shining mirrors and the heavily frosted devices. Census: 14 in 64 Cameo, 21 finer (7/08). (#85303)

Toned 1878 Twenty Cent, PR62

1814 **1878 PR62 PCGS.** The final issue of the denomination, struck only in proof, with a total production of 600 coins. While the fields exhibit a few faint hairlines, the rich gold, blue, and violet toning adds exceptional eye appeal. A delightful example for the specialist or type collector. (#5306)

Famous Key 1796 Quarter XF40, B-2

1815 **1796 XF40 NGC.** High 6. B-2, R.3. Two varieties are known for the Draped Bust, Small Eagle quarter dollar coinage, a single year design and the first year of issue for the denomination. The two varieties can be quickly distinguished by the position of the digit 6, high and almost touching the bust on this B-2 variety, and lower, nearly centered between the bust and border, on the rarer B-1 variety. The next quarter dollar issue, struck eight years later in 1804, has the new Heraldic Eagle design. Mintage of these early issues was limited with just 6,146 quarters produced in 1796 and 6,738 more in 1804. It is reasonable to assume that the 1796 calendar year mintage corresponds with the actual production of coins bearing the 1796 date. One researcher, Robert Hilt, claimed that the 1796 B-1 variety was actually struck in 1804! He further claimed that the survival rate for the early quarter dollars was only 1.32%, a figure that is much too low. His figures suggest that only about 170 quarter dollars survive from both years, 1796 and 1804. The actual survival rate is probably more in the order of 8% to 10%, or about 1,000 to 1,200 examples for both years.

The present example is an attractive, well balanced, copper-gray representative, perfectly centered, with strong dentils around both sides, which is typical for the issue. Faint mint luster still radiates from some of the recessed areas, and examination under a loupe reveals no marks worthy of singular mention. For possible pedigree purposes, we point out a small linear mark equidistant between star two and the dentils, and another just to the left of the middle of the right ribbon coming out of the bowknot. Nice definition is displayed in most of Liberty's hair, and in the eagle's wing feathers. A desirable coin sure to appeal to a number of audiences.

From The Menlo Park Collection. (#5310)

1816 **1804 Fair 2 NGC.** B-1, R.4. The 1804 is the scarcest date of the brief Draped Bust, Heraldic Eagle quarter series. Two varieties are identified by the relationship between the top of the 4 and the bust, with B-1 having the 4 clearly separated. This piece has considerable wear, but does have a complete date. The obverse is fully AG3, the reverse barely Fair 2. (#5312)

1817 **1804 Good 4—Bent—NCS. Good Details.** B-1, R.4. The right-side borders are bent, and the surfaces are granular. The reverse has dark blue-gray toning. All legends are clear aside from a few letters in E PLURIBUS UNUM.
From The Morton J. Greene Collection. (#5312)

XF Sharpness 1804 Quarter, B-1

1818 **1804—Reverse Damage—NCS. XF Details.** B-1, R.4. The die marker between stars 8 and 9 confirms the variety. While this piece has been "gently pummeled" on the reverse by some contemporary malefactor, it nonetheless has many commendable features. Shades of powder-gray and pinkish-gold grace both sides in an irregular fashion, much detail remains on both sides, and the coin displays well. The "gentle pummeling" is a series of smallish, shallow, round indentations inflicted on the eagle's neck, the shield, a couple of the stars above, and in the right (facing) field. The damage is worse than it sounds, however; the reverse actually shows a good deal more luster than does the obverse, and without a loupe the noted damage, confined to less than 20% of the reverse surface area, is not readily apparent. (#5312)

1819 **1805 Fine 12 PCGS.** B-2, R.3. A pleasing example of this scarce variety with strong outlines and remaining detail on the major devices. Deep blue-gray toning at the margins lightens at the centers and the peripheral lettering. (#5313)

1820 **1805 Fine 15 PCGS.** B-2, R.3. The R in LIBERTY is usually weak on its right side for this variety, and the 5 in the date touches the bust. On the reverse, there is a wide gap in the dentils above the E in STATES. Heavy clash marks are apparent on the reverse, which is typical of Browning-2. Both sides are evenly worn and minimally marked, with dove-gray toning on the centers that yields to deeper color around the perimeter. (#5313)

1821 **1806 Fine 12 ANACS.** B-9, R.1. The obverse has a vertical bisecting crack from the lower border through the 1 and right half of the low curl, all of Liberty's hair, and finally to the upright of the E and the border above. The obverse is mostly light gray with splashes of light gold toning, and the reverse is deeper gray, also with light gold. (#5314)

Terminal 1806 B-9 Quarter, XF40

1822 **1806 XF40 PCGS.** B-9-A, R.1. Breen Die State XI. This variety is usually recognized by the vertical bisecting obverse die crack from the 1 through Liberty's hair to the E. The reverse now has narrow rim breaks over OF and A. Both dies show clash marks, and the obverse has been lapped, the bottom half of the lowest curl entirely missing. Both sides have deep gray and steel toning with lighter gray on Liberty's shoulder. Aside from the usual faint handling marks, the surfaces are smooth and pleasing. (#5314)

Delightful 1806 Quarter, B-3, Choice XF

1823 **1806 XF45 PCGS.** B-3, R.1. Die State II. The feet of the 1 in the date and the I and T in LIBERTY are defective, identifying this obverse. The reverse is distinguished because the 5 in the denomination does not touch the arrows. Numerous adjustment marks are visible on the obverse, which accounts for the weakness at the center of both sides. Plenty of luster remains and enhances the eye appeal of this light gray representative. (#5314)

Interesting 1806 Quarter, B-9, MS62

1824 **1806 MS62 PCGS.** B-9, R.1. This variety is easily identified by the vertical die crack that bisects the obverse, but other diagnostic points include an unevenly spaced date and the position of the denomination. There are 11 die states of Bolender-9, and this piece is State IX, according to the rubric by Breen. The crack extends from rim to rim on the obverse, and both sides show pronounced clash marks, which have not yet been removed by relapping. A small rim break is apparent above OF.

Pleasing silver-gray patina drapes the surfaces of this interesting specimen, with a waft of hazel toning is the field. The centers and several stars are soft, as typically seen, but there is plenty of flashy luster throughout. Both sides are minimally marked with just a few minuscule spots. This impressive example has lovely eye appeal and is housed in a green label PCGS holder. (#5314)

1825 **1807 Fine 12 NGC.** B-1, R.3. Although both varieties of 1807 quarter are rated R.3, the B-1 variety with a broken I in AMERICA is more often seen. This piece is original with deep lilac-gray fields and lighter silver-tan devices.
From The Morton J. Greene Collection. (#5316)

BUST QUARTERS

Uncirculated Sharpness 1815 Quarter, B-1

1826 **1815—Improperly Cleaned—NCS. Unc Details.** B-1, R.1, the only dies. This Capped Bust half is glossy from a long-ago wipe, and has since acquired deep forest-green and rose-gold patina. A suitable strike with the expected minor blending on the forehead curl and on the eagle's claws. (#5321)

1827 **1818/5 XF45 NGC.** B-1, R.2. The overdate is undesignated on the NGC insert. Dove-gray and chestnut-gold with aquamarine toning along the obverse border. Ample luster glimmers from design crevices. A prominent die crack passes through the eagle's beak.
From The Morton J. Greene Collection. (#5323)

1828 **1818 VF35 PCGS. CAC.** B-2, R.1. The date is noticeably wide and star 13 is obviously repunched, identifying the obverse. The reverse is distinguished by the location of the scroll and the letters in the motto. This piece is Breen Die State II, with a die crack from the field above Liberty's cap and through stars 8, 9, and 10. Although Browning wrote that there were several die flaws by the 2 in the denomination, on this piece it appears that the 2 was actually repunched. Pale gray toning drapes the devices, which contrast nicely against the gunmetal-gray fields. A couple of nearly imperceptible scratches behind Liberty's head are barely worthy of note. (#5322)

1829 **1819 Large 9 AU53 NGC.** B-2, R.3. A low D in UNITED aids attribution. A golden-brown and gunmetal-blue example with few marks and only moderate highpoint wear. The obverse has slender peripheral die cracks. (#5326)

1830 **1821 XF45 PCGS. CAC.** B-4, R.3. The first S in STATES is centered above the PL in PLURIBUS, and the second S is directly above the S in PLURIBUS. This piece is Breen Die State II, as evidenced by the clash marks from the shield near Liberty's ear. Traces of luster shine beneath the medium gray patina. Most of the details are crisply defined and there are no marks of any significance. (#5331)

Remarkable 1821 Quarter, B-1, MS62

1831 **1821 MS62 NGC.** B-1, High R.2. Star 7 points to the cap and the date is unevenly spaced, which helps identify the obverse. The reverse was reused from 1820 B-4 and has numerous die chips in the field to the left of the 2 in the denomination. Also, the R in PLURIBUS is centered under the right side of the A in STATES. Deep gunmetal-gray patina envelops both sides of this remarkably clean representative. Crisply struck with pleasing eye appeal.
From The Menlo Park Collection. (#5331)

1832 **1824/2—Improperly Cleaned—NCS. Fine Details.** B-1, R.3, the only dies. Cream-gray with glimpses of tan and olive. Somewhat glossy from a wipe, but all legends are clear, and the eagle exhibits considerable plumage.
From The Morton J. Greene Collection. (#5335)

Charming 1824/2 Quarter, AU55 Details, B-1

1833 **1824/2—Cleaned—ANACS. AU55 Details.** B-1, R.3. The only variety known. A trace of the underdigit is visible at the top and bottom of the 4. Numerous hairlines on both sides are an unfortunate side effect of the cleaning, but there are no prominent marks otherwise. A touch of gold toning in the periphery accents the mostly silver-gray surfaces. The stars are a trifle weak, as typically seen, but the rest of the details are sharp. Although the exact mintage is unknown, it is estimated that fewer than 24,000 examples were struck, despite the exorbitant figure listed in the *Guide Book*. (#5335)

1834 **1828 AU55 NGC.** B-1, R.1. Minor highpoint wear leaves intact most design details. The moderately toned surfaces have lavender-gray and greenish-gold accents. Noticeable luster remains, and there are no consequential marks. (#5342)

1835 **1833 AU50 NGC.** B-2, R.1. Just two 1833 quarter varieties are known, B-1 with a period after 25 C., and B-2 with no period after the denomination. This pleasing AU example has evenly distributed gray-brown patina with splashes of darker brown toning. (#5352)

1836 1834 AU53 ANACS. B-1, R.1. The reverse has no period after the denomination, and it is the same die that was earlier used for 1833 B-2. Both sides have deep steel and ebony surfaces with a few minor marks. (#5353)

1837 1834—Improperly Cleaned—NCS. Unc Details. B-1, R.1. The only variety for the year that has no period after the C in the denomination. This piece is Die State III, as evidenced by the numerous die cracks on the obverse (the most prominent being an arc across the bottom of the bust) and by the clash marks from the shield that are readily apparent around Liberty's ear. Deep steel-gray toning drapes the surfaces of this minimally marked representative. Sharply struck save for minor weakness on the drapery. (#5353)

Impressive MS64 1836 Quarter, B-2

1838 1836 MS64 PCGS. B-2, R.2. Lushly toned in apricot, electric-blue, and olive colors, this flashy near-Gem has exceptional eye appeal when viewed with the unaided eye. In its appearance in the Isaac Edmunds auction, the lot was described, in part, as "At first glance, this has the appearance of a nice cameo Proof. Indeed, Proof examples were struck from this die pair." Well struck aside from the centers of stars 4 and 7. Four lengthy, slender die cracks journey across the obverse, one of which bisects the portrait. A few wispy marks are detected in the fields, only visible upon close inspection under a loupe, and a small aqua spot is noted just beneath the neck. Population: 6 in 64, 1 finer (8/08).
Ex: Isaac Edmunds Collection (Bowers and Merena, 6/02), lot 479, where it realized $6,900.
From The Bell Collection. (#5355)

Alluring 1838 Capped Bust Quarter, MS62, B-1

1839 1838 MS62 NGC. B-1, R.1. The only Capped Bust quarter variety known for the year. Die State II, as evidenced by the clash marks on the reverse. A lovely layer of frost covers the surfaces of this untoned and attractive specimen. Several light abrasions are located in the fields, but overall this piece is exceptionally unmarked for the grade. There is just a trace of weakness on the stars, but the reverse is outstanding and nearly full throughout. This was the final issue of Kneass' Capped Bust design, which was replaced when the Mint switched to a 90% silver standard. Census: 16 in 62, 42 finer (7/08). (#5357)

Splendid 1838 B-1 Capped Bust Quarter, MS63

1840 1838 MS63 NGC. B-1, R.1. The only known Capped Bust quarter variety struck during the transition from the Capped Bust to the Seated Liberty design. Minted during most years since 1815, the design was about to be replaced by Christian Gobrecht who developed the famous and long-lived design for silver dollars first produced in 1836. Deeply toned in variegated gold, russet, and sea-green Census: 18 in 63, 24 finer (7/08). (#5357)

SEATED QUARTERS

Select 1838 Seated Quarter

1841 1838 No Drapery MS63 NGC. This issue of under half a million pieces marked the beginning of the Seated Liberty quarter design, which would remain in place (with minor variations) for over half a century. The present piece is well-defined and strongly lustrous beneath subtle peach and silver-gray patina. Census: 18 in 63, 31 finer (7/08). (#5391)

1842 1839 No Drapery AU55 NGC. Breen-3936, Briggs-1A. This is the Open Claws reverse that is described as "presently very rare" by Breen in his *Complete Encyclopedia*. Larry Briggs notes that this variety is scarcer than the Closed Claws reverse. Although we do not have further data on the rarity of this variety, it is certainly an important opportunity for the specialist.

This piece is also an example of the late die state with a horizontal bisecting crack across the eagle, from the T in UNITED to the R in AMERICA. The central obverse and reverse have pale heather toning surrounded by peripheral sea-green. The surfaces are lightly marked as expected for the grade. (#5392)

1843 1839 No Drapery MS61 NGC. Bright and untoned, with an intense semi-prooflike sheen. Light hairlines are noted in the fields, and Liberty's head is softly struck. A few tiny field marks are seen on each side. Census: 4 in 61, 24 finer (7/08). (#5392)

1844 1847-O AU53 NGC. Deep steel and gray toning is evident over nearly full luster on each side of this boldly detailed piece. No unusual die characteristics are noted, except that the bottom horizontal line of the shield extends into the left wing. An important date in the Seated quarter series. (#5411)

Toned 1847-O Quarter, MS63

1845 **1847-O MS63 PCGS.** Briggs 1-A. Numerous reverse die cracks are evident, as usual for this reverse die. The 1847-O is a rarity in the Seated quarter series, especially in Mint State grades. In fact, Larry Briggs was only aware of one Mint State piece in 1991. Today, it is probably correct to say that only eight of nine examples are known.

This intriguing coin has mottled ivory and dark iridescent toning. Both sides are similar, the reverse slightly brighter. The upper obverse stars and head details are weak as usual for this date. Population: 2 in 63, 1 finer (7/08). (#5411)

Conditionally Rare 1852 Quarter, Gem Uncirculated

1846 **1852 MS65 PCGS.** Variegated lilac, amber, slate-gray, and teal toning embraces the surfaces of this powerfully struck Gem. Flashes of luster penetrate the deep patina. The surfaces appear pristine to the unaided eye, and the appeal is excellent. This conditionally rare specimen is housed in a green label PCGS holder. Population: 3 in 65, 3 finer (8/08). (#5419)

1847 **1853 Arrows and Rays MS62 NGC.** A pleasing Mint State example of the brief Arrows and Rays quarter type. Lustrous and essentially untoned, save for brief hints of border toning. Free of distracting marks and well struck for the issue, with typical weakness on Liberty's head and the upper obverse stars. (#5426)

1848 **1853 Arrows and Rays MS62 NGC.** Though light, wispy abrasions cross parts of the obverse, this Arrows and Rays quarter offers powerfully lustrous surfaces with no trace of wear. A great, minimally toned representative of the one-year type.
From The Menlo Park Collection. (#5426)

Splendid 1853 Arrows and Rays Quarter, Choice Mint State

1849 **1853 Arrows and Rays MS64 NGC.** A hint of rose toning accents the mostly medium gray surfaces of this boldly impressed near-Gem specimen. The nearly full details are complemented by dazzling satiny luster in the fields. The reverse is remarkably unabraded, while the obverse has only a few minuscule signs of handling. A pleasing example of this one-year type. NGC has certified only 36 examples finer (8/08). (#5426)

Collectible Fine 1854-O Huge O Quarter

1850 **1854-O Huge O Fine 12 PCGS.** FS-004. Briggs 1-A. The popular 'Huge O' quarter has an uncommonly high relief, and its borders are unduly thick, as well. Specialists believe the mintmark was hand-engraved into the working reverse die, probably because no one at Philadelphia entered the mintmark before the die was hardened. No thought was given to discarding the die, since heavy production of new tenor silver coins was needed to replace hoarded old tenor examples. This slate-gray example has nearly a full LIBERTY, and drapery and plumage detail is evident. Population: 4 in 12, 24 finer (8/08). (#5434)

Popular 1854-O Huge O Quarter, Fine 15

1851 **1854-O Huge O Fine 15 PCGS.** FS-004. Briggs 1-A. The only die pairing. Lovely medium gray patina drapes the surfaces of this evenly worn specimen. The devices are crisply outlined, and the mintmark is bold. The surfaces are remarkably clean save for a tiny spot of verdigris inside the opening of the mintmark. This interesting variety is listed in the *Guide Book* and is believed to have been caused when a worker engraved the mintmark by hand, which accounts for its large size and unusual thickness. Population: 6 in 15, 18 finer (7/08). (#5434)

Lightly Toned Gem 1857 Quarter

1852 **1857 MS65 NGC.** This charming No Motto type coin has only wisps of light chestnut-gold toning. Cartwheel luster dominates the open fields, and the strike is bold with the exception of the stars. Marks are virtually absent aside from a faint V-shaped graze near star 4. Census: 53 in 65, 59 finer (7/08). (#5442)

Shining Gem 1857 Quarter

1853 **1857 MS65 NGC.** While the 1857 quarter is readily available in most grades, thanks to a mintage of over 9.6 million pieces, Gem and better survivors are elusive. This MS65 piece is well-defined in the centers, if a trifle softly struck at the margins, with strongly lustrous, minimally toned surfaces. Pleasingly preserved and attractive. (#5442)

1854 **1858 MS64 NGC.** Delicate gold and pink shadings embrace much of this delightful near-Gem. Pleasingly detailed save for trifling softness on the right obverse stars.
From The Menlo Park Collection. (#5445)

1855 **1861 MS64 PCGS.** Subtle lavender and pink-gold shadings enrich the shining surfaces of this Civil War-era near-Gem. Boldly struck with amazing luster and eye appeal. (#5454)

Formidable XF40 1861-S Seated Quarter

1856 **1861-S XF40 PCGS.** Briggs 2-B. In the Jan. 11, 2008, issue of the *Coin Dealer Newsletter*, Larry Briggs calls the 1861-S Seated quarter a low-mintage issue in two varieties that is "plagued by problems" whose rarity escalates with grade, with XF coins rare, AU pieces very rare, and true Mint State coins unknown. This example offers powder-gray surfaces with some charcoal rim toning, and shows the late die state of the reverse with the mintmark about to connect to the fletchings. A still-lustrous piece with some mint-green accents on the lower reverse. Population: 2 in 40, 11 finer (8/08). (#5455)

Elusive 1862-S Seated Quarter, AU53

1857 **1862-S AU53 PCGS.** This coin offers considerable rarity for a relatively modest price. A peripheral gathering of golden-brown patina interrupts the otherwise medium steel-gray patina. A few scattered marks are noted in the right obverse field. An original, well defined survivor from a mintage of only 67,000 pieces. Population: 1 in 53, 18 finer (8/08). (#5457)

1858 **1864-S Fine 12 PCGS.** Light to medium gray patina occupies both sides of this S-mint quarter. Nicely defined, with a strong LIBERTY. An old linear mark occurs on the lower legs, and some faint pinscratches are visible on the eagle's neck. (#5460)

1859 **1865-S XF40 PCGS.** A boldly defined gunmetal-gray rare date Seated quarter that has glimpses of obverse russet toning and a few stray field marks on each side. Population: 4 in 40, 16 finer (8/08). (#5462)

Rare 1872-CC Seated Quarter, VF30

1860 **1872-CC VF30 PCGS.** A rare issue from the third year of Carson City Mint coinage, the 1872-CC shows diagonal die scratches from the base of the rock through the lower shield stripes on all known examples, as here. This piece shows the moderate wear expected, but there are few singular abrasions. The pretty pinkish-gold surfaces with blue accents are a plus. Population: 7 in 30, 7 finer (8/08). (#5482)

Elusive 1873-CC Arrows Quarter, Fine 12

1861 **1873-CC Arrows Fine 12 PCGS.** This appealing example displays originally toned surfaces that show even, moderate wear consistent with the Fine 12 grade designation. The rims are essentially intact on both sides, and considerable design detail remains. Just a few tiny marks are found, under low magnification. This elusive issue is the target of date as well as type collectors, as the only Arrows CC-mint Seated quarter. The second Arrows type of the Seated quarter series was made only in 1873 and 1874, with the Carson City Mint abstaining from quarter dollar production in the latter year. (#5492)

1862 **1875 MS64 PCGS.** Charcoal-gray patina gravitates to the margins of this near-Gem. Lustrous surfaces exhibit well struck design elements, and are devoid of significant contacts. Population: 62 in 64, 48 finer (8/08). (#5498)

Glorious 1876-CC Quarter, MS66

1863 **1876-CC MS66 NGC.** After the limited Carson City quarter dollar mintages of the first few years, production spiked substantially upward, with numerous high grade survivors. Beginning in 1875, most Carson City mint coins are much more plentiful than earlier-dated issues. This beautiful Premium Gem is fully lustrous with bold design details and satin surfaces, enhanced by gold, blue, and iridescent toning. Census: 9 in 66, 2 finer (7/08). (#5502)

Attractive 1877-S Quarter, MS66

1864 **1877-S MS66 NGC.** Even for a generous mintage of nearly 9 million pieces, the present Premium Gem must be a serious contender for the most attractive from an aesthetic viewpoint, if not absolutely the finest from a technical standpoint. The silver-white surfaces show just the barest suggestion of champagne patina, and full cartwheel luster bursts forth from each side. A loupe reveals both a bold strike, and the few tiny ticks that apparently prevent a Superb Gem grade. Census: 4 in 66, 5 finer (7/08). (#5506)

Impressive 1879 Quarter, MS66

1865 **1879 MS66 NGC.** While NGC has not certified this piece Prooflike, it shows moderate cameo contrast between the decidedly prooflike fields and frosted devices. The strike is bold, with only slight weakness on several stars. Tremendous satiny luster is barely affected by a few light grazes. A tiny nick is noted between the O and D of GOD. This brilliant and appealing example is one of just 13,600 pieces minted. (#5511)

Thickly Frosted 1879 Seated Quarter, MS66

1866 1879 MS66 PCGS. Unsurprisingly for a coinage of only 13,600 pieces, this example offers wonderful prooflike surfaces, even though they are unacknowledged on the PCGS slab. But both sides show copious cartwheel luster, with thick mint frost coating the devices and high reflectivity in the fields. Tinges of iridescent pink and ice-blue dance near the obverse rim, with lilac hues on the reverse periphery. Population: 29 in 66, 23 finer (8/08). (#5511)

Beautiful Gem 1881 Seated Quarter

1867 1881 MS65 ANACS. A low mintage and a low survival rate are characteristic of the 1881 Seated quarter issue. Just 12,000 coins were produced, and only a few hundred of those pieces are known to still exist. This fabulous Gem is one of the most stunningly attractive coins that we have seen in recent years, from any date or type. The amazingly intense toning variations across each side include shades of electric-blue, crimson, and burnt-orange. Well struck and free of distractions.
From The Morton J. Greene Collection. (#5513)

Amazing 1883 Seated Quarter, MS67

1868 1883 MS67 PCGS. An absolutely stunning Superb Gem, this 1883 quarter has full silver brilliance with wispy toning that is barely visible on each side. The strike is impeccable with full gown, head, and star details on the obverse, and complete eagle details on the reverse. No finer examples of this low mintage issue have been certified. Population: 2 in 67, 0 finer (8/08).
From The Bell Collection. (#5515)

Magnificent 1888 Quarter, Superb Gem

1869 1888 MS67 NGC. With the mint focusing on Morgan dollar production, the number of quarters coined at Philadelphia was limited to just 10,001 business strikes and 832 proofs. This carefully preserved Superb Gem has impressive cartwheel luster and captivating fully white surfaces. Sharply struck save for the star centrils. Census: 14 in 67, 4 finer (7/08). (#5520)

1870 1891-S MS64 PCGS. This issue is not rare at the MS64 grade tier, but it immediately becomes much scarcer at the Gem level of preservation. This near-Gem exhibits some striking softness and accompanying bits of die rust on the central and lower parts of Liberty, including the shield area. Creamy, somewhat milky patina prevents the piece from being brilliant, but does not keep it from being an attractive example for the grade. (#5526)

PROOF SEATED QUARTERS

Lightly Toned 1859 Quarter, PR64

1871 1859 PR64 PCGS. From a mintage of 800 pieces. A pinpoint-sharp near-Gem with consistent medium chestnut-gold toning. A few faint obverse field hairlines are all that limit the grade. PCGS and NGC have certified approximately 250 proofs of this date. Population: 46 in 64, 13 finer (8/08). (#5555)

Scarce PR65 1859 Quarter

1872 1859 PR65 NGC. The razor sharp striking definition and shimmering fields are indicative of proof production methods. The dominant colors on both sides of this richly toned example are cobalt-blue and lilac-gray in shade, but a blush of sunset-red patina is noted on the reverse over the eagle's portrait. High quality representatives of this earlier proof Seated quarter are anything but common. Census: 16 in 65, 17 finer (7/08). (#5555)

Splendid 1859 Quarter, PR65 Cameo

1873 1859 PR65 Cameo NGC. An extremely difficult proof issue to find, especially with Cameo contrast. This remarkable Gem is untoned with fully mirrored fields and excellent eye appeal. According to the *Guide Book*, 800 proof quarters were struck in 1959, but the actual number was probably quite a bit less. (#85555)

1874 1863 PR63 Cameo NGC. The 1863 quarter had relatively low mintages of 191,600 business strikes and 460 proofs. A delightful ring of brown toning encircles the brilliant centers on the present piece. There are a few minor marks in the fields, but they hardly affect the excellent eye appeal. Fully struck with a splendid cameo appearance. Census: 4 in 63 Cameo, 15 finer (7/08). (#85559)

Amazing 1864 Seated Quarter, PR66 Cameo

1875 1864 PR66 Cameo NGC. Due to the demands of hoarders during the Civil War, silver and gold coins, including proofs, had limited mintages. An impressive Premium Gem proof with exceptional cameo contrast beneath amazing sea-green and violet toning at the obverse, lighter gold around the reverse. Census: 3 in 66 Cameo, 1 finer (7/08).
From The Malibu Collection. (#85560)

1876 1866 Motto PR64 NGC. Gold-orange surfaces are accented with various shades of blue, and a solid strike emboldens the design elements. A hair-thin mark is visible in the lower right obverse quadrant. Census: 40 in 64, 27 finer (7/08). (#5565)

Vibrant 1867 Quarter, Superb Proof Cameo

1877 1867 PR67 Cameo NGC. Vibrant rainbow toning covers both sides of this deeply mirrored Superb Gem, with electric-blue, magenta, gold, and violet present throughout the fields. The highly reflective fields and frosted devices create a startling cameo appearance. This nearly perfect piece would make an outstanding representative. One of just 625 proofs struck. Census: 3 in 67 Cameo, 0 finer (7/08). (#85566)

Wonderful 1872 Seated Quarter, PR68

1878 1872 PR68 NGC. The reverse has a raised die line, over 1 mm. in length, crossing the left shield border, and identifying this as a proof die, used also on proofs from 1873 through 1880.

An amazing proof with mostly brilliant silvery-white centers, framed by russet, violet, and deep blue toning closer to the borders. Considerable contrast is evident on both sides, giving the appearance that the central devices are floating above the surface, although NGC did not designate this piece as a cameo proof. This is the finest example that NGC has certified.
From The Malibu Collection. (#5571)

Attractive 1874 Arrows Quarter, Premium Gem Proof

1879 1874 Arrows PR66 NGC. CAC. A dramatic array of colors endows the surfaces, with a ring of deep cobalt-blue around the rims and streaks of hazel and rose-red across the centers. The strike is full save for softness on the stars. Watery, deeply mirrored fields give this piece outstanding eye appeal. Only 700 proofs were struck. Census: 14 in 66, 7 finer (7/08). (#5575)

1880 **1875 PR64 PCGS.** Type One Reverse. This deeply toned Choice proof displays cobalt-blue and chocolate-brown when it is rotated beneath a light. The strike is needle-sharp, and no marks are evident beneath the patina. Encased in a green label holder. Population: 34 in 64, 10 finer (8/08). (#5576)

1881 **1875 PR63 Cameo NGC.** Pleasingly reflective with mild, yet distinct contrast on each side. The minimally toned surfaces show faint, scattered hairlines that account for the grade. Census: 4 in 63 Cameo, 24 finer (7/08). (#85576)

1882 **1880 PR64 PCGS.** Though a handful of tiny contact marks visit each side, this minimally toned proof Seated quarter retains excellent eye appeal. Strongly mirrored with mild obverse contrast. (#5581)

1883 **1880 PR64 ANACS.** Type One Reverse. Deeply toned in dusky peach, rose-red, and powder-blue. A needle-sharp Choice proof with an unabraded appearance. A low mintage date due to the inordinate number of Morgan dollars coined that year.
From The Morton J. Greene Collection. (#5581)

Magnificent 1880 Quarter, Superb Proof

1884 **1880 PR67 NGC.** The low number of 1880 business strikes (13,600 pieces) is complemented by a diminutive number of proofs (1,355 coins), which makes this a scarce issue in both Mint State and Proof. This fully struck Superb Gem exhibits deep electric-blue, rose-red, yellow, and amber toning on both sides. Powerful reflectivity gives this specimen outstanding eye appeal. Census: 14 in 67, 4 finer (7/08). (#5581)

Extraordinary 1880 Quarter, PR68 Cameo

1885 **1880 PR68 Cameo NGC.** The 1880 is the second in a series of low mintage proof and business strike Liberty Seated quarters. A total of 1,355 proofs were struck and, of course, any specimen that grades PR68 is truly exceptional. Only a select few 19th century proofs exhibit such remarkable preservation, and the present piece would make a tremendous addition to any collection.

An arc of violet and maroon toning graces the upper reaches of the obverse and surrounds the entire reverse. The virtually immaculate fields are deeply mirrored and show spectacular cameo contrast against the vividly frosted devices. A full strike only adds to the appeal of this fantastic representative. Census: 5 in 68 Cameo, 1 finer (8/08).
From The Malibu Collection. (#85581)

1886 **1882 PR63 NGC.** Enchanting silver-gray, steel-blue, and rose-gold shadings consume each side. Marvelous eye appeal from the patina, though faint hairlines appear through the toning. (#5583)

Magnificent 1883 Quarter, PR68 Cameo

1887 **1883 PR68 Cameo NGC. CAC.** Business strike mintage of quarters in 1883 was a minuscule 14,400 pieces. Treasury vaults were bursting with hoards of minor silver coins that had returned to the United States from offshore havens where they had been secreted during the Civil War. The unexpected influx of those minor coins, together with large mintages during the 1870s, completely satisfied public demand for the coins in everyday commerce. Treasury Secretary John Sherman, in accordance with the Mint Act of 1873, halted production of minor coinage early in 1878. For the next decade, the Mint adhered to a policy of small mintages of quarters and half dollars. All available resources were concentrated on production of Morgan silver dollars.

Fortunately, numismatic demand for quarters and half dollars continued unabated, and the Mint produced proof coins in numbers large enough to satisfy collector demand. The result of this policy was a mintage of 1,039 proof quarters in 1883. Only one die combination was needed to produce the entire mintage. In 1991 Seated quarter specialist Larry Briggs detected the remains of a blundered date in the 1883 obverse proof die. The tops of the numerals 83 can be seen in the dentils below 88 in the date. This is an important distinction; business strikes use the same reverse die, and early strikes have prooflike surfaces that can be mistaken for genuine proofs.

The present coin is a magnificent example of this scarce issue. Brightly reflective fields show through delicate shades of green toning, with an accent of cerulean blue at the rims. The strike is impeccable on both sides, with sharp cameo contrast between the field and devices. Virtually perfect surfaces complement the beautiful toning to yield outstanding eye appeal. A great prize for the Seated Liberty Seated specialist. (#85584)

Vibrantly Toned 1884 Quarter, PR66

1888 **1884 PR66 NGC.** Sharp design details and deeply mirrored fields are evident beneath wonderful lilac-gold, sea-green, and iridescent toning on both sides. The boldly rendered design motifs are lustrous with hidden cameo contrast. A desirable proof quarter due to the rarity of circulation strikes. Census: 36 in 66, 18 finer (7/08). (#5585)

Colorful PR67 ★ Cameo 1884 Quarter

1889 **1884 PR67 ★ Cameo NGC.** The present Superb Gem is the sole proof 1884 quarter to secure a Star designation from NGC, as of (8/08). Undoubtedly, the dramatic navy-blue, cherry-red, and orange-gold toning inspired the NGC Star. The patina is especially eye-catching on the reverse. Boldly struck with pleasing cameo contrast and unabraded surfaces. (#85585)

1890 **1885 PR64 PCGS.** Deep gray and beige patina occupies the centers of this near-Gem proof quarter, flanked by a sliver of light yellow-green and sky-blue coloration at the margins. Well struck, save for weakness in most of the star centers. Housed in an old green-label holder. Population: 87 in 64, 49 finer (8/08). (#5586)

1891 **1885 PR64 NGC.** Enchanting violet, gold-orange, and ruby shadings embrace each side of this gleaming Choice proof. The strike is crisp, and only minor hairlines affect the fields. (#5586)

1892 **1885 PR64 NGC.** The frosty, sharply defined motifs stand out against the mirrored fields. Electric-blue, purple, and golden-brown patination clings to the reverse margins, while the same color palette is randomly distributed over the obverse. Impeccably preserved throughout. Housed in a prior generation holder. (#5586)

1893 **1886 PR63 Cameo PCGS.** Dramatic violet toning encircles the obverse, while the reverse exhibits an attractive ring of russet and lavender in the periphery. The deeply mirrored fields show impressive cameo contrast against the icy-frosted devices. This fully struck piece has only a couple of small blemishes and virtually no marks. A mere 886 proofs were struck. Population: 9 in 63 Cameo, 23 finer (8/08). (#85587)

Gorgeous 1886 Quarter, PR67 Ultra Cameo

1894 **1886 PR67 Ultra Cameo NGC.** An essentially untoned Superb Gem with amazing contrast between the heavily frosted devices and the fathomless mirrors of the fields. The preservation is excellent, and the eye appeal is a perfect match. A top-notch condition rarity. Census: 5 in 67 Ultra Cameo, 1 finer (7/08). (#95587)

Glamorous 1889 Quarter, PR68 ★ NGC

1895 **1889 PR68 ★ NGC.** The star designation for exceptional quality is undoubtedly a result of the spectacular eye appeal created through the lovely toned surfaces. Both sides have excellent cameo contrast and deeply mirrored fields that shine through the blue-green, amber, and iridescent toning.

It is doubtful that more than a few of the 711 proof quarters minted in 1889 are any finer than this piece. Only five coins have been certified finer at NGC. This amazing, superlative proof will prove to be a highlight of the new owner's cabinet.
From The Malibu Collection. (#5590)

Extraordinary 1890 Quarter, PR68 ★ Ultra Cameo

1896 **1890 PR68 ★ Ultra Cameo NGC.** Only 590 proof quarters were minted in 1890 to complement the 80,000 business strikes of that year, the smallest proof quarter mintage since 1877 and the third smallest of the Liberty Seated With Motto design. The Sherman Silver Purchase Act, passed on July 14, 1890, replaced the Bland-Allison Act of 1878. Under the new legislation, the Mint reversed its policy of small mintages for quarters and half dollars. While silver dollars continued to be produced in huge numbers, the other silver denominations were not neglected from 1891 on. Thus, 1890 is the last year in which the small supply of business strikes puts severe pricing pressure on the surviving proof mintage.

This coin features spectacular eye appeal. The beautiful, mirrored fields contrast with the thickly frosted design elements to produce a startling, three-dimensional cameo effect. The untoned, brilliant surfaces of the coin are devoid of blemishes and provide the stark white-on-black contrast that is typical of the Ultra Cameo designation. A virtually unimprovable example of this scarce date. (#95591)

Impeccable 1891 Quarter, PR67 Cameo

1897 **1891 PR67 Cameo NGC.** An amazing Superb Gem proof with exceptional cameo contrast. The designation is unusual inasmuch as this coin is moderate to deep peripheral toning with only a small area of lighter silver or ivory on each side. The border toning includes russet, violet, and sky-blue. Census: 9 in 67 Cameo, 1 finer (7/08). *From The Malibu Collection.* (#85592)

BARBER QUARTERS

1898 **1892 MS64 PCGS.** A gorgeous first year specimen, pale gray in the centers with delightful reddish-gold and russet peripheral accents. Typically well struck, with unmarked surfaces. A conservatively graded near-Gem. (#5601)

1899 **1892-S MS64 PCGS.** Mottled deep violet toning covers the obverse, which contrasts nicely against the lightly toned purple-red reverse. Pleasing satiny luster graces both sides and appears semiprooflike, especially on the obverse. Minimally abraded and boldly struck. Population: 17 in 64, 12 finer (7/08). (#5603)

Elegant Gem 1894 Quarter

1900 **1894 MS65 PCGS.** Strong, swirling luster enlivens the dusky surfaces, which show attractive peach, green-gold, and sapphire accents. Well-defined and pleasingly preserved. Like many circulation-strike Barber issues, the 1894 quarter was little saved at the time of release and is a condition rarity any finer. Population: 25 in 65, 11 finer (8/08). (#5607)

1901 **1896 MS65 PCGS.** The 6 in the date is lightly repunched. A lustrous, lavishly toned Gem, with deep purple, rose, and turquoise-green toning. Well struck with minimal marks. There is a faint luster graze on Liberty's eyebrow. Population: 28 in 65, 9 finer (8/08). (#5613)

1902 **1896-O AU58 ANACS.** Only a trace of friction keeps this attractive O-mint quarter from a substantially higher (and much more expensive) grade. Amply lustrous with delightful blue-green, peach, and gold-orange peripheral toning. Housed in a small-format holder. (#5614)

1903 **1896-S Good 4 PCGS.** The 1896-S boasts a diminutive mintage of just 188,039 pieces, which is many multiples lower than the typical Barber quarter. This example has fully outlined design elements, with even medium gray toning throughout save for a patch of charcoal color on the reverse rim. There are no mentionable marks, and a tiny spot of verdigris in the obverse field is barely worthy of note. Encapsulated in a green label PCGS holder. (#5615)

1904 **1896-S VG10 PCGS.** An evenly worn and appealing example of this key-date Barber quarter. The dove-gray surfaces have hints of golden-brown at the periphery. Minimally marked with the four outermost letters of LIBERTY clearly visible. (#5615)

1905 **1901 MS65 PCGS.** Smooth luster and excellent striking definition for the grade. Generally silver-gray centers cede to gold-orange and lavender-violet patina at the margins. Population: 26 in 65, 10 finer (8/08). (#5628)

Collectible 1901-S Quarter, AG3

1906 **1901-S AG3 PCGS.** Light to medium gray patina in the fields highlight the central devices of this '01-S quarter. All elements are outlined on the obverse, and portions of the ear and eye show on Liberty. The reverse central device displays a modicum of internal detail, and the rim has worn into one-half to two-thirds of the legend. The date and mintmark are both strong. The surfaces reveal a few of the expected circulation marks, but these are neither serious nor detracting. A great specimen for the budget-minded collector, that will fit comfortably in a low to mid-grade collection. (#5630)

Original 1901-S Quarter, Good 6

1907 **1901-S Good 6 PCGS.** A nice original example of this key-date. Light grayish-blue patination resides in the fields, somewhat more so on the reverse, leaving the devices lighter silver-gray. The Y in LIBERTY shows, as do portions of the ear and eye, and the rim is virtually fully outlined. The reverse rim is weaker, but does *not* merge with any letters of the legend. The shield-wing borders show clearly, and three or four letters are visible in the motto. Both sides are remarkably clean for a piece that has seen heavy circulation. (#5630)

Amazing 1903-S Barber Quarter, MS66

1908 **1903-S MS66 PCGS.** Ex: Duckor/Friend. Dr. Steven Duckor and Dale Friend each owned this amazing piece, including it among some of the finest of its peers in their collections. The date is rare and undervalued, and especially elusive in grades higher than MS65. This beauty has deep lilac and blue toning on the obverse, accompanying warm iridescent tones, and it is similar but somewhat brighter on the reverse. An outstanding example for the connoisseur. Population: 8 in 66, 2 finer (8/08). (#5636)

1909 **1905-S MS63 PCGS.** Hints of dappled gold color visit the lustrous surfaces of this Select quarter, and a well executed strike sharpens the design features. Some minute obverse marks define the grade. Housed in a first generation holder. (#5641)

1910 **1905-S MS64 PCGS.** Violet, olive-brown, and silver-gray intermingle on the surfaces of this lustrous Choice specimen. The strike is nearly full and there are only a few light abrasions on Liberty's cheek. Population: 22 in 64, 16 finer (8/08). (#5641)

Frosty Premium Gem 1907 Barber Quarter

1911 **1907 MS66 PCGS.** One would not think the 1907 Barber quarter, with a generous mintage exceeding 7 million pieces, would be elusive, even in the finer Mint State grades. One would be wrong: PCGS and NGC combined have certified only two dozen examples in this grade, with less than a half-dozen finer (8/08). Frosty luster emanates from this splendid silver-gray example, with just a touch of iridescent cinnamon toning near the rims on each side. Population: 15 in 66, 1 finer (8/08).
From The Bell Collection. (#5645)

1912 **1909 MS65 NGC.** Magnificent satiny luster shimmers across the frosty and untoned surfaces. Patches of light hazel toning cover the reverse, which has virtually no marks. Several abrasions on the bust of Liberty keep this attractive piece from an even higher grade. Census: 32 in 65, 14 finer (7/08). (#5653)

1913 **1909 MS66 PCGS.** Vibrant orange-gold toning with accents of lavender covers both sides of this conditionally scarce example. This powerfully struck piece has just a trace of softness on the eagle's shield and right wingtip, as often seen. Remarkable satiny luster shimmers throughout and enhances the spectacular eye appeal. Population: 16 in 66, 2 finer (7/08). (#5653)

1914 **1909-D MS65 PCGS.** Milky white toning covers the surfaces of this minimally marked Gem with plenty of luster visible beneath. The reverse has two notable die cracks connected to either side of the banner, and there is a small break on the right side. A couple of stars and the bottoms of the arrows are soft, but the rest of the design is powerfully impressed. Population: 25 in 65, 18 finer (7/08). (#5654)

1915 **1909-D MS65 PCGS.** This is a gorgeous Gem Barber quarter, with mottled, original purple and teal patina on both sides. Sharply struck and highly lustrous, without a single noteworthy mark or blemish on either side. Population: 25 in 65, 18 finer (8/08). (#5654)

1916 **1910 MS65 PCGS.** Deep golden-brown and lavender toning covers both sides of this lustrous Gem. The strike is sharp save for a trace of softness on the eagle's claws. A loupe locates only a few trivial handling marks. Population: 38 in 65, 19 finer (7/08). (#5657)

1917 **1912 MS64 PCGS.** Splashes of medium gray, a shade deeper on the reverse, reside on the lustrous surfaces of this near-Gem. A well executed strike brings out nice detail on the design elements. A couple of minor marks preclude full Gem. (#5662)

Pleasing 1913 Quarter, Gem Uncirculated

1918 **1913 MS65 NGC.** Light tan patina accents the obverse, which contrasts nicely against the ivory-gray toned reverse. Impressive satiny luster complements the powerfully impressed design elements. A conditionally scarce and minimally marked example with great eye appeal. Census: 8 in 65, 3 finer (7/08). (#5664)

1919 **1913-D MS65 PCGS.** The design elements are boldly struck, especially on the obverse. Speckled olive and charcoal patina partially overlies the fundamental rose and creamy-gray coloration. A pleasing, well preserved, blemish-free Gem. Population: 29 in 65, 10 finer (8/08). (#5665)

Elusive 1913-S Quarter, VG10

1920 **1913-S VG10 PCGS.** The 1913-S is one of the three keys to the Barber quarter series, and has its lowest mintage (40,000 business strikes). The Choice VG example presented in this lot will fit ideally in a low to mid-grade Barber quarter collection. Slightly darker gray-blue fields highlight somewhat the design features, especially on the reverse. Each side portrays good detail for the grade: most of the leaves on the obverse wreath show, as do the letters LI and Y in LIBERTY (the T partially shows). On the reverse, most of the motto letters are clear, and there is some detail left in the eagle's wings, legs, and shield. Full rims exhibit relatively strong dentilation on the reverse. Wispy circulation marks on the obverse portrait are mentioned for complete accuracy. (#5666)

1921 **1914 MS65 NGC.** Satiny with full mint frost on the devices and virtually no toning on either side. Boldly impressed and immensely attractive. Census: 52 in 65, 13 finer (7/08). (#5667)

1922 **1914-D MS65 PCGS.** Uncommon in Choice, this issue is truly rare at the Gem level. The detail on this lightly toned example is sharp, and there are only a few marks visible to the naked eye. Population: 43 in 65, 10 finer (8/08). (#5668)

1923 **1916 MS65 PCGS.** Both Barber and Standing Liberty quarters were struck in 1916, and although the former is significantly more available, it is nonetheless conditionally scarce in high Uncirculated grades. Mottled russet and deep green toning surrounds the perimeter of the obverse, which contrasts nicely against the lightly toned reverse. A trace of softness on the tip of the right (facing) wing is the only perceptible sign of weakness on this satiny Gem. Population: 45 in 65, 24 finer (7/08). (#5673)

1924 **1916-D MS65 PCGS.** Speckles of russet and sky-blue are scattered over the lustrous surfaces of this D-mint quarter. Well struck and minimally marked. (#5674)

1925 **1916-D MS65 PCGS. CAC.** Dappled blue-green and tan toning drapes the immensely lustrous surfaces of this delightful Gem. Well-defined for the final Denver issue of the design. PCGS has graded 94 finer pieces (8/08). (#5674)

1926 **1916-D MS65 PCGS.** Delicate golden tints grace the obverse fields, while the rest of the coin is generally pale silver-gray. Softly lustrous and well struck for this final-year issue. (#5674)

1927 **1916-D MS65 NGC.** Glowing luster shines through the golden-gray patina of this sharply struck Gem. A well preserved piece. (#5674)

Outstanding 1916-D Barber Quarter, MS66

1928 **1916-D MS66 PCGS. CAC.** A wonderful acquisition for collectors working on a last-year-of-issue type set, this 1916-D Barber quarter boasts splendid cartwheel luster over radiant silver-white surfaces that appear completely devoid of coloration. Under a loupe a couple of small die cracks appear on each side, signs of die fatigue. PCGS has certified six coins finer (8/08). (#5674)

1929 **1916-D MS66 PCGS.** With the Standing Liberty design delayed so much during 1916, the vast majority of quarters from that year are of the Barber design, with over three-quarters of the total production taking place at Denver. This strongly lustrous Premium Gem is exquisitely preserved beneath vivid, dappled russet, ocean-blue, and amber patina. Population: 88 in 66, 6 finer (8/08). (#5674)

PROOF BARBER QUARTERS

1930 **1892 PR65 PCGS.** A magnificent first-year representative with lightly frosted devices and deeply mirrored fields that create a moderate cameo appearance. Several nearly imperceptible contact marks in the fields limit the grade, but the strike is full. A patch of russet on the rim of the reverse is the only area of color on this otherwise brilliant Gem. One of only 1,245 proofs struck. (#5678)

Cameo Gem Proof 1892 Quarter

1931 **1892 PR65 Cameo NGC.** Type Two Reverse. While both major devices are frosty, the portrait of Liberty is particularly luminous when compared to the glassy field. The strike is essentially unimprovable, and the nearly untoned surfaces are devoid of distractions. Census: 25 in 65 Cameo, 40 finer (7/08). (#85678)

Exquisite PR66 Cameo 1892 Quarter

1932 **1892 PR66 Cameo NGC.** Type Two Reverse, as nearly always for this proof issue. A lovely Premium Gem with frosty devices, glassy fields, and light tan toning. Intricately impressed, with memorable sharpness on the shield corners and fletchings. A worthy first year proof type coin. Census: 21 in 66 Cameo, 19 finer (7/08). (#85678)

1933 **1895 PR64 NGC.** A simply amazing near-Gem brilliant proof, with just a touch of smoky gold-gray color. The design elements are perfectly brought up, and both sides are nicely preserved. (#5681)

1934 **1896 PR64 PCGS.** This near-Gem proof displays a good deal of field-device contrast. Essentially untoned, and sharply struck. Some light handling marks define the grade. (#5682)

1935 **1897 PR64 PCGS.** Lovely pearl-gray devices are surrounded by captivating violet-crimson and deep blue toning. A couple of nearly imperceptible handling marks preclude a Gem designation. This highly lustrous and appealing specimen is one of only 731 proofs struck. (#5683)

Brilliant 1899 Barber Quarter, PR66 Cameo

1936 **1899 PR66 Cameo NGC.** Only 846 proof quarters were coined in 1899, and probably a little less than half that mintage still exist today. An amazing Premium Gem with fully brilliant, untoned silver surfaces. Both sides have deeply mirrored fields around frosty devices, creating a wonderful Cameo appearance as designated on the NGC holder. Census: 5 in 66 Cameo, 12 finer (7/08). (#85685)

Outstanding 1900 PR68 ★ Quarter

1937 **1900 PR68 ★ NGC. CAC.** Electric-blue, purple, and golden-tan patina concentrates at the obverse margins, leaving the central area and most of the reverse light golden-tan. An attentive strike leaves crisp definition on the design elements, including the upper right shield corner, which is often soft. Immaculately preserved throughout. The outstanding eye appeal confirms the lofty numeric grade, Star designation, and CAC sticker. Census: 2 in 68 ★, 0 finer (7/08). (#5686)

Spectacular 1900 Quarter, PR67 Cameo

1938 **1900 PR67 Cameo NGC.** The surfaces are nearly immaculate with only a couple of pinpoint contact marks visible under magnification. Immensely mirrored fields show impressive black and white cameo contrast against the vividly frosted devices. This fully struck piece is an outstanding representative. Only 912 proofs were struck. Census: 11 in 67 Cameo, 4 finer (8/08). (#85686)

Untoned 1901 Quarter, PR67 Cameo

1939 **1901 PR67 Cameo NGC.** The untoned surfaces of this Superb Gem Cameo display excellent contrast between the deeply mirrored fields and mildly frosted motifs. A well executed strike leaves excellent definition on the design features, save for minor weakness on the upper right corner of the shield. Both sides are impeccably preserved. Census: 14 in 67 Cameo, 4 finer (7/08) (#85687)

Immaculate 1903 Quarter, PR68

1940 **1903 PR68 NGC.** Medium intensity multi-colored toning bathes both sides of this Superb Gem, but does not diminish the field-motif contrast when the coin is tilted ever so slightly under a light source. An impressive strike leaves bold definition on the design features. Immaculately preserved throughout. Census: 10 in 68, 0 finer (7/08). (#5689)

1941 **1906 PR64 Cameo PCGS.** A conditionally scarce, fully struck, and minimally marked representative. The surfaces are mostly brilliant save for a few minor blemishes. The frosted devices and highly lustrous fields show a delightful cameo appearance. Population: 3 in 64 Cameo, 3 finer (7/08). (#85692)

1942 **1907 PR63 PCGS.** Mostly brilliant with a touch of lavender in the periphery. The upper left (facing) corner of the shield, the tip of the eagle's left wing, and star 11 are soft, but the rest of the details are nearly full. The fields are highly reflective and have only a few minor contact marks. One of just 575 proofs struck. (#5693)

1943 **1907 PR65 Cameo PCGS.** Iridescent multicolored toning bathes both ides of this lovely Gem Cameo proof. An attentive strike brings out top-level detail on the design elements, save for the usual softness on the upper right corner of the shield. Carefully preserved and delightful. Population: 12 in 65 Cameo, 15 finer (8/08). (#85693)

Exemplary 1910 Barber Quarter, PR68 ★ Cameo

1944 **1910 PR68 ★ Cameo NGC.** A stunning early 20th century Barber quarter proof, one of only 551 produced in 1910. The number of Barber quarter proofs steadily declined from a high of 1,245 coins in 1892, falling below 600 pieces per year in six years of the early 20th century. This example is fully struck with deep mirror surfaces and sharply contrasting frosty devices. This untoned silver-white specimen shows no distracting marks or spots, as expected for the Superb Gem grade. It is, remarkably, one of five PR68 Cameo 1910 quarters awarded the Star designation by NGC for exceptional eye appeal. Census: 6 in 68 Cameo, 2 finer (8/08). (#85696)

1945 **1911 PR64 PCGS.** Decisively struck with wafts of champagne toning over the highly reflective surfaces. A few faint hairlines are visible under a glass, but to the unaided eye this Barber quarter appears remarkably clean. One of only 543 proofs struck. (#5697)

1946 **1912 PR65 Cameo NGC.** Though the devices show little frost, as usual for later proof Barber quarters, the powerful mirrors supply solid contrast. Essentially untoned save for hints of champagne near the rims. Census: 12 in 65 Cameo, 14 finer (7/08). (#85698)

STANDING LIBERTY QUARTERS

1947 **1916 Fair 2 ANACS.** 1916 was a transitional year for quarters, and production of the Standing Liberty design did not begin until December 16 of that year. As a result, only 52,000 pieces were struck, which is the lowest mintage of any issue in the series save for the 1918/7-S overdate. This lovely, evenly worn specimen has no marks worthy of specific mention and would make a great first-year representative. (#5704)

Lovely Choice 1916 Standing Liberty Quarter

1948 **1916 MS64 PCGS.** Both sides of this pleasing Choice coin offer soft, attractive luster that shines through subtle mustard-gold, orange, and silver-gray patina. Though the head is a trifle soft, the rest of this piece shows pleasing detail, and the rivets of the shield are complete. Only a handful of tiny flaws combine to preclude Gem status. Though all three of the minor silver denominations underwent several iterations in their redesigns, the Standing Liberty quarter proved the most troublesome, and the 1916 issue saw production of just 52,000 pieces, which were released alongside Philadelphia Type One coins dated 1917. (#5704)

Scarce 1916 Standing Liberty Quarter MS63 Full Head

1949 **1916 MS63 Full Head PCGS.** Hermon MacNeil's Standing Liberty design is acclaimed as one of the most artistic U.S. coins. With a series-low mintage of 52,000 pieces, and as the first year of the type, the 1916 quarter is in demand in all grades. MacNeil's original style lasted just two years before exposed Liberty was covered with a coat of chain mail, though there is debate about whether the change was made primarily to cover the partial nudity. This coin is a lustrous example with no significant abrasions or spots. Though there is typical softness in the feathers on the eagle's left wing and breast and in the rivets and stripes of the shield, sufficient detail remains in Liberty's helmet for the coin to be certified as a Full Head example. Muted silver-gray patina on both sides and a few darker pinkish-gold highlights near the rim combine to produce a pleasing example of this popular early 20th century type. (#5705)

1950 **1916 MS66 Full Head NGC.** Ex: Richmond Collection. This Premium Gem Full Head first-year key-date 1916 quarter is virtually in the finest quality obtainable in the numismatic marketplace. The current population of 1916 Standing Liberty quarters certified MS66 Full Head is 17 coins at NGC, with three finer, and 10 at PCGS, with four finer (8/08)—and it is likely that any higher-grade pieces are held in strong hands, indeed, as the Registry Set phenomenon appears to be growing in intensity.

The surfaces of this coin are silver-white, without so much as a hint of discernible color. The texture is deeply frosted, with incredible luster emanating from both sides. As expected of the grade, there is virtually no sign of visible contact, save for a single nick in the belly of the eagle. The head details are full as defined within the context of the issue, and even more remarkably, most of the shield rivets and lines are in place.

It was not only gold, but the minor denominations of silver and copper, that saw the noted coinage renaissance of American numismatic researcher Roger Burdette. First came the Lincoln cent of Victor D. Brenner replacing the Indian cent, followed four years later by James Earle Fraser's Buffalo nickel replacing the Liberty Head nickel. The reinvigoration of the minor coinage concluded in 1916 with the near-simultaneous launches of the Mercury dime and Walking Liberty half dollar designs of A.A. Weinman, and the introduction of Hermon MacNeil's Standing Liberty design.

Next year, 2009, will see the Mint's special issues related to the centenary of the release of the Lincoln cent. One wonders, with the proliferation of Lincolns and Buffalos from the current Mint nearly 100 years after their launch, might the Mint similarly produce centenary commemorations of the Mercury dime, Walking Liberty Half and Standing Liberty quarter a few years later, in 2016? If that turns out to be so, the 1916-dated issues will see feverish demand similar to that currently prevailing for the 1909 cent issues.

Ex: Richmond Sale, Part II (DLRC Auctions, 11/2004), lot 1346, which realized $33,925. (#5705)

1951 **1917 Type One MS65 PCGS.** Sky-blue and russet patina is more extensive and deeper on the reverse of this lustrous Gem. Sharply struck, including near-complete detail on the horizontal and vertical stripes of the shield. A few grade-consistent obverse marks are noted. (#5706)

1952 **1917 Type One MS64 Full Head PCGS.** Both sides of this near-Gem are awash in potent luster, and are in receipt of an attentive strike, culminating in Full Head definition. Subtle hints of gold-tan patina show up at the reverse margins. A few trivial marks preclude Gem status.
From The Menlo Park Collection. (#5707)

1953 **1917 Type One MS64 Full Head PCGS.** Numerous lines of dark toning cross the light gold surfaces on both sides of this boldly defined near-Gem. (#5707)

1954 **1917 Type One MS65 Full Head NGC.** A solid strike leaves exquisite definition on the design features of this Gem quarter. In addition to the Full Head, the vertical and horizontal stripes in the shield are visible. Lustrous surfaces yield a hint of light tan-gray color at the margins. A pin-point spot is noted in the upper right obverse quadrant. (#5707)

1955 **1917 Type One MS65 Full Head NGC.** A sharply struck Gem example of this popular type issue, impressively lustrous with subtle gold and silver-blue patina. Pleasingly preserved and attractive. (#5707)

1956 **1917 Type One MS65 Full Head NGC.** The shining centers are essentially silver-white, while the margins show bands of golden-tan and violet. Delightfully detailed and an excellent candidate for a similarly graded type set. (#5707)

1957 **1917 Type One MS66 Full Head NGC.** Intricately struck with full details and great eye appeal. Deep frost covers both sides of this brilliant piece, which has almost a matte appearance. Several minuscule spots and abrasions are barely worthy of note. (#5707)

1958 **1917 Type One MS66 Full Head NGC.** Pink and orange-gold shadings prevail, though a crescent of silver-gray frames Liberty's well-defined head. Carefully preserved with satiny luster. (#5707)

1959 **1917 Type One MS66 Full Head NGC.** Subtly lustrous beneath heavy golden-brown and medium gray patina. The strike is bold, and the overall effect is delightful. Seldom can a Standing Liberty quarter be described as fully struck, but a close examination shows virtually no areas of weakness. A perfect example for any type set. (#5707)

1960 **1917 Type One MS66 Full Head PCGS. CAC.** This is a visually enticing Premium Gem, with radiant luster and a light, even golden cast across both sides. Sharply struck with crisp details on Liberty's head and shield rivets, and also on the eagle's breast feathers. The Type One quarter is a brief type that was only produced in 1916 and part of 1917. (#5707)

Delightful Full Head MS67 1917 Quarter, Type One

1961 **1917 Type One MS67 Full Head PCGS.** Shades of amber-gold embrace the margins of this thoroughly lustrous Superb Gem. Exactly struck and devoid of visible abrasions. A wonderful silver type coin, produced for only two years. Certified in a green label holder. Population: 56 in 67, 0 finer (8/08). (#5707)

1962 **1917-D Type One MS65 Full Head PCGS.** This gorgeously preserved Gem is precisely struck and exhibits dappled chestnut-brown patina. A desirable example of the sole Type One Denver issue. (#5709)

1963 **1917-S Type One MS65 PCGS.** A lustrous honey-gold Gem that has lovingly preserved surfaces. Liberty's head and the upper shield show slight softness, but the devices are otherwise bold. Population: 35 in 65, 15 finer (8/08). (#5710)

Stunning 1917-S Type One Quarter, MS67

1964 **1917-S Type One MS67 NGC.** White surfaces (save for wisps of light gray on the upper reverse) are embraced in full luster, and an exacting strike imparts sharp definition to the design features, including the rivets, the inner shield, Liberty's toes, and the eagle's plumage. A couple of grade-consistent marks concealed on Liberty do not detract. (#5710)

Scarce 1917-S Type One Quarter, MS67

1965 **1917-S Type One MS67 PCGS.** The Hermon MacNeil Type One Standing Liberty quarter is among the small group of milestone coin issues from the early 20th century renaissance in U.S. coin design. This Superb Gem example is an opportunity to own a near-flawless example of MacNeil's original concept for the coin. NGC and PCGS have certified only three pieces in MS67, with none finer among non-Full Head examples (8/08). Appealing champagne-gold and silver-gray patina adorns the obverse, while much of the reverse is brilliant, save for a dark crescent of reddish-brown on the left side. Crisply struck overall, as expected for this Type One issue, with a hint of satin on the obverse and powerful luster on the reverse. (#5710)

Gem Full Head 1917-S Quarter, Type One

1966 **1917-S Type One MS65 Full Head PCGS.** Exquisitely struck with complete shield rivets and feathers on the eagle. Light golden-brown toning visits the lower left obverse, while this lustrous Gem is otherwise nearly brilliant. Housed in a green label holder. *Ex: FUN Signature (Heritage, 1/2004), lot 6185.* (#5711)

1967 **1917 Type Two MS64 Full Head PCGS.** A penetrating strike goes beyond the Full Head to include virtual completeness in the horizontal and vertical shield stripes. A lustrous piece with dapples of russet at the margins. A handful of trivial marks is fewer than what might be expected for the grade designation. *From The Menlo Park Collection.* (#5715)

Resplendent 1917-S Type Two Quarter, MS66

1968 **1917-S Type Two MS66 NGC.** Only one finer non-full head example of this issue has been certified by NGC. This grading company has also graded 12 Full Head pieces in MS66 or finer quality. Despite noticeable design weakness, this piece has exceptional frosty silver luster with wispy gold toning. Population: 15 in 66, 0 finer (8/07). *From The Beau Clerc Collection.* (#5718)

1969 **1918-S MS65 NGC.** This early Type Two example is boldly struck and nicely preserved, with pleasing satin luster and silver surfaces that are partially imbued with light gold and apricot patina. There are no significant marks on either side of this attractive Gem. Census: 58 in 65, 30 finer (7/08). (#5724)

Scarce Full Head 1918-S Quarter MS63

1970 **1918-S MS63 Full Head PCGS.** Light butter-gold toning adorns this highly lustrous and attractively preserved quarter. A pair of faint slide marks on the waist were present prior to the strike. A pleasing strike for the issue aside from a trio of indistinct shield rivets. Housed in a green label holder. (#5725)

Popular 1918/7-S Quarter, XF40

1971 **1918/7-S XF40 ANACS.** Even with 20 points of wear, this piece displays several of the authenticating diagnostics visible on this popular overdate variety. Chief among them is the prominent E clash mark at Liberty's left (facing) knee, produced from the E in E PLURIBUS UNUM on the reverse. Another parallel die lines, actually clashes from the eagle's wing, that run southeast from the top left serif of the first T in TRVST. The diagonal downstroke of the 7 is clear under the 8, although wear has joined the area to the rear of the 7 with the 8. This piece has attractive pinkish-silver surfaces on both sides, with some glints of amber and ice-blue. *From The Morton J. Greene Collection.* (#5726)

Lustrous Mint State 1918/7-S
Standing Liberty Quarter

1972 **1918/7-S MS61 NGC.** This coin has much to commend itself, and is nicer-looking than the conservative MS61 grade might lead the reader to believe. Neither side reveals any abrasions that are worthy of singular mention, and indeed there are remarkably few contact marks of any size appearing, even under a loupe. Splendid luster is visible on both sides, although the golden-gray toning in some places cedes to a more-dense powder-gray that somewhat obscures the luster in limited areas. The strike is a bit blunt on Liberty's face and some of the usually weak shield rivets—but this coin will be a surprising find and a worthy addition to a fine collection of Standing Liberty quarters, or to that overdate type set you have always wanted to work on. (#5726)

Outstanding 1918/7-S Quarter, MS62

1973 **1918/7-S MS62 PCGS.** The 1918/7-S overdate is the only Standing Liberty quarter that successfully competes with the first-year 1916 issue in terms of desirability and rarity. Most references state that this variety was unknown to collectors until 1937. Walter Breen (1988) notes that many rolls of quarters were retrieved from cash reserves of failed banks during the 1930s. Perhaps the two events are linked, with collector scrutiny at the time bringing to light this previously unpublicized variety? In any case, this coin is a beautiful Mint State example of a highly desirable type with an unknown mintage. The downstroke of the 7 is clearly visible through the bottom loop of the 8 in the date. Though the strike is somewhat soft in the usual reverse and obverse locations, this is an amazingly clean coin with no abrasions or spots of concern. The surfaces shows abundant luster, overall bright silver-gray patina with a hint of bronze, and darker toning highlights near the rims. Population: 12 in 62, 42 finer (8/08). (#5726)

1974 **1919 MS64 Full Head PCGS.** An exquisitely struck near-Gem. In addition to the Full Head, the chain mail and rivets are bold. Highly lustrous surfaces show localized russet freckles, especially on the reverse. (#5729)

1975 **1919 MS65 Full Head PCGS.** Solidly detailed with surprising eye appeal, even by Gem standards. The surfaces are essentially untoned with uncommonly vibrant luster. PCGS has graded 70 finer Full Head pieces (8/08). (#5729)

1976 **1920 MS65 Full Head PCGS.** This crisply struck Gem offers elegant luster and impressive eye appeal. The carefully preserved surfaces are entirely deserving of the grade assigned. PCGS has graded just 19 finer Full Head pieces (8/08). (#5735)

Rare 1920-S Quarter, MS63 Full Head

1977 **1920-S MS63 Full Head NGC.** In the third edition of his reference *Standing Liberty Quarters,* author Jay Cline stated that the 1920-S is very rare with full head details, and boldly suggested that it should be the second or third most valuable quarter in the entire Standing Liberty series. Both obverse and reverse have frosty luster with light iridescent toning. This splendid specimen exhibits considerable eye appeal and total originality. (#5739)

Well Struck 1921 Gem Quarter

1978 **1921 MS65 PCGS.** Exquisitely struck, with strong (though not full) definition on Liberty's head. The stripes on the inner shield are complete, as is the chain mail and eagle's plumage. Whispers of light gray run over the highly lustrous surfaces that reveal nice preservation. Population: 91 in 65, 15 finer (8/08). (#5740)

Vibrant 1921 Quarter, MS64 Full Head

1979 **1921 MS64 Full Head PCGS.** Nearly 38 million quarters combined were minted in 1920 at the Philadelphia, Denver, and San Francisco mints. The following year the total number of quarters produced dropped to less than 2 million coins, all minted at Philadelphia. This example has radiant luster with clean silver surfaces accenting subtle bronze toning along the rims. Head detail is excellent, as expected from the designation, but there is some weakness in the shield and feather details. PCGS has graded only 20 Full Head examples finer (8/08). (#5741)

1980 **1923-S Fine 15 PCGS.** A charming evenly worn example of this scarce issue. Lovely silver-gray patina covers most of the surfaces, with accents of yellow and russet toning on the reverse. Several patches of verdigris, mostly on the obverse, are noted on this otherwise minimally marked representative. (#5744)

1981 **1923-S XF40 PCGS.** Vibrant electric-blue undercurrents charge the luminous silver-gray surfaces. Minimally marked with only light, even wear across the centers. (#5744)

1982 **1923-S XF40 ICG.** Soft remnants of luster glimmer at the margins. Well struck with few marks on light silver-gray surfaces that show a deepening to slate around the central devices. *From The Morton J. Greene Collection.* (#5744)

Sharp 1923-S Standing Quarter, MS64 Full Head

1983 **1923-S MS64 Full Head NGC.** The 1923-S is an important key date in the Standing Liberty quarter series. MS65 Full Head examples are scarce (J.H. Cline, 2007), and even near-Gem Full Heads, such as the piece in the current lot, are tough to locate. Whispers of copper-gold color are scattered about, concentrating at the borders, and dazzling luster exudes from both sides. An attentive strike transcends Liberty's Full Head to brings out sharp definition in the other design elements, including the chain mail, the inner shield, and all but two of the rivets. Close scrutiny reveals no significant marks. (#5745)

1984 **1925 MS65 Full Head PCGS.** Whispers of russet and sky-blue patina are occasionally seen on the lustrous surfaces of this Gem. A solid strike goes beyond the Full Head to bring out strong definition on the chain mail, rivets, and eagle's plumage. A well preserved piece. (#5753)

1985 **1926 MS65 Full Head PCGS.** This is a marvelous Gem example, with crisply struck devices and even satin luster that illuminates silver-gray surfaces. A small degree of russet color emerges near the upper obverse border, near ERT. There are no mentionable marks on either side. (#5755)

1986 **1927 MS64 Full Head NGC.** Highly lustrous surfaces display dapples of faint tan patina, more noticeable on the reverse. An attentive strike culminates in a Full Head. A few minute marks define the grade. (#5761)

1987 **1927 MS65 Full Head PCGS.** This lustrous gunmetal-gray and honey Gem is magnificently preserved, and exhibits impressive definition on the obverse highpoints. Certified in a green label holder. *Ex: Central States Signature (Heritage, 4/2006), lot 1674.* (#5761)

1988 **1927-D MS66 PCGS.** A patch of cherry-red patina appears to the left of Liberty's head, but aside from a few scattered spots in the periphery of the obverse, this highly appealing piece is brilliant. Well-struck save for the often-seen softness on Liberty's head and shield. Population: 24 in 66, 0 finer (8/08). (#5762)

Coveted Choice 1927-S Quarter

1989 **1927-S MS64 PCGS. CAC.** This low mintage semi-key quarter provides scintillating luster. Light almond-gold patina visits smooth surfaces. The obverse is particularly free from marks. Nicely struck despite the usual incompleteness on a couple of shield rivets and the center of the head. Boldly clashed near Liberty's legs. (#5764)

1990 **1928-S MS65 Full Head PCGS.** Large S. Ultra frosty with tinges of golden color at the margins. Liberty's head is full, while the centers show selected softness. Well preserved and original. *Ex: FUN Signature (Heritage, 1/2004), lot 6274.* (#5771)

1991 **1929 MS65 Full Head PCGS.** This frosty Gem is boldly detailed and fully lustrous, with faint heather and light olive toning on each side. (#5773)

Gem Full Head 1929-D Quarter

1992 **1929-D MS65 Full Head PCGS.** Light almond-gold and gunmetal-blue patina embraces this highly lustrous and splendidly preserved Gem. A very good strike, since even the shield rivets closest to the waist are outlined. Certified in a green label holder. Population: 35 in 65 Full Head, 10 finer (8/08). (#5775)

1993 **1929-S MS66 Full Head PCGS.** Eye-catching satiny luster radiates from surfaces of this carefully preserved quarter. Most S-mint Standing Liberty quarters were weakly struck, but this Full Head representative is exceptional with sharply struck details save for some softness on several rivets. Minor flecks on each side and a couple of tiny abrasions keep this piece from an even higher grade. PCGS has certified only 10 Full Head examples finer (7/08). (#5777)

1994 **1930 MS65 Full Head NGC.** Boldly impressed overall with only trifling softness on the rivets of Liberty's shield. Strongly lustrous and carefully preserved with only occasional whispers of golden patina. (#5779)

1995 **1930 MS66 Full Head PCGS.** Many 1930 quarters are available with Full Heads for a price, but the present piece is among the finest. A dusting of hazel and russet toning covers each side, with darker areas around the rims. The surfaces are nearly perfect, and a couple of softly struck rivets are the only areas of weakness. A great piece for a type collector. (#5779)

1996 **1930 MS66 Full Head PCGS.** Strong overall detail for this final-year issue with only slight softness on the rivets of the shield. Immensely lustrous and carefully preserved, even by Premium Gem standards. PCGS has graded 28 finer Full Head coins (8/08). *From The Bell Collection.* (#5779)

1997 **1930 MS66 Full Head NGC.** Crisply struck save for typical weakness on three of the shield rivets. The satiny surfaces exhibit pale greenish-gray toning, modified by speckled russet-red patina near the lower obverse border, and faint streaks of russet across the center of the reverse. Carefully preserved and mark-free; a lovely Premium Gem quarter. (#5779)

Spectacular 1930 Standing Liberty Quarter, MS67 Full Head

1998 **1930 MS67 Full Head NGC.** This outstanding piece is certainly among the finest 1930 Standing Liberty quarters. While this is a relatively common date, as one would expect the number of survivors in MS67 Full Head is quite low. Neither NGC nor PCGS has certified any examples finer than the present piece, and NGC reports just 24 pieces at the MS67 Full Head level. This highly lustrous specimen is fully struck save for a touch of weakness on a couple of rivets, as is almost always the case. Entirely brilliant, minimally marked, and exceptionally attractive. (#5779)

Full Head Superb Gem 1930 Quarter

1999 **1930 MS67 Full Head PCGS.** Potent luster dominates this exceptionally preserved Superb Gem. Pastel gold and sky-blue toning ensures the eye appeal. Well struck except for a pair of shield rivets near the waist. The final date of the prematurely ended series. Housed in a green label holder. Population: 28 in 67 Full Head, 0 finer (8/08). (#5779)

2000 **1930-S MS67 ★ NGC.** Although a common date in low grades, the 1930-S is a condition rarity above Gem Uncirculated. The head is slightly weak on this piece, but it is better than average for the issue, and the only other area of softness is on a couple of rivets. Pleasing hazel toning graces the surfaces of this minimally marked specimen. NGC has certified only one other 1930-S (also a Superb Gem) with the coveted Star designation (7/08). (#5780)

2001 **1930-S MS67 PCGS.** Reddish-gold and russet patina concentrates at the margins of this S-mint Superb Gem. Well defined and nicely preserved. Housed in a green-label holder. (#5780)

Magnificent 1930-S Quarter, Superb Gem Full Head

2002 **1930-S MS67 Full Head NGC. CAC.** Although a common issue in lower grades, the 1930-S is seldom seen in Superb Gem. Mottled cobalt-blue, olive, and russet toning drapes the frosted surfaces of this virtually pristine specimen. A trace of softness on the rivets is typical, but the rest of the details are powerfully impressed. This attractive and highly lustrous representative is housed in an old NGC holder. Census: 20 in 67 Full Head, 2 finer (7/08). (#5781)

EARLY HALF DOLLARS

2003 **1795 Two Leaves, O-116, R.4—Improperly Cleaned—NCS. VG Details.** Finely hairlined and a bit bright, this Flowing Hair half has parallel adjustment marks on each side of the profile and minor rim irregularities on the reverse. The centers are ivory-gray while the borders are olive-green and navy-blue.
From The Morton J. Greene Collection. (#6052)

2004 **1795 2 Leaves VG8 NGC.** O-128, R.5. Wonderful pewter-gray surfaces for the grade, with slightly lighter patina on the devices. A well centered impression, noticeably worn but still very attractive. (#6052)

Charming 1795 Half Dollar, O-126a, Choice Very Good

2005 **1795 2 Leaves VG10 PCGS.** O-126a, R.4. The bust is small, and the reverse has a 9-8 berry arrangement in the wreath, with only two berries below the eagle's right wing, both of which are on the inside. This variety is distinguished from Overton-126 because of the die cracks through the E in UNITED and the left (facing) ribbon of the wreath. Pleasing olive-green patina overlies the surfaces. The details are fully outlined and there are no particularly bothersome marks. (#6052)

Significant 1795 Half Dollar, 2 Leaves, O-106, VG10

2006 **1795 2 Leaves VG10 PCGS.** O-106, R.6. This rare variety is easily identified by the reverse, which features the distinctive 9-10 berry pattern, with four berries below the eagle's right (facing) wing. An oddly shaped die break is also notable and completely bisects the reverse. Several shallow adjustment marks on the obverse translate to minor weakness on part of the reverse lettering. Pale gray patina covers the minimally marked surfaces of this desirable representative. (#6052)

Fine 12 1795 Two Leaves Half, O-104

2007 **1795 2 Leaves, O-104, R.4, Fine 12 NGC.** Deep cobalt-blue and olive toning envelops this Flowing Hair collector coin. Marks are surprisingly minor aside from a solitary pinscratch on the neck and a few faint slide marks on the forehead. A vertical die break through the right (facing) wing, as often seen. (#6052)

2008 **1795 2 Leaves Fine 12 NGC.** O-116, R.4. Wonderful pewter-gray surfaces with lighter tan on the devices. The reverse is rotated 45 degrees counterclockwise. The obverse has clash marks from UNITED behind star 8 and LIBERTY. (#6052)

2009 **1795 2 Leaves—Genuine—PCGS.** O-108, R.4. We grade this piece Fine 12. Doubled M in AMERICA. Lightly cracked through the right serifs of I in UNITED, to the wreath, but no evidence of the O-108a crack through AME. PCGS certified as "Genuine," the grade assigned by Heritage. Deep heather and gray toning with pleasing surfaces, marred only by a few faint scratches on each side. (#6052)

Rare 1795 Half Dollar, 2 Leaves, O-120, Genuine

2010 **1795 2 Leaves—Genuine—PCGS.** O-120, R.6. We grade this piece Fine 15. Star 1 pierces the first hair curl and star 2 is point-to-point with the second hair curl, identifying the obverse. Overton-120 has the only reverse that features a 9-8 berry pattern with three berries on the inside of the wreath below the eagle's right (facing) wing and one on the outside. Deep gray toning envelops the surfaces, which show no mentionable marks. The details are well-outlined. Overall, a nice example of this seldom-seen variety. (#6052)

2011 **1795 2 Leaves Fine 12 ANACS.** O-119, R.4. Deep gray-brown surfaces with even darker patina near the reverse border. This attractive and fully original piece has excellent, mark-free surfaces. (#6052)

Late State 1795 O-105a Half, VF25

2012 **1795 Two Leaves, O-105a, R.4 VF25 NGC.** Ex: Brown. A late die state with obverse die cracks through most stars, especially at the right. Another crack extends from the border through the B to the top of the head, and an additional crack from the bust tip crosses the lower point of the last star to the border.

A beautiful and fully original deep gray example with blue, lilac, and tan on both sides, accompanying light ivory surfaces. Most collectors think of Robinson S. Brown, Jr., as an advanced large cent collector, which he certainly was, but he also assembled an excellent collection of early half dollar varieties.
From the Robinson S. Brown, Jr. Collection. (#6052)

Appealing 1795 Half Dollar, O-104, Choice XF

2013 **1795 2 Leaves, O-104, R.4, XF45 NGC.** A small die lump below star 15 identifies the obverse, while the reverse has the useful diagnostic of a die defect that connects the knot of the ribbon to the rock above. Only 1794 and 1795 half dollars feature the Flowing Head design, and examples from the first year are quite rare. Although all 1795 halves are scarce, they can be obtained at a more affordable price and would be a perfect representative for a type collector without unlimited funds.

Both sides of the present piece have traces of luster, which is remarkable given the condition. Scattered abrasions on the surfaces limit the grade of this otherwise excellent example. The reverse has numerous shallow adjustment marks at the center. Lovely pale gray toning covers the surfaces, with hints of gold and steel in the margins. A well-detailed piece with charming eye appeal. *From The Menlo Park Collection.* (#6052)

Lovely 1795 O-122 Half, XF45

2014 **1795 2 Leaves XF45 NGC.** O-122, R.5. Medium aqua-blue, pearl-gray, and olive colors embrace this refreshingly unmarked and attractively defined Half Dollar. For Overton-122, the eagle's wings are boldly clashed beneath Liberty's chin and behind her head, and a heavy arc-shaped die crack from 2:30 to 5:30 threatens the integrity of the reverse die. Unimportant mint-made clashmarks are noted on the upper reverse border. (#6052)

Imposing AU53 1795 Flowing Hair Half
Two Leaves Reverse, O-110

2015 **1795 Two Leaves, O-110, R.3, AU53 PCGS.** The Flowing Hair half is enormously popular, as it represents the first silver design of the U.S. Mint. Struck for just two years, mintages were low in 1794 but (fortunately for collectors) more generous in 1795. Examples went into circulation and remained there for decades, which accounts for the five pieces graded Fair 2 by PCGS. Few who encountered the new Federal type had the foresight or means to set aside high grade examples, which means most survivors are VG to VF. The present silver-gray piece is noteworthy for its ample shimmering luster and bold hair definition. Impressively undisturbed by abrasions apart from a hair-thin mark near the TAT in STATES. Struck from prominently clashed dies, as usually seen with this variety. Population: 10 in 53, 57 finer (8/08). (#6052)

Seldom-Offered 1795 Small Head Half Dollar, O-127, VG10

2016 **1795 Small Head VG10 PCGS.** O-127, R.6. The bust is narrow, although it is not quite as small as on Overton-126. The reverse has nine berries on the left and eight on the right, and the position of the leaf below the upright of the F in OF is diagnostic. Light gray toning on the devices contrasts nicely against the slightly darker fields. The upper left corner of the obverse shows several adjustment marks, and stars 6 and 7 are soft. The remaining details are fairly well-outlined, and there are no marks worthy of mention. A splendid example of this rare variety. (#6054)

Pleasing 1796 Half Dollar
VF25, O-101, R.5

2017   **1796 15 Stars VF25 PCGS.** O-101, R.5. Following a relatively high production for the 1795 Flowing Hair half dollar (nearly 300,000 pieces), mintage of the 1796-1797 Draped Bust Small Eagle design type totaled only 3,918 coins. No half dollars at all were minted in 1798 through 1800, and when the denomination resumed in 1801, the Small Eagle reverse was replaced with a Heraldic Eagle.

The small mintage of 1796 and 1797 halves presents a significant obstacle to collectors seeking to complete a type set of U.S. coinage. Indeed, many, if not most, type collections lack this important key. Date and variety specialists create additional demand.

Ocean-blue shades embrace the fields of the present offering, while the lightly toned devices are pearl-gray. This example is sharp for its designated grade, since the denticles are individually distinctive, and Liberty's hair and the eagle's wings exhibit considerable inner detail. No adjustment marks are evident, and the few contacts scattered about are in line with what is expected for a coin that has seen light to moderate circulation. For pedigree purposes, we mention a couple of marks on Liberty's middle chest, another to the upper left of star 11, and a small cluster between the eagle's head and right (facing) wing.

As seen on most survivors of the O-101 marriage, a die crack begins at the rim near 3:30 and reaches star 13, then continues down through stars 14 and 15 into the curve of an inner drapery fold, with a bold branch crack to the rim at 5 o'clock. A second arc-shaped die crack is noted above Liberty's shoulder. This latter crack is not mentioned in the standard Overton reference, but is visible on the plate coin for O-101. The above reference also mentions a "small die defect" in the lower fold of Liberty's drapery (just above the 6 in the date). This "defect" is actually part of the network of aforementioned cracks.

This is a pleasing specimen that will delight the new owner. Encapsulated in a green label PCGS holder.
Ex: James Kelly (11/1957), lot 1588; R.E. Cox, Jr. Collection, Metro New York Numismatic Convention (Stack's, 4/1992), lot 1756. From The Menlo Park Collection. (#6057)

Wonderful 1796 15 Stars Half Dollar
AU58, O-101, R.5

2018 **1796 15 Stars AU58 PCGS.** O-101, R.5. The Draped Bust Small Eagle half dollar, bearing the date 1796 or 1797, is rare in any level of preservation. This is not unexpected, as the mintage for this two-year type coin was a relatively sparse 3,918 pieces.

Its rarity was well known at an early date in American numismatic history. For example, in a little known, four-page July 1858 publication by Joseph J. Mickley titled *Dates of United States Coins and Their Degrees of Rarity*, the author says the 1796 half dollar is "Rare" and the 1797 "Very Rare" (Mickley employed a three-point scale to denote the degree of rarity of all U.S. gold, silver, and copper coins between 1793 and 1858—Common, Rare, and Very Rare). And in one of the first books on numismatics written in America, *American Numismatical Manual* by Dr. Montroville W. Dickeson (1859), the author says of the 1796 issue: "They are rare" (Dickeson was apparently unaware of the 1797 half dollar, for he makes no mention of it).

Empirically derived evidence of the awareness of the 1796-1797 half dollar's rarity in the earlier stages of American numismatics is gleaned from auction prices realized in sales conducted during the 1850s, 1860s, and 1870s. The 1796-1797 half, along with various early cents, the 1802 half dime, the 1823 quarter, the 1794 dollar, and a few other issues, consistently ranks among the highest prices realized for regular-issue U.S. coins in early auction sales.

About Uncirculated 1796 15 Stars half dollars in general, and high-end AU coins in particular, such as the AU58 PCGS offered here, are far and few between. Indeed, NGC and PCGS have, to date, certified seven 1796 15 Star halves in AU grades, only two of which rate AU58.

Light to medium steel-gray toning, imbued with occasional blushes of sky-blue, graces both sides of this near-Mint example, with brighter undertones evident as the coin is rotated under a light source. A well-executed strike imparts sharp definition to the design elements, especially Liberty's hair, ribbon, and drapery, and to most of the star centrils. Strong detail is evident on the eagle's wing and tail feathers, while those on the breast and legs exhibit the usual weakness. The motifs are well-centered, and all of the dentilation shows. A few light adjustment marks on the eagle's lower torso and legs and the clouds are not at all detracting. We mention some scattered marks that are consistent with light circulation. Two to the right of star 2, and a few more on the forehead and in the field to its right, serve to identify the coin.

The die crack from the rim at 5 o'clock branches to the left and to the right through the drapery. This crack, which is visible on most known 1796 15 Stars half dollar specimens, is finer than seen on most examples. Moreover, while the right-branch crack shows a faint extension to star 15, it does not travel through stars 14 and 13 to the edge, as seen on most coins of this issue. A faint crack also runs from the upper upright of the second T in STATES through the tops of ES, and then nearly to the O in OF.

This is a wonderful Draped Bust Small Eagle half dollar example that will delight the new owner.

Ex: The Douglas L. Noblet Collection (Bowers and Merena Rarities Sale, 1/1999), lot 4; The Richard Genaitis Collection (Heritage 2001 Atlanta ANA, 8/2001), lot 6090. (#6057)

2019 **1802 O-101, R.3—Improperly Cleaned—NCS. Good Details.** The peripheral legends and stars are distinct from the rim, and surprising hair detail is present. The slate-gray surfaces are mildly granular, but many collectors would relish the opportunity to add this rare date to their holdings. (#6065)

XF Details 1802 Draped Bust Half, O-101

2020 **1802 O-101, R.3—Genuine—PCGS.** The only dies for this challenging date. The present piece has XF sharpness, and the surfaces are cloudy and subdued from an unobtrusive cleaning. Evenly retoned gray-brown. No marks are evident, and most collectors would be proud to have such a richly detailed example within their holdings. (#6065)

Important XF O-107 1805 Half Dollar

2021 **1805 O-107, R.5, XF40 PCGS.** An impressive example of this scarce variety. Luster shimmers across the borders and devices, and there are no noticeable marks. The obverse margin is autumn-gold and forest-green, while the remainder of this desirable piece is pearl-gray. Encapsulated in an old doily label holder. (#6069)

2022 **1806/5 XF45 PCGS.** O-103, R.2. A splendid light gray example with traces of luster visible on both sides. Subtle splashes of light gold add to its overall eye appeal.
From The Menlo Park Collection. (#6077)

Worthy Choice XF 1806/5 Half Dollar, O-101

2023 **1806/5 XF45 PCGS.** O-101, R.3. Predominantly cream-gray with peripheral orange-red and aquamarine. A good strike for the type with even definition, although the stars lack centril detail. Thorough study fails to locate any abrasions worthy of comment. Scarcer than the common O-109, yet an excellent candidate for a date or type set. Population: 11 in 45, 31 finer (8/08). (#6077)

2024 **1806 Pointed 6, No Stem VF25 PCGS.** O-109, R.1. The date has a pointed 6, and there is no stem through the eagle's right (facing) claw. An appealing VF example, with even medium-gray coloration across both sides. Typically worn for the grade, without any undue surface marks. (#6073)

2025 **1806 Pointed 6, No Stem—Cleaned—ICG. AU50 Details.** O-109, R.1. This variety has a pointed 6 in the date, and there is no stem through the eagle's right (facing) claw. This lightly cleaned example displays aqua-green and gray-lavender color. Nicely defined throughout. (#6073)

2026 **1806 Pointed 6, Stem XF40 PCGS.** O-115, R.1. The obverse has a die crack through the bottom of the date and the first five stars. It also has prominent repunching on the TY in LIBERTY, which is diagnostic for this die. On the reverse, the ME in AMERICA is joined at the base, a point of a star is firmly attached to the top of the eagle's beak, and the lowest berry does not have a stem. Pale gray patina on the devices contrasts against darker gray toning around the perimeter. The centers and stars are a little soft, as typically seen, but the surfaces are remarkably clean. (#6071)

2027 **1806 Pointed 6, Stem XF45 NGC.** O-115a, R.1. Cracked through the top of STATES. The additional crack through UNITED is currently unknown. A lovely example with deep lilac-gray surfaces that gradually give way to deeper steel at the borders. Lighter silver appears on the obverse motif. (#6071)

2028 **1807 O-102, R.2 VF25 ANACS.** Deep olive-brown with cream-gray highpoints. A couple of marks near the far left reverse stars, but otherwise minimally abraded. All of E PLURIBUS UNUM is legible, although several letters are faint. (#6079)

2029 **1807 Draped Bust VF30 PCGS.** O-106, R.3. The 1 in the date is joined to Liberty's lowest hair curl; there are five berries on the reverse, and the uppermost one is half-buried in a leaf. An attractively original example of this scarcer variety, from the final year of the Draped Bust half dollar design type. Evenly worn with smooth surfaces that have few marks on either side. (#6079)

2030 **1807 Draped Bust—Scratched—ICG. VF30 Details.** O-102, R.2. Light silver surfaces with pale gray-gold patina and lighter silvery highlights. A short vertical scratch in the right obverse field is just right of the nose and mouth. (#6079)

2031 **1807 Draped Bust XF40 NGC.** O-102, R.2. An appealing XF example of this final-year Draped Bust half dollar variety. Brownish-gold and champagne colors increase the coin's eye appeal. (#6079)

AU 1807 Draped Bust Half, O-105

2032 **1807 O-105, R.1, AU50 ANACS.** O-105, R.1. This impressive Draped Bust type coin is toned olive-gray aside from a blush of milky tan beneath the hair ribbon and a streak of brown near Liberty's nose. Luster dominates design recesses, and no marks merit individual discussion. (#6079)

Choice AU 1807 Draped Bust Half, O-110a

2033 **1807 O-110a, R.2, AU55 PCGS.** The later die state with a descending die crack to the cloud between STATES and OF. This partly lustrous half dollar is shaded in rich apple-green, gunmetal-gray, and orange-gold. The strike is bold for the type, and a thorough scrutiny beneath a loupe locates only minor contact. (#6079)

BUST HALF DOLLARS

Famous 'Bearded Goddess' O-111b
1807 50 Over 20 Half Dollar, VF Details

2034 **1807 Bearded Goddess, Large Stars, 50/20, O-111b, R.5— Improperly Cleaned—NCS. VF Details.** One of the few die states of *any* denomination separately listed in the Guide Book, the 'Bearded Goddess' commands a huge premium over the common O-112 50/20 variety. The 'beard' is actually a heavy die crack between the chin and bust. This slate-gray example provides glimpses of luster across the reverse. The obverse is moderately hairlined. (#6086)

2035 **1807 Large Stars, 50/20, O-112, R.1, VF35 NGC.** Dusky almond-gold and slate toning embraces this nicely detailed example, which displays traces of its introductory luster within peripheral recesses. Both sides are devoid of consequential contact. (#6086)

Charlton Meyer's 1807 O-112 Half, AU50

2036 **1807 Large Stars, 50 Over 20 AU50 PCGS.** Ex: Meyer Collection. O-112, R.1. The blundered denomination occurred when the engraver mistakenly grabbed the punch for a 2 instead of a 5. Either he thought he was working on a quarter die, or he simply grabbed the wrong punch due to a similarity in appearance. This lilac and medium gray piece has considerable lighter silver luster. Traces of an unknown black substance adhere to the reverse, but could probably be removed with little effort. (#6086)

Toned 1807 Capped Bust Half AU53
Large Stars, 50/20, O-112

2037 **1807 Large Stars, 50/20, O-112, R.1, AU53 NGC.** Blended tan-brown, gunmetal-gray, and aqua-blue toning embraces this well detailed Bust half. The subdued surfaces have relatively few marks. The popular blundered denomination variety, caused when the engraver briefly believed he was making a quarter dollar reverse die. (#6086)

2038 **1807 Capped Bust, Small Stars VF35 NGC.** O-113, R.2. The stars are small and distant from the rim, and the denomination is widely spaced, with the C exceptionally far from the 50. Lovely gunmetal-gray patina coats each side save for patches of light toning on parts of the devices. Evenly worn with wonderful definition particularly on the stars. A splendid type coin from a transitional year. (#6087)

1807 Small Stars Half, O-113a, AU58

2039 **1807 Small Stars, O-113a, R.3 AU58 NGC.** The 'a' subvariety is distinguished by extensive die cracking on each side. On the obverse, most notably a crack from the end of the bust through all the stars on the left, another from the milling through the 0 in the date up to the drapery. On the reverse, several die cracks encircle most of the periphery of that side. Better struck on the obverse than the reverse, the centers are bright and nearly untoned and surrounded by a thin band of russet at the margins. (#6087)

2040 **1807 Large Stars, O-114, R.3—Improperly Cleaned—NCS. VF Details.** Die flaws beneath the 7 in the date identify this scarcer 1807 Capped Bust variety, seen less often than the ubiquitous O-112. O-114 receives its own *Guide Book* listing, as the sole Large Stars, normal 50 C variety. A bit bright and mildly granular, but some luster is present, and no marks merit comment. (#6088)

2041 **1808 XF45 PCGS.** O-104, R.2. Original gray surfaces with deep steel toning at the borders, blended with faint traces of gold. (#6090)

2042 **1808 AU50 NGC.** O-109a, R.3. A number of die cracks on the obverse identify this die marriage, the most prominent a crack from the second 8 through the bust, and ending at the rim next to star 6. Clash marks are visible, and an impression of the shield is especially pronounced inside the upright of the L in LIBERTY, which appears serrated. The bust and eagle's wings are somewhat flat, as typically seen, but the stars are nicely detailed. Delightful luster gives this light gray piece excellent eye appeal. (#6090)

2043 **1808 AU50 NGC.** O-108, R.3. A die crack through portions of the reverse legend may be sufficient to call this O-108a. Pleasing gray-gold surfaces with hints of lighter silver luster. (#6090)

2044 **1808/7 XF40 NGC.** O-101, R.1. This nearly untoned half dollar has plentiful peripheral luster, although the portrait exhibits wear on the face on hair. Smooth overall despite a faint horizontal mark near the chin. (#6091)

Rare 1809 O-113a Half, VF Details

2045 **1809 Normal Edge—Improperly Cleaned—NCS. VF Details.** O-113a, R.5. The reverse has several fine peripheral die cracks. An elusive variety that is usually found only in low grades, with less than 10 pieces known finer than this coin. Deep gray surfaces with pale gold toning over lightly hairlined surfaces that retain traces of luster on the obverse. The sharpness grade that NCS assigned is somewhat conservative, in our opinion, despite a typical strike with the left (facing) wing nearly flat. (#6092)

Difficult XF O-114a 1809 Half

2046 **1809 Normal Edge XF40 NGC.** O-114a, R.5. A very scarce and distinctive variety with numerous die cracks and die chips along the reverse border. The devices show moderate wear consistent with the grade, but luster illuminates the margins. A few wispy marks on the field near the beak are of little import. (#6092)

2047 **1809 Normal Edge AU50 ICG.** O-115a, R.3. Luster emerges from protected regions of this lightly toned almond-gold Capped Bust half. No marks are consequential, although portions of the left (facing) wing are softly brought up. (#6092)

Pleasing 1809 Half Dollar, O-102, AU58

2048 **1809 AU58 PCGS.** O-102, R.1. Star 13 is close to the hair curl and there are a number of clash marks above the eagle's heads, identifying this variety. The edge features the distinctive XXX pattern as typically seen on Overton-102. Traces of luster accent the gunmetal-gray patina that covers both sides. Scattered abrasions define the grade, but none are particularly detracting. Sharply struck with lovely eye appeal. (#6092)

Attractive MS62 1809 Bust Half O-102a

2049 **1809 Normal Edge MS62 NGC.** O-102a, R.1. One of the curious varieties with clashed denticles in the field, here located beneath the scroll. Medium dove-gray toning is accompanied by peripheral powder-blue, lime, and russet. A couple of pale charcoal spots on the left obverse, but surprisingly unabraded. (#6092)

2050 **1810 AU55 PCGS.** O-102a, R.1. Star 12 has a trace of recutting, and there is a small die defect on Liberty's upper lip, identifying the obverse. The T in UNITED is also recut, which is diagnostic for the reverse. This later die state example has a die crack that encircles nearly all of the reverse lettering, in addition to several other cracks emanating from the date. A shallow scratch through Liberty's cheek is barely worthy of mention. Slate-gray and medium brown surround the perimeter, with a streak of russet across the reverse. Several darker spots are noted on the reverse. The top of the eagle's left wing is weakly struck, as usual, but the rest of the details are sharp. Flashy luster gives this piece delightful eye appeal. (#6095)

2051 **1810 AU58 NGC.** O-110, R.2. Star 13 has a blundered point that is close to the bust, which identifies the obverse. The reverse has the diagnostic joined AM in AMERICA, with the M slightly higher than the A. An arc of charcoal toning encircles the right side of the obverse, which contrasts sharply against the lightly toned remainder. The stars and dentils are weakly struck, as typically seen, but the rest of the details are well defined. (#6095)

2052 **1811 Large 8 AU55 NGC.** O-104, R.1. A die crack starts at the rim near star 7, crosses the cap, and encircles the bust on the right side, terminating below the lowest point of the bust. The reverse has a small center dot between crossbars 4 and 5. Plenty of luster gleams from the steel-gray surfaces. A couple of stars show excellent definition, and the only prominent area of weakness is the hair beneath the cap. Minimally marked with great eye appeal. (#6096)

2053 **1811 Small 8 AU55 PCGS.** O-110a, R.1. The date slants sharply to the left on this variety, and the reverse has a die crack from the edge near the olive leaves through the top of UNITED and ending at the rim above the first S in STATES. Medium gray and amber patina in the recesses accents the charming light silver toning. Significant luster throughout enhances the eye appeal of this crisply struck representative. (#6097)

2054 **1811 Small 8 AU55 PCGS.** O-111, R.1. Incorrectly designated by PCGS as a Large 8 variety. The borders are originally toned in golden-brown and ocean-blue. Luster shimmers from the design when this unblemished example is rotated. Liberty's chin is widely strike doubled. (#6097)

2055 **1811 Small 8 AU58 PCGS.** O-111, R.1. A faint die lump below Liberty's ear identifies the obverse, and the IT in UNITED are touching, which is diagnostic for the reverse. Plenty of eye-catching luster radiates from the light gray surfaces of this carefully preserved piece. The stars on the right are sharp, as are the dentils, but there is the typical weakness on the left stars and the tops of the eagle's wings. Both sides show clashmarks in the fields, in addition to a number of tiny die lumps throughout. An interesting and appealing example. (#6097)

2056 1811 Small 8 AU58 PCGS. O-108, R.2. The 8 is crudely engraved with two overlapping circles, which identifies the obverse. A tiny spike at the tip of the eagle's right (facing) wing is diagnostic for the reverse. Outstanding luster enhances the eye appeal of this attractive, silver-gray piece. The reverse is exceptionally sharp, while the obverse exhibits the typical weakness on the stars and several hair curls. (#6097)

Pleasing Select O-103 1812 Half

2057 1812 MS63 PCGS. O-103, R.1. Faint vertical die lines beneath the beak decide the variety. Delicate gold toning adorns this lustrous and unblemished Bust half dollar. All design elements are crisply impressed aside from the right-side stars. Multiply clashed beneath UNUM. Population: 46 in 63, 72 finer (8/08). (#6100)

2058 1813 Over UNI AU53 NGC. O-101, High R.3. A trace of an inverted UNI is visible at the denomination, which is diagnostic for this variety. There are also prominent clashmarks on both sides, and several outlines of a retrograde LIBERTY are visible beneath the eagle's right (facing) wing, which indicates that the dies clashed on more than one occasion. Mottled deep gray and brown toning covers both sides of this interesting specimen. The stars on the right are sharply struck, while the left stars are weak, as usual. The same pattern of softness is noted on the eagle's wings, but the rest of the details are well defined. A couple of marks on each side are masked by the dramatic toning. (#6104)

2059 1813 AU50 PCGS. O-102, High R.3. The dentils are nearly flat, as typically seen for this variety, and on the reverse the upright of the E in the motto is centered under the D in UNITED. An arc of purple toning at the lower left of the reverse contrasts nicely against the medium gray patina, while the reverse has accents of gold toning around the rims. The obverse shows clashmarks from the eagle, with the vertical lines of the shield visible on Liberty's temple and partially obscuring the bottom of the motto. Traces of mint luster sparkle in the fields. (#6103)

2060 1813 AU55 PCGS. O-106a, R.2. Star 7 is recut and UNITED is exceptionally weak, which are the two major diagnostics for this die marriage. O-106a differs slightly with two faint die cracks: one from the rim through the bottom of UNITED, the other joining the olive branch and the denomination. The surfaces are mostly brilliant save for a trace of hazel around the perimeter. Prominent clashmarks are visible on both sides with a retrograde LIBERTY fully apparent on the reverse. An interesting and lustrous example with great eye appeal. (#6103)

Impressive 1813 Half Dollar, O-107, MS63

2061 1813 MS63 NGC. CAC. O-107, R.1. Star 10 is recut, which is diagnostic for the obverse, while the reverse is easily identified by a die line from the rim to the leaves. Pleasing violet and gunmetal-gray toning surrounds the silver-gray centers of this lustrous piece. The details are nearly full, and there are no bothersome marks on either side. A wonderful representative for a type collector. Housed in an old NGC holder. (#6103)

2062 1814 AU50 NGC. O-103, R.1. The heavy vertical die line beneath the left scroll end is diagnostic. This pleasing silver-gray half dollar has noticeable cartwheel luster, and both sides lack any detectable marks. Struck from boldly clashed dies. (#6105)

Important Gem 1814 O-109 Half Dollar

2063 1814 MS65 PCGS. CAC. O-109, R.2. Golden-brown hints visit peripheral elements, but this fully lustrous Gem is only lightly toned. All stars are fully struck, and a trace of incomplete definition is only encountered on the top of the eagle's head and the leftmost portion of the scroll. This well preserved beauty is certain to hold a place of honor within an advanced collection. Population: 9 in 65, 2 finer (8/08). (#6105)

2064 1815/2—Improperly Cleaned—NCS. AG Details. O-101, High R.2. The only known die variety. This is a heavily worn item which has been improperly cleaned, at some point in its history. An affordable piece, from a scarce, low mintage issue. (#6108)

2065 1815/2—Plugged, Improperly Cleaned—NCS. VF Details. O-101, High R.2. The only die marriage known. With a mintage (47,150 pieces) many multiples lower than every other Capped Bust half dollar, the 1815/2 is by far the scarcest issue in the series. Myriad abrasions cover the surfaces of this pale silver-gray example. The plug above Liberty does not affect the obverse details, but the denomination on the reverse has been poorly re-engraved. Verdigris obscures some tooling in the field above Liberty, and also partially covers the cap. An evenly worn and affordable representative. (#6108)

Desirable 1815/2 Half Dollar, XF Sharpness

2066 **1815/2—Improperly Cleaned—NCS. XF Details.** O-101, High R.2. The overdate instantly identifies this variety. Deep patina envelops both sides because of a prior cleaning, but the surfaces are remarkably unabraded. Several clash marks are noted on the reverse. The strike is crisp, and a small blemish near star 13 is barely worthy of mention. Still a lovely example of this popular variety. (#6108)

Popular 1815/2 Half Dollar, XF Sharpness

2067 **1815/2—Improperly Cleaned—NCS. XF Details.** O-101, High R.2. The only variety known. Deep gunmetal-gray patina covers both sides. The stars are soft, as typical, but the rest of the details are boldly defined. The surfaces appear remarkably smooth to the unaided eye, and a close examination reveals no significant marks. A splendid example of this desirable variety despite cleaning. *From The Morton J. Greene Collection.* (#6108)

Delightful 1817/3 Half Dollar, O-101, Choice AU

2068 **1817/3 AU55 NGC.** O-101, R.3. This is the only variety that features the 17 over 13 overdate, and it is distinguished from O-101a because it has no die cracks on the reverse. The underdigit 3 is exceptionally clear. Lovely medium gray patina graces this sharply struck and carefully preserved representative. A few minute marks on Liberty's cheek do not detract from the splendid eye appeal. (#6111)

2069 **1817 AU55 PCGS.** O-110a, R.2. Both dies have the cracks listed in Overton for O-110a. This lovely Choice AU piece has bright silver luster and traces of peripheral gold. (#6109)

2070 **1818 AU58 PCGS. CAC.** O-107, R.1. The mouth is slightly open and the date is closely spaced, which is diagnostic for the obverse. Two minuscule tines at the top of the eagle's beak identify the reverse. The usual clashmarks from the reverse are especially pronounced on this piece, with an impression of the vertical lines of the shield on Liberty's ear, hair, and the motto. Gold to medium brown toning encircles the mostly brilliant centers, and pleasing satiny luster radiates from the minimally marked surfaces. The strike is sharp save for slight weakness on a couple of hair curls and the arrowheads. (#6113)

2071 **1818/7 Small 8 AU53 NGC.** O-102a, R.2. The first 8 is small, and the second 8 is not only punched over a 7, but now also has a small die break in the upper loop. Pleasing violet patina in the periphery accents the silver-gray centers. Liberty's hair and the tops of the eagle's wings are a trifle soft, but the rest of the details are boldly defined. A minimally marked and significantly lustrous representative. (#6114)

2072 **1818/7 Large 8 AU55 PCGS.** O-101, R.1. PCGS incorrectly labeled this piece as a Small 8 overdate. Both sides have wonderful silver surfaces with frosty luster and peripheral gold toning, accented by cobalt-blue. (#6115)

2073 **1819 AU58 NGC.** O-114, R.3. NGC misattributed this piece as O-111. It is a lovely near-Mint example with a trace of highpoint wear on both sides. The surfaces have virtually complete satin luster with brilliant gold toning. (#6117)

Vibrant 1819/8, Small 9, Half Dollar, O-101, Choice Mint State

2074 **1819/8 Small 9 MS64 NGC.** O-101. A small 9 is punched over an 8, which is clearly visible underneath. The reverse is identified by the triple dentil below the 0 in the denomination. Vibrant rainbow toning covers both sides, with arcs of gold, teal, lavender, and slate-gray that give this piece spectacular eye appeal. This minimally marked example exhibits a sharp strike and impressive satiny luster. (#6118)

Colorful MS62 1819/8 Half Dollar Large 9, Scarce O-103 Marriage

2075 **1819/8 Large 9 MS62 PCGS.** O-103, R.5 for the major die state, R.4 for the die marriage. Beautifully toned in jade-green, golden-brown, and dove-gray. Splendidly devoid of consequential contact, and luster encompasses the open fields. Housed in a green label holder. Population: 4 in 62, 11 finer (8/08). (#6119)

Splendid 1819/8 O-104 Half, MS63

2076 **1819/8 Large 9 MS63 PCGS.** O-104, R.1. Probably a Census level example of the variety, one of only half a dozen pieces known in Mint State grades. A boldly defined representative, this half dollar has satiny silver luster with attractive gold, russet, and iridescent toning. (#6119)

Lovely 1820 Half Dollar, O-107, Choice Very Fine

2077 **1820 No Serifs on Es VF35 NGC.** O-107, R.5. This scarce and interesting variety is easily distinguished because none of the A's have right serifs and likewise all of the E's are missing their left serifs. Pale gray patina endows the surfaces of this evenly worn specimen. Traces of luster remain in the protected areas, which is remarkable given the grade. Scattered abrasions and a tiny spot below the eagle's head keep this charming piece from a higher grade. (#6124)

2078 **1821 AU58 NGC.** O-105, R.1. Nearly full satin luster is intermingled with pale gray and gold toning on this lovely half dollar. The 1821 is an excellent earlier date for type collectors. (#6128)

2079 **1821 MS61 PCGS.** O-103, R.2. The obverse has a prominent center dot, and stars 1 and 13 nearly touch the bust. The reverse is easily identified because the right serifs of the A's and the left serifs of the E's are missing. Delightful gunmetal-gray patina drapes the surfaces of this intricately preserved specimen. Flashes of luster give this piece wonderful eye appeal. (#6128)

Attractive 1822 Half Dollar, O-105, MS63

2080 **1822 MS63 NGC.** O-105, R.3. This is the only use of this reverse, which has several diagnostic die dots to the right of the eagle's neck. A delicate die crack extends through OF AMERIC and is often seen in various stages on this variety. Accents of gold around the perimeter mix with the mottled slate and silver-gray patina that covers the remainder of the surfaces. The strike is bold, and there are no marks of any significance. Plenty of luster throughout gives this piece excellent eye appeal.
From The Menlo Park Collection. (#6129)

2081 **1823 AU58 NGC.** O-112, R.1. The 3 is normal, but much taller than usual for the 1823 half dollars. Nearly full satin luster can be seen beneath the moderate gray-gold toning. This piece has a remarkably sharp double profile. (#6131)

2082 **1824/4 AU55 NGC.** O-110, R.2. This gunmetal-gray Choice AU half has plentiful mint sheen, and a thorough pass beneath a loupe fails to locate marks. Well struck except for the stars. (#6140)

2083 **1825 AU58 PCGS.** O-108, Low R.4. The 2 in the date has a thick base, which identifies the obverse, and the M in AMERICA is recut and slightly higher than the first A, which it touches. Dazzling cartwheel luster glides across the exceptionally clean surfaces. A touch of light tan toning at the rims is the only hint of color on this silver-gray representative. An attractive, solidly struck example with just a trace of softness on the stars and hair. (#6142)

2084 **1825 AU58 PCGS.** O-112, R.3. The stars are large and close to the dentils, and AME in AMERICA is connected at the bottoms of the letters. Flashy luster accents the boldly struck devices, with slight weakness on the stars and a couple of hair curls. Mostly brilliant save for a few light spots of toning. This minimally marked and briefly circulated specimen would make an excellent representative. (#6142)

2085 **1826 MS61 NGC.** O-114, High R.4. This obverse is also used for O-113, so this variety can best be identified by the reverse. The denticles on the obverse of O-114, however, are typically flat, which is a good indication of the variety. On the reverse, the upper angle of the N in UNITED is partially filled, and there is a tiny center dot between crossbars 3 and 4. The fields are exceptionally clean on this bright, light gray representative, which exhibits impressive luster throughout. The milling and stars are flat, as usual, and the outermost tips of the stars and letters are fading into the rims, which is typical of this late die state. (#6143)

Satiny Choice 1826 Half Dollar, O-117

2086 **1826 MS64 PCGS.** O-117, R.2. This nondescript variety is confirmed by the first line in the fifth vertical shield stripe, which extends to the third horizontal line. A satiny cream-gray and apple-green near-Gem. Uncommonly void of marks, and sharply struck aside from a few star centers. A beautiful representative of the Capped Bust type. (#6143)

2087 **1827 Square Base 2 AU55 PCGS.** O-120, R.2. Multiple die lines beneath the left side of the bust are characteristic the obverse, while the reverse has a high C in the denomination that nearly touches the stem. The left side of the I in PLURIBUS is centered under the right side of the upright of the T in STATES. Lavender, red, and lemon toning in the fields enhances the eye appeal of this lustrous piece. The strike is crisp save for the usual weakness on the stars. (#6144)

2088 **1827 Square Base 2 AU58 PCGS.** O-138, R.4. Straight die lines below the eagle's head identify the reverse, and the C in the denomination is the smallest used for this date. This is the only use of this reverse die. Hints of yellow and lilac toning accent the steel-gray centers, and splendid cartwheel luster highlights the boldly struck devices, save for the usual softness on the highest hair curls and the stars. The surfaces have virtually no marks and the eye appeal is excellent. (#6144)

2089 **1827 Square Base 2 AU58 PCGS.** O-105, R.3. Splashes of copper-gold toning enrich the peripheries of this shimmering example. The stars are blunt, but all other design details are sharply struck. Marks are surprisingly scarce. Produced from clashed dies. (#6144)

Well Struck 1827 Square Base 2 Fifty Cent MS62, O-133

2090 **1827 Square Base 2 MS62 NGC.** O-133, R.4. The scarce Overton-133 has several diagnostics, such as several repunched stars, a diagonal die line in the field above the right (facing) claw, two "spikes" extending from the top of the left (facing) wing into the field (these show clearly on the 2005 Parsley/Overton plate coin), and a line above the LI in LIBERTY. Splashes of electric-blue and purple toning visit the luminous surfaces of this well struck specimen. A few trivial obverse marks are not bothersome. (#6144)

Charming 1827 Square Base 2 Half Dollar, O-126, MS63

2091 **1827 Square Base 2 MS63 PCGS.** O-126, R.2. A die break through the lowest hair curl helps identify the obverse, and there is also a thin die crack through the 182 in the date. Several vertical lines in the shield extend as far as crossbars 2 and 3 (from the bottom). Pleasing violet toning drapes the obverse, while the reverse exhibits lilac and rose in the margins. Dazzling satiny luster complements the sharply defined details of this attractive specimen. (#6144)

2092 **1828 Square Base 2, Small 8, Large Letters AU58 NGC.** O-113, R.3. This interesting variety has a slightly raised area around the olive leaves due to unfinished die work. The stars are drawn close to the edge, and the obverse, which was also used to strike O-112, no longer has die lines near the date. Silver-gray centers contrast nicely against the medium gray and gold toning around the rims. This briefly circulated representative has a few insignificant marks and lots of flashy luster. (#6151)

Lovely 1828 Square Base 2, Small 8 Half Dollar, O-115, MS63

2093 **1828 Square Base 2, Small 8, Large Letters MS63 PCGS.** O-115, R.2. This variety can best be distinguished by the reverse, which has a number of die lines from the motto to the top of the left wing, including a "spike" at the outer edge of the wing. On the obverse, star 13 nearly touches the hair curl. Medium and silver-gray toning mix across the surfaces of this carefully preserved piece. A few darker spots of toning are noted on the obverse, but both sides are nearly devoid of marks. The strike is bold save for the usual weakness on the stars. Several die cracks are noted on the reverse. A handsome piece with lots of luster. (#6151)

Delightful 1828 Square Base 2 Half Dollar, O-122, MS63

2094 **1828 Square Base 2, Small 8, Large Letters MS63 NGC.** O-122, R.3. A broken rim between stars 5 and 6 identifies the obverse, and there is a small patch of die defect lines to the left of the date. The M in AMERICA is noticeably lower than the adjacent E, which is diagnostic for the reverse. Charming violet toning encircles the perimeter, while lovely rose color graces the centers. Bright luster shines beneath the attractive toning and complements the sharply struck details. Housed in an old NGC holder. (#6151)

2095 **1829/7 AU55 PCGS.** O-101a, R.1. A large 5 in the denomination is diagnostic for this die marriage, which is one of only two varieties that feature an overdate. O-101a was struck from a relapped reverse die, and the shafts of the arrows are now barely visible. The bottoms of the 2 and 7 are visible at the bases of the 2 and the 9. Deep amber, brown, and dark purple toning covers both sides of this magnificent specimen. The surfaces are clean save for a couple of inconsequential marks, and the stars are sharply defined. Slight weakness is noted on the hair below the Liberty Cap. (#6155)

2096 **1829/1827 AU55 NGC.** O-102, R.2. A partly lustrous Choice AU Bust half that has an unabraded pearl-gray appearance. A crisply struck example of the popular *Guide Book* overdate. (#6155)

2097 **1829/7 AU58 NGC.** O-102, R.2. For many years this overdate was called "1829/1" but it is now recognized as an 1829/7 overdate. Actually, 1829/1827 would be more accurate, as all four digits show clear doubling. Fully lustrous light gray surfaces exhibit reflective silver fields. (#6155)

2098 **1829/7 MS61 NGC.** O-101a, R.1. A later die state with the reverse showing signs of lapping or resurfacing, including missing tail feathers and arrow shafts. This delightful half dollar has frosty silver luster beneath gray, gold, and steel patina. (#6155)

2099 **1829 Small Letters AU58 NGC.** O-105, R.1. Luster fills the borders and eagle of this briefly circulated Bust half. Light golden-brown overall with glimpses of aqua-blue across the obverse. The surfaces are pleasantly devoid of marks, and the eye appeal is exemplary. (#6154)

2100 **1829 Small Letters MS62 PCGS.** O-112a, R.2. Light caramel-gold toning is uniform aside from glimpses of forest-green and fire-red near the peripheries. A satiny and generally smooth piece that is well struck save for the center of the first star. (#6154)

2101 **1830 Small 0 AU58 NGC.** O-115, R.2. The 3 in the date is lower than the other three digits, and there are numerous die defect lines below the bust, identifying this variety. On the reverse, the eagle's left (facing) tailfeather extends slightly below the olive branch. Although not mentioned in Overton, there is a faint trace of repunching above the 8 in the date. Splendid violet and hazel toning surrounds the silver-gray centers of this lustrous and sharply struck piece. There are no detracting marks save for a small spot below Liberty's chin, and a retained lamination is noted to the right of the date. (#6156)

2102 **1830 Small 0 MS62 PCGS.** O-102, R.3. Ocean-blue, yellow-gold, stone-gray, and russet-red enrich this satiny and minimally abraded Bust half. Crisply struck except for softness on the center of star 8. (#6156)

Elegant 1830 O-119 Medium 0 Half, MS63

2103 **1830 Medium 0 MS63 PCGS.** O-119, R.1. Incorrectly described as a Small 0 on the holder. One of the common varieties of 1830, yet elusive in Mint State grades. This example probably ranks as one of the 10 finest representatives of the die marriage. There are three distinct sizes of the 0 in the date, called Small, Medium, and Large, although usually only the Small 0 and Large 0 are recognized. The Small 0 is smaller than the adjacent 3, the Medium 0 is about the same size as the 3, and the Large 0 is taller than the 3. Lustrous ivory and cream with champagne and iridescent toning on both sides. A wonderful example. (#6156)

Choice 1830 Small 0 Half Dollar, O-109

2104 **1830 Small 0 MS64 PCGS.** O-109, R.3. The 8 in the date is widely recut within the upper loop. Variegated golden-brown enriches this lustrous near-Gem. The strike is sharp, and the fields are impressively devoid of contact. The portrait has minor marks, but the eye appeal is undeniable. Population: 78 in 64, 19 finer (8/08). (#6156)

2105 **1830 Large 0 AU58 NGC.** O-120, R.1. The 0 is large and higher than the other three digits of the date, and the left side of the second T in STATES is aligned above the right side of the I in PLURIBUS. Medium gray patina shows lovely accents of gold around the rims. Nearly all the stars have fully defined centrils, and the strike is sharp save for the usual weakness on the highest points of the hair. Magnificent luster shimmers across the minimally marked fields. (#6157)

2106 **1831 AU58 NGC.** O-104, R.1. A number of die lines below the bust identify the obverse, and another die defect through the upper berry of the olive branch is diagnostic for the reverse. This briefly circulated example has a peppering of light hazel toning across the bright silver-gray surfaces, which exhibit dazzling luster throughout. The URI in PLURIBUS and a couple of hair curls are weak, as usual, but the stars are all sharply struck. A close inspection with a loupe reveals only a couple of tiny marks on the obverse. (#6159)

2107 **1831 AU58 NGC.** O-119, R.3. Partial cartwheel luster confirms the proximity to Mint State, although the cheek and bust tip show light wear. This crisply struck and charming half dollar has no mentionable marks. (#6159)

2108 **1831 AU58 NGC.** O-109, R.1. This satiny deep dove-gray Borderline Uncirculated half lacks consequential marks, and the strike is bold apart from bluntness on the star centers. (#6159)

2109 **1831 AU58 NGC.** O-104, R.1. Distinguished by die lines below the bust and a line through the leftmost olive berry. A pleasing piece that shows ample luster with just a touch of friction on the high points and splashes of violet and green-gold at the margins. The center of the word PLURIBUS is missing, possibly due to a filled die. (#6159)

2110 **1831 MS61 NGC.** O-101, R.2. Light chestnut toning visits this lustrous and undisturbed representative. The overall strike is good, despite a few flat stars and some weakness near the E in STATES. (#6159)

2111 **1831 MS62 NGC.** O-110, R.2. The 18 is noticeably higher than the 31 in the date, and the stars are typically drawn to the edge, which is diagnostic for this obverse die. On the reverse, the base of the A in STATES is noticeably lower than the second T. Dramatic gold, blue, and violet toning endows the obverse, which contrasts sharply against the mostly brilliant reverse. Several stars are soft, as usual, but the rest of the details are powerfully impressed. A lightly abraded, vividly lustrous, and attractive piece. (#6159)

Lovely Select 1831 Half Dollar, O-104

2112 **1831 MS63 PCGS.** O-104, R.1. A faint die defect line pierces the upper olive berry and the first 1 in the date is notably higher than the 8. This is a late die state example of Overton-104: the top of the 5 in the denomination is barely visible and the die lines that are normally apparent below the bust are no longer there. Streaks of lemon-yellow, hazel, and slate-gray drape both sides of this carefully preserved specimen. The centers are sharply struck, while the stars show the usual weakness and are drawn to the edge. There are no mentionable marks and plenty of flashy luster. (#6159)

Charming Select O-119 1831 Half Dollar

2113 **1831 MS63 PCGS.** O-119, R.3. This intricately struck half dollar provides unbroken cartwheel sheen and displays attractive chestnut-tan and ivory-gray toning. No marks are remotely worthy of comment. The population reports suggest higher graded pieces are available, but those in search of a quality example of the 1831 need look no further. (#6159)

Lightly Toned Choice 1831 Half, O-119

2114 **1831 MS64 NGC.** O-119, R.3. A later die state without obverse die lines at 7:30. This lustrous near-Gem has light tan toning and is precisely struck near the centers. A few peripheral elements lack a full impression. Careful inspection fails to locate any remotely mentionable marks. (#6159)

2115 **1832 Small Letters AU55 PCGS.** O-118, R.1. An essentially brilliant Choice AU half that boasts substantial luster and nearly unblemished surfaces. Housed in an old green label holder. (#6160)

2116 **1832 Small Letters AU58 NGC.** O-116, R.3. Golden-brown and ocean-blue toning graces the margins of this lustrous half dollar. Friction is minimal, and the fields and devices are unblemished. (#6160)

2117 **1832 Small Letters AU58 NGC.** O-106, R.1. Luster sweeps the open fields, and only telltale friction on the cheek precludes designation as Mint State. Boldly struck and lightly toned with marks noted near star 10 and the upper arrow. (#6160)

2118 **1832 Small Letters AU58 NGC.** O-102, R.1. Wispy golden-brown and pale gray patina appears over satiny silver luster on this pleasing near-Mint example. (#6160)

2119 **1832 Small Letters AU58 NGC.** O-118, R.1. Just a trace of wear appears at the highpoints of the design on this lustrous near-Mint example of the Laced Lips variety. Both sides are untoned with frosty silver luster. (#6160)

2120 **1832 Small Letters AU58 NGC.** O-107, R.2. Rich russet-red, apple-green, and pearl-gray encompasses this satiny and nearly unabraded near-Mint half. The stars are generally flat, but the strike is otherwise good. (#6160)

2121 **1832 Small Letters AU58 NGC.** O-118, R.1. Known as the "laced lips" variety for the vertical die line through Liberty's lips. Fully lustrous and delightful, exhibiting brilliant silver surfaces with a faint trace of subliminal toning. A plentiful variety, apparently always from perfect dies. (#6160)

2122 **1832 Small Letters MS61 NGC.** O-102, R.1. On the reverse, the arrowheads are malformed and solidly joined. A tiny die lump is noted at the tip of the eagle's right (facing) wing. A weakly struck example with greenish-gold toning near the peripheries. (#6160)

2123 **1832 Small Letters MS61 NGC.** O-110, R.1. A spike at the top of the cap identifies the obverse, and the 5 in the denomination is slightly recut on the outer curve. Significant luster shimmers beneath the gunmetal-gray patina, which has splendid accents of rose and russet toning around the perimeter. A streak of darker toning bisects the reverse. The details are boldly impressed with excellent sharpness on several stars and the motto on the reverse, save for the usual weakness on the A in STATES. Several marks define the grade, and a shallow dig is noted near star 10. (#6160)

2124 **1832 Small Letters MS61 NGC.** O-103, R.1. A satiny Mint State piece with pale gray patina, framed by amber, russet, and iridescent toning. (#6160)

Lustrous 1832 Small Letters Half Dollar, O-110, MS63

2125 **1832 Small Letters MS63 PCGS.** O-110, R.1. A "spike" at the top of the cap typically identifies the obverse, but one must be careful because this same defect is sometimes seen on O-109, which shares the same obverse. The 5 in the denomination is slightly recut on the outer curve, which is diagnostic for the reverse. This bright silver-gray piece has a brilliant obverse that contrasts nicely against the lightly toned reverse. Several tiny dark toning spots on each side barely affect the magnificent satiny luster that graces both sides of this minimally marked specimen. The central design elements are sharply struck, with the typical softness on the stars and the LURIB in PLURIBUS. (#6160)

Impressive 1832 Small Letters Half Dollar, O-103, MS64

2126 **1832 Small Letters MS64 NGC.** O-103, R.1. Star 8 is closely spaced to the cap, which is a helpful diagnostic for the obverse. The 5 in the denomination is recut and the AM in AMERICA are nearly touching, which identifies the reverse. Faint clash marks are visible in the reverse field. Lavender and rose-gold toning in the periphery accents the silver-gray that drapes the centers. Impressive satiny luster shimmers throughout and highlights the exquisitely detailed design elements. An appealing near-Gem specimen. (#6160)

2127 **1833 AU58 NGC.** O-102, R.1. An impressive cream-gray example with satiny luster and no remotely mentionable marks. A lovely near-Mint Capped Bust half. (#6163)

2128 **1833 AU58 PCGS.** O-110, R.1. A sharply struck near-Mint half dollar with original pearl-gray and olive-gold toning. The fields have a few faint marks. Encapsulated in a first generation holder. (#6163)

2129 **1833 MS61 NGC.** O-104, R.1. The date is low and evenly spaced as opposed to the exceptionally high denomination. Impressive satiny luster accents the powerfully impressed design elements. A trace of charcoal toning on the rims is the only area of color on this otherwise brilliant representative. Scattered abrasions on the bust limit the grade, but none merit individual mention. (#6163)

2130 **1833 MS62 PCGS.** O-105, R.2. A recut second S in STATES makes positive attribution a cinch. Chestnut-gold and gunmetal-blue toning enriches this satiny and unmarked example. Some incompleteness of strike is present on the claws and facial curls. (#6163)

Pleasing 1833 Half Dollar, O-106, Choice Uncirculated

2131 **1833 MS64 NGC.** O-106, R.2. A delicate vertical line joins Liberty's lips (often called "laced lips") and chin, distinguishing the obverse. The 50 in the denomination is closely spaced and the top of 5 is unusually tapered, which is diagnostic for the reverse. Another identifier is the slight filling in the upper curve of the S in PLURIBUS. A dusting of russet and violet accents the obverse, while the reverse is entirely brilliant. Liberty's hair, the top of the eagle's right (facing) wing, and several letters in PLURIBUS are soft, as typically seen. A highly lustrous and handsome representative. (#6163)

2132 **1834 Large Date, Large Letters AU58 NGC.** O-103, R.3. The 1 in the date is significantly higher than the 8, and the tip of the eagle's left tail feather crosses the olive branch. Splendid satiny luster shimmers beneath the light to medium gray toning. All of the stars are sharply defined, and the only areas of weakness are minor, with several hair curls, part of the eagle's left (facing) wing, and the IBU in PLURIBUS soft. A lightly abraded and appealing example. (#6164)

2133 **1834 Large Date, Large Letters AU58 NGC.** O-102, R.1. A shimmering gunmetal-gray half with peripheral glimpses of chestnut toning. Splendidly free from marks. With careful purchases, the AU58 grade provides good value for this type, since one receives a coin with nearly full luster and detail for about one-third the price of an MS63. (#6164)

2134 **1834 Large Date, Large Letters AU58 NGC.** O-102, R.1. Golden-brown enriches the obverse margin, although the obverse center and the reverse are only faintly toned. This lustrous half is attentively struck aside from a few blunt right-side stars. A strike-through is noted within the space between STATES and OF. (#6164)

2135 **1834 Large Date, Large Letters MS61 NGC.** O-101, R.1. The obverse has Liberty's forecurl joined to form one solid piece, rather than the usual separate curls. This pleasing piece has satiny luster beneath gray and gold toning with faint traces of blue. (#6164)

2136 **1834 Large Date, Small Letters AU58 NGC.** O-107, R.1. Light autumn-gold patina congregates along the margins of this satiny and nearly Uncirculated Capped Bust half. The absence of detrimental marks ensures the eye appeal. (#6165)

2137 **1834 Large Date, Small Letters AU58 PCGS.** O-106, R.1. A large crude 4 in the date is cut over a small 4. The M in AMERICA is recut along the left side. This is a lustrous, slightly toned representative, with a faint golden cast across both sides. Traces of highpoint wear keep it from receiving a Mint State grade, but surface marks are minimal. (#6165)

2138 **1834 Large Date, Small Letters MS62 NGC.** O-105, R.1. A tall, recut 4 identifies this obverse, while the reverse is distinguished by a recut ATES and a die line between STATES and OF. Lovely shades of maroon, cobalt blue, teal, and violet border this impressive specimen. Dazzling luster shimmers from the minimally marked fields. A little weakness is noted on the stars, hair curls, and eagle's wings, as typically seen. (#6165)

2139 **1834 Small Date, Small Letters AU58 NGC.** O-116, R.2. Although the mouth is typically open, this piece is a trifle soft in that area and the lips appear joined. Nonetheless, the obverse can be identified by the small and close date. Crossbars 4 and 5 extend into the right wing on the reverse, and the A in STATES and the URI in PLURIBUS are weakly struck, which is typical for this variety. A touch of rose toning in the fields accents the silver-gray patina that covers the rest of the surfaces. Several abrasions in the fields are entirely inconsequential. (#6166)

2140 **1834 Small Date, Small Letters AU58 NGC.** O-113, R.1. This variety can be difficult to attribute, especially when several of the key diagnostic areas are weakly defined. A sharply curled upper lip aids in the attribution of the obverse. On the reverse, a trace of a first engraving of the E in the motto is visible to the right of its present location. The URI in PLURIBUS is flat, as often seen, and the stars and hair curls are also soft. Hints of amber toning in the periphery accent the medium gray devices. A small patch of charcoal toning is noted to the left of the eagle's head for identification purposes. This minimally marked and attractive example would make a wonderful representative of a late Bust half dollar. (#6166)

2141 **1834 Small Date, Small Letters AU58 NGC.** O-121, R.3. Rich aquamarine and pearl-gray graces this well defined and lightly abraded near-Mint half. The reverse has nearly full luster, as do the stars and hair. (#6166)

2142 **1834 Small Date, Small Letters MS62 PCGS.** O-113, R.1. There are several key diagnostics for this variety: star 13 is recut, there are die lines under the clasp on Liberty's shoulder, and a trace of an E is visible between E and PLURIBUS. An arc of teal, maroon, blue, and gold toning graces the lower right obverse rim, while a faint yellow hue imbues the remainder of the perimeter. Several hair curls, the stars, the URIB in PLURIBUS, and the tops of the eagle's wings are weakly struck, as typically seen. Charming satiny luster shimmers across the minimally marked surfaces. (#6166)

2143 **1835 AU58 PCGS.** O-106, R.1. The recut 5 in the date helps identify the variety. Dusky lavender, sea-green, gold, and ruby-red envelop this crisply impressed and moderately abraded near-Mint half. (#6168)

Colorful Gem 1835 Half Dollar, O-103

2144 **1835 MS65 NGC.** O-103, R.2. Sea-green and cherry-red embrace this deeply toned and lustrous Gem. Splendidly free from marks, and the strike is good with only moderate blending on the curls near the ear and on the junction of the left (facing) wing with the shield. Surely among the finest survivors of the variety. Census: 14 in 65, 6 finer (7/08). (#6168)

2145 **1836 Lettered Edge MS62 PCGS.** O-101a, R.1. A small die spur attached to the bottom of the 6 in the date, as well as a recut star 6, is diagnostic for this obverse. Stars 7 and 11 are also recut, but it is less evident on this specimen. The loop of the 5 in the denomination is nearly closed, and a die crack from the edge through the tip of the left (facing) wing and two olive leaves identifies this later die state example. Flashy luster accents the light to medium gray toned surfaces. The hair beneath the cap is a trifle soft, and the crossbars on the shield lack definition, which is typical for this variety. The rest of the design elements, however, are nearly full. An attractive example of this late Bust half dollar issue. (#6169)

2146 **1836 Lettered Edge MS62 PCGS.** O-122, R.2. A small tine extends to the left of the upper serif of the E in STATES, distinguishing this die marriage. Violet and gold toning surrounds the silver-gray centers of both sides, but the reverse is particularly vibrant. Flashy luster radiates from the minimally marked surfaces. Sharply struck with fully defined stars and boldly impressed devices. (#6169)

2147 **1836 Lettered Edge MS62 NGC.** O-110, R.1. Star 7 shows faint recutting, as does the end of the olive branch directly above the C in the denomination. A number of vertical stripes connect to the second crossbar, which is another diagnostic for the reverse. Deep gunmetal-gray patina envelops the surfaces of this minimally marked representative. A nearly imperceptible scratch is noted above the date, but the rest of the fields are smooth. The left stars and several letters in LIBERTY are softly struck, but the rest of the details are razor-sharp. (#6169)

2148 **1836 Lettered Edge MS62 PCGS.** A frosty mint state piece with brilliant silver luster and strong design details at the centers. Heavy flow lines are evident, creating exceptional luster. (#6169)

Richly Toned Gem 1836 Half Dollar, O-114

2149 **1836 Lettered Edge MS65 NGC.** O-114, R.2. A honey-gold Gem that has glimpses of russet throughout the margins. The cheekbone has moderate contact, but the overall preservation is impeccable. The cartwheel luster is booming, and the strike is crisp save for the RIB in PLURIBUS. (#6169)

REEDED EDGE HALF DOLLARS

Transitional 1836 Reeded Edge Half, VF30

2150 **1836 Reeded Edge VF30 PCGS. CAC.** An attractive, originally toned example of the transitional Capped Bust, Reeded Edge half dollar, with pewter gray fields and lighter tan devices. Although listed in the *Guide Book* and collected along other regular issue half dollars, this variety is also listed in the pattern references as Judd-57 or Pollock-60. (#6175)

Pleasing 1836 Reeded Edge Half, XF40

2151 **1836 Reeded Edge XF40 PCGS.** Discussing the 1836 Reeded Edge halves, Andrew Pollock, III, wrote: "Although Davis, Adams-Woodin, and Judd included them as part of the pattern series, many others have considered them to be a regular-issue, struck for circulation, possibly in 1837, using planchets of the fineness specified by the Act of January 18, 1837." This example has smooth surfaces with deep steel-gray on both sides, and splashes of lighter silver on the highpoints of the design. (#6175)

Appealing 1836 Reeded Edge Half Dollar, AU55

2152 **1836 Reeded Edge AU55 NGC.** The Reeded Edge 50 CENTS reverse came with a mintage of 1,200 or so pieces in 1836. This Choice AU example displays silver-gray surfaces that retain luster in the recessed areas, and the design features are well defined, save for minor softness in the left (facing) claw. A few minute circulation marks do not detract from the overall eye appeal (#6175)

2153 **1837 AU58 NGC.** Well-defined with strong, satiny luster and minimal patina. Only a touch of friction and the occasional faint abrasion visit the otherwise pleasingly preserved surfaces. (#6176)

2154 **1837 AU58 NGC.** A light layer of golden-tan toning embraces the highly lustrous surfaces, which show only scant evidence of friction. Pleasingly detailed with the reverse rotated approximately 45 degrees counterclockwise. (#6176)

2155 **1837 AU58 NGC.** Nearly full luster can be seen beneath pleasing bluish-gray luster with traces of gold on the reverse. First-year type collectors could make a case to include this issue, rather than the 1836 that is technically a pattern. *From The Menlo Park Collection.* (#6176)

2156 **1837 MS61 NGC.** Light to medium gray surfaces are framed by electric-blue peripheries, and an attentive strike brings out sharp definition on the design elements. A few light marks occur on each side. (#6176)

Lustrous MS65 1837 Reeded Edge Half 50 CENTS Variant

2157 **1837 MS65 NGC.** Second year of the new Reeded Edge half, struck by steam power rather than by "blood power," a term used by Mint Director Patterson. According to Robert Julian in his article "Coins of Evolution" in the October 1998 issue of *Coins* magazine:

> "The coins of 1837 have some interesting characteristics. Even though the steam coinage was clearly working, there were some minor technical problems involved with ejecting the coins from the closed collar. For this reason there was some experimentation with collar size, resulting in coins of slightly different diameter for this year."

Certainly an interesting and little-known fact about these pivotal half dollars. However, with the prevalence of encapsulation in the coin market today such variation in diameter is all-but-impossible to determine. The surfaces of this piece are highly lustrous and glow brightly beneath the overlay of golden-gray toning that covers each side. The strike is full, and there are no noticeable abrasions on either side of this splendid Gem. Census: 37 in 65, 12 finer (7/08). (#6176)

2158 **1838 MS62 PCGS. CAC.** Deep gray toning covers the obverse, which contrasts sharply against the peppered russet and silver-gray reverse. Although the luster is partly obscured on the obverse, the reverse exhibits scintillating satiny luster. The stars are weakly struck, but the rest of the details are essentially full. A number of horizontal striations are noted at the bottom of the reverse. (#6177)

Appealing 1838 Capped Bust, Reeded Edge Half, MS64

2159 **1838 MS64 PCGS.** A two-year type coin with the Capped Bust obverse, reeded edge, and HALF DOL. denomination, superseded in 1839 by the Seated Liberty half dollar. This piece shows generous luster over the silver-gold surfaces, with a sharp strike (save for star 12, often seen weak) and some striations near the obverse rim from 4 to 6 o'clock and correspondingly on the reverse, a phenomenon also frequently seen on this issue. Scattered traces of die rust appear, without in the least detracting from the premium appeal of this near-Gem coin.
From The Bell Collection. (#6177)

2160 **1839 AU58 PCGS.** Only a whisper of friction affects the high points, and this minimally toned Reeded Edge half retains virtually all of its original luster. Well-defined and highly appealing. (#6179)

2161 **1839-O—Improperly Cleaned—NCS. AU Details.** Slate-gray with hints of chestnut-gold and olive-green. Subdued by a cleaning, but splendidly detailed. The mintmark is repunched, although the initial impression is faint. Both sides have a series of bold die cracks across the peripheries.
From The Morton J. Greene Collection. (#6181)

2162 **1839-O AU55 PCGS.** Speckles of charcoal-gray gravitate to the margins of this Choice AU O-mint half, and traces of luster reside in the recessed areas. A few small marks are visible over each side. (#6181)

Extremely Rare 1839-O Capped Bust Half Dollar, PR62

Please visit <u>HA.com</u> to view other collectibles auctions
A 15% Buyer's Premium ($9 min.) Applies To All Lots

2163 **1839-O Capped Bust, Reeded Edge PR62 NGC.** Substantially rarer than the 1838-O proof half dollars are the similarly designed 1839-O proof halves. About a dozen of the former are known, but only about five of the latter are known. While the 1838-O is a celebrated rarity in American numismatics, the 1839-O proof is only recognized by a small number of specialists.

The 1838-O and 1839-O proof halves show a remarkable number of similarities. Both were apparently struck in proof format at about the same time in early 1839. Both have the popular Obverse Mintmark style only produced in those two years, making them a two-year subtype. There is no record of proof coins being struck of either year, in keeping with typical Mint practice of the era. Of course, an obvious difference is that, while the 1838-O halves were only struck in proof to the extent of about 20 pieces, with 11 pieces known today, the 1839-O halves are even rarer in proof format, with only four or five pieces known. Despite their greater rarity, the proof 1839-O halves are relatively unknown to the numismatic community, perhaps because of a fairly large production of 1839-O business strikes.

Variety and Die State

The obverse has a boldly doubled mintmark that was repunched north of its original position. The mintmark is nearly centered over the space between the 8 and 3, slightly favoring the 3. A faint die crack connects stars 3 through 6, and another connects stars 9 through 12. A third crack connects all four digits of the date at their centers. All three of these die cracks are virtually invisible without a magnifier and a good light source.

The reverse has several similar fine and nearly invisible die cracks connecting most of the letters. Perhaps the easiest to view is the segment of a die crack through AMERICA that connects the left upright of the R to the crossbar of the E. The ER crack, along with several others, exactly matches die cracks observed on the reverse of known 1838-O half dollars.

Sharing a common reverse die in a nearly identical die state, the 1838-O and 1839-O proof half dollars were produced at about the same time, probably circa January 1839 in both cases. Some have suggested that the 1838-O half dollars were mere test coins, struck as press trials before the proof 1839-O coins were minted. In his *Complete Encyclopedia*, Breen cited a note in the National Archives that he had located in 1951, suggesting that a "few half dollars were coined to test a new press."

Die Alignment

Walter Breen reported in his *Proof Encyclopedia* that the Straus coin he examined in 1951 had the dies aligned in medal turn orientation, and questioned the others, writing: "is this constant for these proofs?" A decade later in his *Complete Encyclopedia*, Breen reported that all five known proofs have medal turn alignment. More recent examination shows Breen's error in his 1988 reference. In the George Byers Catalog, Stack's notes that the Byers coin has normal alignment, and we observe that the present piece also has normal alignment.

This Specimen

Deeply toned in steel-blue that is intermingled with dark tan around the devices. The underlying fields are fully reflective, and all of the design elements are boldly defined. A few scattered surface marks and faint hairlines are evident on each side, accounting for the assigned numerical grade.

2164 1839-O Capped Bust, Reeded Edge PR63 NGC. When discussing the hidden jewels of the numismatic world, the subject of the 1839-O proof half dollars is sure to arise. Unfortunately, relatively little is known about this enigmatic issue. The written contributions on the subject by noted specialist Walter Breen are ambiguous and modern day researches have dedicated little time and effort to unraveling the mysteries of the 1839-O proof fifty cent pieces. However, two things are certain about this issue—they are indubitably specially struck coins and there are only four confirmed examples extant. The current auction is a landmark event in that we are offering two pieces in the same sale! Considering that only 10 or so examples have crossed the auction block in the past century, this is an amazing occurrence. Having two proof 1839-O halves available for examination concurrently, coupled with the fact that we sold yet a third specimen in our July 2008 sale, affords us the opportunity to shed more light on this mysterious issue.

Perhaps the biggest question regarding the 1839-O proofs relates to the quantity of coins minted. There are no Mint records pertaining to the issue and over the years as many as 10 different pieces have been reported, though not confirmed. Census information included in auction lot descriptions has varied from four to six examples, although the latter figure includes an erroneous duplication and an unconfirmed coin. Breen suggested the existence of five specimens in his 1988 *Complete Encyclopedia*, but only documents four halves in his revised *Encyclopedia of Proof Coins* (1989); although he makes it clear in the latter reference that he was uncertain about his census. The earliest evidence relating to the mintage of proof 1839-O halves can be found in New York Coin and Stamp Company's June 1890 description of an 1838-O proof fifty cent piece (now known as the Norweb coin). In that catalog the writer notes:

"We have seen a letter from Dr. Riddell, superintendent N.O. Mint, 1838, which accompanied a similar half dollar, in which it was stated that only four half dollars of this date and mintage were issued ..."

Dr. John Riddell was never superintendent of the New Orleans Mint. He was, however, the melter and refiner and in that position he would have been intimately involved with advanced coining operations at the new branch mint. Dr. Riddell was appointed to his position by President Martin Van Buren in 1839 (Doug Winter, 2006), although the exact date is unknown. Researcher David Lange notes that "a particularly severe outbreak of yellow fever caused the mint to suspend operations from July 1 to November 30, 1839," so we can safely assume that Dr. Riddell began work at the New Orleans Mint sometime during the first quarter of 1839. This fact is important in that the Riddell letter referenced in the June 1890 auction catalog must have been dated 1839 and, as such, was referring to 1839-O proof half dollars-not the 1838-O pieces, even though the latter pieces were also struck in the first quarter of 1839—not 1838. Carefully dissecting the 1890 catalog entry, we note that the letter "accompanied a similar half dollar." Since the cataloger associated the letter to the Norweb 1838-O proof half, the word "similar" is immensely significant. It is likely Riddell was referring to 1839-dated coins. To further substantiate this logic, consider that only four 1839-O proof halves are known, whereas 11 1838-O proof fifty cent pieces have been traced. Conveniently, as of (8/08) NGC has certified four different 1839-O proof half dollars and we have traced each piece to previously reported examples (see our census at the end of this description). That fact, together with the aforementioned Riddell letter, lends credence to the belief that only four 1839-O halves were struck in proof format.

Another bit of misinformation that has been propagated through the last several decades is the fact that 1839-O proof haves were struck in medal-turn orientation. Breen (1988) stated that the five known examples "have dies aligned 180 degrees from normal, so that date is nearest to HALF DOL." Since Breen cataloged the Krouner-Byers coin, the specimen offered here, which is also the plate coin in his *Encyclopedia of Proof Coins*, we are dumbfounded since this piece was unequivocally struck in coin-turn orientation. In fact, all four 1839-O proof halves that we have traced, including the three that we have handled within the past few months, have normal obverse to reverse positioning. Yet another mystery unraveled, thanks to the reemergence of all four specimens within the past year.

In terms of technical grade, the current offering is now ranked as the third finest of the four 1839-O proof half dollars thus traced, although the eye appeal of this piece arguably places it higher within the census. Variegated russet coloration is suitably complemented by electric-blue and sea-green toning at the peripheries on both the obverse and reverse. Unsurprisingly for a proof issue, the strike is bold and the fields are delightfully reflective. Scattered hairlines in the delicate fields are observed through close scrutiny, yet the aesthetically pleasing patina does well to conceal them. A minuscule dark spot above the eagle's head shall serve as a pedigree marker for the sake of posterity.

Census of Proof 1839-O Half Dollars

New information has come to light since our July 2008 offering of the PR64 piece, so we have revised our roster slightly from that catalog. We list four distinctly different pieces, along with two additional appearances that may be duplicates of the four individual specimens.

1. PR65 NGC. Robison Collection (Stack's, 2/1982), lot 1607; Queller Family Collection (Stack's, 10/2002), lot 448; Goldberg Coins (2/2008), lot 2177.

2. PR64 NGC. Bowers and Merena (9/1994), lot 1214; Heritage (7/2008), lot 1690.

3. PR63 NGC. The present specimen and the Breen *Proof Encyclopedia* Plate Coin. Krouner Collection (Lester Merkin, 2/1971), lot 736; Stack's (9/1992), lot 358; George Byers Collection (Stack's, 10/2006), lot 1098; Heritage (9/2008).

4. PR62 NGC. Heritage (9/2008), lot 2163 in the present auction.

A. Proof. F.C.C. Boyd; World's Greatest Collection (Numismatic Gallery, 5/1945), lot 411; Christian Allenburger (B. Max Mehl, 3/1948); R.E. Cox (Stack's, 4/1962), lot 1875. The Boyd-Cox piece may be the same as one of the above coins.

B. Proof. An unverified example that Breen reported in the Philip G. Straus Collection, circa 1951. The coin remains unseen since that time and is likely one of the four listed above. (#6227)

Stunning 1839 No Drapery Half Dollar, MS63

2165 1839 No Drapery MS63 PCGS. The half dollar was the last of five denominations to receive Christian Gobrecht's neoclassical Seated Liberty design. The No Drapery style lacks drapery folds extending from Liberty's left elbow to the knee, but a second diagnostic is that the left edge of the boulder is much closer to star 1 than on the Drapery version. As a first-year issue and a one-year type, No Drapery half dollars are always in demand, but Mint State examples are rare. A couple of shallow abrasions to the right of Liberty and a small spot above I in UNITED are noted, but neither stands out. Both sides display stunning aquamarine and blue toning, particularly on the reverse, with apricot-tinted silver in the centers and around the stars. There is some softness of strike in the center devices, along with a considerable number of parallel roller marks on the center obverse, but the overall appearance is stunning. PCGS has graded just 10 coins finer (8/08).
From The Sundance Collection. (#6230)

Richly Toned Choice 1839 Drapery Seated Half

2166 1839 Drapery MS64 PCGS. Apple-green and sun-gold alternate across this lustrous and sharply struck near-Gem. Occasional moderate field marks fail to distract. 1839 was a transitional year from the Capped Bust to the Seated series. The first Seated halves lacked drapery beneath Liberty's elbow, but drapery folds were added shortly thereafter. Population: 15 in 64, 2 finer (8/08).
From The Sundance Collection. (#6232)

Beautifully Toned Gem 1839 Drapery Half Dollar

2167 1839 Drapery MS65 NGC. Considering the seven-figure mintage of 1839 With Drapery half dollars and the fact that 1839-dated Seated Liberty halves represented the first-year of production of a major new design, one would expect that high grade survivors of this issue would be more plentiful. Such is not the case. Although the No Drapery variant is slightly less available than With Drapery halves in Mint State, both types are equally rare in Gem or better condition. As of (8/08), NGC has certified only four pieces at the MS65 level and PCGS has graded a mere two at the same grade, with none finer at either service. An awe-inspiring blend of rose, amber, and electric-blue toning blankets the lustrous surfaces on both sides of this truly special coin. The current offering is more than a solid Gem survivor—it is also a eye-appealing specimen that will surely elicit aggressive bidding competition.
From The Sundance Collection. (#6232)

Eliasberg's MS63 1841-O Seated Half

2168 **1841-O MS63 PCGS.** Ex: Eliasberg. Large O. WB-101. The rich dove-gray centers are framed with butter-gold and apple-green. Sharply struck, and smooth aside from an inconspicuous curved mark near star 13. The reverse has numerous slender die cracks. Population: 7 in 63, 6 finer (8/08).
Ex: Nicholas Petry Collection; S.H. and H. Chapman, 5/1993; J.M. Clapp; John H. Clapp; Clapp estate, 1942, to Eliasberg; Louis E. Eliasberg, Sr. Collection (Bowers and Merena, 4/1997), lot 1920.
From The Sundance Collection. (#6237)

Rare Small Date, Small Letters 1842-O Half VF25

2169 **1842-O Small Date, Small Letters VF25 PCGS.** A rare variety identified by a Plain 4 in the date. The (comparatively) common Large Date has a Crosslet 4. The Guide Book reports a mintage of 203,000 pieces, but it seems likely that much of that production belongs instead to the Large Date. Pearl-gray and light golden-brown centers are framed by rich sea-green and power-blue peripheries. LIBERTY is bold, and there are few noticeable marks. Population: 6 in 25, 30 finer (8/08). (#6238)

Original AU 1842-O Small Date, Small Letters Half

2170 **1842-O Small Date, Small Letters AU50 NGC.** WB-101. This reverse style has been identified on all 1839 Seated Liberty, 1840 (P), 1840-O, 1841, and 1841-O Half Dollars, as well as on a portion of the 1842-O mintage. Most survivors are well circulated, placing this AU50 at or very near a Condition Census rating. The slate-gray surfaces display generous amount of underlying luster. Ancient marks are present near the raised arm and to the left of the beak, but these are scarcely visible due to the coin's originality.
Ex: Long Beach Signature (Heritage, 9/2003).
From The Sundance Collection. (#6238)

Peripherally Toned Gem 1842 Half
Medium Date, Large Letters, WB-106

2171 **1842 Medium Date, Large Letters MS65 NGC.** WB-106. The 8 in the date is repunched, and a misplaced digit is right of the shield point. Cobalt-blue and golden-brown bands grace the borders, while the fields and devices are nearly brilliant. Well struck with modest field reflectivity and a few minor marks. Census: 4 in 65, 0 finer (7/08).
From The Sundance Collection. (#6239)

Richly Toned Choice 1843 Half

2172 **1843 MS64 NGC.** WB-103. The 4 is lightly recut along its crossbar. This boldly struck and satiny Choice No Motto half is dramatically toned in navy-blue, orange-gold, plum-red, and ivory-gray. The surfaces appear smooth even when studied beneath magnification. Census: 15 in 64, 3 finer (7/08).
From The Sundance Collection. (#6243)

Choice AU Double Date 1844-O Half, FS-301

2173 **1844-O Double Date AU55 PCGS.** WB-103. FS-301, formerly FS-001. This dramatic repunched date variety became even more famous when it appeared on the cover of the Wiley-Bugert volume, the standard reference to the series. Most examples are well worn, but the present piece has only minor friction on Liberty's legs and other highpoints. Lightly toned and partly lustrous. Population: 3 in 55, 3 finer (8/08).
From The Sundance Collection. (#6247)

2174 **1846-O Tall Date XF40 PCGS.** A much more difficult coin to locate in any grade than its Medium Date counterpart, this example features light gray toning over bright surfaces that are relatively clean, with very few marks. The design elements reveal considerable detail. (#6256)

2175 **1849 AU58 NGC.** This is a decidedly scarce Philadelphia Mint issue in higher grades, despite its substantial original mintage of more than 1.25 million coins. This near-Mint specimen has a satiny, somewhat muted appearance, with medium-gray color that is modified by speckled olive patina, mainly near the borders. Boldly struck and abrasion-free. Census: 19 in 58, 38 finer (7/08).
From The Morton J. Greene Collection. (#6262)

Boldly Repunched Date AU58
1849 Half, FS-301, WB-102

2176 **1849 Doubled Date AU58 PCGS.** FS-301, formerly FS-004.5. WB-102. The date is repunched east, with ample remnants of bases of the prior logotype. An errant 9 also protrudes from the bottom of Liberty's rock. Boldly struck except for the left (facing) claw. Abundant silver-gray luster penetrates the medium mauve patina. Population for all 1849 varieties: 11 in 58, 29 finer (8/08).
Ex: Baltimore Signature (Heritage, 7/2003), lot 7554, which realized $7,130.
From The Sundance Collection. (#6262)

Prooflike Near-Gem 1849 Half Dollar
Repunched Date, WB-103

2177 **1849 MS64 Prooflike NGC.** WB-103. The 1 in the date is repunched south. Powder-blue and caramel-gold endow this precisely struck near-Gem. The fields are moderately reflective, and inspection beneath a loupe fails to locate any relevant marks. Census: 2 in 64 Prooflike, 0 finer as Prooflike (7/08).
From The Sundance Collection. (#6262)

Lovely Gem 1849-O Half

2178 **1849-O MS65 NGC.** Despite a mintage of over 2.3 million pieces, like many antebellum minor silver issues, this heavily circulated New Orleans half dollar is immensely elusive in the better Mint State grades, particularly at the Choice and Gem levels. In the latter state, auction appearances are markedly infrequent. This highly lustrous survivor is one of the latter, well-defined and minimally marked beneath thin, yet ample green-gold, sage, and marble-pink patina. It is tied with two others at NGC and one at PCGS for numerically finest in the combined certified population (8/08).
From The Sundance Collection. (#6263)

2179 **1850 AU50 PCGS.** This issue has a low mintage of only 227,000 pieces, and was extensively melted, so survivors are few, especially in AU and Mint State. Softly detailed on a few of the obverse stars, but bold elsewhere, with a trace of wear on the highpoints, drab olive-gray color, and a modicum of scattered surface blemishes. Population: 8 in 50, 51 finer (8/08). (#6264)

Toned 1850 Select Half Dollar

2180 **1850 MS63 NGC.** A medley of cobalt-blue, lavender, gray, and yellow-gold patination covers the lustrous surfaces of this Select half dollar. A concise strike brings out uniform definition on the design elements, except for minor softness on the left (facing) claw. There are fewer marks than what might be expected for the grade. Census: 13 in 63, 4 finer (7/08).
From The Sundance Collection. (#6264)

2181 **1851 VF35 PCGS.** Delicate mocha-gray toning reveals a few pale-blue accents. Pleasingly detailed for the grade assigned with only trifling flaws, as befits the Choice VF designation. Population: 2 in 35, 51 finer (8/08). (#6266)

Enchanting Gem 1851-O Half

2182 **1851-O MS65 NGC.** The 1851-O half dollar was heavily minted for the era, with production of 402,000 pieces; it was also heavily circulated, though lesser Mint State examples are available for a price. The appearance of a Gem at auction, however, is an infrequent occurrence. This captivating coin offers soft, pleasing luster that filters through rich violet, rose-gold, and silver-blue patina. Crisply struck and pleasingly preserved. The certified populations at NGC and PCGS mirror each other, with three MS65 examples graded by each service and one coin finer (8/08).
From The Sundance Collection. (#6267)

2183 **1852 VF35 NGC.** With only 77,130 pieces struck, the 1852 has the lowest mintage of all Variety One Liberty Seated half dollars. Pleasing medium gray toning in the fields is surrounded by a darker patina on the perimeter. This evenly worn example shows no marks worthy of individual mention. (#6268)

2184 **1852 AU50 PCGS.** Only a trace of wear crosses the central devices of the obverse, and the eagle is virtually untouched. Splashes of silver-blue and sun-gold patina grace the otherwise steel-gray surfaces. Minor ticks appear on Liberty's shield arm, but the coin is minimally marked elsewhere. Population: 3 in 50, 58 finer (8/08). (#6268)

Scarce 1852-O Fifty Cent, AU55

2185 **1852-O AU55 PCGS.** The 1852-O is scarce in AU and nearly unknown in Mint State. The bright champagne-gold surfaces of this Choice AU specimen exhibit traces of luster in the protected areas, along with well struck design features. A pleasing, minimally marked piece. Population: 9 in 55, 7 finer (8/08). (#6269)

Challenging Near-Mint 1852-O Half Dollar

2186 **1852-O AU58 PCGS.** This well defined near-Mint example is richly toned in steel-gray, aquamarine, and straw-gold. The only mark of any relevance is relegated near the final A in AMERICA. Only 144,000 pieces were struck, and presumably a large portion of the mintage was melted by bullion speculators. Population: 4 in 58, 3 finer (8/08). (#6269)

2187 **1853 Arrows and Rays AU58 NGC.** Aside from a hint of friction on the uppermost design elements, this Arrows and Rays half is surprisingly flawless. No overt abrasions appear on either side, and the peach-gold surfaces sport impressive luster. (#6275)

Impressive 1853 Arrows and Rays Half, MS64

2188 **1853 Arrows and Rays MS64 PCGS.** A one-year type coin, the 1853 Arrows and Rays coins (both quarters and half dollars) are extremely important and rare. A slightly reduced weight meant that these coins began to circulate more freely, with the result that few have survived in Mint State grades. This lovely piece is mostly silver-white, with a crescent of deep lilac on the obverse and peripheral gold on the reverse. (#6275)

Outstanding Gem 1853 Arrows and Rays Half

2189 **1853 Arrows and Rays MS65 NGC.** Arrows and Rays halves are abundant in circulated grades, and even lower grade Mint State examples can be found in any major auction. Gems, by contrast, are highly elusive and appear only irregularly in the numismatic marketplace. This is a splendid and obviously original example that has light steel-gray surfaces with somewhat darker accents over the highpoints. A couple of marks are located on the lower area of the legs of Liberty, but these are insignificant, and the overall surfaces are clean and problem-free with soft, frosted mint luster. Boldly impressed and delightful. Census: 27 in 65, 15 finer (7/08). *From The Sundance Collection.* (#6275)

2190 **1853-O Arrows and Rays AU58 NGC.** Both sides of this near-Mint half yield a bright silver-gray appearance, and are remarkably clean. An attentive strike leaves strong detail on the design elements. Less common than its Philadelphia Mint counterpart, due in part to its lower mintage (less than 1.4 million as opposed to over 3.5 million), and probably fewer collectors actively saving mint-marked coins. *From The Menlo Park Collection.* (#6276)

2191 **1854-O Arrows MS62 PCGS.** Splotches of olive-green, russet, and sky-blue patina visit each side of this O-mint half. Fairly well struck, with a few light obverse marks. (#6280)

2192 **1854-O Arrows MS62 PCGS.** A highly lustrous example of this popular type coin, one of only two years struck with arrows and without rays. Delightful russet toning surrounds the mostly silver-gray centers. Both sides are minimally marked for the grade, and there is just a trace of weakness on Liberty's head and a few stars. (#6280)

Eliasberg's 1854-O Arrows Half, MS64

2193 **1854-O Arrows MS64 NGC.** Ex: Eliasberg. Wisps of golden-brown and ocean-blue fill the borders, although the open fields and devices are cream-gray. This well struck and minimally abraded half dollar possesses one of the most desirable pedigrees in all numismatics. *Ex: Mumford Collection, New York Coin & Stamp, 4/1896; J.M. Clapp; John H. Clapp; Clapp Estate, 1942 to Eliasberg; Louis E. Eliasberg, Sr. Collection (Bowers and Merena, 4/1997), lot 1961. From The Sundance Collection.* (#6280)

2194 **1855-O Arrows MS63 PCGS.** This Select New Orleans Mint half displays splashes of cobalt-blue, pale violet, orange-gold, and yellow-gold on the obverse, and light tan-gray and blue-green peripheral toning on the reverse. Lustrous surfaces exhibit well struck design features, and are minimally marked. *From The Menlo Park Collection.* (#6283)

Richly Toned 1855-O Arrows Half MS64

2195 **1855-O Arrows MS64 NGC.** Lavishly toned in sun-gold, sky-blue, rose-red, and forest-green. A satiny New Orleans half with unmarked surfaces beneath the rich patina. A good strike despite a few softly brought up stars. A briefly issued branch mint Seated type coin, certified in a former generation holder. Census: 47 in 64, 24 finer (7/08). (#6283)

2196 **1856-S—Genuine—PCGS.** In-house graded XF40, cleaned. Gray-tan surfaces exhibit traces of luster in the recesses. The design elements are well defined. Some minute circulation marks are scattered over each side. (#6289)

Condition Rarity 1857 Half Dollar, MS66

2197 **1857 MS66 NGC.** Soft luster emanates from light to medium gray surfaces accented with electric-blue and lavender. A well executed strike leaves bold definition on all but the eagle's left (facing) leg and claw. A couple of grade-consistent obverse marks do not disturb. A common date, except for the better levels of Mint State. Census: 3 in 66, 0 finer (7/08). *From The Sundance Collection.* (#6290)

Elusive 1857-O MS64 Half Dollar

2198 **1857-O MS64 PCGS.** Light beige-gold and blue-gray patination resides on the highly lustrous surfaces of this near-Gem. The design elements are sharply defined, as is characteristic of most '57-Os. A handful of minute contacts precludes Gem classification. Scarce in all levels of preservation, and elusive in the better Mint State grades. Population: 6 in 64, 0 finer (8/08). *From The Sundance Collection.* (#6291)

2199 **1857-S XF45 PCGS.** Dots of dappled silver-blue and green-gold grace the lightly worn surfaces of this minimally marked Choice XF coin. Despite a mintage of 158,000 pieces, few survivors remain for this early San Francisco minor silver issue. (#6292)

2200 **1858 MS63 PCGS.** Splendid lilac, lemon, and green toning graces the obverse, which contrasts nicely against the light gold reverse. There is slight weakness on the head and nearby stars, as typically seen, and there is some softness on the eagle's left (facing) claw, also as usual. Minimally marked for the grade, this piece would make an excellent and relatively affordable type coin. (#6293)

Striking Gem 1858 Seated Half Dollar

2201 **1858 MS65 PCGS. CAC.** WB-101. Tail Hub Variety One, Normal Date. This is a strikingly original Gem, with a pleasing layer of variegated, natural patina across both sides. Vibrant, satiny luster emerges from beneath the rich toning. The design elements are sharply defined, except for the top of Liberty's head and a few of the upper obverse stars, and the surfaces reveal excellent preservation. Population: 10 in 65, 5 finer (8/08). (#6293)

2202 **1858-S AU55 NGC.** Freckles of golden-tan visit portions of the reverse of this well defined half. Traces of luster reside in the recessed areas. Minimally marked. (#6295)

Better-Date 1858-S Select Half Dollar

2203 **1858-S MS63 NGC.** This better date half dollar is "very scarce in mint state" (Wiley and Bugert, 1993). Light champagne-gold patina is accented by freckles of russet, somewhat more so on the reverse, and a penetrating strike imparts bold definition to the design elements. A few unobtrusive marks occur over each side. Census: 4 in 63, 5 finer (7/08).
From The Sundance Collection. (#6295)

Highly Lustrous 1859 Fifty Cent, MS64

2204 **1859 MS64 NGC.** Both sides of this near-Gem are awash with potent luster, and each displays light to medium orange-gold patina, accented with an occasional splash of sky-blue. Excellent delineation shows on the design features, save for minor softness on the eagle's left (facing) leg and claw. A handful of minute marks defines the grade. Census: 19 in 64, 10 finer (7/08).
From The Sundance Collection. (#6296)

2205 **1860-O MS62 ANACS.** Breen-4898, Type Two reverse. A lovely Mint State piece with bold design elements and satiny luster beneath pale champagne toning. A trace of recutting appears inside the 0. (#6300)

2206 **1860-O MS63 PCGS.** Lovely gold and slate-gray patina surrounds the frosted and untoned devices. The remarkably clean fields exhibit flashy luster, which complements the sharp details. Only the head and a couple of nearby stars show a trace of softness. Population: 18 in 63, 48 finer (7/08). (#6300)

Richly Toned Near-Gem 1860-O Half

2207 **1860-O MS64 PCGS. CAC.** Dappled golden-tan, aquamarine, fire-red, and olive embrace this satiny Choice type coin. The strike is needle-sharp save for the centers of a couple of upper left stars. The reverse is beautifully preserved, and the obverse has only minor field chatter. Population: 30 in 64, 19 finer (8/08). (#6300)

Desirable Near-Gem 1860-S Half Dollar

2208 **1860-S MS64 PCGS.** WB-101, Large S. This caramel-gold near-Gem has a precise strike and impeccably preserved surfaces. It is doubtful that a nicer example can be found, yet the present lot should still hammer for a reasonable amount. Population: 5 in 64, 0 finer (8/08).
From The Sundance Collection. (#6301)

Attractively Toned Gem 1861 Half

2209 **1861 MS65 PCGS.** A beautiful No Motto half with untoned centers and dusky autumn-gold, cobalt-blue, and lilac-red margins. The strike is penetrating, and the lustrous fields and devices are free from obtrusive marks. This Civil War date is available in AU55 through MS64, but Gems are difficult to procure. Population: 15 in 65, 12 finer (8/08).
From The Bell Collection. (#6302)

Originally Toned Gem 1861 Half

2210 **1861 MS65 PCGS.** Golden-brown and forest-green compete for territory across this lustrous and meticulously struck Gem. Only careful evaluation can locate the few faint field grazes. A popular Civil War date. Encapsulated in a green label holder. Population: 15 in 65, 12 finer (8/08).
From The Sundance Collection. (#6302)

Near-Gem 1861 CSA Restrike Half

2211 **1861 Scott Restrike MS64 NGC.** Breen-8002. While restrikes often diminish the rarity of original strikings, that is certainly not the case with the Scott Restrikes of the Confederate half. Scott struck (or restruck, as the case may be) 500 impressions on planed off reverses of 1861-O halves. These pieces are easily distinguished from the four known originals as the restriking process greatly weakened the details on the obverse. On the originals, the obverse was sharply defined. This obvious and well-known fact was overlooked by none other than John Ford. Many years ago, he was offered what he thought was a CSA Restrike, paid the man a fair price, and then his partner said, "Didn't you look at the obverse?" He had inadvertently bought one of the four originals!

As expected, the reverse on this piece is sharply defined while the obverse is weak from the striking process. The obverse is deeply toned in shades of rose and deep blue, while the reverse is light gray overall. A problem-free example of this highly collectible restrike. (#340402)

2212 **1864 MS63 NGC.** Silver-gray shadings with varying levels of blue grace the satiny surfaces of this Select Seated half. Well-defined with no overt flaws on the obverse. Census: 11 in 63, 33 finer (7/08). (#6311)

Well Struck 1865-S Near-Gem Half Dollar
Rare WB-101, 'Broken Mintmark'

2213 **1865-S MS64 NGC.** WB-101. Small Wide "Broken" Mintmark. Wiley-Bugert (1993) assign a low R.8 to this variety (we note, however, that the authors suggest caution when using these values, and write that "with time and public exposure, most R values should decrease"). This well struck, lustrous piece displays dapples of light golden-tan, and is nicely preserved. Census: 7 in 64, 2 finer (7/08). *From The Sundance Collection.* (#6314)

2214 **1866-S No Motto VF35 PCGS.** Subtle lilac, silver-blue, and golden-brown elements grace the otherwise steel-gray surfaces. Solid detail for the grade assigned and surprisingly few flaws. Population: 6 in 35, 28 finer (8/08). (#6315)

2215 **1866-S No Motto—Cleaned—ICG. XF40 Details.** Well struck with muted luster that comes from moderately hairlined surfaces. Medium-gray peripheral toning surrounds slivers of lighter silver-gray that are scattered in the centers. *From The Morton J. Greene Collection.* (#6315)

2216 **1866-S No Motto—Improperly Cleaned—NCS. XF Details.** A rare San Francisco issue that was little saved despite a mintage of only 60,000 pieces, since there were no serious West Coast coin collectors at the time. A slate-gray representative with a minor bend at 5:30 on the obverse and an occasional glimpse of peripheral porosity. (#6315)

Elusive 1866-S No Motto Half Dollar, Choice XF

2217 **1866-S No Motto XF45 PCGS.** The vast majority of 1866-S half dollars were struck using a new reverse die that featured the IN GOD WE TRUST motto above the eagle, and only 60,000 examples without the motto were minted. Charming gunmetal-gray patina drapes the surfaces of this well-defined representative, which boasts traces of luster in the fields. Both sides are minimally abraded, and a few small digs through the first 6 in the date are barely worthy of note. A lovely example of this elusive issue. Population: 9 in 45, 12 finer (8/08). (#6315)

Important No Motto 1866-S Half, MS62

2218 **1866-S No Motto MS62 PCGS.** The No Motto half dollars struck at San Francisco in 1866 make up just a tiny fraction of the original mintage, 60,000 pieces versus the nearly one million recorded for the With Motto variety. Combined with a low survival rate, this means high demand for a limited supply of pieces, particularly at higher grades. This noteworthy Mint State beauty offers frosty luster beneath light gray-gold patina. Scattered, wispy flaws in the fields blend with the minor clash marks present on the reverse. All things considered, an impressive survivor. Population: 1 in 62, 3 finer (8/08).
From The Sundance Collection. (#6315)

Attractively Toned 1866 Select Half Dollar

2219 **1866 Motto MS63 PCGS.** Electric-blue, purple, and golden-brown toning at the peripheries, somewhat more extensive on the obverse, frames subtle champagne-gold central areas. Numerous die polish lines impart prooflike tendencies to the field, thus establishing pleasing contrast with the devices. A sharply struck coin, with just a few marks that keep from near-Gem.
From The Sundance Collection. (#6319)

2220 **1868 AU58 NGC.** The highly reflective fields appear watery and semiprooflike. A number of minute scratches are noted in the left obverse field, but the surfaces are otherwise well-preserved. The strike is sharp and there is lovely violet and gold toning throughout. Census: 6 in 58, 16 finer (8/08). (#6323)

Sharply Struck 1870 Half Dollar, MS64

2221 **1870 MS64 PCGS.** A delicate mix of light green, orange-gold, light gray, and golden-tan patination resides on the lustrous surfaces of both sides, and a well executed strike results in strong definition on the design features. A few unimportant marks keeps this lovely piece from Gem status. Population: 4 in 64, 4 finer (8/08).
From The Sundance Collection. (#6327)

2222 **1870-CC VG8 PCGS.** The 1870-CC was the first half dollar struck at the Carson City Mint and virtually all were extensively circulated. A patch of charcoal color covers the field around stars 1 and 2, but the rest of the surfaces are medium gray. The details are clearly outlined and, although LIBERTY is not readable, IN GOD WE TRUST is plain. One of only 54,617 pieces minted. (#6328)

2223 **1870-CC VG8 PCGS.** The L, T, and Y are visible on the shield. A starkly contrasted piece with deep blue-gray fields and lighter silver-gray devices. A notable representative of this initial Carson City half dollar issue. Population: 6 in 8, 63 finer (8/08). (#6328)

2224 **1870-CC AU50 NGC.** As is the case with the many other issues struck in the first year of operation for the Carson City Mint, the 1870-CC halves rank as the most challenging and desirable within their series, though their high production compared to other denominations (54,617 pieces) means that they are relatively affordable in most grades. While collectors in the 1970s and earlier considered the 1870-CC a rarity in any grade, according to Rusty Goe's *The Mint on Carson Street*, after the rumors of a hoard of nearly 100 1870-CC halves proved true, numismatists revised their estimates.

Though the issue became "scarce in all grades" instead of rare, most of the survivors in that hoard were low-grade pieces, and the populations of high-end (XF and better) coins remained nearly stable. The 1980s also saw a marked rise in collector interest in the coins of Carson City, and though this interest extended through all grade levels, the best pieces gained the most from this added attention, and even in the past decade, one can chart the dramatic spike in price for better circulated pieces in general and About Uncirculated coins in particular.

The present coin is surprisingly well-defined for an early Carson City product, particularly on Liberty's hair and foot and on the eagle's feathers. Modest, yet distinct wear affects Liberty's upper body on the obverse and the eagle's beak and arrowheads on the reverse. The fields remain softly lustrous beneath elegant green-gold and sage patina. Minimally marked and highly attractive, a winning candidate for the discerning Carson City silver specialist. Census: 3 in 50, 2 finer (7/08). (#6328)

2225 **1870-CC AU50 PCGS.** WB-101. Extremely scarce overall and of the utmost rarity in high grades, the 1870-CC Seated half dollar is an important key date in the series. Randy Wiley and Bill Bugert (1993) make the following observations:

"Many 1870-CC Liberty Seated Half Dollars are not well struck. This is probably due to the fact that this was the first year of operation at the Carson City Mint. The letters BER in LIBERTY show signs of premature wear and the eagle's left leg and feathers are often flatly struck. Advanced die abrasion is well documented with 1 of 3 head dies (2 of the marriages) having a partial or no drapery. Our research indicates that about 14% of all 1870-CC half dollars have partial drapery and 40% have no drapery at all. We do not consider the 'no drapery' feature significant enough for a separate listing."

The current offering is a conditionally rare AU example that shows just a bit of drapery: a small enough amount that it might easily be mistaken for a die chip if it were placed in a different location on the coin. Light rose-tan, lilac-gray, and gold toning over the surfaces is very pleasing to the eye and obviously original. This piece does not suffer from the premature wear mentioned by Wiley-Bugert on BER in LIBERTY, or on the eagle's left leg and neck feathers. It does show slight indications of striking weakness on Liberty's head, and on the eagle's left talons. A handful of small marks are noted on each side of the piece, and there are traces of highpoint wear on the major devices that seem entirely consistent with the grade level assigned by PCGS. Just seven examples are currently certified at AU50, by NGC and PCGS combined, and only eight pieces are graded finer, as of (8/08). Of course, these numbers may not account for possible resubmissions, which are usually a factor when such rare numismatic issues are involved.

This is a coin of obvious importance to any specialist in the Seated half dollar series. It is an item that many will covet, when it crosses the auction block, and one that will serve as the centerpiece of a remarkable collection. (#6328)

Impressive Gem 1870-S Half

2226 **1870-S MS65 NGC.** WB-101, Breen-4953. There is no drapery visible at Liberty's elbow, a popular variant with Seated Liberty half dollar collectors. This is the usually seen variety with a small and complete mintmark. The S mintmark is located below the arrow feather with only the extreme left curve of this letter extending past the left tip of the feather. Very sharply struck with satiny silver luster and hints of pale gold toning over the otherwise brilliant silver surfaces. A delightful and desirable Gem. Both sides have light planchet roller marks, created during planchet production. In most cases, such lines were obliterated during the actual striking process. The single finest survivor known to NGC, and tied with two others at PCGS at the summit of the combined certified population (8/08). *From The Sundance Collection.* (#6329)

Lustrous AU53 1871-CC Seated Half

2227 **1871-CC AU53 NGC.** A rare issue from the second year of operation of the Carson City Mint, the 1871-CC is rated R.5 by Seated half pundits Wiley and Bugert in XF-AU grades. While this coin does not show a repunched final digit in the date, an obverse with that feature was paired, apparently with this same reverse, to produce some one-sided proofs or, possibly, some two-sided branch mint proofs. The reverse, left over from 1870, is distinguished by a die crack that joins the final A in AMERICA with the topmost arrowhead, as well as a crack through the MER, both of which are plain on this silver-gray example. Some die doubling is also noted on the reverse, most visible through DOL. and RICA. Considerable luster remains on each side of this attractive, problem-free piece, a choice find for Seated Liberty specialists. (#6331)

Well Struck 1871-S Select Half Dollar

2228 **1871-S MS63 PCGS.** The 1871-S is common in circulated grades, but rare in Mint State (Randy Wiley and Bill Bugert, 1993). Golden-gray patination dominates this Select example, accented with aqua-blue at the margins. A well struck piece that shows no hints of weakness. Inoffensive handling marks in the fields define the grade. Population: 6 in 63, 10 finer (8/08). *From The Sundance Collection.* (#6332)

2229 **1872 MS63 NGC.** Orange and mauve patina blankets lustrous surfaces that display well struck design elements. Only a handful of modest abrasions are present on each side. Census: 4 in 63, 11 finer (7/08). (#6333)

Sharply Struck 1872 Fifty Cent, MS64

2230 **1872 MS64 PCGS.** The 1872 half dollar is available in circulated grades, but challenging in Mint State. Satiny luster adorns this near-Gem that displays whispers of light tan at the margins. An exacting strike leaves exquisite definition on the design elements, further heightening the eye appeal. Trivial obverse handling marks prevent Gem status. Population: 10 in 64, 8 finer (8/08). *From The Sundance Collection.* (#6333)

2231 1872-CC VF35 PCGS. Like most other Carson City halves, the 1872-CC is typically seen heavily circulated, and even a Choice Very Fine example ranks among the finer pieces. A glance at the *Population Report* shows just how scarce this issue is in any grade. Gunmetal-gray toning covers both sides, with darker areas around the rims. This evenly worn example has no noteworthy marks and would make an excellent representative. Population: 7 in 35, 48 finer (7/08). (#6334)

2232 1873-CC No Arrows VF25 PCGS. Evenly worn with most of the major design devices still evident, and appealing rose-gray coloration over each side. A very scarce issue with a low mintage of 122,500 pieces, most of which were melted. (#6338)

2233 1873 Arrows MS62 PCGS. The 1873 with Arrows is a two-year type coin. Splashes of pastel bluish-gray patina visit both sides, each of which exhibits well struck design elements, including complete separation of the sandal, straps, and Liberty's foot. A few light handling marks occur over each side.
From The Menlo Park Collection. (#6343)

2234 1873-CC Arrows XF40 PCGS. 1873-CC half dollars were struck both with and without arrows, and a total of 214,560 examples of the Arrows at Date variety were minted. This medium gray representative has no mentionable marks and is well-defined save for a little weakness on the shield. An excellent example of this popular type coin. Population: 18 in 40, 63 finer (8/08). (#6344)

2235 1875 MS64 PCGS. Light to medium multicolored toning bathes lustrous surfaces that exhibit well struck design features. Some faint slide marks are visible on the obverse. Population: 33 in 64, 18 finer (8/08). (#6349)

Splendid Gem 1875 Seated Half

2236 1875 MS65 PCGS. More than 6 million half dollars were struck in 1875. Yet the issue is hardly common in Uncirculated condition, and full Gems are rare. The present lustrous example has pleasing lime-green and copper-gold toning, and the strike is unimprovably sharp. Abrasions are virtually absent, and the eye appeal is exceptional. An excellent candidate for an enviable type set. Population: 13 in 65, 5 finer (8/08).
From The Sundance Collection. (#6349)

2237 1875-S MS64 PCGS. An array of colors intermingle on the obverse, with gold, russet, red, and purple present. Liberty's head and the adjacent stars are a little weak, as usual, but the rest of the details are razor-sharp. This satiny and carefully preserved piece would make an excellent type coin. (#6351)

2238 1875-S MS64 PCGS. A brilliant and frosty Choice representative. The stars lack full centrils, as typically seen, and the N in UNITED is soft, but the rest of the details are razor-sharp. A number of delicate die cracks are noted around the perimeter of the reverse. Highly lustrous with excellent eye appeal. Population: 71 in 64, 59 finer (7/08). (#6351)

2239 1876 MS64 PCGS. Electric-blue, purple, and golden-brown patina gravitates to the margins of this lustrous near-Gem half. An attentive strike leaves strong definition on the design elements. A few minute obverse marks are noted, as is a dark spot on Liberty's abdomen. Population: 52 in 64, 18 finer (8/08). (#6352)

2240 1876-CC MS61 NGC. Type One Obverse. A hint of golden toning accompanies this lustrous and precisely struck Carson City half. The few faint field marks do not appear to limit the grade. (#6353)

Superlative 1877-S Half Dollar, MS67

2241 1877-S MS67 NGC. San Francisco minted a generous 5,356,000 half dollars in 1877, the highest total of Seated halves for any year from that mint. Most 1877-S certified half dollars are graded AU58 through MS64, with a small number of Gems and Premium Gems. But only three pieces are classified Superb Gem by NGC, with none finer, and PCGS has graded a single MS67 (8/08). This piece not only tops the certified population, but it also displays beautiful toning. A sunset blaze of crimson dominates both surfaces, with jade, russet, and copper highlights surrounding essentially untoned centers. Clean, well struck surfaces prevail. This is an uncommon opportunity for the discriminating Seated Liberty or type collector.
From The Sundance Collection. (#6357)

Attractively Toned 1879 Half Dollar, MS66

2242 **1879 MS66 PCGS.** The 1879 half dollar saw a minuscule mintage of 4,800 circulation strikes, likely due to the implementation of the Bland-Allison Act of 1878 that required mints to purchase large amounts of silver bullion for producing vast quantities of silver dollars. Waves of cobalt-blue, purple, and golden-orange patina concentrate at the obverse margin, ceding to silver-gray in the center. The same color scheme is randomly distributed over the reverse. Partially prooflike fields establish modest contrast with the satiny motifs. Generally well defined and cared for. Population: 43 in 66, 15 finer (8/08).
From The Sundance Collection. (#6361)

Charming 1887 Half Dollar, MS66

2243 **1887 MS66 NGC.** Variegated aqua-blue, silver-gray, and pale purple toning resides on the lustrous surfaces of this Premium Gem, and a well executed strike leaves strong definition on the design elements, except for weakness in the hair atop Liberty's head and the adjacent stars. Impeccably preserved throughout. Census: 16 in 66, 3 finer (7/08).
From The Sundance Collection. (#6369)

2244 **1888 MS63 (PR63?) PCGS.** The date positioning and the spur from the rim under the F of HALF seem to indicate that this coin is a proof (compare with the 1888 PR67 in our July-August 2008 ANA sale, lot 589). The mirrored fields of this Select example establish noticeable contrast with the satiny devices. A powerful strike results in bold definition on the design elements, save for softness in the left (facing) claw. A splash or two of light gold-tan color visit each side. Wispy handling marks in the fields define the numerical grade. (#6370)

Well-Preserved 1888 Half Dollar, MS66

2245 **1888 MS66 PCGS. CAC.** Half dollar mintage numbers dropped dramatically in the last two years of the 1870s and stayed low for all of the 1880s, as silver bullion was used primarily to produce Morgan dollars. Though the 1888 mintage was the highest for the decade, that total was just 12,001 coins. The fields of this high-end example are smooth and reflective, with a few bronze patches accenting a blush of magenta and sea-green toning. Population: 19 in 66, 4 finer (8/08). (#6370)

Important and Extremely Rare Choice Proof 1848 Half Dollar
The Second Finest Known, From the Eliasberg Collection

2246 1848 PR64 NGC. Ex: Eliasberg. The extraordinarily rare 1848 proof half dollar. Only one finer specimen of this elusive issue is known: an NGC MS66 specimen sold by Heritage on July 30, 2008 for the princely sum of nearly $75,000 as part of the Phil Kaufman Collection of Early Proof Sets, Part Four. That piece was described as "one of the rarest coins in the Phil Kaufman collection, and the finest known of an exceedingly sparse population." It is an immense pleasure to have the opportunity to present another representative of this rare issue less than two months later.

The exact number of survivors is unknown, and estimates range from a low of three to a high of eight specimens. Wiley and Bugert (1993) write that fewer than four proofs are known (i.e. three, at the most). Breen (1988) lists six examples, one of which is housed in the Smithsonian, and Akers (1998) gives a similar figure of five to six survivors. The cataloger of the Eliasberg coin speculated that "fewer than seven or eight Proofs are known." NGC and PCGS combined report just four submissions. In the description for the Kaufman specimen (lot 1819) we provided a list of five distinct 1848 proof half dollars, along with three additional appearances. This important piece may be one of only four coins in private hands.

Matching the present coin to the plate of the Eliasberg example has left us certain that they are the same specimen. Although the photos in the Eliasberg catalog leave something to be desired, several toning spots on both sides are unquestionably identical. This remarkable coin has light hazel toning in the periphery that encircles the silver-gray centers, with wafts of medium gray that help distinguish this piece. Deeply mirrored fields complement the powerfully impressed design elements. Several pinpoint handling marks are only minor disturbances. This is a spectacular opportunity for the collector to obtain the second finest known example of this rare issue.

Ex: Eliasberg Collection (Bowers and Merena, 4/1997), lot 1944. From The Sundance Collection. (#6392)

Impressive 1849 Seated Half, PR66
From the Pittman and Byers Collections

2247 **1849 PR66 NGC.** Ex: Pittman. We believe this piece is the finest of just six or seven 1849 proof half dollars currently traced. In 1977, Walter Breen recorded five examples, including a badly impaired piece that he saw over 20 years earlier. Wiley and Bugert stated that at least five are known, and David Akers noted exactly five known when he cataloged this coin as part of the Pittman sale.

Expanding on the roster that appeared in our Kaufman Collection offering (April 2008), we trace the following proofs:

1. **PR66 NGC. The present specimen.** Paramount (1967 Grand Central Sale), lot 1017; John Jay Pittman (David Akers, 5/1998), lot 1536; Bowers and Merena (8/1999), lot 205; George "Buddy" Byers (Stack's, 10/2006), lot 1150; Heritage (7/2008), lot 1701; to our present consignor.

2. **PR65 NGC.** F.C.C. Boyd; World's Greatest Collection (Numismatic Gallery, 4/1945), lot 296; Floyd T. Starr (Stack's, 10/1992), lot 549; Superior (7/1993), lot 421; Phil Kaufman (Heritage, 4/2008), lot 2391. Breen suggested that this coin was possibly earlier in the Parmelee (lot 1201) and Earle (lot 2997) sales.

3. **PR64 NGC.** The Richmond Sale, Part III (David Lawrence, 3/2005), lot 1793.

4. **PR64 PCGS.** Randall Collection, lot 409; Garrett Collection (Stack's, 3/1976), lot 214; Auction '88 (RARCOA, 7/1988), lot 1725; Heritage (9/2005), lot 3265.

5. **PR64.** Louis E. Eliasberg, Sr. (Bowers and Merena, 4/1997), lot 1947.

A. **Proof.** James A. Stack (Stack's, 3/1975), lot 453. Apparently different from any of those listed above. In fact, the only piece it could be is #3, the Richmond specimen.

B. **Proof.** Kagin's (7/1978), lot 622. Possibly the Richmond coin (3), the Garrett coin (4), or the Stack coin (A).

C. **Proof.** Amwest (7/1981). The catalog is unavailable. Possibly the Richmond coin (3), the Garrett coin (4), the Stack coin (A), or the Kagin coin (B).

A boldly detailed example with sharp stars, head, foot, and gown details on the obverse, and strong eagle, claw, and leaf details on the reverse, this gorgeous proof has amazing aesthetic appeal. Both sides have brilliant silver proof surfaces, with deep peripheral sea-green, russet, violet, and gold. Aside from a few wispy hairlines, there are no contact marks or other blemishes. An exceptional example that provides an important opportunity for an advanced Seated half dollar or type specialist. *From The Malibu Collection.* (#6393)

Magnificent 1850 Half Dollar, PR64

Very Rare Choice Proof 1855/54 Half Attractively Toned, FS-301, WB-102

2248 **1850 PR64 NGC.** WB-102, with the lower right curve of the 0 doubled. The 1850 proof half dollar comes from an unknown, but extremely small mintage. Randy Wiley and Bill Bugert, in their *The Complete Guide to Liberty Seated Half Dollars*, suggest that at least four examples are known. In our January 2008 FUN sale, we listed four separate pieces in the roster developed as part of the Phil Kaufman 1850 proof half dollar writeup, along with seven "additional appearances" that may or may not be duplicates of one another, or of the four aforementioned coins. In any event, we are unable to conclusively match the current near-Gem with any 1850 proof halves in our plated catalogs.

Dappled cobalt-blue and russet patina races over luminous surfaces, and a solid strike leaves bold definition on the design elements. Only the left (facing) claw exhibits minor softness. A few minute marks preclude Gem classification; we mention the following solely for pedigree purposes: a milling mark in the right obverse field, a series of horizontal ticks on Liberty's abdomen, and a couple of grazes at the left (facing) elbow.

This is a magnificent representative of this classic Seated Liberty proof. The new owner will be delighted with its technical quality and aesthetic appeal, and will take pride in owning one of America's rarest coins.

From The Sundance Collection. (#6394)

2249 **1855/54 PR64 PCGS.** FS-301, formerly FS-005, WB-102. The 1855/54 is very rare in proof format. Heritage recently conducted extensive pedigree research for the proof issue, published under lot 2398 in our 2008 Central States Signature, and located seven different examples. The present piece does not match any of those, and thus becomes the eighth known proof. Future pedigree researches should note two pinpoint spots beneath the beak, and mint-made roller marks on the softly impressed star 7. The strike is otherwise very sharp.

This is a lovely Gem with golden-brown, jade-green, and gunmetal-gray toning. Each side has a few minute lintmarks, as produced, but no abrasions are present. All pre-1858 proof halves are rare, and its overdate status only enhances its importance. Population: 2 in 64, 1 finer (8/08).
From The Sundance Collection. (#6409)

Challenging 1856 Half Dollar, Gem Proof

2250 **1856 PR65 NGC.** Although the exact number of survivors is unknown, no more than 25 proof 1856 half dollars are considered to exist. Wiley and Bugert (1993) speculated that "less than 25 are known," while Breen estimated 14 specimens extant in 1977 and then raised that figure to 20 or 25 examples in 1988. Regardless of the precise number, this impressive coin is certainly one of the finest known representatives of this rare issue.

Pleasing amber and violet toning encircles the perimeter, which contrasts nicely against the silver-gray centers. Both sides exhibit deeply mirrored fields and there is moderate cameo contrast on the reverse. Several minuscule contact marks are visible under magnification, but they are nearly imperceptible to the unaided eye. PCGS has certified just two example in PR65 (one is Cameo) with none finer. Census: 3 in 65, 2 finer (7/08). (#6410)

Attractive 1857 Half Dollar, PR64

2251 **1857 PR64 PCGS.** The population of 1857 proof half dollars is probably about 50 coins, but this is only an estimate. PCGS and NGC have graded about 70 examples, an unknown number of which are likely resubmissions. This exquisitely struck near-Gem displays whispers of delicate golden toning, accented with hints of electric-blue and lavender at the margins The location of a few minuscule obverse flecks appears to match those on the Louis E Eliasberg, Sr. specimen (Bowers and Merena/Stack's, 4/1997), lot 1970. *From The Sundance Collection.* (#6411)

Charming 1858 Half Dollar, Choice Proof

2252 **1858 PR64 NGC.** The 1858 is the first collectible proof issue in the Liberty Seated half dollar series following the extremely low production of previous years. This is also the first date that the *Guide Book* attempts to give an estimate for the number of proofs minted, which it places at 300+ pieces. Delightful cobalt-blue surrounds the light gray toning that covers the top half of the obverse. An arc of tan and lavender toning graces the bottom of the obverse and surrounds the rim of the reverse. A carefully preserved and sharply struck representative. Census: 10 in 64, 10 finer (7/08). *From The Sundance Collection.* (#6412)

Appealing 1863 Half Dollar, PR64 Cameo

2253 **1863 PR64 Cameo PCGS.** This Civil War era half comes with a relatively low mintage of 460 proofs. Perusal of PCGS/NGC population data indicates a fair number have survived to the present day. The two services have seen about 30 Cameos. This near-Gem Cameo exhibits a barely discernible film of champagne color, and outstanding field-motif contrast. An exacting strike imparts bold definition to the design elements, further enhancing the coin's eye appeal. A few trivial handling marks preclude Gem status. Population: 6 in 64 Cameo, 4 finer (8/08). *From The Sundance Collection.* (#86417)

Spectacular 1865 Half Dollar, PR67 Cameo

2254 **1865 PR67 Cameo NGC.** In the introduction to *April 1865: The Month That Saved America,* author Jay Winik states that "... what emerges from the panorama of April 1865 is that the whole of our national history could have been altered but for a few decisions, a quirk of fate, a sudden shift in luck." The year that marked the end of the Civil War was also the last year No Motto proof half dollars were minted. This example displays remarkable toning. Splashes of aquamarine and sky-blue near the obverse rim, outlined by copper and mahogany to the inside, focus attention to the dove-gray center. The same blues and greens form a toning halo on the reverse, rimmed on the inside by dark copper that fades to an untoned silver-gray center. NGC has certified just 33 1865 Cameo proofs, with this piece tied with only one other at the Superb Gem level, and none finer (8/08).
From The Sundance Collection. (#86419)

Amazing 1866 Motto PR66 Fifty Cent

2255 **1866 Motto PR66 NGC.** The satiny motifs stand out against the mirrored fields of this Premium Gem proof, especially when the coin is tilted slightly under a light source. Soft cobalt-blue and gold-beige patina concentrates in the fields, joined by purple and violet in those of the reverse. Light silver-gray dominates the central devices. A solid strike emboldens the design features, and impeccable preservation characterizes both faces. Census: 7 in 66, 1 finer (7/08).
From The Sundance Collection. (#6424)

Beautiful 1867 Gem Cameo Proof Half Dollar

2256 **1867 PR65 Cameo PCGS.** Mildly frosted design elements appear to be suspended above the glassy fields of this beautiful Cameo. A powerful strike seems to enhance the field-motif contrast even more, regardless of the angle of view. Electric-blue, lavender, and golden-tan at the obverse margin yields to soft gold-champagne in the center. The latter dominates the reverse, transitioning to deeper reddish-gold at the periphery. A few trivial obverse field marks may well preclude an even higher grade. Population: 6 in 65 Cameo, 3 finer (8/08).
From The Sundance Collection. (#86425)

2257 **1868 PR64 NGC.** A lightly frosted, brilliant, and deeply mirrored Choice representative. Close inspection with a loupe reveals only a couple of tiny contact marks. This fully struck specimen is one of just 600 proofs minted. (#6426)

Exquisite 1869 Half Dollar, PR65

2258   **1869 PR65 PCGS.** The half dollar saw 600 proofs coined in 1869. PCGS and NGC have graded approximately 300 pieces, the vast majority through PR64. Gunmetal-blue adorns the Liberty motif on this Gem, yielding to sky-blue and golden-brown in the fields. Champagne-gold dominates the reverse central device, while the fields assume a mix of sky-blue, purple, and soft beige-gold. Exquisitely struck and well preserved throughout. Population: 12 in 65, 4 finer (8/08).
From The Sundance Collection. (#6427)

Attractively Toned 1870 PR64 Half Dollar

2259   **1870 PR64 NGC.** An attractive blend of medium intensity cobalt-blue, purple, yellow-gold, and orange patina bathes this near-Gem proof half, and an exacting strike imparts crisp definition to the design elements, save for a touch of softness on the left (facing) claw. A few unobtrusive handling marks preclude Gem classification. Census: 32 in 64, 22 finer (7/08). (#6428)

Lightly Toned 1870 Fifty Cent, PR66

2260   **1870 PR66 PCGS.** Soft champagne color dominates the obverse, while the same color palette takes on slightly deeper hues on the reverse. Incompleteness of strike occurs on Liberty's breasts and the eagle's left (facing) leg and claw and adjacent arrow feathers, while the remaining design elements are sharply defined. Both sides are nicely preserved. Population: 4 in 66, 0 finer (8/08).
From The Sundance Collection. (#6428)

Colorful Choice Proof 1871 Half

2261   **1871 PR64 PCGS.** Exquisite orange-gold, fire-red, powder-blue, and mauve envelops this flashy and unblemished near-Gem. Well struck apart from the usual inexactness on the eagle's left (facing) ankle. Certified in an old green label holder. A mere 960 proofs were struck. Population: 24 in 64, 14 finer (8/08).
From The Sundance Collection. (#6429)

Delightful 1872 Half Dollar, PR66 Cameo

2262   **1872 PR66 Cameo NGC.** Concentric rings of deep electric-blue, purple, and gold-orange patina, slightly more extensive on the obverse, cling to the rim areas of this Premium Gem Cameo, framing soft champagne centers. The design features exhibit crisp definition, and both sides are nicely preserved.
From The Sundance Collection. (#86430)

2263   **1873 No Arrows, Closed 3 PR64 Cameo PCGS.** Warm gold-gray and sunset-orange patina graces much of each side, though this toning leaves the coin's essential contrast undimmed. Only a few minor hairlines affect the fields. Population: 11 in 64 Cameo, 4 finer (8/08). (#86431)

Extravagantly Toned PR66 ★ 1873 Arrows Half

2264 **1873 Arrows PR66 ★ NGC.** Lush ocean-blue, honey-gold, apricot, and cherry-red invigorate this precisely struck and unabraded Premium Gem. A small oval lamination near Liberty's raised elbow is of mint origin. An elusive proof subtype, the 1873 Arrows has a proof mintage of just 550 pieces, and its only successor, the 1874, contributes only an additional 700 proofs. Arrows were added to signify a minor weight change to correspond with the metric system. Those in search of a gorgeously toned specimen need look no further. Census: 3 in 66 ★, 1 finer with a Star designation (as MS66 ★ Cameo) (7/08). *From The Malibu Collection.* (#6434)

Select Proof 1874 Arrows Half

2265 **1874 Arrows PR63 PCGS.** An attractive example of this two-year type. The obverse is sharply divided between the lovely hazel toning that covers the upper four-fifths and the untoned region at the bottom. In contrast, the reverse has a light dusting of toning at the margins. This powerfully struck piece has only a couple of minor contact marks and is one of just 700 proofs struck. (#6435)

Lavishly Toned PR66 ★ Cameo 1876 Half

2266 **1876 PR66 ★ Cameo NGC.** FS-401 with a partial impression of an S on Liberty's throat, presumably from a dropped letter punch. Type One Reverse. Iridescent navy-blue, plum-red, and caramel-gold endows this proof type coin. The strike is exacting save for slight blending on the eagle's left (facing) ankle. A thin mark near star 12, but otherwise flawless. Census: 2 in 66 ★ Cameo, none finer with a Star designation (7/08). *From The Malibu Collection.* (#86437)

Pleasing 1878 Half Dollar, PR65 Cameo

2267 **1878 PR65 Cameo NGC.** Type Two Reverse. Deeply reflective with a touch of haze over the obverse fields. This scarcely dims the contrast between the lightly frosted devices and the mirrors. A well executed strike brings up excellent definition in all of the design elements. This well-preserved and aesthetically appealing Gem, one of just 800 specimens, is a testament to the heights the 19th century minting process could achieve. Census: 10 in 65 Cameo, 10 finer (7/08). (#86439)

Appealing 1879 Half Dollar, PR66 Cameo

2268 **1879 PR66 Cameo NGC.** Type One Reverse. An exceptionally reflective and practically untoned Premium Gem. Thick mint frost is consistent throughout the devices and legends. An unobtrusive fingerprint is noted on AMERICA. Great overall appeal. Census: 7 in 66 Cameo, 12 finer (7/08). (#86440)

Premium 1879 Half Dollar, PR67 Cameo

2269 **1879 PR67 Cameo NGC.** The proof mintage of 1879 Seated half dollars, at 1,100 pieces, was nearly one-quarter that of the business strike total—only 4,800 coins. Boldly struck devices contrast sharply against the unblemished and untoned fields of this coin, earning it the well-deserved Cameo designation. Census: 11 in 67, 1 finer (7/08). (#86440)

Wondrous 1880 Half Dollar, PR65

2270 **1880 PR65 PCGS.** Housed in a green-label PCGS holder, this Gem is an extraordinary example of the PR65 grade. It is also clearly a full Cameo and deserves such a designation from one of the grading services. With frosty devices and fully mirrored fields, both sides have peripheral gold accents with deep blue along the right reverse border. Population: 28 in 65, 17 finer (8/08). (#6441)

Lushly Toned PR66 ★ 1880 Half

2271 **1880 PR66 ★ NGC.** Splendid lemon-gold, cherry-red, and ocean-blue toning invigorates this crisply struck Premium Gem. For proofs and business strikes combined, fewer than 10,000 pieces were struck. NGC has awarded three proof 1880 halves with a ★ designation, the present piece and two others graded PR66 Prooflike (8/08). *From The Sundance Collection.* (#6441)

2272 **1881 PR64 PCGS.** Elegant gold-orange and violet patina of varying thickness drapes the moderate mirrors of this Choice proof. Minimally flawed for the grade assigned. PCGS has graded 32 finer pieces (8/08). (#6442)

Pleasing 1881 PR64 Half Dollar

2273 **1881 PR64 PCGS.** Concentric rings of iridescent multicolored toning around the borders frame light silver-gray central areas. An impressive strike results in strong definition on the design elements, save for minor softness on Liberty's breasts and adjacent hair curls, and the reverse arrow feathers. A few light marks keeps from full Gem. *From The Sundance Collection.* (#6442)

Glassy PR64 Cameo 1881 Half

2274 **1881 PR64 Cameo NGC. CAC.** The icy devices provide blatant contrast with the glassy fields. A hint of rose-gold toning clings to the rims, but the remainder of this Choice proof half is brilliant. A good strike with only minor incompleteness on the fletchings and claws. A slender diagonal planchet streak passes through the shield. Census: 27 in 64 Cameo, 30 finer (7/08). (#86442)

Elusive 1881 PR66 Cameo Half Dollar

2275 **1881 PR66 Cameo NGC.** 1881 half dollars in proof format are readily available (Randy Wiley and Bill Bugert, 1993). Better-grade Cameos, however, remain elusive. Such is the case with the current Premium Gem. Both sides reveal strong field-motif contrast. Hints of gold color gravitate to the rims, slightly more so on the reverse. An attentive strike leaves sharp definition on the design elements, and both faces are well preserved. Census: 12 in 66 Cameo, 3 finer (7/08). (#86442)

2276 **1883 PR65 PCGS.** Ex: Eliasberg. The obverse is close to brilliant, while pastel tan-gold toning clings to the reverse periphery. The strike is precise aside from a hint of incompleteness on Liberty's forehead curls. Flashy fields and nicely frosted motifs suggest a Cameo designation is due. Housed in a green label holder. Population: 32 in 65, 9 finer (8/08).
Ex: Louis E. Eliasberg, Sr. Collection (Bowers and Merena, 4/1997). From The Sundance Collection. (#6444)

2277 **1884 PR64 NGC.** A remarkable specimen with vivid violet toning around the devices. The devices are lightly frosted and, although this piece is not designated as such by NGC, there is lovely cameo contrast against the deeply mirrored fields. A few minor contact marks keep this piece from an even higher grade. The 1884 was part of a series of low mintage Philadelphia issues from 1879 to 1890. A mere 4,400 circulation strikes were minted, along with just 875 proofs. (#6445)

2278 **1884 PR66 PCGS.** This coin was previously offered as lot 6877 in our September 2002 Long Beach Signature Sale, where it was cataloged as: "This is an interesting example from the standpoint of toning. The majority of the surface area displays silver-gray color, but there are irregular splashes of orange-gold, lilac-gray, and cobalt-blue iridescence scattered about. Shining powerfully through this toning one can discern reflective fields, and the smooth, fully brought up devices are no less evident. A lone spot at 5 o'clock on the obverse periphery is noted for accuracy." Population: 8 in 66, 3 finer (8/08).
From The Sundance Collection. (#6445)

2279 **1884 PR67 Cameo NGC.** Just over 5,000 1884 Seated Liberty half dollars were produced in any form. Of those, a mere 875 were proofs. Of those proofs, just a few dozen have been designated as Cameo by either NGC or PCGS. And of those Cameos, NGC and PCGS have combined to certify but five 67s, with none finer (7/08). While 1884 proof half dollars were preserved at a high rate, it is clear that this coin stands strong among the elite not only for the date and series, but for the type. That being the case, general collectors and series enthusiasts alike should look at this Superb Gem Cameo as a unique opportunity to own a conditional rarity. The surfaces are brilliant throughout and the fields deeply reflective. This reflectivity sets up a strong cameo contrast against the frosted devices on each side. An essentially flawless Superb Gem. (#86445)

Exquisitely Toned PR66 ★ Cameo 1885 Half

2280 **1885 PR66 ★ Cameo NGC.** Rose-red, yellow, and sky-blue enriches this pristine Premium Gem. The strike is complete aside from Liberty's forehead curls. A scant 930 proofs and 5,200 business strikes were coined. Census: 1 in 66 ★ Cameo, 2 finer as Cameo with a Star designation (7/08).
From The Sundance Collection. (#86446)

Outstanding 1886 Half Dollar, PR66 Cameo

2281 **1886 PR66 Cameo NGC.** The 1886 Half is a rare issue in both business strike and proof formats with only 5,000 and 886 pieces produced of each, respectively. The fields of this piece are deeply reflective and have wondrous "black-on-white" cameo contrast against the heavy mint frost on the devices. A fully struck and impeccably preserved specimen. Census: 5 in 66 Cameo, 2 finer (7/08). (#86447)

Gorgeous 1887 Seated Half, PR65

2282 **1887 PR65 PCGS.** Delightful patina on this Gem captures the viewer's gaze. Both sides are nicely mirrored with lustrous devices, under ivory, gold, and iridescent toning. In the late 19th century, collectors preferred proof coins for their collections, while the few circulation strikes of the 1880s mostly escaped into commerce. Mintages were low as the Mint tried to keep up with silver dollar production required by law. Today, collectors relish the chance to acquire the proof half dollars of the decade, perhaps the only opportunity to add a particular date to an advanced cabinet. (#6448)

2283 **1888 PR63 PCGS.** Lovely pearl-gray toning endows the surfaces, with accents of gold in the periphery. The strike is full save for a touch of softness on Liberty's hair. Scattered hairlines limit the grade, but none merit specific mention. A highly reflective and appealing example. One of only 832 proofs struck. (#6449)

2284 **1891 PR63 PCGS.** Remarkable iridescent blue toning surrounds the rose and steel colored centers. The highly reflective fields show minor lint marks but none are consequential. A sharply struck and handsome final year of issue. One of just 600 proofs struck. (#6452)

BARBER HALF DOLLARS

Richly Toned MS65 1892 Barber Half

2285 **1892 MS65 PCGS.** The first year of issue for the design created by Charles Barber, and highly sought by both date and type collectors. An exquisite and frosty Gem with gold, steel, and light brown toning on each side. Design elements on both sides are sharply defined, from freshly created hubs and dies. PCGS has only graded 50 finer pieces (8/08). (#6461)

Appealing 1892-S Half Dollar, Choice Mint State

2286 **1892-S MS64 PCGS.** A vibrantly toned representative of the first Barber half dollar. Amber, violet, and rose colors drape both sides of this carefully preserved specimen. The surfaces appear remarkably pristine for the grade, and the strike is nearly full. Fabulous satiny luster penetrates the appealing toning. Population: 32 in 64, 15 finer (8/08). (#6464)

Spectacular 1893-O Half Dollar, Premium Gem

2287 **1893-O MS66 NGC.** Although not rare in the absolute sense, the 1893-O is a condition rarity in high Mint State grades. A look at the population reports reveals that the number of 1893-O halves drops significantly above the MS63 grade level. Only five MS66 pieces have been certified by both NGC and PCGS combined, with none finer (8/08). This is a rare opportunity for a collector to obtain one of the finest representatives of this early Barber half.

Pleasing green-gray toning in the periphery encircles the lighter silver-gray centers. The strike is razor-sharp with no notable weakness on either side. Powerful luster radiates beneath the vibrant toning and enhances the eye appeal. This virtually pristine specimen would make a perfect addition to a registry set. (#6466)

2288 **1894 MS63 NGC.** Beautifully detailed, impressively lustrous, and highly appealing. Only occasional golden accents visit the minimally abraded surfaces. Census: 26 in 63, 54 finer (7/08). (#6468)

2289 **1894-O MS63 PCGS.** Well struck with strong, slightly frosty luster beneath subtle gold, silver, and powder-blue shadings. Minimally marked for the grade and highly appealing. Population: 30 in 63, 60 finer (8/08). (#6469)

2290 **1894-O MS63 NGC.** Vibrant gold, rose-red, and violet toning embraces both sides of this highly lustrous Barber half. Scattered abrasions limit the grade, but all are insignificant. An attractive and fully struck representative. Census: 21 in 63, 41 finer (8/08). (#6469)

2291 **1895 MS64 PCGS.** Pleasing medium-gray patina covers the obverse, which contrasts sharply against the silver-gray reverse. Enticing luster gleams beneath the toning and accents the razor-sharp details. A loupe locates several minor abrasions on this conditionally scarce representative. Population: 30 in 64, 22 finer (7/08). (#6471)

2292 **1895-S MS63 NGC.** Dense charcoal-gray and greenish-brown toning covers both sides. Well struck with nearly mark-free surfaces. (#6473)

Patinated Choice 1896 Half Dollar

2293 **1896 MS64 PCGS.** This satiny Choice Barber half is lushly toned in olive-green and rose-red. The strike is virtually full, even near the right shield corner. Beautifully preserved aside from a faded thin horizontal mark on the neck. Lower mintage than usual for a Philadelphia issue. Population: 26 in 64, 18 finer (8/08). (#6474)

Captivating 1896 Half Dollar, MS67 ★
Tied With One Other For Finest
Certified With Star

2294 1896 MS67 ★ NGC. The 1896 has one of the lowest business strike mintages (950,000 pieces) in the Barber half dollar series, and is scarce in all levels of preservation. In the better Mint State grades (MS65 and finer), NGC and PCGS have certified just 29 coins: 21 examples in MS65, five in MS66, and three in MS67, including two Superb Gems with Star.

The present MS67 ★ offering displays intense luster radiating from surfaces splashed with delicate cobalt-blue, beige-gold, magenta, sky-blue, and violet patination. A penetrating strike leaves virtually complete delineation on the design elements, heightening even more the outstanding eye appeal. Close inspection reveals a handful of trivial, grade-consistent marks, barely precluding an MS68 numerical grade. This captivating piece will delight the new owner! (#6474)

2295 1896-O—Artificial Toning—NCS. AU Details. Deep ocean-blue envelops this semi-key half dollar, although the reverse periphery is golden-brown. The reverse luster is complete, while the obverse luster is subdued only across the open field. Portions of the eagle lack a bold strike, and a brief diagonal mark is noted east of Liberty's ear. (#6475)

Outstanding 1897 Half Dollar, MS65

2296 1897 MS65 NGC. Despite a mintage of nearly 2.5 million business strikes, the 1897 is surprisingly scarce in high Uncirculated grades. At the MS65 level NGC has certified only 18 pieces, with just five coins finer (8/08). Enticing satiny luster shimmers beneath the pleasing mint frost that covers the untoned surfaces. The strike is nearly full and there are only a couple of microscopic handling marks. (#6477)

2297 1898 MS64 PCGS. Flashy luster radiates beneath the gunmetal-gray patina. The strike is nearly full, and there are only a few trivial marks on each side. Population: 44 in 64, 22 finer (7/08). (#6480)

Delightful Gem 1900 Half Dollar

2298 1900 MS65 PCGS. Jade-green, rose-red, and slate-gray compete for territory across this lustrous Gem. The obverse border has the richest toning, while much of the reverse has only light freckled patina. The strike is decisive, even on the fletchings, and both sides are impressively devoid of marks. Population: 21 in 65, 6 finer (8/08). (#6486)

2299 1901-S—Genuine—PCGS. In-house graded AU58 Details, lightly cleaned. Silver-gray surfaces display considerable luster, and reveal some fine hairlines under magnification. Well struck, except localized softness on the shield and eagle. (#6491)

Eye-Catching 1902-O Half Dollar, Choice Uncirculated

2300 1902-O MS64 PCGS. A ring of violet toning encircles the centers, which have a lovely dusting of rose-red patina. Alluring satiny luster enhances the eye appeal of this sharply struck near-Gem specimen. Several minuscule handling marks are nearly imperceptible. Population: 15 in 64, 6 finer (8/08). (#6493)

Pleasing 1903-O Half Dollar, Choice Uncirculated

2301 **1903-O MS64 PCGS.** Slate-gray patina across the devices yields to violet and cobalt-blue toning around the rims. Coruscating mint luster glimmers beneath the deep toning. A few small reeding marks on the obverse account for the grade, but the reverse is remarkably clean. NGC has certified only 12 coins finer than this attractive example (8/08). (#6496)

2302 **1906-D MS64 NGC.** Lovely ivory-white toning drapes the surfaces, with captivating satiny luster beneath. A few nearly imperceptible grazes keep this razor-sharp piece from being flawless. Census: 27 in 64, 10 finer (8/08). (#6505)

Sharply Struck 1906-O Fifty Cent, MS64

2303 **1906-O MS64 PCGS.** The 1906-O tends to come poorly struck (David Lawrence, *The Complete Guide to Barber Halves*). The present near-Gem is a pleasant exception, as none of the design elements reveal hints of weakness. Light gray-tan patina, somewhat thicker on the reverse, adorns highly lustrous surfaces. A few inoffensive handling marks define the grade. Population: 23 in 64, 12 finer (8/08). (#6506)

Gem 1907-D Barber Half

2304 **1907-D MS65 PCGS.** Hints of straw-gold toning deny full brilliance, but booming luster and smooth surfaces ensure the eye appeal. A precisely struck example of an issue that is scarce in Mint State and rare as a Gem. Encased in an old green label holder. Population: 15 in 65, 12 finer (8/08). (#6509)

2305 **1907-O MS64 NGC.** A milky white representative of one of the final New Orleans Mint issues. Typical for an O-mint issue of this era, the right corner of the shield, the tips of the wings, and several stars exhibit softness. The surfaces are surprisingly clean with splendid satiny luster on each side. A conditionally scarce piece; NGC has certified only 28 coins finer (7/08). (#6510)

Dazzling 1907-S Gem Half Dollar

2306 **1907-S MS65 NGC.** The 1907-S half dollar comes from a mintage of 1,250,000. David Lawrence writes in his *The Complete Guide To Barber Halves* reference: "Very scarce in XF and above." He goes on to say: "This is the scarcest late date of the series in MS." Lawrence assigns an R.5 value to Mint State pieces.

Both sides of this Gem are awash in dazzling luster. Untoned surfaces have a silky finish, and a well executed strike leaves strong definition on the design elements, with the sole exception of the usual softness on the upper right corner of the shield and the adjacent feathers. A couple of minor obverse marks likely preclude an even finer grade. A fine die crack runs across the lower edge of the bust to the last star (mentioned in Lawrence). Census: 6 in 65, 3 finer (7/08). (#6511)

Bright, Lustrous MS66 1908-O Barber Half

2307 **1908-O MS66 PCGS.** This is a beautifully preserved representative of this popular O-mint issue with a slightly above average strike. Both sides are essentially brilliant, save for the slightest hint of pale rose color. The obverse is unusually well defined, however, the eagle's neck, right talon, and right shoulder are slightly weak. The surfaces are smooth and shimmer displaying full, frosty luster. Despite its incomplete strike, this is an attractive, original Premium Gem that would fit nicely into a high grade collection. Population: 16 in 66, 12 finer (8/08).
From The Bell Collection. (#6514)

Outstanding 1909 Half Dollar, MS66

2308 **1909 MS66 PCGS.** Lovely rose, hazel, and violet colors intermingle on the surfaces of this carefully preserved Premium Gem. Both sides are remarkably clean and a loupe locates only a couple of microscopic handling marks. A conditionally rare and vividly toned specimen. Neither NGC nor PCGS have certified any pieces finer than the present examples, and NGC reports just six submissions at the MS66 level (8/08). (#6516)

Well Struck 1909-S Half Dollar, MS64

2309 **1909-S MS64 PCGS.** Lustrous silver-gray surfaces display whispers of light tan-gold color, and a well executed strike imparts bold definition to the design elements. The word LIBERTY is especially strong (see David Lawrence, 1991, pp. 83 and 85). A few minute handling marks preclude Gem classification. (#6518)

Interesting 1909-S Half Dollar, MS65

2310 **1909-S MS65 NGC.** Inverted S. The mintmark was obviously punched upside-down. An outstanding, brilliant, and highly lustrous Gem. The surfaces are remarkably pristine for the grade, and there are just a few light grazes on Liberty. Captivating satiny luster sparkles on both sides and accents the nearly fully struck details. This often overlooked issue is rare in Gem and extremely difficult to locate in grades finer. Census: 8 in 65, 5 finer (7/08). (#6518)

Impressive 1910 Half Dollar, Gem Mint State

2311 **1910 MS65 PCGS.** With just 418,000 pieces struck, the 1910 had a mintage that is significantly lower than most Barber halves, which typically had distributions well into the millions. In addition, the 1910 is seldom seen in Gem and is virtually impossible to locate any finer. The present example is untoned and sharply struck, save for the often-seen weakness on a few stars. Both sides show only minor marks, and these barely affect the watery reflectivity of the semiprooflike fields. An attractive and conditionally scarce representative. Population: 21 in 65, 4 finer (8/08). (#6519)

Radiant 1910-S Half Dollar, MS64

2312 **1910-S MS64 PCGS.** Radiantly lustrous surfaces display traces of golden-tan color, most noticeable in the left obverse margins. The only weakness occurs on the right (facing) claw and the adjacent arrows. A handful of minute marks keep from full Gem status. Population: 18 in 64, 25 finer (8/08). (#6520)

2313 **1911 MS63 PCGS.** Dusky gold, orange, and rose patina embraces the luminous surfaces of this Select survivor. Minimally marked for the grade with strong visual appeal. (#6521)

Stunning 1911 Barber Half, MS65

2314 **1911 MS65 PCGS. CAC.** A stunning Gem with fully brilliant, untoned silver surfaces and frosty luster. This lovely half dollar is highly appealing, a numismatic treat for the connoisseur. It is sharply detailed on both sides, with bold star, leaf, and hair details on the obverse, and bold definition on all aspects of the reverse. Population: 41 in 65, 9 finer (8/08). (#6521)

Important Gem 1911 Barber Half Dollar

2315 **1911 MS65 PCGS.** A boldly defined Gem with brilliant and frosty luster that is enhanced through splashes of delicate lilac, gold, and iridescent toning on each side. The 1911 and 1912 Barber half dollars are underrated, as they fall between the elusive 1910 and the key-date 1913, 1914, and 1915 Philadelphia Mint issues. Population: 41 in 65, 9 finer (8/08). (#6521)

Brilliant 1912 Barber Half, MS65

2316 **1912 MS65 PCGS.** Essentially brilliant with a bright, monochromatic cartwheel finish and strong definition overall. Carefully preserved and visually impressive. While the 1912 has a higher mintage than its later Philadelphia half dollar counterparts, it is no less elusive than those issues in Gem condition. Population: 18 in 65, 2 finer (8/08). (#6524)

2317 **1912-D MS64 PCGS.** Swirling luster engulfs this near-Gem Barber half, and whispers of barely discernible light gold run over each side. Well struck, save for softness in a couple of obverse star centers, and on the upper right corner of the shield. A few minute obverse marks define the grade.
From The Menlo Park Collection. (#6525)

Vibrant 1912-D Half Dollar, Gem Mint State

2318 **1912-D MS65 PCGS.** Deep russet, gold, and violet toning envelops both sides, with soft luster that gleams beneath. The strike is nearly full, and the surfaces appear pristine to the unaided eye. The 1912-D is difficult to locate in a higher grade. Population: 50 in 65, 14 finer (7/08). (#6525)

Sharp, Lustrous 1912-S Barber Half, MS65

2319 **1912-S MS65 PCGS.** A Gem-condition example of the 1912-S is just about as nice as most collectors could ever hope to find, as only seven coins at PCGS and eight coins at NGC—minus the inevitable duplications—have been certified finer (8/08). This specimen displays mottled olive and powder-gray patina on both sides, with a nearly full strike and considerable luster. (#6526)

2320 **1913 AU58 NGC.** With just 188,000 pieces struck, the 1913 has one of the lowest mintages of the series. This briefly circulated example is significantly finer than most, and has no marks worthy of individual mention. The strike is crisp and the fields have plenty of luster. Census: 11 in 58, 47 finer (7/08). (#6527)

2321 **1913-D MS64 PCGS.** Light creamy toning with a peppering of hazel covers each side of this satiny specimen. The stars and the tips of the eagle's wings are a little soft, but the rest of the details are crisply defined. With 534,000 pieces struck, the 1913-D is on the low side compared to the typical mintage of several million coins. PCGS has certified only 13 examples finer (7/08). (#6528)

Delightful 1913-S Half Dollar, Choice Mint State

2322 **1913-S MS64 NGC.** Peppered russet toning in the margins accents the mostly brilliant surfaces. Exquisite satiny luster shimmers throughout and gives this example impressive eye appeal. A few minor reeding marks keep this sharply struck piece from an even higher grade. Census: 26 in 64, 15 finer (7/08). (#6529)

Scarce 1913-S Barber Half, MS64

2323 **1913-S MS64 PCGS.** The 1913-S half dollar is not a famous rarity, unlike the 1913-S quarter, but it is a scarcer date in the series. Just above 600,000 pieces were struck, and while pieces are not too difficult to find in worn-out circulated grades, Mint State pieces are few and far between. This lustrous and nearly brilliant near-Gem is well preserved, and is perhaps limited in grade by slight striking weakness on the cheek and right shield corner. Population: 22 in 64, 18 finer (6/08). (#6529)

2324 **1915-S MS64 PCGS.** Peppered russet toning graces the obverse, and just a hint of color is visible on the reverse. The remarkable satiny luster is particularly eye-catching. This crisply struck representative has only insignificant marks in the fields and would make a lovely final-year type coin. (#6534)

2325 **1915-S MS64 NGC.** An arc of deep violet toning covers the left side of the obverse, while a touch of rose accents the remaining silver-gray surfaces. Pleasing satiny luster shimmers on both sides and is barely affected by a couple of light grazes. (#6534)

2326 **1915-S MS64 NGC.** An attractive near-Gem with light olive-gray toning and speckled russet patina on both sides, mainly near the borders. The striking details are rather soft on the eagle's tail feathers and talons, and on two or three of the obverse stars, but surface marks are virtually nonexistent. (#6534)

2327 **1915-S MS64 PCGS.** Freckles of faint gold-tan color are distributed over the lustrous surfaces of this near-Gem half. The design features are well defined, save for the usual softness in the upper right corner of the shield. A few minute handling marks define the grade. Population: 87 in 64, 44 finer (8/08). (#6534)

2328 **1915-S MS64 PCGS.** Sharply struck with scintillating luster and a slight golden cast over both sides. A handful of faint marks on the obverse keep it from grading finer. An attractive near-Gem from the final year of the Barber half dollar series, housed in a green label PCGS holder. (#6534)

Eye-Catching 1915-S Half Dollar, Gem Mint State

2329 **1915-S MS65 NGC.** Mostly brilliant with a dusting of russet on the reverse. The sharp strike is complemented by impressive satiny luster throughout. There are several wispy abrasions, but none detract from the great eye appeal. This conditionally scarce Gem would make a wonderful type coin of the final year of issue. Census: 35 in 65, 8 finer (7/08). (#6534)

Lustrous 1915-S Half Dollar, MS65

2330 **1915-S MS65 NGC.** Impressive satiny luster complements the sharply struck details. Peppered reddish-purple toning accents the obverse, which appears brilliant at first glance. A few minor marks are visible on the obverse, but the reverse looks pristine to the unaided eye. NGC has certified only 35 pieces in MS65 and eight finer, while PCGS reports a nearly identical figure (8/08). (#6534)

PROOF BARBER HALF DOLLARS

2331 **1894 PR64 PCGS. CAC.** Vibrant rose, orange, and violet toning drapes the deeply mirrored surfaces of this carefully preserved specimen. A number of lint marks (as made) limit the grade. Sharply struck save for softness on the eagle's right wing. Only 972 proofs were struck. (#6541)

2332 **1894 PR64 NGC.** Dappled sky-blue and golden-tan patina bathes both sides of this near-Gem proof, and a well executed strike imparts crisp definition to the design elements. A handful of obverse marks defines the grade. (#6541)

Amazing 1894 Half, PR65 Cameo

2333 **1894 PR65 Cameo ICG.** The centers offer powerful, essentially untoned mirrors and solid contrast with the mildly frosted devices. At the margins, gold-orange toning visits the obverse, while deeper russet, gold, and violet shadings prevail near the peripheries on the reverse. (#86541)

Splendid 1894 Barber Half PR66 Cameo

2334 **1894 PR66 Cameo NGC.** This is an outstanding proof Barber half dollar, with a combination of exceptional technical quality and eye appeal. All of the design elements are reproduced with razor-sharp precision, as is expected but not always delivered on proof specimens. The watery, deeply reflective fields provide a splendid backdrop for the frosted silver devices, and lovely cobalt-blue and gold-tan peripheral toning further increases the visual allure of this conditionally scarce example. Census: 15 in 66 Cameo, 12 finer (7/08). (#86541)

2335 **1897 PR64 PCGS.** Well-defined and strikingly toned. Chalk-white and champagne-gold shadings appear on each side, and the obverse sports salmon accents as well. Strongly mirrored beneath the patina. (#6544)

Spectacular 1897 Barber Half, PR68 Ultra Cameo

2336 **1897 PR68 Ultra Cameo NGC.** From a proof mintage of only 731 coins, the lowest proof mintage of the decade for any Barber half. This wonderful coin has been perfectly preserved for more than a century. The brilliant flash of the deeply mirrored fields contrasts vividly with the frosty luster of the design elements. The full strike brings up every detail of Barber's design in bold three-dimensional relief. The surfaces are free of hairlines and contact marks, as expected in the PR68 grade. The brilliant, untoned surfaces glow with exquisite eye appeal. For the advanced collector, this combination of rarity, historical interest, and aesthetic appeal should be irresistible. (#96544)

Impressive 1898 Barber Half, PR66

2337 **1898 PR66 PCGS.** The design elements are reproduced with razor-sharp precision, on both sides, and the surfaces are adorned in deep, variegated shades of rose, gold, and electric-blue. Partial (and very faint) fingerprint fragments appear on the obverse, but there are no distracting contact marks or hairlines noted on either the obverse or the reverse. Population: 26 in 66, 14 finer (8/08). (#6545)

Gem Proof 1900 Barber Half Dollar

2338 **1900 PR65 PCGS.** Light cameo contrast is evident on both sides of this Gem proof with its lovely faint champagne toning. It is boldly detailed as all proofs should be, with fully defined central motifs. Coins bearing the 1900 date are extremely popular with collectors, even though the 20th century didn't start until 1901. Population: 40 in 65, 19 finer (8/08). (#6547)

2339 **1901 PR63 PCGS.** Just 813 proofs were struck. Dramatic rings of charcoal, teal-green, violet, and gold yield to silver-gray on the centers. The fields are powerfully reflective and there is moderate cameo contrast on the reverse. Nearly fully struck with great eye appeal. (#6548)

2340 **1901 PR63 PCGS.** Rich violet, gold, and blue shades appear in a narrow band around the inner rim, while the rest of the coin is primarily silver-gray. Well-defined with minor hairlines consistent with the Select grade. (#6548)

2341 **1902 PR63 NGC.** Vivid russet, hazel, and indigo toning around the perimeter accents the deeply mirrored fields. Several hairlines across Liberty's cheek, and a couple of contact marks in the fields keep this sharply struck representative from an even higher grade. Only 777 proofs were struck. (#6549)

2342 **1902 PR63 PCGS.** Rich gold-orange toning graces the margins, while the centers offer deep silver-gray patina. Powerful luster radiates beneath the toning and the eye appeal is barely affected by scattered hairlines in the fields. (#6549)

2343 **1902 PR63 NGC.** Light gold toning visits this nicely struck specimen. The devices appear frosted when rotated at select angles. The cheek has a few nearly imperceptible slide marks. A scant 777 proofs were struck. In a prior generation holder. (#6549)

Superlative 1902 Half Dollar, PR67 ★
Finest Certified With ★

2344 **1902 PR67 ★ NGC.** Gleaming surfaces set off boldly struck devices on this essentially untoned proof specimen, one of 777 coined this year. Traces of crimson arc along the top and bottom edges of the obverse, while the reverse shows a highlight of copper, rose, and sky-blue across the legend at the top. Although several hundred proof 1902 halves have been certified in all grades, a Superb Gem with ★ such as this coin is an extraordinary find. Census: 1 in 67, 0 finer (8/08). (#6549)

2345 **1902 PR63 Cameo PCGS.** The design elements are reproduced with pinpoint sharpness on both sides. The fields are watery and deeply reflective, contrasting nicely with the mildly frosted devices. Population: 5 in 63 Cameo, 13 finer (8/08). (#86549)

Toned 1903 Half Dollar, PR65

2346 **1903 PR65 NGC.** A moderately toned Gem, both sides exhibiting delicate gold, framed by deeper blue and lilac. Like most proof coins, the devices are boldly defined. Struck during an era of diminished cameo contrast, this piece actually has good contrast between the devices and the fields. (#6550)

Brilliant PR66 ★ 1903 Barber Half

2347 **1903 PR66 ★ NGC.** One of only two proof 1903 Barber halves to merit a Star designation from NGC (8/08). This is a brilliant Premium Gem with undisturbed glassy fields and fully struck devices. The eagle is nicely icy, although Liberty's bust lacks sufficient frost to command a rare (for this issue) Cameo designation. A mere 755 proofs were issued. (#6550)

2348 **1905 PR64 PCGS.** Deep gunmetal gray, violet, orange, and yellow toning envelops the obverse, which contrasts sharply against the lighter violet, maroon, and yellow toning on the reverse. Although the luster is subdued on the obverse, the reverse is highly reflective. A fully struck and attractive representative. A mere 727 proofs were struck. (#6552)

Impressive PR67 ★ 1906 Half Dollar

2349 **1906 PR67 ★ NGC.** As of (8/08), only three proof 1906 half dollars have received a Star designation from NGC. The present crisply struck Superb Gem is stone-white without a trace of toning, just as it fell from the dies more than a century ago. White on black contrast is noticeable, particularly on the reverse, although the frost on the portrait apparently falls just short of a Cameo designation. (#6553)

2350 **1907 PR64 NGC.** Splashes of gold and sea-green toning grace the margins of this strongly mirrored Choice proof. Solid detail with surprisingly few overt hairlines in the fields. (#6554)

Sharp 1907 Gem Proof Half Dollar

2351 **1907 PR65 NGC.** Splashes of gold-tan visit this Gem proof, and are slightly more extensive and deeper on the reverse, where they are joined with accents of powder-blue at the margins. A penetrating strike leaves strong definition on the design elements, except for minor softness in the upper right corner of the shield. A shallow hair-thin mark is noted in the upper reverse field. Census: 32 in 65, 33 finer (7/08). (#6554)

Moderately Toned 1908 PR67 Fifty Cent

2352 **1908 PR67 PCGS.** The 545-piece proof mintage in 1908 results in one of the lowest in the Barber half dollar series. Light to medium intensity olive-green patination dominates the obverse of this Superb Gem, and is joined on the reverse with orange, violet, apple-green, and lavender. A solid strike brings virtual completeness to the design elements. Some light toning streaks are noted, more so on the reverse. A well preserved specimen. Population: 7 in 67, 3 finer (8/08). (#6555)

Superb Proof 1910 Barber Half Dollar

2353 **1910 PR67 PCGS. CAC.** Circulation strike 1910 half dollars are highly elusive coins, especially in Choice and Gem Mint State grades, adding additional demand for proofs when they appear for sale. This Superb Gem has readily apparent cameo contrast beneath lovely lilac, blue, and gold toning, with several lighter toning lines on the obverse. Population: 12 in 67, 1 finer (8/08). (#6557)

Toned Proof 1910 Half, PR64 Cameo

2354 **1910 PR64 Cameo PCGS.** This specimen is a pleasure to examine closely, as the myriad design elements are each crisply defined on both sides, as they always should be on a proof striking but sometimes are not. Lovely original toning covers obverse and reverse, in a pleasing display of many variegated colors. Handling marks and hairlines are virtually nonexistent. Population: 6 in 64 Cameo, 15 finer (8/08). (#86557)

2355 **1912 PR64 PCGS.** Subtle champagne and gold-gray shadings grace the minimally disturbed surfaces of this Choice specimen. Well-defined with strong mirrors. Housed in a prior-generation holder. (#6559)

2356 **1912 PR64 PCGS.** This flashy Choice proof has medium gold toning, and is well struck despite minor inexactness on the right shield corner. Certified in a first generation holder. A mere 700 proofs were issued. Population: 51 in 64, 36 finer (8/08). (#6559)

Deeply Reflective PR65 1912 Barber Half

2357 **1912 PR65 PCGS.** A lovely Gem with deeply mirrored fields around satiny devices, exhibiting a trace of contrast on each side, although not sufficient to warrant the Cameo designation. The obverse is lightly toned and the reverse is mostly brilliant with a trace of champagne about the perimeter. Population: 15 in 65, 21 finer (8/08). (#6559)

Attractive Gem Proof 1912 Barber Half Dollar

2358 **1912 PR65 PCGS.** This attractive Gem proof is from an original mintage of just 700 pieces, and approximately half of that number have been certified by NGC and PCGS combined. Relatively few have been certified as Gems, however. This specimen is sharply struck and well preserved, with a light coating of speckled patina across each side attesting to the originality of the piece. Population: 15 in 65, 21 finer (8/08). (#6559)

Delightful 1912 Barber Half, PR66

2359 1912 PR66 PCGS. CAC. This delightful Premium Gem proof has deeply mirrored fields surrounding fully lustrous and frosty devices, creating excellent contrast. Both sides exhibit a kaleidoscope of toning, with considerable bright silver remaining on the obverse. Population: 16 in 66, 5 finer (8/08). (#6559)

EARLY DOLLARS

2360 1795 Flowing Hair, Three Leaves, B-7, BB-18, R.3—Scratched—NCS. VG Details. Die State I. All legends are readable on this well circulated stone-gray example. The date and STATES OF has greater wear, perhaps partly due to the die alignment when the piece was struck. The centers show wispy slide marks, and the right obverse field has three relatively inconspicuous pinscratches. *Ex: FUN Signature (Heritage, 1/2005), lot 8097.* (#6852)

Pleasing 1795 Flowing Hair Dollar, B-5, BB-27, VG10

2361 1795 Flowing Hair, Three Leaves VG10 NGC. B-5, BB-27, R.1. This variety is easily identified by the die lump just to the left of Liberty, and that defect is particularly obvious on this specimen. Deep gray patina covers the fields, which contrast nicely against the light gray devices. The details are well-outlined, and there are no bothersome abrasions on either side. This charming example would make a relatively affordable type coin of the second silver dollar issue. (#6852)

VF Details 1795 Flowing Hair Dollar, B-5, BB-27

2362 1795 Flowing Hair, Three Leaves, B-5, BB-27, R.1—Altered Surfaces—ANACS. VF20 Details. The surfaces appear to have been lightly whizzed and retoned an even, dark gray color, possibly to cover a few scrapes visible on the lower hair curls and the profile of Liberty, with a few others on the lower eagle's feathers. A pleasing level of deep detail remains, however, on this most common Flowing Hair variety. (#6852)

2363 1795 Flowing Hair, Three Leaves, B-5, BB-27, R.1—Improperly Cleaned—NCS. VF20 Details. A "bar" or die lump extends into the field near the uppermost hair curl, which is diagnostic for this die marriage. Deep charcoal toning surrounds the medium gray centers of this evenly worn piece. A number of small marks are typical for the grade, and none are particularly detracting. (#6852)

Desirable 1795 Flowing Hair Dollar, B-5, BB-27, VF20

2364 1795 Flowing Hair, Three Leaves, B-5, BB-27, R.1, VF20 PCGS. A "bar" or die lump in the field to the left of the uppermost hair curl identifies the obverse, which also has the lowest curl distant from the first star. The reverse is distinguished by the three leaves under each of the eagle's wings, and there is a total of 13 berries in the wreath. Pale gray patina covers the devices, which contrast nicely against the medium gray fields. A deeper area of toning is noted by Liberty's forehead. Scattered marks are typical for the grade, and a couple of shallow pinscratches on the obverse are barely worthy of mention. A small rim disturbance above the I in UNITED is noted. Two distinct dollar types were minted in 1795, and this variety features the popular Flowing Hair design that was used on the first dollars struck at the Mint in the previous year. *From The Menlo Park Collection.* (#6852)

Splendid 1795 Flowing Hair Dollar, B-5, BB-27, VF30 Details

2365 1795 Flowing Hair, Three Leaves—Corroded—ICG. VF30 Details. B-5, BB-27, R.1. The obverse, which was used only to strike this variety, is quickly identified by a die lump in the left field. Although ICG has certified this piece as "corroded," the surfaces are actually fairly smooth, but there is some discoloration on the devices. Overall, a minimally marked and relatively affordable representative of this popular variety. (#6852)

Charming 1795 Flowing Hair Dollar, B-6, BB-25, XF Sharpness

2366 **1795 Flowing Hair, Three Leaves—Damaged—ICG. XF40 Details.** B-6, BB-25, R.3. The obverse is distinguished by the wide date, with the 7 and 9 closer than the other digits. There are three leaves under each of the eagle's wings and 13 berries in the wreath, identifying the reverse. Medium gray patina drapes the surfaces, with a lighter color in the protected areas. The reverse is remarkably clean, but the obverse has a gouge and several shallow scratches on Liberty's cheek that account for the "damaged" moniker. Still, a well-defined example of this desirable issue. (#6852)

Original Choice XF 1795 Flowing Hair Dollar Three Leaves Reverse, B-5, BB-27

2367 **1795 Flowing Hair, Three Leaves, B-5, BB-27, R.1, XF45 NGC.** Bowers-Borckardt Die State III. The tell-tale 'bar' or die line behind the highest neck curl is diagnostic for Bolender-5, the usually encountered Flowing Hair dollar variety. This example has dove-gray devices and lighter cream-gray fields. Satin luster shimmers from the design, and the surfaces are minimally abraded save for a small reverse rim nick at 11 o'clock. BB-27 is the final Flowing Hair marriage listed in Bowers' *Silver Dollar Encyclopedia.* Since its 1993 publication, however, two additional varieties have been discovered, the extremely rare BB-28 and BB-29. (#6852)

Popular 1795 B-5, BB-27 Dollar Three Leaves, AU53

2368 **1795 Flowing Hair, Three Leaves, B-5, BB-27, R.1 AU53 PCGS. CAC.** The plentiful and popular 1795 B-5, BB-27 silver dollar is the variety most often chosen for date or type collections. In comparison with other varieties, probably close to 50% of all 1795 Flowing Hair dollars are from the single die combination that is seen here. Pleasing and natural grayish-gold toning on both sides slightly masks the luster that remains. The surfaces are smooth and pleasing, with a few faint adjustment marks on the obverse. The strike is nicely centered and the rims are full and sharp, without rim bumps or bruises on either side. (#6852)

2369 **1795 Flowing Hair, Two Leaves—Damaged, Polished—ANACS. VG8 Details** B-1, BB-21, R.1. A plentiful blundered date variety, with 1795 over 1195. Unnatural silver surfaces are accompanied by a clear surface mark across Liberty's chin and neck. (#6853)

Pleasing VF 1795 Flowing Hair Dollar Two Leaves, B-1, BB-21

2370 **1795 Flowing Hair, Two Leaves, B-1, BB-21, R.2, VF20 NGC.** Golden-brown overlies the borders of this dove-gray representative. No marks are consequential, and the wings, tail, and hair display ample remaining definition. The Flowing Hair type is increasingly popular, and was only struck for two years with the first year beyond the means of most collectors. (#6853)

The Ostheimer 1795 B-3, BB-11 Dollar
Unc Details

2371 **1795 Flowing Hair, Two Leaves, B-3, BB-11, R.5—Repaired, Improperly Cleaned—NCS. Unc Details.** Die State I, perfect dies as always. The 7 and 5 are each clearly repunched with remnants of the first punch to the right of the 7 and above the 5. The surfaces have light silver-gray patina with deeper gold and iridescent toning on both sides. This piece is boldly defined with full definition on both sides. At some time between 1968 and 1977, this example was repaired, with initials SEP removed from the obverse fields. In the September 1968 Lester Merkin catalog, the initials are clearly visible in the plate. In the June 1977 Bowers and Ruddy catalog, the initials are no longer evident, having been carefully removed. Despite the repair, we feel that this piece may still qualify as the finest known example of the variety.

In 1968, the cataloger for Lester Merkin (probably Walter Breen) stated exactly how he felt: "Would be of almost gem quality but for some idiot's having faintly scratched his initials SEP on obv., these being visible only at a certain angle." Earlier, in Stack's 1954 sale of the Davis-Graves Collection, the cataloger wrote: "Some fool put his initials in front of and in back of head."

From The Aspen Collection. Ex: Davis-Graves Collection (Stack's, 4/1954), lot 1268; A.J. Ostheimer, 3rd (Lester Merkin, 9/1968), lot 226; Doolittle Collection (Bowers and Ruddy, 6/1977), lot 2834. (#6853)

Elusive 1795 B-1, BB-21 Silver Plug Dollar

2372 **1795 Flowing Hair, Silver Plug—Genuine—PCGS. VF20 Details.** B-1, BB-21. Certified as genuine but ungraded by PCGS, the grade assigned by Heritage. The right obverse field is repaired with considerable tooling and smoothing. The surfaces are faint grayish-gold with a few hairlines and a minor reverse rim bump.

The 1795 silver plug dollars have one of the most interesting stories in American numismatics. Planchets that were above standard weight were adjusted by simply filing away excess silver, but underweight planchets were not so easily adjusted. Essentially, they had to be melted and formed into new planchets. In 1795, the Mint experimented with small silver plugs to increase the weight back to standard. A small hole was punched in the center of the flan, and a short piece of silver was inserted. When the planchet was struck, the silver piece spread over the surface and picked up the designs. Only a few of these pieces survive, and today they are highly collectible. (#6854)

Double Struck 1795 Draped Bust Dollar
VF Details, B-15, BB-52

2373 **1795 Draped Bust, Centered, B-15, BB-52, R.2—Double Struck, Cleaned—ANACS. VF Details, Net Fine 15.** The coin was struck twice by the dies, rotating slightly between blows. Doubling is present on the profile and peripheral legends. Glossy, and a bit bright despite subsequent tan toning that is deepest near the rims. *Ex: Dr. Douglas Roane Collection (Heritage, 9/2003), lot 7459.* (#6858)

Charming VF30 1795 Draped Bust Dollar
Centered Bust, B-15, BB-52

2374 1795 Draped Bust, Centered, B-15, BB-52, R.2, VF30 ANACS.
A pearl-gray first year Draped Bust dollar that has peripheral hints of
olive and aqua. Surprisingly free from abrasions, although moderate
adjustment marks on the lower right reverse are noted, as made by
the mint. Substantial hair detail remains despite wear on the eagle's
breast. (#6858)

Defective Flan 1795 B-15, BB-52 Dollar, XF45

2375 1795 Draped Bust, Centered—Defective Planchet—XF45 PCGS.
B-15, BB-52, R.2. A lovely piece called a Mint error by PCGS. Both
sides have faint traces of blue and gold toning with excellent eye
appeal. The flan defect is located at 5 o'clock on the obverse or 1
o'clock on the reverse. (#6858)

AU Details 1796 Bust Dollar
Small Date, Large Letters, B-4, BB-61

**2376 1796 Small Date, Large Letters, B-4, BB-61, R.3—Artificial
Toning—NCS. AU Details.** Bowers-Borckardt Die State II. Sea-
green and autumn-brown alternate across this boldly detailed Small
Eagle dollar. The fields are moderately abraded, and the cleavage
has a pair of pinscratches, but the piece is attractive to the unaided
eye, and luster glistens from design recesses. (#6860)

Difficult AU 1796 Large Letters Dollar
Small Date, B-4, BB-61

**2377 1796 Small Date, Large Letters, B-4, BB-61, R.3, AU50
PCGS.** Bowers-Borckardt Die State I. Most easily attributed by
the die dot over the 1 in the date and the location of a berry under
the first T in STATES on the reverse. Glossy, minimally worn
surfaces are well toned in gunmetal-gray and golden hues and
there is a series of widely spaced adjustment marks (as produced)
across the portrait. Perusal beneath a loupe locates only one
consequential mark, which is inconspicuous and located beneath
the eagle's left (facing) wing. Population: 6 in 50, 8 finer (8/08).
Ex: Long Beach Signature (Heritage, 5/2003), lot 6451.
(#6860)

Pleasing 1796 B-4, BB-61 Dollar, VF30 Details

**2378 1796 Small Date, Small Letters—Cleaned—ANACS. VF30
Details.** B-4, BB-61, R.4. Light silver surfaces are enhanced by a
hint of gold and iridescent peripheral toning on each side. Faint
hairlines are left from the cleaning. A delightful high grade example
for the advanced specialist or date collector. (#6859)

Collectible Fine 1797 Dollar
10x6 Stars, Large Letters, B-3, BB-71

2379 **1797 10x6 Stars, Large Letters, B-3, BB-71, R.2, Fine 12 ANACS.** Bowers-Borckardt Die State III. This popular variety has 16 stars on the obverse: 10 on the left and 6 on the right. This star arrangement is not seen on any other early silver dollar. The unique star arrangement on the obverse makes this variety in demand by both type and die variety collectors. The medium-gray fields illustrated on this example highlight lighter-gray design elements. Pleasing detail remains for the designated grade, especially on the obverse. The only notable blemishes on this specimen are numerous light to moderate shallow ticks on Liberty's neck.
Ex: Paulsboro Collection, Part Two (Heritage, 7/2004), lot 6867.
(#6865)

Pleasing 1797 Dollar, 10x6, Large Letters, B-3, BB-71, VF25

2380 **1797 10x6 Stars, Large Letters, B-3, BB-71, R.2, VF25 PCGS.** Die State II. This interesting variety features an obverse that has 10 stars crowded to the left of Liberty and 6 stars to the right. A faint die dot to the right of the first 7 in the date is obvious under a glass and makes the date appear to be 17.97. The strike is average for the variety. This specimen has a mix of medium gray and gold toning, with the highpoints of Liberty a light shade of gray. Numerous light adjustment marks are apparent on the reverse. Scattered abrasions define the grade, and a faint pinscratch through Liberty's hair and neck is noted. Still, a charming example of this interesting variety.
From The Menlo Park Collection. (#6865)

Scarce XF 1797 Dollar
9 x 7 Stars, Large Letters, B-1, BB-73

2381 **1797 9x7 Stars, Large Letters, B-1, BB-73, R.3, XF40 ANACS.** Bowers-Borckardt Die State III. Rich cobalt-blue, olive, and lilac-gray envelops the obverse, while the reverse is lightly toned golden-gray aside from a blush of deeper blue along the lower border. A tiny clip on the reverse at 3:30 appears to be of mint origin. Encased in an ANA cache holder. (#6863)

Patinated XF 1797 9x7 Stars Dollar
Large Letters, B-1, BB-73

2382 **1797 9x7 Stars, Large Letters, B-1, BB-73, R.3, XF40 NGC.** Bowers-Borckardt Die State I. Deep walnut-brown toning envelops this moderately circulated Small Eagle dollar. Prolonged examination with a lens fails to find any reportable marks. The eagle's breast retains significant plumage detail. (#6863)

VF 1798 Small Eagle Dollar
15 Stars, B-2, BB-81

2383 **1798 Small Eagle, 15 Stars, B-2, BB-81, R.3, VF20 ANACS.** Bowers-Borckardt Die State II with minor lapping on the upper hair curl. An attractively detailed final year Small Eagle dollar with pastel apricot and gunmetal-blue toning. Mildly granular and surprisingly unabraded. (#6868)

Splendid 1798 Small Eagle Dollar
15 Stars, B-2, BB-81, VF30

2384 **1798 Small Eagle, 15 Stars VF30 PCGS.** B-2, BB-81, R.3. This is the only variety with 15 stars on the obverse. Charming medium gray patina drapes both sides of this minimally marked representative. Scattered abrasions define the grade, but none are particularly bothersome. A minor rim disturbance at the top of the obverse is barely worthy of mention. A crisply defined example of this interesting variety. (#6868)

Delightful 1798 Small Eagle Dollar, 13 Stars, B-1, BB-82, XF40

2385 **1798 Small Eagle, 13 Stars XF40 PCGS.** B-1, BB-82, R.3. Only two varieties of 1798 dollars featured a small eagle on the reverse, and B-1 is easily identified because it has the standard number (13) of stars on the obverse. Gunmetal-gray patina envelops the obverse, which contrasts nicely against the light gray reverse. Both sides are remarkably smooth and a careful inspection reveals only trivial marks. This attractive piece would make a wonderful type coin. (#6867)

2386 **1798 Large Eagle, Knob 9, 4 Vertical Lines, B-7, BB-95, R.5, VG10 NGC.** A better variety, and one of three (the others are BB-93 and BB-94) with a Knob 9 in the date, four lines in each vertical shield stripes. A well circulated slate-gray dollar with a few blushes of deeper steel-gray. Some hair and shield definition is present. (#6875)

XF 1798 Large Eagle Dollar Knob 9, 5 Lines, 10 Arrows, B-6, BB-96

2387 **1798 Large Eagle, Knob 9, 5 Vertical Lines, 10 Arrows, B-6, BB-96, R.3, XF40 PCGS.** Medium olive and sky-blue toning embraces this well defined XF Bust dollar. A few faint adjustment marks are concealed within the hair, but post-strike abrasions are minimal. Luster glimmers from the legends, plumage, and hair. Housed in an old green label holder. (#6875)

VF 1798 Large Eagle Dollar Pointed 9, Wide Date, B-23, BB-105

2388 **1798 Large Eagle, Pointed 9, Wide Date, B-23, BB-105, R.3, VF20 NGC.** Ocean-blue and apple-green toning blankets this evenly circulated Heraldic Eagle dollar. The centers have a few small ticks, an obverse rim nick is noted at 2:30, and the obverse dentils are softly defined at 8 o'clock. (#6877)

2389 **1798 Large Eagle, Wide Date, Pointed 9—Cleaned—ANACS. VF20 Details** B-11, BB-111, R.3. The obverse has parallel cracks through star 13 to Liberty's chin. This lovely piece has deep grayish-violet surfaces with splashes of lighter tan and gold. (#6877)

Popular 1798 Heraldic Eagle Dollar VF25 Pointed 9, Wide Date, B-23, BB-105

2390 **1798 Large Eagle, Pointed 9, Wide Date, B-23, BB-105, R.3, VF25 PCGS.** The pearl-gray centers gradually cede to cobalt-blue borders. Although the portrait displays wear consistent with the grade, the reverse appears sharper, since all letters in E PLURIBUS UNUM are bold, as are the wing and tail feathers. Encapsulated in an old green label holder. (#6877)

Near-Mint 1798 Large Eagle Dollar Wide Date, Pointed 9, B-23, BB-105

2391 **1798 Large Eagle, Pointed 9, Wide Date, B-23, BB-105, R.3, AU58 NGC.** The top of the 8 is joined to the drapery, and the top row of reverse stars is well below the clouds. The B-23 die marriage is among the more available 1798 varieties, an excellent candidate for a date or type collection. An impressive near-Mint example with substantial luster beneath natural golden-brown patina, enhanced by pale blue and iridescent toning. Peripheral design elements are well struck, and the centers show only moderate incompleteness. This piece just misses the Condition Census for the variety, but probably still ranks among the top dozen known. (#6877)

2392 **1798 Large Eagle, Pointed 9 Fine 12 PCGS.** B-15, BB-112, R.3. Although considerably worn, this lovely light gray and tan specimen has smooth surfaces and excellent eye appeal. (#6873)

2393 **1798 Large Eagle, Pointed 9, B-12, BB-120, R.4—Cleaned— ANACS. VF30 Details.** The 17 in the date is closely spaced while the other two digits are distant. On the reverse a point of a star touches the lower part of the eagle's beak. This piece is Die State III, as evidenced by the crack between the 7 and 9 of the date, as well as one through UNITED ST, ending at the rim above the AT in STATES. Light gray toning covers each side of this lightly marked representative. Well-detailed save for several unstruck stars on the reverse. (#6873)

XF40 1798 Large Eagle, Pointed 9, B-28, BB-118

2394 **1798 Large Eagle, Pointed 9, B-28, BB-118, R.3, XF40 NGC.** Pointed 9, Close Date. Digit 8 out of position, high and leaning slightly right; point of leaf below right half of C. A heavy die crack begins on the obverse rim at 6 o'clock, extending upward through the 9 in the date; to the left through the first two points of star 2 ending in the field; and to the right curving up to meet the lower edge of Liberty's bust.

There is a lengthy planchet lamination in the left obverse field, traveling from a point of star 6 to Liberty's lowest hair ribbon. Deep mauve-gray patina covers the lightly worn surfaces, where no untoward marks are found. A faint pinscratch is noted from the highest point of star 13, through the field, and up to Liberty's eye. (#6873)

1798 Large Eagle, Pointed 9, B-15, BB-112, XF40 Interesting Flawed Planchet Error Striking

2395 **1798 Large Eagle, Pointed 9, B-15, BB-112, R.3, XF40 NGC.** Bowers Die State II. A fascinating coin that will appeal to the error enthusiasts as much as to the early dollar specialists. Stars 6 and 7, as well as LI in LIBERTY are absent on the obverse, with all but the first and last letters of UNITED on the reverse missing. Closer examination reveals that the planchet is out of round, with the vertical axis being slightly shorter than the horizontal axis. It is obvious that the missing design details are the result of improper metal flow, but a conclusive determination cannot be made until this coin is removed from its holder and examined more closely. Of particular interest is the weight of the coin and the details present—or absent—from the edge. One thing for certain is that the current coin was struck on a flawed planchet and the resulting anomaly is not to be confused with postmint damage. NGC agreed and certified this piece as XF40, an accurate determination in our opinion. Medium gray toning reveals subtle hues of rose and gold when viewed at various angles. A couple of small rim ticks on the reverse at 12 o'clock are the only problems that are worthy of mention. (#6873)

Choice XF 1798 B-28, BB-118 Dollar

2396 **1798 Large Eagle, Pointed 9 XF45 NGC.** B-28, BB-118, R.2. A relatively plentiful dollar variety that is identified by the leaf below the right tail of R in AMERICA. Pleasing silvery-gray surfaces are accented by pale rose toning on the design highpoints. A few faint obverse and reverse marks are consistent with the grade. (#6873)

Impressive and Conditionally Rare 1798 Dollar Heraldic Eagle, Pointed 9, B-13, BB-108, MS61

2397 1798 Large Eagle, Pointed 9, B-13, BB-108, R.3, MS61 NGC. The obverse is easily identified by a die flaw between the bust and star 13, and there is a die crack from the rim to the lower right serif of the L in LIBERTY. Only 10 arrowheads are visible on the reverse, which is a telltale diagnostic for this die. After striking BB-107 the reverse die was lapped, and the five small berries now have faint or nonexistent stems. Although this variety is relatively available in grades through XF, the Bowers-Borckardt reference states that it is "exceedingly rare" in Mint State. Their list of notable specimens, while not quite a condition census, features only three Uncirculated examples, two of which grade MS60.

Hints of gold and rose around the margins accent the mostly medium gray surfaces of this exquisitely preserved representative. There are prominent adjustment marks at the center of the reverse, with a corresponding area of weakness on Liberty's hair on the obverse. Plenty of luster radiates throughout the fields and enhances the eye appeal. This piece is Die State IV, with a die crack from the rim below the 17 in the date that progresses through the first five stars. A spectacular representative from the first year of the Heraldic Eagle reverse. (#6873)

2398 1799 7x6 Stars Fine 12 ICG. B-11, BB-161, R.3. Extremely dark field patina with light silver highlights on the devices creates The reverse die is extensively cracked as usual for the variety. (#6878)

2399 1799 7x6 Stars, B-22, BB-168, R.5—Improperly Cleaned—NCS. VF20 Details. Die State II, with a faint die crack connecting the final three stars. This variety can be easily identified by the horizontal die crack that bisects the reverse. Pale silver-gray patina shows accents of hazel toning around the perimeter, with streaks of charcoal color on the reverse. A scarce variety with no marks worthy of specific mention. (#6878)

2400 1799 7x6 Stars—Repaired, Cleaned—ANACS. VF20 Details. B-6, BB-162, R.4. Pleasing light gray surfaces, somewhat deeper on the reverse. While this piece has been cleaned, it is still finer than most, with pleasing surfaces. (#6878)

2401 1799 7x6 Stars—Improperly Cleaned—NCS. VF Details. B-11, BB-161, R.3. Numerous die cracks on the reverse are typical for the variety, and the olive branch has no berries, which is an important diagnostic. The surfaces show no mentionable marks save for a nearly imperceptible pinscratch at the upper right of the obverse. A lovely, pale gray example despite cleaning. (#6878)

Charming 1799 Dollar, B-12a, BB-160, VF25

2402 1799 7x6 Stars, B-12a, BB-160, R.3, VF25 NGC. The first star is distant from the hair curl, identifying the obverse, while the reverse has no berries and only a tiny remnant of a stem. Although NGC labels this piece B-12, it is Die State III, with the diagnostic die cracks through the date, which Bolender categorizes as 12a. Lovely gunmetal-gray fields contrast nicely against the light silver devices. A shallow mark below the Y in LIBERTY is noted, but the rest of the surfaces are smooth and lightly abraded. An evenly worn and handsome representative. (#6878)

1799 7 x 6 Stars Dollar VF25
Scarce Late Dies B-7, BB-156 Variety

2403 1799 7x6 Stars, B-7, BB-156, R.4, VF25 PCGS. Bowers-Borckardt Die State III with numerous reverse cracks and a sinking die near the eagle's head. Light golden-tan toning graces this bright and lightly abraded example. Luster glimmers from selected regions, but wear is concentrated on the upper central reverse, where the reverse die is failing. (#6878)

Interesting 1799 Dollar, B-21, BB-169, Choice Very Fine

2404   **1799 7x6 Stars, B-21, BB-169, R.3 VF35 NGC.** The second star is repunched and a die crack goes from the rim to the bust, through the 99 in the date. On the reverse, the right foot of the A in STATES is centered over the junction of clouds 3 and 4. This piece is Die State IV, as evidenced by the additional die cracks from the bust through the right stars and the TY in LIBERTY. It is interesting how much die rust is present on this late die state example. Delightful medium gray patina graces both sides, with patches of lighter toning on the devices. There are no mentionable marks on either side, and the details are crisply defined. (#6878)

2405   **1799 7x6 Stars, B-17, BB-164, R.2—Whizzed—ICG. XF40 Details.** Die State III. Reverse with hairline die crack beginning from the right side of U, through the bottom of N, all the way up through eagle's left (facing) wing feathers, and through the top of the first T in STATES. This is a heavily whizzed example that displays a typical degree of wear for the XF grade level. (#6878)

Elusive 1799 Dollar, B-12b, BB-160, XF40

2406   **1799 7x6 Stars XF40 PCGS. CAC.** B-12b, BB-160, R.3. Die cracks on the obverse help distinguish this variety. On the reverse, there are no berries on the olive branch and the left serif of the U in UNITED is defective. The numerous die cracks on the obverse identify this piece as Die State IV, which is considered scarce in the Bowers-Borckardt reference. Lovely gunmetal-gray patina in the fields contrasts nicely against the lighter toning that covers the devices. The reverse stars are soft, as usually seen, but the rest of the details are well-defined. An elusive terminal die state example. (#6878)

Important Mint State 1799 7x6 Stars Dollar, B-8, BB-165

2407   **1799 7x6 Stars, B-8, BB-165, R.3, MS60 NGC.** The lower right corner of the N on the reverse shows an extraneous serif from an erroneous original punching; this feature is diagnostic for the reverse die and for the variety. This die pairing is scarce in an absolute sense, and as one might presume by its age, Mint State examples are highly elusive.

Rich blue, sage, and violet-rose patina drapes the subtly lustrous surfaces of this representative. The overall level of detail is surprisingly strong, though the eagle's neck feathers are indistinct. The general visual appeal is far greater than the MS60 designation might suggest, though under magnification, a number of wispy abrasions appear. For all 7x6 Stars varieties, Census: 5 in 60, 73 finer (11/07). (#6878)

Interesting 1799/8 Dollar, 15 Star Reverse
B-3, BB-141, XF45 Details

2408 **1799/8 15 Stars Reverse, B-3, BB-141—Cleaned—ANACS. XF45 Details.** This interesting 15 star reverse variety was created when the engraver punched one too many stars in both the top and second rows. Realizing his mistake, he then tried to disguise the extra stars by engraving clouds on top of the stars, but he failed to cover the innermost tips of those two stars, which are protruding from clouds 1 and 8. The obverse, of course, features an overdate. Steel-gray toning covers both sides, with darker areas around the lettering. A small lamination (as made) is noted inside the reverse stars, and is accompanied by another smaller planchet flaw. Neither of these, however, adversely affects any part of the design. Despite cleaning, the surfaces are relatively unabraded and attractive. *From The Jerry Kochel Collection.* (#6883)

Lustrous AU 1799/8 Dollar
15 Stars Reverse, B-3, BB-141

2409 **1799/8 15 Stars Reverse, B-3, BB-141, R.3, AU50 PCGS.** Bowers-Borckardt Die State III. Light honey-gold borders encompass the powder-blue and ivory-gray centers. Luster dominates the legends and devices. The obverse has a few unimportant marks, but the eye appeal is undeniable. The popular overdate variety with enlarged first and last clouds that nearly conceal errantly engraved stars. *From The Bell Collection.* (#6883)

1799/8 15 Stars Reverse Dollar
B-3, BB-141, AU58

2410 **1799/8 15 Stars Reverse, B-3, BB-141, R.3, AU58 NGC.** Bowers-Borckardt Die State III. Die crack from right ribbon through AMERIC.

According to the Bowers-Borckardt silver dollar *Encyclopedia* (1993), the most definitive reference work for these early dollars: "The overdate, from a common obverse die, occurs in three varieties created through the combination with as many different reverse dies, known as BB-141, BB-142, and BB-143. Specimens are known in all grade levels, including Mint State, but higher grade examples are elusive."

This near-Mint example is very attractive, and boasts a dappled layer of russet-gold patina across each side that will undoubtedly appeal to the connoisseur of original toning. Well struck with traces of highpoint wear on Liberty's hair and cheek, and a milling mark on her jaw. A few other trivial blemishes are scattered over the still-lustrous surfaces. (#6883)

2411 **1799 8x5 Stars, B-23, BB-159, R.4—Cleaned—ANACS. VF20 Details.** This variety is instantly recognizable because it is the only 1799 dollar with the eight stars left, five stars right arrangement on the obverse. Pale gray patina endows the surfaces, which are fairly smooth and have no prominent marks. A pleasing evenly worn example of an interesting variety. (#6881)

Magnificent 1800 Dollar, B-13, BB-193, XF40

2412 **1800 B-13, BB-193, R.4, XF40 NGC.** The obverse, which was used for this variety only, is attributed by the E in LIBERTY, which is slightly higher than the B, and also by the spacing of the stars. Severe clash marks on the reverse through the F in OF and the nearby stars, however, instantly identify this die marriage and indicate that it is Die State III. A die crack connects the tops of AMERICA and extends into the field, but the obverse has no cracks. Pleasing gunmetal-gray patina covers both sides of this interesting piece, with a few streaks of darker toning on each side. This minimally marked example has great eye appeal. (#6887)

Splendid 1800 Dollar, B-13, BB-193, Extremely Fine

2413 **1800 XF40 PCGS. CAC.** B-13, BB-193, R.4. This variety is best identified by the reverse, which features pronounced clash marks around OF, clouds 7 and 8, and several stars. The clash marks are not as pronounced as often seen, which indicates that this piece is Die State II, and there are no longer clash marks visible on the obverse. A hint of lavender toning in the periphery accents the dusting of russet that covers the mostly medium gray surfaces. The details are crisply outlined and there are no noteworthy marks on either side. A lovely example of this interesting variety. (#6887)

2414 **1800 Dotted Date, B-14, BB-194, R.3—Improperly Cleaned—NCS. VF20 Details.** This peculiar variety has several tiny dotlike die breaks around the first 0 in the date, and this is the only use of this obverse die. A delicate die crack from the border through star 1 into the field indicates that this piece is the scarce Die State III. A shallow scratch across Liberty's jaw is noted, but the rest of the surfaces are fairly clean. The tops of ERTY are weakly struck, as typically seen. Overall a pleasing example despite cleaning. (#6889)

VF25 Dotted Date 1800 Dollar, B-14, BB-194

2415 **1800 Dotted Date, B-14, BB-194, R.3, VF25 NGC.** The popular Dotted Date variety, named for curiously arranged die dots about the first 0 in the date. Toned medium dove-gray with lighter ivory shades on the devices. The right obverse has faint hairlines, but no marks are apparent to the unaided eye. All letters in E PLURIBUS UNUM are at least partly legible. *Ex: Ira & Larry Goldberg, 9/2005, lot 1848, which realized $2,530.* (#6889)

AU 1800 Silver Dollar, 12 Arrows, B-17, BB-196

2416 **1800 12 Arrows, B-17, BB-196, R.1, AU50 PCGS.** Struck from clashed and cracked dies, as usual for this die pairing. BB-196 receives its own Guide Book listing, as the sole 1800 variety with 12 arrows. Golden-brown fields and devices are bordered by aquamarine. A loupe and careful scrutiny reveals a few inconspicuous thin marks on each side. Population: 3 in 50, 8 finer (8/08). (#6890)

2417 **1801 B-4, BB-214, R.4, Fine 12 NGC.** Bowers-Borckardt Die State III. An attractive and lightly abraded dove-gray example. Most letters in E PLURIBUS UNUM are legible, and substantial wing plumage remains. In an older NGC holder. *Ex: Long Beach Signature (Heritage, 6/2005), lot 6636, which realized $1,667.50.* (#6893)

Delightful 1801 Dollar, B-3, BB-213, XF40

2418 **1801 B-3, BB-213, R.3, XF40 NGC.** A tiny dot is visible under magnification just to the left of the center dot, identifying the obverse. On the reverse, a point of a star touches the outside of the eagle's beak and the right foot of the T's is missing. Pleasing slate-gray overlies the devices, which contrast nicely against the deep amber toning that drapes the fields. This evenly worn representative is well-defined with only minor softness on the eagle's wings and Liberty's hair. Plenty of luster remains in the fields and gives this piece great eye appeal.
From The Menlo Park Collection. (#6893)

2419 **1802 Narrow Date, B-6, BB-241, R.1—Improperly Cleaned— NCS. VF Details.** The 8 and 0 in the date are widely spaced, and the third cloud on the reverse has a small die spur. Hazy, light gray patina covers the both sides, with several darker spots on the reverse. Scattered abrasions throughout are entirely insignificant. (#6895)

Lustrous AU53 1802 Dollar
Narrow Date, B-6, BB-241

2420 **1802 Narrow Date, B-6, BB-241, R.1, AU53 PCGS.** Bowers-Borckardt Die State III. Considerable luster dominates design details and penetrates the open fields. The borders are sea-green, while light golden-gray visits the fields and devices. Smooth save for a thin mark beneath the hair ribbon and a bright slender mark near star 7. (#6895)

2421 **1803 Large 3, B-6, BB-255, R.2—Improperly Cleaned—NCS. VF Details.** The 3 in the date is double punched, which is most noticeable at the bottom curve. The reverse has several diagnostics, among them the top of the eagle's beak touches the point of a star. Cleaning has given the surfaces a dull gray complexion, and a glass reveals a number of hairlines in the fields. A tiny rim nick is noted at the bottom of the reverse. Nonetheless, plenty of detail remains and this piece would make an affordable representative. (#6901)

Borderline Uncirculated 1803 Dollar
Large 3, B-6, BB-255

2422 **1803 Large 3, B-6, BB-255, R.2, AU58 NGC.** Bowers-Borckardt Die State II with a hair thin die crack between stars 10 and 11. Generally silver-gray with deep cream-gray on the devices. As expected for the grade, luster shimmers across the borders and within the hair and shield. Liberty's cheek and shoulder has slight wear, but the surfaces are impressively void of abrasions. An interesting lintmark between the U in UNITED and the fletchings provides an identifier. Mint records indicate that 19,570 silver dollars were delivered in 1804. Most of these were likely BB-255, the sole Large 3 variety aside from the novodel proof made decades later. (#6901)

Famous 1836 Name Below Base Gobrecht Dollar
Judd-58, PR55

2423 **1836 Name Below Base, Judd-58 Restrike, Pollock-61, R.6(?), PR55 NGC.** Silver. Die Alignment III: Center of Liberty's head opposite N in ONE. A great deal of research has been done in the Gobrecht dollar series over the past several years. We planned to publish a book on this series four years ago, but new findings have caused postponement of its publication until we are fairly confident that what is published will be correct and current information for several years.

A significant amount of research has been done regarding the Starry Reverse Name Below Base 1836 dollars. An unpublished paper by John Dannreuther addresses the series in general and specifically on the Judd-58 coins. The great debate is over when the coins were struck. The story that has been handed down over generations is that Gobrecht placed his name too prominently below the base and he was forced to move it to the lower part of the rock. The problem with this story is that the Name Below Base coins were struck from a die created from the same die that had the name mostly effaced from the hub used on 1838 and 1839 dies. The Name Below Base coins were struck from this name-effaced hub, and this places the striking period sometime after the 1838 and 1839 dollars. JD points out that the 1851 Roper Sale had both an 1838 and 1839 dollar, but that auction did not contain a Name Below Base. Also, all Name Below Base dollars are only seen in Die Alignment III or IV and with a cracked reverse. Therefore, the striking period must be significantly later than the date on the coin.

The usually microscopic die cracks on the reverse are significantly more visible on this particular coin. The striking details are also more pronounced than one would expect from a PR55 coin. Liberty's hair and extended foot show complete definition, and there is just the slightest friction on the high point of the eagle's breast. Evidence of light handling is apparent in the fields on each side. The light gray surfaces are accented by a thin accent of russet around the devices. A light grease stain is located just below the 3 o'clock position on the obverse rim. (#11217)

2424 **1836 Name on Base, Judd-60 Original, Pollock-65, R.1, PR40
PCGS.** Silver. Plain Edge. Die Alignment I. Original Issue of 1836
with the eagle flying upward. This piece was produced during the
second striking period in December 1836 after the reverse die was
inadvertently scratched above the eagle's wing. On this coin the die
scratch is very faint. All 600 coins that are believed to have been
struck of these later die state dollars were distributed to the public
via a local Philadelphia bank. This is a bright coin that shows only
modest gray accents with deeper accents around the devices. There
is a noticeable splotch of charcoal-gray in the area of the Phrygian
Cap.
From The Menlo Park Collection. (#11225)

2425 **1836 Name on Base, Judd-60 Original, Pollock-65, R.1, PR55
NGC.** Silver. Plain Edge. Die Alignment I (Center of Liberty's
head opposite DO in DOLLAR). No die scratch above the eagle,
indicating an early December striking. Often confused with
patterns, when initially issued, it was clear to the Mint Director
Robert Patterson and other government officials including
President Andrew Jackson that the 1836 dollars were regular issue
coins. In fact, many of these coins, such as this piece, show signs
of circulation wear. Also, their mintage was officially recorded
in the U.S. mintage records; whereas, the mintage of patterns
was not reported. Another reason for this confusion appears to
be due to the Gobrecht dollar format and the small mintage. All
Gobrecht dollars were struck with a proof finish. This is a nearly
unique situation. U.S. coins are generally not struck and issued
for circulation in proof format, although some proof coins have
circulated. However, in 1836, Robert Patterson wanted to impress
the public with the new coin design, and therefore decided to issue
this coin in the best possible condition (i.e., as proofs).

This is an impressive striking that shows just a hint of friction
over the high points and in the fields. The devices are sharply
defined throughout, and each side shows pale golden color in the
centers with ever deepening gray-golden patina toward the margins.
(#11225)

Richly Toned 1836 Gobrecht Dollar
PR61 Die Alignment I

VF Details 1836 Gobrecht Dollar
Judd-60 Restrike, Die Alignment IV

2426 **1836 Name on Base, Judd-60 Original, Pollock-65, R.1, PR61 NGC.** Silver. Plain Edge. Die Alignment I (Center of Liberty's head opposite DO in DOLLAR). Mint Director Robert Patterson worked with artist Thomas Sully to give him an idea of the concept he had for what would eventually become the Gobrecht dollar. Patterson's sketched his idea directly from contemporary British coinage—an adaptation of the Britannia reverse. This design had in turn been adapted from the Britannia on Roman coinage, which in turn was based on ancient Greek coins. Director Patterson instructed Christian Gobrecht to make a copperplate etching of the best drawing which was ready by October 1835.

This is one of the so-called First Original strikings from late December 1836 which is distinguished by the accidental die scratch above the wing of the eagle. The surfaces are deeply toned in shades of rose, blue, and gray. The reverse is noticeably lighter in the center with deeper, irregular color at the top of that side. Numerous tiny contact marks account for the grade but none are worthy of individual mention. (#11225)

2427 **1836 Name on Base, Judd-60 Restrike, Pollock-65, R.5— Holed—NCS. VF Detail.** Silver. Die Alignment IV (Center of Liberty's head opposite the right side of F in OF). Because of the heavy wear the die scratch above the eagle's wing is not visible. This piece was neatly drilled just above the head of Liberty and the hole is positioned between the O and F in OF on the reverse. Obviously used as a watch fob or another similar jewelry item. The fields are deep in color with an almost charcoal appearance while the devices are brilliantish-silver and present a stark two-toned contrast. Surprisingly well detailed still, especially so on the eagle's wings. (#11227)

2428 **1836 Name on Base, Judd-60 Restrike, Pollock-65, R.5, PR63 NGC.** Silver. Die Alignment IV (Center of Liberty's head opposite the right side of F in OF). The accidental die scratch above the eagle's wing is evident to the unaided eye. These pieces are related to the medallic-oriented Die Alignment II pieces, and each is a so-called Second Original from March 1837. Recent research by Saul Teichman and John Dannreuther have demonstrated that there were four states of the Starry Reverse die. This particular coin is from a later state of the dies as seen by die lapping that increasingly separates the denticles, as well as the lack of the scribe line. These diagnostics place this as a later Restrike. The striking period of these pieces is still uncertain. Another, more easily seen characteristic on later Restrikes is the depth of mirroring in the fields. While all Gobrecht dollars were struck in proof format, those from the 1836-1838 time frame are not as reflective as those pieces struck beginning in 1858. Those coins are comparable to proofs of other denominations struck in that time period.

This piece shows unfathomably deep mirrors in the fields. The striking definition is generally strong throughout with complete details on Liberty's hair and the eagle's breast. Liberty's foot, however, lacks complete definition—a trait common to many Gobrecht dollars. The centers of each side are noticeably lighter in hue than the margins which pick up increasing golden-gray patina toward the rims. Light hairlines explain the grade. A lovely, high grade example of this important 19th century type coin. (#11227)

2429 **1836 Name on Base, Judd-60 Restrike, Pollock-65, R.5, PR63 NGC.** Silver. Die Alignment III (Center of Liberty's head opposite the N in ONE). No reverse die scratch is apparent on this piece as the dies were repolished prior to striking, thus eliminating the scratch. Jim Gray and Mike Carboneau have roughly classified Die Alignment III coins into three striking periods. The first is from the late 1850s and these coins show some reverse die cracks, but no die rust on the obverse. The second period is believed to date to the late 1860s and these pieces show extensive reverse die cracks and possibly some die rust around OF, but no obverse die rust. Coins from the third period show extensive reverse die cracks and obverse die rust. It is believed that these pieces may have been struck sometime in the 1870s.

This piece is from the third striking period, and in our experience such coins are seldom seen. Die cracks are heavy relative to other Gobrecht dollars and seen through NITED STATES O and then again at OLLA. But most interesting is the patch of die rust that was transferred to the obverse die in the field to the left of Liberty's head. Die Alignment III dollars are usually seen in high grades. This would make sense as they were struck as collector pieces, and as such they would have been better preserved than, say, Die Alignment I pieces from 1836 which were dropped into circulation. This coin has the deeply mirrored reflectivity one would expect of a proof coin from the 1870s, when these pieces are believed to have been struck. Light hairlining accounts for the grade, and undoubtedly was the result of a collector who wished to "improve" the coin at some point in the past 130 years. Each side is generally brilliant with just a hint of light golden toning, and the striking details are full in all areas. Many may overlook the significance of this coin, but the wise collector of this interesting series will understand the rare opportunity this coin presents. (#11227)

2430 **1838 Name Omitted, Judd-84 Restrike, Pollock-93, R.5, PR63 PCGS.** Silver. Reeded Edge. Die Alignment III (head of Liberty opposite the NE of ONE; or equivalently, coin-turn with the eagle flying level). There are two widely separated time periods for the striking of 1838 Gobrecht dollars. The first is in the actual year on the coin, 1838. These are generally considered patterns and probably no more than 10 pieces were made. These major rarities were struck in Die Alignment IV (head of Liberty opposite the F in OF) and there are no reverse die cracks. The 1838 in the Smithsonian is such a coin. All others are struck in Die Alignment III or IV. The Die Alignment III coins show die cracks through MERI and TE, and in later states through the base of LAR. This is one such piece. Because of the depth of the toning strong magnification and a good light source is necessary to locate the microscopic die cracks through MERI and TE, which places this as a Restrike most likely made in the late 1850s. The removal of GOBRECHT F. is almost complete on this piece. This nearly complete effacement of the name on 1838 dollars is more advanced than that on 1839 dollars, strongly suggesting that 1839 dollars were struck prior to 1838 coins.

Again, because of the depth of toning on each side, the flashy reflectivity in the fields is not as apparent as one might expect. The striking details on each side also show a noticeable lack of high point detail, perhaps indicative of hurried manufacture of this piece. Deep rose and emerald-green toning is splashed over each side, and to the casual observer there are no obvious contact marks. (#11352)

2431 **1838 Name Omitted, Judd-84 Restrike, Pollock-93, R.5, PR64 NGC.** Silver. Reeded Edge. Die Alignment III (head of Liberty opposite the NE of ONE). The majority of 1838 dollars are known in Die Alignment III. It is estimated that perhaps 250-300 of these restrikes were produced and they may have spanned as many as three striking periods. These striking periods can roughly be determined by the presence and strength of the die cracks on the reverse. It has been asserted (by Jim Gray and Mike Carboneau) that these dollars were struck during the tenure of Mint Director James Ross Snowden (1858-1861), or during one of Henry Linderman's terms as director (1867-1869 and 1873-1878). This piece is undoubtedly from one of Linderman's terms as the reverse shows die cracks through the tops of MERIC, ITE, and the bottoms of LAR.

One of the more interesting recent discoveries in Gobrecht dollars was by Saul Teichman. He noticed a group of extra feathers along the neck of the eagle on the Starless reverse for the 1838 and 1839 issues—indicating an alteration to the master die.

The relatively untoned surfaces of this piece make it easier to find the die cracks on the reverse. In fact, two of the cracks extend slightly further than usually encountered, enabling identification of this coin as a later striking. There is, however, just a bit of light toning present, mostly around and within the peripheral devices. Sharply, but not fully struck, the head of Liberty and the eagle's breast feathers are completely brought up but the extended foot of Liberty is flat, as often seen. A few light hairlines keep this lovely piece from the Gem category. The only other surface imperfections are Mint-made: slight porosity in the right obverse field. Sure to be of interest to the collector of this fascinating series. (#11352)

2432 **1839 Name Omitted, Judd-104 Restrike, Pollock-116, R.3, PR64 NGC.** Silver. Die Alignment IV (Center of Liberty's head opposite the right side of F in OF). Restrikes are known in both Die Alignment III and IV, and both show faint die cracks through the tops of MERI, TE, and on later strikings cracks connect LAR. Two hub changes were made to the 1839 dollars. One was the addition of feathers along the eagle's neck, the other was the effacement of Gobrecht's name from the base of the rock. The effacement was incompletely done for the 1839 dollars with shadowy remnants still in evidence. When the 1838 dollars were struck (after the 1839 coins!) the job was much more thoroughly done.

Gobrecht dollars have always been highly prized by collectors, which accounts for the various striking periods of restrikes. In the Fewsmith Sale of 1870, an 1839 brought $29. Curiously, in that same sale a Name Below Base only realized $10.50, while the 1838 was the most expensive Gobrecht at $45.

This is a lovely 1839 dollar. The fields are deeply reflective, suggestive of a later striking period, and each side is covered with spectacular toning. The obverse displays reddish-golden toning of varying intensity. The reverse has just a bit of that color on the left part of that side, the remainder is a mixture of thalo blue and violet. Still, the fields are deeply mirrored enough to forcefully flash through the layers of color. There are no noticeable or mentionable contact marks on either side of this near-Gem 1839. A coin worthy of consideration for a high-grade 19th century type set or set of Gobrecht dollars. (#11446)

SEATED DOLLARS

2433 **1841 AU50 NGC.** Despite light wear, this generally silver-white coin sports a degree of reflectivity in the fields. Well struck with small, scattered abrasions on each side. (#6927)

2434 **1841 AU55 PCGS.** Modestly reflective beneath the orange-gold and violet shadings across each side, though the slight striking softness on the central devices attests to this coin's business-strike origins. Minimally worn and pleasing. (#6927)

2435 **1841 AU58 NGC.** Only a touch of friction affects the high points of this earlier Seated dollar. The surfaces are subtly lustrous beneath ample violet, gold-orange, and silver-gray patina. Census: 42 in 58, 44 finer (7/08). (#6927)

Elusive Uncirculated 1843 Dollar

2436 **1843 MS61 NGC.** A shimmering silver-gray and almond-gold silver dollar that has a good strike and moderately abraded fields. The obverse has a hair-thin mark near the first two stars and a tiny rim nick at 6 o'clock. The 1843 has a plentiful mintage by No Motto Seated dollar standards, yet remains very scarce in Mint State. Census: 21 in 61, 31 finer (7/08). (#6929)

Challenging Choice AU 1845 Seated Dollar

2437 **1845 AU55 NGC.** Luster shimmers across the devices and borders of this low mintage No Motto silver dollar. The obverse is ocean-blue with glimpses of plum-red, while the reverse is lightly toned except for golden-brown and russet-red near the right border. Minor field marks pose no distraction. Census: 22 in 55, 43 finer (7/08). (#6931)

2438 **1846 AU50 PCGS.** Pleasing violet toning encircles the perimeter, which contrasts nicely against the silver-gray devices. Both sides are highly reflective despite the abrasions typical for the AU50 grade. (#6932)

2439 **1846 AU55 NGC.** Light to medium grayish-purple toning dominates this Choice AU dollar, joined by splashes of aqua-green and rose at the borders, especially on the obverse. This is a well defined piece, with a minimum of contacts. Nice for a high-grade type set. (#6932)

Condition Rarity 1846 Select Dollar

2440 **1846 MS63 NGC.** The 1846 is similar in both overall and high grade rarity to the 1843: examples are generally obtainable in circulated grades, but rare in Mint State, and excessively rare in grades above the MS63 level. This Select representative is lightly overlaid in golden and silver-gray iridescence. Some roller marks have remained through the central obverse, but the strike is bold, if not sharp in virtually all areas. A few scattered abrasions, none of which are worthy of individual mention, account for the MS63 designation. (#6932)

Original 1846-O Dollar, AU58

2441 **1846-O AU58 NGC.** The first year that silver dollars were produced at the New Orleans Mint, and one of only four years of O-mint issues in the entire Seated dollar series. Original dove-gray surfaces show uniform wear and abrasions from a brief time in circulation, including a couple of barely noticeable rim bumps. A trace of luster remains in the fields of this scarce example from a low mintage of 59,000 pieces. Census: 28 in 58, 20 finer (8/08). (#6933)

Lovely Select 1847 Seated Dollar

2442 **1847 MS63 NGC.** Soft, pleasing luster shines through delicate layers of gold and silver-gray patina. The strike is pleasing, save for a touch of weakness on the right stars, and the surfaces are minimally marked for the Select designation. Conditionally rare any finer, with just 11 such pieces known to NGC (8/08). (#6934)

Low Mintage 1848 Silver Dollar AU53

2443 **1848 AU53 PCGS.** Steel-gray and pastel straw-gold visit this briefly circulated Seated dollar. Nicely struck, and minimally abraded aside from a few ticks on the right obverse field. A tiny mintage of 15,000 pieces ensures the rarity of this No Motto date. Housed in a green label holder. Population: 14 in 53, 59 finer (8/08). (#6935)

Lightly Circulated AU53 1848 Seated Dollar

2444 **1848 AU53 PCGS.** This lightly circulated dollar has pastel chestnut-gold and steel-gray toning. Evenly struck, and without more than the usual number of small field marks. The 1848 has a mintage of a mere 15,000 pieces, and only a handful are known in Uncirculated grades. Population: 14 in 53, 59 finer (8/08). (#6935)

2445 **1848 AU55 NGC.** Modest wear across the high points has left the luster of the pale silver-gray fields largely intact. Well struck and a pleasing survivor. Census: 17 in 55, 29 finer (7/08). (#6935)

Shining 1849 Seated Dollar, MS63

2446 **1849 MS63 NGC.** Impressive eye appeal for this mid-19th century issue. The luster is strong, and whispers of golden toning grace the margins. Central detail is crisp, though the peripheral elements show trifling softness, and though a handful of wispy abrasions are present in the fields, the surfaces are devoid of overt flaws. Census: 14 in 63, 6 finer (7/08). (#6936)

2447 **1850-O—Genuine—PCGS.** AU Details in the opinion of our graders. The surfaces are lightly hairlined beneath rose-gray patina, suggestive of a past cleaning, and a significant cut appears to the left of Liberty's head. Still, an important example of this challenging O-mint Seated dollar issue. (#6938)

2448 **1853 AU50 NGC.** Boldly struck and essentially untoned, with silvery-gray surface that show even wear and few noticeable marks. A deep rim nick is noted near 5 o'clock on the obverse. An attractive AU representative. (#6941)

Brilliant 1859-O Seated Dollar, MS63

2449 **1859-O MS63 PCGS.** Prior to the Treasury releases of the early 1960s, the 1859-O was a scarce, yet not rare coin in Mint State. By 1964, however, multiple 1,000-coin bags of Mint State 1859-O and 1860-O Seated dollars emerged from Treasury Department vaults and found their way into the hands of the public. These coins were uniformly frosty in texture with mostly untoned surfaces and enough scattered bagmarks to net grades in the MS60-62 range. This example fits the bill with a nice strike, full mint frost, lightly abraded surfaces and a completely brilliant appearance. Population: 42 in 63, 16 finer (8/08).
From The Bell Collection. (#6947)

2450 **1859-S—Cleaned—ANACS. AU Details, Net XF45.** The majority of the 20,000 1859-S dollars minted were sent to China where they were subsequently melted, and today this issue is exceptionally scarce in grades finer than VF. Magnification reveals fine hairlines on the golden-gray surfaces, where traces of luster still reside in the protected areas. Strong definition is apparent on the motifs. (#6948)

Choice XF 1859-S Dollar

2451 **1859-S XF45 PCGS.** The 18 in the date is repunched south. Toned light golden-gray and richly detailed. Luster illuminates protected areas, especially on the reverse. The fields have scattered small marks, none of which are individually distracting. A mere 20,000 pieces were struck, presumably for export purposes. Encapsulated in an old green label holder. (#6948)

Scarce AU55 1859-S Dollar

2452 **1859-S AU55 NGC.** The 1859-S dollar is fairly scarce, and usually found in Very Fine and Extremely Fine grades. About Uncirculated pieces are scarce, and Mint State coins are rare. Light to medium bluish-gray patina visits the surfaces of this Choice AU example that displays traces of luster in the recesses. Nicely struck and lightly abraded. (#6948)

Undisturbed 1860 Seated Dollar MS63

2453 **1860 MS63 PCGS.** This mildly prooflike Select Seated dollar exhibits medium caramel-gold toning. The strike is precise, lacking absolute definition only on Liberty's hair and a nearby star. Scattered small marks are appropriate for the grade. Encased in a green label holder. Population: 17 in 63, 30 finer (8/08). (#6949)

Scintillating MS62 1860-O Dollar

2454 **1860-O MS62 PCGS.** This lustrous No Motto type coin is virtually untoned save for a wisp of charcoal-gray along the lower reverse border. The right obverse field and the upper reverse field have the small marks expected of the grade, but the preservation is superior to the usually seen bagmarked 1860-O.
From The Menlo Park Collection. (#6950)

Satiny 1860-O Dollar MS62

2455 **1860-O MS62 PCGS.** A lightly toned Mint State example of this New Orleans issue. Both sides have lustrous satin surfaces with a few splashes of gold and brown color. Small spots are noted on the obverse field near the knees and on the reverse field above the eagle's left (facing) wing.
Ex: FUN Signature (Heritage, 1/2006), lot 4398. (#6950)

Lustrous 1860-O Silver Dollar, MS64

2456 **1860-O MS64 PCGS.** This lustrous Choice Seated dollar has delicate chestnut-gold toning with glimpses of navy-blue, sea-green, and rose-red along the left reverse periphery. As is usual for the 1860-O, the fields display a number of small marks. Population: 16 in 64, 9 finer (8/08). (#6950)

Sharp and Elusive 1861 Seated Dollar, MS63

2457 **1861 MS63 PCGS.** A Select Mint State Seated Liberty dollar from the first year of the Civil War, which saw a small original mintage of 77,500 coins and subsequent melting of many pieces that same year. The issue is seldom seen in Mint State, nor even in the higher circulated grades. The present example has satiny luster over pinkish-golden surfaces on both sides. A few light abrasions account for the grade, but the sharp strike and excellent eye appeal are noteworthy. (#6951)

Fabulous Choice 1867 Seated Dollar

2458 **1867 MS64 NGC.** A solidly struck near-Gem survivor from this post-Civil War Seated dollar issue, pleasingly lustrous beneath captivating patina. Elements of reddish-gold, violet, and tan embrace much of each side. This issue is elusive in almost all grades and a condition rarity so fine. Census: 8 in 64, 4 finer (7/08). (#6960)

2459 **1869 AU55 PCGS.** Medium chestnut-gold and lime toning graces this richly detailed Seated dollar. Curious hair-thin lines near the TES in STATES appear to be mint-made. The fields are moderately prooflike, and the date location is identical to that of a Gem proof that appeared as lot 1374 in our 2007 June Long Beach Signature. Certified in an old green label holder. (#6962)

2460 **1870 AU58 NGC.** This is an originally toned near-Mint example of the 1870 Seated dollar, a popular and relatively common issue. This piece has a coating of original brown-gray and mauve patina over both sides. Surface marks and highpoint wear are only minor, for the grade. (#6963)

Worthy XF 1870-CC Silver Dollar

2461 **1870-CC XF40 PCGS.** Breen-5485, "rare." Variety 1-A. The mintmark is closely spaced. A stone-gray example of the introductory Carson City issue. LIBERTY is full readable, and all but the B is sharp. The right obverse has distributed small marks, and tiny rim dings are noted on the obverse at 2 o'clock, and on the reverse at 1 o'clock and 6:30. (#6964)

Popular XF 1870-CC Dollar

2462 **1870-CC XF40 PCGS.** Variety 3-C. The first issue struck at the Carson City Mint was the 1870-CC Seated dollar. Eventually, 12,462 examples were issued, a low mintage but greater in number than the 1871-CC to 1873-CC Seated dollars. Thus, type demand from CC-mint collectors is focused on the 1870-CC. The present cream-gray piece has light wear, some remaining luster, and moderately abraded fields. (#6964)

2463 **1870-CC—Obverse Graffiti, Polished—NCS. AU Details.** The heavily polished silver-gray and orange surfaces give off an unnatural sheen. Little actual wear shows, and the scratches that NCS has characterized as "graffiti" seem more random than deliberate. (#6964)

2464 **1870-CC—Cleaned, Damaged—ICG. AU55 Details.** Well struck for the issue with only minor wear, though the chromelike sheen that comes from the light silver-gray surfaces is clearly unnatural. Light marks pepper the obverse. (#6964)

2465 **1871 AU50 NGC.** Lovely medium gray patina embraces the surfaces, which show no noteworthy marks. A minor rim disturbance is noted at the bottom of the reverse. This well-detailed example would make a relatively affordable representative of one of the final Liberty Seated dollars. (#6966)

2466 **1871 AU53 NGC.** Flashy luster emanates from the light gray surfaces of this boldly defined piece. A hint of gold and lavender graces the margins. Numerous abrasions define the grade. A tiny spot on the Y in LIBERTY is noted for future identification purposes. (#6966)

Attractive MS63 1871 Seated Dollar

2467 **1871 MS63 NGC.** Impressively detailed for this late-date Seated dollar. Both sides offer considerable luster with a hint of frostiness beneath subtle gold and silver-gray patina. A handful of shallow, scattered abrasions on each side contribute to the grade. Census: 37 in 63, 41 finer (7/08). (#6966)

Luminous Near-Gem 1871 Seated Dollar

2468 **1871 MS64 PCGS.** A heavily toned Choice representative of this later Liberty Seated silver dollar issue, well struck with glimmers of luster at the obverse margins and on the reverse. Green-gold and orange shadings are translucent, while the violet-gray toning that dominates the obverse is largely opaque. Population: 33 in 64, 6 finer (8/08). (#6966)

2469 **1872 AU53 NGC.** A pleasing, lightly abraded example of the penultimate issue in the series. Plenty of luster resides in the fields. The strike is crisp save for the typical softness on the stars. There are no mentionable marks on either side, and a touch of deep purple by the date adds color to the otherwise pale gray surfaces. (#6968)

Rare 1872-CC Dollar, AU53

2470 **1872-CC AU53 NGC.** Congress approved the Carson City Mint in 1863, but the Civil War delayed completion of the facility until 1869. The branch mint struck Seated dollars starting in 1870 and every year thereafter through 1873, though never in great quantities. Production was 3,150 coins in 1872, and the date is the third rarest CC-mint Seated dollar after the 1873-CC and the 1871-CC. Breen (1988) considered the 1872-CC rare and believed many were melted after the Mint Act of Feb. 12, 1873, became law.

The present coin is a pleasing example though some features are softly struck, and there are a few insignificant marks from its moderate time in circulation. Both surfaces have medium-gray toning, the reverse a bit lighter, with darker outlines around some of the features. A few spots of emerald are tucked into the corners of the letters and devices. NGC has graded only 26 coins finer (8/08). (#6969)

2471 **1872-S XF40 PCGS.** A challenging issue in all grades with an original mintage of only 9,000 pieces. Light in color overall, although streaky gray toning is seen over portions of the obverse. Noticeable luster is present, and marks are mostly confined to the right obverse field. *Ex: FUN Signature (Heritage, 1/2004), lot 6327. From The Menlo Park Collection.* (#6970)

Remarkable 1872-S Dollar, Choice AU

2472 **1872-S AU55 PCGS.** The 1872-S is effectively the only collectible With Motto Liberty Seated dollar from the San Francisco Mint, considering that the 1870-S is extremely rare and the '73-S is unknown in any collection. Only 9,000 examples were struck, and the number of survivors drops precipitously in high grades. Dusted hazel toning in the margins accents the pale gray patina that envelops both sides. The abrasions are entirely trivial, and there are no prominent areas of weakness. Plenty of luster in the fields adds to the appeal of this briefly circulated representative. Population: 10 in 55, 10 finer (8/08). (#6970)

Highly Desirable 1858
Liberty Seated Dollar, PR63

2473 **1858 PR63 PCGS.** Although the *Guide Book* gives an estimated mintage for the 1858 of at least 300 proofs, Bowers' *Encyclopedia* estimates that 225 to 300+ proofs were struck. The actual mintage has been the subject of debate within the numismatic community for the past 150 years, with estimates varying widely. NGC and PCGS report a combined total of 156 specimens, some of which are undoubtedly resubmissions. Perhaps the actual surviving population numbers slightly over 100 pieces.

This is the sole proof-only issue in the Liberty Seated dollar series, with the exception of the 1866 No Motto, of which only two are known. Highly desired by many collectors, some of whom are not even interested in the series, the 1858 is one of the most famous numismatic rarities of all time. The present piece is brilliant and boldly struck, with eye-catching deeply mirrored fields. Scattered hairlines limit the grade and there is a tiny blemish below the date. A number of minuscule milk spots are noted on the reverse. This is an excellent opportunity to acquire this popular and seldom-seen issue. (#7001)

2474 **1858 PR65 Cameo NGC.** This brilliant Gem possesses icy devices that exhibit obvious contrast with the unperturbed and glassy fields. The 1858 is the final proof date without a recorded mintage, and is from the first year that proofs were made available to collectors (earlier-dated proofs are principally restrikes, coined at a later time). More importantly, it is a proof-only date, the only such date in the series. Breen (1988) estimated that the proof 1858 has a mintage of 80 pieces, but Duncan Lee (2006) states it is 300+ pieces. Census: 2 in 65 Cameo, 1 finer (7/08). (#87001)

2475 1859 PR66 NGC. Although glimpses of navy-blue and mauve adorn the peripheries, the fields and devices display rich golden-brown toning. This superior No Motto type coin exhibits a penetrating strike, and the surfaces are nearly bereft of contact. A slender, subtle planchet streak to the E in UNITED provides an identifier for future pedigree researchers. The base of the 1 in the date is lightly repunched. A prize for the connoisseur of patinated silver proof coinage, and an opportunity not to be missed. A mere 800 proofs were struck. Census: 18 in 66, 4 finer (7/08). (#7002)

2476   **1859 PR67 ★ NGC.** The 2009 *Red Book* reports that 800 dollars were struck in proof format in 1859. David Bowers writes in his 1993 *Silver Dollars and Trade Dollars of the United States* that:

> "... many Proofs were made this year in the hope that the public, which was becoming increasingly interested in numismatics, would buy them. Today, the issue is quite rare, and it is likely that 450 or fewer were actually distributed. Even that figure might be on the high side. There were hardly 450 numismatists in 1859 interested in buying Proof dollars from the Mint. However, enough coins survive today to indicate that 450 is a reasonable estimate of distribution."

In any event, NGC and PCGS have certified approximately 290 1859 proof dollars, ranging in grade from PR50 to PR67, with the vast majority falling within the PR61 to PR64 range. The two services have assigned the Cameo designation to a few pieces. NGC has given the coveted Star label to a mere three pieces, a PR66 and two PR67s.

The Superb Gem with ★ offered in this lot displays light gold-beige patination around the peripheries that transitions into medium intensity cobalt-blue in the central areas. A splash of purple is visible on the lower half of Liberty, and a blush of lilac occupies the area around the eagle's head and neck. Complementing the exquisite toning pattern is a penetrating strike that brings out virtually complete delineation on the design elements. Both faces are impeccably preserved, and yield modest field-motif contrast when the coin is tilted slightly under a light source. A wonderful coin overall. (#7002)

Appealingly Toned 1859 Seated Dollar, PR63 Cameo

2477 **1859 PR63 Cameo PCGS.** An appealing Seated dollar proof from the first year of publicly offered proof coinage at the Philadelphia Mint. Seldom does one see a proof so deeply toned yet still showing cameo contrast, yet here it is: The surfaces are honey-gold and light brown in the center, yielding to deeper iridescent lavender and electric blue near the rims on each side. Despite the fairly intense patina, the devices show much frost and contrast against the translucent color, sufficient both for the Cameo designation and generous eye appeal. Population: 8 in 63 Cameo, 9 finer (8/08). (#87002)

Choice Cameo Proof 1859 Silver Dollar

2478 **1859 PR64 Cameo NGC.** Cameo contrast is unmistakable despite light honey-gold toning. A needle-sharp Choice proof with a well preserved reverse and a few faint hairlines on the right obverse field. 1859 was the first year that proof mintages were recorded. 800 pieces were struck, although survivors appear scarcer than the lower mintage 1862 to 1865 No Motto proofs. Probably, a portion of the 1859 mintage went unsold and was melted at the Mint. Census: 8 in 64 Cameo, 6 finer (8/08). (#87002)

Toned Gem Cameo Proof 1860 Seated Dollar

2479 **1860 PR65 Cameo NGC.** With a published mintage of 1,330 pieces, the 1860 Seated dollar had the highest mintage for any dollar-sized proof issue until the Trade dollars of 1879; however, only 527 of those pieces actually sold, according to *Silver Dollars and Trade Dollars of the United States* by Q. David Bowers, with the rest melted. As a result, the issue is much more elusive than the mintage figure might suggest, and it commands a greater premium than a number of later issues with lower gross mintages but higher net sales. This Gem offers rich rose, violet, and gold shadings over strong mirrors and mildly frosted, sharply struck devices. Delightful contrast and powerful eye appeal. Census: 3 in 65 Cameo, 10 finer (7/08). (#87003)

2480 **1861 PR66 Cameo NGC.** The 1,000-coin proof mintage of the 1861 Seated dollar was the second highest annual total of the No Motto type. The proof dollar was originally offered as part of proof sets, but both Bowers (2006) and Breen (1988) estimate than only 300-350 coins were sold, and the rest melted. This coin exhibits a sharp strike and clean surfaces, except for a few minor marks on and around Liberty's knees. Rings of iridescent copper and electric-blue on both sides frame pinkish-golden centers. Over 200 proof coins have been certified for the date by both NGC and PCGS, 29 receiving the Cameo designation. NGC has graded two as PR66 Cameo, with none finer from either service (8/08). (#87004)

2481 **1863 PR65 NGC.** This exquisite Gem proof Seated dollar has a mintage of just 460 pieces. The strike is razor-sharp, even on the claws, Liberty's hair, and the upper stars. Rotation of the coin reveals ocean-blue, rose, caramel-gold, and slate-gray. The preservation is exemplary. A tiny strike-through near star 5 provides an identifier. A beautiful and important representative of the Motto subtype. 1863 was the year of Gettysburg, the turning point of the Civil War. Census: 12 in 65, 12 finer without a Cameo designation, 4 in higher grades as Cameo (7/08). (#7006)

Desirable 1864 Seated Dollar, PR63

2482 **1864 PR63 PCGS.** A Seated dollar from the Civil War era that surprisingly is more available as a proof than as an Uncirculated business strike, even though only 470 proofs were minted in 1864. This example has a strong strike with just a touch of softness in the impression of Liberty. Gold and lavender toning dusts the obverse, with some ice-blue showing along the device edges. The reverse displays emerald and dusty gray toning, with highlights of turquoise around the eagle and the legends. (#7007)

Sharply Struck 1864 Dollar, PR61 Cameo

2483 **1864 PR61 Cameo NGC.** Whispers of light gold-tan color make occasional visits to both sides of this PR61 Cameo, each of which exhibits pronounced field-motif contrast. A well executed strike leaves bold definition on the design elements. Some fine hairlines show up under magnification, especially on the reverse. (#87007)

Sharp Gem Proof Cameo 1864 Seated Dollar

2484 **1864 PR65 Cameo NGC.** The 1864 Seated dollar saw a production of 470 proofs, a fair number of which survive today. Indeed, NGC and PCGS combined report more than 300 certified examples. Only about 25 proofs have been assigned the Cameo designation, however. The current PR65 Cameo displays near white-on-black contrast and is essentially devoid of toning, save for the merest suggestion of golden rim toning. The strike is simply outstanding, manifesting itself in bold detail on Liberty's head, the stars, and the eagle's feathers. A few wispy handling marks prevent an even higher grade. Interesting lint marks are noted on Liberty's left hand and arm. Census: 4 in 65, 3 finer (8/08). (#87007)

Elusive PR62 1865 Silver Dollar

2485 **1865 PR62 PCGS.** Variegated caramel-gold and steel-blue embraces this penetratingly struck specimen. Faint field abrasions and minor granularity near 6 o'clock on the reverse corresponds to the grade. Only 500 pieces were struck for this final Civil War proof issue. Certified in a green label holder. (#7008)

Exceptional 1865 PR66
Ultra Cameo Seated Dollar

2486 **1865 PR66 Ultra Cameo NGC.** On April 2, 1865, the government of the Confederacy evacuated Richmond after Petersburg fell to Union forces. President Abraham Lincoln visited fire-ravaged Richmond just two days later, and stopped at Jefferson Davis' abandoned residence. Less than a week after, Lee surrendered to Grant near the Appomattox Court House.

In that same year, the Philadelphia Mint produced 500 proof silver dollars, the final year of the Seated Liberty, No Motto type. This coin is a fitting tribute to a year of significant endings. NGC has graded only seven 1865 PR66 Ultra Cameo examples, with none finer from either service (8/08). Exceptionally clean fields contrast dramatically with sharply struck devices. Bright silver like-new surfaces dominate, with just a whisper of gold toning. (#97008)

Delightful 1866 Motto Dollar, PR63

2487 **1866 Motto PR63 ANACS.** Gunmetal-gray toning envelops the surfaces, which are remarkably clean for the grade. Although the deep patina partially obscures the reflectivity, there are still flashes of luster under a lamp. This fully struck piece is a lovely representative of the first With Motto Liberty Seated dollar. A mere 725 proofs were struck, along with a business strike mintage of just 48,900 pieces. (#7014)

Wonderful 1866 Motto
Seated Dollar, PR65 Cameo

2488 **1866 Motto PR65 Cameo PCGS.** For the Seated silver dollar, 1866 is the first year that the motto IN GOD WE TRUST was added to the reverse and this addition created a new type coin. Many collectors desire the first year of issue, and the present example is a desirable Gem level coin which has the elusive Cameo contrast. As a date, the 1866 Seated dollar is seldom found with the Cameo or Deep Cameo contrast, with approximately fifteen percent of the known coins showing this desirable feature. The color is bright gray in the fields, with a hint of gold over the white, frosted devices. Slightly muted in intensity with hints of cloudy toning in the fields. There are no distracting nicks or cuts in the fields or on the devices, and this is a solid coin for the grade.

America was just coming out of the disastrous Civil War in 1866, with most of the South in emotional, physical and economic ruins, and the Industrial North was struggling with their own appalling losses. This Gem proof Seated dollar is a reminder of those darker days when Andrew Johnson was swept into the Presidency after the assassination of Lincoln in 1865, and struggled to bring his own state of Tennessee and the entire South back into the United States with his ideals of reconstruction. The political tides shifted in 1867 and Johnson was impeached by the Senate, and clung to the Presidency by a single Senator's vote. (#87014)

Patinated Choice Proof 1867 Seated Dollar

2489 1867 PR64 PCGS. Electric-blue, apricot, rose, and plum-mauve patina envelops this intricately struck Choice Motto proof. The holder is a bit scuffy, but the coin itself has pleasing preservation. A mere 625 proofs were struck, and most of the 46,900 business strikes were exported and eventually melted. Population: 67 in 64, 17 finer (4/08). (#7015)

Attractive 1867 Seated Dollar, PR65 Cameo

2490 1867 PR65 Cameo NGC. Annual production of business strike Seated Liberty dollars remained low for the first two years after the addition of IN GOD WE TRUST to the reverse. However, the number of proofs minted bumped up slightly from the 500-coin total of the last year of the No Motto issue, to 725 coins in 1866 and then 625 pieces in 1867. NGC has certified over 200 1867 Gem proof Seated dollars, about a fourth of them Cameo, but only 55 Gem business strikes for the year.

  For many collectors, a proof 1867 is an alternative to the scarce business strike, and this example is a splendid choice. Both sides display gleaming silver surfaces with a modest hint of golden toning. The strike is sharp, with a few scattered marks defining the grade, though none is prominent. Census: 10 in 65 Cameo, 11 finer (8/08). (#87015)

2491 1868—Obverse Scratched—NCS. Proof. Minor evidence of rub affects the high points, and a shallow near-vertical scratch runs just above Liberty's outstretched foot. Moderate mirrors show a number of small, scattered hairlines. (#7016)

Impressive PR67 Cameo 1868 Seated Dollar

2492 1868 PR67 Cameo NGC. Exceptionally mirrored with a touch of golden toning in the centers that lightens to near-brilliance on the reverse. Surrounding the major devices are rich, colorful cobalt-blue and copper-gold shadings, along with softer pink hues. Well-defined aside from trifling softness seen on the tops of the eagle's wings and on Liberty's lower locks. This issue's extreme difficulty is finer Mint State grades has long placed added importance on high-end proofs such as the present coin. It is one of the more visually impressive specimens of this sought-after type we have ever offered, a captivating, utterly Superb specimen that offers the advanced collector an opportunity to acquire the single finest Cameo proof 1868 dollar certified by either major grading service. Census: 1 in 67 Cameo, 0 finer (8/08). (#87016)

2493 1869—Artificial Toning—NCS. Proof. Streaks of hazel patina intermingle with silver-gray toning across the surfaces of this highly reflective representative. Although NCS has only called this specimen "Proof," the details are powerfully struck and there are few detracting marks. Only 600 proofs were issued. (#7017)

2494 **1869 PR67 ★ Cameo NGC.** The proof Seated dollars dated 1869 are in high demand, not only as representatives from a pool of proofs only 600 pieces strong, but also as substitutes for the business strikes of the same year, which are famously challenging in Mint State. Curiously, that year saw production of the denomination more than double from 1868's tally, with 423,700 coins struck for circulation. Still, heavy melting and other forms of attrition claimed the vast majority of the original population. Proofs, on the other hand, were generally well-conserved and more readily available in many cases.

Out of 600 proofs coined for 1869, most of the pieces (400 specimens) were struck and delivered in February and March of that year. Other, small deliveries came later in the year: 50 pieces on May 12; 50 more coins on July 12; and a final batch of 100 specimens came in the fourth quarter of the calendar year, with delivery on October 8.

NGC has graded just two Cameo coins as PR67, while PCGS acknowledges none; in addition, this is the only one of the two to have received the Star designation (8/08). Though this issue may be popular among collectors as a business-strike substitute, there is no mistaking the present example for a Mint State piece. For a coin only designated as Cameo, the contrast level is astonishing, with rich frost across the devices that stands out boldly from the lightly toned silver-gray fields. Powerful mirrors further fuel the cameo effect. Even under close scrutiny, the surfaces appear virtually flawless. All factors considered, a simply marvelous survivor, easily one of the most appealing proof 1869 Seated dollars available today. (#87017)

Charming 1870 Seated Liberty Dollar, PR62

2495 1870 PR62 PCGS. Oak-gray toning drapes the surfaces of this fully struck specimen. Although the deep patina partly affects the luster, there is still a great amount of reflectivity. A few shallow scratches are noted in the right obverse field, but the rest of the surfaces display only minuscule contact marks. One of just 1,000 proofs struck. (#7018)

Notable Select Proof 1870 Seated Dollar

2496 1870 PR63 NGC. Both sides of this Select proof show mild contrast, though predominantly silver-gray patina has formed over the lightly hairlined mirrors. The sharply struck obverse shows subtle steel-blue and lavender elements, while the reverse displays attractive blue-green and sage accents. (#7018)

Patinated Choice Proof 1870 Silver Dollar

2497 1870 PR64 PCGS. Although its published mintage is 1,000 pieces, "many were melted at year's end, making the [proof] 1870 scarcer than its mintage would indicate," per Duncan Lee in the August 11, 2006 CDN *Newsletter*. The reverse is lightly die doubled, as often seen on Motto proofs. Well struck save for the left (facing) claw, and toned golden-brown and sea-green. The left corner of the rock has a small lamination, as made. Population: 51 in 64, 22 finer (8/08). (#7018)

Glittering 1871 Dollar, PR64 Cameo

2498 1871 PR64 Cameo PCGS. This specimen's glittering surfaces boast enormous eye appeal that is generated by the stark contrast between fields and devices. The essentially untoned obverse cedes to barely discernible champagne color on the reverse. Sharply struck, with just a few minor grade-defining marks. Only a small percentage of proofs from this year have received a cameo designation. Population: 8 in 64 Cameo, 1 finer (8/08). (#87019)

Beautiful 1871 Dollar, PR66 Ultra Cameo

2499 1871 PR66 Ultra Cameo NGC. Annual mintage totals for the 1871 Seated dollar were the second highest for both proof and circulation coins of the With Motto type. Of the 960 proof coins minted, this is one of just two pieces certified by NGC as PR66 Ultra Cameo, with only three finer (8/08). As expected from the grade, pristine surfaces contrast sharply with frosted devices, and no marks or spots detract from the commanding presentation of this coin, an untoned silver-white piece with just the faintest suggestion of golden color. A beautiful and striking representative of the type, and a fine addition to a high-end Seated dollar collection. (#97019)

Beautifully Toned 1873 Seated Dollar, PR64 Cameo

2500 **1873 PR64 Cameo NGC.** The Mint Act of 1873 abolished the circulating silver dollar in favor of the Trade dollar, an action deemed the "Crime of '73" by silver mining interests enriched by the production of this largest of all U.S. silver coins. Adding insult to injury, in 1874 Congress demonetized silver dollars, revoking their legal tender status. Within this milieu of competing and factious political interests 600 proof Seated Liberty dollars were minted in 1873, the lowest total since 1869. The present coin is a beautiful representative of the last year of the type. Blue and turquoise accents at the rim frame soft plum and apricot toning that transitions to dove-gray at the obverse center. The reverse offers blue, turquoise, apricot and plum toning with a bright, untoned central circle. Census: 18 in 64 Cameo, 5 finer (8/08). (#87021)

TRADE DOLLARS

2501 **1873 MS61 NGC.** Sharply struck with crisp definition on Liberty's head and the obverse stars. Only a handful of minor marks are noted on either side. A satiny example with pleasing shades of original lilac and tan coloration across the carefully preserved surfaces. (#7031)

Desirable Choice AU 1873-CC Trade Dollar

2502 **1873-CC AU55 NGC.** This low mintage issue of 124,500 pieces is a key date in the Trade dollar series. This Carson City production was consigned almost entirely to China; just as this type was intended to do from the outset. Some were released to local depositors, however, and another small number were eventually repatriated from Asia back to American coin collectors. This example displays pleasing, even tan coloration across both sides. Boldly struck and lightly worn on the highpoints, this desirable Choice AU representative is free of any distracting surface marks. (#7032)

2503 **1873-S MS62 PCGS.** Traces of gold and russet toning highlight the satiny fields. Liberty's head is a trifle soft, but the rest of the details are boldly impressed. Scattered abrasions limit the grade but none merit individual mention. A tiny retained lamination is noted on the left side of the reverse. Encapsulated in a green label PCGS holder. (#7033)

2504 **1874 MS61 NGC.** Well struck and nicely preserved, with a dense coating of brownish-green toning across both sides. A few minor marks and luster grazes restrict the grade. Census: 16 in 61, 53 finer (7/08). (#7034)

Elusive 1874 Trade Dollar, MS64

2505 **1874 MS64 PCGS. CAC.** Warm pink and champagne undertones enliven the surfaces of this scarce issue. The luster is perhaps less flashy than seen on peer examples, but the clean surfaces and bolder than normal strike more than compensates. While the total mintage of the 1874 is not on the large side for the Trade dollar series, it is impressive for a coin of this type from the Philadelphia Mint. In fact, the delivery of 987,100 Trade dollars in 1874 is the second highest for this coinage facility trailing only 1877's output. As one might expect for an early date Trade dollar, the 1874 saw very little domestic circulation. Scarce in circulated grades, the issue is rare in Mint State. Population: 23 in 64, 7 finer (8/08). (#7034)

2506 **1874-CC Chop Mark MS61 PCGS.** Untoned surfaces exhibit well struck devices. Scattered marks result in localized interruptions on the luster flow. A chop mark is concealed in the top rear of the wheat sheaf. (#87035)

2507 **1874-CC—Improperly Cleaned—NCS. AU Details.** Dotted milk-white and russet cover the mostly silver-gray surfaces. The scattered abrasions are entirely trivial, and the strike is sharp save for the usual weakness on Liberty's head and the final few stars. (#7035)

Lovely 1874-CC Trade Dollar, Mint State

2508 **1874-CC MS60 ANACS.** Despite a fairly high mintage of nearly 1.4 million pieces, the 1874-CC was shipped overseas in large quantities and is relatively scarce in Mint State today. A hint of maroon and light brown toning graces the margins, while the balance is silver-gray. Liberty's head and a few stars are a trifle soft, but the rest of the details are crisp. Minimally marked with plenty of luster throughout. (#7035)

Pleasing 1874-CC Trade Dollar, MS61

2509 **1874-CC MS61 NGC.** A hint of golden toning on the rims accents the mostly brilliant centers. Myriad abrasions limit the grade but minimally affect the flow of the stunning satiny luster. Crisply struck save for the typical weakness on Liberty's head and the adjacent stars. Delicate die cracks are noted by the date. (#7035)

Bright MS65 1874-CC Trade Dollar

2510 1874-CC MS65 NGC. A seldom-seen Trade dollar in mint condition as most of the 1.3 million struck were shipped to the Orient. Bowers states that in the mid-1970s a hoard of about 15 pieces was located in the Far East by World Wide Coin Investments. In fact, a large quantity of Uncirculated Trade dollars were found by Warren Tucker, partner in World Wide at the time, who paid approximately $200 per coin. Virtually all dates and mintmarks were represented in this hoard except the 1878-CC. These pieces were quickly dispersed among U.S. collectors. This is a lovely, bright example that is fully struck in all areas. Apparently the full strike was achieved by setting the striking pressure too high as both sides show extensive peripheral die cracks. Flashy mint luster rolls around each side of this lovely Gem. Census: 4 in 65, 0 finer (7/08). *From The Laredo Collection.* (#7035)

2511 1874-S MS61 PCGS. An intense, frosty sheen radiates from the mostly untoned, ice-white surfaces of this alluring Mint State specimen. Trace amounts of speckled olive patina occur over the lower half of the reverse. A few noticeable abrasions in the obverse fields limit the grade. (#7036)

Splendid Choice 1874-S Trade Dollar

2512 1874-S MS64 NGC. Medium S. No period after FINE. Attractive chestnut-gold, sky-blue, and rose toning invigorates this lustrous and impressively mark-free near-Gem. Crisply struck despite a hint of softness on the eagle's right (facing) claw. Much nicer than the usual Mint State Trade dollar. Census: 19 in 64, 2 finer (7/08). (#7036)

Brilliant Choice 1874-S Trade Dollar

2513 1874-S MS64 NGC. Breen-5785. Large S, which Breen considered rare. No period after FINE, apparently inadvertently removed from a working hub since the mint error appears on other reverse dies. This is a brilliant and satiny near-Gem with surprisingly smooth surfaces. Much scarcer than the 1877-S in this grade. Census: 19 in 64, 2 finer (7/08). (#7036)

2514 1875-CC MS60 NGC. Type 1 Obverse, Type 1 Reverse. Alluring luster radiates from both sides of this lightly toned specimen. Liberty's head is a trifle soft, as usually seen, but the rest of the details are razor-sharp. A minimally marked and attractive example. (#7038)

2515 1875-S MS61 NGC. Type One Reverse. Large S. Touches of amber and russet toning accent the mostly brilliant surfaces. Several stars, Liberty's head, and the eagle's right (facing) claw are a little soft. Delightful satiny luster enhances the eye appeal of this minimally marked representative. Housed in an old NGC holder. (#7039)

2516 1875-S MS61 PCGS. Dusky hazel and gray patina partly subdues the full mint luster. The strike is crisp, save for the usual weakness on Liberty's head, and the surfaces are remarkably well-preserved for the grade. A faint pinscratch in the left obverse field is the only distraction. (#7039)

2517 1875-S MS62 PCGS. A shining, unworn representative of this popular Trade dollar type issue, well-defined with only occasional whispers of gray-gold patina in the fields. Wispy abrasions appear in the fields, though overt flaws are few. (#7039)

Glowing Select 1875-S Trade Dollar

2518 **1875-S MS63 PCGS.** Type One Reverse. Large S. Luster dominates the open fields of this lightly toned and carefully preserved Trade dollar. As is usual for the type, Liberty's hair and the eagle's right (facing) leg show incompleteness, although the strike is otherwise exemplary. (#7039)

Impressive 1875-S Trade Dollar, Choice Uncirculated

2519 **1875-S MS64 PCGS.** Type One Reverse, Large S. A hint of hazel toning at the margins accents the mostly silver-gray surfaces of this resplendent piece. Vibrant satiny luster shimmers across the surfaces and complements the boldly struck design elements. Only a few areas (namely the eagle's left claw) show some softness. Several minor marks are visible under magnification, but none are of any consequence. PCGS has certified just 33 examples finer (8/08). (#7039)

Dazzling Choice 1875-S Trade Dollar

2520 **1875-S MS64 PCGS. CAC.** Type One Reverse. Large S. The light golden-gray toning is most prevalent across the lower reverse. This lustrous near-Gem has a good strike aside from Liberty's hair and a pair of nearby stars. Only infrequent minor field marks prevent an even finer grade. (#7039)

2521 **1875-S/CC XF45 NGC.** FS-501, formerly FS-012.5. Faint remnants of a prior CC mintmark are evident beneath the S. A popular *Guide Book* variety that is very scarce at all grade levels. This is a well detailed XF example with brownish-gray toning over smooth, unabraded surfaces that show a few wispy hairlines in the fields. (#7040)

Lustrous 1875-S/CC Trade Dollar MS62

2522 **1875-S/CC MS62 PCGS.** FS-501, formerly FS-012.5. Type One Reverse. The more prominent of the two S/CC varieties, which shows traces of a Carson City mintmark on each side of the S. The right C has greater definition, and is relatively distant from the S. Lustrous and lightly toned with minor field marks consistent with the grade. Population: 10 in 62, 13 finer (8/08). (#7040)

2523 **1876 MS61 NGC.** Untoned and boldly struck with a bright, semi-frosty finish. A few wispy hairlines and small abrasions are noted in the fields. The most common of the Philadelphia Mint Trade dollars in Mint State, and a good choice for an uncirculated type collection. (#7041)

2524 **1876 MS62 NGC.** Type One Obverse. Type Two Reverse. This is the seldom-encountered transitional variety from the obverse hub of 1873 to 1876 and the reverse hub of 1876 to 1883. Satiny luster shines beneath deep blue and light gray patina. Boldly struck with only minor reeding marks. (#7041)

Uncirculated 1876-CC Trade Dollar

2525 **1876-CC MS60 NGC.** Type One Obverse, Type Two Reverse. The tall CC mintmark is widely spaced. Pastel powder-blue and apricot colors grace this slightly subdued Carson City Trade Dollar. Field marks are present, but are minimal for the grade. This is a surprisingly difficult coin to encounter in Mint State grades. Census: 9 in 60, 37 finer (7/08).
Ex: Long Beach Signature Sale (Heritage, 10/01), lot 7229. (#7042)

2526 **1876-S MS61 PCGS.** A small streak of charcoal toning and a hint of purple toning above Liberty add color to the lightly toned surfaces. Pleasing satiny luster is minimally affected by a number of grade-defining marks throughout. The strike is bold save for a little weakness on Liberty's head. (#7043)

2527 **1876-S MS62 NGC.** Type One Obverse and Reverse. A hint of light yellow patina complements the flashy luster that shimmers throughout this minimally marked specimen. This attractive piece is sharply struck except for minor softness on Liberty's head, as usual. (#7043)

Impressive MS63 1876-S Trade Dollar

2528 **1876-S MS63 PCGS.** Type Two Obverse and Reverse. Minute S. Breen-5803, "very rare." The 1876-S usually has a Type One obverse, identified by a left-pointing lower scroll end, but here the scroll points down. Brilliant and lustrous with pleasing preservation and an exacting strike. Certainly a worthy representative that will cause many to raise their bidding paddles. (#7043)

2529 **1877 MS62 NGC.** Liberty's head and the obverse stars are softly struck, as usual, but the reverse design elements are sharply defined. The silver-gray toning yields to golden peripheral accents on each side. Scattered small abrasions are consistent with the grade. (#7044)

2530 **1877 MS62 PCGS.** The design elements are boldly rendered on this Mint State Trade dollar, except for typical softness on the upper obverse stars and on Liberty's head. Full silver-gray luster emanates from each side, and champagne highlights visit the peripheries. Strong eye appeal for the grade. (#7044)

2531 **1877 MS62 PCGS.** Nearly all 1877 Trade dollars are weakly struck (David Bowers, 2006). This MS62 example displays somewhat better definition than most; with the exception of softness in Liberty's hair and the centrils of three or four of the adjacent stars, the design elements exhibit sharp impressions. Silver-gray surfaces reveal a few minute marks. (#7044)

2532 **1877 MS62 PCGS.** Lustrous, untoned surfaces exhibit well struck design elements, including complete definition on the eagle's plumage. Minute marks are scattered about both sides. (#7044)

2533 **1877-CC VF35 PCGS.** A steel-gray scarce date Carson City trade dollar with reasonable remaining definition and a couple of small ebony spots above the knee and mintmark. (#7045)

Delightful 1877-CC Trade Dollar, Uncirculated

2534 **1877-CC MS60 NGC.** Mostly brilliant and highly lustrous with a hint of red toning at the bottom of the obverse. The strike is sharp save for the usual softness of Liberty's head. Numerous abrasions define the grade, and none merit specific mention. The 1877-CC is surprisingly scarce in Mint State, as a look at our auction records reveals. Census: 4 in 60, 58 finer (7/08). (#7045)

2535 **1877-S Chop Mark MS63 PCGS.** Pale steel-gray toning accents the bright silver-gray patina that covers both sides. Peppered abrasions limit the grade, and a small area of granularity in the right obverse field is noted. A tiny carbon spot on the obverse rim is barely worthy of mention. An interesting chop mark touches the eagle's right (facing) wing. (#87046)

2536 **1877-S MS61 NGC.** Well struck and nicely preserved, with shimmering mint frost across the icy-white surfaces. A few minor marks and wispy hairlines appear on each side, limiting the grade. (#7046)

2537 **1877-S MS62 NGC.** The splendid, dazzling mint frost that emanates from the surfaces of this San Francisco Mint Trade dollar is its most noteworthy attribute. The design details are crisply produced, and only scattered, superficial marks preclude a finer grade assessment. (#7046)

Appealing 1877-S Trade Dollar, MS63

2538 **1877-S MS63 PCGS.** Excellent luster and eye appeal for this amazing piece, one that offers substantially better viewing than the Select designation might suggest. If not for a thin mark to the left of the olive branch on the reverse, this minimally toned survivor would be assured of an even finer designation. (#7046)

Handsome 1877-S Trade Dollar MS64

2539 **1877-S MS64 PCGS. CAC.** Large S. Splashes of peripheral caramel-gold patina enhance this frosty silver trade dollar. All of the design elements are bold, and the surfaces are carefully preserved. Cartwheel luster dominates the open fields. The mintage of the 1877-S exceeded 9.5 million pieces, since many were coined for introduction in American circulation to profit from the difference between bullion value and face. (#7046)

Richly Toned MS64 1877-S Trade Dollar

2540 **1877-S MS64 PCGS.** With its gargantuan mintage of 9,519,000 pieces, the 1877-S is the Trade dollar most often selected by type collectors. The present piece, with its dappled peach, rose, and navy-blue patina, is an excellent candidate for such a set. Well-preserved aside from a handful of light marks and solidly struck with attractive luster. (#7046)

Well Struck 1877-S Trade Dollar, MS64

2541 **1877-S MS64 PCGS.** The 1877-S is the highest-mintage Trade dollar (9.519 million pieces), and is the most common in circulated grades. Even Mint State pieces are available through the Select level, after which they become more difficult to locate. Dappled gold-tan patina is somewhat deeper and more extensive on the obverse of this near-Gem coin. The fields are partially prooflike, yielding mild contrast with the well struck design features. Minute handling marks preclude Gem status. Housed in a green-label holder. (#7046)

Vibrant Gem 1877-S Trade Dollar

2542 **1877-S MS65 NGC.** This wonderful S-mint Gem Trade dollar, which hails from the issue with the highest mintage for the series, would make an excellent addition to a date or type set. Each side offers crisp detail at both the centers and the margins, and the generally silver-white surfaces show glimpses of reddish-tan toning near the rims. The luster offers interesting contrast between the strong cartwheels of the obverse and the striking mirrors of the reverse. Both the figure of Liberty and the eagle exhibit considerable frostiness. Census: 29 in 65, 5 finer (7/08). (#7046)

Pleasing 1878-CC Trade Dollar, XF45

2543 **1878-CC XF45 ANACS.** Although Carson City minted 97,000 Trade dollars in 1878, the comparative scarcity of the issue has led some to speculate that many were melted later in the 1870s. This example is not chopmarked, perhaps indicating its considerable time in circulation was Stateside rather than in the Orient. This is a yeoman's example of a desirable type, with even circulation wear but no significant abrasions or spots. Dusky gray toning covers both sides, with occasional rose highlights. (#7047)

Dazzling Choice 1878-S Trade Dollar

2544 **1878-S MS64 PCGS.** Light gold toning enriches this thoroughly lustrous near-Gem. The reverse is virtually pristine, while the obverse has only scattered minor abrasions. Exactingly struck, and a worthy representative of the final year of Trade dollar production. Population: 71 in 64, 35 finer (8/08). *From The Bell Collection.* (#7048)

Uniformly Toned 1878-S Trade Dollar, MS64

2545 **1878-S MS64 PCGS.** The 1878-S is one of the more common issues in all grades of the Trade dollar series, though the certified population drops off between MS63 and MS64. Uniform light to medium intensity golden-gray patina bathes the lustrous surfaces of this near-Gem specimen, and an attentive strike imparts strong definition to the design features. A few unobtrusive marks preclude Gem status. Population: 72 in 64, 36 finer (8/08). (#7048)

Remarkable 1878-S Trade Dollar, MS65

2546 1878-S MS65 PCGS. The year 1878 marked both a beginning and an end in U.S. coinage history. Congress passed the Bland-Allison Act on February 28, 1878, which was a boon to silver mining interests. Bland-Allison required the Treasury to purchase millions of ounces of silver bullion, and the end result was obvious: there would be a new circulating silver coin, George T. Morgan's dollar. Buffeted by changing market and political winds, the Trade dollar became the orphan no one wanted, and the last circulation issues were minted in 1878. Over 4.1 million coins were produced at San Francisco that year, and though many were likely melted, the 1878-S Trade dollar is a common issue in lower grades. However, it is rare in Gem or finer grades.

This coin is a wonderful example of the last year of Trade dollar production. Light strokes of pastel cinnamon and rose are brushed over a taupe underlay, both yielding to untoned centers. The strike is sharp, and radiant luster complements the moderate patina. This is an uncommonly preserved representative of a unique chapter in the history of U.S. coinage. Population: 18 in 65, 18 finer (8/08). (#7048)

PROOF TRADE DOLLARS

Impressive 1873 Trade Dollar, Gem Proof

2547 1873 PR65 NGC. Authorized by the Coinage Act of February 12, 1873, Trade dollar production began shortly thereafter. Despite a plentiful mintage of business strikes (396,635 pieces), there was little demand for proofs, so only 865 specimens were struck, which is low compared to the four-figure proof mintages for later years. Vibrant toning endows the surfaces of the present piece, with rose and gold at the centers and cobalt-blue in the margins. The deeply reflective fields are remarkably pristine, and a loupe locates only a couple of nearly imperceptible contact marks. A sharply struck and exceptionally attractive representative. Census: 14 in 65, 3 finer (7/08). (#7053)

Lovely 1873 Trade Dollar, PR64 Cameo

2548 1873 PR64 Cameo PCGS. CAC. Production of trade dollars began shortly after the end of the Seated dollar series in 1873, with the intention of creating a coin that would compete with Mexican dollars and other trade coins in the orient. This proof is a lovely Cameo example of the first year of issue, a fitting representative of the design for type collectors. All of the design features are bold, and both sides display full cameo contrast beneath pale gold toning. Population: 6 in 64 Cameo, 0 finer (8/08). (#87053)

Patinated Choice Proof 1876 Trade Dollar

2549 1876 PR64 NGC. Type One Obverse, Type Two Reverse. This proof type coin is deeply toned, and reveals golden-brown, electric-blue, plum-red, and straw-gold when it is rotated beneath a light. A small spot and wispy contact is noted above the date, and a faint graze is present near star 8. Census: 49 in 64, 19 finer (7/08). (#7056)

Magnificent 1876 Trade Dollar, PR63 Cameo

2550 **1876 PR63 Cameo NGC.** Type One Obverse, Type Two Reverse. Enticing deeply mirrored fields have a pleasing medium gray complexion and show powerful cameo contrast against the light silver-gray devices. A number of hairlines in the fields limit the grade, but they are nearly imperceptible without a loupe. This fully struck piece has exceptional eye appeal. Only 1,150 proofs were minted. Census: 14 in 63 Cameo, 31 finer (7/08). (#87056)

Luminous PR62 1879 Trade Dollar

2551 **1879 PR62 PCGS.** Both sides offer mild contrast, though the softly frosted devices and the lightly toned mirrors do not combine for a full Cameo designation. Silver-gray patina drapes the mirrors, while elements of tan visit the margins. A sharply struck piece that displays well, with few abrasions in the obverse fields. (#7059)

Splendid 1879 Trade Dollar, Choice Proof

2552 **1879 PR64 PCGS.** Deep gunmetal-gray patina covers the remarkably unabraded surfaces. Although the toning partly obscures the luster, a watery sheen becomes clear under a lamp. This fully struck near-Gem specimen is one of only 1,541 proofs minted. The 1879 was the first of the six proof-only issues that closed the Trade dollar series. (#7059)

Colorful Gem Proof 1880 Trade Dollar

2553 **1880 PR65 NGC.** A pleasingly preserved, delightfully toned specimen from the most populous of the proof Trade dollar issues. Deep, dusky violet and sapphire patina prevails over much of each side, while the obverse shows lighter peach and gold elements in the centers. NGC has graded 62 numerically finer representatives (8/08). (#7060)

Extraordinary 1880 Trade Dollar, Superb Proof Cameo

2554 **1880 PR67 Cameo NGC.** The 1880 was the second proof-only Trade dollar issue and a total of 1,987 specimens were minted. Bowers (1993) is perhaps a little generous when he estimates that between 1,300 and 1,700 proofs survive. NGC and PCGS report a combined 1,339 submissions, but that does not count the number of unique specimens. Regardless of the exact number of survivors, this issue, as one might expect, is a true condition rarity in high grades.

Eye-catching deeply mirrored fields appear watery and show strong cameo contrast against the frosted devices. Close examination with a loupe reveals only a few minute hairlines. The strike is full and the eye appeal is extraordinary. PCGS reports six pieces in PR67 Cameo, with none finer. NGC has certified 10 specimens in PR67 Cameo and the same number one point above (8/08). It is a rare pleasure to offer a Superb Proof Cameo at auction. (#87060)

Brilliant PR66 Ultra Cameo 1880 Trade Dollar

2555 **1880 PR66 Ultra Cameo NGC.** It would be difficult to surpass the cameo contrast generated by this outstanding proof-only specimen. The frosted motifs appear to float over deep, watery fields, and provide a white-on-black appearance when the coin is viewed from a direct angle. All of the detail on the design elements appears to be brought out, including excellent delineation in Liberty's hair and on the eagle's feathers and claws. An unobtrusive hairline or two may show in the obverse fields, but the essentially untoned surfaces are near-pristine. Census: 1 in 66 Ultra Cameo, 4 finer (7/08).
Ex: Columbus Central States Signature (Heritage, 4/2006), lot 2238.
(#97060)

2556 **1881—Corroded, Cleaned—ICG. PR60 Details.** The 1881 was a proof-only issue from the waning years of the Trade dollar series and had a mintage of just 960 pieces. Deep gunmetal-gray toning covers both sides of this sharply struck specimen. The speckled corrosion is generally minor. (#7061)

2557 **1881 PR61 PCGS.** Reflective fields highlight the motifs of this proof-only Trade dollar, and a well executed strike leaves bold definition throughout, an unusual attribute for this issue that is typically flat in several areas. Hints of purple cling to the margins, and wisps of tan-gold visit the centers. Some fine hairlines in the fields limit the grade. Overall, an exceptional 1881, housed in a green label holder. (#7061)

Exemplary PR66 Deep Cameo 1882 Trade Dollar

2558 **1882 PR66 Deep Cameo PCGS.** The Trade dollar was unpopular with the general public in 1882, who remembered that those stuck with examples could only receive bullion value for them. It was a different story for collectors of the day, who pursued the run of proof-only dates that began in 1879 (the 1878 was proof-only, but the 1878-S Trade dollar was plentiful). Proof set mintages dropped in 1884 once the proof Trade dollar was no longer offered. The present piece helps explain the perennial popularity of the proof type. Frosted devices contrast with the darkly mirrored fields. The strike is exacting, and light golden toning further confirms the originality. Population: 4 in 66 Deep Cameo, 0 finer (8/08). (#97062)

End of Session Three

SESSION FOUR

Live, Internet, and Mail Bid Signature® Auction #1116
Friday, September 19, 2008, 9:30 AM PT, Lots 2559 - 3104
Long Beach, California

A 15% Buyer's Premium ($9 minimum) Will Be Added To All Lots

Visit HA.com to view full-color images and bid.

MORGAN DOLLARS

2559 **1878 8TF MS65 PCGS.** VAM-16. This crisply struck Morgan dollar has sweeping luster, and is brilliant aside from infrequent wisps of tan toning. Well preserved except for a few faint grazes. (#7072)

Scarce 1878 7/8TF Strong Morgan Dollar
VAM-44, Choice XF

2560 **1878 7/8TF Strong XF45 ANACS.** VAM-44. A Top 100 Variety. LIBERTY is slightly doubled, which is most noticeable at the B, and the cotton blossoms and leaves are tripled on the right side. This key 7/8TF variety is scarce in all grades, and is categorized as R-7 in the fourth edition of the VAM *Encyclopedia*. A ring of lilac and maroon surrounds the medium gray centers. Minimally marked and well detailed. (#7078)

2561 **1878 7/8TF Strong MS64 NGC.** Deep copper, sage, gold, and russet tints on both sides of this near-Gem provide strong appeal. This popular first-year variety is much more elusive at the next grade level, but this example should prove to be a satisfying acquisition. (#7078)

2562 **1878 7/8TF Weak MS62 NGC.** VAM-34. A Hot 50 Variety. A very scarce 7/8TF VAM. Lustrous and virtually brilliant with a bold strike. The cheek has a faint vertical graze, and the reverse field is abraded above the branch leaves. (#7070)

2563 **1878 7/8TF Weak MS63 NGC.** VAM-30. 7/0TF. A Long Nock reverse VAM that shows no tailfeather doubling. The lower obverse margin has an arc of canary-gold, while the remainder of this satiny and meticulously struck silver dollar is pearl-gray. (#7070)

2564 **1878 7/8TF Weak MS62 Deep Mirror Prooflike PCGS.** VAM-32. A Top 100 Variety. A diagonal die line through the right-side tail feathers identifies this challenging 7/3TF VAM. Brilliant and well struck with dazzling field reflectivity. The obverse has marks that correspond to the grade. Housed in a green label holder. (#97071)

2565 **1878 7TF Reverse of 1878 MS65 PCGS.** The right (facing) leg of the eagle shows obvious doubling, and there are numerous raised die lines that surround the opposite claw. Several die cracks are also noticeable on each side. Both sides are brilliant and highly reflective, and the flow of the luster is barely affected by a couple of minor bagmarks. A wonderful choice for the variety specialist. (#7074)

2566 **1878 7TF Reverse of 1878 MS65 PCGS. CAC.** Charming orange-gold, violet, and cobalt-blue toning in the periphery is especially vivid on the obverse, and surrounds the brilliant silver-gray centers. Powerful luster radiates from the semiprooflike fields. The surfaces are remarkably clean for the grade, and only several faint grazes are visible. PCGS has certified just 18 pieces finer (7/08). (#7074)

2567 **1878 7TF Reverse of 1878 MS65 PCGS.** Ex: Ray George. A hint of gold toning is present, but most collectors would consider this lustrous Gem to be brilliant. The strike is penetrating, and the fields are remarkably clean. (#7074)

2568 **1878 7TF Reverse of 1878 MS65 PCGS.** This is a gorgeous Gem with luscious russet-red peripheral toning on each side, and flashy coruscating luster in the untoned fields and centers. Sharply struck throughout, with a single shallow abrasion directly beneath D WE TR, on the upper reverse, as the only minor detraction. (#7074)

2569 **1878 7TF Reverse of 1878 MS65 PCGS.** VAM-84. A 'Washed Out L' variety with a dash below the first 8 and a broken base to the D in DOLLAR. Not to be confused with the Reverse of 1879 VAM-223, a Top 100 Variety that also has a Washed Out L. Lustrous and attractively preserved with lavish autumn-gold and aquamarine patina. (#7074)

2570 **1878 7TF Reverse of 1878 MS64 Deep Mirror Prooflike NGC.** A single mark in the left obverse field accounts for the grade of this important piece. Both sides have deeply mirrored fields and faint cameo contrast. (#97075)

Gem Deep Mirror Prooflike 1878 7 Tailfeathers
Reverse of '78 Dollar, Tied for Finest Certified

2571 **1878 7TF Reverse of 1878 MS65 Deep Mirror Prooflike PCGS. CAC.** The 1878 7 Tailfeathers with Reverse of 1878 is considerably more common than the Reverse of 1879, but the issue is not at all common with Deep Mirror Prooflike surfaces, as here. Some coins show a moderate degree of prooflikeness, but this piece shows wonderfully bold reflectivity and the coveted black-on-silver contrast seldom seen for the issue. Deep Mirror Prooflike Morgans are not only among the most attractive and sought-after silver dollars, they have also held up quite well in most numismatic markets. A sharply struck and thoroughly delightful Gem example, among the dozen finest graded at PCGS, with 11 more at NGC and none finer (8/08). (#97075)

Attractive 1878 7TF Morgan Dollar
Reverse of 1879, Gem Uncirculated

2572 **1878 7TF Reverse of 1879 MS65 NGC.** A slanted top arrow feather and rounded eagle's breast identifies the Reverse of 1879, which is significantly scarcer than its Reverse of 1878 counterpart. This brilliant and frosty Gem has a few light grazes on Liberty's cheek, but overall exhibits a remarkable level of preservation. NGC has certified only a dozen pieces finer (7/08). (#7076)

Gem 1878 Third Reverse Silver Dollar with 7TF

2573 **1878 7TF Reverse of 1879 MS65 PCGS.** A hint of tan toning near the centers denies absolute brilliance, but the booming luster and unblemished appearance confirm status as a Gem. Boldly struck and beautiful. The Third Reverse or Reverse of 1879 with a high relief eagle's breast and a slanted upper arrow feather. (#7076)

2574 **1878-CC MS65 NGC.** A frosty and lustrous Gem with a circle of russet and deep violet toning around the rims. This sharply struck and minimally marked piece would make a splendid representative of the first Morgan dollar. (#7080)

2575 **1878-CC MS65 NGC.** The design elements are reproduced with razor-sharp precision, especially on the central details, including the hair detail just above Liberty's ear and the eagle's breast feathers. Mottled sea-green, gold, and turquoise toning adorns the vibrantly lustrous surfaces. A gorgeous, nicely preserved Gem. (#7080)

2576 **1878-CC MS65 NGC.** A sharply struck Gem with potent luster and an occasional wisp of golden toning. The obverse has only a few faint grazes, while the reverse is exceptional smooth. (#7080)

Beautiful Premium Gem 1878-CC Morgan Dollar

2577 **1878-CC MS66 PCGS.** Take the first year of Morgan dollar production, the coveted Carson City mintmark, and the eye appeal of a brilliant Premium Gem Morgan dollar, and one has the present coin. Radiant with satiny cartwheel luster and premium eye appeal, this piece is exceeded by only a handful of Superb Gems at both services combined (8/08). The strike is bold, save for some softness on the lower eagle, and swirling die finishing lines, raised on the coin, are noted in that same area under a loupe. A beautiful example. (#7080)

Thickly Frosted MS66 1878-CC Dollar

2578 **1878-CC MS66 NGC.** This example of the premier Carson City Morgan dollar offering boasts the sharp details so often seen from the earlier issues from this storied mint. The lustrous fields only hint at reflectivity, with ample mint frost providing a pleasing visual effect. Bright silver surfaces are accented with a light gold tint. (#7080)

Exciting 1878-CC Morgan Dollar, MS65 Prooflike

2579 **1878-CC MS65 Prooflike PCGS.** Remarkable prooflike fields show exciting cameo contrast against the frosted devices. Flashy luster accents the nearly fully struck design elements. A few wispy abrasions limit the grade, but they barely affect the spectacular eye appeal. Several tiny toning spots are the only signs of color on this otherwise brilliant representative. PCGS has certified just 12 Prooflike examples finer (7/08). (#7081)

2580 **1878-CC MS63 Deep Mirror Prooflike NGC.** An impressive, deeply mirrored example with a moderate cameo appearance. The obverse is mostly brilliant, while the reverse has a vibrant ring of russet toning around the perimeter. Scattered grazes minimally affect the splendid eye appeal. (#97081)

2581　**1878-CC MS63 Deep Mirror Prooflike PCGS.** Prominently reflective fields and powerfully struck devices distinguish this first-year Carson City Morgan dollar. Smooth for the grade, but the left obverse has a fingerprint. Encased in an old green label holder. (#97081)

1878-CC Dollar, MS65 Deep Mirror Prooflike

2582　**1878-CC MS65 Deep Mirror Prooflike ANACS.** The combination of first-year issue, Carson City mintmark, and Deep Mirror Prooflike surfaces should prove irresistible for the legions of collectors of this popular series. Rim toning in shades of pink and blue and deep field-device contrast makes this a memorable example in this popular series. (#97081)

2583　**1878-S MS65 PCGS. CAC.** This is a richly toned Gem example of this first-year San Francisco Mint issue, with lavender and sapphire patina in generous supply on the obverse, while the reverse shows silver centers tinged with sage at the rims. Generous luster proceeds from each side, despite the moderate toning. A prize for color collectors. (#7082)

2584　**1878-S MS66 PCGS.** Bright luster radiates from the untoned surfaces of this S-mint Premium Gem. An impressive strike leaves strong definition on the design elements, including the hair over Liberty's ear and the eagle's breast feathers. Some minor obverse grazes are noted. (#7082)

2585　**1878-S MS66 PCGS.** Meticulously struck and virtually brilliant with potent luster and nearly immaculate fields. Encapsulated in an old green label holder. (#7082)

2586　**1879 MS65 PCGS.** Well struck for the issue and carefully preserved. The immensely lustrous obverse shows ample gold-orange and cerulean peripheral toning, while the reverse shows only occasional glints of gold. (#7084)

2587　**1879 MS65 PCGS.** This delicately toned olive-gray Gem displays vibrant luster and has a nearly immaculate cheek. Nicely struck, and clean overall despite faint left obverse field grazes. In a green label holder. (#7084)

2588　**1879 MS65 PCGS.** Although the reverse is nearly brilliant, the obverse has medium chestnut-gold toning with a blush of lemon-gold and cherry-red near 1 o'clock. Potent luster sweeps the impressively unabraded surfaces. (#7084)

2589　**1879 MS65 Prooflike NGC.** This is a lovely Gem Prooflike offering. Crisp definition characterizes the design elements, including the hair over Liberty's ear and the eagle's breast feathers. A few minor grazes on the untoned surfaces might preclude an even higher grade. Census: 14 in 65 Prooflike, 0 finer (7/08). (#7085)

2590　**1879-CC AU53 NGC.** This is the desirable Normal Mintmark variety, and it is an attractive, lightly worn example with nearly full satin luster and pale golden-brown toning. (#7086)

Brilliant 1879-CC Normal Mintmark Dollar, MS62

2591　**1879-CC MS62 PCGS.** Normal Mintmark. A few stray abrasions and reeding marks on Liberty's cheek likely account for the grade, but much appeal is present. The satiny silver surfaces show radiant cartwheel luster, and the surfaces show a remarkable consistency of texture. Light die clashing appears on the reverse, with a small die crack connecting NITED with the eagle's nearby wingtip. A nice example of this popular key date, seemingly high-end for the assigned grade. (#7086)

Charming 1879-CC Morgan Dollar, MS62

2592　**1879-CC MS62 NGC.** While its mintage of 756,000 pieces does not suggest a scarce issue, the 1879-CC is one of the more difficult Carson City dollars to locate in Mint State grades. Dazzling cartwheel luster radiates beneath the lightly frosted and untoned surfaces. The hair above Liberty's ear is slightly weak, as typical, and there are scattered light grazes throughout. An attractive and relatively affordable example of this popular issue. (#7086)

Semikey 1879-CC Morgan Dollar, MS62

2593　**1879-CC MS62 PCGS.** Normal Mintmark. Powerful semiprooflike luster graces the fields and complements the sharply defined design elements. Myriad abrasions cover each side, as typical for the grade, but none merit specific mention. The 1879-CC is a semikey issue in the series and Bowers (2005) estimates that hundreds of thousands were melted under the 1918 Pittman Act. (#7086)

Exceptional MS64 1879-CC Dollar

2594 **1879-CC MS64 PCGS.** The low mintage and low availability make the 1879-CC the key to the early Carson City dollars. Only 756,000 pieces were struck and high grade examples are exceptionally scarce. The surfaces on this piece are bright and highly lustrous with the usual semireflective gleam in the fields. The striking details are strong throughout, and the only mark of any note is located on the reverse to the right of the eagle's right (facing) wing. (#7086)

Splendid 1879-CC Morgan Dollar, Choice Mint State

2595 **1879-CC MS64 NGC. CAC.** Normal Mintmark. Outstanding semiprooflike fields reflect incredible amounts of luster and show moderate contrast against the frosted devices. Light lemon-yellow toning accents the crisply struck design elements. The reverse is remarkably clean, and the obverse has only trivial abrasions. This issue ranks among the scarcer Carson City Morgan dollars and is particularly difficult in high Uncirculated grades. NGC reports just 38 examples finer (7/08). (#7086)

Prooflike MS62 1879-CC Morgan

2596 **1879-CC MS62 Prooflike PCGS.** When this brilliant Carson City dollar is rotated just so, the frosty devices display pleasing contrast with the reflective fields. The strike is crisp and the coin is attractive, despite the faint distributed grazes that determine the grade. The 1879-CC is the key Morgan issue of the first period (1870 to 1885) of the Nevada facility's production. (#7087)

Magnificent 1879-CC Morgan Dollar, MS63 Prooflike

2597 **1879-CC MS63 Prooflike NGC.** Normal Mintmark. In *A Guide Book of Morgan Silver Dollars*, Bowers (2005) writes that "the 1879-CC is the first key or rare variety in the Morgan dollar series and is the second rarest (after 1889-CC) of all Carson City Morgans." The present piece is nearly brilliant and has a prominent retained lamination from the rim to the O in ONE. A small patch of verdigris surrounds the lamination. The fields are highly reflective and show moderate contrast against the frosted devices. A minimally marked and crisply struck representative. (#7087)

2598 **1879-CC Capped Die—Scratched, Cleaned—ANACS. AU50 Details.** VAM-3. A Top 100 Variety. Light gray patina covers both sides, with traces of luster in the protected areas. Several pinscratches in the left obverse field and a few shallow digs on Liberty's cheek account for the designation from ANACS. (#7088)

Sharp 1879-CC Capped Die Morgan Dollar, MS62

2599 **1879-CC Capped Die MS62 PCGS.** VAM-3. A Top 100 Variety. While the Capped Die (Medium over Small Mintmark) variety is less popular than its Perfect Mintmark counterpart, it is actually scarcer, particularly in high grades. The present piece has a touch of violet and russet toning at the upper right quadrant of both sides. Scintillating luster in the fields highlights the powerfully impressed design elements. Myriad abrasions limit the grade, but none are particularly significant. (#7088)

Condition Scarcity 1879-CC Capped Die Dollar MS62 Prooflike

2600 **1879-CC Capped Die MS62 Prooflike ANACS.** VAM-3. A Top 100 Variety. This well mirrored example offers moderate mint frost over the devices. The surfaces are untoned, save for a thin ring of gold around the rims on each side, and relatively sharp definition shows on the design features. Numerous light to moderate abrasions, more so on the obverse than reverse, confirm the grade. Although it is less popular than the Perfect Mintmark variant, is it scarcer in high grades. (#7089)

2601 **1879-S MS67 PCGS.** Immensely lustrous with considerable frost evident on Liberty's portrait. While the center of the obverse is generally silver-gray, the rest of the piece displays ample tan-gold, blue-green, and reddish-orange patina. (#7092)

2602 **1879-S MS67 PCGS.** Razor-sharp striking definition and flashy luster characterize each side of this beautifully preserved Superb Gem. The obverse has Prooflike-level reflectivity, though the reverse falls just shy of the standard. (#7092)

2603 **1879-S MS67 NGC.** Alluring semiprooflike reflectivity in the fields complements the icy-frosted devices. A thin streak of tan-gray on the reverse is the only color on this otherwise brilliant representative. Carefully preserved and highly appealing. (#7092)

2604 **1879-S MS67 NGC.** Exquisitely detailed with hints of twinkling frost on the high points. This shining Superb Gem is essentially untoned aside from hints of yellow-orange at the obverse rims. (#7092)

2605 **1879-S MS67 PCGS.** An attractive arc of violet, red, and gold graces the left half of the obverse, with pleasing light reddish-brown across the remainder. The reverse, however, is entirely brilliant. Both sides have only a few pinpoint handling marks and exhibit a razor-sharp strike. Eye-catching luster enhances the eye appeal of this vibrant specimen. (#7092)

2606 **1879-S MS67 PCGS.** The reverse of this attractive piece is decidedly prooflike, while the obverse is nearly so. Several wispy abrasions and a couple of tiny milk spots barely affect the excellent eye appeal and immense reflectivity. (#7092)

2607 **1879-S MS65 Deep Mirror Prooflike ANACS.** Despite moderate blue, indigo, and champagne patina across each side, the immense reflectivity of the fields shines through. The boldly struck central devices are beautifully frosted. (#97093)

2608 **1879-S Reverse of 1878 MS61 Deep Mirror Prooflike NGC.** A Top 100 Variety. The boldly impressed devices on both sides offer rich frost that starkly contrasts with the essentially untoned, intensely reflective fields. Distributed minor abrasions on the obverse account for the grade. Census: 2 in 61 Deep Mirror Prooflike, 10 finer (8/08). (#97095)

2609 **1880 MS65 PCGS.** Dazzling cartwheel luster drapes the minimally marked surfaces. The strike is above-average for this Philadelphia issue and the details are nearly full. A wonderful piece with great eye appeal. (#7096)

2610 **1880 MS65 PCGS.** Vibrant rainbow toning adds a dramatic flair to this minimally marked specimen. Rings of cobalt-blue, teal-green, maroon, and gold cover both sides, with only a small area of silver-gray at the center of the reverse. Captivating luster shines beneath the enticing toning and enhances the outstanding eye appeal. (#7096)

2611 **1880 MS65 PCGS.** Splashes of electric-blue, golden-tan, and purple toning are more extensive on the obverse of this Gem. Lustrous surfaces exhibit well struck devices, and are minimally abraded. (#7096)

Snowy 1880 Morgan Dollar, MS66

2612 **1880 MS66 PCGS.** A remarkable Premium Gem, tied for the finest that PCGS has certified, with frosty white luster and only a trace of peripheral gold toning. The hair over Liberty's ear is a trifle weak, but all other design features are sharp. Population: 79 in 66, 0 finer (7/08). (#7096)

2613 **1880 MS64 Deep Mirror Prooflike PCGS.** Mostly brilliant save for a circle of gold and lavender toning around the rims. The deeply mirrored fields appear watery, and contrast sharply against the frosted devices. Wispy abrasions throughout are typical for the grade. An appealing Choice representative. (#97097)

2614 **1880-CC MS64 PCGS.** A largely untoned silver-white reverse complements a lavish obverse in shades of lilac and sage. Generous luster proceeds from each side, and only a few stray abrasions apparently keep this piece from the Gem level. (#7100)

2615 **1880-CC MS65 NGC.** Sharply struck with intense mint frost and dazzling reflectivity in the fields, on both sides. Some cloudiness precludes a Prooflike grade designation, but surface flaws are minor otherwise. (#7100)

2616 **1880-CC MS65 PCGS.** Dazzling cartwheel luster flows throughout the fields, which contrast nicely against the frosted devices. Several light grazes keep this powerfully impressed Gem from an even higher grade. (#7100)

2617 **1880-CC MS65 PCGS.** Extravagant copper-gold, silver-gray, and ice-blue envelop this satiny Carson City Gem. The obverse shows only light tan toning. The reverse is well preserved, and the obverse has only faint grazes made nearly imperceptible by the patina. (#7100)

Frosty 1880-CC Morgan, MS66

2618 **1880-CC MS66 PCGS.** Superb frosty mint luster and minimal surface marks for this typically abraded issue. Natural molten silver surfaces with an untoned appearance overall. Boldly defined with nearly full details over the ear. PCGS has only certified 31 finer examples, including all different varieties of the date (7/08). (#7100)

2619 **1880-CC 8 Over High 7 MS65 PCGS.** VAM-5. A Top 100 Variety. The 7 underdigit is all too obvious. The crossbar, downstroke, base, and 'horns' are evident above, within, and below the second 8. Lustrous and impressively unabraded with light golden-gray toning and only minor indifference of strike above Liberty's ear. (#7102)

2620 **1880/79-CC Reverse of 1878 MS64 PCGS.** VAM-4. A Top 100 Variety. A fairly obvious overdate identifies the obverse, while the Reverse of 1878 is distinguished by a flat top arrow feather (as opposed to a slanted feather). This resplendent Choice specimen is crisply struck and has no mentionable marks. (#7108)

2621 **1880/79-CC Reverse of 1878 MS64 PCGS. CAC.** VAM-4. A Top 100 Variety. A touch of gold and rose-red toning graces the margins, which contrast nicely against the brilliant centers. The surfaces are minimally marked and the strike is sharp, with a plain overdate visible under magnification. A lovely example of this popular variety. (#7108)

Interesting 1880/79-CC, Reverse of 1878, Gem Mint State

2622 **1880/79-CC Reverse of 1878 MS65 PCGS. CAC.** VAM-5. A Top 100 Variety. A trace of the underdigit 7 just below the second 8 in the date identifies this variety. Although the overdate is not as pronounced on other specimens, it is easily distinguishable under a loupe. Pleasing frost overlies the untoned surfaces of this lightly abraded and sharply struck specimen. Housed in a green label holder. PCGS reports just 50 examples finer (8/08). (#7108)

Appealing Gem 1880/79-CC Reverse of '78 Dollar

2623 **1880/79-CC Reverse of 1878 MS65 PCGS.** VAM-4. A Top 100 Variety. One could say that the present coin has evidence of three different years on its surfaces: the parallel arrow feathers Reverse of 1878, and the underdigits 79 that on this Van Allen-Mallis variety are bold underneath the overlying 80. Gem examples of this are near the top of many Morgan dollar variety collectors' want lists, but there are insufficient numbers to serve the demand. This is a silver-white piece with good luster and tremendous eye appeal. Only a series of small reeding marks in the right obverse field that require singular mention. (#7108)

Splendid MS66 VAM-4 1880/79-CC Reverse of 1878 Dollar

2624 **1880/79-CC Reverse of 1878 MS66 NGC.** VAM-4. A Top 100 Variety. Although undesignated as such on the NGC slab, this is actually the so-called "major overdate" for the series, with bold traces of the underlying 79 visible inside the final 80 in the date. The Reverse of 1878, of course, features the first-year reverse with parallel top arrow feathers in the fletchings and flat-breasted eagle. This silver-white example boasts splendidly smooth surfaces with thick mint frost, and only a few tiny luster grazes apparently limit an even finer grade. (#7108)

1880/79-CC Reverse of 1878 Dollar, VAM-4, MS66

2625 **1880/79-CC Reverse of 1878 MS66 PCGS.** VAM-4. A Top 100 Variety, and worth a premium for its use of the earlier "B" reverse from 1878. The surfaces are brilliant and frosty white with a dash of iridescence at the top of the obverse and pale gold at the lower right reverse. Population: 50 in 66, 0 finer (7/08). (#7108)

2626 **1880-O MS64 PCGS.** Sharply struck and delightfully lustrous with highly reflective, semiprooflike fields. This is a lovely example of this issue, which is seldom found any finer. PCGS has certified a mere 21 examples finer (7/08). (#7114)

2627 **1880-O MS64 NGC.** Both sides are covered in patches of violet, dove-gray, olive-green, and amber, which complement the sharply struck details. Some grade-defining marks are noted on Liberty's cheek, on the eagle's breast, and in the upper reverse field. NGC reports just 19 examples finer (7/08). Housed in an old holder. (#7114)

2628 **1880-O MS64 PCGS. CAC.** Micro O. This well struck near-Gem displays vibrant cartwheel luster, and has only a hint of golden toning on each side. The reverse is beautifully preserved, and the face has only minor abrasions. (#7114)

2629 **1880-O MS64 PCGS.** Well-defined for this New Orleans issue with occasional elements of rose and pink-peach across parts of the reverse. Strongly lustrous and attractive. PCGS has graded just 21 finer examples (8/08). (#7114)

2630 **1880-O MS64 PCGS.** Dramatic steel, lemon, teal, and lilac toning envelops the obverse, which contrasts sharply against the brilliant and frosty reverse. Semiprooflike luster on the obverse radiates beneath the vivid toning, and the reverse shows a splendid cartwheel effect throughout. Scattered bagmarks are visible in the fields, but there are none of any significance. PCGS has certified a mere 21 pieces finer (6/08). (#7114)

2631 **1880-O MS64 PCGS.** This well struck near-Gem features potent luster and clean fields. A dab of golden-brown color is at 9 o'clock on the obverse. A beautiful New Orleans silver dollar. (#7114)

Near-Gem 1880-O Morgan Dollar, Prooflike

2632 **1880-O MS64 Prooflike NGC.** The 1880-O Morgan dollar is a two-fold condition rarity. It is elusive in MS64 or finer grades, and it is also hard to locate with any degree of prooflike mirrored surfaces. This piece is fully brilliant with excellent mirrored fields that surround the frosty and highly lustrous obverse and reverse devices. Census: 17 in 64 Prooflike, 1 finer (7/08). (#7115)

2633 **1880-S MS65 ★ NGC.** An arc of yellow-gold, ruby-red, and ocean-blue dominates the right obverse border and garners the coveted Star designated from NGC. The reverse remains brilliant. The Large S mintmark has a repunched upper serif. A faint fingerprint is seen near Liberty's jaw, but the only discernible contact is on the upper left obverse field. (#7118)

2634 **1880-S MS67 NGC. CAC.** Although not designated as such by NGC, the fields are decidedly Deep Mirrored and Prooflike, and along with the frosted devices create a startling cameo appearance. Orange-gold toning surrounds the brilliant centers. Several light grazes on Liberty's cheek keep this piece from an even higher grade. (#7118)

2635 **1880-S MS67 PCGS. CAC.** Decidedly prooflike fields show moderate cameo contrast against the frosted devices. Enticing satiny luster graces both sides. This resplendent, near-perfect coin is housed in a green label holder. (#7118)

2636 **1880-S MS67 PCGS. CAC.** An impeccably preserved specimen with only a couple of nearly imperceptible grazes. Scattered toning spots on the obverse are noted, with a hint of rose on Liberty's cheek and a splash of gold on the reverse. Nearly fully struck with splendid satiny luster throughout. Housed in a green label PCGS holder. (#7118)

2637 **1880-S MS67 NGC. CAC.** Medium S. Lustrous surfaces are dominated by aqua and purple on the obverse, and by russet and reddish-gold color on the reverse. Nicely struck, with no significant contact marks noted. (#7118)

2638 **1880-S MS67 NGC.** Large S. An impeccably preserved and fully brilliant representative. Impressive cartwheel luster accents the nearly full details. A few minuscule marks on each side keep this piece from being absolutely flawless. (#7118)

2639 **1880-S MS67 PCGS. CAC.** Large S. This is a beautiful Superb Gem example with impressive satiny luster and delightful pearly-white surfaces and hints of color on each side. A sharply struck and immaculately preserved representative. Certified in a green label PCGS holder. (#7118)

Magnificent MS68 1880-S Morgan

2640 **1880-S MS68 PCGS.** Medium S. Wisps of gold toning are here and there, but this penetratingly struck Superb Gem is otherwise brilliant. Potent luster sweeps essentially immaculate surfaces. Those in search of an extraordinary quality Morgan dollar for their silver type set need look no further. (#7118)

Exemplary MS68 1880-S Dollar

2641 **1880-S MS68 PCGS.** Ex: Gold River. Medium S. This magnificent silver type coin is brilliant aside from a wisp of two of faint chestnut-tan toning. The strike is razor-sharp, and the preservation is outstanding. PCGS has certified only 6 pieces in higher grades, as of (8/08). *From The Bell Collection.* (#7118)

2642 **1880-S MS67 Prooflike PCGS.** The impressively mirrored fields and exactly struck devices are untoned. Remarkably free from marks, even for an '80-S, which often comes nice. The large S mintmark was entered with an unusual slant to the left. Housed in a green label holder. (#7119)

2643 **1880-S MS67 Prooflike NGC.** Medium S. A virtually stone-white Superb Gem with beautifully smooth surfaces and moderate field reflectivity. A nicely struck high quality silver type coin. (#7119)

2644 **1880-S 8 Over 7 MS65 Prooflike PCGS. CAC.** VAM-8. A Top 100 Variety. Medium S. This brilliant overdated Gem has impressive field reflectivity, and the strike is exacting. Occasional small marks fail to challenge the grade. Population: 9 in 65 Prooflike, 4 finer (8/08). (#7121)

2645 **1880-S 8 Over 7 MS65 Prooflike NGC.** VAM-9. Diagonal Overdate, Large S. A Top 100 Variety. The diagonal markings through the upper loop of the 8 are traces of the underdigit 7, and the Large S shows a top that is about at the height of the bottom of the bowloops, with a peculiar two-pointed serif on the top of the S. A pretty, Prooflike Gem with silver centers and lilac at the rims. (#7121)

2646 **1880/9-S MS65 Deep Mirror Prooflike PCGS.** VAM-11. A Hot 50 Variety. Medium S. Spectacular field reflectivity combines with frosty devices to provide exemplary eye appeal. The reverse is well preserved, and the obverse has only a few wispy grazes on the field and portrait. Population: 23 in 65, 10 finer (8/08). (#97123)

2647 **1881 MS65 NGC.** Though Liberty's portrait shows minor softness, the eagle is boldly impressed. Strong, pleasing luster and noteworthy eye appeal with only occasional hints of gold-orange toning. NGC has graded 52 numerically superior examples (8/08). (#7124)

2648 **1881 MS65 NGC.** A frosted, untoned, and remarkably clean Gem. Only a few minor luster grazes on Liberty's cheek keep this outstanding representative from an even higher grade. Boldly struck with great eye appeal. (#7124)

2649 **1881-CC MS65 NGC. CAC.** Medium gray toning drapes the obverse, which contrasts sharply against the hazel toning around the perimeter of the highly reflective and lightly frosted reverse. A couple of tiny bagmarks are noted on each side, but are barely visible without magnification. Only 296,000 pieces were minted. (#7126)

2650 **1881-CC MS65 PCGS.** Slight tan toning across the top of the obverse is the only area of color on this brilliant and frosted Gem. A few wispy grazes on Liberty's cheek and a couple of bagmarks in the fields keep this attractive specimen from an even higher grade. Several die cracks encircle nearly all of the reverse lettering, and another faint crack bisects the date. (#7126)

2651 **1881-CC MS65 PCGS.** A hint of golden toning at the edge is the only trace of color on this brilliant and frosty Gem. Dazzling cartwheel luster enhances the eye appeal, and is barely affected by a few trivial abrasions. (#7126)

2652 **1881-CC MS65 NGC.** Frosty and immensely lustrous, a delightful Gem example of this popular Carson City issue. Razor-sharp detail and minimal patina make this coin a winner. (#7126)

2653 **1881-CC MS66 NGC.** A visually alluring Premium Gem example of this common date Carson City dollar. An arc of deep teal-blue, burnt-orange, and purple-red toning covers the left side of the reverse, while the obverse is essentially untoned. A gorgeous Morgan dollar, with a coating of intense mint frost across each side. (#7126)

2654 **1881-CC MS66 PCGS.** Sparkling frost enhances the eye appeal of this shining Carson City dollar. Occasional hints of cloud-gray patina visit otherwise untoned and carefully preserved surfaces. (#7126)

2655 **1881-CC MS66 NGC.** An outstanding piece with pleasing maroon accents in the margins. Eye-catching cartwheel luster graces the fields, and the devices are vividly frosted. The reverse is nearly immaculate, while the obverse has only minor pinpoint marks. (#7126)

2656 **1881-CC MS64 Deep Mirror Prooflike PCGS.** Razor-sharp detail is the most impressive feature of this vibrant Choice example. Despite areas of gold, orange, and aquamarine patina over the obverse, it and the minimally toned reverse boast captivating mirrored fields. (#97127)

2657 **1881-CC MS64 Deep Mirror Prooflike PCGS.** VAM-2. The 8s in the date have die fill suggestive of repunching. Brilliant and intricately brought up with prominently reflective fields and only minor marks. Encased in an old green label holder. (#97127)

Deep Mirror Prooflike MS66 1881-CC Dollar

2658 **1881-CC MS66 Deep Mirror Prooflike PCGS.** Ex: DCT Collection. Here is a pleasing coin for the grade, with well-frosted devices that stand out from the mirrored fields. The coin is faintly toned almond-gold. Basically the same quality as encountered on proofs, although not quite as perfectly struck. The reverse has a few trivial specks, not unexpected for a coin of this period. Worthy of a top-notch collection. Population: 43 in 66, 1 finer (8/08).
Ex: Long Beach Signature (Heritage, 2/2005), lot 10041; Long Beach Signature (Heritage, 6/2006), lot 2260. (#97127)

2659 **1881-O MS65 PCGS.** Although common in low grades, the 1881-O can be difficult to locate in Gem, and is exceedingly rare in any grade finer. Delightful light brown toning encircles the rims, which contrasts nicely against the brilliant and frosty centers. Several light grazes and minor reeding marks keep this lovely piece from an even higher grade. PCGS has certified only 12 coins finer (7/08). (#7128)

2660 **1881-O MS65 PCGS.** The peripheral golden-brown and aqua-blue patina is attractive, and contrasts nicely against the brilliant centers. Sharply struck with remarkably clean surfaces and captivating cartwheel luster. (#7128)

2661 **1881-O MS65 NGC.** A brilliant Gem, minimally toned with blazing luster. Excellent eye appeal with only the most trivial of faults away from the well struck portrait. NGC has graded only seven numerically finer pieces (8/08). (#7128)

2662 **1881-O MS65 PCGS. CAC.** Dramatic slate-gray, blue, and maroon toning covers both sides, with a delightful ring of lemon and orange colors around the rims. Several light grazes on Liberty's cheek are barely noticeable, and there is impressive luster throughout. A boldly impressed and attractive example. (#7128)

2663 **1881-S MS67 NGC.** Exactingly struck on almost all of the design elements, as usual for this well produced, high-mintage San Francisco Mint issue. Gorgeous variations of deep electric-blue, golden-brown, and crimson iridescence appear on both sides. The surfaces are impressively preserved. (#7130)

2664 **1881-S MS67 NGC.** A dazzling, razor-sharp, and highly reflective Superb Gem. The fields are undoubtedly prooflike, although NGC has not designated this piece as such. This utterly brilliant piece has only a couple of nearly imperceptible marks. (#7130)

2665 **1881-S MS67 NGC.** The enchanting obverse offers gorgeous diamond-white frost on the portrait and outstanding, essentially untoned mirrors. The equally well-preserved reverse's prominent cartwheel luster is attractive in its own right. (#7130)

Marvelous 1881-S Dollar, MS68

2666 **1881-S MS68 NGC.** This is simply a marvelous example of the coiner's art, and like most S-mint Morgans from early in the series, it is virtually unparalleled by issues from later in the collection. Full cartwheel luster radiates from both sides, and the reverse on its own verges on a Prooflike designation. The obverse offers a bit less field-device contrast, however, but there are no mentionable abrasions on either side. None finer at NGC, and only two pieces at PCGS (8/08). (#7130)

Impressive MS68 1881-S Dollar

2667 **1881-S MS68 PCGS.** This sharply struck Superb Gem has dazzling luster and an essentially pristine obverse. A hint of gold toning along the upper obverse border denies full brilliance. The upper obverse has a pair of unimportant marks. Certified in an old green label holder. (#7130)

2668 **1881-S MS67 Prooflike NGC.** This is a brilliant and beautiful Superb Gem, with watery prooflikeness in the fields, and softly frosted devices. One of the most common dates in the Morgan dollar series, but scarce at the MS67 Prooflike grade level. (#7131)

2669 **1881-S MS67 Prooflike NGC.** A brilliant and intricately struck Superb Gem that boasts dazzling luster and a pristine cheek. The 1881-S is commonplace in Mint State, but truly exceptional pieces remain scarce. (#7131)

2670 **1881-S MS66 Deep Mirror Prooflike NGC.** Rich golden-brown and fire-red color dominates the reverse margin, and the upper right quadrant of the obverse has vivid cobalt-blue, gold, and violet patina. The deeply mirrored fields show splendid cameo contrast against the snow-white devices. A sharply struck and carefully preserved example. (#97131)

2671 **1882 MS66 PCGS. CAC.** Electric-blue, purple, and golden-brown toning clings to the margins of this highly lustrous Premium Gem. These attributes are accompanied by strongly impressed design features, including nearly complete separation in the hair at Liberty's ear. A few minor reverse marks do not disturb. (#7132)

2672 **1882 MS66 PCGS.** Pleasing luster emanates from the silver-gray surfaces of this attractive Premium Gem Morgan. The design features reveal sharp definition, including good detail in the hair at Liberty's ear and on the eagle's breast feathers. (#7132)

2673 **1882-CC MS66 NGC.** White surfaces reveal radiant luster, and just an occasional graze. A well executed strike imparts sharp definition to the design features, including partial detail in the hair at Liberty's ear. (#7134)

2674 **1882-CC MS66 ★ NGC.** Pleasing luster shows through the layer of apple-green and plum toning that is somewhat deeper on the obverse. The design elements are generally well impressed, and just a few minor marks are noted on the reverse. Census: 14 in 66 ★, 4 finer (7/08). (#7134)

2675 **1882-CC MS66 NGC.** An attentive strike manifests itself in strong definition on the design features, including the hair over Liberty's ear. The only color visible on the well preserved surfaces is a splash or two of faint gold on the reverse. (#7134)

2676 **1882-CC MS66 PCGS.** Boldly impressed with just a touch of patina on the portrait. An exquisitely preserved Carson City representative with vibrant luster and excellent eye appeal. PCGS has graded 49 finer pieces (8/08). (#7134)

2677 **1882-CC MS66 Prooflike PCGS.** This high grade Carson City type coin has sweeping luster and peripheral peach and apple-green toning. The strike is precise throughout. Encapsulated in an old green label holder. Population: 60 in 66 Prooflike, 1 finer (8/08). (#7135)

2678 **1882-CC MS66 Prooflike NGC.** Although common in nearly all grades, the 1882-S is virtually impossible to find above MS66 Prooflike. The brilliant fields appear watery under a light and show pleasing contrast against the frosted devices. A powerfully impressed and vibrant Premium Gem. NGC and PCGS combined report just two examples finer (8/08). (#7135)

2679 **1882-CC MS64 Deep Mirror Prooflike PCGS.** A stunning and attractive example with watery, deeply mirrored fields and snow-white devices that create an outstanding cameo appearance. Scattered abrasions minimally detract from the resplendent fields. A number of die breaks in the periphery of both sides are noted. (#97135)

2680 **1882-CC MS65 Deep Mirror Prooflike NGC.** This is a gorgeous Gem from the Carson City Mint, with deep mirror fields and nicely frosted devices. Well struck and free of any significant surface marks. Census: 86 in 65 Deep Mirror Prooflike, 4 finer (7/08). (#97135)

2681 **1882-O MS65 NGC.** Subtle golden tints visit the otherwise silver-white surfaces of this O-mint Morgan dollar. Well-defined overall with only trifling softness at the uppermost design elements. NGC has graded only 10 numerically finer pieces (8/08). (#7136)

2682 **1882-O MS65 NGC.** Faint yellow toning accents the mostly brilliant surfaces of this carefully preserved Gem. The luminous fields complement the razor-sharp design elements. The 1882-O is seldom-seen in a higher grade. NGC reports just 10 pieces finer (8/08). (#7136)

2683 **1882-O MS65 Prooflike PCGS.** This New Orleans Gem has flashy fields and light chestnut toning. Only the hair above the ear lacks precise definition. Lustrous and attractively preserved. Population: 32 in 65, 1 finer (8/08). (#7137)

2684 **1882-O/S MS61 PCGS. VAM-4. A Top 100 Variety.** The 'Recessed' O/S VAM, which has a bold diagonal line within the lower half of the opening of the New Orleans mintmark. This lustrous Mint State example has honey-gold toning, clean fields, and unobtrusive facial marks. (#7138)

2685 **1882-O O/S Recessed MS63 PCGS. VAM-4. A Top 100 Variety.** This desirable VAM is identified by the recessed diagonal crossbar inside of the O mintmark. Lovely cartwheel luster glides across the lightly abraded surfaces and enhances the eye appeal of this boldly defined piece. (#7138)

Desirable 1882-O/S VAM-4 Dollar, MS64

2686 **1882-O/S MS64 PCGS. VAM-4.** The recessed S under the O is characteristic of VAM-4, one of three different die varieties of the 1882-O/S mintmark variety. This brilliant specimen is just shy of the Gem category. It is well defined with frosty white luster and wispy toning. PCGS has only certified a single finer example (8/08). (#7138)

2687 **1882-S MS67 NGC.** Exquisitely detailed, particularly on the highest design elements, with soft frost across much of the central devices. Delicate golden tints grace parts of the fields, most noticeably at the left obverse. (#7140)

2688 **1882-S MS67 NGC.** Sharply struck with pale silver-gray centers that yield to gold, orange, and violet-rose at the margins. Impressively lustrous and beautifully preserved. (#7140)

2689 **1882-S MS65 Deep Mirror Prooflike NGC.** A stunning Gem with bright silver surfaces and no evidence of toning. It is sharply defined with deep mirrors and frosty devices. Census: 71 in 65 Deep Prooflike, 8 finer (7/08). (#97141)

Superb Gem 1883 Morgan Dollar

2690 **1883 MS67 NGC. CAC.** Many of the so-called "common date" Morgan silver dollars are anything but common in high grades, and this 1883 is just one of those coins, as the NGC Census date indicates. This piece is a gorgeous Morgan dollar with brilliant silver surfaces, frosty luster, and a hint of pale gold and iridescent toning along the borders. (#7142)

2691 **1883-CC MS66 NGC.** The Carson City Mint produced just over 1.2 million silver dollars in 1883, and enough of them have survived to make this a suitable issue for type purposes. The bright, flashy representative displays intense mint frost over both sides, and the surfaces are essentially brilliant. (#7144)

2692 **1883-CC MS66 PCGS.** A brilliant and boldly impressed example with lovely luster. Marvelously preserved with only a handful of trivial luster grazes away from the gently frosted portrait. (#7144)

2693 **1883-CC MS66 NGC.** A flashy and slightly frosty representative of this Carson City Morgan dollar issue, crisply struck with russet-peach patina restricted to the rims and essentially untoned surfaces elsewhere. One of slightly over 1.2 million examples coined. (#7144)

2694 **1883-CC MS66 PCGS.** Amazingly vibrant layers of crimson, gold, and green iridescence cover the entire obverse of this exquisitely preserved dollar. The reverse is mostly white, save for mere hints of lilac and gold coloration. Well struck and nearly blemish-free. (#7144)

2695 **1883-CC MS66 Prooflike NGC.** Magnificent prooflike fields show impressive cameo contrast against the frosted devices. The design elements are sharply struck save for weakness in the hair over Liberty's ear. Traces of light gold and gray patina visit selected areas, and Liberty's cheek and neck reveal just a few minor scuffs. Census: 61 in 66 Prooflike, 2 finer (7/08). (#7145)

2696 **1883-CC MS66 Prooflike PCGS.** Dazzling reflectivity and a nearly immaculate cheek proclaim the stellar quality of this sharply struck and lightly toned premium Gem. The 1883-CC is commonly seen with numerous bagmarks, and a minimally abraded example such as the present coin is a pleasant surprise. A small carbon spot to the right of Liberty's eye is noted for identification purposes. PCGS has certified just eight Prooflike pieces finer (7/08). (#7145)

Superb Gem 1883-CC Morgan, MS67 Prooflike

2697 **1883-CC MS67 Prooflike PCGS. CAC.** The 1883-CC, like all Morgan dollars from this branch mint, is a noteworthy condition rarity in the finest Mint State grades. A decent percentage of those coins extant display a prooflike finish (NGC and PCGS have certified several thousand in all PL grades), but, once again, the number of Superb Gems is severely limited. Originally toned, the obverse is overlaid in mostly even, apricot-gray colors. The reverse, on the other hand, is more extensively patinated in mottled olive-russet and silver-gray shades that yield to swirls of electric-blue iridescence at direct angles. The glistening, reflective fields are readily evident as the coin rotates into the light, and the smooth features exhibit overall bold definition. Population: 8 in 67 prooflike, 0 finer (8/08). (#7145)

2698 **1883-CC MS63 Deep Mirror Prooflike ICG.** Wonderful deeply mirrored fields show stark cameo contrast against the white devices. Scattered abrasions limit the grade, but none merit specific mention. A crisply struck and eye-catching piece. (#97145)

2699 **1883-CC MS65 Deep Mirror Prooflike PCGS.** Mostly brilliant, crisply struck, and minimally marked. Eye-catching deeply mirrored fields create stunning black and white cameo contrast against the frosted devices. A number of fine die lines are noted around the eagle. Housed in a green label PCGS holder. (#97145)

2700 **1883-CC MS65 Deep Mirror Prooflike PCGS.** An arc of russet toning around the right side of the reverse is the only sign of color on this brilliant Gem. Deeply mirrored fields and frosty devices create an outstanding cameo appearance. Several light grazes define the grade. (#97145)

2701 **1883-CC MS65 Deep Mirror Prooflike NGC.** Both sides of this deeply mirrored prooflike dollar have lustrous and frosty devices, with brilliant, untoned surfaces and bold designs. An aesthetically desirable piece for the advanced collector. NGC has only certified 40 finer examples (8/08). (#97145)

2702 **1883-S MS61 PCGS.** Lightly toned and lustrous with a cleaner than expected appearance despite a few marks on the face. Unlike its 1878 to 1882 S-mint predecessors, the 1883-S is a better date in Mint State. Housed in a green label holder. (#7148)

2703 **1883-S MS62 PCGS.** Sharply struck and well defined on the central design elements, with amazingly intense, coruscating mint frost over both sides. Minor scuffiness limits the grade. Fully untoned and very attractive. (#7148)

2704 **1883-S MS62 PCGS.** While the 1883-S is common in almost all grades, it is significantly less available in Mint State compared to most Morgan dollars. This sharply struck example is nearly brilliant, with just a touch of hazel toning on the obverse. No marks merit specific mention, and this piece exhibits impressive luster throughout. (#7148)

2705 **1883-S MS63 NGC.** Golden-brown patination, impressed with dapples of electric-blue and purple, dominates the obverse, yielding to a nearly untoned reverse. Lustrous surfaces reveal a few minute grade-defining marks, and nice detail is apparent on the design elements. (#7148)

2706 **1883-S MS63 NGC.** Warm yellow and orange tones prevail at the peripheries, while the centers of this Select coin are virtually brilliant. Immense eye appeal and crisp detail. (#7148)

2707 **1883-S MS63 PCGS.** Impressively detailed with spectacular luster and vibrant visual appeal. Only light, scattered ticks appear on the obverse, though an abrasion crosses the eagle's breast. (#7148)

2708 **1883-S MS63 PCGS.** Pleasingly detailed for this issue, which shows weak strikes more frequently than earlier S-mint dates. Gold and silver-gray shadings across the obverse yield to deeper reddish-orange shadings on the reverse. (#7148)

Brilliant Near-Gem 1883-S Dollar

2709 **1883-S MS64 PCGS. CAC.** This near-Gem has blazing luster and is nearly bereft of toning. The strike is decisive, and neither side has any individually mentionable marks. The 1883-S is less well known than the famous 1884-S conditional rarity, but the 1883-S is also exceptionally costly above the MS64 level. (#7148)

Worthy Near-Gem 1883-S Silver Dollar

2710 **1883-S MS64 PCGS.** Golden-brown and rose toning clings to the peripheries of this highly lustrous and exactly struck near-Gem. The reverse is nearly pristine, and the obverse field also has minimal contact. The 1883-S is much scarcer in Mint State than prior San Francisco Morgan issues. (#7148)

2711 **1884 MS65 Prooflike NGC.** Splashes of lemon patina invigorate this beautiful Gem. The fields are highly lustrous, and the reverse on its own merits an even finer grade. Certified in a prior generation NGC holder. (#7151)

Sharp 1884 Gem Deep Mirror Prooflike Dollar

2712 **1884 MS65 Deep Mirror Prooflike NGC.** The fields are nicely reflective and yield pronounced contrast with the lightly frosted devices, especially on the reverse. Bright, with light gray freckles on the obverse. The design elements are sharply impressed, including good detail in the hair over Liberty's ear and the eagle's breast feathers. Well preserved. Census: 14 in 65 Deep Mirror Prooflike, 0 finer (7/08). (#97151)

2713 **1884-CC MS65 ★ NGC. CAC.** The left obverse has a splendid arc of lemon-gold, cherry-red, and apple-green that undoubtedly wrested the Star designation from NGC. A lustrous and precisely struck Carson City Gem that has a nearly brilliant reverse. (#7152)

2714 **1884-CC MS66 PCGS.** Sharply struck with beautiful and lustrous silver-gray surfaces. Although common in virtually all grades, the 1884-CC is seldom available finer than the present piece. This minimally marked Premium Gem is a perfect coin for a type collector. (#7152)

2715 **1884-CC MS66 PCGS.** A flashy and essentially brilliant example with light frost on the boldly struck devices. The fields exhibit a degree of reflectivity that falls just shy of warranting a Prooflike designation. (#7152)

Extraordinary 1884-CC Morgan Dollar, Superb Gem

2716 **1884-CC MS67 NGC.** While the 1884-CC is one of the most common Carson City Morgan dollars in almost all grades, it is seldom seen in Superb Gem and is virtually impossible to locate any finer. A few wispy luster grazes keep this outstanding piece from being flawless. The strike is nearly full and the eye appeal is spectacular. PCGS has certified just three examples finer and NGC reports none above MS67 (8/08). (#7152)

2717 **1884-CC MS65 Deep Mirror Prooflike NGC.** This delightful Carson City Gem has flashy fields, frosty devices, and original peripheral orange-gold and powder-blue patina. A few light field marks decide the grade. Housed in a prior generation holder. (#97153)

2718 **1884-CC MS65 Deep Mirror Prooflike NGC.** VAM-2. The 18 in the date is clearly repunched northwest. Well struck and thoroughly lustrous with honey-gold toning along the reverse periphery. The fields are splendidly preserved, and the cheek has only faint grazes. (#97153)

2719 **1884-CC MS65 Deep Mirror Prooflike NGC.** A richly frosted Gem that has splendid cameo contrast with minimally marked, deeply mirrored fields. Boldly struck and entirely brilliant, this piece is a great representative of the popular Carson City Mint. (#97153)

2720 **1884-CC MS66 Deep Mirror Prooflike NGC.** Impressive deeply mirrored fields and icy-frosted devices create a dazzling cameo appearance, which is accented by a hint of hazel toning around the perimeter. Several light grazes and tiny blemishes limit the grade, but barely affect the spectacular eye appeal of this razor-sharp Premium Gem. Census: 41 in 66 Deep Mirror Prooflike, 3 finer (7/08). (#97153)

2721 **1884-O MS67 NGC.** Though the hair over Liberty's ear is a trifle soft, the rest of this Superb Gem is unusually well-defined. Both sides sport impressive, creamy luster with narrow bands of orange and blue peripheral toning around gold-gray centers. Tied for numerically finest known to NGC (8/08). (#7154)

2722 **1884-S AU58 PCGS. CAC.** Most 1884-S dollars saw extensive circulation, and today they are difficult to find in Uncirculated condition, and are virtually impossible to locate in grades finer than MS62. This briefly circulated piece has delightful hazel toning around the perimeter, with medium gray patina across the central design elements. Splendid cartwheel luster shines from each side, and there are only minimal abrasions throughout. (#7156)

2723 **1884-S AU58 NGC.** Crispy struck and mostly untoned, save for a hint of rose color on the reverse. Both sides exhibit highly reflective semiprooflike surfaces. A number of faint hairlines are noted, along with a few small milling marks. The 1884-S is among the most difficult Morgan dollars to find in grades higher than About Uncirculated. (#7156)

2724 **1884-S AU58 NGC.** Light golden patina drapes much of each side on this attractive near-Mint Morgan dollar. Immensely lustrous and well-defined with glimmers of reflectivity at the margins. (#7156)

2725 **1884-S AU58 NGC.** A briefly circulated and lightly toned representative with enticing cartwheel luster. The strike is sharp save for the usual softness on the hair above Liberty's ear. Numerous abrasions in the fields are typical for the grade, and all are minor. (#7156)

2726 **1884-S AU58 NGC.** Well-defined with considerable luster and a degree of flashiness despite the light marks and wear present in the fields. Attractive for the grade and issue. (#7156)

2727 **1884-S AU58 NGC.** This minimally toned near-Mint piece retains virtually all of its original luster. Well struck save for trifling softness at the highest parts of the obverse design. (#7156)

2728 **1884-S AU58 NGC.** Despite a touch of friction on the high points, this S-mint dollar offers appreciable reflectivity on each side and hints of yellow-orange patina near the rims. Minimally marked and attractive. (#7156)

1884-S Morgan Dollar, Sharpness of MS60

2729 **1884-S—Genuine—PCGS.** The present piece is certified "Genuine" by PCGS but it ungraded by that service. We call it an MS60 Cleaned piece, due to the somewhat flat, diffuse luster visible on the silver-white surfaces, with tinges of grayish-gold near the rims. The overall effect is not too displeasing, and the 1884-S remains a rare issue in Mint State. (#7156)

Conditionally Scarce 1884-S Dollar, MS60

2730 **1884-S MS60 ANACS.** One of the best known condition rarities in the Morgan dollar series. Very few Uncirculated examples are known of this issue in MS60 and better grades. This piece has an especially strong strike on each side, and the surfaces are enveloped with even gray-rose toning. Minimally abraded for an MS60. (#7156)

2731 **1885 MS67 NGC.** A highly lustrous Superb Gem with sharply struck motifs. Untoned surfaces are impeccably preserved. (#7158)

2732 **1885 MS67 NGC.** An amazing Superb Gem with frosty silver luster on both sides, enhanced through light gold and iridescent toning along the obverse border, and even lighter gold on the reverse. NGC has only certified five finer examples of the date. (#7158)

2733 **1885 MS66 Deep Mirror Prooflike NGC.** Sharply struck and brilliant with a frame of peripheral gold and iridescent toning on each side. Considered a common date, the 1885 is a difficult issue with deep mirror prooflike surfaces. Census: 54 in 66, 5 finer (7/08). (#97159)

2734 **1885-CC MS65 PCGS.** Untoned and frosted, this magnificent Gem has scattered light grazes on the obverse, while the reverse is nearly pristine. A delicate die crack connects the tops of the letters in UNITED STATES OF. Fully struck and certified in a first-generation PCGS holder. (#7160)

2735 **1885-CC MS65 ANACS.** Satiny luster radiates from this sharply struck Gem and gives it outstanding eye appeal. The creamy surfaces have accents of hazel toning in the periphery. Several light grazes on the obverse limit the grade, but the reverse is remarkably pristine. (#7160)

2736 **1885-CC MS65 PCGS.** Dramatic arcs of lavender, yellow, pale green, blue, and maroon toning covers the majority of the obverse, which contrasts sharply against the lighted toned and frosty reverse. This impeccably preserved Gem has exquisite satiny luster that shines beneath the vibrant toning. (#7160)

2737 **1885-CC MS65 PCGS.** Ex: GSA. A sharply struck and resplendent Gem. Eye-catching cartwheel luster radiates from the mostly brilliant and lightly abraded surfaces. The devices are nicely frosted, and a small spot of brown toning beneath the eagle's beak is the only area of color. (#7160)

2738 **1885-CC MS66 NGC.** A brilliant, lightly frosted Premium Gem. The reverse is nearly perfect, and a few light grazes on Liberty's cheek preclude a Superb designation. Enticing cartwheel luster gives this piece wonderful eye appeal. A tiny spot above Liberty's head is noted for future identification purposes. (#7160)

2739 **1885-CC MS66 NGC.** Silver-gray surfaces radiate intense luster, and sharp definition shows on the design elements. A nicely preserved Premium Gem. (#7160)

2740 **1885-CC MS66 NGC.** Wisps of light apricot visit the radiantly lustrous surfaces of this Premium Gem CC dollar, and an attentive strike imparts strong definition to the design features. A few minor luster grazes do not disturb. (#7160)

2741 **1885-CC MS66 PCGS.** This low-mintage Carson City representative displays a narrow zone of attractive electric-blue, purple, and golden-tan patina at the margins. Additionally, partially prooflike fields establish pleasing contrast with the satiny motifs. Sharply struck, including the hair over Liberty's ear and the eagle's breast feathers. A few minor grazes do not detract. (#7160)

2742 **1885-CC MS66 PCGS.** An immensely lustrous Premium Gem with whispers of frostiness across the high points. Highly appealing, minimally toned, and carefully preserved. (#7160)

2743 **1885-CC MS66 NGC. CAC.** Excellent detail on the central design elements with whispers of twinkling frost over them. Shallow, yet elegant orange-gold and rose shadings drape each side. (#7160)

2744 **1885-CC MS66 NGC.** An impressively lustrous example of this low-mintage Carson City issue. The frostiness of the obverse portrait shines through gold and green-blue patina, while the near-brilliance of the reverse puts the frost across the eagle on full display. NGC has graded 60 numerically finer pieces (8/08). (#7160)

2745 **1885-CC MS66 PCGS.** An attractive piece with lustrous white centers that give way to golden-orange toning near the rims. The design elements are well struck throughout. The surfaces have only a few marks, as one might expect from the grade. Thin die cracks wander through the reverse lettering, most prominently at STATES OF. (#7160)

2746 **1885-CC MS66 PCGS.** Lustrous silver-gray surfaces display partially prooflike fields that offer a mild contrast with frosty design elements that are sharply impressed, though the hair over Liberty's ear and the eagle's breast feathers are a tad soft in places. Both sides are impeccably preserved, revealing just a few minor luster grazes in the left (facing) obverse fields. PCGS has certified only 38 coins finer (8/08). (#7160)

352   Please visit HA.com to view other collectibles auctions

A 15% Buyer's Premium ($9 min.) Applies To All Lots

2747 **1885-CC MS66 PCGS.** This is a lovely Gem with faint blue color on the obverse and pale gold on the reverse. Lustrous surfaces exhibit well struck design elements, including the hair at Liberty's ear and the eagle's breast feathers. A low-mintage Carson City issue (228,000 pieces). (#7160)

Richly Toned Superb Gem 1885-CC Dollar

2748 **1885-CC MS67 PCGS.** The reverse shows just a whisper of golden rim color, but the obverse is richly toned in translucent sunset-orange, ceding near the rim to deeper violet and fuchsia. Despite the deep color there is enormous cartwheel luster present, and singular abrasions are simply absent from the picture. A real prize for the color aficionados. (#7160)

2749 **1885-CC MS64 Deep Mirror Prooflike NGC.** Vibrant russet and lavender toning surrounds the periphery of this outstanding specimen. The deeply mirrored and lightly abraded fields create a stunning cameo contrast against the icy frosted devices. This razor-sharp example has impressive eye appeal and is one of just 228,000 pieces struck. Housed in an old NGC holder. (#97161)

2750 **1885-CC MS64 Deep Mirror Prooflike PCGS.** Splendid field reflectivity and lightly iced motifs ensure the beauty of this boldly struck Carson City near-Gem. The reverse is impressively unabraded, and the obverse has only faint distributed marks. Housed in a green label holder. (#97161)

2751 **1885-S MS65 PCGS.** Light gray-gold toning endows this boldly struck Gem, which boasts dazzling cartwheel luster. Minimally marked and encased in a first-generation PCGS holder. The 1885-S is seldom seen in finer grades. (#7164)

2752 **1885-S MS65 PCGS.** Traces of golden toning in the margins accents the mostly brilliant surfaces of this exquisitely detailed Gem. The surfaces are remarkably clean for the grade with only a couple of light grazes. Enticing cartwheel luster gives this piece excellent eye appeal. PCGS has certified just 27 coins finer (8/08). (#7164)

2753 **1885-S MS65 PCGS.** The lightly toned surfaces of this lovely Gem are nearly prooflike and the reverse is especially reflective. The strike is bold and there are only a couple of light abrasions on each side. (#7164)

2754 **1885-S MS64 Prooflike NGC.** Flashy fields and an intricate strike confirm the eye appeal of this lightly abraded near-Gem. The obverse is brilliant, while the lower reverse border is rose-red. In a prior generation holder. (#7165)

2755 **1886-O MS61 NGC.** No trace of wear appears on this O-mint Morgan dollar, though a number of significant flaws affect the obverse. The well-defined and strongly lustrous reverse is comparatively clean. (#7168)

2756 **1886-O MS61 NGC.** VAM-1A. A Top 100 Variety. One set of clashmarks inside the upper right portion of the wreath. The E in LIBERTY is dramatically clashed beneath the eagle's tail, but any Mint State 1886-O is desirable. Lustrous and nicely struck with nearly untoned surfaces and the expected faint grazes on the left obverse. (#7168)

2757 **1886-O MS62 NGC.** Boldly impressed with powerful, swirling luster. A generally silver-gray coin that shows faint whispers of iridescence close to the rims. Faintly abraded, yet attractive. (#7168)

Lustrous 1886-O Morgan, MS63

2758 **1886-O MS63 PCGS.** Despite its heavy production of more than 10.7 million pieces, the 1886-O is scarce in Mint State, and becomes one of the keys to the series at the MS65 level. The centers are softly defined, as usual for a New Orleans dollar from the era, but the luster is comprehensive, and the medium rose-gold toning is attractive. (#7168)

Extraordinary 1886-O Morgan, MS64

2759 **1886-O MS64 PCGS. CAC.** Both sides of this entirely untoned near-Gem have frosty silver luster and nearly full design details with only slight weakness above the ear. Although a few scattered marks are evident, they are entirely consistent with the grade. In fact, this piece has exceptional aesthetic appeal equal to that of many full Gem Morgan dollars. The '86-O is noted for its conditional rarity in higher grades, with a PCGS population of just four full Gem specimens (8/08). (#7168)

Wonderful Gem 1886-S Morgan Dollar, MS65

2760 **1886-S MS65 PCGS.** Housed in an older green-label holder, the surfaces of this brilliant Gem are exceptional, with hardly a mark on either side. Just a trace of pale gold toning follows the obverse and reverse borders. The strike is bold, including partial separation of the hair strands over the ear. PCGS has only certified 33 circulation strike dollars finer than this piece, in a green-label holder (8/08). (#7170)

2761 **1887 MS67 NGC.** This entirely brilliant and highly lustrous Superb Gem has incredible eye appeal. Satiny luster highlights the razor-sharp devices, and there are only a couple of minor grazes. NGC and PCGS have certified a combined three pieces finer (7/08). (#7172)

2762 **1887 MS67 PCGS.** Well struck with uncharacteristically flashy luster and minimal patina. This beautifully preserved Superb Gem is nearly unsurpassed for the issue, with just one finer example known to PCGS (8/08). (#7172)

2763 **1887 MS66 Prooflike NGC.** Attractively toned, with ice-blue, peach, and plum-red along the upper obverse and golden-russet throughout the reverse periphery. Certified in a former generation holder. Census: 41 in 66 Prooflike, 5 finer (8/08). (#7173)

Eye-Catching 1887 Morgan Dollar MS66 Deep Mirror Prooflike

2764 **1887 MS66 Deep Mirror Prooflike PCGS.** Razor-sharp and mostly brilliant, with an accent of gold toning around the perimeter of the reverse. The deeply mirrored fields appear watery and create a vivid cameo contrast against the frosted devices. Scattered abrasions keep this piece from an even higher grade, but none merit specific mention. This dazzling Premium Gem is housed in a green label PCGS holder. (#97173)

2765 **1887/6 MS64 PCGS.** VAM-2. A Top 100 Variety. A brilliant and highly lustrous example of this popular and fairly elusive overdate. The semiprooflike fields exhibit dazzling satiny luster that accents the boldly struck devices. Scattered abrasions limit the grade but none are noteworthy. (#7174)

2766 **1887/6 MS64 PCGS.** VAM-2. A Top 100 Variety. Characteristic of this popular overdate, the outline of the base of a 6 bookends the base of the 7. Lightly toned and lustrous with a smooth reverse and a few faint obverse marks. (#7174)

2767 **1887/6 MS64 PCGS.** VAM-2. A Top 100 Variety. This untoned and lustrous overdated Morgan dollar retains a hint of granularity on the reverse, as struck on an improperly prepared planchet. The few faint obverse grazes are inconsequential for the grade. Certified in a green label holder. (#7174)

Attractive 1887/6 Morgan Dollar, Gem Mint State

2768 **1887/6 MS65 PCGS.** VAM-2. A Top 100 Variety. While PCGS has not designated this piece Prooflike, the fields are unquestionably so. Besides the highly reflective surfaces, this brilliant specimen exhibits a bold strike and frosty devices. Scattered reeding marks and light grazes define the grade, although none merit individual mention. A trace of the underdigit 6 is easily visible under magnification. PCGS has certified a mere seven coins finer (7/08). (#7174)

Elusive 1887-S Gem Dollar

2769 **1887-S MS65 PCGS.** The only recorded quantities of Mint State 1887-S Morgan dollars that entered the numismatic market did so in the 1940s and 1950s. These releases (mostly from storage in the San Francisco Mint) have resulted in a significant number of MS60-MS64 examples in today's market, but Gems remain elusive. Typically well produced for the issue, both sides are sharply struck throughout, with swirling, frosty cartwheel luster. There are no singularly distracting abrasions, and the otherwise untoned features reveal original peripheral toning in reddish-golden shades. (#7180)

Brilliant 1887-S Morgan Dollar, MS65

2770 **1887-S MS65 PCGS.** An absolutely stunning, spectacular Gem Morgan dollar with fully brilliant silver surfaces on both sides, enhanced by splendid pale gold toning at the peripheral areas. All design elements are sharp, and the overall eye appeal is exceptional. PCGS has only certified 20 finer non-prooflike pieces. (#7180)

Spectacular MS67 1888 Morgan Dollar

2771 **1888 MS67 NGC.** The prodigious mintage of the 1888 Morgan dollar approached the 20 million-coin mark, but despite that overwhelming number, only a few dozen business strikes at NGC and PCGS combined attain the Superb Gem level. This silver-white piece is among the chosen few, with spectacular cartwheel luster and nary a blemish in sight on either side. NGC has graded a single coin finer of the issue (8/08). (#7182)

2772 **1888-O AU55 ANACS.** VAM-4. A Top 100 Variety. This popular variety listed in the *Guide Book* features pronounced doubling not only on Liberty's lips (a.k.a. "hot lips"), but also on the nose and chin. The medium-gray surfaces have patches of russet toning on each side. A sharply defined, lightly marked, and desirable representative. (#7184)

Captivating 1888-O Morgan Dollar
MS65 Deep Mirror Prooflike

2773 **1888-O MS65 Deep Mirror Prooflike PCGS.** This brilliant Gem features incredible deeply mirrored fields that show outstanding cameo contrast against the white devices. Scattered abrasions in the fields barely affect the captivating reflectivity. Sharply struck and housed in a green label PCGS holder. Population: 56 in 65, 4 finer (7/08). (#97185)

2774 **1888-O Doubled Die Obverse AU53 PCGS.** VAM-4. A Top 100 Variety. The famous "Hot Lips" variety, listed in the *Guide Book*, is named for the pronounced doubling on Liberty's lips. Numerous abrasions limit the grade, but none merit individual mention. A lustrous example of this popular and scarce variety. (#7308)

Popular AU53 "Hot Lips" 1888-O Dollar

2775 **1888-O Doubled Die Obverse AU53 NGC.** VAM-4. A Top 100 Variety. VAM-4 is better known as the 'Hot Lips' variety. Indeed, her lips and chin exhibit strong die doubling. This example features dusky pearl-gray and almond-gold patina. Surprisingly smooth aside from minor grazes on the cheek. Census: 13 in 53, 49 finer (7/08). (#7308)

2776 **1888-S MS64 NGC.** Well struck and surprisingly reflective for a piece not designated as Prooflike. Excellent overall eye appeal with occasional whispers of ice-blue patina in the fields. (#7186)

2777 **1888-S MS64 PCGS.** Whispers of frostiness appear on the high points of the devices, and the fields are essentially brilliant. Minor, scattered flaws account for the grade. Housed in a green label holder. (#7186)

Radiant Silver-White Gem Prooflike 1888-S Dollar

2778 **1888-S MS65 Prooflike NGC.** The radiant silver-white fields of this lovely Gem show just a trace of gold toning, with blinding reflectivity in the mirrored fields, thick mint frost, and cartwheel luster lavishly spread on both sides. Some of the certified Prooflike and Deep Mirror Prooflike coins today hailed originally from the famed Nevada hoard of LaVere Redfield. Census: 7 in 65 Prooflike, 0 finer (7/08). (#7187)

2779 **1888-S MS63 Deep Mirror Prooflike NGC.** Well-defined with a striking, chromelike gleam across the silver-white surfaces. Light, wispy abrasions leave the reflectivity of the fields undimmed. Census: 39 in 63 Deep Mirror Prooflike, 19 finer (7/08). (#97187)

2780 **1889 MS66 PCGS.** A few tiny dark spots of toning accent the otherwise brilliant and lightly frosted surfaces. Alluring cartwheel luster gives this minimally marked and sharply struck Premium Gem great eye appeal. It is nearly impossible to find an 1889 in a higher grade, as NGC and PCGS combined have certified just seven coins finer (7/08). (#7188)

2781 **1889 MS66 PCGS. CAC.** Lovely crimson, hazel, and deep purple toning surrounds the silver-gray centers of this carefully preserved Premium Gem. The strike is nearly full, and the flow of the magnificent satiny luster is barely affected by several minor abrasions. PCGS has certified a mere five pieces finer (7/08). (#7188)

Sharp 1889 Dollar
MS65 Deep Mirror Prooflike

2782 **1889 MS65 Deep Mirror Prooflike PCGS.** Mostly brilliant, with traces of gold and sky-gray emerging near the rims. This is a lustrous, well struck and carefully preserved representative of this issue, one that is common without prooflike fields in MS63 to MS64 grades, but surprisingly rare as a Gem with prominent mirrors. Certified in a green label holder. Population: 30 in 65 Deep Mirror Prooflike, 3 finer (6/08). (#97189)

2783 **1889-CC—Improperly Cleaned—NCS. VG8 Details.** An evenly worn, medium gray example of this popular key-date Carson City dollar. There are no particularly noteworthy marks on this gently cleaned piece, and LIBERTY is boldly defined. A small die crack connects star 1 to the date. (#7190)

2784 **1889-CC Fine 12 ANACS.** Pale brown and ice-blue toning grace this collector grade key date Carson City dollar. There are no consequential marks, and the eagle's wings display much feather detail. (#7190)

2785 **1889-CC Fine 15 PCGS.** Original light to medium gray patination resides on the relatively clean surfaces of both sides. A pleasing Choice Fine example of this desirable Carson City issue. (#7190)

2786 **1889-CC—Obverse Scratched—NCS. VF Details.** Because a relatively low mintage of 350,000 pieces and only a small number being released by the Treasury as part of the GSA sale, the 1889-CC is a scarce and highly desirable issue today. Several shallow scratches on the obverse minimally detract from the well-defined design elements. Charming medium gray patina covers both sides of this popular key date. (#7190)

2787 **1889-CC VF25 PCGS.** Pleasing gunmetal-gray patina endows the surfaces, with deeper areas of toning in the periphery. Scattered abrasions are typical for the grade, and a couple of tiny digs near the UN in UNUM are barely worthy of note. (#7190)

2788 **1889-CC VF25 NGC.** Deep steel-gray toning overall with hints of gold-orange and rose. Though a handful of minor abrasions affect the portrait, this remains a pleasing mid-range representative of its challenging key issue. (#7190)

2789 **1889-CC VF30 PCGS.** Subtle rose accents grace the pearl-gray and seal-gray surfaces of this mid-range Carson City key. Only a handful of minor abrasions are present on the portrait. (#7190)

2790 **1889-CC—Rim Filed, Polished—NCS. XF Details.** The 1889-CC is not only the rarest Carson City Mint issue in the series, but it is also one of the scarcest Morgan dollars from any mint. This piece has numerous hairlines from polishing, but the fields are free of any significant marks save for a small dig by the second A in AMERICA. Nonetheless, there is plenty of detail remaining, and this would make a relatively affordable example of a highly desirable issue. (#7190)

2791 **1889-CC—Scratched, Improperly Cleaned—NCS. XF Details.** Despite a past cleaning, the silver-white surfaces retain a degree of original luster at the margins. Modestly worn with a thin, arcing scratch that runs from the rim at 9 o'clock to Liberty's neck. (#7190)

2792 **1889-CC—Improperly Cleaned—NCS. XF Details.** This example is bright from improper cleaning, and the centers (Liberty's cheek and the eagle's breast) appear to have been whizzed, or polished. A few sizeable abrasions are also noted, on each side. An affordable example of this important key date in the Morgan dollar series. (#7190)

2793 **1889-CC—Improperly Cleaned—NCS. XF Details.** A wealth of detail is present on this key date Carson City dollar. The centers show light wear, and the nose and chin have a few bagmarks. A bit bright from cleaning, although retoned in deep brown and gunmetal shades. (#7190)

Luminous XF 1889-CC Dollar

2794 **1889-CC XF40 PCGS.** This key Carson City Morgan dollar issue has a mean combined certified population grade of 33.9, which puts the XF40 example offered here above the curve. The fields are subtly luminous beneath generally silver-gray surfaces that show flecks of tan-gold and blue. Generally well struck with only small, isolated flaws. (#7190)

Key-Date 1889-CC Morgan, XF45

2795 **1889-CC XF45 PCGS.** This Choice XF is an attractive example of this key-date issue, displaying a delicate blend of dusky gray, sky-blue, and golden-tan patination. Nice definition is apparent on the design elements, as this coin exhibits a better-than-average strike. Both sides are remarkably clean for a coin that has seen some circulation. (#7190)

Charming 1889-CC Morgan Dollar, About Uncirculated

2796 **1889-CC AU50 NGC.** A lightly circulated example of the key Carson City Morgan dollar. The 1889-CC is quite rare in Mint State, and AU examples are highly desired by collectors. A couple of tiny digs on the obverse are barely worthy of mention, and the rest of the surfaces have only minuscule abrasions. Plenty of luster remains in the fields and enhances the eye appeal of this brilliant representative. (#7190)

1889-CC Morgan, MS62, Rarest CC-Mint Dollar

2797 1889-CC MS62 NGC. After being closed for four years, the Carson City Mint reopened on July 1, 1889. The facility required extensive repairs after its long period of inactivity, and coinage did not resume until October. This circumstance resulted in a low mintage of 350,000 silver dollars. Judging from the small number of circulated coins known today, few of those silver dollars were released at the time. In later years, the majority of the mintage was stored at the San Francisco Mint and in bank vaults throughout the West. Natural attrition and the well-known silver melts of later years drastically reduced the already small supply of the coins. Few 1889-CCs were distributed through the great Treasury releases in Washington. David Bowers relates that when the government decided to hold back Carson City dollars in 1964 to prepare for the GSA sales, only one 1889-CC dollar could be found in the Treasury vaults. Today the issue is acknowledged as the rarest Carson City silver dollar by a wide margin.

The present example boasts splendid cartwheel luster on both sides, with silvery centers accenting a ring of gold at the rims. A few stray contact marks on the cheek and the obverse fields account for the grade, but in terms of strike, rarity, and overall eye appeal, this piece has much to commend itself. (#7190)

2798 1889-O MS63 Deep Mirror Prooflike NGC. Outstanding contrast between the heavily frosted devices and fields that are reflective even at arm's length. A hint of golden-tan toning adds color to the rims of this Select beauty. Census: 18 in 63 Deep Mirror Prooflike, 12 finer (7/08). (#97193)

2799 1889-S MS64 PCGS. Essentially untoned surfaces reveal partially prooflike fields that highlight the motifs. Crisply impressed, including the hair at Liberty's ear and the eagle's breast feathers. A few minute marks preclude Gem status. (#7194)

2800 1889-S MS65 PCGS. Whispers of golden-tan, electric-blue, and purple toning gravitate to the margins of this well struck Morgan. Some minor luster grazes do not detract. (#7194)

2801 1889-S MS65 NGC. Whispers of sky-blue, gold-tan, and purple color visit the lustrous surfaces of this S-mint Gem. The design elements are well impressed, including nice definition in the hair at Liberty's ear. A few light marks preclude an even higher grade. (#7194)

2802 1890 MS65 PCGS. Although most 1890 dollars have a notoriously weak strike, this piece is sharply defined with above-average details. Delightful satiny luster enhances the eye appeal of this outstanding Gem. PCGS has certified only one coin finer (7/08). (#7196)

2803 1890 MS65 NGC. Strongly lustrous with occasional hints of golden toning in the otherwise light silver-gray fields. Well struck and pleasing. Though the 1890 dollar is available in grades through Gem, anything finer is extremely rare. (#7196)

White MS64 ★ Deep Mirror Prooflike 1890 Morgan

2804 1890 MS64 ★ Deep Mirror Prooflike NGC. CAC. The present near-Gem is the only Deep Mirror Prooflike 1890 Morgan dollar that has received a Star designation from NGC. Both sides are fully brilliant, and the strike is above average. No marks merit mention, and the sweet spot of the cheek is especially smooth. (#97197)

1890-CC 'Tail Bar' Morgan Dollar, VAM-4, MS62

2805 1890-CC Tail Bar MS62 PCGS. VAM-4. A Top 100 Variety. A prominent die break below the eagle's tail accounts for the "tail bar" moniker. The reverse is remarkably clean for the grade, although the obverse does have a number of reeding marks and light grazes. An arc of gold toning graces the perimeter of the obverse, which contrasts sharply against the brilliant reverse. This piece is essentially prooflike, although not designated as such by PCGS. A lovely example of this popular variety. (#87198)

2806 1890-CC MS63 PCGS. Well struck with intense, satiny luster, and a slight degree of golden color on the obverse. Normally abraded for the Select uncirculated grade level. A scarcer Carson City Morgan dollar issue; not as plentiful as its original mintage of over 2.3 million pieces would suggest. (#7198)

2807 1890-CC MS64 NGC. A boldly struck and lustrous example of this late Carson City issue. Scattered grade-defining grazes minimally affect the flow of the impressive cartwheel luster. A small patch of charcoal toning above the ON in ONE is noted for identification purposes. (#7198)

2808 **1890-CC MS64 PCGS. CAC.** Pleasing hazel toning surrounds the untoned centers of this fully struck representative. Wonderful cartwheel luster radiates from the lightly marked surfaces and gives this piece excellent eye appeal. (#7198)

2809 **1890-CC MS64 PCGS.** A touch of golden toning on the rims accents the brilliant and frosty centers. The strike is nearly full, and the cartwheel luster is outstanding. Several reeding marks on Liberty's face keep this piece from an even higher grade. (#7198)

2810 **1890-CC MS64 PCGS.** Enticing cartwheel luster graces the untoned surfaces of this well-preserved and boldly struck representative. Scattered abrasions limit the grade, but all are minor, and a couple of microscopic toning spots are noted. Despite a high mintage, the 1890-CC is less available in Choice Mint State than some of its Carson City dollar counterparts. (#7198)

2811 **1890-CC MS64 NGC.** VAM-3, with prominent recutting on the 90 in the date. This lustrous near-Gem has only light peripheral gold toning on the obverse, but the reverse is luxuriously patinated in ocean-blue, cherry-red, and honey-gold. A few light marks limit the grade. (#7198)

2812 **1890-CC MS64 PCGS.** Warm gold-orange and pink patina graces most of the obverse and the reverse periphery. A well struck and strongly lustrous Choice example of this later Carson City Morgan dollar issue. (#7198)

2813 **1890-CC MS64 NGC.** A fresh, immensely lustrous representative of this popular Carson City dollar. Only occasional glimpses of rose and gold patina keep it from absolute brilliance. NGC has graded 63 numerically finer pieces (8/08). (#7198)

2814 **1890-CC MS64 PCGS.** Essentially untoned aside from occasional hints of silver-gray close to the margins. Well struck everywhere save the highest parts of the design. The pleasingly preserved fields offer creamy luster. (#7198)

2815 **1890-CC MS64 NGC.** Ex: Fitzgerald Collection, Nevada Club Reno Hoard. Luxurious mint frost over suitably preserved snow-white surfaces. A band of deep burnt-orange and gold toning appears along the upper left reverse border between 9 o'clock and 11:30. Marks are generally confined to the cheek and left obverse field. (#7198)

2816 **1890-CC MS64 PCGS.** Medium shades of gray, blue, and sunset-golden toning fail to conceal the underlying luster on this near-Gem specimen. Well struck with a minimum of marks for the assigned grade.
Ex: Palm Beach Signature (Heritage, 3/2005), lot 6195 (#7198)

Impressively Toned 1890-CC Dollar, MS65

2817 **1890-CC MS65 PCGS.** Splendid hues of translucent, pastel lilac and ice-blue evenly coat each side of this impressively toned Gem. A few ticks on the reverse apparently limit a finer grade. Despite the intense toning, much luster remains visible, and a passable strike only adds to the considerable allure. (#7198)

Brilliant MS65 1890-CC Dollar

2818 **1890-CC MS65 NGC.** With a mintage of nearly 2.4 million coins, the 1890-CC dollar has a larger emission than any other CC-mint Morgan. It remains elusive at the Gem level and above, however. NGC has certified only two pieces finer than the present Gem example (8/08). This piece is brilliant throughout, and it shows the coruscating mint luster usually seen on Carson City coinage. (#7198)

2819 **1890-CC MS63 Deep Mirror Prooflike PCGS.** Delicate gray-gold patina drapes each side, and splashes of cloud-white appear in the immensely reflective fields. Boldly impressed with only light, scattered abrasions. (#97199)

2820 **1890-CC MS63 Deep Mirror Prooflike PCGS.** VAM-3. The 90 in the date is lightly recut. This brilliant Carson City dollar has dazzling field reflectivity. The strike is precise, and there are no mentionable marks. Certified in a green label holder. (#97199)

2821 **1890-O MS64 PCGS.** Shades of amber, gold, and iridescent ice-blue complement an untoned reverse of silver-white. There are few singular abrasions, but the strike is somewhat soft on the hair over the ear. A pretty near-Gem piece nonetheless. (#7200)

2822 **1890-O MS65 PCGS.** Light frost covers the highly lustrous and mostly brilliant surfaces, with just a few spots of russet toning on the reverse, most notably on the eagle's neck. Liberty's cheek has only a couple of microscopic abrasions below the eye, and the rest of the surfaces are remarkably clean. Housed in a green label PCGS holder. (#7200)

2823 **1890-S MS65 NGC.** Mostly brilliant with a small streak of russet across the left obverse field. The strike is sharp with no signs of weakness. A carefully preserved and moderately prooflike example. (#7202)

2824 **1891-CC MS63 PCGS.** VAM-3. A Top 100 Variety. Lustrous and boldly struck, with scintillating mint frost on both sides. Creamy-white in the centers with lovely golden color around the peripheries. Moderate luster grazes on Liberty's cheek, and in the lower right reverse field, limit the grade. (#7206)

2825 **1891-CC MS64 PCGS.** An exquisite representative from the popular Carson City Mint. Dazzling cartwheel luster radiates from the surfaces of this handsome, fully struck piece. A number of light grazes on Liberty's cheek are typical for the grade. (#7206)

2826 **1891-CC MS64 PCGS.** This dazzling, untoned representative exhibits a remarkably clean reverse and a lightly abraded obverse. Several faint clash marks and die cracks are noted on the reverse. The strike is razor-sharp save for the usual minor weakness on the hair above Liberty's ear. (#7206)

2827 **1891-CC MS64 PCGS.** Delightfully frosted and mostly brilliant with eye-catching luster throughout. This sharply struck Choice specimen has several light grazes, but none of any consequence. A faded spot is noted to the left of Liberty's nose. (#7206)

2828 **1891-CC MS64 NGC.** Subtle frostiness on the central devices filters through rich silver-gray, violet, and green-gold patina. Well struck with just a few shallow reed marks close to the eye that preclude an even finer designation. (#7206)

2829 1891-CC MS64 PCGS. VAM-3. A Top 100 Variety. The "Spitting Eagle," though this is not noted on the holder. Boldly struck and highly lustrous, with bright, frosty, untoned surfaces that only show a few trivial blemishes, mainly on Liberty's face and neck. Borderline Gem quality for this popular VAM variety. (#7206)

2830 1891-CC MS64 PCGS. This late-series CC-mint near-Gem has basically untoned silver-white surfaces, with just a hint of gold near the rims on each side. Abundant luster and premium eye appeal will make this piece a prize acquisition. (#7206)

Attractive, Semireflective MS65 1891-CC Dollar

2831 1891-CC MS65 PCGS. While many of the 1880s Carson City dates are fairly common in MS65, despite a moderate mintage the 1891-CC remains scarce in the higher Mint State grades, due largely to its minuscule representation in the GSA-Treasury sales of a few decades ago. Only three dozen PCGS-certified coins exceed the grade of the present Gem example (8/08). The devices are sharply defined on each side and brilliant throughout, and the fields display a noticeable semireflectivity. (#7206)

Lustrous 1891-CC Morgan, MS65

2832 1891-CC MS65 PCGS. CAC. Housed in an older green-label holder, this amazing piece is really quite special, even at the Gem grade assigned. Both sides have a full quota of frosty mint luster with faint traces of pale gold confined to the borders. PCGS has only certified 40 finer examples of the date (8/08). (#7206)

Elusive 1891-CC Morgan Dollar, MS65

2833 1891-CC MS65 PCGS. An elusive Carson City date in Gem quality, and an exceptional piece with lovely ivory surfaces and impressive gold and violet toning on both sides. Sharply defined, even including the hair over the ear that is almost fully detailed. Population: 443 in 65, 38 finer (7/08). (#7206)

2834 1891-O MS64 PCGS. Dappled golden-brown and electric-blue patina runs over lustrous surfaces. Well struck, except for weakness in the centers, a typical characteristic of the issue. Generally well preserved. (#7208)

2835 1891-O MS64 PCGS. An outstanding near-Gem, weak at the centers as usual for the date, but fully brilliant with highly lustrous, untoned surfaces. A lovely example. (#7208)

Impressive 1891-O Morgan, MS64 Prooflike

2836 1891-O MS64 Prooflike PCGS. A wonderful prooflike piece, tied for the finest prooflike 1891-O Morgans that NGC or PCGS have certified. Both sides are entirely brilliant with a trace of faint gold toning on Liberty's cheek. No toning appears on the reverse. Population: 11 in 64, 0 finer (7/08). (#7209)

2837 1891-S MS65 NGC. Solidly struck with strong luster beneath the dusky silver-gray and gold-gray shadings that embrace each side. Well-defined and pleasingly preserved. (#7210)

2838 1891-S MS64 Deep Mirror Prooflike NGC. Flashy, chromelike fields and richly frosted devices are the most striking characteristics of this near-Gem. Decisively struck with small, scattered marks and areas of haze in the fields. NGC has certified a mere five finer Deep Mirror Prooflike representatives (8/08). (#97211)

2839 1892 MS64 NGC. Powerful, creamy luster with whispers of frost that enliven the well struck portrait. Minimally marked with elegant eye appeal. NGC has graded 85 numerically finer examples (8/08). (#7212)

2840 1892-CC—Improperly Cleaned—NCS. Unc Details. Somewhat bright and improperly cleaned, according to NCS. Well struck and minimally abraded, however, with an appealing light golden cast over the fundamentally silver-gray surfaces. (#7214)

2841 1892-CC MS60 ANACS. Bright surfaces with wisps of light gold-tan color at the margins, more so on the reverse, exhibit well struck design features. Light handling marks are scattered about. (#7214)

2842 1892-CC MS62 PCGS. A frosty, pale gray representative of this desirable Carson City Mint issue. Several reeding marks are noted on Liberty's cheek and in the right obverse field. Crisply struck, with a number of die cracks in the periphery of the obverse. (#7214)

Radiant 1892-CC Select Dollar

2843 1892-CC MS63 NGC. Radiantly lustrous surfaces are home to whispers of gold-tan and light purple toning around the peripheries, and a well executed strike imparts sharp definition to the design elements. A few minute obverse marks limit the grade; nevertheless, this is still a pleasing specimen. (#7214)

Handsome 1892-CC Morgan Dollar, MS64

2844 **1892-CC MS64 PCGS.** This brilliant near-Gem piece is complemented by enticing luster that radiates from the decidedly prooflike fields. Scattered grazes barely affect the impressive eye appeal of the highly reflective surfaces. A streak of pearl-gray is noted on the reverse, and the devices are nicely frosted. Delicate die cracks surround the perimeter of both sides. A magnificent example of the penultimate CC-mint issue. (#7214)

Interesting 1892-CC Dollar, MS64

2845 **1892-CC MS64 PCGS.** One of the more popular dates in the Carson City series, the 1892-CC has a relatively low mintage of only 1.35 million coins, which was likely further reduced by Pittman Act meltings. This silver-gray and lustrous piece is well-struck, although it does show light roller marks at the center of the obverse under magnification. Contact marks are minimal. This piece also shows an interesting die break/fill on the lower loop of the 2 in the date with a die crack that joins stars 13-11, 9-8 with the (UNU)M, and on the left another one join the other date digits, the rim, and stars 2-4. A nice piece for the grade, and one that should see a good premium as a variety. (#7214)

High-End MS64 1892-CC Dollar

2846 **1892-CC MS64 PCGS.** A popular issue from the final years of the Carson City Mint, and a difficult one to encounter in nice shape, the 1892-CC is often seen bagmarked. The issue is otherwise well-produced, however. This example offers frosty silver-gray surfaces with good cartwheel luster. The strike is somewhat soft on the hair above the ear, and some old die clashing is noted on the reverse. A nice one, close to Gem quality. (#7214)

Sharp, Delightfully Toned Near-Gem 1892-CC Morgan Dollar

2847 **1892-CC MS64 PCGS.** Iridescent ice-blue and cinnamon rim toning cedes to untoned silver centers on this splendid near-Gem example of the penultimate Carson City Morgan issue. The strike is sharp save for the hair just over the ear, and only under a loupe do a few marks appear that likely prevented a Gem grade. Interestingly, the reverse shows a couple of wispy die cracks, including one connecting the two C's of the mintmark. A prize for the color aficionados. (#7214)

Remarkable 1892-CC Dollar, Choice Uncirculated

2848 **1892-CC MS64 NGC.** A sizeable percentage of 1892-CC dollars saw some circulation, especially when compared to other Carson City Mint Morgans, and today this issue is relatively scarce in Mint State, particularly in Choice or finer. Dazzling cartwheel luster radiates from this brilliant and lightly abraded specimen. The strike is bold and the eye appeal is excellent. (#7214)

Smooth Near-Gem 1892-CC Dollar

2849 **1892-CC MS64 PCGS.** This better date Carson City dollar has dazzling luster and a good strike. Brilliant save for a blush of peach-gold along the upper right reverse margin. A die chip fills the lower opening of the 2 in the date, as often seen with this non-GSA issue. The fields are well preserved, while the cheek has faint grazes. Encapsulated in a first generation holder. (#7214)

Lovely 1892-CC Dollar, Choice Mint State

2850 **1892-CC MS64 PCGS.** Deep pearl-gray toning covers the devices, with pleasing rose and hazel tints in the fields. Several minor grazes define the grade, and none are particularly bothersome. Plenty of luster flashes beneath the patina and enhances the eye appeal. A sharply struck and carefully preserved specimen. (#7214)

Appealing 1892-CC Gem Dollar

2851 **1892-CC MS65 PCGS.** Fully brilliant and sharply struck with excellent eye appeal. Only slight weakness is visible over Liberty's hair. This is a remarkable example with few peers. Both sides have frosty white luster without any indication of toning. A few light grazes likely precludes an even higher grade. (#7214)

Eye-Catching 1892-CC Dollar, MS63 Deep Mirror Prooflike

2852 **1892-CC MS63 Deep Mirror Prooflike NGC.** A ring of lilac and hazel toning encircles the brilliant centers of this boldly struck specimen. Heavy frost covers the devices and creates a splendid cameo appearance with the deeply mirrored fields. Scattered light grazes limit the grade, but overall this piece has no bothersome marks and exhibits outstanding eye appeal. (#97215)

2853 **1892-O MS64 ICG.** Crisply detailed on the central devices with hints of frostiness at the high points. Powerfully lustrous with splashes of orange-gold and cloud-white patina close to the margins. (#7216)

2854 **1892-S XF45 PCGS.** The 1892-S is another issue in the Morgan dollar series that circulated extensively and is seldom found in grades above MS60. Myriad abrasions are visible throughout, but none are particularly detracting. A brilliant and surprisingly lustrous example; housed in a green label PCGS holder. (#7218)

2855 **1892-S XF45 PCGS.** Untoned silver-gray surfaces retain splendid amounts of luster. This piece is well-defined save for the typical softness above Liberty's ear. Myriad abrasions are typical for the grade, but none are of any significance. (#7218)

2856 **1892-S AU50 PCGS.** Impressively lustrous for the issue and the grade assigned. Minor wear is concentrated at the softly struck high points, though certain traces of circulation are noted in the gold-gray fields. (#7218)

Enticing 1892-S Morgan Dollar, AU55

2857 **1892-S AU55 PCGS. CAC.** For collectors of Mint State Morgan silver dollars, the 1892-S and 1893-S coins, along with a few other dates such as 1895-O and 1901, present major hurdles. Merely finding such a coin is extremely difficult, and finding one that is also attractive or appealing substantially increases the challenge. Once those two hurdles have been cleared, the next object is price. Those who have such coins for sale are simply not going to be pressured into discount selling.

  To solve those challenges, many collectors are delighted when an attractive, properly graded Choice AU example appears in the market place. The present piece is just one of those coins, with nearly full luster, excellent design details, and faint peripheral gold toning on otherwise brilliant, untoned silver surfaces. (#7218)

Lustrous Near-Mint 1892-S Morgan

2858 **1892-S AU58 NGC.** Just a whisper of light rub separates this attractive coin from Mint State, and as a high-end circulated piece, it offers a wonderful alternative to a low-end Mint State piece. The surfaces are silver-white with a bare suggestion of golden toning, and generous cartwheel luster radiates from both sides. While a few contact marks are visible and consistent with a short spate in circulation, there are no singular marks. NGC has certified 49 coins finer for the issue (8/08). (#7218)

2859 1892-S MS60 NGC. The 1892-S Morgan dollar, with its mintage of 1.2 million pieces, was not an issue that attracted particular notice for many years. Circulated examples have long been readily available, and premiums through XF are modest compared to other challenging dates with similar mintages. Following the Treasury releases of the early to mid-1960s, though numerous Morgan dollar dates experienced known population explosions, the 1892-S never turned up in appreciable quantities, and collectors began to recognize it as conditionally elusive in AU and better.

Throughout the 1960s and 1970s (and to a certain extent, the 1980s, as exemplified by passages in Wayne Miller's *The Morgan and Peace Dollar Textbook*), prior to the widespread acceptance of certification services and their grading standards, the 1892-S was often subject to misgrading, willful and accidental, with near-Mint State pieces the most frequent subjects. As a result, many knowledgeable collectors shied away from all but the highest-quality survivors, and the resulting lack of demand depressed prices. Since the 1990s, however, the greater confidence placed in certified grading has increased the popularity of this issue.

The present piece is strictly Mint State, with no trace of wear on any part of the design. While the MS60 designation may suggest an unattractive coin, this example is remarkably pleasing, and no abrasions merit individual mention, though a number of fine marks on each side confirm the grade's accuracy. Well struck and strongly lustrous beneath generally silver-white patina that shows occasional golden tints. Census: 6 in 60, 43 finer (7/08). (#7218)

2860 **1893 MS62 PCGS.** A brilliant and frosty specimen. Several shallow hairlines run across Liberty's cheek, but the rest of the surfaces show only light grazes and minor marks. A sharply struck representative with lovely eye appeal; housed in a green label PCGS holder. (#7220)

2861 **1893 MS63 NGC.** Shining and solidly struck with delightful eye appeal for the Select grade. The portrait is notably free of overt distractions. A pleasing example of this lower-mintage issue. (#7220)

2862 **1893 MS63 PCGS.** Boldly detailed with strong, shining luster and surprising eye appeal for the Select grade. A subtly gold-toned example of this popular semi-key issue. (#7220)

2863 **1893 MS64 PCGS.** The reverse of this Choice example is remarkably clean for the grade, and only a couple of wispy abrasions on Liberty's cheek keep this piece from Gem. Exciting cartwheel luster drapes the brilliant surfaces and enhances the great eye appeal. (#7220)

Lustrous MS64 1893 Morgan Dollar

2864 **1893 MS64 NGC.** With a mintage of less than 400,000 business strikes, the 1893-P Morgan dollar is a difficult issue to find in the higher Mint State grades, given the considerable demand for them. This piece shows silver-white surfaces with good luster and a clean appearance overall. The certified population at both NGC and PCGS thins out by an order of magnitude one grade point finer, making this an optimal collector grade. (#7220)

Impressive 1893 VAM-2 Dollar, MS64

2865 **1893 MS64 PCGS. CAC.** VAM-2. The top of the 3 is slightly doubled, and that digit is open with its upper loop separated from the center. A low-mintage issue, surviving from a total production of 389,792 coins, many having entered circulation. This wonderful near-Gem has all the quality and aesthetic desirability of a finer grade coin. (#7220)

Splendid 1893 Morgan Dollar, MS65

2866 **1893 MS65 PCGS.** Bowers (1993) advises cherrypicking for quality when it comes to the 1893. The present Gem is certainly among the more appealing survivors of this issue, with sharp striking detail throughout and a pleasing satin finish. The obverse is champagne tinged with some more extensive color along the left border. The reverse, on the other hand, is richly toned with blushes of cobalt-blue, lavender, and apricot patina over a base of medium gray color. The reverse is lightly die doubled, most noticeably along the bottom of the wreath. PCGS has only graded four examples of this issue finer than MS65 (8/08). (#7220)

Rare Prooflike 1893 Dollar MS61

2867 **1893 MS61 Prooflike NGC.** The low mintage 1893 is extremely rare in Prooflike format. This untoned example has flashy fields and a sharp strike. The fields are somewhat scuffy, consistent with the grade. NGC has certified only a single Deep Mirror Prooflike, an AU55. Census: 2 in 61 Prooflike, 2 finer (7/08). (#7221)

2868 **1893-CC XF45 PCGS.** Light silver-gray surfaces show glimmers of original luster at the gold-kissed peripheries. Well struck with modest wear concentrated at the high points. (#7222)

2869 **1893-CC—Cleaned—ICG. AU50 Details.** An untoned and hairlined example of this semi-key Carson City issue. Liberty's neck has light pinscratches, and an unobtrusive scratch is noted above the right wreath end. (#7222)

Brilliant 1893-CC Dollar, MS61

2870 **1893-CC MS61 PCGS.** A brilliant and frosty example of the highly popular final issue 1893-CC Morgan dollar. This piece has reflective fields with scattered obverse marks and few reverse marks. Like usual, the reverse seems to be two points finer than the obverse. While the central details are lacking, all other design elements are bold. (#7222)

2871 1893-CC MS62 PCGS. An outstanding, crisply struck representative of the final Carson City dollar. This brilliant specimen exhibits captivating prooflike fields that show moderate contrast against the frosted devices. Scattered abrasions define the grade, although the reverse is remarkably clean. (#7222)

2877 1893-O MS63 NGC. The 1893-O has an impressively low mintage of only 300,000 pieces—the lowest mintage of any New Orleans Mint Morgan dollar. A bit softly struck in the centers, as always, the fields are bright and semi-prooflike, and each side has a light, speckled overlay of rose-gray patination. (#7224)

Pretty MS62 1893-CC Morgan Dollar

Exceptional 1893-O Morgan Dollar, MS64

2872 1893-CC MS62 NGC. This pretty coin appears silver-white and untoned at first glance, but both sides offer a faint suggestion of sage coloration. The appearance is somewhat prooflike, more so on the reverse than the obverse. There are numerous bagmarks on this piece, like so many of this popular issue, that define the grade. (#7222)

Lustrous 1893-CC Morgan, MS63

2873 1893-CC MS63 PCGS. Typical of nearly all 1893-CC dollars, the obverse is a solid MS63 with some scattered marks, and the reverse is easily MS65 with pristine surfaces. Both sides have natural ivory-white luster with hints of lemon-yellow toning along the right obverse and at the reverse borders. (#7222)

2874 1893-O AU58 NGC. 1893-O dollars are typically seen circulated and can be exceptionally difficult to locate in high Uncirculated grades. This minimally abraded example shows traces of light rub on Liberty's cheek and in the fields, but exhibits splendid luster throughout. One of just 300,000 pieces struck. (#7224)

2875 1893-O AU58 NGC. Well struck with considerable luster remnants, and attractive light toning on both sides. The fields show moderate hairlines, and there a few noticeable marks on Liberty's cheek. (#7224)

2876 1893-O—Cleaned—ICG. MS60 Details. The cartwheel luster is undiminished and the strike is precise, but the obverse of this nearly brilliant key date New Orleans dollar displays wispy hairlines. The eagle has concealed abrasions, and Liberty's cheek has a few marks. (#7224)

2878 1893-O MS64 PCGS. CAC. Reading down the list of annual mintage numbers for New Orleans silver dollars, one sees multiple millions of coins produced every year until 1893. Just 300,000 Morgans were minted at New Orleans in 1893. Along with low quantity, there is also an issue of quality. Q. David Bowers (2005) notes that it is a challenge to find an 1893-O dollar without bagmarks, adding humorously that "the easy way out is to buy a certified coin and forget it." The present coin, however, answers that challenge without compromise. Except for a few small abrasions behind Liberty's eye, the surfaces of this coin are exceptionally clean. There is virtually no toning to obscure the strong, as-new luster, and though minor softness of strike in the centers is apparent, the remaining details are solid. This is a wonderful coin for the type or Morgan collector. PCGS has certified only seven pieces finer (8/08). (#7224)

2879 **1893-S AG3 NGC.** Pale gray devices contrast nicely against the gunmetal-gray fields. The rims are flat, and the outer part of the lettering is obscured, but the central design elements are completely outlined and LIBERTY is bold. A pleasing, evenly worn example of this key-date Morgan dollar. (#7226)

Popular 1893-S Dollar, Good 4

2880 **1893-S Good 4 NGC.** The surfaces are pinkish-silver and golden-tinged, and a bit of rim weakness is noted from 4 to 6 o'clock on the obverse, and from 12 to 3 on the reverse. There is a small rim bump below stars 3 and 4 on the obverse. A popular issue, in demand in all grades. (#7226)

2881 **1893-S—Improperly Cleaned—NCS. Good 4 Details.** The 1893-S has always been one of the most desirable Morgan dollars, and it is scarce in any grade. The surfaces are exceptionally clean and LIBERTY is sharp. A collectible example of this low-mintage issue. (#7226)

Attractive Good 4 1893-S Morgan

2882 **1893-S Good 4 ANACS.** In this grade, of course, only the deep detail remains, but there are no singular distractions. The rims are full, although weak on the obverse above E PLUR and on the reverse below LLAR. A bit of buildup is noted between stars 12 and 13. The surfaces show attractive silver-gold hues throughout. (#7226)

2883 **1893-S—Bent—NCS. Good Details.** 1893-S dollars are highly sought after in all grades. This example is slightly bent, and appears to have been improperly cleaned, but sufficient details remain to readily identify it as a genuine example. (#7226)

Affordable VG Details 1893-S Dollar

2884 **1893-S—Cleaned—ANACS. VG8 Details.** A slightly glossy and lightly hairlined example of this famous Morgan issue, which has the lowest business strike mintage of the series. Toned canary-gold and void of distressing marks, although a minor obverse rim nick is noted at 2:30. More than half of the wing feathers are still visible. (#7226)

Coveted VG Details 1893-S Dollar

2885 **1893-S—Improperly Cleaned—NCS. VG Details.** This steel-gray key date Morgan may be moderately granular, but it will be acceptable to many collectors who have long wished to fill that final hole. The lower half of the wings display ample feather detail, and there are no obtrusive abrasions. (#7226)

2886 **1893-S—Cleaned—ANACS. VG8 Details.** Charcoal-gray patina outlines the slate-gray design elements. A few tiny rim dings, but a worthy key date representative despite a subdued appearance from a cleaning. (#7226)

Desirable 1893-S Dollar, VG10

2887 **1893-S VG10 NGC.** Ex: Fitzgerald Collection, Fitzgerald's Nevada Club Reno Hoard. A Choice VG example of this key date issue. Light silver-gray surfaces display good detail for the grade designation, and reveal the expected number of marks for a moderately to heavily circulated coin. (#7226)

Fine Sharpness 1893-S Morgan Dollar

2888 **1893-S—Scratched, Improperly Cleaned—NCS. Fine Details.** A long, straight scratch runs from star 4 on the obverse up before Liberty's face and to the first U in UNUM, but it is mostly hidden under a layer of deep golden-gray toning and is not overly distracting. The surfaces are a bit flat and light-diffusing, characteristic of the noted cleaning, but overall the piece still has a lot of appeal for a midgrade example of this key coin. (#7226)

VF Sharpness Key 1893-S Dollar

2889 **1893-S—Improperly Cleaned—NCS. VF Details.** This lightly toned rare date dollar is clouded by a cleaning, but careful rotation fails to locate oppressive hairlines or heavy bagmarks. A majority of the wing feathers are bold, although the hair above the ear is smooth. Key diagnostics are present, such as the minute diagonal die line within the center top of the T in LIBERTY. (#7226)

Challenging VF Details Key 1893-S Dollar

2890 **1893-S—Improperly Cleaned—NCS. VF Details.** Deep cream-gray toning envelops this key date dollar. About three-fourths of the wing feathers remain clear. Portions of the lower reverse are slightly bright from a wipe, and a couple of faded vertical marks are noted beneath the left (facing) wing. A collectible example of the most challenging business strike of the series. (#7226)

Delightful 1893-S Morgan, VF20

2891 **1893-S VF20 PCGS.** A delightful 1893-S Morgan dollar with medium to dark gray surfaces, exactly as an old circulated silver dollar should look. Even with a glass, there are no marks aside from the usual handling marks that accumulate over a period in circulation. An excellent mid-grade example of the key Morgan dollar issue. (#7226)

VF Details 1893-S Dollar

2892 **1893-S—Improperly Cleaned—NCS. VF Details.** The surfaces show light hairlines when the coin is closely examined; however, the overall appearance is not one of a harshly cleaned piece. The fields and recesses are light to medium gray and set up a noticeable contrast against the brilliantish-silver color over the high points. (#7226)

Pleasing 1893-S Morgan Dollar, VF25

2893 **1893-S VF25 NGC.** The fields are dusky smoke-gray on this piece, but they are remarkably clean on both sides and free to the naked eye of distracting abrasions, large or small. Hints of pink and gold appear when the coin is rotated, and much pleasing detail remains for the assigned grade level. (#7226)

Wonderful 1893-S Morgan, VF25

2894 1893-S VF25 PCGS. This piece has the kind of sharp detail and problem-free appearance that almost ensures that it traded hands in the past "raw" as high as an XF40. Plenty of detail remains in the hair and the flora of Liberty's cap, and almost all of the wing feathers are present. Muted luster remains on the pinkish-gold and silver-gray surfaces, along with much eye appeal. Even now, this wonderful key-date piece would fit nicely in a high-grade circulated set. (#7226)

Desirable 1893-S Dollar, XF45

2895 1893-S XF45 NGC. The 1893-S is generally considered to be the most desirable single Morgan dollar issue struck at a branch mint. In a September 5, 2005 *Coin World* article entitled "1893-S Morgans Hot Market Commodity," Paul Gilkes writes: "Morgan dollar collectors desire the 1893-S Morgan dollar ... in all grades. The demand-supply ratio is such that the issue is valued in four figures even in lower grades."

The Choice XF example offered in this lot displays silver-colored surfaces that retain traces of luster in the protected areas. The expected light wear is seen on portions of Liberty's hair, the eagle's breast, and other highpoints, but great device detail is still visible. The contact marks scattered over each side are not out of line with what would be expected for a lightly circulated, large and heavy coin such as the Morgan dollar. (#7226)

Appealing 1893-S Dollar, AU50

2896 1893-S AU50 NGC. This glowing key-date Morgan dollar would be the pride of an advanced, high grade collection. The surfaces retain much of the original luster, complementing the light-golden cast seen at the rims on each side, with a dash of russet and ice-blue near the lower reverse rim. While grade-consistent rub appears in the center of the eagle's breast and the wing highpoints, on Liberty's cheek, and on the highest hair above Liberty's ear and below LIBERTY, much pleasing detail remains. The overall appeal of this piece is undeniable, and many a collector will no doubt vie for the privilege of adding this lovely coin to her/his holdings. (#7226)

2897 1894—Cleaned—ANACS. VF Details. Net Fine 15. This is a nicely detailed example with few noticeable abrasions ion either side. The surfaces display an even coating of drab brown-gray toning, and the piece appears to have been cleaned or whizzed, at some point. (#7228)

2898 1894—Improperly Cleaned—NCS. VF Details. The 1894 had a relatively low mintage of 110,000 pieces, which ranks it among the scarcest of all Morgan dollars. Cleaning has left the surfaces pale silver-gray, and there are several shallow nicks on Liberty's cheek and neck. Nonetheless, this piece is a well-detailed and affordable example of this key date. (#7228)

2899 **1894—Improperly Cleaned—NCS. VF Details.** Medium gray patina covers both sides, with peppered charcoal toning throughout. The details are nicely outlined, and there are no mentionable marks one either side. A relatively affordable example of this key date. (#7228)

2900 **1894—Improperly Cleaned—NCS. VF Details.** This low mintage Morgan dollar exhibits blended cream-gray and chestnut-brown toning. Hairlined, but the only remotely mentionable mark is a tiny rim bruise on the reverse at 11 o'clock. (#7228)

2901 **1894—Improperly Cleaned—NCS. VF Details.** Light to medium gray surfaces reveal fine hairlines under magnification, along with some minute circulation marks. Nice detail for the grade. (#7228)

2902 **1894 VF25 NGC.** Generally medium-gray with a degree of darkening around the central devices. A minimally marked mid-range piece that shows occasional coffee tints. (#7228)

2903 **1894—Improperly Cleaned—NCS. XF Details.** A mix of bluish-gray, olive-green, and golden-green patina rests on each side of this lightly cleaned Morgan. Light to moderately abraded, and relatively well defined. (#7228)

2904 **1894—Improperly Cleaned—NCS. XF Details.** Untoned surfaces reveal fine hairlines and a scattering of contact marks. Generally well defined. (#7228)

2905 **1894—Improperly Cleaned—NCS. XF Details.** Light silver surfaces with traces of wear and hints of gold toning at the upper obverse. Lightly cleaned, but still a delightful example. (#7228)

2906 **1894—Scratched—NCS. XF Details.** Aside from a handful of unfortunate scratches in the left obverse field and at the eagle's breast, the overall eye appeal of this key-date Morgan dollar is excellent. Well struck with ample remaining luster at the margins, which show glimmers of rose and champagne patina. (#7228)

2907 **1894—Improperly Cleaned—NCS. XF Details.** This is one of the scarcest Philadelphia Mint issues in the Morgan dollar series, and a key date by any standard. The current example is bright and hairlined from improper cleaning, but exhibits well struck design elements and a good degree of remaining detail, in line with the XF Details designation by NCS. (#7228)

2908 **1894—Improperly Cleaned—NCS. AU details.** A fully brilliant example, save for slight luster breaks on the highpoints. Although certainly cleaned at least once in its life, this lovely dollar is still an attractive, appealing example of the elusive date. (#7228)

2909 **1894 AU55 PCGS.** The 1894 has the lowest mintage of all Philadelphia issues, aside from the proof-only 1895. The present untoned example has virtually complete mint luster, and the absence of noticeable marks ensures the eye appeal. The upper reverse legends are minutely die doubled, as usually seen on quality examples of this desirable date. (#7228)

Lustrous AU58 1894 Dollar

2910 **1894 AU58 NGC.** One of the lowest mintages in the Morgan series, but there were a number recovered from the Treasury Morgan dollar release of the early 1960s. Frosty surfaces display barely discernible whispers of beige and ice-blue patina in selected areas. The design elements are sharply defined, the only exception being softness in the hair over Liberty's ear. The surfaces are relatively clean and show just a few minute marks on Liberty's cheek and in the right (facing) reverse field. (#7228)

2911 **1894—Improperly Cleaned—NCS. Unc. Details.** Pearl-gray save for glimpses of honey-gold along the right obverse border. The cartwheel luster is unbroken but subdued. A sharply struck and moderately abraded better grade example of this coveted low mintage issue. (#7228)

MS62 1894 Morgan Dollar

2912 **1894 MS62 NGC.** The 1894 Philadelphia Mint Morgan is a perennially popular piece, with its memorable 110,000-piece mintage second only to the famous 1893-S dollar. This example offers silver-white surfaces with lots of eye appeal, despite the few contact marks, consistent with the grade, that prevent an even finer Mint State grade. Only a trace of peach rim toning occurs on the reverse rim. (#7228)

Appealing 1894-O Dollar, MS63

2913 **1894-O MS63 NGC.** Plenty of appeal attracts the viewer of this coin, with well-mirrored silver centers that complement rings of pink-champagne and gold near the rims on each side. The reverse is rotated about 15 degrees counterclockwise with respect to the obverse. A loupe reveals a few light contact marks and luster grazes, but this piece has much to commend itself. (#7230)

2914 **1894-S MS64 NGC.** Beautifully detailed, particularly in the often-weak centers, with few flaws in the fields. Immensely lustrous with occasional silver-gray and golden elements splashed across each side. (#7232)

2915 **1894-S MS64 PCGS. CAC.** Dappled caramel-gold and sky-blue patina endows this satiny and assertively struck near-Gem. Liberty's jaw has faint roller marks, but the surfaces are pleasantly free from abrasions. (#7232)

2916 **1894-S MS64 PCGS.** In Select and finer grades, the 1894-S is the most available of the three silver dollar issues for that year, though attractive examples can be elusive. This near-Gem has strong luster and notable detail overall. Lightly gold-toned in the fields with a few spots of opaque chalk-white color on the obverse. (#7232)

Pleasing 1895-O Dollar, AU58

2917 **1895-O AU58 PCGS. CAC.** This briefly circulated piece is mostly medium gray, with just a hint of golden toning around the rims. A number of shallow marks are typical for the grade, but none merit individual mention. The strike is crisp save for the usual weakness on the hair above Liberty's ear. A lovely, borderline Uncirculated example of this issue, which is seldom seen in Mint State. (#7236)

AU58 ★ Key 1895-O Dollar

2918 **1895-O AU58 ★ NGC.** The 1895-O is the key date of the New Orleans Morgan dollars, and attractively toned examples are highly elusive. But this Borderline Uncirculated representative features peach-gold toning that ripens near the rims. The right reverse margin also has an arc of sky-blue patina. The cheek is moderately abraded and has a trace of friction. (#7236)

Gorgeous 1895-O Morgan, AU58

2919 **1895-O AU58 PCGS. CAC.** At current market levels, the price difference between an AU58 and an MS60 example of this date is considerable, while the quality difference is slight. In fact, many collectors prefer an exceptional AU58 example with excellent surfaces to a beat-up old MS60. The present example is just one of those exceptional AU58 coins, with brilliant silver luster, pleasing and slightly reflective fields, and wonderful surfaces. (#7236)

Lustrous 1895-O Morgan Dollar, AU58

2920 **1895-O AU58 PCGS. CAC.** Only a slight trace of highpoint wear on the obverse separates this lovely near-Mint coin from others that are full Mint State. It has brilliant silver surfaces with frosty luster and only a slight number of tiny surface marks, certainly less than usual. Highly desirable and destined for an excellent Morgan dollar collection. (#7236)

2921 1895-O AU58 ICG. A touch of wear at the highest part of the portrait is the only barrier to a Mint State designation. The highly lustrous surfaces are primarily silver-white with gold-orange patina around the obverse margins. (#7236)

Luminous Mint State 1895-O Dollar

2922 1895-O MS60 PCGS. CAC. Each side offers soft, pleasing luster with a hint of satin, far from the "dull, insipid luster" Q. David Bowers describes as common in his *A Guide Book of Morgan Silver Dollars*. The strike, however, is more typical, with significant softness noted around Liberty's ear and the eagle's breast. Variable silver-rose and golden-tan toning crosses much of each side. The MS60 designation is a fair grade, considering the numerous wispy abrasions that populate the fields, yet the coin retains appreciable eye appeal and shows no trace of wear, as attested to by the PCGS certification grade and the CAC sticker. (#7236)

Appealing MS61 1895-O Dollar

2923 1895-O MS61 PCGS. CAC. In 1895, the New Orleans Mint struck silver dollars in only four months of the year, January, February, April, and May, for a total mintage of just 450,000 coins. The present piece is an appealing Mint State survivor of this popular issue, one that is relatively available in most circulated states but surprisingly elusive in unworn grades. The luminous surfaces are primarily silver-gray, though hints of rose and sage dot parts of the portrait and the nearby fields. Well-defined at the margins, though the hair over Liberty's ear and the eagle's breast show the softness that is characteristic for the date. (#7236)

2924 **1895-O MS62 PCGS.** While the 1895-O has always been something of a darling among Morgan dollar enthusiasts, particularly in higher grades, enough circulated examples have been through the marketplace that collectors have been able to assume its ready availability in almost all non-Mint State grades. As noted by Q. David Bowers in his *A Guide Book of Morgan Silver Dollars*, "There are scads of high EF and AU coins around, indicating that many 1895-O dollars must have been in circulation for only a short time ... "

Also noteworthy is that almost all of the 1895-O dollars were paid out, with virtually none left to languish in Treasury vaults, unlike the majority of Morgan dollar issues. In the *Guide Book*, Bowers further notes: "The 1895-O emerged as the single circulation-strike variety that is not known to have been a part of any Treasury releases via bags." He later clarifies that he has " ... found no account or even a rumor of any [1895-O dollars] being a part of the 1962 through 1964 Treasury release."

With so many survivors showing evidence of circulation, Mint State representatives of this issue are treasures, and the present coin is no exception. The strike is surprisingly bold, with individual feathers showing on the eagle's breast, and the highly lustrous surfaces show only occasional hints of golden patina. While an abrasion at Liberty's upper hair and smaller, scattered marks preclude Select status, the overall eye appeal remains high. An excellent choice for the Morgan dollar aficionado. Population: 37 in 62, 36 finer (8/08). (#7236)

2925 **1895-O MS63 ANACS.** While the 1893-S issue is arguably the most important and widely recognized of all business strike Morgan silver dollars, the 1895-O follows closely behind. Similarly rare dates include 1884-S, 1892-S, and 1901. All of these dates have a similar theme, that of relative availability in circulated grades, but not in Mint State. These dates had varying mintages from 100,000 coins for the 1893-S to nearly 7 million examples of the 1901 dollar. The 1895-O Morgan dollar had a mintage of 450,000 coins, and it seems that most of those pieces entered circulation. There were no hoards of any substance, and none were found in the Treasury vaults when Morgan dollars were released some 40 years ago (David Bowers, *Silver Dollars and Trade dollars of the United States*, 2006, p. 241).

This particular example has generally sharp design elements with slight weakness over Liberty's ear and on the eagle's breast. Both sides are fully lustrous with frosty silver surfaces. There is no evidence of toning on the brilliant white obverse and reverse. A few minor field marks are visible on each side, as well as a few other tiny blemishes on the devices. It is important to realize that this is at once an important date and also a rarity in all Mint State grades. Since the beginning of our auction record keeping in 1993, we have only handled 12 examples at this grade level and 15 finer coins. Given the extraordinary population of Morgan dollars in all grades as a type, these population figures for the 1895-O are exceptionally important. (#7236)

Alluring 1895-O Dollar, AU58 Prooflike

2926 **1895-O AU58 Prooflike NGC.** The 1895-O has the distinction of being the only circulation strike Morgan dollar that is not known to have been part of any Treasury releases. This attractive example has vivid amber toning in the periphery that surrounds the brilliant centers. Myriad abrasions lightly affect the impressive reflectivity of the fields. A relatively low 450,000 pieces were struck, and only a select few have received a Prooflike designation from either NGC or PCGS. NGC reports just four finer Prooflike examples. (#7237)

2927 **1895-S XF40 NGC.** Though each side shows light to moderate wear across the silver-gray centers, the green-gold and cerulean margins are surprisingly flashy. Striking eye appeal. (#7238)

2928 **1895-S—Scratched—ICG. AU50 Details.** A crisply detailed example of one of the keys to the Morgan dollar series. The surfaces are a trifle dull, and there are scattered scratches on the obverse. The reverse, however, displays no prominent marks. (#7238)

Vibrant MS62 1895-S Dollar

2929 **1895-S MS62 PCGS.** VAM-3. A Hot 50 Variety. The initial mintmark was entered too high with an extraordinary slant to the left, and was only partially effaced before a second mintmark was better placed. Of course, any Mint State '95-S dollar is desirable, since just 400,000 pieces were struck. This lustrous and boldly struck example has light obverse tan toning and a smattering of small marks on the portrait. (#7238)

Splendid 1895-S Morgan, MS63

2930 **1895-S MS63 PCGS.** The 1895-S Morgan is the only moderately priced dollar of the date. The 1895-O is a major condition rarity and the 1895 is only available as a proof. This piece has exceptional silver luster with excellent satin surfaces and bold design features. An excellent opportunity to add this date to a Morgan dollar registry set. (#7238)

Impressive 1895-S Dollar, MS63

2931 **1895-S MS63 NGC.** The 1895-S dollar's mintage of just 400,000 pieces is significantly lower than the typical issue in the series. Like many San Francisco Morgan dollars, a large number saw some circulation, and today Mint State pieces are relatively scarce. Numerous grazes cover the obverse, although the reverse is remarkably clean. This untoned and crisply struck example would make a lovely representative. (#7238)

2932 **1896 MS66 Prooflike NGC.** Excellent striking definition with subtle golden patina over the powerful, pleasingly preserved mirrors. Light frost across the portrait supplies a degree of contrast. Census: 8 in 66 Prooflike, 1 finer (7/08). (#7241)

2933 **1896 MS65 Deep Mirror Prooflike NGC.** Each side exhibits powerful mirrors beneath a thin layer of silver-gray haze. Whispers of golden patina grace the obverse margins, and the portrait is delightfully frosted. NGC has graded only one finer Deep Mirror Prooflike piece (8/08). (#97241)

2934 **1896 MS65 Deep Mirror Prooflike PCGS.** Outstanding mirrors beneath delicate silver-gray and gold-orange patina. Boldly struck with amazing preservation and eye appeal to match. PCGS has graded just 11 finer Deep Mirror Prooflike pieces (8/08). (#97241)

2935 **1896-O MS61 NGC.** Aside from trifling softness at the high points of the obverse, this O-mint dollar is well-defined. Strongly lustrous with wispy abrasions that render the grade accurate, yet misleading on its high eye appeal. (#7242)

2936 **1896-O MS61 NGC.** Subtle gold-gray and pink tints enliven the lustrous surfaces of this modestly abraded O-mint dollar. Well struck with solid eye appeal for the grade. (#7242)

Lovely 1896-O Morgan, MS62

2937 **1896-O MS62 PCGS.** A frosty Mint State piece with brilliant silver surfaces and a splash of gold at the center of the obverse. A scarce issue in Mint State grades, always in demand from advanced collectors. The strike is excellent for the issue, with only modest central weakness. (#7242)

Conditionally Scarce 1896-O Dollar, MS63

2938 1896-O MS63 NGC. Dave Bowers (2005) writes that most of the mintage of the 1896-O must have been released into circulation because this date is difficult to find in Mint State. Choice examples are quite rare and whenever a Gem specimen comes to the market it fetches a six-figure price. This brilliant representative is sharply struck, but has a number of grade-defining abrasions on both sides. A tiny blemish is noted by Liberty's chin. An attractive piece that would be worth many multiples more just one numerical grade finer. NGC has certified only 15 finer examples (8/08). (#7242)

MS63 1896-O Dollar, An Important Condition Rarity

2939 1896-O MS63 PCGS. This conditionally rare O-mint Morgan has golden-brown borders and cream-gray fields and devices. The satiny surfaces are clean for the grade, and the reverse on its own has the look of a finer grade. The strike is slightly soft on the eagle's breast, customary for New Orleans dollars from this era. (#7242)

Remarkable 1896-S Dollar, Choice Uncirculated

2940 1896-S MS64 NGC. Like many of the late S-mint Morgan dollars, the 1896-S is elusive in high Mint State grades. Examples of this issue can be easily found in most circulated grades, but even AU specimens have a substantial premium. A few patches of light tan toning accent the mostly silver-gray surfaces of this highly lustrous piece. The reverse is remarkably pristine for the grade and the obverse has only trivial abrasions. NGC has certified a mere 24 coins finer (8/08). (#7244)

2941 1897-O MS61 NGC. Generally well struck save for slight weakness above Liberty's ear. Strongly lustrous with pleasing surfaces for the MS61 grade level. The obverse displays pale violet-red toning, while the reverse has a pale golden-silver cast. (#7248)

2942 1897-O MS62 NGC. Pleasingly detailed for this later O-mint issue with bands of gold-orange at the margins and otherwise silver-gray surfaces. Luminous with few overt flaws. (#7248)

2943 1897-O MS62 PCGS. Light tan color is more prominent on the reverse, where it is joined by whispers of light blue. The obverse center reveals some softness, a characteristic of the issue. Some light grazes and marks result in occasional breaks in the luster flow. (#7248)

2944 1897-O MS62 PCGS. This '97-O exhibits a thin veil of champagne-gold toning with subtle accents of magenta and lilac over soft luster. The design elements are sharply struck, though the hair above Liberty's ear is a touch soft. Liberty's cheek displays a few light marks. (#7248)

Delightful 1897-O Dollar, Select Mint State

2945 1897-O MS63 PCGS. An arc of sea-green, lilac, and gold toning graces the obverse periphery, while streaks of tan patina adorn much of the reverse. This well-struck piece has shimmering mint luster and nicely preserved surfaces that show only a few wispy abrasions. A die crack encircles the reverse lettering. Boldly struck and quite attractive. (#7248)

2946 1897-S MS66 NGC. A well-defined beauty with powerful, swirling luster and carefully preserved surfaces. Virtually brilliant and delightful in all respects. NGC has graded just 11 numerically finer pieces (8/08). (#7250)

2947 1898 MS66 Deep Mirror Prooflike NGC. Deeply mirrored fields yield pronounced contrast with the motifs of this Premium Gem. A solid strike imparts strong definition on the design features, including the hair over the ear and the eagle's breast feathers. Untoned save for a couple of light gold-tan splashes on the obverse and well-preserved throughout. Census: 4 in 66 Deep Mirror Prooflike, 0 finer (8/08). (#97253)

Captivating 1898-O Morgan Dollar, MS67

2948 1898-O MS67 NGC. A frosty Superb Gem with exceptional aesthetic appeal created through a combination of ivory luster and splashes of gold and iridescent toning. Considered common in all grades, the present example of this one-time rarity is exceeded at NGC by just one higher grade coin. (#7254)

2949 **1898-S MS65 PCGS.** Bright luster exudes from both sides, and light tan-gold color hugs the margins, especially those of the reverse. Generally well struck. Some minute marks are visible on both sides. (#7256)

2950 **1899 MS65 PCGS.** This low mintage Gem has light caramel-gold patina and splendidly smooth fields. Even the cheekbone has only minor contact. Lustrous and lovely. It is one of the anomalies of the series that the high mintage 1901 is vastly rarer than the 1899 in better Mint State grades. (#7258)

Highly Lustrous MS67 1899-O Dollar

2951 **1899-O MS67 PCGS.** A lustrous and brilliant Superb Gem with impressive luster and exquisite surfaces. The centers are slightly soft in strike, while the often-weak bow of the wreath has excellent detail. By no means a rare issue, it would take an exhaustive search to find another any finer. Population: 80 in 67, 1 finer (8/08). (#7260)

2952 **1899-O MS67 NGC.** A Superb and frosty Gem with creamy silver luster and peripheral green, rose, and gold toning on both sides. An exceptional example, and tied for the finest NGC has graded (8/08). (#7260)

2953 **1899-O Micro O MS61 ANACS.** VAM-6. A Top 100 Variety. A tiny mintmark, slanted slightly to the right, identifies this variety. Dazzling cartwheel luster radiates from this brilliant and lightly abraded piece. The strike is a little soft at the centers, as typical, but most of the details are fully defined. (#87260)

2954 **1899-S MS65 PCGS.** Sharply struck with the vibrant visual appeal only a Gem can provide. Essentially brilliant aside from occasional hints of peach-gold patina at the obverse margins. (#7262)

Elusive 1899-S Gem Deep Mirror Prooflike Dollar

2955 **1899-S MS65 Deep Mirror Prooflike NGC.** The 1899-S dollar, with a mintage of 2.562 million pieces, is a relatively plentiful issue in Mint State through the MS65 level. David Bowers, in his 1993 *Silver Dollars & Trade Dollars of the United States*, partially accounts for this: "A steady stream of Uncirculated 1899-S dollars ... was paid out by the San Francisco Mint during the period from 1942 through the mid-1950s."

Bowers goes on to say that Prooflike coins are abundant. Indeed, NGC and PCGS have graded approximately 300 Prooflike specimens. On the other hand, the two services have seen only about 85 Deep Mirror Prooflike examples, mostly through the near-Gem grade levels. A mere five Gem DMPLs have been seen, and four finer.

A sliver of electric-blue and russet patina clings to the rim areas of the present MS65 DMPL coin, and an attentive strike nicely defines the design features, including partial detail in the hair over Liberty's ear and on the breast feathers. A few minor grade-consistent marks are visible, more so on the reverse. Census: 3 in 65 Deep Mirror Prooflike, 0 finer (7/08). (#97263)

Exquisite 1900 Morgan, MS67

2956 **1900 MS67 NGC.** This Superb Gem is tied for the finest that either NGC or PCGS has graded. It has brilliant and satiny silver surfaces with untoned brilliance on both sides. The strike is bold and the overall aesthetic appeal is exceptional. Census: 31 in 67, 0 finer (8/08). (#7264)

Exceptional MS67 1900-O Dollar

2957 **1900-O MS67 NGC.** While one of the more frequently encountered late-date Morgans, few examples are known of the 1900-O in Superb condition. This splendid coin has the usual thick, satiny mint luster and each side is covered with rich golden toning and faint flecks of lilac are interspersed. Sharply struck. Census: 56 in 67, 0 finer (7/08). *From The Mississippi Collection.* (#7266)

2958 **1900-O/CC MS63 ANACS.** VAM-11. A Top 100 Variety. Traces of the CC mintmark are easily visible under magnification. Hints of orange-gold toning around the periphery accent the silver-gray centers. The splendid cartwheel luster is barely affected by a few wispy abrasions. A sharply struck piece with excellent eye appeal. (#7268)

2959 **1900-O/CC MS63 ANACS.** VAM-8. A Top 100 Variety. Remnants of the partially effaced CC mintmark are clearly visible under a glass. Alluring cartwheel luster graces each side of this carefully preserved example. A little weakness on the hair above Liberty's ear is noted. Mostly brilliant save for a trace of light brown toning near the rims. (#7268)

2960 **1900-O/CC MS64 PCGS.** VAM-8. A Top 100 Variety. Faint olive toning visits this highly lustrous and boldly impressed near-Gem. Marks require patience to locate. The reverse field is nearly immaculate. (#7268)

2961 **1900-O/CC MS64 ANACS.** VAM-10A. A Top 100 Variety. The n in IN is faintly clashed near Liberty's neck. A scarcer O/CC variety, since most are VAM-8 or VAM-11. A lustrous example with well preserved fields and peripheral honey-gold toning. A graze is noted to the right of the mouth. (#7268)

2962 **1900-O/CC MS64 PCGS.** VAM-8. A Top 100 Variety. Essentially untoned except for a dash of charcoal between the RI in AMERICA. Lustrous and boldly impressed with pleasing preservation. Certified in a green label holder. (#7268)

Premium Gem 1900-O/CC Dollar

2963 **1900-O/CC MS66 PCGS. CAC.** VAM-11. A Top 100 Variety. Fragments of the partially effaced Carson City mintmark bookend the prominent New Orleans mintmark. This well struck and essentially brilliant premium Gem has booming cartwheel luster on each side. An exceptionally preserved representative of this popular variety. Encased in an old green label holder. Population: 74 in 66, 2 finer (7/08). (#7268)

2964 **1900-S MS65 PCGS.** Light honey toning visits this lustrous and clean-cheeked Gem. A good strike with incompleteness confined to the hair above the ear. The obverse is beautifully preserved, while the reverse field has minor marks. (#7270)

Sharp 1901 Morgan, MS61

2965 **1901 MS61 NGC.** An abundant issue in AU, but one quite scarce in the higher realms of Mint State, the 1901 is seldom seen with prooflike surfaces, and no DMPL pieces have ever been reported. This flashy silver-white coin has generous cartwheel luster, with quite a few shallow ticks and contact marks that account for the grade. The strike is well-executed, and the eye appeal is high. (#7272)

Conditionally Scarce 1901 Morgan Dollar, MS62

2966 **1901 MS62 NGC.** According to Bowers (1993): "Of all Philadelphia Mint business strike dollars, excepting the spectral 1895, the 1901 is the rarest in Mint State." This is a lovely, satiny example with russet-red and cobalt peripheral toning, and surfaces that are only lightly abraded on both sides. (#7272)

2967 **1901-S MS63 NGC.** Subtle silver-gray and peach shadings embrace the immensely lustrous surfaces of this Select coin. Well-defined with only faint abrasions that score the frost of the portrait. (#7276)

Rare Prooflike 1901-S Dollar MS64

2968 1901-S MS64 Prooflike NGC. Russet-red and navy-blue embrace the borders of this lustrous and nicely struck Gem. Marks are refreshingly few in number. The 1901-S is elusive in Mint State, and decidedly rare with prooflike fields. Encased in a former generation holder. Census: 8 in 64 Prooflike, 1 finer (7/08). (#7277)

2969 1902 MS66 ★ NGC. Gorgeous golden-brown, plum-red, and navy-blue patina graces the borders of this sharply struck and lustrous Premium Gem. An exquisitely preserved and beautiful silver type coin. Only two business strike 1902 dollars have received a Star designation from NGC, the present piece and an MS66 Prooflike example (8/08). (#7278)

2970 1902-S MS64 NGC. A shining and sharply struck example of this popular 20th century Morgan dollar issue. Occasional glimmers of peach patina visit the well-preserved margins. (#7282)

Impressive 1902-S Dollar, MS65

2971 1902-S MS65 PCGS. The 1902-S Morgan dollar is seldom seen finer than this attractive specimen. Rings of violet, amber, and gold toning encircle both sides and contrast nicely against the eye-catching silver-gray centers. Pleasing cartwheel luster graces both sides and accents the sharply struck details. PCGS has certified only 31 examples finer (8/08). (#7282)

Brilliant 1902-S Morgan Dollar, MS65

2972 1902-S MS65 PCGS. A satiny Gem with fully brilliant silver luster on both sides. It is boldly struck for the issue, with only slight weakness on the hair strands over the ear, and on the eagle's breast. All other details are boldly brought up. Near vertical striae across Liberty's cheek is the result of planchet preparation and has no effect on the grade. An important piece, exceeded by only 30 finer PCGS certified examples. (#7282)

2973 1902-S MS63 Prooflike PCGS. Pleasingly reflective, if not absolutely mirrored, with light silver-gray patina across much of each side. The strike is generally strong, with only a trace of weakness at the highest part of Liberty's hair. (#7283)

Bright, Satiny 1903 Dollar, MS67

2974 1903 MS67 PCGS. Ex: R. Dier Collection. This uncommonly well preserved, frosty Superb Gem would be deemed immaculate by many collectors, and only thorough scrutiny beneath a loupe locates even trivial imperfections. The 1903 is not rare, but few survivors can challenge the Superb quality of the present well struck, satiny piece. Population: 61 in 67, 0 finer (8/08). (#7284)

2975 1903 MS63 Deep Mirror Prooflike NGC. Pleasing violet and russet toning encircles the perimeter of this highly lustrous specimen. The strike is razor-sharp save for minor weakness on the hair above Liberty's ear. A number of grade-defining grazes cover both sides, although the reverse has significantly fewer marks than the obverse. (#97285)

2976 1903-S—Cleaned—ANACS. AU Details, Net XF40. VAM-2. A Top 100 Variety. A small, centered, and upright mintmark identifies this variety. Cleaning has given the surfaces a dull gray complexion, although there are accents of red toning near the rims. Scattered abrasions throughout are typical of the grade. Still, a lovely example of this collectible VAM variety. (#7288)

Dazzling Select Mint State 1903-S Dollar

2977 1903-S MS63 NGC. Dazzling, coruscant luster flashes over the surfaces of this bright, brilliant example. Well struck with scattered small to moderate marks on each side. According to Bowers' silver dollar *Encyclopedia:* "This is an important, key issue. I have never handled a quantity of them, and few other dealers have either." (#7288)

Elusive 1903-S Dollar, Choice Mint State

2978 1903-S MS64 PCGS. A desirable semi-key Morgan dollar, the 1903-S is particularly elusive in Mint State, especially in Choice or finer. This brilliant near-Gem representative exhibits flashy luster that highlights the powerfully impressed devices. Several minor reeding marks preclude a higher grade, but this dazzling piece has great eye appeal nonetheless. (#7288)

Highly Lustrous MS66 1903-S Dollar

2979 1903-S MS66 NGC. A beautiful example of this sought-after date. The 1903-S is known to be one of the rarest silver dollars in Mint State. Q. David Bowers estimated that only 400-800 examples are extant at the MS65 and above level. The mintage of 1.2 million pieces is fairly small for a Morgan dollar. It is likely that hundreds of thousands of 1903-S dollars were melted under the 1918 Pittman Act. They were not given out in the 1962-1964 Treasury release in any large quantity. Prooflike coins are prohibitively rare so even the most discriminating collector will be glad to obtain a Premium Gem example of this date.

This breathtaking coin displays heather and gray toning over satiny, lustrous fields, and there are splashes of blue near the rims. The coin is well struck, with only a little softness on the eagle's feathers. The fields are free of distractions, with none visible to the unaided eye. Census: 8 in 66, 1 finer (7/08). (#7288)

2980 1904-O MS65 Deep Mirror Prooflike PCGS. A brilliant and flashy Gem that has a pleasing strike and only infrequent small marks. The 1904-O is common in Mint State, but deeply mirrored pieces are scarce. Housed in an old green label holder. (#97293)

Flashy MS63 1904-S Dollar

2981 1904-S MS63 NGC. A semikey issue in the Morgan dollar series, and the last S-mint Morgan of the "traditional" design, as the 1921 issues were a redesign. This silver-white coin is essentially devoid of color save for a tiny splash of lilac at 1:30 on the obverse rim. Plenty of luster emanates from both sides of this flashy piece, and the few small abrasions noted are grade-consistent. (#7294)

Lustrous Gem 1904-S Dollar

2982 1904-S MS65 PCGS. A rarity in properly graded Gem condition, as here, the 1904-S is also in heavy demand from date collectors of the popular Morgan dollar series. Generous cartwheel luster flows from both sides of this splendid silver-white example, and the few tiny contact marks are consistent with an MS65 grade. The reverse is rotated about 20 degrees clockwise with respect to the obverse. PCGS has certified only 11 pieces finer (9 in MS66, 2 in MS67) (8/08). (#7294)

2983 1921 MS66 ★ NGC. Shimmering white surfaces exhibit sharply struck design elements, including strong definition in the hair over Liberty's ear. A minuscule mark or two is noted over each side. Census: 5 in 66 ★, 0 finer (7/08). (#7296)

Lofty PR66 Cameo 1878 8 Tailfeathers Dollar

2984 **1921-S Morgan Dollar—Double Struck, Second Strike 90% Off Center—AU58 PCGS.** The first strike was normal, but the piece failed to fully eject from the dies, and was struck a second time 90% off center toward 6 o'clock. The second strike is at 6 o'clock relative to the first strike, but the top of the date is apparent, and its status as a 1921-S is confirmed by the minute mintmark and spade-shaped eagle's breast. No additional planchet was fed in between the two strikes. A satiny cream-gray silver dollar with a typical strike and a mere whisper of highpoint friction. Surprisingly lustrous for a near-Mint coin, no doubt due to the unusually strong mint frost usually found on 1921-S dollars.

2985 **1878 8TF PR66 Cameo NGC.** VAM-14.8. This sharply defined Premium Gem has a luminous portrait and wreath that provide noticeable contrast with the darkly reflective fields. A small roundish strikethrough near the E in E PLURIBUS UNUM, a tiny spot near the T in UNITED, and a nearly imperceptible graze near obverse star 2 provide identifiers for pedigree researchers. Minor roller marks near the chin are of Mint origin, on the planchet prior to the strike. A difficult proof subtype, since just 500 pieces were struck. A wonderful opportunity for the advanced specialist. Census: 8 in 66 Cameo, 5 finer (7/08). (#87311)

Charming Choice Proof 1880 Morgan

2986 **1880 PR64 PCGS.** Light honey-gold toning congregated near the borders of this needle-sharp near-Gem. The devices are nicely frosted, but the age of the old green label holder precludes a Cameo designation. Business strike 1880 silver dollars are commonplace in Mint State, but proofs are comparatively rare. (#7315)

2987 1881 PR62 PCGS. Richly toned over moderately hairlined surfaces. Both sides offer deep lavender-gray, silver, and green-gold shadings. The portrait is a trifle soft, but the eagle shows decisive detail. (#7316)

Attractive Superb Gem Cameo Proof
1881 Morgan Dollar

2988 1881 PR67 Cameo NGC. One of only 984 proofs struck this year. There were two sets of dies made but all known examples are from a single obverse (VAM-8) mated to two reverses. This example is the slightly more common variety with a wavy die scratch across the eagle's right leg.

The coin exhibits fully reflective fields in stark contrast to the frosty cameo devices. Proof Morgans are rarely found in such superb condition and Bowers estimates only 90 examples above PR65 for 1881. The bright, white fields are predictably free of contact marks. There are small areas of russet toning between Liberty's hair and the stars on the obverse and below the wreath on the reverse. Near-perfect surfaces, bright color, and outstanding contrast make this coin a collector's dream. Census: 11 in 67, 8 finer (7/08). (#87316)

2989 1882 PR62 PCGS. Dramatic violet, gold, and red toning covers the fields, which contrast sharply against the gunmetal-gray devices. This boldly impressed specimen is surprisingly clean for the grade, and has just a few insignificant hairlines and contact marks. One of a mere 1,100 proofs struck. (#7317)

PR63 Cameo 1882 Silver Dollar

2990 1882 PR63 Cameo NGC. This intricately struck Select proof Morgan dollar is unabraded aside from faint hairlines on the right obverse field. Light gold toning with infrequent tiny spots. The devices are pleasingly frosted and present noticeable cameo contrast against the reflectivity on each side. Census: 5 in 63, 66 finer (8/08). (#87317)

Attractive 1885 Morgan Dollar, PR64

2991 1885 PR64 PCGS. The proof mintage of 1885 Morgan dollars was 930 pieces, of which there are an estimated 300 survivors. A pleasing mid-1880s example of one of the most popular collector series today, this specimen displays a strong strike, though a bit of softness is noted in the central reverse. There are a couple of toning spots and contact marks, including a stray lint impression to the right of Liberty, but none is detracting. Both sides show light golden toning, with a few areas of darker rose and gray along the rims. PCGS has graded just 30 pieces finer (8/08). (#7320)

2992 1886 PR60 ANACS. Pearl-gray toning covers both sides of this highly reflective specimen. There are no prominent marks, although numerous hairlines are noted on both sides. This sharply struck example is one of 886 proofs struck. (#7321)

Wonderful 1887 Morgan, PR63

2993 1887 PR63 PCGS. A lovely Select proof, this dollar has a touch of cameo contrast beneath pale champagne toning. Hints of deep peripheral toning can be seen along the border on each side. This proof Morgan is an exceptional example for its modest certified grade, an ideal candidate for a type collector. (#7322)

Brilliant Choice Proof 1888 Dollar

2994 **1888 PR64 NGC.** This snow-white and nicely mirrored near-Gem is boldly struck aside from the usually-seen incompleteness on the hair above the ear. Although business strike 1888 dollars are plentiful, proofs are very scarce, since only 832 pieces were struck. Census: 51 in 64, 38 finer (7/08). (#7323)

Cameo Choice Proof 1891 Dollar

2995 **1891 PR64 Cameo PCGS.** The portrait, eagle, and wreath exhibit obvious contrast with the glassy fields, despite a light veneer of canary-gold toning. The strike is exemplary, the reverse is exquisitely preserved, and the obverse field has only a few faint hairlines. Population: 17 in 64 Cameo, 12 finer (8/08). (#87326)

Attractive 1893 Dollar, PR63 Cameo

2996 **1893 PR63 Cameo NGC.** From a proof mintage of 792 dollars, this piece shows a few light hairlines and contact marks in the fields that prevent a finer grade. There is still plenty of appeal, however, and the silver-white surfaces ringed with gold will make this piece an attractive acquisition. The reverse appears high-end for the assigned grade. Census: 6 in 63 Cameo, 33 finer (7/08). (#87328)

Splendid 1894 Dollar, PR62

2997 **1894 PR62 NGC.** Because of the rarity of 1894 business strikes, proofs of this year as especially popular. Only 110,000 business strikes were minted, along with just 972 proofs. Deep violet-gray patina surrounds the perimeter, which contrasts nicely against the steel-gray centers. The toning is a little streaky in some areas and partially obscures the luster, but there is still nice reflectivity under a light. The strike is sharp, and the surfaces are remarkably unabraded for the grade. Housed in an old NGC holder. (#7329)

Sharp PR66 Cameo 1896 Silver Dollar

2998 **1896 PR66 Cameo NGC.** A razor-sharp Premium Gem that boasts honey-gold toning and pleasing white-on-black contrast. A couple of trivial hairlines near the profile are nearly imperceptible. Separated a year from the famous proof-only 1895, but the proof mintage of the 1896 is actually lower at just 762 pieces. Census: 11 in 66 Cameo, 24 finer (7/08). (#87331)

Outstanding 1896 PR67 Cameo Dollar

2999 **1896 PR67 Cameo NGC.** Commenting on the 1896 proof dollars in his Morgan silver dollar *Guide Book* (2005, p. 227), David Bowers says: "Good strike. Deep cameo contrast. Some nice ones are around. Whew! Those nasty years of weak striking, beginning in 1888, are over!"

And over the weak strikes were, at least for the Superb Gem Cameo being offered in this lot! The design elements are well brought up, including sharp (though just a tad short of full) delineation in the hair over Liberty's ear. All of the eagle's plumage is bold, including that on the breast. Fantastic field-motif contrast is noted on both sides, as are impeccably preserved and essentially untoned surfaces. All in all, great technical quality and aesthetic eye appeal. Census: 18 in 67 Cameo, 6 finer (7/08). (#87331)

Luminous Select Proof 1897 Dollar

3000 **1897 PR63 PCGS.** A boldly struck and strongly mirrored Select proof, gold-orange near the margins and on the devices with glimmers of steel-blue in the fields. Light hairlines in the fields contribute to the grade. This issue of 731 pieces enjoys popularity with both type and date collectors. (#7332)

Pristine PR66 1897 Morgan Dollar

3001 **1897 PR66 ICG.** The reflective fields have a blush of golden and lavender on both sides, deepening a bit at the lower reverse, but there is little contrast against the devices, which are not deeply frosted. The extreme rims show a tinge of gold. Except for the lack of contrast, however, the surfaces are essentially untroubled, and show no obvious contact at all. From a proof emission of 731 coins. (#7332)

3002 **1898 PR67 Ultra Cameo NGC.** From a proof mintage of only 735 coins. Proof Morgan silver dollars minted in the years 1895-1898 are known for their high technical quality and beautiful appearance. The dollars of 1898 are particularly noteworthy in this respect. Most examples seen are boldly struck on high quality, polished planchets. It is evident that the engravers and diesinkers at the Mint had perfected the proof die production process to a high state of the art. Proofs of later years seldom show the deep cameo contrast that is characteristic of examples from this period. Michael Fuljenz states, "This date was probably the best made in the entire series."

While production values were at a peak in 1898, coin collecting in general was in the doldrums. The public was distracted by the dramatic events of the Spanish-American War and the Klondike gold rush. There were no new coin designs, and most people felt that existing designs were drab and uninspiring. In the November issue of *The Numismatist*, Dr. Heath indicated that the ANA had been in a state of "innocuous disquietude" since the autumn of 1896. Proof sets sold slowly in that environment. When proof dollars were offered individually at auction, they often sold at face value. Proof Trade dollars fared even worse. At the S.H. and H. Chapman sale of July 7, 1899, a run of proof Trade dollars from 1874-1883 sold for only 90 cents each. It is a testament to the few devoted numismatists of the period that a handful of the beautiful proof silver dollars from 1898 were preserved in their original splendor.

The 1895 proof dollar has often been called the "King" of the Morgan dollars because there are no known business strikes. The proof mintage of 880 coins has been under extreme pressure to meet collector demand for the 1895 since the circumstances of its production were first realized. It is worth noting that the proof dollars of 1898 have a smaller mintage and a lower survival rate than the 1895. David Bowers estimates that only 55-80 examples are extant at the PR67 level and above.

The present coin is a masterpiece of the minter's art. The strike is perfect, with every detail of the design elements fully brought up. The richly frosted devices contrast dramatically with the virtually flawless fields. The deeply mirrored surfaces produce a chromium effect, and the white-on-black contrast of the issue is a match for present-day proof coins. There is no detectable color on either side, save for the slightest tinge of gold near the extreme rims. Eye appeal is outstanding. A great prize for the collector of pre-modern proofs as well as the Morgan dollar specialist. Census: 16 in 67 Ultra Cameo, 2 finer (8/08). (#97333)

Amazing PR67 Cameo 1900 Morgan Dollar

3003 **1900 PR67 Cameo NGC.** The 1900 is a popular proof Morgan dollar issue among type collectors; in his *The Morgan and Peace Dollar Textbook*, Wayne Miller writes: "Not all proofs of this date are cameos, but deep mirror frosty cameos do exist, and are very beautiful." The sentence is apt, particularly when one examines the present Superb Gem. The strike is bold, the mirrors are deep, and the moderate frost on the devices supplies excellent (though not Ultra Cameo-level) contrast. Light golden overtones drape the surfaces, and small dots of deeper patina appear at the margins. Census: 13 in 67 Cameo, 7 finer (7/08). (#87335)

Brilliant PR64 1901 Morgan Dollar

3004 **1901 PR64 NGC. CAC.** This stone-white near-Gem has an exacting strike and only a few trivial field hairlines. DOLLAR is lightly die doubled, diagnostic for proofs of this date. The rarity of the 1901 in Mint State adds to the demand for quality proofs as a substitute. Only 813 proofs were issued. (#7336)

Scarce Choice Proof 1901 Morgan

3005 **1901 PR64 PCGS.** Delicate gold toning visits this undisturbed near-Gem. The strike is exacting save for slight blending above Liberty's ear. ONE DOLLAR is minutely die doubled, diagnostic for proofs of this better date. Only 813 proofs were struck. Population: 74 in 64, 28 finer (8/08). (#7336)

Appealing Gem Proof 1901 Morgan Dollar

3006 **1901 PR65 NGC.** A hint of gold patina confirms the originality of this beautifully preserved and nicely struck Gem. Dashes of cherry-red are limited to the lower right obverse periphery. As on all proofs seen, DOLLAR has minor die doubling. Census: 38 in 65, 38 finer (7/08). (#7336)

Brilliant 1903 Morgan Dollar, PR64

3007 **1903 PR64 PCGS.** This Choice proof example has fully brilliant silver surfaces with no trace of toning on either side. A few faint hairlines and other tiny imperfections are all that keep it from the Gem grade level. Just 755 proof dollars were coined in 1903, and most of those that survive today are in similar grade to this one. (#7338)

3008 **1904 PR62 PCGS.** Patches of hazel and cobalt-blue grace the mostly silver-gray surfaces. Scattered hairlines limit the grade but barely affect the impressive watery reflectivity of the fields. Boldly struck with great eye appeal. One of only 650 proofs struck. (#7339)

The Childs Collection 1904 Gem Proof Morgan Dollar

3009 **1904 PR65 PCGS.** Ex: Childs Collection. This is a splendid Gem Morgan dollar proof with iridescent ice-blue and gold patina on both sides, with complementing shades of mint-green and violet. Of course the Walter H. Childs Collection is one of the most famous in U.S. numismatics, chiefly for its 1804 Original or Class I silver dollar graded PR68 by PCGS.

From a low mintage of only 650 proofs for the year, this is one of 29 PR65 coins so graded at PCGS, with 18 finer (8/08). The cataloger in the Bowers and Merena sale noted that Walter H. Childs was believed to have purchased it directly from the Mint. *Ex: Walter H. Childs Collection (Bowers and Merena, 8/1999), lot 520.* (#7339)

PEACE DOLLARS

3010 **1921 MS64 NGC.** Fully brilliant with magnificent satiny luster. The surfaces are remarkably clean for the grade with only a few minor luster grazes. A boldly impressed and attractive example of this popular issue. (#7356)

3011 **1921 MS64 NGC.** Very well struck, except for typical flatness over the centers, with appealing satin luster and creamy mint-green and rose coloration intermingled with ivory toning. This was the first year of the Peace dollar series, which would only continue through 1935. (#7356)

3012 **1921 MS64 NGC.** Vibrant luster and light gold toning ensure the originality of this attractively preserved near-Gem. The hair over the ear has above average detail for the date, although the definition is incomplete. (#7356)

3013 **1921 MS65 NGC.** Champagne-gold and pastel blue-gray patina rests on the highly lustrous surfaces of this attractive Gem Peace dollar. The central obverse reveals the usual weak strike. (#7356)

3014 **1921 MS65 NGC.** Lustrous surfaces display a veneer of light champagne color on the obverse, and medium gray patination on the reverse. Typical design softness shows in the obverse center. A few grade-consistent marks do not detract. (#7356)

3015 **1921 MS65 PCGS.** The strike is unexpectedly crisp on this lustrous and delicately toned Gem. Wisps of honey toning deny full brilliance. Carefully preserved, and a worthwhile representative of this introductory issue. (#7356)

3016 **1921 MS65 PCGS.** VAM-3. A Top 50 Variety. Although undesignated on the holder, this is the famous 'Line Through L' variety, which features a re-engraved ray through the first L in DOLLAR. Rich autumn-gold and steel-blue toning embraces satiny and smooth surfaces. (#7356)

3017 **1921 MS65 NGC.** A popular, first-year Peace dollar, struck in high relief as Anthony de Francisci's gorgeous design was meant to appear. A pleasing layer of frost covers on each side, and there is just a trace of violet toning near the rims. Flashy luster enhances the outstanding eye appeal. (#7356)

3018 **1921 MS65 NGC.** This is an absolutely gorgeous first-year Gem Peace dollar. An original coating of champagne-tan coloration covers each side, and surface blemishes are minimal. The striking details are exceptional. (#7356)

3019 **1921 MS65 PCGS.** Lovely rose-gold toning overlies each side of this wonderful high relief Peace dollar. A couple of scattered abrasions and a little weakness on the hair is noted on this appealing Gem. Frosty luster shimmers beneath the pleasing toning. An attractive first year of issue. (#7356)

3020 **1921 MS65 NGC.** A hint of gold toning graces lustrous and splendidly smooth surfaces. As usual for this high relief issue, the hair over the ear is incompletely brought up. A desirable first year Gem. (#7356)

Vivid 1921 Peace Dollar, Premium Gem

3021 **1921 MS66 NGC.** A razor-sharp Premium Gem with vivid russet, violet, and gold toning on both sides, which appears mottled on the reverse. The surfaces seem pristine to the unaided eye, and only a few tiny handling marks are visible under magnification. Dazzling satiny luster gives this piece wonderful eye appeal. A popular first-year issue. (#7356)

Outstanding Premium Gem 1921 Peace Dollar

3022 **1921 MS66 NGC.** The 1921 Peace dollar is a conditionally scarce issue at the Premium Gem grade level, and it is rare any finer. Currently, just 236 pieces (from an original mintage of 1,006,473 coins) are graded at MS66 by NGC and PCGS combined, and only 12 pieces are certified as MS67 (with none finer) by the two companies (8/08). The current example is a splendid representative with untoned surfaces and shimmering, satin luster. It is well struck and minimally abraded, with just a couple of trivial marks on each side. (#7356)

3023 **1921 Peace, Ray Through L MS65 NGC.** VAM-3. A Top 50 Variety. This seldom seen VAM variety is significant because the ray through the first L in DOLLAR has been hand-engraved on the working die, such that the ray passes *over* rather than under the letter. A number of tiny die lines are visible around the adjacent rays. Honey, sky-blue, and charcoal colors visit this lustrous and minimally marked Gem. The hair is a trifle weak, but the rest of the details are fully struck. NGC VAM-3 Census: 2 in 65, one finer (7/08). (#133734)

3024 **1922 MS66 PCGS.** The surfaces of this resplendent Premium Gem appear remarkably pristine to the unaided eye. Several tiny russet toning spots are noted on the mostly brilliant reverse. Boldly struck with appealing satiny luster. (#7357)

3025 **1922 MS66 PCGS.** Crisply struck with subtle frostiness across the high points of the eagle. Amazing visual appeal, even by Premium Gem standards, thanks to the vibrantly lustrous, minimally toned surfaces. PCGS has graded 20 finer pieces (8/08). *From The Bell Collection.* (#7357)

3026 **1922-D MS64 PCGS.** Streaks of pale gray and silver color intermingle on the obverse, but both sides are untoned. Pleasing satiny luster graces both sides and complements the bold details. (#7358)

3027 **1922-D MS64 PCGS.** Whispers of light gray adhere to the lustrous surfaces of this near-Gem. Generally well struck, and revealing a few minute marks that prevent Gem status. (#7358)

3028 **1922-D MS66 NGC.** A stunning, brilliant, and entirely white Premium Gem. The resplendent surfaces appear watery as impressive luster shimmers in the light. Speckled deep purple around the rims accents the untoned centers. An outstanding and minimally marked example. (#7358)

Exceptional Premium Gem 1922-D Peace Dollar

3029 **1922-D MS66 NGC.** Sharply struck and mostly untoned, except for a light layer of milkiness over each side. Peace dollars from any year are rarely seen with full, or nearly full striking definition on all of the design elements, but this Premium Gem is an exception. Lustrous and well preserved, save for a couple of small milling marks on the eagle's back and tail feathers. (#7358)

3030 **1922-S MS64 NGC.** Generous luster and silver-white rims complement a swath of light gold coloration in the center of each side. An available issue in MS64, but much more elusive only one grade point finer. (#7359)

3031 **1922-S MS65 PCGS.** Faint almond-gold toning enriches this highly lustrous and suitably struck Gem. A few wispy grazes are of little import. PCGS has certified just six pieces finer (8/08). (#7359)

3032 **1922-S MS65 NGC.** Delicate olive-gold and sky-blue toning graces this nicely impressed Gem. Luster sweeps the smooth surfaces, and the eye appeal is attractive. (#7359)

3033 **1923 MS66 PCGS. CAC.** Spectacular satiny luster shimmers across the surfaces of this gorgeous white-toned specimen. A couple of minuscule marks on the obverse barely affect the impressive, lightly frosted luster. A die crack is noted from Liberty's hair bun to the Y in LIBERTY. This crisply struck Premium Gem representative is housed in a green label PCGS holder. (#7360)

3034 **1923 MS66 NGC. CAC.** Captivating satiny luster radiates from the fields and highlights the sharply defined details. Several inconsequential marks keep this Premium Gem from an even higher grade. A pronounced die crack runs from the truncation of the bust to the ends of Liberty's hair, and a smaller one connects the hair bun to the Y in LIBERTY. NGC has certified 49 pieces finer (7/08). (#7360)

3035 **1923 MS66 PCGS.** Gold, reddish-brown, and medium gray toning appears at the periphery of this highly lustrous specimen. Well struck with a few light ticks on the devices that have only minor impact on the eye appeal. A captivating type issue that has an original mintage above 30 million pieces. (#7360)

3036 **1923 MS66 NGC. CAC.** VAM-1a. A thick die break resides at the juncture of Liberty's neck and jawline. A pretty Premium Gem with great cartwheel luster and a pleasing yellow-golden cast on each side. A few brief marks are too minor to disturb the coin's considerable eye appeal. (#7360)

3037 **1923-D MS65 PCGS.** An exactingly struck Gem that boasts potent luster and only a hint of caramel-gold toning. The occasional minor graze is all that limits the grade. The cheek is particularly smooth. (#7361)

3038 **1923-D MS65 NGC.** Delicate chestnut-gold toning visits this thoroughly lustrous and nicely struck Gem. The portrait is particularly free from marks. Common in typical Mint State grades, but scarce in the present quality. (#7361)

3039 **1924 MS62 PCGS.** VAM-2. A Top 50 Variety. Doubled Reverse. Fully brilliant with impressive cartwheel luster throughout. Scattered abrasions are noted on each side, but the surfaces seen exceptionally clean for the MS62 grade. (#7363)

3040 **1924 MS65 PCGS.** Faint olive-gold toning visits this lustrous, powerfully struck, and lightly abraded Gem. Struck from moderately rotated dies, and housed in a green label holder. (#7363)

3041 **1924 MS66 PCGS.** Light olive-gray patina rests on the lustrous surfaces of this Premium Gem. Nicely struck, with just a few light ticks. (#7363)

3042 **1924 MS66 NGC.** VAM-2. A Top 50 Variety. The eagle's back and rear feathers show pronounced doubling. Entirely brilliant and lustrous, this Premium Gem has only a couple of microscopic abrasions. Sharply struck with delightful eye appeal. (#133765)

3043 **1924-S MS64 NGC.** White and untoned, this highly lustrous piece has only inconsequential bagmarks. A sharply struck example with outstanding eye appeal. NGC has certified 63 pieces finer (7/08). (#7364)

3044 **1924-S MS64 PCGS.** Patches of light hazel toning accent the mostly silver-gray surfaces of this near-Gem representative. Several minor abrasions limit the grade, but none merit specific mention. Captivating satiny luster shimmers across both sides and gives this piece great eye appeal. (#7364)

Conditionally Scarce 1924-S Dollar, Gem Mint State

3045 **1924-S MS65 NGC.** Powerful satiny luster graces the surfaces of this sharply struck representative. Pale yellow toning covers the obverse, while the reverse has a spotted milky-orange and russet complexion. Scattered grazes define the grade, but none merit individual mention. The 1924-S is difficult to locate Gem, and is virtually impossible to find in a higher grade. Census: 62 in 65, 1 finer (7/08). (#7364)

Amazing 1924-S Peace Dollar, MS65

3046 **1924-S MS65 PCGS.** The relatively low mintage (1.728 million pieces) and, according to David Bowers in his *Silver Dollars and Trade Dollars of the United States*, "... the relative unavailability of mint-sealed bags combine to make this one of the scarcest issues of the early part of the Peace dollar series ..." In full Gem condition, a little more than 120 examples have been certified by PCGS and NGC combined, and just six pieces grade finer.

The Gem we offer in this lot displays dazzling luster, and just a whisper of light tan color on the Liberty and the eagle motifs. The design elements are fairly well impressed, including on the reverse, which is often weak. A few minute marks on the central devices do not distract. Population: 68 in 65, 5 finer (7/08). (#7364)

3047 **1925 MS64 PCGS.** VAM-5. A Top 50 Variety. The 'Missing Ray' VAM. The reverse die was lapped at the Philadelphia Mint to remove clashmarks, and the ray northeast of the leg feathers was inadvertently scrubbed completely from the die. Deeply toned in lilac, autumn-brown, and sea-green. A horizontal mark is noted on the eagle above DOLLAR.

3048 **1925 MS66 NGC. CAC.** A spectacular Premium Gem example with a light milky toning across the satiny surfaces. The strike is razor-sharp, and a few minor marks in the fields do not detract from the impressive eye appeal. (#7365)

3049 **1925 MS66 NGC. CAC.** This sharply struck and minutely abraded example would make an excellent type coin. Spectacular satiny luster radiates from both sides of this cream-colored Premium Gem. Mostly brilliant save for a couple of minor milk spots. (#7365)

Impeccable 1925 Dollar, Superb Gem

3050 **1925 MS67 NGC.** Flashy luster radiates from both sides of this untoned and impeccably preserved specimen. Several minor marks on Liberty's neck and the eagle's wings limit the grade, but do not detract from the flow of the incredible satiny luster. A tiny spot above the 2 in the date is noted for future identification purposes. NGC has certified just one piece finer (7/08). (#7365)

Incredible MS67 1925 Peace Dollar

3051 **1925 MS67 NGC.** Peace dollars of any stripe are elusive in Superb Gem condition. A quick look at the NGC and PCGS population data show that in percentage terms, only about one-tenth as many Peace dollars as Morgans are certified MS67 at each service. This incredible coin has frosty silver-white, fine-grained, mattelike surfaces on both sides, with radiant cartwheel luster and enormous eye appeal. Thorough perusal with a loupe locates only the most picayune evidence of contact, along with a few wispy obverse die cracks. Census: 43 in 67, 1 finer (7/08). (#7365)

3052 **1925-S MS64 NGC.** A delightfully lustrous and essentially brilliant piece save for a thin grease stain on the reverse. Scattered reeding marks keep this powerfully detailed representative from a Gem designation. This issue is seldom seen finer than the present piece. (#7366)

3053 **1925-S MS64 NGC.** A light coating of kelly-green and coral patina blankets each side of this attractive near-Gem. Vibrantly lustrous, with a few field abrasions that keep it from a higher grade. (#7366)

3054 **1925-S MS64 NGC.** Lustrous silver-gray surfaces display hints of light gold on the obverse. Nicely defined, save for minor softness in the centers. Some minute marks define the grade. (#7366)

3055 **1925-S MS64 PCGS.** Though slight striking softness affects the portrait, the overall eye appeal of this slightly frosty near-Gem is grand. Minimally toned and delightful. (#7366)

3056 **1925-S MS64 PCGS.** Pale gold toning subdues the satiny silver luster of this near-Gem. Although typically weak at the center, it is better struck than many of the date. (#7366)

3057 **1925-S MS64 NGC.** VAM-3. A Top 50 Variety. The VAM is undesignated on the NGC insert, but confirmation of the obverse diagnostics at vamworld.com confirms the variety. This is the 'Doubled Wing' variety, undoubtedly scarce in better Mint State grades. Lustrous with sun-gold toning and a few faint field grazes. Well struck at the borders, with minor blending at the centers. (#7366)

Vibrant 1925-S Gem Dollar

3058 **1925-S MS65 NGC.** The 1925-S is surprisingly rare in MS65 grade. Indeed, David Bowers, in his *Silver Dollars and Trade Dollars of the U.S.*, writes: "It and the 1928-S are the two toughest varieties to find in this grade (MS65) in the entire Peace dollar series."

The present Gem displays a trace of light gold color on the right reverse, along with vibrant luster throughout. The design elements are sharply struck, and the surfaces are generally well preserved. Just a few tiny, unobtrusive marks are noted on Liberty's jaw and on the eagle. Census: 55 in 65, 0 finer (7/08). (#7366)

3059 **1926 MS65 PCGS.** Delicate honey-gold toning enriches this lustrous and sharply struck Gem. Well preserved overall, although a few small marks are present on the wing. In a green label holder. *Ex: September Long Beach Signature (Heritage, 9/2004), lot 8987.* (#7367)

3060 **1926-D MS65 PCGS.** Apricot-gold, olive, and steel-blue intermingle on this lustrous and impressively clean Gem. The details are razor-sharp save for some incompleteness on the E in LIBERTY. A common coin in an uncommon grade. (#7368)

3061 **1926-D MS65 PCGS.** Blushes of pale chestnut toning are most evident on the lower reverse. A lustrous and needle-sharp Gem with exceptionally unabraded surfaces. (#7368)

3062 **1926-D MS65 NGC.** The centers are needle-sharp, while the peripheries show a band of incompleteness due to convex dies. Pastel lemon, olive, and sky-blue enrich this lustrous Gem. Struck from moderately rotated dies. (#7368)

3063 **1926-D MS65 NGC.** This boldly struck Gem has light gold toning most apparent on the left obverse field. The fields are beautifully preserved, and the cheek has only unobtrusive grazes. The dies are lightly rotated. (#7368)

3064 **1926-S MS63 PCGS.** Clean-cheeked and lustrous with pleasing golden-brown and forest-green obverse toning. (#7369)

Pleasing Gem 1926-S Dollar

3065 **1926-S MS65 NGC.** Light honey toning adorns this thoroughly lustrous Gem. The strike is surprisingly bold, and the absence of mentionable marks confirms its designated grade. A relatively high mintage issue, yet difficult to locate in such quality. Housed in a former generation holder. (#7369)

3066 **1926-S MS65 NGC.** Light gold and sky-blue toning visits the mostly brilliant surfaces of this boldly struck piece. Several trivial abrasions define the grade, but they do not affect the flow of the eye-catching luster. NGC has certified only 37 example finer (8/08). (#7369)

3067 **1926-S MS65 NGC.** This pleasing Gem has light gold toning and dynamic cartwheel luster. Exactingly struck and refreshingly smooth. Only the most competitive specialist will feel the need to upgrade this splendid representative. (#7369)

Beautiful 1927 Peace Dollar, MS65

3068 **1927 MS65 PCGS.** A satiny Gem with impressive, untoned silver surfaces. Both sides are exquisitely detailed. A great condition rarity in higher grades, as PCGS has only certified five finer examples. The 1927 is one of those elusive issues that was completely underrated until recent times. (#7370)

Attractive Gem 1927-D Dollar

3069 **1927-D MS65 PCGS. CAC.** Lustrous and untoned with an exemplary strike and pleasing preservation. The designer's monogram is die doubled. At 1,268,900 pieces, a low mintage issue, although its 1927 and 1927-S counterparts each failed to reach 900,000 pieces. Certified in an old green label holder. PCGS has certified a mere nine pieces finer (8/08). (#7371)

Lightly Toned 1927-D Gem Dollar

3070 **1927-D MS65 PCGS.** The 1927-D is the rarest Denver Mint Peace dollar in Mint State (David Bowers, 2006). Lustrous tan-gray surfaces of this Gem display well struck design elements. A few minute marks may well preclude an even higher grade. PCGS has seen only nine coins finer (8/08). (#7371)

3071 **1927-S MS64 PCGS.** Mostly brilliant, this attractive piece has hints of lemon and gold color on each side, with a deeper layer of milky frost that covers the surfaces. Flashy luster enhances the eye appeal of this boldly struck example. The 1927-S has the third lowest mintage of the series with just 866,000 coins struck. (#7372)

3072 **1927-S MS64 PCGS.** This low mintage Peace dollar possesses delicate gold toning and unencumbered satin sheen. The strike is precise, better than typically seen for the issue. Well preserved for the grade designation. (#7372)

3073 **1927-S MS64 NGC.** Primarily silver-gray centers yield to rose, violet, and tan tints at the margins. Well struck with only a few small digs on the cheek that preclude Gem status. (#7372)

3074 **1927-S MS64 PCGS.** VAM-3. A Top 50 Variety. The VAM is unlisted on the insert, but the die doubling on the leaves, in addition to the mintmark location, confirm the variety. Medium tan-gold toning enriches the lower obverse and central reverse. Well struck, lustrous, and clean-cheeked. (#7372)

Conditionally Scarce 1927-S Dollar, Gem Uncirculated

3075 **1927-S MS65 NGC.** The 1927-S has the third lowest mintage in the Peace dollar series with only 866,000 pieces struck. It is also a significant condition rarity that is infrequently offered in Gem condition and is virtually impossible to locate any finer. This sharply struck example has smooth surfaces with flashy mint luster and no mentionable abrasions on either side. Census: 69 in 65, 1 finer (8/08). (#7372)

3076 **1928 MS63 PCGS.** A solidly struck, surprisingly flashy example of this popular lower-mintage Peace dollar issue. Splashes of milky toning dot otherwise silver-white surfaces, which show faint, scattered abrasions and reed marks. (#7373)

3077 **1928 MS63 PCGS.** A minimally toned and attractive Select example of this popular key-date Peace dollar issue. If not for a handful of reed marks on the cheek, this piece could lay claim to Choice or better status. (#7373)

3078 **1928 MS64 NGC.** Solidly detailed and shining with the beginnings of golden toning close to the margins. Only a handful of small, stray marks affect the central devices. (#7373)

Remarkable Key-Date 1928 Dollar, MS65

3079 **1928 MS65 PCGS.** Wafts of lavender, russet, and gold accent the mostly silver-gray surfaces of this carefully preserved Gem. The strike is sharp, and there are no mentionable marks. Pleasing cartwheel luster gives this piece excellent eye appeal. With the lowest mintage in the series (just 360,649 pieces), the 1928 is easily one of the key dates. PCGS reports only 11 pieces finer (8/08). (#7373)

Gleaming Gem 1928 Peace Dollar

3080 1928 MS65 PCGS. The 1928 Peace dollar, long recognized as a key for the series, is generally available for a price in grades through MS64, though Gems are elusive, and anything finer is a rarity. This MS65 piece is well struck with dappled blue-green and gold field toning around a silver-white center on the obverse, and similar, more even coloration prevails on the pleasingly preserved reverse. (#7373)

Lightly Toned 1928 Peace Dollar, MS65

3081 1928 MS65 PCGS. A wonderful Gem with exceptional satin luster beneath faint champagne toning, a bit more intense on the reverse. The 1928 is considered a key-date in the Peace dollar series from a mintage of only about 360,000 coins. Quite a number of Gems have been certified, but PCGS has only graded 11 finer pieces. (#7373)

3082 1928-S MS64 PCGS. Bright luster exudes from both sides, each of which displays speckles of light gold-tan color, which is a tad deeper in hue on the obverse. Typical softness in the centers, especially on the reverse. Minuscule marks define the grade. (#7374)

3083 1928-S MS64 PCGS. An attractive near-Gem example of this scarce, semi-key Peace dollar. Sharply struck with the obverse mostly brilliant, while the reverse is subtly orange-toned. (#7374)

3084 1928-S MS64 NGC. Gold, orange, crimson, and silver-gray shadings drape the highly lustrous surfaces in varying measures. Well struck and elusive any finer, with just 39 numerically superior pieces known to NGC (8/08). (#7374)

3085 1928-S MS64 NGC. Although common in circulated grades, the 1928-S is one of the scarcest Peace dollars in Mint State. NGC reports only 39 pieces finer (7/08), and a glance at the *Guide Book* shows just how valuable this piece would be only one numerical grade higher. Patches of hazel toning accent the mostly brilliant surfaces. A sharply struck piece with sparkling cartwheel luster. (#7374)

3086 1928-S MS64 PCGS. Essentially brilliant, except for faint champagne toning over part of the obverse. Sharply struck with frosty silver surfaces. (#7374)

3087 1928-S MS64 PCGS. An important frosty near-Gem, rarely seen any finer. In fact, PCGS has only certified 47 higher grade examples. Both sides are brilliant, bold, and beautiful. (#7374)

3088 1928-S MS64 NGC. Impressively lustrous with hints of golden toning in parts of the otherwise silver-white fields. The strike is crisp, and the eye appeal is strong. This challenging issue is a condition rarity any finer. (#7374)

3089 1934 MS65 NGC. This lovely Gem from the next-to-last year of the Peace dollar series features splendid luster and warm patination in shades of amber and gold, somewhat more intense on the reverse than the obverse. NGC has certified only 29 examples finer (8/08). (#7375)

3090 1934 MS65 NGC. Although the reverse is essentially brilliant, the obverse displays caramel-gold patina. This decisively struck Gem has dazzling luster and exceptional preservation. (#7375)

3091 1934 MS65 NGC. Booming luster, a crisp strike, and exquisitely preserved surfaces confirm the quality of this low mintage Gem. The obverse has medium apricot toning with a blush of ice-blue on the cheek. (#7375)

Magnificent 1934 Dollar, Premium Gem

3092 1934 MS66 PCGS. The 1934 is scarce in Premium Gem and virtually impossible to locate in a higher grade. Creamy surfaces are accented by pale rose toning in the fields, which complements the sharp strike and delightful cartwheel luster. A loupe locates a couple of nearly imperceptible marks. PCGS has certified just three examples finer (7/08). (#7375)

3093 1934-D MS65 NGC. Medium D. VAM-3. A Top 50 Variety. Liberty's profile and GOD WE exhibit strong die doubling. The variety is undesignated on the NGC insert, but is unmistakable. A crisply struck Gem with vibrant luster and infrequent wisps of gold toning. (#7376)

3094 **1934-S AU58 PCGS.** Only trifling softness and a hint of friction affect the high points of this near-Mint beauty. Essentially silver-white surfaces offer vibrant luster and striking eye appeal. (#7377)

3095 **1934-S MS62 NGC.** Stone-gray and straw-gold blend throughout this precisely struck key date dollar. The surfaces lack noticeable marks, and although the luster is unremarkable, the grade appears conservatively assessed. (#7377)

Pleasing 1934-S Peace Dollar, MS63

3096 **1934-S MS63 PCGS.** A lustrous example of the key 1934-S Peace dollar, with brilliant silver luster and splashes of gold and iridescent toning on the obverse, pale champagne on the reverse. The strike is generally strong, with only slight weakness on Liberty's hair and the eagle's body. (#7377)

Marvelous 1934-S Dollar, MS64

3097 **1934-S MS64 PCGS.** A brilliant and highly lustrous near-Gem representative. While the strike is a trifle soft on Liberty's hair, as usually seen, the remaining details are boldly impressed. The fields appear remarkable clean for the grade and a careful inspection reveals only minor marks on the devices. An appealing example of this late Peace dollar issue. (#7377)

Brilliant Gem 1934-S Dollar, Light Champagne Toning

3098 **1934-S MS65 PCGS.** The 1934-S Peace dollar is from a mintage of only 1.01 million coins, and few have survived in the highest grades. This sharp Gem has satiny silver luster with gorgeous light champagne toning on both sides. Only 23 finer pieces have crossed the PCGS grading desk. (#7377)

3099 **1935 MS65 NGC.** A crisply struck and thoroughly lustrous Gem that has exemplary preservation along with a hint of gold toning. The final Philadelphia issue, which has a low mintage. (#7378)

3100 **1935-S MS65 NGC.** Three rays beneath ONE, which are minutely die doubled. A lustrous Gem that exhibits gorgeously smooth fields and a penetrating strike. The cheekbone has a moderate reeding mark, but the preservation is otherwise outstanding. (#7379)

PROOF EISENHOWER DOLLAR

Magnificent 1977-S Eisenhower Dollar, PR70 Deep Cameo

3101 **1977-S PR70 Deep Cameo PCGS.** An outstanding, technically perfect 1977-S Eisenhower dollar. The deeply mirrored fields show exciting cameo contrast against the icy-frosted devices. This eye-catching specimen showcases the pre-Bicentennial reverse and is the penultimate issue in the series. PCGS has certified only 13 pieces at the PR70 Deep Cameo level (8/08). (#97437)

Popular Superb Gem 2000-P 'Cheerios' Dollar

3102 2000-P Cheerios MS67 PCGS. FS-901, though listed as FS-401 on the holder. This is one of the 5,500 2000-P Sacagawea dollars randomly placed inside Cheerios-brand cereal products during a 2000 General Mills advertising promotion. The 5,500 coins were struck with a reverse die produced from a different hub than that used for the regular issue Sacs. The "Cheerios" variety coins show greater definition on the eagle's tail feathers, and the line on the central tail feather is raised, whereas it is incuse on the regular issue coins (Paul Gilkes, " 'Cheerios' 2000-P Dollars Have Different Reverse," *Coin World*, July 4, 2005).

This Superb Gem displays gorgeous brass-gold surfaces and radiant luster. A well executed strike imparts bold definition to the design elements, and both faces are virtually flawless. A small as-made indentation is visible in the right obverse field.

This lot also includes a **2000 Cheerios Lincoln Cent, MS66 Red PCGS,** that was part of the same promotion. Both sides exhibit copper-gold luster and razor-sharp motifs. A few minor spots at the margins do not unduly detract from the pleasing eye appeal. (Total: 2 coins) (#147231)

3103 2000-P Goodacre MS68 PCGS. One of 5,000 "golden dollars" paid to sculptor Glenna Goodacre in compensation for designing the obverse of the Sacagawea dollar. These pieces had a special finish and are entirely prooflike with no cameo contrast. Fully struck and virtually pristine. An ICG label, included, indicates that this was number 2,665 out of 5,000 examples certified. (#99584)

PROOF SACAGAWEA DOLLAR

3104 2000-S Sacagawea PR70 Deep Cameo PCGS. A technically perfect example of the first year of Sacagawea dollars. Powerfully impressed with spectacular deeply mirrored fields and incredible cameo contrast. An outstanding specimen in all regards. (#99598)

End of Session Four

SESSION FIVE

Live, Internet, and Mail Bid Signature® Auction #1116
Friday, September 19, 2008, 3:00 PM PT, Lots 3105 - 3422
Long Beach, California

A 15% Buyer's Premium ($9 minimum) Will Be Added To All Lots

Visit HA.com to view full-color images and bid.

GOLD DOLLARS

3105 **1849 Closed Wreath MS62 NGC.** Large Head, With L. A bright lemon-gold example from the first year of the denomination. A vertical strike-through (as made) on the neck merits mention, although it blends in well with the design. (#7503)

Choice AU 1849-C Closed Wreath Gold Dollar

3106 **1849-C Closed Wreath AU55 NGC.** Variety 2-B. The only collectible variety for this first year Charlotte issue. The straw-gold surfaces have plenty of luster, and study beneath a loupe can find only a few minor field marks. A crisply struck example that has light wear on the hair curls. (#7505)

3107 **1849-D—Bent—NCS. AU Details.** Variety 1-A. Distributed tiny digs affect this shimmering and glossy tan-gold example. A slightly wavy representative of the only Open Wreath Dahlonega gold dollar issue. (#7507)

Pleasing 1849-D Gold Dollar, AU55

3108 **1849-D AU55 NGC.** Variety 1-A. The more available of two varieties for the issue, with the mintmark shifted to the left compared to 1-B. Bright yellow-gold surfaces display hints of light tan. The design elements are generally well defined, except for the usual softness on the curls below LIBERTY. Both sides are devoid of significant marks. (#7507)

Borderline Uncirculated 1849-D Dollar

3109 **1849-D AU58 PCGS.** Variety 1-A. A crisply struck slider that has just a trace of wear on the hair above the ear. The smooth surfaces display original orange-gold toning. Very similar in appearance to an MS62, but for less than half the cost. The sole Dahlonega issue of the Open Wreath subtype. Population: 40 in 58, 45 finer (8/08). (#7507)

Scarce 1849-D Gold Dollar, MS62

3110 **1849-D MS62 NGC.** Variety 1-B. The mintmark is centered below the bow, which identifies this scarce variety. Charming yellow-gold patina endows the surfaces, which exhibit pleasing luster throughout. Liberty's hair is a trifle soft, but the rest of the details are boldly defined. An attractive example of this elusive variety. Census: 33 in 62, 25 finer (8/08). (#7507)

3111 **1850 MS63 PCGS.** An attractive example of the second gold dollar issue. Despite a relatively high mintage, Garrett and Guth (2006) write that the 1850 is much scarcer in high grades than other P-mint Type One gold dollars. The present piece has splendid yellow-gold patina and lots of luster. The centers show minor weakness, but the surfaces are remarkably clean. Population: 41 in 63, 45 finer (8/08). (#7509)

3112 **1850 MS64 PCGS.** Although nearly 500,000 pieces were minted, the 1850 is scarcer in high grades compared to other P-mint Type One gold dollars. Enchanting yellow-gold patina coats the surfaces, which exhibit tremendous, flashy luster throughout. There is some softness on the upper left quadrant of the obverse, but the bust is unaffected by the weak areas. A die crack bisects the reverse from the T in UNITED to the final A in AMERICA. (#7509)

3113 **1850-C—Whizzed—NCS. AU Details.** Variety 3-C. Little actual wear is present on the devices, though a past whizzing has created unnatural lemon-gold luster. Close inspection reveals a degree of porosity. Still, a collectible representative of this lower-mintage Charlotte gold dollar variety. (#7510)

Bold 1850-C Gold Dollar AU53

3114 **1850-C AU53 PCGS.** Variety 3-C, the usual dies for this rare low mintage issue. An intricately struck Charlotte gold dollar that has rich butter-gold toning. A faded thin mark above UNITED is distant from the focal points. A mere 6,966 pieces were struck. Population: 6 in 53, 31 finer (8/08). (#7510)

1850-C Gold Dollar, Uncirculated Details

3115 **1850-C—Cleaned—ICG. MS60 Details.** Variety 3-C. This sharply struck Charlotte gold dollar has light lime and orange toning. Parallel hairlines are present but nearly imperceptible. A minor mark on the cheek and another on the jaw, but surprisingly free from other contact. A stingy 6,966 pieces were produced. (#7510)

3116 **1850-O AU58 NGC.** The 1850-O is a scarce issue from a mintage of only 14,000 coins, and it is especially elusive in higher grades. Well struck with frosty yellow luster and faint traces of green patina. Just one variety is known with a small, round O mintmark that is slightly left of center between the ribbon ends. (#7512)

Low Mintage 1850-O Gold Dollar MS61

3117 **1850-O MS61 NGC.** All of the O-mint Type One gold dollars have plentiful mintages, with one exception. The 1850-O has a meager production of 14,000 pieces, perhaps because Seated dollars were also struck at New Orleans that year. This is a well struck and satiny example with original khaki-gold toning. Faint vertical marks near the profile limit the grade, but are difficult to see with the unaided eye. Census: 36 in 61, 30 finer (7/08). (#7512)

3118 **1851 MS64 PCGS.** A lustrous peach-gold near-Gem. Beautifully unabraded, and crisply struck save for minor incompleteness on the hair above the ear. Housed in a green label holder. (#7513)

3119 **1851-C AU55 ANACS.** Variety 4-D. A well struck Charlotte type coin that has plentiful luster and little indication of highpoint wear. Surprisingly unabraded, although careful rotation locates a few faint reverse hairlines. (#7514)

Well Struck 1851-C Gold Dollar AU58, Variety 4-D

3120 **1851-C AU58 NGC. CAC.** Variety 4-D. The reverse date has the bases of the 1's below the leaf tips, the stars are recut, and clashmarks from the head are visible within the wreath, all of which confirm the variety. Yellow-gold surfaces display ample luster, and are minimally marked. Nice detail is seen on the design elements, including those of the reverse, that are often weak. (#7514)

3121 **1851-C—Improperly Cleaned—NCS. Unc Details.** Variety 4-D. The stars show recutting, and the mintmark is nearly centered under the bow. There are also traces of clash marks from Liberty's head within the wreath. A delightfully sharp Charlotte Mint piece, one of just 41,267 pieces minted. Lemon-gold surfaces have numerous hairlines in the fields, evidence of a prior cleaning, but none are particularly noteworthy. Still, a lovely example of a Type One gold dollar. (#7514)

Unblemished Near-Mint 1851-D Gold Dollar

3122 **1851-D AU58 NGC.** Variety 3-E. This luminous sun-gold near-Mint gold dollar has a wealth of detail, although the hair near the ear exhibits slight wear. Void of consequential marks. The usual variety for this challenging Dahlonega date, although a different (and rare) reverse is known. Only 9,882 pieces were produced. (#7515)

3123 **1851-O MS60 NGC.** Nicely detailed and lustrous with a few faint lines and abrasions on the reverse. The '51-O is a plentiful date from a mintage of 290,000 coins, likely struck from freshly mined gold transported from California. (#7516)

3124 **1852 MS64 PCGS.** Scintillating satiny luster radiates from the charming lemon-yellow surfaces. The strike is nearly full and both sides are remarkably clean for the grade. This attractive example would make a perfect type coin. (#7517)

3125 **1852 MS64 PCGS.** Captivating luster shimmers across the lemon-yellow surfaces of this carefully preserved near-Gem representative. The reverse die was clearly relapped sometime before striking this specimen, as there is some loss of detail on the left side of the wreath. Nonetheless, the obverse is boldly defined and both sides have great eye appeal. (#7517)

3126 **1852-C—Improperly Cleaned—NCS. AU Details.** Variety 7-H. Though the coin's original luster is all but gone, the portrait shows only minor wear with slight blurriness from the soft strike. An interesting example of this lower-mintage North Carolina issue. (#7518)

3127 1852-C AU55 NGC. Variety 7-H. The centers on each side show significant softness; Liberty's hair shows blending despite only light wear, and the reverse exhibits a planchet void at the second L of DOLLAR. Still, judging by the nearly intact luster, this yellow-gold piece is well-preserved. (#7518)

Condition Census 1852-C Gold Dollar, MS65

3128 1852-C MS65 NGC. Variety 7-H. Charlotte produced fewer than 10,000 gold dollars in 1852, and though NGC and PCGS combined report over 200 certifications, many authors suggest the survival rate is closer to 100 pieces. This example has the common Mint-made planchet or die problem in the center of the reverse that blurs the definition of LA in DOLLAR. However, from a mint notorious for striking problems, this is a beautiful coin. Liberty's hair, the centers of the obverse stars (save for one below the point of the neck), and the reverse wreath are all strongly defined, though the dentils on the obverse are mushy. This amazing coin also displays vibrant luster and bright honey-gold color. The surfaces are exceptionally clean for the grade; a couple of areas of roughness on the lower neck and before and behind Liberty's neck, and through the reverse denomination, are typical for the issue and neither particularly distracting nor grade-affecting.

The second (1998) edition of Winter's reference on Charlotte Mint gold enumerates one MS66 NGC example as the finest known, with one each certified at NGC and PCGS in MS65. PCGS no longer lists an MS65 in its online *Population Report*, while the NGC *Census Report* shows five MS65 examples—some likely duplications. While we cannot determine whether this MS65 NGC piece is a crossover from PCGS or another coin certified since the Winter reference was published, it definitely appears tied for second finest in the Condition Census with a handful of other coins. (#7518)

3129 1852-D—Whizzed—NCS. AU Details. Variety 4-F. This rare Dahlonega gold dollar has little actual circulation wear, but the surfaces are bright and somewhat blurry due to metal movement from a mechanical brush. (#7519)

3130 1853 MS64 PCGS. Vibrant satiny luster shimmers beneath the charming yellow-gold patina of this carefully preserved representative. The centers are a trifle soft, as typically seen, and several stars show minor weakness. An attractive example of the penultimate Type One gold dollar. Housed in a green label PCGS holder. (#7521)

3131 1853 MS64 PCGS. This remarkably attractive example would make an outstanding type coin. Vivid satiny luster gleams beneath the apricot-gold patina. Faint clash marks are noted on the reverse, and a prominent die gouge extends from the bottom of the bust. Sharply struck with no marks of any significance. Housed in a green label PCGS holder. (#7521)

Splendid Gem 1853 Gold Dollar

3132 1853 MS65 PCGS. The most numerous gold dollar type coin, the 1853 Type One is occasionally found in Gem and even finer grades. This splendid Gem example boasts frosty surfaces with a bold strike, good luster, and splendid orange-gold color. PCGS has certified 35 pieces finer (8/08).
From The Bell Collection. (#7521)

Desirable MS65 1853 Gold Dollar

3133 1853 MS65 NGC. CAC. Original lime and honey toning visits this shimmering and undisturbed Gem. Expertly struck, and worthy of bidder attention. Mintages of gold dollars peaked in 1853, as the Mint sought to replace silver coins removed from circulation as their bullion value exceeded face. (#7521)

Beautiful Premium Gem 1853 Gold Dollar

3134 1853 MS66 PCGS. Sharply struck with vibrant, satiny luster and delightful reddish-gold coloration over the two sides. Interesting die lines emerge from just below Liberty's ear to the jawline. Exquisitely preserved and blemish-free, a beautiful example of this early Type One gold dollar. Population: 24 in 66, 11 finer (8/08). (#7521)

Challenging 1853-C Gold Dollar AU53

3135 **1853-C AU53 NGC.** Variety 8-I. A generous amount of orange-tinted luster outlines design elements. Free from consequential marks, and the stars are well struck. The centers show minor softness, typical of the mint and type. A rare Charlotte issue that has a mintage of just 11,515 pieces. (#7522)

Handsome MS62 1853-C Gold Dollar

3136 **1853-C MS62 PCGS.** Variety 8-I. A radiant yellow-gold Charlotte representative with intricately struck stars and only slight inexactness of strike on the hair near the ear. A hair-thin mark above the coronet tip is of little consequence. Just 11,515 pieces were struck. Population: 11 in 62, 3 finer (8/08). (#7522)

Avidly Pursued AU 1853-D Gold Dollar

3137 **1853-D AU50 NGC.** Variety 5-G. This olive-gold Dahlonega dollar displays more than its share of luster once rotated beneath a light. A good strike with only minor central weakness. The fields are smooth and appear slightly sunken in places. A mere 6,583 pieces were struck. (#7523)

Appealing Near-Gem 1853-O Gold Dollar

3138 **1853-O MS64 NGC.** An obtainable O-mint Type One gold dollar, the 1853-O is seldom found in Gem condition, making near-Gems such as the present piece popular. This example is fairly well struck, save for one mushy star at 4:30 on the obverse, and abrasions are few. The color is a pretty peach-gold, with much luster and appeal. Census: 42 in 64, 12 finer (8/08). (#7524)

3139 **1854 Type One MS64 NGC.** 1854 was a transitional year for gold dollars, and this bright and lustrous piece is an excellent representative of the final year of Type One issues. The orange-patinated surfaces of this boldly struck example are remarkably clean and exceptionally attractive. A number of die polish lines are noted on the reverse. (#7525)

Scarce 1854-S Gold Dollar, MS62

3140 **1854-S MS62 NGC.** The 1854-S gold dollar, with a mintage of 14,632 pieces, is moderately scarce in all grades. An attentive strike sharpens the design elements of this MS62 example, including well defined star centers and separation of Liberty's hair strands. Yellow-gold surfaces display soft luster, and reveal a few minute handling marks. Census: 21 in 62, 14 finer (7/08). (#7527)

3141 **1854 Type Two AU58 NGC.** A popular first-year Type Two gold dollar. Pleasing yellow-orange patina drapes the lustrous surfaces. There are no marks worthy of specific mention, and prominent clash marks are visible on both sides. (#7531)

3142 **1854 Type Two AU58 PCGS.** Midway through 1854 Longacre was asked to redesign his Type One gold dollar and increase the diameter of the planchet. He chose a design similar to his three dollar piece, which debuted that same year. The present specimen has pronounced clash marks on both sides, with roller marks noted in the lower left of the obverse. Coruscating mint luster shines beneath the milky-gold patina and gives this well-defined piece lovely eye appeal. (#7531)

3143 **1854 Type Two AU58 NGC.** Luminous khaki-gold shadings prevail on this briefly circulated piece. Only a handful of trivial flaws and minor friction account for the grade. An excellent type coin. (#7531)

Mint State 1854 Type Two Gold Dollar

3144 **1854 Type Two MS61 PCGS.** A more common Type Two P-mint along with the 1855, the 1854 is sometimes preferred by first-year-of-type collectors. This piece shows antique-gold coloration and some bold clash marks, with a few small contact marks that determine the grade, which nonetheless seems a bit conservative. (#7531)

Delightful 1854 Type Two Gold Dollar, MS61

3145 **1854 Type Two MS61 NGC. CAC.** Despite a mintage of 783,943 pieces, the 1854 is usually seen circulated, and examples are relatively elusive in Mint State. Dusky yellow patina embraces the lustrous surfaces. There are extremely pronounced clash marks on both sides, and several of the reverse letters are visible on the obverse. An interesting and handsome representative. (#7531)

3146 **1854 Type Two MS62 NGC.** Yellow-gold surfaces are tinted with light tan. Generally well struck, with no significant marks. Both sides show clash marks. (#7531)

Popular 1854 Type Two Gold Dollar, MS63

3147 **1854 Type Two MS63 PCGS.** In mid-1854, the Mint attempted to rectify problems caused by the small size of the Type One gold dollar. The planchet diameter was increased by 2 mm, and the thickness was reduced accordingly to maintain weight and fineness standards. Chief Engraver James Longacre also introduced an elegant new design, featuring the head of an Indian princess on the obverse. Unfortunately, the highest points of this design were directly opposite the high relief of the reverse design. Coupled with the thinner planchet, the juxtaposition of the designs led to striking difficulties that were never resolved. Most 1854 Type Two dollars show softness in the details of the hair on the obverse and corresponding weakness in LL of DOLLAR and 85 of the date on the reverse. The issue is often seen with clash marks. The coins wore down easily in commerce, and the design was discontinued after only three years. The average grade seen is AU55.

The present coin displays unbroken, but slightly subdued luster, set off by lovely orange-gold color. The strike is typical for the date. The fields are unblemished except for a few clash marks, mostly on the reverse. The short life of this design type makes this date attractive as a type coin, and the relatively high grade should appeal to the gold dollar specialist.
From The Bell Collection. (#7531)

Select Type Two 1854 Gold Dollar

3148 **1854 Type Two MS63 PCGS.** A well struck example of this widely pursued and briefly issued gold type. Luster rolls unencumbered across the pleasing surfaces. Both sides are boldly clashed, customary for the Type Two. Apricot gold in color with glimpses of lime here and there. (#7531)

3149 **1855 AU58 NGC.** The 1855 is popular among type collectors because of its relative availability and its status as one of the few issues of Type Two gold dollars. Alluring luster radiates beneath the yellow-gold patina. A few minor marks are nearly imperceptible without a loupe. (#7532)

3150 **1855 AU58 NGC.** Pleasing butter-yellow patina drapes the surfaces of this briefly circulated representative. Pronounced clash marks are visible on both sides. Liberty's hair is a trifle soft, as usual, but the rest of the details are sharp. A well-preserved and lustrous example. (#7532)

3151 **1855 AU58 NGC.** Lovely orange-gold patina graces the surfaces, with splendid lemon color in the recesses. Save for a shallow scratch to the right of the bust, the numerous marks are entirely insignificant. Multiple clash marks are noted on each side. (#7532)

3152 **1855 AU58 NGC.** Primarily sun-gold with lighter yellow shadings that glimmer at the margins. Minimally flawed and pleasingly detailed overall, though a degree of striking softness appears at the bow of the wreath. (#7532)

3153 **1855 AU58 NGC.** Well struck with crisp details on DOLLAR and the date. Attractive straw-gold toning adorns the satiny surfaces, which retain a good deal of luster for the grade. There are typical, moderate clash marks on each side, and a shallow pinscratch extends from the bottom of O in OF through the A to the left side of M in AMERICA, near the upper right obverse border. Just a touch of rub on Liberty's upper hair detail prevents a Mint State grade assessment. (#7532)

Pleasing 1855 Gold Dollar, MS61

3154 **1855 MS61 NGC.** Numerous die polish lines account for the impressive luster that graces both sides of this yellow-orange piece. While there are scattered marks throughout, none are particularly detracting. A touch of weakness of Liberty's hair is the only area of softness on this otherwise crisply defined representative. (#7532)

Popular MS62 1855 Gold Dollar

3155 **1855 MS62 NGC.** A lustrous sun-gold example of this famous and scarce gold type coin. The strike is pleasing, with only minor incompleteness on the 8 in the date and the forehead curls. No abrasions merit individual mention, but a double set of bold clashmarks from the portrait bookends the denomination. (#7532)

Lustrous 1855 Select Gold Dollar

3156 **1855 MS63 NGC. CAC.** Lustrous yellow-gold surfaces display tints of light tan. The design elements exhibit the typical softness in the central reverse, particularly on the first L of DOLLAR and the 8 in the date. Light clash marks are visible on both sides. A couple of minor grazes define the grade. (#7532)

Vibrant 1855 Gold Dollar, Near-Gem

3157 **1855 MS64 NGC.** As found on many 1855 gold dollars, the current offer displays strike weakness in the central reverse design and bold clash marks. The redeeming qualities are the vibrant luster, well preserved surfaces, and attractive straw-gold coloration throughout. The 1854 and 1855 gold dollars are typically selected by those building type sets since both dates were struck in relatively large quantities and are the most available of the six different Type Two issues. However, in near-Gem or better condition neither date is common. NGC has graded a mere 44 pieces finer than the current MS64 example as of (8/08). (#7532)

Exceptional 1855-C Gold Dollar, AU50

3158 **1855-C AU50 NGC.** Variety 9-K, the only known. Light yellow-gold with slight wear visible on both sides. A few minor imperfections are noted, including a faint pin scratch in the upper left obverse. Virtually all known survivors are poorly struck (Douglas Winter, 1998). This example, however, is a tad better defined than most; all of LIBERTY shows in the headband, and some of the leaf ribbing is visible. All in all, an exceptional piece. *From The Laredo Collection.* (#7533)

3159 **1855-D—Plugged, Improperly Cleaned—NCS. XF Details.** Variety 7-I. Not only is the 1855-D an extremely low mintage issue, it is also requisite for a Dahlonega gold type set. This is a harshly cleaned straw-gold example with noticeable wear on the portrait and a possible repaired plug between the ES in STATES. (#7534)

3160 **1855-O XF40 NGC.** A popular type coin, the 1855-O is the only Type Two gold dollar struck at the New Orleans Mint. Charming olive-green patina overlies the fairly smooth surfaces. The centers are soft, as typically seen, but there is still plenty of detail throughout. (#7535)

Bright 1855-O Near-Mint Gold Dollar

3161 **1855-O AU58 NGC.** Ample luster resides on the yellow-gold surfaces of this near-Mint New Orleans representative. The design elements are generally well defined, except for softness in portions of Liberty's hair and on the 8 in the date. A few small obverse circulation marks are noted. (#7535)

Pleasing Near-Mint 1855-O Gold Dollar

3162 **1855-O AU58 NGC. CAC.** Generally yellow-gold with faint orange elements in the fields. This well struck Type Two gold dollar, one of just 55,000 pieces coined, shows a single fleck of alloy in the left obverse field and minor friction across the high points. NGC has certified 67 finer pieces (8/08). (#7535)

Uncirculated Details 1855-O Gold Dollar

3163 **1855-O—Scratched—NCS. Unc. Details.** The 1855-O is the sole New Orleans issue of the desirable Type Two design. It is much rarer than either of the two Philadelphia issues of the type. This straw-gold example has well-struck devices, but the obverse is moderately hairlined and exhibits fine pinscratches near the first T in STATES. The reverse has several pinscratches and a number of pinpoint marks. (#7535)

Scarce 1856-S Type Two Gold Dollar
AU58, Breen-6045, Double S

3164 **1856-S Type Two AU58 NGC.** Breen-6045, Double S. The first S mintmark was punched too high and to the right. The 1856-S is scarce in grades above Extremely Fine. Variegated apricot and yellow-gold patina covers both sides of this AU58 specimen, and a precise strike brings out nice detail on the design features. The surfaces retain considerable luster, and are lightly marked. A couple of obverse cracks are noted. (#7536)

Normal S 1856-S Type Two Gold Dollar, MS61

3165 **1856-S Type Two MS61 NGC.** Breen-6044, with a normal mintmark. The obverse of this late state example has several fine die cracks in the fields. The last 25 examples that have appeared in our Signature sales included 15 of the Normal Mintmark variety and 10 of the Doubled Mintmark variety, showing that their populations are relatively similar. This satiny Mint State piece has rich orange luster and few faint surface marks. A wonderful example that will please the advanced collector. Census: 21 in 61, 16 finer (8/08). (#7536)

Dazzling 1856 Slanted 5 Gold Dollar, MS66

3166 **1856 Slanted 5 MS66 NGC.** Dazzling mint frost radiates over the beautifully toned surfaces of this Premium Gem gold dollar. The 1856 issue features two varieties: the normal 5 and this, the Slanted 5. This piece offers generally good striking detail, although there is typical weakness on OLL and 85, near the center of the reverse. Shallow planchet flaws appear beside the large denominational 1 and near the lower left reverse border at 8 o'clock; but post-striking defects are minimal. (#7540)

3167 **1856-D—Ex-Jewelry—ANACS. XF45 Details.** Variety 8-K. Mildly granular and somewhat bright with a bulge at 5 o'clock on the reverse and a bend on the second S in STATES. A mere 1,460 pieces were issued, which places the 1856 Dahlonega among the lowest mintage gold dollars. (#7543)

Key-Date 1856-D Gold Dollar, AU58

3168 **1856-D AU58 NGC.** Variety 8-K, the only known variety. The 1856-D is one of the keys to the series, and always in demand. Douglas Winter (*Gold Coins of the Dahlonega Mint*) estimates 80 to 90 pieces known. It is most often seen in Very Fine and Extremely Fine grades. Winter writes that it is extremely rare in the higher About Uncirculated levels of preservation, and is one of the rarest Dahlonega issues in Mint State.

This near-Mint specimen retains a good amount of luster on its yellow-gold surfaces. The overall design impression is relatively sharp, except for the usual softness in the hair, the U of UNITED, and the 5 in the date. Both sides are remarkably clean. Census: 18 in 58, 6 finer (7/08). (#7543)

3169 **1857-C—Mount Removed—NCS. AU Details.** Variety 10-L. The only variety known. A soldered mount to the top of the bust has been removed, but only the denticles have been affected, and all of the central design elements are well-defined. Peppered marks on Liberty's cheek are minor, and the rest of the surfaces are fairly clean. A tiny blemish is noted at the bottom of the wreath. One of just two Charlotte Mint Type Three gold dollars, with a mintage of just 13,200 pieces. (#7545)

Worthy 1857-C Gold Dollar AU53

3170 **1857-C AU53 NGC.** Variety 10-L. The issue is almost always found with prominent planchet defects (Douglas Winter, 1998), and this AU53 coin is no exception. The bright yellow-gold surfaces exhibit three shallow linear depressions on the obverse, and another on the reverse. The design elements are relatively well defined, better so than usually seen on this poorly struck date. (#7545)

Conditionally Rare 1857-C Dollar, MS61

3171 **1857-C MS61 NGC.** Variety 10-L. The only variety known. Although the mint issued the first Type Three gold dollars in 1856, the first examples were not struck in Charlotte until the following year. It is interesting that while the 1857-C dollar's mintage of 13,280 pieces is on the high side when compared to most dates in the series, this issue is among the rarest in Mint State. This is partially because the 1857-C is, on average, one of the worst produced gold coins in United States history, which is a major reason for the lack of high grade specimens. Only a select few examples have been certified in Mint State, with none above MS62. This is an excellent opportunity to acquire one of the finest representatives of this desirable issue.

Pleasing olive-gold patina endows the surfaces of this lightly marked specimen. Although the quality of this issue is notoriously poor, this piece exhibits a significantly sharper strike and fewer defects than typically seen. The fields have a wavy appearance, as usual, and there is minor deterioration on the rims. Nonetheless, the surfaces are fairly smooth overall, and there are patches of luster throughout, which is remarkable for the issue. A number of die cracks are noted on both sides. This piece has great eye quality compared to the average 1857-C, which is usually seen dull and rather rough. PCGS has certified just one example at the MS61 level, with none finer. NGC reports four MS61 representatives, which may represent multiple submissions of the same coin, along with only two MS62 specimens (8/08). (#7545)

Lovely 1857-D Gold Dollar, VF20

3172 **1857-D VF20 PCGS.** Variety 9-L, the only known die pairing. Housed in a green-label PCGS holder, this low-mintage issue is most desirable, surviving from a production of just 3,500 coins. An intriguing coin, as the obverse appears to grade much higher than the reverse. The wreath is essentially flat. Both sides have pleasing green-gold with traces of pale orange patina. (#7546)

Scarce 1857-D Gold Dollar, AU55

3173 **1857-D AU55 PCGS.** Variety 9-L, the only variety for the year. Lustrous light yellow-gold surfaces with a hint of green color. Both sides have high point weakness, typical of this issue. Slight imperfections are present on both sides, as usual for this issue and for all Southern Mint gold coinage. This is an important opportunity for the collector to acquire a pleasing example of this low mintage issue. (#7546)

Condition Rarity 1857-D Gold Dollar, AU55

3174 **1857-D AU55 NGC.** Variety 9-L, the only one known. The 1857-D is most often seen in Very Fine and Extremely Fine grades. It is rare in About Uncirculated, and extremely rare in Mint State (Douglas Winter, 2003). This Choice AU specimen displays ample luster on yellow-gold surfaces. The design elements exhibits the usual weakness on the top of the bonnet and hair curls, and on portions of the rims. (#7546)

Lustrous Near-Mint 1857-S Gold Dollar

3175 **1857-S AU58 NGC.** This is one of those early U.S. gold issues that is just loaded with "character." The fledgling U.S. Mint in San Francisco had been open only three years when this piece was produced, and in terms of rarity it is on par with contemporary C- and D-mint issues, despite a larger emission. This piece offers pretty, lustrous yellow-gold surfaces with just a few light abrasions that attest to a short spate in circulation. Census: 35 in 58, 16 finer (8/08). (#7547)

Well Struck 1857-S Gold Dollar, AU58

3176 **1857-S AU58 PCGS.** The 1857-S, with a mintage of 10,000 pieces, is scarce in AU grades and rare in Mint State. This near-Mint specimen is well struck, and retains a good amount of luster on its apricot-gold surfaces that have a greenish cast. Each side reveals a few minor circulation marks. (#7547)

3177 **1858-S AU50 NGC.** Light highpoint wear is evident on both sides of this moderately lustrous piece. The yellow-gold surfaces are smooth and attractive. A large S mintmark is close to the ribbon knot, and virtually the same size as the date digits. (#7550)

3178 **1859-C—Improperly Cleaned, Bent—NCS. VF Details.** Variety 11-M. A wavy and thickly hairlined caramel-gold example of this challenging Charlotte issue. Just 5,235 pieces were coined. (#7552)

Attractive, Scarce 1859-C Gold Dollar, AU55

3179 **1859-C AU55 PCGS.** Variety 11-M. The 1859-C is the final gold dollar minted at the Charlotte Mint, and with just 5,200 pieces struck, it also has the lowest mintage of any C-mint dollar. This eye-catching piece has magnificent luster that is complemented by charming yellow-gold patina. The strike is weak at the centers, as always, and the O in DOLLAR is exceptionally soft. A small dig is noted at the U in UNITED, but the rest of the abrasions are minor. Overall, an attractive example of this scarce issue. Population: 15 in 55, 21 finer (7/08). (#7552)

Difficult Choice AU 1859-C Gold Dollar

3180 **1859-C AU55 NGC.** Variety 11-M. This nearly unmarked Charlotte gold dollar is iridescently toned in peach-gold and ice-blue. Liberty's hair shows some merging of detail, but the strike is generally sharp. Only 5,235 pieces were struck, and examples with ample remaining luster are rare. (#7552)

3181 **1859-S AU53 ANACS.** A scarce issue with a mintage of 15,000 pieces, the 1859-S is particularly elusive in high grades. The centers of this yellow-orange specimen are a trifle soft, as often seen, but there are no prominent marks on either side. (#7554)

Sharp 1859-S Gold Dollar, AU58

3182 **1859-S AU58 NGC.** The relatively small 15,000-piece mintage of 1859-S gold dollars was quickly circulated, with very few survivors (Jeff Garrett and Ron Guth, 2006). This AU58 example features well defined motifs, and exhibits luster in the recesses. Yellow-gold surfaces are quite clean. Census: 41 in 58, 14 finer (7/08). (#7554)

Important 1859-S Gold Dollar, MS61

3183 **1859-S MS61 NGC.** Lustrous light yellow surfaces exhibit a few small scattered surface marks on each side. Most design definition is bold, although slight highpoint weakness is evident on the obverse and reverse design motifs. The 1859-S is elusive in high grades, and NGC has only certified one finer example (8/08). (#7554)

3184 **1860-D—Ex-Jewelry, Damaged—ANACS. AU50 Details.** Variety 12-P. This rare Dahlonega gold dollar is bright from polishing. Solder residue is noted on the obverse at 12 o'clock, and a mount appears to have been removed from the lower left reverse border. Somewhat wavy, and a few faint pinscratches are present on the central reverse. Only 1,566 pieces were struck. (#7556)

Scarce 1860-S Gold Dollar, MS61

3185 **1860-S MS61 NGC.** The 1860-S gold dollar, coming from a mintage of 13,000 pieces quickly entered the channels of commerce, and has a low survival rate. The peach-gold surfaces of this MS61 specimen display wisps of tan, and the design elements are well defined, save for minor softness in Liberty's hair. Minute handling marks are scattered over each side. Census: 19 in 61, 14 finer (7/08). (#7557)

Green-Gold 1863 Gold Dollar, AU58

3186 **1863 AU58 NGC.** This Civil War era gold dollar is scarce in all grades. Rich green-gold patina adorns both sides of this AU58 specimen, each of which possesses a good amount of luster. The design elements are sharply defined, further enhancing the coin's eye appeal. A few minor circulation marks do not detract. Census: 7 in 58, 32 finer (7/08). (#7562)

View color images of virtually every lot and place bids at HA.com

Shining 1865 Gold Dollar, MS61

3187 **1865 MS61 NGC.** Apricot and orange-gold surfaces display traces of light bluish-green, especially noticeable on the reverse, and yield a cameo-like effect when the coin is rotated under a light source. The design elements are quite well impressed. Wispy slide marks occur over each side, but do not seriously distract. (#7564)

Dazzling MS63 Prooflike 1868 Gold Dollar

3188 **1868 MS63 Prooflike NGC.** Impressively reflective fields contrast with lightly frosted devices. Well struck, and smooth save for a tick on the cheek and a thin mark near the C in AMERICA. A low mintage issue that is difficult to find in any Mint State grade. Census: 2 in 63 Prooflike, none finer as Prooflike, 1 finer as Deep Mirror Prooflike and 7 finer without a Prooflike designation (7/08). (#77567)

3189 **1869 MS61 NGC.** Bright yellow patina overlies the surfaces of this sharply struck representative. The semiprooflike fields emit impressive reflectivity, which is barely affected by myriad grade-defining abrasions. Only 5,900 examples were struck. (#7568)

3190 **1870 MS61 PCGS.** The 1870 is elusive in Uncirculated grades because of its low mintage of 6,300 pieces. The 0 in the date is lightly repunched at the base. The cheek has a light graze, but there are no particularly unpleasant abrasions. This crisply struck specimen exudes powerful luster throughout.
Ex: Bowers and Merena (3/2003), lot 2055, where it realized $805. Earlier authenticated by ANACS with the serial number E-4126-G. (#7569)

Reflective 1870 Gold Dollar, MS64

3191 **1870 MS64 PCGS.** Unsurprisingly for a survivor from a mintage of only 6,300 gold dollars, this piece shows surfaces that are decidedly prooflike on each side. The fields are highly reflective, and thick frost coats the devices. A couple of parallel lines on Liberty's cheek are the apparent grade-limiting factor. Population: 19 in 64, 20 finer (7/08). (#7569)

Appealing 1870-S Gold Dollar, MS61

3192 **1870-S MS61 PCGS.** Variegated orange-gold and yellow-gold patina is joined by an occasional splash of purple, and well struck design elements stand out from partially prooflike fields. A few obverse contact marks define the grade. Nevertheless, this piece generates considerable eye appeal. Housed in a green-label holder. (#7570)

3193 **1871 MS63 PCGS.** This piece is decidedly Prooflike, although PCGS does not use that designation, and there is powerful contrast between the fields and the yellow-gold devices. A number of wispy abrasions limit the grade of this eye-catching and sharply struck piece. Population: 21 in 63, 42 finer (8/08). (#7571)

3194 **1874 MS63 NGC.** Solidly defined for the issue with vibrant luster and excellent eye appeal. Only a handful of tiny marks in the fields preclude a finer designation.
From The Menlo Park Collection. (#7575)

Rare 1875 Gold Dollar, MS60 Details

3195 1875—Damaged—ANACS. MS60 Details. A large contact mark is seen across Liberty's chin that appears to have buckled the planchet. The 1875 is one of the best known scarcities in the gold dollar series, its notoriety derived from the original mintage of 420 pieces, 20 struck as proofs. Like all 1875 business strikes, a tiny "spine" projects downward into the field from Liberty's throat, this still being visible despite the aforementioned mark. Normally the fields are prooflike, a characteristic that is still very much in evidence on this minimally-worn, watery example. Appealing golden patina overall. (#7576)

Shimmering MS67 1880 Gold Dollar

3196 1880 MS67 PCGS. CAC. Only 1,636 gold dollars were produced in 1880 (including 36 proofs), making this a highly desirable, low mintage date in the series. This particular coin displays bright, semi-prooflike fields, as one would expect from such a low mintage. The surfaces shimmer with golden mint luster and each side has a rich overlay of reddish-orange patina that adds even more to the overall appeal of this scarce coin. The surfaces are free from any troubling abrasions. (#7581)

Spectacular 1880 Gold Dollar, MS68

3197 1880 MS68 PCGS. An extraordinary, highly lustrous, and impeccably preserved representative. It is a rare pleasure to catalog a gold dollar that is virtually flawless in every respect. The present piece is powerfully struck with captivating satiny luster throughout the fields. Even with the aid of a loupe it is difficult to locate any handling marks and just a couple of pinpoint abrasions keep this piece from being absolutely perfect. This yellow-gold specimen has outstanding eye appeal and is one of only 1,600 coins struck. Housed in a green label PCGS holder. A excellent piece for an advanced collector. Population: 23 in 68, 1 finer (8/08). *From The Bell Collection.* (#7581)

3198 1880 MS62 Prooflike NGC. The gleaming fields are unsurprising, given this issue's tiny business strike mintage of 1,600 pieces, but the overall eye appeal is much stronger than the norm. Beautifully detailed with no overt abrasions, though a scattering of minor flaws precludes Select status. (#77581)

3199 1880 MS62 Prooflike NGC. The honey-gold surfaces are amply reflective, and a hint of frostiness on the portrait supplies a degree of mild contrast. A handful of fine abrasions in the fields account for the grade. Census: 4 in 62, 28 finer (7/08). (#77581)

Dazzling 1880 Gold Dollar, MS67 ★ Prooflike

3200 1880 MS67 ★ Prooflike NGC. Although most Type Three gold dollars were struck in small quantities, the 1880's mintage of just 1,600 pieces is significantly lower than usual. Delightful lemon-yellow patina endows the surfaces of this powerfully impressed specimen. Intense mint frost illuminates the devices, which contrast nicely against the satiny and essentially pristine fields of this handsome example. Census: 7 in 67 ★ Prooflike, 0 finer (7/08). (#77581)

3201 1882 MS63 NGC. A boldly struck example with rich sun-gold toning and good luster. Careful inspection fails to locate consequential marks. A meager 5,000 pieces were struck. (#7583)

3202 1884 MS64 Prooflike NGC. This low-mintage issue (5,200 pieces) is seldom seen in Prooflike, and NGC has certified just 21 examples as such. Charming sun-gold patina covers both sides, which appear nearly pristine to the unaided eye. A sharply struck and attractive specimen. Census: 9 in 64, 7 finer (8/08). (#77585)

Magnificent 1885 Gold Dollar, MS68

3203 1885 MS68 NGC. Despite having a higher mintage than some of the other late gold dollar issues, the 1885 presents a greater challenge than many in high Mint State grades. Any year, however, would be truly remarkable and extremely rare in MS68. Many collectors are forced to wait years before given the opportunity to acquire such a spectacular example, and it is essentially impossible to find a representative any finer. The present specimen is powerfully struck, and the butter-yellow surfaces exhibit vibrant satiny luster throughout. This simply breathtaking representative appears flawless, even under magnification. PCGS has not certified any examples at this level, and NGC reports just three pieces in MS68, with none finer (8/08). (#7586)

3204 **1885 MS64 Prooflike NGC.** Attractive rose-orange patina drapes the immensely prooflike fields, which show impressive contrast against the yellow-gold devices. Scattered pinpoint abrasions keep this remarkable razor-sharp piece from an even higher grade. Census: 7 in 64, 11 finer (8/08). (#77586)

Intriguing Clashed 1886 Gold Dollar, MS64

3205 **1886 MS64 NGC.** Quite a number of these have been graded in comparison to the 5,000-coin mintage, easily explained by a lack of circulation when they were first coined. Most of the dates in the 1880s never entered circulation, and quite a few survive today. This lovely example has satiny orange-gold surfaces and sharp design details.

Both dies are clashed, but careful examination shows that the reverse was rotated slightly clockwise when the die clashing occurred, and now it is rotated slightly counterclockwise. (#7587)

Spectacular 1886 Gold Dollar, Superb Gem

3206 **1886 MS67 NGC.** With just 5,000 business strikes produced, the 1886 ranks as the scarcest issue from the final decade of gold dollars. This impeccably preserved Superb Gem has spectacular satiny luster that shimmers beneath the yellow-gold patina. A loupe locates a couple of nearly imperceptible handling marks, and also reveals clash marks on both sides. Neither NGC nor PCGS have certified any pieces finer than this attractive representative. Census: 12 in 67, 0 finer (7/08). (#7587)

Prooflike MS66 1886 Gold Dollar

3207 **1886 MS66 Prooflike NGC.** A needle-sharp Premium Gem with mirrored fields and nearly immaculate preservation. A minute planchet flake near 6 o'clock will identify the present piece. A tiny mintage of 5,000 pieces ensures a paucity of high grade survivors. Census: 4 in 66 Prooflike, 4 finer (8/08). (#77587)

3208 **1887 MS62 Prooflike NGC.** Splendid prooflike fields enhance the eye appeal of this delightful yellow-gold representative. The C in AMERICA is softly defined, but the rest of the details are sharp. A minimally marked and attractive example. Census: 6 in 62, 17 finer (8/08). (#77588)

Marvelous 1887 Gold Dollar, MS66 Prooflike

3209 **1887 MS66 Prooflike NGC.** The 1887 is one of the final gold dollars and boasts a low mintage of just 7,500 pieces. Eye-catching prooflike fields have only a few minor abrasions, and the butter-yellow devices are similarly devoid of significant marks. Sharply struck with wonderful eye appeal. Census: 3 in 66, 4 finer (8/08). (#77588)

Appealing Premium Gem 1888 Gold Dollar

3210 **1888 MS66 PCGS.** This wonderful Premium Gem shows deep apricot-gold surfaces delicately tinged with ice-blue on both sides, and splendid luster completes the unusual but thoroughly appealing package. By this time in the gold dollar series its fate was writ large upon the wall, and the mintage of only 15,500 business strikes in this penultimate year was yet another chapter. (#7589)

3211 **1889 MS64 PCGS.** Vibrant satiny luster shimmers beneath the yellow-gold patina. The obverse appears pristine to the unaided eye and the reverse has only a few light grazes. A boldly impressed example of this final-year issue. (#7590)

Alluring 1889 Gold Dollar, Gem Mint State

3212 **1889 MS65 PCGS.** Several nearly imperceptible luster grazes on the yellow surfaces keep this Gem from an even higher grade. A few minuscule toning spots barely hinder the excellent eye appeal. Dazzling satiny luster graces both sides and highlights the nearly full details. This impressive piece is housed in a green label PCGS holder (#7590)

Outstanding 1889 Gold Dollar, MS66 ★

3213 **1889 MS66 ★ NGC.** Although its relatively low 28,950-piece business strike mintage suggests a rarity, 1889 gold dollars are readily available in most grades. Jeff Garrett and Ron Guth (2006) point out that small hoards have turned up over the years. They also suggest that the date's high survival rate is probably due to its status as the last year of gold dollars. Considering the high availability of the issue, it is noteworthy that this Premium Gem example is the *only* 1889 MS66 gold dollar given the coveted Star designation by NGC (7/08). Spectacular reddish-gold orange patina graces the satiny and lightly frosted surfaces. The strike is razor-sharp with even the most intricate details fully visible. A glass reveals only a couple of inoffensive handling marks. An eye-catching and handsome piece. (#7590)

Gorgeous 1889 Gold Dollar, MS66

3214 **1889 MS66 NGC.** Bold design features and exquisite surfaces unite with satiny yellow-gold luster to create an exceptional visual presentation. Although the mintage was limited to 29,000 coins, the date is rather plentiful, making the 1889 an ideal choice for type collectors. (#7590)

Remarkable 1889 Gold Dollar, Premium Gem

3215 **1889 MS66 NGC.** A spectacular, impeccably preserved, final year of issue gold dollar. The yellow-gold surfaces are virtually immaculate, and only a couple of tiny handling marks are visible under magnification. A number of planchet striations on the obverse are also visible with a loupe, and there are a few delicate die cracks around the perimeter of the reverse. Impressive satiny luster gives this piece excellent eye appeal. (#7590)

3216 **1889 MS64 Prooflike NGC.** A flashy and meticulously preserved near-Gem example with beautifully smooth and highly reflective fields. The ER in LIBERTY is weak because of relapping. Census: 5 in 64 Prooflike, 11 finer (8/07). (#77590)

PROOF GOLD DOLLAR

Spectacular 1882 Gold Dollar, PR65 Deep Cameo

3217 **1882 PR65 Deep Cameo ANACS.** Of the 125 proof 1882 gold dollars struck, it is generally thought that somewhere between 45 and 55 pieces still exist. Gold specialist David Akers (1975) wrote of surviving specimens that " ... an abnormally high percentage ... are not particularly choice." The Deep Cameo Gem that we offer in this lot, therefore, is a very uncommon appearance. The overall apricot-gold surfaces have outstanding contrast between the frosted devices and the deeply mirrored fields, which appear black when viewed from above. The design elements are powerfully impressed, further enhancing the outstanding eye appeal of this piece. An impeccably preserved and handsome example. (#97632)

Elusive 1798 BD-2 Quarter Eagle, AU50

3218 **1798 AU50 PCGS.** BD-2, Low R.5. The top of the 8 slightly overlaps the lower edge of the drapery. The branch has five berries. Either feature is diagnostic for the elusive 1798 BD-2 quarter eagle. The other variety, that is even rarer, has the 8 distant from the drapery and only four berries in the branch. Both dies are perfect on this example, as they apparently are on all known 1798 BD-2 quarter eagles. The reverse die remained in used for 1798 JR-4 and 1800 JR-1 dimes. Since both of the dime varieties were actually struck in 1800, it seems likely that these five berries quarter eagles were coined about the same time. The actual mintage of the five berries pieces probably included mint deliveries dated May 15, 1798 (298), April 15, 1798 (60), and December 28, 1799 (480), for a total of 838 coins.

The present piece, housed in a green-label PCGS holder, is moderately abraded, but exhibits lovely green-gold luster with reflective fields. Splashes of violet toning appear in the obverse fields, with pale rose toning about the reverse. The strike is adequate, with especially bold details on the reverse. In the Ed Price catalog, we estimated about 80 to 90 survivors exist of the variety, although that number may be a little high. Perhaps only 60 to 70 still exist, more in keeping with our Low R.5 rarity rating. This piece is probably one of the ten finest examples of the variety known today. It seems that there are about five Mint State examples and five more AU grade coins in existence. (#7649)

Pleasing 1804 14 Star Reverse
Quarter Eagle, BD-2, AU53

Lovely 1804 BD-2 14 Stars Quarter Eagle, AU55

3219 **1804 14 Star Reverse AU53 NGC.** BD-2, R.4. A classic blundered die variety. Instead of a proper count of 13 stars to represent the original colonies, this reverse die was sunk with 14 stars. Breen believed that the die was cut in 1798 and set aside due to the error, only to be used six years later—inadvertently or not—to strike 1804 quarter eagles and, subsequently, the 1804 JR-2 dimes. Bass, however, felt that the small size of the stars on the 1804 BD-2 reverse die would not have been engraved by Scot in 1798 and was actually created at a later date. Regardless of the origin of the die, this variety is tangible evidence of the struggles encountered by our first Mint. Reasonably struck for the issue with light straw-gold coloration throughout, although adjustment marks on the reverse between 7 and 11 o'clock has resulted in localized weakness on the corresponding area of the obverse rim. An eye-appealing coin nonetheless. Census: 5 in 53, 49 finer (8/08). (#7652)

3220 **1804 14 Star Reverse AU55 NGC.** B-2, R.4. In 1804 two dime varieties and two quarter eagles were coined, using just two reverse dies, one with 13 stars and the other with 14 stars. Each reverse die was used for both denominations. The 13 Stars quarter eagle is a rarity, so this 14 Star variety is the only reasonable option for date collectors. Probably about 125 to 150 examples of both varieties are known, about the same total population as the 1804 dimes. This lovely green-gold example has nice design details with satiny luster and only insignificant marks. (#7652)

Attractive 1807 Quarter Eagle, BD-1, VF35

3221 **1807 VF35 PCGS.** BD-1, R.3. The only variety known. The low mintage (estimated at 6,812 pieces) of this issue exemplifies the fact that the Quarter Eagle was not a favored denomination during the early 19th century. This piece exhibits splendid orange-gold patina with accents of olive-green and tan. Although the obverse denticles are incomplete at the top, the rest of the features are clearly defined. Scattered abrasions define the grade, and a few shallow abrasions in the right obverse field are barely worthy of note. An attractive and fully original example of this scarce issue. *From The Menlo Park Collection.* (#7656)

Splendid 1807 Quarter Eagle, BD-1, XF Details

3222 **1807—Damaged, Cleaned—ANACS. XF40 Details.** BD-1, R.3. The only variety known. Apricot-gold patina graces both sides and is complemented by a surprisingly amount of luster in the fields. The obverse is moderately pitted and there is a slightly unnatural hue to the surfaces because of cleaning. Nonetheless, this is a boldly detailed example that would make a lovely and relatively affordable type coin. (#7656)

Scarce 1825 BD-2 Quarter Eagle, XF45

3223 **1825 XF45 NGC.** BD-2, High R.4. Light green-gold with reflective surfaces and minor marks consistent with the grade. The obverse exhibits slight wear on the highpoints that substantially diminishes the detail. The die was cut shallow, resulting in a worn appearance even with only the slightest actual use or handling. The reverse is slightly sharper, and overall this piece may actually be a full AU. *From The Menlo Park Collection.* (#7664)

3224 **1825 MS61 PCGS.** BD-2, R.4. The obverse has a recut 5, and the reverse has the stem ending over the upright of the D. Both dies appear to be perfect with no die cracks or clash marks. Approximately 80 to 100 examples still exist in all grades, with only about a dozen that grade MS60 or finer, including this piece.

There are three different varieties of 1825 quarter eagles known, rather significant for a date with a mintage of just 4,434 coins. BD-1 is a new discovery by Harry Bass who identified the variety from a remarkable double struck piece. The present cataloger identified the second known piece in the Bowers and Merena January 2000 Rarities Sale. Since that time, John Dannreuther has identified several other examples, with a present population estimated at 12 to 15 known. BD-2 is the common die marriage, earlier known as Breen-1. Perhaps as many as 100 examples in known in all grades. BD-3 is the other rarity in the series a population about the same as BD-1.

Housed in a green-label PCGS holder, this brilliant and reflective piece has limited surface marks and presents excellent eye appeal. The details are well defined and there is no evidence of weakness on either side. Proof examples were coined from this die pair, and those struck immediately after the proofs were most likely to have reflective, mirrored obverse and reverse surfaces. Population: 10 in 61, 13 finer (7/08). (#7664)

Luminous AU55 Details 1830 BD-1 Quarter Eagle

3225 **1830—Altered Surfaces—ANACS. AU55 Details.** BD-1, R.4. The only variety for the year and a very scarce issue in any grade. This well-defined piece has strong overall detail, though the yellow-gold and orange-gold surfaces exhibit unnatural luster and a degree of porosity. Still, an eminently collectible survivor of this Capped Bust Left quarter eagle issue. (#7670)

Scarce 1830 Quarter Eagle, BD-1, AU58

3226 **1830 AU58 NGC.** Breen-6133, BD-1, R.4. All Capped Head quarter eagles are scarce or rare. In 1830 only 4,540 coins of the denomination were minted, but the number of survivors is estimated to be just 80 to 100 pieces. In the early 1800s many gold coins were melted as bullion, and the few that survive likely saw little time in commerce. Only one variety is known for the date, identified by the repunched U in UNITED from a reverse die that was used every year from 1830 through the end of the type in 1834. In spite of this example's brief sojourn as perhaps a carry piece or a treasured keepsake there are no spots and virtually no abrasions, except for an almost imperceptible rim bump below the date. The coin is well struck, displaying a warm orange-gold color on both sides. This exceptional Capped Head quarter eagle, a type that is infrequently available and avidly sought, is sure to highlight an advanced collection. Census: 18 in 58, 21 finer (7/08).
From The Menlo Park Collection. (#7670)

1831 Quarter Eagle
Struck on a Dime Planchet, Good 6

3227 **1831 Quarter Eagle—Struck on a Dime Planchet—Good 6 NGC.** 2.33 gm. Over the years we have handled many, many error coins, but this is undoubtedly the most strikingly obvious and interesting error we have ever handled. It is classified in the rather pedestrian category of an off-metal striking. Such coins are common among error coins, but this is such an unusual piece that it immediately grabs the attention of any coin collector.

At the Summer ANA we offered the Ed Price Collection of Dime and Quarter Eagle Varieties. The crux of that collection was the interchangeability of dime and quarter eagle dies. For those who lack a copy of the catalog, it is a worthy addition to any numismatic library. In the earliest years of the Mint, dime and quarter eagle reverse dies were used on each denomination—apparently a conscious decision. The planchet sizes were close, 19 mm for the dimes and 20 mm for the quarter eagles. The diameter of each denomination was later reduced when new machinery was introduced. The dime's diameter was reduced to 18.5 mm beginning in 1809, and the quarter eagle to 18.2 mm in 1829. It is not a stretch to imagine the Mint striking a batch of dimes with a few unstruck planchets remaining in the hopper, then striking a run of quarter eagles, a couple of which were struck on leftover dime planchets. Only 0.3 mm separated the size of the two planchets, an imperceptible difference to the casual inspector.

What happened next is fairly obvious: nothing. This piece entered the channels of commerce and circulated as a dime for many years. Only recently and after 54 points of wear did someone notice that the design was inconsistent with that of an 1831 dime. This piece was found in a bag of silver in North Texas, in May of this year. It is always interesting to scan the "Found in Rolls" column in *Coin World*. Foreign coins, tokens, silver coins are constantly found in rolls. But an 1831 quarter eagle struck on a dime planchet in a bag of silver?

This is the second example of this off-metal striking that is known. The other piece is high-grade and has a distinguished pedigree including Brand, Opezzo, Farouk, Judd, and Sloss. It has been off the market since 1974, when it was traded privately, then it was withdrawn from the 1979 ANA Sale. Over the years that piece has been listed and delisted as a possible pattern. It has been listed in the Judd book as Judd-49, and in Andrew Pollock's reference as Pollock-50. It was also listed in the 1913 Adams-Woodin pattern reference as AW-39. Don Taxay listed it in the 1976 *Scott Catalogue* as an error.

Regardless of its listing in pattern references, no one seems to have taken the previously known piece seriously as a pattern. Both of the two known coins were struck 30-40 years before the "made to order" rarities were produced by the Mint, so chicanery would seem to be out of the question, especially when one considers the extensive circulation on this example. There seems to be no confusion about the status of this piece as the USPatterns.com website states: "Although listed by Judd as a regular dies trial piece struck in silver, Taxay describes this as a mint error, struck on a dime planchet which your editor believes is the more likely scenario. At least 2 examples are known ... The other [this coin] is the illustrated example where it was slabbed by NGC as a Mint Error."

As one would expect from a Good 6 coin, the surfaces show extensive signs of circulation. Several planchet flaws are still apparent on each side and serve to identify this piece. The devices are silvery and serve as an accent against the charcoal-gray fields.

This piece is a cataloger's favorite. It is a wonderful coin to preface with, "What's wrong with this picture?" and is even more dramatic when seen alongside a true 1831 silver dime in similar grade. It is jarring to see this quarter eagle design in silver. In a photograph the coin certainly looks unusual, but in person it is even more impressive. Truly a must-see lot.

CLASSIC QUARTER EAGLES

3228 **1834 Classic AU50 NGC.** Breen-6138, R.1. The Small Head variety, characterized by flattened curls atop Liberty's head. Well struck and briefly circulated with radiant, lightly abraded lemon-gold surfaces. (#7692)

3229 **1834 Classic—Scratched, Cleaned—ICG. AU58 Details.** Breen-6138, his 'Small Head' variety. This splendidly detailed type coin is slightly subdued and has a few faded pinscratches in the fields. Luster glints from the design and legends. (#7692)

Uncirculated 1834 Classic Quarter Eagle

3230 **1834 Classic MS61 NGC.** Large Head, Breen-6140, McCloskey-C, R.3. This well struck Classic two and a half has a slender strike-through near star 12, but no abrasions are visible to the unaided eye. A loupe reveals wispy field marks. Bright luster dominates the borders and devices. (#7692)

3231 **1835 AU58 NGC.** McCloskey-1, R.2, the variety with the widely spaced AM in AMERICA. The reverse die was also used to strike 1834 quarter eagles. The stars are intricately struck, while the centers show only moderate incompleteness. Luster dominates the borders, eagle, and hair. (#7693)

3232 **1835—Improperly Cleaned—NCS. Unc. Details.** McCloskey-1, R.2. The "Wide AM" variety. Lightly hairlined, but the eye appeal is substantial since there are no bagmarks and the devices are void of friction. A crisp strike with only unimportant blending of detail at the centers. (#7693)

3233 **1836 Script 8 XF45 NGC.** Head of 1837, Breen-6144, McCloskey-C, R.2. Lovely olive-orange patina is entirely original and covers the lightly abraded surfaces. The motto is a trifle soft, but the rest of the details are well-defined. A pleasing example of this transitional variety. *From The Menlo Park Collection.* (#7694)

Brilliant 1836 Classic Quarter Eagle, MS62

3234 **1836 Script 8 MS62 PCGS.** McCloskey-D, Head of 1835, Breen-6143, R.2. This piece is from a late die state, as the nearest point of star 6 is joined to the rim by a light crack, and a second crack connects a second point to the front of Liberty's ribbon, down through the foot of the L in LIBERTY, and into the highpoint hair. Lustrous orange-gold surfaces with glints of apricot. Population: 58 in 62, 48 finer (8/08). *From The Bell Collection.* (#7694)

3235 **1836 Block 8 AU50 PCGS.** Head of 1834, Breen-6142, McCloskey-B, R.3. A thin center line of the 8 in the date distinguishes this example from the Script 8 variety. Both types are listed in the Red Book, although there are several minor variations of each. Most notably, this piece features the Head of 1834, which is identified by the large first hair curl above Liberty's forehead. Numerous abrasions define the grade, but none are particularly bothersome. Dazzling luster sparkles throughout and complements the pleasing yellow-gold patina. The strike is bold save for minor weakness on several stars and a couple of letters in STATES. This attractive specimen is housed in a green label PCGS holder. (#97694)

Pleasing 1837 Quarter Eagle, Choice AU

3236 **1837 AU55 NGC.** McCloskey-B, R.2. Each vertical stripe of the shield has three distinct lines, and the lowest arrowhead touches the second A in AMERICA, identifying this variety. The stars and Liberty's hair are soft, as typically seen, but there are no noteworthy marks. Plenty of luster remains in the fields and enhances the eye appeal. An excellent type coin. (#7695)

Challenging 1837 Quarter Eagle MS61

3237 **1837 MS61 NGC.** McCloskey-B, R.2., distinguished by three lines in the stripes of the shield, and overlapping of the right foot of the last A in AMERICA and the arrowhead. Variegated apricot and yellow-gold patina graces lightly marked surfaces. Partially prooflike fields yield mild contrast with nicely defined devices. Examples can be located in XF and AU, but Mint State coins are challenging. (#7695)

Scarce 1837 Two and a Half MS62

3238 **1837 MS62 NGC.** McCloskey-B, R.2. A lustrous example that has a good strike save for minor blending on the center of the shield. Smooth save for a small mark beneath the chin. A low mintage date, since commercial need was met by a large 1836 production. Census: 19 in 62, 4 finer (7/08). (#7695)

3239 **1838 AU53 NGC.** Breen-6146, R.2. With just 47,030 pieces struck, the 1838 has a mintage of less than one-tenth of its 1836 predecessor. Dazzling luster radiates from the yellow-gold surfaces. A shallow mark is noted to the left of Liberty's nose. The stars and eagle's wings are soft, as typically seen, but the remaining details are well defined. (#7696)

Crisp 1838-C Quarter Eagle, AU50

3240 **1838-C AU50 NGC.** Breen-6147, Variety 1-A. A striking survivor from this initial Charlotte quarter eagle issue, impressively detailed on Liberty's curls and the eagle's feathers. Dusky orange-gold centers yield to deeper reddish-orange close to the rims. Light, even wear crosses the surfaces, minimally marked save for a handful of minor abrasions in the reverse fields. (#7697)

AU55 Details 1838-C Quarter Eagle

3241 **1838-C—Altered Surfaces—ANACS. AU55 Details.** Variety 1-A. This first-year Charlotte quarter eagle issue is scarce in any grade and immensely popular. Though the present piece is softly struck with unnatural luster on each side, the surfaces show little actual wear. Yellow-gold centers fade to deeper orange near the margins. (#7697)

Late State AU Details 1839-C Two and a Half

3242 **1839-C—Improperly Cleaned—NCS. AU Details.** Recut 39, Winter 3-C, McCloskey-C, Breen-6150, R.3. Three different die varieties are known despite a tiny mintage of 18,140 pieces. A late die state with several heavy, lengthy cracks on each side. A well defined example, but thickly hairlined and bright from cleaning. (#7699)

Scarce 1839-C Quarter Eagle, AU55

3243 **1839-C AU55 NGC.** Recut 39, Winter 3-C, McCloskey-C, Breen-6150, R.3. The C mintmark is over the space between 83 in the date. The 1839-C is a low-mintage, scarce date. Bright yellow-gold surfaces of this Choice AU specimen exhibit well defined design features, except for the usually soft star centers. Light marks are evenly distributed over each side. (#7699)

Near-Mint 1839-C Two and a Half

3244 **1839-C AU58 NGC.** Recut 39, Winter 3-C, McCloskey-C, Breen-6150, R.3. Formerly thought to be an overdate, the final digits have now been proven to be recut instead. Two obverse dies were used for this issue and only one reverse die was employed. The reverse die was the same one used on the 1838-C, thus it has more extensive die cracking. The surfaces are bright green-gold with a faint overlay of reddish patina. Slightly soft on the high points on the obverse, the reverse is better detailed. Only tiny handling marks are seen on each side, none of which merit individual mention. (#7699)

Charming 1839-O Quarter Eagle, AU53

3245 **1839-O AU53 NGC.** High Date, Wide Fraction, Breen-6152, McCloskey-A, R.3. Charming olive-orange patina drapes the surfaces of this early O-mint quarter eagle. The stars are weakly struck, as typically seen, but the rest of the details are boldly defined. Numerous abrasions cover the fields, and all are minor save for a shallow scratch across Liberty's head. One of just 17,781 pieces minted. (#7701)

Choice AU 1839-O McCloskey-A Quarter Eagle

3246 **1839-O AU55 PCGS.** High Date, Wide Fraction, Breen-6152, McCloskey-A, R.3. As the first quarter eagle mintage from the New Orleans Mint that had only opened the year before, in 1838, the 1839-Os must have been saved by the local populace. Despite their meager mintage of less than 18,000 pieces, today they are available for a price up through the lower Mint State grades. This Choice AU piece displays lustrous yellow-gold surfaces with only a few shallow, sprinkled contact marks. (#7701)

Scarce Uncirculated 1839-O Quarter Eagle

3247 **1839-O MS61 NGC.** Low Date, Close Fraction, Breen-6153, McCloskey-B, R.4. This distinctive variety not only has the date placed low in the exergual area but it also shows a disconnected berry on the reverse and malformed arrowheads. Interestingly, most examples of this variety have a medallic alignment, as does this piece. The reverse of this coin shows extensive, almost terminal die cracking. Well, but not fully struck up, the surfaces are bright orange-gold. A couple of marks limit the grade to the MS61 level, one behind the hair curls on the obverse and another in the reverse field between the eagle's head and left (facing) wing. (#7701)

LIBERTY QUARTER EAGLES

3248 **1840 XF40 PCGS.** A splendid first-year example of Christian Gobrecht's Liberty Head quarter eagle. Surprisingly, these pieces were not saved at the time, and this statement is supported by the current population data. Lovely orange patina graces the perimeter and surrounds the yellow-gold centers. Myriad marks limit the grade, but none are of any consequence save for a small dig above the eagle's left (facing) wing. A lovely piece for a type collection. (#7717)

3249 **1840 AU50 NGC.** Though it is not the most heavily minted quarter eagle issue for the year, the 1840 commands a surprisingly small premium in grades through XF. Only AU and better pieces, such as the present coin, command better prices. The bright yellow-gold surfaces of this well struck piece show subtle crescents of orange along the margins. (#7717)

Splendid 1840 Quarter Eagle, AU53

3250　**1840 AU53 NGC.** This briefly circulated piece has lots of eye-catching luster and no marks worthy of individual mention. The star above the point of Liberty's coronet and the eagle's left (facing) leg are soft, but the rest of the details are bold. This conditionally scarce example would make an excellent first-year representative. One of just 18,800 pieces minted. Census: 11 in 53, 31 finer (7/08). (#7717)

3251　**1840-C—Obverse Repaired, Improperly Cleaned—NCS. AU Details.** Variety 1-A. The initial Coronet quarter eagle issue struck at Charlotte. Scratches in the right obverse field have been smoothed out, and the yellow-gold surfaces show distinct evidence of cleaning. Still, a strangely pleasing, minimally worn coin. (#7718)

Luminous Choice AU 1840-C Two and a Half

3252　**1840-C AU55 NGC.** Variety 1-A. A radiant yellow-gold Choice AU example with a surprisingly unabraded reverse and no singularly important obverse marks. The introductory Charlotte Mint Liberty quarter eagle issue has a typically minimal mintage of only 12,822 pieces. Census: 28 in 55, 39 finer (7/08). (#7718)

3253　**1841-C Fine 12 PCGS.** Variety 2-B. The only variety known. Winter (1998) writes that the "1841-C is one of the rarest Charlotte quarter eagles" and has a mintage of just 10,281 pieces. Lovely original orange patina drapes the surfaces of this elusive piece. The devices are clearly outlined and there are no marks worthy of mention. (#7721)

Well-Defined 1842-O Quarter Eagle, AU53

3254　**1842-O AU53 NGC.** Representatives of this issue are most often seen in the VF to XF range. AU examples are scarce, and Mint State coins are quite rare. The present AU53 offering displays honey-gold patina with tints of light tan. The design elements exhibit above-average definition, as evidenced by sharp centrils on all stars. Some minor roughness is noted on portions of the rims. (#7726)

Conditionally Rare 1842-O Two and a Half, MS60

3255　**1842-O MS60 NGC.** When specialists discuss high grade 1842-O two and a half dollar pieces they are typically speaking of AU examples. Doug Winter states in his *Gold Coins of the New Orleans Mint* (2006): "The 1842-O quarter eagle is an issue that was, as recently as a few years ago, nearly impossible to find in grades above AU55." The current offering provides the opportunity to acquire a Mint State specimen of this conditionally challenging issue without entering into the extreme price levels of the few finer known pieces. Most 1842-O quarter eagles are weakly struck and this example is no exception. Pale gold with subdued luster throughout and pleasing overall. Census: 3 in 60, 11 finer (8/08). (#7726)

Important MS61 1842-O Quarter Eagle

3256　**1842-O MS61 PCGS.** Softly struck as usual in the centers, though the luster of the yellow-orange surfaces shows no disturbances. Minimally marked for the grade with its own brand of eye appeal. This issue of 19,800 pieces is highly elusive in better grades and a rarity in Mint State. Population: 4 in 61, 6 finer (7/08). (#7726)

3257 **1843 AU58 NGC.** Well struck with light greenish color and glints of golden luster remaining near the borders. Wispy hairlines are observed in the fields, and a pinscratch is noted just behind Liberty's hair bun that passes between obverse stars 10 and 11, and almost to the rim. Extremely scarce in Mint State. Census: 53 in 58, 19 finer (7/08). (#7727)

3258 **1843-C Large Date, Plain 4 VF30 NGC.** Variety 5-D. Despite the mid-range assigned grade, the modestly alloyed tan-gold surfaces offer considerable luster. A degree of striking softness is noted in the centers, which are minimally marked. (#7728)

3259 **1843-C Large Date, Plain 4 XF40 NGC.** Variety 5-D. A luminous XF representative of this more available 1843-C quarter eagle variety. Subtly luminous honey-gold surfaces show glimmers of luster at the margins. (#7728)

3260 **1843-C Large Date, Plain 4—Improperly Cleaned—NCS. AU Details.** Variety 5-D, distinguished by the large, sans-serif 4 in the date. Well-defined with oddly bright yellow-orange surfaces that retain vestiges of original luster at the margins. (#7728)

Popular 1843-D Small D Quarter Eagle, AU55

3261 **1843-D Small D AU55 NGC.** Variety 4-D. Moderately abraded greenish-gold surfaces display nearly full satin luster. Hints of pale orange patina add to the impressive aesthetic appeal of this Choice AU quarter eagle. Both sides have some typical weakness at the central areas Census: 49 in 55, 64 finer (8/08). (#7730)

Pleasing 1843-D Small D Quarter Eagle, AU58

3262 **1843-D Small D AU58 NGC.** Variety 4-D. The "low mintmark" Small D variety. The bright yellow-gold surfaces of this near-Mint example display considerable luster, and an attentive strike imparts sharp definition to the design features, except for the usual softness on the eagle's left (facing) leg. The surfaces are devoid of significant abrasions, that are visible on many '43-Ds (Douglas Winter, 2003). (#7730)

3263 **1843-O Small Date, Crosslet 4 AU50 ANACS.** This well struck orange-gold two and a half has only faint friction on the portrait highpoints. Luster glimmers from protected areas, and neither side displays detracting marks. (#7731)

3264 **1843-O Small Date, Crosslet 4 AU58 NGC.** This attractive piece would make a great type coin. The strike is sharp and there is powerful luster throughout. Charming yellow-gold patina covers the surfaces, which show no significant abrasions. (#7731)

3265 **1843-O Small Date, Crosslet 4—Damaged—NCS. Unc Details.** Pleasing yellow-gold patina drapes the resplendent surfaces. The centers are just a little soft, but the rest of the details are razor-sharp. A few small gouges at the bottom of the bust and several hairlines in the right reverse field are noted. (#7731)

Attractive 1843-O Small Date, Crosslet 4 Quarter Eagle, MS62

3266 **1843-O Small Date, Crosslet 4 MS62 NGC.** The 1843-O Small Date is the most common quarter eagle from the New Orleans Mint, and is easily located through About Uncirculated. It is scarce to rare in the lower Mint State grades (Douglas Winter, 2006). Soft frosty luster shows on both sides, each with attractive yellow-gold color. Well struck, save for minor softness on the eagle's neck and the upper shield. A few minute handling marks are scattered about. Census: 25 in 62, 12 finer (7/08). (#7731)

Bright 1843-O Large Date, Plain 4 Quarter Eagle, AU53

3267 **1843-O Large Date, Plain 4 AU53 NGC.** The 1843-O Large Date, from a mintage of 76,000 pieces, is the rarest of the two varieties of quarter eagle struck this year at the New Orleans Mint. The bright yellow-gold surfaces of this AU53 example exhibit traces of luster in the protected areas. The design features are generally well defined, except for the usual softness on portions of the eagle. A few minor circulation marks do not disturb. (#7732)

Charming AU 1845-D Two and a Half

3268 **1845-D AU50 NGC.** Variety 6-I. Luster glints from protected regions of this green-gold rare date quarter eagle. The eagle's neck and the curls near the ear show selected softness, but the stars have crisp centrils. This Dahlonega issue has a scant emission of just 19,460 pieces. (#7738)

Incredible 1846-C Quarter Eagle, MS62

Condition Rarity 1846-D Quarter Eagle
MS62, Variety 7-J

3269 **1846-C MS62 NGC.** Winter 7-F. The 1846-C is a very scarce coin in any grade with only 4,808 pieces struck, and high grade examples are especially difficult. Once again (as in 1844), the fire that closed down the Charlotte mint for a year and a half is responsible for the dearth of collectible examples of this issue. It is also presumably responsible for the extensive die rust seen on each side of all surviving 1846-C quarter eagles. After the fire in July 1844, the dies lay around unused and rust accumulated on their surfaces, which of course transferred to each of the coins of this issue. Only four or five pieces are believed known in Mint State and this coin is tied with several others as fourth finest known on the Condition Census. The striking details are not complete but better than one might imagine given the state of the dies used. The surfaces are bright overall with lighter green-gold color that shows an attractive intermingling of orange. Distinguished by a shallow scratch above star 12, which should be helpful for pedigree purposes.
Ex: 2001 Long Beach Sale (Heritage, 2/01), lot 6859, where it brought $23,575.
From The Mississippi Collection. (#7741)

3270 **1846-D—Cleaned—ICG. AU53 Details.** Variety 7-J. One of four die combinations known for this issue, despite its low mintage of 19,303 pieces. This example is glossy, but appears pleasing to the unaided eye. The centers are typically brought up, but all stars are crisp. (#7742)

3271 **1846-D MS62 NGC.** Variety 7-J, identified by a die crack that begins at the rim at the right side of the E in AMERICA and runs through the field and into the feathers. A second crack runs from the first S in STATES through to the rim.

    The 1846-D is usually seen in Very Fine and Extremely Fine grades. It is scarce to rare in About Uncirculated, and is an extremely rare issue in Mint State. Indeed, NGC and PCGS have certified only 17 such coins, the highest being a single MS64.

    The bright peach-gold surfaces of this MS62 specimen exhibit well struck design elements, the only exception being softness in the eagle's legs and neck. A few small marks are visible, slightly more so on the obverse. This is the highest grade most collectors can hope to own. Census: 3 in 62, 2 finer (7/08).
From The Mississippi Collection. (#7742)

3272 **1846-O AU50 NGC.** Despite a recorded mintage of 62,000 coins, few examples of the date appear on the market at any one time, and those that do are apt to be in lower grades. This example shows little actual wear, though the soft strike contributes to the overall impression. (#7743)

Rarely Seen 1846-O Quarter Eagle, MS64
Probably Third Finest Known

3273 1846-O MS64 NGC. Variety Two. The mintage of 62,000 pieces for the 1846-O quarter eagle belies its true scarcity. Only 100-110 pieces are believed known today in all grades. High grade examples are difficult to locate, but there are several notable high grade pieces that were obviously set aside at the time of production. The finest known is an MS66 from the Pittman Collection, and it is considered the finest O-mint quarter eagle known. Second finest is the Bass MS64. This seems to be a coin that was unknown to Doug Winter when he wrote his 2006 update of his O-mint gold reference as it does not appear in the Significant Pieces Known section.

Variety Two 1846-O quarter eagles are recognized by the arrow feathers that enter the top of the mintmark. Coins of this variety are often seen with weak central details. Both the hair curls around Liberty's face and the feathers on the eagle are notably soft. Otherwise, the surfaces have resplendent mint luster and a hint of semiprooflikeness in the fields. The most obvious mark for tracing the pedigree of this coin is a short, shallow abrasion in front of the ear of Liberty. The bright yellow-gold color has a light overlay of reddish patina. (#7743)

3274 1847-D VF30 PCGS. Variety 9-M. Deep orange patina covers the majority of the surfaces, with yellow accents on the highpoints and a few tiny areas of detritus. Two small pinscratches in the right obverse field are barely worthy of note. This pleasing example is one of only 15,784 pieces struck. (#7746)

Smooth Choice AU 1847-D Quarter Eagle

3275 1847-D AU55 NGC. Variety 9-M. A pleasing olive-gold representative with minimally marked surfaces. The strike is above average for the Dahlonega Mint, and luster connects the reverse legends and individually illuminates the stars. A mere 15,784 pieces were coined. Census: 17 in 55, 59 finer (7/08). (#7746)

Conditionally Rare 1848 Quarter Eagle, MS62

3276 1848 MS62 NGC. Jeff Garrett and Ron Guth note that the "1848 quarter eagle is actually much rarer than the 1848, CAL. Above Eagle variety in Mint State." An interesting observation, although rarity, as always, is a combination of demand and supply. This example offers attractive greenish-gold surfaces, with parallel planchet striations visible on both sides. A few stray abrasions constitute the grade, but much appeal is present. The strike is soft on the eagle's left (facing) leg, but sharp elsewhere. A rare and attractive coin. Census: 5 in 62, 3 finer (8/08).
From The Mississippi Collection. (#7748)

3277 1848-C—Ex-Jewelry, Rims Filed—ICG. AU50 Details. Variety 9-F. The field above the eagle's head is repaired, as is Liberty's cheek and jaw. The field beneath the chin and the right obverse field are also smoothed. Some scratches remain on the upper reverse field. The rims appear unimpaired where visible from within the holder. (#7750)

Popular 1848-C Two and a Half AU53

3278 1848-C AU53 NGC. Variety 9-F. This low mintage Charlotte Mint quarter eagle displays straw-gold and pale lime patina. The strike is above average despite blending on the lowest portion of the eagle. There are no reportable abrasions. Difficult to find with such original color, as most pieces have been dipped in recent decades. (#7750)

Near-Mint 1848-C Quarter Eagle

3279 **1848-C AU58 NGC.** Variety 9-F. A splendid near-Mint example with pastel green-gold surfaces, faint bluish patina, and excellent eye appeal. The fields are slightly prooflike on both sides. A few scattered surface marks are mostly concentrated on the reverse of this piece. Census: 36 in 58, 16 finer (8/08). (#7750)

3280 **1848-D XF40 PCGS.** Variety 10-M. This reverse die was used on nearly all Dahlonega quarter eagles from 1847 on, and features the top of the fraction bar centered below the mintmark. Copper-orange patina graces the surfaces of this lovely representative. Both sides show wear typical of the grade, but there are no prominent marks or blemishes. A mere 13,771 pieces were minted. (#7751)

Pleasing 1848-D Quarter Eagle, AU50

3281 **1848-D AU50 PCGS.** Variety 10-M. The end of the fraction bar does not cross the middle of the mintmark's opening, which is diagnostic for this variety. This variety is occasionally seen with rotated dies, and on this piece the reverse is rotated approximately 30 degrees. Delightful yellow-gold patina is accented by impressive luster throughout. Several minor marks limit the grade, but none merit individual mention. The eagle's wings and legs are soft, as often seen, but the rest of the details are bold. Population: 20 in 50, 68 finer (7/08). (#7751)

Lustrous AU53 1848-D Quarter Eagle

3282 **1848-D AU53 NGC.** Variety 10-M. Luminous yellow-orange obverse fields pale to lighter lemon-gold on the portrait, while the reverse has even, dusky orange-gold shadings. A well struck example of this mid-date Dahlonega quarter eagle issue, minimally marked and luminous with light, even wear across the central devices. (#7751)

Sharp 1850-C Quarter Eagle, AU53

3283 **1850-C AU53 NGC. CAC.** Variety 12-H. Two reverse dies were employed in the production of this Charlotte Mint quarter eagle issue. The mintmark on this variety is nearly centered above the diagonal fraction bar of 1/2. Reddish-gold patina bathes this AU53 example. The strike is above average, including strong radials on all stars. The usual softness is apparent on portions of the eagle. The surfaces retain luster in the recesses, and are quite clean. A sharp piece, evidenced by the CAC label. (#7756)

Interesting AU53 1850-D Quarter Eagle

3284 **1850-D AU53 NGC.** Variety 13-M. Primarily yellow-gold with occasional elements of green and orange. Softly struck on the hair below the coronet, as often seen, yet only mildly worn with appreciable luster in the modestly abraded fields. Attractive and desirable. Census: 15 in 53, 84 finer (8/08). (#7757)

Delightful 1850-D Quarter Eagle, AU58

3285 **1850-D AU58 PCGS.** Variety 13-M. The only variety known. With a mintage of just 12,148 pieces, the 1850-D is a scarce issue in any grade. Mint State coins are decidedly rare, and NGC and PCGS report a combined 24 pieces at that level. This impressive near-Uncirculated example displays a delightful mix of apricot-gold and mint-green color on both sides. Enticing semiprooflike luster accents the sharply defined design elements, which are full save for a trace of weakness on the eagle's legs. Population: 13 in 58, 6 finer (8/08). (#7757)

Difficult XF 1851-C Quarter Eagle

3286 **1851-C XF40 PCGS.** Variety 13-G. A orange-gold example with noticeable luster and the expected number of inconspicuous field marks. Moderate horizontal roller marks across the centers of both sides are strictly as made. Like all Charlotte quarter eagles, the 1851-C has a meager mintage. Only 14,923 pieces were struck. (#7760)

Lovely 1851-C Quarter Eagle, AU50

3287 **1851-C AU50 PCGS.** Variety 13-G. A scarce Southern branch mint issue, a scant 14,923 pieces were struck. Minor marks on Liberty's jaw and above the first star are hardly worthy of mention. The strike is, as expected, not full on the eagle's shield and plumage, or on the hair curls, but the impression from the dies is suitable for a Charlotte Mint product. Population: 13 in 50, 18 finer (8/08). (#7760)

Charming 1851-C Quarter Eagle, Choice AU

3288 **1851-C AU55 NGC.** Variety 13-G. The only variety known. The 1851-C has a mintage of just 14,923 pieces, and while that is actually higher than most C-mint quarter eagles, this issue is actually scarcer than most. Delightful olive-yellow patina covers both sides of this minimally marked specimen. The strike is crisp save for minor weakness on a couple of stars and the shield. Census: 15 in 55, 34 finer (7/08). (#7760)

3289 **1851-D—Scratched—ANACS. XF Details.** Variety 14-M. Sharp for the designated grade, and the apricot-gold surfaces are generally pleasing, but a thin diagonal scratch nearly connects the base of the hairbun with star 12. (#7761)

Rare Choice AU 1851-D Two and a Half

3290 **1851-D AU55 NGC.** Variety 14-M. Substantial luster fills the margins and devices of this low mintage Dahlonega quarter eagle. The luminous surfaces lack detrimental marks. A crisp strike with only slight weakness on the claws and Liberty's forehead curls. Census: 13 in 55, 18 finer (7/08). (#7761)

3291 **1851-O AU55 NGC.** An early die state, with doubling on all four digits of the date. The date was first punched too low and leaning down too far towards the left. Douglas Winter (2006) writes that examples with strong repunching on all four digits (such as the present AU55 piece) are scarce and should sell for a premium. Bright peach-gold surfaces display fairly well defined motifs, though the usual softness is visible on the left (facing) leg and neck feathers of the eagle. A few light marks do not detract. (#7762)

MS61 1851-O Quarter Eagle With Boldly Repunched Date

3292 **1851-O MS61 PCGS.** Breen-6214, Doubled Date. The mintage of O-mint quarter eagles was nearly twice that of the previous year's emission, despite which the 1851-O is still rare in Mint State. This example has pretty green-gold surfaces with good luster and a few moderate abrasions.

This is an early state of the Doubled Date obverse, in which all four numerals are significantly doubling from a first punching that was too low and sloping downward from left to right. The effect is that the first 1 shows tips of second serifs to the left of the final serifs, while the last 1 shows an entire digit, considerably lower and out of line with the final 1. Douglas Winter says of the variety, "Examples with strong repunching on all four digits are scarce and should sell for a premium over those that have it on only the 51 or the final digit." (#7762)

3293 **1852-O AU58 NGC.** A briefly circulated example with bright, semiprooflike surfaces. There are a number of minor abrasions on each side, but none merit specific mention. Plenty of captivating luster gives this untoned and boldly struck specimen impressive eye appeal. NGC reports a mere 30 pieces in Mint State (7/08). (#7766)

Flashy MS62 1852-O Two and a Half

3294 **1852-O MS62 NGC.** Breen-6219, his 'extra heavy O' variety, which he considered very rare but makes up a significant portion of the issue. The mintmark is unusually thick and tall, reminiscent of the 1854-O 'Huge O' quarter which is believed to have been entered by hand into the die. This is a moderately prooflike example with a pleasantly unmarked appearance. The strike is precise except on the eagle's left (facing) leg. Census: 7 in 62, 4 finer (7/08). (#7766)

3295 **1853 MS64 PCGS.** Although common in most grades, the 1853 quarter eagle is seldom seen in Choice Mint State, and is extremely difficult to locate any finer. This minimally marked piece has attractive yellow-gold patina on both sides. The strike is sharp save for a touch of weakness on LIBERTY. Dazzling satiny luster shimmers in the fields and gives this piece great eye appeal. Population: 68 in 64, 5 finer (7/08). (#7767)

3296 **1854 MS63 PCGS.** Enticing satiny luster shimmers beneath the charming yellow-gold patina. A few minor marks limit the grade, but the details are razor-sharp. Both sides show obvious clash marks and it appears that the dies clashed at least twice. PCGS has certified only 23 examples finer (8/08). (#7769)

3297 **1854-C—Improperly Cleaned—NCS. XF Details.** Variety 15-I. Moderately hairlined surfaces are dusky butter-yellow with occasional glimpses of alloy. Only light wear crosses the high points of the design. (#7770)

Attractive Uncirculated 1854-O Quarter Eagle

3298 **1854-O MS61 NGC.** A bright yellow-gold representative that lacks the field marks often associated with the MS61 grade. Luster is especially active throughout the peripheries. A slender strike-through (as made) is noted above the eagle's head, and the obverse die is sinking (also as struck) between stars 5 and 8. Census: 21 in 61, 7 finer (7/08). (#7772)

3299 **1856 MS63 NGC.** Interestingly, the date on 1856 quarter eagles is significantly smaller than on previous issues. This yellow-gold representative exhibits a razor-sharp strike and impressively lustrous fields. A conditionally scarce and lightly abraded representative. Census: 37 in 63, 18 finer (7/08). (#7777)

Gem 1856 Quarter Eagle, Ex: Bass

3300 **1856 MS65 PCGS.** Ex: Bass. A beautifully preserved pumpkin-gold Gem that exhibits vibrant luster and a desirable pedigree. LIBERTY and portions of the lower half of the eagle lack a full impression. Population: 4 in 65, 4 finer (8/08).
Ex: Fairfield Collection (Bowers and Ruddy, 10/1977), lot 1549; Harry W. Bass, Jr. Collection, Part IV (Bowers and Merena, 11/2000), lot 193; Heritage, 4/2001, lot 21043, which realized $5,250. (#7777)

Important Premium Gem 1856 Quarter Eagle Ex: Bass

3301 **1856 MS66 PCGS.** This heavily minted pre-Civil War issue has a handful of pieces above the Gem level in the PCGS *Population Report*, which increases its importance to the collector who wishes to assemble the ultimate gold type set. This famously pedigreed piece is primarily yellow-gold with only a single, trivial fault below Liberty's chin. The present cataloger sees no need to disagree with the coin's description in Bass II: "A splendid eye-appealing coin with rich, smooth, satiny lustre on obverse and reverse, the latter side challenging perfection." Population: 3 in 66, 1 finer (7/08).
Ex: Purchased from Julian Leidman, 7/28/72; The Harry W. Bass, Jr. Collection, Part II (10/99), lot 479. (#7777)

Elusive Near-Mint 1856-C Quarter Eagle

3302 **1856-C AU58 NGC.** Variety 17-J. 1856 was one of the years in which the lowly and little-respected quarter eagle denomination was produced at five different U.S. mints, including the Mother Mint in Philadelphia; the original branch mints of New Orleans, Charlotte, and Dahlonega; and the fledgling San Francisco Mint, which had opened only two years previously. The 1856-C quarter eagle is seldom offered, however, and the coins were poorly struck on roughly made planchets. This piece is no exception, but it does show copious luster remaining on orange-gold surfaces, and there is only a sprinkling of tiny post-strike abrasions. Census: 23 in 58, 13 finer (7/08). (#7778)

Lovely AU58 1856-C Quarter Eagle

3303 **1856-C AU58 NGC.** Variety 17-J, the only die pair for the year. The 1856-C is a challenging issue that is slightly underrated today, due to its proximity to the famously low-mintage 1856-D quarter eagle. Still, series enthusiasts know the difficulty in procuring a near-Mint example. The radiant yellow-gold surfaces of this piece are minimally marked with pillowy detail on the portrait. Census: 23 in 58, 13 finer (8/08). (#7778)

Shining Near-Mint 1856-O Quarter Eagle

3304 **1856-O AU58 NGC.** An uncommonly appealing, scarcely worn survivor of this popular antebellum issue. The generally lemon-gold surfaces offer considerable luster with few marks, and the central and peripheral devices are equally well-defined. Elusive any finer; NGC has graded just 14 Mint State pieces (8/08). (#7780)

Conditionally Scarce 1856-S Quarter Eagle, MS60

3305 **1856-S MS60 NGC.** According to the *Encyclopedia of U.S. Gold Coins, 1795-1933*, by Jeff Garrett and Ron Guth (2006): "The 1856-S Liberty Head quarter eagle is the first truly collectible quarter eagle from the San Francisco Mint. With a moderate mintage of 72,120 pieces, the issue is fairly available in the lower grades up to the About Uncirculated level." This conditionally scarce Mint State specimen is bright and highly lustrous, with lovely lime-green and peach toning. Boldly struck with scattered field marks that are mostly superficial. Census: 8 in 60, 20 finer (8/08). (#7781)

3306 **1857 MS62 PCGS.** Warm gold-orange surfaces show subtle variations from sun to rose. Pleasingly detailed with minor, wispy flaws across each side that account for the grade. Population: 44 in 62, 28 finer (8/08). (#7782)

3307 **1857 MS62 NGC.** Despite a relatively high mintage, the 1857 can be surprisingly difficult to locate higher than low Mint State grades. Delightful sun-gold patina graces both sides of this lustrous piece. Sharply struck and minimally marked. (#7782)

3308 **1857 MS63 NGC.** Warm orange-gold surfaces offer delightful luster and occasional peach accents. Pleasingly detailed and minimally marked by Select standards. Census: 30 in 63, 16 finer (7/08). (#7782)

Attractive 1857-O Quarter Eagle, AU58

3309 **1857-O AU58 NGC.** The 1857-O is one of the more available New Orleans quarter eagles, though Douglas Winter (2006) writes: "... original, properly graded AU55s and AU58s are becoming scarce. This date is rare in Uncirculated ... ." Attractive peach-gold color adorns this near-Mint specimen, and it is better struck than most, evidenced by strong star radials and sharp hair on Liberty. The eagle's left (facing) leg and neck show the typical softness. A few minute marks are not serious. (#7784)

Radiantly Lustrous 1857-S Quarter Eagle, Unc Details

3310 **1857-S—Scratched—NCS. Unc Details.** A Choice piece but for the few shallow scratches on the reverse. The bold strike is enhanced by the satiny luster underneath the orange-gold patina. In 1857 the San Francisco Mint was focusing on double eagle production and struck only 69,200 quarter eagles. Of the pieces that survived, most are seen with considerable wear. An excellent piece for the specialist. (#7785)

3311 **1858 MS60 NGC.** A flashy lemon-gold piece with no trace of wear. The well struck devices and nearby fields show a number of faint to overt abrasions that account for the grade. Census: 2 in 60, 62 finer (7/08). (#7786)

3312 **1858 MS62 NGC.** An amazing yellow-gold Mint State example of this moderately low-mintage issue, one of fewer than 50,000 pieces struck. Highly elusive and underrated, particularly in better circulated and unworn states. Census: 14 in 62, 17 finer (7/08). (#7786)

Choice AU 1858-C Two and a Half

3313 **1858-C AU55 NGC.** Variety 18-J. This yellow-gold Charlotte representative has a wealth of detail, since the strike is superior for the mint and there is only marginal wear. The surfaces are pleasantly smooth, and traces of dirt within protected areas confirm the originality. A mere 9,056 pieces were struck. (#7787)

3314 **1859 Old Reverse, Type One AU55 NGC.** Two distinct quarter eagle varieties were coined in 1859 because of the introduction of a new reverse hub. This piece features the old design, which was used intermittently for two more years. Scattered abrasions define the grade, but none are particularly bothersome. Crisply struck with lovely yellow-gold patina. (#97788)

Rare MS62 Type One Reverse 1859 Two and a Half

3315 **1859 Old Reverse, Type One MS62 PCGS.** The broad arrowheads confirm the rare Type One reverse, which comprises a small minority of the mintage of less than 20,000 pieces. The strike is sharp save for the portions of the lower half of the eagle. Generally well preserved, although a curved mark near star 1 limits the grade. Population: 5 in 62, 7 finer (8/08). (#97788)

Delightful 1860-C Quarter Eagle, XF45

3316 **1860-C XF45 PCGS.** *Ex: Stecher Collection.* Variety 19-J. The 1860-C Liberty Head quarter eagle, with a mintage of 7,469 pieces, was the final quarter eagle struck by the Charlotte Mint. Jeff Garrett and Ron Guth (2006) write that it is always seen weakly struck on rough planchets. This Choice XF example, while having some inoffensive contact marks scattered over each side, exhibits rather pleasing apricot-gold surfaces tinted with wisps of red at the margins. The initial strike was relatively strong, as most of the star centers are sharp, as is most of Liberty's hair. Some softness is noted on the eagle's neck and legs. Purchased in the 1930's at face value by Karl Stecher Sr. from coins turned in by the public as per President Roosevelt's March 9, 1933 directive. (#7792)

Scarce Old Reverse 1861 Two and a Half, MS63

3317 1861 Old Reverse, Type One MS63 NGC. Final year to use the Reverse of 1858, and as such a very scarce hubbing variant. The old hub is distinguished by the lowest arrowhead almost touching the CA in AMERICA. The space between the arrowheads is also more closed than on the new hub, the lettering is larger and less chunky, and the period after the D is more distant. The surfaces are bright and lustrous with just a tinge of reddish peripheral color. Well struck, there are no mentionable abrasions present on either side. Census: 5 in 63, 5 finer (8/08). (#97794)

Gem 1861 Quarter Eagle, New Reverse

3318 1861 New Reverse, Type Two MS65 PCGS. CAC. The New Reverse, featuring smaller lettering and arrowheads, is much more common than the Old Reverse, used for the last time in 1861 on P-mint quarter eagles and distinguishable by the larger arrowheads that nearly touch the R and C in RICA. This Gem example of the New Reverse shows boldly struck surfaces with orange-gold coloration and good luster. A small die crack does run from the smaller middle arrowhead to R, and of apparent Mint origin are a couple of small planchet flakes on the lower reverse. Population: 20 in 65, 10 finer (7/08). (#7794)

3319 1866—Rim Filed, Bent—NCS. VF Details. File marks on the rim are most evident on the obverse between 7 and 8 o'clock. That area is slightly bent as well, and both sides are glossy from cleaning. Moderate marks on the reverse further suggest former use as jewelry. Still a rare low mintage date. (#7803)

3320 1866—Improperly Cleaned—NCS. VF Details. A slightly bright green-gold example of this challenging Reconstruction-era issue. About one-third of the feathers show within the wings. A mark is noted beneath the left (facing) wing. A mere 3,080 pieces were struck. (#7803)

Fantastic MS61 1866 Quarter Eagle

3321 1866 MS61 NGC. This issue's business strike mintage of 3,080 pieces is part of a string of four-figure production for Philadelphia quarter eagles that runs from 1864 (only proofs were struck in 1863) to 1872. It was also little-saved, and as a result, Mint State survivors are particularly elusive. This captivating piece, well struck with deep orange-gold and sun-yellow surfaces overall, shows occasional wispy abrasions in the fields that contribute to the grade. Still, an attractive and important coin. Census: 1 in 61, 4 finer (8/08). *From The Mississippi Collection.* (#7803)

3322 1866-S AU50 NGC. The 1866-S has a mintage of only 38,960 pieces, and most survivors are heavily worn. The surfaces display an even, reddish-gold appearance with a few noticeable abrasions. Trifling softness is noted on the eagle. Census: 19 in 50, 66 finer (7/08). (#7804)

Conditionally Scarce 1866-S Quarter Eagle, AU58

3323 **1866-S AU58 NGC.** Although slightly more available than earlier S-Mint quarter eagles, the 1866-S circulated extensively and only a select few survive in About Uncirculated and Mint State. Plenty of luster graces the yellow-gold surfaces of this briefly circulated piece. Minimally marked and quite handsome. Census: 19 in 58, 7 finer (8/08). (#7804)

3324 **1868 AU58 NGC.** A briefly circulated representative with eye-catching semiprooflike reflectivity. Bright yellow patina overlies the minimally marked surfaces. With a mintage of just 3,600 pieces, the 1868 is scarce in any grade and is quite elusive in Mint State. NGC and PCGS combined report just 29 examples finer (8/08). (#7807)

3325 **1868-S AU55 NGC.** With a mintage of just 34,000 pieces, the 1868-S is a difficult piece in nearly any grade, and it is seldom encountered in Mint State. Garrett and Guth (2006) estimate that there are fewer than two dozen Uncirculated coins remaining. Lovely orange patina graces the surfaces of this briefly circulated example. Several minor abrasions are present in the fields, and a small dig is noted on Liberty's hair. A sharply defined and appealing representative. (#7808)

3326 **1869 AU58 NGC.** The 1869 quarter eagle is an often underrated issue with a diminutive mintage of just 4,320 pieces. Examples are particularly rare in Mint State, which increases collector demand for nice About Uncirculated specimens. A trace of light rub keeps this highly lustrous piece from an Uncirculated grade. Pleasing yellow-gold patina drapes the minimally marked surfaces and complements the sharp design elements. (#7809)

3327 **1872-S AU58 NGC.** One of just 18,000 pieces minted. Delightful yellow-gold patina graces both sides, with a few minuscule areas of charcoal color around the reverse devices. Flashy luster accents the powerfully struck design elements. NGC has certified only 16 pieces finer (8/08). (#7816)

Original Gem 1873 Open 3 Quarter Eagle

3328 **1873 Open 3 MS65 PCGS.** This penetratingly struck representative has original dusky orange-gold toning and vibrant cartwheel sheen. Well preserved despite a pair of minor marks above the portrait. The Open 3 variety comprises about 70% of the issue, although early deliveries were Closed 3. Encapsulated in an old green label holder. Population: 10 in 65, 1 finer (8/08). (#7817)

Underrated 1875 Quarter Eagle Rarity
Near-Mint State
One of Fewer Than 30 Examples Known

3329 **1875 AU58 NGC.** Specialists suggest that approximately 25 1875 quarter eagles have survived from the original mintage of 400 pieces, making the date one of the rarest in the entire series. Another challenging Liberty two and a half is the 1854-S, of which 12 or so specimens are believed to be extant from a mintage of 246 coins. Interestingly, the 1854-S—when sold at auction—realizes healthy six-figure price tags, while the 1875 quarter eagles tend to bring low five-figure amounts. The conclusion is that the 1875 quarter eagle is drastically underrated and undervalued. The current near-Mint State offering displays a prooflikeness observed on all known 1875 two and a half survivors and the visual appeal is substantial, considering the assigned grade. A classic numismatic rarity that will one day receive the attention it so deserves. (#7822)

3330 **1876 AU53 NGC.** An attractive AU specimen with pale green and peach coloration and clean surfaces that are free of any noticeable blemishes. Moderate, even wear across the highpoints, and wispy hairlines in the fields define the grade of this better-than-average survivor. (#7824)

Shining MS61 1876 Quarter Eagle

3331 **1876 MS61 NGC.** Though proof issues of 1876 saw a boost of interest from centennial-year celebrations, the business strikes of that year did not see a similar spike, and well coinage of quarter eagles remained low. This strongly lustrous, well struck Mint State survivor shows light abrasions and scattered, wispy marks in the yellow-gold fields, though series enthusiast know that the apparent flaw at Liberty's upper neck is actually a die diagnostic for the issue. Census: 7 in 61, 7 finer (8/08). (#7824)

MS61 ★ 1877 Quarter Eagle, Prooflike Surfaces

3332 **1877 MS61 ★ NGC.** A wonderful example with prooflike fields and bold design features. Both sides exhibit brilliant yellow-gold luster. Just 1,652 of these pieces were coined, and Mint State survivors are rare. A few scattered surface marks are evident on each side of this example. (#7826)

3333 **1877-S MS62 NGC.** Bright yellow patina covers both sides, which feature nearly fully struck details. A number of trivial abrasions define the grade, but they barely affect the eye-catching luster. NGC has certified only 12 pieces finer (8/08). (#7827)

Gorgeous 1878 Gem Quarter Eagle

3334 **1878 MS65 PCGS.** The 1878 is available in the lower Mint State grades, but MS65 pieces are scarce, and anything finer is quite rare. Pleasing silk-like luster adorns the honey-gold surfaces of the present Gem, and a precise strike leaves uniform definition on the design features. Some minute marks might well preclude an even higher grade. Population: 27 in 65, 4 finer (8/08). (#7828)

3335 **1878 MS64 Prooflike NGC.** Impressive prooflike fields contrast nicely against the frosty devices. The strike is razor-sharp, and spectacular luster radiates beneath the bright yellow patina. A tiny mark on Liberty's neck is barely worth noting. NGC has certified only five coins in 64 Prooflike and this piece is the finest (7/08). (#77828)

Famously Rare 1881 Quarter Eagle, MS61

3336 **1881 MS61 PCGS.** An Uncirculated survivor from a minuscule mintage of 640 coins. Garrett-Guth (2006) expound on the importance of the 1881 two and a half: "Of the small number of quarter eagles produced, most entered circulation, with the average survivor being in only Extremely Fine to About Uncirculated condition. Mint State coins are very rare." The current offering is a boldly impressed piece with prooflike surfaces and orange-gold coloration. A tiny toning spot in the field between Liberty's nose and star 3 serves as a pedigree marker for future generations. As of (8/08), PCGS has graded a mere seven examples as MS61, with four finer specimens at the MS62 level. (#7833)

3337 **1886 MS62 PCGS.** Vibrant orange-gold patina coats the surfaces, which have outstanding prooflike fields. The hair above Liberty's forehead is a trifle weak, but the rest of the details are razor-sharp. The 1882 has a low mintage of just 4,000 coins, and this piece ranks among the finest. Population: 14 in 62, 16 finer (7/08). (#7838)

3338 **1886 MS62 NGC.** The 1886 is elusive in MS62, with the typical grade for the issue ranging from About Uncirculated to MS60 or 61 (Garrett and Guth, 2006). Vividly reflective fields complement the yellow-gold patina. A sharply struck piece with great eye appeal. (#7838)

3339 **1887 MS62 NGC.** An outstanding representative with eye-catching, semiprooflike fields. Scattered marks limit the grade, but none merit individual mention. A little weakness is noted on the stars, but the rest of the details are sharply defined. The 1887 is a scarce coin in any grade with a mintage of just 6,160 pieces, and it is a pleasant surprise to come across a well-preserved example such as the present piece. (#7839)

Pretty 1887 Quarter Eagle, MS63
Low-Mintage P-Mint Rarity

3340 **1887 MS63 PCGS.** The 1887 quarter eagle hails from a string of unheralded low-mintage issues of the denomination in the 1860s through mid-1890s, a period when the nation's mints were largely concentrating on other denominations of more significance, both larger and smaller. The 1887 saw a stingy production of only 6,160 coins, and today most certified examples grade only about AU58. The surfaces are unsurprisingly prooflike on this pretty orange-gold piece, which under a loupe reveals the tiny abrasions that prevent an even finer grade. This MS63 example is one of 16 pieces so graded at PCGS, with 13 finer (8/08). (#7839)

3341 **1891 MS63 PCGS.** Yellow-orange patina with slate-gray accents endows both sides of this lustrous piece. The strike is bold and the surfaces have only a few minor abrasions. Housed in a green label PCGS holder. Population: 28 in 63, 29 finer (8/08). (#7843)

Magnificent 1893 Quarter Eagle, Premium Gem

3342 **1893 MS66 PCGS.** Although the 1893 quarter eagle's mintage of 30,000 pieces is a sharp increase from previous years, it is still quite low compared to other denominations. This remarkable specimen is one of the finest certified and would be an excellent piece for a connoisseur. Lovely lemon-yellow patina covers both sides of this satiny Premium Gem. A couple of pinpoint handling marks keep this piece from an even higher grade. Fully struck with outstanding eye appeal. Population: 14 in 66, 0 finer (8/08). (#7845)

MS64 ★ Prooflike 1894 Two and a Half

3343 **1894 MS64 ★ Prooflike NGC.** A penetratingly struck Choice quarter eagle that boasts flashy fields and substantial cameo contrast. The fields are unblemished, and the portrait exhibits only minimal contact. Underrated, as only 4,000 pieces were struck. Census: 1 in 64 ★ Prooflike, 1 finer as Prooflike without a Star designation (7/08). (#77846)

Extraordinary 1898 Quarter Eagle, Superb Gem

3344 **1898 MS67 NGC.** One of just 24,000 pieces struck. Neither NGC nor PCGS has certified any examples finer this impeccably preserved Superb Gem (8/08). Dazzling satiny luster shimmers beneath the yellow-gold patina. The obverse is essentially flawless, while the reverse has only a couple of tiny marks. An outstanding, fully struck representative.
From The Mississippi Collection. (#7850)

Imposing 1903 Quarter Eagle MS66

3345 **1903 MS66 NGC.** An exquisite gold type coin that boasts a needle-sharp strike. A strong loupe is required to locate even trivial surface imperfections. This Premium Gem has dazzling luster, and the eye appeal is virtually unimprovable. Housed in a prior generation holder. (#7855)

3346 **1903 MS63 Prooflike NGC.** Exquisitely struck design elements display pleasing contrast with prooflike fields on this handsome quarter eagle. A few wispy handling marks are visible under magnification. The 1903 quarter eagle is seldom seen in prooflike condition. Census: 2 in 63 Prooflike, 2 finer (7/08). (#77855)

Impressive 1904 Quarter Eagle, MS66 Prooflike

3347 **1904 MS66 Prooflike NGC.** This razor-sharp beauty has flashy prooflike fields and exceptional eye appeal. The surfaces are essentially pristine, and the only detected contact is concealed on the jaw. A faint grease stain is noted on the M in AMERICA. NGC has certified only 11 pieces in Prooflike, with three MS66 examples tied for the finest. (#77856)

Outstanding Premium Gem 1905 Quarter Eagle

3348 **1905 MS66 PCGS.** This exquisitely preserved specimen exhibits blazing luster and lovely yellow-gold toning that yields to faint accents of rose near the margins. The design elements are sharply and fully struck on both sides. This date is a very common one in the series, but the current example is outstanding and decidedly uncommon in terms of both technical and aesthetic merit. *From The Bell Collection.* (#7857)

Glorious MS66 1907 Quarter Eagle

3349 **1907 MS66 NGC.** One of the glorious late-series Liberty Head quarter eagle issues that can occasionally be found in grades up to the Superb Gem level. This Premium Gem coin boasts splendid luster over distraction-free orange-gold surfaces, with a bold strike and only the most minuscule marks apparently precluding an even finer grade (8/08). (#7859)

PROOF LIBERTY QUARTER EAGLES

Low-Mintage 1873 Closed 3 Quarter Eagle, PR58

3350 **1873 Closed 3 PR58 ANACS.** The 1873 quarter eagle proof has a minuscule mintage of 25 coins, one of the lowest of the series. These are all of the Close 3 variety. The yellow-gold surfaces of this PR58 specimen exhibit occasional whispers of apricot, and the design elements are crisply defined. Each side reveals a few minor circulation marks. (#7899)

Amazing PR65 Ultra Cameo 1875 Quarter Eagle

3351 1875 PR65 Ultra Cameo NGC. Since both business strikes and proofs of the 1875 quarter eagle are low-mintage issues, at 400 pieces and 20 specimens respectively, the already-small population of proof survivors faces added pressure from numismatists seeking a business-strike substitute. This spectacular example could not be mistaken for a business strike, however; the outstanding contrast between the heavily frosted, boldly impressed lemon-gold devices and the highly reflective mirrors borders on absolute. A handful of small, isolated flaws in the fields are consistent with the grade. Census: 2 in 65 Ultra Cameo, 0 finer (8/08). (#97901)

Singular PR64 Deep Cameo 1884 Quarter Eagle

3352 1884 PR64 Deep Cameo PCGS. The 1884 quarter eagle proof comes with a mintage of 73 coins. It is a very rare issue, with probably 30 to 40 pieces known in all grades. Though contrast is relatively common on proof 1884 quarter eagles, only the present piece has the impressive reflectivity and strong cameo effect to qualify for the Deep Cameo designation, as awarded by PCGS (8/08). The peach-gold surfaces of this near-Gem example display beautiful gold-on-black contrast, and the design elements are crisply and uniformly struck. Close examination reveals no significant flaws. The only pedigree markers visible are a couple of alloy spots below the I in AMERICA. (#97910)

3353 **1898 PR67 ★ Ultra Cameo NGC.** Proof gold coins have held a place of honor in many of the greatest collections to come across the auction block in the past several decades. Names such as Bass, Pittman, and Trompeter are forever attached to the spectacular specimens that they had the pleasure of owning. Each of those renowned numismatists possessed an outstanding proof 1898 quarter eagle, and the present piece is certain to be treasured by the next great collector.

From an original mintage of just 165 specimens, it is estimated that between 80 and 100 examples still exist—a truly miraculous survival rate. Unfortunately, as Garrett and Guth (2006) are quick to point out, many of those pieces are impaired or otherwise less-than-stellar. Of course, a few virtually perfect pieces do exist, but they seldom come to market. Ultra Cameo coins are even rarer, and NGC reports that just 37 submissions have received that designation. While they have certified 10 pieces finer than this example (one of which is a spectacular PR69), only one of those has received the coveted star designation (8/08). The PR67★ Ultra Cameo grade indicates that this piece is truly among the cream of the crop.

Frosted yellow-gold patina covers the devices, which show stunning cameo contrast against the bottomless, deeply mirrored fields. A minuscule mark between the date and star 13 is noted for future pedigree purposes. The rest of the surfaces are virtually immaculate, although a few small milky patches are visible on the reverse. The full strike further adds to the appeal of this resplendent Superb Gem. This piece is undoubtedly one of the finest known. A discerning collector trying to assemble one of the next important gold collections should not miss the opportunity to acquire this magnificent specimen. (#97924)

Stunning 1900 Quarter Eagle, PR64 Cameo

3354 **1900 PR64 Cameo NGC. CAC.** From a proof mintage of 205 pieces, the 1900 is probably the most available issue of the Liberty Head design type in proof. The date has long been a favorite with proof type collectors. The radiant devices provide dramatic contrast with the darkly mirrored fields. The strike is remarkable, with full detail on the hair above the ear and on the eagle's legs. Since the eye appeal is formidable and there are no post-strike abrasions, the grade must be limited only by a pair of curly mint-made obverse lintmarks, which are found near stars 2 and 12. Proof gold has long been regarded as "the caviar of numismatics," and the present gorgeous specimen provides further supporting evidence for such a statement. (#87926)

Dazzling 1903 Quarter Eagle, PR60

3355 **1903 PR60 NGC.** The population data for this piece, like for many other scarce issues, is inaccurate on the high side due to resubmissions. NGC and PCGS combined have certified well over 200 examples, while the mintage of proof 1903 quarter eagles is only 197 coins! The bright yellow surfaces of this example boast fully struck details and highly reflective surfaces. Several shallow digs and numerous minor abrasions limit the grade of this charming specimen. (#7929)

Remarkable 1904 Quarter Eagle, PR64 Cameo

3356 **1904 PR64 Cameo NGC.** With a mintage of just 170 specimens, the 1904 is the rarest proof quarter eagle from 1900 to 1907. Impressive deeply mirrored fields and frosted yellow devices create an eye-catching cameo appearance. A few peppered contact marks preclude a higher grade, but this fully struck piece is quite attractive for the grade. Census: 23 in 64 Cameo, 44 finer (8/08). (#87930)

Sharp 1905 Quarter Eagle, PR61

3357 **1905 PR61 NGC. CAC.** One of just 144 proof quarter eagles struck in 1905. This specimen displays bright brass-gold surfaces that actually have a fair degree of field-motif contrast, and a solid strike leaves virtual completeness on the design features. This lovely piece would grade significantly higher were it not for a few minor handling marks. Still, much better looking than the designated grade would suggest, as evidenced by the CAC label. (#7931)

INDIAN QUARTER EAGLES

3358 **1908 MS64 NGC.** Alluring yellow-gold patina drapes each side of this crisply struck example. The surfaces are remarkably clean and have only a couple of microscopic abrasions. This interesting series was unpopular at the time but has gradually become more desirable among collectors. (#7939)

3359 **1908 MS64 NGC.** A popular first-year issue. Charming yellow-gold patina covers both sides of this well-preserved specimen. Close inspection reveals scattered yet minor marks, which barely affect the flow of the glowing luster. (#7939)

3360 **1908 MS64 PCGS.** Peach-gold surfaces give off pleasing luster, and the design elements are well defined, except for weakness on the eagle's shoulder. David Akers (1988) writes that this is not the result of a weak strike, but of a lack of die detail. The die work was improved on later issues. (#7939)

3361 **1908 MS64 NGC.** Peach-gold luster is seen on both sides of this near-Gem. Nicely struck, except for the typical softness on the eagle's shoulder. Some light handling marks define the grade. (#7939)

Desirable Gem 1908 Two and a Half

3362 **1908 MS65 PCGS.** This radiant lemon-gold Gem has coruscating luster, and a loupe is required to locate even the most trivial abrasions. Headdress definition is intricate, as is the eagle's plumage. This first year type coin will satisfy even the most demanding collector. Certified in a green label holder. (#7939)

Satiny 1908 Quarter Eagle Premium Gem Uncirculated

3363 **1908 MS66 PCGS.** Although the 1908 two and a half is a relatively common date in the Indian quarter eagle series, finding Premium Gem Uncirculated or better examples can be challenging, especially when the eye appeal of an offering is nicer than one would expect for the assigned technical grade. This amber-gold piece is blanketed in rich, satiny luster and boasts pleasing, distraction-free surfaces. The resulting aesthetic qualities of this example exceeds what is typically encountered at the MS66 grade level and the next owner will likely view this coin as unimprovable for the issue. Only two examples have been graded finer as of (8/08) by PCGS. (#7939)

3364 **1909 MS63 NGC.** The yellow-gold surfaces appear remarkably clean to the unaided eye. Pleasing luster complements the boldly defined design elements. An attractive representative of this second-year issue. (#7940)

Lovely 1909 Quarter Eagle, MS64

3365 **1909 MS64 NGC.** Traces of light-green tint the apricot-gold surfaces of this near-Gem quarter eagle, and a solid strike brings out excellent detail on the design elements. Some minor handling marks are visible under magnification. This attractive quarter eagle would make a delightful type coin. (#7940)

Lustrous 1909 Quarter Eagle, MS64

3366 **1909 MS64 PCGS. CAC.** The 1909 quarter eagle, with a business strike mintage of 441,760 pieces, is a readily available issue, even in the better Mint State grades. The greenish-gold surfaces of this near-Gem example display nice luster and sharply defined motifs. A few minute marks prevent Gem classification. (#7940)

3367 **1911 MS64 NGC.** A nearly fully struck Choice representative with lovely wafts of olive-green and orange patina. Vibrant luster shimmers on each side. Several light grazes preclude Gem status, but overall this piece has tremendous eye appeal. (#7942)

3368 **1911 MS64 NGC.** A precise strike brings out sharp definition on the motifs of this near-Gem quarter eagle. Peach-gold patina, imbued with traces of light tan, adorns lightly marked, lustrous surfaces. (#7942)

Key XF 1911-D Two and a Half

3369 **1911-D XF40 PCGS.** This khaki-gold quarter eagle has light wear on the headdress and wing, but there are no relevant marks. The Denver mintmark is weak but its outline is evident by changes in color. Long acknowledged as the key to this widely collected series. Encapsulated in a first generation holder. (#7943)

AU Details 1911-D Quarter Eagle

3370 **1911-D—Improperly Cleaned—NCS. AU Details.** A bold mintmark example of this widely pursued key date. The devices are well defined, and the cheekbone has only faint friction. The green-gold surfaces are subdued but appear unabraded. An interesting, slender strike-through is noted beneath the MER in AMERICA. (#7943)

Desirable AU Sharpness 1911-D Quarter Eagle

3371 **1911-D—Improperly Cleaned—NCS. AU Details.** This lightly circulated key date quarter eagle has a sharply defined mintmark and a good strike. The peach-gold surfaces are faintly hairlined, but many collectors would be delighted to use the present lot to complete their long-outstanding sets. (#7943)

Pretty AU 1911-D Quarter Eagle

3372 **1911-D AU50 PCGS.** The slight color change on the forward wingtip of the eagle, the Indian's cheek, and the headdress ribbons are all signs of the slight wear association with 10 points of circulation, but there is little evidence of contact, and the mintmark is easily discernible, if not exactly bold. The surfaces show pretty khaki-gold patina on each side. (#7943)

3373 **1911-D—Mount Removed, Polished—NCS. AU Details.** Bright yellow patina overlies the surfaces, which are extremely reflective because of polishing. The bottom half of the obverse has some minor damage in the margins from the mount. Still, the details are quite sharp, and the mintmark is surprisingly bold. A relatively affordable and well-defined example of this key issue. (#7943)

Bold AU 1911-D Two and a Half

3374 **1911-D AU50 PCGS.** The cheekbone and the left border of the headdress exhibit slight friction, but luster glimmers from the design. Star 5 is abraded, but the mildly bright surfaces are generally smooth. The Denver mintmark is low relief but is unmistakable. An appealing example of this low mintage collector favorite. (#7943)

Attractive 1911-D Quarter Eagle, AU53

3375 **1911-D AU53 PCGS.** Rich apricot-gold color graces both sides of this key-date representative, with a splash of light violet visiting the lower left reverse. Save for some high-point wear, nice detail is visible on the design features. The surfaces retain a good amount of luster, and show no marks out of the ordinary for a lightly circulated coin. The mintmark, while not bold, shows clearly. (#7943)

Choice AU 1911-D Two and a Half

3376 **1911-D AU55 NGC.** The 1911-D is the rarest Indian Head quarter eagle, and the margin is not even close. The 1914 claims the second-lowest production at 240,000 items, which is more than four times the meager 55,600 1911-D coins minted. A few field marks are present, especially on the reverse, and the coin has a brown-gold hue. This Choice AU represents great value, with good eye appeal and only slight wear. (#7943)

Bright 1911-D Quarter Eagle, AU55

3377 **1911-D AU55 ANACS.** Bright brassy-gold surfaces display subtle hints of light tan on this Choice AU specimen, and they still retain a good amount of luster. A well executed strike leaves sharp definition on the design elements, except for minor softness on the eagle's shoulder. (#7943)

Sharp AU58 1911-D Quarter Eagle

3378 **1911-D AU58 NGC.** The 1911-D Indian Head quarter eagle stands alone as the rarest and most desirable date in a series that saw no single issue surpassing a yearly production of three-quarters of a million pieces. This near-Mint State coin is a desirable example and displays bright lemon-yellow color. The features are sharply struck (except on the mintmark), and the usual field marks are present. (#7943)

Popular 1911-D Quarter Eagle, MS61

3379 **1911-D MS61 NGC.** A highly desirable Mint State representative of the unquestionable key to the Indian Head quarter eagle series. Plenty of luster shines beneath the attractive butter-gold patina that coats both sides. Scattered abrasions limit the grade, but all are insignificant. Crisply struck with great eye appeal. (#7943)

Well-Defined 1911-D Quarter Eagle, MS62

3380 **1911-D MS62 NGC.** The 1911-D is the undisputed key to the Indian Head quarter eagle series. Fuljenz and Winter write in their *A Collector's Guide to Indian Quarter Eagles* that there are a number of other factors that make it the single most desirable coin in the set:

> "It has the lowest mintage by a huge margin and is the only issue whose mintage is below 100,000. It is the first Indian Head Quarter Eagle to be produced at a mint other than Philadelphia and one of just three non-Philadelphia issues of this design."

The lustrous brass-gold surfaces of this MS62 coin exhibit well struck design elements, including most of the feathers in the bonnet and on the eagle. The mintmark is strong. A few light marks are noted, including a hair-thin one in the upper right reverse field. Nevertheless, a nice looking coin overall.
From The Mississippi Collection. (#7943)

Near-Gem 1911-D Quarter Eagle

Near-Mint 1911-D Weak D Quarter Eagle

3383   1911-D Weak D AU58 NGC. The Denver mintmark has low relief, but is unmistakable when viewed beneath a loupe. The vertical oval center of the mintmark is gray, and contrasts with the light gold mintmark itself, which is fully outlined. The Indian's cheekbone and the eagle's shoulder display a trace of wear, but luster shimmers throughout the smooth straw-gold surfaces. The unchallenged key to the series. (#7954)

3384   1913 MS64 NGC. Delightful yellow-gold patina covers the surfaces of this bright and lustrous representative. This sharply struck piece is remarkably clean for the grade, with only a couple of microscopic marks in the fields. A wonderful type coin. NGC has certified only 52 pieces finer (7/08). (#7945)

Charming 1913 Quarter Eagle, Choice Mint State

3385   1913 MS64 NGC. Attractive orange-gold patina endows the satiny surfaces of this carefully preserved Choice representative. Both sides appear pristine to the unaided eye, and a loupe locates only a couple of grazes. The strike is nearly full and the eye appeal is excellent. The 1913 quarter eagle can be difficult to locate in grades finer than the present piece. (#7945)

3386   1913 MS64 PCGS. CAC. Enticing luster shimmers beneath the pleasing apricot-gold patina. The strike is crisp and there are no marks of any significance. This attractive near-Gem example is seldom available finer and would make a perfect type coin. (#7945)

3387   1913 MS64 PCGS. Warm honey-gold surfaces show occasional glimpses of mustard-gold and peach. Crisply struck with ample luster. PCGS has graded 91 finer pieces (8/08). (#7945)

3388   1913 MS64 PCGS. Precisely struck with shimmering luster and rich sun-gold and peach toning. The obverse is beautifully preserved, and the reverse field has only a few subtle marks. Certified in a green label holder. (#7945)

3389   1914 MS62 NGC. Predominantly yellow-orange with occasional variations that come close to either color in a "pure" state. Well struck with a number of short, shallow abrasions that define the grade. (#7946)

3381   1911-D MS64 PCGS. The rarest and most valuable quarter eagle in the Indian Head series. Numismatists failed to appreciate the issue when it was released. The small mintage of 55,680 pieces was somehow overlooked, and few pieces were saved at the time of release. Perhaps this is not so strange, since collecting U.S. gold coins by date and mintmark did not become truly popular until the 1940s. Today the Indian Head quarter eagle type is avidly collected, and this issue is universally acknowledged as the key to the series.

    Most survivors of the 1911-D are in lower Uncirculated grades. The mintmark is often weak, and abrasions in the fields limit the grade on many coins. There is a diagnostic partial wire rim on the upper right obverse of all known examples.

    The present example reveals only the most minute ticks on the Indian's cheek that limit a finer grade, but the exposed fields elsewhere reveal no mentionable distractions. The rich amber-gold coloration and bold mintmark will be other pluses for collectors. Certified in a green-label holder. (#7943)

3382   1911-D Weak D XF45 PCGS. The mintmark is nearly invisible, but close examination with a lamp and loupe reveals just a trace of the opening of the mintmark. Charming orange-gold patina drapes the surfaces of this minimally marked and well-defined example. With a mintage of just 55,680 pieces, the 1911-D is by far the scarcest issue in the series. (#7954)

3390 1914 MS62 NGC. The 1914 has the second-lowest mintage in the series (240,000 pieces) after the rare 1911-D. Coruscating luster shines beneath the lemon-yellow patina. The surfaces show no noteworthy marks save for a shallow scratch below AMERICA on the reverse.
From The Mississippi Collection. (#7946)

3391 1914 MS62 PCGS. This surprisingly unabraded gold type coin has satin luster, and is crisply impressed aside from unimportant blending of detail on the lowest headdress feathers. (#7946)

Semi-Key 1914 Quarter Eagle, MS63

3392 1914 MS63 ICG. Garrett and Guth (2006) state that "even in lower Mint State grades, this coin is a challenge, with fewer coins reported than almost any other issue besides the 1911-D." Delightful luster radiates beneath the pleasing pumpkin-orange patina that covers both sides. There are no mentionable marks, the details are sharp, and the eye appeal is excellent. (#7946)

Flashy 1914 Two and a Half MS63

3393 1914 MS63 NGC. The fields are moderately prooflike, an uncommon occurrence for the Indian quarter eagle series. The strike is meticulous, even within the headdress, and both sides are splendidly devoid of visible abrasions. A worthy example of Bela Lyon Pratt's novel recessed relief design. (#7946)

Beautiful Near-Gem 1914 Quarter Eagle

3394 1914 MS64 PCGS. The second-lowest mintage of the entire series, the 1914 Indian Head is rare in Gem grades and elusive even in lower grades. This piece offers beautiful orange-gold surfaces that display relatively few marks, save for the couple on the high points that determine the near-Gem grade. Much appeal is present, however, and this coin should be given serious consideration. PCGS has certified 47 examples finer (8/08). (#7946)

Exceptional 1914-D Quarter Eagle, MS64

3395 The PCGS insert states this is a 1914, but it is actually a 1914-D. Yellow-gold surfaces are imbued with traces of light green, and reveal soft luster with a somewhat granular appearance, which is typical for the issue (Michael Fuljenz and Douglas Winter, 2000, p. 26). Sharply struck throughout, with well preserved, exceptional surfaces. In this regard, the above authors indicate that this issue is typically heavily abraded and shows mint-made spots. (#7946)

3396 1914-D MS63 PCGS. Light wheat-gold centers cede to sun-yellow near the margins. Minor, scattered marks on the lustrous surfaces are consistent with the Select designation. (#7947)

3397 1914-D MS63 PCGS. An exquisitely detailed and carefully preserved specimen. The lustrous fields have only a few marks visible to the unaided eye. Charming pale yellow patina graces both sides of this lovely representative. (#7947)

3398 1914-D MS63 NGC. A ring of light olive-gold encircles the mostly yellow-gold centers. Several wispy abrasions define the grade, but none are of any significance. Boldly struck with charming eye appeal. (#7947)

Lustrous Near-Gem 1914-D Quarter Eagle

3399 1914-D MS64 NGC. Areas of khaki-gold and greenish-gold alternate on the lustrous surfaces of this near-Gem, but there are remarkably few signs of contact on the obverse. The reverse shows some light planchet roughness before the eagle, apparently as made, and a couple of stray abrasions that preclude the Gem level. (#7947)

3400 1915 MS64 PCGS. Alluring red and orange patina drapes the surfaces of this minimally marked representative. Soft luster enhances the appeal of this handsome example, which was the last quarter eagle issue for a decade. (#7948)

3401 1915 MS64 NGC. An impeccably preserved specimen with pleasing apricot-gold patina throughout. The surfaces are exceptionally clean for the grade and the details are boldly defined. An attractive and lustrous example that would be perfect for a type collector. (#7948)

3402 1915 MS64 NGC. Magnificent frosty luster covers the orange-gold surfaces of this near-Gem example. The strike is razor-sharp, and there are only a few minor abrasions on each side. This midseries issue can be somewhat difficult to find in grades finer than Choice. (#7948)

3403 **1915 MS64 NGC.** Vibrant yellow-gold patina graces the surfaces of this crisply struck example. A few light marks on each side are noted, but they are virtually invisible without a loupe. This lustrous and attractive piece would make a wonderful type coin. (#7948)

3404 **1915 MS64 PCGS.** The yellow-gold surfaces of this attractive specimen are remarkably clean, even for the MS64 grade. This boldly struck piece exhibits powerful luster that adds to the great eye appeal. Encapsulated in a green label PCGS holder. (#7948)

3405 **1925-D MS64 NGC.** Splendid orange-gold patina with streaks of lemon color graces the surfaces of this lustrous, near-Gem example. A couple of microscopic marks limit the grade, but overall this sharply struck piece has clean and attractive surfaces. (#7949)

3406 **1925-D MS64 PCGS.** The 1925-D was the first quarter eagle struck in a decade, and the Denver Mint produced a total of 578,000 pieces. This enticing near-Gem has scintillating satiny luster beneath lovely butter-yellow patina. A minimally marked and sharply struck representative. (#7949)

3407 **1925-D MS64 PCGS.** Luminous sun-gold and orange-gold surfaces show few flaws. This well struck near-Gem was struck in 1925, the first year for coinage of the denomination in a decade. (#7949)

3408 **1925-D MS64 PCGS.** Dusky orange-gold surfaces show occasional peach and violet elements. A lustrous and well struck survivor from the last of the branch mint quarter eagle issues. (#7949)

3409 **1925-D MS64 PCGS.** The strongly lustrous obverse is primarily wheat-gold, while the reverse shows a stronger yellow-gold influence. Minimally marked and attractive. (#7949)

3410 **1925-D MS64 PCGS.** Magnificent luster shines throughout the apricot patinated surfaces. The surfaces are remarkably clean for the grade and have only minuscule luster grazes. This sharply struck piece would make a wonderful type coin. (#7949)

3411 **1925-D MS64 NGC.** Brass-gold surfaces radiate bright luster, and exhibit sharply struck design elements. Some minor contacts and grazes prevent Gem classification. (#7949)

Colorful MS65 1925-D Two and a Half

3412 **1925-D MS65 PCGS.** The final five quarter eagle issues, those of 1925-1929, are the most commonly collected for type purposes. While the 1925-D, the highest-mintage of those issues, is common in lesser grades, even it is elusive as a Gem. The present piece is one such coin. The frosty amber-gold surfaces have a touch of green, and the devices are well struck. A cursory inspection indicates a high-quality coin, yet it is not until one looks closely that this example's comparative lack of marks stands out. A wonderful representative of this daringly designed series. *From The Bell Collection.* (#7949)

3413 **1926 MS64 NGC.** An excellent opportunity for the type collector. This razor-sharp 1926 quarter eagle exhibits delightful apricot and yellow patina on each side. Several minimal abrasions barely affect the flow of the tremendous luster. (#7950)

3414 **1926 MS64 PCGS.** An interesting piece, generally wheat-gold with hints of sun and frostiness on the high points. Minimally marked with a tiny area of alloy in the feathers of the headdress. (#7950)

3415 **1927 MS64 PCGS.** Vibrant sun-gold surfaces show whispers of orange near the margins. A well-defined piece with a single, shallow abrasion noted to the left of the portrait. (#7951)

Enticing 1927 Quarter Eagle, Gem Mint State

3416 **1927 MS65 PCGS.** Although common in most grades, the 1927 is seldom seen finer than Gem. Warm yellow-gold patina covers the highly lustrous surfaces. A loupe locates a couple of trivial marks, but both sides are quite pleasing. Encapsulated in a green-label PCGS holder. Population: 337 in 65, 17 finer (8/08). *From The Mississippi Collection.* (#7951)

3417 **1929 MS64 PCGS.** The final year of the Indian quarter eagle series, the 1929 is not a scarce date, but can be difficult to locate in grades finer than the present piece. This resplendent example features a sharp strike, and has only minor marks on each side. An excellent choice for the type collector. (#7953)

3418 **1929 MS64 NGC.** Splendid sun-gold patina covers the fields and contrasts nicely against the pale lemon accents on the devices. A few light abrasions limit the grade, but none merit specific mention. Significant luster gives this piece outstanding eye appeal. (#7953)

3419 **1929 MS64 NGC.** A delightful final-year issue. This enticing lemon-yellow representative has wafts of peach-gold patina across the surfaces. Satiny luster ripples throughout and highlights the boldly struck design. A few abrasions in the fields keep this piece from an even higher grade. (#7953)

3420 **1929 MS64 PCGS.** Impressive luster for this final quarter eagle issue, and the strike is pleasing. Choice with few flaws across the attractive yellow-orange surfaces. (#7953)

Elusive Gem Proof Roman Finish
1909 Indian Head Quarter Eagle

3421 **1909 PR65 NGC.** It was not only Bela Lyon Pratt's innovative incused design for the Indian Head quarter and half eagles that collectors mostly disdained in 1908, the year of their introduction onto an unsuspecting populace. The Mint also chose to foist the unpopular matte proof format for all gold coinage onto collectors at the same time, a heavy, non-lustrous, grainy texture that most numismatists of the era loathed.

After the proof mintage of quarter eagles reached 236 pieces recorded for the premiere year of 1908—from collectors who likely had never seen and had no knowledge of what they were ordering—the second-year proof emission plummeted to a low 136 pieces.

Although the second-year issues were modified to something called the Roman or Satin Finish, in between the matte proofs and the traditional mirrored proofs of earlier (pre-1902) years. Those coins were not much liked by proof gold connoisseurs, either. A quick look at the NGC *Census Report* will confirm that the 1909 is by far the most elusive of the eight proof issues from 19008 through 1915. It is also the rarest issue in Gem proof or finer grades. The situation is the same at PCGS, which, although it has graded less proofs of the 1912 and 1913, has certified only a single Gem proof 1909, with none finer.

The present Gem NGC-certified coin does indeed appear as somewhat of a hybrid between the matte and reflective proofs. While it is noticeably brighter than a matte piece, it is not what one would think of as "lustrous" in the sense of radiance, and examination under a loupe will reveal a microscopic, fine-grained surface, somewhat like a matte proof but with much finer texture. Although collectors of the era may not have valued them, today a collector would find this lovely Gem to be a real treasure. A couple of hair-thin marks on the reverse above the eagle are the only mentionable contact on this delightful and attractive piece, a historic example of early proof gold experimentation during the renaissance period of U.S. coinage. (#7958)

Rare Matte PR63 1913 Quarter Eagle

3422 **1913 PR63 PCGS.** A rare issue in proof format, like all matte proof coinage, the 1913 matte proof shows a combined mintage between NGC and PCGS of 92 coins. The 1913 issue was struck with a fine-grained, multifaceted surface like the 1912 pieces; this example shows deep color somewhere between olive-green and olive-brown, but except for the intense color it is difficult to see why this piece failed to achieve a finer grade. Population: 3 in 63, 28 finer (7/08). (#7962)

End of Session Five

SESSION SIX

Live, Internet, and Mail Bid Signature® Auction #1116
Friday, September 19, 2008, 6:00 PM PT, Lots 3423 - 4546
Long Beach, California

A 15% Buyer's Premium ($9 minimum) Will Be Added To All Lots

Visit HA.com to view full-color images and bid.

PATTERNS

PR61 1850 Three Cent Silver Pattern, Judd-125 Original

3423   **1850 Three Cent Silver, Judd-125 Original, Pollock-147, R.4, PR61 NGC.** The design for this three cent silver is similar to the famous Judd-67 gold dollar pattern from 1836, but the date has been moved to the obverse below the cap, and the denomination within the palm frond is expressed with a large Roman numeral III. Struck in silver with a plain edge. This popular design was executed by Franklin Peale from designs by James Longacre. This silver-gold piece with tinges of ice-blue and lilac shows good luster and eye appeal, but is lightly hairlined. (#11536)

Choice Proof 1858 Flying Eagle Cent
Judd-202, Pollock-245

3424   **1858 Flying Eagle Cent, Judd-202, Pollock-245, R.5, PR64 PCGS.** The obverse resembles the contemporary Flying Eagle cent, but the eagle is smaller in scale. The reverse is close to the issued 1859 Indian cent. The five leaf cluster Pollock variant of this popular pattern. Struck in copper-nickel with a plain edge. Well struck and mark free with light chestnut-gold obverse toning and deep olive-brown shading on the reverse. Housed in an old green label holder. Population: 17 in 64, 8 finer (8/08). (#11867)

3425   **1858 Indian Cent, Judd-212, Pollock-263, R.4—Polished—ICG. PR60 Details.** Obverse similar to the Indian Head cent, but dated 1858. The reverse has an oak wreath with a large shield bordered by scrollwork at the top. Struck in copper-nickel with a plain edge. On the present specimen, the violet-tinged surfaces are unnaturally lustrous from polishing, though there is no detail loss. (#11895)

Transitional 1859 Indian Cent Pattern, Judd-228, MS65

3426   **1859 Indian Cent, Judd-228, Pollock-272, R.1, MS65 PCGS.** The famous transitional cent with the design as adopted in 1860, but here dated 1859. These pieces were struck in both proof and business strike format. The 1859 patterns of this design have the oak wreath with shield design on the reverse, with the regular Indian cent obverse. Struck in copper-nickel with a plain edge. This sharply struck piece offers light tan-gold surfaces with glints of lilac and jade on each side. The Judd pattern reference comments: "Rarer than an 1856 Flying Eagle cent, another transitional pattern. The good news is that, unlike the latter, the 1859 is not listed in *A Guide Book of United States Coins*. Otherwise, it would become so popular that it would cost tens of thousands of dollars!" (#10362)

Gem Proof Judd-237 1859 Half Dollar

3427   **1859 Half Dollar, Judd-237, Pollock-293, R.4, PR65 NGC.** Liberty faces right with laurel and vine in her hair. A ribbon below the bust is inscribed LIBERTY, with UNITED STATES OF AMERICA around, and the date below. The reverse has an agricultural wreath around the denomination HALF DOLLAR. Struck in silver with a reeded edge. This needle-sharp Gem proof features luxurious ocean-blue toning, along with glimpses of straw-gold and lavender. Census: 4 in 65, 4 finer (7/08). (#11966)

Gilt 1860 Five Dollar, Judd-272, PR63

3428 1860 Five Dollar, Judd-272, Pollock-320, Low R.6, PR63 Gilt NGC. Ex: Bass. Thin planchet. 65.2 grains. The obverse introduces the right facing bust of Liberty with three large stars on her cap, a motif familiar to Standard Silver collectors but first used on Judd-271 and Judd-272. The date is quite small. The reverse features an eagle with raised wing, carrying the banner E PLURIBUS UNUM with its beak and clutching arrows and an olive branch within its claws. Struck in copper with a reeded edge, later gilt, probably outside the Mint. Identical to Judd-283 except for the change in date. This pattern was for a large diameter, thin planchet half eagle, designed to keep unethical individuals from hollowing out gold coins and replacing their content with a less valuable metal. The thicker planchet variant of this pattern varies in weight from 120 to 140 grains. This piece is identifiable as the DiBello-Bass example (Bass owned three of these gilt pieces) by two small contact marks, one in the reverse field below the TE of UNITED and another above the second L in DOLLAR. The gilt is intact throughout and the only mentionable defect is a haziness in the right obverse field that extends on to Liberty's face.
Ex: Gaston DiBello (Stack's, 5/1970), lot 484; Bass I (Bowers and Merena, 5/1999), lot 1350; American Numismatic Rarities, 8/2006), lot 923. From The Mississippi Collection. (#12078)

Impressive 1862 GOD OUR TRUST Pattern Half Dollar
Judd-293, Pollock-351, Choice Proof

3429 1862 Half Dollar, Judd-293, Pollock-351, R.5, PR64 PCGS. Struck in silver with a reeded edge. The obverse is the same die used to strike regular-issue 1862 Liberty Seated halves. The reverse is nearly identical to the standard die as well, except that there is the motto GOD OUR TRUST above the eagle's head. Pollock notes that the W.E. Woodward catalog of May 1863 claims that 25 original sets of this combined with a copper eagle pattern were produced. Vibrant lavender and blue toning drapes the centers, which contrast nicely against the hazel and russet toned margins. Sharply struck and intricately preserved. (#60443)

Rare 1863 Ten Cents, Judd-325, Pollock-390, Low R.6, PR63

3430 1863 Ten Cents, Judd-325, Pollock-390, Low R.6, PR63 PCGS. The obverse depicts an ornamental shield with an inverted laurel wreath suspended from a ring. A pair of crossed arrows is behind the shield, with EXCHANGED FOR U.S. NOTES around the perimeter. The reverse has 10 CENTS 1863 in the center, with * POSTAGE CURRENCY * ACT JULY 1862 around. Struck in silver with a plain edge. Richly and originally toned, both sides display a base of dove-gray toning over which mottled copper-russet shadings have developed. The surfaces, while a little subdued by the patination, are free of noticeable handling marks. There are, however, several interesting mint-made features (as struck) that should help trace the pedigree of this rare and important example. The most important are a die crack from the upper rim to the tip of the ring, on the obverse, and a faint lint mark on the reverse, out from the right side of the 0 in 10. (#60482)

3431 1863 Half Dollar, Judd-338, Pollock-410, R.5, PR50 PCGS. Essentially identical to the regular design in production during the Civil War, with only the addition of a scroll inscribed GOD OUR TRUST. Struck in silver with a reeded edge. Noticeable mirrors remain on both sides, with brilliant silver surfaces and only a few slight marks. A trace of rub on the highpoints accounts for the grade. (#60500)

3432 1864 Two Cents, Judd-371, Pollock-440, Low R.6—Damaged—ANACS. PR60 Details. This pattern is produced from the regular Large Motto dies, but it is struck in copper-nickel as opposed to copper. The edge is plain. It is possible that these pieces were restrikes, but there is no conclusive evidence as to when and why they were struck. Mottled medium brown and orange-tan toning covers the reflective surfaces. A nearly imperceptible mark by the OF accounts for the "damaged" moniker, but it is possible that this is simply a planchet flaw. (#60541)

Select Proof Copper-Nickel 1864 Two Cent Piece
Judd-371, Struck With a Partial Collar

3433 1864 Two Cents, Judd-371, Pollock-440, Low R.6—Partial Collar—PR63 NGC. From regular issue Large Motto dies, but struck in copper-nickel instead of bronze. Well struck and unabraded with golden-brown toning and a small spot to the left of prominent 2. The partial collar error is difficult to see because the edge is obscured by the holder. However, both sides exhibit a wire rim that varies considerably in height and thickness. The wire rim is especially prominent on the obverse near 12 o'clock. (#60541)

PR55 1865 Seated Dollar in Copper, Judd-437

3434 **1865 Dollar, Judd-437, Pollock-510, High R.7, PR55 PCGS.** Both sides feature the same die design that was used on regular issue 1865 (No Motto) Dollars, and as such is scarcer than the retro-dated With Motto pieces made of this date. Struck in copper with a reeded edge. This well struck deep golden-brown specimen has slight wear on Liberty's legs and the fields have scattered tiny marks in addition to a couple of faded pinscratches on the upper reverse. Population: 1 in 55, 2 finer (8/08).
Ex: New York Connoisseur's Collection (American Numismatic Rarities, 3/2006), lot 1341. (#60622)

PR64 Red and Brown Judd-462
1866 Washington Five Cent

3435 **1866 Washington Five Cents, Judd-462, Pollock-536, Low R.7, PR64 Red and Brown PCGS.** A five cent pattern featuring George Washington in profile, facing right, on the obverse. The date has minute digits. The reverse has the 5 of the denomination central on that side, surrounded by a laurel wreath. Struck in copper with a plain edge. Lovely orange-red dominates but cedes to rose-lilac on the central reverse. Well struck and mark-free with a solitary small spot on the reverse rim at 9 o'clock. (#70657)

R.7 1866 Washington Head
Five Cent Pattern in Copper
Judd-468, PR63 Red

3436 **1866 Five Cents, Judd-468, Pollock-561, R.7, PR63 Red PCGS.** The obverse bears a bust of a pigtailed George Washington facing right, with IN GOD WE TRUST over his head at the rim. The reverse is a tall 5 in a wreath (olive or laurel, with berries) joined by a bowknot, UNITED STATES OF AMERICA around. There is no denominator. Struck in copper with a plain edge. The Judd pattern reference lists the copper issue as R.8, but www.USPatterns.com lumps the "copper and/or bronze" Judd-468 and 469 patterns together, saying "about a half-dozen known" and giving an R.7 listing.

   This piece is fully Red within the context of early copper, with attractive pinkish-orange coloration on both sides and splendid luster. PCGS lists only three examples: PR63 Red (this coin), PR64 Red, and PR63 Brown (8/08). (#80664)

Cameo Gem Proof 1867 Five Cent Pattern, Judd-566

3437 **1867 Five Cents, Judd-566, Pollock-627, Low R.6, PR65 Cameo PCGS.** The obverse features a bust of Liberty facing left, wearing a coronet, surrounded by the legend and date. The denomination is within a laurel wreath that is close to the edges on the reverse, with a tiny IN GOD WE TRUST above. Struck in nickel with a plain edge. One of many similar five cent patterns of the year based on the contemporary three cent nickel design, Judd-566 features CENTS in straight rather than curved letters, and Liberty's coronet does not have a star. Brilliant throughout, the striated fields give this pattern a deep reflectivity that sets off the lightly frosted devices with a mild cameo contrast. A delightful example of this popular design. *Ex: Western Hills Collection (Heritage, 6/2005), lot 7399.* (#60776)

Interesting 1868 Ten Cent Pattern in Nickel, Judd-641, PR65

3438 **1868 Ten Cents, Judd-641, Pollock-713, Low R.7, PR65 PCGS.** A curious pattern coin, the Judd-641 almost appears as though it was decided to put as many elements as possible on the reverse while putting as few as possible on the obverse. The obverse includes just the usual Seated Liberty motif and UNITED STATES OF AMERICA on the periphery, with nothing in the exergue. The reverse appears much the same as on a Seated Liberty dime, with the addition of the date below ONE DIME and a large six-pointed star joining the two halves of the agricultural wreath. Struck in nickel with a reeded edge. The Judd ninth edition notes that "research by David Cassel has revealed that these coins were struck in 1863 from a die erroneously dated 1868. The obverse without date is the same as that used in 1863 to strike [Judd]-331." This example is a problem-free silver-gray Gem, with considerable cameo contrast and certified in a green-label holder. (#60859)

3439 **1869 Three Cent Nickel, Judd-676, Pollock-753, R.4, PR62 NGC.** This piece is quite similar to the circulating three cent nickel, and is distinguished by a slightly reduced bust and flat, plain denomination columns. It is struck in nickel with a plain edge. Lovely soft luster is accented by hints of lemon and lilac toning in the fields. A carefully preserved specimen with only a couple of tiny handling marks. (#60901)

3440 1869 Five Cents, Judd-688, Pollock-769, High R.7, PR66 PCGS. Aluminum is a common element, the third most widely found in the Earth's crust after silicon and oxygen. But because of its extreme reactivity it is rare in its pure, free form, instead found in more than 270 mineral compounds, most abundantly as bauxite ore.

The use of pure aluminum—even more so the use of pure aluminum in coinage—is a recent phenomenon. Pure aluminum used to be considered a precious metal, more prized than gold. The Emperor Napoleon is said to have given a banquet at which only the most honored guests were given aluminum utensils; the others had to settle for gold.

When the Washington Monument was completed in 1884, its 100-ounce pure aluminum capstone was the largest single piece of aluminum cast at that time, and the lightweight metal was considered more expensive than gold, silver, or platinum at that time. The Hall-Héroult process for extracting aluminum from its ore was discovered around 1884, making the pure metal much less expensive than before and widening its commercial availability.

That greater availability, of course, also extended to coins and medals, and only during the late 1880s and early 1890s are such pieces generally seen. In fact, a famous series of so-called dollars from the 1892-93 World's Columbian Exposition touts the many newly discovered attributes of aluminum for coinage: "malleable, tasteless, sonorous, ductile, untarnishable."

It is against the above background that the present pattern Shield nickel in aluminum, Judd-688, must be viewed. Dated 1869, this piece was produced at a time (presumably the year it bears, or not much later) when aluminum was among the *most precious of metals*. The design is the same as the regular-issue Shield nickel, although in the pure aluminum context this piece is starkly silver-white, rather than gray. The piece is certified in an old-style PCGS green-label holder, and it certainly appears qualified for a Cameo designation, with thickly frosted devices and splendidly reflective fields that show the coveted black-on-silver appearance of cameo proof coinage at the proper angle.

According to the www.USPatterns.com website, this pattern in aluminum, Judd-688, is part of a series of similar 1869-dated patterns that, despite their listing as die trials, were actually deliberately struck for sale to collectors as part of complete off-metal sets.

Apparently only two or three pieces of the Judd-688 in aluminum are known. The PCGS *Population Report* shows three pieces certified at that service, one each in PR63, PR65, and PR66, this piece the finest of the three. Besides its status as a fabulously rare pattern, it is a quite beautiful and interesting one—like so many patterns, little is actually known concerning its manufacture, but much research remains to be done, and much will likely remain the subject of conjecture ... (#60913)

Deeply Toned 1869 Standard Silver Dime
Judd-708, PR64

3441 **1869 Standard Silver Ten Cents, Judd-708, Pollock-787, R.5, PR64 PCGS.** Liberty faces right and wears a band ornamented with a star. IN GOD WE TRUST is placed on a banner beneath the bust. On the reverse, an undersized wreath crowds the 10/CENTS denomination. The reverse periphery displays STANDARD SILVER and the date. Struck in silver with a reeded edge. An attractive example of this fairly common Standard Silver pattern. Both sides are enveloped with deep blue toning that shows a significant amount of rose color in the centers. (#60933)

Aluminum 1869 Standard Silver Quarter
Judd-725, High R.7, PR64

3442 **1869 Standard Silver Quarter Dollar, Judd-725, Pollock-806, High R.7, PR64 PCGS.** Liberty faces left, and is adorned with a large cap with stars along the lower front border. IN GOD WE TRUST is featured in a scroll below the portrait. The reverse has a wreath of oak and laurel leaves, with 25 CENTS crowded inside while the date is below and STANDARD SILVER is centered above. Struck in aluminum with a reeded edge. The right obverse field has an area of slightly granular surface, as made, while the reverse has a couple of retained mint-made laminations. A few wisps of charcoal patina grace each side. The finest of only two examples of Judd-725 certified by PCGS. NGC has also encapsulated a single piece as PR63 Cameo (8/08).
Ex: FUN Signature (Heritage, 1/2004), lot 8451, which realized $5,405. (#60952)

Colorful Gem Proof Judd-727
1869 Standard Silver Quarter

3443 **1869 Standard Silver Quarter Dollar, Judd-727, Pollock-808, R.5, PR65 PCGS.** Liberty's hair is bound, and she wears a diadem. The obverse exergue displays IN GOD WE TRUST within a scroll. The date is instead on the reverse exergue. A small oak and laurel wreath crowds the centrally placed 25 CENTS. STANDARD SILVER dominates the upper reverse border. Struck in silver with a reeded edge. The obverse center is toned orange and fire-red, while apple-green fills the obverse margin and aquamarine encompasses the reverse. Population: 5 in 65, 5 finer (8/08). (#60954)

1869 Standard Silver Quarter
Judd-736, PR63 Brown

3444 **1869 Standard Silver Quarter Dollar, Judd-736, Pollock-817, Low R.7, PR63 Brown NGC.** This Standard Silver entry features a high relief portrait of Liberty with a large star above her forehead. The date is on the reverse exergue, and the denomination is crowded within a wreath. Struck in copper with a plain edge. Boldly struck and minimally abraded with rich olive, aquamarine, gold, and plum-red patina. (#60963)

Appealing PR64 Cameo Judd-755
1869 Standard Silver Half

3445 **1869 Standard Silver Half Dollar, Judd-755, Pollock-839, High R.6, PR64 Cameo PCGS.** Standard Silver design for the half dollar with Liberty wearing a ribbon inscribed LIBERTY on the obverse. The ribbon is ornamented with a star, the legend UNITED STATES OF AMERICA is around the periphery, and the motto IN GOD WE TRUST is on a scroll below. On the reverse, the denomination 50 CENTS is positioned within a wreath of oak and laurel. STANDARD SILVER is above, the date, 1869, is below. Struck in silver with a plain edge. This brilliant near-Gem has good white-on-black contrast, and is well struck save for slight incompleteness on the cheek. (#60985)

Impressive 1870 Standard Silver Half Dime
Judd-809, PR65

3446 **1870 Standard Silver Half Dime, Judd-809, Pollock-897, Low R.7, PR65 PCGS.** William Barber's Seated Liberty design is paired with a familiar Standard Silver reverse motif, a wreath of corn and cotton. The obverse die appears identical to that used to strike the Judd-796 through Judd-801 trime patterns. As of (8/08), PCGS has certified seven pieces of this Judd variety, this is the single finest certified example. (#61053)

PR66 1870 Standard Silver Quarter
Judd-888

3447 **1870 Standard Silver Quarter Dollar, Judd-888, Pollock-987, R.5, PR66 NGC.** A bust of Liberty wears a cap ornamented with three stars and faces right, the legend UNITED STATES OF AMERICA surrounds the figure, and a scroll with IN GOD WE TRUST is below. The reverse reads 25 CENTS 1870 in the center and is surrounded by a wreath of cotton and corn. Struck in silver with a reeded edge. A splendid, richly toned pattern with shades of rose, deep blue, and gray on each side. (#61132)

Gem 1870 Standard Silver Half in Copper
Judd-942, High R.7, PR64 Red

3448 **1870 Standard Silver Half Dollar, Judd-942, Pollock-1069, High R.7, PR64 Red PCGS.** Standard Silver design with a bust of Liberty facing right on the obverse. Liberty wears a cap that is ornamented with two stars, and the word LIBERTY is on a ribbon over her shoulder. The legend UNITED STATES OF AMERICA is at the upper border, while the motto IN GOD WE TRUST is on a scroll below. On the reverse, one can see the denomination 50 CENTS and the date 1870 within a wreath of cotton and corn. the word STANDARD is at the upper border. Struck in copper with a plain edge. In the 1994 book *United States Pattern and Related Issues*, Andrew W. Pollock III actually breaks down examples of Judd-942 into two separate varieties. The present example, a Pollock-1069 coin, is distinguishable from Pollock-1055 by the position of the tip of Liberty's cap relative to the final S in STATES. On this coin, it is under the left side of that letter. The author was aware of two examples of Pollock-1069:

1. Ex: Winthrop Collection Sale (Bowers and Ruddy, 9/1975), lot 1026.

2. Ex: Sieck Collection Sale (Bowers and Ruddy, 10/1981), lot 2411.

The two lots were imaged in their respective catalogs, and neither appears to be the present coin. In addition, an NGC PR65 Brown example appeared as lot 1462 in our 2006 Denver ANA Signature. Both sides of the present piece are fully lustrous with rich reddish-olive coloration. A few scattered carbon spots seem to bar this coin from a full Gem grade, the most readily evident of which is located at the top of Liberty's neck in the center of the obverse. Population: 1 in 64 Red, 0 finer (8/08).
Ex: Trane Collection (Heritage, 1/2003), lot 9925. (#81188)

1870 Seated Dollar in Copper
Judd-1020, PR60 Details

3449 **1870 Dollar, Judd-1020, Pollock-1155, Low R.7—Altered Surface—NCS. Proof (PR60 Details).** The regular dies for the 1870 Seated Liberty dollar, but struck in copper with a reeded edge. The obverse field is thickly hairlined, and the Seated Liberty has an unnatural matte texture. Retoned in deep sea-green, apricot, and fire-red, with the latter color dominating the reverse. (#61268)

Longacre's 1871 'Indian Princess' Standard Silver Dollar
Judd-1133, PR66

3450 **1871 Standard Silver Dollar, Judd-1133, Pollock-1270, High R.6, PR66 NGC.** A dollar pattern with Longacre's modified design with only 13 stars on the flag and the first and thirteenth peripheral stars closer to the base. The reverse has 1 DOLLAR as the central design element which is surrounded by a wreath of cotton and corn, and the word STANDARD above. Struck in silver with a reeded edge. Possibly more than a dozen pieces are known of this variant. The striking definition is razor sharp in all areas and the fields are deeply mirrored beneath rich orange and blue iridescent accents. (#61393)

Judd-1147 PR64 Red and Brown
1871 Longacre Silver Dollar in Copper

3451 **1871 One Dollar, Judd-1147, Pollock-1289, High R.6, PR64 Red and Brown PCGS.** Ex: The New Millennium Collection. The Longacre design is used on the obverse that features Liberty seated with conjoined flags behind, left hand resting on a globe, and right hand holding a Phrygian cap on top. The reverse is of the regular die. Struck in copper with a reeded edge. This is the most common of the Longacre dollar designs of the year. It is often called the obverse of 1870 although it does not have Longacre's name in the right corner. The fields are deeply reflective and most of the original fiery-red luster is still evident on each side—there is a very fine line between full red and full red color that has slightly mellowed enough to be called Red and Brown, as seen on this coin. Fully and intricately detailed, there are a few tiny specks of carbon on each side that serve to limit this piece to the PR64 category.
Ex: New Millennium Collection (Heritage, 11/2003), lot 11187, which realized $6,785. (#71409)

Rare and Highly Desirable 1880 Stella
Judd-1658, Copper Striking, Gilt

3452 **1880 Flowing Hair Four Dollar, Judd-1658, Pollock-1858, Low R.7—Copper, Gilt—Genuine PCGS.** Struck in copper with a reeded edge. Although not graded by PCGS and simply labeled as Genuine, we believe this piece to be PR60 with altered surfaces. The gilt overlay is nicely done, with no apparent flakes or prominent blemishes. Many collectors are familiar with the design of the stella, which features a flowing haired Liberty facing left on the obverse and a five-pointed star surrounded by text on the reverse. It is interesting that the denomination is written in three different ways on the reverse: ONE STELLA, 400 CENTS, and FOUR DOL.

The incomparable Flowing Hair stella, designed by Charles Barber, was proposed to serve as an alternative for several foreign coins of the same size. One of several Congressional proposals for an international trade coin, the stella was never adopted for a variety of reasons, not the least of which is its odd-denomination that is so popular among collectors today. The 1880 stellas are often overshadowed by their 1879-dated counterpart, which is significantly more available in gold. Copper examples are extremely rare, with a population of only 10 examples of the present variety known according to the ninth edition of *United States Pattern Coins*. In nearly 15 years of record-keeping, this is only the eighth time a Judd-1658 has been offered at auction by Heritage.

This desirable piece still has lovely eye appeal despite altered surfaces. Pleasing lemon-yellow patina encircles the perimeter and contrasts against the streaks of milky-gold across the centers. Liberty's hair is a trifle soft, but the rest of the details are powerfully impressed. Strong, watery reflectivity shimmers throughout the surfaces. Nearly any collector can speak to the desirability of a stella, and most can only dream of owning one. Serious consideration should be given before the opportunity to acquire this seldom-offered rarity is missed. (#62043)

1881 Liberty Head Nickel Pattern, Judd-1671, PR66

3453 **1881 Liberty Head Five Cents, Judd-1671, Pollock-1872, High R.6 PR66 NGC.** Although resembling the Liberty nickel's final design as adopted two years later, this version differs in several ways: On the obverse UNITED STATES OF AMERICA encircles the rim in place of the stars, while on the reverse a wreath surrounds a large V, with no statutory inscriptions around the rim. Struck in nickel with a plain edge. The surfaces are lustrous pearl-gray, with lots of appeal. (#62067)

Zinc-Coated Steel 1942 Pattern Cent, Judd-2054

3454 **1942 One Cent, Zinc-Coated Steel, Judd-2054, High R.7, MS62 NGC.** The obverse features the female head from the Colombian two centavos, with LIBERTY left, JUSTICE right, date 1942 at bottom. The reverse shows UNITED STATES MINT in center, with a wreath surrounding, struck in medal turn on zinc-coated steel (same apparent composition as the 1943 Lincoln cents). Struck in zinc-coated steel with a plain edge. One of the wartime cent experiments in off-metal (and no-metal) composition, struck as an alternative to the copper needed for the war effort. Many similar pieces, all R.7 to R.8, were produced in various compositions, including plastic, glass, Bakelite, rubber, and manganese. The surfaces are dark charcoal-gray on this interesting and rare pattern.

Choice 1759-Dated Martha Washington 'Nickel', Judd-2182

3455 **"1759" Martha Washington "Five Cent" Test Token, Judd-2182, R.7, MS64 NGC.** 5.0 gm. Unlike other U.S. coin denominations, the alloy for the five cent piece or nickel has remained the same since it was first issued in 1866, except for the World War II alloy of copper, silver, and manganese. Martha Washington dies of five cent size were apparently made to test presses instead of compositions. The dies were likely made before 1999, because the design for the "golden" dollar dies exhibit minor differences, such as missing designer initials below the shoulder. This a satiny near-Gem that has light golden toning and a sharp strike. Minute carbon and contact are present but of little import.

1759-Dated Martha Washington 'Dollar' Judd-2185, MS66

3456 **(1999) Martha Washington "Dollar," Judd-2185, Low R.7, MS66 NGC.** The 1759-dated obverse has a portrait of Martha Washington facing right, while the reverse shows a view of Mount Vernon. These dies, which omit a denomination and the UNITED STATES OF AMERICA, have been used by the Mint to test coinage alloys since 1965. Struck in magnesium brass-coated copper-clad metal with a plain edge. The consistent green-gold color is similar to that of the Sacagawea dollar, which succeeded the Anthony dollar in 2000. A lustrous and intricately impressed Premium Gem that possesses immaculate fields. (#62401)

THREE DOLLAR GOLD PIECES

3457 **1854—Improperly Cleaned—NCS. XF Details.** This moderately circulated representative has a uniform sheen and a minutely pebbled texture. An affordable example of this scarce gold type. (#7969)

3458 **1854—Improperly Cleaned—NCS. XF Details.** This first-year type coin has a glossy and slightly bright appearance. Inspection beneath a lens reveals countless minute marks. (#7969)

3459 **1854—Mount Removed, Improperly Cleaned—NCS. AU Details.** There is no obvious sign of a removed mount, but both sides have a cloudy appearance and a couple of abrasions are near the CA in AMERICA. (#7969)

3460 **1854—Scratched—ICG. AU53 Details.** A couple of wispy pinscratches bookend the 3 in the denomination. Still a partly lustrous example of the single-year Small Letters subtype. (#7969)

3461 **1854 AU53 NGC.** Satiny luster is visible but subdued beneath pale orange toning on both sides of this popular three, representing the first year of issue for the denomination. (#7969)

Impressive 1854 Three Dollar, MS62

3462 **1854 MS62 NGC.** The 1854 is popular as the first year of the denomination, and thanks to a high mintage it is also relatively available. This highly lustrous yellow-gold representative is truly exceptional and has outstanding eye appeal. Scattered abrasions limit the grade, but all are minor. A crisply struck and impeccably preserved representative. (#7969)

Splendid 1854 Three Dollar Gold, MS64

3463 **1854 MS64 PCGS.** This first-year Philadelphia three dollar gold issue was the denomination's high-water mark, the only one to have a six-figure mintage. The novelty of the three dollar gold piece also encouraged saving, and the 1854 is relatively available in grades through Select, though Choice examples are elusive and Gems are conditionally rare. This near-Gem is immensely lustrous with an interesting blend of yellow-gold and peach-gold on the minimally marked surfaces. Well struck and highly appealing. PCGS has certified just 25 finer representatives (8/08). (#7969)

3464 **1854-O—Scratched—NCS. VF Details.** The obverse has numerous thin marks, all of which are inconspicuous aside from a relatively lengthy pinscratch on the neck. Luster still shimmers from protected crevices. (#7971)

3465 **1854-O—Improperly Cleaned—NCS. XF Details.** The New Orleans Mint struck three cent silver only in 1851, and coined the three dollar denomination only in 1854. Half dollars, though, were struck annually at the facility until the Civil War. This example is cloudy from faint hairlines, but noticeable luster remains and there are no distracting marks. (#7971)

3466 **1855 XF40 PCGS.** Considerable luster clings to the margins of this lightly circulated piece, honey-gold with ample violet-rose accents. Surprisingly few overt marks for the grade. (#7972)

3467 **1855—Improperly Cleaned—NCS. XF Details.** This green-gold second year three dollar gold piece is lackluster and the color is slightly off, but neither side exhibits any consequential marks. (#7972)

3468 **1855—Scratched, Improperly Cleaned—NCS. XF Details.** A dull thin scratch travels from the cheek to the neck, and circular fine hairlines are present on the reverse, particularly near 12:30. Luster glimmers from the legends despite rub on Liberty's hair. (#7972)

3469 **1855 XF45 NGC.** Light but distinct wear affects the high points of this dusky khaki-gold survivor. Well struck with a few wispy horizontal abrasions present to the left of Liberty's face. (#7972)

3470 **1855 XF45 NGC.** Light yellow surfaces with considerable remaining luster suggest this piece has been carefully conserved. A delightful example for a date or type collector. (#7972)

3471 **1855—Reverse Scratched—ICG. AU53 Details.** Traces of luster accent the olive-yellow patina that drapes both sides. A number of abrasions are typical for the grade, and there are only two shallow scratches on the reverse. A lovely example despite the "scratched" designation. (#7972)

3472 **1856—Improperly Cleaned—NCS. XF Details.** Cloudy from a moderate cleaning, but there are no conspicuous marks and the headdress plumes retain ample detail. (#7974)

3473 **1856—Improperly Cleaned—NCS. XF Details.** The pale yellow surfaces have been gently cleaned, but are surprisingly pleasant. There are no bothersome marks on either side, although some minor verdigris is retained in the obverse lettering. (#7974)

3474 **1856—Reverse Repaired, Improperly Cleaned—NCS. AU Details.** The surfaces are polished with tooling in places on the reverse, probably from removal of a jewelry mount. (#7974)

3475 **1856 AU55 PCGS.** Briefly circulated with delightful orange-gold patina and accents of bright yellow luster in the protected areas. Scattered abrasions limit the grade, but none are particularly bothersome. A pleasing, boldly struck example. (#7974)

Remarkable 1856 Three Dollar
Choice Uncirculated

3476 1856 MS64 NGC. In *The United States $3 Gold Pieces,* Bowers (2005) writes that "in Mint State the rarity of the 1856 is not widely appreciated. Truly choice and gem pieces are seldom seen in the marketplace now, nor were they ever plentiful." Garrett and Guth succinctly describe this issue when they say: "Circulated examples are very common, but Mint State examples are very rare." This sharp contrast is supported by the population data from both NGC and PCGS.

Flashy luster radiates from the yellow-gold surfaces of this carefully preserved piece. Scattered grazes are nearly imperceptible to the unaided eye. A few tiny toning spots barely detract from outstanding eye appeal. It is virtually impossible to find an 1856 three dollar nicer than the present specimen. NGC and PCGS combined report just three pieces finer (8/08). (#7974)

Beautiful 1856 Three Dollar Gold, MS64

3477 1856 MS64 PCGS. In 1856 the Philadelphia Mint produced 26,010 three dollar gold pieces. This is not a small mintage by three dollar gold standards, but the date is rare in Mint State grades. The three dollar gold piece was entering its third year of production and was no longer a novelty to be saved by the public at large. Few coin collectors were active at the time, so the survival of Mint State coins of the issue was a matter of chance. In *The United States $3 Gold Pieces 1854-1889*, David Bowers and Douglas Winter estimate that only 90-120 examples are extant in Mint State grades.

This sharply struck, near-Gem example is a rare find for the knowledgeable collector. The surfaces have wonderful luster complementing apricot-gold coloration with tinges of pinkish and lilac, and neither side reveals any mentionable distractions, as expected for the near-Gem grade. Seldom seen finer: Both NGC and PCGS have each certified only a single Gem finer (8/08). *From The Bell Collection.* (#7974)

3478 1856-S VF35 PCGS. The olive-orange coloration is quite attractive. All of the design features are bold, if moderately worn across the highpoints. (#7975)

3479 1856-S—Scratched—NCS. XF Details. Small S, the scarcer of the two mintmark sizes for the issue. Faint field abrasions are strictly assessed by NCS. Luster persists in recessed portions of the design, although wear is noticeable on the wreath and hair. (#7975)

3480 1856-S—Improperly Cleaned—NCS. AU Details. The 1856-S is a popular type coin because of its relative availability. Lemon-yellow patina drapes the present piece, which has numerous hairlines consistent with cleaning. Nonetheless, the details are well-defined. (#7975)

In-Demand 1856-S Three Dollar, AU50

3481 **1856-S AU50 NGC.** One of the few available S-mint three dollar gold issues, and in demand as such, the 1856-S saw a healthy emission of 34,500 coins. This example shows a single straight scrape in the left obverse field before Liberty's face, but elsewhere the surfaces are largely unperturbed, with pretty yellow-gold color and about half of the luster remaining. (#7975)

Lustrous AU53 1856-S Three Dollar

3482 **1856-S AU53 PCGS.** The light abrasions visible under a loupe are consistent with a short spate in circulation, but there is little actual wear visible. Considerable luster covers the orange-gold surfaces of this popular S-mint issue, one of only four available (and excluding the unique 1870-S) in the series. (#7975)

Meritorious AU53 1856-S Three Dollar

3483 **1856-S AU53 PCGS.** Medium S. Similar to the 1856-S half eagle and eagle, two different mintmark sizes are known for the 1856-S three dollar. This is a charming San Francisco type coin that has light gold toning and no obtrusive abrasions. Luster shimmers from protected regions, and wear is generally confined to Liberty's hair and the center of the corn stalks. (#7975)

Near-Mint 1856-S Three Dollar

3484 **1856-S AU58 NGC.** Medium S. Although Philadelphia struck three dollar gold pieces annually between 1854 and 1889, San Francisco coinage was limited to only five issues, excluding the unique 1870-S. The combined mintage of the denomination at San Francisco was 62,100 pieces, which is less than the 1856-S quarter eagle mintage, and approximately 5% of the mintage of the 1856-S double eagle. This is a surprisingly mark-free example that has substantial luster and only faint wear on the hair and eyebrow. (#7975)

3485 **1857—Improperly Cleaned—NCS. VF Details.** The portrait displays wear consistent with the grade, yet luster is unmistakable throughout the lettering and the border of the wreath. The fields are cloudy from a chemical cleaning, but there are no obtrusive marks. (#7976)

3486 **1857—Improperly Cleaned—NCS. XF Details.** Evenly worn with lovely yellow-orange patina. Scattered abrasions limit the grade, but none are of any significance. Faint clash marks are noted on the reverse. A relatively affordable, well-detailed representative. (#7976)

Charming 1857 Three Dollar, AU58

3487 **1857 AU58 NGC.** Only 28,891 pieces were struck and today examples are scarce any finer than the present piece. Splendid apricot-gold patina embraces both sides of this briefly circulated specimen. Scattered abrasions limit the grade, but they barely affect the impressive luster. Clash marks are noted on each side. *From The Menlo Park Collection.* (#7976)

Impressive 1857 Three Dollar, MS62

3488 **1857 MS62 NGC.** Although the 1857 is easily located in most grades, it is elusive even in low Mint State. The present piece has delightful sun-gold patina and captivating satiny luster throughout. The strike is crisp, and the surfaces appear remarkably clean to the unaided eye. Light clash marks are noted on each side. Census: 34 in 62, 19 finer (8/08). (#7976)

3489 **1857-S—Improperly Cleaned—NCS. XF Details.** Dusky yellow-orange patina envelops both sides. A few shallow marks on the obverse are barely worthy of note, but the date is unusually soft. Bowers (2005) believes that the 1857-S is "very scarce in any grade" and estimates that only 160 to 225 examples still exist. (#7977)

3490 **1858—Improperly Cleaned—NCS. XF Details.** Luster brightens the legends, headdress, and wreath. A bit glossy, but suitable for many collectors. After comparatively large mintages between 1854 and 1857, a mere 2,133 business strikes were coined in 1858. (#7978)

3491 **1858—Reverse Graffiti—NCS. AU Details.** Enticing luster in the margins accents the straw-gold patina that covers the centers. A small X has been etched into the reverse field, but there are no significant marks otherwise. One of just 2,133 examples struck. (#7978)

3492 **1859—Damaged—NCS. XF Details.** The obverse field is typically abraded and Liberty's cheek has a minor scratch, but perhaps the NCS assessment is unduly strict. A 'dirty gold' example that retains glimpses of crud in protected areas, an indication that the piece is original. (#7979)

3493 **1859—Improperly Cleaned—NCS. AU Details.** Charming orange-gold patina endows the lightly marked surfaces. A light cleaning minimally affects the lovely eye appeal. A crisply defined example with hints of luster throughout. (#7979)

3494 **1859 AU55 ANACS.** A pale apricot-gold coin with more than its share of rich luster throughout the wreath, obverse legend, and other protected regions. Free from obtrusive marks. A scant 15,558 pieces were struck. (#7979)

3495 **1860-S—Improperly Cleaned—NCS. XF Details.** The 1860-S is a great rarity in Mint State, and even circulated pieces are difficult to acquire. Significantly scarcer than the '56-S. Mildly cleaned, but this olive-gold example has noticeable luster and moderately abraded fields. (#7981)

3496 **1860-S—Mount Removed, Improperly Cleaned—NCS. AU Details.** Mounts have been removed from the reverse at 3 and 9 o'clock, where the piece was once affixed to jewelry. The dusky orange toning appears artificial, and the underlying surfaces are subdued and faintly hairlined. Still a collectible example of this rare San Francisco issue, which had a little-saved mintage of just 7,000 pieces. (#7981)

3497 **1861 VF25 NGC.** 1861 was the last year that the Philadelphia Mint paid out three dollar gold pieces at face value until 1879. For this reason, a signification number of the mintage of 5,959 business strikes saw circulation. This yellow-orange representative has no mentionable marks and just a few tiny areas of verdigris and toning spots. Only a couple hundred examples of this issue are believed to exist. (#7982)

3498 **1861 VF35 NGC.** Splashes of rose in the margins accent the mostly yellow-gold patina that drapes both sides. Myriad abrasions limit the grade, but none merit specific mention. A lovely, well-defined example. (#7982)

3499 **1861—Improperly Cleaned—NCS. XF Details.** Pale straw-gold patina embraces both sides of this evenly worn representative. Traces of luster remain in the margins. Myriad abrasions cover the surfaces, but none merit individual mention. (#7982)

3500 **1862—Improperly Cleaned—NCS. AU Details.** The mintage of gold dollars soared in 1862, but three dollar production was again neglected that Civil War year, reaching only 5,750 pieces. This lightly circulated example is glossy from a wipe, but will meet the needs of many assemblers of the series. (#7983)

3501 **1862—Improperly Cleaned—NCS. AU Details.** The 1862 is elusive in all grades with a mintage of just 5,750 pieces. The present piece has delightful yellow-gold patina that covers the surfaces, which have numerous hairlines but no significant problems otherwise. Light clash marks are noted on each side. (#7983)

3502 **1862—Cleaned—ANACS. AU50 Details.** This briefly circulated example retains substantial luster. The surfaces are only slightly bright, and there are no obvious hairlines. The left obverse field has a faint thin diagonal mark. (#7983)

Pleasing Select 1862 Three Dollar Gold

3503 **1862 MS63 PCGS.** With the onset of the Civil War, gold and silver coinage rapidly disappeared from circulation, and the already-unpopular three dollar gold pieces were no exception. The 1862 issue is no exception, and coins such as the present Select piece are highly prized. Warm honey-gold surfaces offer lovely luster with blushes of peach and rose. The strike offers a wealth of detail, and Liberty's hair shows all of its fine strands. Lines to the left of the portrait and wreath are die striations that were present when the coin was struck. Population: 9 in 63, 18 finer (8/08). (#7983)

3504 **1863—Scratched, Improperly Cleaned—NCS. AU Details.** Pronounced clash marks are visible on both sides of this butter-yellow specimen. Several shallow scratches are noted on the obverse, but the reverse has no bothersome marks. (#7984)

3505 **1864 XF40 NGC.** Deep orange patina covers both sides, but there are traces of yellow luster in the protected areas. The surfaces are quite clean and the details are well-defined. Housed in an old NGC holder. (#7985)

3506 **1864—Improperly Cleaned—NCS. XF Details.** This low mintage Civil War gold piece has pleasing definition and noticeable remaining luster. The cleaning is relatively mild. The date is lightly repunched, and the dies are moderately rotated. (#7985)

3507 **1864—Polished—NCS. AU Details.** Polishing has left the yellow-gold surfaces unnaturally reflective, but there are no noteworthy marks on either side. The usual weakness is seen on Liberty's hair. Only 2,630 pieces were minted. (#7985)

Scarce 1865 Three Dollar, About Uncirculated

3508 **1865 AU50 PCGS.** Bowers (2006) estimates that fewer than 100 examples of the 1865 survive in any grade, out of an original mintage of just 1,140 coins. Attractive orange-gold patina endows the surfaces, with a lovely rose tint on the obverse. Significant luster shines throughout the fields, and the strike is sharp save for minor weakness on Liberty's hair. Although minimally abraded for the most part, there is a shallow scratch between the bust and the U in UNITED, with a similar mark on the reverse above the date. Population: 5 in 50, 43 finer (7/08). (#7986)

Challenging Mint State 1865 Three Dollar

3509 **1865 MS61 NGC.** The 1865 three dollar is one of the scarcest dates, regardless of condition, in an already challenging series. Of course with a puny mintage of 1,140 pieces, the aforementioned fact is no surprise. With less than 100 examples believed to be extant in all grades, we can only imagine what the auction hammer prices would be for this issue if more people collected three dollar gold pieces by date. In Mint State condition, the availability of 1865 threes is even more bleak. To make this point clear, we note that NGC has certified eight pieces at the MS61 level, with only 12 listed at higher grades (8/08). The lovely peach-gold example offered here boasts a solid strike and ample eye appeal. (#7986)

3510 **1866—Improperly Cleaned—NCS. AU Details.** A low-mintage issue with just 4,000 pieces struck. The 1866 is scarce in all grades, and Bowers (2005) estimates that just 125 to 180 circulated examples have survived. The present piece has splendid orange-gold patina patina across the minimally marked surfaces. (#7987)

Splendid 1866 Three Dollar, AU58

3511 **1866 AU58 PCGS. CAC.** Bowers (2005) calls the 1866 a rarity at all levels and estimates that only 200 or so pieces exist in any grade, with only 25 to 40 Mint State examples. Charming orange-gold patina overlies the lightly hairlined surfaces. Powerful luster radiates throughout and enhances the eye appeal. This boldly struck specimen is one of just 4,000 coins minted. PCGS has certified a mere 33 pieces finer, some of which are undoubtedly resubmissions (8/08). (#7987)

Appealing Mint State 1866 Three Dollar Gold

3512 **1866 MS60 NGC.** The post-Civil War mintage of the 1866 three dollar gold was a skimpy 4,000 pieces, and today the average certified survivor grades only AU53 or thereabouts. Mint State examples are available, but seldom seen above MS62. This coin has surprisingly strong appeal for an MS60-graded piece, with strong luster and pretty tinges of peripheral peach against yellow-gold centers. The numerous abrasions appearing on both sides determine the grade, but the piece is commendable nonetheless. (#7987)

3513 **1867—Obverse Planchet Flaw, Improperly Cleaned—NCS. AU Details.** Lightly cleaned, with traces of luster in the periphery of this yellow-gold specimen. A piece of wire was struck in the coining chamber and has left a gouge at the bottom of the obverse. This interesting example is one of only 2,600 pieces struck. (#7988)

3514 **1868—Obverse Damage, Improperly Cleaned—NCS. AU Details.** Pale sun-gold patina embraces both sides of this well-defined piece. Two small digs on the obverse account for the "damage" moniker, but the reverse has only minor abrasions. (#7989)

3515 **1868 AU53 NGC.** A mere 4,850 pieces were minted. Remarkably reflective fields complement the pleasing yellow-gold patina that endows the surfaces. Myriad abrasions define the grade, but the strike is bold. (#7989)

3516 **1868 AU58 NGC.** A nice near-Mint example of this three dollar gold issue, with a satiny appearance and enticing green-gold and orange toning. Boldly struck with minimal wear on the highpoints, and a few wispy hairlines. (#7989)

3517 **1868 AU58 NGC.** Both sides of this important near-Mint example show rich orange toning in the fields. Both sides have virtually full frosty yellow luster. Many of the 4,850 pieces coined have survived, so examples are often available with only a little searching. (#7989)

Attractive and Scarce 1868 Three Dollar, MS63

3518 **1868 MS63 PCGS.** Scarce in any grade, the 1868 had a mintage of just 4,850 pieces. Although this number is higher than some of the later issues in the series, the 1868 is essentially on par with those years in terms of present-day survivors. In *The United States $3 Gold Pieces*, Bowers (2005) speaks of the rarity of the 1868 and estimates that between 70 and 90 Mint State coins exist, mostly in MS60 to MS62.

This yellow-gold representative exhibits fantastic satiny luster throughout the fields, which are nearly prooflike. A couple of tiny blemishes are noted at the top of the obverse. Scattered abrasions define the grade, but none merit individual mention. A sharply struck piece with impressive eye appeal. Population: 25 in 63, 19 finer (8/08). (#7989)

3519 **1869—Polished—NCS. AU Details.** Circulation wear is minimal, but the fields are artificially reflective from polishing. Just 2,500 pieces were produced, and survivors are highly elusive. (#7990)

3520 **1869—Improperly Cleaned—NCS. AU Details.** Unnaturally prooflike from a past wipe, and the left obverse field has numeral minor abrasions. The devices show only slight friction. A difficult date with a low production of 2,500 pieces. (#7990)

3521 **1869 AU53 NGC.** The 1869 three dollar is rare in all grades, according to Bowers (2005), and he believes that between 160 and 240 still exist in all grades. This charming yellow-gold piece is boldly defined and has flashy luster throughout. There are no bothersome abrasions on either side, and the eye appeal is excellent. (#7990)

3522 **1870 AU50 NGC.** A mere 3,500 business strikes of the 1870 were minted and Bowers (2005) states that examples are rare in all grades. Pleasing orange-yellow patina covers the relatively unabraded surfaces. Traces of luster in the fields accent the well-defined devices. (#7991)

3523 **1870—Obverse Damage—NCS. AU Details.** Liberty's neck has a small but somewhat deep mark, and a couple of dull, unobtrusive pinscratches are noted on the lower reverse field. A mere 3,500 pieces were struck. (#7991)

3524 **1870—Improperly Cleaned—NCS. AU Details.** The yellow-gold surfaces appear extremely reflective because of prior polishing. Scattered abrasions limit the grade, but none are particularly bothersome. The scarcity of the 1870, with its mintage of just 3,500 pieces, is often underappreciated. (#7991)

3525 **1870 AU55 NGC.** A late die state with the top of the reverse slightly bulged. This pleasing example survives from a mintage of only 3,500 coins. The surfaces show considerable light yellow luster with traces of rose toning. (#7991)

3526 **1871—Scratched—NCS. XF Details.** All gold denominations struck at Philadelphia in 1871 have low mintages, but the three dollar production was particularly minimal. Just 1,300 pieces were struck. This example has ample luster and moderate wear. A small cluster of pinscratches near the first T in STATES explains the NCS designation. (#7993)

3527 **1871—Improperly Cleaned—NCS. AU Details.** Traces of luster in the protected areas accent the dull apricot-gold patina that covers the majority of the surfaces. Liberty's hair is a trifle soft, but the rest of the details are boldly defined. (#7993)

3528 **1874—Mount Removed, Improperly Cleaned—NCS. AU Details.** A glimpse of solder is visible on the reverse edge near 6:30, although the damage is largely obscured by the holder. The surfaces have an unnatural matte sheen, but the devices have only minimal actual wear. (#7998)

3529 **1874—Improperly Cleaned—NCS. AU Details.** A slightly glossy green-gold type coin that lacks mentionable marks. Liberty's hair and eyebrow show slight wear. Luster glimmers from design crevices. (#7998)

3530 **1874—Polished—NCS. AU Details.** A faintly hairlined and somewhat luminous gold type coin that lacks the bright mirrored fields associated with the polished designation. Liberty's cheek and hair has minor rub. (#7998)

3531 **1874 AU55 PCGS.** A lightly circulated but pretty example of this available date, with tinges of lavender toning near the upper obverse rim and strong field-device contrast. Certified in a small-size PCGS first-generation holder. (#7998)

Charming 1874 Three Dollar, AU58

3532 **1874 AU58 NGC.** The 1874 is an excellent year for a type collector because of its relatively high mintage of 41,800 pieces, which allows examples to be purchased at a fairly affordable price. Bright yellow-gold patina drapes both sides of this resplendent specimen. Although the highpoints show light rub, bright mint luster dominates the remarkably clean surfaces. Well-struck except for a small area of the wreath to the right of the bow. (#7998)

3533 **1874—Improperly Cleaned—NCS. Unc Details.** Delightful satiny luster shimmers across the hazy yellow surfaces. A number of faint hairlines are noted in the fields, but there are no significant marks otherwise. Sharply struck with better-than-expected eye appeal. (#7998)

Pleasing 1874 Three Dollar, MS61

3534 **1874 MS61 NGC.** Pleasing lemon color in the periphery accents the deeper yellow-gold patina in the fields. Liberty's hair is a little soft, but the reverse is sharply defined. The scattered abrasions on both sides are entirely minor and barely affect the strong satiny luster. An attractive example for the grade. (#7998)

Splendid 1874 Three Dollar, MS61

3535 **1874 MS61 PCGS.** The 1874 would make an excellent type coin with its relatively high mintage of 41,800 coins. This yellow-gold piece has great eye appeal, which is enhanced by the shimmering satiny luster in the fields. The strike is crisp, and there are no mentionable marks on either side.
From The Mississippi Collection. (#7998)

Captivating 1874 Three Dollar, MS64

3536 **1874 MS64 NGC.** Impressive satiny luster shimmers throughout the yellow-gold surfaces of this impeccably preserved specimen. A number of pinpoint abrasions on both sides limit the grade, but none are particularly detracting. This sharply struck piece exhibits excellent eye appeal. NGC has certified a mere 13 coins finer (8/08). (#7998)

Charming 1874 Three Dollar, Choice AU Prooflike

3537 **1874 AU55 Prooflike NGC.** Only 18 examples have been certified Prooflike by NGC, and this yellow-gold example has definite glassy reflectivity throughout despite brief circulation. Numerous marks limit the grade, but none merit specific mention. A crisply defined representative with lovely eye appeal. Census: 1 in 55, 16 finer (8/08). (#77998)

3538 **1877—Bent, Polished—NCS. XF Details.** The 1877 is one of the key issue in the series and boasts a diminutive mintage of just 1,468 pieces. Numerous hairlines account for the polished appearance of this bright yellow specimen. A shallow dig is noted on Liberty's jaw, but the bend is nearly imperceptible. (#7999)

3539 **1878—Improperly Cleaned—NCS. VF Details.** The obverse is faintly hairlined and has a few wispy pinscratches. The central reverse has a blurred, matte-like appearance. Bold for the VF level, luster still glimmers from the obverse legend. (#8000)

3540 **1878 AU55 PCGS.** An attractive, lightly circulated example of this popular odd-denomination type issue. The yellow-gold fields retain excellent luster, though a shallow diagonal abrasion crosses Liberty's cheek. (#8000)

3541 **1878 AU58 NGC.** An outstanding opportunity for the type collector to acquire a lovely three dollar piece, in this case with frosty yellow luster and traces of wear limited to the highest design points. (#8000)

3542 **1878—Reverse Rim Damage—NCS. Unc Details.** Two minuscule rim nicks on the reverse have kept this attractive piece from an NGC holder. Dazzling satiny luster shimmers across the smooth surfaces. The well-defined details are complemented by pleasing yellow-gold patina. Scattered light grazes in the fields are typical of a Choice grade, with a couple of tiny digs noted on the reverse. An attractive piece despite minor rim damage. (#8000)

Subtly Colored Uncirculated 1878 Three Dollar

3543 **1878 MS61 NGC.** The 1878 three dollar gold is the last of the three series entries generally considered "common," which includes the 1854 and 1874 issues. But all issues in the series are quite desirable, and it is a challenge to find problem-free Mint State coins such as the present specimen. The devices are well but not fully struck, and the mint luster is untampered with attractive rose and lilac shades. (#8000)

Eye-Catching 1878 Three Dollar, Choice Mint State

3544 **1878 MS64 PCGS. CAC.** Magnificent satiny luster shimmers beneath the light yellow patina that drapes the surfaces. A few minor abrasions barely hinder the impressive reflectivity. Only a touch of weakness on Liberty's hair keeps this piece from being fully struck. This attractive example would make a wonderful representative of the three dollar series. (#8000)

3545 **1880—Improperly Cleaned—NCS. Unc. Details.** Among the lowest mintage dates with a tiny commercial emission of 1,000 pieces, one-third of the 1879 production. By 1880, Philadelphia-area dealers were setting examples aside, but the date is nonetheless rare. This friction-free representative has smooth fields whose slight reflectivity has been enhanced by a long-ago wipe. (#8002)

3546 **1880—Environmental Damage, Cleaned—ANACS. MS60 Details.** The lower reverse border has glimpses of mauve verdigris, and an attempt at removal has left hairlines within the area. Still a thoroughly lustrous and sharply struck representative of this rare date, which has a mintage of only 1,000 pieces. (#8002)

Handsome 1880 Three Dollar, MS61

3547 **1880 MS61 NGC.** Eye-catching luster flashes from the butter-yellow surfaces. A touch of weakness on Liberty's hair limits the grade of this impressive piece. Several pinpoint abrasions in the fields are entirely inconsequential. This enticing specimen is one of only 1,000 coins struck. (#8002)

3548 **1882—Improperly Cleaned—NCS. AU Details.** This briefly circulated gold piece has been wiped, perhaps to reduce the impact of a trio of thin marks on the cheek. The 2 in the date is widely recut, as usual for business strikes of this low mintage date. (#8004)

3549 **1882—Improperly Cleaned—NCS. AU Details.** Flashes of luster accent the dusky yellow-orange surfaces. There are no marks worthy of mention, and the strike is crisp. A charming example of this scarce issue. A mere 1,500 examples were struck. (#8004)

3550 **1882—Scratched—NCS. Unc Details.** Pleasing luster radiates from the yellow-gold surfaces. Several shallow scratches on each side account for the designation by NCS. The design elements are well-defined, and the reverse is particularly sharp. (#8004)

3551 **1883 VF20 NGC.** A well-worn example of the low-mintage 1883 three-dollar gold piece, with just 900 circulation strike pieces minted. An additional 89 proofs were coined, but that still keeps the total mintage below the magical 1,000 coin barrier. (#8005)

Appealing 1884 Three Dollar, MS63

3552 **1884 MS63 NGC.** Although Bass considered the 1884 to be the rarest circulation strike of the decade, Bowers (2005) writes that while it is certainly "very rare," he would not consider it to be the rarest. He believes that between 80 and 110 examples survive in any grade from a mintage of only 1,000 pieces. Perhaps three-quarters of the survivors are in Mint State condition.

Delightful pumpkin-orange patina graces both sides of this powerfully lustrous specimen. The reverse is especially attractive, although both sides are lightly abraded and have great eye appeal. This crisply struck specimen is housed in an old NGC holder. Census: 5 in 63, 28 finer (7/08). (#8006)

Prooflike 1884 Three, MS61

3553 **1884 MS61 Prooflike NGC.** At first glance, this beauty looks just like a proof, but only on closer examination do the tell-tale signs of a circulation strike become obvious. The strike is excellent, but falls short of full. The fields are mirrored, but fail to show the depth of true proofs. The die was undoubtedly polished, but the planchet was probably unpolished. The tiny field spaces inside the ribbon bows show satin luster, but are not mirrored.

With a mintage of only 1,000 circulation strikes, examples are rare and desirable in either format. This lovely piece has bright yellow surfaces and few minor marks that prevent a higher grade. Census: 1 in 61 prooflike, 2 finer (8/08). (#78006)

3554 **1885—Mount Removed—NCS. XF Details.** Possibly tooled west of the 1 in the date and beneath the TA in STATES, and the surfaces are bright and have myriad tiny marks. Some luster remains, and an opportunity to acquire a sharp example of this extremely low mintage date. (#8007)

Impressive 1885 Three Dollar, AU58

3555 **1885 AU58 NGC.** A trace of light rub keeps this lustrous piece from an Uncirculated grade. Lovely orange-gold patina drapes the surfaces, which have no marks worthy of specific mention. Liberty's hair is a trifle soft, but the rest of the details are sharply struck. An attractive example of this elusive issue. Only 801 pieces were struck. (#8007)

3556 **1886—Improperly Cleaned—NCS. AU Details.** Charming pumpkin-orange patina covers both sides, with faint lemon-yellow accents in the protected areas. There are no mentionable marks on either side, although the surfaces appear to have been wiped. A scarce issue with a mintage of only 1,000 pieces. (#8008)

3557 **1887 XF45 NGC.** A degree of reflectivity remains at the margins, though light wear across the yellow-gold centers has claimed much of the coin's original luster. Little-marked and pleasing. (#8009)

3558 **1887—Improperly Cleaned—NCS. AU Details.** Only slight wear is seen on the left border of Liberty's hair, and luster beckons from the design when the piece is rotated beneath a light. Subdued from a cleaning, but nonetheless compelling. A scant 6,000 pieces were struck. (#8009)

3559 **1887 AU53 NGC.** Luster brightens the coronet, plumes, legends, and wreath of this better date three dollar piece. Light wear on the portrait confirms brief circulation. The reverse has a gray spot at 7:30. A mere 6,000 pieces were struck. (#8009)

3560 **1887 AU55 NGC.** Highly lustrous with brilliant yellow satin surfaces and reflective fields. It is an attractive example of the date, surviving from a 6,000 coin mintage. (#8009)

3561 **1887—Altered Surfaces—ANACS. MS60 Details.** This lustrous example has sun-gold centers and peripheral rose toning. Each side has glimpses of struck-in grease, as made. The fields are uncommonly unabraded, and may have been carefully smoothed here and there. Portions of LIBERTY and AMERICA are nicely die doubled, characteristic of this low mintage date. (#8009)

Radiant MS63 1887 Three Dollar Gold

3562 **1887 MS63 PCGS.** A survivor from near the series' end, one of only 6,000 examples produced. Wonderful coloration is this coin's chief attribute, exhibiting glimpses of sage-green in the obverse fields and peach-gold in the peripheral lettering and on the reverse. Radiant cartwheel luster cascades from both sides, and it appears to be only a couple of parallel scrapes within the wreath on the reverse that keep this piece from an even finer grade. (#8009)

3563 **1888 VF20 NGC.** An unusually well-circulated example of this penultimate three dollar gold issue, possibly one kept as a pocket piece. Hints of original luster cling to the mustard-gold margins. One of just 5,00 business strikes coined. (#8010)

3564 **1888—Damaged, Improperly Cleaned—NCS. AU Details.** No damage is readily evident, but this low mintage three dollar piece is whizzed and has a luminous appearance and microgranular surfaces. (#8010)

3565 **1888—Scratched, Improperly Cleaned—NCS. AU Details.** Virtually Mint State in terms of wear, this low mintage example is lightly polished and has an intermittent slender scratch between the ST in STATES, through the portrait, and to the E in AMERICA. (#8010)

3566 **1888—Obverse Improperly Cleaned—NCS. Unc Details.** Vibrant satiny luster shimmers beneath the splendid yellow-gold patina. A gentle cleaning on the obverse keeps this crisply defined piece from an NGC holder. The reverse is remarkably unabraded, while the obverse has only insignificant marks. (#8010)

3567 **1889—Improperly Cleaned—NCS. AU Details.** Traces of dirt cling to design crevices, but the surfaces are slightly glossy from a wipe. The devices show only a whisper of wear. Just 2,300 pieces were struck. (#8011)

3568 **1889—Reverse Scratched—NCS. AU Details.** A popular final-year type coin. Pleasing olive-gold patina covers both sides, which are surprisingly clean save for a shallow scratch on the left side of the reverse. Although this mark keeps this piece from an NGC holder, it is not as bothersome as one might expect. (#8011)

Splendid Near-Gem 1889 Three Dollar Gold

3569 **1889 MS64 PCGS.** A glory from the last year of the unusual three dollar series, and one for which numerous examples were saved, despite the tiny mintage of 2,300 coins. This near-Gem boasts splendid reddish-orange coloration with tremendous eye appeal, and only a few tiny, picayune contact marks seemingly preclude the Gem grade. Population: 49 in 64, 37 finer (7/08). (#8011)

Desirable 1879 Flowing Hair Stella
Judd-1635, PR64 ★ Cameo

3570 **1879 Flowing Hair, Judd-1635, Pollock-1833, R.3, PR64 ★ Cameo NGC.** Numismatic riddle: What do the half cent, two cent, three cent, twenty cent, three dollar gold, and four dollar stella have to do with each other? Alert numismatists probably picked up on the answer at the second coin: They are the odd denominations of U.S. coinage, neither fish nor fowl. While not quite fitting into the mainstream of the United States' numismatic history, each denomination has still taken a part at one time or another, some merely bit players, some with more substantial roles ranging from the significant to the merely "curious."

It is also well worth mentioning that the perception of most of those denominations and their importance in numismatic history has, in most cases, changed greatly over time.

The half cent was produced in mostly small numbers at sporadic intervals from 1793 until 1857—sometimes in proof format only for certain years. It was a denomination with little purchasing power, one that took a back seat to the large cent, a workhorse of early U.S. commerce along with the half dollar. Today, of course, both the half cent and large cent are the beloved "old coppers" of numismatic lore.

The copper two cent (1864-1873) and silver twenty cent piece (1875-1878) were much more bit players in coinage history, the former enduring less than a decade and the latter lasting only four years before numerous personality problems ended its brief career.

With some overlap during the 19th century, first the three cent silver (1851-1873) and then the three cent nickel (1865-1889) took their turns on the numismatic stage. The three cent silver was detested due to its diminutive size (giving rise to the term "fish scales"); the three cent nickel had a slightly longer life but performed past its prime in 1883, when lower rates for letter postage obviated the need for a three cent coin. The three cent nickels' career finally ended with a whimper in 1889, after a series of proof-only issues that have so often in U.S. numismatics signaled the final curtain for various denominations.

The three dollar gold (1854-1889) was another numismatic curiosity, one whose career roughly coincided with the minor three cent denominations. Although some modern-day numismatists suppose the denomination would have been useful to buy sheets of 100 three cent postage stamps or 100 three cent silvers, the series was unable to perform any role that a quarter eagle and half dollar could not do just as well. The mintages of the denomination reflect considerable ambivalence over its desirability, and as often happens with numismatic actors whose careers are doomed, the business strike emissions became progressively less before coming to a halt in 1889.

Finally we come to the four dollar denomination. This is likely the oddest and most curious denomination of all. While the four dollar coin was intended as a unit of international commerce—and a metric one, at that—it was not a precise equivalent for any of the denominations it was supposed to replace. And while the inscriptions on the coin claim an even number of metric grams as composition, most numismatists today believe that, as a pattern proposal for a coinage that was never launched, the planchets used to strike the coins were of the normal gold composition, on planchets 80% of the thickness of a half eagle to produce the intrinsic value of four dollars. While the 1879 Coiled Hair and both of the 1880 issues were produced in extremely tiny numbers, the 1879 Flowing Hair was —so the story goes—produced to the extent of 15 "originals" in 1879 with an unknown number of "restrikes," variously estimated from 300 to 700 pieces, in 1879 or 1880. The supposition about "restrikes" comes from Akers' 1976 gold reference, Volume III, where he notes that the "restrikes" have "light adjustment marks or striations on the head of Liberty."

In practice, all of the 1879 gold stellas we have cataloged at Heritage have shown the striations, which are roller marks from a shaved planchet, thinner than a regular half eagle planchet, that did not strike out during impression of the coins.

The present example displays the roller marks or planchet striations through Liberty's lower hair and her profile to the jawline. This desirable coin appears quite close to an Ultra/Deep Cameo designation, and tilting the piece at the proper angle produces the black-on-gold appearance so coveted in proof gold. Viewed head-on, the specimen appears greenish-gold with a lot of eye appeal, and only under a loupe do a few tiny contact marks appear.

Although the stella is considered strictly a pattern, the number of estimated pieces produced has allowed many numismatists of means to collect one alongside their regular U.S. coinage. In this respect, the 1879 Flowing Hair stella has similarities to yet another U.S. coin—the 1856 Flying Eagle cent. Both are among the most memorable and desirable issues in all of U.S. numismatics.

From The Laredo Collection. (#88057)

3571 1879 Flowing Hair, Judd-1635, Pollock-1833, R.3, PR65 Cameo NGC. The 1879 four dollar stella is the most popular gold pattern of all time. It is properly considered a pattern, but conventional gold collectors have adopted the issue as well. The stella is pursued passionately by collectors from many different disciplines and backgrounds. An example is considered a highlight of any collection that features one.

The stella was originally intended to function as a medium of international exchange, much as the euro does today. The Honorable John A. Kasson conceived of the coin as a handy denomination, nearly equivalent to the Austrian eight florin, French twenty franc, Italian twenty lire, Spanish twenty peseta, and Dutch eight florin coins. Having traveled extensively in Europe in political assignments as an envoy and minister plenipotentiary, Kasson understood the financial difficulties faced by international travelers in his day. Banks charged a significant premium to exchange one currency for another. Repeatedly changing money as one journeyed from country to country would result in substantial loss through the repeated fees. Money-changers would usually refuse to exchange minor coins, causing further drain on the traveler's funds. Kasson hoped to facilitate travel overseas and foreign trade by developing a coin that could be used in many countries without the expense and inconvenience of monetary exchange. Kasson had impressive credentials as a former chairman of the Committee of Coinage, Weights and Measures in Congress. Using his political connections, the former chairman convinced the sitting Committee of Coinage, Weights and Measures to consider his project. The result was the stella.

Engravers Charles Barber and George Morgan both developed a pattern four dollar gold coin in 1879. Barber produced the Flowing Hair obverse design, which was similar to a half eagle pattern design from 1878, Judd-1574. Morgan created an elegant design known as the Coiled Hair stella, with Liberty's hair gathered up in braids atop her head. The designs used a common reverse, with a five-pointed star as the central element, from which the pattern takes its name. It is believed that 15 Flowing Hair stellas were coined in 1879, but demand from Congressmen and Mint officials caused the issue to be restruck in 1880. The restrikes were from the original dies and may have numbered as many as 600-700 examples. All examples seen in modern times have parallel striations across the obverse design, usually in the hair, and it is impossible to differentiate between restrikes and originals. Morgan's Coiled Hair design was produced in extremely small quantities and was not given out to congressmen for examination. The design was not restruck and remains very rare today. Experts believe that 400-500 specimens of the Flowing Hair stella have survived. Both Flowing Hair and Coiled Hair varieties were later reproduced in small numbers, with new dies dated 1880, to satisfy numismatic demand from favored collectors.

Kasson's idea was ahead of its time, but it was fatally flawed. The different currencies that he sought to exchange with the stella were not exact equivalents and varied against each other over time. Congress realized that the stella was impractical, and no regular mintage was ever authorized. Many stellas did circulate in this country, and popular stories relate that members of Congress used the coins they obtained as exotic gifts for their mistresses.

As a result of their colorful history as gifts and circulating coins, many stellas are seen in impaired condition today. Gem Cameo examples are rare and desirable. The present example is a fine representative of this much-loved design. The deeply mirrored fields contrast boldly with the frosty devices to produce a dramatic cameo effect. The strike is strong, and all design elements are brought up in great detail. The lovely green-gold color accents the virtually flawless surfaces. A classic rarity that will appeal to the pattern specialist and the mainstream collector. Census: 14 in 65 Cameo, 26 finer (8/08). (#88057)

Desirable and Scarce 1795 Small Eagle Five Dollar
BD-4, AU Sharpness

3572 **1795 Small Eagle—Plugged, Whizzed—NCS. AU Details.** Breen-6412, BD-4, R.5. Lovely butter-yellow patina drapes the surfaces of this well-defined representative. Although this piece has been whizzed, the surfaces show no significant marks or blemishes. The plug is surprisingly well-done and minimally detracts from the design elements. A die crack from the rim to star 12 indicates that this piece is obverse die state d, which is always paired with reverse die state a.

Dannreuther (2006) estimates that between 1,000 and 1,500 BD-4 specimens were struck out of a total mintage of 8,707 to 12,106 coins. Only 60 to 75 examples of this variety are believed to have survived. Speaking to the desirability of this issue, Garrett and Guth (2006) write: "The 1795, Small Eagle gold piece is an extremely popular coin, being the first year of the type and denomination." Despite several flaws, the present piece is an impressive and fairly attractive representative of this important issue. (#8066)

3573 **1795 Small Eagle AU55 PCGS.** Breen-6412, BD-3, High R.3. The Bass-Dannreuther *Early U.S. Gold Coin Varieties: A Study of Die States, 1795-1834* lists 12 varieties for the 1795 Small Eagle five dollar, plus a 1796/5 overdate. Varieties BD-2, BD-3, and BD-4 show overlapping obverse stars 11 and 12, and star 11 over the Y of LIBERTY. The reverse wreath of BD-4 has three berries, while BD-2 and BD-3 each have four berries. The present coin, an example of the BD-3, is distinguished from BD-2 by the palm leaf that extends past N in UNITED, a higher inside right berry on the wreath, and by the tips of the wreath that are roughly centered between the S of STATES and the O of OF.

The Mint produced half eagles from 1795 through 1929, although not during every year of that period. The 2009 *Guide Book* notes that with the production of five dollar commemorative and bullion coins at West Point in the late 20th century "this is the only U.S. denomination made at each of the eight mints." Only 8,707 1795 half eagles were minted, with 175-225 of this variety known today. As Dannreuther notes, "Although this is the common variety of 1795 Small Eagle coinage, one must realize *common* is a very relative term. Even if there are 200 extant for this pairing, it is still a rare coin."

The obverse of the present example displays a sharp strike, but there is softness in the central part of the eagle from the head to the right (facing) leg. A bit of detritus clings to a few letters on both sides, and there is a tiny dig below the eagle on the reverse; neither is bothersome. Both sides display red-gold toning, slightly darker on the obverse, with a contrasting yellow-gold halo surrounding the stars and letters. This pleasing example of the first-year half eagle issue is an ideal coin for the type or early gold collector. *From The Menlo Park Collection.* (#8066)

3574 **1795 Small Eagle AU55 NGC.** Breen-6412, BD-4, R.5. A number of diagnostics easily identify this variety. On the obverse, a point of star 1 touches the hair curl, the tip of the 5 in the date connects to the bust, and star 11 overlaps the Y in LIBERTY. The reverse is distinguished by the central location of the wreath under the O in OF and by the position of the olive branch in relation to the UNI in UNITED.

The obverse of this variant is shared with two other Bass-Dannreuther varieties, namely BD-2 and BD-3, on which it saw earlier use. Thus the earliest die state is die state c, the state of the latest BD-3. In this slightly later die state a crack runs from the rim through star 12 and slightly into the field, but star 1 just barely touches the lowest curl; later in this die state lapping separates the two. (Bass-Dannreuther note that, since this is the last use of this obverse, some pieces [which may have been melted hundreds of years ago] should exist in the terminal die state, presumably showing shattering of the die.)

The reverse of this die marriage, BD Reverse C, is unique to this variety and can be easily distinguished not only by the diagnostics above, but because there are only three berries on the small wreath that the eagle holds in its beak—two outside and one inside.

Bass-Dannreuther estimate that 60 to 75 specimens of this variety exist, making the present coin an attractive potential acquisition for the variety or type collector. From the 30,000-foot perspective, all of the 1795 Small Eagles are important as the first gold coins struck by the U.S. Mint, even if this variety cannot possibly be the absolutely first of that important beginning.

The charming surfaces of this Choice AU example show lovely orange-gold coloration, with a few minor surface ticks consistent with the grade. A small patch of adjustment marks appears from above stars 14 and 15 to below the tip of the bust. Much luster remains, and the overall impression of one of high quality, despite some strike softness on the eagle's head and neck that is usual for the variety. (#8066)

1795 Small Eagle Five Dollar, BD-1, MS62
Likely the First U.S. Gold Coin Variety

1795

3575 **1795 Small Eagle MS62 NGC.** Breen-6412, BD-1, R.5. This coin is of immense historical importance. Not only is it a high-grade specimen of the first U.S. gold coinage, it is an odds-on favorite as the first of the 12 different varieties of 1795 Small Eagle struck.

Even though the Philadelphia Mint was established in 1793 and struck copper half cents and cents during its first calendar year—the latter in three different styles—the Mint Act of 1792 set an onerous requirement that the treasurer, chief coiner, and assayer each post surety bonds in the amount of $10,000 before coinage of the precious metals, gold and silver, could commence. Congress in 1794 lowered the requirements to $5,000 for the chief coiner and to $1,000 for the assayer, and those lower bonds were paid. But the Mint in its early years (until 1837) had no bullion fund of its own. It produced gold and silver coinage only on demand for depositors of bullion (or foreign coins, also considered just so much bullion). It was late in 1794 before silver dollars were produced on a coinage press of sufficient size. The first deposit of gold for coinage was on July 21, 1795. Accordingly, on July 31 of that year, Warrant 1 was for the production of 744 half eagles, of course dated 1795 and using the Capped Bust to right, Small Eagle motif of designer Robert Scot.

The Bass-Dannreuther early gold reference asserts Harry Bass Jr.'s belief that the BD-1 variety of the present example, included in (or possibly all of) that first delivery of half eagles, signifies the first gold coins produced by the Mint of the United States. In the early days of the Mint, the coinage personnel had not yet learned how to properly harden dies; many of them cracked within a short time after entering production. And dies were used until they failed, regardless of the date they bore.

It took eight obverse dies and nine reverse dies to produce those 12 known varieties of 1795 Small Eagle. A good number of them may have been produced in 1796; the reported mintage of 6,196 half eagles is too high for the single die pairing known for 1796.

The BD-1 die pairing has several characteristics that lead one to reasonably believe it could be the first variety struck, including a wide date, four berries on the reverse (two inside the wreath, two outside), and of course the Small Eagle reverse that later in the year was supplanted by the Large Eagle varieties (BD-12 through BD-15). On the obverse the flag of the 5 in the date is embedded in Liberty's lower drapery, while a point of star 15 is into the front of the bustline. Star 11 is clearly separated from the Y in LIBERTY, and BERTY is repunched. Bass-Dannreuther notes, "Rust on both dies may be due to the delay in striking gold coins, noted elsewhere, due to the high bonds that had to be reduced and posted by three Mint officials."

On this piece the die rust is prominent (although, of course, not grade-affecting) in the lower and rear hair curls, the lower drapery, and the left (facing) field on the obverse, and on the reverse as a small patch of roughness above and right of the F in OF. A loupe also reveals a few light, scattered contact marks that account for the grade, although only a thin scrape behind Liberty's head, near the cap tip, requires mention. The yellow-gold surfaces reveal considerable field reflectivity and frosted devices, yielding a moderate prooflike effect. The eye appeal of this coin is every bit as high as its historical importance.
From The Laredo Collection. (#8066)

3576   **1798 Large Eagle, Large 8, 14 Star Reverse—Scratched—NCS. AU Details.** Breen-6427, BD-3, R.5. This is the only variety to feature the unusual 14 star reverse. Although the *Early U.S. Gold Coin Varieties* reference indicates that all BD-3 examples were struck from a perfect obverse die (state a), this specimen shows a delicate die crack that connects the tops of the TY in LIBERTY. This pieces exhibits the terminal reverse die state (state d), and has numerous bisecting cracks. It is presumed that this die shattered fairly early, which explains the relative rarity of this variety.

Charming orange-gold patina drapes both sides of this peculiar early half eagle. The eagle's left (facing) claw and wing are soft, and the center of the obverse is a trifle weak, as typically seen. The rest of the details, however, are crisply defined. While there are myriad shallow scratches on both sides, they are mostly in the fields and hardly affect the central design elements.

John Dannreuther (2006) states that there are only three dozen BD-3 survivors from a total mintage of an estimated 2,500 to 3,500 pieces. The Bass collection had four examples, which seems to indicate that he liked this unusual issue. According to Garrett and Guth (2006) this popular variety averages one appearance at auction each year, and there are only about a dozen About Uncirculated representatives, with one known Mint State specimen. This interesting and seldom-offered variety would make a wonderful addition to any collection. (#8080)

3577 **1799 Large Stars Reverse MS61 NGC. CAC.** BD-5, R.5. Only two of the nine known die varieties of 1799 half eagles had large stars on the reverse, and both are rare. Actually, all nine varieties of this elusive date are rare. John Dannreuther estimates that only 190 to 250 1799 half eagles still exist. The two Large Stars varieties are only known by their appearance for BD-5 and BD 8, with less than 60 pieces known for both varieties combined. The large star punch remained unused until 1807 when it was used for all known varieties except BD-1. We are currently aware of just three or four Mint State examples of this variety, including the present piece.

Both sides have excellent design details, with all individual elements boldly defined with the sole exception of the drapery over Liberty's bosom.. Extremely faint adjustment marks can be seen at the right obverse border. The surfaces are brilliant with greenish-gold patina and the fields are fully reflective, creating a cameo appearance.

An intriguing die state is presented, with a perfect obverse die, and heavy clash marks on the reverse. Usually, when dies clashed, the clash marks were picked up on both sides. After the dies clashed, the obverse must have been removed from the press and repolished before being replaced for more strikes with the clashed reverse die.

The very existence of such a die state is one of those situations that makes numismatic research so enjoyable. Census: 8 in 61, 3 finer (7/08). (#98081)

Marvelous 1800 Half Eagle, BD-5, Choice AU

Desirable 1802/1 BD-2 Half Eagle, AU55

3578 **1800 AU55 NGC.** Breen-6438, BD-5, High R.3. The obverse, which was used on four out of the five varieties for 1800, features the distinctive blunt 1. This variety is distinguished by the reverse, on which a point of star 13 touches the eagle's neck and the second A in AMERICA is firmly joined to the right (facing) claw. Numerous die cracks on the reverse are also diagnostic for BD-5. This piece is a transitional die state example (between Bass-Dannreuther d/b and e/c), with a faint crack on the obverse between the I and B in LIBERTY.

Impressive luster penetrates the lovely olive-gold patina. The strike is a trifle weak at the centers, as typically seen, although the stars show excellent definition. Dannreuther estimates that between 175 and 250 examples of this variety exist, and fewer than 8 pieces appear at auction, on average, each year. An attractive representative of this early issue. (#8082)

3579 **1802/1 AU55 NGC.** BD-2, R.4. all 1802 half eagles are overdates from two different obverse dies. Those dies were combined with several reverse dies to create eight known die marriages. Four of the eight varieties are common enough, either R-4 or R.5, while the other four are rated R.7.

A plentiful variety, BD-2 combines the low centered overdate obverse die with a defective reverse die that has die chips over the left (facing) wing and between the tops of TA in STATES, visible on all known examples. The reverse also has a missing ribbon loop in the eagle's mouth. This attractive representative has smooth green-gold surfaces with nearly full luster and hints of attractive iridescent toning. (#8083)

Very Rare BD-4 1802/1 Five Dollar AU58

3580   **1802/1 AU58 NGC.** Breen-6440, BD-4, R.7. Bass-Dannreuther Die State c/b. A very rare die marriage with two pick-up points. A leaf tip points between the RI in AMERICA, and the 1 underdigit is centered within the 2. The date is double clashed within STATES, and the left obverse border is slightly buckled. This is a generally lustrous straw-gold half eagle with a precise strike and only a hint of friction, limited to the forehead and cloud centers. Despite the recent publication of the well made Bass-Dannreuther reference, collecting early half eagles by die pairing has yet to catch on. Nonetheless, varieties of the greatest rarity have enormous market potential, and the present piece should be the subject of enthusiastic bidding. (#8083)

Scarce 1802/1 Half Eagle, BD-1, Mint State Sharpness

3581   **1802/1—Improperly Cleaned—NCS. Unc Details.** BD-1, High R.4. Since all eight known varieties of 1802 half eagles feature the overdate (although two different obverse dies were employed), this piece can best be identified by the reverse. A star points to the lower beak tip and a leaf points to the I in AMERICA, identifying this variety. Despite a gentle cleaning, the yellow-gold surfaces are remarkably pleasing and have only minor abrasions. Sharply defined with lovely eye appeal. (#8083)

Lovely Mint State 1802/1 Half Eagle, BD-1

3582   **1802/1 MS61 NGC.** Breen-6440, BD-1, High R.4. Key diagnostics include a previous 1 centered within the 2 in the date; and a reverse leaf tip that points directly to the center of I in AMERICA.

This is a lovely Mint State example that retains full mint luster and displays alluring lime-green and yellow-gold toning. The design elements are crisply defined, except for slight softness on the eagle's head and breast feathers, and there are only small, superficial marks on either side of the piece. The fields have a flashy, semireflective appearance. This is a popular issue that is considered to be relatively common within the context of early gold coinage, but Bass-Dannreuther (2006) give an estimate of just 75 to 100 survivors for the BD-1 variety at all grade levels. (#8083)

VF Details 1803/2 Five Dollar, BD-4

3583   **1803/2—Improperly Cleaned—NCS. VF Details.** Breen-6441, BD-4, R.4. Bass-Dannreuther Die State b/c. The T in LIBERTY is perfect, diagnostic for BD-4. A green-gold representative that has a glossy appearance and wear on the portrait. Close inspection locates thin marks near the AM in AMERICA and the ED in UNITED. An opportunity to acquire an example of the difficult Bust Left type at an affordable price. (#8084)

Worthy AU53 1804 Small 8 Five Dollar, BD-1

3584 **1804 Small 8 AU53 NGC.** Breen-6443, BD-1, High R.4. The small 4 in the date is lightly repunched near the left corner, and a die line extends from the left shield corner. This generally lustrous example shows only minor rub from brief circulation, along with a few faded obverse marks. A scarce Heraldic Eagle date. *From The Menlo Park Collection.* (#8085)

Difficult AU Details 1805 Half Eagle, BD-1

3585 **1805—Mount Removed, Improperly Cleaned—NCS. AU Details.** Close Date, Breen-6445, BD-1, High R.3. Liberty's hair and shoulder has only a whisper of friction, but both sides are hairlined, and tooling near the LI in LIBERTY and opposite on the lower tail feathers suggest a repaired plug. The cheek has a pair of wispy marks. A bold example of this popular early gold type. (#8088)

Splendid 1805 Half Eagle, BD-3, MS62

3586 **1805 MS62 NGC.** Wide Date. Breen-6444, BD-3, High R.5. Dannreuther-Bass (2006) list five varieties of the 1805 half eagle. Varieties BD-3, BD-4, and BD-5 have an "imperfect 1" in the date (the left base serif is incomplete) and more widely spaced date digits than on BD-1 and BD-2. BD-3 is distinguished from BD-5 by star 1 positioned farther away from Liberty's hair curl, and from BD-4 by star 9 located closer to the Y of LIBERTY. Dannreuther's study of a reverse rim break above the last S in STATES on 1805 and early 1806 half eagles indicates that "... most of the 1805 coins that employed this reverse were struck in 1806!"

This example has tremendous eye appeal, displaying warm honey-gold surfaces tinted with reddish highlights. Some luster remains, and though the center devices have softness typical for the date, there are no detracting abrasions or spots to compromise the overall impression. A few light adjustment marks are well-hidden in Liberty's cap. The present coin is a pleasing and scarce early 19th century half eagle that is sure to appeal to the early gold specialist. (#8088)

1805 Close Date Five, BD-2

3587 **1805 MS65 NGC.** Close Date, Breen-6445, BD-2, R.4. Bass-Dannreuther Obverse State e/f, Reverse State b. The BD-1 and BD-2 1805 half eagle varieties are the so-called Perfect 1, Close Date types, sharing a common obverse and with different reverses. The other three known varieties for the 1805-dated issue are the Imperfect 1, Wide Date variants, BD-3 through BD-5.

Of the two Close Date combinations, the Bass-Dannreuther *Early U.S. Gold Coin Varieties: A Study of Die States, 1795-1834* pegs the BD-1 at High R.3 (175-225 known in all grades), while the BD-2 is set at R.4 (100-200 known). In other words, the BD-2 is about twice as rare as the BD-1. In the broader context of this difficult early U.S. gold coin series, however, the BD-2 is considered very scarce, and the Gem quality of the present offering catapults it into the very rare to extremely rare category, conditionally speaking.

On the obverse of this variety, which is shared with the BD-1, the 1 in the date is perfect, of course, and its top serif touches the lowest curl of the hair. The flag of the 5 is buried in the drapery, and star 13 is embedded in the bust of Liberty. Star 8 is quite close to but not touching the cap, and star 9 touches the right branch of the Y in LIBERTY.

The reverse die is shared among the BD-2 *and* the three Imperfect 1, Wide Date 1805 varieties, as mentioned, *plus* the 1806 Pointed 6, BD-1. The I in AMERICA is free of the nearby leaf, and IT in UNITED are separated.

Harry Bass, Jr., never having to confine his collecting interests due to budgetary concerns, owned a remarkable seven examples of this variety. According to Bass-Dannreuther, "The attraction no doubt was due to the fact that this hardy reverse die was used for *four* more varieties and the obverse die shattered. Seeing varieties progress through states, especially those with multiple die combinations, enthralled Harry Bass. He put the *pieces* together like a jigsaw puzzle and every time a new state was encountered, he could put another notch on his numismatic belt."

At this particular *stage* in the life of the dies, the obverse die crack through the 0 in the date, running up through the hair and to Liberty's cap, is prominent. A second crack extends from star 13 through the center, but the crack through its ultimate destination, star 4, is not yet seen. Die rust appears boldly through the LI, and much of LIBERTY shows clashing from the reverse. The reverse, as well, shows considerable clashing through the lower tail feathers from the obverse.

This charming and interesting coin shows remarkably few abrasions of any size on either side, and its generous eye appeal and reflective fields more than merit the Gem grade assigned by NGC. Only under a loupe do a few tiny, undistracting ticks appear, mostly in the right obverse field but scarcely worthy of mention. The color is a consistent golden-orange, with a touch of hazel on the obverse high points. The strike is well-executed overall, although a touch of bluntness appears on the eagle's left wing near the shield and the claw and arrows below. A fascinating Gem example for the specialist in early die states, as well as for the date collectors of the series. *From The Laredo Collection.* (#8088)

Impressive 1806 Knobbed 6 Half Eagle
BD-6, Choice AU

3588 1806 Round Top 6, 7x6 Stars AU55 NGC. BD-6, R.2. This is the only variety with the Knobbed or "Round Top" 6 in the date. BD-6 is relatively available compared to the other die marriages for the year, and this variety is perhaps the most common of any Heraldic Eagle five. The strike is sharp for the most part, although the arrows are rather soft. Impressive luster enhances the eye appeal of this delightful yellow-gold example. This attractive piece has no mentionable marks and would make a splendid type coin. (#8089)

Upper-End MS63 1806 Knobbed 6
Five Dollar, BD-6

3589 1806 Round Top 6, 7x6 Stars MS63 NGC. CAC. Breen-6448, BD-6, R.2. Mint State examples of the 1806 Capped Bust Right (or Turban Head) five dollar are relatively plentiful within the context of early gold. In fact, when early type collectors begin their search for early fives, the 1806 Knob 6 is likely the first coin that comes to mind. However, at the MS63 level the field thins out rapidly and drops precipitously above that. This discrepancy makes solid examples like this Select coin all the more desirable. Additionally, though the date is relatively common for its type, the Knob 6 (also known as the Round Top 6) is the only die pair among half eagles to incorporate the 7x6 star split as opposed to the usual 8x5. Thus, this high-end coin is also worthy of interest because of its auspicious design variation. The surfaces display bright, even yellow-gold color with rich mint frost. A few light abrasions in the obverse fields explain the grade. An outstanding early gold type coin. (#8089)

3590 **1807 Bust Right MS62 PCGS.** BD-1, High R.4. This is the only known variety that features small stars on the reverse. All varieties of 1807 half eagles are scarce, and fewer than 100 examples of BD-1 are believed to exist. Amazingly, Harry Bass owned three representatives of this variety. The present piece is Bass-Dannreuther die state b/c, and has several faint cracks in the obverse margins along with a number of more pronounced die cracks on the reverse. Wonderful satiny luster highlights the crisply struck design elements. The reverse has numerous adjustment marks throughout, but that translates only to minor weakness on parts of the obverse. A remarkably clean and attractive specimen.
From The Bell Collection. (#8092)

3591 **1807 Bust Right MS62 NGC.** Small Date, Small Obverse Stars, Large Reverse Stars, Breen-6450, BD-4, High R.4. Bass Dannreuther Die State c/a. This is a crisply struck sun-gold final year example of the Draped Bust Right type. Luster fills the reverse and dominates the portrait, stars, and legends. Through examination reveals inconspicuous marks on the lower right obverse field and Liberty's cheek. Most 1807 half eagles are the John Reich Bust Left type, and attractive Mint State examples of the Bust Right design are eagerly pursued by early gold specialists. (#8092)

3592 **1807 Bust Right MS64 NGC.** BD-1, High R.4. Bass-Dannreuther die state b/b. It is believed that the reverse die used in this marriage was a leftover die from the 1806 production run, based on the combination of the large letters and small stars. Of the six varieties of 1807-dated half eagles, all except BD-1 feature large stars in the reverse design.

The fact that we offer two examples of BD-1 in this sale may lead some to believe that it is a common variety. In reality, fewer than 100 examples of this die marriage are believed extant in all grades. Both the NGC *Census Report* and the PCGS *Population Report* combine the population data for all six 1807 Bust Right five dollar varieties into one total, so auction records become a more reliable source for determining the true rarity of this issue. Bass and Dannreuther documented 53 auction appearances of this variety between 1990 and 2005. In other words, this is a scarce variety.

Due to the ambiguity of the population data, we cannot be certain of the finest graded BD-1 half eagle, but the current offering must be near the top of the Condition Census for the variety. NGC has certified eight pieces as MS64 with one finer—an MS65 specimen. The numbers at PCGS are similar, with only four MS64 examples and a lone MS65 coin (8/08). The current offering is fully brilliant, with frosty luster and lovely yellow-gold coloration. All of the design elements on each side are sharply struck, with the exception of star 13 on the reverse. Insignificant adjustment marks on the obverse rim and a nearly invisible hairline scratch in the right field from the chin to star 8 are noted for the sake of accuracy. The reverse is void of mentionable flaws and would achieve Gem status if graded separately. (#8092)

XF Definition 1807 Bust Left Five Dollar, BD-8

3593 **1807 Bust Left—Mount Removed—NCS. XF Details.** Bust Left, Breen-6453, BD-8, R.2. This first year Bust Left half eagle has a thickly hairlined obverse and a whizzed reverse. Mildly wavy, and damage near 3 and 9 o'clock on the reverse suggests the removal of solder where the piece was once affixed to jewelry. The fields have a few faded pinscratches. (#8101)

1807 Bust Left Five Dollar, BD-8, AU53

3594 **1807 Bust Left AU53 NGC.** Breen-6453, BD-8, R.2. Luster fills the reverse and dominates the obverse periphery. Originally toned canary-gold with a shade of lime along the reverse margin. This sharply struck early gold type coin has excellent eye appeal. A loupe is required to locate wispy field marks. Certified in a prior generation holder. (#8101)

Remarkable 1807 Capped Bust Half Eagle, AU55, BD-8

3595 **1807 Bust Left AU55 PCGS.** Breen-6453, BD-8, R.2. The reverse identifies this variety, and is distinguished by the location of the feather tip, which points to the tip of the 5 in the denomination. This piece is obverse state d/reverse state b, and features fairly prominent clash marks on both sides, most notably in Liberty's hair from the shield. Pleasing yellow-gold patina graces both sides of this boldly defined representative. Scattered abrasions define the grade, but none are worthy of note. An attractive and lustrous example from the first year of John Reich's Capped Bust design. Housed in a green label PCGS holder. (#8101)

Exciting 1807 Capped Bust Left Half Eagle BD-8, MS62

3596 **1807 Bust Left MS62 PCGS.** Breen-6453, BD-8, R.2. First year of issue, from a mintage of 51,605 pieces. John Reich engraved two varieties of this design in 1807. This is the more available variety, identified by the position of the arrow feather on the reverse. Reich left his secret signature on the design, a notch on the outermost point of star 13. In *Collecting & Investing Strategies for United States Gold Coins*, Jeff Ambio endorses the 1807 half eagle as a most desirable issue to represent the Capped Bust Left half eagle in a type set. The MS62 grade of the present specimen is in line with Ambio's recommendation for most desirable Mint State grade.

The coin offered here is difficult to improve upon. The strike is extraordinary for a coin made with open collar technology. All star centers are strongly delineated, and there is full detail in the hair. Abrasions are minimal for the grade. Smooth, frosty luster complements the sharp strike. A prize for the type collector or early gold specialist.
From The Laredo Collection. (#8101)

3597 **1808—Improperly Cleaned—NCS. Unc. Details.** Wide 5D, Breen-6457, BD-4, High R.3. An unworn olive-green half eagle that has faint obverse hairlines and a couple of unobtrusive abrasions on the obverse field. The obverse has a small edge nick at 2 o'clock. An opportunity to acquire an example with full details without writing a check for five figures. (#8102)

Wonderful 1809/8 BD-1 Half Eagle, AU55

3598 **1809/8 AU55 PCGS.** Breen-6458, BD-1, High R.3, the only 1809-dated dies. A honey-gold representative that has extensive shimmering luster and only a hint of rub on the hair above the ear and on Liberty's drapery. Refreshingly unabraded, it is a raised die line (as made) that crosses the middle arrow head and reaches the eagle's wing. Faint clash marks, also of mint origin, are present on the reverse field. All 1809 Half Eagles are from a single die pairing, which has the lower curve of an apparent 8 within the 9 in the date. This lovely example has greater eye appeal than many higher graded pieces, and would provide a formidable contribution to an advanced early type set.
From The Menlo Park Collection. (#8104)

Interesting 1809/8 Half Eagle, BD-1, Mint State Sharpness

3599 **1809/8—Improperly Cleaned—NCS. Unc Details.** BD-1, High R.3. Only one variety is known for the year and it is debatable whether this "overdate" features a 9 over 8, or a 9 over 9. Bass' doubts were seconded by Dannreuther, who agreed that the underdigit is most likely a misplaced 9. Bright yellow-gold patina embraces both sides of this boldly defined specimen. There are a number of die rust lumps on the bust, but there are no significant abrasions. This piece is Bass-Dannreuther die state b/b, as evidenced by the clash marks on the reverse and the die cracks through several of the obverse stars. A pleasing example despite cleaning. Just 250 to 325 examples are believed to exist. (#8104)

Smooth MS62 1809/8 Five Dollar BD-1

3600 1809/8 MS62 NGC. Breen-6458, BD-1, High R.3. Bass-Dannreuther Die State b/b. The sole die variety for the date. The 9 in the date is large and is accompanied by small lumps of raised metal traditionally associated with an underdigit 8, although this consensus is by no means definitive. The reverse die is the Wide 5D carried over from 1808 BD-4. This unmarked and original Capped Bust half eagle is sharply struck and has substantial luster. The planchet is completely problem-free. Given the rapid rise in value with each succeeding grade, the best value for the type may be found in MS62. (#8104)

Uncirculated 1810 Capped Bust Five Large Date, Large 5, BD-4

3601 1810 Large Date, Large 5 MS61 NGC. Breen-6459, BD-4, R.2. Bass-Dannreuther a/a, the dies are perfect except for a raised area near star 4 caused by an obverse die depression of unknown origin. The 1810 comes with three different date logotypes and three different logotypes for the 5 in the denomination. Although BD-1 and BD-2 are both considered Small Date varieties, the 0 punch is clearly larger on BD-2 than on BD-1. The present Large Date example is yellow-gold with pleasantly smooth surfaces. The strike is exacting save for incompleteness on the claws. Luster illuminates the devices and legends. A desirable early half eagle that will fulfill a difficult obligation within an advanced gold type set.
From The Mississippi Collection. (#8108)

3602 1810 Large Date, Large 5 MS64 PCGS. Large Date, Large 5, Breen-6459, BD-4, R.2. The date is large, with a near-horizontal flag atop the first 1 in the date. The reverse shows a large, squat 5 with the top right portion of its flag pointing directly at the lowest feather tip on the fletchings.

The obverse of this die combination is shared with the extremely rare 1810 Large Date, Small 5 variant, BD-3, estimated at High R.7 or four to six pieces known according to Bass-Dannreuther. But with the Large 5 reverse, this 1801 variety is among the most available of this difficult U.S. coin series, along with the 1806 Knobbed 6 (BD-6), the 1807 BD-8, and the 1813 BD-1. Bass-Dannreuther notes that this variety is the most frequently seen early half eagle in MS64 (the grade of the present piece) or finer condition. That reference notes that the estimated upper range for the mintage is some 90,000 pieces, and that the dies "remained in great shape with nearly every example examined either in the perfect state or clashed."

The piece appears to be a fresh strike from new dies, as there is no visible clashing on either side, and considerable frosty luster emanates from each side of this orange-gold near-Gem. A few light adjustment marks appear on Liberty's cheek, so faint that they are scarcely visible without magnification. The strike is sharp if a trifle short of full, and neither side reveals anything more than the most minute, scattered signs of contact. This piece would make a wonderful type coin for the collector who desires a nice near-Gem piece without seeking one of the rarer varieties that so abound in the series.
From The Laredo Collection. (#8108)

3603 **1811 Small 5 MS61 NGC.** Breen-6464, BD-2, R.3. The 1811 Small 5 half eagle shares a mintage of 98,851 pieces with the other variety of this date, the Tall 5. The Small 5 is slightly more common and ranks as one of the most available Capped Bust Left half eagles. In *Collecting & Investing Strategies for United States Gold Coins,* Jeff Ambio recommends this date for inclusion in a complete type set. The characteristic Small 5 numeral punch was previously used on two rare half eagle varieties in 1810 (BD-2, BD-3) and continued to be used in 1812 (BD-1, BD-2).

This Mint State coin will attract the attention of type collectors and early half eagle specialists alike. The coin appears high-end for the assigned grade, with only light field chatter visible on both sides but no singularly mentionable abrasions. Tiny adjustment marks are noted at the obverse rim above stars 6 and 7, scarcely visible without a glass. (#8109)

Outstanding 1812 Half Eagle, BD-1, Choice Mint State

3604 **1812 MS64 PCGS. CAC.** Wide 5D, Breen-6466, BD-1, R.3. The two known 1812 half eagle varieties feature the same obverse and are distinguished by the spacing of the denomination. This piece is Bass-Dannreuther die state a/a, as evidenced by the absence of clash marks on either side. The reverse of BD-1 has two peculiar die defect lines, which were either accidental graver's marks or some sort of damage. One is located just before the first A in AMERICA from the rim to the eagle's right (facing) wing, and another bisects the shield and the eagle's left wing. The unknown nature of these die lines makes this piece an excellent candidate for further research.

Dannreuther estimates that between 45,000 to 60,000 examples of this variety were minted, but there are only between 300 and 450 survivors. Although not as scarce as its Close 5D counterpart, BD-1 is seldom seen in Choice condition, and it is extremely difficult to locate in Gem. On July 30, 2008 we sold another PCGS MS64 specimen, but the present piece is unquestionably more attractive than that coin. PCGS reports only five examples finer, four of which are just one point higher (8/08).

An interesting characteristic of this piece is the fairly obvious strike doubling on the reverse. Minor die chatter has caused most of the letters to be slightly wider than normal. There are also several light adjustment marks on the obverse, which translate to minor weakness on the eagle's left (facing) wing. The rest of the details, however, are quite sharp. Impressive satiny luster shimmers beneath the sun-gold patina. A few minuscule marks in the fields preclude an even higher grade. This handsome piece is a wonderful representative of the final issue before alterations were made to John Reich's Capped Bust design. (#8112)

Scarce Choice AU 1813 Half Eagle, BD-1

3605 **1813 AU55 NGC.** Breen-6467, BD-1, R.2. Perhaps no series is more difficult to assemble by date than the Capped Head Left half eagle. The 1813 is the first year of the type, and is also among the few comparatively available dates. Thus, it is under heavy demand from gold type set collectors. This partly lustrous Choice AU representative has a hint of wear on the forehead, hair, and cap, but there are no obtrusive marks, and the light green-gold toning is original.
From The Menlo Park Collection. (#8116)

Select Mint State 1813 Five Dollar
Better BD-2 Variety

3606 **1813 MS63 NGC.** Breen-6467, BD-2, R.4. The scarcer of only two known varieties of this introductory Capped Head Left date. This type is essentially impossible to complete, since only one 1822 is known outside of the Smithsonian and the 1815, 1825/4, and 1828/7 are extremely rare. Fortunately, the type itself is collectible, due in large part to the 1813 BD-1. The availability of that specific variety allows the astute collector to on occasion obtain the difficult BD-2 for a type price. The present example has energetic luster and undisturbed olive-gold toning. Sharply struck save for the claws, and consequential marks are limited to a trio of faint lines on the cheek. (#8116)

Rare 5D Over 50 1818 Half Eagle
Borderline Uncirculated, BD-3

3607 **1818 5D Over 50 AU58 NGC.** Breen-6472, BD-3, R.5. Bass-Dannreuther b/b with clashed letters from LIBERTY within the shield. The rarest of the three die pairings known for the date. Each receives a separate *Guide Book* listing, since BD-2 is the STATESOF variety, while the D in the denomination for BD-3 is entered over an errant 0. The engraver was presumably in the habit of cutting half dollar dies, which were certainly more prevalent than their half eagle counterparts. This is a boldly struck piece that has only minimal friction on the eyebrow and forecurl. The green-gold surfaces lack noticeable marks, and the extent of luster throughout the margins and devices is consistent with that of higher certified grades for this difficult type. (#8120)

3608 **1833 Large Date MS61 PCGS.** Breen-6498, BD-1, High R.5. Mislabeled on the PCGS insert as a Small Date, the digits in the date are definitely more widely spaced than on the Small Date variant. The actual size of the digits is just barely noticeable, but the style of the number punches is distinctively different. The 3s on the Large Date have pronounced knobs and the 8 is more block-like rather than the italic (or belted) style seen on the Small Date.

An article by Paul Gilkes in the June 26, 2000 issue of *Coin World* deals directly with the rarity of the 1829 half eagle, but the explanation applies just as effectively to the 1833:

> "The main reason the 1829 Capped Head, Large Planchet half eagle is so difficult to obtain is that it and many of its predecessors fell victim to the great melts, a byproduct of the flood of Mexican and Peruvian silver. The influx of silver on the world market compared to gold supplies lowered the silver price, but appeared as an unstoppable increase in the value of gold reckoned in Mexican dollars. The result was widespread hoarding and melting of older gold coins when their bullion value exceeded their face value by enough to warrant a profit over the cost of melting. Tens of thousands of half eagles and other gold denominations of recent vintage were melted soon after their production and reclaimed..."

As a result, few people in the 1820s and 1830s ever saw or handled a U.S. quarter eagle or half eagle. The few that did survive are often encountered in relatively high grades. For the 1833, the average grade is 57.4. This coin is noticeably finer at the MS61 level. It would, in fact, grade higher but there is a long, vertical abrasion on the shield on the reverse, and we are at a loss to explain its origin. A bit softly struck on the obverse stars and the left portion of the eagle's wing, the surfaces otherwise are bright and the fields semireflective. Even, light reddish-yellow color is seen over each side of this rarely seen Capped Head issue. Population: 2 in 61, 9 finer (8/08).
From The Laredo Collection. (#8157)

CLASSIC HALF EAGLES

3609 **1834 Plain 4—Improperly Cleaned—NCS. AU Details.** Second Head, Breen-6502, McCloskey 2-A, R.2. The 4 in the date is triple-punched. Although the obverse has been cleaned, the reverse is surprisingly pleasant with plenty of luster in the fields. Both sides are well-defined, and there are no particularly bothersome marks. (#8171)

3610 **1834 Plain 4 AU53 NGC.** Second Head, Breen-6502, McCloskey 2-B, R.3. This yellow-gold piece is identified by the triple-punched 4 in the date and the absence of the eagle's tongue. Flashes of luster accent the lightly abraded the surfaces. The strike is crisp save for the typical weakness on the hair by Liberty's ear.
From The Menlo Park Collection. (#8171)

3611 **1834 Plain 4 AU53 NGC.** First Head, Breen-6501, McCloskey 3-B, R.2. A nicely struck introductory year type coin that has more than its share of peach-tinted luster. The green-gold fields are smooth save for faded marks beneath OF. In a former generation holder. (#8171)

Popular 1834 Plain 4 Classic Head Half Eagle, AU58

3612 **1834 Plain 4 AU58 NGC.** Second Head, Breen-6502, McCloskey 4-C, R.3. 1834 was a transitional year for half eagles, and both Capped and Classic Head type were minted, along with Plain and Crosslet 4 varieties for each. This piece is the most available issue of the year, and is arguably the most common of the Classic Head series. Boldly struck save for minor weakness on the hair by Liberty's temple. Plenty of luster radiates from the fields and enhances the eye appeal. A wonderful type coin. (#8171)

Radiant AU58 Classic Head 1834 Five

3613 **1834 Plain 4 AU58 NGC.** First Head, Breen-6501, McCloskey 3-B, R.2. Radiant yellow-gold surfaces exhibit only a trace of friction on the softly struck high points. Minimally flawed otherwise. (#8171)

Near-Mint 1834 Plain 4 Classic Five

3614 **1834 Plain 4 AU58 NGC.** Second Head, Breen-6502, McCloskey 2-A, R.2. A honey-gold Classic half eagle with plentiful luster across the margins and central devices. The strike is good, since only the forehead curls and the vertical shield stripes exhibit blending. A faint hair-thin vertical mark near the profile, otherwise uncommonly free from visible abrasions. (#8171)

Exquisite 1834 Plain 4 Classic Head Half Eagle, MS62

3615 **1834 Plain 4 MS62 NGC.** First Head, Breen-6501, McCloskey 3-B, R.2. A plain 4, with the 34 in the date comparatively distant, identifies the obverse. On the reverse, the eagle has no tongue, and there is no motto above its head. There are a number of varieties of 1834 half eagles, and the 1834 Plain 4 Classic Head is probably the most available. Perhaps the strongest quality of the present piece is its flashy, semiprooflike luster, which gives it tremendous eye appeal. Enticing yellow-gold patina overlies the surfaces and is complemented by powerfully struck details. This exquisitely preserved and attractive piece would make a wonderful representative for a type collection. (#8171)

Exceptional Reflective MS64 ★ 1834 Classic Five

3616 1834 Plain 4 MS64 ★ NGC. CAC. First Head, Breen 6501, McCloskey 3-B, R.2. Congress acted on June 28, 1834 to reduce both the weight and fineness of United States gold coins to bring their intrinsic value into line with their face value. A new design was needed to distinguish the new tenor gold coins from the old. Chief engraver William Kneass created the Classic Head design to be used on all United States gold coins.

Nine varieties of 1834 Classic Head half eagles have been identified by Dr. John McCloskey. The present coin is variety 3-B. Obverse 3 is identified by characteristics of the numerals in the date. The numeral 1 has a long, sloping serif at the top. The 4 is distant from the curl with a crossbar that extends the same distance beyond the upright as the base. On reverse B, the eagle has no tongue and the 5 is nearly centered under the arrow feather. Although this is a common variety, it is unusual to find an example as nice as the present coin.

This coin has great eye appeal. The strike is just a little weak at the center of both sides, as almost always seen, with all the surrounding elements sharply outlined. The surfaces are brightly reflective and have only a moderate number of abrasions. The luxuriant yellow-gold color is virtually unblemished. (#8171)

3617 1835 XF45 ICG. First Head, Breen-6504, McCloskey 1-B, R.3. The 5 in the denomination is to the left of the arrow feathers, and the olive leaves are distant from the U in UNITED. Splendid orange-gold patina drapes the surfaces of this lovely representative. Myriad marks are typical for the grade, but none save for a shallow scratch on the reverse merit specific mention. Several stars and hair curls are soft, as usual. Clashmarks are visible on the obverse, with a prominent outline of the shield in Liberty's hair. (#8173)

3618 1835 AU50 NGC. First Head, Breen-6504, McCloskey 1-A, R.2. Lovely straw-gold patina embraces the minimally marked surfaces. Plenty of luster remains in the fields and enhances the eye appeal. The stars are somewhat soft, as typically seen, but the rest of the details are crisply defined. (#8173)

3619 1836 AU50 ANACS. Second Head, Large Date, Breen-6509, McCloskey 4-D, R.2. A modestly worn piece that retains ample luster in the yellow-orange fields. Minor, scattered abrasions affect the portrait and nearby fields. (#8174)

3620 1836 AU53 PCGS. Second Head, Large Date, Breen-6509, McCloskey 2-B, R.4. A scarce variety identified by a die break within the upper loop of the first S in STATES and a bold bisecting obverse die crack between the 6 in the date and star 8. Original, partly lustrous, and well defined. The upper reverse field has a few faded marks. (#8174)

1836 Five Dollar, McCloskey 3-C, Choice AU

3621 1836 AU55 NGC. Third Head, Breen-6510, McCloskey 3-C, R.2. The large 1 in the date, the 6 somewhat distant from the lowest hair curl, and the D. in the denomination about halfway left under the stem tip diagnose this available variety. The present example boasts much luster remaining over the orange-gold fields, with good eye appeal. A few tiny abrasions appear under a loupe, consistent with a short stay in commerce. (#8174)

3622 1836 AU55 NGC. Second Head, Large Date, Breen-6509, McCloskey 4-C, R.3. A problem-free green-gold Classic five that is well struck aside from the left-side stars. The cheek and curls show only slight wear. (#8174)

Resplendent 1836 Half Eagle, AU58

3623 **1836 AU58 PCGS.** Second Head, Large Date, Breen-6509, McCloskey 4-D, R.2. The 1 in the date is significantly larger than the other digits, identifying this obverse, and the right side of the D in the denomination is nearly centered under the stem. Flashy of luster radiates throughout this briefly circulated specimen. There are no marks on either side, and the strike is razor-sharp. (#8174)

MS62 1836 Half Eagle, McCloskey 4-D

3624 **1836 MS62 NGC.** Second Head, Large Date, Breen-6509, McCloskey 4-D, R.2. The large digit 1 in the date, much larger than the other digits, identifies the obverse, and on the reverse the TES is tight, with a wide OF, and the D in the denomination is almost entirely under the stem. This lustrous greenish-gold piece shows light field chatter under a loupe, but there are no singular abrasions, and good eye appeal is present. (#8174)

3625 **1837 XF40 PCGS.** Large Date, Large 5, Breen-6512, McCloskey 2-B, R.3. Sharply defined for the grade, and rotation reveals remnants of luster. A few faint marks are east of the date, and a shallow strike-through is at 5 o'clock on the reverse. (#8175)

3626 **1838—Improperly Cleaned—NCS. XF Details.** McCloskey 1-A, R.2. Dusky, moderately hairlined orange-gold surfaces show significant evidence of a past cleaning. Otherwise, well struck with light to moderate wear focused on the high points. (#8176)

Appealing 1838 Five Dollar, McCloskey 1-A, AU55

3627 **1838 AU55 NGC.** Large Arrows, Small 5, Breen-6514, McCloskey 1-A, R.2. In the few years following the redesign and reduced metal content of gold coinage, the U.S. Mint was scrupulous about producing an abundant number of circulation strikes, in order to "jump start" their circulation. Most examples of this issue are about Choice AU or so. This AU55 piece shows pretty yellow-gold, clean surfaces with premium eye appeal. (#8176)

3628 **1838—Improperly Cleaned—NCS. Unc Details.** Large Arrows, Small 5, Breen-6514, McCloskey 1-A, R.2. The end of the stem is to the right of the D in the denomination, identifying this variety. Despite cleaning, the surfaces are remarkably pleasant, with bright yellow-gold patina that covers both sides. The strike is razor-sharp save for the typical weakness on several stars. A lovely representative of William Kneass' short-lived Classic Head design. (#8176)

AU Details 1838-D Five Dollar

3629 **1838-D—Obverse Repaired, Improperly Cleaned—NCS. AU Details.** McCloskey 1-A, R.3, the only dies. This first-year Dahlonega half eagle has been smoothed near Liberty's eye, and both sides are thickly hairlined. Nonetheless, a bold example that still possesses some mint luster. The mintmark is on the obverse above the date, its location prior to 1840. (#8178)

LIBERTY HALF EAGLES

3630 **1839 AU50 NGC.** A boldly defined light yellow-gold example of the first Liberty half eagle that Christian Gobrecht designed. This date is always popular with type collectors, and is even considered a one-year design type by advanced collectors. (#8191)

3631 **1839-C MS63 NGC.** Variety 1-A. The only variety known. This piece is Die State I, with no die defects on either side. In 1839 the design of the half eagle was changed to feature Gobrecht's new stylization of Liberty. Although this basic type lasted for many decades, noticeable alterations were made in 1840, which makes the 1839 a popular representative not only because it was a first-year issue, but also due to its status as a one-year type. The mintmark was moved to the reverse with the 1840 issue, and the hairbun was slightly modified.

Bright lemon-yellow patina endows the surfaces of this conditionally scarce representative. This issue often features an irregular strike, but the present example is sharply struck throughout save for minor softness on several of the star centrils. Scattered abrasions are entirely trivial and barely affect the flow of the flashy luster. Numerous die polish lines are noted on the obverse, particularly near the date, which explains the impressive luster that enhances the excellent eye appeal.

A mere 17,205 examples were struck, and the 1839-C is seldom seen in grades above Extremely Fine. Garrett and Guth (2006) generously estimate that 30 to 40 coins exist in About Uncirculated, with an even smaller number of Mint State representatives. Two pieces have been certified MS64 by PCGS, one of which exhibits deeply prooflike surfaces, possibly because it was a presentation issue. No specimens have been certified finer than the present piece by NGC, and both services report a combined four pieces at the MS63 level (8/08). This outstanding piece is among the finest known and would make a spectacular addition to any of the finest collections. (#8192)

3632 1840 Narrow Mill AU53 NGC. The 1840 half eagle's mintage of 137,382 pieces is divided among the Narrow Mill and Broad Mill varieties, which are distinguished by the width of the outer rim. Lots of luster radiates from the fields of this yellow-gold example. There is a little weakness on the hair above Liberty's forehead, but the remaining details are sharply defined. (#8194)

3633 1840 Broad Mill AU55 NGC. A luster connects the peripheral legend of the reverse, and surrounds individual stars. Nicely detailed and lightly abraded with slightly subdued green-gold surfaces. (#8194)

3634 1840-C—Polished—NCS. AU Details. Variety 2-B. The only variety known. Despite a relatively high mintage (18,992 pieces), the 1840-C is one of the scarcest Charlotte Mint half eagles. Although this piece has been polished, there is still lots of detail. Mottled bright yellow and dusky orange patina covers both sides. (#8196)

3635 1840-D Tall D Fine 12 PCGS. Variety 3-B. This variety is easily distinguished because of the large mintmark. Delightful pumpkin-orange patina drapes both sides, which show no prominent marks. Liberty's cheek is soft, but the eagle is actually well-defined. A charming example of this scarce issue. Only 22,896 pieces were struck of both mintmark varieties. (#8198)

3636 1840-O Broad Mill VF30 NGC. A circulated but relatively unabraded New Orleans half eagle with red-russet toning along the borders. The eagle's wings display substantial plumage definition. (#8200)

3637 1840-O Narrow Mill XF45 NGC. The 1840-O was the first half eagle struck at the New Orleans Mint, and the Narrow Mill variety is the more common of the two distinct types for this issue. A mere 40,120 pieces were minted of both varieties. This orange-gold example is a little weak at the centers, as is often the case, but it is boldly defined around the perimeter. Plenty of luster shimmers in the fields and there are no significant marks to report. (#8200)

3638 1842-C Large Date VF35 PCGS. Variety 5-C. The only Large Date variety known. Subdued green-gold patina graces the surfaces, with pale orange accents around the devices. Both sides are lightly abraded, as typical for the grade, but there are no marks of any significance. Although not as rare as its Small Date counterpart, the 1842-C Large Date is a scarce issue in any grade with a mintage of just 23,589 pieces. (#8209)

3639 1842-C Large Date—Cleaned—ICG. AU53 Details. Variety 5-C. A well detailed Charlotte five dollar piece, but the reverse is overly bright, and the obverse is thickly hairlined. A solitary pinscratch is noted above the right (facing) wing. Still worthwhile for its sharpness and scarcity. (#8209)

Rare AU Details 1842-D Large Date Five

3640 1842-D Large Date—Improperly Cleaned—NCS. AU Details. Variety 9-G. Large Letters reverse. Splendidly detailed, but hairlined and subdued. Still desirable for its sharpness. Much rarer than its Small Date counterpart, which constituted the majority of the mintage of 59,608 pieces. (#8211)

Sharp Mint State 1843 Half Eagle

3641 1843 MS61 NGC. This is an available P-mint issue from the 1840s, but as this example proves it is also a well-produced one, with a bold strike and appealing surfaces. A few dozen Mint State coins are known. This piece has good luster, with some light smoky gray-gold haze in the fields. There are few mentionable distractions, save for a couple of tiny dotlike indentations beneath the eagle's beak. Census: 22 in 61, 33 finer (8/08). (#8213)

Pleasing, Highly Lustrous MS64 1843 Five Dollar

3642 1843 MS64 NGC. CAC. As a date, the 1843 half eagle is the second most common issue of the 1840s. David Akers states that it is only moderately rare in the lower Uncirculated grades. However, at the MS64 level, the coin is very elusive. In *The Official Red Book of Auction Records 1994-2003*, Jeff Garrett and John Dannreuther were able to find only four offerings of MS64 coins during that ten-year period. A few more coins may have surfaced since then but the issue remains very challenging at this level. Harry Bass settled for an MS61 and the John J. Pittman coin was called Uncirculated, nearly Choice.

The present coin would be a great addition to a type set or a date-mintmark collection of No Motto Liberty half eagles. The striking details are razor-sharp on both sides. The color is a pleasing, misty, orange-gold with red patina on the reverse. There are virtually no abrasions visible to the naked eye. Census: 10 in 64, 1 finer (7/08). (#8213)

Near-Mint 1843-C Half Eagle

3643 1843-C AU58 NGC. Variety 6-C, the only variety described for the issue, although two minutely different mintmark positions are known. One has the point of the projecting arrow feather over the left inside curve of the C as seen on this piece, and the other has the point of the arrow feather over the center of the C. This lovely half eagle has a trace of highpoint wear with lightly abraded greenish-gold surfaces and brilliant luster. (#8214)

Important and Highly Desirable 1843-D Small D Half Eagle, MS62

3644 1843-D Small D MS62 PCGS. Variety 10-G. The rare Small D variety, which is significantly more elusive than its Medium D counterpart. The surfaces of this immensely appealing example offer vibrant luster, semiprooflike in the centers with frosty margins. The color on the piece is attractive and displays peripheral orange patina that frames the rich yellow-gold interiors. Lightly abraded in the fields but with a clean appearance overall, this coin is impressive for the grade.

This outstanding Small D piece is undoubtedly among the finest known and is the sole MS62 example of this variant graded by PCGS, with none finer (8/08). In fact, PCGS has graded only two Uncirculated specimens. NGC does not distinguish the Medium D and Small D variants, so one of the five Select pieces or the lone Choice coin at that service could possibly be a Small D as well. Regardless, this gorgeous coin is an important example that belongs in a collection of the finest Dahlonega gold. (#98215)

Interesting Late-State 1843-O Large Letters Five, MS60

3645 1843-O Large Letters MS60 NGC. This is a spectacular grade for this well-known O-mint rarity, one that is quite scarce in grades above XF and rare in Mint State. The finest example known was the Bass coin, which graded MS64. Both the Bass coin and the present example were in late die states. This piece shows many spidery die cracks on both sides, including one from the rim through the 1 in the date and to the bust; cracks from 11 of the 13 stars; and a crack from the 3 in the date to the bust. On the reverse, which shows the normal weak strike on the periphery, most of the bases of UNITED STATES OF AMERICA are joined by various cracks that are more advanced than those on the obverse.

Another crack joins the tops of FIVE D, the nearby period, and the rim, and IC in AMERICA are nearly obliterated on this failing die. The centers of this coin are actually remarkably well struck, and both sides show somewhat prooflike luster. If you are seeking gold coins with interesting die state characteristics and tons of character, this piece should be high on your list. (#8216)

3646 1844-D MS64 NGC. Gold was discovered in a big way in the Appalachian regions of Georgia and North Carolina during the 1820s. At the time, transporting the gold ore from the mining regions to the Mint at Philadelphia was an arduous and dangerous task. Several private mints were established near the gold fields to allow the miners to avoid the risk and expense of shipping their gold overland to Philadelphia. Jealous of their coining powers and anxious to properly exploit this new source of wealth, Congress decided to establish branch mints at convenient locations near the gold fields. The Act of March 3, 1835, created the three Southern branch mints at New Orleans, Charlotte, and Dahlonega. Construction delays and personnel problems plagued all the new mints, and coinage finally commenced in 1838. The mints at Charlotte and Dahlonega coined only gold denominations during their short careers. The gold deposits of the region were gradually depleted, and the great California Gold Rush of 1849 enticed many local miners to abandon their claims and go West. The Confederacy seized the mints at the start of the Civil War but lacked the resources to operate them after the supply of coin blanks was used up. The mints at Charlotte and Dahlonega were never reopened after the war and produced no coinage after 1861. Today, advanced collectors highly prize gold coins with the coveted C and D mintmarks.

From an original mintage of 88,982 pieces, the 1844-D is one of the more available issues from the Dahlonega Mint in circulated grades. About Uncirculated examples are encountered with some regularity. The situation changes dramatically at the Mint State level. There are eight to 10 survivors in lower Mint State grades; Gem coins are unknown. The present near-Gem coin qualifies as one of the three finest certified by the leading grading services. Many dates from the Dahlonega Mint display characteristic weak strikes. The 1844 issue is one of the few that is generally seen with above-average striking quality. The coin offered here has an outstanding strike, with strong detail in the stars, hair, and eagle. The fields are semiprooflike, with delicate shades of orange and green toning. The accent of green toning near the rim is reminiscent of the Pittman coin. There are few distractions, none worthy of individual notice. A breathtaking coin overall, certainly one of the finest examples known. Census: 2 in 64, 0 finer (8/08). (#8221)

3647 **1844-O AU53 NGC.** Ex: Ashland City. This luminous yellow-gold New Orleans No Motto five has a wealth of detail and is only moderately abraded. Luster outlines individual stars and dominates the reverse legends. (#8222)

3648 **1844-O AU55 NGC.** Bright luster fills the reverse legends and outlines individual stars. Neither side has any noticeable marks, and only the fletchings and the curl below the ear lack a crisp impression. (#8222)

MS62 1844-O Half Eagle

3649 **1844-O MS62 NGC.** Variety Two. The 1844-O half eagle had the largest mintage of any O-mint half eagle, and the second-largest emission of any O-mint gold coin behind the 1847-O eagle. Most examples circulated extensively, however, and certified survivors average only XF45 or AU50. This piece shows some planchet roughness and die rust, not unusual for the issue, and stars 5 through 10 are notably weak due to the die lapping for which the issue is known (per Doug Winter). A couple of canal-shaped planchet flaws appear, one from Liberty's chin to star 2 on the obverse, a second on the reverse from between OF downward into the field above the eagle's wing. None of the reverse die cracks Winter describes are obvious, however. Census: 5 in 62, 11 finer (8/08). (#8222)

Appealing 1844-O Half Eagle, MS63

3650 **1844-O MS63 NGC.** As a date, the 1844-O is the most available New Orleans half eagle. Most examples are found in circulated grades from VF20 to AU55. Douglas Winter states that fully Uncirculated coins are rare, and coins at the Choice level are extremely rare. In *Collecting & Investing Strategies for United States Gold Coins*, Jeff Ambio recommends the 1844-O as the best choice for an O-mint No Motto Liberty half eagle in a type set from each issuing mint (just makes it clearer).

The coin offered here is well struck, with just the slightest weakness on the curls that is often seen with this issue. The surfaces have only minimal abrasions for the grade, none individually distracting. The frosty mint luster of the devices underscores the bright, orange-gold color of the fields. This coin combines excellent eye appeal, condition rarity, and the cachet of the old Southern mint. A great opportunity for the type collector and the specialist. Census: 10 in 63, 6 finer (7/08). (#8222)

Attractive 1845 Half Eagle, MS62

3651 1845 MS62 NGC. Garrett and Guth (2006) write: "As can be expected from an issue with a fairly large mintage, the 1845 half eagle can be found with relative ease in grades below Mint State." Uncirculated examples, however, are seldom seen and are quite desirable when they come to market. Powerful reflectivity is barely affect by peppered abrasions in the fields. The razor-sharp strike is complemented by pleasing butter-yellow patina. Census: 10 in 62, 14 finer (8/08). (#8223)

Choice XF 1845-D Five Dollar

3652 1845-D XF45 NGC. CAC. Variety 13-I. Well-defined for the grade with original, dusky orange-gold surfaces. Light, even wear and few faint marks overall, though an abrasion is present near the corner of Liberty's mouth. The '45-D is the most frequently encountered D-mint five, and this piece is an excellent candidate as a type representative of Dahlonega gold. (#8224)

Interesting 1846 Large Date Five, MS62

3653 1846 Large Date MS62 NGC. Another sharp example of the Large Date 1846 half eagle, rare in Mint State. This piece displays pretty yellow-gold patina with good luster and a few stray contact marks and light scrapes that account for the grade. This is one of several examples of the 1846 Large Date in the present sale that feature several different and interesting die states. The present piece shows wispy obverse die cracks through stars 6-11, but there are none of the dramatic die cracks and clash marks on the reverse that later appear on some examples. Another interesting piece for the die state specialist. (#8226)

High Grade 1846 Large Date Five, MS63

3654 1846 Large Date MS63 NGC. CAC. The 1846 half eagle is relatively scarce in all grades and quite rare in Mint State. The MS63 coin in the Harry Bass Collection was considered the finest known when that landmark collection crossed the auction block. Since then a few more coins have been certified at the MS64 level. The coin offered here, one of two MS63 coins in the present offering, is a realistic candidate for Condition Census.

The 1846 half eagle is a delight for the student of varieties and die states. Two major varieties have been identified, Large Date and Small Date. The present coin is the more common Large Date variety. The obverse features a long die crack running from the rim near star 5, through all stars 6-11, and back to the rim. The reverse has an even more dramatic crack running from the E in STATES through the eagle, shield, lowest arrowhead, and touching the foot of the second A in AMERICA. The reverse die also shows prominent clash marks in the field.

The surfaces are semiprooflike, with beautiful reddish-gold color overall that darkens slightly around the periphery. Some light chatter is evident in the fields on both sides. The strike is extraordinary, and all details of the design are fully realized. This coin combines rarity, beauty, and special interest for the die student in one total package. (#8226)

Tremendous 1846 Large Date Half Eagle, MS63

Impressive 1846-D/D Half Eagle, MS62

3655 **1846 Large Date MS63 NGC.** There are two major varieties of the 1846 half eagle, the Small Date and Large Date, although the actual difference in date size is slight. The Large Date is the more common of the two, but both varieties are scarce in Mint State. Harry Bass Jr. owned *eight* examples of the issue.

The easiest way to distinguish between the two variants is to examine the position of the 1 in the date against the forward truncation of the bust—although even this method requires a side-by-side comparison. The Large Date has the left top serif of the 1 more nearly aligned with the left edge of the truncation, and the entire date, of course, fills more of the space underneath the bust.

The surfaces are markedly prooflike on this splendid MS63 piece, with lustrous yellow-gold coloration and much overall eye appeal. Wispy die cracks run through stars 5 through 10, and only a few light contact marks on both sides seemingly preclude an even finer grade. The strike is bold, and generous luster washes from each side. In MS63, this coin is one of only two so certified at NGC, and there are only two pieces finer (8/08). Simply a tremendous example! (#8226)

3656 **1846 Small Date AU58 NGC.** This straw-gold Borderline Uncirculated has an exacting strike, noticeable luster, and subdued, lightly abraded surfaces. Heavy die cracks over the AME in AMERICA threaten to form a retained die break. (#88226)

3657 **1846-D/D XF40 PCGS.** Variety 16-L. The mintmark is prominently repunched northeast, although the feature is undesignated on the green label insert. Luster is unexpectedly plentiful for the grade, and softness on Liberty's hair is chiefly due to the strike. (#8229)

3658 **1846-D/D MS62 NGC.** Variety 16-L. In 1846 the Dahlonega Mint produced several different varieties including this prominent and popular doubled mintmark variety. In the second edition of *Gold Coins of the Dahlonega Mint 1838-1861*, Doug Winter describes three obverse dies and three reverse dies.

The three obverse dies are quite similar in appearance, and rather easily confused. Obverse 14 has the 1 closer to the bust, obverse 15 has the 1 centered between the bust and border, and obverse 16 has the 1 slightly closer to the border. The reverse dies include Reverse I that was carried over from 1845 with the upright of the D nearly over the center of the V below, Reverse J with the mintmark high, nearly touching the stem and point of the arrowfeather, Reverse K with the mintmark nearly centered between the stem, arrowfeather, and E, and Reverse L, actually an early die state of Reverse J with the mintmark boldly doubled.

This frosty green-gold specimen is about sixth or seventh finest for the D over D variety, and is similarly ranked when all 1846-D half eagles of any die variety are considered. Several of the scattered abrasions may remain from the original planchet. It is a bold strike with essentially full details, and possesses excellent eye appeal. Census: 1 in 62, 3 finer (8/08). (#8229)

3659 **1847 MS61 NGC.** Gleaming yellow-gold surfaces show glimmers of reflectivity at the margins. Minimally marked for the grade with excellent detail aside from slight softness at the eagle's neck. (#8231)

Elusive 1847 MS64 Half Eagle

3660 **1847 MS64 NGC.** With an abundant mintage of nearly one million pieces, the 1847 half eagle is the most common date of the 1840s. Lower level Mint State coins can be located with patient searching, but better-grade examples are elusive. This near-Gem displays partially prooflike fields, and except for softness on portions of the eagle, the design elements are well brought up. Peach-gold surfaces reveal a few minor, grade-defining handling marks. Census: 8 in 64, 0 finer (7/08).
From The Mississippi Collection. (#8231)

Flashy MS64 1847 Five Dollar

3661 **1847 MS64 PCGS.** A dazzling, heavily striated Mint State example with nearly complete sharpness in the centers. A cluster of field marks can be seen to the right of the portrait and a few abrasions are also noted on Liberty's cheek. There is an interesting die crack down much of the portrait, piercing the left serif of the 7 and into the border to the right of 6 o'clock. The 1847 is one of the more commonly encountered dates from the 1840s, even in Uncirculated condition, but near-Gems are elusive and their difficulty as a No Motto type coin far outweighs the scarcity of this particular issue. Population: 3 in 64, 2 finer (8/08). (#8231)

3662 **1847-C—Improperly Cleaned—NCS. AU Details.** Variety 9-E. Whispers of original luster cling to the margins of the lightly hairlined yellow-orange surfaces. Well struck with only modest wear on the central devices. (#8233)

Desirable 1847-D Five Dollar XF45

3663 **1847-D XF45 NGC.** Variety 16-M. This Dahlonega date is known with one obverse die and two different reverses, which are roughly equal in scarcity. The present piece has luminous peripheral luster and only minimal highpoint wear. The eagle's neck and Liberty's hair show moderate merging of detail, but the strike is generally good. (#8234)

Pleasing 1847-D Five, XF45

3664 **1847-D XF45 ANACS.** Variety 16-M. The upright of the mintmark is over the upright of the E, while the other known variety has the upright of the mintmark over the space between V and E. This piece has remarkably bright yellow surfaces for the grade, with only a few standard marks that are expected. (#8234)

Unheralded 1847-O Half Eagle, XF40

3665 **1847-O XF40 NGC.** The 1847-O half eagle is one of those unheralded early O-mint rarities that would likely be much more recognized and sought-after if it bore a C or D mintmark rather than an O. The meager emission of only 12,000 pieces in antebellum New Orleans ensured its rarity. This piece is about in the average grade for certified survivors, with antique-gold surfaces that show tinges of reddish-lilac in the protected areas of the lettering and devices. There is, of course, moderate wear, but there are few abrasions of any import. Census: 4 in 40, 25 finer (7/08). (#8235)

Coveted Choice XF 1848-C Five

3666 **1848-C XF45 NGC.** Variety 11-E. This Choice XF Charlotte half eagle exudes glimmers of apricot luster around design elements, particularly across the reverse peripheral legend. Small marks are scattered, but none individually distract. The centers show moderate inexactness of strike, characteristic of the issue. (#8237)

Remarkable 1848-C Half Eagle, AU55

3667 **1848-C AU55 NGC.** Variety 11-E. The only variety known. Dazzling luster radiates beneath the yellow-gold patina. There are no significant abrasions save for a shallow scratch in the field to the right of the eagle's head. Liberty's hair and several stars are soft, but the rest of the details are well-defined. A pleasing, conditionally scarce example. Census: 29 in 55, 24 finer (7/08). (#8237)

Delightful 1850-C, Weak C, Half Eagle, AU53

3668 **1850-C Weak C AU53 PCGS.** Variety 15-G. The date is high, but the 1 is well-centered between the bust and the dentils. This variety is sometimes seen with a weak mintmark, as is the case with the present piece, which Winter (1998) describes as Die State II. While the C mintmark is faint, it is still readily apparent under a loupe. The rest of the details are crisply defined, and there are no marks of any significance. Flashy luster glimmers throughout the yellow-gold surfaces. Population: 4 in 53 Weak C, 1 finer (8/08). (#98244)

Scarce 1850-D AU50 Half Eagle

3669 **1850-D AU50 PCGS.** Variety 23-O. The mintmark is away from the stem, and its upper serif is joined to the feather. The D is weak at the bottom. Diagnostic cracks run through UNITED STATES and FIVE D. The 1850-D is scarce in AU and very rare in Mint State. PCGS and NGC have seen only seven such pieces, all in MS60 and MS61. The bright yellow-gold surfaces of this AU50 coin display partially prooflike fields, and exhibit a better-than-average strike, though the first four or five stars reveal the typical softness. Only lightly abraded. (#8245)

Splendid 1850-D Half Eagle, AU55

3670 **1850-D AU55 PCGS.** Variety 23-O. The obverse has a tall date with the 1 close to the bust and the border. The reverse has the mintmark high over VE, with its left serif joined to the feather and its upper right curve separated from the branch. The other obverse, number 24, has the top of the 1 lightly joined to the bust, with the bottom left foot well above the border. The other reverse, letter P, has the mintmark touching the stem but distant from the feather, according to Doug Winter's description.

This pleasing Choice AU has lovely greenish yellow-gold luster with deeper patina in the fields on both sides. The strike is weak at the centers, as usual, but the mintmark is bold. Population: 16 in 55, 10 finer (7/08). (#8245)

Borderline Uncirculated 1850-D Five

3671 **1850-D AU58 NGC.** Variety 24-P. A yellow-gold near-Mint Dahlonega five with ample luster, particularly on the reverse. Crisply struck save for the low relief mintmark, which has a complete outline. Lightly abraded apart from a slender tick on the forehead and a raised reverse rim at 4:30. Census: 24 in 58, 4 finer (7/08). (#8245)

Elusive Mint State 1851 Half Eagle

3672 **1851 MS61 PCGS.** A seldom-seen Mint State example of this scarce issue. Flashy luster radiates beneath the yellow-gold patina. Liberty's hair is a trifle soft, as typically seen, but the rest of the details are boldly defined. Several minor luster grazes barely affect the great eye appeal. Population: 12 in 61, 21 finer (8/08). (#8246)

Pleasing 1851-C Half Eagle, XF45

3673 **1851-C XF45 NGC.** Variety 16-G with the mintmark below the crotch formed by the stem and point of the arrow feather. A second reverse die is known with the mintmark far to the left, over the left top of the V. A pleasing light yellow example, enhanced by pale orange toning on each side. Scattered surface marks are consistent with the grade. (#8247)

1851-D Weak D Half Eagle AU53, Variety 26-O

3674 **1851-D Weak D AU53 PCGS.** Variety 26-O. The first 1 in the date is imbedded in a denticle and shows noticeable repunching. An additional diagnostic for this variety is the die crack running from the lower serif of D in the denomination through the bottom part of FIVE and the upper portions of UNITED STATE. Only the upper right curve of the D mintmark is barely visible on this AU53 specimen. Peach-gold surfaces display hints of light green, and traces of luster in the recesses. This piece is slightly better defined than most 1851-Ds, that is rated as one of the more poorly struck Dahlonega half eagles from the 1850s (Douglas Winter, 2003). A few inoffensive circulation marks are noted on each side. (#98248)

3675 **1851-O XF40 NGC.** A bright example that has no unpleasant marks. Quite sharp on the stars and the central reverse, while Liberty's hair and the eagle's claws and fletchings show some merging of detail. Scarcer than implied by the production of 41,000 pieces. *Ex: Long Beach Signature (Heritage, 2/2006), lot 2900.* (#8249)

Delightful 1852 Half Eagle, MS62

3676 **1852 MS62 NGC.** Although common in circulated grades due to a mintage of 573,901 pieces, the 1852 is scarce in Mint State. A pleasing rose tint accents this butter-yellow representative. The strike is razor-sharp, and there is eye-catching satiny luster throughout. Census: 34 in 62, 37 finer (7/08). (#8250)

3677 **1852-C Improperly Cleaned, Reverse Scratched—NCS. XF Details.** Variety 18-H. The more common of two varieties for the year, distinguished by the 2 in the date being close to the truncation of the bust. The variable yellow-gold surfaces are moderately abraded and suspiciously radiant. A pair of scratches appear in the fields around the eagle's head. (#8251)

Lovely 1852-C Half Eagle, AU50

3678 **1852-C AU50 NGC.** Variety 18-H. The 1 in the date touches the bust and the 2 is nearly as high. Charming orange-gold patina drapes both sides of this well-defined piece. A couple of stars are soft, and there is the usual weakness on some of Liberty's hair. Myriad abrasions cover both sides, as typically seen, but plenty of luster still resides in the fields. A tiny dig below the M in AMERICA is noted. With a mintage of 72,574 pieces, the 1852-C is more available than other Charlotte Mint half eagles, and this piece would make a wonderful type coin. (#8251)

Choice AU 1852-C Five Dollar

3679 **1852-C AU55 NGC.** Variety 18-H. A partly lustrous Charlotte example that retains its original pale peach and straw-gold color. A good strike despite the usual blending of detail on the eagle's neck. The reverse field is abraded above the eagle's right (facing) shoulder, and the obverse rim is slightly raised at 6 o'clock. (#8251)

Pleasing Near-Mint 1852-D Five

3680 **1852-D AU58 NGC.** Variety 27-U. The reverse luster is close to complete, and the obverse also provides plentiful coruscation. This lightly abraded Dahlonega gold piece has only minor marks, and hints of apricot toning contribute further to the eye appeal. Liberty's curls and the lower half of the eagle display moderate incompleteness. (#8252)

3681 **1853 AU58 PCGS.** This is an interestingly, yet appealingly colored example with dominant crimson-gold shading. A few highlights of lilac tinting appear when the coin is tilted under the light. With as few marks as this piece has, it is only a trace of friction away from Select or better status. Population: 30 in 58, 66 finer (8/08).
From The Menlo Park Collection. (#8253)

3682 **1853-C—Improperly Cleaned—NCS. XF Details.** Variety 20-H. The 1 in the date is closer to the bust than the denticles, which is diagnostic for this variety. Bright lemon-yellow patina overlies the surfaces, with a tiny spot of detritus noted to the right of Liberty's neck. Myriad marks cover each side although none are particularly bothersome. An affordable type coin. (#8254)

3683 **1853-C XF40 ANACS.** Variety 20-H. The most available variety of this popular Charlotte gold type issue. Though the present lemon-gold piece is softly struck in the centers, the fields offer considerable radiance for the grade. (#8254)

Exceptional 1853-C Five Dollar, AU50

3684 **1853-C AU50 NGC.** Variety 20-H. The digit 1 is close to the bust, with a small curved notch in the lower bust line. This lightly worn example possesses bright yellow-gold surfaces that show traces of luster in the protected areas. The design elements are well defined, except for softness in three or four of the star centers. Unlike most examples that "... are very heavily abraded," (Douglas Winter, 1998), the current specimen reveals just a few small marks over each side. (#8254)

Spectacular 1853-C Five Dollar AU50 Variety 21-H Reverse Retained Cud

3685 **1853-C AU50 PCGS.** Variety 21-H. Bold mintmark. The 1 in the date is totally free of the bust, and the 3 is slightly closer to the denticles than to the bust. Housed in a green-label PCGS holder, this AU specimen displays well defined design elements, and lightly marked yellow-gold surfaces that retain luster in the recesses.

This fascinating piece has a spectacular retained cud on the reverse below VE D. A heavy die crack begins at the border below the right base of I in FIVE, angles up to the right to entirely cover the bottom of the E, touches the lower left corner of the D, then returns to the border below that letter. The crack forms a retained cud, with the border dentils dramatically shifted out of alignment, indicating that the break in the die was still attached to the die shaft, pivoting below the die surface.

Doug Winter states that the die break (or crack) forms below FIVE on late states of the 20-H die combination, with the mintmark somewhat weak. For variety 21-H, he mentions that examples exist with both weak and strong mintmarks. It appears that the weak or bold mintmark is not a function of die state. Obverses 20 and 21 are similar enough that they can be easily confused. But obverse 20 eventually forms two rim breaks after the reverse crack first appears. Still later cracked states of reverse H exist from a second obverse die without rim breaks.

It appears that the order of striking was:
1. Variety 20-H. Early state without obverse or reverse die cracks.
2. Variety 20-H. Intermediate state with light reverse die cracks.
3. Variety 20-H. Late state with obverse rim breaks and light reverse cracks.
4. Variety 21-H. Early state with light reverse cracks.
5. Variety 21-H. Intermediate state with heavier reverse cracks.
6. Variety 21-H. Late state with retained cud on reverse.

Unrecognized by Winter, the late state 21-H with the retained cud at VE D seems to be quite rare, with only two or three examples appearing in our auction archives. (#8254)

Important 1853-D Half Eagle, AU55

3686 **1853-D Large D AU55 NGC.** Variety 29-V. Four die varieties are known from a single obverse die and four different reverse dies. This reverse has the mintmark high above VE, but clearly separated from VE. This wonderful green-gold example is boldly defined with excellent surfaces for the grade. It is highly attractive and will easily delight the connoisseur (#8255)

Unblemished 1853-D Five Dollar MS62

3687 **1853-D Large D MS62 PCGS.** Variety 29-U. The mintmark is deeply entered and is lightly repunched at its base. The apricot-gold surfaces are only lightly abraded, and the strike is pleasing given its Dahlonega origin. Luster glimmers from design elements. An attractive addition to an advanced Southern gold collection. Population: 8 in 62, 6 finer (8/08). (#8255)

Scarce 1854-C Half Eagle, AU Sharpness

3688 **1854-C—Improperly Cleaned—NCS. AU Details.** Variety 22-I. The mintmark is centered over the left half of the V in FIVE, identifying this variety. Mottled lemon-yellow and orange-gold patina covers both sides of this lightly abraded piece. The 1854-C is an underrated issue and is one of the scarcest Charlotte half eagles. Just 39,200 pieces were minted. (#8257)

3689 **1854-O AU55 NGC.** Luster peers from the legends, coronet, and stars. Inspection beneath a loupe fails to locate relevant marks. A low mintage of 46,000 pieces ensures the rarity of better grade survivors. Census: 32 in 55, 53 finer (7/08). (#8259)

3690 **1855 MS61 NGC.** A pleasing No Motto issue with eye-catching semiprooflike fields. The 1855 half eagle is seldom seen in Mint State, and this bright yellow example would make an excellent representative. The stars show fully defined centrils, but there is a little weakness on Liberty's hair and the eagle's head. A number of shallow marks are typical for the grade. Census: 9 in 61, 13 finer (7/08). (#8261)

Condition Rarity 1855 Five Dollar, MS61

3691 **1855 MS61 NGC.** The 1851 half eagle is rare in Mint State (Jeff Garrett and Ron Guth, 2006). The 48 Uncirculated examples graded by NGC and PCGS likely consist of several resubmissions. The brass-gold surfaces of this MS61 specimen display partially prooflike fields that establish modest contrast with the motifs. Well struck, save for softness on the arrow feathers. The few minuscule marks visible are less than what might be expected for the grade. Census: 9 in 61, 13 finer (7/08). (#8261)

3692 **1855-C—Obverse Damage—NCS. XF Details.** Variety 23-J, the only recorded die pair for the 1855-C half eagles. Both sides have the usual circulation marks with a small punch mark in front of Liberty's mouth. Pleasing greenish-yellow gold. (#8262)

Choice XF 1855-C Half Eagle

3693 **1855-C XF45 PCGS.** Variety 23-J. This Choice XF Charlotte Mint five dollar piece has an impressive strike, with softness generally limited to the eagle's neck. The surfaces are untoned and offer plentiful glimpses of luster. Tiny marks are distributed, consistent for a gold coin with mid-19th century circulation. Population: 26 in 45, 49 finer (8/08). (#8262)

Broken Die 1855-C Five, MS61

3694 **1855-C MS61 NGC.** Variety 23-I. In spite of a substantial mintage of 39,789 pieces, the 1855-C is seldom located in AU or Uncirculated grades. While this piece is labeled as a mint error, it is actually from the terminal state of the dies. A rim-to-rim die crack formed and the curved crack finally fell away from the die, leaving the blobby die break seen on this piece. Such pieces are rare. Winter stated he had seen at least two such coins. Otherwise, the surfaces are bright orange-gold with strong striking definition, as usually seen on this issue. *From The Mississippi Collection.* (#8262)

Desirable 1855-D Half Eagle, VF30

3695 **1855-D Large D VF30 PCGS.** Variety 32-AA. Housed in a green-label holder, this pleasing half eagle is sharply detailed for the assigned grade, with pleasing pale yellow surfaces, and it is void of unexpected marks. Deep orange patina adheres to the protected peripheral fields. (#8263)

Challenging 1855-O Half Eagle, AU53

3696 **1855-O AU53 NGC.** Bright yellow surfaces show captivating semiprooflike reflectivity. Numerous abrasions cover each side, but all are inconsequential save for a shallow scratch at the bottom of the bust. This piece exhibits impressive sharpness, with the hair just a trifle soft. A mere 11,100 coins were struck, and most were heavily circulated. The 1855-O ranks among the scarcest New Orleans half eagles and is especially challenging in high grades. Census: 12 in 53, 21 finer (7/08). (#8264)

Elusive 1856 Liberty Five, MS62

3697 **1856 MS62 NGC.** The mintage of 197,990 coins hardly draws attention to the elusive nature of 1856 half eagles, especially in Mint State grades. NGC has only certified 38 examples of the date in all Mint State grades from MS60 to MS65. Compare those figures to a date such as 1854-D, with a mintage of only 56,413 coins, but a NGC Mint State total of 53 coins from MS60 to MS67, for just one example. There are a number of surprising rarities in the Liberty half eagle series. This wonderful specimen has brilliant orange-gold luster with excellent details, minimal surface marks, and remarkable eye appeal. Census: 8 in 62, 8 finer (8/08). (#8266)

3698 **1856-C—Reverse Scratched, Improperly Cleaned—NCS. AU Details.** Variety 24-J. The luminous sun-gold surfaces exhibit moderate hairlines. Well struck overall with only a trace of weakness at the modestly worn portrait. (#8267)

Lovely 1856-C Half Eagle, AU58

3699 **1856-C AU58 NGC.** Variety 24-J, the only known die pair for the date. This boldly define piece has deep orange-gold color with satiny luster. A few surface marks on each side include a tiny reverse rim nick at 12 o'clock, and they are all consistent with the grade. The reverse is rotated about 45 degrees clockwise. (#8267)

3700 **1856-O XF45 NGC.** Somewhat weakly defined but attractive with bright yellow and orange-gold surfaces. Considerable luster remains for the grade. (#8269)

Outstanding 1856-O Half Eagle, MS61

3701 **1856-O MS61 NGC.** The New Orleans Mint produced only 10,000 Half Eagles in 1856, which ties this issue with the 1892-O for lowest mintage honors among New Orleans half eagles. Only a select few Uncirculated 1856-O fives are extant, and the rarity of this issue in Mint State is such that even Eliasberg and Bass had to settle for circulated representatives. This example is powerfully struck, indeed almost full, and subtle reflectivity can be seen in the fields, which is only slightly diminished by light grazes. Pleasing yellow-gold patina with a hint of rose-red drapes the surfaces and adds to the aura of originality. This spectacular piece is nearly the finest known example of this elusive date. Census: 2 in 61, 1 finer (8/08). (#8269)

Attractive and Conditionally Rare 1856-S Half Eagle, Mint State

3702 **1856-S MS60 NGC.** Nearly all 1856-S half eagles saw circulation and Mint State examples are seldom seen. In fact, NGC and PCGS combined have certified only a dozen Uncirculated pieces, and a PCGS MS64 example is the finest known by two points. Delightful orange-gold patina embraces the astonishingly lustrous surfaces. Peppered abrasions limit the grade, but none are of any significance. This fully struck specimen has outstanding eye appeal and would make a wonderful addition to a collection. Census: 3 in 60, 6 finer (8/08). (#8270)

Scarce MS62 1857 Five Dollar

3703 **1857 MS62 PCGS.** Even though 98,188 pieces were struck of the 1857, it was not widely saved at the time of issue. Similarly, it is often an overlooked date by all but the most serious 19th century gold specialists. In spite of the MS62 grade, the main attraction of this coin is its outstanding mint luster. The luster is thick and softly frosted, the same as one would expect on a Gem coin. A few small abrasions are peppered over each side, which account for the grade. Sharply and evenly defined on each side. Population: 13 in 62, 15 finer (7/08). (#8271)

Impressive 1857 Half Eagle, MS63

3704 **1857 MS63 PCGS.** While PCGS does not use a Prooflike designation, the fields of this highly lustrous piece are unquestionably so. The impressive reflectivity complements the razor-sharp design elements. Numerous die polish lines are visible throughout, but there are no bothersome abrasions on either side. The 1857 is seldom seen in such a remarkable level of preservation. Population: 12 in 63, 3 finer (8/08). (#8271)

Elusive AU 1857-C Five Dollar

3705 **1857-C AU50 ANACS.** Variety 25-J. This yellow gold Charlotte Mint five has an above average strike and luminous, moderately abraded surfaces. The extent of luster about the obverse stars is substantial. Struck from perfect dies. A mintage of only 31,360 pieces ensures the scarcity of the issue. (#8272)

Splendid 1857-C Half Eagle, Choice AU

3706   1857-C AU55 NGC. Variety 27-J. The only variety known. Lots of luster shines beneath the delightful yellow-gold patina. The details are crisply defined and there are no mentionable marks on either side. Several minuscule planchet defects are noted, as well as a few tiny blemishes on the obverse. A lovely and relatively affordable type coin. Just 31,360 pieces were minted. (#8272)

Borderline Uncirculated 1857-C Half Eagle

3707   1857-C AU58 NGC. Variety 25-J. The borders glimmer with bright luster, as do the major devices. The strike is crisp despite minor merging of plumage on the eagle's neck. The honey-gold surfaces are refreshingly unabraded, although the right shield border has a concealed mark. (#8272)

3708   1857-O VF35 PCGS. Somewhat weakly struck on the eagle's talons and arrow fletchings, but boldly detailed otherwise. Khaki-green and reddish patina combine over the two sides. Just 13,000 examples of this final New Orleans Mint No Motto half eagle were struck, and survivors are scarce at any grade level. (#8274)

3709   1857-O—Improperly Cleaned—NCS. AU50 Details. The final No Motto New Orleans half eagle, the 1857-O boasts a diminutive mintage of just 13,000 pieces. Scarce in all grades, most '57-Os are seen heavily circulated, and it is virtually impossible to find a Mint State example. The present piece exhibits a sharp strike save for slight weakness at the centers. Trivial abrasions throughout are typical for the grade, and there are no marks worthy of individual mention. The yellow-gold surfaces have charming eye appeal despite a gentle cleaning. (#8274)

Extremely Rare 1858-C Variety 26-L Half Eagle, XF45

3710   1858-C XF45 PCGS. Variety 26-L was described in Doug Winter's *Gold Coins of the Charlotte Mint 1838-1861,* as quite scarce, but more recently was believed nonexistent. Now we present an example of variety 26-L.

Reverse K has the mintmark mostly over the V in FIVE, with its right edge over the left edge of the upright of E. The point of the arrow feather is over the inner curve of the C.

Reverse L has the mintmark mostly over the E in FIVE, with the right edge of the mintmark nearly over the center of that letter. The point of the arrow feather is entirely left of the mintmark, and this is the easiest diagnostic. This die also has a bold crack from the border below the left edge of the F in FIVE, across two dentils and through the field to the upper left serif of the U in UNITED. The crack seems to end at that letter, but might possibly continue across UNITED in later die states. It appears that reverse L was only used for this single variety, and the possibility of a terminal die state with extended die cracks or even a rim break certainly exists.

A review of the Heritage Permanent Auction Archives shows that we have previously handled three examples of 26-L, one misattributed and two others unattributed: 1) NGC AU55. Heritage (9/2006), lot 3533. 2) NGC AU50. Heritage (11/2002), lot 7600. 3) PCGS AU50. Heritage (1/2000), lot 7760.

This piece has excellent detail with pleasing medium yellow surfaces and splashes of deep orange patina in the protected field areas close to the devices. Both sides have moderately abraded surfaces, consistent with the grade. The die variety specialist of Southern mint gold coinage should carefully consider this important opportunity. (#8277)

3711   1858-C XF45 ANACS. Variety 26-K. The only confirmed variety. Evenly worn with crisp detail remaining. Original orange-gold patina drapes the lightly abraded surfaces. A pronounced lamination is noted by star 9. (#8277)

3712   1858-S—Improperly Cleaned—NCS. XF Details. The oddly bright yellow-orange fields show numerous short, fine lines. Well struck overall with scattered abrasions and light wear across the high points. (#8279)

Condition Rarity 1858-S Half Eagle
Near-Mint State

3713 **1858-S AU58 NGC.** Jeff Garrett and Ron Guth, in their *Encyclopedia of U.S. Gold Coins*, state that the "1858-S half eagle is a major condition rarity. The date is currently unknown in Mint State." Since the 2006 release of their book, one coin has been certified above the AU58 level—a solitary MS61 piece graded by PCGS. The lone Uncirculated 1858-S was offered in our August 2008 ANA Signature Sale where it realized $28,877. How the only known Mint State example of a classic coin could sell for so little can only be explained by the lack of pressure from those collecting Liberty half eagles by date and mintmark. It would be an understatement to say that the 1858-S five dollar is an underrated issue. The day will come when collectors and investors alike will realize the importance of this date—of which only 88 examples have been graded by NGC and PCGS combined—and the prices of today will represent the missed opportunities of tomorrow. A few scattered ticks are observed in the right obverse field, as well as one abrasion below the mintmark. The strike of this peach-gold representative is crisp and the overall eye appeal is above average for the assigned grade. Census: 13 in 58, 0 finer (8/08). (#8279)

Popular 1861 Five Dollar, MS61

3714 **1861 MS61 NGC.** The 1861 five dollar is popular due to its Civil War date. Semibright surfaces yield yellow-gold and light tan patina, and exhibit well struck design features, except for minor softness on the arrow feathers. Distributed light contact marks occasionally disrupt the luster flow.
From The Mississippi Collection. (#8288)

3715 **1865-S VF20 NGC.** The 1865-S is rare in any condition (Jeff Garrett and Ron Guth, 2006). This VF specimen displays peach-gold surfaces laced with traces of light green. Relatively clean, with good remaining detail. (#8299)

Singular Select 1866 Motto Five

3716 **1866 MS63 NGC.** All 1866 half eagles struck at Philadelphia were of the With Motto variety. While the denomination had healthy, if modest mintages at San Francisco in the 1860s, production at the mother Mint was consistently low, in the four-figures, and with business strike production of just 6,700 pieces, the 1866 is no exception. Garrett and Guth (2006) describe it as " ... very rare in all grades, and Very Fine or Extremely Fine is the usual grade seen."

As one might infer, this issue is a prize regardless of condition, and Mint State examples are especially elusive and desirable. Between them, NGC and PCGS have had just eight certification events for Mint State examples of the 1866 Motto half eagle (8/08), six of which are at NGC: one in MS60, four in MS61, and the present piece in MS63, not only the finest known to NGC, but finer than either of the grades awarded by PCGS (an MS61 and an MS62). It is a recently certified piece, one that does not appear in the 2006 edition of Garrett and Guth, which lists MS61 as the finest grade known.

Like many of the other top examples of this issue, the Select representative offered here shows a degree of reflectivity in the fields, as well as characteristic sharpness on the portrait and eagle. The radiant yellow-gold surfaces cede to champagne-orange close to the margins. Though wispy abrasions and a handful of shallow reed marks affect the fields, the central devices are remarkably clean, and the overall visual appeal is highly impressive. For the Liberty half eagle collector who demands the finest, this is the only option. (#8311)

Scarce 1866-S Motto Five Dollar, VF25

3717 **1866-S Motto VF25 PCGS.** The 1866-S with Motto five dollar circulated extensively on the West Coast, thus most surviving examples come well worn. The bright honey-gold surfaces of this VF25 example display whispers of reddish-tan, along with nicely defined design features. LIBERTY is strong, and most of the letters in the reverse motto are clear. The expected number of light marks are visible on both sides. Quite scarce at this level. (#8312)

Delightful 1867 Half Eagle, AU53

3718 **1867 AU53 NGC.** While the San Francisco Mint was striking a decent number of half eagles in the 1860s, production at the Philadelphia Mint was quite low. Only 6,870 fives were struck in Philadelphia in 1867. Although this issue is rare in all grades, AU and finer examples are particularly difficult to locate. Scattered abrasions minimally affect the pleasing luster that graces the pale yellow surfaces of this sharply struck specimen. An excellent example in an uncommonly nice condition. Census: 12 in 53, 20 finer (8/08). (#8313)

Sharp XF 1867-S Five Dollar

3719 **1867-S XF40 PCGS.** The 1867-S has a tiny mintage of 29,000 pieces, since the San Francisco Mint preferred to strike double eagles prior to 1878, when the Federal paper dollar finally achieved parity with its gold counterpart. This orange-tinted example is sharply defined and has substantial luster for its designated grade. Encased in an old green label holder. Population: 6 in 40, 22 finer (8/08). (#8314)

Choice AU 1867-S Half Eagle Rarity

3720 **1867-S AU55 NGC.** Despite a mintage of 29,000 coins, this is an extremely rare and underrated date in the Liberty half eagle series. Neither NGC or PCGS have graded a single Mint State example and both services have only graded a total of 38 pieces better than XF45. This lovely light yellow-gold example has a few scattered marks and traces of highpoint wear that are consistent with the grade. Census: 7 in 55, 3 finer (8/08). (#8314)

3721 **1868-S XF40 PCGS.** The 1868-S is surprisingly scarce even in Extremely Fine condition, as a look at the population data indicates. Pleasing olive-orange patina drapes both sides of this evenly worn and handsome specimen. Population: 11 in 40, 37 finer (8/08). (#8316)

Pleasing 1872-CC Half Eagle, VF25

3722 **1872-CC VF25 PCGS.** With a mintage of just 16,980 pieces, the 1872-CC is scarce in all grades, and is almost always seen heavily circulated. Pleasing olive-orange patina drapes the surfaces of this evenly worn example. There are no marks worthy of specific mention, and the details are well-defined. Population: 5 in 25, 39 finer (7/08). (#8326)

3723 **1873 Open 3 MS62 PCGS.** Delightful yellow-gold patina overlies the minimally marked surfaces. The fields have pleasing semiprooflike reflectivity, which complements the crisply struck details. Population: 11 in 62, 18 finer (7/08). (#8328)

Conditionally Rare 1874-S Half Eagle, Choice AU

3724 1874-S AU55 PCGS. With a mintage of just 16,000 pieces, the 1874-S is scarce in any grade, and most of the examples that have appeared at auction are graded Very Fine or Extremely Fine. Garrett and Guth (2006) state: "The 1874-S is a true condition rarity. There are currently no known examples in Mint State." As the population data shows, this issue is exceedingly rare even in About Uncirculated. Charming orange-gold patina drapes the surfaces of this minimally marked example. The stars on the right are particularly soft, and the mintmark is lightly struck, as usual, but the rest of the details are well-defined. Plenty of luster in the fields enhances the eye appeal. Population: 4 in 55, 2 finer (7/08). (#8335)

AU Sharpness 1875-CC Half Eagle

3725 1875-CC—Improperly Cleaned—NCS. AU Details. A rare Carson City issue with a mintage of only 11,828 pieces. NGC and PCGS have each certified only a single example as Mint State. Richly detailed and partly lustrous but subdued and somewhat glossy from a past wipe. The fields have a few small marks unworthy of individual description. (#8337)

Low Mintage 1876 Half Eagle, AU50 Details

3726 1876—Scratched—ANACS. AU50 Details. During the Civil War, federal paper money replaced gold coins in circulation, except in the remote West. Gold coins rarely appeared again in commerce until 1878, when paper money finally traded at par with gold coinage. Low mintages were the rule for Philadelphia issues, and a scant 1,432 half eagles were struck in 1876. The present example has a number of small scratches in the reverse fields. Otherwise, this is a well defined reddish-golden example with an overall pleasing appearance. (#8339)

Important 1876-CC Half Eagle, XF40

3727 1876-CC XF40 ICG. A key coin, the mintage of 6,887 was the lowest of any Carson City half eagle issue. Considerable pale blue patina is blended with the warm honey-gold surfaces of this pleasing half eagle. The surfaces are remarkably well preserved with only a few grade-consistent abrasions. (#8340)

Pleasing 1877-CC Half Eagle, AU55

3728 1877-CC AU55 NGC. From a mintage of only 8,680 pieces, the 1877-CC is an uncommon coin in all grades, and most examples seen are in the VF-XF range. In overall rarity, Doug Winter rates the 1877-CC tied for eighth in the 19-coin series. In high-grade rarity, it ranks seventh. Mint State examples are prohibitively rare, and a nice AU example is the best a realistic collector can hope for.

The coin offered here shows only slight wear on the highest points of the design. The strike is better than average, with Liberty's hair and the eagle's neck showing only typical softness for the issue. A couple of planchet flaws on the obverse rim between 7 and 9 o'clock appear to be as made. The surfaces are remarkably free of distractions, and much original mint luster remains. Overall, an extremely attractive example of this rare date. Census: 13 in 55, 6 finer (8/08). (#8343)

Desirable 1879-CC Liberty Five, XF45

3729 **1879-CC XF45 NGC.** A pleasing Choice XF example of this comparatively available 1870s Carson City issue, well struck with lightly abraded butter-yellow surfaces that display a touch of emerald color. Lightly circulated with faint remnants of original luster at the reverse margins. (#8349)

3730 **1879-S MS62 PCGS.** Crisply struck and highly lustrous, with a pleasing mixture of apricot-gold and lime coloration. Scattered small abrasions define the grade. A surprisingly difficult issue to find in Mint State. Population: 42 in 62, 29 finer (8/08). (#8350)

3731 **1879-S MS62 PCGS.** Lustrous and precisely struck with rich pumpkin-gold toning and unexpectedly few marks. A conditionally scarce issue whose census is topped by a solitary MS65 example. Population: 42 in 62, 29 finer (8/08). (#8350)

3732 **1880-CC XF45 NGC.** This is a well struck piece that displays a reasonable degree of wear, for the grade. Small abrasions and wispy pinscratches appear on both sides, and a couple of moderate marks are noted just above the eagle's head. This coin would be a good choice for type purposes, from a more available Carson City issue. (#8352)

Splendid 1880-CC Half Eagle, Choice AU

3733 **1880-CC AU55 NGC. CAC.** An appealing, briefly circulated representative, this piece would make a splendid type coin. Although plentiful in most grades, the number of survivors drops significantly in AU and this issue is seldom-seen in Mint State. Flashy luster throughout the yellow-gold surfaces complements the boldly defined details. (#8352)

3734 **1881-S MS64 NGC. CAC.** Splashes of delicate greenish-gray find their way onto apricot-gold, lustrous surfaces. Evenly struck, with just a few minor marks. (#8357)

3735 **1881-S MS64 PCGS.** Lustrous surfaces show traces of light blue and pale lavender, and a relatively sharp strike nicely defines the design elements. A couple of copper alloy spots are visible on the reverse. (#8357)

3736 **1881-S MS64 PCGS.** This is one of the more common dates of the Liberty Head with Motto half eagle series, though there is a significant drop in the certified population between the MS63 and MS64 levels. Pleasing luster radiates from the greenish-gold surfaces of this near-Gem. A few minute marks define the grade. Population: 72 in 64, 2 finer (8/08). (#8357)

Amazing Gem 1881-S Half Eagle Tied for Finest PCGS Graded

3737 **1881-S MS65 PCGS.** An extraordinary Gem, this 1881-S half eagle is tied with just one other coin for the best PCGS has certified. Of course, there is always the possibility that the two submissions PCGS has grade represent just this single coin. Both sides are boldly detailed with exceptional surfaces. Satiny yellow luster is enhanced through splashes of pale orange toning. Population: 2 in 65, 0 finer (7/08). (#8357)

3738 **1882-CC AU53 NGC.** Although its mintage of 82,817 pieces is relatively high compared to other CC-mint half eagles, the 1882-CC is scarce when compared to almost any Philadelphia issue. Pleasing yellow-gold patina covers both sides of this minimally marked specimen. A few tiny areas of detritus are noted on the reverse. Sharply struck with flashy luster throughout. (#8359)

3739 **1882-CC AU53 NGC.** This apricot-gold Carson City half eagle is surprisingly unabraded save for a thin mark above the R in TRUST. The eagle's neck feathers are incompletely brought up, but the strike is otherwise sharp. (#8359)

Attractive 1882-CC Five Dollar, AU55

3740 **1882-CC AU55 NGC.** Variety 1-A, the only one known. Yellow-gold surfaces are imbued with tints of light tan, and good definition is apparent on the design features. A few minute contacts are noted over each side, but these are fewer and of less severity that typically seen (Douglas Winter, 2001). A diagnostic die scratch is located between IB of LIBERTY. (#8359)

Scarce 1883-CC Half Eagle, AU58

3741 **1883-CC AU58 NGC.** Winter (2001) estimates that 23 to 28 examples of the 1883-CC have survived in About Uncirculated, with only a few pieces in Mint State. This specimen displays charming brassy-gold surfaces with lots of luster throughout. The design elements are sharply defined save for minor softness on the eagle's neck. A few tiny, unobtrusive marks scattered about both sides do not detract from the coin's overall eye appeal. One of only 12,958 pieces minted. Census: 32 in 58, 5 finer (7/08). (#8362)

Attractive 1884-CC Half Eagle, AU58

3742 1884-CC AU58 NGC. At first glance, this piece appears to be uncirculated, and even under close inspection the surfaces fail to reveal any noteworthy highpoint wear. Rich orange-gold toning increases the coin's eye appeal, along with shimmering mint luster. Garrett and Guth (2006) note that this issue is reasonably available in AU condition, but is very rare in Mint State. Census: 43 in 58, 3 finer (7/08). (#8365)

3743 1884-S MS63 PCGS. The 1884-S is moderately scarce in all grades. Pleasing luster endows this Select example, and a well executed strike imparts strong definition to the design elements. A few minuscule marks define the grade. Population: 42 in 63, 8 finer (8/08). (#8366)

3744 1885-S MS64 NGC. Lime-green peripheries encompass the orange-tinged centers. This lustrous and intricately impressed Choice gold type coin is pleasantly free from blemishes. (#8368)

3745 1886-S MS64 PCGS. Beautifully detailed with strong luster that exhibits elements of satin. Excellent overall preservation and eye appeal to match. PCGS has graded nine finer pieces (8/08). (#8370)

3746 1886-S MS64 PCGS. MS64 is the highest grade most collectors will see. PCGS has seen a mere nine pieces finer! Peach-gold and mint-green compete for territory on this near-Gem, and an attentive strike leaves strong definition on the design features. A few minor marks preclude Gem status. (#8370)

3747 1888 MS62 PCGS. Following a mintage of 388,360 half eagles at the Philadelphia Mint in 1886, no business strikes were produced in 1887, and only 18,296 pieces were struck in 1888. This underrated issue is scarce in any grade and PCGS reports just 27 examples finer than the present piece (8/08). A hint of rose in the fields accents this appealing butter-yellow representative. The strike is sharp and there are no marks of any significance. (#8372)

3748 1889 AU58 NGC. Decisively struck with only a trace of friction on the high points. The luster of the beautifully preserved honey-gold fields is virtually intact. Census: 41 in 58, 56 finer (7/08). (#8374)

Splendid 1890-CC Half Eagle, MS62

3749 1890-CC MS62 PCGS. Scintillating satiny luster sparkles beneath the pleasing yellow-gold patina. Scattered abrasions limit the grade, but none are of any consequence. The strike is sharp save for the typically seen weakness on the centers. A scarce issue in Mint State, and quite desirable as a type coin. (#8376)

Appealing 1890-CC Liberty Half Eagle, MS62

3750 1890-CC MS62 PCGS. Lustrous and well struck, with variegated khaki and copper-orange coloration. The surfaces are modestly marked, as expected for the grade. Garrett and Guth (2006) comment, regarding the 1890-CC half eagle, that it is "scarce, but mostly desirable by collectors desiring a coin struck at the popular Carson City Mint." (#8376)

Select Mint State 1890-CC Five Dollar

3751 1890-CC MS63 PCGS. The year 1890 saw the first coinage of any kind in Carson City in five years, since 1885. Half eagles saw a decent emission, if still smallish, of 53,800 coins, but AU and Choice AU examples are plentiful today. The present example boasts splendid antique-gold coloration and luster, with a decent strike and the few light contact marks that constitute the grade. This Select Mint State piece is one of 25 graded at PCGS, with 35 finer (8/08). (#8376)

Lovely 1890-CC Half Eagle, MS62 Prooflike

3752 **1890-CC MS62 Prooflike NGC.** The first half eagle coined in Carson City since 1884, this issue followed the 1886 to 1888 temporary closing of the Mint. Finally, the Mint ceased operations after its production of 1893 coinage. This desirable half eagle survives from a mintage of 53,800 coins, and retains fully prooflike fields. The central design details are typically weak, but overall, this is an attractive example. Census: 2 in 62 prooflike, 0 finer (8/08). (#78376)

3753 **1891-CC AU58 PCGS.** A whisper of friction on the eyebrow, nose, and coronet tip preclude a Mint State assessment, but the smooth surfaces will please its next owner. The flag of the second 1 in the date is lightly repunched. (#8378)

3754 **1891-CC AU58 PCGS.** This lustrous orange-gold CC-mint half eagle has the look of Mint State, although the eyebrow may have light friction. Marks are surprisingly few in number. Encapsulated in an old green label holder. (#8378)

3755 **1891-CC MS62 PCGS.** A lustrous, yellow-gold example of one of the final Carson City Mint half eagles. Myriad marks limit the grade, but none are worthy of individual mention. Sharply struck with lovely eye appeal. (#8378)

3756 **1891-CC MS62 PCGS.** A sharply struck and shimmering Carson City type coin that boasts a clean appearance and original apricot and olive-green toning. (#8378)

Splendid 1891-CC Half Eagle, MS63

3757 **1891-CC MS63 PCGS.** Bright yellow-gold surfaces exude satiny luster. This boldly struck piece has several small abrasions, but none are of any significance. With a mintage of 208,000 pieces, the 1891-CC is the most common Carson City half eagle and because of its relative availability in Mint State it is immensely popular among type collectors. Nonetheless, PCGS has certified just 44 pieces finer (7/08). (#8378)

Sharp 1891-CC Half Eagle, MS63

3758 **1891-CC MS63 PCGS.** A frequently seen offering from late in the career of the fabled Carson City Mint, the 1891-CC half eagle averages a bit better than Choice AU among the certified survivors. This Select Mint State example show deep orange-gold coloration with some light chatter on the fields and devices and a generally well-delivered strike that together account for the grade. (#8378)

3759 **1892-O AU58 NGC.** A gorgeous example with brilliant yellow and green-gold surfaces and barely detectable wear on the highpoints of the design. The surfaces of this appealing piece have light abrasions, but they are trumped by the exceptional eye appeal. (#8381)

Appealing 1893-CC Half Eagle, MS61

3760 **1893-CC MS61 NGC.** This date is very popular as the final Carson City five dollar gold issue, produced in the last year of the fabled Nevada mint facility. Somewhat scarce, if not rare, in Mint State. This example displays boldly struck design elements and a pleasing, even satiny sheen across each side. Scattered small marks define the grade. (#8384)

3761 **1893-CC MS61 ICG.** A boldly detailed example of the final Carson City coinage, with frosty surfaces and splendid orange luster. (#8384)

Interesting 1893-O Half Eagle, MS62

3762 **1893-O MS62 PCGS.** The 1893-O half eagle is the most common O-mint half eagle in Mint State, and has the second highest mintage, at 110,000 coins, of any New Orleans half eagle, behind the 1844-O's 364,000 pieces. This is an interesting specimen, with several zigzagging peripheral die cracks on the obverse and somewhat prooflike luster beneath a few scuffs that determine the grade. Numerous other die cracks, if a bit less dramatic, join some of the reverse letters. It appears as though the dies, even in their advanced states, had been freshly polished before this coin was struck. Population: 43 in 62, 9 finer (7/08). (#8385)

3763 **1893-S MS62 NGC.** A brilliant yellow-gold example with sharp design details and excellent surfaces for the grade. (#8386)

3764 **1894-S AU58 NGC.** A well-defined and impressively lustrous yellow-gold piece that appears Mint State at first glance. Only close inspection reveals the modest friction that precludes such a grade. Census: 43 in 58, 22 finer (7/08). (#8389)

Desirable 1894-S Five, MS60

3765 **1894-S MS60 NGC.** The mintmark is repunched. Well struck with full even luster and a pleasing, flashy sheen. Numerous small abrasions and a shallow scrape, in the left obverse field, define the grade. Only 55,900 pieces were struck, few if any of which were set aside at the time of issue. Census: 3 in 60, 18 finer (7/08). (#8389)

3766 **1895-S AU58 NGC.** A well-defined piece with only a touch of friction on the uppermost design elements. The yellow-gold margins remain amply lustrous, and hints of pink appear close to the portrait. (#8391)

3767 **1895-S MS61 NGC.** An elusive late-date S-mint five, highly challenging in grades finer than XF. The surfaces of this unworn piece are strongly lustrous, dusky copper-gold. Census: 12 in 61, 8 finer (7/08). (#8391)

3768 **1897 MS64 PCGS.** The 1897 is seldom seen in grades higher than Choice, and PCGS reports only 12 examples finer than the present piece (7/08). This example boasts fantastic satiny luster that shimmers beneath the yellow-gold patina. A razor-sharp example with only a few minor grazes and spots. Housed in a green label PCGS holder. (#8394)

Outstanding 1897 Half Eagle, MS66

3769 **1897 MS66 NGC.** Despite a mintage of over 800,000 pieces, the 1897 is not as available in Gem as many of the later date issues. Garrett and Guth (2006) report that the finest they have seen is an NGC MS66 specimen that sold at auction nearly a decade ago. This delightful piece is tied for the finest certified and NGC reports just nine coins in MS66, with none finer. PCGS has certified none above MS65, at which level they have graded a dozen examples (8/08). Pleasing yellow-orange patina endows the surfaces, which exhibit only minuscule handling marks. Eye-catching satiny luster enhances the wonderful eye appeal. (#8394)

Alluring 1899 Half Eagle, MS66

3770 **1899 MS66 NGC.** This attractive yellow-gold piece has splendid satiny luster that glimmers throughout the fields and highlights the boldly impressed design elements. Only insignificant luster grazes are visible on either side, even with the aid of a loupe. A wonderful representative that would suit even the pickiest collector. (#8398)

Impressive 1899 Half Eagle, Premium Gem

3771   1899 MS66 NGC. A wonderful representative for a type collector, this piece exhibits flashes of luster beneath the lightly frosted, yellow-gold surfaces. Hints of rose in the fields complement the appealing patina. The strike is razor-sharp, and only a couple of tiny handling marks and microscopic blemishes are visible under a glass. NGC reports just seven pieces finer (8/08). (#8398)

3772   1900-S MS64 NGC. Decisively struck with highly lustrous yellow-orange surfaces that show occasional honey accents. Excellent eye appeal for the grade. NGC has certified just four numerically finer examples (8/08). (#8401)

3773   1901 MS64 PCGS. The obverse has frosty yellow-gold luster with hints of pink, while the reverse has rich pink-gold luster with hints of yellow. (#8402)

Exceptional 1901-S Five Dollar, MS66

3774   1901-S MS66 NGC. The 1901-S five dollar has a mintage of 3.648 million pieces, and shows a relatively high survival rate. Walter Breen (1988) writes that the issue is: "Plentiful in choice Unc. from old hoards." The NGC/PCGS population data corroborate this. Premium Gem and finer coins, however, are another matter, as the population figures below indicate. This MS66 example displays dazzling luster and attractive peach-gold surfaces imbued with tints of light green. An attentive strike imparts complete definition to the design elements, and a few trivial marks may well preclude an even higher grade. Census: 73 in 66, 14 finer (7/08). (#8404)

3775   1902-S MS64 NGC. A bright, satiny Choice uncirculated example of this late-date Liberty eagle issue. Lime and apricot color adorns the surfaces. Two or three tiny contact marks are found on each side, under magnification. (#8406)

3776   1903-S MS64 PCGS. Bright, flashy yellow-gold surfaces are the prime feature of this 20th century S-mint half eagle. Crisply struck with few flaws for the grade. (#8408)

3777   1905-S MS62 NGC. Despite its high mintage, many 1905-S half eagles were destroyed and today it is scarce in all grades. The hair and stars are rather soft, as typically seen, but the reverse is sharply defined. The surfaces are minimally abraded for the grade, and flashy luster gives this piece wonderful eye appeal. Census: 47 in 62, 28 finer (7/08). (#8412)

3778   1906-D MS64 PCGS. CAC. Having previously functioned as an assay office, in April 1906 the Denver Mint began coining operations, striking a total of 320,000 half eagles. Although plentiful in most grades, the number of survivors drops significantly above the MS64 level. The present piece features bright yellow-gold surfaces with accents of rose in the fields. This minimally marked specimen boasts a razor-sharp strike and delightful satiny luster. PCGS has certified just 38 pieces finer (7/08). (#8414)

Desirable 1907-D Liberty Head Half Eagle, MS66

3779   1907-D MS66 PCGS. CAC. This is a frosty, immaculately struck Premium Gem, originating from a sizeable mintage of 888,000 pieces. The 1907-D is noteworthy, along with the '06-D, as one of just two Liberty Head half eagles produced at the Denver Mint; and is a desirable choice for type collectors. This piece displays lovely honey-gold coloration and outstanding surface preservation. Population: 14 in 66, 1 finer (8/08).
From The Bell Collection. (#8417)

Attractive 1908 Liberty Head Half Eagle, Gem Mint State

3780   1908 MS65 PCGS. An appealing example of the final Liberty Head half eagle. Bright yellow patina show accents of orange in the fields, along with a few deep red toning spots. The strike is nearly full, and the captivating luster is minimally affected by a number of minuscule abrasions. Just 32 pieces have been certified finer by PCGS (7/08). (#8418)

Extremely Rare 1862 Half Eagle, PR64 Ultra Cameo

3781 **1862 PR64 Ultra Cameo NGC.** The economic conditions of the Civil War had a profound effect on the coinage of the time. The public hoarded any coins with intrinsic value, and only tokens and paper money were willingly used in commerce. Specie payments were suspended, and the small amount of hard money that was available was used to pay off foreign creditors, who would accept nothing else. Under the circumstances, the government found it impractical to mint large quantities of coins that would not circulate. Mint records indicate that only 4,430 business strike and 35 proof half eagles were produced in 1862. Survivorship of both issues is extremely low, with perhaps a dozen proof specimens and only a handful of Uncirculated business strikes extant. The small number of business strikes puts even more pressure on the minuscule supply of proof coins to satisfy collector demand.

The beauty and rarity of the issue cause the 1862 proof half eagle to stand out, even when surrounded by other remarkable coins. Louis Eliasberg made numismatic history by forming the only complete collection of U.S. coins. He included a Gem proof example of the 1862 half eagle in his fabulous collection. Ed Trompeter assembled perhaps the most impressive collection of proof U.S. gold coins of any era. His 1862 half eagle was a magnificent PR64 Cameo. The Trompeter coin later graced the wonderful collection of Dr. Robert Loewinger, which was sold by Heritage on January 4, 2007.

The present coin may eclipse the other remarkable coins discussed above. The devices are even more richly frosted than the Trompeter coin, as evidenced by the Ultra Cameo designation. The stark gold-on-black contrast between the reflective fields and the frosted devices is spectacular. The surfaces of the devices are slightly granular in places and there are a few hairlines in the reverse field, but nothing individually distracting. The strike is sharp, and overall eye appeal is stunning. A magnificent coin and a rare opportunity for the advanced collector. Census: 4 in 64 Ultra Cameo, 2 finer (8/08). (#98452)

3782 **1864 PR64 Deep Cameo PCGS.** The 1864 proof five has a mintage of 50 pieces. While this is a tiny output, the survivorship is higher than other dates from the era and as such it is considered the most "common" date as a proof in the No Motto series. In spite of the multiple resubmissions that have artificially inflated the population data, with more than 30 pieces certified today, probably only 12-15 individual proofs are actually still extant. This number includes three pieces that are held in institutional collections—two in the Smithsonian and one in the ANS. The heavily contrasted coin offered here is in the middle of the pack for surface quality.

Proofs of this date all show a common diagnostic: a die scratch (or is it a short die break?) below Liberty's ear. According to Breen (1988) this diagnostic was observed on the Auction '80 and the Clapp/Eliasberg coins.

This is a lovely example and one that also is numismatically interesting. A streak of slight granularity is seen in the lower obverse field that extends to the rim and then runs between the denticles and stars 10-13. Otherwise, the surfaces display the deeply reflective fields one would expect from a proof gold coin. Also, given the limited mintage of this date, the devices are heavily frosted and present a strong gold-on-black contrast on both obverse and reverse. A few small, stray marks keep the coin from a full Gem classification, but this is a singularly impressive No Motto proof five that will undoubtedly be included in a high grade proof type set. Population: 1 in 64 Deep Cameo, 1 finer (8/08). (#98454)

3783 **1887 PR64 Cameo NGC.** The 1887 proof five has the easy-to-remember mintage of the last two years of the date, 87. Writing 20+ years ago, Walter Breen stated: "Coins offered in lower grade must be authenticated because many forgeries were made by removing S from 1887 S coins, and some of these have date position same as the proofs." Frankly, it is difficult to imagine that the mintmark area could be effectively effaced and that the fields would have strong enough remaining reflectivity to resemble a proof, but such items were more frequently forged in the "bad old days" before third-party certification.

Most of the proofs struck did not survive. A reasonable estimate of the number extant is around 30 pieces in all grades. Bringing scholarship of rare gold coins forward 20 years from Breen's reference, Garrett and Guth point out that: "Many probably entered circulation, as this date has the largest number of impaired examples seen for Proof issues of the 1880s." Another interesting aspect of the 1887 is offered: "Though more examples of this date than of others of the 1880s have been offered at auction, none have been at the gem level." That is no longer true, but our records indicate that only one Cameo Gem has been sold at public auction in recent years, a piece we sold at our 2007 FUN Auction for $103,500. This lovely Cameo example is one of only seven that have been certified by both of the major services in PR64, and a mere three Gems have been graded (8/08).

The fields on this piece are deeply reflective, as one would expect, and show noticeable orange-peel texture when closely examined. The devices are moderately frosted and give the coin its Cameo designation. Even reddish-gold color is seen over each side and there are no mentionable contact marks. (#88482)

Pleasing 1902 Half Eagle, PR61

3784 **1902 PR61 PCGS.** Rich lemon-yellow surfaces, mirrored fields, and reflective devices are accented by wispy orange toning to present exceptional aesthetic appeal for the grade. The surfaces have faint hairlines, but are entirely absent any contact marks or other imperfections. (#8497)

3785 **1906 PR50 PCGS.** Only 85 proofs were struck, but a surprising number of examples have survived. Although this piece has been briefly circulated, it has only trivial abrasions and retains plenty of reflectivity. Pleasing lemon-yellow in the margins surrounds the pumpkin-orange patina that drapes the majority of the surfaces. A relatively affordable and boldly detailed representative. Housed in a first-generation PCGS holder. (#8501)

Low-Mintage 1906 Half Eagle, PR55

3786 **1906 PR55 PCGS.** While the surfaces are somewhat subdued by many dark toning spots, both sides retain bright yellow mirrors. After six years of higher proof mintages that exceeded 100 coins each year, the mintage dipped to just 85 proofs in 1906, the lowest since 1898. An excellent opportunity for the type collector who desires an affordable proof half eagle. (#8501)

INDIAN HALF EAGLES

Lustrous 1908 Five Dollar, MS64

3787 **1908 MS64 PCGS.** The 1908 Indian Head half eagle is relatively common in Mint Sate grades, as many were saved as the first year of issue. This near-Gem possesses nice luster on its peach-gold surfaces, and exhibits well struck design features, save for minor softness on the eagle's shoulder. Minuscule marks on the raised fields, especially of the upper reverse, prevent Gem status. (#8510)

Popular First Year 1908 Indian Half Eagle, MS64

3788 **1908 MS64 PCGS.** This bright, satiny near-Gem displays rich honey-gold coloration and surprisingly intense mint luster for the type. Well struck with a Gemlike appearance on the obverse, and just a couple of wispy field marks on the reverse that prevent a finer grade assessment. An extremely popular first-year issue of the new Indian Head design type. (#8510)

Delightful 1908-D Indian Five, MS64

3789 **1908-D MS64 PCGS. CAC.** The 1908 Indian half eagles are among the most plentiful in the series, but even these coins are hard to locate in top grades. Indeed, PCGS has only certified nine finer examples of this issue in over 20 years of coin certification. Both sides have fully orange-gold luster, and minimal surface marks that are consistent with the grade. (#8511)

3790 **1909 MS62 PCGS.** Delightful yellow-orange patina drapes the surfaces of this lustrous example. The surfaces are minimally marked for the grade, and the eye appeal is outstanding. A lovely type coin. (#8513)

Desirable 1909 Indian Five, MS64

3791 **1909 MS64 NGC.** A gorgeous Choice Mint State example of the Indian design half eagle, scarce at this grade level regardless of the date. This example is boldly defined with essentially full detail on both sides. It exhibits exceptional yellow-gold luster with satiny surfaces. NGC has only certified 52 finer examples of the date (7/08). (#8513)

Lovely 1909 Half Eagle, Choice Uncirculated

3792 **1909 MS64 NGC.** 1909 half eagles are seldom seen in higher grades, and NGC has certified only 52 coins finer than the present piece (7/08). Flashy luster gleams from the attractive yellow-gold surfaces and gives this example splendid eye appeal. A powerfully struck representative with minimal abrasions. (#8513)

3793 **1909-D MS63 PCGS.** Pockets of slate-gray toning accent the vivid yellow patina that covers the majority of the surfaces. Several light marks keep this lustrous piece from an even higher grade. Housed in a green label PCGS holder.
From The Menlo Park Collection. (#8514)

Delightful 1909-D Half Eagle, MS64

3794 **1909-D MS64 NGC.** The 1909-D is a popular type coin but can be difficult to locate in grades finer than Choice Uncirculated. Flashy luster accents the delightful orange-gold patina that covers each side of this remarkable specimen. This smooth and minimally marked example has razor-sharp details and great eye appeal. (#8514)

Handsome 1909-D Half Eagle, Choice Mint State

3795 **1909-D MS64 NGC.** Lovely sun-yellow patina drapes the surfaces of this handsome and well-preserved example. Frosty luster shimmers on each side and accents the sharply struck devices. Although the 1909-D has the highest mintage of the series, it is surprisingly scarce in grades finer than the present piece. NGC has certified 64 pieces finer (7/08). (#8514)

Satiny Choice 1909-D Indian Five

3796 **1909-D MS64 PCGS.** This pleasing Choice Indian gold type coin has satin luster and orange-gold toning. Careful inspection is requisite to locate the few delicate field grazes. Meticulously struck, even within the crevices of the headdress and the eagle's shoulder. Housed in a green label holder. (#8514)

Enchanting 1909-D Half Eagle, Choice Uncirculated

3797 **1909-D MS64 NGC.** Dazzling satiny luster graces the attractive apricot and yellow surfaces. A few small toning spots add color to the obverse. The strike is nearly full, and there are only minuscule abrasions on either side. Although common in nearly all grades, the population of 1909-D half eagles drops precipitously above Choice Mint State. (#8514)

Charming 1909-D Half Eagle, Choice Uncirculated

3798 **1909-D MS64 NGC. CAC.** Pleasing yellow-gold patina with accents of apricot endow the surfaces of this powerfully struck piece. There are a number of grade-defining abrasions, but none are of any significance. Dazzling satiny-luster gives this piece excellent eye appeal. NGC has certified just 64 examples finer (7/08). A perfect coin for the type collector. (#8514)

Near-Gem 1909-D Half Eagle

3799 1909-D MS64 PCGS. The '09-D is by far the most available five dollar Indian issue in Mint State, but the vast majority of survivors fall into the MS60 to MS63 grade range. This sharply defined example is very well struck and shows only minimal surface marks. PCGS has only graded 91 finer examples (7/08). *From The Bell Collection.* (#8514)

3800 1909-O—Improperly Cleaned—NCS. XF Details. The 1909-O is the most famous of the Indian half eagle issues, and though this honey-gold piece shows hairlines from a past cleaning, it remains highly collectible. The surfaces exhibit minimal wear. (#8515)

Significant 1909-O Half Eagle, AU53 Sharpness

3801 1909-O—Cleaned—ICG. AU53 Details. With a mintage of just 34,200 pieces, combined with its status as the only New Orleans Mint product with the Indian Head design, the 1909-O half eagle holds a great deal of numismatic significance. Although the yellow-gold surfaces appear to have been polished, there are no particularly bothersome marks. It is also important to note that the details are quite sharp. (#8515)

Key Date 1909-O Indian Half Eagle, AU58

3802 1909-O AU58 NGC. The 1909-O is the only Indian half eagle from the New Orleans Mint. It is also easily the lowest mintage date in the series at 34,200 pieces. Collectors completing a type set by issuing mint have to obtain an example of this issue to complete their set. For collectors completing a set of Indian half eagles, this issue is the prized key date. Two varieties are known, distinguished by their mintmarks. The present coin is the variety characterized by a weak mintmark that has been recut on the left side. The other variety has a bold mintmark without doubling. Mint State survivors are rare, and eye appeal is often marginal because of heavy abrasions and impaired luster.

The example offered here has good strike detail and retains much frosty mint luster. There is a scattering of small abrasions, expected for the grade, including some thin scratches near the Indian's chin. The fields and design elements are generally well preserved, and the eye appeal is much better than average for the issue. (#8515)

3803 1910 MS63 NGC. Sharply defined with hints of steel-gray color on the reverse of this orange-gold specimen. Bright luster reflects off the surfaces, and there are minimal abrasions in the fields. (#8517)

Resplendent 1911 Half Eagle, Gem Mint State

3804 **1911 MS65 PCGS.** With a mintage of over 900,000 pieces, the 1911 half eagle ranks as one of the more common issues in the series in most grades. The critical statement is "most grades," as the 1911 is seldom seen in Gem Uncirculated and is virtually impossible to locate any finer. Although NGC and PCGS report a combined 90 pieces in grades above Choice, a significant portion of that number is undoubtedly the result of resubmissions. In addition, the immense desirability of this issue in MS65 causes any such example that appears on the market to fetch a hefty sum.

This resplendent yellow-orange specimen displays impressive satiny luster that sparkles throughout. Although most pieces have minor weakness on the headdress with average luster, this piece is sharply defined and has tremendous mint bloom, which places it at a level above the vast majority of its counterparts. Several minuscule grazes limit the grade, but overall this example has been remarkably well-preserved. NGC and PCGS combined have certified only two pieces finer than this appealing Gem (8/08), which is housed in a green label holder. (#8520)

Elusive 1911-S Half Eagle, MS63

3805 **1911-S MS63 PCGS. CAC.** While the mintage of the 1911-S was nearly 1.5 million coins, the date failed to survive in high grades, with the PCGS population report showing just 26 finer coins. This pleasing piece has attractive orange and green-gold surfaces with frosty luster and few scattered marks. (#8522)

Wonderful 1912 Half Eagle, MS63

3806 **1912 MS63 PCGS.** Enticing satiny luster shimmers beneath the attractive yellow-gold patina, with just a few tiny toning spots noted on the reverse. The strike is razor-sharp, and the surfaces are remarkably clean for the grade. This impressively luminous piece has great eye appeal and is encapsulated in a first-generation PCGS holder. (#8523)

Choice 1913 Indian Five

3807 **1913 MS64 NGC.** A lovely, brilliant honey-gold example, this Indian half eagle exhibits frosty luster on both sides. Hints of pale orange toning add to its aesthetic desirability, as does the above average design definition. NGC has only certified 42 finer examples of the date (7/08). (#8525)

Sumptuous 1913 Indian Half Eagle, MS65

3808 **1913 MS65 PCGS. CAC.** A superlative example of singular and significant importance to the advanced specialist! The 1913 is one of the great condition rarities in the Indian half eagle series, common enough in lower Mint State grades through about MS63, but scarce in MS64, and rare in MS65 grades. The surfaces show excellent, frosty luster qualities with appealing green-gold color tinged in orange patina. A faint line below UNITE and a few other insignificant surface marks are the only imperfections. As PCGS has only graded one coin finer than MS65, this piece effectively represents the finest obtainable quality. Our consignor, an advanced gold specialist, is thrilled to provide others with a chance to enjoy this beautiful and memorable coin. Population: 49 in 65, 1 finer (8/08). (#8525)

Delightful 1913-S Half Eagle MS61

3809 **1913-S MS61 NGC.** The reverse is remarkably clean for the grade, while the obverse shows only trivial marks. Vivid yellow-gold patina embraces the surfaces. The details are a trifle soft, as typically seen, but there is a surprising abundance of luster on both sides. A well-struck and appealing representative. (#8526)

3810 **1914 MS63 PCGS.** Flashy luster emanates from the apricot-orange surfaces. Both sides are minimally marked and have great eye appeal. The strike is razor-sharp save for a touch of softness on the Indian's headdress. A total of 247,000 pieces were struck, which is somewhat below average. This attractive piece is encapsulated in a green label PCGS holder. (#8527)

Impressive 1914 Half Eagle, MS64

3811 **1914 MS64 PCGS.** A wonderful example of the relatively high mintage 1914 half eagle, with a production of 247,000 coins. All three mints had similar mintages in 1914, as Denver tied the Philadelphia mintage of 247,000 coins, and San Francisco minted 263,000 pieces. This representative has bold and frosty honey-gold luster that creates excellent eye appeal. Rather plentiful at the present grade level, the 1914 half eagle is a rarity any finer, with just 23 better pieces graded at PCGS. (#8527)

3812 **1914-D MS64 ICG.** A bold example with vibrant yellow frost and traces of faint rose and blue toning. (#8528)

3813 **1914-S AU58 NGC.** A trace of light rub keeps this highly lustrous and minimally abraded piece from Uncirculated. The strike is sharp, and there are no significant marks. (#8529)

Wonderful 1914-S Half Eagle, MS62

3814 **1914-S MS62 PCGS.** Like other San Francisco Indian Head half eagles, the 1914-S is relatively scarce in low Uncirculated grades and is extremely rare in high Mint State. Flashes of luster accent the apricot-gold patina that envelops both sides. The surfaces are remarkably clean for the grade, and the strike is sharp. PCGS has certified only 23 pieces finer (8/08). (#8529)

1795 BD-2 Eagle, XF40 Details

3815 **1795 13 Leaves—Genuine—PCGS.** Breen-6830, Taraszka-2, BD-2, High R.4. We give this piece an XF40 grade, but note that considerable graffiti appears on the reverse. It has probably also been lightly cleaned, with a bright yellow appearance.

The BD-2 die combination is substantially rarer than the BD-1 eagle, with only between 90 and 110 known, compared to an estimated 225 to 325 known for BD-1. Both varieties share a common reverse with a leaf touching the left bottom of U in UNITED. The obverse of BD-1 has a star nearly touching the Y in LIBERTY, while the obverse of BD-2 has a star distant from the Y. (#8551)

3816 **1795 13 Leaves—Improperly Cleaned—NCS. AU Details.** Breen-6830, Taraszka-5, BD-5, R.5. Bass-Dannreuther Die State e/c. The rarest die marriage for the Small Eagle type, aside from the famous 9 Leaves BD-3 variety. BD-1 and (less often) BD-2 are the usually seen 1795 ten dollar varieties.

The present piece has bright luster across the stars, wings, hair, and legends. The eagle's breast shows slight wear, but the design is otherwise bold save for some softness on the right-side dentils. The honey-gold surfaces are lightly hairlined, and the right obverse field has a couple of faded, inconspicuous pinscratches. Minor adjustment marks are present on the obverse dentils, and, to a much lesser extent, are concealed in the hair. A prize for the alert numismatist who seeks additional value (in the form of a much better die variety) from a type purchase. (#8551)

526   Please visit HA.com to view other collectibles auctions

A 15% Buyer's Premium ($9 min.) Applies To All Lots

3817 **1796 AU55 NGC.** Breen-6832, Taraszka-6, BD-1, R.4. The only known die pair for coinage of 1796. Mint delivery records indicate that 2,795 eagles were coined in 1795, followed by 6,934 in 1796, but that fails to explain why 1795 had five different die marriages, compared to just one die marriage for 1796. The obvious and simple explanation is that some of the 1795 varieties were actually coined in 1796. The total of 9,729 coins delivered in the two years yields an average of 1,621 coins per die marriage.

We disagree with the mintages reported in the *Guide Book* and elsewhere for the Small Eagle tens. The *Guide Book* reports 5,583 eagles coined for 1795, 4,146 for 1796, and 3,615 for 1797, suggesting that those mintages are the actual total of coins bearing those dates. For those same dates, NGC and PCGS have combined to certify 370 dated 1795, 139 dated 1796, and 50 dated 1797. Based on a comparison of Mint delivery records and current population totals, we feel that the actual approximate mintages were: 8,875 coins dated 1795, struck from September 22, 1795 through June 21, 1796; 3,320 coins dated 1796, struck from December 22, 1796 until April 20, 1797; and 1,149 coins dated 1797, struck on May 2, 1797.

The 1796 eagles featured an unusual star layout, with eight stars to the left and eight to the right. In 1795, 15 stars were arranged 10 left and five right, in 1797 for the Small Eagle coins, the stars were arranged 12 left and four right, and in 1797 for the Heraldic Eagle coins, stars were arranged with 10 left and six right. All remaining eagles had 13 stars on the obverse. (#8554)

3818 **1797 Large Eagle VF25 NGC.** Breen-6834, Taraszka-12, BD-4, High R.4. The only obverse used with the Large Eagle reverses, ten stars to the left and six right. The eagle has long thick neck and a thick breast area. The arrowheads are past the center of N in UNITED with one nearly to the end. Later dies with a faint crack left of the R in AMERICA. John Dannreuther and Harry Bass, Jr., in their treatise on *Early U.S. Gold Coin Varieties*, write that 90 to 110 examples of this variety are known.

The subdued yellow-gold surfaces of this VF25 example possess a slight green cast, and yield hints of luster in the protected areas. The design features exhibit nice detail, and the dentilation is strong, especially on the reverse. The few minute marks that are present are not bothersome. Overall, a pleasing early gold ten dollar piece. (#8559)

3819 1797 Large Eagle AU58 NGC. Breen-6834, Taraszka-8, BD-2, High R.4. The year 1797 was one of transitions, both at the U.S. Mint and in the United States as a whole. George Washington finished his second term, refused to serve a third, and retired to his beloved Mount Vernon. John Adams took up the mantle as our nation's second president. At the Mint, after producing every authorized coinage denomination the year before from the half cent through ten dollar gold, in 1797 the facility came close to doing it again, omitting only quarters entirely from the lineup (and making some other types in minuscule quantities).

But the focus was on redesign. Tennessee joined the Union on June 1, 1796, and some coinage dies had a 16th star added in commemoration. Mint officials realized, however, that they could not continue adding stars for each new state, and the process of reversion to 13 stars began. Some denominations, such as the Draped Bust, Small Eagle half dime, show 15 stars, 16 stars, and 13 stars on different varieties. In gold and silver coinage, Mint Director Elias Boudinot was overseeing the replacement of the original Small Eagle reverse designs by the Large Eagle (or Heraldic Eagle) reverse, as on the present coin. The 1797 Large Eagle ten dollar, while far from a common early gold type, was produced to the extent of an estimated 10,940 coins, or about three times the 3,615 pieces given for the 1797 Small Eagle ten.

On this variety the obverse stars are arranged 10 x 6 on the left and right, respectively. There is a star on the reverse under the eagle's beak, and the eagle's neck ends in a rather abrupt truncation that is not triangular. Stars 3, 9, 10, and 11 on the reverse are nearly in a straight line. On the obverse star 11 nearly touches the Y in LIBERTY. This same obverse die is paired with all three reverse dies known for the 1797 Large Eagle. Two small cracks pass from the rim below the last 7 through that digit and to the lower bust.

This piece offers exuberant luster radiating from the greenish-gold surfaces, which show little actual wear. There are no distracting abrasions, just some extremely light field chatter. Adjustment marks are mostly struck out, although with a loupe the diligent searcher can discern some well-hidden in the lower hair tresses. The reverse die is rotated about 20 degrees clockwise with respect to the obverse. In the present near-Mint State grade, this example should prove to be a superior acquisition for some astute bidder, as an excellent alternative to a lower-Mint State example. (#8559)

3820 **1798/7 9x4 Stars XF40 PCGS.** BD-1, High R.4. BD Die State c/b. The only early gold issue, regardless of denomination, bearing the 9+4 star arrangement. The odd layout of the obverse devices, together with the bold overdate, is a testimonial to the fact that our infant first Mint was more concerned with quantity than quality. Someone at the Mint must have been displeased with the layout of BD-1 as BD-2—and all subsequent eagles—have a more balanced design. Collectors today, however, are thankful for such quirkiness as it adds to the intrigue and charm of early American coinage issues. Of course few will ever have the chance of owning this particular variety, as fewer than 100 coins are believed to be extant in all grades. In fact, PCGS has certified a mere 33 pieces as of (8/08) and the population at NGC is slightly lower. Considering that only 300 to 842 BD-1 tens were struck (per the Bass-Dannreuther reference), the low population today is not at all surprising.

Straw-gold fields are framed by lovely russet patination that clings heavily to the devices on both sides of this early ten. At first glance the details are what one would expect to find on a piece grading finer, although the conservative designation by PCGS, all factors considered, is accurate. Not affecting the grade, but mentioned for the sake of completeness, are minor adjustment marks observed on the eagle's left wing. Overall, the current offering is a pleasant example of a scarce—and by some measures, rare—early ten dollar gold piece struck when George Washington was still alive. (#8560)

3821 **1799 Large Stars Obverse MS63 PCGS.** BD-10, R.3. Bass-Dannreuther Die State a/a. Traditionally, the 1799 Small Stars ten has been considered scarcer than the Large Stars variety of the same year. Recent research and empirical data sheds light on the relative nature of the two 1799 eagle sub-types—or does it? The important Bass-Dannreuther reference on early gold (2006) provides estimates, by variety, pertaining to mintage, extant population, and auction appearances (1990-2005). For the eight Small Star varieties, Bass and Dannreuther suggest a mintage of between 18,500 to 27,500 pieces, with 416 to 564 survivors, and 258 auction appearances. Regarding the two Large Star die marriages, the same authors estimate a mintage of between 13,250 and 18,750 coins, of which 314 to 418 are extant, with approximately 173 appearances at public sales. The above numbers indicate that the 1799 Large Star tens are scarcer in all categories than their Small Star counterparts. However, the PCGS *Population Report* documents a total of 121 Small Star coins in all grades compared to 435 certified Large Star examples (8/08). To complicate matters, the 2006 Garrett-Guth *Encyclopedia of U.S. Gold Coins* shows that 118 Small Star coins appeared at auction from 1991 to 2005 compared to 177 showings for the Large Star pieces, thus pointing to the Small Star coins as the less available of the two sub-types. So which version is scarcer?

Clearly one—or both—of the above references have put forth imperfect technical data regarding the 1799 eagles. Perhaps we can compromise and agree that both are of comparable rarity, especially considering that fewer than 500 pieces are believed to exist for either type. Of course when dealing with a high grade specimen such as current offering, the matter is less relevant and we simply focus on the splendor of such a fine survivor. Orange-gold coloration combines with vibrantly lustrous surfaces to define this Select Uncirculated beauty. Minor strike weakness is noted in the usual lower portion of the obverse and central area of the stars on the reverse. Light adjustment marks are observed on the lower stars and Liberty's bust, although the affect on the eye appeal of this magnificent offering is negligible. (#8562)

3822 **1799 Small Stars Obverse AU58 NGC.** Breen-6839, Taraszka-14, BD-2, High R.5. BD Obverse State b/Reverse State b. Stars 1 and 13 are away from the bust and star 9 is away from the Y in LIBERTY. A small die crack runs from the rim through the left serifs of the L in LIBERTY, and lightly into the top of the cap. The reverse, previously used on the extremely rare BD-1 pairing, shows a small "rust-like crack" within C, through A, the talon, stem end, and tail feathers; another shows faintly through the O in OF to cloud 7.

Glorious mint luster cascades from both sides of this yellow-gold piece, which shows few abrasions but does have a couple of milky dark-gray toning spots. Nonetheless the piece is quite attractive, and it would make a superb acquisition for a type or date set. (#98562)

Handsome 1800 Eagle, BD-1, VF35

3823 **1800 VF35 PCGS.** Breen-6842, BD-1, High R.3. BD-1 is the only known variety for 1800 eagles. All examples have star 7 double-punched, and many display a die crack along the top of LIBERTY. Both diagnostics are visible on this example. There is an additional minor die crack extending under the base of the olive branch to the eagle's tail feathers.

The Capped Bust design, by Chief Engraver Robert Scot, had been used on the eagle from the first issue in 1795. The Heraldic Eagle reverse debuted in 1797 and—in what has been described as either a blunder or poor judgment—Scot placed the arrows (a symbol of war) in the eagle's right or honorable claw, and the olive branch (the symbol of peace) in the left or sinister claw. Thus the image was supposedly a promotion of war instead of peace, though Scot's actual intentions are unknown. Gold eagles were intended to be a coin of commerce but as Q. David Bowers notes (2005), "In their own time, eagles of the 1795 to 1804 era were seldom seen in everyday circulation, as the face value was equivalent to a week or more of wages for the typical person. Instead, these pieces were the coins of choice for large transactions and international commerce. Government accounts indicate that most were exported and melted, thus being of little value to the intended purpose of establishing a circulating federal coinage."

Certainly some eagles did circulate, as shown by the wear on this coin, notably a small mark on the bust near star 13 and a few short scratches clustered below the arrows on the reverse. However, the overall appearance is excellent. Both sides display warm gold patina, with red highlights near the rims and darker accents around the date. The centers boast a blush of bright yellow-gold, and all devices and lettering are clear. With 200-300 known specimens, 1800 eagles are considered an available variety of the type, but as with all early gold "available" is a relative term. This coin is a handsome and scarce representative of a popular early gold type.
From The Menlo Park Collection. (#8563)

Scarce XF Details 1800 Ten Dollar, BD-1

3824 **1800—Damaged—NCS. XF Details.** Breen-6842, Taraszka-23, BD-1, High R.3. The only dies for this difficult date, which has a *Guide Book* mintage of just 5,999 pieces. Those in need of the formidable Heraldic Eagle type should consider an 1800, since the 1799 and 1801 are similarly priced but decidedly more plentiful. This example has moderate wear on the portrait but the eagle is bold and some luster remains. Slightly glossy, and the obverse field is abraded. A minor rim ding is present on the obverse at 11:30. (#8563)

Fantastic 1800 Eagle, BD-1
Choice About Uncirculated

3825 **1800 AU55 NGC.** BD-1, High R.3. The only variety known. This piece is Bass-Dannreuther die state b/c, with a die crack through LIBERTY and another on the reverse near the olive branch. Although the exact mintage is unknown, the *Guide Book* lists that 5,999 pieces were struck, which is perhaps a little on the low side. Nonetheless, only a couple hundred examples are believed to exist.

Radiant luster enhances the lemon-yellow surfaces of this crisply struck piece. Numerous abrasions limit the grade and a few small marks are noted on the obverse. This appealing Choice AU piece would make a fabulous example of this early eagle in a type collection. (#8563)

Charming 1801 Eagle, BD-2, XF Sharpness

3826 **1801—Damaged, Improperly Cleaned—NCS. XF Details.** Breen-6843, Taraszka-25, BD-2, R.2. The obverse is easily identified because stars 8 and 13 are close to Liberty. Only two varieties for 1801 are known, and this reverse die was used to strike BD-2 in 1801 and then BD-3 in 1803. On this reverse, the top of the eagle's beak nearly touches a star below its point. Lovely orange-gold patina embraces the surfaces of this appealing specimen. The obverse stars are soft, as typically seen, but the rest of the details are sharp. Myriad abrasions on the obverse account for the damaged moniker, although the reverse is remarkably clean. BD-2 is significantly more available than its BD-1 counterpart and would make a perfect choice for a collector. (#8564)

AU Definition BD-2 1801 Eagle

3827 1801—Improperly Cleaned—NCS. AU Details. Breen-6843, Taraszka-25, BD-2, R.2. Obverse star 1 is distant from the bust, characteristic of BD-2. The open fields are faintly hairlined, and the remaining luster is subdued. Nonetheless, this is a bold example with essentially complete definition on the eagle's breast feathers. The highpoints of the cap, shoulder, and forehead have only a trace of friction. No quarter eagles or half eagles were struck in 1801, while production of eagles peaked that year. Bullion depositors preferred the largest possible denomination, which was the most convenient for foreign trade. (#8564)

1801 Eagle, AU Details, BD-2

3828 1801—Obverse Scratched—NCS. AU Details. Breen-6843, Taraszka-25, BD-2, R.2. Easily the most plentiful early eagle variety, the 1801 BD-2 is an excellent choice for type collectors. Aside from the usual moderate circulation marks, this piece has a thin horizontal scratch from Liberty's mouth toward star 10. Bright greenish-gold, it is otherwise an attractive representative of the design. (#8564)

Lovely 1801 BD-2 Eagle, AU53

3829 1801 AU53 PCGS. Breen-6843, Taraszka-25, BD-2, R.2. Two die varieties are known for the 1801 eagles, and they are easily distinguished with one glance toward the obverse. The relative position of the bottom and top left stars will be sufficient. On the BD-1 variety, which is an important rarity, star 1 is closer to the curl than star 8 is to the cap. The BD-2 variety, offered here, has star 1 farther from the curl and star 8 closer to the cap. This variety is arguably the single most common die variety of all early eagles, and it is an ideal choice for the date or type collector. A few light hairlines and minor abrasions are seen in the fields. It is an attractive example with bright surfaces and attractive reddish-gold coloration, particularly on the reverse.
From The Bell Collection. (#8564)

Imposing Choice AU 1801 Ten Dollar, BD-2

Reflective 1801 BD-2 Eagle, AU58

3830 1801 AU55 PCGS. Breen-6843, Taraszka-25, BD-2, R.2. Luster shimmers across the devices and legends of this lemon-tinged representative. Portions of the reverse border offer cherry-wine toning. The strike is exacting, and the eagle's breast feathers have full definition. Given its soft alloy and large size, marks are minor given its brief stint in commerce. A thin vertical mark hidden within the hair and nearly imperceptible marks near the 0 in the date barely merit mention. Certainly, this is a handsome Heraldic Eagle ten that will provide the cornerstone for a gold type collection. (#8564)

3831 1801 AU58 NGC. Breen-6843, Taraszka-25, BD-2, R.2. The present sale offers collectors quite a choice between eight different 1801 eagles in a wide range of quality, a remarkable lineup. This piece has brilliant and lustrous green-gold surfaces with faint traces of pale orange toning in the fields. Myriad tiny abrasions and a trace of high point wear prevent a full Mint State grade, but the coin exhibits excellent eye appeal. The fastidious collector may want to know about a tiny obverse rim nick at 10 o'clock. Both sides have reflective fields, the reverse fully prooflike. (#8564)

Well Detailed AU58 1801 Ten Dollar, BD-2

3832 **1801 AU58 NGC. CAC.** Breen-6843, Taraszka-25, BD-2, R.2. Two star points oriented close to Liberty's cap provide the primary diagnostic for this "plentiful" variety, the most frequently encountered die marriage of all early eagles. Traces of wear are only evident on the high points of this lovely piece. Both sides display brilliant green-gold color and exceptional surfaces. The fields are faintly reflective, and a tiny rim bump at 4 o'clock on the reverse is the only distraction. All design elements are sharply detailed, and the strike is nicely centered with complete borders. Outstanding quality for the date or type collector. (#8564)

3833 **1801 MS63 NGC.** Breen-6843, Taraszka-25, BD-2, R.2. At 44,344 coins, the year 1801 has the highest recorded mintage of eagles than any other date from 1795 to 1804. Even more amazing is the fact that the large emission of 1801-dated tens occurred with only two die pairings. 1799 saw the second highest mintage of early eagles at 37,449 coins, although it took 10 die marriages to get the job done. One would assume that the two die marriages for 1801 would have struck an equal amount of coins, considering the relatively large production volume that year. Not so. Based on research by Bass-Dannreuther (2006), it is believed that the BD-2 die marriage was responsible for producing as many as 40,000 1801-dated tens, or nearly the entire mintage of coins that year. The second highest producing die pair was 1799 BD-10, from which Bass-Dannreuther estimate that 12,500 to 17,500 coins were struck. The fact that neither of the BD-2 dies cracked during the massive production of 40,000 eagles is noteworthy since we know that other dies from the same era broke after striking fewer than 1,000 coins. Eventually the reverse die was married with another obverse die to strike approximately 10,000 1803 BD-3 eagles and subsequently failed toward the end of that production. In total, this reverse die helped to produce as many as 50,000 early eagles—more than any other die in the series. Were the BD-2 dies specially prepared, or was it simply luck? We will never know for certain, but such mysteries are what make numismatics so enjoyable.

Lemon-gold coloration and lustrous surfaces define this Select Uncirculated early eagle. Strike weakness at star 2—common to this issue—is noted, as are a few scattered abrasions commensurate with the assigned grade. Unlike many gold coins of the era, the current offering is pleasantly free of adjustment marks. Overall, this specimen is above average for the series and is sure to see aggressive bidding activity. *From The Mississippi Collection.* (#8564)

3834 **1803 Small Stars Reverse—Reverse Damage, Improperly Cleaned—NCS. AU Details.** BD-3, R.4. An attractive green-gold eagle despite light cleaning. The reverse is lightly stippled with numerous microscopic surface marks. Both sides have survived with considerable luster and excellent eye appeal. (#8565)

3835 **1803 Small Stars Reverse AU53 NGC.** Breen-6844, Taraszka-26, BD-1, High R.5. Official records indicate a mintage of 15,017 eagles for the year 1803. This mintage is shared between six different die marriages, all with the same obverse die. Anthony Taraszka and Harry Bass both concluded that the present variety was first in the die emission sequence because of the number of edge reeds. Eagles from 1799 through 1801 all have 131 edge reeds. There are no eagles dated 1802. The 1803 BD-1 eagle has 131 edge reeds, in keeping with the earlier years. All other 1803 eagle varieties and the eagles of 1804 have either 130 or 126 edge reeds, indicating a break in the production series after BD-1. The variety is very scarce today, with an only 30-40 survivors extant.

The obverse die is perfect, with no clashing, lapping or cracks. The reverse can be distinguished by the small stars combined with the long arrows (one extending past N and another extending to the foot of I in UNITED). The reverse die must have failed quickly because the obverse was still perfect when paired with the BD-2 reverse.

The surfaces are even and bright with some luster remaining on both sides. Both sides have attractive, green-gold color and a moderate number of abrasions. A few adjustment marks can be seen on the reverse, primarily in the dentils. (#8565)

Charming 1803 BD-3 Eagle, Choice AU
Small Stars Reverse

3836 **1803 Small Stars Reverse AU55 PCGS.** Breen-6844, Taraszka-28, BD-3, R.4. Of the six known 1803 ten dollar varieties, four are of the Small Stars Reverse type, with the remaining two variants having large stars. Bass-Dannreuther provide numerous methods of identifying the four Small Stars varieties, but perhaps the quickest pick-up point is the star adjacent to the eagle's beak. BD-3 is the only variety in which the lower point of the star points to the center of the left upright of the second U in PLURIBUS.

While BD-3 is the most available of the four 1803 Small Stars Reverse tens, it is anything but common. If fact, specialists believe that fewer than 200 examples are extant, regardless of condition. The strength of strike is variable on this piece and adjustment marks are noted on the obverse rims—both characteristics being common to the issue. The aforementioned shortcomings are dutifully redeemed by the charming straw-gold coloration and smooth surfaces observed on both sides of this numismatic treasure. (#8565)

LIBERTY EAGLES

Elusive 1839 Eagle, XF40
Type of 1840, Small Letters

3837 **1839 Type of 1840, Small Letters XF40 PCGS.** The 1839 Type of 1840 comes from a small mintage of 12,447 pieces. Few examples of this type have survived in any condition, as is evident from the approximately 60 coins graded by PCGS and NGC. The services have seen only two Mint State examples! Bright yellow-gold surfaces characterize this XF specimen, and they retain well defined devices, except for the star centers. Light contacts are evenly distributed over each side. (#8580)

3838 **1841 AU53 NGC.** Mild reflectivity at the margins hints at this lightly worn yellow-gold example's former luster. Well struck with numerous fine abrasions noted in the fields. (#8582)

Lovely Choice AU 1841 Eagle

3839 **1841 AU55 NGC.** This sharply struck sun-gold example possesses noticeable prooflike luster. Tiny marks frequent the fields and portrait, as often seen on lightly circulated No Motto tens, but the overall visual appeal is excellent. A better date with a small production of 63,131 pieces. Census: 28 in 55, 28 finer (8/08). (#8582)

3840 **1842 Large Date AU50 NGC.** Solidly detailed for this elusive issue, characterized by a larger date (more properly a Medium Date, judging from others) than the Small Date 1842 ten. Light yellow-orange surfaces offer glimpses of luster and hints of honey. Census: 11 in 50, 20 finer (7/08). (#8584)

Important 1842 Large Date No Motto Ten MS64

3841 **1842 Large Date MS64 NGC.** This wonderful No Motto gold coin has radiant luster and an excellent strike. Only the final star lacks complete detail. Untoned and attractive with a minimally abraded obverse and only a few unimportant reverse marks, near the beak and on the shield.

All No Motto tens, even the relatively high mintage 1847, are extremely rare in MS64 or higher. The sole exception is the 1849, which is merely very rare in MS64. The denomination was too costly to be collected by 19th century numismatists, and shipwreck hoards of Uncirculated No Motto gold coins have generally consisted of double eagles.

No Small Date examples have achieved a grade of MS64 or higher. NGC and PCGS have each certified one Large Date as MS64, and another as MS65. The pedigrees for those four coins are likely those listed below, although one of the PCGS MS64 pieces is now graded MS65 PCGS, and another is now graded MS65 by NGC:
1. NGC MS64. Franklinton Collection, Part II (Stack's, 1/2008), lot 1010. The present lot.
2. PCGS MS64. FUN Bullet (Heritage, 1/2001), lot 638.
3. PCGS MS64. Warren Miller Collection (Heritage, 10/1995), lot 6239; Harry W. Bass, Jr. Collection, Part IV (Bowers and Merena, 11/2000), lot 593.
4. PCGS MS64. Central States Signature (Heritage, 5/2000), lot 7741.
From The Mississippi Collection. (#8584)

3842 **1842 Small Date XF45 PCGS.** Olive-green and sun-gold intermingle across this moderately abraded and attractively detailed Liberty ten. The Small Date has a *Guide Book* mintage of 18,623 pieces and is scarce in all grades. Population: 9 in 45, 22 finer (8/08). (#8585)

Seldom-Offered 1842 Small Date Eagle, Mint State Sharpness

3843 **1842 Small Date—Polished—NCS. Unc Details.** There are two distinct varieties of 1842 eagles, and the Small Date type has a mintage of less than one-third of its Large date counterpart. This variety is rare in Mint State and, despite cleaning, this piece is a desirable representative. The strike is sharp, and there are only a few small marks. Bright yellow-gold patina covers the surfaces, which unfortunately have been polished. (#8585)

3844 **1842-O XF40 ANACS.** Only 27,400 pieces were struck for this scarce New Orleans issue. A bright and moderately abraded example with pleasing sharpness on the devices. A slight rim bruise is noted at 1 o'clock. (#8587)

3845 **1842-O XF45 PCGS.** A peach-tinged New Orleans eagle with pleasing definition and bright, moderately abraded fields. Although less rare than the 1841-O, the 1842-O is certainly rarer than the 1843-O. A scant 27,400 pieces were struck. Population: 29 in 45, 35 finer (8/08). (#8587)

Remarkable 1842-O Eagle, About Uncirculated

3846 **1842-O AU50 NGC.** Although not nearly as rare as the first eagle struck at the New Orleans Mint (the 1841-O, which had a mintage of 2,500 pieces), the 1842-O is quite scarce in high grades. Most examples were heavily circulated and prior to the discovery of the *S.S. Republic* it was difficult for collectors to locate an AU example. Charming orange-gold patina embraces the lustrous and minimally marked surfaces. An evenly worn and handsome representative. (#8587)

Desirable Choice AU 1843-O Gold Eagle

3847 **1843-O AU55 NGC.** This is a visually appealing and conditionally desirable Choice AU representative of the 1843-O gold eagle, which is described by Winter (2006) thus: "it is the second most available New Orleans eagle from the 1840s, trailing only the 1847-O. Unlike the 1847-O, it is very rare in higher grades and it compares favorably to such issues as the 1845-O and the 1848-O in AU55 and above." Well struck and still lustrous, with rich coloration and a few noticeable marks. Lightly worn on the highest points of the design. (#8589)

3848 **1844-O AU50 NGC.** Subtly radiant yellow-gold and sun-orange surfaces show light wear on the high points and even, scattered abrasions. A more significant mark is noted on the cheek. (#8591)

Charming 1844-O Eagle, AU55

3849 **1844-O AU55 NGC.** Plenty of luster accents the yellow-orange surfaces of this minimally marked representative. The stars are a trifle weak, as is Liberty's hair, which is typical for this issue. Although more than 100,000 pieces were minted, the 1844-O can be difficult to locate in About Uncirculated. This piece would make an excellent type coin. (#8591)

Condition Rarity 1844-O Ten Dollar, MS60

3850 **1844-O MS60 NGC.** Writing of the 1844-O ten dollar in his *New Orleans Mint Gold Coins* reference, Douglas Winter says this date can be found in Very Fine and Extremely Fine grades. It is rare in About Uncirculated, and exceedingly rare in Mint State.

A well executed strike leaves strong definition on the design features of this MS60 specimen, with the sole exception of weakness in the hair above Liberty's ear. Yellow-gold patina reveals hints of greenish-tan. Light grazes and contacts scattered over both sides result in occasional breaks in the luster. The mintmark is recut slightly at its left and upper inner border. Overall, a nice looking piece for the grade designation. Census: 5 in 60, 3 finer (7/08). (#8591)

3851 **1846 AU50 NGC.** Quite a scarce date in the early Liberty eagle series, with a mintage of only 20,095 coins, and seldom encountered in top grades. Although the surfaces are noticeably abraded, this pleasing AU has light yellow luster and excellent design definition. Census: 15 in 50, 27 finer (8/08). (#8594)

Technical Mint State 1846 Eagle

3852 **1846—Reverse Rim Damage, Improperly Cleaned—NCS. Mint State Details.** Actually a remarkable coin despite minor hairlines, rim filing, and other small scrapes on the reverse. It is fully lustrous with satiny surfaces and no trace of wear on either side. The brilliant yellow fields have considerable reflectivity. Coined before the California Gold Rush, the 1846 is far from common, with a mintage of just 20,095 coins. Consider that PCGS has never graded a Mint State 1846 eagle, and NGC has only graded five examples in MS60 through MS62. An ideal example for the collector with a little forgiveness. (#8594)

3853 **1846 MS62 NGC.** The year is 1846. Mormon pioneers begin their trek West from Illinois toward "Deseret," present-day Salt Lake City. Californians, Nuevo Mexicans, and Texians are in conflict with Mexico over various issues, leading to the the Bear Flag Revolt and the Mexican-American War. U.S. President James K. Polk addresses Congress concerning the tension with Mexico, while General Zachary Taylor leads American troops in Texas. The 1846-48 war ultimately leads to the Mexican loss of Alta California and Nuevo Mexico. (The United States has already annexed Texas, in 1845.)

At the U.S. Mint in Philadelphia, the concentration is on minor coinage and the utilitarian half eagle. The Philadelphia Mint strikes some 4.12 million large cents in the year, along with more than a half-million Liberty Seated quarters and 2.2 million Seated halves. For 1846 half eagles, the mintage is nearly 400,000 coins—a total that exceeds the combined gold coinage totals for all other mints and denominations for the year.

Astute numismatists will note that the year is actually a portrait of a "typical" year from the pre-1857 era in U.S. numismatics. The copper large cent, silver half dollar, and gold half eagle are the workhorses of early U.S. commerce, produced in much greater numbers than their cousins in other denominations.

So it is that the Philadelphia Mint produced only a meager 20,095 business strikes of the 1846 Liberty Head eagle. Only five examples from the entire issue have been certified in Mint State, all at NGC: one in MS60 and two each in MS61 and MS62 (8/08).

The present piece in MS62 is tied for the finest certified, as the highest-graded PCGS examples are four AU58 coins. This specimen offers commendable yellow-gold surfaces, with a clean, pleasing appearance and prooflike luster on both sides. The few light ticks and reeding marks are consistent with the grade, but the strike is extremely well-impressed, if a trifle short of full on the eagle's left leg, and this coin has plenty of appeal in numerous categories. Census: 2 in 62, 0 finer (8/08). (#8594)

3854 **1846-O XF40 NGC.** Significant luster accents the apricot-gold surfaces. Myriad abrasions cover both sides, but none merit specific mention. The 1846-O is popular because of the existence of normal date and overdate varieties, but the normal date is actually considered to be slightly scarcer. (#8595)

Delightful 1846-O Eagle, AU53

3855 **1846-O AU53 NGC.** The 1846-O is scarce in About Uncirculated and is virtually impossible to locate in Mint State. Charming orange color embraces both sides, with a few small patches of green patina on the obverse. There are no marks worthy of mention, and the strike is sharp save for the typical weakness on the stars and the hair curl above Liberty's ear. Census: 18 in 53, 17 finer (8/08). (#8595)

Luminous AU53 1846-O Eagle

3856 **1846-O AU53 NGC.** The mildly reflective surfaces, deep yellow-orange with elements of peach at the margins, bespeak originality. The high points are pleasingly detailed for the grade with just minor wear, and an abrasion over the eagle's head is the only individually mentionable mark. A great example of this popular antebellum issue. Census: 18 in 53, 17 finer (8/08). (#8595)

Unworn So-Called 1846/5-O Eagle

3857 **1846/5-O—Improperly Cleaned—NCS. Unc Details.** Breen-6875. The so-called 1846/5-O overdate eagle has a small circular die lump inside the loop of the 6, that Breen called the "knob of a 5." Many experts believe that it is a die defect rather than a true overdate. But it is listed in the *Guide Book*, assuring its popularity as an important variety.

Perhaps equally important, and seldom mentioned, is the sharply repunched mintmark, with the top of the first punch visible above the final entry. The obverse is harshly cleaned with heavy hairline, despite the retention of full yellow-gold luster. The reverse has a subdued, matte appearance with dull brownish patina. (#8596)

3858 **1846/5-O MS62 NGC.** Although undesignated as such on the NGC holder, this is actually an unrecognized 1846/5-O eagle, and as such it is a great rarity in this condition. Indeed, both the 1846-O and the 1846/5-O are great rarities in the MS62 grade of the present coin: A quick perusal through our Permanent Auction Archives reveals that the finest example of either variant we have previously offered is an AU55, and the finest certified 1846/5-O we have offered is an XF45 PCGS coin from our 2005 St. Louis CSNS Signature Auction #372 (5/2005, lot 8754).

As mentioned, both the overdate and nonoverdate varieties are extremely rare in Mint State, and in fact Extremely Fine examples are very rare. While some numismatists question whether it is a 5 or something else under the 6, there is clearly "something there," and this is a popular variety whose fame has been increased by its listing in the *Guide Book*.

A comparison of the overdate and nonoverdate varieties reveals several key differences that are useful in attribution: Most obvious is the ball of an apparent 5 in the lower loop of the 6, and that underdigit portion is frosted. The area under the top loop of the 6 is also frosted. There are also remnants of an underdigit beneath the 4 in the date, and the enclosed area within the triangle of the 4 is also frosted. The downstroke of the 4 is quite thick, and the thick, long serif on the cross-stroke of the 4 meets the right serif of the downstroke, enclosing an oval area that is also frosted.

This piece reveals considerable prooflike luster when turned under a light, and while there is some light field chatter on both sides, there are no singular abrasions. The color is a delightful medium yellow-gold, and the strike is close to full. PCGS has certified one each of the 1846-O and 1846/5-O in MS64, with the next highest some AU55s. NGC appears not to certify the overdate, but the finest 1846-Os are a single MS63 Prooflike and one MS62 (8/08). This overdate coin appears clearly to be well within the Condition Census. (#8596)

3859 **1847 AU55 NGC.** Pleasing orange-gold patina endows the surfaces, with a rose hue throughout the reverse. Myriad abrasions cover both sides but none merit specific mention. Crisply defined with splendid eye appeal.
From The Menlo Park Collection. (#8597)

Exceptional 1847 Eagle, MS61

3860 **1847 MS61 NGC.** Mint State No Motto eagles are scarce, and despite a plentiful mintage (862,258 pieces), the 1847 is difficult to locate in Uncirculated, as a look at the population data shows. This lovely yellow-gold piece has lots of luster throughout. Myriad marks on each side are typical for the grade and issue. Although the stars and tips of the eagle's wings are soft, the rest of the details are boldly struck. An excellent No Motto type coin. Census: 30 in 61, 20 finer (7/08). (#8597)

Conditionally Scarce 1850 Large Date Eagle, MS61

3861 **1850 Large Date MS61 NGC.** While the Large Date 1850 eagle is more available than its Small Date counterpart by a ratio of 3 to 1, a look at the population data indicates how scarce this variety is in Mint State. Coruscating luster radiates from the bright yellow-gold surfaces of the present piece. The strike is sharp save for the typical weakness on the stars, and there are no mentionable marks on either side. Census: 7 in 61, 11 finer (7/08). (#8603)

Challenging 1850 Small Date Eagle, AU58

3862 **1850 Small Date AU58 PCGS.** The 1850 Small Date ten dollar can be located, with some patience, in Very Fine and Extremely Fine grades. About Uncirculated coins are scarce, and Mint State pieces rare. Yellow-gold patina transitions to reddish-gold at the margins of this near-Mint example. Except for softness in the star centers, the design elements are well defined. The surfaces exhibit considerable luster and are minimally abraded. Population: 6 in 58, 5 finer (8/08). (#8604)

3863 **1851-O AU53 NGC.** Mint State 1851-O eagles are extremely rare and an attractive About Uncirculated example such as the present piece would make a wonderful representative. Lovely olive-orange patina drapes the lightly abraded surfaces and is complemented by traces of luster in the fields. The peripheral design elements are soft, as usually seen. (#8607)

Lovely 1851-O Eagle, AU58

3864 **1851-O AU58 NGC.** A glance at the population data indicates how scarce this issue is in high grades. Barely 100 pieces have been certified in AU58 by NGC and PCGS combined, many of which are undoubtedly resubmissions. Fewer than 20 Mint State examples are reported from both grading services, and NGC has graded a mere 11 pieces finer than the present piece (7/08). This sun-gold ten has myriad marks, which is typical for the issue, and all are minor. The only noteworthy softness is on the stars, as usual, and the tips of the eagle's wings. This lustrous piece would make an excellent representative. (#8607)

Shining Near-Mint 1851-O Eagle

3865 **1851-O AU58 NGC.** A better example of this heavily minted New Orleans eagle issue, one that is highly popular with Southern gold type collectors. The pale lemon-gold surfaces are radiant, and aside from a shallow scrape to the left of Liberty's chin, the fields show only minor marks. A touch of friction visits the high points of the well struck central devices. NGC has graded 11 finer examples (8/08). (#8607)

Flashy Near-Mint 1851-O Ten Dollar Gold

3866 **1851-O AU58 NGC.** Breen-6898. Hollow ring atop second stripe. Well struck with a great deal of luster still evident on both sides, this flashy green-gold example almost has the appearance of a Mint State piece. Small hairlines are noted in the fields, but there are no severe abrasions or any obvious highpoint wear on either side of the coin. An attractive near-Mint specimen, from an issue that becomes very elusive in uncirculated condition. (#8607)

Attractive 1853 Eagle, AU58

3867 **1853 AU58 PCGS.** A frosty near-Mint example of the popular 1853 eagle with moderately abraded surfaces. Both sides have nice details with little apparent weakness. Considered one of the common issues in the Liberty eagle series, the mintage was undoubtedly influenced by the California gold discovery. The massive influx of newly mined gold in the early 1850s meant that all of the mint branches had plenty to keep them busy. Population: 21 in 58, 24 finer (7/08). (#8610)

Scarce AU55 1853/2 Ten Dollar

3868 **1853/2 AU55 NGC. CAC.** FS-301, formerly FS-007. Struck the same year as the 1853/2 double eagle, which like the 1853/2 eagle is the only widely accepted overdate of its respective series. The 1839/8 and 1846/5-O are believed by many specialists to be repunched dates or from defective logotype punches. This is a pleasing example with ample luster and original dusky yellow-gold color. Well defined and without heavy marks. (#8611)

Choice AU 1853/2 Eagle

3869 **1853/2 AU55 NGC.** FS-301. The remnants of a 2 are distinct beneath the 3, but the *Cherrypickers'* fourth edition also mentions a rust spot beneath the R of LIBERTY that appears just to be in the process of forming on this piece. This is a no-questions example of the overdate, however, and certified as such by NGC, with two clear curving arcs within the bottom loop of the 3. The lustrous orange-gold surfaces show tinges of pinkish-orange around the peripheral elements. Census: 38 in 55, 22 finer (8/08). (#8611)

Well Defined 1853/2 Ten Dollar, AU58

3870 **1853/2 AU58 NGC.** FS-301. The fourth edition of the *Cherrypickers' Guide* says "the 3 of the primary date is punched over a clearly visible 2." These diagnostics show clearly on the present AU58 offering. Most certified examples are in the VF to lower AU range. Peach-gold surfaces display luster in the recessed areas, and a relatively even distribution of minute marks. Well defined, save for softness in some of the star centers. Census: 21 in 58, 1 finer (7/08). *From The Mississippi Collection.* (#8611)

3871 **1853-O AU50 NGC.** Bright yellow-gold surfaces show traces of luster residing in the protected areas. Nicely defined, with just a few light scattered marks. (#8612)

3872 **1854-O Small Date AU53 NGC.** Though the date seems large in isolation, it is distinctly smaller than that of the Large Date when seen side-by-side. This lightly worn orange-gold piece shows only a few significant abrasions, one on the portrait and another in the right obverse field. (#8614)

Sharp 1854-O Small Date Eagle, Choice AU

3873 **1854-O Small Date AU55 NGC.** Although the Large Date is usually considered to be less available than its Small Date counterpart, the Small date may actually be scarcer in high grades. Delightful luster shines beneath the orange-gold patina. There are no marks worthy of mention, and the strike is sharp save for weakness on the stars. Census: 49 in 55, 43 finer (7/08). (#8614)

Conditionally Scarce 1854-S Eagle, AU58

3874 **1854-S AU58 NGC.** The 1854-S is the first eagle struck in San Francisco and a total of 123,826 pieces were minted. While this issue is relatively available in circulated grades, it is scarce in About Uncirculated and is virtually impossible to find in Mint State. NGC and PCGS each report only four examples finer than the present piece (8/08). Strong mint luster accents the olive-orange surfaces. The dies were clearly relapped as the lower hair curls are not fully outlined. A charming, lightly circulated example. (#8615)

Delightful 1854-S Eagle, AU58

3875 1854-S AU58 NGC. The San Francisco Mint began operating in 1854, striking a small number of quarter eagles and half eagles, along with a substantial production of eagles and double eagles. This light yellow example is boldly detailed with nearly full luster. The reverse is extensively cracked through the legend, with a small triangular die chip over the left side of the M. Census: 52 in 58, 4 finer (8/08). (#8615)

3876 1855 AU55 NGC. Well struck except for the high relief stars. Luster beckons from design recesses, and although abrasions are distributed, none individually distract.
Ex: St. Louis Signature (Heritage, 5/2005), lot 8769. (#8616)

3877 1855 AU58 PCGS. This No Motto ten has plentiful luster, and the strike is precise throughout. The fields have the customary small marks, none of which merit mention aside from a pair of lines below the left (facing) claw. Population: 17 in 58, 16 finer (8/08). (#8616)

Low-Mintage 1855-O Ten Dollar, VF30

3878 1855-O VF30 PCGS. Just 18,000 pieces were struck for this No Motto New Orleans issue. The obverse portrait is significantly sharper than the assigned grade, but the star centers and the eagle's neck are somewhat soft. Bright yellow-gold surfaces display traces of luster in some of the recesses. Several minute circulation marks are scattered over each side. Encased in an old green label holder. (#8617)

3879 1856 AU58 NGC. An attractive mixture of lime-green and orange toning covers the still-lustrous surfaces of this near-Mint gold eagle. Well struck and only slightly worn, with some hair-thin lines in the obverse and reverse fields. (#8619)

3880 1856 AU58 PCGS. Strong luster emanates from the minimally marked, yellow-gold surfaces. The stars are nearly flat, but the central details are razor-sharp. A handsome example of this scarce issue. Population: 18 in 58, 18 finer (8/08). (#8619)

3881 1856 AU58 NGC. Substantial luster and a crisp strike combine with lightly abraded fields for good eye appeal. A scarcer date infrequently encountered this close to Mint State. (#8619)

Lovely 1856-O Eagle, AU53

3882 1856-O AU53 NGC. Although there exist several 1856-O eagles in higher numerical grades, few could match this coin's aesthetic desirability. Pale orange toning at the borders frame the brilliant yellow-gold surfaces. All design elements are sharply detailed, and the fields retain slight reflectivity. The obverse has minor die rust through LIBERTY and along the back of the neck, and the reverse has strong clash marks on either side of the eagle's head and neck. Census: 19 in 53, 41 finer (8/08). (#8620)

Beautiful 1856-O Eagle, AU55

3883 1856-O AU55 NGC. The New Orleans Mint struck few gold coins in 1856 as the San Francisco Mint picked up the pace to convert newly mined gold into specie. In fact, New Orleans coined just 47,850 gold coins of all denominations throughout the year, using a little over 14,000 ounces of gold. In the same year, San Francisco struck almost 1.5 million gold coins, using 1.22 million ounces of gold!

This delightful Choice AU eagle has excellent light yellow-gold luster with traces of orange patina. The fields retain some reflective appearance especially close to the devices. Census: 21 in 55, 20 finer (8/08). (#8620)

3884 1856-S AU53 NGC. Breen-6922. Medium S. Luster shimmers from the borders of this well defined and typically abraded example. All pre-1879 San Francisco eagles are scarce in AU, since that facility concentrated on double eagle production for its first quarter century of operation. (#8621)

3885 1857 AU50 NGC. Luster shimmers across the reverse periphery, and is otherwise visible here and there. The fields display diverse minor marks appropriate for the type. Only 16,606 pieces were coined. (#8622)

3886 1858-O XF40 ANACS. Charming orange-gold patina endows the lightly abraded surfaces. A shallow mark above Liberty's hairbun is barely worthy of mention. Significant luster remains in the fields, which is remarkable given the grade. (#8626)

Challenging Choice AU 1858-O Ten

3887 **1858-O AU55 PCGS.** Luster shimmers from the borders and devices of this richly detailed No Motto ten. Moderately abraded overall with a few marks clustered on the field beneath the chin. A scarce New Orleans issue with a mintage of just 20,000 pieces. Population: 14 in 55, 14 finer (7/08). (#8626)

Important 1865-S Over Inverted 186 Eagle, VG10

3888 **1865-S 865 Over Inverted 186 VG10 PCGS.** All 1865-S eagles, both normal date and inverted date varieties, are elusive in any grade. The mintage of 16,700 coins for the date includes both varieties, and they are similar in rarity, although the inverted date variety seems slightly more available. The present piece is really quite exceptional for its well-worn condition. The medium yellow surfaces are smooth and essentially mark-free, aside from the usual tiny handling marks that accumulated from time in circulation. Deep steel patina around the border devices, including the stars and legend, provide excellent eye appeal. It is quite a delightful piece for the grade. (#8643)

Pleasing 1865-S Over Inverted Date Ten, Fine 12

3889 **1865-S 865 Over Inverted 186 Fine 12 NGC.** Although called a Normal Date on the NGC holder, this is actually an example of the intriguing 1865/Inverted 186 variety. The engraver accidentally punched the three digit 186 logotype in the die upside down, then corrected his mistake before adding the final 5. This lovely piece has smooth light yellow-gold surfaces, a most attractive example. (#8643)

3890 **1868 AU50 NGC.** A bright yellow-gold example of this elusive issue. The luster extent is pleasing, and the obverse has only light, scattered flaws. Just 10,630 pieces were struck, and only a tiny fraction of the original mintage escaped the smelter. Census: 12 in 50, 53 finer (7/08). (#8653)

3891 **1868 AU53 NGC.** Honey-gold surfaces reveal traces of luster in the recesses, and are generally well defined. Distributed light marks occur over each side. AU coins are not that common, and Mint State pieces are virtually unobtainable. (#8653)

3892 **1868 AU53 NGC.** This low-mintage issue is usually seen in VF or XF grades; AU coins are elusive, and Mint State pieces are virtually non-existent. Traces of luster reside in the recesses of this AU53 example, and the design elements are relatively well defined. Several minute marks are distributed over each side. (#8653)

3893 **1868 AU53 NGC.** The 1868 eagle boasts a low mintage of just 10,665 pieces, and is seldom seen in About Uncirculated. Although there are myriad abrasions throughout, none are of any significance. Well-defined with charming yellow-gold patina. Census: 15 in 53, 37 finer (7/08). (#8653)

Elusive Choice AU 1868 Ten Dollar

3894 **1868 AU55 NGC.** A well struck example with sun-gold and pale olive toning. Luster fills design recesses, and the scattered small marks are unobtrusive. All Philadelphia issues between 1862 and 1873 are rare, although the 1868 has a mintage of 10,630 pieces, which is relatively high for the era. Census: 16 in 55, 21 finer (7/08). (#8653)

Rare Reconstruction-Era 1869 Eagle, AU58

3895 **1869 AU58 NGC.** Liberty Head eagle production was low from 1861 until the end of the 1870s. In 1869 Philadelphia minted just 1,830 business strikes. The rarity of this date is such that 1869-S tens with weak mintmarks have been offered as Philadelphia examples, though both issues are rare in all grades and virtually unknown in Mint State. Of the Philadelphia issue Garrett and Guth (2006) note that "Extremely Fine examples are very rare, and About Uncirculated examples are extremely rare."

This example displays uniform honey-gold color with a hint of cinnamon toning. As expected from the assigned grade, there are minor abrasions collected from the time in circulation, a short scratch above the date the most obvious. Even so this is an attractive coin, desirable both from the standpoint of rarity and as a representative from the historic but often troubled post-Civil War era of U.S. history. Census: 6 in 58, 1 finer (8/08). (#8655)

Fantastic Uncirculated 1869 Ten Dollar

3896 **1869 MS60 PCGS.** There are no proof-only Liberty eagle dates, but there are many Philadelphia business strikes with tiny emissions. The 1869 has a mintage of just 1,830 pieces, and only three examples have been certified as Mint State by either PCGS or NGC. The other two coins are a PCGS MS62 and an NGC MS63, and neither have appeared at auction since 1995.

The present piece is prooflike, not unexpected given the low mintage. A few faint marks beneath the eagle's left wings determine the grade. Sun-gold overall with splashes of lemon-gold on the right fields. An important opportunity to acquire a Condition Census example that has been off the market for a number of years. Housed in a green label holder. Population: 1 in 60, 1 finer (8/08). (#8655)

Remarkable 1870 Eagle, About Uncirculated

3897 **1870 AU50 NGC.** Although both sides exhibit traces of luster, the reverse is remarkably resplendent, with watery reflectivity that is barely obscured by peppered abrasions. The impressive luster shimmers beneath the pale straw-yellow patina that covers both sides. The stars are a trifle soft, but the rest of the details are crisply defined. One of only 3,990 pieces struck. Census: 11 in 50, 36 finer (8/08). (#8657)

3898 **1870-S VF25 PCGS.** The 1870-S has a tiny mintage of 8,000 pieces, actually the largest mintage of eagles at any facility that year. This almond-gold example is bereft of mentionable marks, and the eagle displays much feather detail. Population: 4 in 25, 36 finer (8/08). (#8659)

3899 **1870-S—Cleaned—ANACS. AU50 Details.** A well detailed example of this rare date eagle. Few from the mintage of 8,000 pieces were set aside, and only the Bass example has achieved a certified Mint State grade. Careful rotation locates distributed hairlines. Minute rim nicks at 9:30 on the obverse and 11 o'clock on the reverse merit only passing mention. (#8659)

Important 1873-S Eagle, XF45

3900 **1873-S XF45 NGC.** Pleasing orange-gold surfaces are free of all but the usual inconsequential handling marks. Considerable luster is still visible in the protected areas near the border and next to the devices. NGC and PCGS have certified 30 pieces at this grade level, 53 others in lower grades, and 49 in higher grades, including a single PCGS MS61, the only Mint State piece graded by either service. (#8668)

Conditionally Rare 1873-S Eagle, About Uncirculated

3901 **1873-S AU50 PCGS.** Garrett and Guth (2006) state that the 1873-S, with a mintage of only 12,000 pieces, is an underrated issue. About Uncirculated examples are rare, and PCGS reports just four pieces at the AU50 level, with nine finer (8/08). Myriad abrasions barely affect the impressive luster that graces both sides. A handsome, crisply struck example with lovely lemon-yellow patina. (#8668)

3902 **1874 MS61 NGC.** This bold example has vibrant peripheral luster and distributed field marks. Philadelphia issues between 1862 and 1877 are laced with rarities. Within this group, the 1874 is comparatively available, but is certainly difficult in Mint State. Census: 27 in 61, 18 finer (7/08). (#8669)

Eye-Catching 1874 Eagle, MS62

3903 **1874 MS62 PCGS.** An excellent example for a type collector. Pleasing satiny luster shimmers beneath the honey-gold patina that overlies the surfaces. Only light grazes are visible on each side, and they barely affect the lovely reflectivity. This sharply struck piece has great eye appeal and is seldom seen in higher grades. Population: 10 in 62, 9 finer (8/08). (#8669)

Lovely Gem 1874 Eagle

3904 **1874 MS65 NGC.** This With Motto Liberty eagle issue hits a middle ground for its decade; it is not so rare as many other contemporaneous dates, though Garrett and Guth point out three issues from the late 1870s that are substantially more available. Garrett and Guth further note that while the 1874 is "easy to find" in almost any circulated grade, " ... Mint State examples are obtainable but they remain scarce."

Gems such as the present piece take that scarcity to another level, since NGC and PCGS have certified just five such coins between them, with none finer (8/08). It is impressively detailed with creamy luster that enlivens the beautifully preserved surfaces, generally pale wheat-gold with occasional deeper accents. (#8669)

Attractive 1874-CC Eagle, VF35

3905 **1874-CC VF35 PCGS.** The mintage of 16,767 eagles at Carson City in 1874 was the highest production total for the denomination through the first 11 years that eagles were coined in Nevada. As such, it is clearly the most easily located of any issue in the 1870s, but it should still be considered a rare issue. This pleasing specimen has smooth light yellow surfaces with a hint of green. The fields remain slightly reflective, and the overall eye appeal is excellent. (#8670)

Desirable 1874-CC Ten, XF45

3906 **1874-CC XF45 PCGS.** A tiny obverse rim nick at 11:30 is the only blemish on otherwise exceptional surfaces for the grade. Both sides have pleasing light yellow surfaces with noticeable luster retained in the protected areas. Although considered one of the more available dates in the Carson City Eagle series, XF examples are scarce and finer grade pieces are rare. (#8670)

Shining Choice AU 1874-S Ten

3907 **1874-S AU55 NGC.** Generally yellow-gold with surprisingly radiant surfaces. This well-defined example shows only a handful of minor, scattered marks on each side, and the lightly worn cheek is comparatively clean. This issue of just 10,000 pieces is a condition rarity even at the AU55 level. Census: 7 in 55, 7 finer (8/08). (#8671)

Elusive AU50 1875-CC Eagle

3908 **1875-CC AU50 NGC.** The 1875-CC is one of the rarest Carson City eagles and boasts a diminutive mintage of just 7,715 pieces. Although this number is actually higher than several other CC-mint eagles, the low survival rate of the 1875-CC has caused it to be difficult to locate today. Like many Carson City eagles, a large percentage saw fairly extensive circulation, and the number of extant pieces drops dramatically above XF. While a couple of Mint State examples have surfaced in the past decade, the 1875-CC remains an extremely elusive issue in high grades.

Significant luster radiates beneath the charming orange-gold patina. A number of wispy abrasions define the grade, but none are of any significance. The details are crisp save for a touch of softness on Liberty's hair. An appealing representative of this key date. Census: 8 in 50, 10 finer (8/08). (#8673)

Rare XF Details 1876-CC Eagle

3909 **1876-CC—Repaired, Improperly Cleaned—NCS. XF Details.** This Carson City issue from the centennial year has an official mintage of just 4,696 pieces, most of which were melted long ago. Repaired near 12:30 on the obverse and opposite at 5:30 on the reverse. The surfaces are glossy from cleaning. (#8675)

3910 **1878-S AU50 NGC.** A charming lemon-gold example with lots of luster on each side. The stars and hair show a little softness, as typically seen, but the eagle is crisply struck. Scattered marks define the grade, but none are particularly detracting. (#8682)

Scarce 1879-O Eagle, Choice AU

3911 **1879-O AU55 NGC.** With a mintage of only 1,500 pieces, the 1879-O eagle has the second lowest mintage of any O-mint ten dollar piece—and of any New Orleans gold issue for that matter. NGC has certified a single Mint State specimen, and PCGS has certified no Uncirculated examples (7/08). It is virtually impossible to find an 1879-O eagle finer than the present Choice About Uncirculated piece. Pleasing yellow-gold patina drapes the surfaces of this seldom offered rarity. Both sides show scattered abrasions, which is typical for the issue, but there are no marks of any significance. This sharply struck representative has just a trace of weakness on the hair above Liberty's ear and on the stars. Significant luster gleams from the protected areas and gives this piece lovely eye appeal. (#8685)

Lovely Select 1880 Ten Dollar

3912 **1880 MS63 NGC.** Beautifully detailed with considerable frostiness evident in the minimally abraded wheat-gold fields. Aside from a shallow vertical flaw on the left cheek, Liberty's portrait is seemingly mark-free. Despite a mintage of over 1.6 million pieces, the 1880 eagle is very scarce in Select and a rarity any finer; NGC has graded only seven such pieces (8/08). (#8687)

3913 **1880-CC—Improperly Cleaned—NCS. XF Details.** Minor, scattered hairlines affect the khaki-gold surfaces of this softly struck Carson City eagle. A handful of shallow abrasions are noted in the fields. (#8688)

Delightful 1880-S Eagle, MS63

3914 **1880-S MS63 NGC. CAC.** This conditionally rare ten dollar piece has undiminished cartwheel luster and an exacting strike. The apricot-gold toning is original, and the portrait and reverse are minimally abraded. The obverse field has only minor marks. An opportunity for the alert specialist. (#8690)

3915 **1881 MS61 Prooflike NGC.** Alertly struck and nicely mirrored with the usual number of small field abrasions. The 8s in the date have substantial die fill, suggestive of repunching. The 1881 has the highest mintage of the series, but because of its relatively early date, prooflike Uncirculated examples are very scarce. Census: 9 in 61 Prooflike, 4 finer (7/08). (#78691)

3916 **1881-CC XF45 NGC.** The 1881-CC has a diminutive mintage of just 24,015 pieces, which is actually a significant increase compared to previous Carson City eagle issues. Pleasing orange-gold patina overlies the surfaces, with some luster still present in the protected areas. Numerous abrasions are noted on each side, but none are of any significance. (#8692)

3917 **1881-CC AU53 NGC.** The borders offer plentiful luster, and the slightly subdued fields are void of distracting marks. A popular Carson City issue that has a low mintage of 24,015 pieces. By comparison, Philadelphia struck more than 3.8 million pieces. (#8692)

Conditionally Scarce 1881-S Eagle, MS63

3918 **1881-S MS63 ICG.** The 1881-S is yet another gold dollar that is easily located in circulated grades, but becomes scarce in Mint State. In fact, no examples have been certified finer than the present piece by either NGC or PCGS (7/08). Enticing semiprooflike fields exude bright luster beneath the pleasing yellow-gold patina. The details have above-average sharpness and there are no marks worthy of individual mention. (#8694)

Wonderful 1883-S Eagle, MS62

3919 **1883-S MS62 PCGS.** This is a wonderfully lustrous example of this low-mintage (38,000 coins) issue, one usually found in AU or Choice AU at best. The orange-gold fields display full cartwheel luster, with a bold strike and tremendous eye appeal. PCGS has certified only three examples finer (8/08). (#8702)

Lustrous 1884-CC Eagle, AU53

3920 **1884-CC AU53 NGC.** A lovely piece with considerable luster retained over medium yellow surfaces. The design definition is bold and the overall appearance is exceptional for the grade. The 1884-CC Eagle is a scarce issue from a mintage of just 9,925 coins, and examples are always in demand in most any grade. Census: 23 in 53, 78 finer (8/08). (#8704)

3921 **1885-S MS62 PCGS.** Splendid orange-gold patina graces both sides of this sharply impressed specimen. Several reeding marks on the obverse limit the grade, and a number of light grazes barely affect the wonderful luster. The 1885-S is seldom seen finer than the present piece. (#8707)

Desirable 1885-S Ten, MS63

3922 **1885-S MS63 NGC.** Straw-gold and olive-green patina bathes each side. Nicely struck, with a few small abrasions. The '85-S ten could not be described as a rarity in lesser grades, but emerges as an extremely challenging issue any finer than the present example. Census: 48 in 63, 1 finer (7/08).
From The Mississippi Collection. (#8707)

3923 **1888-O MS62 PCGS.** Although relatively available compared to most O-mint eagles, the 1888-O still has a mintage of just 21,335 pieces. Dazzling luster sparkles beneath the charming yellow-gold patina. The details are nearly full, and there are no significant marks on each side. PCGS has certified a mere 18 examples finer (7/08). (#8713)

3924 **1888-O MS62 NGC.** Rich orange-gold shadings dominate the centers, while dots of crimson and areas of yellow-orange prevail at the margins. Pleasingly detailed with only a handful of overt marks, though these are enough to preclude Select status. (#8713)

3925 **1888-O MS62 NGC.** Powerful semiprooflike luster graces both sides and complements the attractive yellow-gold patina. The stars are soft, but the central design elements are crisply defined. An excellent type coin. (#8713)

3926 **1889 AU53 PCGS.** The 1889 is the lowest mintage post-1883 Liberty eagle. The mintage is actually less than the famous 1870-CC. An original orange-gold example with the expected moderate obverse abrasions. In an old green label holder.
Ex: Century Collection Sale (Superior, 2/1992), lot 2848. (#8715)

3927 **1889-S MS63 PCGS.** Charming yellow-gold patina complements the dazzling satiny luster. The strike is sharp, and there are only insignificant grazes on each side. The 1889-S is seldom seen finer and PCGS reports just 15 such examples (8/08). (#8716)

3928 **1889-S MS63 PCGS.** Impressively lustrous gold-orange surfaces show occasional glimpses of tan. Satiny and well-defined with only minor, scattered abrasions on each side. (#8716)

Challenging 1891 Eagle, MS63

3929 **1891 MS63 PCGS.** A relatively low mintage issue (91,820 pieces), the 1891 is available in Mint State but typically comes thoroughly abraded. The present sharply struck pink-gold example lacks noticeable contact aside from a typical number of scattered, wispy blemishes. The luster is satiny, and is especially prominent on the reverse. Population: 32 in 63, 2 finer (8/08). (#8719)

Eye-Appealing MS62 1891-CC Eagle

3930 1891-CC MS62 NGC. Although the plentiful emission and large subsequent survival rate mean that examples can be found in all grades up through MS65, the average certified survivor is only about AU55 or AU58. This nice MS62 piece displays semiprooflike surfaces with some light field chatter and a bold strike, an eye-appealing and collectible combination. (#8720)

3931 1892 MS61 Prooflike NGC. A lovely orange-gold example with fully mirrored fields. A few too many marks are present for a higher numerical grade, but it is still highly desirable. In all grades, NGC has certified 23 prooflike examples, with only six of those finer than this piece (8/08). (#78721)

3932 1892-CC XF45 NGC. Only 40,000 examples were struck of the 1892-CC, the second-to-last issue at the Carson City Mint. Plenty of luster remains beneath the pleasing orange patina. The strike is crisp, and there are no mentionable marks on either side. (#8722)

3933 1892-O MS60 NGC. A few stars are softly impressed, but the strike is generally good. Luster dominates the reverse and fills the obverse margin and portrait. NGC has yet to certify any examples above MS62. (#8723)

Attractive MS62 1892-O Eagle

3934 1892-O MS62 PCGS. CAC. Though the 1892-O is a lower-mintage issue among New Orleans eagles, Mint State pieces are surprisingly accessible, though MS62 coins are elusive and just four Select or better coins are noted in the PCGS *Population Report* (8/08). This well-defined survivor combines a solid strike with immensely lustrous sun-yellow and orange-gold surfaces. (#8723)

3935 1893 MS61 Prooflike NGC. The fields are flashy, although scattered minor marks affect the reflectivity. Well struck, and the borders display honey-gold toning. Census: 23 in 61 Prooflike, 50 finer (7/08). (#78725)

3936 1893-CC XF45 NGC. The 1893-CC is the final eagle produced at the Carson City Mint, and with a mintage of only 14,000 pieces it is also fairly scarce. Deep orange-gold patina covers each side of this lightly abraded piece. The details are above average, with impressive definition on the stars and hair. (#8726)

Lovely 1893-CC Eagle, AU53

3937 1893-CC AU53 NGC. A popular issue from the final year of the Carson City Mint, the 1893-CC has a diminutive mintage of just 14,000 pieces. Pleasing orange-gold patina endows this well-defined example, with plenty of luster in the fields. A shallow dig on the right side of the 3 in the date is the only mark worthy of mention. Census: 29 in 53, 76 finer (7/08). (#8726)

3938 1893-O MS62 PCGS. The 1893-O eagle has a low mintage of only 17,000 coins, and it is seldom seen in grades finer than the present piece. Eye-catching, lightly frosted luster shines beneath the yellow-orange patina. Scattered abrasions are typical of the grade, and this example boasts a powerful strike. A lamination is noted at the rim by the eagle's left (facing) wing. (#8727)

Conditionally Elusive 1896 Gold Eagle, MS63

3939 1896 MS63 PCGS. Sharply struck and intensely lustrous, with lovely, variegated yellow-gold, steel-green, and copper-rose coloration and nicely preserved surfaces for the grade. This Philadelphia Mint issue had a low mintage of just 76,200 pieces, and remains conditionally elusive in grades any finer than MS63. (#8735)

3940 1896 MS61 Prooflike NGC. Well struck and impressively reflective with glossy, typically abraded fields. The 1896 is low mintage, but because of its Philadelphia Mint origin, it carries little premium. Prooflike pieces are rare. Census: 3 in 61 Prooflike, 0 finer (7/08). (#78735)

3941 1897 MS64 NGC. Although its mintage of slightly over 1 million pieces suggests a common issue, the 1897 is conditionally scarce in Choice Uncirculated and finer. Rose and yellow-gold patina overlies the eye-catching satiny luster. NGC reports a mere 24 examples finer (7/08). (#8737)

3942 1897-O MS62 PCGS. CAC. The 1897-O has a mintage of 42,500 pieces yet it is even scarcer than the 1893-O, of which 17,000 pieces were struck. As is the rule for New Orleans eagles from this era, the issue is available in abraded Mint State, but attractive pieces without heavy marks are hard to locate. This boldly struck and lustrous apricot-gold example should please the dedicated but budget-minded specialist. Population: 37 in 62, 34 finer (8/08). (#8738)

Delightful 1899-S Eagle, Select Mint State

3943 **1899-S MS63 PCGS.** The 1899-S is another issue that is relatively available through low Uncirculated grades, but becomes quite difficult to locate in higher grades. Light rose-red patina in the fields accents the yellow-gold that drapes both sides. Dazzling cartwheel luster gives this piece excellent eye appeal. PCGS has certified only 17 specimens finer (8/08). (#8744)

3944 **1901 MS64 NGC.** A frosty and lustrous yellow-gold ten with lovely rose accents in the fields. This nearly fully struck example shows scattered grazes typical for the grade, but has no significant marks. A handsome representative for the type collector. (#8747)

3945 **1901 MS64 PCGS.** Original peach-gold toning graces this lustrous and powerfully impressed Choice gold type coin. Minor field grazes are all that preclude an even finer assessment. (#8747)

3946 **1901 MS64 PCGS. CAC.** This decisively struck Choice ten dollar piece has exemplary luster and attractive surfaces. The 1901 is among the more available issues of the type, but high quality examples are always in demand. (#8747)

Challenging 1901-O Eagle, MS63

3947 **1901-O MS63 NGC.** As noted by Winter in the second edition of his *Gold Coins of the New Orleans Mint, 1839-1909* (2006), this later gold eagle issue has become relatively available in grade levels up to and including MS62. Select Mint State specimens, however, like the currently offered example, remain conditionally scarce. This piece has a richly satiny appearance, with appealing green-gold coloration and a very clean obverse. The reverse shows a handful of minor field marks that limit the grade. Census: 22 in 63, 6 finer (8/08). (#8748)

Lovely Gem 1901-S Eagle

3948 **1901-S MS65 PCGS.** An enormous mintage exceeding 2.8 million coins in San Francisco in 1901 ensured that this piece would one day assume a favored position among collectors of high-grade gold type. This lovely Gem example displays full cartwheel luster on both sides, and both the strike and the relative lack of abrasions make this a remarkable coin.
From The Bell Collection. (#8749)

3949 **1902-S MS64 NGC.** This Choice Liberty Motto ten has booming luster and a precise strike. The smooth, radiant pumpkin-gold surfaces offer glimpses of sea-green across the peripheries. (#8751)

3950 **1903 MS63 PCGS.** Dazzling luster complements the pleasing yellow-gold patina. This sharply struck specimen has scattered abrasions, but all are insignificant. While the 1903 ten is common in low grades, it is surprisingly scarce is MS63. Population: 87 in 63, 44 finer (7/08). (#8752)

Outstanding 1903-O Eagle, Choice Uncirculated

3951 **1903-O MS64 NGC.** Numerous 1903-O eagles have returned to the United States from overseas bank vaults, which enables this piece to be obtained without much difficulty in grades up to MS63. It is, however, exceptionally difficult to locate just one numerical grade finer, with only 17 examples certified in any grade above Select. This is an excellent opportunity to acquire a seldom-offered Choice Uncirculated example. Enticing yellow-gold patina graces the surfaces and is complemented by razor-sharp design elements. Scattered light abrasions define the grade, but barely affect the flow of the dazzling satiny luster. Census: 5 in 64, 1 finer (7/08). (#8753)

Captivating 1906 Eagle, Choice Uncirculated

3952 **1906 MS64 PCGS.** Enticing satiny luster shimmers throughout the attractive yellow-gold surfaces. The strike is razor-sharp, and both sides have only trivial abrasions. Although the 1906 is relatively common in most grades, the number of survivors drops precipitously in grades above MS63. Population: 19 in 64, 7 finer (8/08). (#8759)

Handsome Choice 1906 Ten

3953 **1906 MS64 PCGS.** A penetratingly struck Choice representative that exhibits coruscating luster, unblemished surfaces, and light green-gold toning. Despite its Philadelphia Mint origin and its proximity to the end of the series, the 1906 is lower mintage and scarce as a near-Gem. Population: 19 in 64, 7 finer (8/08). (#8759)

Spectacular 1906-D Eagle, Gem Mint State

3954 **1906-D MS65 PCGS.** Eye-catching satiny luster shimmers beneath the charming yellow-gold patina. The details are powerfully impressed with only a trace of weakness on the hair above Liberty's ear. Several minute grazes do not affect the flow of the impressive luster. Population: 22 in 65, 3 finer (8/08). (#8760)

Conditionally Scarce 1907-D Eagle, MS64

3955 **1907-D MS64 NGC.** The 1907-D was the second issue from the Denver Mint, and is the final Liberty Head eagle. This attractive piece has fantastic satiny luster that shimmers across the yellow-gold surfaces. Several light marks are noted on the obverse, but the reverse is remarkably clean. The strike is sharp, and the eye appeal is excellent. Garrett and Guth (2006) write that while the mintage of more than a million pieces makes this issue seem common, it is actually fairly scarce in most grades. At the time of writing, they reported that no MS65 examples had been auctioned since 1994, but in our April 2006 auction we sold a Gem for nearly $11,000. This conditionally scarce piece would make a wonderful addition to any collection. (#8764)

PROOF LIBERTY EAGLES

Rare 1895 Eagle, PR61 Cameo

3956 **1895 PR61 Cameo PCGS.** In only three years between 1866 and 1907 did the production of proof Liberty With Motto eagles exceed 100 coins. In fact, it was 1885 before the annual mintage of proof eagles topped 50 coins. Walter Breen (1988) estimated 18-20 survivors of proof 1895 tens from a mintage of 56 pieces. With that in mind, it is interesting to look at current certification totals. NGC and PCGS combined list a total of 47 proof submissions for the date, just nine coins shy of the total mintage. It would be a remarkable situation if in the last century nearly all of the original mintage survived, but multiple grading submissions is a more likely explanation. In any case, the strong appeal of 19th century proof gold coins is undeniable, and this is a fine example. There are no major abrasions or spots, but a close look reveals numerous hairlines. Sharply struck devices contrast nicely against mirrored fields, and the honey-gold surfaces display a trace of orange highlights. Population: 1 in 61 Cameo, 4 finer (8/08). (#88835)

3957 **1906 PR67 ★ Cameo NGC.** In 1906, the penultimate year of the Liberty Head ten dollar series, the Philadelphia Mint struck a meager 77 proofs. These pieces have a diagnostic die dot at the center of the right curve of the 9 in the date, although the proof nature of the present specimen is unmistakable. Additionally, Breen wrote in his *Encyclopedia of United States and Colonial Proof Coins* that most specimens are impaired, and even those examples seldom come to market. This specimen, however, is not only tied for the finest certified, but is also virtually flawless.

Estimates vary of the total number of survivors of proof 1906 eagles, and current research indicates that around half of the original number has survived. Previously, Akers (1980) wrote that between 25 and 30 pieces are known, and in 1988 Breen estimated 30 to 35 examples have survived. As with most proof gold issues, the population data is unreliable because of resubmissions. NGC and PCGS combined report a total of 68 submissions in all designations. Only three pieces certified by NGC are considered Ultra Cameo and 20 have been labeled Cameo. Just three grade PR67 Cameo, with none finer, and two of those (the present piece included) have received the coveted Star designation (8/08).

Powerful deeply mirrored fields on this spectacular coin show impressive contrast against the frosted devices. It is difficult to ascertain what keeps this piece from NGC's Ultra Cameo designation and it is hard to imagine a specimen with a greater cameo appearance. Bright yellow patina graces both sides, although the highly reflective fields seem nearly black under a lamp. Careful examination with a loupe reveals only a couple of inconsequential contact marks and virtually imperceptible toning spots. This fully struck piece exhibits outstanding eye appeal.

The *Official Red Book of Auction Records, U.S. Gold Coinage, 2003-2007* indicates that there were 11 appearances of the proof 1906 eagle at auction during that five-year span, of which the two finest were graded PR65 Cameo by NGC. In our February 2003 Long Beach auction we had a PCGS PR66 Cameo specimen that was not sold. These records indicate the infrequency at which this issue appears at auction, and highlight the extreme rarity of a PR67 ★ Cameo example. This magnificent coin deserves a place in one of the finest collections. (#88846)

Important Gem 1907 Wire Rim Saint-Gaudens Eagle

3958 **1907 Wire Rim MS65 PCGS. CAC.** Before the pendulum of official sentiment would swing completely against pattern collectors later in the 20th century, the Mint tradition of making patterns available to collectors enjoyed a brief revival, spurred by the enthusiasm of President Theodore Roosevelt for the coinage designs of Augustus Saint-Gaudens. George Roberts, in one of his last official correspondences as Director of the Mint, mentioned Roosevelt's involvement in the production and distribution of the experimental pieces that would later become known as the Wire Rim, Periods variety. As quoted in Roger W. Burdette's *Renaissance of American Coinage 1905 - 1908*:

> "In connection with the new coinage I intend to also refer to the President's wish to have a number of coins struck from the high relief experimental dies. ... In considering the number authorized I would suggest that to strike only a few will be to give them a very high money value and very likely occasion criticism. ... It would be better, in my opinion, to strike several hundred and to at least allow the public collections of the country to obtain copies."

The traditional mintage figure of 500 pieces, however well-intentioned, is not nearly enough to keep up with today's demand for this beautiful issue, and Gems such as the present coin are particularly valuable and prized. The devices are pleasingly detailed and free of significant distractions, as are the satiny sun-yellow fields. The namesake wire rim is visible on each sides, though an arc above Liberty's head is the most prominent. Population: 45 in 65, 19 finer (7/08). (#8850)

3959 **1907 No Periods—Altered Surfaces—ANACS. MS60 Details.** At first glance, this appears to be an unabraded caramel-gold example. Close scrutiny under a loupe locates careful smoothing on the cheekbone. (#8852)

3960 **1907 No Periods MS61 PCGS.** A charming first-year representative of this popular series. Saint-Gaudens' original design was modified by Charles Barber early in the year and, among other slight changes, the periods bordering the legends were removed. The reverse of the present piece has a number of shallow marks, but the obverse is exceptionally clean for the grade. Delightful luster radiates from the bright yellow surfaces. Crisply struck save for a little softness at the centers. (#8852)

3961 **1907 No Periods MS61 NGC.** Subtle green-gold elements offer an interesting counterpoint to the otherwise brassy surfaces. Modestly marked for the grade with well struck central devices. (#8852)

3962 **1907 No Periods MS62 PCGS.** Charming yellow-gold surfaces and flashy luster catch the viewer's eyes immediately, and a careful examination reveals only insignificant marks on the high points. The strike is nearly full and the appeal is excellent. (#8852)

3963 **1907 No Periods MS62 NGC.** Various yellow-gold, orange, and rose shadings converge on this brightly lustrous first-year Saint-Gaudens eagle. Minor flaws appear in the fields and at the high points. *From The Menlo Park Collection.* (#8852)

3964 **1907 No Periods MS63 PCGS.** Vivid yellow-gold shadings combine with impressive luster on this Select representative. Well struck for the first-year issue with solid overall visual appeal. (#8852)

Outstanding 1907 No Periods Eagle, MS64

3965 **1907 No Periods MS64 NGC.** Wondrous satiny luster graces the yellow-gold surfaces of this impeccably preserved specimen. This sharply struck piece appears pristine, and a careful examination yields only a couple of trivial abrasions. The 1907 No Periods is a perennial favorite among type collectors, and this attractive piece would make an excellent representative. (#8852)

Lovely 1907 No Periods Ten, MS64

3966 **1907 No Periods MS64 PCGS.** The first regular-issue Indian eagle, after the two With Periods pattern coins were struck, although the latter are often collected as part of the regular series. This wonderful near-Gem is a frosty and brilliant yellow-gold piece with traces of deep orange patina on the highest design points. (#8852)

Handsome Gem 1907 Indian Eagle

3967 **1907 No Periods MS65 NGC.** Scintillating luster sweeps the uncommonly mark-free fields and devices. Boldly struck and beautiful. 1907 witnessed numerous major and minor changes to the ten dollar design, yet it would change again in 1908 to add the motto. Encased in a prior generation holder. (#8852)

Conditionally Rare and Highly Desirable
1907 No Periods Eagle, Superb Gem

3968 **1907 No Periods MS67 NGC.** The 1907 No Periods eagle was the third Indian Head type ten struck at the Philadelphia Mint. The first examples were special issues of Saint-Gaudens' original concept and were struck in limited quantities. These pieces, however, had a Wire Rim, which was considered a serious flaw by Mint officials, who realized that it would prevent the coins from stacking properly. After modifications to the rim were made, Charles Barber insisted—almost certainly out of jealousy—that production of these so-called Round Rim pieces be halted so that he could further alter the design. Barber made several minute changes, which included the removal of the periods that bordered the reverse legends.

Collectors familiar with Indian Head eagles know that these first business strikes were probably the best produced of any date in the series. From a mintage of 239,406 pieces, many have survived in high grades. While the population data shows that there are quite a few Gems available, it also reveals that that Superb Gem examples are extremely rare. These pieces are seldom offered at auction, and when they are, they cause a considerable stir. It is amazing that NGC and PCGS have each certified an MS68 example (8/08). Any collector lucky enough to own a specimen of that quality, however, would surely be reluctant to part with it.

Enticing satiny luster glides across the virtually immaculate surfaces. The surfaces are seemingly perfect, even under magnification. Pleasing yellow-gold patina embraces both sides and complements the powerfully impressed design elements. The 1907 No Periods is a favorite among type collectors because of its status as a first-year issue, its relative availability, and its attractive design. Any collector with deep enough pockets should own an outstanding representative of this issue. (#8852)

Notable Select 1908-D No Motto Eagle

3969 **1908-D No Motto MS63 PCGS.** Though this issue's mintage is comparable to the 1907 No Periods variety, it is far more elusive in Mint State grades, particularly Select and finer, where its price eclipses even that of the low-mintage 1908 No Motto ten. This strongly lustrous wheat-gold piece, housed in a green label holder, is well struck with few overt flaws. PCGS has graded 41 finer examples (8/08). (#8854)

3970 **1908 Motto MS62 NGC.** A Congressional mandate required that the IN GOD WE TRUST motto be restored to the eagle after it was omitted by Saint-Gaudens. Both No Motto and Motto types were struck in 1908, which makes this a popular year among type collectors. Delightful yellow-gold patina endows the minimally marked surfaces, with small streaks of darker toning throughout. Captivating luster highlights the powerfully impressed design elements. (#8859)

Pleasing 1908 Motto Ten Dollar, MS64

3971 **1908 Motto MS64 PCGS.** Pleasing luster exudes from both sides of this near-Gem With Motto ten dollar, and a well directed strike imparts strong detail to the design features. Each side displays pleasing apricot-gold color, with occasional hints of light violet, and some variegated toning on the lower portions. A few unobtrusive marks prevent Gem classification. (#8859)

Fabulous Gem 1908 Motto Ten

3972 **1908 Motto MS65 PCGS. CAC.** This heavily minted first-year Motto issue is generally available in grades through Select, though examples are elusive in Choice and scarce in Gem. This shining MS65 beauty has impressively lustrous surfaces, pale yellow-gold and pleasingly preserved. The striking definition on the central devices is bold. Population: 61 in 65, 35 finer (7/08). (#8859)

3973 **1908-D Motto MS60 NGC.** Both Motto and No Motto 1908-D eagles were struck, and although the former had a mintage of nearly four times the latter, it is actually slightly scarcer in Uncirculated grades. Charming bright yellow patina covers the surfaces, with a small patch of deep green toning around the mintmark. The hair and arrows are a little soft, and several marks on each side define the grade. (#8860)

Lustrous 1908-S Indian Ten, MS64

3974 **1908-S MS64 PCGS.** While the mintage of just 59,850 coins ranks the '08-S as one of the important issues in the Indian eagle series, enough are available in higher grades that nearly any enthusiast can own an attractive example. The lustrous and frosty surfaces are finely granular, an appearance that Jeff Garrett and Ron Guth note as typical for many examples of the date. The surfaces are brilliant yellow with hints of orange toning. Both sides have excellent design definition that adds to its exceptional aesthetic appeal. Population: 28 in 64, 32 finer (7/08). (#8861)

3975 **1909 MS62 PCGS.** A lustrous and only faintly abraded example of this lower mintage Indian issue. A sharp strike with just a hint of blending on the forehead curls. (#8862)

3976 **1909 MS62 PCGS.** Sweeping luster and lemon coloration ensure the eye appeal of this smooth and luminous example. A low mintage issue by Philadelphia standards. Encapsulated in a green label holder. (#8862)

Dazzling 1909-S Eagle, MS62

3977   **1909-S MS62 PCGS.** Magnificent satiny luster gleams beneath the pleasing yellow-gold patina. Several wispy abrasions are visible, although the fields are remarkably clean for the grade. The tips of the feathers on the headdress are a trifle soft, but the rest of the details are boldly defined. A prominent lamination is noted in the left reverse field. (#8864)

Condition Scarcity 1909-S Ten Dollar, MS64

3978   **1909-S MS64 PCGS. CAC.** The 1909-S is one of the most difficult issues in the entire Indian Head ten dollar series to locate in Gem condition. Even obtaining a near-Gem example will take patient searching. Strong luster adorns the peach-gold surfaces of this MS64 piece, and an attentive strike leaves nice detail on the design elements. A hair-thin mark on the cheek and another in the left obverse field keep from the MS65 level. Population: 42 in 64, 22 finer (8/08). (#8864)

3979   **1910 MS63 PCGS.** This Select Indian ten has dazzling luster and an assertive strike. Thorough inspection locates a faint graze on the cheekbone, but the preservation is nonetheless imposing. (#8865)

Elegant 1910 Eagle, Choice Uncirculated

3980   **1910 MS64 PCGS.** This attractive and carefully preserved piece would make an excellent type coin. Charming lemon-yellow patina drapes the surfaces, with a couple of orange toning spots noted on the reverse. The bold strike is highlighted by dazzling luster in the fields. PCGS reports 67 pieces finer, some of which are undoubtedly resubmissions (8/08). (#8865)

3981   **1910 MS64 PCGS.** A well-defined and shining representative of this popular Philadelphia Saint-Gaudens eagle issue, yellow-gold and wheat-gold with modest granularity in the reverse fields. Attractively preserved and surprisingly challenging any finer, with just 67 finer pieces known to PCGS (8/08). (#8865)

3982   **1910-D MS63 NGC.** A dazzling lemon-yellow representative with pleasing satiny luster. The strike is mostly sharp, and a slight scratch on Liberty's jaw is barely worthy of note. A wonderful type coin. (#8866)

Lovely 1910-D Eagle, MS64

3983   **1910-D MS64 NGC. CAC.** The most available date in the Indian ten dollar series, the 1910-D would make a perfect representative for a type collector. This piece has a delightful butter-yellow patina with a faint ring of olive-green in the periphery. Splendid satiny luster shines throughout the minimally marked surfaces. (#8866)

Appealing 1910-D Eagle, MS66

3984   **1910-D MS66 NGC.** David Akers states that the 1910-D is the most common branch mint Indian eagle. That seems to be true through the MS63 grade level, and even near-Gems are available with patience and a little searching. Gems are more difficult to locate, and Premium Gems are very scarce. The issue's availability makes it an outstanding type coin. Jeff Ambio recommends it as the best choice for a Denver Mint example in a type set by issuing mint.

   This example features radiant luster and the finely granular surfaces usually seen on this issue. The coin is fully struck, with fine detail in the hair and headdress feathers. A few minute marks on the Indian's cheek are noted for accuracy. A sharp-looking coin overall, with bright color and excellent eye appeal. Census: 47 in 66, 8 finer (7/08).
   (#8866)

Pleasing 1911-D Indian Head Eagle, AU58

3985 1911-D AU58 NGC. Sharply struck with crisp detailing on all of the headdress feathers, and on all of the eagle's leg and wing feathers. Just a trace of wear is evident on Liberty's cheekbone and on the eagle's shoulder. An appealing near-Mint example of this conditionally scarce issue, with smooth surfaces that are virtually unmarked. (#8869)

Desirable 1911-D Eagle, MS61

3986 1911-D MS61 NGC. Only 30,100 pieces of the 1911-D Indian Head eagle were minted, making this the lowest mintage of the With Motto series. As such, it is scarce and desirable in all Mint State grades. The honey-gold surfaces of this MS61 coin display soft luster and sharply struck design elements. Small marks are visible on the cheek and in the reverse fields. (#8869)

3987 1911-S AU58 ANACS. The 1911-S had a diminutive mintage of just 51,000 pieces, which is lower than all With Motto Indian Head eagles save for the '11-D. Flashy luster radiates beneath the pumpkin-orange patina. A couple of abrasions on each side are nearly imperceptible without a loupe. (#8870)

3988 1911-S MS61 PCGS. For many years the 1911-S was considered a great rarity in Mint State and while that has changed with the repatriation of numerous gold coins from Europe, this low mintage issue is still scarcer in high grades than most Indian Head eagles. Attractive yellow-gold patina graces both sides of this boldly defined piece. Scattered abrasions limit the grade, but all are trivial. (#8870)

Low-Mintage 1911-S Eagle, Select Mint State

3989 1911-S MS63 PCGS. Faint splashes of gray accent the butter-yellow patina that drapes the surfaces. The obverse is remarkably pristine for the grade, but the reverse has only a few pinpoint marks. With just 51,000 pieces struck, the 1911-S has the second-lowest mintage in the series. Encased in a green label PCGS holder. Population: 17 in 63, 55 finer (8/08). (#8870)

Frosty 1912 Indian Ten, MS64

3990 1912 MS64 PCGS. Frosty olive-gold surfaces and bold design motifs on this near-Gem immediately greet the connoisseur's eye. Both sides have faint pinkish toning to further enhance its eye appeal. PCGS has only certified 31 finer examples of this conditionally rare issue. (#8871)

Remarkable 1913 Eagle, Near-Gem

3991 1913 MS64 NGC. Magnificent butter-yellow patina covers the surfaces of this resplendent specimen. Several light grazes on Liberty's cheek limit the grade, but they barely affect the impressive eye appeal. The reverse is particularly stunning with vibrant streaks of orange and pale green across the eagle. This razor-sharp, near-Gem example would make an ideal type coin. (#8873)

Gem 1914 Indian Ten

3992 1914 MS65 NGC. The bright honey-gold surfaces are illuminated by intense mint frost over both sides. The fields have a distinctly matte-like texture, and the devices are crisply struck, with just a trace of softness noted on the hair detail beneath LIBE. Impressively preserved, with only two or three small milling marks observed on the eagle's back. Census: 41 in 65, 9 finer (7/08). (#8875)

3993 1914-D MS62 PCGS. CAC. This is a bright, satiny piece with matte-like fields and minimally abraded surfaces overall, for the grade. An appealing yellow-gold example that would admirably as a type representative. (#8876)

3994 1914-S AU58 ICG. A trace of rub keeps this lustrous and minimally marked piece from Mint State. The strike is a little weak at the centers, but is otherwise sharp. One of just 208,000 coins minted. (#8877)

3995 1915 MS63 PCGS. A boldly struck example with original honey-gold and aqua toning. Luster is comprehensive, and the reverse is well preserved. Moderate marks are concealed within the hair. Encased in a green label holder. (#8878)

Sharp 1915-S Ten Dollar, AU58

3996 1915-S AU58 NGC. Most of the 59,000-piece 1915-S ten dollar mintage apparently ended up in the melting pots (Jeff Garrett and Ron Guth, 2006). This near-Mint survivor displays sharply struck devices, and retains considerable luster on its yellow-gold surfaces. A few minute circulation marks do not detract. (#8879)

3997 1926 MS64 PCGS. Charming yellow-gold patina drapes the surfaces of this carefully preserved piece, with splendid satiny luster throughout. This sharply struck specimen is encapsulated in a green label PCGS holder. (#8882)

3998 1926 MS64 PCGS. Strongly detailed, particularly on the high points, which often appear weak for examples of this popular type issue. The yellow-gold fields sport impressive luster. (#8882)

3999 1926 MS64 PCGS. This green-gold Choice Indian ten has exemplary luster, and is perhaps kept from a finer grade by only a hair-thin vertical line to the right of the mouth. Certified in a green label holder. (#8882)

4000 1926 MS64 PCGS. This well struck eagle exhibits pleasing luster emanating from greenish-gold surfaces. Some light handling marks keep from a higher grade. (#8882)

4001 1926 MS64 NGC. A sharply struck and lightly abraded representative. There is a peculiar die defect on Liberty's chin. Exquisite satiny luster throughout gives this piece wonderful eye appeal. (#8882)

Condition Rarity 1926 Eagle MS66

4002 1926 MS66 NGC. As a date, the 1926 eagle is the second most common of all the Indian Head ten dollar gold coins. Gems are not difficult to locate. However, the situation changes dramatically at the MS66 level. In *The Official Red Book of Auction Records 1994-2003*, Jeff Garrett and John Dannreuther list only three auction appearances of a 1926 MS66 in the entire ten-year period. The 1926 eagle defines condition rarity!

The present coin is a particularly pleasing example of this Premium Gem rarity. The fields are virtually free of abrasions, with only a short "dig" above D in the denomination to serve as a pedigree marker. The obverse displays thick, frosted mint luster with intense red-gold color and generous portions of lilac interspersed over each each side. The strike is strong and crisp overall with all of the details of Saint-Gaudens beautiful design shown to best advantage. This exquisite Premium Gem eagle represents the highest goal a collector can aspire to for this date (#8882)

Fabulous Premium Gem 1926 Eagle

4003 1926 MS66 NGC. The 1926, with its mintage of slightly over a million pieces, is one of the most famous and popular type issues among Saint-Gaudens eagles, particularly through Choice grades; interestingly enough, while a handful of Superb Gem coins are known for other issues in the series, the finest grade for a 1926 eagle is MS66, according to both NGC and PCGS (8/08). This beauty certified by the former firm is well-defined with elegant luster. The yellow-gold fields and devices show none of the overt flaws that appear so often on lesser examples. Spectacular in all respects. (#8882)

4004 1932 MS64 NGC. The 1932 is a longtime favorite among type collectors, and this crisply struck eagle would make an excellent representative. Satiny luster creates a watery appearance on the surfaces, and gives this piece excellent eye appeal. A couple of light grazes define the grade. (#8884)

4005 1932 MS64 NGC. Rich apricot-gold patina adorns both sides of this near-Gem eagle, each of which displays shimmering luster and well struck devices. A handful of minute marks define the grade. (#8884)

4006 1932 MS64 PCGS. Fully brilliant and highly lustrous yellow surfaces with exceptional mint frost. A delightful example of the common date Indian eagle, the only collectible gold piece from the 1930s. (#8884)

Dazzling 1932 Indian Ten, MS65

4007 1932 MS65 PCGS. CAC. Housed in an older green-label PCGS holder, this 1932 eagle is an exceptional coin for the grade, with brilliant and frosty lemon-yellow luster on the obverse, and subdued buttery-yellow toning on the reverse. Considered a common date in the series, this issue is extremely popular with collectors as the only readily available U.S. gold coin of the 1930s. (#8884)

Frosty Gem 1932 Indian Eagle

4008 1932 MS65 PCGS. The glistening surfaces exhibit lovely, variegated khaki-gold and rose toning. The boldly struck design motifs show typical slight weakness on the hair detail below LIBERTY. A few small marks are noted on the reverse, but the obverse is blemish-free. PCGS has only certified 82 finer pieces (7/08). *From The Bell Collection.* (#8884)

Lustrous 1932 Indian Ten MS65

4009 1932 MS65 NGC. Potent luster illuminates this alertly struck gold type coin. Minor contact on Liberty's jaw and the center of the eagle merits only passing mention. Most gold issues from the 1930s are very rare, but the 1932 is the exception, within the budget of most numismatists. (#8884)

Appealing 1932 Eagle, MS65

4010 **1932 MS65 PCGS. CAC.** Apricot-gold and mint-green colors compete for territory on this radiantly lustrous Gem. Moreover, an impressive strike brings out strong delineation on the design features, including the Indian's hair and bonnet feathers and the eagle's plumage. Some minute reverse marks do not take away from the incredible eye appeal of this coin. (#8884)

Exceptional 1932 Gem Ten Dollar

4011 **1932 MS65 PCGS. CAC.** Although the 1932 is the most common issue of the Indian Head ten dollar series, this Gem specimen is especially desirable. The surfaces display outstanding luster and beautiful yellow-gold color. A well executed strike complements these attributes, and were it not for a few minuscule marks, this piece might well grade even higher. This will be a lovely coin for a high-grade type collection. (#8884)

LIBERTY DOUBLE EAGLES

4012 **1850 VF35 PCGS.** Dusky butter-yellow and khaki-gold surfaces show minor, scattered abrasions. Light to moderate wear is even across each side. The stars show well-defined centers. (#8902)

Choice XF 1850 Double Eagle

4013 **1850 XF45 PCGS.** Ever popular as the first year of issue, the 1850 double eagle is nearly as much a souvenir of the California Gold Rush as any 1851 Humbert or U.S. Assay Office octagonal fifty, as it is all but certain the denomination would never have come into existence were it not for the fabled grab for gold. Philadelphia was also the recipient of much of that "Forty-Niner" gold, which it promptly turned into double eagles. Numerous abrasions pepper each side of this still-lustrous coin, with attractive orange-gold coloration. (#8902)

Desirable 1850 Double Eagle, AU53

4014 **1850 AU53 PCGS.** Splendid olive-gold patina covers the lightly abraded surfaces of this lustrous coin. The details are boldly defined and there are no mentionable marks on either side. Despite a high mintage, the 1850 had a lower survival rate than many of the later issues. These pieces are now extremely popular as a type coins because of their status as the first regular issue double eagles. (#8902)

4015 **1850—Cleaned—ANACS. AU53 Details.** Upon rotation to a certain degree, a patch of hairlines appears on the cheek of this briefly circulated first year double eagle. Luster is extensive, particularly on the reverse. There are no heavy marks. (#8902)

4016 **1850—Cleaned—ANACS. AU55 Details.** The pale gold surfaces exude subdued luster in recessed areas, but the typically abraded fields are slightly bright and granular. Still a sharp representative of the first collectible date. (#8902)

Appealing 1850-O Twenty Dollar, XF45

4017 **1850-O XF45 NGC. CAC.** The 1850-O double eagle can be located in Extremely Fine and About Uncirculated, but is extremely rare in Mint State, that has a certified population of just three pieces. This Choice XF example exhibits a good amount of luster for the grade. Yellow-gold surfaces have a slight greenish cast, and display well defined motifs. The handful of light circulation marks are not detracting. (#8903)

Pleasing MS61 1851 Double Eagle

4018 **1851 MS61 NGC.** This satiny piece is generally yellow-gold on the obverse aside from a touch of reddish-alloy below the date, while the reverse offers considerable orange elements. Though a number of fine abrasions preclude a finer designation, this coin is appealing nonetheless. Census: 28 in 61, 36 finer (8/08). (#8904)

Delightful Choice XF 1851-O Double Eagle

4019 **1851-O XF45 PCGS.** Evenly worn across both sides, with delightful reddish-khaki color that increases the coin's eye appeal. With the near-absence of any noteworthy surface marks, this piece could have claims to a finer grade designation. A high-end Choice XF example of this popular early double eagle issue from the New Orleans Mint. (#8905)

Alluring 1851-O Double Eagle, Choice AU

4020 **1851-O AU55 PCGS.** Although common in low grades, the 1851-O becomes scarce in Choice AU and rare in Mint State. Nonetheless, it is relatively affordable compared to most New Orleans double eagles, which makes it an ideal type coin. Lovely orange-yellow patina drapes the surfaces of this minimally marked representative. Both sides exhibit delightful luster, and the reverse has captivating semiprooflike fields. Sharply struck save for a little softness on Liberty's hair. Population: 27 in 55, 25 finer (7/08). (#8905)

Lustrous AU55 Details 1851-O Twenty

4021 **1851-O—Cleaned—ANACS. AU55 Details.** Well-defined for this higher-mintage New Orleans double eagle issue with only minor, scattered marks on each side. The lemon-gold and green-gold surfaces display radiant, unnatural luster, as well as numerous minor hairlines. Still, this is a collectible and desirable survivor. (#8905)

4022 **1852/1852 VF25 NGC.** FS-301, Breen-7152. The date is clearly repunched directly north. An unblemished apricot-gold double eagle that still has traces of luster in protected areas despite noticeable wear on the portrait. (#8906)

4023 **1852 XF45 PCGS.** This yellow-gold Choice XF double eagle retains traces of luster in the protected areas. Save for highpoint wear on Liberty's curls, the design elements display nice detail. The expected number of contact marks are scattered over each side. (#8906)

4024 **1852 AU50 PCGS.** Peach-gold surfaces are light to moderately abraded. Relatively strong definition is apparent on the design elements. (#8906)

4025 **1852 AU53 NGC.** The yellow-orange surfaces are surprisingly vibrant. A pleasingly detailed coin for this early Philadelphia issue with only modest wear across the lightly abraded high points. (#8906)

4026 **1852 AU55 NGC.** Soft luster radiates from the lovely orange-gold surfaces. A few shallow marks are noted on Liberty's chin, but the rest of the abrasions are trivial. This sharply struck piece would make a wonderful and affordable example of an early Type One double eagle. (#8906)

Interesting 1853/2 Double Eagle, Choice AU

4027 **1853/2 AU55 PCGS.** FS-301. Numismatists have debated the nature of this issue for many years, and its status as an "overdate" has been quite controversial. Nonetheless, the bottom of the underdigit 2 is plain on this piece, and this rare variety is confirmed by the small die lump beneath the R in LIBERTY, which is present on all true 3/2 overdates. Pleasing yellow-gold patina endows the surfaces of this interesting specimen. The right stars have weak centrils, but the rest of the details are crisply defined. Captivating luster gives this piece great eye appeal. Population: 13 in 55, 17 finer (7/08). (#8909)

4028 **1854 Small Date AU50 NGC.** Satiny overall with bits of pink coloration about some of the yellow-gold devices. Modest, even wear on the high points leaves the luster of the minimally marked fields virtually untouched.
From The Menlo Park Collection. (#8911)

4029 **1854 Small Date AU55 NGC.** 1854 double eagles were produced with two distinct date punches, and although the Small Date variety is more available than its Large Date counterpart, it can be difficult to locate in AU and finer grades. Splendid orange-gold patina graces the surfaces of this sharply struck piece. (#8911)

Magnificent 1854 Small Date Double Eagle, AU58

4030 **1854 Small Date AU58 PCGS.** Both Small Date and Large Date double eagles are seldom seen in Mint State, although the Small Date variety is more available. Peppered abrasions on the yellow-gold surfaces are entirely inconsequential. Dazzling luster shines across both sides and complements the razor-sharp design elements. PCGS has certified only 22 pieces finer (8/08). (#8911)

4031 **1854-S Broken A AU53 PCGS.** Ex: *S.S. Central America.* 17A. Slight friction is evident in the fields and over the high points, but this is an attractive coin for the grade. Undoubtedly much of the reason is because the coin rested for 130 years at the bottom of the ocean and was not subject to any further handling marks from circulation. There is considerable mint luster remaining in the reverse fields. Remarkably clean with rich orange-gold color. Also included are the Blanchard box, COA, and booklet. (#8913)

MS61 1855-S Double Eagle
Ex: *S.S. Central America*

4032 **1855-S Broken A, Full E MS61 PCGS.** SSCA 6262. Though the 1857-S double eagles that went down with the *S.S. Central America* make up the most famous issue salvaged from that ship, other dates were present in its official gold stores as well, including the 1855-S. The present survivor, unworn though with wispy abrasions in the lemon-gold fields and several marks on the cheek, is crisply detailed with impressive luster. Strongly appealing and immensely desirable. Comes with faux-book case, certificate of authenticity, and blue outer box from distributor Blanchard.

4033 **1855-S AU50 NGC.** Generally wheat-gold with scattered elements of straw and honey. This second-year S-mint twenty is well struck for the issue with light, scattered abrasions and minor, even wear. (#8916)

Remarkable 1855-S Double Eagle, AU53
Ex: *S.S. Central America*

4034 **1855-S AU53 PCGS.** Ex: *S.S. Central America.* SSCA 6449. Variety 14D, S Tilted Left. More than 300 1855-S twenties were found in the wreckage of the SSCA and a number of die varieties were discovered among those pieces. Pleasing straw-gold patina drapes the surfaces of this resplendent specimen. Powerfully impressed with great eye appeal. (#8916)

Charming 1855-S Double Eagle, AU55

4035 **1855-S AU55 NGC.** The 1855-S twenty is typically seen in Very Fine or Extremely Fine, and despite a mintage of 879,675 pieces it is actually rather scarce in About Uncirculated and finer. Delightful orange-gold patina overlies the surfaces of this crisply struck representative. There are no mentionable marks, and scattered abrasions are typical for the grade. (#8916)

Enticing 1855-S Double Eagle, AU58

4036 **1855-S AU58 NGC.** The 1855-S is elusive in Mint State, as a look at the population data reveals. NGC reports just 26 examples finer than this lustrous, lemon-yellow representative. Scattered abrasions define the grade, but all are trivial. A crisp strike further enhances the wonderful eye appeal. (#8916)

Important 1856 Twenty, AU58

4037 **1856 AU58 PCGS.** Sharply defined with fairly numerous abrasions that break of the flow of satiny luster on the obverse. Tinges of reddish patina cling to the devices. Often overlooked because of its P-mint origin, the 1856 is the most challenging Type One twenty from the Philadelphia facility and is particularly scarce in grades approaching Mint State and higher. Population: 8 in 58, 24 finer (8/08). (#8917)

Scarce 1856 Double Eagle, Mint State Sharpness

4038 **1856—Damaged—ICG. MS60 Details.** Bright lemon-yellow patina graces the surfaces of this lustrous and sharply defined specimen. There are a number of abrasions in the fields with what appear to be test marks on Liberty's cheek and between TWENTY and UNITED, which account for the "damaged" moniker. The 1856 is scarce in all grades, but is decidedly rare in Mint State. (#8917)

4039 **1856—Scratched, Cleaned—ICG. MS60 Details.** Although the 1856-S was recovered in some quantity from the *S.S. Central America*, the 1856 remains rare in Uncirculated condition. The obverse is somewhat bright, however, and appears slightly granular adjacent to the three obverse scratches, located near the chin, star 6, and the lower right field. (#8917)

4040 **1856-S XF45 NGC.** A slightly scuffy example that only shows a small degree of highpoint wear on either side. This issue is not rare, making it a good selection for type collectors. (#8919)

4041 **1856-S AU50 ICG.** Plenty of luster remains on this pleasing yellow-gold representative. Liberty's hair is a little soft, but the rest of the details are sharply defined. Myriad abrasions are on each side, but none merit specific mention. (#8919)

4042 **1856-S AU53 PCGS.** Considerable luster remains on both sides of this medium to dark yellow example. With an entirely different look from the recent treasure coins, we suspect that this piece may have predated the treasure discoveries of the past decade. (#8919)

Lustrous 1856-S Double Eagle, AU58

4043 **1856-S AU58 NGC.** Prior to the discovery of the *S.S. Central America* and several other shipwrecks, the 1856-S was virtually impossible to locate in Mint State and was scarce in About Uncirculated. Nonetheless, it remains difficult in grades finer than the present piece. Charming yellow-gold patina endows the surfaces of this crisply defined piece. Scattered abrasions limit the grade, but none are of any significance. NGC has certified a mere 32 examples finer (7/08). (#8919)

S.S. Central America MS62 1856-S Twenty

4044 **1856-S No Serif, Spiked F MS62 PCGS.** Ex: *S.S. Central America.* 17K. Fully struck in all areas, even the stars in the oval on the reverse show complete centril definition. Beautiful, frosted mint luster rolls over both obverse and reverse and is interrupted by minimal abrasions. The only one worthy of singular mention is in the obverse field out from the point of Liberty's chin. Accompanied by the complete Blanchard box and packaging. (#8919)

Stunning 1856-S Double Eagle, MS63

4045 **1856-S MS63 PCGS.** An absolutely stunning Type One double eagle, probably from the *S.S. Central America* treasure, although it is not designated as such. It has the familiar deep yellow luster with hints of orange and lemon yellow toning, the latter following the borders on each side. Prior to discovery of the *S.S. Central America* treasure, the 1856-S double eagle was an extreme rarity in Mint State grades. Today, enough are available that any date or type collector can aspire to own one, ranging from basic MS60, through Select MS63, to Gem MS65. (#8919)

Lustrous Near-Gem 1856-S Double Eagle

4046 1856-S MS64 PCGS. The 1856-S twenty is the third most available Type One double eagle, and there are many examples in Mint State grades. The large mintage of 1.2 million coins is not enough to account for the high degree of availability by itself. Twenty dollar gold pieces were not widely collected in the 19th century, and collecting by mintmark did not become popular until after 1893, with the publication of Augustus Heaton's famous treatise on the subject. The few collectors who did collect double eagles usually just purchased a proof example from the Philadelphia Mint every year.

The key to the high rate of survival for the issue is its inclusion in several shipwreck hoards. There were 1,085 examples of the 1856-S recovered from the *S.S. Central America*, many in Uncirculated condition. Another find off the coast of Florida in the 1970s yielded a substantial number of pieces. While not all 1856-S double eagles are pedigreed to shipwrecks, the romantic association of the issue to those dramatic events has greatly enhanced its reputation. The easy availability of Mint State examples makes the 1856-S an ideal type coin.

The present example is certainly no exception, with two examples certified in MS64 at PCGS and only a single coin finer. Wonderful cartwheel luster emanates from the orange-gold surfaces on both sides, and only the most minute abrasions—including one near Liberty's eye, but otherwise away from the focal points—appear to limit an even finer grade. The reverse is high-end for the grade. (#8919)

4047 1857 AU55 NGC. This is an unusually attractive Choice AU double eagle, for the grade. The luster and coloration are exceptional for an AU coin. Numerous small to moderate abrasions limit the grade. (#8920)

Scarce 1857-O Double Eagle, VF30

4048 1857-O VF30 NGC. The 1857-O is scarce in any grade with a mintage of just 30,000 pieces. While this number is actually an increase compared to some of the previous New Orleans issues, it is many multiples lower than the typical Philadelphia output. Myriad abrasions cover both sides, as typical for the issue, although none merit specific mention. Pleasing orange-green patina drapes the surfaces and is complemented by well-defined design elements. An affordable example of this scarce issue. (#8921)

4079 1857-S XF45 ICG. Moderately worn with pleasing orange-gold patina on each side. There are no significant marks and some luster still resides in the protected areas. A well-defined and affordable representative. (#8922)

4050 1857-S AU53 NGC. Honey-gold surfaces display wisps of tan, and traces of luster in the recessed areas. Light marks are scattered about, including a hair-thin one in the lower right obverse quadrant. (#8922)

4051 1857-S AU55 PCGS. The pale straw-gold surfaces offer shining luster, and the portrait shows only a hint of wear. Scattered marks cross each side, though a pair of small depressions at the lower neck are the only flaws deserving particular mention. (#8922)

Shining Choice S.S. *Central America* 1857-S Twenty

4052 1857-S Spiked Shield MS64 PCGS. SSCA 0275. A boldly detailed and attractive survivor from this popular shipwreck issue. Its vibrant luster is its prime attribute, with impressive swirls and flashiness on each side. The center of the obverse is generally pale yellow-gold, while the margins of that side and the reverse show deeper sun-yellow and orange-gold shadings. (#70000)

Vibrant MS64 S.S. Central America 1857-S Twenty

4053 **1857-S Spiked Shield MS64 PCGS.** SSCA 7326. Well-defined with powerfully lustrous yellow-gold fields that show hints of alloy at the margins. Strong definition, eye appeal, and preservation, even by Choice standards. This shipwreck treasure coin comes with a certificate of authenticity, faux-book case, and brown outer box from Blanchard. (#70000)

Fantastic Gem 1857-S Double Eagle
From the *S.S. Central America*

4054 **1857-S Spiked Shield MS65 PCGS.** SSCA 1095. Though a number of Select and even Choice survivors of the 1857-S double eagle issue came from the wreckage of the *S.S. Central America*, Gems were far more elusive and are highly prized by type enthusiasts, date collectors, and sunken-treasure devotees alike. This piece offers all the hallmarks of a *Central America* Gem, including the bold detail, radiant yellow-gold surfaces, and astonishingly high preservation with eye appeal to match. Comes with certificate of authenticity, faux-book case, brown Blanchard outer box, and the receipt for the coin's original purchase.

Gorgeous Gem 1857-S Double Eagle
Ex: *S.S. Central America*

4055 **1857-S Bold S MS65 PCGS.** SSCA 5728. Both sides offer the characteristically vibrant luster and sharp detail that distinguish the finest survivors from the wreck of the *S.S. Central America*. Seemingly flawless with delightful straw-gold centers that yield to slightly deeper yellow-gold close to the rims. Though thousands of fresh, virtually untouched double eagles came to light with the *Central America* salvage operations, few examples can match the eye appeal or condition of this delightful Gem. For the 20B or Bold S variety, PCGS has certified a mere 48 finer representatives (8/08). (#70001)

Brilliant 1857-S S.S. Central America Twenty, MS65

4056 **1857-S Narrow Serif MS65 PCGS.** Ex: *S.S. Central America.* Housed in the special gold label holder that PCGS created exclusively for these treasure coins. Bold details and frosty luster are hallmarks of this brilliant light yellow Gem. Both sides exhibit prominent splashes of deep orange patina along the right obverse and right reverse borders. The left outside serif of the U in UNITED is shorter and thinner than the others, giving the variety its name. The obverse has a few short spikes extending from the front edge of Liberty's neck. An outstanding example for the treasure hunter or connoisseur. (#70002)

Scarce 1858-O 'Genuine' Double Eagle In-House Graded AU Details

4057 **1858-O—Genuine—PCGS.** We give this coin an AU50 Details grade. The design elements are in receipt of a sharp strike, as Liberty's hair and the star centers are strong. The surfaces have a greenish-yellow cast, and have been subdued as a result of cleaning. A few minute contact marks are visible, as are light roller marks in the lower right obverse field. This issue is scarce in any grade, and is difficult to obtain any better than VF. A mere four coins have been rated Mint State (#8924)

Original Choice AU 1858-S Twenty

4058 **1858-S AU55 NGC.** A wide band of luster connects the reverse legends and outlines individual obverse stars. An original Choice AU twenty with relatively smooth surfaces aside from a slender mark on the cheek. Struck one year too late to participate in the famous hoard of the denomination recovered from the *S.S. Central America.* (#8925)

Luminous AU55 Details 1859 Twenty

4059 **1859—Damaged, Cleaned—ANACS. AU55 Details.** The well struck devices show little actual wear, and remnants of original luster cling to the reverse margins. The oddly luminous yellow-gold surfaces show a mix of significant abrasions, more shallow marks, and hairlines from a past cleaning. Still, a readily collectible example of this lower-mintage Philadelphia double eagle issue. (#8926)

Choice AU 1859-S Double Eagle

4060 **1859-S AU55 NGC.** A generous mintage exceeding 600,000 coins make this early S-mint issue widely available, although most examples are heavily bagmarked. This piece shows generous luster over the yellow-gold surfaces, but there are numerous small abrasions consistent with the grade and a short spate in circulation. *From The Menlo Park Collection.* (#8928)

4061 **1860 AU50 NGC.** Impressively lustrous, briefly circulated yellow-gold surfaces show only isolated abrasions. Softly struck as usual, though the overall eye appeal is strong for the grade. *From The Menlo Park Collection.* (#8929)

4062 **1860 AU55 NGC.** Splendid yellow and orange patina drapes the surfaces of this lustrous specimen. Scattered abrasions cover each side, but none are particularly detracting. A crisply struck and affordable representative. (#8929)

Worthy Near-Mint 1860 Double Eagle

4063 **1860 AU58 NGC.** The reverse appears fully lustrous, and obverse luster is diminished only on the cheek and open field. A charming near-Mint double eagle from the year of the Pony Express. No marks are noticeable apart from a small reverse rim ding at 5 o'clock. Subtle alloy spots on the shield will be ignored by most collectors. (#8929)

Lustrous Near-Mint 1860 Double Eagle

4064 **1860 AU58 NGC.** A lightly circulated example of this P-mint issue, one that generally averages only AU or so. There are a few moderate abrasions on each side, with pretty orange-gold patina and splendid mint luster radiating forth. The S.S. *Republic* recovery yielded quite a few hoard coins, including some spectacular Mint State pieces. (#8929)

Impressive 1860 Double Eagle, AU58

4065 **1860 AU58 NGC.** Although plentiful in circulated grades, the 1860 double eagle becomes scarce in Mint State. A trace of light rub keeps this crisply struck piece from Uncirculated. Lots of eye-catching luster radiates beneath the lovely butter-yellow patina. Numerous roller marks are noted across the obverse, with a number of die cracks around the periphery. There are no mentionable marks, and the eye appeal is excellent. (#8929)

Splendid 1860-S Double Eagle, Choice AU

4066 **1860-S AU55 NGC.** Garrett and Guth (2006) call the 1860-S a "workhorse of commerce" and explain that most coins seen have been heavily circulated. About Uncirculated examples can be difficult to locate, and this lustrous piece would make an excellent representative. Delightful yellow-gold patina drapes both sides. Sharply struck with no mentionable marks. (#8931)

Charming 1860-S Double Eagle, AU58

4067 **1860-S AU58 PCGS.** Most 1860-S twenties saw extensive circulation and today examples are surprisingly scarce in high grades. Numerous abrasions cover both sides, which is typical of the issue, but none merit specific mention. This piece is sharply struck with lovely yellow-gold patina. Plenty of luster throughout enhances the eye appeal. (#8931)

4068 **1861 XF45 PCGS.** A boldly struck, olive-orange example with significant luster in the protected areas. Although there are numerous abrasions on each side, none are significant. A charming and relatively affordable type coin. (#8932)

4069 **1861 AU50 PCGS.** A crisply defined piece with yellow-gold and olive-orange patina on both sides. Myriad bagmarks cover the surfaces, but there are no marks worthy of individual mention. (#8932)

4070 **1861 AU50 NGC.** Lustrous light yellow surfaces with nearly full mint frost, broken only by slight wear and minor abrasions. A plentiful date, often chosen for type sets. (#8932)

4071 **1861 AU55 NGC.** Powerfully lustrous fields show scattered marks but none are worthy of individual mention. Delightful honey-gold patina coats the surfaces of this impressive Type One double eagle. (#8932)

4072 **1861 AU55 NGC.** A gorgeous Type One twenty with lovely lime-green and rose toning and considerable remnants of original mint luster. A grease streak extends from near obverse star 3 to just below star 5. Wispy hairlines are noted in the fields, but abrasions are minimal for the Choice AU grade level. (#8932)

4073 **1861 AU55 NGC.** Warm yellow-gold surfaces show undercurrents of honey. A briefly circulated, minimally marked example of this heavily minted issue, popular with type collectors. (#8932)

4074 **1861 AU55 NGC.** Nearly full luster and frosty lemon-yellow surfaces characterize this Choice AU early double eagle. Slight highpoint wear prevents a full Mint State grade, but it has the aesthetic appeal of a much higher numerical quality. (#8932)

4075 **1861 AU58 PCGS.** The 1861 double eagle is a perfect choice for a type collector. It is not only one of the most available Type One twenties, but it is also popular as a Civil War issue. This briefly circulated representative has a trace of softness on Liberty's hair, but the rest of the details are boldly defined. Scattered abrasions are typical for the grade, and none merit individual mention. Delightful yellow-gold patina drapes the surfaces of this lustrous piece. (#8932)

Spectacularly Toned MS61 1861 Twenty

4076 **1861 MS61 NGC.** With the highest production figure of any double eagle until the 1904 (and 1904-S) issues, the 1861 is nonetheless available in Mint State grades for a price, up through the MS65 level—and PCGS has certified a single, incredible MS67 example! This example has much appeal and exuberant luster for the MS61 grade, with beautiful, mellow red-orange patina deepening to amber near the obverse rim. A couple of tinges of ice-blue appear around the stars, and the reverse has a similar palette. The abrasions on Liberty's cheek preclude a finer grade, but this is a spectacular coin nonetheless in aesthetic terms.
From The Menlo Park Collection. (#8932)

Rare 1862 Double Eagle, AU53

4077 **1862 AU53 PCGS.** This Civil War-era twenty is one of the scarcest Type 1 double eagles from the Philadelphia Mint with a mintage of just 92,098 pieces. Adding to its elusiveness, this issue was notably absent from all of the recently discovered shipwrecks save for the S.S. *Republic*, which had only nine examples. Delightful luster radiates beneath the yellow-gold patina that covers the surfaces of the present piece. Liberty's hair is a trifle soft, but the rest of the details are powerfully impressed. Myriad abrasions are typical for the grade, and none merit specific mention. A better example of this rare issue. Population: 8 in 53, 14 finer (7/08). (#8937)

4078 **1863-S XF40 NGC.** Charming yellow-orange patina graces both sides of this early double eagle. Significant luster remains in the recesses, especially considering the grade. Myriad marks cover the surfaces, but none are of any consequence. Housed in an old NGC holder. (#8940)

4079 **1863-S—Altered Surfaces—ANACS. AU55 Details.** A color and texture change near the bust tip suggests mechanical enhancement, but this Civil War double eagle has plentiful remaining luster, particularly on the reverse. (#8940)

S.S. *Republic* 1863-S Twenty, MS61

4080 **1863-S MS61 PCGS.** Ex: *S.S. Republic.* Large S. The mintmark is positioned close to the tail feathers, with its left serif over the left upright of the N. Two different treasure discoveries, those of the *S.S. Brother Jonathan* and the *S.S. Republic*, are responsible for nearly all of the higher grade examples of the date that exist today. This frosty and lustrous light yellow specimen has a few scattered marks on each side that prevent a higher grade, but it presents excellent eye appeal. Population: 58 in 61, 52 finer (7/08). (#8940)

Lovely 1864 Double Eagle, AU58

4081 **1864 AU58 NGC.** An impressive example of the elusive 1864 double eagle that survived the hoarding activities during and after the Civil War. Perhaps some 19th century coin collector set this piece aside for today's collectors. The surfaces are almost fully lustrous with rich orange-gold patina. NGC has only certified eight finer examples. (#8941)

4082 **1864-S AU53 NGC.** Despite a relatively high mintage (more than 3/4 million pieces), the '64-S was once one of the scarcest Type I Liberty double eagles, judging by condition rarity. Since the recovery of the SS *Brother Jonathan* and SS *Republic* shipwrecks, this issue is much easier to locate in grades higher than XF. This piece is slightly bright, probably due to long-term immersion in sea water, but overall it is quite an attractive piece for the grade. (#8942)

4083 **1864-S—Cleaned—ANACS. AU53 Details.** A gentle cleaning minimally detracts from this delightful yellow-gold representative. Myriad abrasions cover each side, but none are particularly bothersome. Boldly struck with traces of luster in the margins. (#8942)

Delightful 1864-S Double Eagle, Choice AU

4084 **1864-S AU55 NGC.** Prior to the discoveries of the *S.S. Brother Jonathan* and the *S.S. Republic*, the 1864-S double eagle was difficult to locate in grades finer than XF. Nonetheless, fewer than 300 examples were found on these shipwrecks, and there is great demand for high grade examples. This charming orange-gold specimen has no mentionable marks and plenty of eye-catching luster. The hair is a little soft, as usual, but the rest of the details are crisp. An attractive representative that would make a great type coin. (#8942)

4085 **1865 AU50 PCGS.** The final No Motto Philadelphia issue, struck during the final year of the Civil War. Luster illuminates protected areas. The obverse rim is slightly raised at 10 o'clock. In an old green label holder. (#8943)

4086 **1865-S AU55 PCGS.** Ex: *Brother Jonathan.* Splendid apricot-gold patina endows the surfaces of this lustrous example. The reverse is remarkably pristine for the grade, while the obverse has scattered light abrasions and a couple of shallow scratches. Sharply struck save for weakness on Liberty's hair. (#8944)

Resplendent 1865-S Double Eagle, Choice AU

4087 **1865-S AU55 PCGS.** Sharply struck with appealing apricot-gold patina. Peppered abrasions are typical for the grade, but they barely affect the impressive reflectivity of the fields. Prior to the discovery of the *S.S. Brother Jonathan* and the *S.S. Republic*, this issue was virtually unobtainable in high grades. Interestingly, even the great collector Harry Bass could only locate an Extremely Fine example. (#8944)

S.S. Brother Jonathan 1865-S Twenty, MS64

4088 **1865-S MS64 PCGS.** Ex: *S.S. Brother Jonathan.* The *S.S. Brother Jonathan* sailed north from San Francisco, bound for Portland, Oregon. After putting in at Crescent City, California, the ship resumed her voyage just after noon on Sunday, July 30, 1865. Sailing into a gail from the northwest, progress came to a standstill, and the ship turned around to return to Crescent City, but never made it as she crashed on a hidden rock, ripping the ship apart.

After a series of explorations, Deep Sea Research, Inc., located the treasure in the 1990s. Bowers and Merena handled an auction of 1,207 coins from the treasure in May 1999. Today, these treasure coins appear infrequently. This double eagle, minted just weeks before, is a wonderful orange-gold example with brilliant surfaces and extraordinary eye appeal. PCGS has only certified 23 finer pieces (8/08). (#8944)

Important Choice 1865-S Twenty
Ex: S.S. *Brother Jonathan*

4089 1865-S MS64 PCGS. Ex: *S.S. Brother Jonathan.* One of the more interesting features of Garrett and Guth's *Encyclopedia of U.S. Gold Coins* is its notation of the finest example of a given issue found in the collection of the Smithsonian Institution. In the case of the 1865-S, it is highly illustrative in showing how the discovery of the shipwrecks *S.S. Brother Jonathan* and *S.S. Republic* affected its availability in high grades: while coins in several Mint State grades are available to collectors today, the best example the Smithsonian owns is an AU50, likely donated decades ago and one of the finest pieces known at that time.

This well struck coin, at MS64 a grade that was unheard-of even a decade ago, offers smooth, creamy luster and peach-tinted straw-gold surfaces. The devices are minimally marked, and the overall eye appeal is excellent. PCGS has graded just 23 finer pieces (8/08). (#8944)

Desirable XF Details 1866-S No Motto Twenty

4090 1866-S No Motto—Scratched, Improperly Cleaned—NCS. XF Details. The No Motto 1866-S double eagle, one of several No Motto variants from that Mint created by the lag in transcontinental communication between San Francisco and Philadelphia, is a popular and elusive coin in all grades. This lightly worn piece, though significantly hairlined and scratched in the yellow-gold fields (particularly near the margins), remains highly desirable. (#8945)

Attractive 1866 Double Eagle, AU55

4091 1866 AU55 NGC. While common in low grades, With Motto 1866 double eagles are scarce About Uncirculated and rare in Mint State. Flashy luster radiates beneath the delightful yellow patina that drapes the surfaces. Scattered grade-defining marks are entirely inconsequential. Sharply struck with great eye appeal. (#8949)

Lovely 1866 Double Eagle, MS60

4092 1866 MS60 PCGS. This issue was the first to feature the IN GOD WE TRUST motto, which was added to the reverse above the eagle. Charming yellow-gold patina overlies the surfaces of this scarce issue. Numerous abrasions define the grade, but they barely obscure the dazzling luster. A sharply struck piece that is seldom seen in higher grades. Population: 10 in 60, 9 finer (7/08). (#8949)

4093　1866-S Motto AU50 NGC. A wheat-gold and honey-gold representative of the first S-mint Type Two double eagle issue. Minimally marked save for a handful of distractions, including an abrasion on the cheek and reed marks to the left of Liberty's neck. *From The Menlo Park Collection.* (#8950)

Lustrous AU53 1866-S Twenty

4094　1866-S Motto AU53 NGC. The first S-mint issue of the With Motto type, the 1866-S Motto double eagle is generally found when certified only about XF or Choice XF. This nice AU53 piece offers the expected light abrasions and slight wear for the grade, with good eye appeal and luster. (#8950)

Exquisite 1866-S Motto Double Eagle, AU55

4095　1866-S Motto AU55 NGC. The 1866-S With Motto double eagle had a mintage that was perhaps eight times as many as its No Motto counterpart, but both saw extensive circulation and are elusive in high grades today. Delightful luster glides across the yellow-orange surfaces of this sharply struck piece. Myriad abrasions limit the grade, but none merit specific mention. (#8950)

4096　1867—Scratched—ANACS. AU58 Details. A thin obverse scratch at 4:30 confirms the ANACS notation. Nevertheless, this early Type Two twenty retains most of its initial semi-prooflike luster, and the strike is above average. (#8951)

4097　1867-S AU50 NGC. Lightly worn with a shallow overlay of rose patination near some of the orange-gold devices. Though a scattering of the usual marks is present, none of these is individually distracting. *From The Menlo Park Collection.* (#8952)

Delightful 1867-S Double Eagle, Choice AU

4098　1867-S AU55 PCGS. Although easily located in most grades, the 1867-S is scarce in About Uncirculated and rare in Mint State. Garrett and Guth (2006) estimate that there are only about a dozen examples known in Uncirculated condition. Numerous bagmarks cover the orange-gold surfaces of the present piece, which is typical for the issue, but there is still plenty of luster in the fields. PCGS has certified only 50 examples finer (8/08). (#8952)

Popular Near-Mint 1867-S Twenty

4099　1867-S AU58 NGC. Subtle honey and peach shadings grace the immensely lustrous, minimally marked yellow-gold surfaces. Only a touch of wear visits the high points. Remarkably appealing for this Type Two S-mint double eagle issue, which is a condition rarity in Mint State. Census: 157 in 58, 19 finer (7/08). (#8952)

Eye-Catching 1867-S Double Eagle, AU58

4100　1867-S AU58 NGC. A great example of a Type Two S-mint twenty, this piece has only a hint of wear and a few shallow marks on Liberty's chin and cheek. Dazzling luster gives this piece great eye appeal and the reverse is particularly resplendent. NGC has certified only 20 pieces finer than this remarkable specimen (8/08). *Ex: Bowers and Merena (10/87), lot 2048.* (#8952)

Outstanding 1867-S Double Eagle, AU58

4101 **1867-S AU58 PCGS.** A trace of light rub keeps this highly lustrous piece from an Uncirculated grade. Only a select few 1867-S twenties have been certified by either NGC or PCGS in Mint State, which increases the demand for briefly circulated specimens. This sharply struck piece has no mentionable marks on either side and has tremendous eye appeal. (#8952)

Conditionally Scarce and Lustrous 1868 Twenty, Choice AU

4102 **1868 AU55 NGC.** The 1868 twenty had a mintage of less than 100,000 pieces, and most of the survivors typically grade Very Fine to Extremely Fine, partly because very few pieces were saved by contemporary collectors. This explains the scarcity of this issue in high grades, and the 1868 is seldom seen in Mint State. Pleasing butter-yellow patina graces both sides of this well-detailed and lustrous piece. There are a number of bag marks on each side, as typically seen, but none merit individual mention. Census: 31 in 55, 49 finer (7/08). (#8953)

4103 **1868-S AU50 NGC.** A lustrous AU representative with lovely lime and peach coloration. The smooth surfaces are largely unmarked, but typical wear is seen on both sides, for the grade. (#8954)

4104 **1868-S AU50 ICG.** Although the 1868-S is easily located in Extremely Fine grades and below, it is scarce in About Uncirculated and nearly impossible to find in Mint State. Significantly lustrous fields accent the pale yellow surfaces of the present piece. A number of abrasions are typical for the issue, and none are particularly prominent. The centers are a trifle soft, but the rest of the details are bold. (#8954)

Pleasing AU55 1868-S Double Eagle

4105 **1868-S AU55 PCGS.** A softly struck Type Two double eagle that offers surprisingly strong luster in the pale yellow-gold fields. Only minor wear is present on the high points, and relatively few flaws are noted in the fields. Despite this issue's mintage of over 800,000 pieces, it is elusive even in better circulated grades. Population: 49 in 55, 50 finer (7/08). (#8954)

1868-S Twenty Dollar, AU55

4106 **1868-S AU55 NGC.** The 1868-S double eagle is readily found in Very Fine and Extremely Fine grades. About Uncirculated pieces, such as the present Choice AU, are much more difficult to locate, and what few Mint State examples that have been certified are primarily MS60 and MS61. Yellow-gold surfaces exhibit tints of light tan, along with traces of luster in some of the recesses. Well struck, save for the usual softness in Liberty's hair and some of the star centers. Several minute marks are noted, especially on the obverse. (#8954)

Elusive, Appealing Near-Mint 1868-S Double Eagle

4107 **1868-S AU58 NGC.** The generous mintage exceeding three-quarters of a million coins belies the rarity of this issue in high grade. The average certified survivor grades only Choice XF or a bit better, and Mint State coins are "exceedingly rare," according to Bowers' reference on the denomination. It appears as though most examples circulated in the hardscrabble West of the era, while those that remained Uncirculated must have been melted at a later date. The present coin, unlike most circulated and Mint State pieces seen, is relatively free of bagmarks, and has wonderful eye appeal emanating from the orange-gold surfaces. The strike is somewhat weak on some of the peripheral stars on the obverse, but the abundant luster and premium appeal more than compensate. (#8954)

Attractive 1868-S Twenty, AU58

4108 **1868-S AU58 NGC.** Only a trace of wear is evident on the highest points of the design, with all other aspects sharp and fully lustrous. While a few surface marks are visible, they are entirely inconsequential. An early Type 2 example, this date like all Type Two double eagles is a major condition rarity in higher grades. This present piece has brilliant yellow luster. (#8954)

4109 **1869-S AU55 NGC.** A lustrous and impressive Choice AU example of this scarce San Francisco Mint double eagle issue. Modest highpoint wear and scattered small marks are noted on both sides. (#8956)

4110 **1869-S AU55 PCGS.** Though the lightly worn obverse is softly struck, the dusky yellow-gold surfaces are radiant, and the minimally abraded reverse offers better detail. PCGS has graded 93 finer examples (8/08). (#8956)

4111 **1869-S AU55 NGC.** Exceptional light yellow luster is evident on each side of this pleasing double eagle. The surfaces are lightly abraded as usual. (#8956)

Desirable 1869-S Twenty, AU58

4112 **1869-S AU58 NGC.** Moderately abraded surfaces include a few marks in the left obverse field of this lustrous orange-gold example. Perhaps technically Mint State, but downgraded due to the blemishes on each side. An early Type Two twenty, from an issue that is usually only found with considerable wear. (#8956)

4113 **1870-S XF45 NGC.** Dusky orange-gold patina covers the surfaces, which still have flashy luster in the margins. There are no noteworthy marks on either side and the details are boldly defined. *From The Menlo Park Collection.* (#8959)

4114 **1870-S AU50 NGC.** Sun-gold luster outlines the stars, letters, feathers, and rays. An attractive piece without singularly obtrusive marks. The 87 in the date is lightly recut. A Type Two issue rarely encountered in Mint State. (#8959)

4115 **1870-S AU53 NGC.** Lustrous light yellow surfaces provide a backdrop for splashes of coppery-orange toning, mostly on the obverse. Minor surface marks are expected. (#8959)

4116 **1870-S AU55 NGC.** Vivid butter-yellow surfaces offer glimpses of sun-gold and reflectivity at the margins. Only a trace of wear crosses the well struck devices, and the fields show few marks. (#8959)

4117 **1871 XF40 NGC.** Lustrous medium yellow surfaces retain traces of luster with splashes of vivid orange toning, especially on the reverse. A single tiny reverse rim nick is evident near 4 o'clock. (#8960)

4118 **1871-CC AU50 NGC.** For collectors today, the CC mintmark carries an undeniable appeal. Carson City's website (www.carson-city.nv.us) gives an appropriate summary: "All of these coins, whatever their rarity or market value, carry romantic associations with the Old West and the great bonanza years of the late 19th century." Discovery of silver and gold deposits, including the well-known Comstock Lode, encouraged local mine owners, abetted by Carson City founder Abraham Curry, to petition Congress for a Nevada branch mint in the early 1860s. Mint Director James Pollock's objections were ignored; Congress approved the Carson City Mint in 1863. Delay caused by the Civil War pushed coin production back to 1870. Even after the commencement of Carson City coinage, the mint's *raison d'être* was in jeopardy. Breen (1988) notes that "authorities and bankers preferred to ship bullion to San Francisco, alleging lower cost ... but their real reasons had to do with who would get the coveted contracts for transporting ores and finished coins." Falling silver prices and allegations of fraud combined with political maneuvering to end Carson City's Mint status in 1899.

The present example represents the second year of double eagle production at Carson City, and though 17,387 coins were minted in 1871, it is a scarce issue. As Garrett and Guth (2006) note, "By a large margin, the 1871-CC double eagle is the second-rarest Carson City issue. The mintage is small, and most of the production was destined for circulation in Nevada and the surrounding areas. Circulation is the key word, as most of the coins found of this issue are well worn and heavily bagmarked. ... The 1871-CC double eagle is scarce in Extremely Fine and About Uncirculated condition."

The lustrous honey-gold surfaces of this coin are accented by a blush of rose and occasional carmine highlights nearly hidden along the edges of the devices. Despite a brief trip through the pockets and cash drawers of commerce, wear is uniform, and there are no significant marks or spots. This is a wonderful Carson City double eagle, perfect for the advanced gold collection. (#8961)

4119   1871-CC AU58 NGC. Though the 1870-CC double eagle is substantially more elusive and exponentially more famous, the 1871-CC twenty is also challenging and low-mintage, though exactly how low is a matter of debate; the figure of 17,387 pieces prevails in the 2009 *Guide Book*, while Rusty Goe's *The Mint on Carson Street* cites a mintage of 14,687 double eagles, though he also acknowledges the higher figure.

Goe highlights an important reason why the earliest double eagles from the Carson City Mint are so elusive, particularly in better grades: while later issues often were shipped overseas and later repatriated, most of the earlier twenties circulated locally and changed hands frequently, wearing out and acquiring numerous abrasions. This is reflected in the certified populations: NGC has identified a mere six examples as Mint State, and PCGS has no coins graded above AU55 in its *Population Report* (8/08). NGC also shows a total of 21 pieces as AU58, though this number likely includes a substantial quantity of resubmission.

The Mint on Carson Street indicates that visual appeal is at a premium for this earlier issue: "Of the surviving 1871-CCs extant, few are inspiring, although there are several AU-55 and AU-58 examples which possess higher than average eye appeal ..." The present coin certainly matches that description, with gleaming yellow-orange fields that offer hints of reflectivity. The portrait and stars are well-defined for the issue, and though a handful of small abrasions are present on the obverse, they are trivial in context. Only a trace of friction stands in the way of an otherwise well-deserved Mint State grade. (#8961)

4120 **1871-S AU55 ICG.** While the 1871-S is common issue with a mintage of nearly 1 million pieces, it can be surprisingly difficult to locate in grades finer than AU. Briefly circulated with substantial satiny luster on each side, this piece has myriad abrasions on each side, as usual. The hair is somewhat soft, as typically seen, and the stars on the right side are also weakly struck. (#8962)

4121 **1871-S AU55 NGC.** Highly attractive with nearly full light yellow luster and relatively few abrasions for the grade. (#8962)

4122 **1871-S AU58 NGC.** Somewhat scuffy and lightly worn on the highpoints, but with considerable luster and attractive lime-green and gold coloration. The first three and last two obverse stars show weak centrils, but the other design elements are boldly defined. (#8962)

4123 **1871-S AU58 NGC.** A delightful near-Mint example with lustrous yellow surfaces. Faint wear on the highpoints and minor field marks prevent a higher grade. (#8962)

Impressive 1871-S Double Eagle, AU58

4124 **1871-S AU58 NGC.** Although common in low grades with a mintage of nearly a million pieces, the 1871-S can be elusive in high AU and is difficult to locate in Mint State. A trace of light rub on the obverse keeps this lightly marked piece from Uncirculated. The above-average eye appeal is enhanced by strong luster throughout. (#8962)

4125 **1872 AU55 NGC.** Vivid yellow patina drapes both sides of this powerfully impressed Choice AU representative. Numerous abrasions partially obscure the luster, but the fields are still highly reflective. A few tiny spots are noted on the obverse. (#8963)

4126 **1872 AU55 ICG.** A splendidly prooflike specimen although ICG does not designate it as such. The reverse is especially dazzling, and the reflectivity of the obverse is only partly obscured by peppered abrasions. Sharply struck save for softness on Liberty's hair and a couple of stars. (#8963)

4127 **1872 AU55 NGC.** Bright and semi-prooflike with meticulously defined devices that show above average eye appeal. Surprisingly undisturbed save for modest wear and a short line of reed marks at Liberty's neck.
From The Menlo Park Collection. (#8963)

4128 **1872 AU58 NGC.** The 1872 is typically encountered in VF or XF grades, and it can be challenging to locate a nice About Uncirculated example. Mint State pieces are decidedly scarce. There are a number of abrasions on each side of this yellow-orange representative, but they are generally minor. Dazzling cartwheel luster accents the sharply struck devices. (#8963)

4129 **1872 AU58 Prooflike NGC.** Magnificently prooflike fields instantly catch the viewer's eyes and highlight the sharp details. Scattered bagmarks in the fields are typical for the issue, but none merit individual mention. NGC has certified two pieces in 58 PL, with one finer (7/08). (#78963)

Choice XF 1872-CC Twenty

4130 **1872-CC XF45 NGC.** Although Carson City had been producing double eagles for only two years previously, the 1872-CC mintage was a respectable 26,900 pieces, and examples today are available in Choice XF to AU condition. This piece shows a single mentionable arcing scrape from below the chin, through the bust truncation and above the 72, but otherwise there are no singular marks. The yellow-gold surfaces display considerable retained luster. (#8964)

Delightful 1872-CC Double Eagle, About Uncirculated

4131 **1872-CC AU50 NGC.** A scarce issue in all grades with a mintage of just 26,900 pieces, the 1872-CC is particularly elusive in About Uncirculated and above. Bright luster radiates beneath the pleasing yellow-gold patina. The surfaces are lightly abraded save for a shallow dig to the left of Liberty's chin. That mark, and a small blemish to the right of the date, can be useful for future identification purposes. (#8964)

Remarkable 1872-CC Double Eagle, About Uncirculated

4132 **1872-CC AU50 PCGS.** In *A Guide Book of Double Eagle Gold Coins*, Bowers (2004) writes: "The 1872-CC double eagle is a rarity in the context of the Carson City series. Most extant pieces are VF, others are EF, but only a few are AU or finer." This briefly circulated piece would make an outstanding representative of this elusive issue. Lovely apricot-gold patina embraces the lustrous and minimally marked surfaces. The centers are soft, as typical, but the rest of the details are crisp. (#8964)

4133 **1872-S AU53 NGC.** Rich lemon-yellow surfaces with mild abrasions that are expected for the grade, especially on a large double eagle gold piece. (#8965)

4134 **1872-S AU55 NGC.** A challenging issue, especially at AU or higher grades. This piece has a rather subdued appearance, and a few small marks on the obverse. A lightly worn Choice AU example. (#8965)

4135 **1872-S AU55 PCGS.** The bright yellow fields are decidedly prooffike, with exciting reflectivity that is minimally affected by light abrasions. Liberty's hair and a few stars are a little soft, but the rest of the details are bold. A handsome better-grade example. (#8965)

4136 **1872-S AU58 NGC.** A sharply struck and generally lustrous Borderline Uncirculated Type Two twenty. The reverse has few marks, while the left obverse is typically abraded, as is the obverse rim at 1:30 and 7 o'clock. (#8965)

4137 **1872-S AU58 NGC.** An attractive example with splashes of pale orange toning over light yellow surfaces. The mintmark is left of its normal position, over the left half of N in TWENTY. (#8965)

Important 1872-S Twenty, MS61

4138 **1872-S MS61 PCGS.** Lustrous and frosty light yellow surfaces with splashes of deeper patina on both sides. A trace of green adds to its overall appeal. Like many west coast issues of its time, the 1872-S double eagle had a high mintage of 780,000 coins, but a small survival rate in high grades. Population: 22 in 61, 4 finer (7/08). (#8965)

4139 **1873 Open 3 MS61 PCGS.** A frosty and highly lustrous Mint State piece with excellent eye appeal. Both sides have brilliant yellow surfaces with traces of darker patina. (#8967)

4140 **1873 Open 3 MS61 ICG.** An unworn wheat-gold representative of the later Open 3 logotype, well struck and appealing despite numerous fine abrasions. A handful of more significant marks dot the fields. (#8967)

4141 **1873 Open 3 MS61 NGC.** A frosty and brilliant yellow-gold example with excellent design definition and excellent surfaces for the grade. Although one of the common dates among the Type Two twenties, any Liberty double eagle of the middle design type is desirable in MS60 or finer grade. (#8967)

Dazzling 1873 Open 3 Double Eagle, MS62

4142 **1873 Open 3 MS62 PCGS.** Wafts of charcoal-gray add color to Liberty's cheek, but both sides are mostly yellow-gold. Myriad abrasions cover the obverse, while the reverse has significantly fewer marks. The sharp strike is complemented by flashy luster. This charming piece is housed in a green label PCGS holder. (#8967)

Lightly Circulated 1873-CC Double Eagle, XF40

4143 **1873-CC XF40 NGC.** This XF Carson City representative exhibits a good amount of luster in the recessed areas for the grade. Additionally, the design elements are generally well defined, including the obverse star centers and the eagle's plumage. While the yellow-gold surfaces reveal some circulation marks, they are not as deep or detracting as usually seen on '73-CC survivors. All in all, a rather nice specimen. (#8968)

Scarce 1873-CC Twenty Dollar, AU53

4144 **1873-CC AU53 NGC.** The 1873-CC double eagle (22,410 mintage) is usually found in Extremely Fine or About Uncirculated condition. Douglas Winter, in his *Carson City Mint* reference, writes that this issue has become more available due to the discovery of some small hoards in the 1990s, but is still scarce in the lower to middle AU grades. This AU53 example is relatively well struck, showing strong radials in all obverse stars. Honey-gold surfaces display races of luster in the protected areas. A number of minute marks are scattered over each side, which is typical for this issue. (#8968)

Attractive 1873-S Closed 3 Twenty Dollar, MS62

4145 **1873-S Closed 3 MS62 NGC.** This variety is rarer than its Open 3 counterpart. An attractive blend of apricot-gold and mint-green enriches the lustrous surfaces of the present offering. This is a well struck piece, especially on the star radials and the eagle's plumage. A handful of minor marks define the grade. (#8969)

4146 **1873-S Open 3 XF40 PCGS.** Incredible amounts of luster remains in the fields, especially on the reverse, which is truly exceptional. This well-defined representative has no marks of any significance and pleasing olive-gold patina. A small lamination is noted to the lower left of the bust. (#8979)

Lovely 1873-S Open 3 Double Eagle, AU58

4147 **1873-S Open 3 AU58 NGC.** Although the Open 3 Philadelphia issue is common, dies with the new date logotype had to travel cross-country to San Francisco. By that time, most of the million-plus mintage for the year had already been struck with Closed 3 dies, which made its Open 3 counterpart significantly scarcer. This lemon-gold example has a light pinscratch on the cheekbone and a faint grease streak beneath the hair bun. (#8979)

Sharp 1873-S Open 3 Double Eagle, AU58

4148 **1873-S Open 3 AU58 NGC.** A good amount of luster is visible in the recessed areas of the bright yellow-gold surfaces laced with hints of light tan. The star centers and the eagle's feathers are sharply defined, save for the typical softness in portions of Liberty's hair. The expected light circulation marks are noted. (#8979)

Mint State 1874 Double Eagle

4149 **1874 MS61 PCGS.** According to Garrett and Guth (2006): "The vast majority of the 1874 double eagles seen fall into the Very Fine to About Uncirculated range." This Mint State specimen offers moderately marked surfaces that display intense satiny luster and straw-gold coloration. The design elements are sharply struck on both sides. Just 22 pieces have been graded finer than MS61, by PCGS (8/08). (#8970)

4150 **1874-CC VF35 PCGS.** This Carson City twenty shows moderate wear on Liberty's curls, but the portrait lacks any detrimental marks. Substantial luster remains, particularly on the reverse. *From The Menlo Park Collection.* (#8971)

4151 **1874-CC XF40 NGC.** Impressive luster remains in the protected areas and accents the mostly yellow-orange patina. A few small patches of charcoal toning add color to the reverse. Boldly defined with no mentionable marks. (#8971)

4152 **1874-CC XF40 PCGS.** Despite the modest wear on each side, this pleasing CC double eagle has attractive medium yellow surfaces that are surprisingly free of blemishes. (#8971)

Pleasing 1874-CC Double Eagle, Choice XF

4153 **1874-CC XF45 PCGS.** Light yellow patina overlies the surfaces of this moderately circulated representative. Liberty's hair and several stars are soft, but the reverse is crisply defined. Scattered abrasions limit the grade, but none are particularly bothersome. A collectible issue with a mintage of 115,085 pieces. (#8971)

4154 **1874-CC—Cleaned—ICG. XF45 Details.** A softly struck khaki-gold survivor from this Type Two Carson City double eagle issue. Moderately hairlined with whispers of original luster that cling to the margins. (#8971)

Early Carson City Twenty, 1874-CC AU53

4155 **1874-CC AU53 PCGS.** This Carson City Mint double eagle is moderately abraded, with the most noticeable marks on Liberty's chin, along with a luster graze in the field before her portrait. Boldly struck and satiny, with plenty of luster for the grade. Deep khaki-orange coloration adorns both sides. A scarce issue in AU condition or finer. This example is housed in a green label PCGS holder. (#8971)

Lustrous Choice AU 1874-CC Twenty

4156 **1874-CC AU55 NGC.** The first CC-mint double eagle issue that is generally available, although the average certified survivor only comes in at XF45 or so. This Choice AU piece boasts strong luster over lightly abraded orange-gold fields, with considerable prooflikeness in the fields and excellent eye appeal. (#8971)

4157 **1874-S AU58 PCGS.** This briefly circulated example has charming yellow and orange patina on each side. Peppered abrasions minimally affect the flow of the impressive luster. A nice, well-defined representative. (#8972)

4158 **1874-S AU58 NGC.** Light yellow-gold and wheat-gold shadings blend on each side of this S-mint double eagle. Moderately abraded overall with just a hint of friction on the well struck high points. (#8972)

4159 **1874-S AU58 NGC.** A brilliant near-Mint piece with lustrous light yellow surfaces and subtle traces of pink patina. (#8972)

Attractive 1874-S Double Eagle, MS61

4160 **1874-S MS61 PCGS. CAC.** Bright lemon patina graces the obverse, which contrasts nicely against the orange-gold reverse. The obverse is particularly resplendent, although both sides exhibit impressive luster. There are no marks worthy of individual mention, and the strike is crisp. Garrett and Guth (2006) state that this issue is "very scarce" in grades finer than MS61. PCGS has certified 40 pieces finer, many of which are undoubtedly resubmissions (7/08). (#8972)

Appealing MS61 1874-S Double Eagle

4161 **1874-S MS61 NGC.** An unworn and pleasingly lustrous survivor from this Type Two S-mint double eagle issue, elusive despite a mintage of over 1.2 million pieces. Though the yellow-gold surfaces show numerous light to moderate abrasions, this well struck coin retains considerable eye appeal. NGC has graded 28 finer pieces (8/08). (#8972)

4162 **1875 MS61 NGC.** Delightful yellow-orange patina graces the surfaces of this crisply defined representative. Numerous abrasions are typical of the grade, but none merit individual mention. Sparkling luster gives this piece great eye appeal. (#8973)

4163 **1875 MS61 NGC.** Ample peach and yellow-orange shadings converge on this Philadelphia double eagle. Delightfully lustrous with fewer overt flaws than the designation might suggest. (#8973)

Lustrous MS62 1875 Double Eagle

4164 **1875 MS62 PCGS.** The double eagle mintage of 1875 is a generous figure approaching 300,000 coins, all the more remarkable when one considers that most of the other gold denominations produced in that pre-Centennial year range from the absurdly low to the nearly unique. The eagle, for example, saw a business strike mintage of only 100 coins, the smallest circulation strike emission of any gold coin.

This is a lustrous MS62 example of the double eagle, with glowing luster radiating from orange-gold surfaces and excellent overall eye appeal. At the MS63 level, the certified population thins out markedly.
From The Menlo Park Collection. (#8973)

4165 **1875-CC XF40 NGC.** Deep orange patina envelops the devices, which contrast nicely to the yellow-gold fields. Myriad abrasions minimally affect the significant luster that remains. The stars are soft, as usual, but the rest of the details are well-defined.
From The Menlo Park Collection. (#8974)

Exceptional 1875-CC Double Eagle, AU58

4166 **1875-CC AU58 PCGS.** While the mintage of the 1875-CC is similar to that of the 1874-CC, it is somewhat more available in high grades. This, however, is a remarkably lustrous coin with just a trace of light rub. The details exhibit above-average sharpness. There are a number of small abrasions, but the reverse is exceptionally clean. (#8974)

Unworn 1875-CC Double Eagle

4167 **1875-CC—Altered Surfaces—ANACS. MS60 Details.** Considerable frostiness clings to the portrait, and the eagle has generally appreciable detail. The primarily yellow-gold surfaces offer considerable luster, though the excessive purplish alloy in and around the reverse glory leads to questions about the coin's originality. Still, it displays beautifully. (#8974)

Pleasing 1875-CC Twenty Dollar, MS62

4168 **1875-CC MS62 NGC.** The Carson City Mint began producing double eagles in its first year of production, 1870. Of all the twenties produced by that mint the 1875 is considered the most common. But, as Garrett and Guth (2006) caution, "As with all With Motto double eagles, the availability drops drastically as the grade increases. The 1875-CC double eagle becomes scarce in MS-62 and MS-63." This coin is generally well struck, though there is softness in the details of Liberty's hair. Vivid luster reflects from red-gold surfaces, and there are no distracting spots or abrasions. This is a well-preserved and scarce example of Carson City gold; NGC has graded only 27 coins finer (8/08). (#8974)

Lustrous 1875-CC Double Eagle, MS62

4169 **1875-CC MS62 PCGS.** From an original mintage of 111,151 coins, the 1875-CC double eagle is the most common Liberty Head, With Motto issue from the Carson City Mint, according to Jeff Garrett and Ron Guth (2006). It should also be mentioned, however, that just 52 examples have been graded finer than MS62, by NGC and PCGS combined, as of (8/08). This piece displays luxuriant mint frost and boldly struck devices. A somewhat scuffy obverse keeps it from grading higher. (#8974)

Beautiful 1875-S Twenty, MS61

4170 **1875-S MS61 PCGS.** Although the obverse and reverse surfaces have quite a few abrasions, the rich green, yellow, and orange luster creates exceptional eye appeal. The 1875-S is a relatively plentiful date, although any Mint State Type Two double eagle is worthy of special attention from specialists. (#8975)

4171 **1875-S MS61 NGC.** Hints of pink and splashes of deep steel toning are present on this desirable, fully lustrous double eagle. (#8975)

4172 **1875-S MS61 NGC.** This Type Two twenty exhibits scintillating luster, and the strike is sharp aside from a few obverse star centers. Faint field grazes and an alloy spot along the left shield border determine the grade. (#8975)

4173 **1875-S MS61 NGC.** Lovely greenish-gold surfaces display a full quota of tiny abrasions, as expected for the grade. Although a tad flat at the peripheries, the central obverse and reverse are sharp. (#8975)

Condition Scarcity 1875-S MS62 Double Eagle

4174 **1875-S MS62 PCGS. CAC.** The 1875-S double eagle is available in Mint State, but usually only in MS60 or MS61. Douglas Winter and Michael Fuljenz (1999) write: "This date is very scarce in MS62 and it becomes very rare in MS63." The rich peach-gold patina of this MS62 example is imbued with tints of light tan. Generally well struck, save for the characteristic softness in Liberty's hair. A scattering of light grazes on the lustrous surfaces preclude the next highest grade. (#8975)

4175 **1876 MS60 PCGS.** The ephemeral Light Motto reverse, known only on this issue. Philadelphia also struck Heavy Motto twenties in 1876. Presumably, the Type Three design prevented further use of this minor subtype. Lustrous and precisely struck with the expected distributed field marks. Certified in a green label holder. (#8976)

4176 **1876 MS61 NGC.** A lovely Mint State example of the last of the Type Two Philadelphia twenties. Ample frosty luster characterizes the mildly abraded yellow-gold and wheat-gold surfaces. *From The Menlo Park Collection.* (#8976)

Well Struck 1876 Twenty Dollar, MS62

4177 **1876 MS62 NGC.** The last P-mint Type Two Liberty double eagle, and a Centennial issue. A well executed strike leaves strong definition on the motifs of this MS62 twenty dollar, including fullness in the star radials and the eagle's plumage. Minor softness occurs in portions of Liberty's hair, as usually seen. Small contacts and grazes define the grade. A couple of light grease marks are visible on the reverse. (#8976)

Attractive 1876 Double Eagle, MS62

4178 **1876 MS62 PCGS. CAC.** The design elements display relatively sharp definition, except for the usual softness in Liberty's hair. Attractive apricot-gold coloration is seen on both sides. While a scattering of small contact marks results in occasional localized interruption of the luster flow, the coin does not possess the "numerous deep, detracting marks" that Douglas Winter and Michael Fuljenz (1999) say are found on the typical 1876. This is likely one of the reasons for the CAC label. (#8976)

4179 **1876-CC—Improperly Cleaned—NCS. XF Details.** An inoffensively cleaned Carson City Type Two twenty that possesses plentiful luster and typically abraded fields. (#8977)

4180 **1876-CC AU50 NGC.** Impressively radiant yellow-gold surfaces despite modest wear across the high points. Well struck on the reverse, though the portrait shows more typical softness. Light abrasions overall. (#8977)

4181 **1876-CC AU50 PCGS. CAC.** Luminous and well struck for this final Carson City Type Two twenty. Minor elements of alloy appear at the high points of the otherwise butter-yellow surfaces, which show minor, scattered flaws. (#8977)

4182 **1876-CC AU53 NGC.** Splendid semiprooflike luster shines beneath the yellow-orange patina. The centers are somewhat soft, but the peripheral details are boldly defined. This lovely example is one of 138,441 pieces minted. (#8977)

Scarce 1876-CC Twenty Dollar AU55

4183 **1876-CC AU55 NGC.** This CC-mint twenty offers light orange toning and a pleasantly unabraded appearance. Luster glimmers from design elements. Wear on the wingtips requires a glass to observe. Problem-free for the grade, and a quality collector coin from our nation's Centennial year. (#8977)

Pleasing Near-Mint 1876-CC Twenty

4184 **1876-CC AU58 NGC.** A Type Two Carson City twenty with pleasantly unblemished surfaces. Only a trace of wear on the cheek and diminished luster across the open fields deny a Mint State assessment. The highest mintage issue from the Nevada facility, but the production was less than one-tenth that of the 1876-S. (#8977)

Brilliant 1876-CC Twenty, AU58

4185 **1876-CC AU58 NGC.** At first glance, this beauty seems to be fully Mint State, with traces of highpoint wear only visible through careful scrutiny. Light abrasions in the fields are typical of these large gold coins, in this case having no singularly distracting marks. Nearly full brilliant yellow-gold luster is present on frosty surfaces. (#8977)

Lustrous AU58 1876-CC Twenty

4186 **1876-CC AU58 PCGS.** Doubly popular with the Centennial year and CC mintmark, the 1876-CC double eagle is the last Type Two from the fabled Nevada mint. This example is just a hair's breadth away from Mint State, with radiant semiprooflike fields and much luster roiling about the orange-yellow surfaces. (#8977)

Delightful 1876-CC Double Eagle, MS61

4187 **1876-CC MS61 NGC.** A seldom-seen Mint State 1876-CC double eagle. Numerous abrasions on the yellow-gold surfaces keep this piece from an even higher grade, and this issue is quite scarce any finer. The details exhibit above-average sharpness, and there is remarkable luster throughout. NGC has certified just 52 examples finer (8/08). *From The Menlo Park Collection.* (#8977)

4188 **1876-S MS60 ICG.** Pleasing yellow patina overlies the surfaces, with dazzling cartwheel luster across both sides. The hair and several stars are soft, as usual, but the reverse is nearly fully defined. A lovely Centennial issue. (#8978)

4189 **1876-S MS60 NGC.** Highly lustrous and generally well struck, except for some softness on Liberty's hair. Several bits of grease appear to have been struck into the coin's surface, on the lower right reverse. Sharply defined throughout but moderately abraded, limiting the grade. (#8978)

4190 **1876-S MS61 NGC.** This Type Two twenty has booming luster and a sharp strike. The obverse displays the expected chatter from coin to coin contact, while the reverse is generally smooth save for a mark within the shield. (#8978)

4191 **1876-S MS61 NGC.** An impressive piece with fully brilliant honey-gold luster, lighter yellow on the devices. The mintmark is farther right than normal, nearly over the upright of the T. (#8978)

4192 **1876-S MS61 PCGS.** Eye-catching cartwheel luster glides across the butter-yellow surfaces. Scattered grade-defining abrasions barely affect the great eye appeal. A sharply struck example from this country's centennial year. (#8978)

Splendid MS62 1876-S Twenty
Popular Type Two Centennial Issue

4193 **1876-S MS62 PCGS.** A popular S-mint Centennial issue, the 1876-S double eagle had a generous mintage that approached 2 million pieces. As a plentiful Type Two issue, the 1876-S is also in great demand, and this piece should fill the bill nicely. With a bold strike and splendid luster radiating from the orange-gold surfaces, the piece shows some moderate contact marks consistent with the grade. It nonetheless offers considerable eye appeal. (#8978)

Gorgeous MS62 1877 Twenty

4194 **1877 MS62 PCGS.** A shining and uncommonly attractive example from the debut year of the Type Three double eagle reverse. The yellow-gold and sun-gold surfaces are immensely lustrous with subtle elements of frost and satin. Only a handful of wispy abrasions preclude Select status. A rarity any finer, with just 15 such pieces known to PCGS (8/08). (#8982)

Pleasing Choice AU 1877-CC Twenty

4195 **1877-CC AU55 NGC.** This issue brought the Type Three double eagle design to Carson City, and it has been popular with collectors for decades. This briefly circulated piece is mildly reflective and generally orange-gold, though areas of alloy or grease are noted around the left obverse stars and at the top of Liberty's hair bun. (#8983)

Lovely 1877-CC Twenty, AU55

4196 **1877-CC AU55 NGC.** A most attractive 1877-CC, representing the start of the modified Type Three twenty design with the denomination spelled out in its entirety. This boldly defined example is highly lustrous with bright yellow-gold surfaces and sharp design features. A small crescent of rainbow iridescence is visible at the top of the reverse. (#8983)

Luminous Near-Mint 1877-CC Twenty

4197 **1877-CC AU58 NGC.** The first Type Three double eagle issue struck at the Carson City Mint has been repatriated in quantity in the last two decades, and so pleasing examples are much more available than they were in the 1970s and early 1980s. Most pieces circulated to some degree before moving into overseas storage. This coin is one of them, though it shows only trifling friction on the high points, and the luminous honey-tinged orange-gold surfaces retain virtually intact luster. Minimally flawed with considerable visual appeal. NGC has graded 21 finer examples (8/08). (#8983)

4198 **1877-S MS61 NGC.** A crisply detailed beauty that offers primarily yellow-gold surfaces with occasional whispers of sun-orange. A moderately abraded, yet appealing representative of the first Type Three S-mint twenty. (#8984)

4199 **1877-S MS61 PCGS.** While the surfaces have a few minor abrasions that are consistent with the grade, the overall appearance is nice, with frosty yellow luster. (#8984)

Lustrous 1877-S Double Eagle, MS62

4200 **1877-S MS62 NGC.** Significant quantities of 1877-S twenties were shipped overseas, and those that have returned are heavily bagmarked and typically grade from AU58 to low Uncirculated. Only a few specimens have been certified finer than MS62, and NGC reports just four such examples (7/08). Lovely yellow-gold patina covers both sides of the present piece, with a streak of deep green on the reverse. This specimen has the usual bagmarks, but none merit individual mention. The strike, however, is razor-sharp, and is complemented by dazzling luster throughout. (#8984)

Important 1877-S Twenty, MS62

4201 **1877-S MS62 PCGS.** Honey-gold patina graces both sides of this moderately lustrous coin that reveals well struck design features. A few heavy marks that are consistent with the grade are evident, particularly on the obverse. PCGS has only certified 25 finer examples (8/08). (#8984)

4202 **1878 MS61 PCGS.** Alluring luster accents the splendid yellow-gold surfaces. The details are crisply defined, but myriad abrasions limit the grade. Nonetheless, the 1878 is scarce in any grade finer (7/08). (#8985)

4203 **1878 MS61 PCGS.** The reverse is lightly die doubled, with the spread perhaps most apparent on the D in DOLLAR. This lustrous peach-gold double eagle has a clean reverse and the expected marks on the left obverse.
From The Menlo Park Collection. (#8985)

Pleasing 1878 Double Eagle, MS62

4204 **1878 MS62 NGC.** A powerful strike is complemented by splendid satiny luster throughout. There are a number of light grazes on each side, as typical for the grade, but only a shallow group of marks below the eagle's right (facing) wing merit specific mention. A bright yellow and handsome specimen. NGC has certified just 32 pieces finer (7/08). (#8985)

Impressive 1878-CC Double Eagle, Choice XF

4205 **1878-CC XF45 NGC.** Significant luster highlights the boldly impressed design elements. Myriad abrasions cover both sides, but none merit specific mention. Charming yellow-gold patina graces the surfaces of this splendid representative. Production of double eagles at the Carson City Mint dropped significantly in 1878 and only 13,180 pieces were struck. (#8986)

Delightful 1878-CC Double Eagle, XF45

4206 **1878-CC XF45 NGC.** Compared to previous years, the number of Carson City double eagles minted in 1878 was significantly lower. Only 13,180 examples struck, and the vast majority of the survivors are circulated. Lots of luster on the present example highlights the yellow-gold surfaces. A couple of clash marks are noted on Liberty's neck. There are no mentionable marks and the design elements are crisply defined. (#8986)

Bold AU 1878-CC Double Eagle

4207 **1878-CC AU50 NGC.** Light field chatter and small abrasions appear on each side of this Carson City Mint rarity—one created by the launch of the Morgan dollar in the same year—but some prooflikeness also appears, along with the light wear expected for the grade. The strike is boldly executed, and the eye appeal is high. (#8986)

4208 **1878-S MS61 NGC.** An attractive orange-gold example of this earlier Type Three twenty with slight evidence of alloy at the high points. Minor, scattered abrasions across each side contribute to the grade. (#8987)

4209 **1879 AU58 PCGS.** A trace of light rub keeps this impressive piece from Mint State. The surfaces are minimally abraded, and there is lots of luster throughout. A sharply struck and handsome representative. (#8988)

Doubled Die 1879 Twenty, AU58

4210 **1879 AU58 PCGS. CAC.** FS-801. Doubled Die Reverse. One of the boldest doubled dies found on any gold issue with bold doubling visible on UNITED STATES, TWENTY, and the left ribbon. PCGS has certified just seven examples of the variety, having just recently started to recognize it as such. Frosty honey-gold surfaces with nearly full luster and hints of pale pink toning. (#8988)

4211 **1879 MS60 PCGS.** An outstanding representative with captivating prooflike fields. Myriad abrasions are visible throughout, but all are insignificant. The 1879 is another condition rarity of the double eagle series with surprisingly few survivors in Mint State. (#8988)

4212 **1879-S AU58 PCGS.** The 1879-S twenties were shipped overseas in large quantities, and the examples that have returned to the United States are typically seen heavily abraded. This piece is no exception, but it does exhibit a sharp strike, along with eye-catching luster beneath charming yellow-gold patina. (#8991)

Remarkable 1879-S Double Eagle, MS61

4213 **1879-S MS61 PCGS.** The 1879-S is another double eagle issue that was sent abroad in large quantities, and although large numbers have returned in recent decades, they are in surprisingly low grades, with the majority in Extremely Fine or About Uncirculated. This issue is relatively scarce in Mint State, and PCGS reports just 51 examples finer than the present piece (7/08). Eye-catching luster radiates beneath the pleasing yellow-gold patina that graces both sides. The surfaces have a number of grade-defining abrasions, but all are inconsequential. The strike is sharp save for minor weakness on several stars. (#8991)

Lustrous Mint State 1879-S Twenty

4214 **1879-S MS61 PCGS.** An excellent example of this important condition rarity, seldom found finer despite a high mintage of 1,233,800 coins. Survivors are generally only found with considerable wear, or with heavily marked fields. PCGS has only certified 52 finer examples of the date. (#8991)

Pleasing 1879-S Double Eagle, MS61

4215 **1879-S MS61 NGC.** According to Garrett and Guth (2006), while many 1879-S twenties have returned to the United States, they remain scarce in Mint State. In grades higher than MS62 the 1879-S is virtually unobtainable. Charming butter-yellow patina embraces the surfaces, with lovely rose accents in the fields. Powerfully struck with impressive luster. NGC has certified just 30 coins finer (8/08). (#8991)

Gorgeous MS61 1880-S Twenty

4216 **1880-S MS61 NGC.** It is hard to look at this double eagle, sharply struck with spectacular luster, and not think of the qualities that make the silver dollars of this date and mint so prized. Though numerous wispy abrasions and light marks are present in the lemon-gold fields, the eye appeal is strong. NGC has graded 50 finer pieces (8/08). (#8993)

4217 **1881-S MS61 PCGS.** Pale yellow patina graces the surfaces, which are actually quite clean for the grade. Alluring satiny luster enhances the eye appeal of this powerfully impressed specimen. A lovely piece for a type collection.
From The Menlo Park Collection. (#8995)

Sharp MS62 1881-S Double Eagle

4218 **1881-S MS62 PCGS.** Although the yellow-gold surfaces of this piece show some light field chatter, there is also considerable prooflikeness apparent on both sides, apparently a fresh strike—and a sharp one, at that—from new dies front and back. Like so many Type Three double eagles, this issue is seldom seen in finer grades: NGC and PCGS combined have certified less than two dozen higher (8/08). (#8995)

Desirable 1881-S Liberty Twenty, MS62

4219 **1881-S MS62 PCGS.** Considering the rarity of the 1881 Philadelphia Mint double eagle, the 1881-S is the only collectible issue of the year. The mintage totaled 727,000, but most survive in circulated grades. In Mint State grades, the date is a rarity that can usually only be found at the MS60 or MS61 grade. Jeff Garrett and Ron Guth write: "Above that [MS61], it becomes scarce, and there are probably just 15 or so coins known in choice condition." Given its aesthetic appeal, the present brilliant and lustrous example is clearly a candidate for the advanced specialist. The surfaces are remarkable for the grade, with only a single significant mark at DO of DOLLAR. PCGS has only graded 19 finer examples (8/08). (#8995)

4220 **1882-CC XF40 NGC.** Moderately worn with light green-gold coloration and a few minor abrasions that are noticeable on the obverse. A relatively available issue at this grade level, despite the low original mintage of just 39,140 pieces. (#8997)

Delightful 1882-CC Twenty, AU53

4221 **1882-CC AU53 PCGS.** A luminous and attractive yellow-orange exemplar from this desirable 1880s Carson City issue, well struck with light, scattered abrasions that pepper the peach-inflected yellow-gold surfaces. A small alloy streak is noted above the eagle's left (facing) wing. (#8997)

Eye-Catching 1882-CC Double Eagle, Uncirculated

4222 **1882-CC MS60 PCGS.** The 1882-CC boasts a diminutive mintage of just 39,140 pieces, and it is virtually impossible to locate finer than low Uncirculated grades. This crisply struck specimen is decidedly Prooflike and features highly reflective surfaces that show remarkable contrast against the frosted devices. Lovely orange-gold patina endows the surfaces, which have numerous light grazes but none that merit individual mention. (#8997)

Frosty 1882-S Double Eagle, MS62

4223 **1882-S MS62 PCGS.** Like many S-mint Type Three double eagles, the 1882-S is readily available in grades through MS62, but elusive finer. Many of the S-mint Type Threes are also underrated in higher grades. The present example offers somewhat prooflike surfaces with good luster and rich orange-gold coloration. PCGS has only certified 31 finer pieces (8/08). (#8998)

Appealing 1883-CC Double Eagle, AU50

4224 **1883-CC AU50 PCGS.** This piece is generally well struck, and only shows a trace of weakness on Liberty's brow. A few of the obverse stars are incomplete in the centers. Appealing lime-gold toning aids the coin's eye appeal, while moderate highpoint wear is noted for the grade. (#8999)

Scarce 1883-CC Double Eagle, MS61

4225 **1883-CC MS61 PCGS. CAC.** The 1883-CC double eagle is easily obtainable through the mid AU grade levels. AU58 through MS61 coins are very scarce, and anything finer remains rare (Michael Fuljenz and Douglas Winter, 1999). The apricot-gold surfaces of this MS61 specimen yield semiprooflike fields that establish mild contrast with the motifs. The design elements are much better defined than ordinarily seen, and the minute marks scattered about are fewer and of less severity that typically found. In sum, this piece generates considerable eye appeal for the grade, to which the CAC label attests. Population: 31 in 61, 14 finer (8/08). (#8999)

4226 **1883-S MS61 PCGS.** Impressive prooflike reflectivity accents the bright yellow patina. A couple of tiny streaks of brown are noted on the reverse. This sharply struck and vividly lustrous example would make an excellent representative. (#9000)

4227 **1883-S MS62 PCGS.** Enchanting cartwheel luster radiates from the yellow-gold surfaces. A few reeding marks on the obverse are barely worthy of note. This boldly struck piece has great eye appeal. (#9000)

4228 **1883-S MS63 PCGS.** Circulation strike double eagles were only coined at Carson City and San Francisco in 1883, as the Philadelphia Mint production was limited to a small number of proofs. Like most other dates, the San Francisco double eagles entered circulation, or they were harshly treated in international trade, and survivors are usually only found worn or heavily marked. The present Select Mint State piece is a lovely exception, with outstanding surfaces that are free of marks. The fields are somewhat reflective, and both sides have subtle rose toning. Just 11 finer pieces have been certified by PCGS. (#9000)

Sharp 1884-CC Double Eagle, AU50

4229 **1884-CC AU50 PCGS.** Bright yellow-gold surfaces exhibit hints of green, along with traces of luster in the recessed areas. The design elements benefited from a relatively sharp strike, manifested in strong definition in most of Liberty's hair, the star centers, and the eagle's plumage. A few light marks are not detractive. Housed in a green-label holder. (#9001)

4230 **1884-CC—Improperly Cleaned—NCS. AU Details.** A charming orange-gold representative with sharply defined design elements. Both sides have been lightly cleaned, but there are no particularly bothersome marks. This piece would make a relatively affordable type coin from the popular Carson City Mint. (#9001)

4231 **1884-CC AU53 NGC.** Bowers (2004) writes that while the 1884-CC is not a rarity, it is not common either. The present piece has plenty of luster beneath the charming yellow-gold patina. The strike is crisp and there are no mentionable marks on either side. A relatively low 81,139 pieces were struck. (#9001)

Pleasing 1884-CC Double Eagle, AU58

4232 **1884-CC AU58 NGC.** A well executed strike leaves its mark on this 1884 Carson City representative. Most of Liberty's hair is individually defined, the star radials on both sides are sharp, and the eagle exhibits strong feather and wingtip detail. Ample luster is apparent on yellow-gold surfaces imbued with hints of light tan. The minute marks scattered about are not out of the ordinary for a lightly circulated, heavy gold coin. (#9001)

Mint State 1884-CC Twenty

4233 **1884-CC MS60 NGC.** Although there are a couple of singular abrasions in the obverse field before Liberty's chin, elsewhere the fields are fairly clean, and splendid luster makes this coin appear undergraded and quite attractive. Usually found only AU or so and, like many Type Three double eagles, seldom seen above MS62. (#9001)

Lustrous MS61 1884-CC Liberty Twenty

4234 **1884-CC MS61 NGC.** The fields are somewhat scuffy on this piece, and pretty antique-gold coloration nicely complements the strong luster emanating each side. The strike through the center is somewhat soft, as often seen on this issue, with weakness on the tops of LIBERTY and the eagle's head. The peripheries are well brought up. *From The Menlo Park Collection.* (#9001)

4235 **1884-S MS61 ICG.** A splendidly frosted specimen with lots of flashy luster beneath the yellow-gold patina. The strike is razor-sharp, but the grade is limited by numerous yet inconsequential marks on each side. (#9002)

4236 **1884-S MS61 ICG.** The 1884-S is typically seen heavily abraded, and this piece is no exception. Nonetheless, its impressive cartwheel luster gives it great eye appeal and the strike is sharp throughout. (#9002)

4237 1884-S MS61 NGC. Outstanding luster radiates from both sides, and the reverse is decidedly prooflike with captivating watery fields. Scattered marks limit the grade but barely detract from the immense eye appeal of this yellow-gold specimen.
From The Menlo Park Collection. (#9002)

4238 1884-S MS62 PCGS. Most 1884-S double eagles were put into circulation, and they are less frequently seen in Mint State than many other years. This yellow-gold piece exhibits numerous abrasions, as typical for the issue, but it has no marks that merit specific mention. A crisply struck representative with charming cartwheel luster. (#9002)

4239 1884-S MS62 NGC. Well-defined with occasional glimpses of alloy that stand out against the sun-gold and yellow-gold surfaces. Scattered, minor abrasions preclude Select status. (#9002)

4240 1884-S MS62 PCGS. A lovely honey-gold Liberty twenty that possesses vibrant luster and a precise strike. Faint obverse grazes are distributed, but are fewer in number than is usual for the grade. (#9002)

Elusive 1885-CC Twenty, AU50

4241 1885-CC AU50 PCGS. This is a pleasing AU example that displays light, even wear over the highpoints and strong definition. Generous portions of mint luster can still be seen around and within the recesses of the devices. The few expected marks scattered about are not bothersome. A scarce issue from a mintage of 9,450 pieces. (#9004)

4242 1885-S MS62 PCGS. Touches of rose blend in with the brass-gold patination on this S-mint twenty. Light marks break the luster flow to some degree. Adequately struck. (#9005)

4243 1885-S MS62 PCGS. A sensational example for the grade with fully reflective fields around the lustrous devices. Traces of green and pink over the yellow-gold surfaces complete the picture. (#9005)

4244 1885-S MS62 PCGS. Dynamic luster, a good strike, and a clean obverse field confirm the eye appeal. The cheek and the right reverse field are moderately abraded.
From The Menlo Park Collection. (#9005)

4245 1885-S MS62 PCGS. Vibrant yellow-orange surfaces are satiny and minimally marked for the grade. Pleasing detail and strong overall visual appeal. Likely a repatriated representative. (#9005)

4246 1885-S MS62 PCGS. A pleasing double eagle whose khaki-gold surfaces are lustrous and only lightly abraded. A good choice to represent the type for those who prefer a better date than the common 1904. (#9005)

Lovely 1885-S Liberty Twenty, MS63

4247 1885-S MS63 PCGS. Here is an important opportunity for the advanced collector to obtain a wonderful 1885-S double eagle. The few small marks on either side are all that separate it from a much higher grade. Both sides are highly lustrous with satiny surfaces and beautiful yellow-gold that is accented by hints of pinkish toning. PCGS has only certified 30 finer pieces (8/08). (#9005)

Attractively Toned 1885-S Select Double Eagle

4248 1885-S MS63 NGC. Variegated orange-gold and mint-green patina residing on lustrous surfaces yields a pleasing overall appearance. An exacting strike leaves strong definition on the design elements, including Liberty's hair strands. Some minute obverse marks limit the grade. NGC has seen only 11 examples finer (8/08).
From The Mississippi Collection. (#9005)

4249 1887-S MS61 PCGS. A green-gold representative with booming luster and no singularly distracting abrasions. A low mintage for the San Francisco Mint, as only 283,000 pieces were coined.
From The Menlo Park Collection. (#9007)

4250 1888 MS61 NGC. Dusky patina is evident on the highpoints of this lovely double eagle. Although rather common at this grade level, the present specimen is an attractive piece for the MS61 grade. (#9008)

4251 1888 MS61 NGC. A narrow band of greenish-yellow at the peripheries frames peach-gold shadings in the central areas. Several light abrasions scattered about account for the grade.
From The Menlo Park Collection. (#9008)

4252 1888 MS61 PCGS. FS-801. An underrated variety, this piece features pronounced doubling throughout the reverse. Numerous abrasions on each side are entirely trivial and barely affect the flashy luster. Charming yellow-gold patina covers both sides and complements the boldly struck details. (#9008)

4253 1888-S MS62 ICG. Pleasing yellow-gold surfaces have accents of rose color in the fields. The design is crisply struck and there are only insignificant grazes scattered throughout. This lustrous piece would make a nice type coin. (#9009)

4254 1888-S MS62 PCGS. Rich yellow-orange surfaces show occasional hints of peach and lavender. The central devices are well-defined, though the right obverse stars show a degree of softness. (#9009)

Important 1889 Twenty, MS62

4255 **1889 MS62 PCGS.** An impressive example for the grade, with exceptional yellow surfaces and frosty gold luster. The 1889 double eagle is one of the unrecognized rarities in the series, with a mintage of only 44,000 coins. This coin has few certified peers, and just 16 finer specimens certified by PCGS. (#9010)

Delightful 1889-CC Double Eagle, AU58

4256 **1889-CC AU58 PCGS.** A touch of light rub on Liberty's cheek keeps this powerfully impressed piece from an Uncirculated grade. Butter-yellow patina coats both sides, although the color is partly obscured by small patches of verdigris and toning spots on the reverse. Flashy luster in the fields enhances the eye appeal. One of only 30,945 pieces struck at the fabled Carson City Mint. (#9011)

4257 **1889-S MS62 PCGS.** This sharply struck S-mint twenty displays honey-gold color on softly lustrous surfaces. Several light marks are scattered over both sides (#9012)

4258 **1889-S MS62 PCGS.** Yellow and peach-gold colors intermingle on the surfaces of this crisply defined piece, with darker areas of patina on Liberty's cheek and hair. The pleasing luster is partly obscured by a number of grazes in the fields. It can be difficult to find an 1889-S in grades finer than MS62. (#9012)

Lustrous 1889-S Twenty, MS63

4259 **1889-S MS63 PCGS.** Like so many other San Francisco twenties, a substantial number of 1889-S twenties were minted, in this case 774,700 pieces. Also like other issues, survivors are apt to be worn or heavily abraded. Select MS63 examples are difficult to locate, and the collector might as well forget about anything nicer, as PCGS has only graded nine better pieces. This one has wonderful lemon-yellow luster with rose highlights, frosty surfaces, and few abrasions of any kind. (#9012)

4260 **1890 MS60 NGC.** The devices are crisply struck, and the yellow-gold fields show surprisingly strong mirrors. Myriad fine abrasions and a handful of more significant marks account for the grade. (#9013)

4261 **1890 MS62 PCGS.** Production of double eagles at the Philadelphia Mint significantly decreased beginning in 1880, and only 75,940 pieces were struck in 1890, which is less than a tenth of the San Francisco production for that year. Seldom seen finer, this MS62 representative has charming yellow and orange patina on each side, with plenty of luster throughout. A sharply struck example with insignificant scattered abrasions. (#9013)

4262 **1890 MS62 PCGS.** Dazzling cartwheel luster radiates from both sides of this sharply struck, low-mintage piece. A number of abrasions on the obverse are typical for the grade, but the reverse is surprisingly well-preserved. PCGS has certified only 31 pieces finer (7/08). (#9013)

4263 **1890 MS62 PCGS.** Lightly frosted devices contrast nicely against the cartwheel luster that graces the fields. Although there numerous marks on each side, the design elements exhibit remarkable sharpness for the grade.
From The Menlo Park Collection. (#9013)

4264 **1890-CC XF45 NGC.** The sunset-orange surfaces of this Carson City twenty are surprisingly vibrant despite light wear. Softly struck at the margins, though the portrait and eagle offer pleasing detail.
From The Menlo Park Collection. (#9014)

4265 **1890-CC AU55 NGC.** The cheek has light wear, but the fields offer substantial mint luster. A pleasing, minimally worn piece with surprisingly few flaws and excellent visual appeal. (#9014)

4266 **1890-CC AU55 PCGS.** A generally lustrous peach-gold example with minor friction on the cheek. TWENTY and PLURIBUS are lightly die doubled, as is customary for the issue. (#9014)

Charming 1890-CC Double Eagle, MS61

4267 **1890-CC MS61 NGC.** The devices have a lovely rose-orange tint, while the fields have bright, butter-yellow patina. Myriad abrasions limit the grade, but they minimally affect the captivating luster. Mint State 1890-CC twenties are surprisingly difficult to locate. NGC has certified only 31 pieces finer. (#9014)

Shining MS61 1890-CC Twenty

4268 **1890-CC MS61 PCGS.** The 1890-CC is one of the most popular Carson City double eagle issues for the type collector, and this unworn representative offers strong, mildly reflective luster in the yellow-orange fields. The strike is crisp in the centers, and though light, scattered abrasions appear on each side, the overall eye appeal is impressive. PCGS has certified 48 finer examples (8/08). (#9014)

4269 **1890-S MS62 PCGS.** Flashy luster radiates beneath the attractive apricot-gold patina, which has a touch of deep green toning on the reverse. Several stars are weakly struck, but the rest of the details are razor-sharp. Numerous abrasions are typical for this issue, which was shipped overseas in large quantities and roughly handled. (#9015)

4270 **1890-S MS62 PCGS.** Many of the 1890-S twenties that have returned to the United States from overseas bank vaults are heavily abraded, and this piece is no exception. Nonetheless, the strike is sharp and there is flashy luster throughout.
From The Menlo Park Collection. (#9015)

Lustrous 1890-S Double Eagle, MS63

4271 **1890-S MS63 PCGS.** Only 802,750 double eagles were coined in San Francisco during the year, and few have survived in better Mint State grades. The present specimen is highly lustrous with excellent, nearly mark-free surfaces. In recent years, large quantities of heavily abraded examples have been returned from overseas, only further emphasizing the importance of Select and Choice Mint State examples. PCGS has only certified 18 finer pieces (8/08). (#9015)

4272 **1891-S MS62 PCGS.** A lovely semiprooflike example with scattered abrasions on each side, which is typical for this issue. The centers are sharply defined and some weakness is noted on the right stars. (#9018)

4273 **1891-S MS63 NGC.** A frosty, yellow gold piece with lovely olive and rose tints in the fields. The strike is razor-sharp, and there is impressive luster throughout. While most 1891-S twenties are seen heavily marked, this piece has only scattered, light abrasions on Liberty's cheek and in the fields. (#9018)

Lovely 1891-S Double Eagle, MS63

4274 **1891-S MS63 PCGS.** The eye appeal of this piece is simply outstanding. The coloration is a combination of deep apricot-gold and greenish toning, illuminated by intense, coruscating mint luster. The design details are well struck, and most of Liberty's hair strands are crisply articulated. A few scattered abrasions limit the grade.
From The Mississippi Collection. (#9018)

Impressive 1891-S Double Eagle, Choice Mint State

4275 **1891-S MS64 PCGS. CAC.** The 1891-S is a relatively obtainable San Francisco double eagle, but MS63 is the upper end of availability without paying a substantial premium. It is elusive in MS64, and only two Gems have been certified by a major service, both by NGC (8/08). This sharply struck example is among the finest certified by PCGS and has bright green-gold patina. Lightly abraded for the grade with eye-catching luster throughout. (#9018)

4276 **1891-S MS61 Prooflike NGC.** Myriad light abrasions on each side are typical for the grade, but they barely affect the enticing prooflike fields. Pleasing bright yellow patina overlies the surfaces of this crisply struck representative. NGC has certified a mere seven coins in 61 Prooflike, with five finer (7/08). (#79018)

4277 **1891-S MS61 Prooflike NGC. CAC.** An absolutely sensational example with fully mirrored fields, excellent contrast, and bold design features. Census: 7 in 61, 5 finer (8/08). (#79018)

Appealing 1892 Double Eagle, AU55

4278 **1892 AU55 NGC.** One of just 4,400 pieces struck, the 1892 was the last low mintage double eagle at the Philadelphia Mint. Splendid yellow patina drapes both sides of this boldly defined specimen. Myriad abrasions cover the surfaces and lightly obscure the still-impressive prooflike fields, although NGC has neglected to designate them as such. A shallow dig is noted to the left of the bust. An eye-catching and highly lustrous representative. (#9019)

4279 **1892-CC XF45 NGC.** Somewhat unevenly worn on the obverse, with numerous wispy hairlines in the fields and a rather muted overall appearance. One of just 27,265 business strikes produced, and a previously rare issue before repatriations from overseas made it more easily available. (#9020)

Low-Mintage 1892-CC Double Eagle, AU53

4280 **1892-CC AU53 PCGS.** Although the 1892-CC is more available than the rare 1891-CC, its low mintage of 27,265 pieces ensures that survivors are very scarce. The present example has surprisingly few marks for a lightly circulated double eagle, and luster beckons from the margins and devices. Encased in a green label holder. (#9020)

Lustrous Choice AU 1892-CC Double Eagle

4281 **1892-CC AU55 PCGS.** Rusty Goe notes in *The Mint on Carson Street* that by 1892 Comstock Lode miners were "beginning to scrape bottom in their search for more gold ore," despite which sufficient bullion was deposited to manage a respectable double eagle mintage of 27,265 pieces. Considerable numbers of the 1892-CC, from the penultimate year of Carson City mintage, appear to have been saved. This piece offers splendid eye appeal over the apricot-gold surfaces, with good luster and relatively few marks for the grade. (#9020)

Prooflike 1892-CC Twenty, AU58

4282 **1892-CC AU58 NGC.** Typical of the 1892-CC twenty, this piece retains considerable prooflike surface in the obverse and reverse fields. Scattered surface marks and tiny blemishes are reflected in the mirrored fields, giving the piece an abraded appearance that is undeserved. (#9020)

Important Near-Mint 1892-CC Twenty

4283 **1892-CC AU58 PCGS.** Wisps of lilac toning accompany natural and highly lustrous green-gold surfaces. Both sides have light abrasions, fully consistent with the grade of this delightful piece. The '92-CC ranks among the plentiful dates in the Liberty double eagle series, an ideal type coin. (#9020)

Attractive 1892-CC Double Eagle, MS61

4284 **1892-CC MS61 NGC.** While the 1892-CC is no longer considered to be as rare as once believed, it remains scarce, especially in high grades, with a mintage of just 27,265 pieces. This example is exceptionally sharp at the centers, and only a couple of stars show minor weakness. A number of light grazes define the grade, but they barely affect the eye-catching reflectivity. NGC has certified only 41 pieces finer (8/08).
From The Menlo Park Collection. (#9020)

Pleasing 1892-S Double Eagle, Select Mint State

4285 **1892-S MS63 PCGS. CAC.** A charming yellow-gold representative with dazzling cartwheel luster on both sides. Scattered light luster grazes limit the grade, but none are of any significance. This sharply struck piece exhibits impressive eye appeal. The 1892-S twenty can be difficult to locate in grades finer than the present piece. (#9021)

Appealing Select 1892-S Twenty

4286 1892-S MS63 PCGS. The obverse is moderately prooflike, although undesignated as such on the PCGS insert. The reverse has flashy cartwheel luster. Well struck and attractive with the usual small marks customary for the grade. Recutting within the 2 in the date may have inspired Breen-7312, his listing for an "1892/1-S." (#9021)

4287 1893 MS63 PCGS. Vibrant sun-gold shadings cross each side, and glimpses of lemon-yellow and orange visit the margins. Well-defined and attractive despite minor scrapes in the left obverse field. (#9022)

Desirable 1893-CC Double Eagle, Choice AU

4288 1893-CC AU55 PCGS. A splendid final-year Carson City double eagle. Coruscating mint luster enhances the yellow-gold surfaces. Myriad abrasions cover both sides, but they minimally affect the impressive luster. The strike is sharp, and there are no particularly detracting marks. One of only 18,402 pieces minted. (#9023)

Alluring 1894-S Double Eagle, MS63

4289 1894-S MS63 PCGS. This Select Uncirculated double eagle displays intense mint luster and semi-reflective fields. The design elements are crisply struck and the overall appearance of the piece is quite pleasing. Bright lime-gold and peach coloration further increases the coin's visual appeal. The usual number of small to moderate marks are seen, for the grade. A scarce issue any finer than MS63. (#9026)

4290 1894-S MS63 PCGS. CAC. A lovely Select representative of this later S-mint double eagle issue, primarily yellow-gold with subtle mint accents near the obverse margins. Modest haze in the fields suggests long-term overseas storage in this piece's past. (#9026)

4291 1894-S MS62 Prooflike NGC. A charming, highly lustrous, and startlingly prooflike piece. Scattered light grazes are visible in the fields, but none merit individual mention. Pleasing yellow patina overlies the sharply struck devices. NGC has certified six coins in 62 Prooflike, with one finer. (#79026)

4292 1895 MS60 Prooflike NGC. A wonderful piece with fully prooflike surfaces and traces of cameo contrast. Dark patina is evident on the obverse and scattered abrasions are on both sides. (#79027)

4293 1895-S MS63 PCGS. Hints of rose color accent the delightful yellow-gold patina of this attractive piece. Garrett and Guth (2006) write that significant numbers of this issue were sent overseas and today examples finer than MS63 are elusive. Pleasing satiny luster shimmers throughout the fields of this sharply struck representative. (#9028)

4294 1897 MS63 NGC. Hints of frostiness grace the high points and the yellow-gold surfaces offer impressive overall luster with occasional alloy. Minor, scattered marks are consistent with the Select grade. *From The Menlo Park Collection.* (#9031)

Charming 1897 Double Eagle, MS64

4295 1897 MS64 PCGS. Although the 1897 double eagle is a common issue in most grades, Choice examples are scarce, and only a select few are available in Gem. Rose and yellow patina graces the surfaces of this sharply struck representative. A couple of light grazes barely affect the flow of the pleasing cartwheel luster. An excellent pre-1900 type coin. (#9031)

Gorgeous 1897-S Twenty Dollar, MS64

4296 1897-S MS64 NGC. The 1897-S double eagle is readily available through the MS63 grade level. Near-Gem examples can be obtained with a degree of patience and searching, but anything finer is rare. A gorgeous medley of apricot, mint-green, and yellow-gold visits the lustrous surfaces of this MS64 specimen, and a well executed strike leaves crisp definition on the design features. Gem status is denied by a few minute handling marks. (#9032)

4297 1897-S MS64 NGC. The sharply struck devices are pleasingly preserved, and the yellow-gold fields offer mild reflectivity along with ample rotational luster. Occasional elements of alloy appear close to the high points of the design. Elusive any finer, with just 19 such pieces known to NGC (8/08). (#9032)

4298 1898 MS62 NGC. Crisply struck with powerfully lustrous straw-gold and yellow-gold surfaces. Though a number of light abrasions appear on each side, the overall eye appeal is high for an MS62 coin. *From The Menlo Park Collection.* (#9033)

Please visit *HA.com* to view other collectibles auctions   *A 15% Buyer's Premium ($9 min.) Applies To All Lots*

4299 **1898-S MS64 NGC.** Thanks to a relatively high mintage of 2.57 million coins and the repatriation in recent decades of double eagles that were stored in overseas bank accounts, the 1898-S is fairly available in grades through Choice and is a favorite among type collectors. Splendid frosty luster graces the surfaces of this orange and yellow patinated example. A sharply struck and minimally marked representative. (#9034)

4300 **1898-S MS64 PCGS.** Crisply detailed with remarkable eye appeal for a 19th century S-mint double eagle. Bright sun-yellow and wheat-gold surfaces are carefully preserved. PCGS has graded 76 finer pieces (8/08). (#9034)

4301 **1898-S MS61 Prooflike NGC.** An outstanding piece with deeply mirrored fields around lustrous and boldly defined devices. Census: 22 in 61, 25 finer (8/08). (#79034)

4302 **1898-S MS62 Prooflike NGC.** An impressive example with rich yellow surfaces that are deeply mirrored around the devices. Boldly defined with excellent eye appeal. Census: 14 in 62, 11 finer (8/08). (#79034)

4303 **1899-S MS63 NGC.** An outstanding representative with brilliant yellow-gold luster and faint traces of green and rose patina. The surfaces are exceptional for the grade. (#9036)

Lovely 1899-S Twenty, MS64

4304 **1899-S MS64 PCGS.** A stunning near-Gem with highly lustrous and frosty yellow-gold surfaces. More than 2 million 1899-S double eagles were coined, yet few have survived as fine as this piece. Higher grade examples are major rarities. In fact PCGS has only certified three finer pieces (8/08). (#9036)

4305 **1899-S MS64 PCGS.** Rich yellow-gold surfaces offer captivating luster, and the boldly detailed devices show only a handful of faint flaws. Virtually unavailable any finer, with just three such pieces known to PCGS (8/08). (#9036)

4306 **1900 MS64 PCGS.** Exciting cartwheel luster accents the pleasing yellow-gold patina. This fully struck piece has a number of light grazes but none that are particularly detracting. An attractive example that would make a splendid type coin. (#9037)

4307 **1900 MS64 PCGS.** Delightful pinkish-orange patina on the central devices contrasts nicely against the bright yellow fields. An immensely lustrous and crisply struck example with minimal abrasions. PCGS has certified 56 pieces finer (7/08). (#9037)

4308 **1900 MS63 Prooflike NGC.** Pleasing yellow-gold patina graces the surfaces of this impressive, fully struck representative. Scattered abrasions in the fields minimally affect the spectacular prooflike reflectivity. Although the 1900 double eagle is common in nearly any condition, it is seldom seen Prooflike, and NGC has certified just five such examples in all grades, with none finer than the present piece (7/08). (#79037)

Conditionally Rare 1900-S Twenty, MS64

4309 **1900-S MS64 PCGS.** A remarkable example of the conditionally rare 1900-S twenty, this piece has satiny luster with reflective reverse fields. Both sides have brilliant yellow luster with traces of pink and faint bluish-green. PCGS has only certified three finer examples of the date. (#9038)

Beautiful Near-Gem 1900-S Double Eagle

4310 **1900-S MS64 PCGS.** This is a popular issue, either as a Type Three double eagle from the San Francisco Mint, or as a turn-of-the-century-date example. This near-Gem displays sumptuous luster and heavenly honey-gold toning. Crisply struck throughout, with a couple of faint luster grazes in the left obverse field the prevent a higher grade. Rare any finer, with just 11 pieces certified above MS64 by NGC and PCGS combined. (#9038)

Popular 1901 Double Eagle, Gem Uncirculated

4311 **1901 MS65 PCGS. CAC.** The 1901 is popular as a type coin because most were exceptionally well-produced. This piece is no exception and features a powerful strike complemented by captivating cartwheel luster. Scattered grazes keep this appealing Gem from an even high grade. Housed in a green label PCGS holder. NGC reports no pieces finer than MS65 and PCGS reports just three such specimens (8/08). (#9039)

Lustrous 1902-S Select Double Eagle

4312   **1902-S MS63 PCGS.** Much of the 1902-S double eagle mintage was sent to Europe or South America for international trade, and many have since returned, making the date easy to obtain in XF to MS62 grades (Jeff Garrett and Ron Guth, 2006). The lustrous, honey-gold surfaces of this MS63 example exhibit well struck design features. A scattering of minute marks limits the grade. (#9042)

4313   **1904 MS64 NGC.** Attractive peach-gold and light green patina rests on the lustrous surfaces of this near-Gem, complementing well struck design elements. A few minute marks precludes Gem status. (#9045)

4314   **1904 MS64 NGC. CAC.** Captivating cartwheel luster radiates beneath the vibrant yellow-gold patina. This sharply struck near-Gem representative has only minuscule grazes. Housed in an old NGC holder. (#9045)

4315   **1904 MS64 PCGS.** A lightly abraded and powerfully impressed near-Gem example. Pleasing satiny luster sparkles throughout the yellow-gold surfaces. This luminous piece in housed in a first-generation PCGS holder. (#9045)

Wonderful 1904 Double Eagle, Gem Uncirculated

4316   **1904 MS65 PCGS.** A great choice for the type collector, this sharply struck 1904 double eagle exhibits resplendent cartwheel luster across both sides. Splendid lemon-yellow patina coats the surfaces, and is accented by a reddish hue in the fields. A couple of light abrasions on the obverse are barely noticeable and hardly affect the outstanding eye appeal. (#9045)

Popular 1904 Liberty Twenty, MS65

4317   **1904 MS65 NGC.** The 1904 double eagle is the highest mintage issue of the design, and it is by far the most easily obtainable date. An ideal example for a type collector, this piece has sharp design details and lovely yellow luster with traces of pinkish toning. A small mark on Liberty's cheek prevents a higher grade. (#9045)

Impressive 1904 Twenty, MS65

4318   **1904 MS65 NGC.** This exceptional Gem has nearly flawless obverse and reverse surfaces, a bold strike, and fully brilliant satin luster. Both sides exhibit lovely yellow-gold surfaces, the reverse with faint iridescent highlights. An outstanding candidate for a type collector, or for someone who simply wants to own an example of our nation's gold coinage. (#9045)

Magnificent 1904 Double Eagle, Gem Uncirculated

4319   **1904 MS65 NGC.** Sparkling cartwheel luster accents the exquisitely defined details. The reverse of this appealing Gem is virtually pristine, and the obverse has only inconsequential grazes. Charming yellow-gold patina covers the surfaces of this magnificently lustrous representative. A handsome piece that would suit even the most discerning eye. (#9045)

Dazzling 1904 Twenty Dollar, MS65

4320   **1904 MS65 NGC.** Pleasing butter-yellow patina coats the surfaces of this lustrous Gem. A couple of minor copper spots and several light grazes limit the grade, but none are particularly noteworthy. This sharply struck piece exhibits dazzling cartwheel luster and has great eye appeal. A lovely representative of a Type Three double eagle. (#9045)

Pleasing Gem 1904 Double Eagle

4321 **1904 MS65 NGC.** A fantastic yellow-gold representative with hints of olive patina in the fields. The razor-sharp strike is accented by dazzling cartwheel luster on each side. Several grade-defining grazes are noted in the fields. 1904 double eagles are common in nearly all grades, but become scarce in grades finer than Gem. (#9045)

Marvelous 1904 Double Eagle, MS65

4322 **1904 MS65 NGC. CAC.** A touch of rose in the periphery complements the handsome yellow-gold patina that covers the majority of the surfaces. Stunning satiny luster graces the fields, which appear remarkably pristine even for the MS65 grade. This powerfully impressed piece would make an outstanding type coin. (#9045)

Wonderful 1904 Double Eagle, Gem Uncirculated

4323 **1904 MS65 NGC.** An exciting, impeccably preserved Gem. Several light grazes barely affect the impressive satiny luster that radiates from the yellow-orange surfaces. The strike is nearly full, which contributes to the immense appeal of this specimen. Although relatively available in most grades, the number of 1904 twenties drops significantly just one grade point finer. (#9045)

Lustrous 1904 Gem Double Eagle

4324 **1904 MS65 NGC.** Tens of thousands of 1904 double eagles have been certified in Mint State, making representatives of the issue popular among type collectors. The present Gem is such a coin. Bright luster endows peach-gold and mint-green surfaces, and a solid strike imparts complete delineation to the motifs. A few minor grazes may well preclude an even finer grade. An excellent candidate for a high-grade type collection. (#9045)

Impressive 1904 Double Eagle, MS65 ★

4325 **1904 MS65 ★ NGC. CAC.** Although common in nearly all grades, only a select few 1904 twenties have received NGC's coveted star designation. In fact, this piece is among only eight certified in MS65★, with none finer (7/08). Dazzling cartwheel luster radiates beneath the pleasing butter and lemon-yellow patina. The obverse has a few wispy abrasions, while the reverse is exceptionally clean and attractive. This boldly struck example would make a wonderful addition to any collection. (#9045)

4326 **1904 MS65 NGC. CAC.** An outstanding Gem representative with marvelous satiny luster that graces the vibrant yellow-gold surfaces. The strike is razor sharp, and there are only a few pinpoint abrasions on either side. This eye-catching piece is housed in an old NGC holder. A spectacular representative for a type collector. (#9045)

4327 **1904 MS63 Prooflike NGC.** Enticing prooflike fields show astonishing reflectivity that highlights the sharply struck details. A number of minor abrasions on the obverse limit the grade, but the reverse is spectacularly clean with only a couple of light grazes. (#79045)

4328 **1904 MS64 Prooflike NGC.** Sharply struck, with bright peach-gold surfaces that display spectacular luster. Minute abrasions in the fields limit the grade but hardly affect the glassy, prooflike fields. NGC has certified only 40 pieces in 64 PL, with 11 finer (7/08). (#79045)

4329 **1904-S MS64 PCGS.** Beautiful orange toning dominates, although the obverse also has blushes of olive-green. Crisply struck and lustrous with a splendidly smooth reverse and a couple of minor marks near the profile. Housed in a green label holder. (#9046)

4330 **1904-S MS64 NGC.** A brilliant near-Gem with amazing, frosty orange luster and exceptional surfaces. While strictly considered a common date, its eye appeal increases desirability. (#9046)

Amazing Gem 1904-S Twenty

4331 **1904-S MS65 PCGS.** Crisply detailed with bright yellow-gold and sun-gold surfaces. Excellent preservation and eye appeal to match. Though the 1904-S is readily available in grades through Choice, this type issue is elusive in Gem and prohibitively rare any finer, with just two such pieces known to PCGS (8/08).
From The Bell Collection. (#9046)

4332 **1904-S MS61 Prooflike NGC.** The surfaces are moderately abraded, with the marks reflected in the fully mirrored fields. Despite the common nature of the date, prooflike examples are seldom seen and most desirable. (#79046)

Pleasing 1905 Double Eagle, MS62

4333 **1905 MS62 PCGS.** Following an enormous mintage for the 1904 double eagle (over 5.1 million pieces), the Philadelphia Mint responded by striking only 58,919 twenties in 1905. This issue is typically seen in grades up to MS61 and the number of survivors drops significantly above that level. Bright yellow patina graces the surfaces of this crisply struck representative. Scattered abrasions define the grade and none are particularly detracting. PCGS has certified just 52 pieces finer (8/08). (#9047)

Crisp 1905-S Twenty, MS63

4334 **1905-S MS63 PCGS.** In 1905 San Francisco struck more than 1 million double eagles, while Philadelphia coined less than 60,000. As such, the San Francisco issue is the only easily collectible representative of the date in higher Mint State grades. This remarkable piece has satiny yellow-gold luster with lovely rose and pink toning. The surfaces are smooth and pleasing with only a few marks that are consistent with the grade. (#9048)

4335 **1906 MS60 NGC.** Highly attractive for the grade, with frosty yellow surfaces and few abrasions on either side. A couple tiny rim bumps may account for the conservative grade. (#9049)

Sharp MS62 1906 Double Eagle

4336 **1906 MS62 PCGS.** The 1906 is one of the scarcer P-mint issue from late in the Liberty Head series, about on a par with the 1902 and 1905 issues, all of which saw five- rather than six-digit mintage figures. This specimen offers deep, rich orange-gold coloration, although a straight scrape in the field before Liberty's nose and another on her cheek require mention. A pretty and well-struck piece.
From The Menlo Park Collection. (#9049)

Strongly Defined 1906-D Double Eagle, MS64

4337 **1906-D MS64 NGC.** This is a pleasing near-Gem example from the first year of operation for the Denver Mint. Lustrous surfaces project a satiny finish, and give off a greenish-gold cast. An exacting strike leaves strong definition on the devices, including Liberty's hair and the star centrils. A handful of grazes preclude full Gem status. (#9050)

4338 **1906-S MS63 NGC. CAC.** A handsome representative of the penultimate Liberty Head double eagle. Fantastic cartwheel luster shines beneath the yellow-gold patina. The strike is nearly full, and there are no noteworthy marks to report. (#9051)

4339 **1906-S MS63 PCGS.** Housed in a green-label holder, this frosty piece has brilliant orange-gold luster. It is sharply struck and possesses excellent luster. (#9051)

Lovely 1907 Double Eagle, Choice Mint State

4340 1907 MS64 PCGS. This powerfully impressed near-Gem representative features delightful yellow-gold patina across both sides. The scattered abrasions are all minor save for one shallow scratch by the last star. This highly lustrous piece has excellent eye appeal. PCGS reports just 10 pieces finer (7/08). Encapsulated in a green label holder. (#9052)

Well Struck 1907-D Double Eagle, MS63

4341 1907-D MS63 PCGS. This MS63 Denver Mint twenty dollar exhibits potent luster, and an attractive mixture of apricot-gold and mint-green patination. A well executed strike imparts strong delineation to the design features, including the star centers, Liberty's hair strands, and the eagle's plumage. A handful of minor contacts and grazes precludes the next highest grade. (#9053)

Lustrous 1907-D Twenty Dollar, MS63

4342 1907-D MS63 PCGS. The 1907-D Liberty Head double eagle is popular as being the last year for the type. A relatively large number of Mint State coins are known, probably the result of having been saved when the series was discontinued. This is a highly lustrous Select example that displays crisp design detail. Peach-gold surfaces reveal a scattering of grade-defining marks. (#9053)

Sharply Struck 1907-D Gem Double Eagle

4343 1907-D MS65 NGC. The 1907-D Liberty Head twenty dollar is common through near-Gem. Gems can be had with patience and searching, and anything finer is rare. On this MS65 coin, satiny luster adorns yellow-gold surfaces imbued with traces of light green, and an attentive strike emboldens the design features. A few minor grazes are all that stand in the way of an even higher grade. (#9053)

4344 1907-S MS63 PCGS. This is a visually appealing representative from the final S-mint issue in the Liberty head double eagle series. Attractive rose toning is intermingled with yellow-gold color on both sides. A trifle soft in the centers, with minimal marks for the grade. (#9054)

4345 1907-S MS63 PCGS. CAC. The 1907-S is relatively scarce just one grade finer than the present piece and it is quite rare in Gem Uncirculated. Scattered abrasions define the grade, but none are particularly bothersome. Wonderful satiny luster flashes beneath the charming yellow-gold patina. (#9054)

4346 1907-S MS63 NGC. Sharply struck and shining with a hint of frostiness. Though a handful of minor, scattered abrasions appear on and near the portrait, the overall visual appeal is strong. (#9054)

HIGH RELIEF DOUBLE EAGLES

XF45 Sharpness MCMVII High Relief Saint-Gaudens

4347 1907 High Relief, Wire Rim—Cleaned, Ex-Jewelry, Scratched—ANACS. XF45 Details. The fields are a bit bright but display only wispy marks aside from a trio of minor pinscratches on the upper obverse. Light wear on the eagle's breast and Liberty's knee suggests moderate non-numismatic handling. The famous High Relief Saint-Gaudens twenty, struck in limited quantity shortly after the death of its designer, ranks high within the want lists of thousands of collectors. (#9135)

Impressive 1907 Double Eagle, High Relief, Wire Rim, XF45

4348 1907 High Relief, Wire Rim XF45 PCGS. The first two-thirds of the 12,367 High Relief 1907 double eagles struck featured a raised "fin," as it was called in the time, around the rim. This wire rim was considered a serious flaw by mint officials and efforts were taken to flatten the rim. Today this type is treasured by collectors, who consider the wire rim to be an important aesthetic element of the design. Perhaps this example served as a pocket piece, which would account for the wear on the high points and the scattered abrasions throughout. Deep yellow-gold patina endows the surfaces, with a milky patch noted at the bottom of the reverse. Significant luster remains in the fields. A handsome representative of Saint-Gaudens' original conception for the double eagle. *From The Menlo Park Collection.* (#9135)

AU Details 1907 High Relief Twenty

4349 1907 High Relief, Wire Rim—Improperly Cleaned—NCS. AU Details. This bold representative has only moderate wear on Liberty's chest and raised knee, and on the crest of the eagle's front wing. The strike is crisp save for base of the reverse rays. Cloudy from a cleaning, but collectible relative to an Uncirculated example. (#9135)

Classic 1907 High Relief, Wire Rim Twenty, MS61

4350 1907 High Relief, Wire Rim MS61 NGC. The undeniable beauty, imbedded history, and relative scarcity of the 1907 High Relief, Roman Numeral twenty makes it an American numismatic masterpiece, regardless of the type of rim (Wire or Flat). This example happens to be the Wire Rim, which is more common than its Flat Rim counterpart, although each type typically sells at comparable price levels. The current offering is a Mint State survivor which displays amber-gold coloration and pleasantly lustrous surfaces throughout. Enough scattered abrasions are visible to limit the grade to MS61, although the immediate eye appeal of this piece suggests a higher designation. (#9135)

Lustrous 1907 High Relief Twenty Wire Rim, MS62

4351 1907 High Relief, Wire Rim MS62 NGC. Intense frosty luster and brilliant lemon-yellow and orange-gold surfaces are the first thing the viewer sees when examining this moderately abraded High Relief double eagle. Multiple blows of the coining press gave this piece its incredible detail. This piece has a modest wire rim around the entire obverse circumference with slight evidence on the reverse as well. This example appears to be a later die state of the wire rim coins, with little of the usually visible die polish evident. An impressive piece that will see considerable bidding interest. (#9135)

Elegant High Relief, Wire Rim Twenty, MS64

4352 1907 High Relief, Wire Rim MS64 PCGS. CAC. Saint-Gaudens' High Relief twenty has been a numismatic icon for more than a century. Public enthusiasm for the coin was infectious and examples were selling for a premium as soon as the coin was released. Henry Chapman offered a specimen of the Wire Rim variety as lot 619 in his public auction sale of February 20, 1908. To quote from Chapman's lot description, "In great demand, and supply very small. $35 to $45 now being paid." Collector enthusiasm for this coin remains undimmed today. It is on the "must- have" lists of collectors from a wide range of disciplines, including those who collect no other gold coins!

The magnificent design that has inspired so much admiration was not easy to conceive, even for an artist of Saint-Gaudens' genius. Roger Burdette relates the story of Saint-Gaudens' struggle in his acclaimed reference *Renaissance of American Coinage 1905-1908.* At different points in the design process, Saint-Gaudens considered an assortment of design elements that can only dismay admirers of his final masterpiece. Imagine Liberty wearing a Native American headdress (Theodore Roosevelt's suggestion) or having full, spreading, angel wings! Thankfully, Saint-Gaudens discarded these anachronisms and settled on the simple, majestic figure of Liberty with her torch and olive branch.

The present coin has the full strike expected on a High Relief. All details are sharp and crisp on both sides. The surfaces are free from distractions and are highlighted by unbroken, satiny mint luster. The rich, yellow-gold color of the obverse is complemented by subtle shades of magenta on the reverse. A beautiful, historic prize. (#9135)

4353   **1907 High Relief, Wire Rim MS64 PCGS.** More than a century after his design for the double eagle first made its way into circulation, Augustus Saint-Gaudens and his coin design legacy have become seemingly permanent fixtures on American coinage. Its initial quarter-century run (26 years, if one counts the 1933 double eagles) began with numismatic acclaim and ended with frantic saving of choice examples.

As repatriation brought increasingly valuable double eagles out of European bank vaults, appreciation for the artistry of Saint-Gaudens increased even further, and in 1986, the year the United States Mint belatedly entered the international bullion coinage sweepstakes with its .900 fine American Eagles, a low-relief rendition of the familiar image of Liberty graced the gold pieces. The 2009-dated pure gold one-ounce bullion pieces recently unveiled by the Mint are further echoes of his vision, this time as, in the words of a Mint press release, "the ultra high relief coin envisioned, but never fully realized, by renowned sculptor Augustus Saint-Gaudens in 1907."

While the novelty and grandeur of the 2009 Ultra High Relief pieces will prove popular, collectors will still continue to admire the 1907 High Relief double eagles, the first encounter many numismatists have had with the Saint-Gaudens image, not merely as a coin design, but as a work of art. This well-preserved Choice piece shows an extensive wire rim around the obverse, which has generally yellow-gold surfaces that show a distinct peach cast in the fields. Minimally marked for the grade and gorgeous. (#9135)

4354 1907 High Relief, Wire Rim MS64 NGC. Two varieties were created at the time the High Relief Saint-Gaudens double eagles were coined. Known as the Wire Rim and Flat Rim, they actually reflect minor changes in Mint apparatus, rather than actual varieties or even die states.

The first 8,000 or so coins struck all had a wire rim, called a fin within the Mint, that was considered less desirable. The fin was a result of metal squeezed between the edge of the die and the collar. The Flat Rim variety was the result of corrections to the combination of milling and planchet diameter. Approximately 4,000 of the Flat Rim coins were minted. Known almost immediately after the coins first appeared, the debate surrounding the Flat Rim and Wire Rim coins continues to this day.

Dave Bowers writes: "In my opinion the wire rim does not constitute a distinctive variety worth collecting. For some reason, these are listed separately in the *Guide Book of United States Coins*, and thus a modest demand has arisen for them."

This piece is highly lustrous with frosty light yellow-gold surfaces and excellent design definition. A few faint surface marks are present, but the overall eye appeal is extraordinary. The wire rim is most evident around the obverse, with some slight evidence on the reverse. An exceptional near-Gem, this piece should see strong bidder interest at the sale.
From The Mississippi Collection. (#9135)

Gem 1907 High Relief, Wire Rim Twenty

4355   1907 High Relief, Wire Rim MS65 PCGS. CAC. While opinions of the artistry exhibited by the Saint-Gaudens coinage designs are nearly uniformly high today, it is important to remember that initial reactions were more mixed, particularly among those who valued practicality and uniformity over aesthetics. While the eagle came in for more extensive criticism, even the now-venerated High Relief double eagle suffered its share of indignities. In his *Renaissance of American Coinage 1905 - 1908*, Roger W. Burdette quotes one Talcott Williams, writing for the February 1908 edition of what he termed "a publication of art and design," *The International Studio*:

> "To those trained by earlier models, the designs of Saint-Gaudens are the only ones in our day above the mere draughtsman's level. Little more depressing has occurred in our day than the baiting these coins have had from newspaper and sciolist. No application of art to familiar objects is possible where men are wedded to their preconceptions and are ignorant of the succession of art."

Today, the High Relief double eagles are virtually irresistible to collectors, especially when they are so well-preserved as this charming Gem. With no significant distractions on either side, one is free to appreciate the sculptural qualities of the beautifully detailed central devices. A prominent wire rim around the obverse further reinforces the bold strike. While the lustrous reverse is generally yellow-gold, subtle peach and orange elements grace the smooth fields to either side of Liberty. PCGS has certified 83 finer examples (8/08). (#9135)

SAINT-GAUDENS DOUBLE EAGLES

4356 1907 Arabic Numerals MS63 NGC. Pleasing yellow-gold patina covers each side of this lustrous specimen. The surfaces are minimally marked, and the strike is bold. A marvelous piece with impressive eye appeal. (#9141)

4357 1907 Arabic Numerals MS63 NGC. Shimmering luster and deep rose-gold toning ensure the alluring visual quality of this Select uncirculated example, from the first year of Saint-Gaudens' twenty dollar gold series. The striking details are generally bold, as small, scattered marks limit the grade. (#9141)

4358 1907 Arabic Numerals MS63 NGC. Originally, the Saint-Gaudens double eagle design featured Roman numerals on the date. That was changed on this, the third version of the new twenty-dollar coins to be produced in 1907; and Arabic numerals were used afterward. This Select example exhibits shimmering luster and enticing lime-gold toning. There are a few small marks on each side that limit the grade. (#9141)

4359 1907 Arabic Numerals MS63 NGC. A honey-gold first year Saint-Gaudens twenty that boasts shimmering luster and is void of memorable abrasions. A good strike with only minor blending of detail on the chest and raised knee. (#9141)

4360 1907 Arabic Numerals MS64 PCGS. A popular first-year issue of Saint-Gaudens' spectacular design, which was modified by Charles Barber to feature a lower relief and Arabic numerals. Delightful satiny luster enhances the great eye appeal. Several bagmarks on Liberty's body limit the grade, and a trace of softness is noted on the eagle's feathers. (#9141)

4361 1907 Arabic Numerals MS64 PCGS. This alluring near-Gem exhibits lovely lime-gold patina, and full satin luster over both sides. Boldly struck with a few scattered marks that keep it from grading as a Gem. Still an attractive first-year representative that should satisfy the needs of a type collector. (#9141)

4362 1907 Arabic Numerals MS64 NGC. An appealing near-Gem from the first year of the Saint-Gaudens double eagle series. Shimmering luster and delicate honey and lime-green toning combine to ensure the coin's high level of eye appeal. Shallow abrasions in the left obverse fields preclude a finer grade. (#9141)

4363 1907 Arabic Numerals MS64 PCGS. A satiny and original piece. The devices are crisply detailed and generally devoid of marks, though the fields have minor abrasions consistent with the grade. (#9141)

Shining 1907 Arabic Numerals Gem Twenty Dollar

4364 1907 Arabic Numerals MS65 PCGS. The highly lustrous surfaces of this Gem possess attractive peach-gold coloration splashed with light grayish-green. An attentive strike imparts strong detail to the design features, including the panes of the Capitol building, Liberty's fingers, facial features, and toes. A few grade-consistent marks are not disturbing. (#9141)

Frosty 1907 Arabic Numerals Twenty, MS65

4365 1907 Arabic Numerals MS65 PCGS. Attractive apricot and orange-gold coloration bathes both sides of this Gem double eagle. An impressive strike brings out sharp definition on the design elements, including separation in the panes of the Capitol building, and on Liberty's fingers and toes. Intensely lustrous surfaces reveal just a few light marks within the confines of the grade designation. (#9141)

Lustrous Gem 1907 Arabic Numerals Twenty

4366 1907 Arabic Numerals MS65 PCGS. The lower-relief version of Saint-Gaudens' design as Charles Barber modified it for production coinage: One wonders how the various 1907-1908 double eagle issues will perform in the next few years, after the 2009 Mint issue of the "piedfort" or double-thick, smaller-diameter version of the original Ultra High Relief, in pure 24-karat gold. This Gem example of the 1907 Arabic Numerals offers wonderfully lustrous orange-gold surfaces, with few abrasions appearing, even under a loupe. (#9141)

Fantastic 1907 Saint-Gaudens Double Eagle, Gem Mint State

4367 1907 Arabic Numerals MS65 PCGS. Warm honey-gold patina covers the smooth surfaces. A nearly full strike is complemented by powerful satiny luster throughout. Both sides are remarkably pristine, even for the Gem grade. An attractive specimen, this piece would make a splendid type coin to represent the first year of the Saint-Gaudens double eagle. (#9141)

4368 1908 No Motto MS66 PCGS. CAC. Well struck with smooth, softly lustrous yellow-orange surfaces. Excellent preservation aside from a single, shallow flaw on Liberty's leg. PCGS has graded just 51 numerically finer pieces (8/08). (#9142)

4369 1908 No Motto MS66 NGC. Vibrant yellow-gold surfaces exhibit subtle traces of orange, peach, and wheat. Well-defined and beautifully preserved with excellent visual appeal. (#9142)

4370 1908 No Motto MS66 PCGS. Luminous yellow-orange surfaces and crisply detailed devices combine with solid preservation for amazing eye appeal. A noteworthy No Motto type piece. (#9142)

4371 1908-D No Motto MS64 PCGS. A medley of yellow-gold, light green, and orange-gold patina races over the lustrous surfaces of this near-Gem. Lightly marked, and well struck. (#9143)

4372 1908-D No Motto MS64 PCGS. A well executed strike leaves strong definition on the design elements of this near-Gem Saint, and brass-gold surfaces exhibit pleasing luster. Kept from full Gem by a few small marks. (#9143)

4373 1908-D No Motto MS64 PCGS. Short Rays Obverse. A sharply struck example with good luster and lightly abraded fields. Unlike its Philadelphia counterpart, the Denver No Motto is somewhat scarce as a near-Gem. (#9143)

4374 1908-D No Motto MS64 PCGS. Bright yellow-gold surfaces show occasional glimpses of orange. A pleasing Choice example of this No Motto issue, surprisingly elusive in finer grades. (#9143)

Reddish Tinged MS65 1908-D No Motto Twenty

4375 1908-D No Motto MS65 PCGS. Q. David Bowers' *A Guide Book of Double Eagle Gold Coins* sums up this issue succinctly: "Today the 1908-D No Motto, while the least plentiful issue of the Type 5 design, is readily available in grades from MS60 to 63 or even 64, but MS65 examples are very rare." The present strictly Gem coin offers all of the requisite characteristics and more, with softly glowing, lustrous fields, few abrasions, and a boldly pleasing strike. As a further indication of this issue's rarity in Gem state, PCGS has graded only nine examples finer, with four at NGC (8/08). (#9143)

Enticing Near-Gem 1908 Motto Twenty

4376 1908 Motto MS64 PCGS. The With Motto is an issue that was mostly melted during the Gold Recall of the 1930s, and today specimens in Gem or finer condition are quite elusive. This enticing near-Gem example offers attractive, fine-grained, mattelike surfaces that are typical for the issue. The sharp strike and relatively abrasion-free surfaces are a plus. (#9147)

Splendid 1908 Motto Double Eagle, Choice Uncirculated

4377 1908 Motto MS64 PCGS. The mintage of Motto 1908 double eagles is many multiples lower than that of its No Motto counterpart. Enchanting satiny luster graces the minimally marked surfaces. Pleasing yellow and gold patina complements the bold strike. The 1908 Motto twenty is elusive in higher grades. (#9147)

Lovely 1908 With Motto Twenty, MS64

4378 1908 Motto MS64 PCGS. A lovely example of the newly modified design with the motto IN GOD WE TRUST added over the sun at the bottom of the reverse. Philadelphia only coined 156,200 examples of the new type in 1908, and most that survive today are in lower grades. PCGS has certified just 48 finer examples. (#9147)

Satiny Gem 1908-D Motto Twenty

4379 1908-D Motto MS65 PCGS. An exceptionally clean example of this conditionally scarce and somewhat underrated issue. The mint frost shows light pinkish-rose color with a subtle interplay of antique-golden. A must-see Saint for the specialist. PCGS has only certified 26 finer coins (8/08). (#9148)

Condition Rarity 1908-D Double Eagle, MS66

4380 **1908-D Motto MS66 PCGS.** Like the earlier Liberty double eagles, there are several issues in the Saint-Gaudens series that are conditionally rare in Gem or finer quality. Issues such as the 1908-D that began with a moderate mintage of 349,500 coins are relatively plentiful in lower Mint State grades, but are nearly impossible to find in higher grades. David Akers considers the issue to be underrated and ranks it 20th in the 55-coin series in terms of rarity.

Both sides of this honey-gold Premium Gem have satiny luster with subdued mint brilliance and subtle reflectivity in the fields. A few tiny toning spots can be seen on the obverse, and the surfaces are virtually free of distractions. A winning combination of eye appeal, condition rarity, and high grade. Population: 23 in 66, 3 finer (8/08). (#9148)

Choice XF 1908-S Double Eagle

4381 **1908-S XF45 PCGS.** The 1908-S twenty has the lowest mintage of any of the With Motto double eagles, although obviously a higher subsequent survival rate than some of the late-series entries. This Choice XF piece displays the moderate wear expected of the grade, and scattered, even, undistracting surface abrasions, with plenty of luster remaining. (#9149)

4382 **1909 MS61 NGC.** Primarily wheat-gold surfaces show occasional sun-orange and ruby accents. Well struck and lustrous with numerous fine flaws that account for the grade.
From The Menlo Park Collection. (#9150)

Attractive MS63 1909 Saint-Gaudens Twenty

4383 **1909 MS63 PCGS.** The 1909 and 1909/8 double eagles show virtually identical certified populations, presumably reflecting a 50:50 split between the overdate and nonoverdate varieties. This regular-date piece shows tinges of orange and green over lustrous, frosty, and lightly abraded surfaces. (#9150)

Scarce 1909 Twenty Dollar, MS64

4384 **1909 MS64 PCGS.** The near-Gem double eagle offered here is the highest grade most collectors will be able to locate, and even MS64s take some patient searching. PCGS and NGC have seen fewer than 40 pieces finer, and a number of those are likely resubmissions. This is a well struck, lustrous piece. Yellow-gold surfaces display hints of light tan, and are minimally abraded. (#9150)

4385 **1909/8 MS61 PCGS.** The dramatic hubbed overdate, also popular because the 1909 is a lower mintage date. A satiny butter-gold Mint State example that has few marks given its grade. Encased in a green label holder. (#9151)

4386 **1909/8 MS61 NGC.** The popular overdate double eagle, in this instance a lower Mint State piece with lustrous yellow-gold surfaces. (#9151)

Notably Lustrous 1909/8 Twenty, MS65

4387   **1909/8 MS65 PCGS.** The only overdate in the Saint-Gaudens series, the 1909/8 is a popular issue that is also of considerable rarity as a Gem. The obverse die was a holdover from the 1908 No Motto issue, and most representatives of this overdate variety are softly defined on the portrait of Liberty. On the other hand, this coin is well struck throughout with swirling mint luster. The surfaces exhibit a rich, frosty texture, and there are no abrasions of note. For pedigree purposes, a single copper-colored toning spot is seen at the intersection of the eagle's tail and the reverse rim. A reddish-gold Gem that offers both condition rarity and superior eye appeal. Population: 14 in 65, 3 finer (8/08). (#9151)

4388   **1909-S MS64 PCGS.** Dazzling luster shines from the yellow-gold surfaces. The details are boldly defined, and there are no marks that merit individual mention. This appealing example would make an excellent type coin. (#9153)

4389   **1909-S MS64 PCGS.** Alluring satiny luster graces the pleasing honey-gold surfaces of this attractive piece. Several wispy bagmarks define the grade, but all are minor. Boldly struck with great eye appeal. (#9153)

4390   **1909-S MS64 PCGS.** Brass-gold surfaces give off a slight greenish cast, and exhibit well struck design features. A few minute marks prevent Gem classification. (#9153)

4391   **1909-S MS64 NGC.** Although the 1909-S has a large mintage of nearly 2.8 million pieces, the number of available pieces drops dramatically in grades finer than the present example. Splendid satiny luster accents the bright yellow surfaces, which have no marks of any significance. A crisply struck near-Gem example. (#9153)

4392   **1910 MS64 PCGS.** Partly satiny surfaces show captivating golden-orange patina with pleasing wafts of rose. The bright and magnificent luster is barely affected by a couple of grazes on the obverse. This fully struck and eye-catching specimen would make an excellent type coin. (#9154)

4393   **1910 MS64 NGC.** Bright orange and yellow patina endows each side, with lovely satiny luster that shimmers throughout. This minimally marked and nearly fully struck Choice representative has great eye appeal. (#9154)

4394   **1910 MS64 PCGS.** Though the sun-gold obverse is slightly subdued, the yellow-gold reverse offers powerful luster. Solidly struck with considerable eye appeal for the grade. (#9154)

4395   **1910 MS64 PCGS. CAC.** The rich yellow-orange of the obverse shows elements of alloy near Liberty's feet, while the paler lemon-gold reverse offers pure color and vibrant luster. Choice and incredibly appealing. (#9154)

Remarkable 1910 Double Eagle, Gem Uncirculated

4396   **1910 MS65 PCGS.** The 1910 is common in nearly all grades, but in MS65 the number of certified specimens drops dramatically. NGC and PCGS combined report just nine coins finer than the present example (7/08). Satiny luster sparkles throughout this handsome rose-yellow representative, which has only a few minuscule abrasions. Sharply defined with spectacular eye appeal. (#9154)

Impressive 1910-D Twenty, MS65

4397   **1910-D MS65 PCGS. CAC.** A boldly detailed and frosty 1910-D twenty, this piece has exceptional surfaces and excellent aesthetic appeal, a coin for the connoisseur to truly appreciate. Like so many of its peers in the Saint-Gaudens series, the 1910-D is a condition rarity in higher grades. PCGS has only certified 96 finer examples (8/08). (#9155)

4398   **1910-S MS64 PCGS.** The satiny and well-preserved surfaces of this piece are essentially free of any noticeable marks. Hints of pale lavender and blue toning visit the otherwise butter-yellow fields. A wonderful type coin. (#9156)

Attractive 1910-S Double Eagle, Choice Mint State

4399 **1910-S MS64 PCGS.** While the 1910-S had a mintage of over 2.1 million pieces, most were either melted or sent overseas. The rough handling of the examples that have returned to the United States has led this issue to be relatively scarce in grades finer than the present piece. Delightful pale yellow patina graces both sides of this specimen, with a couple of tiny blemishes noted. This minimally marked representative exhibits splendid eye appeal. (#9156)

4400 **1910-S MS64 PCGS.** A pleasing Saint-Gaudens double eagle with traces of pink toning over the lustrous yellow-gold surfaces. Both sides are frosty with few distracting marks. (#9156)

4401 **1910-S MS64 PCGS.** 1910-S double eagles are less available than other similarly high mintage twenties because many were sent to the melting pot during the 1930s. Delightful satiny luster shines from the surfaces, which are minimally marked for the grade. Crisply struck with lovely yellow-gold patina. (#9156)

4402 **1910-S MS64 PCGS.** It is impossible to overstate the spectacular eye appeal of this sun-yellow, highly lustrous representative. A close examination yields a couple of tiny handling marks on Liberty's dress, but overall this sharply struck piece has been impeccably preserved. (#9156)

Desirable Choice 1910-S Twenty

4403 **1910-S MS64 PCGS.** Warm orange-gold surfaces offer glimmers of peach in the fields. Minimally marked and crisply struck with soft, pleasing luster. Despite a mintage of over 2.1 million pieces, the 1910-S is a surprisingly elusive issue in better Mint State grades, with a mean certified grade for the combined certified population of just 61.9 (8/08). (#9156)

4404 **1911 MS62 PCGS.** Attractive apricot-gold color covers both sides, each of which displays frosty luster and well-defined motifs. A handful of minute marks limit the grade, but none are particularly bothersome. (#9157)

Outstanding 1911 Double Eagle, MS64

4405 **1911 MS64 PCGS.** The 1911 double eagle is seldom seen finer than the present piece, and this highly lustrous example has above-average eye appeal. A few trivial grades barely affect the flow of the satiny luster, which accents the sharply struck details. This attractive yellow-gold representative would suit even the most discerning eye. PCGS has certified 42 pieces finer (7/08). (#9157)

Lovely 1911 Double Eagle, MS64

4406 **1911 MS64 PCGS.** Patches of olive-green patina cover the figure of Liberty, while the fields have a lovely yellow-gold complexion. There are no mentionable abrasions on either side. The obverse is heavily frosted, which contrasts nicely against the more satiny reverse. PCGS reports a mere 42 pieces finer (8/08). (#9157)

Pleasing 1911 Double Eagle, MS64

4407 **1911 MS64 PCGS.** The lustrous surfaces of this near-Gem twenty dollar display yellow-gold patination with a greenish tint. Sharp impressions characterize the design elements, which is evident in Liberty's fingers, the Capitol building, and the eagle's plumage. A handful of minute marks preclude Gem classification. PCGS has graded only 42 pieces finer. (#9157)

Exceptional MS65 1911 Saint-Gaudens Twenty

4408 **1911 MS65 PCGS. CAC.** This is a beautiful example of a rare and underrated coin. The 1911 double eagle is surprisingly difficult to locate at the Gem level. In *The Official Red Book of Auction Records 1995-2003*, Jeff Garrett and John Dannreuther found only six auction records for a 1911 double eagle in MS65 and none higher. David Akers notes that a large hoard of 1911 twenties appeared on the market in the 1990s but Gem quality coins were noticeably absent.

The present example is fully struck with exquisite detail on all the design elements. The coin has exceptional luster, a quality not found on many coins of this year. The fields are pristine and the only blemish worthy of mention is a thin scratch on Liberty's outstretched arm. Vivid, orange-gold color radiates from the coin's superb surfaces. In addition to its obvious qualities, this coin has all the subtle intangibles that make for remarkable eye appeal. This high-end Gem is a rare opportunity for the discerning collector. Population: 33 in 65, 9 finer (7/08). (#9157)

Compelling 1911-D Twenty, MS66

4409 **1911-D MS66 PCGS.** An issue that is well-known for its overall excellent production values, the 1911-D is a popular mintmarked twenty from early in the Saint-Gaudens series. Frosty luster emanates from the mattelike surfaces on both sides, with lovely antique-gold patina and premium appeal in evidence throughout. PCGS has certified only nine examples finer than the present specimen (8/08). (#9158)

Splendid Premium Gem 1911-D Saint-Gaudens Twenty

4410 **1911-D MS66 NGC.** One of the more available mintmarked issues from early in the Saint-Gaudens series, the 1911-D is well-known for a popular overmintmark variety. This example is not the variety, but it demonstrate the other characteristic for which the issue is known, generous production values. The fields on each side are of the full cartwheel variety, and the strike is nearly full. Even under a loupe the surfaces reveal essentially no distractions, along with mattelike luster and tremendous appeal. (#9158)

Elegant 1911-D Double Eagle, MS66

4411 **1911-D MS66 PCGS.** The 1911-D is, fortunately, one of the early-series issues that can be occasionally found in Gem and finer grades, as here. This piece displays remarkably few contact marks of any significance, and splendid cartwheel luster roils around each side of this orange-gold piece. Seldom seen finer, as PCGS has certified only nine coins at the next level higher (8/08). *From The Bell Collection.* (#9158)

4412 **1911-D/D MS64 PCGS.** FS-901. The mintmark is clearly repunched east, as often seen on this Taft-era issue. This is a well struck and minimally abraded near-Gem with superior eye appeal for the designated grade. (#145010)

4413 **1911-D/D RPM FS-501 MS65 PCGS.** Under magnification it becomes apparent that the original D was punched slightly to the right of its current location. This crisply struck Gem has lovely orange-yellow patina with only a few insignificant grazes on each side. Flashy luster enhances the terrific eye appeal. A great choice for the double eagle specialist. (#145010)

4414 **1911-D/D MS65 NGC.** FS-501. The mintmark is boldly repunched east. This is a beautiful Gem with blazing luster and radiant sun-gold color. The use of a loupe fails to locate relevant marks. Sharply struck and exceptional in quality. (#145010)

Sharp MS66 1911-D/D Double Eagle, FS-501

4415 **1911-D/D RPM FS-501 MS66 NGC.** VP-001. The mintmark is boldly and broadly repunched east of the final punch, an RPM variety that is nearly of the "naked-eye" sort. That it occurs on such a high-grade and well-preserved Saint-Gaudens double eagle is a doubly felicitous happenstance. The coin is smoothly lustrous, with plenty of fire and flash emanating from the orange-gold surfaces. This piece shows the bold strike and mattelike appearance characteristic of the issue. (#145010)

4416 **1911-S MS64 PCGS.** A charming early series San Francisco issue, with pleasing butter-yellow patina that envelops both sides. The sharp strike is complemented by eye-catching luster. This minimally marked specimen would make an excellent type coin. (#9159)

Lustrous 1911-S Gem Double Eagle

4417 **1911-S MS65 PCGS.** The 1911-S is one of the more available dates in the Saint-Gaudens double eagle series, right through the near-Gem level. MS65 pieces are obtainable with patient searching, but anything finer is much more challenging. The lustrous surfaces of this Gem display honey-gold patina and nicely defined devices. A few minor grade-consistent marks are seen over each side. (#9159)

Conditionally Scarce Gem 1911-S Saint-Gaudens Twenty

4418 **1911-S MS65 PCGS.** This San Francisco Mint issue is conditionally scarce at the Gem grade level, and relatively rare any finer. The luster is exceptional, and light orange-gold and champagne toning increases the eye appeal of the piece. A well struck, minimally abraded Gem Saint-Gaudens double eagle. (#9159)

Vibrant MS66 1911-S Twenty, Ex: Brahin

4419 **1911-S MS66 PCGS.** Ex: Brahin. Though its mintage was not in the millions, the 1911-S double eagle has long been considered one of the more available Saint-Gaudens twenties, and Garrett and Guth describe it as " ... available up to and including grades of MS-65." At the Premium Gem level, however, the numbers change, and the 1911-S is a condition rarity. This impressively lustrous, slightly satiny piece offers an interesting blend of sun-gold and wheat shadings. Excellent detail, particularly on the finer elements of Liberty's branch hand, and remarkable preservation. PCGS has graded only one finer example (8/08). (#9159)

4420 **1912 MS63 PCGS.** This is a lustrous and lightly abraded Select Mint State example of this scarcer Philadelphia Mint issue. Housed in a green label PCGS holder. (#9160)

4421 **1912 MS63 NGC.** Solid strike and eye appeal for the grade with excellent luster. Though a handful of scattered marks affect the fields and devices, none of them are individually distracting. *From The Menlo Park Collection.* (#9160)

Lovely 1912 Saint-Gaudens Twenty, MS64

4422 **1912 MS64 PCGS.** A frosty near-Gem example of the scarce, low-mintage 1912 double eagle, surviving from a production of just 149,700 coins. This piece has splendid bright yellow-gold surfaces with a few tiny splashes of copper toning on each side. PCGS has only certified 31 finer examples (8/08). (#9160)

Elusive 1912 Double Eagle, MS64

4423 **1912 MS64 PCGS.** An attractively preserved near-Gem that has a precise strike and clean surfaces. The 1912 is part of a run of low mintage Philadelphia double eagles struck between 1911 and 1915. 1912 was the first date with 48 obverse stars, due to the Union admission of New Mexico and Arizona. (#9160)

4424 **1913 MS61 NGC.** Captivating satiny luster graces the butter-yellow surfaces. The scattered abrasions are all minor save for a shallow scrape below Liberty's right (facing) arm. Boldly struck with the usual weakness on the high points of Liberty. (#9161)

4425 **1913 MS62 NGC.** A lustrous example with pleasing yellow-gold patina that has traces of deep purple toning on the rims. This boldly struck specimen has a number of scattered marks, typical for the grade. (#9161)

Select 1913 Saint-Gaudens Twenty

4426 **1913 MS63 PCGS.** An original green-gold example of this lower mintage Philadelphia issue. Shimmering luster sweeps the lightly marked surfaces. Liberty's face and the Capitol building are well struck, although the fingers of the torch hand show slight merging. The pre-1920 portion of the series is readily collectible, and makes an impressive short set. (#9161)

Captivating Near-Gem 1913 Double Eagle

4427 **1913 MS64 NGC.** This popular Philadelphia is highly challenging any finer, with only 18 numerically superior pieces known to NGC (8/08). The present example, deep yellow-gold with rich, satiny luster, is well-defined overall and pleasingly preserved. Only a handful of isolated abrasions on the obverse preclude an even finer designation. (#9161)

Frosty 1913 Double Eagle, MS64

4428 **1913 MS64 PCGS. CAC.** Splendid light yellow surfaces with brilliant, frosty golden luster and bold design motifs. Only a few faint toning spots and occasional marks are visible on either side. The 1913 is a major condition rarity in the series, especially any finer than the present piece. PCGS has only certified eight MS65 or finer coins since 1986. (#9161)

Lustrous Choice 1913 Double Eagle

4429 **1913 MS64 PCGS.** This lower-mintage Philadelphia issue is readily available in grades through MS63, though Choice coins prove elusive and anything finer is a condition rarity. The present MS64 coin is generally sun-gold with occasional hints of green-gold in the minimally marked fields. Well struck and lustrous with a touch of alloy on the high points. (#9161)

4430 **1913-D MS64 PCGS.** Primarily yellow-gold with a touch of green in the lustrous fields. This mid-date Denver double eagle offers pleasing detail and excellent eye appeal for the grade. (#9162)

Shining MS62 1913-S Twenty

4431 **1913-S MS62 PCGS.** Among the With Motto double eagles the 1913-S is second in terms of low mintage only to the 1908-S, and their easily remembered five-digit mintages (34,000 and 22,000 coins, respectively) serve to increase their popularity among collectors. A few moderate abrasions on Liberty's exposed left (facing) thigh are chiefly responsible for the grade, with lesser contact marks visible elsewhere, none particularly distracting. Bold cartwheel luster radiates from the yellow-gold surfaces, and the strike is well-executed. (#9163)

Lovely Select 1913-S Twenty

4432 **1913-S MS63 PCGS.** This San Francisco issue's original mintage was a scant 34,000 pieces, and there are few survivors to go around. The present Select piece has soft, yet pleasing luster that graces surfaces with only faint, scattered abrasions. Well struck with solid visual appeal for the grade. (#9163)

Formidable Gem 1913-S Twenty, Ex: Brahin

4433 **1913-S MS65 PCGS. CAC.** Ex: Jay Brahin. Booming luster, radiant yellow-gold surfaces, and a paucity of tiny marks confirm the exemplary quality of this desirable Gem. The mintage, a mere 34,000 pieces, ensures that the 1913-S will command collector attention. Among Motto issues, only the 1909-S has a lower production. The patient set assembler can locate a Mint State 1913-S, but Gems are rare and are eagerly contested by Registry competitors. The present piece, from an important collection and CAC-approved, is particularly desirable. Only one finer example is known, a PCGS MS66 from the Phillip H. Morse Collection that brought $149,500 in our November 2005 Signature. Population: 19 in 65, 1 finer (8/08). (#9163)

Well Struck 1914 Double Eagle, MS63

4434 **1914 MS63 PCGS.** The Philadelphia Mint apparently upped its standards this year, as most examples are sharply struck and lustrous (Jeff Garrett and Ron Guth, 2006). This Select example is no exception, as it possesses great luster and strongly defined design features. Yellow-gold surfaces reveal a few grade-defining marks. (#9164)

Marvelous 1914 Double Eagle, MS63

4435 **1914 MS63 PCGS.** Splashes of orange endow the yellow-gold surfaces. Enticing satiny luster graces both sides and complements the powerfully impressed design elements. Scattered marks limit the grade, but none merit specific mention. The 1914 twenty's mintage of just 95,250 pieces is significantly lower than the typical Saint-Gaudens double eagle.
From The Menlo Park Collection. (#9164)

Sharp 1914 Twenty Dollar, MS63

4436 **1914 MS63 NGC.** This Select example yields pleasing luster and attractive honey-gold color. The strike is sharp, displaying, for example, crisp delineation in the Capitol building panes, Liberty's branch hand, and on the eagle's feathers. A scattering of minute marks defines the grade. (#9164)

Pleasing 1914 Double Eagle, MS63

4437 **1914 MS63 NGC.** With the appearance of a number of high-quality coins from a large hoard in recent years (David Akers, The Thaine Price Collection, May 1998, p. 50), the 1914 twenty has become more available. That said, this Select example displays pleasing luster on its yellow-gold surfaces. The design features, including Liberty's facial features and branch hand, are sharply impressed. A few minuscule marks, more so on the reverse, account for the grade. (#9164)

Enticing 1914 Double Eagle, Choice Mint State

4438 **1914 MS64 PCGS.** The 1914 double eagle has a relatively low mintage of 95,250 pieces, and it is elusive in grades finer than the present piece. Delightful yellow-gold patina shows accents of rose on each side, with captivating cartwheel luster throughout. There are several grade-defining abrasions on the obverse, but none merit individual mention. A sharply struck and attractive representative. (#9164)

Lustrous 1914 Twenty, MS64

4439 **1914 MS64 PCGS. CAC.** The 1914 double eagle is not at all a common issue among early Saint-Gaudens twenties, but when found it is apt to be highly attractive, as here. Splendid cartwheel luster emanates from orange-gold surfaces that are somewhat mattelike, even though under a loupe a few minor abrasions on Liberty appear that account for the grade. PCGS has certified only 39 coins finer (8/08). (#9164)

Dazzling 1914 Double Eagle, Choice Mint State

4440 **1914 MS64 PCGS. CAC.** A hint of olive-green graces the mostly yellow-gold surfaces. Enticing satiny luster radiates from both sides and enhances the eye appeal of this sharply struck representative. The surfaces are remarkably clean with only a few pinpoint abrasions. PCGS has certified just 39 coins finer (8/08). (#9164)

Splendid Gem 1914 Twenty

4441 **1914 MS65 PCGS.** The circulation strike mintage is on the low side at 95,200 coins in this first year of World War I, but fortunately enough piece survived the mass meltings of later dates that today the issue is still available up to Gem grade, with an occasional piece even finer. The population data, however, thin out markedly—by an order of magnitude or more—above the MS65 level.

This splendid Gem offers cascading cartwheel luster emanating from both sides. The orange-gold surfaces are mattelike and well-struck, and just a couple of nicks on Liberty's exposed thighs are in line with the grade. The reverse is choice for the grade. Population: 36 in 65, 3 finer (7/08). (#9164)

4442 **1914-D MS64 PCGS.** This resplendent near-Gem would make a perfect example for a type collector. Powerful satiny luster shimmers beneath the bright yellow patina. Minimally marked and razor-sharp.
From The Menlo Park Collection. (#9165)

Pleasing 1914-D Double Eagle, Gem Mint State

4443 **1914-D MS65 PCGS.** A bright and lustrous Gem with a razor-sharp strike. Delightful yellow-gold patina overlies the surfaces of this flashy specimen. The only mark worthy of mention is on the eagle's beak, and the rest of the abrasions are insignificant. This eye-catching example would make a wonderful and relatively affordable type coin. (#9165)

4444 **1914-D MS65 PCGS.** Dazzling luster graces bright yellow-gold surfaces with splashes of orange. Decisively struck with captivating eye appeal. This D-mint issue is elusive any finer, with just 56 such pieces known to PCGS (8/08). (#9165)

Delightful Gem 1914-D Twenty

4445 **1914-D MS65 NGC.** After striking double eagles in most of the prior years it had been in operation, the Denver Mint halted production of the denomination after the 1914 issue and did not restart until 1923. This Gem from the former year is well struck with attractive luster. The surfaces are generally yellow-gold with splashes of peach. NGC has graded 32 numerically finer pieces (8/08). (#9165)

4446 **1914-S MS65 PCGS.** Bright luster emanates from peach-gold surfaces that exhibit nicely struck design elements. Devoid of significant abrasions. (#9166)

Dazzling 1914-S Double Eagle, MS66

4447 **1914-S MS66 NGC.** The 1914-S is one of the most common dates of the Saint-Gaudens twenty dollar series, due in part from overseas hoards. Dazzling luster characterizes this Premium Gem, as does an attentive strike that leaves strong definition on the design elements. Nicely preserved throughout. (#9166)

Impeccably Preserved 1914-S Double Eagle
The Finest Certified, Superb Gem

4448 **1914-S MS67 NGC.** With one exception, no 1914-S has been certified by either NGC or PCGS above MS66. That exception is the present coin, which stands alone as the single finest certified. The 1914-S has the highest mintage of any issue from the teens, but few collectors even considered setting aside examples of such a high denomination, aside from Philadelphia Mint proofs and the highly popular High Relief issue.

A sizeable majority of 1914-S twenties were eventually melted, particularly after the 1933 gold recall. However, hard money advocates also acquired quantities, many of which came from foreign bank vault hoards, which have been widely disbursed in recent decades. Those pieces had one thing in common: bagmarks, caused by coin to coin contact within sealed bags as they were moved from one location to another, including a likely journey by ship overseas.

The large size and soft gold alloy of double eagles made it nearly impossible for examples to survive in high grades under such circumstances, but a few pieces faced better odds than their peers. Those were placed into advanced cabinets, such as the Connecticut State Library or John Clapp collections. Even so, it is miraculous that any Superb Gems exist today, since indifferent handling at the San Francisco Mint itself would cause abrasions before any possible collector intervention.

The present piece, then, is a marvel. It is one in a million, or more explicitly, one in 1.498 million. Those familiar with MS65 1914-S twenties know that they have numerous small marks, which are unacceptable for the MS67 grade. But this coin is remarkably smooth. Only one or two minute marks on each side are visible with the unaided eye, and these are concealed within the devices. The yellow-gold surfaces are lustrous and crisply struck, but it is the exceptional preservation that makes the current lot so important to those who demand only the finest for their collection. (#9166)

4449 **1915 MS61 NGC.** With just 152,000 pieces struck, the 1915 is yet another low mintage P-mint double eagle. Splendid yellow-gold patina graces the surfaces, which have scattered grade-defining abrasions. There are traces of softness on Liberty's head and body, but the rest of the details are sharply pronounced. Impressive cartwheel luster shines from each side. (#9167)

4450 **1915 MS63 NGC.** Charming yellow-gold patina endows the surfaces of this razor-sharp specimen. Scattered marks define the grade, although none detract from the swirling luster. This piece would make a wonderful type coin. (#9167)

4451 **1915 MS63 PCGS.** An attractive piece for the grade, this straw-gold specimen has only light luster grazes that barely affect the pleasing satiny luster. The 1915's mintage of 152,000 pieces ranks in the middle of the series.
From The Menlo Park Collection. (#9167)

Delightful Near-Gem 1915 Double Eagle

4452 **1915 MS64 PCGS.** Most certified survivors average only MS62 or so, but examples are occasionally found at the near-Gem level, with only a few dozen Gems certified. This piece displays bold, radiant luster as its chief attribute, with mattelike antique-gold patina ceding to amber and smoky-gold at the rims, with some tinges of sage. A delightful example. (#9167)

Pleasing 1915 Double Eagle, Choice Mint State

4453 **1915 MS64 PCGS.** Garrett and Guth (2006) speak to the outstanding quality of the 1915 double eagles. This piece is no exception, and boasts eye-catching luster beneath light rose and yellow patina. The strike is razor sharp, and there are only a few wispy abrasions on either side. A small milky patch in the field to the left of Liberty is barely worthy of mention. PCGS has certified just 32 pieces finer (8/08). (#9167)

4454 **1915 MS65 PCGS.** The 1915 Philadelphia issue, with a mintage of only 152,000 business strikes, is moderately scarce in all grades, as are all of the With Motto Philadelphia double eagles from the 1908 to 1915 period. David Akers (1988) writes: "...although the 1915 is certainly not rare in grades below the Gem level, it is a classic condition rarity and is definitely rare in full Gem condition. It is nearly identical in terms of overall rarity to the 1908 With Motto, although Gems of the 1915 do seem to be available somewhat more often than those of the 1908 With Motto. This issue is considerably rarer than the lower mintage 1914 (95,250 business strikes), once again showing that mintage figures, especially among 20th Century gold issues, are not a very accurate barometer of the relative rarity of any given issues."

This coin presents a rich, satiny finish that is accented with pronounced yellow-golden patina. All details are well struck including the often-weak Capitol building. Just a few insignificant marks are seen on the reverse that limit the grade. An elusive opportunity for the 20th Century gold specialist. Population: 31 in 65, 0 finer (8/08). (#9167)

4455 **1915-S MS64 NGC.** The 1915-S is popular among type collectors because of its relative availability, sharp strike, and magnificent satiny luster. This minimally marked piece is no exception and would make a wonderful representative. (#9168)

4456 **1915-S MS65 PCGS.** This frosty Gem has rich honey-gold luster with excellent surfaces. The devices are exceptionally well detailed. (#9168)

4457 **1915-S MS65 PCGS.** A gorgeous Gem with frosty yellow luster and excellent eye appeal. Both sides are boldly defined and almost entirely void of marks. (#9168)

Exemplary MS66 1915-S Twenty Dollar

4458 **1915-S MS66 PCGS. Ex: Jay Brahin.** Mr. Brahin currently has the #1 NGC Registry of Saint-Gaudens double eagles, and this lustrous Premium Gem once belonged to his famous collection. Original honey-gold and lime toning invigorates the boldly struck and nearly mark-free Premium Gem. Only a single example (an NGC MS67) has been certified finer by either major service (8/08). (#9168)

4459 **1916-S MS64 NGC.** A crisply struck example of this midseries issue, with lovely yellow-gold patina that has accents of olive-green on the reverse. Several light grazes in the fields barely affect the delightful satiny luster. An excellent type coin. (#9169)

4460 **1916-S MS65 PCGS.** Well struck and highly lustrous, with a radiant frosty sheen across each side, and lovely rose-gold color that heightens the visual allure of the piece. Carefully preserved with just a few minuscule nicks that keep it from grading even higher. (#9169)

4461 **1916-S MS65 PCGS.** A sensational Gem with bold design definition and frosty yellow luster, highlighted by subtle rose, violet, and blue toning. (#9169)

Original Gem 1916-S Twenty Dollar

4462 **1916-S MS65 PCGS.** Lustrous and well impressed with peach-gold toning and a couple of unimportant obverse alloy spots. The final gold issue prior to the 1920s, as there was no domestic demand and foreign trade was diminished by the World War. Housed in a green label holder. (#9169)

Marvelous 1916-S Twenty, MS66

4463 **1916-S MS66 PCGS. Ex: Brahin.** The 1915-S and 1916-S double eagles are among the most popular in the Saint-Gaudens series, a combination of their coveted mintmark and excellent production values. Lower-quality coins of the issue, however, are likely to show numerous bagmarks. This piece shows no such complaints, with marvelous luster and lovely peach-gold coloration, complemented on the reverse by some patches of hazel. This piece is tied among several dozen at PCGS for the honor of finest certified (8/08). (#9169)

4464 **1920 MS62 NGC.** Lustrous and original with orange and lime toning and a few tiny alloy spots. Due to the unpredictable nature of the Treasury releases prior to the 1933 gold recall, the 1920 is relatively available, while the much higher mintage 1920-S and 1921 are famous rarities. (#9170)

4465 **1920 MS63 NGC.** The strike is crisp with only minor weakness on the highest points of Liberty. A number of grazes on each side are typical of the grade, but none are worthy of individual mention. Flashy luster and lovely yellow patina give this piece great eye appeal. (#9170)

4466　1920 MS63 PCGS. This boldly defined yellow-gold piece has enticing satiny luster throughout. There are no bothersome abrasions on either side, which further enhances the splendid eye appeal. *From The Menlo Park Collection.* (#9170)

4467　1920 MS63 PCGS. Orange-gold surfaces are accented by hints of lilac. Both sides exhibit dazzling luster along with sharply struck design elements. A few minute contact marks define the grade. (#9170)

Appealing Near-Gem 1920 Double Eagle

4468　1920 MS64 PCGS. Despite the relatively low mintage of the 1920 Saint-Gaudens, many survivors exist today, with certified survivors averaging MS62 or thereabouts. This near-Gem example offers generous appeal, a combination of the radiant cartwheel luster, relatively clean surfaces, and bold strike. Almost never seen finer: PCGS has certified a single Gem (8/08). (#9170)

Vibrant 1920 Double Eagle, MS64

4469　1920 MS64 NGC. MS64 is the highest grade most collectors will be able to acquire of the 1920 double eagle. NGC and PCGS have seen a total of eight coins finer, all MS65s. Vibrant luster radiates from the honey-gold surfaces of this lovely example. Well struck, and revealing a few marks denying Gem status. (#9170)

Gorgeous 1920 Double Eagle, MS64

4470　1920 MS64 NGC. A fully brilliant near-Gem with rich honey-gold color and frosty luster, this wonderful piece features a bold strike and exceptional aesthetic appeal. NGC and PCGS have combined to certify just eight finer examples of the date. The surfaces are pristine and the overall presentation is exceptional. (#9170)

Desirable Choice 1920 Double Eagle

4471　1920 MS64 PCGS. A challenging post-World War I issue that is essentially unavailable any finer, with just one such coin known to PCGS (8/08). Both sides are yellow-gold with strong detail and few flaws. The obverse has strong, satiny luster, while the reverse luster is more swirling and vibrant. (#9170)

4472　1922 MS64 NGC. A delightful representative with a mix of rose and yellow patina on each side. Several light grazes define the grade, but overall the eye appeal is outstanding. Nearly fully struck with pleasing satiny luster. (#9173)

Pleasing 1922 Gem Twenty Dollar

4473　1922 MS65 PCGS. The discovery of various hoards has made the 1922 double eagle one of the most plentiful issues in the entire series. Pleasing luster adorns apricot-gold surfaces imbued with hints of khaki-green. Generally well struck and minimally abraded. Gem coins such as this are the finest most collectors will acquire; PCGS and NGC have seen only 15 coins finer (8/08). (#9173)

Lustrous 1922 Gem Double Eagle

4474 **1922 MS65 PCGS.** The 1922 is a common and readily obtainable coin through the near-Gem level. MS65 pieces are more challenging, and anything finer is quite rare. Pleasing luster emanates from the peach-gold surfaces of this Gem, and a well executed strike leaves strong delineation on the design features. A few minute marks are consistent with the grade level. (#9173)

Scarcer MS65 1922 Twenty

4475 **1922 MS65 PCGS.** A highly lustrous and solidly struck Gem representative of this mid-date issue. The peach-gold surfaces have only a handful of marks. While the 1922 is usually not considered a scarce issue, MS65 is the finest generally attainable. PCGS has certified only seven coins finer (8/08). (#9173)

Dynamic Gem 1922 Double Eagle

4476 **1922 MS65 PCGS. CAC.** The obverse center and most of the reverse is peach-gold, while the obverse border is olive-green. Scintillating luster and splendidly unmarked surfaces confirm status as a Gem. Housed in an old green label holder. PCGS and NGC combined have certified only 15 pieces finer (8/08). (#9173)

Beautiful Gem 1922 Saint-Gaudens Twenty Dollar

4477 **1922 MS65 PCGS.** This Gem Saint-Gaudens double eagle possesses simply extraordinary eye appeal, by any standard. Coruscating mint frost in the fields is unusually intense, for the type, and beautifully complements the variegated lime-green and peach-gold toning across each side. Surface marks are only minor, as expected for the grade. Just seven examples have been certified at finer levels, by PCGS (8/08). (#9173)

Attractive MS62 1922-S Double Eagle

4478 **1922-S MS62 PCGS.** Most survivors of the original 2.6 million-coin mintage are those that were exported overseas and later repatriated, as many millions that remained Stateside were melted in the 1930s. MS62 is the average grade of certified specimens of the issue; the present example displays pretty yellow-gold surfaces with some light field chatter and a few abrasions on the focal points that determine the grade. The eye appeal is nonetheless high, however, with excellent luster and a reverse that is slightly rotated clockwise with respect to the obverse. (#9174)

4479 1922-S MS65 NGC. After a three-year hiatus in double eagle production from 1917 to 1919, mintages resumed with two years of tentative striking in 1920 and 1921, and not until 1922 did official mintages return to the millions, as it did in San Francisco. While the 1922 Philadelphia issue, with its mintage of under 1.4 million pieces, is available in most grades thanks to extensive repatriation, the 1922-S double eagle was not so fortunate, and as Garrett and Guth described it, the issue " ... suffered tremendously from the massive meltings of gold coins in the 1930s."

In this sense, the 1922-S has more in common with the substantially rarer issues struck in 1920 and 1921 than its Philadelphia contemporary. Garrett and Guth continue by noting the existing combined certified population of under 2,000 pieces, a tiny figure that surely includes resubmissions, and they point out that " ... most of those are in lower Mint State grades or circulated." They laud Gem and better survivors, which now show a combined certified population of just 21 examples of the former and a mere five pieces in the latter category (8/08).

The present survivor's luster is stronger than the norm, though it also shows an undercurrent of the more typical satin. Striking quality is excellent, and the generally yellow-gold surfaces show hints of green-gold and sun. All things considered, this is a delightful example of an already challenging issue, made even more desirable by its conditionally rare state, and a coin that virtually any collector of the series would be proud to own. (#9174)

Compelling Gem 1923 Double Eagle

4480 **1923 MS65 PCGS.** Although several of the P-mint Saint-Gaudens twenties are relatively available, the 1924 and 1928 are the most abundant in high grades. The 1923 is not a rare coin, but it is one that is quite well-produced, and in Gem condition is in great demand. The present example displays generous luster with a two-toned effect, orange-gold on the higher points and some hazel-gray in the lower fields. A compelling and startlingly original Gem. (#9175)

4481 **1923-D MS66 PCGS. CAC.** Rich butter-yellow fields cede to paler straw-gold centers on this immensely lustrous Premium Gem. Crisply struck and carefully preserved, an exciting survivor of this Denver issue. PCGS has certified 58 numerically finer representatives (8/08). (#9176)

4482 **1923-D MS66 PCGS.** Marvelous detail and visual appeal. This captivating Premium Gem has strong, satiny luster that swirls across primarily butter-yellow surfaces that exhibit scattered orange and wheat elements. This Denver issue is highly elusive any finer, with just 58 such pieces certified by PCGS (8/08). (#9176)

Outstanding Superb Gem 1923-D Twenty

4483 **1923-D MS67 PCGS. CAC.** Fortunately for type collectors, a fairly substantial portion of the Mint State population of this D-mint issue has survived in Gem condition. Why this should be the case for the 1923-D, while other issues are predominantly bagmarked or scuffed, is likely to be a topic for spirited discussion among Saint-Gaudens double eagle enthusiasts. The 1923-D is one of the best-produced of the available issues in the Saint-Gaudens series, and all of those attributes are on full display on this Superb example. The surfaces boast an intense satiny sheen, crisp definition, and terrific yellow-gold color with slightly deeper orange-golden peripheral accents. This piece is in a tie for the finest certified by PCGS (8/08). (#9176)

4484 1924 MS66 NGC. This is a visually delightful Premium Gem example of one of the most common of all Saint-Gaudens double eagle issues. Intense mint frost and magical champagne-gold toning combine to guarantee the splendid eye appeal of this captivating piece. Sharply struck and nearly pristine. (#9177)

Bold 1924-D MS62 Double Eagle

4485 1924-D MS62 PCGS. Mint State coins of the 1924-D double eagle are available through near-Gem. The lustrous surfaces of this MS62 piece exhibit well struck design elements, including Liberty's facial features and branch hand, and the eagle's feathers. Attractive peach-gold color graces both sides, each of which is only lightly abraded. (#9178)

Pleasing MS62 1924-D Double Eagle

4486 1924-D MS62 NGC. Strong, almost brassy luster shines from the yellow-gold fields, and the figure of Liberty is generally well-defined. A well struck, lightly abraded representative of this challenging Denver issue, one of the earliest melt rarities from that Mint. *From The Mississippi Collection.* (#9178)

Attractive 1924-S Double Eagle, MS64

4487 1924-S MS64 NGC. During the first half of the 20th century, the 1924-S was considered the rarest Saint-Gaudens double eagle. The Pierce Collection example was the first to appear at public auction, as lot 711 in the 1947 ANA auction. Abe Kosoff's lot description took 17 lines to describe the virtues of the issue, which was only 23 years old at the time! Fortunately, later numismatists found specimens of the 1924-S included in several hoards that surfaced in Europe in the 1950s and 1960s. Today the coin is still considered scarce, with David Akers ranking it the 14th-rarest issue in the 55-coin series. Most survivors are in lower Mint State grades, and the typical example has numerous bagmarks and abrasions. Gem specimens are still extremely rare.

The present coin is a pleasing example of this scarce date. The fields are much better than average, with a minimal number of abrasions for the grade. The devices are virtually free from distractions. Unbroken, frosty mint luster accents the bright, yellow-gold color. The mystique of its once-great rarity still clings to the 1924-S, and the discerning collector will recognize this near-Gem example as a singular opportunity. (#9179)

Choice 1924-S Double Eagle
Ex: Akers, Duckor, Brahin

4490 **1925-S AU58 PCGS.** Vast quantities of the 3.77 million 1925-S twenties struck were melted during the 1930s, and the high mintage figure does not represent the true scarcity of this issue. A relatively low number have emerged from European bank vaults, which makes this date difficult to locate in Mint State. This briefly circulated example has lovely yellow-gold patina and boldly defined details. Flashy luster gives this piece excellent eye appeal. (#9182)

Lovely Select 1925-S Double Eagle

4488 **1924-S MS64 PCGS.** Ex: Jay Brahin, Dr. Steven L. Duckor, David W. Akers. The 1924-S has a mintage of nearly 3 million pieces, but that figure is misleading. A large majority of the issue never left Treasury holdings, and was eventually melted after President Roosevelt ended the issue of gold coins in 1933. It was a different story for the 1924, which like other Philadelphia dates from the mid-1920s was paid out in quantity, principally for payments of imports.

Less a thousand 1924-S double eagles escaped the mass meltings. Most resided in foreign vaults as bank reserves at the time of the recall, and examples have trickled back to the United States once the rarity of the issue was known. The typical 1924-S grades MS62 to MS63. The issue is extremely rare as a Gem, and few pieces are MS60 or lower, since gold coins seldom circulated after World War I. The present coin is boldly struck and has beautiful orange toning. As one might expect from its illustrious pedigree, marks are difficult to find. Population: 86 in 64, 3 finer (8/08). (#9179)

4489 **1925 MS66 PCGS.** Shining, crisply struck, and virtually unimprovable. The rich sun-yellow surfaces show glints of straw at the left and right obverse. Essentially unavailable any finer, with just five such pieces known to PCGS (8/08). (#9180)

4491 **1925-S MS63 PCGS.** As is often the case for later mintmarked Saint-Gaudens double eagle issues, the original mintage (almost 3.8 million pieces) is out the window, and the small combined certified population takes precedence. This striking Select survivor has a potent, almost brassy sheen to the bright yellow-gold surfaces. The overall detail is strong, and though a few marks of varying intensity are present on each side, the eye appeal is notable. On the reverse, a thin but noticeable die crack arcs through the eagle's beak. PCGS has certified 33 finer examples (8/08). (#9182)

Scarce Uncirculated Details 1926-S Twenty

4492 1926-S—Improperly Cleaned—NCS. Unc. Details. Lustrous, sharply struck, and nearly free from bagmarks. Slightly glossy, but there are no obvious hairlines. More than 2 million 1926-S double eagles were struck, but most were retained by the Treasury and eventually melted following the 1933 gold recall. (#9185)

Charming 1926-S Double Eagle, MS64

4493 1926-S MS64 PCGS. CAC. Two PCGS certified 1926-S double eagles in the present sale have different mintmark positions, clearly illustrating the use of multiple obverse dies to coin more than 2 million examples of the date. Both sides have frosty yellow-gold luster with splashes of rose and faint green on the reverse. (#9185)

Dazzling 1926-S Double Eagle, MS64

4494 1926-S MS64 NGC. CAC. The 1926-S is seldom seen finer than the present piece, and this lovely yellow-orange example would make a wonderful representative. Powerful cartwheel luster graces both sides and is barely affected by several grade-defining handling marks. The strike is bold save for minor weakness on the BER in LIBERTY. NGC has certified just 24 coins finer (7/08). (#9185)

Wonderful 1926-S Twenty, MS64

4495 1926-S MS64 PCGS. CAC. One of the important and elusive dates in the Saint-Gaudens series, the 1926-S double eagle had an original mintage of more than 2 million coins, but few were actually released to banks and circulation. The majority of coins struck remained in vaults until the mid- to late-1930s, when they were melted. This example is fully brilliant with magnificent yellow-gold luster and only a few entirely insignificant marks. PCGS has only graded 29 finer examples of the date (8/08). (#9185)

Exceptional 1926-S Double Eagle, MS64

4496 1926-S MS64 PCGS. This near-Gem twenty has several outstanding features: its design elements are crisply impressed, including the panes of the Capitol building, Liberty's fingers and toes, and the eagle's feathers; it radiates potent luster and possesses attractive yellow-gold color; and its surfaces are minimally abraded. This piece would grade higher were it not for some minuscule rim marks that are actually difficult to see in the holder. (#9185)

4497 1927 MS64 PCGS. Yellow-gold throughout with distinct orange accents across the reverse fields. Pleasing for the grade with strong luster, although the surfaces show just a few marks that preclude a higher grade. (#9186)

4498 1927 MS65 PCGS. A splendid Gem with brilliant and highly lustrous butter-yellow surfaces and bold design details on both side. A plentiful date along with the other P-Mint issues from 1924 to 1928, ideal for date or type collectors. (#9186)

4499 1927 MS66 NGC. CAC. The 1927 double eagle is a popular coin among type collectors because of its relative availability with impressive eye appeal and luster. This handsome orange-gold piece is no exception, and exhibits a razor-sharp strike that is highlighted by blazing luster throughout. (#9186)

Delightful 1927 Double Eagle, MS66

4500 **1927 MS66 NGC. CAC.** Captivating cartwheel luster shines throughout the lightly frosted surfaces. A couple of nearly imperceptible abrasions keep this spectacular piece from an even higher grade. It is exceptionally difficult to find a 1927 any finer than Premium Gem, and NGC reports only 43 pieces at the MS67 level, some of which are undoubtedly resubmissions (7/08). (#9186)

4501 **1927 MS66 NGC. CAC.** An eye-catching Premium Gem with dazzling cartwheel luster throughout. This fully struck piece is nearly flawless, with only a couple of wispy abrasions in the obverse field. Faint streaks of deep russet accent the bright yellow-gold patina. A perfect choice for a type collector. (#9186)

Dazzling MS66 ★ 1927 Twenty Dollar

4502 **1927 MS66 ★ NGC. CAC.** The obverse field is semi-prooflike, and the light peach-gold toning is highly attractive. Vibrant luster sweeps uncommonly mark-free surfaces. The 1927 is a plentiful issue despite Roosevelt's gold recall, but those who can see this coin in person will consider it special. Census: 32 in 66 ★, 2 finer with a Star designation (7/08). (#9186)

The White House, Circa 1920s

Desirable MS62 1927-S Double Eagle

4503 1927-S MS62 PCGS. Though Mint records show over 3.1 million double eagles produced at San Francisco in 1927, that figure is utterly disconnected from the numismatic reality of today. While it is not of the supreme rarity that characterizes its Denver counterpart, it is nonetheless highly prized and elusive. As recounted in Garrett and Guth: "This tremendous mintage did little to provide coins for future collectors. Virtually the entire mintage was destroyed in the 1930s, leaving just a few hundred around today for collectors to fight over."

Interestingly for an issue that saw little circulation, the 1927-S appears frequently in worn grades, as shown by the NGC *Census Report* and the PCGS *Population Report*. In fact, the mean grade for the combined certified population is a mere 60.1, which puts virtually any Mint State coin, including the present MS62 piece, ahead of the curve.

Deep sun-gold shadings prevail on this desirable and satiny 1927-S twenty, though a hint of orange is present on the reverse. It is well struck overall, though the edges show a degree of the usual beveling and the peripheral stars are a trifle soft. A number of wispy abrasions are present in the fields and a handful of small digs appear on the central devices, yet the overall eye appeal is far better than the MS62 grade might suggest. It would make an excellent candidate for most double eagle cabinets, even one that has mainly Select or better pieces. Population: 36 in 62, 42 finer (7/08). (#9188)

Magnificent 1927-S Double Eagle, MS65
Ex: Duckor, Brahin

4504 **1927-S MS65 PCGS.** The 1927-S has long been recognized as a key date in the Saint-Gaudens double eagle series. In 1949, Max Mehl believed there were only three or four specimens known. The coin was generally regarded as the fourth rarest date of the design type, behind the 1924-S, 1926-D and 1926-S. This issue gradually became more available as individual examples leaked out of European bank holdings in the 1950s and 1960s. The issue never surfaced in hoard quantities, however, and its decline in the rarity rankings has been gradual. In recent times, David Akers ranks it as the 10th rarest coin in the 55-coin series. Most examples are in AU or lower Mint State grades. At the Gem level, this issue remains very rare and sought after.

Prominent collector Stephen Duckor was kind enough to provide an account of this coin's history while it was in his remarkable collection. Dr. Duckor remembers purchasing the coin from New England Rare Coin Auctions sometime around 1979 (actually Boston Jubilee Auction, 7/1980, lot 367). At that time, the cataloger graded this specimen MS66 and stated, "Possibly the finest known." Third-party grading was still far in the future, and Dr. Duckor was able to examine the coin in its natural state. He found it to be completely natural, undipped, and noted a beveled rim on the reverse. This beveled rim is a characteristic that occurs frequently on coins produced at the San Francisco Mint during the 1920s. Dr. Duckor retained this coin in his collection for 26 years before selling it to Jay Brahin in 2006. Brahin retained it in his collection until he sold it to the current consignor a year later. A pedigree to either the Duckor or Brahin Collections is extremely important. A pedigree to both collections is a mark of distinction for any coin.

The present coin features a strong strike, with good detail in all the design elements. This is an important consideration with the issue; many examples display a weak strike and crumbling rims. Smooth, satiny luster radiates from the coin's surfaces. The rich coloration is predominantly orange-gold, but shades of mint-green and reddish-orange play on each side, more boldly on the reverse. The fields have minimal distractions, as expected at the MS65 level. A tiny bit of struck-in die grease, between the eagle's wing and the letters DO of DOLLARS, can be used as a pedigree marker. Overall, this example displays outstanding eye appeal. Beauty, rarity, and an illustrious pedigree make this coin a prize for the advanced collector.
Ex: New England Rare Coin Auctions (7/1980), lot 367; Dr. Steven Duckor (2006); Jay Brahin (2007). (#9188)

Outstanding 1928 Double Eagle, Premium Gem

4505 1928 MS66 PCGS. CAC. The 1928 boasts the highest mintage of any U.S. gold coin, but the number of survivors drops precipitously in grades finer than the present piece. This razor-sharp Premium Gem has magnificent satiny luster and pleasing rose-yellow patina, with only a few wispy abrasions. An excellent piece for a type collector. PCGS has certified just 64 coins finer (7/08). (#9189)

Enchanting Superb Gem 1928 Double Eagle

4506 1928 MS67 PCGS. CAC. One could hardly wish for a more attractive type coin from the Saint-Gaudens series than a high-grade 1928, and the fortunate winner of this lot should consider it a wish granted. The surfaces are immensely lustrous and thickly frosted, the norm for this popular later issue. The strike is similarly bold, particularly on Liberty's flowing hair. On the obverse, soft peach and rose elements add color to the otherwise yellow-gold fields, while the reverse exhibits delightful lilac accents. The Registry enthusiast should note that this coin is tied for the finest certified by either NGC or PCGS (8/08). (#9189)

4507 **1929 MS64 PCGS. CAC.** Widely recognized as the first of the key issues at the end of the Saint-Gaudens series of twenties, a series that includes such fabled rarities as the 1930-S, 1931, 1931-D, and 1932. The scarcity of this date was commented upon by Paul Green in the October 24, 2006 issue of *Numismatic News:*

> "While not at the top of the list in terms of dates destroyed, the large mintage of the 1929 suggests that in terms of actual numbers it might well have been one of the dates most heavily destroyed. Our supply today appears to be in large part thanks to examples found in European banks. While the 1929 is expensive, the situation could have actually been much worse."

The MS64 level represents the greatest availability for the 1929 as well as the best value. With 161 submission events representing approximately 120-130 individual coins at this grade level, an MS64 is only 20-30% more than an MS63 coin.

The CAC sticker on this coin is a meaningful expression of the upper end appearance of this piece. This is, to a great extent because the surfaces are untampered as one can tell from the rich reddish-gold and lilac color on each side. The softly frosted mint luster gives the piece a pleasing glow and the coloration adds even more to the appeal of this rarity. Sharply defined throughout with no meaningful or mentionable abrasions, just the few tiny marks one would expect from a near-Gem coin. (#9190)

Key 1929 Saint-Gaudens Twenty, MS66
One of the Finest Examples Known

4508 **1929 MS66 PCGS. CAC.** Like so many other issues in this fabled and fabulous series, the 1929 Saint-Gaudens was once considered a major rarity, only to see its position somewhat eroded over time as the repatriations of overseas caches of coins occur. Today it is still a scarcity and expensive, but examples are available for a price, as nearly 300 examples are certified between NGC and PCGS. Most of those coins, in fact the vast majority, are MS64 or less, although the MS64 grade represents the bulk of the certified coinage for the issue. Between NGC and PCGS, 149 pieces fall into that near-Gem grade level. At the Gem or MS65 level the number certified plummets sharply, and in MS66 the total drops even more radically. There are 26 Gem pieces certified, and only six coins at both services combined have achieved the Premium Gem or MS66 level, including the present piece. All of the above totals, of course, almost certainly include unknown but considerable numbers of resubmissions.

Bowers' *Guide Book of Double Eagle Gold Coins* aptly calls the 1929 issue a "changing rarity in modern times," although we disagree with his lumping it with the common 1922-1928 Saint-Gaudens pieces when he says, "Now, many collections will end with the 1929 date instead of 1928 as formerly." *Au contraire,* we believe the 1929 date will always remain associated with the various legendary issues including the 1930-S, 1931, 1931-D, and 1932. While the latter pieces are notably rarer than the 1929, the association is apt for two reasons: First, because all of the group were issued during the Great Depression, and second, the 1929 is orders of magnitude rarer than the earlier Philadelphia Mint dates from 1922 to 1928.

Bowers' estimate of 1,250 to 1,750 pieces extant also appears wildly optimistic, given the certified totals and the distant probability of many more examples remaining undiscovered. In *The Coinage of Augustus Saint-Gaudens as Illustrated by the Phillip H. Morse Collection,* the authors note, "It seems highly unlikely that any sizeable quantity of an expensive coin such as the 1929 Saint could exist without being certified. Around 40 pieces were discovered in England in 1984, but we are not aware of any other sizeable holdings of this issue that have been uncovered recently."

It is extremely telling and significant that the present MS66 specimen is even finer than either of the Morse Collection pieces, an MS65 that brought $97,750 and an MS64 that yielded $35,938 in the 2005 FUN Auction (Heritage, 11/2005, lots 6707-6708). In point of fact, this is one of only five MS66 pieces certified at PCGS, with a single MS66 at NGC, and there are none finer at either service (8/08).

Exuberant cartwheel luster, more frosty than satiny, radiates from each side of this lovely coin. The centers are apricot-gold, while the peripheries on each side show tinges of mint-green. There are no singular abrasions on either side, and the strike is pleasingly bold. The latter characteristic is typical of the 1929 issue, which generally comes well struck. (#9190)

Lovely 1910 Saint-Gaudens Twenty, PR63

4509 **1910 PR63 PCGS.** For the type collector who desires a single proof Saint-Gaudens double eagle, either the 1909 or 1910 are ideal candidates. Those two dates are found with the so-called Roman Finish, with a soft, satiny appearance. They have the closest appearance to a brilliant proof gold coin, and they were the most popular with contemporary collectors. In 1908, the dark and dull matte finish was introduced and proved unpopular with collectors who then stayed away in 1909 when the Mint introduced the Roman or Satin Finish gold proofs. Those proved more popular with collectors, who returned to buy similar pieces in 1910. The mintage more than doubled with 167 proofs struck in 1910, by far the highest annual production of proof Saint-Gaudens double eagles. Of course, the high mintage meant that many more survived for collectors today.

The present specimen is a lovely proof with brilliant lemon-yellow surfaces, bold design features, and slightly reflective fields. Some minor surface marks appear on both sides, and they are more noticeable on the reverse. An extraordinarily attractive proof, this double eagle should see considerable bidding activity when it crosses the auction block. Interest will be shown by type collectors and advanced specialists alike. Furthermore, the combination of an attractive piece and a modest technical grade should provide an excellent value for the winning bidder. (#9207)

4510 (1842-52) A. Bechtler Dollar, 27G. 21C., Plain Edge—Scratched—NCS. AU Details. Luster outlines the letters and digits, but the central obverse has a cluster of dull scratches, and the reverse field has faint scuffs. Listed on page 359 of the 2009 *Guide Book*. (#10040)

AU53 A. Bechtler Dollar, 27G. 21C., K-24

4511 (1842-52) A. Bechtler Dollar, 27G. 21C., Plain Edge AU53 PCGS. K-24, R.3. The Bechtler family struck the first Territorial gold coins in the United States for two decades, from 1831 until 1852, with two generations sharing the family business. The opening of branch mints in North Carolina and Georgia in 1838, however, decreased the demand for private gold coinage. This piece offers a clean appearance, with lustrous, greenish-gold surfaces that are somewhat prooflike and show relatively few abrasions for the grade, save for a single old, toned-over scrape on the lower reverse through the C in CAROLINA and 21C. Certified in a small-size first-generation PCGS holder, and listed on page 359 of the 2009 *Guide Book*. (#10040)

Lovely AU58 A. Bechtler Gold Dollar, 27G. 21C., K-24

4512 (1842-52) A. Bechtler Dollar, 27G. 21C., Plain Edge AU58 PCGS. K-24, R.3. Among the more available of the Bechtler family issues, the A. Bechtler dollar coinage was trusted and circulated widely among the local North Carolina populace, so that Uncirculated examples are scarce today. This near-Mint piece exhibits the typical greenish-gold surfaces of the Bechtler issues, with good luster and some planchet roughness, as made. An old crack partway through the planchet, moving inward from the obverse rim at 4 o'clock perhaps a third of the way toward the center, is also apparently as made. Listed on page 359 of the 2009 *Guide Book*. Population: 39 in 58, 26 finer (7/08). (#10040)

Desirable K-24 A. Bechtler Dollar, Plain Edge, MS63

4513 (1842-52) A. Bechtler Dollar, 27G. 21C., Plain Edge MS63 NGC. Kagin-24, R.3. This variety is distinguished from K-25 by its plain edge. The first coins struck by the Bechtlers were minted in Rutherford County, North Carolina in 1830 by Christopher Bechtler. Preempting the U.S. Mint by 18 years, the Bechtlers began to strike gold dollars in 1831 and continued to produce them until the mint's close in 1852. In 1842, Christopher's son August took over the operations, hence the A. Bechtler that appears on the coins from the mint's final decade. Charming lemon-yellow patina drapes the surfaces of this minimally marked specimen. Several letters of Carolina are a trifle soft, but the rest of the details are bold. This attractive example is an excellent representative of this popular and numismatically important mint. Listed on page 359 of the 2009 *Guide Book*. (#10040)

Pleasing Near-Mint A. Bechtler Five Dollar 134 G., 21 Carats, K-27

4514 (1842-52) A. Bechtler Five Dollar, 134G. 21C. AU58 NGC. K-27, Low R.5. Moderately abraded with tinges of reddish patina at the margins. Much semi-reflective luster survives in the protected areas. Produced by August Bechtler circa 1842-1846 and an important companion piece to the half eagles produced at the Charlotte Mint during this era. So respected was Bechtler coinage that many pre-Civil War Southern contracts specified payment in Bechtler gold. Listed on page 359 of the 2009 *Guide Book*. Census: 10 in 58, 2 finer (7/08). *Ex: FUN Signature (Heritage, 1/2006), lot 3662.* (#10046)

4515 **(1837-42) C. Bechtler Quarter Eagle, 70G. 20C. AU58 NGC.** K-13, R.6. Plain Edge. From the seventh series of Bechtler gold. This Territorial was struck using South Carolina gold and shares the same obverse die as the K-11 two and a half in this sale, although the latter piece was struck from Georgia bullion. The obverse die is easily recognizable by the die break extending from the rim through T in BECHTLER. The Bechtler's were prolific private gold minters and their coins were greatly respected by the general public of their time for being of the true weight and fineness stated, and the gold value was typically worth more than the face value. The specimen offered here is sharply and evenly struck throughout. The green-gold surfaces are lightly abraded with the only notable distractions being a series of faint pinscratches below 250 on the obverse. Listed on page 358 of the 2009 *Guide Book*. Census: 3 in 58, 5 finer (8/08). (#10070)

4516 **(1837-42) C. Bechtler Quarter Eagle, 64G. 22C. AU58 NGC.** K-11, R.6. Reverse: GEORGIA GOLD, uneven 22. Deeply patinated in milky golden-brown hues, with darker encrustations about the lettering. The strike and quality of the planchet are both excellent. As of (8/08), NGC has certified three pieces at the AU58 level, with only nine coins grading finer, although the census data is likely inflated due to multiple submissions of the same coin. The numbers at PCGS are similar and the total population for this issue at both services—all grades included—is a mere 36 coins. This is one of the two quarter eagle varieties in Bechtler's sixth series of Territorial gold coinage and is listed on page 358 of the 2009 *Guide Book*. (#10073)

4517 **1834 C. Bechtler Five Dollar, Plain Edge—Improperly Cleaned—NCS. XF Details.** K-17, R.5. This piece was struck by Christopher Bechtler sometime between 1834 and 1837. Although this variety is one of the more available Bechtler fives, it is by no means common, and examples are seldom seen in any grade. Pleasing pumpkin-orange patina drapes both sides, with a few patches of verdigris noted on the obverse. The centers are a trifle soft, as usually seen, but the rest of the details are well-defined. A minimally marked example of this desirable Territorial. Listed on page 359 of the 2009 *Guide Book.* (#10091)

4518 **(1837-42) C. Bechtler Five Dollar, 134G, With Star—Improperly Cleaned—NCS. AU Details.** K-20, R.4. This canary-gold pioneer five dollar piece is a bit bright, and has a few slender gray streaks on each side from mint-produced retained laminations. One unobtrusive pinscratch before the H in BECHTLER, but there are fewer marks than typically seen. A scarce Bechtler denomination, more difficult than the gold dollar. Listed on page 359 of the 2009 *Guide Book.* (#10097)

4519 **(1834-37) C. Bechtler Five Dollar, RUTHERF:—Damaged—NCS. XF Details.** K-23, High R.6. Some luster remains on this rare variety C. Bechtler five. A dig following the A in GEORGIA caused a bend and uneven wear on the C (for Christopher) initial. Small but relatively deep marks above the 1 in 128 and the H in BECHTLER merit mention, and olive-gold surfaces are subdued. Listed on page 359 of the 2009 *Guide Book.* (#10109)

4520 **(1834-37) C. Bechtler Five Dollar, 140G. 20C RUTHERF. AU55 NGC.** K-18, R.6. Plain Edge. The Bechtler family made its first gold coins—gold dollars, quarter eagles, and half eagles—in 1831, predating the U.S. Mint by some 18 years. In 1834, when the melt value of federal gold coins exceeded its face value, the gold content was adjusted, and gold coins actually began circulating for the first time in many years, rather than being hoarded or melted. Treasury officials advised the Mint to put the date of the authorizing legislation on the federal coins, but they were redesigned instead. Christopher Bechtler chose a different path, putting the date on the family coinage but keeping the familiar appearance that helped ensure their trusted status and circulation in the local economy.

There are several variants of the 1834-37 five dollars, including reeded edge and plain edge varieties. **This is an example of the rarer K-18 variant, with 20 close to CARATS and plain edge, but RUTHERF. is abbreviated rather than spelled out.** Given the current certified populations, we would call this at least R.6 (13-30 pieces known) rather than the R.7 ranking Don Kagin assigned in 1981. This piece is also in spectacular condition. The still-lustrous greenish-gold surfaces are remarkably clean and free of singular abrasions, with some areas of prooflikeness around the peripheral lettering and some hazy smoky-gold patina on the obverse. Both sides, however, have an overall frosty appearance and generous eye appeal. A loupe reveals only tiny ticks and contact marks consistent with a short stay in circulation. In AU55 this is one of three pieces of the variety so graded at NGC, with eight coins finer (8/08). The PCGS certified figures do not clearly distinguish between the 140G. 20C varieties, so we consider them irrelevant. Listed on page 359 of the 2009 *Guide Book.* (#10112)

K-19 Near-Mint C. Bechtler Five
RUTHERF:, 20 Distant

4521   (1834-37) C. Bechtler Five Dollar, 20 Distant, RUTHERF AU58 NGC. K-19, High R.6. This North Carolina gold variety has the 20 placed distant from CARATS, which distinguishes it from the less rare Kagin-17. Presumably more relevant, RUTHERFORD is spelled out on K-17 but is abbreviated as RUTHERF on K-19. Semi-prooflike luster accompanies the legends, and the pale green-gold surfaces display glimpses of russet patina near the RO in CAROLINA. There are no consequential abrasions. Listed on page 359 of the 2009 *Guide Book*. Census: 4 in 58, 1 finer (7/08). (#10115)

Near-Mint 1861 Clark, Gruber Quarter Eagle, K-5a

4522   1861 Clark, Gruber & Co. Quarter Eagle AU58 PCGS. K-5a, R.4. The star is recut on the star above the peak of Liberty, and we believe this is a characteristic of all examples known (on later die states the recutting fades). The 1861 Clark, Gruber five dollar is roughly modeled on the federal half eagle, although PIKES PEAK replaces LIBERTY on the coronet, and the details are rustic. This lustrous piece has nice green-gold surfaces that are close to Mint State. Listed on page 376 of the 2009 *Guide Book*. (#10139)

Worthy Near-Mint 1861 Clark, Gruber Ten, K-7

4523   1861 Clark, Gruber & Co. Ten Dollar AU58 PCGS. K-7, R.4. From the second and final year of Clark, Gruber & Co. private gold coinage. The distinctive volcano-like Pike's Peak obverse of the 1860 ten dollar issue was replaced with a more readily accepted imitation of the Federal eagle. This is a lightly toned green-gold example with clean surfaces and the customary inexactness of strike on the eagle's extremities. The numerous slender die cracks, particularly through GRUBER, may be of interest to the specialist. Encapsulated in a green label holder, and listed on page 363 of the 2009 *Guide Book*. Population: 15 in 58, 1 finer (8/08). (#10141)

Choice AU 1852 Humbert Ten Dollar
Normal Date, Kagin-10

4524   1852 Humbert Ten Dollar AU55 NGC. K-10, Low R.4. From a late in life obverse die with crumbling on UNITED. An orange-tinted example that boasts noticeable luster and has less abraded surfaces than is characteristic of the type. The top of the shield and the fletchings exhibit moderate wear. Listed on page 363 of the 2009 *Guide Book*. Census: 5 in 55, 10 finer (7/08). (#10187)

4525 1851 Humbert Fifty Dollar, Reeded Edge, 880 Thous.—Obverse Damage—NCS. AU Details. K-5, Low R.5. Portions of the obverse field have wispy pinscratches from an attempt to remove tiny planchet flaws. The obverse is slightly bright. The corners lack the edge knocks usually seen, and luster is present on the wings and the reverse. 1851 was the first year of production at the U.S. Assay Office of Gold, and for the first time during the California Gold Rush, gold dust could be locally transformed into coin bearing the stamp of the Federal government. Listed on page 362 of the 2009 *Guide Book*. (#10211)

4526 1852 Humbert Fifty Dollar, 887 Thous. AU50 NGC. K-11, R.5. A relic of the great California Gold Rush and an iconic product of the U.S. Assay Office while under the direction of Moffat & Company, of which Augustus Humbert was the assayer. This particular variant was struck just prior the turnover of management to Curtis, Perry, & Ward in early 1852. The wording around the outer of circle on this piece reads "AUGUSTUS HUMBERT UNITED STATES ASSAYER OF GOLD CALIFORNIA" with the date at bottom. This would later be changed to read "UNITED STATES ASSAY OFFICE OF GOLD SAN FRANCISCO CALIFORNIA" under the order of Curtis, Perry, & Ward. Both 1852 .887 varieties are listed as R.5, but K-11—the variety offered here—is less available by a substantial margin. This accurately graded AU50 specimen displays the typical strike weakness common to the issue, but no major visual distractions. Census: 3 in 50, 23 finer (7/08). (#10217)

AU 1853 Assay Office Twenty, 900 Thous., K-18

Impressive 1853 U.S. Assay Office Twenty K-18, MS64

4527 **1853 Assay Office Twenty Dollar, 900 Thous. AU50 NGC.** K-18, R.2. The 1853 U.S. Assay Office twenty dollar pieces are among the most common of the various Territorial gold issues, because they were made in great numbers from March through October 1853, as Kagin says "from some 30 different dies destroyed in the fire of 1906." As testament to the great utility to which those dies were put, this late-state example shows a retained rim cud on the reverse at about 8:45, at the corner of the inset text window. A few scrapes and a couple of minor rim bumps attest to a short stint in circulation, but considerable luster remains on this AU yellow-gold example. Listed on page 365 of the 2009 *Guide Book*. (#10013)

4528 **1853 Assay Office Twenty Dollar, 900 Thous. MS64 NGC. CAC.** K-18, R.2. An outstanding example of this popular U.S. Assay Office issue. The .900 was punched over .880, and the second 8 is clearly visible beneath the 0 on this specimen. These pieces have always posed a bit of a numismatic conundrum: are they Territorials, branch mint issues, or something entirely different? By 1853 California had already achieved statehood, but although the San Francisco Assay Office effectively served as a mint, the assayer reported to the secretary of the Treasury as opposed to the director of the mint. While they are not strictly speaking "Territorials," they are not regular U.S. issues either. Regardless, these important coins will continue to pique the interest of future generations of numismatists.

A delightful layer of frost covers the yellow-gold surfaces. The strike is nearly full, and there are only a few nearly imperceptible grazes on either side. Alluring luster further enhances the eye appeal of this outstanding representative. NGC and PCGS each report just five pieces finer (8/08). Listed on page 365 of the 2009 *Guide Book*. (#10013)

4529 **1849 Moffat & Co. Five Dollar AU55 NGC.** K-4a, R.4. The late die state with a cud above the D in GOLD. Luster shimmers from design elements, and the pale straw-gold have surprisingly few marks for a pioneer gold coin. A good strike with the usual blending of detail on the device highpoints. Listed on page 361 of the 2009 *Guide Book*. Census: 14 in 55, 37 finer (7/08). (#10240)

Lustrous AU53 1850 Moffat Five, 'K-7c'

4530 **1850 Moffat & Co. Five Dollar AU53 NGC.** "K-7c," R.4. Although this die variety matches the photos for Breen-7786 in his *Complete Encyclopedia*, it does not match the Kagin-7a coin on page 296, although the die breaks under OL he describes there. The difference is visible in the leaf trio, which terminates under the M. of S.M.V. rather than the S. in the Kagin photo. In this late die state, the break has turned into a rather interesting retained cud. The rather crude die work makes this variety hard to grade, but the considerable luster gleaming from the yellow-gold surfaces and relatively few mentionable abrasions make the AU53 grade appropriate. Listed on page 361 of the 2009 *Guide Book*. (#10243)

Impressive 1849 Moffat & Co. Ten TEN DOL., K-6a, AU53

4531 **1849 Moffat & Co. Ten Dollar, "Ten Dol." AU53 PCGS.** K-6a, High R.5. This pleasing territorial gold piece has apricot-gold fields and lime-tinted luster within design crevices. The cheek and the hair above the ear shows only slight wear, and although minor marks are distributed, none are of singular importance. One of three different TEN DOL die varieties. The other two, K-6 and the currently unlisted K-6b, are extremely rare. K-6 is known only from its appearance as lot 925 in the Garrett:II auction, and the sole known K-6b was lot 7973 in our 2005 San Francisco ANA Signature. Encapsulated in an old green label holder, and listed on page 361 of the 2009 *Guide Book*. Population: 2 in 53, 4 finer (8/08). (#10246)

Rare AU53 1852 Moffat & Co. Ten Dollar Wide Date Kagin-9 Variety

K-5 1850 Mormon Five Dollar, XF Details

4532 **1852 Moffat & Co. Wide Date Ten Dollar AU53 NGC.** K-9, R.6. Less abraded than is typically found on these heavy, higher denomination territorial issues, with pleasing reddish accents and the normal softness of strike over the design elements. The firm of Moffat & Co. was one of the earliest issuers of California gold coinage. Only one other firm, Norris Gregg and Norris, was producing gold coinage at the time. Moffat & Co. struck ten dollar coins in 1849 and again in 1852. The 1852 pieces come in Close Date and Wide Date varieties; these are of approximately equal rarity. Listed on page 361 of the 2009 *Guide Book*.
Ex: FUN Signature (Heritage, 1/2006), lot 3686. (#10254)

4533 **1850 Mormon Five Dollar—Mount Removed—NCS. XF Details.** K-5, High R.5. The only denomination struck in 1850 at the Salt Lake City Mint under the direction of Brigham Young. All issues of Mormon gold (1849 through 1860) are challenging, but the half eagles were the favored denomination and are slightly more available than the two and a half, ten, or twenty dollar pieces. Even so, finding an example can be challenging. As of (8/08) NGC and PCGS combined have certified less than 100 Mormon half eagles dated 1850. The current piece provides a cost effective alternative for those seeking an example of gold from the Mormon Territory. Signs of the mount mentioned by NCS are difficult to see and the overall eye appeal of this specimen—relative to the assigned grade—will surely result in aggressive bidding. (#10265)

Choice Fine 1852 Wass Molitor Ten
Very Rare Small Head, K-3

4534　**1852 Wass Molitor Ten Dollar, Small Head Fine 15 PCGS.** K-3, R.7. The very rare Small Head variety, much more difficult to locate than the usual Kagin-4 1852 Wass Molitor ten dollar variety. A tan-gold representative with a slightly buckled appearance and uneven wear on the S.M.V. initials. The fields before the profile and above the eagle are abraded. Listed on Page 370 of the 2009 *Guide Book*. Population: 3 in 15, 18 finer (8/08). (#10345)

Choice VF 1852 Wass Molitor Ten
Small Head, K-3, Ex: *S.S. Central America*

4535　**1852 Wass Molitor Ten Dollar, Small Head VF35 PCGS.** Ex: *S.S. Central America*. K-3, R.7. SSCA 7254. The *S.S. Central America* shipwreck is best known for its humongous hoard of 1857-S double eagles, but among its treasure was the present lot, a Wass Molitor ten undoubtedly abandoned with much regret by a passenger more concerned with personal survival. This straw-gold piece has glimpses of remaining luster, although the softly impressed devices give the appearance of greater wear than it actually has. The surfaces have numerous tiny marks from Gold Rush commerce. Housed in a gold label holder, and listed on Page 370 of the 2009 Guide Book. Population: 6 in 35, 7 finer (8/08). (#10345)

S.S.C.A. RELIC GOLD MEDALS

4536　**1857/0 SSCA Relic Gold Medal Baldwin & Co. Ten Dollar Deep Cameo Proof PCGS.** The famous 1850 Baldwin "Horseman" Territorial ten dollar issue serves as the design inspiration for this 2002 restrike. An immaculate example with unimprovable cameo contrast. Dated 1857/0 on the obverse, and 2002 on the reverse. The source bullion came from a Justh & Hunter ingot recovered from the *S.S. Central America* shipwreck. Counterstamped JUSTH & HUNTER/4258 on the reverse. The presentation box of issue accompanies the lot. (#10361)

4537　**1857/0 SSCA Relic Gold Medal Baldwin & Co. Ten Dollar Deep Cameo Proof PCGS.** An impressive modern commemorative featuring a design based on the famous 1857/0 Baldwin & Co. "Horseman" ten dollar. Although PCGS has only graded this piece "Deep Cameo Proof," the surfaces are essentially immaculate. This piece was struck in .906 fine gold from Justh & Hunter ingot # 4050, which was recovered from the wreck of the *S.S. Central America*. Serial number 718. (#10361)

4538　**1857/0 SSCA Relic Gold Medal Baldwin & Co. Ten Dollar Deep Cameo Proof PCGS.** This modern commemorative gold restrike is based on the 1857/0 Baldwin & Co. "Horseman" or Vaquero ten dollar. PCGS has graded all of these pieces as "Deep Cameo Proof," but the surfaces are pristine. Struck in .906 fine California gold from Justh & Hunter ingot # 4050, recovered from the wreck of the *S.S. Central America*. Serial number 595, complete with presentation box (#10361)

4539　**1855 SSCA Relic Gold Medal "1855 Kellogg & Co. Fifty" Gem Proof PCGS.** Struck August 20, 2001. Housed in a copper, glass, and plush purple velvet frame with commemorative screwdriver, sturdy outer box, and California Historical Society slipcase. (#10358)

4540　**1855 SSCA Relic Gold Medal "1855 Kellogg & Co. Fifty" Gem Proof PCGS.** Struck on August 20, 2001. This California Historical Society modern restrike, deeply mirrored and sharply detailed, comes with a copper-and-glass case reminiscent of the Shreve & Co. cases made for the Panama-Pacific commemoratives, as well as an outer box, slipcover, and celebratory screwdriver. (#10358)

4541 1855 SSCA Relic Gold Medal "1855 Kellogg & Co. Fifty" Gem Proof PCGS. Struck August 20, 2001. This "Gem Proof" comes with its regular California Historical Society outer cases and a Phillips-head screwdriver, should one wish to remove the piece from its attractive copper-and-glass frame. (#10358)

4542 1855 SSCA Relic Gold Medal "1855 Kellogg & Co. Fifty" Gem Proof PCGS. Minted on August 28, 2001. This gleaming commemorative restrike contains gold taken from ingots salvaged from the wreck of the *S.S. Central America*. Comes in an attractive copper and glass case and has associated literature and box. (#10358)

Interesting 1855 SSCA Relic Gold Medal, Gem Proof

4543 1855 SSCA Relic Gold Medal "1855 Kellogg & Co. Fifty" Gem Proof PCGS. The California Historical Society struck this piece on September 1, 2001 in gold recovered from the shipwreck of the *S.S. Central America*. Although PCGS has only graded this piece "Gem Proof," it is virtually flawless with a magnificent deep cameo appearance. An attractive example of this interesting commemorative. (#10358)

4544 1855 SSCA Relic Gold Medal "1855 Kellogg & Co. Fifty" Gem Uncirculated PCGS. Struck September 7, 2001. Far fewer Uncirculated-finish Kellogg & Co. *S.S. Central America* commemorative restrikes were made than proofs. This example comes in the customary copper-and-glass frame and includes a certificate of authenticity, though the typical screwdriver is strangely absent. (#10359)

Remarkable 1855 *S.S. Central America* $50 Relic Gold Medal, Gem Proof

4545 1855 SSCA Relic Gold Medal "1855 Kellogg & Co. Fifty" Gem Proof PCGS. A relic medal made from Kellogg & Humbert gold ingots recovered from the *S.S. Central America* shipwreck, and struck on August 20, 2001 near San Francisco. Struck by copy dies made from the original Kellogg & Co. fifty dollar dies. Although PCGS has certified all of these strikes as "Gem Proof," the present piece is essentially perfect, with deeply mirrored fields and frosted devices that create a spectacular cameo appearance. A waft of orange color on the obverse accents the bright yellow patina that covers the surfaces. This exquisite, impeccably preserved specimen is an excellent souvenir of the "Ship of Gold." (#10359)

INGOT

Cripple Creek, Colorado One Ounce Gold Ingot

4546 Undated Cripple Creek, Colorado Gold Ingot. One troy ounce. .999 fine. A modern memento from this historic mining district. Rectangular in shape, this small ingot measures 28 x 16 mm. Only the top side is stamped, the back side appears to have an imprint of some sort of cloth.

End of Session Six

Heritage Auction Galleries Staff

Steve Ivy - Co-Chairman and CEO

Steve Ivy began collecting and studying rare coins in his youth, and as a teenager in 1963 began advertising coins for sale in national publications. Seven years later, at the age of twenty, he opened Steve Ivy Rare Coins in downtown Dallas, and in 1976, Steve Ivy Numismatic Auctions was incorporated. Steve managed the business as well as serving as chief numismatist, buying and selling hundreds of millions of dollars of coins during the 1970s and early 1980s. In early 1983, James Halperin became a full partner, and the name of the corporation was changed to Heritage Rare Coin Galleries. Steve's primary responsibilities now include management of the marketing and selling efforts of the company, the formation of corporate policy for long-term growth, and corporate relations with financial institutions. He remains intimately involved in numismatics, attending all major national shows. Steve engages in daily discourse with industry leaders on all aspects of the rare coin/currency business, and his views on grading, market trends and hobby developments are respected throughout the industry. He serves on the Board of Directors of the Professional Numismatists Guild (and was immediate past president), is the current Chairman of The Industry Council for Tangible Assets, and is a member of most leading numismatic organizations. Steve's keen appreciation of history is reflected in his active participation in other organizations, including past or present board positions on the Texas Historical Foundation and the Dallas Historical Society (where he also served as Exhibits Chairman). Steve is an avid collector of Texas books, manuscripts, and national currency, and he owns one of the largest and finest collections in private hands. He is also a past Board Chair of Dallas Challenge, and is currently the Finance Chair of the Phoenix House of Texas.

James Halperin - Co-Chairman

Jim Halperin and the traders under his supervision have transacted billions of dollars in rare coin business, and have outsold all other numismatic firms every year for over two decades. Born in Boston in 1952, Jim attended Middlesex School in Concord from 1966 to 1970. At the age of 15, he formed a part-time rare coin business after discovering that he had a knack (along with a nearly photographic memory) for coins. Jim scored a perfect 800 on his math SATs and received early acceptance to Harvard College, but after attending three semesters, he took a permanent leave of absence to pursue his full-time numismatic career. In 1975, Jim personally supervised the protocols for the first mainframe computer system in the numismatic business, which would catapult New England Rare Coin Galleries to the top of the industry in less than four years. In 1983, Jim merged with his friend and former archrival Steve Ivy, whom Jim had long admired. Their partnership has become the world's largest and most successful numismatic company, as well as the third-largest auctioneer in America. Jim remains arguably the best "eye" in the coin business today (he won the professional division of the PCGS World Series of Grading). In the mid-1980s, he authored "How to Grade U.S. Coins" (now posted on the web at www.CoinGrading.com), a highly-acclaimed text upon which the NGC and PCGS grading standards would ultimately be based. Jim is a bit of a Renaissance man, as a well-known futurist, an active collector of EC comics and early 20th-century American art (visit www.jhalpe.com), venture capital investor, philanthropist (he endows a multimillion-dollar health education foundation), and part-time novelist. His first fictional novel, "The Truth Machine," was published in 1996 and became an international science fiction bestseller, and was optioned for movie development by Warner Brothers. Jim's second novel, "The First Immortal," was published in early 1998 and immediately optioned as a Hallmark Hall of Fame television miniseries. Jim is married to Gayle Ziaks, and they have two sons, David and Michael. In 1996, with funding from Jim and Gayle's foundation, Gayle founded Dallas' Dance for the Planet, which has grown to become the largest free dance festival in the world.

Greg Rohan - President

At the age of eight, Greg Rohan started collecting coins as well as buying them for resale to his schoolmates. By 1971, at the age of ten, he was already buying and selling coins from a dealer's table at trade shows in his hometown of Seattle. His business grew rapidly, and by 1985 he had offices in both Seattle and Minneapolis. He joined Heritage in 1987 as Executive Vice-President and Manager of the firm's rare coin business. Today, as an owner and as President of Heritage, his responsibilities include overseeing the firm's private client group and working with top collectors in every field in which Heritage is active. Greg has been involved with many of the rarest items and most important collections handled by the firm, including the purchase and/or sale of the Ed Trompeter Collection (the world's largest numismatic purchase according to the Guinness Book of World Records), the legendary 1894 San Francisco Dime, the 1838 New Orleans Half Dollar, and the 1804 Silver Dollar. During his career, Greg has handled more than $1 billion of rare coins, collectibles and art, and provided expert consultation concerning the authenticity and grade condition of coins for the Professional Coin Grading Service (PCGS). He has provided expert testimony for the United States Attorneys in San Francisco, Dallas, and Philadelphia, and for the Federal Trade Commission (FTC). He has worked with collectors, consignors, and their advisors regarding significant collections of books, manuscripts, comics, currency, jewelry, vintage movie posters, sports and entertainment memorabilia, decorative arts, and fine art. Additionally, Greg is a Sage Society member of the American Numismatic Society, and a member/life member of the PNG, ANA, and most other leading numismatic organizations. Greg is also Chapter Chairman for North Texas of the Young Presidents' Organization (YPO), and is an active supporter of the arts. Greg co-authored "The Collectors Estate Handbook," winner of the NLG's Robert Friedberg Award for numismatic book of the year. Mr. Rohan currently serves on the seven-person Advisory Board to the Federal Reserve Bank of Dallas, in his second appointed term. He and his wife, Lysa, are avid collectors of rare wine, Native American artifacts, and American art.

Paul Minshull - Chief Operating Officer

As Chief Operating Officer, Paul Minshull's managerial responsibilities include integrating sales, personnel, inventory, security and MIS for Heritage. His major accomplishments include overseeing the hardware migration from mainframe to PC, the software migration of all inventory and sales systems, and implementation of a major Internet presence. Heritage's successful employee-suggestion program has generated 200 or more ideas each month since 1995, and has helped increase employee productivity, expand business, and improve employee retention. Paul oversees the company's highly-regarded IT department, and has been the driving force behind Heritage's web development, now a significant portion of Heritage's future plans. As the only numismatic auction house that combines traditional floor bidding with active Internet bidding, the totally interactive system has catapulted Heritage to the top rare coin website (according to Forbes Magazine's "Best of the Web"). Paul was born in Michigan and came to Heritage in 1984 after 12 years as the General Manager of a plastics manufacturing company in Ann Arbor. Since 1987, he has been a general partner in Heritage Capital Properties, Sales Manager, Vice President of Operations, and Chief Operating Officer for all Heritage companies and affiliates since 1996. Paul maintains an active interest in sports and physical fitness, and he and his wife have three children.

Todd Imhof - Vice President

Todd Imhof did not start collecting coins in his teens, unlike most professional numismatists. Shortly after graduating college, Todd declined an offer from a prestigious Wall Street bank to join a former high school classmate in his small rare coin firm in the Seattle area. In the mid-1980s, the rare coin industry was rapidly changing, with the advent of third-party grading and growing computer technologies; as a newcomer, Todd more easily embraced these new dynamics. He soon discovered a personal passion for rare coins, and for working with high-level collectors; in 1991, he co-founded Pinnacle Rarities, a firm specialized in servicing the savviest and most prominent collectors in numismatics. At 25, he was accepted into the PNG, and currently serves on its Consumer Protection Committee and its Legislation/Taxation Issues Committee. In 1992, he was invited to join the Board of Directors for the Industry Council for Tangible Assets, later serving as its Chairman (2002-2005).

Todd enjoys a reputation that is envied by the entire numismatic community, and his relationship with Heritage's most prominent clients, who seek his expertise and integrity, has only strengthened over the years. Clients and colleagues are impressed by his ability to navigate complex deals with unsurpassed professionalism. By understanding what each collector is trying to accomplish, Todd has the uncanny ability to identify the perfect coins at the right prices. In the famous Phillip Morse Auction, he became the only person in history to purchase two separate $1mm+ coins during a single auction session! Todd is an avid competitive sailor, and collector of fine wines and Olympic medals. He and his wife have two sons and a daughter.

Leo Frese - Vice President

Leo has been involved in numismatics for nearly 40 years, a professional numismatist since 1971, and has been with Heritage for over 20 years. He literally worked his way up the Heritage "ladder" through dedication, hard work, and a belief that the client is the most important asset Heritage has. He worked with Bob Merrill for nearly 15 years and now is the Director of Consignments. Leo has been actively involved in assisting clients sell nearly $500,000,000 in numismatic material. Leo was recently accepted as a member of PNG, is a life member of the ANA, and holds membership in FUN, CSNS, and other numismatic organizations. He believes education is the foremost building block in numismatics. Leo encourages all collectors to broaden their horizons, be actively involved in the hobby, and donate freely to YN organizations. Leo's interests include collecting Minnesota pottery and elegant Depression glass. Although travel is an important element of his job, he relishes time with his wife Wendy, children Alicen and Adam, and son-in-law Jeff.

Norma L. Gonzalez - VP of Auction Operations

Born in Dallas, Texas, Norma joined the U.S. Navy in August of 1993. During her five-year enlistment, she received her Bachelor's Degree in Resource Management and traveled to Japan, Singapore, Thailand and lived in Cuba for three years. After her enlistment, she moved back to Dallas where her family resides. Norma joined Heritage in 1998; always ready for a challenge, she spent her days at Heritage and her nights obtaining an M. B. A. She was promoted to Vice President in 2003. She currently manages the operations departments, including Coins, Currency, World & Ancient Coins, Sportscards & Memorabilia, Comics, Movie Posters, Pop Culture and Political Memorabilia. Norma enjoys running, biking and spending time with her family. In February 2004 she ran a 26.2-mile marathon in Austin, Texas and later, in March she accomplished a 100-mile bike ride in California.

Debbie Rexing - VP - Marketing

Debbie's marketing credentials include degrees in Business Administration in Marketing and Human Resource Management from The Ohio State University, as well as sales and brand development experience for General Foods and Proctor & Gamble. After joining Heritage in 2001, Debbie rapidly became an integral part of the marketing teams involved with Heritage's most exciting and successful specialties, including U.S. Coins, World Coins, Currency, Music & Entertainment, Vintage Movie Posters, Americana, and U.S. Tangibles Inc. Her varied responsibilities included cross-functional coordination of photography, auction logistics, and marketing. Debbie has been active in coin auctions, staffing the podium, executing client bids, and in lot viewing. Her wide experience in many aspects of the business has provided her with a broad perspective of Heritage's activities. She and her husband Rick have three children -- Trent, Abbey, and Claire -- and her hobbies include interior design, entertaining and exercise, the beach and water activities, and watching Ohio State football.

Kelley Norwine - VP - Media and Client Relations

Born and raised in South Carolina, Kelley pursued a double major at Southern Wesleyan University, earning a BA in Music Education and a BS in Business Management. A contestant in the Miss South Carolina pageant, Kelley was later Regional Manager & Director of Training at Bank of Travelers Rest in South Carolina. Relocating to Los Angeles, Kelley became the Regional Manager and Client Services Director for NAS-McCann World Group, an international Advertising & Communications Agency where she was responsible for running one of the largest offices in the country. During her years with NAS Kelley was the recipient of numerous awards including Regional Manager of the Quarter and the NAS Courage and Dedication award. After relocating to Dallas, Kelley took a job as Director of Client Services for TMP/Monster Worldwide and joined Heritage in 2005 as Director of Client Development. She was named VP of Marketing for Heritage in 2007. A cancer survivor, Kelley is an often-requested motivational speaker for the American Cancer Society. In her spare time, she writes music, sings, and plays the piano.

Patricia Gonzalez - Director of Auctions & Client Service

Patricia Gonzalez lived all over the country before settling down in Ferris, Texas, near Dallas. She began her career working in Customer Service, and in 2001 joined the Heritage family assisting in Client Services and live auctions. Patricia's knowledge grew with the company, and her hard work led to her promotion to Director of Auctions and Client Services. Patricia is directly involved in the training and management of the Client Services team. A cancer survivor, Patricia enjoys spending time with her two beautiful little girls, attending softball games, and spending time with family and friends.

Andrea Voss - Live-Auction & Event Coordinator

Andrea Voss is a true Texas native – born and educated in the Dallas area, with a degree in Journalism from the University of North Texas in Denton. Andrea joined the Heritage family in 2004, and after assisting Client Services with e-mail inquiries, she earned the opportunity to become the Auction Supervisor. Her responsibilities have grown with her experiences, and she is now the Live-Auction & Event Coordinator. Clients may see her in the back of the live auction room supervising, or in the front using her Auctioneer license. In her off hours, Andrea enjoys time on her patio with her dog and cat, and still dreams of one day being a writer..

Devin Jackson - Auction Client Services/Live Auction Supervisor

Devin Jackson joined Heritage in 2005 as a member of the Client Services Group. Devin is a native Texan, growing up in a small suburb south of Dallas. Devin later attended the University of North Texas and graduated with a Bachelor's Degree in Kinesiology. A life long sports fanatic, Devin briefly coached high school football, basketball, and track in his home town of Ferris, TX after graduating from college. Devin later joined the staff of Heritage Auction Galleries, assisting with Live Auctions and Client Services. Devin has collected sports cards and memorabilia since he was a young boy and he continues to collect memorabilia from his favorite professional sports teams, including the San Francisco 49ers.

Marti Korver - Manager - Credit/Collections

Marti has been working in numismatics for more than three decades. She was recruited out of the banking profession by Jim Ruddy, and she worked with Paul Rynearson, Karl Stephens, and Judy Cahn on ancients and world coins at Bowers & Ruddy Galleries, in Hollywood, CA. She migrated into the coin auction business, running the bid books for such memorable sales as the Garrett Collection and representing bidders as agent at B&R auctions for 10 years. She also worked as a research assistant for Q. David Bowers for several years. Memorable events included such clients (and friends) as Richard Lobel, John Ford, Harry Bass, and John J. Pittman. She is married to noted professional numismatist and writer, Robert Korver, (who is sometimes seen auctioneering at coin shows) and they migrated to Heritage in Dallas in 1996. She has an RN daughter (who worked her way through college showing lots for Heritage) and a son (who is currently a college student and sometimes a Heritage employee) and a type set of dogs (one black and one white). She currently collects kitschy English teapots and compliments.

Cataloged by: Mark Van Winkle, Chief Cataloger; Jon Amato, John Beety, Mark Borckardt, George Huber, Brian Koller, John Salyer, Max Spiegel, David Stone, Dennis Tarrant

Edited by: Mark Van Winkle, John Beety, George Huber, Stewart Huckaby, Bob Korver

Operations Support by: Cristina Gonzales, Miguel Reynaga Sr., Edna Lopez, Alma Villa, Maria Flores, Celeste Robertson, Manuela Bueno, Cristina Ibarra, Maria Jimenez

Catalog and Internet Imaging by: Tony Webb, Travis Awalt, Jason Young, Colleen McInerney, Darnell McCown, Joel Gonzalez, Lori McKay, Maribel Cazarez, Sharon Johnson

Production and Design by: Tim Hose, Mary Hermann, Mark Masat, Debbie Rexing

U.S. Coin Specialists

David Mayfield - Vice President

David has been collecting and trading rare coins and currency for over 35 years. A chance encounter with his father's coin collection at the age of nine led to his lifetime interest. David has been buying and selling at coin shows since the age of 10. He became a full time coin & currency dealer in the mid-80s. David's main collecting interest is in all things Texas, specializing in currency and documents from the Republic of Texas. Being a sixth generation Texan whose family fought for Texas' independence has only increased the value and meaning of these historical artifacts for him. After more than two decades of marriage, David and Tammy have two wonderful sons, Brian and Michael.

Jim Jelinski - Consignment Director

A collector since age 8, Jim has been involved in numismatics over 5 decades, progressing from humble collector to professional dealer and educator. He is a Life Member of the *American Numismatic Association*, the *American Numismatic Society*, and other state and national organizations. Starting as Buyer for Paramount International Coin Corporation in 1972, he opened Essex Numismatic Properties in 1975 in New Hampshire. Later, positions at M.B. Simmons & Associates of Narberth, Pennsylvania included Director of Sales, Director of Marketing and Advertising, and Executive Vice President. In 1979, he reorganized Essex in Connecticut and, as Essex Numismatics, Inc., worked as COO and CFO. He joined the staff at Heritage as Senior Numismatist and Consignment Coordinator. Jim has two sons, and is actively involved in his church, and community; he just completed his 20th season of coaching youth athletics, and working in Boy Scouting as a troop leader and merit badge counselor. He has been a fund raiser for Paul Newman's "Hole in the Wall Gang" camp for terminally ill children, and for Boy Scouts. His personal diversions include fly fishing, sky diving, cooking, and wine collecting.

Sam Foose - Consignment Director and Auctioneer

Sam's professional career at Heritage divides neatly into two parts. Sam joined Heritage Numismatic Auctions, Inc. in 1993 as an Auction Coordinator. Over the next five years, Sam ran the day-to-day auction operations, ultimately rising to Assistant Auction Director, and began calling auctions. After serving as a Senior Manager and Consignment Director in other collectible fields outside of numismatics, Sam returned to Heritage in 2002 as a Consignment Director in time to help Heritage's expansion into other collectibles. Sam travels the country assisting clients who wish to liquidate their collections of coins, paper money, decorative arts, and sports collectibles. To Sam, helping consignors make the best decisions to maximize their returns from auctioning their properties is the most rewarding part of his job. Sam holds auction licenses in several jurisdictions, and has hammered in excess of $250 million in collectibles as one of Heritage's primary auctioneers. During his free time, Sam enjoys his wife (Heather) and two children (Jackson and Caroline), gardening, golf, grilling, and sports.

David Lisot - Consignment Director

David Lisot is in his fourth decade as a numismatist, writer, researcher, publisher, cataloger, public speaker, and website creator. His expertise includes US & world coins and paper money, gemstones, jewelry, stamps, pocket watches, art, postcards, cigar label art, and antique advertising. David is Director of Heritage's Coin Club Outreach program and a Consignment Director. An accomplished videographer and television producer, David produced the award-winning documentaries, *Money, History in Your Hands, Era of Hometown Bank Notes* for the Higgins Money Museum, and video productions for Heritage. He has videotaped over 750 lectures and presentations about coins and collecting as seen on Coinvideo.com. David was featured in the PBS series, *Money Moves* with Jack Gallagher, as a reporter for FNN, and as founder of CoinTelevision.com. David served as an ANA Governor and is a member of many numismatic organizations. He is a Philosophy graduate of the University of Colorado in Boulder, and a Graduate Gemologist from the GIA. David is married with two children, and enjoys travel, history, exercise, and religious studies.

Bob Marino - Consignment Director & Senior Numismatist

Bob started collecting coins in his youth, and started selling through eBay as the Internet became a serious collector resource. He joined Heritage in 1999, managing and developing Internet coin sales, and building Heritage's client base through eBay and other Internet auction websites. He has successfully concluded more than 40,000 transactions on eBay, selling millions of dollars of rare coins to satisfied clients. Many collectors were first introduced to Heritage through Bob's efforts, and he takes pride in dealing with each client on a personal level. Bob is now a Consignment Director, assisting consignors in placing their coins and collectibles in the best of the many Heritage venues – in short, maximizing their return on many of the coins that he sold to them previously! Bob and his family moved to the DFW area from the Bitterroot Valley in Western Montana. He enjoys spending time with his family, woodworking (building furniture), and remodeling his house.

Charles Clifford - Consignment Director

Charles has been involved with collectibles for over 35 years. His first venture with coins began in the 1970s when he drove to banks all over North Texas buying bags of half dollars to search for the 40% silver clad coins. He has worked as a bullion trader, a rare coin buyer, worked in both wholesale and retail sales, served as a cataloger, and has traveled to hundreds of coin and sports card conventions across the country. Charles also has the distinction of working with Steve Ivy over four decades! Currently he is assisting clients obtain top dollar for the items they have for sale, either by direct purchase or by placing their material in auction. He appreciates Heritage's total commitment to "World Class Client Service" and the "Can Do - Nothing is Impossible" attitude of management and each and every employee. He enjoys collecting hand-blown Depression glass and antique aquarium statues.

Mike Sadler - Consignment Director

Mike Sadler joined the Heritage team in September 2003. Mike attended the United States Air Force Academy, earning a degree in civil engineering and pinned on his silver wings in June 1985. After seven years flying various aircraft, he joined American Airlines where he still pilots. More than once, Mike has surprised Heritage employees serving as their pilot while they flew to shows, conventions, and to visit clients. Like so many of our clients, Mike started putting together sets of coins from circulation when he was a small boy, and that collection grew to go to the auction block with Heritage in January 2004. Before coming to Heritage, his unlimited access to air travel enabled him to attend coin shows all around the country. He gained a tremendous knowledge of rare coins and developed an outstanding eye for quality. He is a trusted friend and colleague to many of today's most active collectors. Having been a collector for so long, and a Heritage consignor himself, Mike understands the needs of the collector and what Heritage can offer. Mike is married, has three children, and enjoys coaching and playing lacrosse

Katherine Kurachek - Consignment Director

Katherine grew up in Sarasota, Florida, graduated from the University of Mississippi in 1993 as an art major, and then resided in Colorado (where she opened a pizzeria!) before moving to Dallas. Acting on a suggestion from her father, an avid collector of type coins and a client of Steve Ivy for more than two decades, Katherine came to Heritage in January 2003. She worked alongside Leo Frese for several years, honing her experience in dealing with the numismatic wholesale trade. Taking care of the needs of our dealer-consignors includes soliciting the consignments, inputting the material into our computer systems, and ensuring the smooth flow of the consignment through the many production processes. Katherine is now frequently traveling to coin shows to represent Heritage and service her dealer accounts. In her spare time, she enjoys gardening, golf, hiking, fly-fishing, and walking her two Akitas (Moses and April). Katherine has finally inherited her father's love of these pieces of history, and currently collects love tokens and counterstamps.

Jason Friedman - Consignment Director

Jason's interest in rare coins began at the age of twelve when he discovered a bag of Wheat cents and Liberty nickels in his garage. His collecting interest expanded to Morgans and dealing in various coinage. Jason's numismatic business allowed him to pay for most of his college tuition while working part time and attending classes full time. Jason earned his degree in business from the University of North Texas in 2005. Shortly after, he joined Heritage and was able to turn his passion for numismatics into a career. His computer skills and coordinator background are invaluable tools in accessing all levels of expertise at Heritage. Jason enjoys interacting with clients and assisting them in every aspect of the auction process. Apart from his director position, Jason finds it particularly gratifying phone bidding on clients' behalf. He is a member of the American Numismatic Association (ANA) and Florida United Numismatists (FUN).

Doug Nyholm - Consignment Director

Doug has been collecting coins since the age of ten and fondly recalls spending Morgan silver dollars to purchase candy as a boy. He worked in the IT industry for 28 years with Unisys, 3Com and Sun Microsystems before joining Heritage. Doug's expertise includes all U.S. coins and varieties. He is also well acquainted with U.S. Federal currency and obsoletes. Doug has a special interest in territorials, and in 2004 he wrote and published *The History of Mormon Currency* and has authored many articles on Kirtland currency, scrip and related Utah items. He is currently writing several additional books including one on Utah National Banknotes. Doug is married, has two daughters, and enjoys mountain climbing and hiking. Doug was the President of the Utah Numismatic Society for 2006-07. His current collecting interests include Capped Bust & Seated half dollars, U.S. Type, and Mormon coins & currency.

Amber Dinh - Consignment Director

Amber joined the team at Heritage Auction Galleries in 2007 and is an active gold, platinum, and silver collector. Prior to starting her numismatic career with Heritage, she was a client specialist for a high volume seller of numismatic coins. In addition to rising to become a Senior Gold and Platinum Specialist, Amber also worked in the audio-video realm; her client-orientation catapulted her to the top of recognition when she was selected among the "Top 40 Under 40" in the country for retail sales. She has been featured in several industry publications for her outstanding client service, and has received numerous awards for her attention to detail. Her love of travel has taken her to amazing places across the globe, including Japan, Saipan, Guam, Okinawa, Korea, Diego Garcia, as well as numerous fascinating places in America. In her spare time, she enjoys working with numerous charities around Dallas and participated in the Susan G. Komen 60 mile, 3-day walk to raise funds to fight breast cancer. Her young daughter is a cancer survivor, so anytime spent with family is truly cherished. She looks forward to provided Heritage's clients "with all the client service they deserve, and more than they expect."

David Lewis - Consignment Director

David Lewis joined Heritage in 2005 as a numismatist, with an extensive numismatic background in wholesale, retail, and internet sales. David's current duties are focused on Heritage's website features, especially "Ask an Expert" and "Coins and Currency Questions", as well as telephone consignments and purchases of rare coins and collections. David is a 22-year veteran of the United States Air Force, and has more than 5000 hours of flight-time as an Airborne Mission Supervisor and Hebrew linguist. David is the winner of the Numismatic Guarantee Corporation's 2004 and 2005 Best Presented Registry Set Awards, and is an avid collector of Washington Quarters and quarter varieties. He holds membership in the ANA, CSNS, and the Barber Coin Collectors Society, among other organizations. David's interests include flying, world travel, history, and collecting Art Deco ceramics and antiques.

David Lindvall - Consignment Director

David is a Life Member of the American Numismatic Association, and it seems at times that he has spent his entire life traveling to coin shows across America. His career in numismatics actually started in 1973 at International Coin of Minneapolis. In 1988, he joined Heritage in their Wholesale Division, ultimately rising to become Manager. David continues to enjoy numismatics, but after three decades of traveling to conventions large and small, he decided to change positions so he could spend more time at home than in airport lounges. He joined Heritage's Consignment Director team, where his lifetime of numismatic experience is benefiting clients who expect the very best service when they consign their coins and notes to auction. David has a BA in History and a Masters of Divinity, and he continues to be active in both areas. Now living on Cedar Creek Lake, his hobbies include boating, fishing, and making his lake home available to family and friends to enjoy the lakeside amenities.

Mark Van Winkle - Chief Cataloger

Mark has worked for Heritage (and Steve Ivy) since 1979. He has been Chief Cataloger since 1990, and has handled some of the premier numismatic rarities sold at public auction. Mark's literary achievements are considerable. He was editor of *Legacy* magazine, won the 1989 NLG award for Best U.S. Commercial Magazine, and the next year won another NLG award for Best Article with his "Interview With John Ford." In 1996 he was awarded the NLG's Best Numismatic Article "Changing Concepts of Liberty," and was accorded a third place Heath Literary Award that same year. He has done extensive research and published his findings on Branch Mint Proof Morgan Dollars, in addition to writing numerous articles for *Coin World* and *Numismatic News*. Mark has also contributed to past editions of the *Red Book*, and helped with the Standard Silver series in Andrew Pollock's *United States Patterns and Related Issues*. He was also a contributor to *The Guide Book of Double Eagle Gold Coins*.

Mark Borckardt - Senior Cataloger

Mark started attending coin shows and conventions as a dealer in 1970, and has been a full-time professional numismatist since 1980. He received the Early American Coppers Literary Award, and the Numismatic Literary Guild's Book of the Year Award, for the *Encyclopedia of Early United States Cents, 1793-1814*, published in 2000. He serves as a contributor to *A Guide Book of United States Coins*, and has contributed to many references, including the Harry W. Bass, Jr. Sylloge, and the *Encyclopedia of Silver Dollars and Trade Dollars of the United States*. Most recently, he was Senior Numismatist with Bowers and Merena Galleries, serving as a major contributor to all of that firm's landmark auctions. Mark is a life member of the A. N. A., and an active member of numerous organizations. He is an avid collector of numismatic literature, holding several thousand volumes in his library, as well as related postcards and ephemera. He is an avid bowler, carrying an 200+ average, and with seven perfect 300 games. Mark is a graduate of the University of Findlay (Ohio) with a Bachelors Degree in Mathematics. Mark and his wife have a 20-something year old son, and twin daughters who are enrolled at Baylor.

Brian Koller - Cataloger

Brian's attention to detail ensures that every catalog, printed and on-line, is as error free as technology and human activity allows. In addition to his coin cataloging duties, he also helps with consignor promises and client service issues. Brian has been a Heritage cataloger since 2001, and before that he worked as a telecom software engineer for 16 years. He is a graduate of Iowa State University with a Bachelor's degree in Computer Engineering, and is an avid collector of U.S. gold coins. Brian's numismatic footnote is as discoverer of a 1944-D half dollar variety that has the designer's monogram engraved by hand onto a working die. In addition to describing many thousands of coins in Heritage catalogs, Brian has written more than one thousand reviews of classic movies, which can be found on his website, filmsgraded.com.

John Salyer - Cataloger

John has been a numismatist and coin cataloger with Heritage since 2002. He began collecting Lincoln Cents, Jefferson Nickels, Mercury and Roosevelt Dimes, and Franklin Halves at the age of eleven, as a sixth-grader in Fort Worth; his best friend was also a collector, and his dad would drive them to coin shops and flea markets in search of numismatic treasures. The two youngsters even mowed lawns together in order to purchase their coins, which were always transferred into Whitman folders. John graduated from the University of Texas with a bachelor's degree in English. Prior to his numismatic employment, he worked primarily within the federal government and for several major airlines. His hobbies include playing guitar and collecting antique postcards; an avid golfer, he also enjoys spending time on the links. John has enjoyed making his former hobby his current occupation.

Dr. Jon Amato - Cataloger

Jon has been with Heritage since 2004. He was previously a Program Manager in the NY State Dept. of Economic Development, and an Adjunct Professor at the State University of New York at Albany, where he taught economic geography, natural disasters assessment, and environmental management. Jon is currently writing a monograph on the draped bust, small eagle half dollars of 1796-1797; his research included surveying more than 4,000 auction catalogs, recording the descriptions, grades, and photos of 1796-1797 halves. He published an article entitled "Surviving 1796-1797 Draped Bust Half Dollars and their Grade Distribution," in the *John Reich Journal*, February 2005, and also wrote "An Analysis of 1796-1797 Draped Bust Half Dollars," in *The Numismatist*, Sept. 2001. Jon belongs to many numismatic organizations, including the ANA, ANS, John Reich Collectors Society, and the Liberty Seated Collectors Club, and has made several presentations at ANA Numismatic Theaters. He earned a bachelor's degree from Arizona State University, an M.A. from the S. U. N. Y. at Buffalo, and a Ph. D. from the University of Toronto.

John Dale Beety - Cataloger

John grew up in Logansport, Indiana, a small town associated with several numismatic luminaries. Highlights as a Young Numismatist include attending Pittman III, four ANA Summer Seminars (thanks to various YN scholarships), and placing third in the 2001 World Series of Numismatics with Eric Li Cheung. He accepted a position with Heritage as a cataloger immediately after graduation from Rose-Hulman Institute of Technology, after serving an internship at Heritage during the summer of 2004. In addition to his numismatic interests, he enjoys many types of games, with two state junior titles in chess and an appearance in the Top 20 Juniors list of the World Blitz Chess Association.

Ron Brackemyre - Operations Manager

Ron Brackemyre began his career at Heritage Auction Galleries in 1998 as the Manager of the Shipping Department, and was promoted to Consignment Operations Manager for Numismatics in 2004. He is responsible for the security of all of Heritage's coin and currency consignments, both at the Dallas world headquarters and at shows. His department also coordinates the photography, scanning, and cataloging of coins for upcoming auctions; coordination of auction planning; security and transportation logistics, and lot-view and auction prep. If you have attended a live Heritage coin auction, you are familiar with Ron's excellent work. Ron and his wife, Denice, have two teen-aged sons, and the family passion is riding dirt bikes.

Terms and Conditions of Auction

Auctioneer and Auction:

1. This Auction is presented by Heritage Auction Galleries, a d/b/a/ of Heritage Auctions, Inc., or its affiliates Heritage Numismatic Auctions, Inc., or Heritage Vintage Sports Auctions, Inc., or Currency Auctions of America, Inc., as identified with the applicable licensing information on the title page of the catalog or on the HA.com Internet site (the "Auctioneer"). The Auction is conducted under these Terms and Conditions of Auction and applicable state and local law. Announcements and corrections from the podium and those made through the Terms and Conditions of Auctions appearing on the Internet at HA.com supersede those in the printed catalog.

Buyer's Premium:

2. On bids placed through Auctioneer, a Buyer's Premium of fifteen percent (15%) will be added to the successful hammer price bid on lots in Coin and Currency auctions, or nineteen and one-half percent (19.5%) on lots in all other auctions. If your bid is placed through eBay Live, a Buyer's Premium equal to the normal Buyer's Premium plus an additional five percent (5%) of the hammer price will be added to the successful bid up to a maximum Buyer's Premium of Twenty Two and one-half percent (22.5%). There is a minimum Buyer's Premium of $9.00 per lot. In Gallery Auctions (sealed bid auctions of mostly bulk numismatic material), the Buyer's Premium is 19.5%.

Auction Venues:

3. The following Auctions are conducted solely on the Internet: Heritage Weekly Internet Coin, Currency, Comics, and Vintage Movie Poster Auctions; Heritage Monthly Internet Sports and Marketplace Auctions; Final Sessions. Signature® Auctions and Grand Format Auctions accept bids the Internet, telephone, fax, or mail first, followed by a floor bidding session; Heritage Live, eBay Live, and real-time telephone bidding are available to registered clients during these auctions.

Bidders:

4. Any person participating or registering for the Auction agrees to be bound by and accepts these Terms and Conditions of Auction ("Bidder(s)").
5. All Bidders must meet Auctioneer's qualifications to bid. Any Bidder who is not a client in good standing of the Auctioneer may be disqualified at Auctioneer's sole option and will not be awarded lots. Such determination may be made by Auctioneer in its sole and unlimited discretion, at any time prior to, during, or even after the close of the Auction. Auctioneer reserves the right to exclude any person from the auction.
6. If an entity places a bid, then the person executing the bid on behalf of the entity agrees to personally guarantee payment for any successful bid.

Credit:

7. Bidders who have not established credit with the Auctioneer must either furnish satisfactory credit information (including two collectibles-related business references) well in advance of the Auction or supply valid credit card information. Bids placed through our Interactive Internet program will only be accepted from pre-registered Bidders; Bidders who are not members of HA.com or affiliates should pre-register at least 48 hours before the start of the first session (exclusive of holidays or weekends) to allow adequate time to contact references. Credit may be granted at the discretion of Auctioneer. Additionally Bidders who have not previously established credit or who wish to bid in excess of their established credit history may be required to provide their social security number or the last four digits thereof to us so a credit check may be performed prior to Auctioneer's acceptance of a bid.

Bidding Options:

8. Bids in Signature® Auctions or Grand Format Auctions may be placed as set forth in the printed catalog section entitled "Choose your bidding method." For auctions held solely on the Internet, see the alternatives on HA.com. Review at HA.com/common/howtobid.php.
9. Presentment of Bids: Non-Internet bids (including but not limited to podium, fax, phone and mail bids) are treated similar to floor bids in that they must be on-increment or at a half increment (called a cut bid). Any podium, fax, phone, or mail bids that do not conform to a full or half increment will be rounded up or down to the nearest full or half increment and this revised amount will be considered your high bid.
10. Auctioneer's Execution of Certain Bids. Auctioneer cannot be responsible for your errors in bidding, so carefully check that every bid is entered correctly. When identical mail or FAX bids are submitted, preference is given to the first received. To ensure the greatest accuracy, your written bids should be entered on the standard printed bid sheet and be received at Auctioneer's place of business at least two business days before the Auction start. Auctioneer is not responsible for executing mail bids or FAX bids received on or after the day the first lot is sold, nor Internet bids submitted after the published closing time; nor is Auctioneer responsible for proper execution of bids submitted by telephone, mail, FAX, e-mail, Internet, or in person once the Auction begins. Internet bids may not be withdrawn until your written request is received and acknowledged by Auctioneer (FAX: 214-4438425); such requests must state the reason, and may constitute grounds for withdrawal of bidding privileges. Lots won by mail Bidders will not be delivered at the Auction unless prearranged.
11. Caveat as to Bid Increments. Bid increments (over the current bid level) determine the lowest amount you may bid on a particular lot. Bids greater than one increment over the current bid can be any whole dollar amount. It is possible under several circumstances for winning bids to be between increments, sometimes only $1 above the previous increment. Please see: "How can I lose by less than an increment?" on our website. Bids will be accepted in whole dollar amounts only. No "buy" or "unlimited" bids will be accepted.

    The following chart governs current bidding increments.

Current Bid	Bid Increment
<$10	$1
$10 - $29	$2
$30 - $49	$3
$50 - $99	$5
$100 - $199	$10
$200 - $299	$20
$300 - $499	$25
$500 - $999	$50
$1,000 - $1,999	$100
$2,000 - $2,999	$200
$3,000 - $4,999	$250
$5,000 - $9,999	$500
$10,000 - $19,999	$1,000

Current Bid	Bid Increment
$20,000 - $29,999	$2,000
$30,000 - $49,999	$2,500
$50,000 - $99,999	$5,000
$100,000 - $199,999	$10,000
$200,000 - $299,999	$20,000
$300,000 - $499,999	$25,000
$500,000 - $999,999	$50,000
$1,000,000 - $1,999,999	$100,000
$2,000,000 - $2,999,999	$200,000
$3,000,000 - $4,999,999	$250,000
$5,000,000 - $9,999,999	$500,000
>$10,000,000	$1,000,000

12. If Auctioneer calls for a full increment, a floor/phone bidder may request Auctioneer to accept a bid at half of the increment ("Cut Bid") which will be that bidders final bid; if the Auctioneer solicits bids other the expected increment, these bids will not be considered Cut Bids, and bidders bidding at such increments may continue to participate. Off-increment bids may be accepted by the Auctioneer at Signature® Auctions and Grand Format Auctions.

Conducting the Auction:

13. Notice of the consignor's liberty to place bids on his lots in the Auction is hereby made in accordance with Article 2 of the Texas Business and Commercial Code. A "Minimum Bid" is an amount below which the lot will not sell. THE CONSIGNOR OF PROPERTY MAY PLACE WRITTEN "Minimum Bids" ON HIS LOTS IN ADVANCE OF THE AUCTION; ON SUCH LOTS, IF THE HAMMER PRICE DOES NOT MEET THE "Minimum Bid", THE CONSIGNOR MAY PAY A REDUCED COMMISSION ON THOSE LOTS. "Minimum Bids" are generally posted online several days prior to the Auction closing. For any successful bid placed by a consignor on his Property on the Auction floor, or by any means during the live session, or after the "Minimum Bid" for an Auction have been posted, we will require the consignor to pay full Buyer's Premium and Seller's Commissions on such lot.
14. The highest qualified Bidder recognized by the Auctioneer shall be the buyer. In the event of any dispute between any Bidders at an Auction, Auctioneer may at his sole discretion reoffer the lot. Auctioneer's decision and declaration of the winning Bidder shall be final and binding upon all Bidders. Bids properly offered, whether by floor Bidder or other means of bidding, may on occasion be missed or go unrecognized; in such cases, the Auctioneer may declare the recognized bid accepted as the winning bid, regardless of whether a competing bid may have been higher.
15. Auctioneer reserves the right to refuse to honor any bid or to limit the amount of any bid, in its sole discretion. A bid is considered not made in "Good Faith" when made by an insolvent or irresponsible person, a person under the age of eighteen, or is not supported by satisfactory credit, collectibles references, or otherwise. Regardless of the disclosure of his identity, any bid by a consignor or his agent on a lot consigned by him is deemed to be made in "Good Faith." Any person apparently appearing on the OFAC list is not eligible to bid.
16. Nominal Bids. The Auctioneer in its sole discretion may reject nominal bids, small opening bids, or very nominal advances. If a lot bearing estimates fails to open for 40–60% of the low estimate, the Auctioneer may pass the item or may place a protective bid on behalf of the consignor.
17. Lots bearing bidding estimates shall open at Auctioneer's discretion (approximately 50% of the low estimate). In the event that no bid meets or exceeds that opening amount, the lot shall pass as unsold.
18. All items are to be purchased per lot as numerically indicated and no lots will be broken. Auctioneer reserves the right to withdraw, prior to the close, any lots from the Auction.
19. Auctioneer reserves the right to rescind the sale in the event of nonpayment, breach of a warranty, disputed ownership, auctioneer's clerical error or omission in exercising bids and reserves, or for any other reason and In Auctioneer's sole discretion. In cases of nonpayment, Auctioneer's election to void a sale does not relieve the Bidder from their obligation to pay Auctioneer its fees (seller's and buyer's premium) and any other damages or expenses pertaining to the lot.
20. Auctioneer occasionally experiences Internet and/or Server service outages, and Auctioneer periodically schedules system downtime for maintenance and other purposes, during which Bidders cannot participate or place bids. If such outages occur, we may at our discretion extend bidding for the Auction. Bidders unable to place their Bids through the Internet are directed to contact Client Services at 1-800-872-6467.
21. The Auctioneer or its affiliates may consign items to be sold in the Auction, and may bid on those lots or any other lots. Auctioneer or affiliates expressly reserve the right to modify any such bids at any time prior to the hammer based upon data made known to the Auctioneer or its affiliates. The Auctioneer may extend advances, guarantees, or loans to certain consignors, and may extend financing or other credits at varying rates to certain Bidders in the auction.
22. The Auctioneer has the right to sell certain unsold items after the close of the Auction. Such lots shall be considered sold during the Auction and all these Terms and Conditions shall apply to such sales including but not limited to the Buyer's Premium, return rights, and disclaimers.

Payment:

23. All sales are strictly for cash in United States dollars (including U.S. currency, bank wire, cashier checks, travelers checks, eChecks, and bank money orders, all subject to reporting requirements). All are subject to clearing and funds being received In Auctioneer's account before delivery of the purchases. Auctioneer reserves the right to determine if a check constitutes "good funds" when drawn on a U.S. bank for ten days, and thirty days when drawn on an international bank. Credit Card (Visa or Master Card only) and PayPal payments may be accepted up to $10,000 from non-dealers at the sole discretion of the Auctioneer, subject to the following limitations: a) sales are only to the cardholder, b) purchases are shipped to the cardholder's registered and verified address, c) Auctioneer may pre-approve the cardholder's credit line, d) a credit card transaction may not be used in conjunction with any other financing or extended terms offered by the Auctioneer, and must transact immediately upon invoice presentation, e) rights of return are governed by these Terms and Conditions, which supersede those conditions promulgated by the card issuer, f) floor Bidders must present their card.
24. Payment is due upon closing of the Auction session, or upon presentment of an invoice. Auctioneer reserves the right to void an invoice if payment in full is not received within 7 days after the close of the Auction. In cases of nonpayment, Auctioneer's election to void a sale does not relieve the Bidder from their obligation to pay Auctioneer its fees (seller's and buyer's premium) on the lot and any other damages pertaining to the lot.
25. Lots delivered in the States of Texas, California, or other states where the Auction may be held, are subject to all applicable state and local taxes, unless appropriate permits are on file with Auctioneer. Bidder agrees to pay Auctioneer the actual amount of tax due in the event that sales tax is not properly collected due to: 1) an expired, inaccurate, inappropriate tax certificate or declaration, 2) an incorrect interpretation of the applicable statute, 3) or any other reason. The appropriate form or certificate must be on file at and verified by Auctioneer five days prior to Auction or tax must be paid; only if such form or certificate is received by Auctioneer within 4 days after the Auction can a refund of tax paid be made. Lots from different Auctions may not be aggregated for sales tax purposes.
26. In the event that a Bidder's payment is dishonored upon presentment(s), Bidder shall pay the maximum statutory processing fee set by applicable state law. If you attempt to pay via eCheck and your financial institution denies this transfer from your bank account, or the payment cannot be completed using the selected funding source, you agree to complete payment using your credit card on file.
27. If any Auction invoice submitted by Auctioneer is not paid in full when due, the unpaid balance will bear interest at the highest rate permitted by law from the date of invoice until paid. If the Auctioneer refers any invoice to an attorney for collection, the buyer agrees to pay attorney's fees, court costs, and other collection costs incurred by Auctioneer. If Auctioneer assigns collection to its in-house legal staff, such attorney's time expended on the matter shall be compensated at a rate comparable to the hourly rate of independent attorneys.

28. In the event a successful Bidder fails to pay all amounts due, Auctioneer reserves the right to resell the merchandise, and such Bidder agrees to pay for the reasonable costs of resale, including a 10% seller's commission, and also to pay any difference between the resale price and the previously successful bid. Auctioneer may sell the merchandise to an under Bidder or at private sale and in such case the Bidder shall be responsible for any deficiency between the original and subsequent sale.
29. Auctioneer reserves the right to require payment in full in good funds before delivery of the merchandise.
30. Auctioneer shall have a lien against the merchandise purchased by the buyer to secure payment of the Auction invoice. Auctioneer is further granted a lien and the right to retain possession of any other property of the buyer then held by the Auctioneer or its affiliates to secure payment of any Auction invoice or any other amounts due the Auctioneer or affiliates from the buyer. With respect to these lien rights, Auctioneer shall have all the rights of a secured creditor under Article 9 of the Texas Uniform Commercial Code, including but not limited to the right of sale. In addition, with respect to payment of the Auction invoice(s), the buyer waives any and all rights of offset he might otherwise have against the Auctioneer and the consignor of the merchandise included on the invoice. If a Bidder owes Auctioneer or its affiliates on any account, Auctioneer and its affiliates shall have the right to offset such unpaid account by any credit balance due Bidder, and it may secure by possessory lien any unpaid amount by any of the Bidder's property in their possession.
31. Title shall not pass to the successful Bidder until all invoices are paid in full. It is the responsibility of the buyer to provide adequate insurance coverage for the items once they have been delivered to a common carrier or third-party shipper.

Delivery; Shipping; and Handling Charges:

32. Buyer is liable for shipping and handling. Please refer to Auctioneer's website www.HA.com/common/shipping.php for the latest charges or call Auctioneer. Auctioneer is unable to combine purchases from other auctions or affiliates into one package for shipping purposes. Lots won will be shipped in a commercially reasonable time after payment in good funds for the merchandise and the shipping fees is received or credit extended, except when third-party shipment occurs.
33. Successful international Bidders shall provide written shipping instructions, including specified customs declarations, to the Auctioneer for any lots to be delivered outside of the United States. NOTE: Declaration value shall be the item'(s) hammer price together with its buyer's premium and Auctioneer shall use the correct harmonized code for the lot. Domestic Buyers on lots designated for third-party shipment must designate the common carrier, accept risk of loss, and prepay shipping costs.
34. All shipping charges will be borne by the successful Bidder. Any risk of loss during shipment will be borne by the buyer following Auctioneer's delivery to the designated common carrier or third-party shipper, regardless of domestic or foreign shipment.
35. Due to the nature of some items sold, it shall be the responsibility for the successful bidder to arrange pick-up and shipping through third-parties; as to such items Auctioneer shall have no liability. Failure to pick-up or arrange shipping in a timely fashion (within ten days) shall subject Lots to storage and moving charges, including a $100 administration fee plus $10 daily storage for larger items and $5.00 daily for smaller items (storage fee per item) after 35 days. In the event the Lot is not removed within ninety days, the Lot may be offered for sale to recover any past due storage or moving fees, including a 10% Seller's Commission.
36. The laws of various countries regulate the import or export of certain plant and animal properties, including (but not limited to) items made of (or including) ivory, whalebone, turtleshell, coral, crocodile, or other wildlife. Transport of such lots may require special licenses for export, import, or both. Bidder is responsible for: 1) obtaining all information on such restricted items for both export and import; 2) obtaining all such licenses and/or permits. Delay or failure to obtain any such license or permit does not relieve the buyer of timely compliance with standard payment terms. For further information, please contact Bill Taylor at 800-872-6467 ext. 1280.
37. Any request for shipping verification for undelivered packages must be made within 30 days of shipment by Auctioneer.

Cataloging, Warranties and Disclaimers:

38. NO WARRANTY, WHETHER EXPRESSED OR IMPLIED, IS MADE WITH RESPECT TO ANY DESCRIPTION CONTAINED IN THIS AUCTION OR ANY SECOND OPINE. Any description of the items or second opine contained in this Auction is for the sole purpose of identifying the items for those Bidders who do not have the opportunity to view the lots prior to bidding, and no description of items has been made part of the basis of the bargain or has created any express warranty that the goods would conform to any description made by Auctioneer. Color variations can be expected in any electronic or printed imaging, and are not grounds for the return of any lot.
39. Auctioneer is selling only such right or title to the items being sold as Auctioneer may have by virtue of consignment agreements on the date of auction and disclaims any warranty of title to the Property. Auctioneer disclaims any warranty of merchantability or fitness for any particular purposes. All images, descriptions, sales data, and archival records are the exclusive property of Auctioneer, and may be used by Auctioneer for advertising, promotion, archival records, and any other uses deemed appropriate.
40. Translations of foreign language documents may be provided as a convenience to interested parties. Auctioneer makes no representation as to the accuracy of those translations and will not be held responsible for errors in bidding arising from inaccuracies in translation.
41. Auctioneer disclaims all liability for damages, consequential or otherwise, arising out of or in connection with the sale of any Property by Auctioneer to Bidder. No third party may rely on any benefit of these Terms and Conditions and any rights, if any, established hereunder are personal to the Bidder and may not be assigned. Any statement made by the Auctioneer is an opinion and does not constitute a warranty or representation. No employee of Auctioneer may alter these Terms and Conditions, and, unless signed by a principal of Auctioneer, any such alteration is null and void.
42. Auctioneer shall not be liable for breakage of glass or damage to frames (patent or latent); such defects, in any event, shall not be a basis for any claim for return or reduction in purchase price.

Release:

43. In consideration of participation in the Auction and the placing of a bid, Bidder expressly releases Auctioneer, its officers, directors and employees, its affiliates, and its outside experts that provide second opines, from any and all claims, cause of action, chose of action, whether at law or equity or any arbitration or mediation rights existing under the rules of any professional society or affiliation based upon the assigned description, or a derivative theory, breach of warranty express or implied, representation or other matter set forth within these Terms and Conditions of Auction or otherwise. In the event of a claim, Bidder agrees that such rights and privileges conferred therein are strictly construed as specifically declared herein; e.g., authenticity, typographical error, etc. and are the exclusive remedy. Bidder, by non-compliance to these express terms of a granted remedy, shall waive any claim against Auctioneer.
44. Notice: Some Property sold by Auctioneer are inherently dangerous e.g. firearms, cannons, and small items that may be swallowed or ingested or may have latent defects all of which may cause harm to a person. Purchaser accepts all risk of loss or damage from its purchase of these items and Auctioneer disclaims any liability whether under contract or tort for damages and losses, direct or inconsequential, and expressly disclaims any warranty as to safety or usage of any lot sold.

Dispute Resolution and Arbitration Provision:

45. By placing a bid or otherwise participating in the auction, Bidder accepts these Terms and Conditions of Auction, and specifically agrees to the alternative dispute resolution provided herein. Arbitration replaces the right to go to court, including the right to a jury trial.
46. Auctioneer in no event shall be responsible for consequential damages, incidental damages, compensatory damages, or any other damages arising or claimed to be arising from the auction of any lot. In the event that Auctioneer cannot deliver the lot or subsequently it is established that the lot lacks title, or other transfer or condition issue is claimed, In such cases the sole remedy shall be limited to rescission of sale and refund of the amount paid by Bidder; in no case shall Auctioneer's maximum liability exceed the high bid on that lot, which bid shall be deemed for all purposes the value of the lot. After one year has elapsed, Auctioneer's maximum liability shall be limited to any commissions and fees Auctioneer earned on that lot.
47. In the event of an attribution error, Auctioneer may at its sole discretion, correct the error on the Internet, or, if discovered at a later date, to refund the buyer's purchase price without further obligation.
48. Arbitration Clause: All controversies or claims under this Agreement or arising from or pertaining to: this Agreement or related documents, or to the Properties consigned hereunder, or the enforcement or interpretation hereof of this or any related agreements, or damage to Properties, payment, or any other matter, or because of an alleged breach, default or misrepresentation under the provisions hereof or otherwise, that cannot be settled amicably within one (1) month from the date of notification of either party to the other of such dispute or question, which notice shall specify the details of such dispute or question, shall be settled by final and binding arbitration by one arbitrator appointed by the American Arbitration Association ("AAA"). The arbitration shall be conducted in Dallas, Dallas County, Texas in accordance with the then existing Commercial Arbitration Rules of the AAA. The arbitration shall be brought within two (2) years of the alleged breach, default or misrepresentation or the claim is waived. The prevailing party (a party that is awarded substantial and material relief on its claim or defense) may be awarded its reasonable attorney's fees and costs. Judgment upon the award rendered by the arbitrator may be entered in any court having jurisdiction thereof; provided, however, that the law applicable to any controversy shall be the law of the State of Texas, regardless of its or any other jurisdiction's choice of law principles and under the provisions of the Federal Arbitration Act.
49. No claims of any kind can be considered after the settlements have been made with the consignors. Any dispute after the settlement date is strictly between the Bidder and consignor without involvement or responsibility of the Auctioneer.
50. In consideration of their participation in or application for the Auction, a person or entity (whether the successful Bidder, a Bidder, a purchaser and/or other Auction participant or registrant) agrees that all disputes in any way relating to, arising under, connected with, or incidental to these Terms and Conditions and purchases, or default in payment thereof, shall be arbitrated pursuant to the arbitration provision. In the event that any matter including actions to compel arbitration, construe the agreement, actions in aid or arbitration or otherwise needs to be litigated, such litigation shall be exclusively in the Courts of the State of Texas, in Dallas County, Texas, and if necessary the corresponding appellate courts. For such actions, the successful Bidder, purchaser, or Auction participant also expressly submits himself to the personal jurisdiction of the State of Texas.
51. These Terms & Conditions provide specific remedies for occurrences in the auction and delivery process. Where such remedies are afforded, they shall be interpreted strictly. Bidder agrees that any claim shall utilize such remedies; Bidder making a claim in excess of those remedies provided in these Terms and Conditions agrees that in no case whatsoever shall Auctioneer's maximum liability exceed the high bid on that lot, which bid shall be deemed for all purposes the value of the lot.

Miscellaneous:

52. Agreements between Bidders and consignors to effectuate a non-sale of an item at Auction, inhibit bidding on a consigned item to enter into a private sale agreement for said item, or to utilize the Auctioneer's Auction to obtain sales for non-selling consigned items subsequent to the Auction, are strictly prohibited. If a subsequent sale of a previously consigned item occurs in violation of this provision, Auctioneer reserves the right to charge Bidder the applicable Buyer's Premium and consignor a Seller's Commission as determined for each auction venue and by the terms of the seller's agreement.
53. Acceptance of these Terms and Conditions qualifies Bidder as a client who has consented to be contacted by Heritage in the future. In conformity with "do-not-call" regulations promulgated by the Federal or State regulatory agencies, participation by the Bidder is affirmative consent to being contacted at the phone number shown in his application and this consent shall remain in effect until it is revoked in writing. Heritage may from time to time contact Bidder concerning sale, purchase, and auction opportunities available through Heritage and its affiliates and subsidiaries.
54. Rules of Construction: Auctioneer presents properties in a number of collectible fields, and as such, specific venues have promulgated supplemental Terms and Conditions. Nothing herein shall be construed to waive the general Terms and Conditions of Auction by these additional rules and shall be construed to give force and effect to the rules in their entirety.

State Notices:

Notice as to an Auction in California. Auctioneer has in compliance with Title 2.95 of the California Civil Code as amended October 11, 1993 Sec. 1812.600, posted with the California Secretary of State its bonds for it and its employees, and the auction is being conducted in compliance with Sec. 2338 of the Commercial Code and Sec. 535 of the Penal Code.

Notice as to an Auction in New York City. These Terms and Conditions are designed to conform to the applicable sections of the New York City Department of Consumer Affairs Rules and Regulations as Amended. This is a Public Auction Sale conducted by Auctioneer. The New York City licensed Auctioneers are Kathleen Guzman, No.0762165, and Samuel W. Foose, No.0952360, who will conduct the Auction on behalf of Heritage Auctions, Inc. ("Auctioneer"). All lots are subject to: the consignor's right to bid thereon in accord with these Terms and Conditions of Auction, consignor's option to receive advances on their consignments, and Auctioneer, in its sole discretion, may offer limited extended financing to registered bidders, in accord with Auctioneer's internal credit standards. A registered bidder may inquire whether a lot is subject to an advance or reserve. Auctioneer has made advances to various consignors in this sale.

Notice as to an Auction in Texas. In compliance with TDLR rule 67.100(c)(1), notice is hereby provided that this auction is covered by a Recovery Fund administered by the Texas Department of Licensing and Regulation, P.O. Box 12157, Austin, Texas 78711 (512) 463-6599. Any complaints may be directed to the same address.

Rev. 5_02_08

Additional Terms & Conditions:
COINS & CURRENCY

COINS and CURRENCY TERM A: Signature₀ Auctions are not on approval. No certified material may be returned because of possible differences of opinion with respect to the grade offered by any third-party organization, dealer, or service. No guarantee of grade is offered for uncertified Property sold and subsequently submitted to a third-party grading service. There are absolutely no exceptions to this policy. Under extremely limited circumstances, (e.g. gross cataloging error) a purchaser, who did not bid from the floor, may request Auctioneer to evaluate voiding a sale: such request must be made in writing detailing the alleged gross error; submission of the lot to the Auctioneer must be pre-approved by the Auctioneer; and bidder must notify Ron Brackemyre (1-800-8726467 Ext. 1312) in writing of such request within three (3) days of the non-floor bidder's receipt of the lot. Any lot that is to be evaluated must be in our offices within 30 days after Auction. Grading or method of manufacture do not qualify for this evaluation process nor do such complaints constitute a basis to challenge the authenticity of a lot. AFTER THAT 30-DAY PERIOD, NO LOTS MAY BE RETURNED FOR REASONS OTHER THAN AUTHENTICITY. Lots returned must be housed intact in their original holder. No lots purchased by floor Bidders may be returned (including those Bidders acting as agents for others) except for authenticity. Late remittance for purchases may be considered just cause to revoke all return privileges.

COINS and CURRENCY TERM B: Auctions conducted solely on the Internet THREE (3) DAY RETURN POLICY: Certified Coin and Uncertified and Certified Currency lots paid for within seven days of the Auction closing are sold with a three (3) day return privilege. You may return lots under the following conditions: Within three days of receipt of the lot, you must first notify Auctioneer by contacting Client Service by phone (1-800-872-6467) or e-mail (Bid@HA.com), and immediately ship the lot(s) fully insured to the attention of Returns, Heritage, 3500 Maple Avenue, 17th Floor, Dallas TX 75219-3941. Lots must be housed intact in their original holder and condition. You are responsible for the insured, safe delivery of any lots. A non-negotiable return fee of 5% of the purchase price ($10 per lot minimum) will be deducted from the refund for each returned lot or billed directly. Postage and handling fees are not refunded. After the three-day period (from receipt), no items may be returned for any reason. Late remittance for purchases revokes these Return privileges.

COINS and CURRENCY TERM C: Bidders who have inspected the lots prior to any Auction, or attended the Auction, or bid through an Agent, will not be granted any return privileges, except for reasons of authenticity.

COINS and CURRENCY TERM D: Coins sold referencing a third-party grading service are sold "as is" without any express or implied warranty, except for a guarantee by Auctioneer that they are genuine. Certain warranties may be available from the grading services and the Bidder is referred to them for further details: Numismatic Guaranty Corporation (NGC), P.O. Box 4776, Sarasota, FL 34230; Professional Coin Grading Service (PCGS), PO Box 9458, Newport Beach, CA 92658; ANACS, 6555 S. Kenton St. Ste. 303, Englewood, CO 80111; and Independent Coin Grading Co. (ICG), 7901 East Belleview Ave., Suite 50, Englewood, CO 80111.

COINS and CURRENCY TERM E: Notes sold referencing a third-party grading service are sold "as is" without any express or implied warranty, except for guarantee by Auctioneer that they are genuine. Grading, condition or other attributes of any lot may have a material effect on its value, and the opinion of others, including third-party grading services such as PCGS Currency, PMG, and CGA may differ with that of Auctioneer. Auctioneer shall not be bound by any prior or subsequent opinion, determination, or certification by any grading service. Bidder specifically waives any claim to right of return of any item because of the opinion, determination, or certification, or lack thereof, by any grading service. Certain warranties may be available from the grading services and the Bidder is referred to them for further details: Paper Money Guaranty (PMG), PO Box 4711, Sarasota FL 34230; PCGS Currency, PO Box 9458, Newport Beach, CA 92658; Currency Grading & Authentication (CGA), PO Box 418, Three Bridges, NJ 08887. Third party graded notes are not returnable for any reason whatsoever.

COINS and CURRENCY TERM F: Since we cannot examine encapsulated coins or notes, they are sold "as is" without our grading opinion, and may not be returned for any reason. Auctioneer shall not be liable for any patent or latent defect or controversy pertaining to or arising from any encapsulated collectible. In any such instance, purchaser's remedy, if any, shall be solely against the service certifying the collectible.

COINS and CURRENCY TERM G: Due to changing grading standards over time, differing interpretations, and to possible mishandling of items by subsequent owners, Auctioneer reserves the right to grade items differently than shown on certificates from any grading service that accompany the items. Auctioneer also reserves the right to grade items differently than the grades shown in the prior catalog should such items be reconsigned to any future auction.

COINS and CURRENCY TERM H: Although consensus grading is employed by most grading services, it should be noted as aforesaid that grading is not an exact science. In fact, it is entirely possible that if a lot is broken out of a plastic holder and resubmitted to another grading service or even to the same service, the lot could come back with a different grade assigned.

COINS and CURRENCY TERM I: Certification does not guarantee protection against the normal risks associated with potentially volatile markets. The degree of liquidity for certified coins and collectibles will vary according to general market conditions and the particular lot involved. For some lots there may be no active market at all at certain points in time.

COINS and CURRENCY TERM J: All non-certified coins and currency are guaranteed genuine, but are not guaranteed as to grade, since grading is a matter of opinion, an art and not a science, and therefore the opinion rendered by the Auctioneer or any third party grading service may not agree with the opinion of others (including trained experts), and the same expert may not grade the same item with the same grade at two different times. Auctioneer has graded the non-certified numismatic items, in the Auctioneer's opinion, to their current interpretation of the American Numismatic Association's standards as of the date the catalog was prepared. There is no guarantee or warranty implied or expressed that the grading standards utilized by the Auctioneer will meet the standards of any grading service at any time in the future.

COINS and CURRENCY TERM K: Storage of purchased coins and currency: Purchasers are advised that certain types of plastic may react with a coin's metal or transfer plasticizer to notes and may cause damage. Caution should be used to avoid storage in materials that are not inert.

COINS and CURRENCY TERM L: NOTE: Purchasers of rare coins or currency through Heritage have available the option of arbitration by the Professional Numismatists Guild (PNG); if an election is not made within ten (10) days of an unresolved dispute, Auctioneer may elect either PNG or A.A.A. Arbitration.

COINS and CURRENCY TERM M: For more information regarding Canadian lots attributed to the Charlton reference guides, please contact: Charlton International, PO Box 820, Station Willowdale B, North York, Ontario M2K 2R1 Canada.

WIRING INSTRUCTIONS:
Bank Information: JP Morgan Chase Bank, N.A., 270 Park Avenue, New York, NY 10017
Account Name: HERITAGE NUMISMATIC AUCTIONS MASTER ACCOUNT
ABA Number: 021000021
Account Number: 1884827674
Swift Code: CHASUS33

Rev. 5_02_08

Your five most effective bidding techniques:

❶ Interactive Internet™ Proxy Bidding
(leave your maximum Bid at HA.com before the auction starts)

Heritage's exclusive Interactive Internet™ system is fun and easy! Before you start, you must register online at HA.com and obtain your Username and Password.

1. Login to the HA.com website, using your Username and Password.

2. Chose the specialty you're interested in at the top of the homepage (i.e. coins, currency, comics, movie posters, fine art, etc.).

3. Search or browse for the lots that interest you. Every auction has search features and a 'drop-down' menu list.

4. Select a lot by clicking on the link or the photo icon. Read the description, and view the full-color photography. Note that clicking on the image will enlarge the photo with amazing detail.

5. View the current opening bid. Below the lot description, note the historic pricing information to help you establish price levels. Clicking on a link will take you directly to our Permanent Auction Archives for more information and images.

6. If the current price is within your range, Bid! At the top of the lot page is a box containing the Current Bid and an entry box for your "Secret Maximum Bid" – the maximum amount you are willing to pay for the item before the Buyer's Premium is added. Click the button marked "Place Bid" (if you are not logged in, a login box will open first so you can enter your username (or e-mail address) and password.

7. After you are satisfied that all the information is correct, confirm your "Secret Maximum Bid" by clicking on the "Confirm Absentee Bid" button. You will receive immediate notification letting you know if you are now the top bidder, or if another bidder had previously bid higher than your amount. If you bid your maximum amount and someone has already bid higher, you will immediately know so you can concentrate on other lots.

8. Before the auction, if another bidder surpasses your "Secret Maximum Bid", you will be notified automatically by e-mail containing a link to review the lot and possibly bid higher.

9. Interactive Internet™ bidding closes at 10 P.M. Central Time the night before the session is offered in a floor event. Interactive Internet™ bidding closes two hours before live sessions where there is no floor bidding.

10. The Interactive Internet™ system generally opens the lot at the next increment above the second highest bid. As the high bidder, your "Secret Maximum Bid" will compete for you during the floor auction. Of course, it is possible in a Signature® or Grand Format live auction that you may be outbid on the floor or by a Heritage Live bidder after Internet bidding closes. Bid early, as the earliest bird wins in the event of a tie bid. For more information about bidding and bid increments, please see the section labeled "Bidding Increments" elsewhere in this catalog.

11. After the auction, you will be notified of your success. It's that easy!

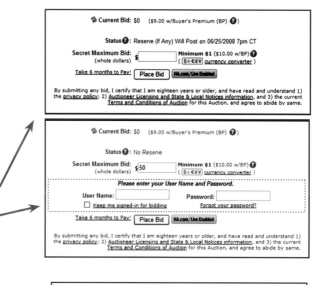

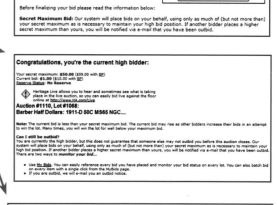

② Heritage Live™ Bidding
(participate in the Live auction via the Internet)

1. Look on each auction's homepage to verify whether that auction is "HA.com/Live Enabled." All Signature® and Grand Format auctions use the Heritage Live™ system, and many feature live audio and/or video. Determine your lots of interest and maximum bids.

2. Note on the auction's homepage the session dates and times (and especially time zones!) so you can plan your participation. You actually have two methods of using Heritage Live™: a) you can leave a proxy bid through this system, much like the Interactive Internet™ (we recommend you do this before the session starts), or b) you can sit in front of your computer much as the audience is sitting in the auction room during the actual auction.

3. Login at HA.com/Live.

4. Until you become experienced (and this happens quickly!) you will want to login well before your lot comes up so you can watch the activity on other lots. It is as intuitive as participating in a live auction.

5. When your lot hits the auction block, you can continue to bid live against the floor and other live bidders by simply clicking the "Bid" button; the amount you are bidding is clearly displayed on the console.

③ Mail Bidding
(deposit your maximum Bid with the U.S.P.S. well before the auction starts)

Mail bidding at auction is fun and easy, but by eliminating the interactivity of our online systems, some of your bids may be outbid before you lick the stamp, and you will have no idea of your overall chances until the auction is over!

1. Look through the printed catalog, and determine your lots of interest.

2. Research their market value by checking price lists and other price guidelines.

3. Fill out your bid sheet, entering your maximum bid on each lot. Bid using whole dollar amounts only. Verify your bids, because you are responsible for any errors you make! Please consult the Bidding Increments chart in the Terms & Conditions.

4. Please fill out your bid sheet completely! We also need: a) Your name and complete address for mailing invoices and lots; b) Your telephone number if any problems or changes arise; c) Your references; if you have not established credit with Heritage, you must send a 25% deposit, or list dealers with whom you have credit established; d) Total your bid sheet; add up all bids and list that total in the box; e) Sign your bid sheet, thereby agreeing to abide by the Terms & Conditions of Auction printed in the catalog.

5. Mail early, because preference is given to the first bid received in case of a tie.

6. When bidding by mail, you frequently purchase items at less than your maximum bid. Bidding generally opens at the next published increment above the second highest mail or Internet bid previously received; if additional floor, phone, or Heritage Live bids are made, we act as your agent, bidding in increments over any additional bid until you win the lot or are outbid. For example, if you submitted a bid of $750, and the second highest bid was $375, bidding would start at $400; if no other bids were placed, you would purchase the lot for $400.

7. You can also Fax your Bid Sheet if time is short. Use our exclusive Fax Hotline: 214-443-8425.

④ Telephone Bidding (when you are traveling, or do not have access to Heritage Live)

1. To participate in an auction by telephone, you must make preliminary arrangements with Client Services (Toll Free 866-835-3243) at least three days before the auction.

2. We strongly recommend that you place preliminary bids by mail or Internet if you intend to participate by telephone. On many occasions, this dual approach has reduced disappointments due to telephone (cell) problems, unexpected travel, late night sessions, and time zone differences. Keep a list of your preliminary bids, and we will help you avoid bidding against yourself.

⑤ Attend in Person (whenever possible)

Auctions are fun, and we encourage you to attend as many as possible – although our Heritage Live™ system brings all of the action right to your computer screen. Auction dates and session times are printed on the title page of each catalog, and appear on the homepage of each auction at HA.com. Join us if you can!

S T R E T C H
Your Budget with Heritage

We're collectors too, and we understand that on occasion there is more to buy than there is cash. Consider Heritage's Extended Payment Plan [EPP] for your purchases totaling $2,500 or more.

Extended Payment Plan [EPP] Conditions

- Minimum invoice total is $2,500.

- Minimum Down Payment is 20% of the total invoice.

- A signed and returned EPP Agreement is required.

- The EPP is subject to a 3% *fully refundable* Set-up Fee (based on the total invoice amount) payable as part of the first monthly payment.

- The 3% Set-up Fee is refundable provided all monthly payments are made by eCheck, bank draft, personal check drawn on good funds, or cash; and if all such payments are made according to the EPP schedule.

- Monthly payments can be automatically processed with an eCheck, Visa, or MasterCard.

- You may take up to six equal monthly payments to pay the balance.

- Interest is calculated at only 1% per month on the unpaid balance.

- Your EPP must be kept current or additional interest may apply.

- There is no penalty for paying off early.

- Shipment will be made when final payment is received.

- All traditional auction and sales policies still apply.

There is no return privilege once you have confirmed your sale, and penalties can be incurred on cancelled invoices. To avoid additional fees, you must make your down payment within 14 days of the auction. All material purchased under the EPP will be physically secured by Heritage until paid in full.

To exercise the EPP option, please notify **Eric Thomas** at **214.409.1241** or email at EricT@HA.com upon receipt of your invoice.

We appreciate your business and wish you good luck with your bidding.